BY JOE CASAD, WAYNE DALTON, EMMETT DULANEY, SHERWOOD LAWRENCE, ROBERT SCRIMGER, STEVEN TATE, ANTHONY TILKE, JOHN WHITE, RAYMOND WILLIAMS, AND KEVIN WOLFORD

MCP+I

TRAINING GUIDE

INTERNET EXAMS

New Riders

MCP+I Training Guide: Internet Exams

By Joe Casad, Wayne Dalton, Emmett Dulaney, Sherwood Lawrence, Robert Scrimger, Steven Tate, Anthony Tilke, John White, Raymond Williams, and Kevin Wolford

Published by:
New Riders Publishing
201 West 103rd Street
Indianapolis, IN 46290 USA

Printed in the United States of America

Library of Congress Catalog Card Number: 97-81212

ISBN: 1-56205-879-7

01 00 99 98   4 3 2 1

Warning and Disclaimer

Executive Editor
Mary Foote

Acquisitions Editors
Julie Fairweather, Nancy Maragioglio, Steve Weiss

Development Editors
Rob Tidrow, Scott Parker, Chris Zahn

Technical Editors
R. Andrew Brice, Robert Bogue, Bob Reinsch, Lance Skok

Managing Editors
Carla Hall, Sarah Kearns

Project Editors
Amy Bezek, Tom Dinse, Theresa Mathias, John Sleeva

Copy Editors
Nancy Albright, Margo Catts, Howard A. Jones, Theresa Mathias, Cliff Shubs

Indexers
Ginny Bess, Kevin Fulcher, Tim Wright

Cover Designer
Karen Ruggles

Book Designer
Glenn Larsen

Production Team
Kim Cofer
Laura A. Knox

About the Authors

Joe Casad is a freelance writer and editor who specializes in programming and networking topics. He was the managing editor of the short-lived but well-received *Network Administrator Magazine*, a journal of practical solutions for network professionals. Mr. Casad received a B.S. in engineering from the University of Kansas in 1980 and, before becoming a full-time writer and editor, spent ten years in the computer-intensive areas of the structural engineering profession. He now lives in Lawrence, Kansas with wife Barb Dineen and a pair of pint-sized hackers named Xander and Mattie.

Emmett Dulaney is a consultant for D. S. Technical Solutions in central Indiana. An MCSE, MCP+Internet, CNE, OS/2 Engineer, and LAN Server Engineer, he has taught continuing education courses for Indiana University-Purdue University of Fort Wayne for more than seven years. Mr. Dulaney has authored or coauthored over a dozen books, including *Teach Yourself MCSE NT Workstation in 14 Days*. He is also the Certification Corner columnist for *NT Systems* magazine. He can be reached at edulaney@iquest.net.

When **Sherwood Lawrence** is not tracing TCP/IP packets and troubleshooting connectivity issues, he spends his time tracking down his free time and troubleshooting why he has so little of it left. He contends that the undeniable proof that black holes exist in the universe sucking up space and time sits squarely in the middle of his desk. He can be contacted through his company's Web site at www.atlasconsulting.com.

For almost 20 years, **Robert Scrimger** has done everything with computers except design the boards (yet) and sell them. In the last eight years, his primary endeavor has been training, starting with many different applications and moving in the last few years to work exclusively with network operating systems and client/server applications. Rob is a Microsoft Certified Systems Engineer on both 3.51 and 4.0 and a Microsoft Certified Trainer.

Anthony Tilke is a network consultant and engineer. He is both Microsoft- and Novell-certified with MCSE and MCNE designations to his credit. After administering his first network in 1987, Anthony started to change his career from an economic analyst to a network engineer. With a transitional period as a statistical programmer and graduate student, Anthony dedicated himself to a career in networking by 1992. His career has included the design, implementation, and management of large networks and messaging systems for public sector clients. More recently, Anthony has been a senior network engineer for a Microsoft Solution Provider, and Novell Platinum reseller in the Pacific Northwest. A 1985 magna cum laude graduate from Pace University in New York, Anthony has written software reviews for *PC* magazine. He can be reached at anthony@compuserve.com.

John White currently works as a senior systems administrator. He is heavily involved in the implementation and support of Windows NT systems worldwide. John was a UNIX and NetWare systems administrator before joining the world of Windows NT. Prior to becoming a systems administrator, he was a biochemistry major at Trent University. He now lives in Ottawa, Canada with his wife Viviana.

Raymond Williams is a Microsoft Certified Trainer (MCT) and consultant. He currently works for GSE Erudite as a network instructor. Raymond is a Microsoft Certified Systems Engineer, as well as a Certified NetWare Instructor and Certified NetWare Engineer. He has worked as a systems analyst and design engineer for many companies during his five years experience. He thoroughly enjoys the computer industry and what it has to offer, and finds pleasure in sharing the information with others.

Kevin B. Wolford is an MCSE, MCT, Master CNE, and CNI. He has had several careers, including technical writer, pension actuary, and trainer. He is the lead Windows NT trainer for GSE Erudite Software in Salt Lake City, Utah. You also can see Kevin in training videos produced by Keystone Learning Systems of Provo, Utah. Kevin enjoys explaining complex, technical things in a simple manner.

Contents at a Glance

Part IV Appendixes 1435

Table of Contents

Part II: TCP/IP   489

Introduction

MCP+I Training Guide: Internet Exams is designed for advanced end users, service technicians, and network administrators with the goal of certification as a Microsoft Certified Professional with a specialization in the Internet (MCP+I). The three exams, "Implementing and Supporting Microsoft Windows NT Server 4.0" (Exam 70-067), "Internetworking with Microsoft TCP/IP on Microsoft Windows NT 4.0" (Exam 70-059), and "Implementing and Supporting Microsoft Internet Information Server 4.0" (Exam 70-087) measure your ability to plan security, install and configure server products, manage server resources, extend servers to run CGI scripts or ISAPI scripts, monitor and analyze performance, and troubleshoot problems.

Who Should Read This Book

This book is designed to help you meet the goal of MCP+I Certification by preparing you for all three exams.

This book is your one-stop shop. Everything you need to know to pass the exams is in here, and Microsoft has approved it as study material. You do not *need* to take a class in addition to buying this book to pass the exam. However, depending on your personal study habits or learning style, you may benefit either from taking a class in addition to the book, or from buying this book in addition to attending a class.

This book can also help advanced users and administrators who are not studying for the exam, but are looking for a single-volume reference on Windows NT Server, Microsoft TCP/IP, or IIS 4.

How This Book Helps You

This book conducts you on a self-guided tour of all the areas covered by the exams and teaches you the specific skills you need to achieve your MCP+I certification. You'll also find helpful hints, tips, real-world examples, exercises, and references to additional study materials. Specifically, this book is set up to help you in the following ways:

✓ Objectives

▶ **Organization.** This book is organized by major exam topics and individual exam objectives. Every objective you need to know for the "Implementing and Supporting Microsoft Windows NT Server 4.0" (Exam 70-067), "Internetworking with Microsoft TCP/IP on Microsoft Windows NT 4.0" (Exam 70-059), and "Implementing and Supporting Microsoft Internet Information Server 4.0" (Exam 70-087) exams is covered in this book; we've included a margin icon, like the one in the margin here, to help you quickly locate these objectives as they are addressed in the chapters.

▶ **Time-management advice.** Quizzes appear at the beginning of each chapter to test your knowledge of the objectives contained within that chapter. If you already know the answers to some or all of these questions, you can make a time-management decision accordingly, adjusting the amount of time you spend on a given topic.

▶ **Extensive practice test options.** Plenty of questions appear at the end of each chapter, as well, to test your comprehension of material covered within that chapter. An answer list follows the questions so you can check yourself. These review questions will help you determine what you understand thoroughly and what topics require further review on your part.

You'll also get a chance to practice for the certification exams by using the TestPrep test engine on the accompanying CD-ROM. The questions on the CD-ROM provide a more thorough and comprehensive look at what the certification exams really are like.

Note

For a complete description of New Riders' newly developed test engine, please see Appendix D, "All About TestPrep."

For a complete description of what you can find on the CD-ROM, see Appendix C, "What's on the CD-ROM."

For more information about the exam or the certification process, contact Microsoft:

Microsoft Education: (800) 636-7544
Internet: ftp://ftp.microsoft.com/Services/MSEdCert
World Wide Web: http://www.microsoft.com/train_cert/default.htm
CompuServe Forum: GO MSEDCERT

Understanding What the MCP+I Exams Cover

The "Implementing and Supporting Microsoft Windows NT Server 4.0" (Exam 70-067), "Internetworking with Microsoft TCP/IP on Microsoft Windows NT 4.0" (Exam 70-059), and "Implementing and Supporting Microsoft Internet Information Server 4.0" (Exam 70-087) exams cover the main topic areas represented by the conceptual groupings of the test objectives. For Windows NT Server 4 and IIS 4, each chapter represents one of these main topic areas. TCP/IP is organized a bit differently. The exam objectives are listed by topic area in the following sections.

Windows NT Server 4

The "Implementing and Supporting Microsoft Windows NT Server 4.0" exam (#70-067) covers six main topic areas.

Planning

Plan the disk drive configuration for various requirements. Requirements include:

- ▶ Choosing a file system
- ▶ Choosing a fault tolerance method

Choose a protocol for various situations. Protocols include:

- ▶ TCP/IP
- ▶ NWLink IPX/SPX Compatible Transport
- ▶ NetBEUI

Installation and Configuration

Install Windows NT Server on Intel-based platforms

Install Windows NT Server to perform various server roles. Server roles include:

- ▶ Primary domain controller
- ▶ Backup domain controller
- ▶ Member server

Install Windows NT Server by using various methods. Installation methods include:

- ▶ CD-ROM
- ▶ Over-the-network
- ▶ Network Client Administrator
- ▶ Express versus custom

Configure protocols and protocol bindings. Protocols include:

- ► TCP/IP

- ► NWLink IPX/SPX Compatible Transport

- ► NetBEUI

Configure network adapters. Considerations include:

- ► Changing IRQ, IObase, and memory addresses

- ► Configuring multiple adapters

Configure Windows NT Server core services. Services include:

- ► Directory Replicator

- ► License Manager

- ► Other services

Configure peripherals and devices. Peripherals and devices include:

- ► Communication devices

- ► SCSI devices

- ► Tape device drivers

- ► UPS devices and UPS service

- ► Mouse drivers, display drivers, and keyboard drivers

Configure hard disks to meet various requirements. Requirements include:

- ► Allocating disk space capacity

- ► Providing redundancy

- ► Improving performance

- ► Providing security

- ► Formatting

Configure printers. Tasks include:

- ▶ Adding and configuring a printer

- ▶ Implementing a printer pool

- ▶ Setting print priorities

Configure a Windows NT Server computer for various types of client computers. Client computer types include:

- ▶ Windows NT Workstation

- ▶ Microsoft Windows 95

- ▶ Microsoft MS-DOS-based

Managing Resources

Managing user and group accounts. Considerations include:

- ▶ Managing Windows NT groups

- ▶ Managing Windows NT user rights

- ▶ Administering account policies

- ▶ Auditing changes to the user account database

Create and manage policies and profiles for various situations. Policies and profiles include:

- ▶ Local user profiles

- ▶ Roaming user profiles

- ▶ System policies

Administer remote servers from various types of client computers. Client computer types include:

- ▶ Windows 95

- ▶ Windows NT Workstation

Manage disk resources. Tasks include:

- ▶ Copying and moving files between file systems
- ▶ Creating and sharing resources
- ▶ Implementing permissions and security
- ▶ Establishing file auditing

Connectivity

Configure Windows NT Server for interoperability with NetWare servers by using various tools. Tools include:

- ▶ Gateway service for NetWare
- ▶ Migration tool for NetWare

Install and configure Remote Access Service (RAS). Configuration options include:

- ▶ Configuring RAS communications
- ▶ Configuring RAS protocols
- ▶ Configuring RAS security
- ▶ Configuring Dial-Up Neworking clients

Monitoring and Optimization

Monitor performance of various functions by using Performance Monitor. Functions include:

- ▶ Processor
- ▶ Memory
- ▶ Disk
- ▶ Network

Identify performance bottlenecks

Troubleshooting

Choose the appropriate course of action to take to resolve installation failures

Choose the appropriate course of action to take to resolve boot failures

Choose the appropriate course of action to take to resolve configuration errors

Choose the appropriate course of action to take to resolve printer problems

Choose the appropriate course of action to take to resolve RAS problems

Choose the appropriate course of action to take to resolve connectivity problems

Choose the appropriate course of action to take to resolve resource access problems and permission problems

Choose the appropriate course of action to take to resolve fault-tolerance failures. Fault tolerance methods include:

- ▶ Tape backup

- ▶ Mirroring

- ▶ Stripe set with parity

- ▶ Disk duplexing

TCP/IP

The "Internetworking Microsoft TCP/IP on Microsoft Windows NT 4.0" exam (# 70-059) covers five main topic areas.

Planning

Given a scenario, identify valid network configurations

Installation and Configuration

Given a scenario, select the appropriate services to install when using Microsoft TCP/IP on a Microsoft Windows NT Server computer

On a Windows NT Server computer, configure Microsoft TCP/IP to support multiple network adapters

Configure scopes by using DHCP Manager

Install and configure a WINS server

- ▶ Import LMHOSTS files to WINS
- ▶ Run WINS on a multihomed computer
- ▶ Configure WINS replication
- ▶ Configure static mappings in the WINS database

Configure subnet masks

Configure a Windows NT Server computer to function as an IP router

- ▶ Install and configure the DHCP Relay Agent

Install and configure the Microsoft DNS Server service on a Windows NT Server computer

- ▶ Integrate DNS with other name servers
- ▶ Connect a DNS server to a DNS root server
- ▶ Configure DNS server roles

Configure HOSTS and LMHOSTS files

Configure a Windows NT Server computer to support TCP/IP printing

Configure SNMP

Connectivity

Given a scenario, identify which utility to use to connect to a TCP/IP-based UNIX host

Configure a RAS server and dial-up networking for use on a TCP/IP network

Configure and support browsing in a multiple-domain routed network

Monitoring and Optimization

Given a scenario, identify which tool to use to monitor TCP/IP traffic

Troubleshooting

Diagnose and resolve IP addressing problems

Use Microsoft TCP/IP utilities to diagnose IP configuration problems

▶ Identify which Microsoft TCP/IP utility to use to diagnose IP configuration problems

Diagnose and resolve name resolution problems

Internet Information Server 4

The "Implementing and Supporting Microsoft Internet Information Server 4.0" exam (# 70-087) covers seven main areas.

Planning

Choose a security strategy for various situations. Security considerations include:

- ▶ Controlling anonymous access

- ▶ Controlling access to known users and groups

- ▶ Controlling access by host or network

- ▶ Configuring SSL to provide encryption and authentication schemes

- ▶ Identifying the appropriate balance between security requirements and performance requirements

Choose an implementation strategy for an Internet site or an intranet site for stand-alone servers, single-domain environments, and multiple-domain environments. Tasks include:

- ▶ Resolving host header name issues by using a HOSTS file or DNS, or both

- ▶ Choosing the appropriate operating system on which to install IIS

Choose the appropriate technology to resolve specified problems. Technology options include:

- ▶ WWW service

- ▶ FTP Service

- ▶ Microsoft Transaction Server

- ▶ Microsoft SMTP Service

- ▶ Microsoft NNTP Service

- ▶ Microsoft Index Server

- ▶ Microsoft Certificate Server

Installation And Configuration

Install IIS. Tasks include:

- ▶ Configuring a Microsoft Windows NT Server 4.0 computer for the installation of IIS

- ▶ Identifying differences to a Windows NT Server 4.0 computer made by the installation of IIS

Configure IIS to support the FTP service. Tasks include:

- ▶ Setting bandwidth and user connections

- ▶ Setting user logon requirements and authentication requirements

- ▶ Modifying port settings

- ▶ Setting directory listing style

- ▶ Configuring virtual directories and servers

Configure IIS to support the WWW service. Tasks include:

- ▶ Setting bandwidth and user connections

- ▶ Setting user logon requirements and authentication requirements

- ▶ Modifying port settings

- ▶ Setting default pages

- ▶ Setting HTTP 1.1 host header names to host multiple Web sites

- ▶ Enabling HTTP Keep-Alives

Configure and save consoles by using Microsoft Management Console

Verify server settings by accessing the metabase

Choose the appropriate administration method

Install and configure Certificate Server

Install and configure Microsoft SMTP Service

Install and configure Microsoft NNTP Service

Customize the installation of Microsoft Site Server Express Content Analyzer

Customize the installation of Microsoft Site Server Express Usage Import and Report Writer

Configuring and Managing Resource Access

Create and share directories with appropriate permissions. Tasks include:

▶ Setting directory-level permissions

▶ Setting file-level permissions

Create and share local and remote virtual directories with appropriate permissions. Tasks include:

▶ Creating a virtual directory and assigning an alias

▶ Setting directory-level permissions

▶ Setting file-level permissions

Create and share virtual servers with appropriate permissions. Tasks include:

▶ Assigning IP addresses

Write scripts to manage the FTP service or the WWW service

Manage a Web site by using Content Analyzer. Tasks include:

▶ Creating, customizing, and navigating WebMaps

▶ Examining a Web site by using the various reports provided by Content Analyzer

▶ Tracking links by using a WebMap

Configure Microsoft SMTP Service to host personal mailboxes

Configure Microsoft NNTP Service to host a newsgroup

Configure Certificate Server to issue certificates

Configure Index Server to index a Web site

Manage MIME types

Manage the FTP service

Manage the WWW service

Integration and Interoperability

Configure IIS to connect to a database. Tasks include:

▶ Configuring ODBC

Configure IIS to integrate with Index Server. Tasks include:

▶ Specifying query parameters by creating the .idq file

▶ Specifying how the query results are formatted and displayed to the user by creating the .htx file

Running Applications

Configure IIS to support server-side scripting

Configure IIS to run ISAPI applications

Configure IIS to support ADO associated with the WWW service

Monitoring and Optimization

Maintain a log for fine-tuning and auditing purposes. Tasks include:

▶ Importing log files into a Usage Import and Report Writer Database

▶ Configuring the logging features of the WWW service

▶ Configuring the logging features of the FTP service

▶ Configuring Usage Import and Report Writer to analyze logs created by the WWW service or the FTP service

▶ Automating the use of Report Writer and Usage Import

Monitor performance of various functions by using Performance Monitor. Functions include HHTP and FTP sessions.

Analyze performance. Performance issues include:

▶ Identifying bottlenecks

▶ Identifying network-related performance issues

▶ Identifying disk-related performance issues

▶ Identifying CPU-related performance issues

Optimize performance of IIS

Optimize performance of Index Server

Optimize performance of Microsoft SMTP Service

Optimize performance of Microsoft NNTP Service

Interpret performance data

Optimize a Web Site by using Content Analyzer

Troubleshooting

Resolve IIS configuration problems

Resolve security problems

Resolve resource access problems

Resolve Index Server query problems

Resolve setup issues when installing IIS on a Windows NT Server 4.0 computer

Use a WebMap to find and repair broken links, hyperlink texts, headings, and titles

Resolve WWW service problems

Resolve FTP service problems

Hardware and Software Needed

As a self-paced study guide, this book was designed with the expectation that you will use Windows NT 4, Microsoft TCP/IP, and IIS 4 as you follow along through the exercises while you learn. Microsoft designed these products to operate in a wide range of actual situations, and the exercises in this book encompass that range. Your computer should meet the following criteria:

- ▶ On the Microsoft Hardware Compatibility List

- ▶ 486DX2 66-Mhz (or better) processor for Windows NT Server

- ▶ Minimum of 32 MB of RAM; 48 MB of RAM is required if SQL Server is installed on the same computer

- ▶ 340-MB (or larger) hard disk for Windows NT Server, 100 MB free and formatted as NTFS

- ▶ 3.5-inch 1.44-MB floppy drive

- ▶ VGA (or Super VGA) video adapter

- ▶ VGA (or Super VGA) monitor

- ▶ Mouse or equivalent pointing device

- ▶ Two-speed (or faster) CD-ROM drive (optional)

- ▶ Network Interface Card (NIC)

- ▶ Presence on an existing network, or use of a 2-port (or more) mini-port hub to create a test network

- ▶ MS-DOS 5.0 or 6.*x* and Microsoft Windows for Workgroups 3.*x* pre-installed

- ▶ Microsoft Windows 95

- ▶ Microsoft Windows NT Server version 4.0 (CD-ROM version)

It is somewhat easier to obtain access to the necessary computer hardware and software in a corporate business environment. It can be difficult, however, to allocate enough time within the busy workday to complete a self-study program. Most of your study time will occur after normal working hours, away from the everyday interruptions and pressures of your regular job.

Tips for the Exam

Remember the following tips as you prepare for the certification exams:

- ▶ **Read all the material.** Microsoft has been known to include material not expressly specified in the objectives. This course has included additional information not required by the objectives in an effort to give you the best possible preparation for the examination, and for the real-world network experiences to come.

▶ **Complete the exercises in each chapter.** They will help you gain experience using the Microsoft product. All Microsoft exams are experienced-based and require you to have used the Microsoft product in a real networking environment. Exercises for each objective are placed at the end of each chapter.

▶ **Take each pre-chapter quiz to evaluate how well you know the topic of the chapter.** Each chapter opens with at least one short answer/essay question per exam objective covered in the chapter. At the very end of the chapter you will find the quiz answers and pointers to where in the chapter that specific objective is covered.

▶ **Complete all the questions in the "Review Questions" sections.** Complete the questions at the end of each chapter—they help you remember key points. The questions are fairly simple, but be warned: some questions require more than one answer.

▶ **Review the exam objectives.** Develop your own questions for each topic listed. If you can make and answer several questions for each topic, you should not find it difficult to pass the exam.

 Note

Although this book is designed to prepare you to take and pass the MCP+I certification exams, there are no guarantees. Read this book, work through the questions and exercises, and when you feel confident, take a practice assessment exam using the TestPrep test engine. This should tell you whether or not you are ready for the real thing.

When taking the actual certification exam, make sure you answer all the questions before your time limit expires. Do not spend too much time on any one question. If you are unsure about an answer, answer the question as best you can and mark it for later review. You can revisit marked items when you have finished the rest of the questions.

Remember, the primary object is not to pass the exam—it is to understand the material. After you understand the material, passing the exam should be simple. Knowledge is a pyramid; to build upward, you need a solid foundation. The Microsoft Certified Professional programs are designed to ensure that you have that solid foundation.

Good luck!

New Riders Publishing

The staff of New Riders Publishing is committed to bringing you the very best in computer reference material. Each New Riders book is the result of months of work by authors and staff who research and refine the information contained within its covers.

As part of this commitment to you, the NRP reader, New Riders invites your input. Please let us know if you enjoy this book, if you have trouble with the information or examples presented, or if you have a suggestion for the next edition.

Please note, however, that New Riders staff cannot serve as a technical resource during your preparation for the Microsoft certification exams or for questions about software- or hardware-related problems. Please refer instead to the documentation that accompanies the software or hardware or to the applications' Help systems.

If you have a question or comment about any New Riders book, there are several ways to contact New Riders Publishing. We will respond to as many readers as we can. Your name, address, or phone number will never become part of a mailing list or be used for any purpose other than to help us continue to bring you the best books possible. You can write to us at the following address:

New Riders Publishing
Attn: Publisher
201 W. 103rd Street
Indianapolis, IN 46290

If you prefer, you can fax New Riders Publishing at (317) 581-4663.

You also can send email to New Riders at the following Internet address:

certification@mcp.com

NRP is an imprint of Macmillan Computer Publishing. To obtain a catalog or information, or to purchase any Macmillan Computer Publishing book, call (800) 428-5331.

Thank you for selecting *MCP+I Training Guide: Internet Exams*!

P a r t 1

Windows NT Server 4

Chapter 1

Stop! Before reading this chapter, test yourself to determine how much study time you will need to devote to this section.

1. Which of the following Windows NT machines can participate in a work-group?

   A. A Windows NT Server Primary Domain Controller (PDC).

   B. A Windows NT Server Backup Domain Controller (BDC).

   C. A Windows NT Server stand-alone server.

   D. None of the above.

2. The _____ partition holds the files needed to boot your computer.

   A. Primary

   B. System

   C. Boot

   D. None of the above

3. The NTFS file system is generally more efficient for partitions larger than _____ MB.

   A. 50

   B. 100

   C. 400

   D. 800

4. The principal disadvantage of the NetBEUI protocol is: _____.

   A. NetBEUI is slow

   B. NetBEUI is difficult to configure

   C. NetBEUI is not routable

   D. NetBEUI is not compatible with Microsoft Client for MS-DOS.

Answers

1. C (see "Workgroups")
2. B (see "Boot and System Partitions")
3. C (see "NTFS")
4. C (see "NetBEUI")

Chapter

Planning

This chapter will help you prepare for the "Planning" section of Microsoft's Exam 70-67, "Implementing and Supporting Microsoft Windows NT Server." Microsoft provides the following objectives for the "Planning" section:

Test Objectives

> ▶ Plan the disk drive configuration for various requirements. Requirements include choosing a file system and choosing a fault-tolerance method.
>
> ▶ Choose a protocol for various situations. Protocols include TCP/IP, NWLink IPX/SPX Compatible Transport, Net-BEUI.

Microsoft grew up around the personal computer industry and as of this writing has established itself as the preeminent maker of software products for computers. Microsoft has a vast portfolio of software products, but is best known for its operating systems.

Microsoft's current operating system products, listed here, are undoubtedly well known to anyone studying for the MCSE exams:

▶ Windows 95

▶ Windows NT Workstation

▶ Windows NT Server

Some older operating system products—namely, MS-DOS, Windows 3.1, and Windows for Workgroups—are still important to the operability of Windows NT Server, so don't be surprised if you hear them mentioned from time to time in this book.

Windows NT is the most powerful, the most secure, and perhaps the most elegant operating system Microsoft has yet produced. It languished for a while after it first appeared (in part because no one was sure why they needed it or what to do with it), but Microsoft has persisted with improving interoperability and performance. With the release of Windows NT 4 and the arrival of a new Windows 95-like user interface, Windows NT seems destined to assume a prominent place in today's world of network-based computing.

This chapter introduces you to Windows NT Server and Windows NT Workstation—the two flavors, you might say, of Windows NT. This chapter compares NT to Windows 95 and also compares the workgroup and the domain, the two basic network archetypes of Windows NT networking. This chapter also examines some planning issues you need to address before you set up your Windows NT network: specifically, choosing a disk configuration and choosing a network protocol.

Windows NT Among Microsoft Operating Systems

As already mentioned, Microsoft has three operating system products now competing in the marketplace—Windows 95, Windows NT Workstation, and Windows NT Server. Each of these operating system products has advantages and each has some disadvantages. These three operating systems have begun to look very much alike with the arrival of Windows NT 4. Each comes with the familiar Windows 95 user interface, featuring the Start button, the Recycling Bin, My Computer, and the ever-useful Explorer, but each is a specific product designed for specific situations. The following sections describe these Microsoft operating systems and delineate their similarities and differences.

Windows NT Server and Windows NT Workstation are essentially the same under the hood, though they include some different utilities and are optimized for different purposes. The term *Windows NT* is a collective name for these two very similar products.

Windows 95

Windows 95 is Microsoft's everyday, workhorse operating system. It provides a 32-bit platform and is designed to operate with a great variety of peripherals. Here are the minimum hardware requirements for Windows 95:

- ▶ 386DX/20 processor or better

- ▶ 4 MB RAM (8 MB is recommended)

- ▶ 40 MB of free disk space

Like Windows NT, Windows 95 supports preemptive multitasking, but unlike Windows NT, doesn't support multiple processors. Windows 95 supports Plug and Play, not to mention a vast number of hardware devices and device drivers (more than Windows NT).

Windows 95 supports 16-bit and 32-bit Windows and MS-DOS applications, including applications that access the hardware directly.

Windows 95 only runs on Intel platforms.

Windows 95 uses the FAT files system, which is less secure than the NTFS file system that Windows NT supports. Windows NT also supports FAT, but NT does not support the FAT32 file system that is supported by recent versions of Windows 95 (OEM Release 2).

You can network a Windows 95 computer in a workgroup (described later in this chapter in the section "Workgroups"), and you can use a Windows 95 computer as a client in a domain-based Windows NT network. However, Windows 95 alone cannot provide a network with centralized authentication and security.

Windows NT Workstation

The original Windows NT operating system has now evolved into a pair of operating system products—Windows NT Workstation and Windows NT Server. These two products are very similar; some might say they are virtually the same except that they include some different tools and are tuned and configured for different roles. NT Server, discussed in the next section, is designed to operate as a network server and domain controller. NT Workstation, like Windows 95, is designed to serve as a network client and desktop operating system.

When Windows 95 first appeared, it seemed that Microsoft planned for Windows 95 to inherit the market of Windows 3.1 (general-use desktop computing for business and consumer), and for Windows NT to focus on the specialty market of professionals, such as programmers who require extra processing power. Now it seems that Windows NT Workstation (with its stability, portability, and airtight security) is poised to assume a large share of the corporate desktop market.

Windows NT Workstation can serve as a stand-alone operating system, act as a client in a domain-based NT network, or participate in a workgroup.

The most striking difference between Windows NT Workstation and Windows 95 is their security. Windows NT Workstation is an extremely secure operating system, and for almost every facet of Windows NT administration and configuration, there are security implications. Windows NT provides security for files, directories, printers, and nearly everything else; in fact, a user must be authenticated to even use Windows NT at all.

Windows NT Workstation requires somewhat more powerful hardware than does Windows 95. Windows NT Workstation's minimum hardware requirements are as follows:

- ▶ 486DX/33 or better processor

- ▶ 12 MB of RAM (16 MB recommended)

- ▶ 120 MB of free disk space

Windows NT is designed to provide system stability; each application can run in its own memory address space. Windows NT supports preemptive multiprocessing and as well as true multiprocessing (more than one processor).

Windows NT doesn't support as many devices as Windows 95 and seems a bit more myopic when it comes to detecting and installing new hardware.

Although Windows NT doesn't support the vast array of devices Windows 95 supports, it supports more processor platforms. Because Windows NT is written mostly in C, it can be compiled separately for different processors. In addition to the Intel platform, versions of Windows NT are available for RISC, MIPS, DEC Alpha, and PowerPC-based systems.

Microsoft designed Windows NT for backward-compatibility with MS-DOS 5.0, Windows 3.1x, OS/2 1.x, and lateral-compatibility with POSIX-based applications. No other operating system supports such a broad spectrum of applications. For security and stability reasons, however, Windows NT doesn't allow applications to directly access the hardware; MS-DOS applications and other legacy applications that attempt to access the hardware directly will run into trouble with Windows NT.

Windows NT Server

When Windows NT 3.1 and Windows NT Advanced Server 3.1 debuted, the marketplace experienced quite a bit of confusion over what the distinction was between the two products. Windows NT Server had some clear advantages, however; unlike Windows NT 3.1, it supported Macintosh clients, for example, and availed its users of RAID fault tolerance. Still, if you just needed a file or print server, Windows NT 3.1 performed just as well as Windows NT Advanced Server 3.1, a situation which resulted in a potentially unprofitable situation for Microsoft.

With the introduction of Windows NT Workstation 3.5 and Windows NT Server 3.5, the two operating systems were tweaked in such a way as to make them different from each other in terms of performance and capacity and features. With version 4, NT Server and NT Workstation continue to differentiate themselves as they adapt to their respective markets. The next few sections go over the major (along with some minor) differences between Windows NT Workstation and Server.

Features

The following features are available on Windows NT Server but not on Windows NT Workstation:

▶ Services for Macintosh

▶ RAID fault tolerance

▶ Domain logon validation

▶ Directory replication

▶ Windows NT Directory Services (NTDS)

▶ Multiprotocol routing and advanced network services, such as DNS, DHCP, and WINS

Capacity

The following facets of Windows NT differ in capacity on Workstation and Server:

▶ **Concurrent Client Sessions.** Windows NT Server supports an unlimited number of inbound sessions; Windows NT Workstation supports no more than 10 active sessions at the same time.

▶ **Remote Access Sessions.** Windows NT Server accommodates an unlimited number of Remote Access connections (although Microsoft only supports up to 256); Windows NT Workstation supports only a single Remote Access connection.

▶ **Multiprocessors.** Although both Windows NT Workstation and Server can support up to 32 processors in an OEM (Original Equipment Manufacturer) configuration, Windows NT Workstation can only support two processors out-of-the-box, whereas Windows NT Server can support four.

▶ **Internet Service.** Both NT Workstation and NT Server come with Internet-type server applications, but the NT Server application (Internet Application Server) is more powerful and better suited to the open Internet than is the

NT Workstation application (Peer Web Services), which is designed primarily for in-house intranets. (Personal Web server software packages are available for Windows 95 systems.)

▶ **BackOffice Support.** Both NT Workstation and NT Server provide support for the Microsoft BackOffice family of software products (SQL Server, Systems Management Server, SNA Server, Exchange Server), but NT Server provides a higher level of support for BackOffice products.

Performance

Microsoft did some performance tuning to both Windows NT Workstation and Server to help them function more appropriately for their intended purposes. Some of the differences are as follows:

▶ Windows NT Workstation preloads a Virtual DOS Machine (VDM), the 32-bit MS-DOS emulator that supports legacy applications. Because older applications are more likely to run on a workstation than a server, the preloading of the VDM speeds up the load time of the first DOS or Win16 application started, at the expense of the RAM used by the VDM, which most likely would need to be loaded anyway. Windows NT Server devotes that RAM to caching and other server operations, because it is not as likely that an MS-DOS- or Win16-based application will be run on a server. This is not to imply that servers cannot run these applications, only that the first such applications executed are slower to load.

▶ Caching is handled differently on workstations and servers, enabling better network throughput on Windows NT Server and better local disk access time on Windows NT Workstation.

▶ Windows NT Server includes a configurable server service that enables you to tune the server as an application server or as a file/print server. Windows NT Workstation does not provide this feature, because it is limited to 10 inbound sessions.

▶ The server files system driver used in both Windows NT Workstation and Server (SRV.SYS) is more subject to paging under Windows NT Workstation than under Windows NT

Server. When Windows NT Workstation runs out of physical RAM, it pages the server code out to disk, which means its network sharing performance takes a hit, but local application performance gets a boost. Windows NT Server does not ever page much of the server code out; it is designed as a server, so it would not make much sense to impair that side of its functionality.

Minimum Hardware Requirements

The minimum requirements for NT Server and NT Workstation are roughly the same, but NT Server needs a little more RAM and a little more disk space, namely:

▶ 486DX/33 processor

▶ 16 MB of RAM

▶ 130 MB of disk space

Workgroups and Domains

Every networked Windows NT-based computer participates in a workgroup or a domain. The difference between a workgroup and a domain boils down to the question of where the user accounts will be stored.

Users must—and it should be stressed that this logon process is completely mandatory—log on to Windows NT to use a Windows NT-based computer.

When a user successfully logs on to Windows NT, it generates an access token, which contains the user's security identifier and group identifiers, as well as the user rights granted through the User Rights policy in User Manager or User Manager for Domains.

The access token identifies the user and all processes spawned by the user. No action can take place on a Windows NT system without somebody's access token attached to it.

Workgroups

A workgroup is a collection of computers in which each computer is like a sovereign state with its own set of security policies and accounts. The security information necessary to verify the user's credentials and generate the access token resides on the local machine. Thus, every Windows NT computer in a workgroup must contain accounts for each person who might ever need to access the workstation (see fig. 1.1). This involves a great deal of administration in workgroups that consist of more than a few members. If a user changes her password on her own workstation, for example, the administrator must connect to every other workstation in the workgroup and change the user's password on those computers as well; otherwise, the user can't access resources beyond her own computer.

Figure 1.1

In a workgroup, each computer is responsible for its own security and each computer maintains its own accounts database.

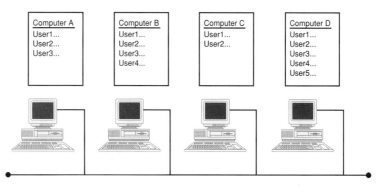

A workgroup is, however, simpler than a domain and easier to install. A workgroup does not require an NT Server machine acting as a domain controller, and the decentralized administration of a workgroup can be an advantage in small networks because it does not depend on the health of a few key server and controller machines.

Unless a Windows NT Server computer is configured as a stand-alone server, it cannot participate in a workgroup (see Chapter 2, "Installation and Configuration"). Windows NT Workstation computers, Windows 95 computers, and older networkable Microsoft systems, such as Windows for Workgroups, can participate in workgroups.

When you log on to a Windows NT machine in a workgroup, you are logging on to that specific machine; the local security database verifies your credentials. The local machine performs the following steps when you log on directly to a Windows NT computer:

1. WinLogon asks for your user name and password, which it then sends to the Local Security Authority (LSA).

2. The LSA sends the user name and password to the Security Accounts Manager (SAM), which looks for the user name and password in the directory database and notifies the LSA whether they are approved.

3. The LSA creates an access token with the user's assigned rights, and passes it to the WinLogon process.

4. The WinLogon process completes the logon, and then starts a new process for the user (usually Explorer.exe). The user's access token is attached to the new process.

Domains

In a domain environment, all nodes must authenticate logon requests with a domain controller that contains the central accounts database for the entire domain (see fig. 1.2). A password needs to be changed only one time to be usable on any member computer of the domain. Likewise, a user needs only a single account to access resources anywhere in the domain. Only Windows NT Server machines can serve as domain controllers in a Windows NT network.

Figure 1.2

In a domain, security and account information resides on one or more domain controllers, and logon requests pass across the network to the domain controller for authentication.

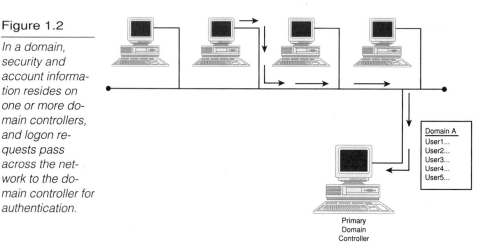

Domain A
User1...
User2...
User3...
User4...
User5...

Primary
Domain
Controller

The logon process is somewhat more complicated for a domain because logon information must pass from the local machine (where the user is sitting) to the domain controller, and back again. This network logon process requires the NetLogon service.

The procedure is as follows:

1. WinLogon sends the user name and password to the Local Security Authority (LSA).

2. The LSA passes the request to the local NetLogon service.

3. The local NetLogon service sends the logon information to the NetLogon service on the domain controller.

4. The NetLogon service on the domain controller passes the information to the domain controller's Security Accounts Manager (SAM).

5. The SAM asks the domain directory database for approval of the user name and password.

6. The SAM passes the result of the approval request to the domain controller's NetLogon service.

7. The domain controller's NetLogon service passes the result of the approval request to the client's NetLogon service.

8. The client's NetLogon service passes the result of the approval request to the LSA.

9. If the logon is approved, the LSA creates an access token and passes it to the WinLogon process.

10. WinLogon completes the logon, thus creating a new process for the user and attaching the access token to the new process.

Choosing a Disk Configuration

One of the first tasks in planning a network is deciding on a disk configuration for each of the computers that will make up the network. Each computer will have its own disk configuration, but this book (and the Windows NT Server exam) targets the disk configuration options available in Windows NT Server systems.

The following sections highlight some specific planning issues related to disk configuration under Windows NT, as follows:

▶ Partitions

▶ Extended and primary partitions

▶ The boot and the system partitions

▶ Windows NT file systems

▶ Windows NT fault-tolerance methods

The topic of hard disks in Windows NT arises again in Chapter 2, which looks at disk configuration issues, and in Chapter 3, "Managing Resources," which looks at managing disk resources. The following sections concentrate on planning issues and provide the background you need to understand the later material.

Microsoft lists the following objective for the Windows NT Server exam:

Plan the disk drive configuration for various requirements. Requirements include choosing a file system and choosing a fault-tolerance method.

Partitions

A *partition* is a logical organization of a physical disk. Such an operating system as Windows NT can subdivide a disk drive into several partitions. Each partition is formatted separately. Windows NT assigns a different drive letter to each of the partitions, and users interact separately with each partition as if each partition were a separate disk drive.

Partitioning is the act of defining a partition and associating that partition with an area (or areas) of free space from a hard disk.

You must partition an area of free space before you can format it with a file system. After you have formatted the partition with a supported file system, you can use the partition for storing files and directories.

As you plan your Windows NT configuration, you must make some decisions about the arrangement of partitions on your disk drive. You must choose whether each partition will be a *primary partition* or an *extended partition*. You also need to designate a *system partition* and a *boot partition* for your Windows NT installation. The following sections discuss some of these concepts.

Primary and Extended Partitions

Windows NT provides the following two types of partitions:

- ▶ **Primary partitions.** A primary partition cannot be subdivided and is capable of supporting a bootable operating system. One hard disk can contain up to four primary partitions. Thus, you can assign up to four drive letters to a disk if you use only primary partitions.

- ▶ **Extended partitions.** An extended partition can be subdivided into smaller logical drives (see fig. 1.3). This feature enables you to assign more than four drive letters to the disk. An extended partition does not support a bootable operating system. The system partition therefore cannot reside on an extended partition (see next section). One hard disk can contain only one extended partition.

If you choose to use an extended partition of a hard disk, you are limited to three (rather than four) primary partitions for that disk.

MS-DOS 5.0 and earlier MS-DOS systems cannot recognize more than one primary partition per disk.

Figure 1.3

A physical disk can consist of up to four primary partitions or up to three primary partitions and one extended partition. An extended partition can be subdivided into logical drives.

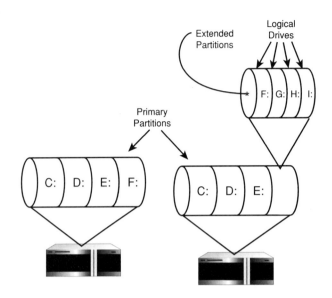

> You do not ever absolutely need to create an extended partition. If you do create one, however, remember that there can never be more than one on each physical disk under any circumstances.

On an Intel-based computer, one primary partition must be marked *active.* The active partition is then used to boot the computer (see the next section). Because any primary partition of sufficient size can support a bootable operating system, one advantage of using multiple primary partitions is that you can isolate different operating systems on different partitions.

> For file-management reasons, it may be advantageous to place the alternative operating system on a separate primary partition. You can, however, also achieve a dual-boot capability with both operating systems on the same partition.

If you install Windows NT on a computer with another operating system in place, the active partition does not change. If you install Windows NT on a new computer, the partition created by Setup becomes the active partition.

Boot and System Partitions

The *system* partition is the partition that contains the files necessary to boot the operating system. (See Chapter 2 for a description of which files these are.) The system partition does not have to be the partition on which Windows NT is installed.

The partition that holds the Windows NT operating system files is called the *boot partition*. If your system boots from drive C, and you install Windows NT on drive D, then drive C is your system partition and drive D is your boot partition (see fig. 1.4). If you boot from drive C, and Windows NT is installed on drive C, then drive C is both the system partition and the boot partition.

Figure 1.4

The partition that boots the computer is the system partition; the partition that holds the Windows NT directory is the boot partition. Note that these names are counterintuitive.

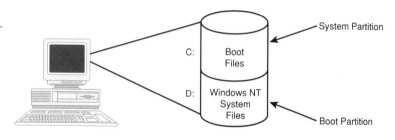

Recall from the preceding section that the active partition is the partition used to boot the system. The system partition must therefore be the active partition.

Yes, it sounds backward, but it is true: Windows NT boots from the system partition and then loads the system from the boot partition.

By the way, active partitions are only a relevant concept for Intel-based computers; RISC-based computers use a hardware configuration utility to designate the system partition.

Windows NT File Systems

After a partition has been created, it must be formatted with a supported *file system*. A file system is a system for organizing and managing the data on a disk. Windows NT supports three file systems: FAT (File Allocation Table), NTFS (NT File System), and CDFS (Compact Disk File System). CDFS is a read-only file system for CD-ROMs, so you can immediately rule it out for hard disk partitions. Each partition must use either the FAT file system or the NTFS file system. You need to understand the advantages and limitations of each file system before you can decide which is best for your system. The following sections introduce you to the FAT and NTFS file systems. Chapter 2 explains more about these file system.

FAT

The venerable File Allocation Table (FAT) file system was originally invented for MS-DOS. FAT is now supported by Windows NT, Windows 95, and OS/2, making it the most universally accepted and supported file system (see fig. 1.5). For this reason alone, you should seriously consider using FAT for your partitions.

Figure 1.5

The FAT file system is accessible from more operating systems than NTFS, but FAT doesn't provide the NTFS advantages.

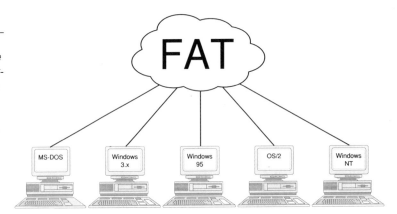

Earlier versions of FAT forced users to use short file names (eight characters plus a three-character extension), but Windows NT overcomes the 8.3 limitation on FAT partitions. Users

continues

can create files with up to 255 characters, as well as spaces
and even multiple extensions in the file name. (Short file
names are still maintained for compatibility with legacy applications and dual-boot systems.)

FAT has a lower overhead than its high-tech counterpart NTFS
(less than 1 MB, compared to an average of 5–10 MB for NTFS),
and FAT is typically the more efficient file system for small partitions (under 200 MB).

Some of the disadvantages of FAT are as follows:

- ▶ FAT is generally slower than NTFS. It takes longer to find
  and access files. For partitions greater than 200 MB, FAT
  performance degrades quickly.

- ▶ The maximum file, directory, or partition size under FAT is
  only 4 GB. Also, because Windows NT does not support any
  FAT compression software, including Microsoft's own
  DriveSpace and DoubleSpace, you cannot conserve space by
  compressing files on a FAT partition.

- ▶ FAT does not offer the security features offered by NTFS
  (see the following section).

- ▶ If the power fails during a disk transaction, the FAT file system may be left with cross-linked files or orphan clusters.

You should use the FAT file system if you will be dual-booting your
computer with another operating system and you wish to access
the partition from the other operating system.

MS-DOS and Windows 95 provide no native support for NTFS;
however, software aids that read NTFS partitions, such as the
NTFSDOS file system driver, have begun to emerge. These
aids are not full implementations of NTFS. They do not, for
example, support NTFS security.

If your Windows NT computer is a RISC-based system, your C drive should be FAT-formatted with at least 2 MB free space.

NTFS

For an exercise testing this information, see end of chapter.

The New Technology File System (NTFS) is designed to fully exploit the features and capabilities of Windows NT. For partitions larger than the range of 200–400 MB, the NTFS file system far outshines the FAT file system. The biggest drawback with using NTFS is that only the Windows NT operating system can access NTFS partitions (see fig. 1.6). If you plan to sometimes boot your computer under a different operating system, such as MS-DOS or Windows 95, you should be aware that the other operating system cannot access an NTFS partition.

Figure 1.6

The NTFS file system is accessible only from Windows NT—it provides a number of advantages for Windows NT users.

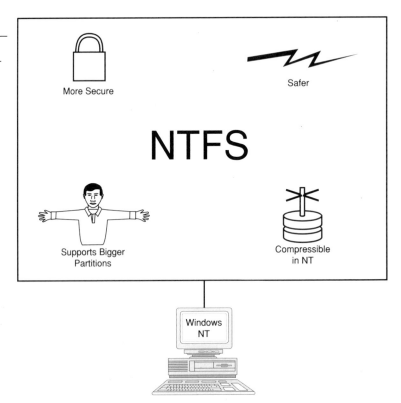

When partitions exceed 400 MB (on average), NTFS is your most reasonable choice. Remember that 400 MB is only an average; actual performance owes more to the number of files than to the size of the files.

NTFS is generally faster than FAT, and NTFS supports bigger partitions. (NTFS files and partitions can be up to 16 exabytes—an exabyte is one billion gigabytes, or 2^{64} bytes.) NTFS is also safer. NTFS supports sector sparing, also known as hot fixing, on SCSI hard drives. If a sector fails on an NTFS partition of a SCSI hard drive, NTFS tries to write the data to a good sector (if the data is still in memory) and map out the bad sector so that it is not reused. NTFS keeps a transaction log while it works. If the power fails, leaving NTFS in a possibly corrupt state, the CHKDSK command that executes when the system boots attempts to redo the transaction (in the case of a delete, for example), or undo the transaction (in the case of a file write where the data is no longer in memory). Two other principal advantages of NTFS are as follows:

▶ **File-level security.** NTFS enables you to assign specific permissions to individual files and directories.

▶ **File compression.** Windows NT provides the capability to compress NTFS files. Traditional FAT compression utilities, including Microsoft's own DriveSpace and DoubleSpace, won't work under Windows NT.

You should use NTFS if you wish to preserve existing permissions when you migrate files and directories from a NetWare server to a Windows NT Server system. Also, if you wish to allow Macintosh computers to access files on the partition through Windows NT's Services for Macintosh, you must format the partition for NTFS.

Like FAT, NTFS can handle long file names, up to 255 unicode characters. (Unicode is a method of including all foreign language characters in a single character set.) NTFS also maintains a short 8.3-compliant file name for compatibility with legacy applications.

Because NTFS has a higher overhead, somewhere between 4.5 and 10 MB for the file system itself, you cannot use the NTFS file system for floppy disks.

Choosing a File System

Here's a quick summary of the differences between file systems:

Feature	FAT	NTFS
File name length	255	255
8.3 file name compatibility	Yes	Yes
File size	4 GB	16 EB
Partition size	4 GB	16 EB
Directory structure	Linked list	B-tree
Local security	No	Yes
Transaction tracking	No	Yes
Hot fixing	No	Yes
Overhead	1 MB	>2 MB (avg. 4.5–10)
Required for RISC-based computers	Yes	No
Accessible from MS-DOS/ Windows 95	Yes	No
Accessible from OS/2	Yes	No
Case-sensitive	No	POSIX only
Case preserving	Yes	Yes
Compression	No	Yes
Efficiency	<200 MB	>400 MB
Windows NT formattable	Yes	Yes
Convertible	To NTFS only	No
Fragmentation level	High	Low
Floppy disk formattable	Yes	No
Extensible attributes	No	Yes
Creation/modification/ access dates	Yes	Yes

Windows NT provides a utility called Convert.exe that converts a FAT partition to NTFS. There is no utility for directly converting an NTFS partition to FAT. To Change an NTFS partition to FAT, back up all files on the partition, reformat the partition, and then restore the files to the reformatted partition (see Chapter 3).

Fault-Tolerance Methods

Fundamentally, *fault tolerance* is the system's capability to compensate in the event of hardware disaster. The standard for fault tolerance is known as Redundant Array of Inexpensive Disks (RAID). RAID consists of several levels (or categories) of protection that offer a mixture of performance, reliability, and cost. One of the steps in planning your Windows NT system may be to decide on a RAID fault-tolerance method. Windows NT Server offers the following two RAID fault-tolerance methods:

▶ **Disk mirroring (RAID Level 1).** Windows NT writes the same data to two physical disks. If one disk fails, the data is still available on the other disk.

▶ **Disk striping with parity (Raid Level 5).** Windows NT writes data across a series of disks (3 to 32). The data is not duplicated on the disks (as it is with disk mirroring), but Windows NT records parity information that it can use to regenerate missing data if a disk should fail.

The following sections introduce you to disk mirroring and disk striping with parity. Chapter 3 explains more about these important fault-tolerance methods.

It is important to note that the fault-tolerance methods available through Windows NT are software-based RAID implementations. Several hardware vendors offer hardware-based RAID solutions. Hardware-based RAID solutions, which, by the way, can be quite expensive, are beyond the scope of this book and beyond the scope of the Windows NT Server exam.

Disk Mirroring (RAID Level 1)

Disk mirroring calls for all data to be written to two physical disks (see fig. 1.7). A mirror is a redundant copy of a disk partition. You can use any partition, including the boot or system partitions, to establish a mirror.

Figure 1.7

How disk mirroring works.

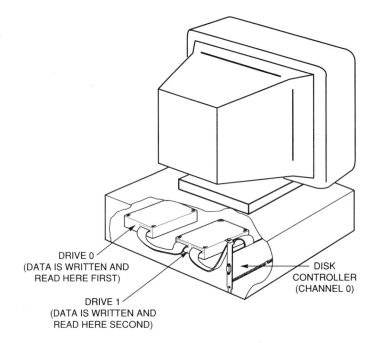

DRIVE 0
(DATA IS WRITTEN AND
READ HERE FIRST)

DRIVE 1
(DATA IS WRITTEN AND
READ HERE SECOND)

DISK
CONTROLLER
(CHANNEL 0)

You can measure the utilization of a fault-tolerance method by the percent of the total disk space devoted to storing the original information. Fifty percent of the data in a disk-mirroring system is redundant data. The percentage utilization is thus also 50 percent, making disk-mirroring less efficient than disk striping with parity. The startup costs for implementing disk mirroring are typically lower, however, because disk mirroring requires only two (rather than 3–32) physical disks.

Disk mirroring slows down write operations slightly (because Windows NT has to write to two disks simultaneously). Read operations are actually slightly faster, because NT can read from both disks simultaneously.

In a typical disk mirroring scenario, a single disk controller writes to both members of the mirror set. If a mirrored disk fails, the user can keep working. If the disk controller fails, however, Windows NT cannot access either disk. *Disk duplexing* is a special kind of disk mirroring that provides a solution for this potential pitfall. In a disk duplexing system, each of the mirrored disks has its own disk controller. The system can therefore endure either a disk failure or a controller failure. Disk duplexing also has some performance advantages, because the two disk controllers can act independently (see fig. 1.8).

Figure 1.8

Disk duplexing.

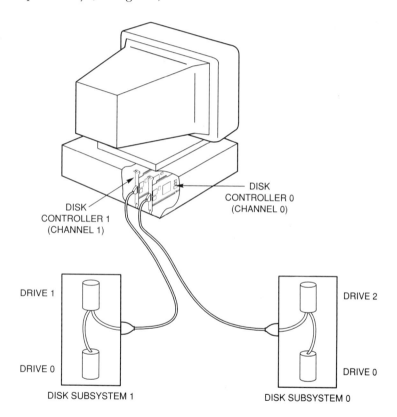

Disk Striping with Parity (RAID Level 5)

A stripe set with parity writes information in *stripes* (or rows) across 3 to 32 disks. For each stripe, there is a parity stripe block on one of the disks. If one of the disks fails, Windows NT can use the parity stripe block to regenerate the missing information. The parity stripe block is the only data that is additional to what the system would need to record the original data without fault tolerance. Disk striping with parity is therefore more efficient than disk mirroring. The percentage of disk space available for storing data is:

$$\% \text{ Utilization} = (\text{no. of disks} - 1) \:/\: \text{no. of disks} \times 100\%$$

If you have five disks, 80 percent of your disk space is available for storing data. This compares with 50 percent for a disk mirroring system. The more disks you add, the more efficient your fault-tolerance becomes. But at the same time, your setup costs also increase as you add more disks.

Windows NT must perform the parity calculations as it writes data to a stripe set with parity. Write operations therefore take three times as much memory if you are using a stripe set with parity. If all disks are working properly, read operations are faster under a stripe set with parity than they are under a mirror set. If a disk fails, however, Windows NT must backfigure the missing data from the parity information, and read operations will slow down considerably.

Any partition except the boot partition and the system partition can be part of a stripe set with parity, provided you have enough other partitions on 3–32 other physical disks.

Choosing a Windows NT Network Protocol

A network protocol is a collection of rules and procedures governing communication among the computers on the a network. In a sense, a protocol is a language your computer uses when speaking to other computers. If two computers don't use the same protocols, they cannot communicate. Windows NT includes several protocols designed for different situations and different networking environments. Later chapters discuss these protocols in more detail. This chapter examines some planning issues relating the three principal Windows NT networking protocols, as follows:

▶ **TCP/IP.** A widely-used, routable protocol that is the basis for communication on the Internet.

▶ **NWLink IPX/SPX Compatible Transport.** Microsoft's rendition of Novell's proprietary IPX/SPX protocol suite. NWLink is a routable protocol designed to enable Windows NT computers to interoperate with Novell NetWare networks.

▶ **NetBEUI.** A very fast but non-routable protocol used on Microsoft networks. Because NetBEUI is non-routable, it is only suitable for Local Area Networks (LANs).

You should learn the advantages and disadvantages of each of these protocols and understand when to use each.

Microsoft lists the following objective for the Windows NT Server exam:

Choose a protocol for various situations. Protocols include TCP/IP, NWLink IPX/SPX Compatible Transport, and NetBEUI.

Protocols and RAS

Windows NT Remote Access Service (RAS) can perform some interesting routing functions. These functions are likely to make their way into the Windows NT Server exam. Chapter 4, "Connectivity," examines RAS in more detail, but for the purposes of preparing for the "Planning" section, keep in mind that RAS can act as a NetBIOS gateway. A RAS client using the NetBEUI protocol can connect to a RAS server and, using the NetBIOS gateway on the RAS server, can gain access to the remote LAN beyond the gateway regardless of which protocol the LAN is using.

RAS can also act as a TCP/IP or IPX router.

TCP/IP

For an exercise testing this information, see end of chapter.

Transmission Control Protocol/Internet Protocol (TCP/IP) is the default protocol for the Intel version of Windows NT. TCP/IP is the only protocol supported on the Internet (which is why it is rocketing toward becoming a global standard protocol).

Windows NT's version of the TCP/IP protocol, Microsoft TCP/IP, is a 32-bit native suite of protocols. It requires more configuration than other protocols, but Microsoft also provides some excellent configuration tools. The end result is a cross-platform, industry-standard, routable network implementation that you can expect only to grow in popularity.

The important things to remember about TCP/IP are as follows:

- ▶ **TCP/IP is routable.** Because TCP/IP packets can be forwarded through routers, you can use TCP/IP on Wide Area Networks (WANs). (The NetBEUI protocol, by contrast, can only be used on Local Area Networks.)

- ▶ **TCP/IP is the language of the Internet.** If your Windows NT computer will be connected to the Internet, you need to use TCP/IP.

- ▶ **TCP/IP is a widely accepted standard.** You can interconnect with more networks worldwide if you are using TCP/IP.

- ▶ **TCP/IP accommodates a wide range of network hardware, operating systems, and applications.**

TCP/IP comes with a number of useful utilities that facilitate network configuration and administration. Chapter 2 explains more about those TCP/IP utilities.

You implement TCP/IP on your network with the help of three important services: Dynamic Host Configuration Protocol (DHCP), Domain Name System (DNS), and Windows Internet Name Service (WINS). To plan your TCP/IP network, you need a basic understanding of these services, especially if you plan to connect your local LAN with a Wide Area Network or with the Internet.

The Internet Protocol (the IP in TCP/IP) sends packets using a computer's IP Address—a unique 32-bit binary number that no other computer on the network can possess. (More precisely, it is not every computer but rather every network adapter card that requires its own IP Address.)

The 32-bit IP address usually is expressed as four octets, or 8-bit numbers, which then are represented in decimal form. An 8-bit number can have a value of anywhere from 0 to 255, so an IP address consists of four numbers between 0 and 255 separated by decimal points (for example, 111.12.3.141).

Every computer on a TCP/IP network must have an IP address. You can configure a permanent IP address for each computer or you can configure each computer to receive a dynamically assigned IP address from a Dynamic Host Protocol (DHCP) server. (See Chapter 2 for more information on configuring TCP/IP.) A DHCP server is assigned a range of IP addresses. The DHCP server then "leases" (assigns for a limited duration) these IP addresses to DHCP clients in the subnet. A computer running Windows NT Server can act as a DHCP server, a DHCP client, or a DHCP relay agent. A DHCP relay agent forwards DHCP broadcast messages across an IP router to a DHCP server on a different subnet.

The decimal octet form of an IP address is easier to remember than its binary equivalent, but even such a number as 111.12.3.141 is not really very easy to remember. The Domain Name System (DNS) is a feature of TCP/IP networks that enables you to map an IP address to an alphanumeric name that is theoretically even easier for humans to remember than the decimal octet. (Internet domain names, such as *newriders.mcp.com*, are now easily recognizable in this age of e-mail.) Windows NT Server's Microsoft DNS Server service can map IP addresses to domain names on a TCP/IP network.

Windows NT's WINS service is similar to DNS except that, rather than mapping IP addresses to domain names, WINS maps IP addresses' NetBIOS names. NetBIOS names are used to identify resources on Microsoft networks. NetBIOS names follow the familiar Universal Naming Convention (UNC) format you use to locate resources from the Windows NT command prompt:

```
\\computername\sharename\path
```

The WINS service is also dynamic. Whereas DNS requires a static listing of all domain name-to-IP-address mappings, the WINS service can automatically associate NetBIOS names with IP addresses.

NWLink

The primary purpose of Microsoft's NWLink/SPX Compatible Transport protocol is to provide connectivity with the many thousands of Novell NetWare networks. NWLink is, however, a fully functional and fully routable protocol. You can use NWLink to network Windows NT machines with or without the involvement of NetWare resources. Because TCP/IP is Internet-ready (and more universally accepted) and NetBEUI is faster and simpler for Microsoft LANs, however, the chances are that if you are using NWLink you will be connecting to NetWare. Chapter 2 describes how to configure NWLink on your Windows NT Server system, and Chapter 4 discusses some issues related to NetWare connectivity.

NWLink provides compatibility with IPX/SPX-based networks, but NWLink alone does not necessarily enable a Windows NT computer to interact with NetWare networks. Windows NT includes several services that provide connectivity with NetWare services after NWLink is in place. Refer to Chapter 4 for more on connecting to NetWare resources using NWLink. Some important points to remember are as follows:

▶ The NWLink protocol provides compatibility with Novell NetWare IPX/SPX networks.

▶ A Windows NT Workstation computer running Client Services for NetWare (CSNW) and the NWLink protocol or a Windows NT Server computer running Gateway Services for NetWare (GSNW) and the NWLink protocol can connect file and print services on a NetWare server.

▶ A Windows NT computer using the NWLink protocol can connect to client/server applications on a NetWare server (without requiring additional NetWare-connectivity services).

▶ Any Microsoft network client that uses Server Message Block (Windows NT, Windows 95, or Windows for Workgroups) can access NetWare resources through a NetWare gateway on a Windows NT Server computer running Gateway Services for NetWare. The NetWare resources will appear to the Microsoft network client as Windows NT resources.

NetBEUI

NetBEUI is the fastest protocol that comes with Windows NT, but it cannot be routed. This means that the NetBEUI protocol is generally only useful for what Microsoft calls "department-sized LANs." The recent emphasis on internetworking means that, in all but the smallest and most isolated networks, NetBEUI is usually not the ideal choice for a primary network protocol. That is why NetBEUI has not been a default protocol for Windows NT since version 3.1 (although Windows NT Server 3.5 and RISC version 3.51 included it for backward-compatibility purposes).

> You cannot use NetBEUI with a router, but you can use a bridge to connect LAN segments operating with the NetBEUI protocol.

NetBEUI was designed for Microsoft networks, and one of the advantages of NetBEUI is that it enables Windows NT machines to interact with older Microsoft network machines that use NetBEUI (for instance, Windows for Workgroups 3.1 or Microsoft LAN Manager).

NetBEUI is also extremely easy to implement. It is self-tuning and self-configuring. (If you try to configure NetBEUI through the Protocols tab of Windows NT's Network application, you receive a message that says, Cannot configure the software component.) Because NetBEUI was designed for an earlier generation of lower-performance computers, it also comes with a smaller memory overhead.

The speed and simplicity of NetBEUI comes with a downside, however: NetBEUI relies heavily on network broadcasts, which can degrade performance on large and busy subnets.

Planning for Network Clients

The Windows NT CD-ROM includes client software for a number of operating systems that are not as naturally networkable as

Windows NT or Windows 95. Some of those client software packages are as follows:

▶ Microsoft Network 3.0 for MS-DOS

▶ LAN Manager 2.2c for MS-DOS client

▶ LAN Manager 2.2c for OS/2 client

Microsoft Network Client 3.0 for MS-DOS enables MS-DOS machines to participate in Windows NT networks. An MS-DOS client using Microsoft Client 3.0 for MS-DOS configured with the full director can perform the following tasks on a Windows NT network:

▶ Log on to a domain

▶ Run logon scripts

▶ Access IPC mechanisms, such as RPCs, named pipes, and WinSock

▶ Use RAS (version 1.1)

A Microsoft Client 3.0 for MS-DOS client cannot browse the network unless a Windows NT computer or a Windows for Workgroups computer is in the same workgroup.

The Windows NT CD-ROM also includes a pair of network client packages that help connect LAN Manager 2.2c systems with Windows NT. Those client packages are LAN Manager 2.2c for MS-DOS client and LAN Manager 2.2c OS/2 client. The LAN Manager 2.2c for MS-DOS client includes some features not found in the OS/2 version, including support for the Remoteboot service (described later in this chapter) and the capability to connect to a NetWare server.

Table 1.1 describes which network protocols and which TCP/IP services each of the client systems supports.

Table 1.1

Network Protocol and TCP/IP Service Support for Various Windows NT Client Systems

Network Protocol	TCP/IP DNS Service	IPX-Compatible	IPX/SPX Compatible	Net-BEUI	TCP/IP	DLC	DHCP	WINS
Network Client for MS-DOS	X	X		X	X	X		
LAN MAN 2.2c for MS-DOS	X			X	X	X		
LAN MAN 2.2c for OS/2	X			X				
Windows 95	X		X	X		X	X	X
Windows NT Workstation	X		X	X	X	X	X	X

Exercise Section

Each chapter of this book contains some exercises that give you first-hand knowledge of the chapter's topics. This chapter does not offer the same opportunities for first-hand exploration that later chapters provide, but the following exercises provide a glimpse of two very important concepts: NTFS file permissions and IP addresses. If you are an experienced NT administrator, you have probably undertaken these exercises many times, and you may want to move on to Chapter 2. If you are just starting to explore Windows NT and its features, try the following exercises.

Exercise 1.1: Exploring NTFS

Exercise 1.1 will help you explore NTFS file permissions—one of the principal features that distinguishes FAT from NTFS.

Estimated Time: 10 minutes

1. Log on as an administrator to a Windows NT Server system.

2. Right-click on the Start button (start Explorer).

3. Scroll to an NTFS partition on your system.

4. Find a file on the NTFS partition and right-click on the file icon. Choose Properties. The File Properties dialog box appears.

5. Click on the Security tab (see fig. 1.9). You will see separate buttons for file Permissions, Auditing, and Ownership. (You will learn more about how to manage and configure file security in later chapters.)

6. Click on the Permissions button. The File Permissions dialog box appears (see fig. 1.10). From within the File Permissions dialog box, you can specify which type of access to the file each user or group will receive. Clicking on the Add button enables you to add new users and groups to the access list.

Figure 1.9

The Security tab of the File Properties dialog box.

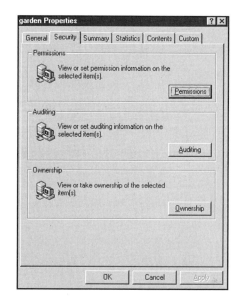

Figure 1.10

The File Permissions dialog box.

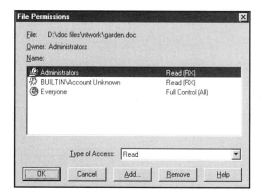

7. Close the File Permissions dialog box and the File Properties dialog box. You return to Explorer. Make sure the file you selected in step 4 is still selected.

8. Pull down the Explorer Edit menu and choose Copy.

9. Scroll the left window of Explorer to a directory on a FAT partition. Select the directory.

10. Pull down the Edit menu and select Paste. A copy of the file you selected in step 4 appears in the FAT directory.

11. Right-click on the new file icon and choose Properties.

12. Examine the File Properties dialog box for the new file. Notice that the Security tab is missing. Because the FAT file system does not enable you to set user and group access to files, you cannot craft a specific security environment for the file as you can through the Security tab and the File Permissions dialog box of the NTFS file. File-level security is one of the biggest advantages of NTFS files.

Exercise 1.2: PING and IPCONFIG

In Exercise 1.2, you will learn how to use the important TCP/IP utilities IPCONFIG and PING to verify your TCP/IP configuration.

Estimated Time: 10 minutes

1. Make sure TCP/IP is installed on your network.

2. Choose Start, Programs, Command Prompt.

3. From the command prompt, type **IPCONFIG**. The IPCONFIG command tells you the IP address, subnet mask, and default gateway for all network adapters to which TCP/IP is bound. (Chapter 2 explains more about TCP/IP configuration and adapter bindings.)

4. If TCP/IP is working properly on your system, the IPCONFIG utility outputs the IP address, subnet mask, and default gateway for your network adapter(s). If your computer obtains an IP address from a DHCP that is not working at this time—for instance, if you have a dial-up adapter that you use to access the Internet with an Internet service provider and you are not presently connected—the IP address and subnet mask appears as 0.0.0.0. If you have a duplicated IP address, the address appears, but the subnet mask appears as 0.0.0.0. Write down your IP address.

continues

5. Type **PING 127.0.0.1**. The Ping utility (Packet INternet Groper) tests your TCP/IP connection. You can specify the IP address of another computer with the command, and Ping makes sure your connection with the other computer is working. The format for the Ping command is:

    ```
    ping <IP address>
    ```

    The address you just typed (127.0.0.1) is a special address called the *loopback address*. The loopback address verifies that TCP/IP is working correctly on your system.

6. Ping the IP address of your own computer. This confirms that your IP address is configured correctly and informs you as to whether any duplicate IP addresses are on your network.

7. Ping the address of another computer on your subnet. If a system has a default gateway (see step 4), it is a common practice to ping the default gateway to ensure that your connection to the gateway is working.

8. If you know the IP address of a computer beyond the gateway, ping the IP address of the remote to ensure that you can connect to remote resources.

Review Questions

The following questions will test your knowledge of the information in this chapter. For additional questions, please see MCP Endeavor and the Microsoft Roadmap/Assessment exam on the CD-ROM that accompanies this book.

1. What are the minimum hardware requirements to run Windows 95?

   A. Intel 286 CPU, 4 MB RAM, 40 MB of disk space

   B. Intel 386 CPU, 4 MB RAM, 40 MB of disk space

   C. Intel 386 CPU or RISC-based processor, 8 MB RAM, 40 MB of disk space

   D. Intel 386 CPU, 8 MB RAM, 45 MB of disk space

2. You need to select an operating system that enables you to run your MS-DOS–based legacy applications. You have been told by your MIS department that these applications are written for speed, and hence sometimes directly access the hardware device. Which of the following operating system(s) should you choose to run these applications? Choose all that apply.

   A. Windows NT Workstation

   B. Windows NT Server

   C. Windows 95

   D. Windows for Workgroups

3. You need an operating system that supports multiple CPUs for a multithreaded database application that your company is developing. Which of the following operating systems support multiple processors? Choose all that apply.

   A. Windows 95

   B. Windows NT Workstation

   C. Windows NT Server

   D. Windows for Workgroups

4. Charles comes to you and says he needs to run a Windows 95 application on his DEC Alpha computer. He wants to know under what circumstances this is possible. Select the best response from the following answers.

   A. It is possible. Windows 95 runs on any RISC-based computer.

   B. It is not possible with his current configuration. He needs to purchase the Windows 95 emulator from Microsoft. After installation, he will be able to run Windows 95 programs on his Alpha.

   C. It is not possible to run Windows 95 on anything but an Intel platform.

   D. Although he can run Windows 95 on a DEC Alpha computer, it violates the license agreement.

5. Your boss comes to you and asks you why, when the company moved to Windows NT, you decided to put Windows NT Workstation rather than Windows NT Server on his computer. What would your explanation be?

   A. Windows NT Workstation is for the average user, whereas NT Server is for power users, such as CAD/CAM users and engineers.

   B. Windows NT Workstation is required on his machine because he is using an Intel-based computer, and NT Server requires a RISC-based CPU for more power.

   C. Windows NT Workstation is specifically tuned for workstation usage, whereas NT Server is tuned more toward being a file and print server.

   D. Tell him that you made a mistake and will load NT Server on his computer as soon as possible.

6. What are the system requirements for running Windows NT Workstation?

    A. Intel CPU, 8 MB of RAM, 120 MB free disk space

    B. Intel CPU, 12 MB of RAM, 85 MB free disk space

    C. Intel CPU or RISC-based computer, 12 MB of RAM, 120 MB free disk space

    D. RISC-based computer, 12 MB of RAM, 120 MB free disk space

7. You need the capability to have Macintosh users connect to and store files on a computer. Which of the following operating systems can serve this purpose? Choose all that apply.

    A. Windows NT Workstation

    B. Windows 95 with the computer to MAC and Back third-party add-on

    C. Windows for Workgroups

    D. Windows NT Server

    E. No version of any Microsoft operating system supports this because of software license issues

8. You get a call from a user stating that he is trying to share a directory with all the users in his office. But not all users can connect to his NT Workstation. His office consists of 15 users all running a mix of NT Workstation and Windows for Workgroups. What could be the potential problem?

    A. The users running Windows for Workgroups need to upgrade to NT Workstation before they can attach his computer.

    B. If he intends on sharing resources, he really should upgrade to NT Server.

    C. He has used up all his licensed sessions. NT Workstation only allows 10 simultaneous sessions.

    D. Tell him to restart his computer and the problem should go away.

9. You are evaluating operating systems for a mission-critical application that your MIS department is in the process of developing. You must choose an operating system that gives you basic data protection features, such as disk mirroring, RAID support, and the capability to secure the data against unauthorized individuals. Which of the following operating systems must you choose? Choose all correct answers.

   A. Windows NT Server

   B. Windows NT Workstation

   C. Windows 95

   D. MS-DOS

10. At a weekly management meeting, the director of the sales department relays concerns from her salespeople that whenever they try to dial in to the network they usually get busy signals. Currently, 10 salespeople are out in the field, but this number is expected to double in the next six months. Currently, all the sales people are accessing the network via RAS (Remote Access Service) running on a dedicated Windows NT Workstation computer. What can you suggest to enable more simultaneous connections?

    A. Nothing more can be done.

    B. Upgrade the dial-in computer to Windows NT Server, which can support up to 256 RAS users. NT Workstation only supports one RAS user at a time.

    C. You must set up a bank of 10 computers all running NT Workstation so that you can provide an adequate number of connections. When the new salespeople are hired, you must purchase an additional 5 to 10 computers.

11. What are the minimum hardware requirements to run Windows NT Server 4?

    A. 386 DX/33 or higher CPU, 16 MB of RAM, 130 MB of disk space

    B. 386 DX2/66 or higher CPU, 12 MB of RAM, 130 MB of disk space

    C. Pentium or higher CPU, 16 MB of RAM, 130 MB of disk space

    D. 486 DX/33 or higher CPU, 16 MB of RAM, 130 MB of disk space

12. Users of the HR workgroup come to you and complain that every time someone joins or leaves their department, they have to delete and re-create user IDs on each one of their 10 workstations. They are running Windows NT Workstation on all their computers. One user asks why this has to be done. Which of the following best describes why this is so?

    A. In a workgroup model, account information is stored on each machine participating in the workgroup. To access a resource on another machine in the workgroup, a user must have an account on the workgroup. To use a single user ID and password for all computers, you must install NT Server in a domain model.

    B. This is known problem in NT Workstation and is easily remedied by downloading a bug fix from Microsoft.

    C. The user needs to designate one of the NT Workstations as the master controller for the workgroup and then transfer all the user account information to that machine. After this is done, users are authenticated by that dedicated workstation and only need one user ID and password.

13. To organize your users and groups in a domain, which type of operating system must you install? Choose all that apply.

    A. NT Workstation—running in dedicated mode

    B. Windows 95

    C. Windows for Workgroups

    D. Windows NT Server

14. You are planning to install Windows NT in a dual-boot configuration on a computer currently running Windows 95. The network users are accustomed to using long file names. The other computers on the network are a mixture of Windows NT and Windows 95 computers, and you have opted for the dual-boot configuration so that users can access file resources from either operating system. Which file system should you use?

    A. NTFS
    B. FAT
    C. HPFS
    D. Either A or B

15. You plan to collect several large directories on to a single partition. The directories require a total of 5 GB in a uncompressed state. You should _____.

    A. Format the partition for the FAT file system
    B. Format the partition for FAT and use DriveSpace file compression
    C. Format the partition for NTFS
    D. Either B or C
    E. All of the above

16. You have a Windows NT Server system with three physical disks. One disk has a single partition that serves as the boot and system partition. The second disk has two partitions of approximately equal size—one formatted for FAT and one for NTFS. The third disk is currently free space. What fault-tolerance method(s) could you use?

    A. Disk mirroring
    B. Disk striping with parity
    C. All of the above
    D. None of the above

17. Users on your Windows NT network occasionally have to exchange messages with users on a Novell NetWare 4.0 network via the Internet. You must use the _____ protocol.

    A. TCP/IP

    B. NWLink

    C. Both A and B

    D. None of the above

18. Your network is a collection of Windows NT machines, Windows 95 machines, and MS-DOS machines running LAN MAN 2.2c Client for MS-DOS. The network, which uses the NetBEUI protocol, used to perform reasonably well, but you recently added additional nodes and noticed a sharp decline in performance. Now you are planning to add to the network again. Which of the following steps might improve network performance?

    A. Keep NetBEUI, but subdivide the network using a bridge

    B. Switch to NWLink

    C. Switch to TCP/IP

    D. A or C

    E. All of the above

Review Answers

1. B	6. C	11. D	16. A
2. C D	7. D	12. A	17. A
3. B C	8. C	13. D	18. D
4. C	9. A	14. B	
5. C	10. B	15. C	

Chapter 2

Stop! Before reading this chapter, test yourself to determine how much study time you will need to devote to this section.

1. To change a member server into a backup domain controller, you must _____.

   A. change the Registry SERVER_TYPE setting in the HKEY_LOCAL_MACHINE Hardware subkey.

   B. change the server type configuration using Server Manager.

   C. configure a domain account database for the server using User Manager for Domains.

   D. reinstall Windows NT Server.

2. The _____ helps you upgrade from a previous version of Windows NT.

   A. WINNT.EXE

   B. WINNT32.EXE

   C. UPGRADE.EXE

   D. WINNTUP.EXE

3. Change the IRQ for a network adapter using the Control Panel _____ application.

   A. System

   B. Adapters

   C. Network

   D. None of the above

4. Which three of the following can act as a directory replication import server?

   A. Windows NT Server

   B. Windows NT Workstation

   C. Windows 95

   D. LAN Manager OS/2 Server

Answers

1. D (see "Choosing a Server Type")
2. B (see "Network Installs")
3. C (see "Configuring Protocols and Protocol Bindings")
4. A B D (see "Directory Replication")

C h a p t e r

Installation and Configuration

2

This chapter will help you prepare for the "Installation and Configuration" section of Microsoft's Exam 70-67, "Implementing and Supporting Windows NT Server 4.0." Microsoft provides the following objectives for the "Installation and Configuration" section:

Test Objectives

- ▶ Install Windows NT Server on Intel-based platforms.

- ▶ Install Windows NT Server to perform various server roles. Server roles include: primary domain controller, backup domain controller, member server.

- ▶ Install Windows NT Server by using various methods. Installation methods include: CD-ROM, Over the network, Network Client Administrator, Express versus Custom.

- ▶ Configure protocols and protocol bindings. Protocols include: TCP/IP, NWLink IPX/SPX Compatible Transport, NetBEUI.

- ▶ Configure network adapters. Considerations include: changing IRQ, I/O base, memory address, configuring multiple adapters.

- ▶ Configure Windows NT Server core services. Services include: Directory Replicator, License Manager, other services.

- ▶ Configure peripherals and devices. Peripherals and devices include: communications devices, SCSI devices, tape device drivers, UPS and UPS service, mouse drivers, display drivers, and keyboard drivers.

▶ Configure hard disks to meet various requirements. Requirements include: allocating disk space capacity, providing redundancy, improving performance, providing security, formatting.

▶ Configure printers. Tasks include: adding and configuring a printer, implementing a printer pool, setting print priorities.

▶ Configure a Windows NT Server computer for various types of client computers. Client computer types include: Windows NT Workstation, Microsoft Windows 95, Microsoft MS-DOS-based.

Installation and configuration is a major thrust of the Windows NT Server exam, so it is a good idea for you to devote time to exploring the installation prerequisites, precautions, and procedures. This chapter traces the installation process start to finish and explains each option you encounter along the way. You will also learn how to configure various components of Windows NT Server—such as protocols, network adapters, services, peripherals, hard disks, and printers—for various situations. Along the way, this chapter will examine some important Windows NT concepts, such as server roles, browser elections, and directory replication.

Installing Windows NT Server

To install Windows NT efficiently, it is best to do some planning in advance. Be prepared with answers to the questions the setup program will ask. And take the time to determine which installation method will work best for you. The following section discusses Windows NT Server installation.

Microsoft lists the following objectives for the Windows NT Server exam:

▶ Install Windows NT Server on Intel-based platforms

▶ Install Windows NT Server to perform various server roles. Server roles include: primary domain controller, backup domain controller, member server.

▶ Install Windows NT Server by using various methods. Installation methods include: CD-ROM, Over the network, Network Client Administrator, Express vs. Custom

Hardware Requirements

Before you install Windows NT, you need to ensure that your hardware can support it. Windows NT doesn't approach the sheer number of devices that Windows 95 supports, so don't assume that Windows NT can support the hardware you currently use for MS-DOS or Windows 95.

You receive lots of advice in this chapter; first and foremost of that advice is to consult the Hardware Compatibility List (HCL) before you try to install Windows NT—certainly before you purchase any new hardware on which to run Windows NT. The HCL includes the vendor and model names for all systems and devices tested and approved for use with Windows NT.

You should know a few things about the HCL, including the following:

▶ The HCL that ships with the product is now obsolete; the HCL is frequently updated and can be found in more recent form on TechNet, Microsoft's monthly product support CD-ROM, as well as on Microsoft Network, CompuServe, the Internet, and other online services.

▶ Just because a product is listed on the HCL doesn't mean it's fully 100 percent compatible. Check the fine print; usually you can find a footnote or endnote that certain caveats apply to supporting a device under Windows NT.

▶ Just because a product isn't listed on the HCL doesn't mean it isn't fully 100 percent compatible. It may just mean it hasn't been tested yet. Before giving up hope, ask the vendor if any drivers are available for Windows NT 4. Recognize, however, that when the device isn't on the HCL, Microsoft probably will just refer you back to the vendor for technical support issues.

▶ If a product isn't on the HCL and the vendor doesn't have a Windows NT 4 driver, ask the vendor if any compatible drivers are available. For instance, the modem may be Hayes-compatible, or the network card may be NE2000-compatible. Should a problem arise down the road, however, chances are you won't be able to rely on Microsoft or the vendor for technical support.

The specific hardware requirements differ depending on the platform on which you intend to install Windows NT.

Intel Requirements

Intel-based computers form the largest segment of the Windows NT installed base, owing to the worldwide predominance of Intel-based computers. If you plan to install Windows NT on an Intel-based computer, make sure that your hardware meets the following minimum requirements:

▶ **Processor.** Intel-based computers require a 32-bit Intel or Intel-compatible CPU (80486 DX-33 or higher); Pentium CPUs give optimal performance.

▶ **Memory.** Windows NT Workstation will install with as few as 8 MB of RAM, but Microsoft's official box specs (and therefore the MCP exam) require 12 MB. Realistically, don't go with less than 16 MB, and expect great performance gains with memory increases up to 32 MB.

▶ **Hard disk.** Windows NT Workstation installation requires at least 110 MB free disk space on the hard drive for Intel-based machines; Windows NT Server installation requires at least 125 MB free. On RISC-based machines, Windows NT

Workstation requires 110 MB and Windows NT Server requires at least 160 MB.

On any platform, cluster size also is important. Microsoft recommends that a Windows NT Server with 32 KB clusters have at least 200 MB free space.

Any supported hard disk suffices, but Windows NT may have a problem addressing IDE drives roomier than 540 MB. If your IDE controller is compatible with the Western Digital WD1003 standard, Windows NT can handle your EIDE drive, but if it isn't, you need to take additional steps. A BIOS upgrade should solve the problem. A utility for MS-DOS called Disk Manager (published by OnTrack Systems) also might do the trick; it alters the BIOS on the hard disk so that MS-DOS (and Windows NT) can correctly handle the drive.

Other Hardware

You need a 3 ½-inch disk drive if you install Windows NT on an Intel-based computer, because Microsoft no longer supplies 5 ¼-inch Setup disks for Windows NT. You also need a VGA (or higher) video card. Other devices, while not mandatory, certainly are quite valuable; for example, a mouse or similar pointing device is hard to get by without these days, as are a CD-ROM drive (optional on Intel only, required for RISC) and a network adapter card. If you're using a PowerPC with an NE-2000 compatible network card, make sure that the computer's firmware is version 1.24 or later.

Multiboot Requirements

You can install Windows NT alongside another operating system on the same machine. You would use a dual boot configuration if you have two operating systems you want to use. If you decide you need or want to do so, you should read the following sections according to the operating systems you want to use.

Windows NT Server

An unlimited number of Windows NT variants can coexist on the same workstation. Be careful to install each operating system in a separate directory. Windows NT-based operating systems will automatically create and update a boot loader menu if other operating systems are found on the system.

Windows 95

Windows 95 and Windows NT can coexist on the same machine, but not in the same directory root, because each OS has files that differ in content but not in name or location. Win95 applications, therefore, must be reinstalled under Windows NT Workstation before you can use them under both operating systems. Again, Windows NT will detect Windows 95 if present and create or update the boot loader menu.

Because Windows 95 and Windows NT have different Registries, and because they support different hardware, no option for upgrading from Windows 95 to Windows NT presently is available; you must perform a full installation.

MS-DOS

If your MS-DOS installation includes Windows 3.x or Windows for Workgroups, you can install Windows NT in the existing Windows root directory. The benefit of this arrangement is a synchronized desktop environment. Also, such an arrangement frees you from having to reinstall your Windows applications before you can use them under Windows NT.

OS/2

You can install Windows NT on a system that currently runs OS/2, but doing so disables OS/2's Boot Manager in favor of the Windows NT Boot Loader. If you want to use the OS/2 Boot Manager, you must re-enable it through Disk Administrator by marking the Boot Manager active after Windows NT successfully installs. When Boot Manager is active, you can boot to Windows NT by choosing MS-DOS from the Boot Manager menu. Choosing MS-DOS invokes the Windows NT Boot Loader, from which you can boot either Windows NT or MS-DOS.

Early versions of OS/2 (version 1.x) don't have Boot Manager. Instead, you must use the BOOT command: type BOOT /DOS from inside OS/2 and reboot to bring up the Windows NT Boot Loader, or type BOOT /OS2 from MS-DOS and reboot to bring up OS/2.

Choosing a Server Type

If you installing Windows NT Server, you must make an important choice; you have to decide on a server role for the computer on which you install Windows NT. You must choose one of three server roles:

▶ **Primary Domain Controller (PDC).** Contains the master copy of the directory database (which contains information on user accounts) for the domain. There can be only one primary domain controller per domain, and the primary domain controller must be the first machine installed.

▶ **Backup Domain Controller (BDC).** Helps the primary domain controller. The primary domain controller copies the directory database to the backup controller(s). The BDC can authenticate users just as the PDC can. If the PDC fails, the BDC can be promoted to a PDC, but if a BDC is promoted, any changes to the directory database since the last time it was copied from the old PDC are lost. A domain can have more than one BDC.

▶ **Member or Stand-alone Server.** A stand-alone server is a Windows NT Server machine that doesn't participate in the system of domain controllers of the domain. A stand-alone server can provide all Windows NT Server function (file service, print service, Internet service, or whatever) but it doesn't maintain a copy of a domain accounts database, and cannot authenticate domain users.

A stand-alone server can be part of a domain or a workgroup. Stand-alone servers that are parts of domains are called member servers, which are useful because keeping a file or print servers free from the overhead of authenticating users often proves cost-effective. You cannot change a stand-alone server into a domain controller after installing it; your only option under such circumstances is to reinstall Windows NT and change the server type to domain controller during the installation process.

After you install a PDC or BDC into a domain, it must remain in that domain unless you reinstall Windows NT, because you can't change the Security Identifier (SID) for the domain after setting it during installation. You can, however, change the name of a domain; change the domain name first on the PDC, then on the other network machines. Windows NT simply maps the new domain name with the old SID for the domain.

Installation Procedure

The user documentation that accompanies Windows NT 4 includes detailed instructions for installing and upgrading to Windows 4.

The following are two possible sources of Windows NT 4 installation files:

▶ The Windows NT Installation CD-ROM (with three setup floppies)

▶ A network sharepoint (with three setup floppies)

Most installation procedures consist of two distinct phases: a file copying phase that takes place under a minimal text-mode version of Windows NT and a configuration phase that runs under the full GUI Windows NT Setup wizard.

The details of the Windows NT installation process depend on the details of your system; different prompts and dialogs may ask you for additional information depending on the devices on your system and the components you want to install.

CD-ROM

The Windows NT Installation CD-ROM, the easiest and most common method for installing NT, comes with three startup floppy disks. To begin the CD-ROM installation process, boot from Setup Disk 1. Setup asks for all three of the setup disks before it asks for the CD-ROM. (You learn how to regenerate these disks should the need arise later in this chapter.)

You also can begin the installation by starting the CD-ROM (from within your existing operating system) and double-clicking on Windows NT Setup. Setup copies the installation files from the CD-ROM to your hard drive and asks you to restart your computer. Don't throw away your Setup floppy disks, however. Even if you initiate the installation from the CD-ROM, Setup asks for Setup Disk 2. (You learn more about the three Windows NT Setup disks later in this chapter.)

If you are initiating the installation from the Setup disks, you must boot from the Setup disks; don't type the standard run a:\setup. Setup is a Windows NT program, so to run it requires that Windows NT be running. When you boot from the initial setup disk, a minimal version of Windows NT loads and initializes.

Network Installs

If you have to roll out many Windows NT Workstations in a short time frame, a CD-ROM-based installation may be impractical. Perhaps not all of your workstations have CD-ROM drives; perhaps you don't have as many copies of the CD-ROM as you do workstations. A network install is really a CD-ROM install; an initial preinstallation phase is added in which the contents of the CD-ROM are copied across the network from the server to the client computer. After all the installation files have been copied, the client computer reboots from the setup disks and proceeds with the installation as if it were a CD-ROM install (in this case, the "CD-ROM" is the hard drive). You can use Windows NT's Client Administrator application to create a network installation startup disk that will enable you to boot the client machine and connect to the shared directory with the installation files. The Client Administrator startup disk is described later in this chapter.

When many workstations are simultaneously downloading the installation files, performance isn't great, but you can still set up many clients at once and let them run while you do other things.

To improve performance, copy the contents of the CD-ROM to the hard drive and share the hard disk's copy rather than the CD's. Hard disks are much faster than CD-ROM drives.

To start an installation across the network, you must first redirect an MS-DOS drive letter to the network sharepoint containing the installation files. From a NetWare client, you use the MAP command; from a Windows 95 client, you utilize the Network Neighborhood and connect to a drive; from an MS-DOS client, you use the NET USE command; from a Windows for Workgroups client, you choose Disk, Connect Network Drive in File Manager. In short, establish network connections however you ordinarily do it.

If you have questions about net commands, type **net help** at the prompt. If you require assistance on the specific command, type **net help** followed by the command, such as **net help view** or **net help logoff**.

After you map a drive to the installation share, change to the drive and run a program called WINNT.EXE. (If you install from a previous version of NT, the system prompts you to run WINNT32.EXE instead of WINNT.EXE.) WINNT.EXE is an MS-DOS program that generates the three necessary Setup disks and copies the Windows NT installation files from the server to the local hard drive. After all the files are copied, WINNT.EXE prompts you to insert Setup Disk 1 so it can reboot the computer and begin the installation process.

note

One interesting quirk about WINNT.EXE: When it asks you to insert each of the three blank, formatted disks necessary to create the setup disks, it does so in reverse order. It asks for Disk 3 first, then Disk 2, and finally Disk 1. Microsoft did this for your convenience, believe it or not: one less disk swap occurs in this scenario—try it and see. Still, it confuses many first-time installers who try to reboot their machine from Disk 3, believing it to be Disk 1.

WINNT.EXE Switches

The following switches enable you to customize how WINNT.EXE begins the setup process.

/B No Boot Floppies

The /B switch instructs WINNT.EXE not to create the three setup disks. Instead, WINNT.EXE creates images of these disks on your system partition, requiring an extra 4 or 5 MB of disk space. The boot sector of the hard disk is modified to point to the temporary directory that contains the images (WIN_NT.~BT).

The /B switch can significantly speed up the installation process. If the computer crashes during Setup, however, you may not be able to reboot to your old operating system. Keeping an MS-DOS or Windows 95 bootable disk around should solve that problem. Simply enter the SYS command for the C drive; your system should boot normally.

/S Source File Location

When WINNT.EXE executes, it immediately asks the user for the location of the Windows NT source files, even if the user is in the same directory from which WINNT.EXE was run. To avoid answering this question, supply the information up-front using the syntax WINNT.EXE /S:<path>.

/U Unattended Installation

The Unattended Installation option automates the installation or upgrade process so you don't have to sit at the keyboard and respond to Setup prompts. Because you're present, you must tell WINNT.exe in advance where to find the installation files, so you must use the /u switch with the /s switch. Normally, the unattended installation only operates unattended through the copy phase, the text mode portion of Setup, and the initial reboot; Setup requires a user to enter the computer name, network settings, and so on. You can, however, enter a colon and a file name after the /u switch, as follows:

```
winnt /u:c:\answer.txt
```

The file answer.txt is an answer file, a file that contains responses to the final Setup prompts. Using the /u switch with an answer file, you can automate the entire installation.

You can use the Setup Manager utility to create an answer file, or you can use any text editor to edit the answer file template unattend.exe (found on the Windows NT installation CD-ROM). You can save the answer file to any legal name.

You can use an answer file in conjunction with the (Uniqueness Database File) /UDF switch.

/UDF Uniqueness Database File

A Uniqueness Database File (UDF) lets you tailor an unattended installation to the specific attributes of specific machines. The UDF contains different sections, each identified with a string called a *uniqueness ID*. Each section contains machine-specific information for a single computer or a group of computers. You can then use a single answer file for all the network installations, and reference machine-specific information by providing the uniqueness ID with the /UDF switch.

/T:drive_letter Temporary Drive

This switch tells winnt or winnt32 to put the installation files on the specified drive.

/OX Only Make Boot Diskettes (Local Install)

Essentially the same command as the /O switch, /OX also creates boot disks. The only difference is that /O creates disks that require the installation files to be in the hard disk's WIN_NT.˜LS temporary directory, and /OX requires the installation files to be on disk or CD-ROM.

The difference between the resulting setup disks is just a single byte on Disk 2. The WINNT.SIF file on Disk 2 is a text file which has an entry of MsDosInitiate= which is set to 1 if the /O command is used, and set to 0 if the /OX command is used. You can actually convert local install disks to network install disks simply by changing this entry in WINNT.SIF.

/F Don't Verify Files

You can shave a bit of time off the installation process by skipping the verification of the files copied to the boot disks, but the savings are negligible. It doesn't take that much time to verify the files, and it certainly takes much longer to restart the installation if the disks are corrupt. Still, such corruption during file copying is rare, so if you aren't averse to the occasional odds-favorable risk, go for it.

/C Don't Check for Free Space

This switch tells WINNT.EXE not to check for the required free space on the setup boot disks. You should not use this switch for two reasons:

▶ The disks are pretty packed; if you have other files on the disks, you probably won't be able to fit all of the required Setup files anyway.

▶ The amount of time you can save by using this switch is approximately equal to the amount of time it takes to type the switch.

The Installation Phases

Microsoft divides the Windows NT installation process into four phases:

▶ Phase 0: Preinstallation

▶ Phase 1: Gathering information about your computer

▶ Phase 2: Installing Windows NT Networking

▶ Phase 3: Finishing Setup

The following sections guide you through these installation phases.

Phase 0: Preinstallation

During preinstallation, Setup copies the necessary installation files to your hard drive and assembles the information it needs for the install by detecting hardware and also by asking the user for configuration information. Before you begin studying the installation process, you should look at what's on the three Windows NT Setup disks.

Setup Disk One

When your computer boots from this disk, the Master Boot Record loads and passes control to NTLDR, the Windows NT Boot Loader. NTLDR, in turn, loads the kernel (NTKRNLMP.EXE). Next, one of three Hardware Abstraction Layers (HAL) is loaded—HAL486C.DLL, HALMCA.DLL, or HALAPIC.DLL—depending on the platform detected.

Setup Disk Two

This disk contains a minimal registry used by Setup, SETUPREG.HIV. This registry contains single entry instructs that tell Windows NT to load the main installation driver, SETUPDD.SYS. After loading SETUPDD.SYS, Windows NT loads generic drivers for video (VIDEOPRT.SYS), keyboard (I8042PRT.SYS, KBDUS.DLL), floppy drive (FLOPPY.SYS), and the FAT file system (FASTFAT.SYS). This disk also includes the setup font (VGAOEM.FON), locale-specific data (C_1252.NLS, \C_437.NLS and L_INTL.NLS), and the first of many SCSI port drivers, which continue on the third Setup disk.

Setup Disk Three

Disk three contains additional SCSI port drivers, of which only one or two are typically loaded (depending on what SCSI adapters are installed, if any). Windows NT loads additional file system drivers, such as NTFS.SYS, from this disk. This disk also includes drivers for specific types of hard disks, specifically ATDISK.SYS for ESDI or IDE and ABIOSDSK.SYS for Micro Channel.

At this point, the SCSI drivers have been loaded, so Windows NT should recognize supported SCSI CD-ROM drives. Windows NT also detects IDE CD-ROM drives, but may not detect proprietary Mitsumi or Panasonic drives; you must manually inform Windows NT of their presence.

The Phase 0 Process

Phase 0 is the same for both Windows NT Server and Windows NT Workstation. In Phase 0, Setup loads a minimal version of Windows NT into memory, and asks if you want to perform an installation or an upgrade.

Between Setup disks two and three, the Welcome screen appears, informing you of your options: installing Windows NT, repairing an existing installation, or learning more about the setup process. Take a moment to read the online help if you want. When you're ready to begin, press Enter to begin the installation.

During this phase of the installation, Setup asks you to verify certain information about your hardware and your hardware-related software components. The following sections describe the questions Setup asks.

Mass Storage Devices

Setup asks if you want it to attempt to detect the mass storage devices attached to your computer. A note informs you that Setup can automatically detect floppy controllers and standard ESDI/IDE hard disks. (Some other mass storage devices, such as SCSI adapters and certain CD-ROM drives can cause the computer to malfunction or become unresponsive.)

Press Enter to let Setup detect mass storage devices on your computer.

Press S to skip mass storage device detection and manually select SCSI adapters, CD-ROM drives, and special disk controllers.

Setup asks for Setup Disk 3 and attempts to detect the mass storage devices. Setup then asks you to verify the list.

Press Enter if you have no additional devices.

Type **S** to specify an additional device.

Hardware and Components

Setup looks for certain hardware and software components, such as a keyboard, a mouse, a video screen, and the accompanying drivers. Setup presents a list of components and asks if you want to make any changes.

Press Enter to accept the list.

To change an item, select the item using the arrow keys and press Enter to see alternatives.

Partitions

After you identify your SCSI adapters and CD-ROM drivers, Windows NT Setup needs to know on which partition it should install Windows NT. Setup displays a screen showing the existing partitions on your hard drive and the space available for creating new partitions.

Press Enter to install Windows NT on the highlighted partition or unpartitioned space.

Type **C** to create a new partition in unpartitioned space.

Type **D** to delete a partition.

NTFS

Setup then presents the following options:

- ▶ Format the partition using the FAT file system.

- ▶ Format the partition using the NTFS file system.

- ▶ Convert the partition to NTFS.

- ▶ Leave the current file system intact.

Specifically designed for Windows NT, NT File System (NTFS) offers some advantages, including better performance and increased security, but NTFS isn't compatible with Windows 95 or earlier versions of DOS and Windows. The other optional file systems for NT hard drives is FAT (for MS-DOS and Windows systems). If you choose FAT, you lose the data currently on the partition.

The conversion to NTFS isn't performed during installation, but rather, after Windows NT is completely installed and the computer reboots for the first time. The end result is the same: before the user can log on to Windows NT, the partition has been converted.

The default choice is to leave the current file system intact. If your system is now running MD-DOS, Windows 3.x, or Windows 95, the current file system is the FAT file system. If you plan on ever accessing the partition from MS-DOS or Windows, select the FAT file system.

See Chapter 3, "Managing Resources," for more on the file systems that Windows NT supports.

NT Root Directory

Setup asks what name you want to give the Windows NT root directory. By default, Setup suggests \WINNT of the system partition as the installation directory.

Windows NT can peacefully coexist with Windows 3.x in the same directory tree, but do not, under any circumstance, install Windows NT in the same directory as Windows 95; currently the two operating systems cannot coexist in the same directory structure.

If Setup detects an installation of Windows NT already in the selected directory, you are given the options to replace the existing installation or choose another location.

Hard Disk Corruption

Setup examines your hard disk(s) for corruption. It automatically performs a basic examination. You can choose whether you want Setup to perform an exhaustive secondary examination, which may take several minutes, by pressing Enter. Press Esc to skip the secondary examination.

Reboot

A progress bar appears as Setup copies files to your hard disk. This may take several minutes.

The last text-mode screen announces that this portion of Setup is complete and asks that you remove the disk from your floppy drive and restart your computer.

Press Enter to restart your computer.

Phase 1: Gathering Information

After your computer restarts, Setup asks you to approve the licensing agreement and begins copying file from the disks, CD-ROM, or network to the Windows NT root directory. The Windows NT Setup Wizard then appears, announcing the three remaining parts of the setup process:

1. Gathering information about your computer.

2. Installing Windows NT Networking

3. Finishing Setup

Name and Company Name

For legal and registration reasons, Setup then asks for your name and organization, which it then uses as the defaults for additional software installed under Windows NT. You must enter a value in the Name field but you can leave the Company Name blank.

Setup also asks for your Product ID number, which is a sticker attached to the CD-ROM sleeve. You must enter this number before you can continue with the installation.

Licensing Mode (NT Server Only)

If you're installing Windows NT Server, you must specify a licensing mode. These are your options:

▶ **Per server license.** Clients are licensed to a particular server, and the number of concurrent connections to the server cannot exceed the maximum specified in the license. When the maximum number of concurrent connections is reached, Windows NT returns an error to a connecting user and prohibits access. An administrator can still connect after the maximum is reached, however.

▶ **Per seat license.** Clients are free to use any server they want, and an unlimited number of clients can connect to a server.

If you can't decide which mode to select, choose Per Server mode. You have a one-time chance to convert the per server license to a per seat license using the Control Panel Licensing application.

Computer Name

Every networked Windows NT-based computer must have a unique computer name, even if the computers are split among multiple domains. The computer name is a typical NetBIOS name: that is, it consists of up to 15 characters. Because workgroup and domain names also use NetBIOS names, the computer name must be unique among all of these names as well. NetBIOS names aren't case-sensitive; they always appear in uppercase.

Server Type (NT Server Only)

If you're installing Windows NT Server, you must specify whether the computer is a primary domain controller, a backup domain controller, or a stand-alone server. These server type options are discussed earlier in this chapter.

Administrator Password

Setup asks you to enter a password for the Administrator account. The length of the password should be 14 characters or less. See Chapter 3, for more on Windows NT accounts. You need the Administrator account to create and manage other accounts within Windows NT.

Don't forget to write down the Administrator account password and store it in a safe place.

Emergency Disk

The Setup Wizard asks if you want to create an emergency repair disk. Chapter 6, "Troubleshooting," discusses the Emergency Repair Disk (ERD) in detail. It's essentially a clone of the information stored in the \REPAIR directory in case that directory or even the hard disk becomes corrupt or inaccessible. Creating an ERD for every computer in your company is a good idea. Label each ERD with the serial number of the computer to which it is paired.

The Wizard then asks whether you want the most common components installed or whether you would prefer to choose the components from a list. (Note that the Microsoft Exchange messaging client may not be in the list of common components.)

If you want to view the list of components, you can always choose the Choose Components option to view the list and then click on Next (leaving the list unchanged and accepting the defaults).

Optional Components

If you're installing Windows NT Server, or if you're installing Windows NT Workstation using the Custom Setup option, Setup asks you to specify which optional components you want to install.

Phase 2: Installing Windows NT Networking

The Wizard then announces that it is ready to begin installing Windows NT Networking. The following sections describe the Networking phase of the setup.

Network Participation

The next screen asks if your computer will participate in a network, and if so, whether it will be wired to the network or whether it will access the network through a modem. If you intend to connect via both a modem and an ISDN adapter or network adapter, check both boxes.

If you click in the No button (your computer will not participate in a network) the Wizard proceeds to Phase 3, "Finishing Setup."

Internet/Intranet Service

If you're installing Windows NT Server, Setup asks if you want to install Internet Information Server (IIS).

If you're installing Windows NT Workstation, Setup asks if you want to install Peer Web Server (PWS).

Network Adapter Card

The next screen asks if you want Setup to search for your network adapter card. Click on Start Search if you want Setup to find your card. Setup stops after it finds the first card and the Start Search button changes into a Find Next button. If you have another network adapter card, choose Find Next. Alternatively, you can choose Select from List to select your Adapter card from a list. The Have Disk button in the Select Network Adapter dialog box enables you to install the software for the adapter card. You need to obtain a Windows NT 4 driver from your vendor and supply the path to the driver in the dialog box.

If Setup successfully autodetects your network adapter card, it displays its findings so that you can confirm the network adapter card and its settings. If it cannot detect the card, Setup expects you to manually select a network adapter card from a list of drivers supplied with Windows NT.

After selecting or confirming your network adapter card, you may see a dialog box with card configuration options. These options may include Interrupt Request (IRQ), Base I/O Address, Transceiver Type, and other card-specific parameters. Confirm these options before proceeding because Windows NT doesn't always pick all of these up correctly, especially if you added your card manually, skipping detection.

If you don't have a network card, you can still install the networking services on top of the remote access service (RAS). You'll only be prompted to install RAS during Setup if you do not select a network card at all. See Chapter 4, "Connectivity," for more information about RAS.

Network Protocols

The next screen enables you to specify networking protocols for your network. You can check TCP/IP, NWLink IPX/SPX Compatible Transport, or NetBEUI. Click on Select from List for a new window with some additional options, including AppleTalk, DLC, Point to Point Tunneling Protocol, and Streams Environment. This new window also provides a Have Disk option you can use if you want to install your own protocol software.

By default, only TCP/IP is installed on an Intel-based computer.

Carefully consider your current network configuration and needs before accepting the default protocols. If your network currently runs mostly NetWare, you may want to use NWLink rather than TCP/IP. If your network uses both NetWare and Unix, you may want both NWLink and TCP/IP. If your network is a small, self-contained workgroup, you may want to use NetBEUI only. See Chapter 1, "Planning," for more information about network transport protocols.

If your clients already use TCP/IP, then you know how easy it is to misconfigure TCP/IP when installing it, especially the subnet mask and default gateway. If you are installing over the network and have copied the install directory (that is, I386) to the hard drive, you can modify IPINFO.INF. This file is a template for TCP/IP configuration parameters. It's a fairly large file, but you're only interested in the section that begins with `[De-faultIPInfo]`. The file consists of mostly comment lines, so make sure that you have found the section that does not have each line preceded by a semicolon (the comment indicator).

After you find the `[DefaultIPInfo]` section, you can modify the following parameters:

▶ `NumberOfIPAddress` = x, in which x is the number of IP Addresses o be assigned. For most workstations, this should simply be set to 1.

▶ `IPAddress1` = 'xxx.xxx.xxx.xxx'. Because this parameter will change from client to client, you might not want to fill this in.

▶ `SubnetMask1` = 'xxx.xxx.xxx.xxx'. All of your clients will probably use the same subnet mask, so this is a smart default to set.

▶ `DefaultGateway` = 'xxx.xxx.xxx.xxx'. Again, all of your clients on a particular subnet should use the same default gateway (router), so this is another smart default.

Of course, users can still override this information during an installation, but at least they won't be guessing parameters out of the blue.

Network Services

If you're installing Windows NT Server, Setup asks what optional network services you want to install.

The other chapters of this book discuss many of the network service options. If you don't install a particular service during Setup, you can always add it later using the Services tab of the Control Panel Network application.

Network Components

Setup then asks if you want to change any of your previous choices, and then proceeds to install your networking components. Depending on the components and options you select, various dialog boxes may appear as the components are installed. The Setup Wizard may try to find your modem, for example, or you may be asked whether you want to use Dynamic Host Configuration Protocol (\DHCP). You also may be prompted for the IP address and default gateway.

After installing the network components, Setup announces that it's ready to start the network so you can complete the network installation. Setup asks for the name of the workgroup or domain to which your computer will belong. (Select Workgroup or Domain, and type the name.) If Setup successfully starts the network, Setup immediately begins to copy additional files for a few minutes. If unsuccessful, Setup asks if you want to change your network adapter card's configuration parameters. It's a good idea not to proceed any further until the network starts correctly, particularly if you're doing a network installation: if your computer doesn't have a CD-ROM drive, you may find yourself unable to load additional drivers after Windows NT restarts. If you cannot get the network to start after multiple attempts, you may proceed with installation, but you can't join a domain until the network services successfully begin at some point.

You must join either a domain or a workgroup, or neither. You cannot join both.

Joining a workgroup requires nothing more than the name of that workgroup. The workgroup doesn't have to exist prior to this point; you can create it just by joining it. In a workgroup, everyone's a chief. Every Windows NT-based computer has its own account database, and sharing resources between computers requires an immense amount of administration or a significant lack of security.

If you're installing a Windows NT workstation or member server and you elect to join a domain, a domain must already exist; that is, a primary domain controller (PDC) must be defined and available on the network. If Setup cannot find a Windows NT Server acting as a primary domain controller for that domain on the network, you can't join the domain.

If the primary domain controller does exist and is available, then an account must be created at the PDC for your workstation or member server. This can occur if the domain administrator manually adds an account for this workstation using the Server Manager application, or if you create the account yourself during workstation installation. Before you can do so, you must know the username and password of the domain administrator or have the user right "Create computer accounts in the domain."

Phase 3: Finishing Setup

After the network components are installed, Setup is almost complete. The Wizard announces that you are ready for Phase 3: Finishing Setup. The following sections describe the Phase 3 installation steps.

Time Zone

You can set your computer's current date and time and select the appropriate time zone through a Setup dialog box. Specify the date and time in the Date & Time tab. Specify a time zone in the Time Zone tab. If you choose a time zone that switches from standard time to daylight savings time and back, you may elect to have Windows NT automatically make this change for you. If so, select the Automatically Adjust Clock for Daylight Savings Changes check box.

Note that certain separate time zone entries for certain individual states simply don't fit within a time zone profile. Arizona, for instance, geographically belongs to the Mountain Standard time zone but, unlike other Mountain Standard time states, does not switch to Daylight Savings Time in the summer. Arizona has a separate entry in the Time Zone list.

Exchange Configuration

If you choose to install Microsoft Exchange as an optional component in Phase 1, Setup requests some information for configuring
Exchange.

Display Settings

Setup detects the video display adapter. If the adapter uses a
chipset for which Windows NT includes a driver, the name of the
chipset appears on-screen.

If this setting is correct, confirm it. If not, choose another driver
by choosing Have Disk and supplying the path to the third-party
driver; or just choose the standard VGA driver. For best performance, use a card-specific driver rather than the standard VGA
driver. Contact your card's vendor for a Windows NT driver if
Windows NT does not detect it correctly.

Setup doesn't let you proceed unless you test the settings you have
selected. Because Windows NT cannot detect your monitor settings, you could pick a resolution or refresh rate that your card
but not your monitor supports. When you click on the Test button, the screen briefly goes blank, to be quickly replaced by a test
pattern. If all looks well, confirm the settings for the card when
the Windows NT Setup interface returns. Otherwise, choose a
new setting and test again. If your test is unsuccessful, odds are
that Windows NT doesn't work right under that setting. A few
monitors go blank and stay blank during testing, even though the
chosen settings are supported. If this is the case with your installation, and you're sure that both adapter card and monitor support
your configuration, you can lie and tell Setup that the test was
successful. If Windows NT restarts in an unusable video state when
you reboot, reboot again and choose Boot Loader, Windows NT
Server 4.0 [VGA mode].

Pentium Patch

The last bit of detection that Setup performs is for the presence of
the Intel Pentium floating-point division error. If you get this error, Setup asks you if you want to disable the floating-point hardware and enable floating-point emulation software.

Disabling the hardware makes your floating-point calculations much more accurate, at the expense of performance (because the software isn't as fast as the native floating-point hardware). The nice thing about this software solution, however, is that Windows NT continues to detect the hardware error every time it boots. If and when the processor is upgraded to an error-free Pentium or higher processor, the emulation software will be automatically disabled and the floating-point hardware re-enabled.

Emergency Repair Directory and Disk

Installation is almost complete. Setup copies files to your Windows NT root directory. The screen then clears, except for a progress gauge called Saving Configuration. At this point, Setup has created a \REPAIR directory in the Windows NT root directory to which it is backing up the configuration registry files. This procedure may take a few minutes, but when it is complete the \REPAIR directory will contain the information necessary to repair most damaged Windows NT installations.

If you previously told Setup you wanted to create an Emergency Repair Disk (refer to the section, "Emergency Disk," earlier in this chapter), Setup now creates an Emergency Repair Disk. Insert a disk into the floppy drive. The disk you supply does not have to be blank or formatted. Setup automatically formats the disk to ensure that it has no media errors. After the disk finishes, Setup informs you that installation is complete and prompts you to reboot.

Uninstalling Windows NT

Uninstalling Windows NT is relatively painless. In most cases, you can remove the operating system without damaging the other applications and documents on your system.

To remove Windows NT from your computer, follow these steps:

1. Boot to another operating system, such as Windows 95 or MS-DOS.

2. Delete the Windows NT installation directory tree.

3. Delete pagefile.sys.

4. Turn off the hidden, system, and read-only attributes for NTBOOTDD.SYS, and then delete them. You might not have all of these on your computer, but if so, you can find them all in the root directory of your drive C.

If you are dual-booting Windows NT and another operating system (such as MS-DOS or Windows 95), create a startup disk for the other operating system before you uninstall Windows NT. If MS-DOS, Windows 3.x, or Windows 95 doesn't boot properly after you remove NT, boot to the startup disk and type **SYS C:** to reinstall your system files onto the hard drive.

To create a startup disk in Windows 95, go to the Add/Remove Programs applet in Control Panel and select the Startup Disk tab.

Client Administrator Installation Aids

The Network Client Administrator application, in the Administrative Tools group, lets you configure your Windows NT Server system to assist you with the process of installing client machines on the network. Figure 2.1 shows the Network Client Administrator.

Figure 2.1

Network Client Administrator.

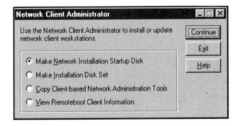

The first two options are designed to help with installing network clients, as follows:

▶ **Make Network Installation Startup Disk.** Shares the client installation files on the network and creates an installation startup disk you can use to connect to the server from the client machine and to download the installation files.

▶ **Make Installation Disk Set.** Creates a set of floppies you can use to install network client software on a client computer.

The following sections discuss these two installation options.

Network Installation Startup Disk

For an exercise testing this information, see end of chapter.

The Make Network Installation Startup Disk option in the Network Client Administrator enables you to set up a share containing installation files and then a create a network startup floppy disk that will enable you to connect to the installation files from the client machine. Client Administrator adds the necessary files to an MS-DOS system disk so that you can boot from the disk and connect to the network share.

You can use this option to create a network startup disk for any of the following operating systems:

▶ Windows NT Server v3.5, 3.51, 4.0

▶ Windows NT Workstation v3.5, 3.51, 4.0

▶ Windows 95

▶ Windows for Workgroups v3.11

▶ Microsoft Network Client for MS-DOS v3.0

The installation files for Windows 95 and Microsoft Network Client for MS-DOS are included on the Windows NT Server CD-ROM, and you'll have the option of copying them to the share you create through Client Administrator. If you plan to install a Windows NT Server, Windows NT Workstation, or Windows for Workgroups system, copy the installation files from the appropriate CD-ROM to to the shared directory on the installation server.

Although Windows 95 installation files are included on the Windows NT Server CD-ROM, you still have to purchase a license for each Windows 95 client you install. The same applies to Windows NT Server, Windows NT Workstation, or Windows for Workgroups installation files that you copy from the appropriate CD-ROM to the installation drive. As with any Windows installation, you are limited to one install per license. You are, however, at liberty to install Microsoft Client for MS-DOS.

note

The Windows NT Server and Workstation startup disks work only for Intel computers.

To create a network installation startup disk:

1. Select the Make Network Installation Startup Disk radio button in the Network Client Administrator dialog box. The Share Network Client Installation Files dialog box appears (see fig. 2.2).

Figure 2.2

The Share Network Client Installation Files dialog box.

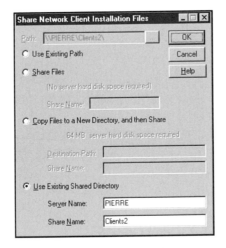

You can either copy the files to your hard disk and share them or share them directly from the Windows NT Server CD-ROM.

The Share Files radio button shares the files directly from the CD-ROM, which doesn't require any hard disk space. Choose the Copy Files to a New Directory, and then Share radio button to copy the files to your hard disk: you'll need 64 MB of hard disk space. The Use Existing Shared Directory radio button tells Client Administrator to set up the installation disk to use an existing share. You can specify a server name and a share name.

When you have configured the location of the installation files, click OK.

2. The Target Workstation Configuration dialog box appears (see fig. 2.3). Specify the size of the floppy disk, the type of network client software, and a network adapter card for the client machine. Click on OK.

Figure 2.3

The Target Work-station Configuration dialog box.

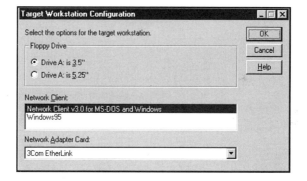

3. The Network Startup Disk Configuration dialog box appears. Specify a computer name, user name, domain, and network protocol for the client machine plus any TCP/IP settings. The Destination Path is the path to the floppy drive.

4. Insert a formatted, high-density MS-DOS system disk in the destination drive and click on OK.

5. You now can use the network installation startup disk to boot the client machine and connect to the installation files.

Make Installation Disk Set

The Make Installation Disk Set radio button in the Network Client Administrator dialog box enables you to create a set of floppy installation disks you can use to install the following network client packages:

▶ Microsoft Network Client 3.0 for MS-DOS and Windows

▶ Microsoft LAN Manager 2.2c for MS-DOS

▶ Microsoft LAN Manager 2.2c for OS/2

▶ Microsoft Remote Access Service Client v1.1 for MS-DOS

▶ Microsoft TCP/IP for Windows for Workgroups

1. Select the Make Installation Disk Set radio button and click on Continue. The Share Network Client Installation Files dialog box appears (refer to fig. 2.2 and discussion in the preceding section).

2. After that, you'll see the Make Installation Disk Set dialog box (see fig. 2.4). Choose the network software you want to install on the client, choose a destination drive, and click on OK.

Figure 2.4

The Make Installation Disk Set dialog box.

Windows NT and the Registry

The Registry is Windows NT's storehouse for configuration information. In order to understand Windows NT, you certainly must have an understanding of what the Registry is and how it works. And yet, direct references to the Registry are conspicuously absent from Microsoft's exam objectives for the Windows NT Server exam. It could be that Microsoft finds it impossible to write an exam question on the hundreds of Registry keys, subkeys, and values that is anything other than pure memorization. Whatever the reason, it is important to know that *any* configuration you do in Windows NT somehow finds its way into the Registry and, because this is a chapter on Windows NT Configuration, it wouldn't be complete without a discussion of the Registry itself.

The Registry is a configuration database, replacing the plethora of INI files used to configure both the operating system and applications under other versions of Windows. Unfortunately, Windows 95, which is on its way to becoming Registry-based, is not quite there yet. The Registry has several advantages over the older system:

> ▶ **Centralized.** Instead of a PROGMAN.INI, CPANEL.INI, and a host of other such files for your applications, Windows NT stores all its configuration data in the Registry. As a result, all Windows NT components and Windows NT-based applications can easily find information about any other aspect of the computer. In addition, the Registry supports remote administration: an administrator, sitting at her own workstation, can alter another computer's configuration by remotely editing its Registry.

> ▶ **Structured.** The Registry can contain subsections within sections, something that was impossible with INI files. The end result is a much more orderly, logical record.

> ▶ **Flexible.** INI files contained ASCII text. The Registry can contain text as well, but it also can hold binary and hexadecimal values. It can even hold executable code or entire text files. The Registry also contains preferences and restrictions for individual users, something that INI files never have done. This provides a configuration database that stores not only computer-specific information but also user-specific information.

> ▶ **Secure.** You can protect the Registry just like any object in Windows NT. An access control list can be defined for any Registry key, and a special set of permissions exists specifically for dealing with the Registry.

When viewed from this perspective, one wonders how users survived without the Registry. However, the Registry has its drawbacks:

> ▶ **Cryptic.** Unlike INI files, the assumption with many parts of the Registry seems to be: humans just don't go here. It isn't always easy to determine why certain entries are present or how to effectively configure them.

> ▶ **Sprawling.** Imagine all the INI files on an average Windows 3.x-based computer merged into a single file, with some additional hardware information as well. The Registry begins its life big, and it only gets bigger. Searching for a specific entry is further complicated by the fact that you cannot search for a specific value in the Registry (which of course you could always do in a plain-text INI file).

> ▶ **Dangerous.** If you make a mistake when editing an INI file, or if you aren't sure about the potential effect of a change, you can always exit the text editor without saving the file. Even a fatal change to an INI file can be fixed by booting to MS-DOS and using a text editor to alter the problematic file. Not so the Registry: Direct changes to the Registry are often dynamic and potentially irreversible.

Windows NT provides the following three tools for editing and managing Registry information:

▶ Registry Editor

▶ Control Panel

▶ System Policy Editor

Later in this chapter, you'll learn more about the Registry Editor and some of the Control Panel applications. (For a guided tour of Control Panel applications, see Appendix B.) Chapter 3 describes System Policy Editor.

How Windows NT Uses the Registry

You now know what the Registry is, at least conceptually. But when and how is it used? The when is easy: constantly. The how is a bit harder to answer, only because the scope of the Registry is so broad.

Windows NT accesses the Registry in the following situations:

> ▶ **Control Panel.** All changes to values in the Control Panel are written to the Registry. Even when the Control Panel

serves merely to confirm values already in place, the information is read from the Registry.

▶ **Setup.** The main Windows NT Setup program or a setup program for a Win32 application always examines the Registry for existing configuration information before entering new configuration information.

▶ **Administrative Tools.** User Manager, Event Viewer, and other Administrative Tools all read and write their information to various parts of the Registry.

▶ **Booting.** When Windows NT boots, hardware information is fed into the Registry. In addition, the kernel reports its version and build number to the Registry and extracts the name and order of the device drivers that must be loaded. These device drivers communicate with the Registry as well, reporting the resources they're using for the current session.

How Users Use the Registry

They don't. Although users can read entries in the Registry, they should not change any of them, and frankly, the Registry should be transparent to them. User settings can be modified indirectly through the Control Panel. Only experienced administrators should work directly with the Registry.

How Administrators Use the Registry

Just because administrators can directly modify the Registry doesn't mean they should do so. Continue to use the Control Panel, Windows NT Setup, and the other front ends whenever possible. Only edit the Registry directly when there is no other option to accomplish the configuration task at hand (which sadly is too often the case). The Registry is so delicate that Microsoft always includes a disclaimer with any instructions about making changes. Edit the Registry only with the specific steps spelled out and only after creating a current emergency repair disk (ERD). For more on the Windows NT Emergency Repair Disk, see Chapter 6.

Using the Registry Editor

REGEDT32.EXE enables you to directly edit the Registry (see fig. 2.5). You can find REGEDT32.EXE, also known as the Registry Editor, in the System32 subdirectory of your Windows NT root directory. The Registry Editor is installed on every Windows NT-based computer, although an icon for it is not placed in any of the program groups, not even Administrative Tools.

Figure 2.5

The Registry Editor REGEDT32.EXE

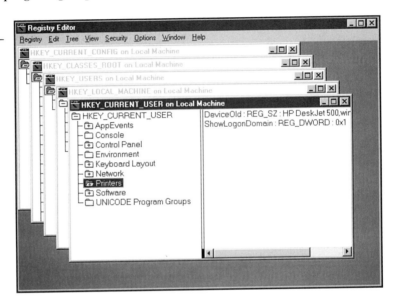

The absence of a Registry Editor icon is your first clue that you just don't toy with the Registry.

Don't confuse Registry Editor with Registry Editor. Unfortunately, two applications have this name in Windows NT. This chapter discusses REGEDT32.EXE. However, Windows 3.x has a Registry Editor, too, retained in Windows NT for compatibility. The old Registry Editor is called REGEDIT.EXE and was used solely for recording file association and OLE information, which information is now contained within a branch of the Windows NT Registry.

Launching the Registry Editor opens a screen similar to the screen shown in figure 2.5.

Before exploring the Registry in the next sections, you should know about a couple of recommendations and one major warning:

▶ From the Registry Editor Options menu, select Read Only Mode. If a check mark precedes the option on the menu, the option is already selected. Working in Read Only mode prevents changes from being recorded to the Registry— which is the safest way to explore the Registry.

▶ Choose Options, Confirm on Delete. As with Read Only Mode, a check mark precedes the option on the menu when it has been selected. If the option isn't selected, pressing the Delete key irretrievably erases the selected Registry key and all its subkeys. By default, Confirm on Delete is selected, and it's automatically enabled when working in Read Only mode. In fact, in Read Only Mode, you cannot turn off Confirm on Delete.

▶ If you're using a production computer to explore the Registry, back up Registry files before you go any further.

Before you change anything using Registry Editor, you should understand that Microsoft washes its hands of its technical support responsibility if you edit the Registry directly. In other words, you're on your own. If after altering the Registry your computer does not boot, you can call Microsoft's Product Support Service Engineers, and they probably will do their best to help you. But their best may not be good enough. You may have to reinstall the operating system, or, at the very least, undertake the emergency repair process described in Chapter 6. Because the Registry Editor writes binary, ASCII, hex, or executable code directly into the Registry, a simple mistyped character can have disastrous consequences.

Navigating the Registry

Refer to the Registry Editor main window shown in figure 2.5 and examine it for a minute. Refer to it as you read the next section, which introduces some important MCSE terminology.

Notice that Registry Editor contains five child windows. If you conceptualize the Registry as a giant tree with branches and sub-branches and leaves, then these five windows are the roots of the tree. In Windows NT-parlance, these roots are called subtrees (and occasionally, predefined key handles). The five subtrees are as follows:

- **HKEY_LOCAL_MACHINE.** Stores all the computer-specific configuration data.

- **HKEY_USERS.** Stores all the user-specific configuration data.

- **HKEY_CURRENT_USER.** Stores all configuration data for the currently logged on user.

- **HKEY_CLASSES_ROOT.** Stores all OLE and file association information.

- **HKEY_CURRENT_CONFIG.** Stores information about the hardware profile specified at startup.

Before delving into a discussion of these subtrees, take a closer look at the foreground window in the Registry Editor. You might find it somewhat similar in appearance to Explorer. This is intentional: conceptually, it helps to picture the Registry as a series of directories, subdirectories, and files. Unfortunately, the Registry doesn't really work that way.

Several files collectively comprise the Registry, but they don't break down as evenly as they do in the interface. In fact, they hardly break down below the top level at all. Some of the data in the Registry actually never gets written to disk: it's dynamically collected every time the system boots and is stored in memory until the system is shut down.

Each of the folders that you see in the left pane of the subtree windows represents a key. A key is a category, a fitting abstraction, because keys don't really exist anywhere outside Registry Editor. As you also can see from the diagram, keys can contain subkeys (or subcategories); there is no limit to how far a branch can reach.

Eventually, however, branches sprout leaves. In the Registry, keys produce values. A value has three components: a name by which it is referenced in the Registry, a data type (text, binary, and so on), and the data itself.

The types of data that can be stored in the Registry have been defined, but look at how these data types are referenced in the Registry Editor:

▶ **REG_BINARY.** Indicates that binary data follows. The binary data, however, actually is stored as a string of hexadecimal pairs, which represent byte values (2 hex digits gives a range of 0 to 255 for each byte).

▶ **REG_DWORD.** Indicates that the data is stored in a word, a term applied to a four-byte number. Words can range in value from 0 to 4,294,967,295 (a 4 GB range, enough to accommodate the full address range of a 32-bit operating system).

▶ **REG_SZ.** Denotes a string value. A string is simply text.

▶ **REG_MULTI_SZ.** Denotes a multiple string, which actually appears as a list in the Registry, with each list item separated by a null character.

▶ **REG_EXPAND_SZ.** Indicates an expandable string, which really is a variable. For instance, %SystemRoot% is an expandable string that Windows NT would interpret as the actual root directory for the operating system.

HKEY_LOCAL_MACHINE

HKEY_LOCAL_MACHINE contains all configuration information relevant to the local machine (see fig. 2.6). Every piece of information that applies to the local computer, regardless of who (if anyone) is logged on, gets stored somewhere in this subtree.

This subtree has five subkeys: HARDWARE, SAM, SECURITY, SOFTWARE, and SYSTEM.

Figure 2.6

The Registry HKEY_LOCAL_MACHINE key.

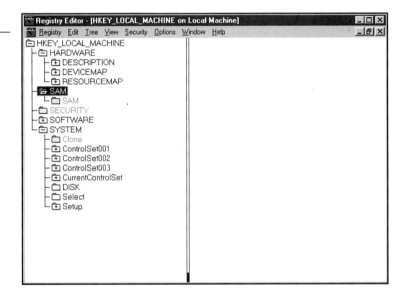

HARDWARE

The Hardware key is the only volatile key in HKEY_LOCAL_MACHINE—its data is never saved to or read from a file. Instead, Windows NT automatically detects the current hardware every time the operating system is booted and stores that information under the Hardware key under the following three subkeys: Description, DeviceMap, and ResourceMap (see fig. 2.7).

Description

The Description subkey contains the hardware database as detected by Windows NT during system boot. On Intel-based computers, the Windows NT hardware recognizer (NTDETECT.COM) autodetects this information. On RISC-based computers, the computer's firmware reads this information.

Figure 2.7

The
*HKEY_LOCAL_*
MACHINE Hard-
ware key.

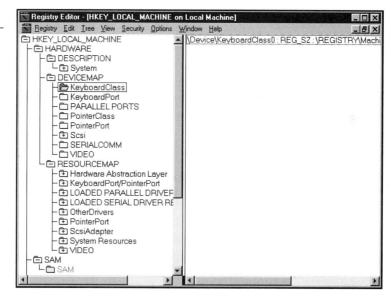

Figure 2.7

The HKEY_LOCAL_MACHINE Hardware key.

Entries for the CPU (CentralProcessor), math coprocessor (FloatingPointProcessor), and <multifunction_adapter>, which is usually called Multifunction Adapter (except in EISA computers, where it is called EisaAdapter) are listed at the top of the following tree:

```
HKEY_LOCAL_MACHINE\HARDWARE\DESCRIPTION\System
```

The <multifunction_adapter> entry enumerates the rest of the devices on the system, including the hard disk controller and serial and parallel ports.

Each device key has an Identifier value, which contains the "name" of each detected device—information that can prove helpful when troubleshooting hardware information.

DeviceMap

The subkeys of this subkey enumerate the Windows NT device drivers currently in use with pointers to the configuration information for each driver contained elsewhere in the Registry; to be exact:

```
HKEY_LOCAL_MACHINE\SYSTEM\CurrentControlSet\Services
```

ResourceMap

The ResourceMap key tracks IRQ, DMA, and other resource allocation for and by each driver. If two devices are competing for a specific resource, the information in ResourceMap can tell you which devices are conflicting—although the information isn't readable; you need to use another front-end, like Windows NT Diagnostics (WINMSD.EXE) to view it in a readable form. (See Chapter 6 for more information on WINMSD.)

SAM

SAM, Security Accounts Manager, is the Registry key that contains the entire user and group account database. As such, it sure is tempting to poke around in it a bit. Unfortunately for would-be techno-predators, but fortunately for administrators, this key is off-limits even to administrators. The only way to modify the data that SAM contains is to use the User Manager utility (or User Manager for Domains on a Windows NT Server domain controller). SAM is actually a subkey of the SECURITY key:

```
HKEY_LOCAL_MACHINE\SECURITY\SAM
```

SECURITY

Besides mirroring the SAM key, SECURITY also contains all the policy information discussed in Chapter 3, well as local group membership information. As with SAM, this key is off-limits to all users (including administrators). To modify this information, an application such as User Manager must make a call to the Windows NT Security API.

SOFTWARE

SOFTWARE is a particularly busy key: it defines and maintains configuration data for all Win32 software on the computer, including Windows NT itself (see fig. 2.8). At least five, and often more, subkeys are available here: Classes, Microsoft, Program Groups, Secure, Windows 3.1 Migration Status, and perhaps additional subkeys for other software vendors besides Microsoft.

Figure 2.8

The HKEY_LOCAL_ MACHINE Soft- ware key.

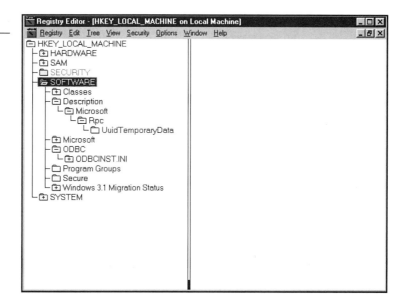

Classes

File association and OLE information is stored in this subkey (see fig. 2.9), which evolved from the old Windows 3.x configuration registry. In fact, to maintain compatibility with the old Win3.x registry addressing scheme, this information is mirrored in the **HKEY_CLASSES_ROOT** subtree. The applications themselves handle OLE configuration, and file association using File Manager hasn't changed since Windows 3.1.

Microsoft

This is one of the more populated keys in the Registry: it contains subkeys for all Microsoft software installed on the Windows NT-based computer (see fig. 2.10). Most of these entries are for Windows NT itself and its related components (Browser, Clipbook Server, Mail, and so on), but others are for Microsoft Office, Cinemania 96, or whatever Microsoft applications you may have installed.

This key sets the rule for other vendors' keys as well. Typically, you can expect to find one key at this level for each software vendor with subkeys for each installed title published by that vendor.

Figure 2.9

First page of the HKEY_LOCAL_ MACHINE\Software\ Classes subkey.

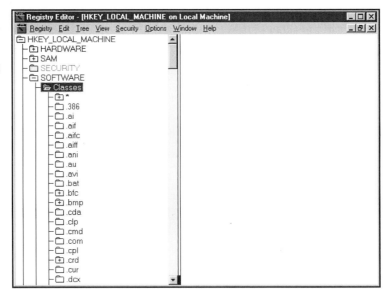

Figure 2.10

The first page of the HKEY_ LOCAL_ MACHINE\ SOFTWARE\ Microsoft subkey.

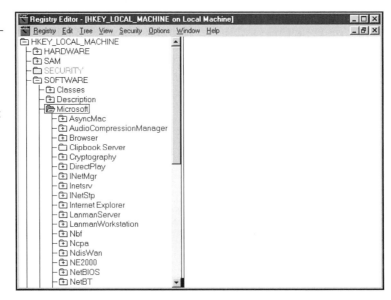

Of particular interest is the following key:

```
HKEY_LOCAL_MACHINE\SOFTWARE\Microsoft\Windows NT\CurrentVersion
```

You can find various useful items under this key, such as the name and company of the user who installed the operating system (which you can change from here), the current build number, the current service pack, and other items specific to Windows NT.

Program Groups

In Windows NT, the program groups in the Programs menu can be personal, in which case they appear only on the desktop of the user that created them, or common, in which case they appear on the desktop of anyone who logs on at the computer. The HKEY_LOCAL_MACHINE\SOFTWARE\Program Groups Registry subkey contains a list of just the common program groups for this computer (the personal program groups are stored under HKEY_USERS because it's user-specific information).

Secure

This key actually goes completely unused by Windows NT, although other applications (such as Microsoft Exchange Server) use it to maintain configuration data restricted to administrator access.

Windows 3.1 Migration Status

If you installed Windows NT Workstation in the same directory as an old copy of Windows 3.x or Windows for Workgroups 3.x, certain computer-specific configuration items from Win3.x were migrated to Windows NT when the system rebooted for the first time. These items include the REG.DAT file and certain WIN.INI settings. The presence of this key indicates that the migration is complete. To force the migration to occur again, you can simply delete this key.

SYSTEM

The critical HKEY_LOCAL_MACHINE\SYSTEM subkey maintains information about the device drivers and services installed on a Windows NT-based computer (see fig. 2.11). The SYSTEM key contains numerous subkeys, most of which are called ControlSets because they contain configuration settings used to control the devices and services on the computer. Each ControlSet contains four subkeys: Control, Enum, Hardware Profiles, and Services.

The Control key maintains information necessary to control the computer, such as the current time zone, the list of drivers to load during system boot, and the name of the computer as seen on the network. The Services key configures background processes that control hardware devices, file systems, network services, and so on.

Figure 2.11

The HKEY_LOCAL_ MACHINE\ SYSTEM\ CurrentControlSet subkey.

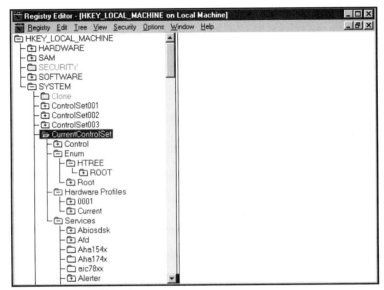

Typically, you see a ControlSet001 and ControlSet002. You also might see a ControlSet003 and even a ControlSet004. Potentially, the four possible ControlSets are as follows:

▶ **Current.** The ControlSet used to successfully boot the computer for the current session.

▶ **Default.** The ControlSet to be used to boot the system the next time the computer reboots.

▶ **Failed.** The ControlSet that attempted but failed to boot the system for this current session.

▶ **LastKnownGood.** The ControlSet that was used to successfully boot the computer for the current session and has been backed up in case the Default ControlSet fails the next time the system is rebooted.

Each of the ControlSet00x entries maps to at least one of these four types of ControlSets. You can view the mappings by examining the HKEY_LOCAL_MACHINE\SYSTEM\Select key. The values for this key are entries for each of the preceding ControlSets. The data for each value is the x in a ControlSet00x entry.

Typically, only two ControlSet00x entries appear. One of these maps to both Current and Default, and because the Current ControlSet was successful, it's used as the Default ControlSet for the next reboot. The other ControlSet00x entry maps to LastKnown-Good.

If you do see a third ControlSet00x entry, it most likely indicates a configuration change made during the current session. Because the Current ControlSet (the one used to boot the system) no longer is the Default ControlSet (the one used to boot the system next time), a separate ControlSet00x entry must exist for Current and Default.

A fourth ControlSet00x entry should exist only if your computer failed to restart and had to resort to the LastKnownGood configuration. In this case, the ControlSet that was Default and would have been Current becomes Failed, and LastKnownGood becomes Current.

The Clone subkey of the SYSTEM key is a temporary holding area that Windows NT uses for creating the LastKnownGood ControlSet, and the CurrentControlSet subkey is a mirror of whichever ControlSet00x entry contains the Current ControlSet. The final subkey is the Setup key, which the Windows NT Setup program uses. Administrators and users have no need to go here.

HKEY_CLASSES_ROOT

As mentioned earlier, the HKEY_CLASSES_ROOT subtree is a mirror of HKEY_LOCAL_MACHINE\SOFTWARE\Classes. It's mirrored here to provide compatibility with the Windows 3.x registration database, which also is accessed using the HKEY_CLASSES_ROOT handle.

HKEY_CURRENT_USER

The HKEY_CURRENT_USER subtree contains the user profile for the currently logged-on user (refer to fig. 2.5). Profiles contain all user preferences and restrictions, including Control Panel settings, personal program groups, printer connections, network drive connections, bookmarks in WinHelp, and even the most recently accessed documents in Microsoft Word. User profiles are discussed in-depth later in this chapter.

HKEY_CURRENT_USER maps to HKEY_USERS\<SID_of_current_user>, in which SID is the lengthy Security Identifier associated with the user. Occasionally, keys in this subtree duplicate keys found in HKEY_LOCAL_MACHINE but with different values. HKEY_CURRENT_USER almost always overrides HKEY_LOCAL_MACHINE.

HKEY_USERS

HKEY_USERS can potentially contain the user profiles for all users defined in the accounts database, although in practice it usually contains only the default user profile (HKEY_USERS\DEFAULT) and the profile for the currently logged on user (HKEY_USERS\<SID_of_current_user>, mapped also to HKEY_CURRENT_USER) (see fig. 2.12).

People frequently ask why Microsoft chose not to load all the user profiles in this subtree. The answer is that it isn't necessary and probably disadvantageous. Remember that the Registry resides in memory. The more data in the Registry, the more memory the Registry uses. Because the only user profile required in memory at any given time is the profile in use by the current user, loading the other users' profiles as well is unnecessary. If you do need to alter another user's profile, however, you can do so.

HKEY_CURRENT_CONFIG

The HKEY_CURRENT_CONFIG subtree contains information about the current hardware profile for the system. You learn more about hardware profiles later in this chapter.

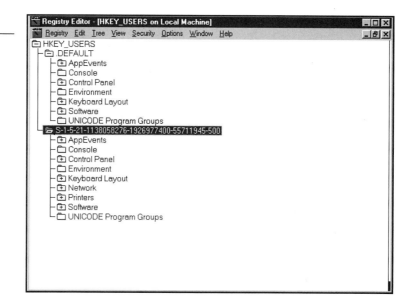

Figure 2.12

The HKEY_USERS subtree.

Editing the Registry

To edit any value in the Registry, simply double-click on the value in Registry Editor. A dialog box appears with the current value selected. You may enter the data for a new value at this point. Choosing OK effectively enters the value in the Registry. Don't look for a "save settings?" prompt message when you close Registry Editor; your changes are saved as soon as you make them.

You must leave Read Only mode to add a Registry value or key. Choose the Options menu and deselect Read Only Mode.

To add a value to an existing key, use the following procedure:

1. Select the key for which you want to add a value.

2. Choose Edit, Add Value to open the Add Value dialog box (see fig. 2.13).

Figure 2.13

Adding a value to an existing key.

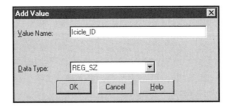

3. In the Value Name text box, enter the name of the new value.

4. Select the appropriate data type from the Data Type combo box and choose OK.

5. In the String Editor dialog box, enter the data for the new value.

To add a new key to the Registry, use this procedure:

1. Select the key under which you want to insert the new key.

2. Choose Edit, Add Key.

3. In the Add Key dialog box, enter a name for the new key in the Key Name box and then choose OK.

To delete a key or a value, simply select the key or value and press Delete. Again, be cautious: you cannot undo deletions any more than you can undo additions or changes. Every action taken in Registry Editor is irreversible (except through manual intervention). Therefore, you should enable Confirm on Delete from the Options menu. If it's already activated, a check mark appears immediately to its left.

Searching the Registry

Unfortunately, Microsoft hasn't included a thorough search utility for use with the Registry (odd, considering the nice facility available for the Windows 95 Registry). Here are your options:

▶ **Find Key.** (Accessed via the View menu.) Searches only the Registry Keys for the desired search string. You can't search for specific values using Find Key. Also, the Find Key command works only in the selected subtree, and in that subtree only from the current key onward. You can't search more than one subtree using a single Find Key command.

▶ **Save Subtree As.** (Accessed via the Registry menu.) Saves up to an entire subtree in a text file that any ASCII text editor or word processor can view. Before choosing this command, choose the key you want to use as the top level of your subtree. Registry Editor populates the text file with that key and its children. From the file, you can then perform a search using a word processor or text editor.

▶ **Print Subtree.** (Accessed via the Registry menu.) Converts the selected key and its descendants into text. Instead of saving it to a text file, however, this command directs its output to a printer.

True masters of Windows NT are true students of the Windows NT Registry, and the best way to study the Registry is to print a copy of each subtree using the Print Subtree command. Armed with a hard copy of your Registry, begin to peruse the Windows NT Resource Guide, which thoroughly documents the major (and most of the minor) Registry entries. Whatever the Resource Guide misses, the REGENTRY.HLP file, which accompanies the Resource Guide on CD-ROM, more than picks up the slack. REGENTRY.HLP is an excellent hypertext guide to the Registry. You can download REGENTRY.HLP free from Microsoft's FTP server: `ftp.microsoft.com`.

Windows NT Control Panel

The Windows NT Control Panel is a collection of small applications that each provide an interface to the Registry for the purpose of editing some specific Windows NT component (see fig. 2.14). The Control Panel is usually the first place to look if you need to make a change to your Windows NT configuration.

Figure 2.14

The Control Panel window.

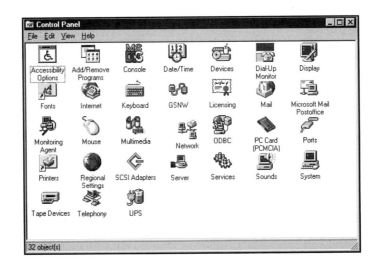

To open the Control Panel, choose Start, Settings, Control Panel. The Control Panel applications each have a specific purpose, and you'll hear them described throughout this book. This section will introduce you to the Control Panel System application. In later sections, you'll learn about the Network application, the Licensing application, and the various Control Panel applications that let you install and configure peripherals and other devices. Refer to Appendix B for a guided tour of Control Panel applications.

The System application is a typical Control Panel application. The System application is a smorgasbord of system-wide configuration parameters. Because the System application is a fairly important configuration tool, and because it doesn't fall very neatly into any of the later section in this chapter, I'll describe it for you here as an example of a Control Panel application.

Double-click on the System application in Control Panel. The System Properties dialog box will appear. The System Properties dialog box tabs are discussed in the following sections.

Startup/Shutdown

The Startup/Shutdown tab enables you to set the default boot menu option for the system startup (see fig. 2.15). It also enables you to define some recovery options in case the system encounters a STOP error.

Figure 2.15

*The System Properties Startup/
Shutdown tab.*

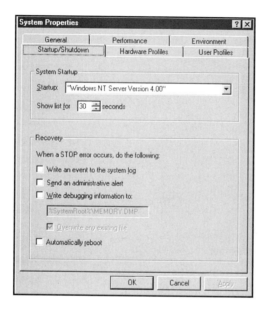

When a Windows NT-based computer is booted, the information in BOOT.INI is used to build the Boot Loader menu that appears before Windows NT loads. Boot Loader menu options typically include Windows NT Workstation 4, Windows NT Workstation 4 [VGA mode], and any other operating system set up to dual-boot with Windows NT. Although BOOT.INI is a text file, you take a risk when you edit it directly; a mistyped character can have disastrous results. The Startup/Shutdown tab provides a safe way to configure the default operating system and the length of time the Boot Loader waits for a selection before proceeding to load the default operating system (the Startup selection).

The Recovery section of the Startup/Shutdown tab determines what happens in the event of a system crash. Any one or all of the four options can be used at any given time:

▶ **Write an event to the system log.** This option records an event that can be viewed using Event Viewer.

▶ **Send an administrative alert.** If the Alerter and Messenger services are running, alerts are sent to designated users and workstations if the system crashes.

▶ **Write debugging information to.** This option launches a program called SAVEDUMP.EXE whenever a system crash occurs. SAVEDUMP.EXE writes the entire contents of the computer's memory to the pagefile and flags it so that when the system reboots, the pagefile will be copied to the file specified in this option. Note that you can overwrite an existing file which may have been generated by an old crash dump. The dump file can then be sent to a debugger or a PSS Engineer for analysis. Before this option can work, your computer's boot partition must have a pagefile of at least the size of your computer's memory.

▶ **Automatically reboot.** This option may be useful if a power surge or an errant application causes a crash (although the latter is extremely unlikely). If the problem is hardware-related, however, the same problem is likely to occur after you restart the system.

Hardware Profiles

The Hardware Profiles tab enables you to create new hardware profiles and change the order of precedence among hardware profiles (see fig. 2.16). Click on the Properties button to define a docking state for a portable computer or to enable/disable network hardware.

To create a new hardware profile, select an existing profile and click on the Copy button. In the subsequent Copy Profile dialog box, enter a name for the new hardware profile. The new hardware profile will appear in the Available Hardware Profiles list.

If you have defined more than one hardware profile, Windows NT displays a menu of hardware profiles at startup and asks which profile you want to use. The profile you specify becomes the active hardware profile. Any changes to your hardware configuration affect the active hardware profile.

Figure 2.16

The System Prop-
erties Hardware
Profiles tab.

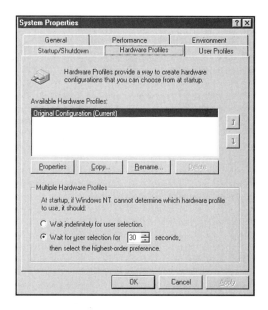

The up and down arrows to the right of the Available Hardware Profiles list let you change the preference order of the hardware profiles. The radio buttons at the bottom of the Hardware Profiles tab let you specify whether Windows NT waits indefinitely for you to choose a hardware profile, or whether the choice defaults to the highest-preference profile after a specific time interval.

Environment

The Environment tab enables you to define system and user environment variables (see fig. 2.17). The system environment variables are written to the following key:

```
HKEY_LOCAL_MACHINESYSTEM\CurrentControlSetControl\Session
Manager\Environment
```

You have to be an administrator before you can alter the System environment variables using Control Panel.

The User Variables section is the only area of this application that non-administrators can access and configure.

To set or change a user environment variable, follow these steps:

Figure 2.17

*The System Prop-
erties Environ-
ment tab.*

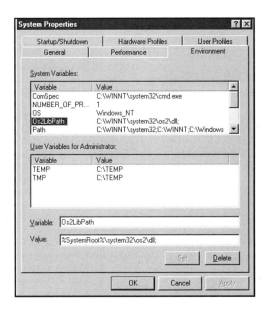

1. Select the environment variable you want to change. (The
   variable and value appear in the Variable and Value text boxes.)

2. Position the cursor at (or tab down to) the Variable or the
   Value text box.

3. Change the variable or value (or both).

4. Click on the Set button.

To create a new environment variable and set its value, do these
steps:

1. Click in the System Variables list box if you want to add a
   system variable; click in the User Variables for Administrator
   list box if you want to add a user variable.

2. Click in the Variable text box and enter the name of the new
   variable.

3. Click in the Value text box and enter the value for the new
   variable.

4. Click on the Set button.

To delete an environment variable, follow these steps:

1. Select the variable in the System Variables list or User Variables for Administrator list.

2. Click on the Delete button.

Performance

The Application Performance setting of the Performance tab enables you to boost the response time for the foreground application (see fig. 2.18). Click on the Change button in the Virtual Memory section to open the Virtual Memory dialog box, which maintains settings for Paging file sizes and Registry size (see fig. 2.19).

Figure 2.18

The System Properties Performance tab.

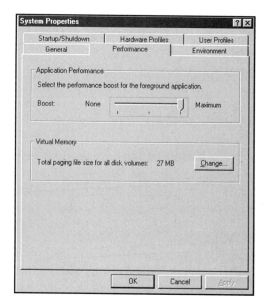

General

The System Properties General tab displays some basic information about your computer: the operating system and version number, the processor type and the amount of RAM, and the registration names from NT Setup.

Figure 2.19

*The Virtual
Memory dialog
box.*

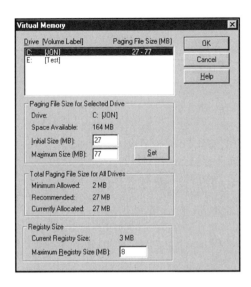

Configuring Protocols and Protocol Bindings

The Control Panel Network application is a central spot for entering and altering network configuration information. The five tabs of the Network application are as follows:

▶ **Identification.** The Identification tab specifies the computer name for the computer and the domain to which it belongs (see fig. 2.20). Click on the Change button to change the values. If your Windows NT computer is a domain controller, you cannot move to a different domain, but you can change domain's name using the Change button. If your Windows NT computer is a workstation or a member server, the Change button offers several alternatives (see fig. 2.21). You can join a workgroup or domain, or you can set up an account for the computer in the domain's security database.

Figure 2.20

The Network application Identification tab.

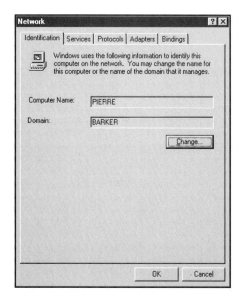

Figure 2.21

The Identification Changes dialog box for a non-domain controller, invoked from the Network application Identification tab.

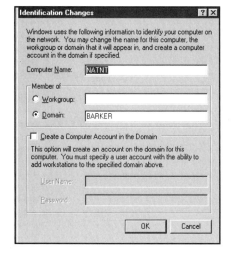

▶ **Services.** The Services tab lets you add, remove, or configure network services (see fig. 2.22). Network services were described earlier in this chapter. Click on the Add button to view a list of available network services. Click on the Properties button to view and configuration information for the service.

Figure 2.22

The Network application Services tab.

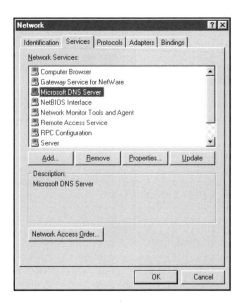

▶ **Protocols.** The Protocols tab lets you add, remove, and configure network protocols (see fig. 2.23). Some of the protocol configuration options are discussed later in this chapter.

Figure 2.23

The Network application Protocols tab.

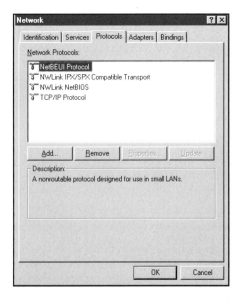

▶ **Adapters.** The Adapters tab lets you add, remove, and configure network adapter cards for the system (see fig. 2.24).

Click on Add to view a list of available network adapter card drivers. The Properties button lets you configure the IRQ and the Port address for the adapter.

Figure 2.24

The Network application Adapters tab.

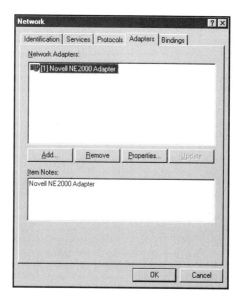

▶ **Bindings.** A binding is a potential pathway from a particular network service to a network protocol to a network adapter. The Bindings tab tabulates the bindings for the system. In figure 2.25, the Workstation service is bound to the Net-BEUI, WINS Client (TCP/IP), and NWLink NetBIOS protocols. Click on the plus sign beside the protocol to reveal the adapters that are bound to the protocol for the particular service. Much of the binding configuration takes place automatically. If you install Remote Access Service and enable TCP/IP, for example, the Remote Access WAN Wrapper appears beneath the WINS Client (TCP/IP) protocol.

Microsoft lists the following objective for the Windows NT Server exam:

Configure protocols and protocol bindings. Protocols include: TCP/IP, NWLink IPX/SPX Compatible Transport, NetBEUI.

Figure 2.25

The Network application Bindings tab.

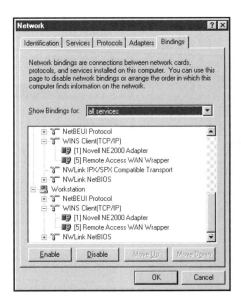

Installing and Configuring NWLink

For an exercise testing this information, see end of chapter.

All Windows NT networking components are installed and configured in the Control Panel Network application. If you want to install the NWLink protocol, choose the Protocols tab and click on the Add button. The message Building Network Protocol Option List appears briefly, and then you are prompted to select a networking component.

Select NWLink IPX/SPX Compatible Transport. You need to steer Setup toward the original source files at this point. (You might need to point Setup to the Microsoft Windows NT Workstation CD-ROM.) If Remote Access Services is installed on your system, Setup asks if you want to configure RAS to support NWLink. After the NWLink files finish installing, an icon labeled NWLink IPX/SPX Compatible Transport appears in the Network Protocols list of the Protocols tab. You must shut down and restart your computer before the changes can take effect.

Figure 2.26 shows the NWLink IPX/SPX Properties dialog box. To reach the NWLink IPX/SPX Properties dialog box, select NWLink IPX/SPX Compatible Transport in the Network application Protocols tab and click on the Properties button. Windows

NT automatically detects your network adapter at Startup. If you know which frame type is in use on your network, you can use this dialog box to manually set Windows NT to match it. By default, Windows NT is configured to autodetect the frame type, which it does by sending out a Routing Information Protocol (RIP) request on all frame types when NWLink is initialized. One of the following scenarios will occur:

Figure 2.26

The NWLink IPX/ SPX Properties dialog box.

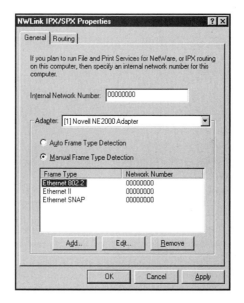

▶ **No response from any of the frame types.** NWLink uses the default frame type, which is 802.2 when Windows NT is first installed.

▶ **A response from one of the frame types.** NWLink uses this frame type, which also becomes the default protocol the next time autodetection occurs.

▶ **Multiple responses are received.** NWLink steps through this list (in order) until it finds a frame type that was one of the multiple responses:

   ▶ Ethernet 802.2

   ▶ Ethernet 802.3

- ▶ Ethernet II

- ▶ SNAP

You can configure both Windows NT Workstation and Windows NT Server for multiple frame types, but you can use Control Panel Network to do so only for Server. If you want Windows NT Workstation to use multiple frame types, you must edit the registry directly with RegEdit. Find the following key and change the PktType value (which is of type REG_MULTI_SZ) to any combination of the following numbers:

```
HKEY_LOCAL_MACHINE\SYSTEM\CurrentControlSet\Services\NWlnkIpx\
~NetConfig\<NIC_Driver>
```

- ▶ 0 Ethernet II

- ▶ 1 Ethernet 802.3

- ▶ 2 Ethernet 802.2

- ▶ 3 Ethernet SNAP

- ▶ 4 ARCnet

Make sure you're using the correct frame type for your network; an incorrect frame type can cause an immense slowdown in network performance. If, because Auto Detected is selected, you cannot determine what frame type your Windows NT-based computer is using, use the IPXROUTE CONFIG command from the command prompt. You get an instant report of the frame type(s) in use.

If you're not sure which frame type(s) your other servers and clients are using, here is a list of which frame types particular servers use:

- ▶ **802.2.** Windows NT Workstation 3.5x, Windows NT Server 3.5x, NetWare 4.x, NetWare, 3.12, Windows for Workgroups 3.11 from the Windows NT Server CD, Microsoft Network Client 3.0

▶ **802.3.** Windows NT 3.1, Windows NT Advanced Server 3.1, NetWare 3.11 and below, Windows for Workgroups 3.x retail.

The preceding are the defaults for the listed operating systems; your mileage, as they say, may vary. To verify the frame type on a NetWare server, check its AUTOEXEC.NCF file.

The Network Number field at the bottom of the NWLink IPX/ SPX Properties dialog box reveals one additional configuration parameter, the Internal Network Number.

The Internal Network Number is similar to a subnet address on a TCP/IP network; that is, it determines which servers are considered "local" and which ones are considered "remote." The default setting here is 0, which forces Windows NT to send out a RIP request and wait for the closest NetWare server to respond with the proper internal network number.

Working with TCP/IP

Of all the protocols that ship with Windows NT, TCP/IP requires the most configuration by the administrator. Nevertheless, TCP/ IP is an integral part of the Internet, and it's becoming an increasingly popular protocol for private networks as well. The section defines some important TCP/IP concepts, describes how to configure TCP/IP on a Windows NT machine, and looks at some of the important commands and tools that will assist you in implementing TCP/IP on your network. This discussion is by no means complete or exhaustive; NRP's *MCSE Study Guide: TCP/IP and SMS* furnishes a thorough discussion of TCP/IP addressing and configuration. This book discusses the basics, the parameters that are necessary to install any TCP/IP network client.

TCP/IP is one of those broad topics that is difficult to position in either the MCSE Server or Enterprise exam. Microsoft's exam objectives include TCP/IP protocols and bindings with the Server exam but reserve TCP/IP-related topics such as DHCP, WINS, and DNS for the Enterprise exam. Nevertheless, it is difficult to even describe how to configure TCP/IP without at least touching on DHCP, WINS, and DNS. Microsoft's Windows NT Core Technologies course includes material on DHCP, WINS, and DNS, and these services are an important component of even smaller Microsoft networks.

IP Address

In any type of network, communication between computers is possible only when you have a bulletproof way for uniquely identifying any computer on the network. At the lowest level, packets are sent from one network card to another, and it's the serial numbers burned into the card itself that serve to identify the sender and receiver.

Most networks cannot see that far down, however, so they apply another level (or perhaps more than one level) of addressing to ensure compatibility across different platforms. The Internet Protocol (the IP in TCP/IP) sends packets using a computer's IP Address (a unique 32-bit binary number that no other computer on the network can possess). Actually, it's about time to stop speaking in terms of computers and begin speaking in terms of network interface cards (NICs): each NIC requires its own IP Address.

Because a 32-bit binary address isn't any easier to remember than the hexadecimal NIC address burned into the card (try 10000011011010110000001011001000 on for size), the 32-bit address usually is expressed as four octets, or eight-bit numbers, which then are represented in decimal form. An eight-bit number can have a value of anywhere from 0 to 255, so an IP address consists of four numbers between 0 and 255 separated by decimal points. The 32-bit binary address in the beginning of this paragraph can also be written like this: 131.107.2.200.

Subnet Mask

Each IP address consists of a netid and a hostid. The netid is the left-most portion of the address and assigns an address every NIC on the same physical network shares. If other physical networks are interconnected via routers (these physical networks are called subnetworks or simply, subnets), each of these networks must have its own unique netid. The hostid is the right-most portion of the IP address, and a unique hostid must be assigned to every network adapter that shares a common netid.

The netid/hostid split isn't always fifty-fifty; a parameter called the Subnet Mask determines how many bits are devoted to each field. The Subnet Mask also is a 32-bit number, and each bit set to 1 denotes a bit assigned to the netid; each bit set to 0 denotes a bit assigned to the hostid.

Some platforms' implementations of TCP/IP do not require the administrator to configure a subnet mask. That doesn't mean that the subnet mask isn't required, just that the operating system is using default subnet masks.

Default subnet masks are defined by the three Internet classes of IP Addresses:

▶ **Class A.** The first octet belongs to the netid and the others to the hostid. Class A netids can range from 0 to 127 (although both 0 and 127 are excluded—see the section "The Rules," later in this chapter), which means that there can only be 126 class A networks in the entire Internet, and because three octets are available for the hostid, each of these 126 networks can host more than 16 million NICs. Odds are, you probably won't be using one of these.

▶ **Class B.** The first two octets define the netid, and the next two octets define the hostid. The first octet of the netid can range from 128 to 191. Combined with the unrestricted second octet, there is room for more than 16,000 Class B networks, each with the capacity for more than 65,000 NICs. These are more common than Class A networks, but still a bit of overkill for most networks.

▶ **Class C.** The first three octets define the netid, and the last octet is the hostid. The first octet of the netid can range from 192 to 223, and combined with the second and third octets, you can have more than two million Class C networks on the Internet. Each of these is restricted to only 254 hosts, however (the extremes in either field are always excluded). This is the most common type of IP address the InterNIC assigns.

You can see that the problem of relying on the default subnets is that if you have more than 254 NICs to support on a single network, you either need to segment your network, or move to a Class B address and probably waste many of the 65,000 hostids that cannot be assigned elsewhere.

That's why the subnet mask comes in handy. Here are the subnet masks for the various classes of networks:

▶ Class A: 255.0.0.0

▶ Class B: 255.255.0.0

▶ Class C: 255.255.255.0

Defaults are an all or nothing deal, but by borrowing some bits from the hostid and tacking them on to the netid, you can take a Class B address and share it among multiple physical networks. You would be well advised to check out the TCP/IP study guide because unless you are already a TCP/IP administrator, you need more depth than this book can devote.

Default Gateway

A default gateway is a router, a device that sends packets on to a remote network. A router can be a device created for that purpose, such as Cisco or 3Com makes, or it can be a Windows NT-based computer that has at least two network cards (for spanning two networks). When a packet is sent to a remote netid, IP forwards the packet to the default gateway in the hopes that it knows where to send the packet. Although strictly speaking, default gateways are optional parameters, without one, communications are limited to the local subnet.

Putting It Together

An important point to remember is that every computer on the internetwork must have a unique IP address. When your internetwork is the Internetwork, that's pretty hard to ensure. Here are a few things to keep in mind:

▶ If you're on the public Internet, apply for a range of addresses from the Internet Network Information Center (InterNIC). The InterNIC is the closest thing the Internet has to a governing body, and it's the organization responsible for tracking and assigning the usage of IP addresses. You can reach the InterNIC via e-mail at hostmaster@internic.net and via the U.S. Postal Service at 505 Huntmar Park Drive, Herndon, VA 22070.

▶ If you aren't on the public Internet, consider applying to the InterNIC anyway. Odds are, you'll be on the Internet sooner or later.

▶ If you're absolutely sure that you don't need Internet connectivity (most likely because you plan to use a proxy server such as Microsoft's forthcoming Catapult project), you may use any IP addresses you like, as long as they're unique within your private internetwork, and as long as they follow the rules.

The Rules

This section doesn't pretend to be a complete discussion of IP addressing requirements, but it does lay out a couple cardinal rules that every TCP/IP administrator must know.

▶ **Rule #1.** Don't go to extremes. Hostids cannot be set to all zeroes or all ones, because these denote broadcast messages rather than a specifically targeted message. An easy rule of thumb is to stay away from 0 and 255 when assigning octets.

▶ **Rule #2.** Don't use 127 as a netid. When 127 is used as the first octet of a netid, TCP/IP recognizes the address as a special diagnostic address called the *loopback address*, so called because any message to this address is returned to its sender. 127 addresses are used to test the configuration of a TCP/IP-based computer.

▶ **Rule #3.** All netids on a subnet must match. If an NIC doesn't have the same netid as the rest of the NICs on its subnet, the host can't communicate with the other hosts on the subnet. Likewise, if a host on a remote subnet is configured using the netid of the local subnet, communication between the two subnets becomes impossible because the packets are never routed because they appear to the local host as the local netid.

▶ **Rule #4.** All hostids in a subnet must be unique. If, on a subnet, two hosts share a hostid, the results are unpredictable—and certainly unwanted. If a Windows NT-based computer attempts to join the network with a duplicate hostid, Windows NT doesn't let it join the network; it sends a message to both the usurper and the usurpee explaining the problem. If a non-Windows NT-based host joins the network with a duplicate hostid, the results can range from the intercepting of the other host's packets, to the locking up of the usurper's computer (and perhaps the usurpee's as well if it isn't a Windows NT-based computer). In short, keep careful tabs on your IP addresses, or use the DHCP protocol described later in this chapter.

Installing TCP/IP

To install TCP/IP, start from the Control Panel Network application. Choose the Protocols tab and click on the Add button. Select TCP/IP Protocol. Choose OK.

Installing and Configuring TCP/IP with DHCP

When you install TCP/IP, Setup asks if you want to use DHCP to dynamically provide IP addresses. DHCP stands for Dynamic Host Configuration Protocol; rather than keep tabs yourself on where your IP addresses have been assigned at any given moment, a Windows NT Server running DHCP can do it for you. A DHCP server leases addresses to clients when they join the network.

If you have a DHCP server on your subnet, or if your routers can forward DHCP packets (ask your vendor if the router is RFC 1542 compliant if you aren't sure) consider choosing Yes for the prompt shown in figure 2.27. The DHCP client is assigned an IP address automatically when it restarts.

Figure 2.27

The DHCP prompt in TCP/IP.

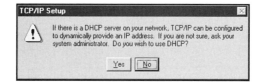

Selecting the DHCP option enables DHCP for all network interface cards in the computer. To selectively assign DHCP to individual NICs in a multihomed computer (a computer with more than one NIC), don't select DHCP at this time. Choose No. You can configure each NIC separately in the Microsoft TCP/IP Properties dialog box.

If Remote Access Services (RAS) is installed on your system, Setup asks if you want to configure RAS to support the TCP/IP protocol. After the installation finishes, choose Close in the Network application main window and the Microsoft TCP/IP Properties dialog box appears (see fig. 2.28).

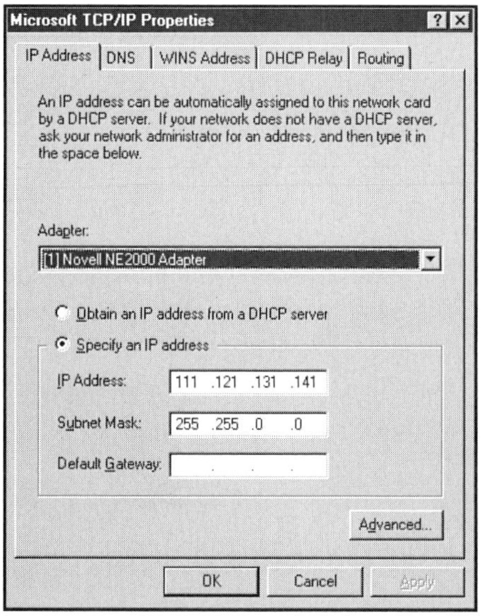

Figure 2.28

The Microsoft TCP/IP Properties dialog box.

In the Adapter drop-down list in the IP Address tab of the Microsoft TCP/IP Properties dialog box, you may select any of the network adapters you have installed on your computer. After you select a network adapter, you have one more chance to Enable Automatic DHCP Configuration. If you enable the Obtain an IP address from a DHCP server radio button, the IP Address and Subnet Mask for this network adapter becomes grayed out, because that information henceforth comes from a DHCP server. You may still specify a Default Gateway by clicking on the Advanced button, but this information can come from a DHCP server as well. Any information you enter at this screen overrides the DHCP-assigned information.

The Advanced button opens the Advanced IP Addressing dialog box (see fig. 2.29). The Advanced IP Addressing dialog box lets you enter multiple IP addresses for a single network adapter, which enables administrators to create logical networks within a single physical network; virtual subnets, you might say. Each IP Address also requires its own Subnet Mask entry. You also may enter multiple Default Gateways for each network adapter. The arrow buttons allow you to adjust the order in which the gateways are tried. If the gateway at the top of the list fails, the second one is used unless it too fails, in which case the third one is used, and so on down the list.

Figure 2.29

The Advanced IP Addressing dialog box.

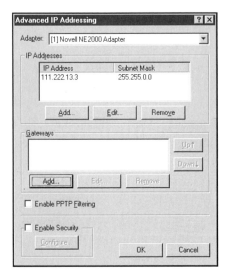

Select the Enable Security check box and click on the Configure button to open the TCP/IP Security dialog box, which lets you selectively enable TCP ports, UDP ports, and IP protocols.

Installing and Configuring TCP/IP Manually

If you really want to configure TCP/IP manually, you must enter an IP Address and Subnet Mask for each NIC. Although Windows NT doesn't consider the Default Gateway mandatory, you probably should enter your router's IP address here (that is, if you want to communicate with remote subnets). To enable IP routing, select the Routing tab in the Microsoft TCP/IP Properties dialog box and enable the Enable IP Routing check box.

What Is WINS?

The WINS Address tab in the Microsoft TCP/IP Properties dialog box lets you specify IP addresses for Primary and Secondary WINS Servers (see fig. 2.30). Although WINS is another service included only with Windows NT Server, as with DHCP, Windows NT Workstations can act as clients to a WINS server.

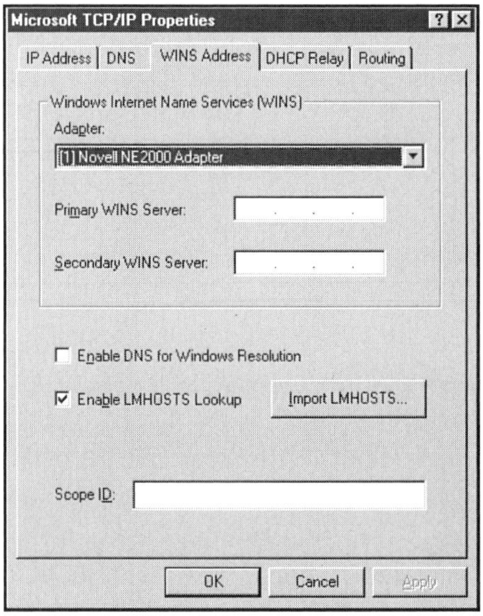

Figure 2.30

The WINS Address tab of the Microsoft TCP/IP Properties dialog box.

WINS stands for Windows Internet Name Service. WINS is a service that maps NetBIOS names to IP addresses. Four decimal octets rather than the full 32-bit binary number are used for configuring IP addresses because it's easier to remember the four decimal octets. Of course, that is a relative concept; it isn't all that easy to remember 131.107.2.200, either.

To make things more user-friendly as well as to maintain the UNC convention across the board, Windows NT includes a NetBIOS layer that resides just above TCP/IP. This component, called Net-BT, allows communication using standard Microsoft NetBIOS computer names, such as \\NTServer.

This is great news for users, but it doesn't change the fact that TCP/IP requires IP addresses to communicate. To resolve the NetBIOS names to IP addresses, Windows NT must broadcast the name of the server and wait for it to respond with its IP address. This takes time, causes network broadcast traffic, and generally doesn't work across subnets (because most routers do not forward broadcast messages).

Here's where WINS comes in. WINS maintains a database of active names on the network. When a WINS client needs to contact another server, the WINS server resolves the NetBIOS name, and responds with the server's IP address.

If you have a WINS server on your network, you may enter its IP address in the Primary WINS Server field. If you have more than one WINS server, you may enter another server's IP address in the Secondary WINS Server field. Again, however, you also can assign this information via DHCP.

The bottom of the WINS Address tab has three Windows Networking parameters:

▶ **Enable DNS for Windows Resolution.** Selecting this check box instructs Windows NT to look up NetBIOS names against a Domain Name Server, which is usually a service running on Windows NT Server, or a daemon running on Unix. DNS is a static database usually reserved for TCP/IP hostnames, such as ftp.microsoft.com, but NT 4.0 provides WINS/DNS integration so that you can use DNS for NetBIOS resolution as well.

- ► **Enable LMHOSTS Lookup.** This check box incorporates a text database mapping of NetBIOS names to IP addresses into the name resolution process. This name resolution technique predates WINS, and although it's harder to keep up-to-date, it causes less network traffic than WINS, because name resolution occurs on the client itself before it attempts to use network name resolution resources.

- ► **Scope ID.** Enables administrators to create logical IP networks that are invisible to each other. Hosts must belong to the same NetBIOS scope before they can communicate.

DNS

To configure DNS, select the DNS tab in the Microsoft TCP/IP Properties dialog box. Enter your domain name. Click on the Add button under the DNS Service Search Order box and enter the addresses of the DNS servers on your network. You can change the search order of the DNS servers using the Up and Down buttons to the right of the box. The DNS tab also allows you to enter a domain suffix search order.

TCP/IP Diagnostics

A host of TCP/IP utilities are included with Windows NT. Some of the more useful ones are IPConfig, Ping, and TRACERT.

IPConfig

IPConfig displays the TCP/IP configuration parameters of the local host. The /ALL switch can be used to display every field, including DHCP and WINS information.

Ping

Ping is a diagnostic utility used to test the connection between two hosts on an internetwork. It uses the Internet Control Message Protocol (ICMP) echo and reply functions to send messages to and from a remote host. If the connection is successful, Ping returns four responses similar to the following:

```
Pinging ftp.microsoft.com [198.105.232.1] with 32 bytes of data:
Reply from 198.105.232.1: bytes=32 time=227ms TTL=51
Reply from 198.105.232.1: bytes=32 time=221ms TTL=51
Request timed out.
Reply from 198.105.232.1: bytes=32 time=205ms TTL=51
```

Note that the third attempt timed out. This can happen on the Internet during busy periods, which is why Ping makes four attempts at a connection. Four timeouts would indicate that a connection is unlikely for the time being.

TRACERT

The TRACERT utility traces the hops that packets take on their way from the local host to a remote host. Here's the route from the Portland, OR MSN, connection, to Microsoft's FTP Server:

```
Tracing route to ftp.microsoft.com [198.105.232.1]
over a maximum of 30 hops:
1    161 ms    154 ms    156 ms   Max3.Seattle.WA.MS.UU.NET
➼[204.177.253.3]
2    198 ms    190 ms    160 ms   Cisco2.San-Francisco.CA.MS.UU.Net
➼[137.39.2.63]
3    185 ms    184 ms    214 ms   San-Jose3.CA.ALTER.NET
➼[137.39.100.17]
4    195 ms    192 ms    213 ms   mae-west.SanFrancisco.mci.net
➼[198.32.136.12]
5    264 ms    191 ms    346 ms   borderx2-hssi2-
➼0.SanFrancisco.mci.net [204.70.158.117]
6    *         212 ms    218 ms   core2-fddi-1.SanFrancisco.mci.net
➼[204.70.158.65]
7    220 ms    229 ms    202 ms   core1-hssi-2.Sacramento.mci.net
➼[204.70.1.146]
8    253 ms    435 ms    269 ms   core-hssi-3.Seattle.mci.net
➼[204.70.1.150]
9    236 ms    263 ms    205 ms   border1-fddi-0.Seattle.mci.net
➼[204.70.2.146]
10   *         204 ms    *        nwnet.Seattle.mci.net
➼[204.70.52.6]
11   242 ms    242 ms    234 ms   seabr1-gw.nwnet.net
➼[192.147.179.5]
12   197 ms    209 ms    199 ms   microsoft-t3-gw.nwnet.net
➼ [198.104.192.9]
```

```
13    *       259 ms   232 ms   131.107.249.3
14   220 ms   245 ms   228 ms   ftp.microsoft.com [198.105.232.1]
Trace complete.
```

Armed with these three utilities, you can troubleshoot connectivity problems between two hosts. Say, for instance, you're trying to reach Microsoft as FTP server, but the connection fails.

First, use IPConfig to confirm that you do indeed have TCP/IP correctly initialized on your computer. Also check the Default Gateway and name resolution information, because incorrect configuration of these items affects your ability to connect to remote hosts.

If everything looks okay, Ping 127.0.0.1, a loopback diagnostic address, and it will confirm that TCP/IP is correctly initialized and bound on your computer. If this step isn't successful, shut down and restart your computer, and try again. If this step still isn't successful, check the network bindings using the Bindings tab of the Control Panel Network application.

Next, ping your own IP address to confirm that your computer is configured with the correct address and to ensure that no other hosts on the network have your IP address. If this step is unsuccessful, use IPCONFIG to check for a typo in your IP address. If the address looks fine but you still cannot ping yourself, check the Event Viewer for a message that indicates another host has your IP address. A message always appears when you do this, but it's easy to dismiss without reading it.

If you successfully ping yourself, try pinging your default gateway. If the router is down, you can't communicate with any remote hosts. If this step is successful, move on to the next step.

Ping the remote host. If this step is successful, you should be able to form a connection. If this step is unsuccessful, a router probably is down somewhere between your default gateway and the remote host. Confirm that by using the TRACERT utility to see where the communication breakdown is occurring.

Configuring Network Adapters

The Adapters tab of the Control Panel Network application lets you add and configure network adapters for your system (refer to fig. 2.24).

To add a new network adapter, click on the Add button. The Select Network Adapter dialog box that appears lets you select an adapter from a list (see fig. 2.31). Click on Have Disk to install an adapter that isn't on the list.

Figure 2.31

The Select Network Adapter dialog box.

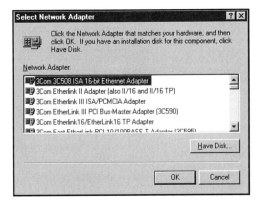

Microsoft lists the following objective for the Windows NT Server exam:

Configure network adapters. Considerations include: changing IRQ, I/O base, memory address, configuring multiple adapters.

To configure the IRQ and/or I/O port address (base-memory I/O address—expressed in decimals), double-click on an adapter in the Network application Adapters tab or select an adapter and click on the Properties button. The Network Card Setup dialog box lets you configure an IRQ and I/O port address (see fig. 2.32).

Figure 2.32

The Network Card Setup dialog box.

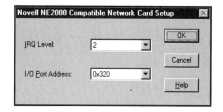

Windows NT Core Services

A service is a built-in application that provides support for other applications or other components of the operating system. Windows NT inlcudes dozens of services, each performing a highly specialized function. Many of Windows NT's services support NT's networking capabilities.

Examples of Windows NT services include:

▶ Windows Internet Name Service (WINS), which maps IP addresses to NetBIOS names.

▶ UPS service, which interacts with an Uninterruptible Power Supply system to prevent your system from abruptly shutting down.

▶ Server service, which accepts I/O requests from the network and routes the requested resources back to the client.

▶ Workstation service, which accepts I/O requests from the local system and redirects the requests to the appropriate computer on the network.

Services are background processes that perform specific functions in Windows NT. Typically, services don't interact with the user interface in any way (including appearing in the Task List), so users shouldn't be aware of their existence. Think of a Windows NT service as the equivalent of Unix daemon, or if you are more comfortable with NetWare, the equivalent of a NetWare Loadable Module (NLM).

This section will take a closer look at some important Windows NT services and how to configure them.

Microsoft lists the following objective for the Window NT Server exam:

Configure Windows NT Server core services. Services include: Directory Replicator, License Manager, other services.

The Services Application

The Control Panel Services application manages the services on your system.

For an exercise testing this information, see end of chapter.

The Services application writes directly to the following key, where configuration data for Windows NT services is maintained:

HKEY_LOCAL_MACHINE\SYSTEM\CurrentControlSet\Control\Services

Double-click on the Services icon in Control Panel to open the Services dialog box (see fig. 2.33). The Services dialog box lists the services on your system, as well as the Status (whether the service is started or not) and the Startup type. The Startup type setting describes whether the service will start automatically or manually, or whether it is disabled. Automatic services start at the very end of the boot process, after the "Welcome: Press Ctrl+Alt+Del to log on" window appears. (Because services are Win32 programs, they require a fully functional operating system before they can be opened.) Manual services start when you select the service in the Services dialog box and click on the Start button.

Figure 2.33

The Control Panel Services application

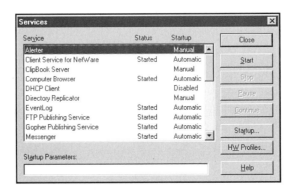

Note that the Services dialog also includes buttons that stop a service, pause a service, or continue a service that has been paused. Pausing a service causes the service to continue handling the processes it's currently serving but not take on any new clients. For example, the Server service is required to run on a server before it can accept connections from a client. Stopping the Server service causes all connections to be immediately dropped, but pausing the service preserves existing connections while rejecting new connection attempts.

To enable a service for a given hardware profile, click on the HW Profiles button in the Services dialog, select a profile, and click on OK.

Double-click on a service to open a configuration dialog box—called the Service dialog (as opposed to the Services dialog)—that enables you to configure a startup type and define a logon account for the service.

The logon account defines a security context for the service. Because services are Win32 programs, they must run under the aegis of a user account. The problem is, services continue to execute even when nobody is logged on to the computer, so the administrator must configure the service to use a specific user account. Here are two options:

▶ **System Account.** An internal account, called SYSTEM, can be used either by the operating system or by the service. This method isn't recommended, however, because you can't fine-tune rights and permissions without possibly affecting the performance and stability of the operating system and other services that may use this account.

▶ **This Account.** You may designate any user account from your account database here. You should create a separate account for each service for which you want to configure rights and permissions.

Network Services

The Services tab of the Control Panel Network application lets you add, configure, and remove services that support network functions (refer to fig. 2.22). The Add button opens the Select Network Service dialog box, which provides a list of available Windows NT network services. Select a service and click OK to add the service to your configuration. Or, click the Have Disk button if you are attempting to install a new service from a disk.

Some of the services in the Network Services list are configurable through the Network application and some are not. Select a service and click on the Properties button to open a configuration dialog box for the service (if there is one). Figure 2.34 shows the configuration dialog box for the Server service.

Figure 2.34

The Server dialog box.

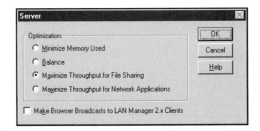

Many of the network components you'll read about elsewhere in this book (DHCP, WINS, DNS, RAS, and Gateway Services for NetWare) are actually services that, though often configured elsewhere, can still be added, started, stopped, and managed through the Network Services tab and the Control Panel Services application. For the most part, anything you do on the network occurs through some form of network service.

The following sections examine some important topics relating to Windows NT services, as follows:

▶ Directory replication

▶ Client license management

▶ The browser process

Directory Replication

For an exercise testing this information, see end of chapter.

Directory Replication is a facility that lets you configure Windows NT Servers to automatically transmit updated versions of important files and directories to other computers on the network.

The purpose of Directory Replication is to simplify the task of distributing updates for logon scripts, system policy files, Help files, phone lists, and other important files. The network administrator updates the file(s) on a single server (called the export server) and the export server automatically distributes the file(s) to other network servers or even to network workstations. The computer receiving the update is called the import computer. A Windows NT Server, a Windows NT Workstation, or a LAN Manager OS/2 server can act as an import computer.

Directory Replication is performed by the Directory Replicator service. You can start and stop the Directory Replicator service from the Control Panel Services application. The parameters for the Directory Replicator service are found in the Registry key:

```
HKEY_LOCAL_MACHINE\SYSTEM\CurrentControlSet\Services\Replicator\
Parameters
```

Most of the parameters in the Registry key HKEY_LOCAL_ MACHINE\SYSTEM\CurrentControlSet\Services\Replicator\ Parameters can be configured within Server Manager (described later in this chapter). Two important exceptions are:

Interval. A REG_WORD value that defines how often an export server checks for updates. The range is from 1 to 60 minutes and the default is 5 minutes.

GuardTime. A REG_WORD value that defines how long a directory must be stable before its files can be replicated. The range is 0 to one half of the Interval value. The default is 2 minutes. See the "Configuring the Export Computer" section later in this chapter for a discussion of the Wait Until Stabilized check box.

The export directory on the export server holds the files and directories are replicated across the network. The default export directory is

`\<winnt_root>\System32\Repl\Export`

For each group of files that set for replication, create a subdirectory in the export directory. When the Directory Replicator service starts, NT shares the export directory with the share name Repl$.

Each import computer has a directory called the import directory, and the default directory is

`\<winnt_root>\System32\Repl\Import`

The Directory Replicator service copies files from the export server's export directory to the import directories of the import computers. In addition to copying files, the Directory Replicator service automatically creates any necessary subdirectories in the import directory so that after each replication the directory structure of the import directory matches the export directory's directory structure.

The process occurs as follows:

1. The export server periodically checks the export directory for changes and, if changes have occurred, sends update notices to the import computers.

2. The import computer receives the update notices and calls the export computer.

3. The import computer reads the export directory on the export server and copies any new or changed files from the export directory to its own import directory.

The following sections describe how to set up the export and import computers for directory replications.

Configuring the Export Computer

To set up the export server for directory replication:

1. Double-click on the Control Panel Services application to start the Directory Replicator service.

2. Create a new account for the Directory Replicator service. (See Chapter 3 for more on creating accounts using User Manager for Domains.) The Directory Replicator account must be a member of the Backup Operator group or the Replicator group for the domain. When you set up the new account, be sure to enable the Password Never Expires option and disable the User Must Change Password at Next Logon option. Also, make sure the account has logon privileges for all hours.

3. Start the Server Manager application in the Administrative Tools program group (see fig. 2.35). Server Manager is a tool for managing network servers and workstations from a single location.

Figure 2.35

The Server Manager main screen.

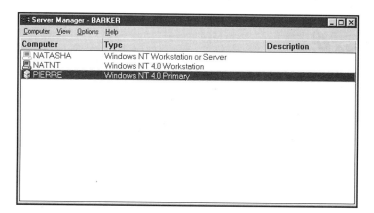

4. In the Server Manager, double-click on the export server to open the Server Properties dialog box (see fig. 2.36).

5. Click on the Replication button to open the Directory Replication dialog box (see fig. 2.37).

Figure 2.36

The Server Prop-erties dialog box

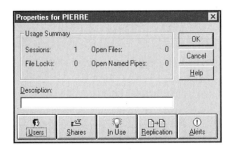

Figure 2.37

The Directory Replication dialog box.

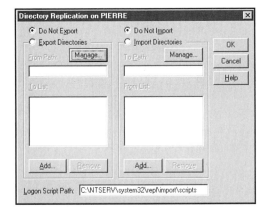

A Windows NT server can serve as an export server, an import computer, or both. The left side of the Directory Replication dialog box defines export properties. The right side of the Directory Export dialog box defines import properties.

6. In the Directory Replication dialog box, select the Export Directories radio button. The default path to the export directory appears in the From Path box. Click on the Add button to open the Select Domain dialog box (see fig. 2.38). Click on a domain to select it. Double-click on a domain to display the computers within that domain (see fig. 2.39). If you select a whole domain, all import servers in the domain receive the replicated data. If you choose a specific computer, only that computer receives the replicated data. You can choose any combination of domains and specific computers.

Figure 2.38

*The Select Do-
main dialog box.*

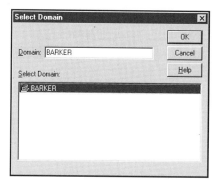

Figure 2.39

*The Select Do-
main dialog box
displaying spe-
cific computers
within the do-
main.*

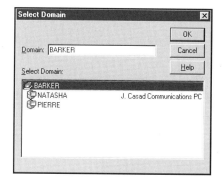

7. Click on the Manage button to open the Manage Exported
   Directories dialog box (see fig. 2.40). Subdirectories within
   the export directory appear in the Sub-Directory list. You
   can add or remove subdirectories from the list by clicking on
   the Add or Remove buttons. Note the check boxes at the
   bottom of the screen. Enabling the Wait Until Stabilized
   check box tells the Directory Replicator service to wait at
   least two minutes after any change to the selected subdirectory tree before exporting. Enabling the Entire Subtree
   check box tells the Directory Replicator service to export all
   subdirectories beneath the selected subdirectory. The Add
   Lock button lets you lock the subdirectory so it can't be exported. More than one user can lock a subdirectory. (Consequently, a subdirectory can have more than one lock.) To
   remove a lock, click on the Remove Lock button.

Figure 2.40

The Manager Exported Directories dialog box.

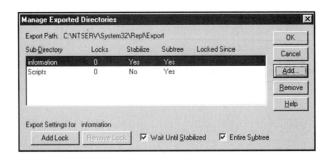

8. Click on OK in the Manage Exported Directories dialog box, the Directory Replication dialog box, and the Server Properties dialog box.

Configuring the Import Computer

To set up the import computer for directory replication:

1. Double-click on the Services icon in the Control Panel. Select the Directory Replicator service and click on the Startup button to open the Service dialog box (see fig. 2.41).

Figure 2.41

The Service dialog box.

2. In the Startup Type frame, select the Automatic radio button. Select the This Account radio button and enter a username and password for the replicator account you created on the export server.

If the import computer and the export server aren't part of the same domain or a trusting domain, you must create a replication user account on the import computer and give that account permission to access the Repl$ share on the export server. Enter this account and password in the Service dialog box in step 2.

3. Start Server Manager, select the computer you're now configuring, and click on the Replication button in the Properties dialog box. The Directory Replication dialog box appears. This time, you're concerned with the import side (the right side) of the dialog box, but the configuration steps are similar to steps for configuring the export side. The default import directory appears in the To Path box. Click on the Add button to add a domain or a specific export server (see step 6 in the preceding section). Click on the Manage button to open the Manage Imported Directories dialog box, which lets you manage the import directories (see fig. 2.42).

Figure 2.42

The Managing Imported Directories dialog box.

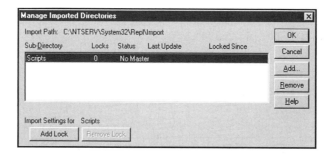

4. In the Manage Imported Directories dialog box, click on Add or Remove to add or remove a subdirectory from the list. Click on Add Lock to add a lock to the subdirectory (see preceding section).

Troubleshooting Directory Replication

The Status parameter in the Manage Exported Directories and the Manager Imported Directories dialog boxes gives the status of the directory replication for a subdirectory. The possible values are as follows:

- ▶ **OK.** The export server is sending regular updates, and the import directory matches the export directory.

- ▶ **No Master.** The import computer isn't receiving updates, which means the export server may not be running, or the Directory Replicator service on the export server may not be running.

- ▶ **No Sync.** The import directory has received updates, but the data in the updates isn't what it should be, which means there could be an export server malfunction, a communication problem, open files on either the import of the export computer, or a problem with the import computer's access permissions.

- ▶ **(Blank).** Replication has never occurred. The cause could be improper configuration on either the import or the export computer.

When the Directory Replication service generates an error, check Event Viewer to learn what you can about the cause.

Microsoft recommends the following solutions for some common replication errors:

- ▶ **Access Denied.** The Directory Replicator service might not be configured to log on to a specific account. Check Event Viewer. Check the Startup dialog box in the Control Panel Services application to see if an account is specified, and use User Manager for Domains to check the permissions for the logon account.

- ▶ **Exporting to Specific Computers.** Designate specific export servers for each import server and specific import computers for each export server. If you just choose a domain in the dialog box opened by clicking on the Add button in the Directory Replication dialog box, every domain computer receives replicated data and every import computer receives updates from every export server in the domain.

▶ **Replication over a WAN link.** When transmitting replication data across a WAN link, specify the computer name rather than just the domain name when you click on the Add button in the Directory Replication dialog box.

▶ **Logon Scripts for Member Servers and Workstations.** NT Workstations and non-controller NT Servers must use the default logon script directory:

```
C:\<winnt_root>\System32\Repl\Import\Scripts
```

Windows NT Client Licenses

Microsoft requires that every client accessing a resource on a computer running Windows NT Server have a Client Access License (CAL). The Client Access License is separate from the license for the client's operating system. Your Windows 95 or Windows NT Workstation doesn't include implied permission to access resources on a Windows NT Server—to access NT Server resources you must have a CAL.

Microsoft provides two options for purchasing Client Access Licenses, as follows:

▶ **Per Server mode.** Client Access Licenses are assigned to each server. A Windows NT Server might be licensed for, say, 10 simultaneous client connections. No more than 10 clients will be able to access the server at one time—additional clients will not be able to connect.

▶ **Per Seat mode.** Client Access Licenses are assigned to each client machine. You purchase a CAL for every client computer on the network. If the total number of simultaneous connections on all Windows NT Servers exceeds the number of per seat licenses, a client can still connect.

Microsoft allows a one-time switch from Per Server to Per Seat licensing mode. If you aren't sure which option to choose, you can choose Per Server mode and change later to Per Seat mode if you determine that Per Seat mode is more cost effective.

If your network has only one server, Microsoft recommends that you choose Per Server licensing mode. If you have more than one server on your network, Microsoft suggests the following formulas:

A=Number of servers

B=number of simultaneous connections to each server

C=total number of seats (clients) accessing computers

If A * B < C use Per Server licensing. Number of CALs=A*B

IF A * B > C use Per Seat licensing. Number of CALs=C

Windows NT Server includes the following tools for managing client licenses:

▶ The Licensing application

▶ License Manager

The following sections describe these Windows NT license-managing tools.

The Licensing Application

The Control Panel Licensing application opens the Choose Licensing Mode dialog box (see fig. 2.43). The Choose Licensing Mode dialog box lets you add or remove client licenses or switch from Per Server to Per Seat licensing mode.

Figure 2.43

The Choose Licensing Mode dialog box.

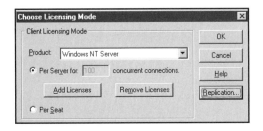

The Replication button opens the Replication Configuration dialog box (see fig. 2.44). The Replication Configuration dialog box lets you configure license replication.

Figure 2.44

The Replication Configuration dialog box.

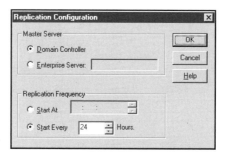

License replication is a convenient feature that lets individual servers send their licensing information to a master server. The master server creates and updates a database of licensing information for the entire network. This provides a single central location for licensing information.

License Manager

License Manager, a tool in the Administrative Tools program group, displays licensing information for the network (see fig. 2.45). You can maintain a history of client licenses, examine your networks Per Server and Per Seat licenses by product, and browse for client license information on particular network clients. You also can monitor server usage by Per Seat clients, and even revoke a client's permission to access a server.

Figure 2.45

The License Manager window.

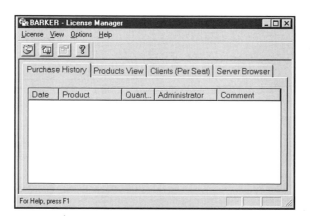

You also can use License Manager to add or edit license groups. A license group is a group of users mapped to a group of Per Seat licenses. License groups are a means of tracking per seat license usage in situations where an organization has more users than computers (or in some cases, more computers than users). For example, a retail outlet may have 10 employees sharing three Per-Seat-licensed computers.

Computer Browser Service

One of the most important network services is the Computer Browser service. The Computer Browser service oversees a hierarchy of computers that serve as browsers for the network. A browser is a computer that maintains a central list of network servers. (In this case, a server is any computer that makes resources available to the network.) That list then becomes available to clients who are "browsing" the network looking for remote computers, printers, and other resources. The list that appears when you open the Network Neighborhood application, for instance, comes from a network browser list.

The advantage of the browser process is that it allows a small number of network computers to maintain browse lists for the whole network, thereby minimizing network traffic and eliminating duplication of efforts. (The alternative would be for all computers to constantly poll the network in order to maintain their own lists.) Before the browser process can function efficiently, however, it must be highly organized so that clients know where to find a list and so that contingencies can take effect when a browser fails.

In a Windows NT domain, each computer assumes one of five browser roles:

> ▶ **Master browser.** Each workgroup or domain subnet must have a master browser. At startup, all computers running the Server service (regardless of whether they have resources available for the network) register themselves with the master browser. The master browser compiles a list of available servers on the workgroup or subnet and forwards the list to the Domain Master Browser. Master browsers then receive a complete browse list for the entire domain from the domain master browser.

▶ **Domain master browser.** The domain master browser requests subnet browse lists from the master browsers and merges the subnet browse lists into a master browse list for the entire domain. It also forwards the domain browse list back to the master browsers. The Primary Domain Controller (PDC) serves as the domain master browser for a Windows NT domain.

▶ **Backup browsers.** The backup browser gets a copy of the browse list from the master browser (on the subnet) and distributes the browse list to subnet clients who request it. If the master browser fails, a backup browser can serve as the master browser for the subnet.

▶ **Potential browser.** A potential browser is a computer that isn't presently serving as a browser but can become a browser at the request of the master browser or as a result of a browser election (described later in this section).

▶ **Non-browser.** A non-browser is a computer that cannot serve as a browser.

The first time a client computer attempts to access the network, it obtains a list of backup browsers for the subnet or workgroup from the master browser. It then asks a backup browser for a copy of the browse list.

If a master browser fails, a new master browser is chosen automatically in what is known as a browser election. A browser election can occur if a client or backup browser cannot access the master browser. A browser election isn't exactly an election; it's really more of a contest. The browsers and potential browsers rank themselves according to a number of criteria, and the machine with the highest ranking becomes the new master browser. Some of the criteria used in a browser election are as follows:

▶ **Operating system.** Windows NT Server gets a higher score than Windows NT Workstation, which gets a higher score than Windows 95.

▶ **Version.** Windows NT Server 4 gets a higher score than Windows NT Server 3.51, and so forth.

▶ **Present browser role.** A backup browser scores higher than a potential browser.

You can configure a Windows NT computer to always, never, or sometimes participate in browser elections, using the Maintain-ServerList parameter in the registry key:

HKEY_Local_Machine\System\CurrentControlSet\Services\Browsr\Parameters

The possible values are as follows:

▶ **Yes.** Always attempt to become a browser in browser elections (default for Windows NT Server domain controllers).

▶ **No.** Never attempt to become a browser in browser elections.

▶ **Auto.** The Auto setting classifies the computer as a potential browser (default for Windows NT Workstations and Windows NT Servers that aren't acting as domain controllers).

To make other domains available to the browser service, select the browser service in the Network application's Services tab and click on the Properties button. The Browser configuration dialog box appears. Enter a domain name in the box on the left and click the Add button; then click on OK.

Configuring Peripherals and Devices

 Control Panel includes several applications that help you install and configure peripherals and devices. You should be familiar with how to use these applications to install drivers and configure peripherals and hardware. The following sections examine these applications:

▶ Devices

▶ Multimedia

▶ Ports

▶ UPS

- ▶ SCSI

- ▶ Tape Devices

- ▶ PC Card

- ▶ Modems

- ▶ Keyboard

- ▶ Mouse

- ▶ Display

You should be familiar with how to use these applications for installing and configuring peripherals and devices. Some of the following sections also appear in the full discussion of Control Panel applications in Appendix A.

Microsoft lists the following objective for the Windows NT Server exam:

Configure peripherals and devices. Peripherals and devices include: communications devices, SCSI devices, tape device drivers, UPS and UPS service, mouse drivers, display drivers, and keyboard drivers.

Devices

The Devices application (SRVMGR.CPL) writes to HKEY_LOCAL_MACHINE\SYSTEM\CurrentControlSet\Services. You can start, stop, or disable device drivers in this Control Panel applet (see fig. 2.46).

Figure 2.46

The Devices application.

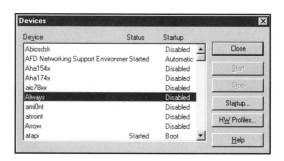

The three columns in the Control Panel Devices main display area are labeled Device, Status, and Startup. The Device column identifies the name of the device driver as it appears in the Registry; the Status column reads "Started" if the driver is active, and otherwise appears blank; the Startup column denotes when each driver is configured to initialize.

To set the Startup value, select the device driver you want to modify and choose the Startup button. In the Device dialog box, shown in figure 2.47, choose one of the following Startup Types:

Figure 2.47

The Device dialog box.

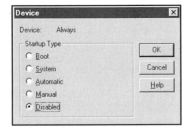

▶ **Boot.** These devices start first, as soon as the kernel is loaded and initialized (see Chapter 6, "Troubleshooting," for more details about the boot process). These devices have a Start value of 0 in the Registry. Atdisk, the hard disk driver, is an example of a boot device.

▶ **System.** These devices start after the boot devices and after the HKEY_LOCAL_MACHINE subtree has begun to be built. These devices have a start value of 1 in the Registry. The video driver is a system device.

▶ **Automatic.** These devices start late in the boot process, after the Registry is almost entirely built, just before the Winlogon screen appears. These devices have a start value of 2 in the Registry. Serial, the serial port driver, is an automatic device.

▶ **Manual.** These devices are never started without administrator intervention. They may be manually started through the Control Panel Devices menu. These devices have a start value of 3 in the Registry.

▶ **Disabled.** These devices cannot be started at all unless their startup Type is changed to something other than Disabled. These devices have a start value of 4 in the Registry. File system drivers are disabled by default (although file system recognizers are started with the system devices; if any file systems are "recognized," the Startup Type of the file system drivers is changed to System as well).

To start a device that isn't active, select the device and choose the Start button. If the Start button is greyed out, the device is already started or disabled.

To stop a device that's active, select the device and choose the Stop button. A greyed out stop button indicates that the device already is inactive.

To enable or disable a device for a given hardware profile, select the device, click on HW Profiles, select enable or disable to change to the desired status, and click on OK. You learn more about hardware profiles later in this chapter.

Multimedia

The Multimedia application (MMSYS.CPL) writes to HKEY_LOCAL_MACHINE\SYSTEM\CurrentControlSet\Services. Multimedia device drivers are added and configured from this Control Panel applet. The Multimedia application also provides settings for CD music, audio, video, and MIDI.

Ports

The Ports application (PORTS.CPL) writes directly to the following key:

```
HKEY_LOCAL_MACHINE\SYSTEM\CurrentControlSet\Services\Serial
```

This Control Panel interface lists only the serial ports that are available but not in use as serial ports. In other words, if a mouse is connected to your COM1 port, COM1 doesn't show up in the

Control Panel Ports dialog box. All serial ports, regardless of whether they appear in Control Panel Ports, are logged in the Registry under the following key:

```
HKEY_LOCAL_MACHINE\HARDWARE\Description\System\<multifunction_
adapter>\0\~SerialController\<COM_port_number>
```

The Settings button displays values for the port's baud rate, data bits, parity, stop bits, and flow control.

If you need an additional port for use under Windows NT, choose the Add button. You may assign a different COM port number, base I/O port address or IRQ, or enable a First In-First Out (FIFO) buffer for that port (see fig. 2.48).

Figure 2.48

Adding a new port using the Ports application's Add button.

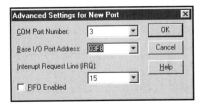

To remove a port, simply select it and click on the Delete button.

UPS

The UPS application (UPS.CPL) writes to the following key:

```
HKEY_LOCAL_MACHINE\SYSTEM\CurrentControlSet\Services\UPS
```

If your computer is equipped with a Universal Power Supply (UPS), Windows NT can be configured to communicate with it. The specific voltages requested in the UPS Configuration area depend on the UPS manufacturer and model. You may need to consult with your vendor to get these values. Armed with the correct information, Windows NT can recognize the following:

▶ **Power failure signal.** The point when an event is logged and the Server service paused. No new connections to this server can be made, but existing connections still function.

▶ **Low battery signal at least 2 minutes before shutdown.**
As the name implies, Windows NT recognizes when the UPS
battery is about to be exhausted.

▶ **Remote UPS Shutdown.** Signals Windows NT that the UPS
is shutting down.

The Execute Command File option enables an administrator to
specify a batch or executable file that runs immediately preceding
a shutdown. The program has 30 seconds before the system shuts
down. The program cannot open a dialog box because that would
require an attendant user.

If no Low Battery Signal is configured, the administrator can enter the Expected Battery Life and the Battery Recharge Time Per
Minute of Run Time in the lower left corner of the dialog box.

After the initial PowerOut alert is raised (the power failure signal
has been received), Windows NT waits until the Time Between
Power Failure and Initial Warning Message has elapsed, and then
sends an alert to all interactive and connected users. Windows NT
continues to send these alerts every time the Delay between Warning Messages elapses.

If the UPS is about to run out of steam, the system shuts down
safely. If power is restored, users are notified, an event is logged,
and the Server service resumes.

SCSI Adapters

This application is one of the great misnomers in Windows NT. As
it suggests, this application opens the SCSI Adapters dialog box,
which is used to install SCSI adapter drivers. However, this dialog
box also is used to install and remove IDE CD-ROM drivers as well
as drivers for CD-ROM drives that use proprietary interfaces, such
as Mitsumi or Panasonic drives. The dialog box should refer to
both SCSI adapters and CD-ROM drives; currently the interface is
completely counter-intuitive.

To add a SCSI adapter or CD-ROM device driver, follow these
procedures:

1. Double-click in the SCSI Adapters application in the Control Panel.

2. In the SCSI Adapters dialog box, choose the Drivers tab and click on the Add button.

3. Select the driver from the list of available drivers in the Install Driver dialog box. If your driver isn't listed but you have a disk from the manufacturer with a Windows NT driver, click on the Have Disk button.

4. Choose OK. You must point Windows NT toward the original installation files (or the disk that contains the driver) and restart the computer in order for the new driver to initialize.

To remove a SCSI adapter or CD-ROM device driver, perform these instructions:

1. Select the Drivers tab in the SCSI Adapters dialog box.

2. Select the driver you want to remove.

3. Choose the Remove button.

Tape Devices

Almost identical to the SCSI Adapter Setup dialog box in both appearance and function, this dialog box allows the installation and removal of tape drives for use with a Windows NT Backup program.

To add a tape drive device driver, use these steps:

1. Double-click on the Tape Devices icon in Control Panel.

2. Select the Drivers tab.

3. Click on the Add button.

4. Select the driver from the list of available drivers. If your driver isn't listed but you have a disk from the manufacturer with a Windows NT Driver, click on the Have Disk button.

5. Choose OK. You must point Windows NT toward the original installation files (or the disk that contains the driver) and restart the computer in order for the new driver to initialize.

To remove a tape drive device driver, do these steps:

1. Select the driver from the list of installed drivers in the Tape Devices dialog box of the Drivers tab.

2. Choose the Remove button.

PC Card (PCMCIA)

The PC Card application helps you install and configure PCMCIA device drivers. Select a PC card and click on Properties. Select the Drivers tab and then choose Add, Remove, or Configure as necessary.

A red X next to a device in the PC card list indicates that NT doesn't support the device.

Modems

The Modems application enables you to add or remove a modem. You can ask NT to detect your modem, or you can select a modem from a list.

To add a modem:

1. Double-click on the Modems application in the Control Panel.

2. Click on Add in the Modem Properties dialog box (see fig. 2.49).

3. In the Install New Modem dialog box, click on Next if you want NT to try to detect your modem. If you want to select your modem from the list, or if you're providing software for a modem not listed, enable the check box and then click on Next (see fig. 2.50).

Figure 2.49

*The Modem Prop-
erties dialog box.*

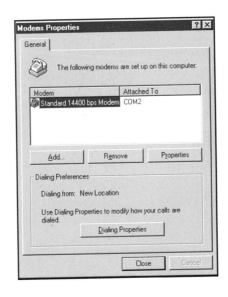

Figure 2.50

*The Install New
Modem dialog
box.*

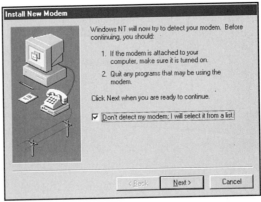

4. Select a manufacturer and a model, and click on Next. Or click on the Have Disk button if you're installing software for a modem not shown on the list.

5. Select a port for the modem, or select All ports. Click on Next.

Select a modem in the Modems list and click on Properties to change the parameters for that modem. A new dialog box opens, with two tabs, General and Connection. The General tab enables you to set the port number and the maximum speed. The Connection tab enables you to define some connection preferences, such as the Data bits, Stop bits, and Parity. Click on Advanced for additional settings.

The Dialing Properties button in the Modem Properties dialog box calls up the My Location tab, which is also in the Telephony application. The My Locations tab enables you to set the dialing characteristics for the modem. If you have a portable computer, you can define additional locations and configure a complete set of dialing properties for each location. If you sometimes travel to a certain hotel in Paris, for instance, you can define a location called Paris and specify the dialing properties you want to use for the Paris hotel. The next time you're in Paris, you only have to change the location setting in the I Am Dialing from box at the top of the My Location tab. The other settings automatically change to the settings you defined for Paris.

To add a new location, follow these steps:

1. Click on the New button at the top of the My Locations tab. (NT announces that a new location has been created.)

2. The new location has the name New Location (followed by a number if you already have a location called New Location). Click on the name and change it if you want to give your location a different name. (NT might not let you erase the old name completely until you add your new name. Add the new name and then backspace over the old text if necessary.)

3. Change any dialing properties. The new properties will apply to your new location.

Keyboard

The Keyboard application opens the Keyboard Properties dialog box, which enables the user to set the keyboard repeat rate, the repeat delay, the cursor blink rate, and the keyboard layout properties. The keyboard driver appears in the General tab in the Keyboard Type text box (see fig. 2.51). To select a new driver, click on the Change button. The Select Device dialog box appears (see fig. 2.52). The Show All Devices radio button will cause a list of available drivers to appear in the Models list. Choose the keyboard model that matches your hardware. If your keyboard comes with its own installation disk for a model that isn't in the list, click on the Have Disk button.

Figure 2.51

The Keyboard Properties dialog box.

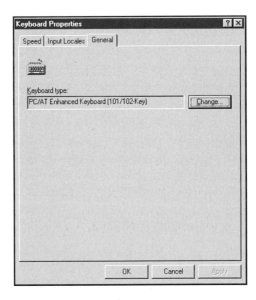

Figure 2.52

The Select Device dialog box.

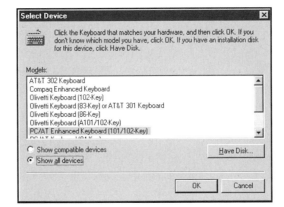

Mouse

The values for this key control the mouse speed, sensitivity, and left- or right-handedness. The one new setting added to this dialog box's Win3.x predecessor is the Snap to Default option in the Motion tab, which instantly positions the pointer over the default button in the active dialog box. In the Pointers tab, you can select a pointer type. The General tab lets you install a new mouse driver. The procedure for selecting a mouse driver is similar to the procedure for selecting a keyboard driver (described in the preceding section).

Display

The Display application configures the values in the following key, including the video driver, screen resolution, color depth, and refresh rate:

```
HKEY_LOCAL_MACHINE\SYSTEM\CurrentControlSet\Services\<video_driver>\
Device0\
```

The five tabs of the Display Properties dialog box, shown in figure 2.53, are as follows:

Figure 2.53

The Display Properties dialog box.

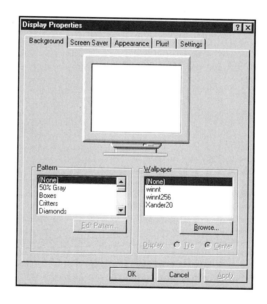

▶ **Background.** Defines the wallpaper for the Desktop.

▶ **Screen Saver.** Defines the screen saver for the Desktop.

▶ **Appearance.** Defines window properties.

▶ **Plus!.** The Visual Enhancements tab from the Microsoft Plus! package for Windows 95 lets you configure the desktop to use large icons or stretch the wallpaper to fit the screen.

▶ **Settings.** Defines desktop colors, refresh frequency, and other screen-related settings.

The Settings tab contains a Test button. You should always test new display settings before making changes permanent. Although Windows NT can detect the capabilities of your video card, it can't do the same with your monitor. Testing these settings before applying them ensures that both video card and monitor can support the new settings.

Unlike Windows 95, Windows NT doesn't let you change video resolution on the fly. The computer must be restarted for the changes to take effect.

All hardware breaks sooner or later, including monitors. When a monitor dies, you often can dig up an older model to use temporarily. Often, however, such a resurrected monitor isn't as advanced as the one that just died, and when you restart Windows NT, such video card settings as the resolution and refresh rate aren't supported. The typical result is that you no longer can view anything on-screen.

If this happens, reboot the computer using the [VGA mode] option on the Boot Loader menu. Windows NT boots using the standard VGA driver at 640x480 resolution. When the system is fully loaded, log on and go to the Settings tab of the Control Panel Display application, so that you can choose optimal settings for your temporary monitor.

To change the video display adapter:

1. Start the Control Panel Display application and click on the Settings tab (see fig. 2.54).

2. Click on the Display Type button. The Display Type dialog box appears (see fig. 2.55).

Figure 2.54

The Display Properties Settings tab.

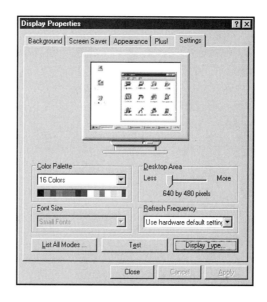

Figure 2.55

The Display Type dialog box.

3. Click on the Change tab in the Adapter Type frame. The Change Display dialog box appears (see fig. 2.56). Select an adapter from the list and click on OK. Or, if you have a manufacturer's installation disk, click on Have Disk.

Figure 2.56

*The Change
Display dialog
box.*

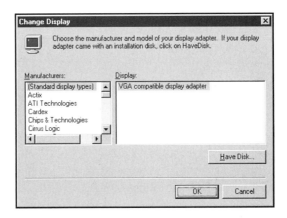

Configuring Hard Disks

Chapter 1 discussed some important concepts related to disk configuration, such as file systems, primary partitions, extended partitions, and fault-tolerance. This section describes how to apply
those concepts to an actual disk configuration using Windows
NT's Disk Administrator disk utility. To access Disk Administrator,
you must be using an administrator account.

Microsoft lists the following objective for the Windows NT
Server exam:

Configure hard disks to meet various requirements. Requirements include: allocating disk space capacity, providing
redundancy, improving performance, providing security,
formatting.

To start the Disk Administrator, choose Start, Programs, Administrative Tools (common), Disk Administrator.

When using the Disk Administrator for the first time, a message
box appears, telling you the following:

```
No signature found on Disk 0.access this disk from other operat-
➥ing systems, such as DOS.
If you choose not to write a signature, the disk will be inacces-
➥sible to the Windows NT Disk Administrator program.
```

```
Do you want to write a signature on Disk 0 so that the Disk Ad-
➡ministrator can access the drive?
```

Choosing Yes has a 32-bit signature that uniquely identifies the disk written to the primary partition. This function makes possible recognition of the disk as the original, even if it is has been used with a different controller or its identification has changed.

If you select any modifications to be performed on a disk(s), a message appears warning that certain changes, such as deleting a partition, are irreversible and require user approval. The changes don't become permanent until you exit the program or choose Partition, Commit Changes Now.

Customizing the Display

The status bar at the bottom of the Disk Administrator's main window displays basic disk information (see fig. 2.57). Along with the status bar, a color-coded legend displays the different representations for partition colors and patterns. When working with multiple disks, hiding one or both of these two options gives you a larger area for viewing information. To do so, choose Options and then select Status Bar or Legend, or both.

Figure 2.57

The Disk Administrator main window.

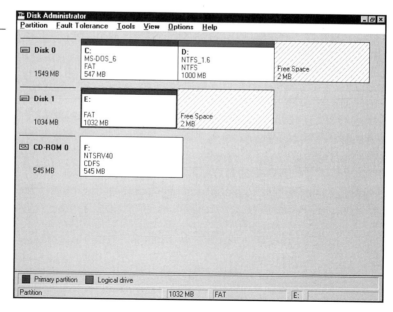

You also can set different colors and patterns to distinguish between different disks and disk characteristics for the primary partition, logical drive, mirror set, and volume set. To change the default settings, choose Options, Colors and Patterns. The Colors and Patterns dialog box appears (see fig. 2.58).

Figure 2.58

Disk Administrator's Colors and Patterns dialog box.

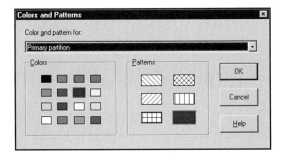

Initially, each disk represented in the display window is sized proportionately. By choosing Options, Region Display, you get several choices in the Region Display Options dialog box for customizing the appearance of each region (see fig. 2.59).

Figure 2.59

Disk Administrator's Region Display Options dialog box.

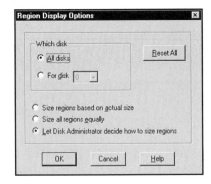

Partitioning

Partitioning refers to the method in which hard disks are made usable. Windows NT includes four options for creating partitions with the Disk Administrator.

To create primary partitions using the Disk Administrator, follow these steps:

1. Select an area of free space on a disk.

2. Choose Partition, Create.

   A message box appears indicating the possible minimum and maximum sizes for a new primary partition.

3. In the Create Primary Partition dialog box, enter the size of the partition you want to create and choose OK.

To create an extended partition using the Disk Administrator, follow these steps:

1. Select an area of free space on a disk.

2. Choose Partition, Create Extended.

   A message box appears indicating the possible minimum and maximum sizes for a new extended partition.

3. In the Create Extended dialog box, enter the size of the extended partition you want to create and choose OK.

To create a logical drive within an extended partition, select the extended partition and choose Partition, Create. If this command is unavailable, you probably have selected another partition rather than the extended one.

To create a volume set using the Disk Administrator, follow these steps:

1. Select the areas of free space you want to include with a volume set.

2. Choose Partition, Create Volume Set.

   A message box appears indicating the possible minimum and maximum sizes for a new extended partition.

3. In the Create Volume Set dialog box, enter the size of the volume set you want to create and choose OK.

After you create a volume set, you must format it before you can use it (NTFS and FAT are both supported). To format the new volume, you must save the changes by choosing Partition menu, Commit Changes Now, or by responding to the prompts when exiting the Disk Administrator. You also must restart the system before formatting.

Before you can reclaim any of the disk space that a volume set uses, you must delete the volume set entirely (although, if formatted with NTFS, you can extend a volume set using other drives without doing additional formatting or losing data).

If NT is configured to support multiple operating systems (such as DOS) when a volume set or stripe set is created, the other systems cannot see the set and, therefore, cannot access it.

The only differences between configuring volume sets and ordinary partitions are as follows:

▶ The system and boot partitions cannot be part of a volume set. Windows NT must be running before these volume sets can be addressed; if Windows NT itself is on a volume set, there is no way to address the volume set.

▶ You can extend an NTFS volume set (but not a FAT volume set) by selecting the volume set in Disk Administrator and simultaneously selecting at least one area of free space (hold down the Ctrl key to select more than one area at a time). Choose the Partition, Extend Volume Set to get a chance to enter a new size for the volume set.

▶ You can never shrink a volume set; after creating or extending it, it's set in stone. You can delete the entire volume set, but not any individual area within it.

If you choose to implement a volume set, be aware of the following drawbacks and dangers:

▶ Only Windows NT supports volume sets; if you're booting between Windows NT and Windows 95, MS-DOS, or another operating system, your volume set is inaccessible if Windows NT isn't active.

▶ Your volume set will break because all drives fail sooner or later, and combining free space from multiple drives increases the chances of a disaster. Be sure to back up your data frequently. If a single member of the volume set fails, you lose a good portion of your data. The rest of the volume set may still be addressable, but don't count on being able to retrieve your data intact. Shut down the system, replace the bad drive, reformat the volume set, and restore your data from backup.

To extend a volume set, both the existing set and the volume you're adding must be formatted with NTFS. To extend a volume set using the Disk Administrator, follow these steps:

1. Select an NTFS volume, then select the area(s) of free space you want to add. (Hold down the Ctrl key while you select the areas of free space.)

2. Choose Partition, Extend Volume Set.

   A dialog box appears indicating the possible minimum and maximum sizes for the creation of an extended partition.

3. In the Create Extended Volume Set dialog box, enter the size of the volume you want to create and choose OK.

Stripe Sets

Stripe sets are similar to volume sets in that they also combine anywhere from 2 to 32 areas of free space into a single logical drive. Stripe sets differ from volume sets in that the free space areas must all be equally sized areas from separate physical disks. Data is read from and written to the stripe set in 64 KB blocks, disk by disk, row by row. If multiple controllers service your stripe set, or if your single controller can perform concurrent I/O requests, you can improve performance dramatically because you can then use multiple drives simultaneously.

Be careful, however—not only do the same dangers apply to stripe sets as apply to volume sets, the potential disaster is even more dire. If any single member of a stripe set fails, the entire volume becomes inaccessible to the point that—because your data is contiguous only for 64 KB at a time—not even a disk editor can help you. If you didn't back up, your data is gone for good.

If all of this scares you, good; preferable alternatives to volume or stripe sets usually are available. Windows NT Server has a more robust method of improving performance while maintaining fault tolerance, called stripe sets with parity. Use a stripe set with parity if you really want the performance boost from striping. If you're using Windows NT Workstation rather than Server, you don't have that option, but you can go with a hardware implementation of striping that offers some method of parity maintenance. This fault tolerant technology is called Redundant Array of Inexpensive Disks (RAID).

The same rules apply for both stripe sets and volume sets—no limits on drive types, no limit for the file system, and no system and boot partitions. You cannot extend a stripe set the way you can volume sets, however, and you cannot shrink one either.

A stripe set can support IDE, EIDE, and SCSI drive types.

When creating a stripe set, the space on each disk must be the same size (see fig. 2.60); if not, the Disk Administrator approximates the sizes for each to make them equal.

To create a stripe set using the Disk Administrator, follow these steps:

1. Select at least two areas of free space on different hard drives.

2. Choose Partition, Create Stripe Set.

   A dialog box appears indicating the possible minimum and maximum sizes for the creation of an extended partition.

3. In the Create Stripe Set dialog box, enter the size of the stripe set you want to create and choose OK.

Figure 2.60

The Disk Admin-istrator main window display-ing stripe set information.

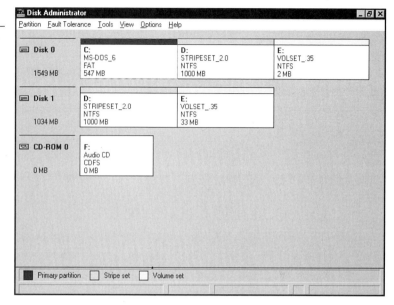

As with a volume set, you must format the stripe set before you can use it. To format the new volume, save the changes by choosing Partition, Commit Changes Now option or by responding to the prompts when exiting the Disk Administrator. You also must restart the system before formatting.

Marking Partition as Active

On a disk(s) using a Windows NT computer, the areas that contain the startup files are called the system and boot partitions. The system partition contains the boot files, and the boot partition contains the system and support files. These denotions appear backwards by conventional terminology, but they accurately describe Windows NT.

With an I386 computer, the system partition is located on the first disk, is marked active, and is designated as the primary partition. You can have only one active partition at a time. To boot between multiple operating systems, you must set the partition as active before restarting the computer.

On RISC-based systems, hard disks aren't marked as active; rather, a manufacturer-supplied hardware configuration utility controls them.

To mark a partition as active using the Disk Administrator, follow these steps:

1. Select a primary partition that contains startup files for a particular OS you want to make active.

2. Choose Partition, Mark Active.

   A dialog box appears indicating that the new partition is active and will be used on startup.

3. Choose OK in the Disk Administrator dialog box.

Notice the asterisk that now appears in the color bar of the new active partition (see fig. 2.61).

Figure 2.61

The Disk Administrator main window depicting active stripe sets (indicated with colored bars).

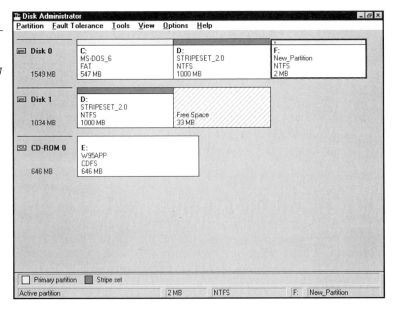

Committing Changes

After you create a partition, you may format it from within Disk Administrator, but only if you choose Partition, Commit Changes Now.

Until you commit changes, your commands aren't actually carried out, so you can change your mind if necessary. If you exit Disk Administrator without first choosing the Commit Changes Now command, Disk Administrator asks you whether it should save your changes (which is the same thing as committing them). That's the last chance you get to back out gracefully.

Deleting Partitions

You can delete any partition except for the system and boot partitions (and you can't delete those because Windows NT is using them) from Disk Administrator. Simply select the partition you want to delete, then choose Partition, Delete. Confirm your action to officially remove the partition from the interface. Again, until you commit changes, nothing officially happens. If you make a mistake, just exit Disk Administrator without saving or committing changes.

Saving and Restoring Configuration Information

The Configuration command on Disk Administrator's Partition menu enables you to save or restore a disk configuration using a floppy disk. You can save the disk configuration to a blank floppy, a floppy with a previous disk configuration, or an emergency repair disk.

You can use the Configuration Save option if you want to change your disk configuration but think you may someday want to return to the configuration you have now. Also, Microsoft recommends that you save a copy of your disk configuration before upgrading Windows NT.

The Configuration Restore option restores a saved disk configuration from a floppy.

The Configuration command includes a third option, Search, which searches your hard drive for other Windows NT installations. If you find any, you can then choose to update your disk configuration to match the configuration of one of the other Windows NT installations on the list.

Both the Restore and Search options come with a warning that you are about to overwrite your disk configuration. The Restore and Search operations don't create or delete partitions, but they do affect drive letters, volume sets, stripe sets, parity stripes, and mirrors.

Tools

The Disk Administrator Tools menu provides some options for further defining and protecting hard disks. The next few sections discuss these options in turn.

Format

A hard disk is divided into logical sections that enable a disk to locate data in a systematic fashion. This process is called formatting.

To format a partition using the Disk Administrator, follow these step:

1. Select the newly created partition you want to format.

2. Choose Partition, Commit Changes Now. Click on Yes to save the changes.

3. Choose Tools, Format.

4. In the Format dialog box, enter the volume label to identify the partition.

5. Select the type of file system to use, then choose OK.

   If you enable the Quick Format check box, the Disk Administrator doesn't scan for bad sectors during the format process. This option isn't available when you format mirror sets or stripe sets with parity.

6. Choose Yes from the Confirmation dialog box to begin the process.

   A dialog box appears indicating the current progress of the format. The format progress window lets you cancel the process, although if you do cancel it, you can't be sure that the volume will be returned to its original state.

You also can format partitions from the command prompt using the syntax

```
FORMAT <drive_letter>: /FS:FAT¦NTFS
```

Assigning a Drive Letter

Normally, Windows NT assigns drive letters starting with the first primary partition on the first physical drive, followed by the logical drives, and finally the remaining primary partitions. After Disk 0 is complete, Windows NT begins assigning drive letters to the partitions on the next physical drive in the same fashion.

If you want to override the normal drive-naming algorithm, choose Tools, Assign Drive Letter. You may change the drive designation to any other unused letter, or you may simply remove the drive letter altogether. The latter option may seem of dubious value, but it allows an administrator to "hide" a partition and its files by not providing the computer a "handle" (drive letter) by which to access it. If the administrator needs to recover the data, the partition can be reassigned a drive letter. This procedure is secure because only Administrators can work with Disk Administrator.

You can manually configure the drive letter of any volume by using the option on the Tools menu. To change a drive letter using the Disk Administrator, follow these steps:

1. Select the partition or logical drive that you want to assign a drive letter.

2. Choose Tools, Assign Drive Letter.

   A message box appears indicating the remaining drive letters for assignment.

3. In the Assign Drive Letter dialog box, select the letter to use and choose OK.

Certain programs make references to a specific drive letter, so be careful when changing drive letter assignments, especially to the active primary partition.

Properties

If you click on a volume and choose Tools, Properties, the Volume Properties dialog box appears (see fig. 2.62). (The Volume Properties dialog box is the same dialog box that will appear if you right-click on the disk in Explorer and choose Properties.) The General tab presents a graphical representation of the free and used space on the volume.

Figure 2.62

The Volume Properties dialog box.

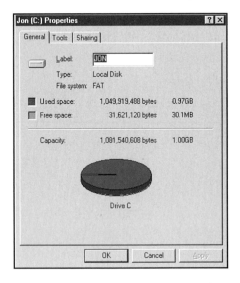

The Sharing tab of the Disk Properties dialog box lets you create and configure a network share for the volume. The Tools tab lets you back up or defragment the volume or check the volume for errors (see fig. 2.63).

Figure 2.63

*The Volume Prop-
erties Tool tab.*

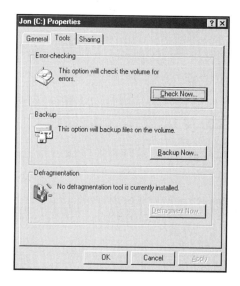

In contrast to earlier versions of NT, in which the only way to scan
a volume for errors was to use CHKDSK (which you had to execute from a VDM), NT 4 provides a graphical method of checking
hard disks for errors.

To check for disk problems from Disk Administrator, select the
partition you want to check, choose Tools, Properties, and select
the Tools tab from the Properties dialog box. Click on the Check
Now button to open the Check Disk dialog box, which offers the
following options:

▶ Automatically fix file system errors

▶ Scan for and attempt recovery of bad sectors

Choose either or both options and click on the Start button to
begin checking the partition.

Fault Tolerance

Fundamentally, fault tolerance is the system's ability to recover in
the event of hardware disaster.

The standard for fault tolerance is known as Redundant Array of Inexpensive Disks (RAID). Chapter 1 introduced the two RAID fault-tolerance methods available with Windows NT, as follows:

▶ Disk Mirroring

▶ Disk Striping with Parity

The following sections describe how to configure these fault-tolerance methods through Disk Administrator.

Creating a Mirror

Disk mirroring is a RAID level 1 fault tolerance method. A mirror is a redundant copy of another disk partition, and it uses the same or a different hard disk controller. You can use any partition, including the boot or system partitions, to establish a mirror.

In the past, disk mirroring was one of the more expensive solutions of protecting against disk failure. However, because a mirror requires only two hard disks for implementation, if you take into account global reductions in pricing, this method now is an effective alternative to other forms of fault tolerance.

To create a mirror using the Disk Administrator, follow these steps:

1. Select at least two areas of free space on different hard drives.

2. Choose Fault Tolerance, Establish Mirror.

The Disk Administrator then creates spaces of equal size on both disks and assigns a drive letter to them.

Creating a Stripe Set with Parity

A stripe set with parity is considered a RAID level 5 fault tolerance method; it differs from other approaches by writing information across all disks in the array. It accomplishes fault tolerance by keeping the data and parity on separate disks.

Parity information exists as a stripe block in each row that spans the array, so three rather than two drives must be used. In the event a single drive fails, enough information is distributed across the drives for it to be completely reconstructed. When creating a stripe set with parity, you may use all partitions except for the boot or system partition. To create a stripe set with parity, follow these steps:

1. Select between 3 and 32 areas of free disk space on each drive.

2. Choose Fault Tolerance, Create Stripe Set with Parity.

   A dialog box appears indicating the possible minimum and maximum sizes for a new extended partition.

3. In the Create Stripe Set with Parity dialog box, enter the size of the stripe set to create and choose OK.

The Disk Administrator calculates the stripe set with parity's total size, based on the number of disks selected, and creates a space that is equal on each disk. It then combines the drives into one logical volume. If you have selected free areas that are disproportionate, the Disk Administrator rounds to the closest value.

As you must with other new volumes, you must format the stripe set before it can be used. To format the new volume, save the changes by choosing Partition, Commit Changes Now or answer the prompts when exiting the Disk Administrator. You also must restart the system before formatting.

Securing System Partition on RISC Machines

The system partition on a RISC computer must be a FAT partition. Because Windows NT cannot provide the same security for a FAT partition that it provides for an NTFS partition, the RISC version of Windows NT includes a special Secure System Partition command that provides an extra layer of security for RISC-based system partitions. This command specifies that only members of the local Administrators group have access to the system partition.

Configuring Printing

The printing process is an important part of an operating system, and network administrators spend a significant amount of time chasing down printing problems. For the NT Server exams, you should become familiar with the following printer-related topics:

- ▶ Understanding Windows NT printing architecture

- ▶ Installing printers

- ▶ Configuring printers

- ▶ Sharing printers

- ▶ Setting up a printer pool

- ▶ Printing from MS-DOS applications

This chapter examines how printing works under Windows NT, both locally and remotely, and examines each of these topics.

Microsoft lists the following objective for the Windows NT Server exam:

Configure printers. Tasks include: adding and configuring a printer, implementing a printer pool, setting print priorities.

Windows NT Printing Architecture

Most of us visualize a printer as a device that receives data from the computer and converts it into a rendered hard copy. In Windows NT, however, the term printer refers to the software that controls a specific printing device or devices.

Windows NT uses the term printing device to refer to the hardware that produces the actual output.

> Other operating systems—NetWare, for example—use the term print queue for what Windows NT calls a printer. Windows NT also uses the term print queue, but in NT, a print queue is simply the list (queue) of documents waiting to print.

It's interesting to note that under Windows NT, a single printer can control more than one printing device. When a single printer (software) controls more than one printing device (hardware), the resulting configuration is called a printer pool. Printer pools are discussed in more detail later in this chapter.

You should become familiar with the components of the Windows NT printing process for the MCSE exam. The process goes roughly as follows:

1. When an application on an NT client sends a print job, Windows NT checks to see if the version of the printer driver on the client is up-to-date with the version on the print server. If it isn't, Windows NT downloads a new version of the printer driver from the print server to the client.

2. The printer driver sends the data to the client spooler. The client spooler spools the data to a file, and makes a remote procedure call to the server spooler, thus transmitting the data to the server spooler on the print server machine.

3. The server spooler sends the data to the Local Print Provider.

4. The Local Print Provider passes the data to a print processor, where it's rendered into a format legible to the printing device. Then, if necessary, the Local Print Provider sends the data to a separator page processor, where a separator page is added to the beginning of the document. The Local Print Provider lastly passes the rendered data to the print monitor.

5. The print monitor points the rendered data to the appropriate printer port and, therefore, to the appropriate printing device.

The following sections discuss the components of the NT printing process.

Printer Drivers

In the first step of the printing process, Windows NT checks to see if the printer driver on the print client is current; if it isn't, Windows NT downloads a new copy of the printer driver from the print server.

> This automatic update of the printer driver on the client is a fundamental element of Windows NT printing. When you set up a Windows NT printer, the Setup wizard asks for the operating systems and hardware platforms of all client machines that are going to access the printer. The wizard then places the appropriate printer drivers on the server so they will be available for downloading.

Because the printer driver is responsible for generating the data stream that forms a print job, the success of the print job relies on the printer driver's health. The Windows NT printer driver is implemented as a combination of two dynamic link libraries (or DLLs) and a printer-specific minidriver or configuration file.

Typically, Microsoft supplies the two dynamic link libraries with Windows NT, and the original equipment manufacturer of the printer supplies the minidriver or configuration file. The following list describes these three files:

▶ **The Printer Graphics Driver DLL.** This dynamic link library consists of the rendering or managing portion of the driver; it's always called by the Graphics Device Interface.

▶ **The Printer Interface Driver.** This dynamic link library consists of the user interface or configuration management portion of the printer driver; it's used by an administrator to configure a printer.

▶ **The Characterization File.** This component contains all the printer-specific information, such as memory, page protection, soft fonts, graphics resolution, paper orientation and size, and so on; it's used by the other two dynamic link libraries whenever they need to gather printer-specific information.

These three components of a printer driver (printer graphics driver, printer interface driver, and configuration file) are all located in the following directory, according to their Windows NT platforms (w32x86, w32mips, w32alpha, and w32ppc) and version numbers (0 = version 3.1, 1 = version 3.5x, 2 = version 4.x):

```
winnt_root\system32\spool\drivers.directory
```

The printer driver is specific to both the operating system and the hardware platform. You can't use a Windows 95 printer driver with Windows NT, and you can't use an Intel Windows NT printer driver on an Alpha Windows NT machine (see fig. 2.64).

Figure 2.64

Choosing a printer driver in the printer Properties Sharing tab.

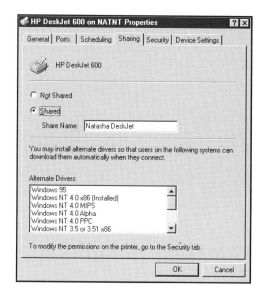

Spooler

The Spooler is a Windows NT service that operates in the background to manage the printing process. The spooler consists of a series of DLLs that work together to accept, process, and distribute print jobs.

You need to understand that the spooler really runs the show. Specifically, the spooler service is responsible for the following functions:

- ▶ Keeping track of what jobs are destined for which printers

- ▶ Keeping track of which ports are connected to which printers

- ▶ Routing print jobs to the correct port

- ▶ Managing printer pools

- ▶ Prioritizing print jobs

The NT Spooler service must be running on both the client and the print server machines for the printing process to function properly. Logically, however, you can think of the print spooler as a single process occurring on the client and on print server machines.

By default, the spool file folder is the `winnt_root\system32\spool\PRINTERS` directory. You can change the spool folder by using the Advanced tab of the printer server Properties dialog box. (The print server Properties dialog box gets more attention later in this chapter.) You also can use Registry Editor to set the spool directory, like so:

For all printers:

```
HKEY_LOCAL_MACHINE\SYSTEM\CurrentControlSet\Control\Print\Printers
DefaultSpoolDirectory:REG_SZ:<New Spool Path>
```

On a per-printer basis:

```
HKEY_LOCAL_MACHINE\SYSTEM\CurrentControlSet\Control\Print\Printers\
<printer>SpoolDirectory:REG_SZ:<New Spool Path>
```

In the event that a print job gets stuck in the spooler to the point that an administrator or print operator cannot delete or purge it, you can stop the Spooler service and restart it using the Control Panel Service application.

You also can start or stop the Spooler service using the following
commands at the command prompt:

```
net start spooler
net stop spooler
```

Router

The print router receives the print job from the spooler and
routes it to the appropriate print processor.

The Print Processor

The process of translating print data into a form that a printing
device can read is called rendering. The rendering process begins
with the printer driver. The print processor is responsible for completing the rendering process. The tasks performed by the print
processor differ depending on the print data's data type.

The primary Windows NT print processor is called
WINPRINT.DLL, and is located in

```
winnt_root\system32\spool\prtprocs\platform
```

WINPRINT.DLL recognizes the following data types:

- ▶ **Raw data.** Fully rendered data that is ready for the printer.
  A postscript command, for instance, reaches the print processor as raw data.

- ▶ **Windows NT Enhanced Metafile (EMF).** A standard file
  format that many different printing devices support. Instead
  of the raw printer data being generated by the printer driver,
  the Graphical Device Interface generates NT EMF information before spooling. After the NT EMF is created, control
  returns to the user. The NT EMF is then interpreted in the
  background on a 32-bit printing subsystem spooler thread
  and sent to the printer driver. This process returns control to
  the user in significantly less time than waiting for the printer
  calls to be directly interpreted by the printer driver.

- ▶ **TEXT.** Raw text with minimal formatting. The TEXT data
  type is designed for printing devices that don't directly

accept ASCII text. The print processor sends TEXT data to the graphics engine.

If you're running Services for Macintosh on a Windows NT server, you also have access to the print processor SFMPSPRT.DLL, which supports the PSCRIPT1 data type. The PSCRIPT1 data type is for print data sent from Macintosh clients to non-PostScript printing devices.

Print Monitors

Print Monitors controls access to a specific device, monitors the status of the device, and communicates this information back to the spooler, which relays the information via the user interface. The print monitor essentially controls the data stream to one or more printer ports; its responsibilities include writing a print job to the output destination and taking care of port access (opening, closing, configuring, reading from, writing to, and acquiring or releasing ports).

To install a new print monitor, click on Add Port in the Ports tab of the printer Properties dialog box. Click on the New Monitor button in the Printer Ports dialog box that appears (see fig. 2.65).

Figure 2.65

The Printer Ports dialog box.

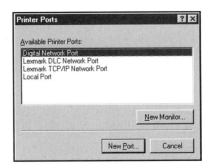

In addition, the print monitor has the following duties:

▶ Detect unsolicited errors (such as Toner Low).

▶ Handle true end-of-job notification. The print monitor waits until the last page has been printed to notify the spooler that the print job has finished and can be discarded.

▶ Monitor printer status to detect printing errors. If necessary, the print monitor notifies the spooler so that the job can continue or be restarted.

Windows NT provides some standard print monitors. These include print monitors for the following:

▶ Local output to LPTx, COMx, remote printer shares and names pipes (\WINNT_ROOT\SYSTEM32\ LOCALMON.DLL).

▶ Output to Hewlett-Packard network interface printing devices (\WINNT_ROOT\SYSTEM32\HPMON.DLL), which can support up to 225 (configured for 64) Hewlett-Packard network interface printing devices. This print monitor requires the DLC protocol.

▶ Output to Digital network port printers (DECPSMON.DLL), supporting both TCP/IP and DECnet protocols. The DECnet protocol doesn't ship with Windows NT.

▶ Output to LPR (Line Printer) Ports (LPRMON.DLL), allowing Windows NT to print directly to UNIX LPD print servers or network interface printing devices over the TCP/IP protocol.

▶ Output to PJL Language printing device (PJLMON.DLL).

▶ Output to Apple Macintosh postscript printers (SFMMON.DLL), for Windows NT servers with services for the Apple Macintosh installed.

Printers Folder

The Printers folder is the Windows NT printing system's primary user interface. The Printers folder replaces Print Manager, the printing interface in previous versions of NT. You can reach the Printers folder through Control Panel, or through the Settings item in the Start menu.

From the Printers folder, you install, configure, administer, and remove printers. You also supervise print queues; pause, purge and restart print jobs; share printers; and set printer defaults. The following sections discuss two of the principal activities managed through the Printers folder: adding printers and configuring printers.

You can install printers on your Windows NT workstation in two ways: install a printer on your own workstation, or connect to a remote printer. Installing your own printer is much more involved than connecting to a remote printer, and it requires Administrative or Power User-level rights. You add a new printer or connect to a remote printer using the Add Printer icon in the Printers folder. You also can connect to a remote printer via Network Neighborhood.

From the Printers folder, double-click on the Add Printer icon to open the Add Printer Wizard (see fig. 2.66).

Figure 2.66

The Add Printer Wizard screen.

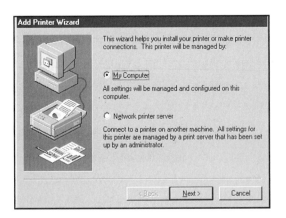

The first screen of the Add Printer Wizard asks if the new printer will be attached to your computer (the My Computer option) or connected to another machine and accessed via the network (the Network printer server option). The My Computer option requires Administrator or Power User rights, whereas the Network printer server option does not; you don't have to be an Administrator or a Power User to connect to a shared printer on another machine.

Adding a Printer on Your Own Machine

If you select the My Computer option from the Add Printer Wizard screen, and then click on Next, the Wizard asks you what port you want to use (see fig. 2.67). You must select a port for the new printer. The Wizard won't let you proceed until you have either checked one of the ports or added a new port.

Figure 2.67

The Add Port button enables you to add a new digital network port, local port, or PJL language monitor to your printing system.

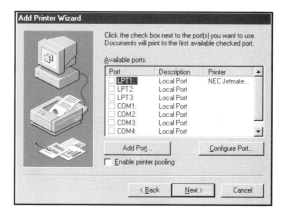

The next screen asks you to specify the manufacturer and model of the new printer (see fig. 2.68). Select a manufacturer, and a list of drivers for printers by that manufacturer appears. Or, if you want to install an unlisted printer driver from a disk, click on the Have Disk button.

Figure 2.68

The manufacturer and model options screen of the Add Printer wizard.

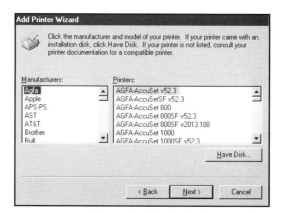

The next screen asks for a printer name, and whether you want the printer to become the default printer for Windows-based programs. As with all objects in Windows NT, a printer requires a name. The printer name can be as long as 32 characters and doesn't have to reflect the name of the driver in use. You should avoid using the full 32 characters, however, because you might sometimes need to type the printer name to connect to it from a remote computer.

The next screen asks if you want to share the printer (see fig. 2.69). If you want to share the printer with other computers on the network, you must also specify a share name (the default share name is the printer name specified in the preceding screen.) The wizard also asks you to specify the operating systems of all computers that will be sharing the printer. Your only choices are Windows 95 and a number of NT versions and platforms.

Figure 2.69

The Add Printer Wizard asks if you want to share the printer.

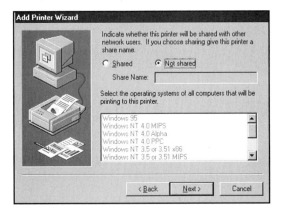

The Add Printer Wizard then attempts to install the printer driver. You may be asked to supply the Windows NT installation disk. (If you designate Windows 95 as the operating system of a computer sharing the printer, you may also be prompted to supply the Windows 95 installation CD-ROM.) The wizard then asks if you want to print a test page.

When the installation is complete, the Add Printer wizard opens the Properties dialog box for the new printer. You can read more about the Properties dialog box later in this chapter.

Adding a Network Print Server

If you choose the work printer server option in the first screen of the Add Printer Wizard, the Wizard opens the Connect to Printer dialog box (see fig. 2.70), which asks for the name of the shared printer to which you want to connect. Click on the workstation to which the printer is attached and then select the printer.

Figure 2.70

The Connect to Printer dialog box.

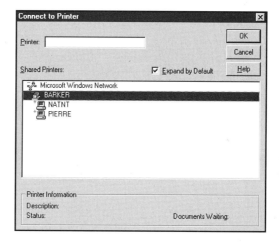

The Add Printer Wizard doesn't know enough to open a network connection for you; if you don't open a connection using the workstation you select in the Connect to Printer dialog box, the printers attached to that workstation don't display. If this situation occurs, double-click on the Network Neighborhood icon and then double-click on the icon for the workstation, to enter your username and password and establish a connection. As long as you're in Network Neighborhood, you might as well establish the printer connection through Network Neighborhood.

The Wizard then asks if you want the printer to serve as a default printer, and completes the installation. If the installation is successful, the icon for the printer appears in the Printers folder.

Configuring Printers

Almost all the configuration settings for a printer in Windows NT 4 are accessible through the following three options of the Printers folder File menu:

▶ Document Defaults

▶ Server Properties

▶ Properties

You also use the Sharing option in the File menu for configuration; specifically, to set up the printer as a shared printer on the network. It's actually just a different path to the Sharing tab of the Properties dialog box.

You find most of the configuration settings for a given printer in the Properties dialog box. The NT 4 printer Properties dialog box is designed to serve as a central location for printer configuration information.

The Server Properties dialog box holds information specific to the computer's print server activities. The Server Properties dialog box thus is independent of any particular printer (which is why Server Properties appears in the File menu regardless of whether a printer is selected.) The Document Defaults option opens the Default Document Properties dialog box, which holds page setup and document settings for a given printer.

You can reach most of the Printers folder File menu options easily; if you right-click on a printer icon in the Printers folder, the File menu options appear in a context menu.

Document Defaults

Choose File, Document Defaults to open the Default Document Properties dialog box (see fig. 2.71). The Default Document Properties dialog box contains document settings for the documents that are to print on the selected printer. A good example of a document setting you can control by using the Default Document Properties dialog box is the Orientation setting.

Figure 2.71

*Page Setup tab
of the Default
Document Prop-
erties dialog box.*

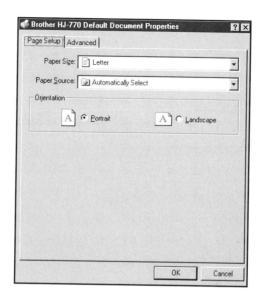

The Page Setup tab defines the Paper Size, Paper Source, and Orientation options for controlling settings for the document you want to print. You change the size, source, and orientation settings in the Advanced tab, which also contains settings for graphics resolution, color adjustment, and print quality (see fig. 2.72).

Figure 2.72

*The Advanced
tab of the Default
Document Prop-
erties dialog box.*

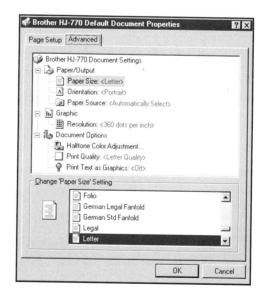

Server Properties

Choose File, Server Properties to open the Print Server Properties dialog box (see fig. 2.73). The following sections discuss the three tabs in the Print Server Properties dialog box.

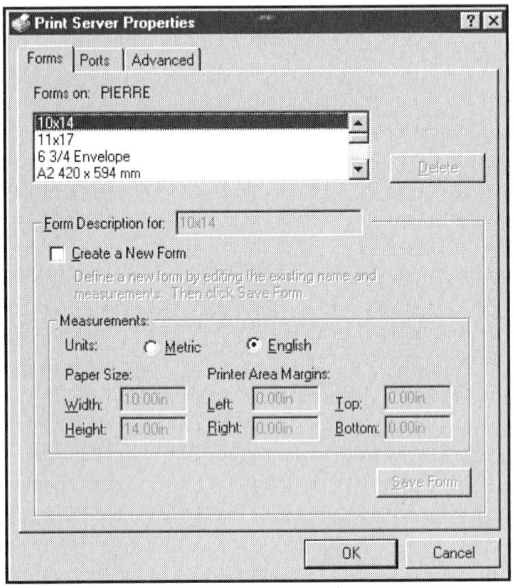

Figure 2.73

The Forms tab of the Print Server Properties dialog box.

Forms

The Forms tab of the Print Server Properties dialog box defines the print forms available on the computer. Think of a print form as a description of a piece of paper that might be in a printer tray. A print form tells NT the size of the paper and where to put the printer margins. The Device Settings tab of the Properties dialog box lets you assign a print form to an actual tray. Thus, you can tell NT the size of the paper in each printer tray, and the size of the printer margins. This facility is useful when you have multiple printer trays with different sizes of paper in each, or when one of your printer trays contains a particular type of paper, such as corporate letterhead paper, which requires a different top or bottom margin from the standard tray.

You can create your own print forms from within the Forms tab. To create your own form, follow these steps:

1. Click on an existing form in the Forms On list.

2. Select the Create a New Form check box.

3. Change the name of the form, and change the form measurements to the new settings.

4. Click on the Save Form button.

Ports

The Ports tab of the Printer Server Properties dialog box maintains a list of available ports. You can add, delete, or configure a port. The Ports tab here is similar to the Add Printer Wizard Ports tab (discussed earlier in this chapter) and the printer Properties Ports tab (discussed later in this chapter) except that, in this case, you don't have to select a port because you aren't associating a port with a particular printer, but rather, are merely viewing the ports that are available for all printers.

Advanced

The Advanced tab of the Printer Server Properties dialog box provides the location of the spooler and an assortment of logging and notification options (see fig. 2.74).

Figure 2.74

The Advanced tab of the Print Server Properties dialog box.

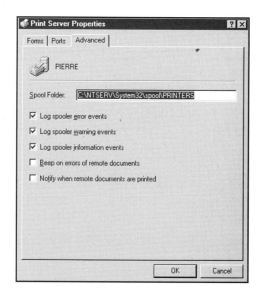

Properties

You can find most of the printer configuration settings in the printer Properties dialog box (see fig. 2.75). To open the printer Properties dialog box, select a printer in the Printers folder and choose File, Properties, or right-click on the printer and choose Properties. The following sections discuss the six tabs of the printer Properties dialog box.

Figure 2.75

*The printer Prop-
erties dialog box.*

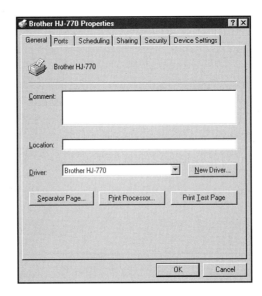

The Printer Properties General Tab

The General tab lets you install a new driver for the printer. The Print Test Page button provides a convenient method for testing whether a printer connection is working. The Separator Page and Print Processor buttons are a bit more complicated.

Separator File

By default, Windows NT doesn't separate print jobs with even a blank sheet of paper; to print a separator page between print jobs, you must configure a separator file, of which three are included with Windows NT. You may use one of these or create your own:

▶ **SYSPRINT.SEP.** Prints a separator page for PostScript printers; stored in the \<winnt_root>\SYSTEM32 directory.

▶ **PSCRIPT.SEP.** Switches Hewlett-Packard printers to Post-Script mode for printers incapable of autoswitching; located in the \<winnt_root>\SYSTEM32 directory.

▶ **PCL.SEP.** Switches Hewlett-Packard printers to PCL mode for printers not capable of autoswitching (and prints a separator page before each document); located in the \<winnt_root>\SYSTEM32 directory.

You also may choose to design your own separator page. If so, use a text editor and consult the escape codes listed in table 2.1. The escape codes are special symbols that prompt Windows NT to replace them with specific pieces of data. For instance, /N is the escape code that instructs Windows NT to print the username of the user who printed the job, and /D represents the date the job was printed.

Table 2.1

Windows NT Printing Escape Codes	
Code	Instruction for Windows NT
\<number>	Skip specified number of lines (0–9)
\B\M	Print text in double-width block mode
\B\S	Print text in single-width block mode
\D	Print current date using Control Panel International format
\E	Eject the page
\F<filename>	Print a file
\H<code>	Send printer-specific hexadecimal ASCII code
\I	Print job number
\L<text>	Print the specified text (use another escape code to end)
\N	Print username of job owner
\T	Print time the job was printed. Use Control Panel International format.
\U	Turn off block mode (see \B\M and \B\S)
\W<width>	Set width of the page (<=256)

To specify a separator file, click on the Separator Page button in the printer Properties General tab and enter the name of the file, or click on Browse and locate the separator file.

Print Processor

Don't mess with the print processor; it's the component of the printing subsystem that actually performs the rendering. Typically, WINPRINT.DLL performs the print processor functions. If it becomes necessary to replace it, Windows NT does it for you.

WINPRINT.DLL supports the following five data types:

▶ Raw Fully rendered data ready for printing

▶ RAW (FF appended)

▶ RAW (FF auto)

▶ NT EMF (enhanced metafile format) A device-independent file format. An EMF file can be spooled directly to the print server and rendered at the server into the correct print format.

▶ TEXT Raw, unformatted ASCII text ready for printing as is.

Printer Properties Ports Tab

The printer Properties Ports tab lets you select a port for the printer, and add or delete a port from the tab (see fig. 2.76). The Configure Port button allows you to specify the Transmission Retry time (the amount of time that must elapse before NT notifies you that the printing device isn't responding). The Transmission Retry setting applies not just to printer you selected but to all printers that use the same driver.

Figure 2.76

*The printer Prop-
erties Ports tab.*

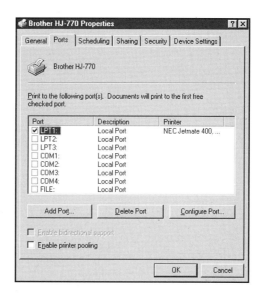

Printer Properties Scheduling Tab

The printer Properties Scheduling tab lets you designate when the
printer is to be available, and to set the printer priority (see fig.
2.77). It also displays some miscellaneous settings that define how
the printer processes print jobs. The next few sections discuss the
important settings of the Scheduling tab.

Figure 2.77

*The printer Prop-
erties Scheduling
tab.*

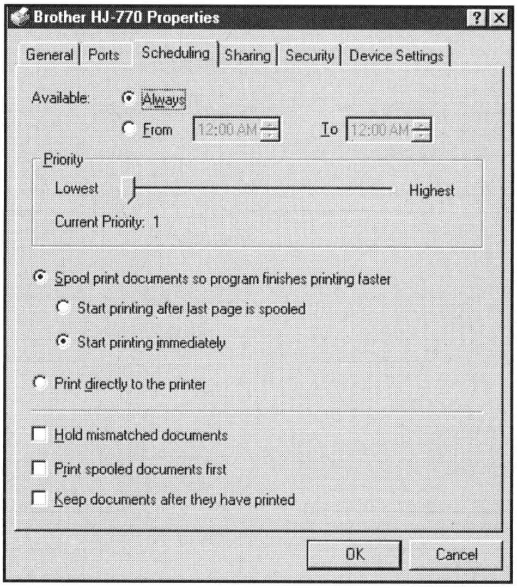

Available

The Available setting lets you limit the availability of a printer to a specific period of time. Note that just because a printer is restricted to a certain period of time doesn't mean the device must be similarly restricted. To keep long monthly reports from monopolizing a device during business hours, for example, you could create two printers for the same printing device, one of which might be used for short print jobs and be available during the day, the other of which might be used for long reports and print only at night.

Priority

The default priority for a printer is 1, but it can be set as high as 99. Changing this setting from its default of 1 is useful in situations in which you have more than one printer printing to the same printing device, in which case the printer with higher priority (99 being the highest) prints before printers of lower priority (1 being the lowest). Note that the Printer Priority is not related to the Print job priority.

Spool Print Documents or Print Directly to Printer

If you spool print documents, the computer and the printer don't have to wait for each other. It's almost always more efficient to spool print documents; you rarely have reason to change this default. One advantage, however, of Print Directly to Printer is that printing directly to the printer might allow you to troubleshoot a problem with the spooler. If you can print to the printer but you can't print via the spooler, you may have a problem with your spooler.

Under the Spool print documents option, there are two other options:

▶ Start printing after the last page is spooled.

▶ Start printing immediately.

The first choice is (in part) a holdover from earlier versions on NT; NT used to wait until a job was completely spooled before beginning to print it. This wait could take a long time for reports hundreds of pages long, so more recent versions offered a "Job prints while spooling" option to let the printer start printing before the spooler finishes. In NT 4, "Start printing immediately" is the default option, but you still have the option of not printing until after the last page spools.

Hold Mismatched Documents

In other Windows-based operating environments, improperly configured print jobs—a print job, for example, requesting a paper tray that isn't present—can be sent to a printer, which usually causes the printer to hang with an error message. But with the Hold Mismatched Documents option selected, Windows NT examines the configuration of both the print job and printer to make sure that they are in agreement before it sends the job.

Print Spooled Documents First

Ordinarily, Windows NT prints documents on a first-come, first-served basis; the document at the top of the queue prints before the documents below it. If the document at the top of the queue takes a long time to spool, and if the Job Prints While Spooling option isn't selected, you might want to enable the Print Spooled Documents First setting. Windows NT always prints the first available completely spooled print job. If this setting is used in conjunction with Job Prints While Spooling, all the completely spooled documents ahead of the spooling document print first. The spooling document is processed next, even if completed documents are waiting behind it in the queue.

Keep Documents After They Have Printed

Normally, Windows NT cleans up after itself as it finishes printing each job. If you enable the Keep documents after they have printed option, however, Windows NT keeps the print document after it prints. One reason to check this box is if you want to have a record of completed print jobs that all users can access. Although you may choose to have completed print jobs recorded in the event logs, non-administrative users cannot view the event logs.

The Printer Properties Sharing Tab

The Sharing tab lets you share the printer with other computers on the network (see fig. 2.78). If you didn't install the printer as a shared printer but decide later to share it, you can change the printer to a shared printer.

Figure 2.78

The printer Properties Sharing tab.

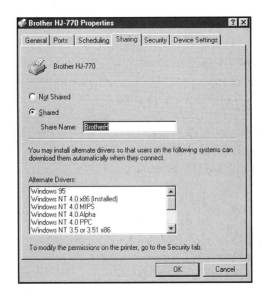

To share a printer, follow these steps:

1. Select Sharing tab in the printer Properties dialog box.

2. Specify a share name (or accept the default, which is the first eight characters of the printer name).

3. Specify what operating systems the other workstations will be using (so NT can automatically download the necessary print drivers to the connecting computers).

4. Click on OK.

You access the Sharing tab directly by clicking on a printer and choosing File, Sharing in the Printers folder, or by right-clicking on a printer and choosing Sharing.

The Printer Properties Security Tab

The Security tab lets you configure permissions, auditing, and ownership for the printer (see fig. 2.79).

Figure 2.79

The printer Properties Security tab.

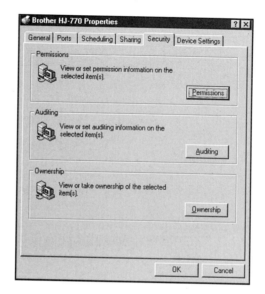

Windows NT printers are Windows NT resources, and Windows NT resources are Windows NT objects. Windows NT objects are protected by the Windows NT security model; that is, they have owners and Access Control Lists that owners can use to protect the printers.

To set or change permissions, a user must be the owner, an Administrator, a Power User, or a user who has Full Control permissions on the printer's ACL.

To set permissions for a printer, select the Security tab in the printer Properties dialog box and click on the Permissions button. You see the Printer Permissions dialog box, which displays common user groups and the permission levels granted to each group for the use of selected printer (see fig. 2.80).

Figure 2.80

The printer Permissions dialog box.

The four possible permission levels are as follows:

▶ **No Access.** Completely restricts access to the printer.

▶ **Print.** Allows a user or group to submit a print job, and to control the settings and print status for that job.

▶ **Manage Documents.** Allows a user or group to submit a print job, and to control the settings and print status for all print jobs.

▶ **Full Control.** Allows a user to submit a print job, and to control the settings and print status for all documents as well as for the printer itself. In addition, the user or group may share, stop sharing, change permissions for, and even delete the printer.

These permissions affect both local and remote users. By default, permissions on newly created printers comply with the following scheme:

Administrators	Full Control
Creator/Owner	Manage Documents
Everyone	Print
Power Users (workstations only)	Full Control and servers
Print Operators (domain only)	Full Control controllers
Server Operators (domain only)	Full Control controllers

To change the permission level for a group, select the group in the Name list and enter a new permission level in the Type of Access combo box, or open the Type of Access combo box and select a permission level. To add a group or user to the permissions list, click on the Add button. The Add Users and Groups dialog box opens (see fig. 2.81).

Figure 2.81

The Add Users and Groups dialog box.

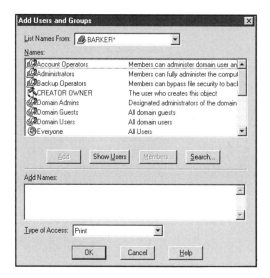

To add a group to the permissions list, select a group in the Names list of the Add Users and Groups dialog box and click on Add. The name of the group appears in the Add Names box. Click on OK to add the name to the permissions list.

To add an individual user to the permissions list, click on the Show Users button in the Add Users and Groups dialog box. This adds users to the Names list. Select the user and click on Add. The name of the user then appears in the Add Names box. Click on OK to add the name to the permissions list.

After you add the group or user to the permissions list, you can change the permission level for that group or user, as described earlier in this section.

The printer Properties Security tab also enables you to set up auditing for the printer and to take ownership of the printer.

Printer Properties Device Settings Tab

The printer Properties Device Settings tab maintains settings for the printing device (see fig. 2.82). These settings differ depending on your printing device. The Form To Tray Assignment setting allows you to associate a print form with an actual paper tray on the printing device.

Figure 2.82

The printer Properties Device Settings tab.

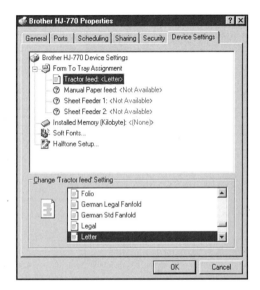

Sharing Printers

As you install a new printer, you can designate as a printer to share over the network. The section "Adding a Printer on Your Own Machine" earlier in this chapter describes how to do this.

You can share a printer that already has been installed using the Sharing tab in the printer Properties dialog box. See the section "The Printer Properties Sharing Tab," earlier in this chapter.

Use the Security tab in the printer Properties dialog box to set or change permissions for printers.

Setting Up a Printer Pool

A printer pool presents interesting possibilities for some office environments. A printer pool is essentially a single logical printer that prints to more than one printing device; it prints jobs sent to it to the first available printing device (and therefore provides the throughput of multiple printing devices with the simplicity of a single printer definition).

> The user has no control over which device prints the job; therefore, printer pools are incredibly annoying if the printing devices aren't located at the same place.

If a printer controls a printer pool, Windows NT ensures that no single device is ever sent more than one document at a time if other devices currently are available. This characteristic ensures the most efficient utilization of your printing devices.

Printer pools are an extremely efficient way of streamlining the printing process, although they don't necessarily fit every environment. Before your network can use a printer pool, it must meet the following criteria:

▶ You must have at least two printing devices capable of using the same printer driver because the entire pool is treated as a single logical device, and is managed by a single printer driver.

▶ The printing devices should be adjacent to each other. Users aren't notified of the actual device that prints their job; users should be able to check all the printing devices rapidly and easily.

To create a printer pool, configure the printer to print to more than one port, and make sure a printing device is attached to each of the ports that the printer is using. You can choose more than one port when you select a printer port at installation (as described earlier in this chapter). Or, you can designate a new port for an existing printer using the Ports tab in the printer Properties dialog box.

Printing from MS-DOS Applications

MS-DOS applications provide their own printer drivers and automatically render printer data to the RAW data type or to straight ASCII text. The print data is then intercepted by the client spooler and routed through the Windows NT printing system.

The MS-DOS application typically isn't equipped to process UNC names, so if it is printing to a remote printer, you should map a physical port to the remote printer, as follows:

```
net use LPTx: \\pserver\printer_name
```

Because the application itself renders the printer data, an MS-DOS application that prints graphics and formatted text must have its own printer driver for the printing device. An MS-DOS application can print ASCII text output without a vendor-supplied printer driver.

Configuring Windows NT Server for Client Computers

The Windows NT CD-ROM includes client software to assist with networking certain common operating systems with Windows NT. Chapter 1 (and the section on "Installing with Client Administrator," earlier in this chapter) discuss some of the client software packages included with Windows NT Server. When you are configuring networking protocols on your Windows NT Server system, it is important to remember that all these software packages don't support all the native Windows NT network protocols and network services.

Microsoft lists the following objective for the Windows NT Server exam:

Configure a Windows NT Server computer for various types of client computers. Client computer types include: Windows NT Workstation, Microsoft Windows 95, Microsoft MS-DOS-based.

Table 2.2 describes which network protocols and which TCP/IP services each of the client systems supports. This table also appears in Chapter 1, in the section entitled "Planning for Network Clients." You must ensure that the Windows NT configuration provides the appropriate protocols for whatever client systems you'll have running on your network. For more on these client system, see Chapter 1.

Table 2.2

Network Protocol and TCP/IP Service Support for Various Windows NT Client Systems

Network Protocol TCP/IP Service

	Net-BEUI	Com-patible	Com-patible	TCP/IP	DLC	DHCP	WINS	DNS
Network Client for MS-DOS	X	X	IPX	X	X	X		
LAN MAN 2.2c for MS-DOS	X		IPX/SPX	X	X			
Lan MAN 2.2c for OS/2	X			X				
Windows 95	X		X	X		X	X	X
Windows NT Workstation	X		X	X	X	X	X	X

Exercise Section

Exercise 2.1: The Server and Workstation Services

In Exercise 2.1, you learn about starting and stopping services using the Services application in the Control Panel, and you study the functions of the Server and Workstation services.

1. Start two Windows NT PCs on your network that each provide shared resources. This exercise will refer to those computers and as Computer A and Computer B.

2. Using Network Neighborhood, browse Computer B from Computer A. Then browse Computer A from Computer B. Make sure the shared resources are available.

3. Start the Control Panel Services application on Computer B. Shut down the Server service. Windows NT will ask if it's OK to shut down the Computer Browser service too. Click OK. Click Close to close the Services application.

4. Now try to browse Computer B from Computer A. You'll get a message that says, "<*computer_name*> is not accessible. The network path was not found."

5. Restart the Server service in the Control Panel Services application. Now try to browse Computer B from Computer A. The shared resources are now available.

6. In the Control Panel Services application, shut down the Workstation service. Notice that you can still browse Computer B from Computer A.

7. With the Computer B Workstation service stopped, try to browse Computer A from Computer B. You'll get a message that says "Unable to browse the network. The network is not present or not started.

8. Restart the Computer B Workstation service. You can now browse computer A from Computer B.

Exercise 2.2: Creating a Network Installation Disk

Exercise 2.2 will show you how to create a network installation disk using Network Client Administrator.

1. Prepare an MS-DOS system disk using the MS-DOS sys command on an MS-DOS machine.

2. Create a network installation startup disk as described in this chapter in the section entitled "Network Installation Startup Disk." Create a share for the installation files using the Share Files option in the Share Network Client Installation Files dialog box, which shares directly from the Windows NT CD-ROM and doesn't require disk space on the installation server.

3. Boot a network computer using the network installation startup disk and attempt to connect to the installation share you created in Step 2.

Exercise 2.3: Directory Replication

In Exercise 2.3, you learn how to set up directory replication on your network.

1. Set up the Windows NT Server export server for directory replication using the procedure described in the "Directory Replication" section of this chapter.

2. Set up an import computer using the procedure described in the "Directory Replication" section of this chapter.

3. Copy some files to the export directory of the export server.

4. Wait a few minutes. See if the files you copied to the export directory in step 3 appear in the import directory of the import computer.

Exercise 2.4: Network Bindings

Just because a protocol is properly installed, it doesn't mean you can use it with a particular network adapter. To use a protocol with an network adapter, a *binding* between the protocol and the adapter must exist. Exercise 2.4 studies the effect of removing a network binding.

1. Logon to a Windows NT Server system that uses the TCP/IP protocol and go to the command prompt.

2. Ping the loopback address: 127.0.0.1 (see Exercise 2 of Chapter 1). The loopback address verifies that TCP/IP is properly configured for your system. You should get four replies.

3. Ping the IP address of the computer you are now using. The IP address is actually associated with your network adapter. You should get four replies.

4. Start Control Panel Network application and select the Bindings tab.

5. In the Show Bindings for: box, select all adapters.

6. Expand the tree for your network adapter. Select the TCP/IP protocol.

7. Click on the Disable button. This will disable the TCP/IP binding for your network adapter card. Click OK.

8. Windows NT will ask if you want to restart your system. Click Yes.

9. Restart your system. Logon and go to the command prompt.

10. Ping the loopback address. You should still get four replies.

11. Ping the IP address of your own computer. You'll get a message that says "Destination host unreachable" four times. Your network adapter is "unreachable" because you have disabled the binding that associates you adapter with the TCP/IP protocol.

12. Ping another computer on your network. You should get the "Destination host unreachable" message for other PCs too, because disabling the binding has disrupted the pathway through which your computer communicates with the network.

13. Return to the Bindings tab of the Network application. In the box labeled Show Bindings for:, select *all adapters*. Expand the tree for your network adapter. Enable the the TCP/IP protocol. Shut down and restart your system.

Review Questions

1. You're considering purchasing a file server for the Accounting department to run Windows NT Server 4. What's the first thing you should do?

    A. Verify that all the hardware to be contained in the server is on Microsoft's Hardware Compatibility List (HCL).

    B. Purchase the parts and put the server together yourself so you know you're obtaining a quality computer.

    C. Buy the server hardware only from a reputable dealer licensed to sell Microsoft Windows NT Server.

    D. Contact Microsoft and ask them to direct you to a Microsoft Certified Hardware vendor in your area.

2. You installed Windows NT Server 4 on a machine that has an existing installation of OS/2. Now, after the final reboot of the installation program, you notice that the OS/2 boot manager menu isn't displaying. What could be the problem?

    A. When you installed NT you actually upgraded from OS/2 to NT, thus overwriting the OS/2 installation.

    B. Nothing, you can't boot OS/2 when Windows NT 4 is installed.

    C. Windows NT has disabled the boot manager and you need to re-enable it via Disk Administrator by marking the Boot Manager active.

    D. Nothing, but you need to install DOS and create a FAT partition and then reinstall OS/2.

3. You installed Windows NT Server 4, but during the installation process you selected Server as the type of installation. You now want to make the Server a backup domain controller. What must you do to convert the server?

    A. Nothing. The next time you restart the server simply select NT Server - Domain Controller from the boot menu.

    B. Under Control Panel, System, change the server type to Domain Controller.

    C. Under Control Panel, Network, change the server type to Domain Controller.

    D. You cannot designate a member server to be a domain controller unless you reinstall NT Server.

4. A domain must have at least one of the following. Select all that apply.

    A. A BDC and a PDC

    B. Only a BDC

    C. A PDC

    D. A PDC and at least one BDC

5. What is the main difference between an NT Server acting as a domain controller and an NT Server not installed as a domain controller?

    A. A domain controller maintains a copy of the directory database, whereas a non-domain controller does not.

    B. A non-domain controller maintains a copy of the directory database, whereas a domain controller does not.

    C. A non-domain controller validates user logons, whereas a domain controller does not.

    D. NT Server 4 cannot be installed as a domain controller.

6. You want to install NT Server on four new servers simultaneously. Which installation method would provide you with the fastest installation?

    A. Floppy disk

    B. CD-ROM

    C. Over the network

7. What must you do to perform an NT installation using the over the network method?

A. Copy the entire CD-ROM contents to a web server and access the server installation files using a web browser installed on the new server.

B. Take the CD-ROM and install it in an existing NT Server and then transfer the program files to the new server by using the NetTransfer program included on the CD-ROM.

C. Copy the I386 directory to a share point on an existing server, connect to the share point using the MS-DOS client software, and then run the WINNT program.

D. Purchase a CD-ROM drive that has an Ethernet card in it and share the CD-ROM over the network. Then run the client software on the computer on which you are going to install NT and run the WINNT program.

8. To save time, you want to install Windows NT without first making the three boot floppies. Which command line switch should you use with the WINNT program.

A. /OX

B. /NF

C. /O

D. /B

9. You're upgrading from Windows NT 3.5 to 4. How should you proceed with the installation?

A. Restart the computer in DOS and run the WINNT program from the CD-ROM.

B. Run the WINNT program from the Program Manager, File, Run command.

C. Run the WINNT32 program from the Program Manager, File, Run command.

D. You cannot directly upgrade to NT 4 because of the new user interface. You must install a fresh copy.

10. If you're installing NT Workstation and you want to be able to specify all the components that should be installed, which installation method should you choose?

    A. Custom

    B. Compact

    C. Typical

    D. Portable

11. While installing NT Server, you were prompted for a Computer Name. Which statement best describes the purpose of the computer name?

    A. The computer name is the NetBIOS name. It identifies the computer on the network. It's okay to have two computers with the same computer name as long as they are separated by a router.

    B. The computer name is the NetBIOS name. It identifies the computer on the network. Under no circumstances should two computers have the same name.

    C. The computer name identifies the computer to the domain controller. The computer name must be at least two characters and must include the domain name as part of the computer name.

    D. Computer names are case-sensitive and must be entered when the user logs on to the computer for the first time.

12. What is the default network protocol installed with Windows NT on an Intel-based platform?

    A. NetBEUI

    B. AppleTalk

    C. IPX/SPX

    D. TCP/IP

13. A user calls you and asks how he can make his NT Workstation a member of a workgroup and domain. He needs to share files with users in his department and access the file server at the same time. How does he make his server a member of the workgroup and the domain at the same time?

    A. He cannot. An NT Workstation computer cannot be a member of a domain and a workgroup at the same time.

    B. Under Control Panel, Network enter the workgroup name and the domain name and then restart the workstation.

    C. He can be a member of both only if the workgroup and domain name are the same.

14. A user calls you and states that during the course of installing NT Workstation, he tried to enter the domain name when prompted, but could not continue. The computer said something on the order of "You do not have sufficient authority to join the domain." What do you need to do so that he can join the domain?

    A. Nothing. A Windows NT Workstation cannot be a member of a domain, only a workgroup.

    B. Grant his domain userid the authority to create computer accounts in the domain and tell him to try it again.

    C. Give him the domain administrator's userid and password and tell him to try it again.

    D. Create a computer account for the user in Server Manager and ask him to try entering the domain name again.

15. You're trying to install Windows NT on a RISC-based computer. Which of the following requirements must you meet?

    A. A Microsoft Certified Hardware Reseller must supply the RISC-based computer and the vender must install NT on the computer.

    B. You must install NT from a SCSI CD-ROM and have at least a 2 MB FAT partition.

    C. You must install NT using the over the network installation method, because NT doesn't support SCSI CD-ROM devices on RISC-based computers.

    D. You must request the special RISC-based CD-ROM when ordering Windows NT.

16. Which of the following outlines the correct procedures for uninstalling Windows NT from a computer that does not have a FAT partition?

   A. You must low-level format the hard drive to remove NT.

   B. You must boot the computer with a DOS bootable disk and then run the SYS.COM program to restore the boot sector files.

   C. You can remove NT by deleting the NTFS partition by using the DOS 6.22 version of FDISK.

   D. You can remove NT by deleting the NTFS partition using a tool such as DELPART or OS/2 version of FDISK.

17. Which statement best describes the differences between a per server and a per seat license mode?

   A. In a per server license mode, a certain number of connections are assigned to the server and in a per seat mode, a license is assigned to each client connecting to the server.

   B. In a per seat mode, a certain number of connections are assigned to the server and in a per seat mode, a license is assigned to each client connecting to the server.

   C. You can convert from a per seat mode license to a per server mode license for a one time charge from Microsoft.

   D. You can convert from a per server license to a per seat license for a one time charge from Microsoft.

18. If you're installing multiple Windows NT Servers, which is the most cost-effective license mode to choose?

   A. Per server

   B. Per seat

   C. It doesn't matter which mode you choose as long as you have a special exemption from Microsoft.

   D. You can install the server in a per seat mode and then later covert to a per server mode if the need arises.

19. Which statement best describes the purpose of the Registry?

    A. The Registry is a configuration database that replaces the INI files used by previous versions of Windows.

    B. The Registry is a configuration database that Windows NT uses to keep domain account information (that is, registered information).

    C. Windows 3.x applications use the Registry rather than INI files to store their configuration information.

20. What is the name of the utility used to directly edit the Registry?

    A. REGEDIT.EXE

    B. EDITREG.EXE

    C. REGEDT32.EXE

    D. CHGREG.EXE

21. What five subtrees make up the Registry?

    A. HKEY_LOCAL_MACHINE; HKEY_ALL_USERS; HKEY_CURRENT_USER; HKEY_ROOT; HKEY_CURRENT_CONFIG

    B. HKEY_LOCAL_MACHINE; HKEY_COMMON; HKEY_CURRENT_USER; HKEY_CLASSES_ROOT; HKEY_CURRENT_CONFIG

    C. HKEY_MACHINE; HKEY_CLASSES_ROOT; HKEY_CURRENT_USER; HKEY_USERS; HKEY_CURRENT_CONFIG

    D. HKEY_LOCAL_MACHINE; HKEY_USERS; HKEY_CURRENT_USER; HKEY_CLASSES_ROOT; HKEY_CURRENT_CONFIG

22. Which Registry subtree contains the information about the current configuration of the computer?

    A. HKEY_CURRENT_USER

    B. HKEY_CURRENT_MACHINE

    C. HKEY_LOCAL_MACHINE

    D. HKEY_CLASSES_ROOT

23. The best way to back up the Registry is to _____.

    A. use the Windows NT Backup utility

    B. choose Registry, Save Key

    C. use the MS-DOS 6.22 Backup program

    D. simply copy the Registry files to a floppy disk using the XCOPY /n command

24. The preferred method of modifying the Registry is to use the _____ utility?

    A. Registry Editor (REGEDT32.EXE)

    B. Control Panel

    C. REGEDIT.EXE

    D. None of the above (The Registry is a system database and should never be directly edited by any users.)

25. A user calls you and tells you that he was trying to verify his hardware settings for his COM ports by looking at Control Panel, Ports, but he doesn't see any listing for his serial mouse, which is on COM1. Why is this?

    A. The user doesn't actually have a serial mouse. He has a bus mouse and that's why the port doesn't show up.

    B. The user is mistaken and probably doesn't have a mouse attached to his system.

    C. The user has a mouse, but needs to look under Control Panel, Mouse to see his device settings.

    D. Control Panel, Ports shows only available ports, not ones in use.

26. You have installed the Remote Access Service (RAS) on your Windows NT Workstation so that you may dial in to your network remotely. However, every time you restart your computer, you must manually restart the RAS service. How can you make this automatic?

    A. Place the RAS icon in the Startup group. This will launch the program every time the workstation is restarted.

B. There is no way to launch this application automatically because it's a system service.

C. Change the following Registry entry to 1 and restart your workstation: HKEY_LOCAL_MACHINE\CurrentControlSet\Microsoft\ Software\LaunchRas

D. Go into Control Panel, Services and select the RAS service and configure it as an automatic service.

27. Your mission critical NT Server just crashed owing to a power failure. You purchase a UPS (Uninterruptible Power Supply) and attach it to the NT Server computer. How can you configure the operating system so that it shuts down gracefully before the UPS runs out of power?

A. You cannot. You must manually shut down the server before the UPS runs out of power.

B. Choose the Control Panel, System option, select UPS, and configure the estimated runtime of the UPS. Be sure to select a number of minutes less than the actual runtime of the UPS.

C. Use the Control Panel, UPS applet and configure the COM Port, Run Time, and signaling methods of the UPS.

D. Because NT is Plug-and-Play compatible, you don't need to configure the UPS. The next time you restart the Server, the device is automatically configured.

28. A user calls you and states that after installing a new hard disk in his computer and partitioning it, he cannot select Format from the Tools menu in Disk Administrator. What does he need to do to be able to format the drive?

A. He must reboot the computer in DOS and then use the Format command to format the hard disk.

B. He has to commit the changes in Disk Administrator before the partition can be formatted.

C. He has to use the low-level format program in the computer's BIOS to prepare the disk.

D. The disk must first be partitioned using FDISK and

then formatted with DOS and then converted to NTFS
before it can be used.

29. You have installed a new hard disk in your NT Server computer and have partitioned it and formatted as a FAT partition. You want to add this disk space onto an existing volume
to extend the disk space. However, when you attempt to extend the volume, you cannot. Why?

    A. The volume that you created must already include four
primary partitions and cannot be extended any further.

    B. You must commit the changes before you can proceed.

    C. You can only extend a volume that has been formatted
or converted to NTFS.

    D. You can only extend volumes that have been formatted
or converted to FAT.

30. What is a disk partitioning scheme that allows equal areas of
disk space to be combined from 2 to 32 physical drives into
one logical drive?

    A. Stripe Set with Parity

    B. Volume Set

    C. NTFS volumes

    D. Stripe Set

31. What is a type of disk system that makes an exact copy of all
data from one disk partition onto another disk partition?

    A. RAID

    B. Disk Saving

    C. Disk Mirroring

    D. Hot Fixing

32. What is the type of disk system that uses 3 to 32 disks and is
also known as RAID level 5?

    A. Disk Striping with Parity.

    B. Disk Striping without Parity.

    C. Disk Mirroring.

D. Striping with Redundant Data.

33. The types of disk systems that are fault-tolerant are: Select all correct answers.

    A. Volume Sets
    B. Disk Striping with Parity
    C. Disk Striping without Parity
    D. Disk Mirroring
    E. RAID level 0

34. In a Windows NT environment, what is the term that refers to the object that performs the actual printing process?

    A. Printer
    B. Printing device
    C. Print queue
    D. Print server

35. A user states that she's trying to load a printer driver for her laser printer but cannot find one specifically written for Windows NT. She wants to know if the one she has for Windows 95 will work. Which statement best describes the relationship between printer drivers for different NT platforms?

    A. The Windows NT printer drivers are platform-specific. You cannot use a Windows 95 driver on an NT computer. You also must be sure to use the printer driver for the platform on which you're running NT.
    B. The NT printer drivers are interchangeable and can be used on any NT platform.
    C. The NT printer drivers and Windows 95 drivers are interchangeable because both operating systems are 32-bit. However, you cannot substitute 16-bit drivers for NT drivers.

36. If print jobs aren't printing properly and you cannot remove print jobs from the printer, what can you do to fix the problem?

A. Nothing.

B. Wait a couple hours; the spooler service will detect the problem and correct it.

C. Take the print server down and restart it.

D. Stop the spooler service on the print server and then restart it.

37. Which statement best describes the procedure for updating the printer driver on all your Windows NT computers?

A. Create a disk with the new printer driver on it and go to each computer and load the new version of the printer driver.

B. You must purchase and configure the SMS product from Microsoft if you want to automatically configure NT computers to update their printer drivers.

C. Load the new driver on the computer acting as the print server. The NT computers will automatically copy down the new printer driver the next time they print.

D. Put the printer driver in a shared directory and have your NT users install the new driver manually.

38. How do you install a new printer driver? Select all correct answers.

A. Choose Start, Settings, Printers. Run the Add Printer Wizard.

B. Start Print Manager and add the printer from the Printer menu.

C. Run Control Panel and click on the Printer icon; then double-click on the Add Printer Wizard.

D. Run the Windows NT Setup program and install the printer driver under the Configuration menu.

39. If you have a printer that has multiple paper trays, how can you make it easier for users to select the proper paper tray for the type of paper they want to print on?

A. Tell the users the type of paper that's in each of the paper trays so that they can select the proper tray when printing.

B. Assign a type of paper to the paper tray under the printer properties. The users can select the type of paper on which to print without knowing which tray the paper is in.

C. The users must select manual feed and then notify the printer operator when they're printing on non-standard paper types.

D. The users must select manual feed and then feed the correct type of paper when they print their documents.

40. If you have a printer set for use only by network users, only during after hours, what's the best way that you can set a schedule so that jobs print only between the hours of 6 p.m. and 6 a.m.?

A. Change the scheduling properties of the printer so that it prints only between the hours that you designate.

B. Only turn on the printer between the hours that you want it to print.

C. Pause the printer until the designated time. Then start the printer and the jobs will print. This way, users can print to the printer during the day and the jobs will accumulate in the printer until the pause is released.

D. Tell your users not to print to the printer until after the designated start time.

41. You have two groups of users who need to print to the same printer. However, one of the groups needs to have priority over the other groups print jobs. How best can you accomplish this arrangement?

A. You must install two separate printing devices and assign each group to print to one of the printing devices.

B. Make the users the higher printing priority printer operators so that they may adjust the order of their print jobs in the printer.

   C. Have the network administrator set up a printing pool with multiple printers.

   D. Install two printers that are connected to the same printing device. Assign different priorities and groups to each printer.

42. Some of the users on your network habitually select the incorrect printer driver when printing to your laser printer. How can you make sure that improperly formatted documents don't print on the printer, possibly causing it to hang?

   A. Tell the users to always check the printer driver selected before printing their documents.

   B. Install a printer that supports both PostScript and PCL printing definition languages.

   C. Select the Hold Mismatched Documents option in the printer properties. This way, the NT print server holds any documents that don't match the printer language.

   D. You shouldn't have to worry about it. The newer printer drivers can automatically translate the page formatting language to match the printer.

43. To set up a printing pool, which of the following criteria must be met? Select all correct answers.

   A. All the printers should be in the same general area.

   B. The printers should be of the same make and model.

   C. The printers must be connected to the same print server.

   D. The printers must be connected to the same type of port.

44. To print from a DOS application to a network printer under Windows NT, what two things must be done?

   A. The LPT device must be redirected to the network printer share using the NET USE command.

   B. The LPT device must be redirected to the network print queue using the CAPTURE command.

   C. The correct printer driver must be selected in Windows NT and it must be set as the default printer before printing from the DOS application.

D. The correct printer driver and LPT port must be selected in the DOS application before printing.

Review Answers

1. A	10. A	19. A	28. B	37. C
2. C	11. B	20. C	29. C	38. A C
3. D	12. D	21. D	30. D	39. B
4. C	13. A	22. C	31. C	40. A
5. A	14. D	23. A	32. A	41. D
6. C	15. B	24. B	33. B D	42. C
7. C	16. D	25. D	34. B	43. A B C
8. D	17. A	26. D	35. A	44. A D
9. C	18. B	27. C	36. D	

Chapter 3

Stop! Before reading this chapter, test yourself to determine how much study time you will need to devote to this section.

1. The capability to perform a particular action on the system without regard to a specific case is a _____.

   A. Permission

   B. Policy

   C. Right

   D. None of the above

2. To enter the roaming profile path, you must first click on the _____ button in the _____ of _____.

   A. Path...Environment Profile...Server Manager

   B. Profile...User Properties...User Manager for Domains

   C. Profile...User Options...Server Manager

   D. Profile...Account Policies...User Manager for Domains

3. Which three of the following are part of Windows NT Server's client-based network administration tools package for Windows 95?

   A. Event Viewer

   B. System Policy Editor

   C. User Manager for Domains

   D. File and Print Services for NetWare

4. If you _____ a file within the same partition, it will retain its original compression attribute.

   A. copy

   B. move

   C. copy or move

   D. None of the above

Managing Resources

3

This chapter will help you prepare for the "Managing Resources" section of Microsoft's Exam 70-67, "Implementing and Supporting Microsoft Windows NT Server." Microsoft provides the following specific objectives for the "Managing Resources" section:

Test Objectives

▶ Manage user and group accounts. Considerations include managing Windows NT groups, managing Windows NT user rights, managing Windows NT account policies, and auditing changes to the user account database.

▶ Policies and profiles for various situations. Policies and profiles include local user profiles, roaming user profiles, and system policies.

▶ Adminster remote servers from various types of client computers. Client computer types include Windows 95 and Windows NT Workstation.

▶ Manage disk resources. Tasks include copying and moving files between file systems, creating and sharing resources, implementing permissions and security, and establishing file auditing.

This chapter examines some important topics related to managing resources on a Windows NT network. *Managing resources* is of course a very broad topic, but Microsoft has narrowed it somewhat in its objectives for the Windows NT Server exam. This chapter considers user and group accounts and the important tool User Manager for Domains, which you will use to manage accounts on an NT domain. This chapter also discusses user profiles, hardware profiles, and system policies—three important features that help administrators define the user environment.

You will learn about the remote administration tools available through Windows NT Server to administer NT resources from client machines. And lastly, this chapter describes some issues relating to administering file and disk resources.

Managing User and Group Accounts

Windows NT users get their rights and permissions in either of two ways: They are explicitly assigned a right or permission through their accounts, or they are members of a group that has been given a right or permission.

When you boot Windows NT, your first interaction with the operating system is with the WinLogon process (see Chapter 1).

An administrator creates an account (maybe more than one) for each person who will use the system. When prompted by WinLogon, the user enters the assigned username and password and logs on to the system. Once on the system, Windows NT checks the user's credentials against the list of valid users and groups for each object to which he or she requests access.

Microsoft lists the following objective for the Windows NT Server exam:

Manage user and group accounts. Considerations include: managing Windows NT groups, managing Windows NT user rights, managing Windows NT account policies, and auditing changes to the user account database.

Users and Groups

Windows NT administrators can create two types of accounts: one for users and one for groups. *User accounts* belong to one person only; rights and permissions assigned to a user account affect only the person who uses that account to log on. A *group* is a collection of users who hold common rights and permissions by way of their association with the group. The number of people who can belong to a group is unlimited, and all members enjoy the rights and permissions (or rue the lack thereof) assigned to the group.

In practice, a group is a vehicle for assigning rights and permissions to an individual user. If you determine that a certain group of users in your environment requires a specific set of rights and permissions, you can create a group that has those rights and permissions and add the users to the new group. It is important to note that there is no order of precedence among user and group accounts. No one group takes priority over any other group, and groups do not take priority over user accounts (or vice versa).

For management purposes, it is easier to use group accounts when assigning rights and permissions. First, it's cleaner: users can be members of as many groups as desired, and group names can be more descriptive than user names. When looking at the permission list for a file, for example, you probably would understand why Vice Presidents have access to sensitive financial information before you would understand why JackS, JanetP, and BillG are allowed in. Second, it's simpler: if you need to give a user the right to back up files and directories, you can find a built-in group, called Backup Operators, specifically designed for that purpose. In fact, you rarely have to create a new group (unless you want to for oversight and management purposes) because Windows NT has built-in groups for almost anything anyone needs to do on the system.

Windows NT has two types of groups: local groups and global groups.

On a Windows NT Workstation or member server of a domain, a *local group* is an entity that exists for the purpose of assigning rights and permissions to resources on the local machine. Remember that these resources consist of drive space and printers on that specific computer. That local group exists only on that computer.

This changes slightly at the domain level—enough to cause quite a bit of confusion. A local group created on a domain controller appears on all domain controllers within that domain. A local group created on one Backup Domain Controller (BDC) appears on the Primary Domain Controller (PDC) and all the BDCs within that domain. You then can assign this local group rights and permissions. Keep in mind that the local share or printer might exist only on that first BDC where the local group was created—and that is where you get the confusion.

A *global group* is a collection of user accounts within the domain. These global groups have *no* power by themselves. These global groups must be assigned to local groups to gain any access to the local resources. You use a global group as a container of users that you then can add to local groups.

When a Windows NT workstation becomes part of a domain, the built-in domain global groups (described later in this chapter) join the corresponding local groups in the workstation's local security database. The global group Domain Admins, for example, becomes a member of the local group Administrators. Each user account in the domain database is a member of an appropriate global group. The Administrator account, for example, is a member of the Domain Admins global group. By nesting global groups in the local groups of individual machines, Windows NT provides users with seamless access to resources across the domain.

A global group must be a member of a local group, but a local group cannot be a member of a global group, nor can a global group be a member of another global group. A global group can contain only user accounts. A local group can contain user accounts and global groups, but putting users in local groups is not good domain management.

Built-In Groups on Domain Controllers

Windows NT domain controllers oversee eight built-in local groups and three built-in global groups. These groups create a wide range of access levels for network resources.

The Windows NT domain local groups are as follows:

- ▶ Administrators

- ▶ Users

- ▶ Guests

- ▶ Backup Operators

- ▶ Replicator

- ▶ Print Operators

- ▶ Server Operators

- ▶ Account Operators

Administrators

Administrators is the most powerful group in Windows NT. Because Administrators has complete control over the entire Windows NT environment, use caution when adding users to this group. If you will be the administrator for a Windows NT machine, consider creating an ordinary user account as well for safety reasons. If an administrator walks away from a computer while still logged on, anyone can walk up to that computer and make unauthorized changes. Even if you are extremely conscientious, mistakes happen. An application that malfunctions and deletes files can wreak more havoc if it runs under an administrative account than if it runs under a user account. Use administrator-level accounts only when necessary.

In the following situations, it is necessary to use administrator-level accounts:

- ▶ To create other administrator-level accounts

- ▶ To modify or delete users, regardless of who created them

- ▶ To manage the membership of built-in groups

- ▶ To unlock workstations, regardless of who locked them

- ▶ To format a hard disk

▶ To upgrade the operating system

▶ To back up or restore files and directories

▶ To change the security policies

▶ To connect to administrative shares

Users

By default, new accounts become members of the Users group automatically. The Users group provides users everything needed to run applications safely and to manage their own local environment—local to the user, that is, not the computer. Users can

▶ Run applications

▶ Manage their own files and directories (but not share them)

▶ Use printers (but not manage them)

▶ Connect to other computers' directories and printers

▶ Save their settings in a personal profile

Because users cannot affect files to which they have not been granted access, and cannot format hard disks, delete accounts, and so on, it is safest to use the Users account unless you need to perform a task that only an administrator or power user has the right to do.

Guests

Windows NT also provides a relatively powerless group called Guests. Because Windows NT Workstation requires accounts for anyone and everyone who accesses the system, you can use the Guest account (described later in this chapter) and the Guests group to allow limited access to users who don't possess an account on your computer. Because the default Guest account does not require a password, it can pose a security risk. The actual extent of the access provided to the Guests group depends on how you implement it. If you are concerned about security, you can disable the Guest account.

Backup Operators

Backup Operators have a singular purpose: to back up files and directories and to restore them later. Although any user can back up and restore files to which he has been granted permissions, backup operators can override the security on resources, but only when using the NTBackup program.

Replicator

The Replicator group is a special group used by the Directory Replication Service. See Chapter 2, "Installing and Configuring Windows NT Server," for more information on this group.

Print Operators

Members of the Print Operators group waive the power to create, manage, and delete print shares on domain controllers.

Server Operators

The members of a Server Operators group have the power to administer primary and backup domain controllers. They can log on to and shut down servers, lock and unlock servers, change the system time, back up and restore files, and manage network shares.

Built-In Global Groups

Windows NT domain controllers also oversee the following three global groups:

▶ **Domain Admins.** Global group of administrator accounts. The Domain Admins group is a member of the Administrators local group for the domain, and is, by default, a member of the local group for every computer in the domain running Windows NT Server or NT Workstation. A domain administrator, therefore, can perform administrative functions on local computers.

▶ **Domain Users.** Global group of user-level accounts. During setup, the domain's Administrator account is part of the

Domain Users global group. All new domain accounts are automatically added to the Domain Users group.

▶ **Domain Guests.** Global group for users with guest-level accounts. The Domain Guest group is automatically a member of the domain's Guest group.

Built-In Groups on Workstations and Member Servers

Windows NT Server member servers (servers that are not domain controllers) and Windows NT Workstations have the following built-in local groups:

▶ Administrators

▶ Backup Operators

▶ Power Users

▶ Guests

▶ Replicator

▶ Users

The descriptions for these groups are the same as the descriptions for their domain-controller counterparts, except for the Power User group, which is not a built-in group on Windows NT domain controllers. Power Users live somewhere between the kingdom of Administrators and the masses of Users. Power users have considerably more power than ordinary users, but not nearly the amount of control that an administrator has. A similar principle applies here: Do not use or give out Power User accounts unless doing so is necessary for performing a task. Power User accounts are ideal for the following types of tasks:

▶ Sharing (and revoking) directories on the network

▶ Creating, managing, and sharing printers

▶ Creating accounts (but not administrator-level)

- ▶ Modifying and deleting accounts (but only the accounts that the power user has created)

- ▶ Setting the date and time on the computer

- ▶ Creating common program groups

Power users cannot touch any of the security policies on a Windows NT system, and their powers are limited in scope. It is best, therefore, to use a Power User account rather than an Administrator account if you can accomplish what you need to as a power user.

Windows NT member servers and workstations don't control any global groups, because global groups can be created and administered only on domain controllers. Global groups nevertheless play an important part in assigning local rights and permissions to server and workstations resources. The following section describes how global groups interact with local accounts.

Member Server and Workstations Accounts

Windows NT Server machines acting as member servers maintain local account databases and manage a set of local accounts and groups independent of any domain affiliations. You can understand the need for these local accounts when you consider the emphasis on security in Windows NT. A user must provide credentials to access a Windows NT system even if that system is not attached to a domain, or even if it has never been attached to a domain. The local account information controls access to the machine's resources.

Domain users can access resources on server and workstation machines logged into the domain because (by default) each domain user is a member of the global group Domain Users, and the global group Domain Users is a member of the machine's local group Users. In the same way, domain administrators are part of the global group Domain Admins, which is part of the machine's local Administrator's group.

Hard-Coded Capabilities

So far, only the hard-coded characteristics of the Windows NT built-in groups have been discussed; in other words, some things you can change and some things you can't. Everything, for example, previously mentioned in the group paragraphs are things that cannot be changed. Users cannot share directories, no matter how hard you might try to change that, and power users cannot be prevented from sharing directories (to which they have access, of course), no matter how hard you might try.

You cannot modify hard-coded capabilities, but you can change user rights. An administrator can grant or revoke a user right at any time. Only administrators have the hard-coded capability to manage this policy. At this point, it is important to clearly distinguish between user rights and resource permissions. *User rights* define what a user can and cannot do on the system. *Resource permissions* establish the scope where these rights can be used. In other words, user rights are stuff you can do, and resource permissions control where you can do it.

Built-In User Accounts

Groups are the center of power in Windows NT, but groups need members to have any effect at all. At least two accounts are created when you install Windows NT Workstation. These users and their group memberships are discussed next.

Administrator

The Administrator account, the first account created during an installation, is a member of the Administrators group. This is an important concept because the Administrator account by itself is powerless—you could remove it from the Administrators group and place it in the Guests group, and you would have a really wimpy administrator. Power in Windows NT comes not from who you are, but from who you know.

The Administrator account is also permanent. You cannot disable or delete it, although it might not be a bad idea to rename it.

Because a username and password are all that is necessary to log on to most Windows NT systems, if you do not rename the Administrator account, a cyber-delinquent has half the information necessary to break into the system.

Guest

The Guest account is another permanent account. It is a member of the Guests group, but this affiliation can be changed. Like the Administrator account, the Guest account itself has no inherent power or lack thereof; it is the group membership for the account that establishes its scope.

Unlike the Administrator account, however, you can disable the Guest account. You might want to disable the account if you are in a secure environment; otherwise, users who don't have an account on your system can log on as guests. At the very least, you should consider adding a password to the Guest account.

User Manager for Domains

Windows NT Server includes a tool called User Manager for Domains that you can use to administer User and Group accounts. User Manager for Domains is similar to the User Manager tool available with Windows NT Workstation, but, whereas User Manager is primarily designed to oversee local Workstation accounts, User Manager for Domains includes additional features that enable it to manage accounts at the domain level and even interact with other domains.

For an exercise testing this information, see end of chapter.

To reach User Manager for Domains, choose Programs in the Start menu, choose Administrative Tools (Common), and then select User Manager for Domains.

Figure 3.1 shows the main screen for User Manager for Domains.

User Manager for Domains enables you to administer any domain over which you have administrative rights. The Select Domain option in the User menu enables you to choose a different domain (see fig. 3.2).

Figure 3.1

Main screen for User Manager.

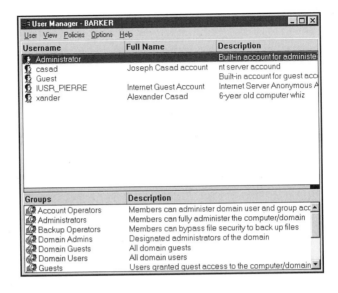

Figure 3.2

Select Domain option in the User menu.

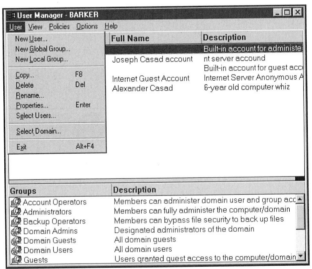

Some of the tasks you can perform with User Manager for Domains include the following:

▶ Creating new user and group accounts

▶ Viewing and configuring the properties of user and group accounts

> ▶ Adding new members to groups and removing members from groups

> ▶ Viewing and configuring account policy restrictions

> ▶ Adding user rights to users and groups

> ▶ Auditing account-related events

> ▶ Establishing, viewing, and configuring trust relationships

You can find most administration and configuration options on the User and Options menus.

Creating a User

Figure 3.2 shows the User menu for User Manager for Domains. To add a new user account, choose User, New User. The New User dialog box opens (see fig. 3.3).

Figure 3.3

The New User dialog box.

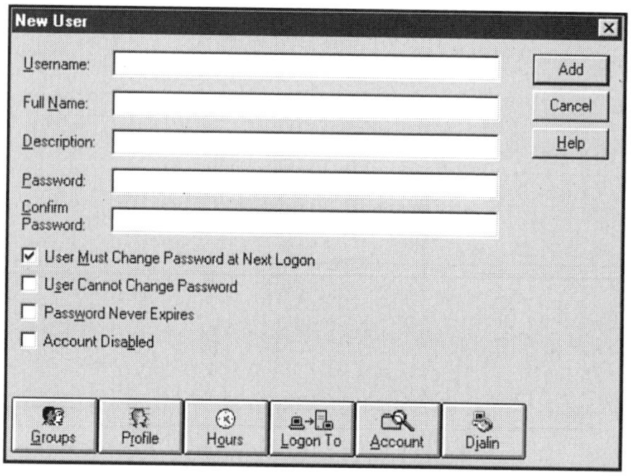

Only two pieces of information are required to create an account: a username and a password. The username is a short "handle" used to identify the user to the system. The password is proof that the user account actually belongs to the person attempting to use it.

The name in the Username field must be unique. No other user or group can have the same username. The username can be as long as twenty characters and is not case-sensitive.

The password entered in the Password field is case-sensitive; in fact, the most common logon-related problem reported by Windows NT users is solved just by pressing the Caps Lock key. The Password field can be left blank (although not recommended for obvious reasons), or it can be as long as fourteen characters. It does not echo on-screen as anything other than asterisks, so you don't need to worry about someone looking over your shoulder. For this reason, however, you must confirm the password just to make certain that you did not mistype a character or two behind those asterisks.

The other parameters in this dialog box are optional but useful. The Full Name is a free text field that can be used for the full name, including spaces and initials, for a particular user. Having both a username and a full name enables users to log on quickly (using the username) but still be listed and available by their full name.

The Description field is also free text. Use it to track the department to which a user belongs, or maybe a location or project team.

Enabling the User Must Change Password at Next Logon check box option is useful when creating an account. Because a new account has a preset password picked by the administrator, this option forces the user to change the password immediately after logging on the first time after setting this option. When the user attempts to log on, the message You are required to change your password at first logon appears. After the user dismisses the message, a Change Password dialog box appears.

Enabling the User Cannot Change Password check box prevents users from making any change to their password at any time. You might want to use this for the Guest account and any other account that several people might share.

Enabling the Password Never Expires check box overrides any blanket password expiration date defined in the Account policy. Again, the Guest account is a likely candidate for this option.

Enabling the Account Disabled check box turns off the account but does not remove it from the database. In general, you should disable rather than remove user accounts. If a person leaves the organization and then later returns, you can reactivate the account. If the user never returns, you can rename the account and reactivate it for the new person replacing the former user. All rights and permissions for the original user are transferred to the new user.

Other serious implications when deleting and disabling accounts are covered later in this chapter; see the section entitled "Deleting versus Disabling."

Clicking on the six buttons at the bottom of the New User dialog box opens the following corresponding dialog boxes:

▶ **Groups.** Enables you to add and remove group memberships for the account. The easiest way to grant rights to a user account is to add that account to a group that possesses those rights.

▶ **Profile.** Enables you to add a user profile path, a logon script name, and a home directory path to the user's environment profile. You learn more about the Profile button in the following section.

▶ **Hours.** Enables you to define specific times when the users can access the account. (The default is always.)

▶ **Logon To.** Enables you to specify the workstations to which the user can log on. (The default is all workstations.)

▶ **Account.** Enables you to provide an expiration date for the account. (The default is never.) You also can specify the account as global (for regular users in this domain) or domain local.

note

Don't confuse a domain local account with a local group membership or a local account on a workstation. A domain local account is designed to enable individual users from un-trusted domains to access to this domain. Unless a domain local account is explicitly granted logon permission, the user must log on normally to a workgroup or domain where he or she has a valid account and then connect to the domain controller that is home to the domain local account.

▶ **Dialin.** Enables you to specify whether the user can access the account via a dial-up connection. You can also configure the call back Properties.

User Environment Profiles

The Profile button invokes the User Environment Profile dialog box, which consists of two frames: User Profiles and Home Directory (see fig. 3.4).

Figure 3.4

The User Environment Profile dialog box.

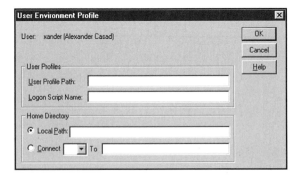

The User Profiles section of the User Environment Profile dialog box enables you to specify the user profile path and the logon script name. The user profile path is for cases in which a roaming or mandatory profile for the user will reside on another computer. If the user will log on to both Windows NT 3.x and Windows NT 4 computers, include the user profile file name in the user profile path. If the user will use only a computer running Windows NT 4, the user profile path should point to the user profile directory and should not include the file name. If the directory does not exist, Windows NT creates it when the roaming profile is created (see the discussion of roaming proiles later in this chapter), but note that the local machine must have access to the roaming profile directory by way of a network share.

The Logon Script Name text box enables you to specify a logon script for the user. *Logon scripts* are CMD or BAT files that contain a series of valid Windows NT commands. A logon script might reestablish a series of network drive connections or display a welcome message. Notice that the dialog box asks only for the name, not the full path. Windows NT already has a directory for logon scripts, but it is buried pretty deep:

```
<winnt_root>\SYSTEM32\REPL\IMPORT\SCRIPTS
```

Typically, logon scripts are not used on Windows NT workstations. User profiles can accomplish most things that logon scripts can.

The Home Directory section of the User Environment Profile dialog box is used whenever a user opens or saves a file in an application, or when the user opens a command prompt window. The default home directory is \USERS\DEFAULT; if a workstation will support more than one user, consider establishing separate home directories for each user. Note that users are not restricted to or from these home directories (unless you establish that security separately); this is just where they start by default when working with documents.

You do not have to create the home directory; User Manager will do it for you as long as you have it create only a single directory at a time. You might have User Manager create a home directory called c:\ken, for example, but it could not create c:\ken\home if the \KEN directory did not already exist. That is just a limitation of User Manager.

Click on the Local Path radio button to specify a local path for the home directory. To specify a home directory on the network, click on the Connect radio button, select a drive letter from the drop-down list, and enter the network path in the To box.

Here's a tip for home directory creation: If you would like the home directory name to be the same as the user's username, you can use a special environment variable in this dialog box: %USERNAME%. The actual username replaces %USER-NAME% after the account is created. This is not really any faster than just typing in the actual username, but it can really save time when copying accounts (described later in this chapter).

When you use User Manager for Domains to create a user's home directory on an NTFS partition, the default permissions for that directory grant that user Full Control and restrict access to all other users.

Creating a Group

You can create new global and local groups by using the New Global Group and New Local Group options on the User Manager for Domains User menu. Figure 3.5 shows the New Global Group dialog box. Note that, by default, the Administrator account is automatically a member of the new group. Only user accounts can be members of a global group. To add a member to the new global group, select a user in the Not Members list and click on the Add button to add the user to the Members list. Click on the Remove button to remove a user account from the Members list.

Figure 3.5

The New Global Group dialog box.

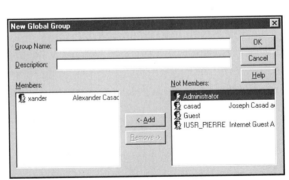

Figure 3.6 shows the New Local Group dialog box. To add additional members to the new local group, click on the Add button. Individual users and global groups both can join a local group.

Figure 3.6

The New Local Group dialog box.

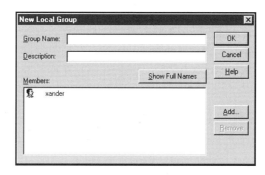

If you select one or more users in the User Manager for Domains main screen, those users automatically appear in the membership list for the new local group. This shortcut can save you a step, but you also need to be careful to make certain that no users are selected in the main screen if you don't want those users to be part of the new group.

You cannot directly add rights to a group. You have to add the group to the list of groups that have a particular right. To add groups to a right, use the User Rights option on the Policies menu (described later in this chapter).

User and Group Properties

The Properties command on User menu of the User Manager opens a Properties dialog box for the selected object. The User Properties dialog box resembles the New User dialog box (refer back to fig. 3.3) except that all the information is filled in. Use the User Properties dialog box to edit user properties after creating an account.

The group Properties dialog boxes for global and local groups also resemble their respective creation dialog boxes (see the preceding section).

Administering Account Policy

Figure 3.7 shows the Policies menu of User Manager for Domains.

Choose the Account option to open the Account Policy dialog box (see fig. 3.8).

Figure 3.7

The User Manager for Domains Policies menu.

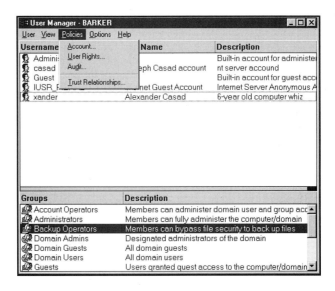

Figure 3.8

The Account Policy dialog box.

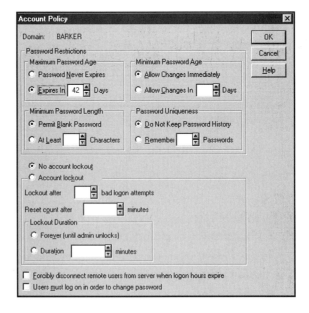

The Account Policy dialog box is pretty busy, but all the options revolve around a single concept: passwords.

Maximum Password Age

In a secure environment, the longer a password is in use, the greater the chance that an unauthorized user will discover it and break in repeatedly. Setting a maximum password age forces users to choose a new password periodically. You have a choice here: If you don't care about password ages, leave the setting at its default of Password Never Expires; if you do want a maximum password age, choose the Expires In radio button and enter the number of days to use as the limit. (The default is 42, but the value can range from 1–999.)

When a maximum password age is in effect, users get a warning 14 days before the password is set to expire.

At the onset of the first warning message, the user can change the password or choose to wait. The password expiration message appears each time the user logs on, until the maximum password age has been reached. At that point, the user cannot access the system until the password has changed. See the section entitled "User Must Log On in Order to Change Password" later in this section for more information.

Minimum Password Age

Users can get very attached to their passwords and resent having to change them. A classic user trick is changing the password when forced and then immediately changing it back, thereby retaining the old password. Setting a minimum password age circumvents this problem. The default, Allow Changes Immediately, enables users to perform the favorite-password sleight-of-hand just mentioned. Allow Changes In forces users to wait anywhere from 1–999 days (at the administrator's discretion) before making changes.

Minimum Password Length

Users also get tired of typing in long passwords. Given the opportunity, many users will use short 3- or 4- (or fewer) character passwords. Setting a minimum password length forces users to choose a longer password. Although you can require up to 14 characters, using 6 to 8 usually suffices.

Password Uniqueness

Even if you force users to set a longer password and wait a week or two before changing it, some tenacious users still swap between two passwords continuously. The Password Uniqueness setting tells Windows NT to remember each password (up to 24) that a user sets. As long as a password is in a user's password history cache, the user cannot reuse it. A Remember setting of 24 combined with a Minimum Password Age of seven days forces users to wait almost six months before reusing a password.

Even all these password options combined won't prevent a user from changing his or her password from "password" to "passworda," "passwordb," "passwordc," and so on. NT can do only so much; the rest is up to you as an administrator.

Account Lockout

The bottom half of the dialog box deals with unauthorized logon attempts.

Windows NT will lock out an account after a certain number of bad logon attempts (that is, an incorrect password for a valid username) within a certain period of time. You can enable this feature by choosing the Account lockout radio button. You must supply a couple of parameters: How many bad attempts should trigger the lockout, how long should the system wait following a bad logon attempt before resetting the counter, and how long should the account stay locked out? If you choose Forever for the last option, the administrator must manually unlock the account in User Manager; otherwise, you can elect to set a duration after which the account will be unlocked.

To set the Account Lockout Policy:

1. In User Manager, choose Policies, Account.

2. Choose the Account lockout radio button.

3. Enter the number of bad logons required to trigger the lockout in the Lockout after bad logon attempts field.

4. Enter the timeout period for resetting the bad logon count in the Reset count after field.

5. Choose a lockout duration: Forever (until admin unlocks) or a specific duration (in minutes).

To unlock an account at any time, perform the following steps:

1. Select the username in User Manager for Domains.

2. Choose User, Properties.

3. To unlock the account, clear the Account Locked Out check box.

Note that, by default, the account lockout feature is turned off. Windows NT has tight security as it is, and the potential is there for this feature to be misused. It is entirely possible, for example, that a user could deliberately lock out a coworker's or supervisor's account by purposefully entering bad passwords with that person's username. For this reason, the built-in Administrator account can never be disabled. Many Administrators don't care for this "out." The Administrator account is arguably the one you need to protect the most. Yet, if the Administrator account was locked out, it is possible that no one else could get on the system to unlock it. Therefore, you should rename the Administrator account after installation. Someone trying to break into the system will have to discover both username and password.

If a user attempts to log on with a locked account, the following message appears:

```
Unable to log you on because your account has been locked out,
please contact your administrator.
```

Forcibly Disconnect Remote Users from the Server After Logon Hours Expire

You can use the Hours button in the New User and User Properties dialog boxes to specify when the user is allowed to access the system. Enable this check box to have the user forcibly disconnected after the specified logon hours expire.

User Must Log On in Order to Change Password

This check box item relates to the password expiration settings discussed earlier. When a user's password nears expiration, the user is prompted at each logon to change it. If the user declines and the password age is exceeded, the user cannot log on until the password is changed. If this selection is cleared (the default), the user is presented with the Change Password dialog box and not allowed to proceed until changing the obsolete password. If this selection is checked, users are allowed to change the password only after logging on. Because an expired password cannot be used to log on, the administrator must change the user's password from within User Manager before the user can log on again. This is a useful option in a secure environment, and the embarrassment of calling the administrator should prompt users to pay more attention to the warnings that precede a lockout.

Assigning Rights to Groups by Assigning Groups to Rights

Choose the User Rights option on Policies menu of User Manager for Domains to open the User Rights Policy dialog box, which enables you to assign groups to a particular right (see fig. 3.9).

Figure 3.9

The User Rights Policy dialog box.

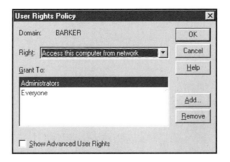

Here you face the most confusing part of User Manager's interface: You cannot view the rights assigned to a particular user. Instead, you must choose a right from the drop-down list so that you can view the users assigned to it. You probably wonder why Microsoft implemented the interface this way. The answer is, "Probably to discourage people from messing with it."

Whereas a *permission* is targeted at a specific object (such as a directory or file), the term *right* refers to a general right to take a particular action on the system. Some Windows NT rights are as follows:

▶ Log on locally

▶ Shut down the system

▶ Restore files and directories

▶ Take ownership of files or other objects

The built-in groups described earlier in this chapter are automatically assigned appropriate user rights. Choose Restore files and directories from the Right combo box in the User Rights Policy dialog box (refer to fig. 3.9). You will see that administrators, backup operators, and server operators all have the right to restore files and directories.

The Add button in the User Rights Policy dialog box enables you to add a user or group to the list of accounts assigned to a particular right. To add a user or group to the rights list for a particular right, perform the following steps:

1. Choose the right from the Right combo box and click on the Add button. The Add Users and Groups dialog box appears (see fig. 3.10).

2. Select the name of a user or group from the Names list and click on the Add button. (By default, only group names appear in the Names list. Click on the Show Users button to include users in the list.)

3. The name(s) you selected appear in the Add Names list in the lower frame. Click on the OK button to add the selected user or group to the list of accounts assigned to the right.

The Remove button in the User Rights Policy dialog box removes an account from the rights list. To deny a right to a user or group account, perform the following steps:

Figure 3.10

The Add Users and Groups dialog box.

1. Choose the right from the Right combo box.

2. Select the user or group from the Grant to list.

3. Click on the Remove button.

You should not need to change user rights policy too often. The built-in groups already are assigned appropriate user rights for most situations. Before you modify the rights policy, make certain that you could not instead simply add or remove a user from an existing group to accomplish the same end.

Note the Show Advanced User Rights check box at the bottom of the User Rights Policy dialog box (refer to fig. 3.9). Advanced user rights are not shown by default, because you rarely need to change them. These rights include creating a pagefile, logging on as a service, and other rights that programs, but not people, need.

Auditing Account-Related Events

The Auditing option in the User Manager for Domains Policy menu invokes the Audit Policy dialog box, which enables you to track certain account-related events (see fig. 3.11). You can track either the success or the failure of the events shown in figure 3.11. Event information is stored in a security log. You can view the security log by using Event Viewer (see Chapter 6, "Troubleshooting").

Figure 3.11

*The Audit Policy
dialog box.*

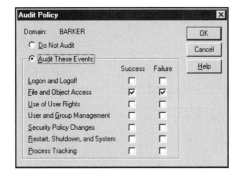

Trust Relationships

The Trust Relationships option on the User Manager for Domains
Policy menu enables you to set up and modify trust relationships
for the domain.

A trust relationship is a relationship between different domains
in which one domain, the *trusting* domain, relinquishes control
of its account database to another domain, called the *trusted*
domain. Trust relationships are commonly used in Wide Area
Network (WAN) situations, and you will get a heavy dose of
them if you ever decide to prepare for the Windows NT Server
Enterprise exam.

Account Administration Tasks

An administrator's job does not end after creating the accounts;
in fact, it just begins. Changes and modifications inevitably are
necessary in day-to-day operations. You can review the properties
of any user account by double-clicking on the username in User
Manager for Domains or by selecting the username and choosing
User, Properties. The User Properties dialog box appears (see fig.
3.12). Although you can change most things about a user in the
User Properties dialog box, you should be aware of a few separate
commands that are launched from the User menu of the User for
Domains main window (see fig. 3.13).

Figure 3.12

*The User Proper-
ties dialog box.*

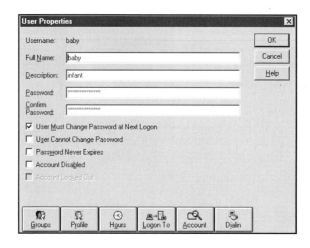

Figure 3.13

*The User menu
of the User
Manager.*

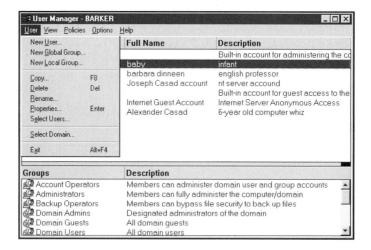

Renaming Users

The User Properties dialog box shows that although you can change a user's full name at any time, the username is fixed. To change the username (remember, the username is the logon name), you must choose User, Rename in the User Manager for Domains main window (refer to fig. 3.13).

When you rename an account, it retains all of its other properties, including user rights and resource permissions. Internally, Windows NT is no more fooled by the new moniker than your family would be if you legally changed your own name. This is because

Windows NT tracks users with an internally defined Security Identifier (SID), which is like a Social Security Number. Once created, an account's SID never changes, even if the account is renamed.

Copying Users

If you need to create many users at one time, consider creating a template account and copying it. When you copy an account by choosing User, Copy in the User Manager, you must enter a new username, full name, and password, but the other properties are retained, including the description, group memberships, and profile information. The only exception is the Account Disabled check box, which is cleared automatically.

Using the home directory tip mentioned earlier, if you copied an account called Ken with a home directory of c:\%USERNAME% and named the new account RyanC, a new directory would be created called \RyanC, in addition to the already existing \Ken directory.

Deleting Versus Disabling

Earlier, Security Identifiers (SIDs) were compared to Social Security Numbers. SIDs, however, go one step further than SSNs. When people die, their SSNs are recycled. SIDs are not recycled. When an account is deleted, that account's SID is never reused. If it were, it would be possible (in fact, probable) that a new account would inherit all the permissions and rights assigned to the account that had previously owned the SID.

This is a cautionary tale: Don't delete accounts if you can at all avoid it; you will have a hard time if you need to re-create it. Consider the following two different scenarios:

Scenario 1

Dan was a consultant with Acme Training Co., with a username of DanR. One day, Dan decided to leave Acme and strike out on his own, so the network administrator deleted Dan's account. Dan struck out, and came crawling back to Acme to his old job. The administrator re-created the account with the exact same name and password, and Dan was able to log back on to the network. Before too long, however, he noticed that he was no longer able to access the files to which he used to have permissions, even his own. Dan had to call each and every person in the company and ask them to please assign permissions to his new account for each file and directory he needed to use. Dan was not a popular person in the office that day.

Scenario 2

Dan tried one more time to make it on his own. This time, suspecting Dan might return, the administrator just disabled the account, leaving its entry in the account database but restricting it from being used to log on to the system. After a few days, Abby was hired to replace Dan. Rather than create a brand new account and face the same problems Dan had faced when he returned to the company in Scenario 1, the administrator just enabled the account and renamed it to AbbyR. Abby suddenly had all the access she needed to all the files, directories, and printers she needed to use. After a week or so, Dan returned and asked for his old job back again. Although the network administrator could have just renamed the account back to DanR, Abby was doing a much better job than Dan ever did, so Abby stayed.

The moral of these stories is that Dan is a loser, but you don't have to be. Disable accounts at least temporarily before you decide to delete them. If you need the account back, re-enable it. If someone else needs it, rename it. If time has passed, and you are certain that you really don't need it anymore, delete it. Life will be much easier.

To disable a user account, perform the following steps:

1. In the User Manager for Domains, select the username of the account you want to disable.

2. Choose User, Properties.

3. In the User Properties dialog box, enable the Account Disabled check box.

To enable a user account that has been disabled, perform the following steps:

1. In the User Manager, select the username of the account you want to enable.

2. Choose User, Properties.

3. In the User Properties dialog box, deselect the Account Disabled check box.

To delete an account, perform the following steps:

1. In the User Manager, select the username of the account you want to delete.

2. Choose User, Delete.

3. A warning message appears (see fig. 3.14). Click on OK to proceed with the deletion.

Figure 3.14

If you attempt to delete a user, you receive this warning.

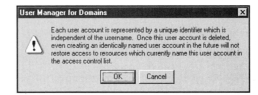

Managing Policies and Profiles

Policies and profiles are two powerful methods for defining the user environment. This section focuses on the following:

▶ User profiles

▶ Hardware profiles

▶ System policies

Microsoft lists the following objective for the Windows NT Server exam:

Create and manage policies and profiles for various situations. Policies and profiles include local user profiles, roaming user profiles, and system policies.

User Profiles

A user profile is the entire collection of configuration data that applies to a specific user and only to that user. Because profiles are maintained for each individual user, users can change their own environment without affecting the environment of other users.

Profiles contain quite a number of items, including the following:

- ▶ Settings for the user-specific Control Panel entries

- ▶ Persistent network drive connections

- ▶ Remote printer connections

- ▶ Personal program groups

- ▶ User environment variables

- ▶ Bookmarks in Help

- ▶ Preferences for Win32 applications

- ▶ Most recently accessed documents in Win32 applications

You can think of a user profile as a bundle of objects in an individual user profile subdirectory that collectively define a desktop environment for the user. The user's profile subdirectory generally consists of an ntuser.dat file (containing Registry information), a transaction log file called ntuser.dat.log (which provides fault tolerance for ntuser.dat), and a series of folders containing other items such as shortcuts and application-specific profile data.

Windows NT provides two types of user profiles: local profiles and roaming profiles. A local profile is stored on a local machine. Because a local profile resides on the local machine, it does not follow the user if the user logs on to the network from a different machine. A roaming profile is a profile that can follow the user to other computers on the network because it is stored at a central location that the other computers can access at logon.

Local Profiles

Unless you specify a roaming profile (see the following section), Windows NT obtains user-specific settings from a local user profile on the workstation the user is currently using. You can find a local user profile subdirectory for each workstation user in the <winnt_root>\profiles directory.

When a user logs on for the first time, the Windows NT logon process checks the user account database to see whether a roaming profile path has been specified for the account (see the following section). If the accounts database doesn't contain a profile path for the user, Windows NT creates a local user profile subdirectory for the user in the <winnt_root>\profiles directory and obtains initial user profile information from the local default user profile, which is stored in the subdirectory:

```
<winnt_root>\profiles\Default User
```

Windows NT saves all changes to the user profile in the new local user profile. The next time a user logs on at the workstation, Windows NT accesses the local user profile and configures all user-specific settings to match the information in the profile.

Roaming Profiles

A *roaming profile* is a centrally located user profile that other workstations on the network can access at logon. You specify a path to a roaming profile subdirectory in User Manager.

When a user logs on to the domain, the Windows NT logon process checks to see whether the account database contains a roaming profile path for the account.

If the account database contains a path to a roaming profile, Windows NT checks whether the user has changed the profile type to Local in the User Profile tab of the Control Panel System application (described later in this chapter). If the profile type is set to Local, Windows NT uses a version of the profile stored locally instead of downloading a new version from the path specified in the account database. If the user has not changed the type to Local in the Control Panel System application, Windows NT compares the local version of the profile with the roaming profile specified in the account database. If the local version is more recent, Windows NT asks whether you would like to use the local version rather than the roaming version. Otherwise, Windows NT downloads the roaming version.

At logoff, if the user is a guest or if the profile is a mandatory profile, Windows NT doesn't save the current user profile to the user profile subdirectory. If the user is not a guest, and if the profile isn't mandatory, Windows NT saves the current profile information. If the profile type has been set to Local in the User Profile tab of the Control Panel Systems application, Windows NT saves the current user profile to the local copy of the profile. If the profile type is set to Roaming, Windows NT saves the current profile information to both the local copy and the version specified in the account database.

A mandatory profile is a preconfigured roaming profile that the user cannot change. To create a mandatory profile, create a roaming profile subdirectory and specify the path to that directory in User Manager for Domains. Then, copy a user profile to the roaming profile subdirectory (using the Copy To command in the User profile tab of the Control Panel System application) and rename the ntuser.dat file to ntuser.man. The MAN extension makes the file a read-only file.

To configure a roaming profile for an account, perform the following steps:

1. Select the account in the User Manager for Domains and choose User, Properties. The User Properties dialog box appears (refer to fig. 3.12). (If you are creating a new

account, choose User, New User. The New User dialog box is similar to the User Properties dialog box.)

2. Click on the Profile button. The User Environment Properties dialog box appears (refer to fig. 3.4).

3. The User Profiles frame of the User Environment Profile dialog box enables you to specify the user profile path and a logon script name. The user profile path is for cases in which the account will use a roaming or mandatory profile. If the user will log on to both Windows NT 3.x and Windows NT 4 computers, include the user profile file name in the user profile path. If the user will use only a computer running Windows NT 4, the user profile path should point to the user profile directory and should not include the file name. If the directory does not exist, Windows NT creates it when the roaming profile is created. Note, however, that the local machine must have access to the roaming profile directory by way of a network share. The User Profile path should include the full UNC path to the profile, including a computer name, a share name, and the directory path. (See the section on the UNC naming convention later in this chapter.)

The User Profiles tab of the Control Panel System application will use a locally stored version of the profile, or whether the computer should download a roaming profile at logon. If you are logged on as an administrator, the user profile list in figure 3.15 displays all user profiles currently stored on the computer. If you are logged on as a user, the list displays only the profile you are currently using. The Change Type button enables you to specify whether to use the local version of the profile, or whether to download a roaming profile at logon. If you choose the roaming profile option, click on the box labeled `Use cached profile on slow connections` if you want Windows NT to use the local profile when the network is running slowly.

Click on the Copy To button box in the User Profiles tab to open the Copy To dialog box, which enables you to copy the user profile to another directory or to another computer on the network. If a different user will use the profile at its new location, you must give that user permission to use the profile. To add a user to the permissions list for the profile, click on the Change button in the Copy To dialog box.

Figure 3.15

The System Prop-erties User Pro-files tab.

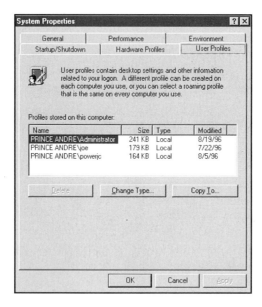

Hardware Profiles

Hardware profiles, a new addition to NT, refers to a collection of information about devices, services, and other hardware-related settings. Hardware profiles were designed for portable computers. The hardware configuration of a portable computer might change each time the portable is attached or removed from a docking station. A hardware profile enables the user to define a set of hardware conditions under which the computer will operate at a given time. A different hardware profile then can define a different set of conditions (see fig. 3.16).

Figure 3.16

Hardware profiles enable the user to predefine hard-ware configura-tions.

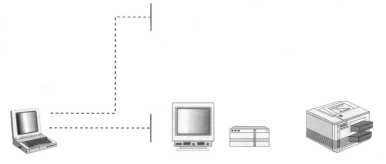

If you have more than one hardware profile, you are asked to specify a hardware profile at startup. The Registry key HKEY_CURRENT_CONFIG contains information about the hardware profile selected at startup.

The Control Panel System application's Hardware Profiles tab enables you to create new hardware profiles and change the order of precedence among hardware profiles (see fig. 3.17). Click on the Properties button to define a docking state for a portable computer or to enable/disable network hardware.

Figure 3.17

The Hardware Profiles tab.

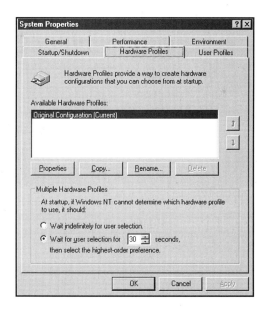

To create a new hardware profile, select an existing profile and click on the Copy button. In the Copy Profile dialog box that appears, enter a name for the new hardware profile. The new hardware profile will appear in the Available Hardware Profiles list in the Hardware Profiles tab.

If you have defined more than one hardware profile, Windows NT displays a menu of hardware profiles at startup and asks which profile you want to use. The profile you specify becomes the active hardware profile. Any changes to your hardware configuration affect the active hardware profile. You can enable or disable a device for a given hardware profile using the Control Panel

Devices application. You can enable or disable a service using the Control Panel Services Application.

The up and down arrows to the right of the Available Hardware Profiles list enable you to change the preference order of the hardware profiles (refer to fig. 3.17). The radio buttons at the bottom of the Hardware Profiles tab enable you to specify whether Windows NT waits indefinitely for you to choose a hardware profile, or whether the choice defaults to the highest-preference profile after a specific time interval.

Managing System Policy with System Policy Editor

System Policy Editor, a powerful configuration tool included with Windows NT Server, enables a network administrator to maintain machine and user configurations for the entire network from a single location.

System Policy Editor can operate in Registry mode or Policy File mode. The following sections discuss these two modes and the two distinct functions associated with both. The exam objectives for the "Managing Resources" section of the NT Server exam specifically mention *system policies*. This implies that, at least for the purposes of the "Managing Resources" section, the Policy mode functions of System Policy Editor are the more significant. The Windows NT Registry, however, is an extremely important part of Windows NT, and System Policy Editor Registry mode is an able and important interface to the Registry.

Registry Mode

For an exercise testing this information, see end of chapter.

In Registry mode, System Policy Editor enables whoever is using it to display and change Registry settings of either the local computer or another computer on the network. In form and function, System Policy Editor's Registry mode stakes out a niche somewhere between Control Panel and Registry Editor. It does not provide the complete Registry access provided that Registry

Editor affords, but it is much easier to use, and it provides powerful access to settings you cannot access via Control Panel. System Policy Editor has a hierarchical structure similar to the Registry, and though it isn't quite as GUI as Control Panel, it is remarkably simple and convenient when you consider its power.

You can use System Policy Editor for the following tasks:

- ▶ Set the maximum number of authentication retries

- ▶ Prohibit NT from creating 8.3 aliases for long file names

- ▶ Define a logon banner to appear prior to logon

- ▶ Enable or disable a computer's capability to create hidden drive shares

- ▶ Hide the Network Neighborhood icon

- ▶ Remove the Run command from the Start menu

- ▶ Require a specific desktop wallpaper

- ▶ Disable Registry editing tools

The best way to get a feel for the kinds of things you set using System Policy Editor is to browse through the Properties dialog boxes yourself (as described later in this section). As you study for the MCSE exam, spend some time familiarizing yourself with System Policy Editor settings.

You can find System Policy Editor in the Administrative Tools program group. Choose Programs in the Start menu, select Administrative Tools, and click on the System Policy Editor icon.

System Policy Editor's Registry mode displays a portfolio of Registry settings that enable the administrator to customize the configuration for a specific machine or a specific local user.

To change Registry settings by using System Policy Editor, follow these steps:

1. Choose File, Open Registry in the System Policy Editor. Figure 3.18 shows the System Policy Editor main screen in Registry mode.

2. Click on the Local Computer icon to configure Registry settings for the computer you are currently using. The Local Computer Properties dialog box appears, showing the hierarchy of the local computer (see fig. 3.19). Click on a plus sign to see settings within each of the categories (see fig. 3.20). Check or uncheck the leaf-level settings to enable or disable the option. If the option requires additional input (such as display text for a logon banner) additional boxes and prompts appear in the space at the bottom of the dialog box. Click on OK to return to the System Policy Editor main window.

Figure 3.18

System Policy Editor Registry mode.

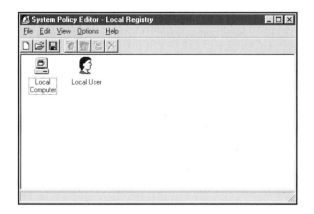

3. Click on the Local User icon to configure Registry settings for the user currently logged on to the computer. The Local User settings differ from the Local Computer settings, but the procedure is the same. Figure 3.21 shows the Local User Properties dialog box. Click on a plus sign to see settings within each of the categories (see fig. 3.22). Check or uncheck the leaf-level settings to enable or disable the option. If the option requires additional input, additional boxes and prompts then appear at the bottom of the dialog box.

Figure 3.19

The Local Computer Properties dialog box in System Policy Editor's Registry mode.

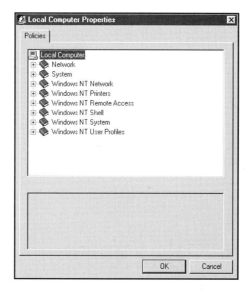

Figure 3.20

The Local Computer Properties dialog box with branches expanded.

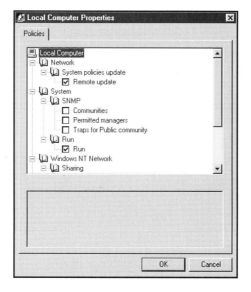

To configure another computer on the network, follow these steps:

1. Choose File, Connect in the System Policy Editor to open the Connect dialog box (see fig. 3.23).

Figure 3.21

The Local User Properties dialog box in System Policy Editor's Registry mode.

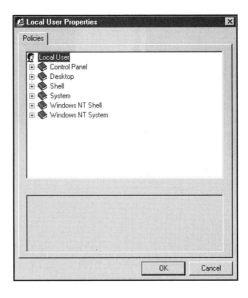

Figure 3.22

The Local User Properties dialog box with branches expanded.

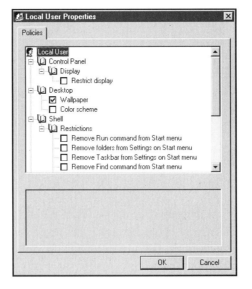

2. Enter the name of the computer you want to reach and click on OK. Another dialog box appears, asking which user account on the remote computer you want to administer. Select an account and click on OK.

Figure 3.23

*The Connect
dialog box.*

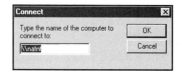

3. The System Policy Editor reappears, looking as it did in figure 3.18, except the name of the remote computer appears in the title bar.

4. Click on the Local Computer icon or the Local User icon, and change the settings as described in the preceding steps.

A typical use of System Policy Editor task is to customize the logon process. The following steps show you how to add a logon banner that appears before you log on to your system:

1. Start the System Policy Editor.

2. Choose File, Open Registry.

3. Double-click on the Local Computer icon.

4. Click on the plus sign next to Windows NT system.

5. Click on the plus sign next to Logon.

6. Select the Logon banner check box. Enter a caption and some text in the text boxes provided at the bottom of the dialog box (see fig. 3.24).

The Logon banner caption and text appears under the LegalNoticeCaption and LegalNoticeText values of the following subkey:

```
\HKEY_LOCAL_MACHINE\Software\Microsoft\Windows NT\
CurrentVersion\Winlogon
```

Figure 3.24

Enabling a logon banner.

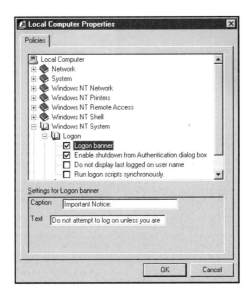

Figure 3.24 also shows another popular System Policy Editor setting. If you select the `Do not display last logged on user name` check box, Windows NT does not display the most recent user in the User Name text box of the Logon dialog box.

Policy File Mode

System Policy Editor's Policy File mode looks similar to Registry mode, but it is significantly different; System Policy is a kind of meta-Registry. The System Policy file can contain settings that override local Registry settings, you can therefore use System Policy Editor to impose a configuration on a user or machine that the user cannot change.

For Windows NT machines, the System Policy file is called NTConfig.pol. To enable system policy, create the NTConfig.pol file (using System Policy Editor) and place it in the \<winnt_root>\System32\Repl\Import\Scripts folder of the Domain controller's boot partition. This directory is shared as \\PDC_servername\Netlogon$. (Store system policy information for Windows 95 machines in the file Config.pol rather than NTConfig.pol.)

When a Windows NT computer attempts to log on, Windows NT looks for the NTConfig.pol file and checks NTConfig.pol for system policy information that affects the user or computer. Windows NT merges the system policy information with local Registry settings, overwriting the Registry information if necessary.

System policy information can come in several different forms. You can define a system policy for a specific computer, user, or group, or you can define default system policies. Default computer policies apply to any computer that does not have specific policy settings. Default user policies apply to any user that does not have specific policy settings or that isn't part of a group with specific policy settings.

Computer system policies modify the HKEY_LOCAL_MACHINE Registry subtree. User and group policies modify the HKEY_CURRENT_USER Registry subtree.

The types of settings you can define through System Policy Editor's Policy File mode are similar to the settings you can define through Registry mode, but system policy settings override Registry settings. Also, because you can apply system policy settings to groups, you can simultaneously set policies for several users, or even for an entire domain.

A complete set of all system policy information for a given configuration is stored in one big system policy file. You can create different system policy files to test different system policy configurations. The active file (for NT machines), however, must be saved as NTConfig.pol. (As mentioned in a previous section, Windows 95 system policies must be saved in Config.pol.)

Windows NT Server includes some System Policy templates, which contain system policy settings and categories. The template files present on Windows NT are as follows:

▶ **c:\<winnt_root>\inf\common.adm.** Settings common to both Windows NT and Windows 95 (and not present on the following two files)

▶ **c:\<winnt_root>\inf\winnt.adm.** Windows NT settings

▶ **c:\<winnt_root>\inf\windows.** Windows 95 settings

To add a System Policy template, choose Options, Policy Template from the System Policy Editor and choose a template from the list.

The System Policy templates are written in a proprietary scripting language. (See the Windows NT Resource kit for more information on the policy template scripting language.)

To define a system policy, perform these steps:

1. Choose File, New Policy in the System Policy Editor.

2. The Default Computer and Default User icons appear. Double-click on one of these icons to set the default computer or default user policy. (The policy settings appear in a tree structure with check boxes at the leaf level.)

3. Use the Edit menu to add specific users, computers, or groups to the policy file (see fig. 3.25). When you add a computer, user, or group, an icon for whatever you choose appears with the Default Computer and Default User icons in the System Policy Editor main window.

4. Double-click on that icon to set or change system policy settings. (Select an icon and choose Edit, Remove to remove that item from the policy file.)

Figure 3.25

The System Policy Editor Edit menu.

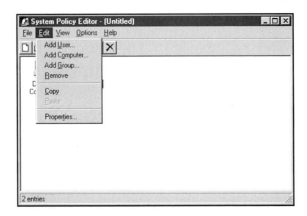

5. After you finish making changes to the Policy file, choose File, Save As. Save the file as the following:

```
\<winnt_root>\System32\Repl\Import\Scripts\NTconfig
```

System Policy Editor appends the POL extension.

Or, if you are only experimenting with the Policy file and don't want to use it yet, save it under a different name. After you save the Policy file, you can open it by choosing File, Open Policy in the System Policy Editor.

Managing Windows NT Server from Client Machines

The Network Client Administrator tool, located in the Administrative Tools program group, makes a set of Windows NT administration tools available to Windows NT clients. The Administration tools enable you to perform network administration functions from a client machine.

Microsoft lists the following objective for the Windows NT Server exam:

Administer remote servers from various types of client computers. Client computer types include Windows 95 and Windows NT Workstation.

There are two packages of client-based network administration tools: one for Windows 95 clients and one for Windows NT Workstation clients.

The Windows 95 client-based network administration tools are as follows:

▶ Event Viewer

▶ File Security tab

▶ Print Security tab

- ▶ Server Manager

- ▶ User Manager for Domains

- ▶ User Manager Extensions for Services for NetWare

- ▶ File and Print Services for NetWare

Before you can use the Windows 95 client-based network administration package, you must have a 486DX/33 or better Windows 95 computer with 8 MB of RAM (highly recommended) and a minimum of 3 MB of free disk space in the system partition. Client for Microsoft Networks must be installed on the Windows 95 computer.

The Windows NT Workstation client-based network administration tools are as follows:

- ▶ DHCP Manager

- ▶ Remote Access Administrator

- ▶ Remoteboot Manager

- ▶ Services for Macintosh

- ▶ Server Manager

- ▶ System Policy Editor

- ▶ User Manager for Domains

- ▶ WINS Manager

Before you can use the client-based network administration package, the Windows NT Workstation must be a 486DX/33 or better with 12 MB of RAM and a minimum of 2.5 MB of free disk space in the system partition. The Workstation and Server services must be installed on the Windows NT Workstation.

To create a share for the client administration tools (so you can access them from the client machine), choose Start, Programs, Administrative Tools, and then click on the Network Client Administrator icon. The Network Client Administrator dialog box appears (see fig. 3.26). Select the Copy Client-based Network Administration Tools radio button, and then click on Continue.

Figure 3.26

The Network Client Administrator dialog box.

Managing Disk Resources

A big part of an NT administrator's job is managing file resources for the network. This might include such things as assigning permissions, creating directory shares, troubleshooting file name problems, and copying or moving files and directories.

The following sections take a close look at working with file resources and working with file permissions and security.

Microsoft lists the following objective for the Windows NT Server exam:

Manage disk resources. Tasks include copying and moving files between file systems, creating and sharing resources, implementing permissions and security, and establishing file auditing.

Working with Windows NT File Resources

File resources are an important aspect of Windows NT administration and, consequently, the file resources topic is an important step in the objective list for the Windows NT Server exam. One significant part of managing file resources is managing NTFS security, which you will get a closer look at later in this chapter. But first, the following sections examine some other important topics you need to understand for the Windows NT Server exam, as follows:

▶ The Universal Naming Convention (UNC)

▶ Copying and moving files

▶ Long file names

▶ Converting a FAT partition to NTFS

▶ NTFS compression

▶ Sharing files

▶ Synchronizing files

The Universal Naming Convention (UNC)

Actually, this is the Microsoft Naming Convention, but when you are Microsoft you can get away with a little hubris. UNC is a common method for referring to servers on a network and the shares published on these servers. A UNC path begins with a double-backslash immediately followed by a server name, like so:

```
\\NTServer
```

To view the shared directories on a computer named NTServer, type the following command from the Windows NT command prompt:

```
net view \\NTServer
```

When you want to refer to a specific shared resource, you refer to the system name, followed by the share name. To map a new drive letter (for example, G) to the documents shared on NTServer, you could type the following command from the Windows NT command prompt:

```
net use G: \\NTServer\Documents
```

You can extend the path even further; from this point forward it looks like an MS-DOS path. To refer to the file README.TXT contained within the PUBLIC subdirectory of the Documents share on NTServer, you could use the following syntax:

```
\\NTServer\Documents\PUBLIC\README.TXT
```

Don't worry about the capitalization; it isn't important here.

To make the connection persistent, (in other words, if you want
Windows NT to reconnect you to this drive every time you log
on), use the /PERSISTENT switch:

```
net use F: \\NTServer\Documents /PERSISTENT:YES
```

To disconnect a network drive, use the /DELETE switch:

```
net use F: /DELETE
```

You can use UNC throughout Windows NT. To view the contents
of the documents shared on NTServer, for example, you could
type the following:

```
dir \\NTServer\Documents
```

To copy README.TXT from its original location on NTServer to
a new location on another server, you could type:

```
copy \\NTServer\Documents\PUBLIC\README.TXT \\ServerTwo\Archive\
```

You don't have to go to the SCS to use UNC, however; you can use
UNC as a time-saver from within the Windows NT GUI. A shortcut
can use a UNC as a target address, for example. From Network
Neighborhood, you can create a shortcut to a file or directory on
a network device just as you would to a file or directory on your
local machine.

In Explorer, if you know the name of the server to which you need
to connect, you don't need to waste time browsing. Choose Tools,
Go To and type the UNC path in the Go To Folder dialog box
(see fig. 3.27). Then click on OK.

Microsoft operating systems use UNC to connect to network resources, regardless of the type of server in use. You can use UNC
to connect from a Windows NT Workstation to a NetWare server,
for example, just as easily as you can connect to a Windows NT
Server.

Figure 3.27

*The Go To Folder
dialog box.*

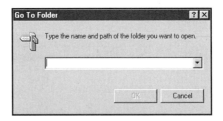

Copying and Moving Files

When you copy a file within or between partitions with the Copy
command, a new instance of that file is created, and the new file
inherits the compression and security attributes of the new parent
directory. (You will learn more about compression and security
later in this chapter.)

The same effect results if a file is moved between partitions by
using the Move command. (Remember that a move between partitions is really a copy followed by a delete.) When a file is moved
within a partition, the file retains its original attributes. The attributes do not change, because the file itself is never altered.
Only the source and target directories change.

Long File Names

*For an exercise
testing this
information, see
end of chapter.*

Although all the Windows NT-supported file systems support long
file names, you should be aware of certain issues.

FAT Long File Names

Although, as explained earlier, the file name length limitations of
the FAT file system has been overcome, one limitation that remains is that only 512 directory entries are permitted in the root
directory of any partition. Because each long file name requires a
directory entry for every thirteen characters (or portion thereof)
in its name and an additional entry for its 8.3 alias, you are in
danger of quickly reaching the entry limit if you use excessively
long file names in a root directory.

Also, if you are dual-booting between Windows NT and Windows 95, you should be aware that although the long file names are compatible with both operating systems, Windows 95 has a path limitation of 260 characters, including the drive letter. If you use a deep hierarchy of subdirectories with long file names, therefore, you may find that Windows 95 cannot access a file buried deep within that directory tree.

The two operating systems also differ in the way they create the 8.3 alias. Both Windows NT and Windows 95 begin by taking the first six legal characters in the LFN (in other words, stripping spaces and punctuation and converting to uppercase) and following them by a tilde (˜) and a number. If the first six legal characters result in a unique identifier for that file, the number following the tilde is 1. If a file in that directory already has the same first six legal characters, the numeric suffix will be 2. For an extension, Windows NT uses the first three legal characters following the last period in the LFN. To give you an idea of what this looks like, here is a sample directory listing:

```
Team Meeting Report #3.Doc          TEAMME˜1.DOC
Team Meeting Report #4.Doc          TEAMME˜2.DOC
Team Meeting Report #5.Doc          TEAMME˜3.DOC
Team Meeting Report #6.Doc          TEAMME˜4.DOC
Nov. 1995 Status Report.Doc         NOV199˜1.DOC
```

Both Windows 95 and Windows NT generate aliases in this fashion until the fifth iteration of the same first six legal characters. At this point, Windows 95 continues to do so, but Windows NT does something altogether different; it takes only the first two legal characters, performs a hash on the file name to produce four hexadecimal characters, and then appends a ˜5. The ˜5 remains for all subsequent aliases of those same initial six characters. If additional reports were saved in the directory used in the preceding example, for example, here is how Windows 95 would and Windows NT might generate the aliases:

	Windows 95	Windows NT
Team Meeting	TEAMME~5.DOC	TEA4F2~5.DOC Report #7.Doc
Team Meeting	TEAMME~6.DOC	TE12B4~5.DOC Report #8.Doc
Team Meeting	TEAMME~7.DOC	TE833E~5.DOC Report #9.Doc

Windows NT does this for performance reasons. It takes a long time to search a directory list for a unique file name if it has to go six or more characters in to find a unique match. Windows 95 eschews this technique, probably assuming that the performance gains are not worth the calls from consumers who can't make heads or tails of their file names from their 16-bit applications.

There are not any problems switching back and forth between Windows 95 and Windows NT on LFN-enabled FAT partitions. Each time you save the file, the LFN remains intact, but you may find that the alias is renamed, depending on the operating system and the file names currently in use in the directory.

If you choose to disable long file name support altogether on a FAT partition, be careful when copying files from a partition that does support LFNs because both the COPY and XCOPY commands always default to using the LFN for their operations. When these commands attempt to write an LFN to an LFN-disabled FAT partition, this error message appears:

```
The file name, directory name, or volume label syntax is incor-
rect.
```

If you are copying from an LFN-enabled FAT partition or from an NTFS partition, you can use the /n switch with both COPY and XCOPY. The /n switch directs the command to use the alias rather than the LFN.

Beware of third-party MS-DOS-based disk utilities. When run under Windows NT, they are harmless because they cannot access the hard disk directly. Run under MS-DOS on a dual-boot system, however, they can wreak havoc on your LFN-enabled FAT partitions. See the sidebar earlier in this chapter for more details. You can use Windows 95-specific disk utilities safely, again, when running Windows 95 on a multiboot system.

NTFS Long File Names

NTFS generates an alias for each LFN the same way that FAT does. This auto-generation takes time, however. If you won't be using 16-bit MS-DOS or Windows 3.x-based applications, you might consider disabling the automatic alias generation by adding a value called NtfsDisable8dot3NameCreation with a type of REG_DWORD and a value of 1 to HKEY_LOCAL_MACHINE\ System\CurrentControlSet\Control\FileSystem. To re-enable alias generation, set the value to 0, or delete the value altogether.

Converting a FAT Partition to NTFS

You can convert a FAT partition to NTFS at any time. You cannot, however, convert an NTFS partition to a FAT partition. Therefore, if you aren't certain about what type of file system to use for a partition, you might want to start with FAT and convert after you are sure there will be no ill effects.

To convert from FAT to NTFS, issue this command from the command prompt (there is no GUI utility for this):

```
CONVERT <drive_letter>: /FS:NTFS
```

The reason for specifying the file system when there has never been more than one choice probably is to accommodate future expansion, perhaps when the new OFS file system is added to Windows NT in the Cairo release.

When you perform a conversion, you do not have to back up your data (although you always should, just in case something goes awry); the conversion is done on the fly. You usually don't even need to shut down and restart the computer, unless another process currently is using the partition you are converting. If so, Windows NT performs the conversion after the system reboots using a special boot-time utility called autoconv. You see it happen when the screen turns blue immediately following the CHKDSK output.

NTFS Compression

Individual files and directories can be marked for compression on NTFS partitions only. (An entire drive can be compressed, too, but all you are really doing is compressing the root directory and the files within it; everything is handled at the file level.)

Compression occurs on the fly. All this is transparent to applications and the rest of the operating system.

Stacker, DoubleSpace, DriveSpace, and the other disk compression products are great products, but you never really know how much disk space you have left. Everything is based on an estimated compression ratio, and because the entire drive is compressed (these products allow no granularity), that compression ratio is applied to all files, DOCs, and ZIPs alike. Sometimes you run out of disk space even though a directory listing says you should have several megabytes remaining.

With NTFS, each file is compressed individually, so you always know the exact amount of disk space you have left. You can also choose which files to compress, so you don't have to waste time compressing the entire drive if you only want keep your Word documents down to size.

NTFS compression does not free up as much disk space as most MS-DOS-compatible compression products. This is not because Microsoft could not write a tight compression algorithm; in fact, they did just that with DriveSpace in Windows 95. The reason for the loose compression in Windows NT is actually to ensure that performance is not affected adversely.

Typically, disk compression products sacrifice performance for extra compression. In Windows NT, you can get a compression ratio almost as good as the MS-DOS 6.22 DriveSpace compression engine, without sacrificing any noticeable performance. When a user marks files to compress, NTFS analyzes the files to see how much disk space will be saved and the amount of time it will take to compress and decompress the file. If NTFS determines that it is not a fair trade, it does not compress the file, no matter how many times the user issues the compress command. NTFS compression is not at all configurable; all parameters are handled exclusively by the file system.

You can compress any file or directory on an NTFS partition, even if it is the system or boot partition. NTLDR, a hidden, system, read-only file in the root of your system partition, is the only file that you cannot compress. NTLDR is the first file loaded when Windows NT boots. NTLDR controls the rest of the boot process, including the loading of a mini-NTFS driver used when the system boots. Until NTLDR loads the NTFS minidriver, compressed files are inaccessible. NTLDR must, therefore, always remain uncompressed.

Not all files compress equally. Document files tend to compress the most. Text-based documents and bitmapped graphics, in particular, can shrink to less than one-eighth of their original size. Program files compress about forty or fifty percent, and already compressed files such as JPG and AVI graphics and videos tend not to compress at all.

Compressing and Uncompressing Files, Directories, and Drives

One of a few ways to compress a file or directory on an NTFS partition is to select the directories and files, and choose File, Compress.

To compress NTFS files, follow these steps:

1. Select the files you want to compress. Use the Ctrl key to select multiple files.

2. Choose File, Properties. The Properties dialog box appears.

3. In the Attributes frame, select the Compressed check box (see fig. 3.28).

Figure 3.28

File Properties dialog box for a file on an NTFS partition.

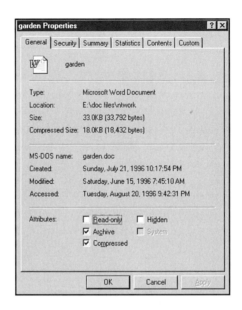

If you select a directory rather than or along with a file, you are asked whether you want to compress all the files and subdirectories within that directory.

To uncompress files or directories, select them and disable the Compressed check box in the Properties dialog box.

When files and directories are compressed, a new Compression attribute is set for those objects. Note that the Compression attribute does not display for non-NTFS partitions.

If you are curious about the amount of disk space NTFS actually is saving you, compare Size to Compressed Size in the General tab of the file Properties dialog box (refer to fig. 3.28).

The procedure for compressing a drive is similar to the procedure for compressing a file or directory. Select the drive in My Computer or Explorer, and then choose File, Properties. Select the Compress check box at the bottom of the General tab of the Properties dialog box (see fig. 3.29).

Figure 3.29

General tab of the drive Properties dialog box.

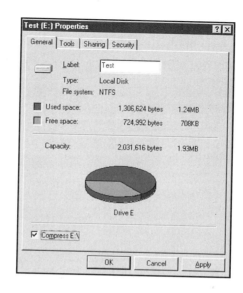

COMPACT.EXE

You also can use a command-line utility to compress files. The COMPACT.EXE command enables a user to compress files and directories from the command prompt. The following table lists switches you can use with the COMPACT command.

Use	To
COMPACT <filelist> /C	Compress
COMPACT <filelist> /U	Uncompress
COMPACT <filelist> /S	Compress an entire directory tree
COMPACT <filelist> /A	Compress hidden and system files
COMPACT <filelist> /I	Ignore errors and continue compressing
COMPACT <filelist> /F	Force compression even if the objects are already compressed
COMPACT <filelist> /Q	Turn on quiet mode; that is, display only summary information

Keep the COMPACT /F command in the back of your mind as a troubleshooting tool because when files are marked for compression, their Compressed attribute is determined and set before the actual file is compressed. Although not usually a big deal, all the selected files would be marked as compressed even though the operation had not been completed if the system were to crash during a compression operation. You could try compressing the files again with the /C switch, but the files would all be skipped because their Compressed attribute has already been set. Using the /F switch forces all files in the list to be recompressed, which should solve the problem.

You also can use the COMPACT command without any switches, in which case it just reports on the compression status, size, and ratio for each file in the file list.

Special Notes About Compressed Directories

Directories do not truly get compressed; the Compressed attribute for a directory just sets a flag to tell Windows NT to compress all current files and all future files created in this directory.

With that in mind, it may be easier to understand that when you copy or move compressed files, the files do not always stay compressed.

When a new file is created in an NTFS directory, it inherits the attributes set for that directory. When a file is created in a "compressed" directory, for example, that file will be compressed. When a file is created in an uncompressed directory, the file will not be compressed. So when a compressed file is copied to an uncompressed directory, the new copy of the file will not be compressed. Likewise, if an uncompressed file is copied to a "compressed" directory, the copy of the file will be compressed even though the original is not.

This much probably makes sense. Windows NT includes a MOVE command, however, that, when used within a single partition, swaps directory pointers so that a single file appears to move from one directory to another. Note the word "appears." The file does not actually go anywhere; it is the source and target directories that actually record a change. When files are moved, attributes do not change. In other words, a compressed file moved into an uncompressed directory stays compressed, and an uncompressed file moved into a compressed directory stays uncompressed.

If you don't think that is complicated enough, Windows NT enables you to use the MOVE command even when the source and target directories are on two different partitions. In this scenario, it is not possible for a directory on one partition to point to a file on another partition. Instead, Windows NT copies the file to the target partition and deletes the original file. Because the target partition now contains a brand-new file, that file inherits the attributes of its new parent directory.

When you copy a file within or between partitions, or move a file between partitions, therefore, the compression attribute of the new copy is inherited from its new parent directory. When you move a file within a single partition, the attributes on the file remain unchanged.

Sharing Directories

Sharing refers to publishing resources on a network for public access. When you share a resource, you make it available to users on other network machines. The Windows NT objects most commonly shared are directories and printers. You learned how to share printers in Chapter 2. This section (and the following subsections) look at how to share directories.

If you are familiar with NetWare but not with Windows NT, you need to understand the concept that, by default, absolutely no Windows NT resources are available to remote users; resources must be explicitly published (shared) on the network to host network users.

If you are familiar with Windows for Workgroups or Windows 95 but not with Windows NT, you also should understand that Windows NT users cannot share directories on their computers; only administrators and power users have this privilege.

Because shares are computer-specific, and because users cannot modify anything that affects the entire computer, shares are off-limits. This restriction is not a default; granting this capability to users is impossible, as is revoking this capability from administrators and power users.

Even if you are an administrator, you must have at least List permissions to the directory before you can share a directory. Any user who has locked you out of a share probably does not want you to publish it on the network.

Three ways to create shared directories are as follows:

▶ Using Explorer or My Computer

▶ Using the command prompt

▶ Using Server Manager

The following sections look at these methods for sharing directories and take a look at two special kinds of shares: hidden shares and administrative shares. You also will get a look at how you can view shared resources and monitor access to them by using the Server Manager and the Control Panel Server application.

Sharing with Explorer and My Computer

You can share directories in Windows NT in a number of ways. The easiest, and usually the most efficient, uses Explorer or My Computer.

Right-click on the directory you want to share and choose Sharing from the shortcut menu to open the Sharing tab of the Properties dialog box (see fig. 3.30). You also can reach the Sharing tab by choosing File, Properties. Or, My Computer enables you to choose Sharing directly from the File menu after you select a directory.

Figure 3.30

The Sharing tab of the directory Properties dialog box.

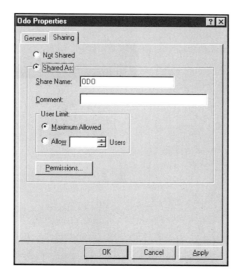

The Share Name defaults to the name of the directory. You can change it; it does not affect the actual directory name at all, it just defines the way the directory appears to network users.

You should never have to change the path. As long as you select the appropriate directory before you choose the Sharing command, the Path box should be set correctly.

The comment is optional. It is nothing more than a free-text tag line that appears next to the share name when browsing in Explorer or Network Neighborhood. (Choose View, Details if you want to see the comments.)

Click on the Permissions button to open the Access Through Share Permissions dialog box, from which you can build an Access Control List for the share to prevent unauthorized network access (see fig. 3.31).

The ATS permissions are completely independent from the local NTFS permissions. In fact, ATS permissions can even be applied to FAT partitions. Because they apply to the entire share, however, you cannot assign granular file-level permissions unless the partition on which the share resides is NTFS.

Figure 3.31

The Access Through Share Permissions dialog box.

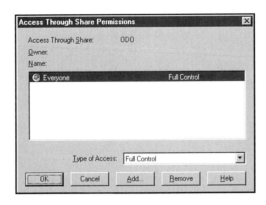

The ATS permissions themselves are not that granular. Here are your choices:

- ▶ **No Access.** Users with No Access to a share can still connect to the share, but nothing appears in File Manager except the message You do not have permission to access this directory.

- ▶ **Read.** Assigns R and X permissions to the share and its contents.

- ▶ **Change.** Assigns R, X, W, and D permissions to the share and its contents.

- ▶ **Full Control.** Assigns R, X, W, and D permissions to the share and its contents. In addition, for NTFS shares, P and O permissions are added.

Just as with local NTFS permissions, user and group permissions accumulate, with the exception of No Access, which instantly overrides all other permissions.

Remember, however, that ATS permissions are completely independent of local NTFS permissions. If both sets of permissions are assigned, only the most restrictive permissions are retained. A user who has Full Control over a file within a share to which only Read access has been granted cannot modify that file. Likewise, a user who has Read access to a file within a Full Control share cannot modify the file.

If you don't require security, you don't have to touch the ATS permissions. The default permissions grant the Everyone group Full Control (just as the default NTFS permissions do).

Choose the OK button to enact sharing of the directory. To modify the share configuration, right-click on the directory again and choose Sharing from the shortcut menu.

The Sharing tab looks identical to the New Share dialog box, with the addition of the New Share button (see fig. 3.32). Click on the New Share button to share the directory again, with a different name and ACL. It does not remove the original share, it just shares the directory again. You can share a single directory an unlimited number of times.

Figure 3.32

The Sharing tab after sharing has been enabled. Note the New Share button.

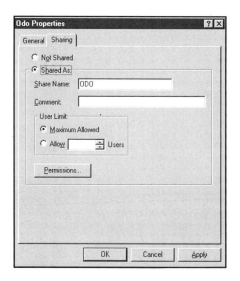

Sharing from the Command Prompt

To share from the Windows NT command prompt, use the NET SHARE command, using this syntax:

```
NET SHARE <share_name>=<drive_letter>:<path>
```

To share the C:\PUBLIC directory as Documents, use the following command:

```
NET SHARE Documents=C:\PUBLIC
```

To add a comment for browsers, use the /REMARK switch:

```
NET SHARE Documents:=C:\PUBLIC /REMARK:"Public Documents"
```

To set the user limit to Maximum allowed, use the /UNLIMITED switch (although this is the default):

```
NET SHARE Documents:=C:\PUBLIC /REMARK:"Public Documents" /
UNLIMITED
```

To set a specific user limit, use the /USERS switch:

```
NET SHARE Documents:=C:\PUBLIC /REMARK:"Public Documents" /
USERS:5
```

To stop a share using the NET SHARE command, use the /DELETE switch:

```
NET SHARE Documents /DELETE
```

Hidden Shares

Regardless of how you created it, you can hide a share by ending the share name with a dollar sign ($):

```
NET SHARE Documents$=C:\Public
```

Users can still connect to these shares, but they must explicitly supply the entire path to do so. And of course, the shares can still be protected using Access Through Share Permissions.

Administrative Shares

Any Windows NT-based computer that has hard-coded ACLs that grant Full Control to Administrators and No Access to everyone else has at least the following two hidden shares:

▶ **C$ shares the root of the computer's drive C.** If other partitions exist on the drive, those partitions also will have similar shares (but not for CD-ROM or disk drives).

Consequently, administrators can easily connect to other computers on the network.

▶ **ADMIN$ shares the root of the Windows NT installation, regardless of where it may have been installed.** It gives administrators easy access to the operating system directory on any Windows NT-based computer.

You can stop these shares if you want to, but they come back the next time you restart your system. You cannot permanently disable them.

Monitoring and Managing Shares

To see a list of all the shares on the system, open the Server application in the Control Panel. Although you cannot stop sharing a resource from the Server application, you can see a complete list of shared resources as well as a list of connected users and other server-related items.

The Server application (SRVMGR.CPL) is a subset of Windows NT Server's Server Manager application. It is a front end for administering connections to your computer. In the Server dialog box, you can view the Usage Summary for your server (see fig. 3.33). The Usage Summary tracks the following statistics:

Figure 3.33

The Control Panel Server application.

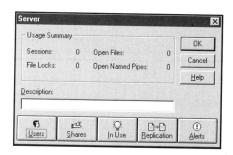

▶ **Sessions.** The number of computers connected to this server.

▶ **Open Files.** The total number of files currently open for access by remote users.

> ▶ **File Locks.** The total number of file locks placed against this computer by remote users.

> ▶ **Open Named Pipes.** The total number of named pipes between this computer and connected workstations. (Named pipes are an interprocess communication (IPC) mechanism.)

The Server dialog box also acts as the launch pad for five other server-configuration dialog boxes, as follows:

> ▶ **Users Sessions.** (Click on the Users button.) Shows detailed information about current user sessions on your Windows NT-based server.

> ▶ **Shared Resources.** (Click on the Shares button.) Displays detailed information about current shares on your server.

> ▶ **Open Resources.** (Click on the In Use button.) Displays the resources of your computer currently being used by remote users.

> ▶ **Directory Replication.** (Click on the Replication button.) You can configure the Directory Replicator service in this window.

> ▶ **Alerts.** (Click on the Alerts button.) Enables an administrator to enter a list of users or workstations to whom messages will be sent in the event of a significant server event.

To view the shared resources on your system, click on the Shares button in the Server application's Server dialog box. The Shared Resources dialog box that appears shows a list of all shares presently configured for your system and the path to each share (see fig. 3.34).

Server Manager, in the Administrative Tools group, offers a similar view of shared resources on the local system and on other network computers as well (see fig. 3.35). Click on a computer icon in the Server Manager main screen to open a dialog box that is similar to the dialog box used for the Control Panel Server application.

Figure 3.34

The Shared Resources dialog box.

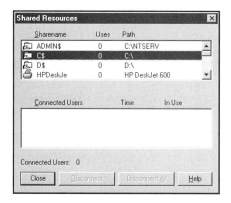

Figure 3.35

The Server Manager main screen.

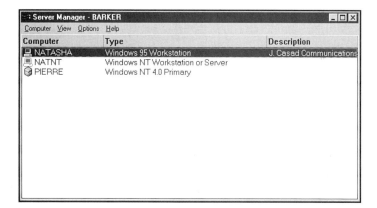

In the Server Manager, not only can you view the share information for a remote PC, you can actually create a new shared directory. Select a computer in the Server Manager and choose Computer, Shared Directories. The Shared Directories dialog box appears (see fig. 3.36). The Shared Directories dialog box shows the shared directories for the computer you selected. Click on the New Share button to add a new share. The New Share dialog box that appears asks you to specify a share name, a path, and an optional comment that will appear in descriptions on the share (see fig. 3.37). You also can limit the number of simultaneous users who can access the share. The Permissions button enables you to specify Access Through Share (ATS) permissions, described earlier in this chapter.

Figure 3.36

The Shared Directories dialog box.

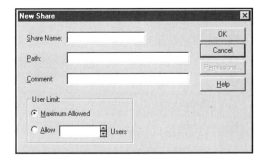

Figure 3.37

The New Share dialog box.

The Stop Sharing button in the Shared Directories dialog box enables you to terminate a share. The Properties button opens the Share Properties dialog box, which is similar to the New Share dialog box.

See Chapter 2 for a discussion of Server Manager's powerful Directory Replication feature.

Synchronizing Files

Windows NT 4, like Windows 95, includes a utility called My Briefcase. My Briefcase helps you synchronize and update files.

My Briefcase is designed to act as a virtual briefcase; you fill it with documents and take it with you when you leave for the office or airport. Of course, you can copy the documents to a disk without the aid of a high-tech virtual briefcase, but as anyone in business knows, keeping multiple copies of important files poses grave dangers. You might forget which version of the file is current and make changes to the non-current version. You might also forget about an update to one of the versions and use an older version as the final document.

My Briefcase solves these problems. Assume, for example, that you copy a document to My Briefcase and take it with you on a business trip. When you return, My Briefcase compares the traveling copy with the original, and tells you whether either or both of the files have changed. Then, you can choose one of the following options:

- ▶ **Replace.** Replaces the old version with the changed version. (Or you can tell My Briefcase to replace the changed version with the unchanged version, and thereby cancel the changes.)

- ▶ **Skip.** Skips the update because both versions have changed. (My Briefcase cannot automatically merge the changes when both files have changed unless the application supports the Briefcase merge feature.)

- ▶ **Merge.** If the application supports the Briefcase merge feature, My Briefcase merges the changes and updates the files so that both copies get the merged version.

- ▶ **Delete.** If either the original or the Briefcase copy has been deleted, Briefcase synchronizes the files by deleting the remaining copy.

To open My Briefcase, double-click on the My Briefcase icon located on the Desktop.

The following steps show you how My Briefcase is typically used:

1. Open My Briefcase (see fig. 3.38).

Figure 3.38

The My Briefcase main screen.

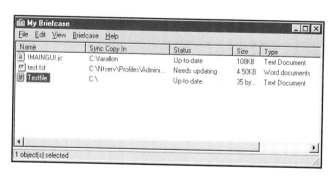

2. Copy a file or a group of files to My Briefcase using Explorer or My Computer. My Briefcase is designed for drag and drop, so drag a file from Explorer to the My Briefcase window or to the My Briefcase icon. You also can use the Clipboard to copy and paste a file to My Briefcase.

3. Put a disk in your disk drive and drag the My Briefcase icon from the Desktop to the disk drive, using Explorer or My Computer.

4. Insert the disk into a different computer. (You can use the same computer if you are just doing this as a test.)

5. Open My Briefcase (on the disk), and then open the copy of the file in My Briefcase and make a change to the file. Close the file.

6. In My Briefcase, choose Briefcase, Update All.

7. The Update My Briefcase dialog box appears, asking whether you want to update the unmodified version (see fig. 3.39). Click on the Update button to synchronize the files, or right-click on a file icon to choose a different action from a shortcut menu (see fig. 3.40).

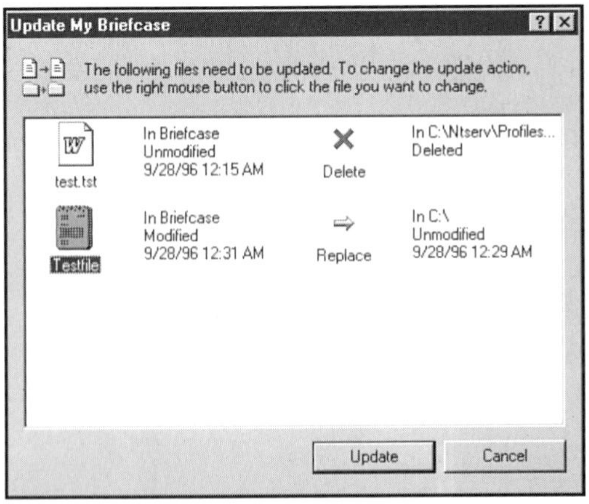

Figure 3.39

The Update My Briefcase dialog box.

Figure 3.40

*Right-click on the
file icon to
choose a differ-
ent update
action.*

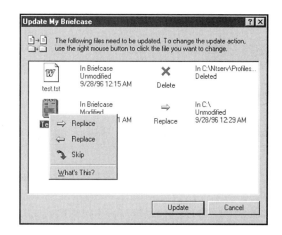

My Briefcase is best known for helping users with portable computers, but you also can use My Briefcase to synchronize files on a
network.

My Briefcase is part of the user profile for a particular user. This
means that each user can have his or her own briefcase, and that a
user's personal briefcase appears on-screen when he or she logs
on. My Briefcase files are stored in the directory:

```
C:\<winnt_root>\Profiles\<username>\Desktop\My Briefcase
```

Working with NTFS File Permissions and Security

The NTFS file system supports a complex arrangement of directory and file security for which there is no equivalent in the FAT file
system.

The following sections examine important aspects of NTFS
security.

Ownership of NTFS Resources

Every NTFS file and directory has one account designated as its
owner. The owner of a resource is the only account that has the

right to access a resource, modify its properties, and secure it from outside access.

By default, the owner of a resource is the user who created the resource. Only one user can own a resource at any given time, except that a user who is a member of the Administrators group cannot be the sole owner of any resource. Any resource created by an administrator, for example, is co-owned by the entire Administrators group. This is part of a checks-and-balances security model in Windows NT that ensures that an administrator cannot irrevocably hoard power and resources—yet another reason administrators should not use administrator-level accounts for day-to-day operations.

To identify the owner of any file or directory, follow these steps:

1. Select the file or directory in My Computer or Windows NT Explorer.

2. Choose File, Properties. The Properties dialog box appears.

3. Click on the Security tab (see fig. 3.41).

Figure 3.41

The file Properties Security tab.

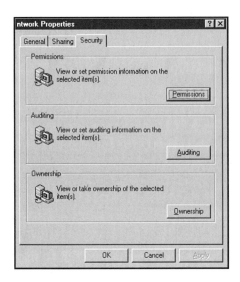

4. Click on the Ownership button. The Owner dialog box appears (see fig. 3.42).

Figure 3.42

The Owner dialog box.

Remember that only NTFS resources have owners.

You also can take ownership away from the current owner by choosing the Take Ownership button in the Owner dialog box. Normally, only administrators can do this—they can take ownership of any resource because they have been granted the Take Ownership of File and Directories user right. You can use User Manager for Domains to revoke the right of administrators to take ownership of files and directories that they did not create or to add another user or group to the list of accounts with the "take ownership" right. It is best, however, not to change this right at all; administrators must have this right if the system is to achieve a C2 security rating.

If you are not an administrator, you may still be able to take ownership if the current owner has granted you permission to take ownership. The important concept to grasp for now, however, is that ownership is taken, never given. Ownership involves responsibility, and that responsibility can never be forced on anyone, even by an administrator. Implications to this rule will surface shortly.

Auditing NTFS Resources

One of the most important aspects of Windows NT security is that system administrators can *audit* access to objects such as directories files. In other words, you can configure NT to track all attempts (successful or not) to access NTFS resources for various purposes. The record of all access attempts then appear in the Security log of the Event Viewer (see Chapter 6).

To configure auditing for a file, follow these steps:

1. Right-click on an NTFS file in Explorer of My Computer and choose Properties.

2. Click on the Security tab of the File Properties dialog box (refer to fig. 3.41).

3. Click on the Auditing button. The File Auditing dialog box appears (see fig. 3.43). You can audit either successful or failed attempts at any of the actions listed, and you can specify which specific groups or users you want to audit.

4. Click on the Add button to add a group or user to the audit list. Click on the Remove button to delete a group or user from the audit list.

Figure 3.43

The File Auditing dialog box.

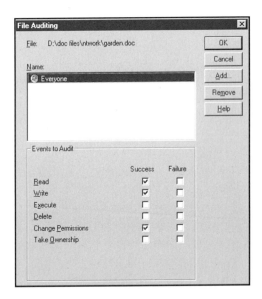

The Directory Auditing dialog box is similar (see fig. 3.44). The procedure for reaching the Directory Auditing dialog box is similar to the procedure for reaching the file Auditing dialog box. Right click on a directory, choose Properties, choose the Directory Properties Security tab, then click on the Auditing button. The Directory Auditing dialog box enables you to choose whether the new auditing arrangement you are configuring will replace the auditing on subdirectories or existing files.

Figure 3.44

The Directory Auditing dialog box.

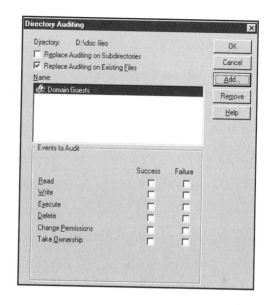

If you copy a file to a directory configured for auditing, the file inherits the directory's auditing configuration. If you move a file (dragging a file in Explorer to another directory in the same partition is a move), the file retains its original auditing configuration.

Securing NTFS Resources

The set of permissions on a file or directory is just another attribute (or stream) attached to the file, called an Access Control List (ACL). Each ACL contains a series of Access Control Entries (ACEs), and each Access Control Entry references a specific user or group SID and a type of access to grant or deny that SID. The end of this section explains how Windows NT checks a user's credentials against the Access Control List. First, this section reviews how permissions are assigned the ACL to begin with.

Discretionary Access

Who gets to assign permissions to a resource? The owner of the resource. Who is the owner of the resource? The user who created it. In other words, unlike other operating systems, security is not the sole domain of the administrator. If you create a file, you, not the administrator, get to secure it. You can, in fact, easily lock administrators out of their resources. And that makes sense in many environments.

Picture a typical company network, for example. Along with memos, reports, and routine documents, there are salary information, personnel files, and other sensitive data that the administrator and MIS department should not have access to just because they run the network. The users who created these files and work with them are the best ones to judge who should and should not have access. This type of access control, called discretionary access, is a hallmark of C2-level security.

Because locking administrators out of files and directories is dangerous, there is a spare key. An administrator cannot be blocked from taking ownership of a resource, and after the administrator owns the resource, he or she can modify the permissions on the resource so that he or she can access it. Remember, though, that ownership can be taken but never given, and that goes for giving back too. When the administrator owns the resource, he can never return ownership to the original user without that user explicitly taking ownership. And that is how it should be for legitimate situations in which a user might be absent from work when a critical file needs to be accessed. The administrator could get into a sticky situation by accessing files without a legitimate reason.

Permissions Versus User Rights

You may remember that resource permissions are not the same thing as user rights. User rights are tasks stored with your account information in the Registry, which you can perform on the system as a whole. NTFS permissions are stored with the resource itself, in the ACL property discussed earlier.

It is important to understand the difference between rights and permissions, because that understanding brings light to why the resource permissions assigned to a user cannot be viewed the way trustee assignments in other operating systems such as Novell NetWare are viewed. Displaying all the permissions assigned to a user would require searching all the NTFS files and directories on all the NTFS partitions on the workstation and on shared directories of any other workstation or server on the network. It also requires searching for incidence of the user's SID or group SIDs on the ACL of each of those files.

Directory-Level Permissions

Permissions can be placed on both directories and files. When they are, you need to resolve the permissions to figure out the effective permissions for a user.

The owner of a directory may grant a user the following permissions:

▶ **No Access.** Restricts the user from accessing the directory by any means. The directory appears in the directory tree, but instead of a file list, you see the message You do not have permissions to access this directory.

▶ **List.** Restricts the user from accessing the directory, although the user may view the contents list for the directory.

▶ **Read.** The user may read data files and execute program files from the directory, but can make no changes of any sort.

▶ **Add.** The user may not read or even view the contents of the directory, but may write files to the directory. If you write a file to the directory, you receive the message You do not have permissions to access this directory, but you still may save or copy files to it.

▶ **Add & Read.** The user may view and read from the directory and save new files into the directory, but may not modify existing files in any way.

▶ **Change.** The user may view and read from the directory and save new files into the directory, may modify and even delete existing files, and may change attributes on the directory and even delete the entire directory. This, by the way, is the most extensive permissions you would ever want assign anyone.

▶ **Full Control.** The user may view, read, save, modify, or delete the directory and its contents. In addition, the user may change permissions on the directory and its contents, even if he or she does not own the resource. The user also has permission to take ownership at any time.

What actually happens with all these levels of permissions is a combination of six basic actions that can be performed against a resource:

▶ Read (R)

▶ Write (W)

▶ Execute (X)

▶ Delete

▶ Change Permissions (P)

▶ Take Ownership (O)

The following table breaks down these permissions by permissions level:

Level	Directory Permissions	File Permissions
No Access	None	None
List	RX	Unspecified
Read	RX	RX
Add	WX	Unspecified
Add & Read	RXW	RX
Change	RXWD	RXWD
Full Control	RXWDPO	RXWDPO

The two custom levels of permissions are Special Directory Access and Special File Access, both of which enable the owner (or any user granted the "P" permission) to custom build an access control entry by using any combination of the six basic actions mentioned here.

To custom build an access control entry for a group or user, follow these steps:

1. Click on the Permissions button on the Security tab of the File or Directory Properties dialog box.

2. In the File Permissions dialog box that appears, select the group or user (see fig. 3.45).

3. Choose Special Directory Access from the Type of Access combo box.

Figure 3.45

The file Permissions dialog box.

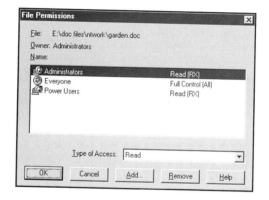

4. Choose the appropriate permissions in the Special Directory Access dialog box that appears (see fig. 3.46).

When an NTFS partition is created, the default permissions are set so that the Everyone group has Full Control. You may want to change this at the root directory level, but see the section, "Special Considerations for the Boot and System Partitions," at the end of this chapter before you do so.

When a new directory or file is created on an NTFS partition, the resource inherits the permissions on its parent directory, the same way it inherits the compression attribute. (See the section, "NTS File Compression," earlier in this chapter.)

File-Level Permissions

Although permissions for files are not as varied as they are for directories, NTFS can store permissions for files also. The owner of a file may grant a user the following permissions:

Figure 3.46

The Special Directory Access dialog box.

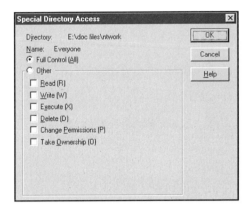

▶ **No Access.** The user may not access this file at all, although the file name and basic attributes still appear in File Manager.

▶ **Read.** The user may read this file if it is a data file, or execute it if it is a program file, but may not modify it in any way.

▶ **Change.** The user may read, execute, modify, or delete this file.

▶ **Full Control.** The user may read or execute, write to, or delete this file, may change permissions on it, as well as take ownership away from the current owner.

The following table breaks down these file permissions:

Level	Permissions
No Access	None
Read	RX
Change	RXWD
Full Control	RXWDPO

As with Directory permissions, a Special Access level allows anyone who has the capability to change permissions to custom build an access control entry for a user or group.

Setting Permissions

To set permissions on a file or directory, first select the resource in Explorer or My Computer, and then choose File, Properties. Click on the Permissions button on the Security tab of the File Properties dialog box to open the File Permissions dialog box (refer to fig. 3.45).

To remove a user or group from the ACL, select the user and click on the Remove button. To add a user or group to the ACL, click on the Add button. Clicking on the Add button opens the Add Users and Groups dialog box, which includes a list of all the groups in your account database (see fig. 3.47).

Figure 3.47

The Add Users and Groups dialog box.

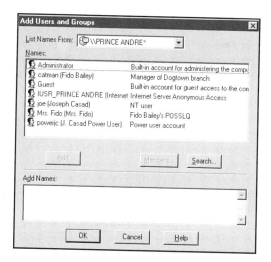

If you want to grant access to a specific user, click on the Show Users button. Otherwise, only the group names are displayed. Choose the users and groups you want to add to the ACL individually or collectively and click on the Add button to enter their names in the Add Names list box at the bottom of the dialog box. Don't try to set their access level here, unless all of these accounts are going to be granted the same access level (this type of access setting is all or nothing). When you click on the OK button, you get another chance to modify the permission level for each individual account on the ACL.

Setting permissions for a directory brings up a slightly different dialog box (see fig. 3.48).

Figure 3.48

*The Directory
Permissions
dialog box.*

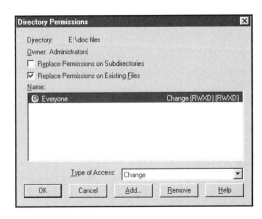

In the Directory Permissions dialog box, you can enable Replace Permissions of Subdirectories or Replace Permissions on Existing Files, the default. If you enable the Replace Permissions on Existing Files check box, the permissions that apply to the directory also apply to the files within the directory, but not to subdirectories or files within subdirectories.

Enabling only the Replace Permissions on Subdirectories check box modifies the permissions on all directories in the directory tree, but not on any files within those directories, even in the top-level directory.

Selecting both check boxes applies these permissions to the entire directory tree and its contents. Enabling neither check box changes the permissions on the top-level directory only.

Local Groups

When working with user rights, assigning rights to user and built-in groups usually suffices. When assigning resource permissions, however, adding individual users may be too time-consuming, and adding built-in groups may be too inclusive. Imagine having a directory that contains meeting minutes for a project on which you are working. You would like to grant permissions to the people on the project team, but the team is more than thirty people strong. Assigning permissions to everybody would take a long time, and assigning permissions to the Users group would give access to too many people.

It is time to introduce local groups, a separate level of user management in Windows NT. Local groups can be created by any user for any purpose (Headquarters, Marketing, Vice Presidents, Portland, Engineering), and once created, can be reused repeatedly. By creating a local group called MyProject and including all the project team members, you need to grant only a single set of permissions for each meeting report.

Local Groups versus Built-In Groups

A *local group* is a group used to assign rights or permissions to a local system and local resources. Local groups are similar to built-in groups in that both can contain many users to address a single purpose. In fact, technically, the built-in groups in Windows NT Workstation are local groups.

Local and built-in groups also have similar structures. Both can contain local users, domain users, and global groups, and users and global groups from trusted domains. The only type of account that cannot be placed inside a local group is another local group.

The difference between local and built-in groups lies in their intended purposes. The built-in groups are predefined and preassigned to specific rights and capabilities for system management. They are not intended for use in managing access to resources. Local groups are impractical for managing the system, but are ideal for assigning permissions to files and directories.

The only other difference between the two types of groups is that built-in groups are permanent members of a computer's account database, whereas local groups can be created and deleted at will.

Defining Local Groups

As with any type of account, you create local groups in User Manager for Domains. To create a local group in User Manager for Domains, follow these steps:

1. Select the user accounts you want to include in the local group (remember to hold down the Ctrl key to select multiple accounts).

2. Choose User, New Local Group to open the New Local Group dialog box (see fig. 3.49).

Figure 3.49

The New Local Group dialog box.

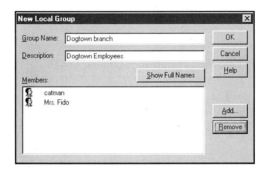

3. Enter a name (required) and a description (optional) for the group. The users you selected before issuing the New Local Group command should already be listed in the Members list.

4. If you want to add additional users, choose the Add button. The Add Users and Groups dialog box appears (refer to fig. 3.47).

   Notice that only users and global groups are displayed, not local groups. Again, local groups cannot be nested, so User Manager does not even tempt you.

5. Choose the users (individual or collective) that you want to add, and click on the Add button to enter their names in the Add Names list at the bottom of the dialog box.

6. Choose OK when you are ready to return to the New Local Group dialog box.

7. If you accidentally choose a user who does not belong in the group, click on the Remove button to delete the account from the group. Otherwise, click on OK to add the local group to the account database.

Managing Local Groups

After you create your local groups, you can manage them much as you manage your user accounts. You should, however, be aware of the following idiosyncrasies concerning local groups:

▶ You cannot rename a group after it has been created. Groups are referenced throughout the system by their Security Identifiers (SIDs), just as users are. Most likely, Microsoft's programmers just never got around to adding this feature to the code. You can copy a local group and give the new group a new name (in fact, you would have to), but that really is not the same as renaming. None of the permissions granted to the original group would apply to the new copy. There just is not a solution for this one.

▶ You cannot disable a group after it has been created. If a group were disabled, some implications would be unclear. Whether members of that group should be unable to log on, or whether the group's permissions and rights just should not apply while it is disabled would be a thorny issue. If you must temporarily disable the effects of a group on the system, remove all the users from the group. Do not delete the group and re-create it later, or your new group will have a new SID and a brand new set of default rights and permissions. All the old properties will be irrevocably lost.

▶ If you do want to delete a group, just select the group in User Manager and choose Delete from the User menu. Be aware that you are deleting only the group itself, not the users within the group. The effect stops here.

▶ You can add or remove members from the group by selecting the group in User Manager and choosing User, Properties.

How User and Group Permissions Interact

At this point, you have probably realized that users are likely to be in many different groups. Abigail's user account, for example, may be a member of the Users group, but also the Marketing group, the Department Managers group, the Philadelphia group, and the Project X group. Each of these user and group accounts are likely to be granted permissions to resources at one time or another, and it is quite likely that some of the accounts might occasionally appear on the same Access Control List. In such scenarios, how should the permissions granted to both a user's user account and group accounts be resolved?

Quite simply, user and group permissions are cumulative; neither takes precedence over the other. If the Marketing group has Read access to a file and the Department Managers group has Change access to the same file, Abigail (a member of both groups) has both—or in other words, Change access, because Change already includes the R and X permissions that Read incorporates.

The one exception to this rule is the No Access permission. No Access overrides all other permissions granted to a user or the user's groups, regardless of where the No Access was assigned. If Abigail were granted Read access to a file but Marketing was granted No Access, for example, Abigail would not be able to access the file. You cannot—and this cannot be emphasized enough—override a No Access permission.

This might seem worrisome at first. Consider a situation in which Beth is thinking about leaving the company and is updating her resume. She doesn't want anyone else to have access to this file, so she assigns the following permissions to the file:

Beth: Full Control

Everyone: No Access

You have probably guessed the result—Beth now can't access her resume because she is a member of the Everyone group, and the No Access she assigned to Everyone overrides the Full Control she assigned to her own account. Can Beth somehow easily retain sole access to her resume, or does she need to create a group called Everyone But Me and assign it No Access?

Yes, there is an easy way, and it involves making the ACL read as follows:

Beth: Full Control

You don't have to specify No Access for a user or group to exclude them from an ACL. The rule in Windows NT is that if you are not on the list, you don't get in. So why does Windows NT include the

No Access command at all if it isn't even necessary to exclude access? Because No Access is intended as a "negator" to remove permissions from a user or group that may already have been implicitly added to the ACL through membership in another group. Beth may not care if her coworkers in the Marketing department know she's thinking about leaving the company, for example, but she would rather her supervisor remain ignorant. She can set the following permissions on her resume's ACL:

> Beth: Full Control

> Marketing: Read

> Abigail: No Access

Because Abigail is a member of the Marketing group, she would have received Read access to Beth's resume if she had not been excluded by a direct No Access.

How Directory and File Permissions Interact

When you have permissions on both directories and files—such is the case on an NTFS partition—things get just a bit more complicated. Fortunately, you can resolve this situation pretty easily, although a few odd circumstances might surround the situation.

Simply put, file permissions override directory permissions. Even if Abigail had Full Control over the directory that contained Beth's resume, she could not read Beth's resume if her account had been granted No Access to that file. Likewise, it is possible to grant a user Read access to a directory and yet still grant Full Control over a single file within that directory.

This can lead to some odd scenarios. Sam may not want anyone to view the contents of his private directory, for example, so he assigns the directory this ACL:

> Sam: Full Control

If Beth tries to view this directory, she gets the `You do not have permission to access this directory` message. Yet Sam may still want to occasionally grant Beth access to one or two of his files. One day, he grants Beth Read access to a document in his private directory. Beth can read that file, but how can she access it? She can't view the directory contents in Explorer, and when she does a File/Open in an application, she cannot view the directory contents there either. Before she can access the file, Beth must type the full path to the file, from the application in which she wants to view it.

File Delete Child

Consider another odd scenario. Sam decides to grant Everyone Full Control to his private directory, and just apply Read permissions to Everyone for the individual files within the directory. Sam knows that although users might be able to copy and save files in his directory, they can't change the ones already present, because those files have only Read permissions. Sam also knows that no one else can change permissions on the existing files, because those files have only Read permissions. Sam, however, thinks that no one can delete his existing files because they only have Read permissions. On this last count, he is wrong.

In addition to the six basic permissions (RXWDPO) granted with Full Control, there is a seventh, implicit permission, called File Delete Child (FDC). FDC is included for POSIX compatibility, and it grants a user who has Full Control over a directory the capability to delete a top-level file within that directory, even if that user does not have delete permissions to the file itself! Only top-level files can be deleted, not subdirectories or files within subdirectories.

There is a workaround, but you must grant Special Directory Access before you can use it. If you grant Special Directory Access and choose all six permissions rather than grant Full Control to a directory, the user granted this level of access won't have the FDC permission. It looks like you are really just assigning the equivalent of Full Control, but you are doing so minus File Delete Child. By the way, don't waste time searching for File Delete Child in the Explorer interface—it is not there. It's an implicit permission granted only when Full Control is granted over a directory.

An even better workaround is to never grant anyone Full Control over anything, unless you grant it to yourself as the owner. After all, you probably don't want anyone else to have the power to change permissions on the file and lock you out. And you certainly don't want someone to have the capability to take ownership of the file at the same time so that you can't even change permissions back to what they were. A good rule of thumb is never to grant anyone any permissions higher than Change. That is high enough, because a user with Change access can delete the resource itself.

Special Considerations for the Boot and System Partitions

When you install Windows NT on an NTFS partition, it is tempting to prevent necessary files from being deleted or overwritten, to try to exclude users from accessing the Windows NT installation directory tree. If you examine the Access Control List for that directory, however, you won't see the customary Everyone/Full Control that you normally find on NTFS resources.

The critical entry on the ACL is the SYSTEM/Full Control ACE. Do not, under any circumstances, remove this ACL from the list, or modify it. Otherwise, Windows NT crashes and you cannot restart the operating system.

If this does happen, don't panic. You can use the Emergency Repair Disk to strip the permissions from the Windows NT installation directory tree. See Chapter 6 for more information on this procedure.

Putting It Together

How does Windows NT make the decision whether to grant access to an NTFS resource?

As you may recall, when a user logs on to a Windows NT-based computer, the security accounts manager generates an access token for the user's current session. The access token contains, among other things, the user's user SID and group SIDs.

When a user requests access to an NTFS resource, the Security Reference Monitor (a component of the security subsystem) examines the SIDs contained in the user's access token. The Security Reference Monitor then parses the Access Control List looking for references to any of the SIDs contained in the user's access token. The search continues until one of the following conditions is met:

▶ The Security Reference Monitor encounters a Deny (the internal representation of No Access) for any SID in the user's access token. At this point, the search stops and access is denied.

▶ The Security Reference Monitor encounters an Allow for any SID in the user's access token. If the Allow specifies the type of access the user seeks, the search stops and access is granted. If the Allow specifies some, but not all the permissions requested, the search continues until all permissions are accumulated, at which point access is granted. If the Allow specifies none of the permissions the user requests, the search continues.

▶ The Security Reference Monitor reaches the end of the Access Control List without accumulating all the requested permissions. Access is denied. No partial access is granted.

What is interesting about this process is that it works only if Denies are placed at the top of the ACL. If any Allows precede a Deny on the ACL, a user can achieve access even if No Access has been granted to one of the SIDs in the user's access token, because the search stops after the requested permissions have been accumulated and before the No Access is encountered.

Luckily, Windows NT does place all Denies before all Allows, at least, in all its built-in applications and interfaces. It is possible for a programmer—to provide maximum compatibility and flexibility in porting existing custom applications to Windows NT—to write a program so that Denies can be placed anywhere within an ACL. You should not have anything to worry about with any professionally sold Windows NT application, but you definitely want to make certain that any programmer hired for custom development knows how structure affects Access Control Lists.

Handles

After the Security Reference Monitor has approved your access to the file resource, the system creates a handle to that resource. (Remember that no user-mode process in Windows NT can access a resource directly.) The handle is entered in the object table of the process that requested the access. The object table contains the list of handles to all resources that process is using, as well as the permissions granted through each handle. When transactions are performed against an open resource, the security subsystem checks the permissions in the object table rather than parsing the entire ACL again, a process which provides both a slight performance boost and guarantees a user's permissions over a file will not refresh until the file is closed and reopened, generating a new handle.

Consider a situation in which you might grant a user Change permissions to a file. The user opens the file that contains the requested and granted Change permissions, and while the file is in use, you decide to change the user's permissions to Read. Although the ACL changes immediately, the security subsystem is not checking the ACL anymore, because the user has an open handle to the file. The user must close and reopen the file before the new permissions can take hold.

Access Tokens Don't Refresh

As is the case with handles, access tokens are generated only when a user logs on. Any changes to a user's rights and group memberships, for example, do not take effect until the user logs off and back on again. You cannot prevent a user logged on as a member of the Marketing group from accessing a resource just by removing him from the group. His access token still reflects Marketing membership until the next time he logs on.

Exercise Section

Exercise 3.1: Creating a User Account

Exercise 3.1 shows you how to configure Windows NT to audit changes to the user account database, create a user account, and then view the audit log.

Estimated time: 20 minutes

1. Log on to the domain as an administrator.

2. Choose Start, Programs, Administrative Tools, and click on User Manager for Domains.

3. In the User Manager for Domains main window, Choose Policies, Audit.

4. In the Audit Policy dialog box that appears, select the Success and Failure check boxes for User and Group Management (refer to fig. 3.11).

5. Click on OK.

6. In the User for Domains main window, choose User, New User. The New User dialog box appears.

7. In the Username text box, type **Exer1**.

8. In the Full Name text box , type **Exercise 1**.

9. For a Description, type **MCSE Training Guide test account**.

10. For the Password, type **exer1**. Type the password again in the Confirm box.

note

You can, of course, make up your own username, password, and description for this test account.

11. Click on the Add button, and then click on the Close button.

continues

The new user account should appear in the user list in the top panel of the User Manager for Domains main window.

12. Double-click on the account icon in the user list (or select the account and choose User, Properties) to open the User Properties dialog box.

13. Browse through each of the buttons at the bottom of the User Properties dialog box. In the Group button, notice that the new account is a member of the Domain Users group. Add the account to other groups by selecting a group in the right panel and clicking on the Add button. Click on Cancel (or OK if you made changes) to return to the User Manager for Domains main window.

14. Choose Start, Programs, Administrative Tools, and select Event Viewer.

15. In the Event View main window, choose Log, Security. Look for three security log entries related to creating the new account at or near the top of the list. The Category column for each of the three entries will be marked Account Manager.

16. Double-click on each of the entries for a detailed look at the audit information.

17. Close Event Viewer.

18. In the User Manager for Domains main window, choose Policies, Audit.

19. Deselect the User and Group Management check boxes (unless you want to keep auditing User and Group Management events).

20. If you plan to continue with Exercise 3.2, close User Manager for Domains. If you don't plan to continue with Exercise 3.2, double-click on the icon for the Exer1 account and select the Account Disabled check box in the User Properties dialog box. The next time you need to set up a user account, you can rename the Exer1 account by choosing User, Rename in the User Manager for Domains main window.

note

As this chapter describes, it is generally a better policy to disable a user account rather than to delete it. Because the Exer1 account created in this exercise was never used, advantages for disabling it are less significant. You also could delete the account by choosing User, Delete in the User Manager for Domains main window.

Exercise 3.2: System Policies

Exercise 3.2 will show you how to use the System Policies Editor to configure a user's Desktop environment.

Estimated time: 20 minutes

1. Log on as an administrator.

2. Choose Start, Programs, Administrative Tools, and then click on System Policy Editor.

3. Choose File, Open Policy.

4. Browse to the <winnt_root.\system32\repl\import\scripts folder and look for an ntconfig.pol file. If the file exists, select the file and click on OK. If the ntconfig.pol file does not exist, click on Cancel, and choose File, New Policy.

5. In the System Policy Editor, choose Edit, Add User.

6. In the Add User dialog box, enter **Exer1** (or whatever name you used for the account you created in Exercise 3.1). Click on OK.

7. The name of the user (Exer1 or whatever name you used) should now appear with an icon in the main window. Double-click on the Exer1 icon.

8. Expand the Shell policy category; then expand the Restrictions subcategory.

9. Select the Remove Run command from the Start menu check box and click on OK.

continues

Exercise 3.2: Continued

10. Choose File, Save.

11. If you started with a New Policy in step 4, Windows NT prompts you to enter a file name. Type **ntconfig** in the File Name text box (NT appends the POL extension) and save the file to the <winnt_root>\system32\Repl\Import\Scripts directory.

12. Log on to the domain from a workstation by using the Exer1 account (or whatever account name you established the policy for in step 6). Use the password you created in step 10 of Exercise 3.1.

13. When the Start button appears, click on the Start button and examine the Start menu. The Run command will be missing from the Start menu.

14. Log off the workstation. Disable or delete the Exer1 account as described in step 21 of Exercise 3.1.

Exercise 3.3: Copying and Moving

Exercise 3.3 will show you how to test the differences between copying and moving for NTFS file.

Estimated Time: 10 minutes

1. Start Windows NT Explorer.

2. Right-click on a directory on an NTFS partition.

3. Choose File, New/Folder.

4. Create a new subdirectory called **compressed**.

5. Right-click on the "compressed" subdirectory and choose Properties. In the directory Properties General tab, select the Compress attribute check box.

6. Right-click on a file in another directory on the NTFS partition and select Properties.

7. Select the file and choose Edit, Copy; then choose Paste. A file called Copy of <filename> will be created.

8. Select this new file and choose File, Rename.

9. Change the file name to **Copy**. Create another copy of the original file and change the name of the new copy to **Move**.

10. Examine the Compress attribute of the Copy and Move files. Make certain the files are not compressed. (Right-click on the file and choose Properties to select the Compress attribute.)

11. Select the file called Copy and choose Edit, Copy.

12. Double-click on the "compressed" directory and choose Edit, Paste. A file called Copy will appear in the "compressed" subdirectory.

13. Drag the file called Move to the "compressed" directory. (Dragging the file within the same partition is a move.)

14. Check the Compress attributes of the Copy and Move files in the "compressed" directory. The Copy file is now compressed. (It inherited the Compress attribute from the parent directory.) The Move file retains its uncompressed state.

Review Questions

The following questions will test your knowledge of the information in this chapter. For additional questions, see MCP Endeavor and the Microsoft Roadmap/Assessment exam on the CD-ROM that accompanies this book.

1. You are the administrator of a Windows NT workgroup. You need to devise a group strategy for the following scenario:

   You have a group of several marketing employees who need access to the contact management database; a second group of people who need to access the accounts receivable program; and a third group of people who need to be able to modify the inventory database and run general programs.

   Keep in mind that you are trying to minimize your account administration time. Management has just informed you that the number of people in your area is expected to double over the next quarter. How would you set up group management for each group?

   Select the best answer from the following:

   A. Create user accounts for each user and assign access permissions based on the requirements laid out in the question.

   B. Create global groups for each unique group, assign the necessary permissions to each group, and then place the users in the appropriate groups.

   C. Create a local group for each unique group, assign the needed permissions to each group, and then place the users in the appropriate groups.

2. Which of the following correctly describes the relationship between deleting and disabling user accounts?

   A. Deleting a user account removes the SID from the directory database, whereas disabling the user account does not remove the SID; it changes the naming property of the user.

   B. Disabling a user account removes the SID from the directory database, whereas deleting the account does not remove the SID; it changes the naming property of the user.

C. After deleting an account, to re-establish the user's permissions and access rights, you just have to re-create the user ID using the same name as it had before, and thus restore the system SID.

3. Which one of the following best describes the differences between local and global groups?

A. A global group is one that resides in an NT Workstation user accounts database and a local group is one that is local to the computer where the resources reside.

B. A local group is a group that resides in an NT Workstation computer and is used to grant access permissions to resources on the workstation. A global group is a group created in an NT domain and used to group domain users into groups with common access needs.

C. Global groups contain local groups that have access to resources on NT Workstation and Windows 95 computers.

D. Local groups are created on NT domain controllers and are used to grant access to domain users to resources in the domain. Global groups are used to give users access to resources in other domains.

4. If you suspect that a user is attempting to gain access to directories that contain sensitive information, which feature can you enable in Windows NT Workstation to create a log of attempted accesses?

A. You can use the System Option in Control Panel to enable the auditing feature of Windows NT.

B. You can use the Windows NT Accounting System.

C. You can use Directory Logging.

D. You can use the User Manager program to enable the Windows NT Audit Policy.

5. A user calls and complains that the system time on his NT Workstation is incorrect and when he tries to fix the time, he gets a message that he doesn't have sufficient permissions.

What is the best way to allow him to change the time on his system?

A. Give him the administrator password and have him log on as administrator and change the system time.

B. Make his userid a member of the Administrator group to give him the permissions he needs to change the time.

C. Grant his user ID the Change system time right in User Manager.

D. Tell him to restart his computer in MS-DOS and change the time and date in DOS.

6. You want to appoint a user the responsibility of backing up all the Windows NT Workstation computers in your workgroup. What is the best way to give the user the permissions necessary to perform this function?

A. Make the user a member of the Administrator group, and thereby give him access to all resources on the NT Workstation computers.

B. Give the user the administrator password and tell him to log on as administrator to perform the backups.

C. Grant the user's account Full Control permissions to all the directories and files that the user needs to back up and restore.

D. Make the user a member of the Backup Operators group, and thereby give him access to all files and directories on the NT Workstation computer without regard to regular NT permissions.

7. You have installed NT Workstation on several computers in your company for use by several temporary employees. You want to prevent the users from changing their passwords. Which step(s) should you take to perform this?

A. Create mandatory profiles on the domain controller.

B. Configure directory, share, and file permissions.

C. Create user accounts that have the correct permissions.

D. Assign appropriate user rights on a user-by-user basis.

E. Enable the User Cannot Change Password option in User Manager.

8. You are the primary user of your NT Workstation computer, but you occasionally share your computer with a couple other users in your department. What is the best way to let them use your computer?

A. Create a user account for each user.

B. Create one account and give each user the password for the new account.

C. Let the users use your account and ask them not to change anything on your computer.

D. Tell them the password to the administrator account on your computer.

9. You share you computer with another user. You need to install Microsoft Word so that it is available to both of you. What type of program group should you create so that the program is available to you and the other user?

A. Personal

B. Local

C. Global

D. Common

10. Your company routinely hires temporary employees around the holidays each year. These temps typically work the last two weeks in November and the entire month of December. How would you design an account policy to maximize the security of your network? Select all correct answers.

A. Set the account policy to lock out users after three bad logon attempts.

B. Set the account policy so that users' passwords never expire.

C. Set the account policy so that users are logged out of the workstation when their time restrictions are exceeded.

D. Modify the temporary users' accounts so that their accounts are disabled after January first.

11. A user calls you and tells you that she accidentally deleted a group that contains several users on her computer. She is worried that this may have affected the users' rights to certain resources on her computer. She knows the name of the group and the users that were members of the group. How can she restore the group and the permissions back to the way they were?

   A. Choose the Undelete option in User Manager to recover the deleted group.

   B. Create a new group with the same name and SID as the deleted group.

   C. Create a new group with the same name, assign the users to the group, and then reassign the permissions to the group.

   D. Re-create the users and group, and reassign the permissions to the group.

12. What are the names of the four special groups in NT Workstation?

   A. Network, Special, Administrators, and Interactive

   B. Administrators, Backup Operators, Network, and Local

   C. Global, Power Users, Macintosh Users, and Network

   D. Network, Creator Owner, Interactive, and Everyone

13. When you connect to a shared directory on another Windows NT Workstation computer, which group do you automatically become a member of?

   A. Network

   B. Administrators

   C. Creator Owner

   D. Interactive

14. You want a user to be able to create user and group accounts, but don't want the user to be able to assign user rights. Of what groups should you make the user a member?

   A. Account Operators

   B. Server Operators

   C. Administrators

   D. Power Users

15. What is the difference between a user account that is locked out and an account that is disabled?

   A. A disabled userid keeps its SID, whereas a locked out user account does not.

   B. The system administrator can lock out a user account, whereas the system administrator cannot disable a user account.

   C. The system administrator can disable a user account, whereas the system administrator cannot lock out a user account.

   D. A locked out userid keeps its SID, whereas a locked out user account does not.

16. You need to create several user accounts that all have the same properties. What is the best method to use?

   A. Create a user who has the correct parameters and use the Replicate option to create as many users as necessary.

   B. Create a user who has the correct parameters and use the Copy function in User Manager to create as many as necessary.

   C. Use the REPLUSER.EXE program to copy a user template that has the correct properties.

   D. Run the RDISK.EXE program to make duplicate user accounts for as many users as necessary.

17. You are using a template to create several user accounts with similar properties. You want to assign home directories, however, to each user based on his or her userid. Which path should you specify for the home directory in the User Environment Profile dialog box?

   A. C:\USERS\DEFAULT

   B. C:\USERS\%HOMEDRIVE%

   C. C:\USERS\%DOMAINUSERS%

   D. C:\USERS\%USERNAME%

18. A user calls you and complains that he cannot log on. Yesterday, he changed his password and now cannot remember it. What can you do to get this user logged on?

   A. Create a new user account with no password and tell him to log on.

   B. Change the user's password and set his account policy so that his password never expires and the password cannot be changed.

   C. Run User Manager and change his password. Set his account policy so that he must change his password at the next logon. Tell the user the password and tell him that he must change it during the logon process.

   D. Tell the user to attempt to log on guessing his password at each attempt and hopefully he will remember it sooner or later.

19. A user is going to be on leave for the next two months. How would you keep anyone from using this account without having to re-create it when the user returns?

   A. Use Server Manager to disable the user's account from logging on to the workstation.

   B. Remove the user's right to log on locally.

   C. Disable the user's account in User Manager.

   D. Delete the user account.

20. Your boss's secretary complains that she cannot log on to her NT Workstation computer. You make a site visit and the user informs you that even though she is entering the correct password, the system tells her that she is either using the incorrect account, or that her password is incorrect. You question her further and find out that yesterday when she logged on she was required to change her password. Which one of the following probably is the cause of her problems?

   A. She is entering her userid in lower case and does not realize that the userid is case-sensitive.

   B. She is entering her password in lower case and does not realize that the password is case-sensitive.

21. You have a user who uses a laptop computer in a docking station at work and uses the laptop at home without the docking station. The laptop is configured with Windows NT Workstation. What is the best way to configure the laptop for each of the different environments.

    A. Use the Control Panel, System, Hardware Profiles tab to create separate hardware profiles for each location. The user can then choose which configuration at bootup time.

    B. There is no way to configure NT with multiple hardware configuration because the operating system does not support Plug and Play.

    C. You don't have to configure the laptop manually. The plug-and-play features of NT automatically detect the difference.

    D. Tell the user to reconfigure the settings for when he is away from the office (before he leaves the office). The next time he reboots, he will have the correct configuration.

22. The easiest way to make a group of users' desktop environments look the same is to use which of the following tools?

    A. Use Registry Editor and then place a copy of the configured Registry in their home directories.

    B. Use User Profile Editor and then place a copy of the configured profile in the user's home directory. Give the profile a MAN extension and it becomes a mandatory profile that the users cannot change.

    C. Use System Policy Editor and create a POL file that all users will use. Place this POL file in the <winnt root>\System32\Repl\Import\Scripts directory, and then assign the policy file for whichever users you want to be able to use it.

    D. You cannot configure a standard desktop automatically, but you can configure each machine manually so that the next time your users log on, they have the configured settings.

23. Which statement is true regarding system policy files between Windows 95 and Windows NT?

    A. The policies are not the same and can't be interchanged.

    B. The policies are the same and can be interchanged.

    C. Windows 95 doesn't have system policies.

    D. Windows 95 policies are local to the machine, whereas Windows NT policies can be stored only on a server.

24. A user calls and complains that every time she changes her desktop, it reverts to its state prior to her changes the next time she logs on. How can you explain what is happening?

    A. Tell the user to choose the Save Settings on Exit option from the Start menu properties.

    B. Tell the user that she doesn't have sufficient rights to save her desktop settings and that she should contact Microsoft to obtain a license to change her desktop.

    C. Her userid probably is set up to use a mandatory profile that she cannot modify.

    D. Tell her she needs to make the changes and save them by using the System Policy Editor. The next time she logs on, the settings should be the same.

25. A user wants to know why when he logs on to a different workstation, his desktop settings are different than when he logs on to his workstation. Which statement best explains this situation?

    A. The user must be set up to use a local policy. This policy is stored on his machine and hence is not available when he moves to a different computer.

    B. The computer policy of the other machine is configured to override his server-based policy.

    C. The user must be logging on with the Ignore Policy setting enabled in the logon dialog box. Tell him to disable this option.

26. You need to copy files from an NT-based computer to a Windows 95 computer. You don't have a direct network connection. Your only option is to copy the files to a disk. The NT-based computer does not have any FAT partitions. Can you copy the file?

    A. Yes, if you format the disk as NTFS and convert it to the FAT file system by using the CONVERT.EXE utility.

    B. No, it cannot be done because Windows 95 doesn't read NTFS formatted floppies.

    C. Yes, copy the files to a FAT formatted disk and the Windows 95 computer can read the files.

    D. Yes, first you must restart the NT-based computer in MS-DOS and then copy the files over from DOS to the disk.

27. The manager of the MIS department comes to you and informs you that you need to connect the graphics department's Macintosh computers to the NT network. Which type of file system enables the Macintosh users to share files and directories with the rest of the NT users?

    A. NTFS

    B. FAT

    C. CDFS

    D. AFP

28. A user calls you in a panic. He says that he cannot create any files on his C drive. You probe further and find out that the user is trying to create a file on the root of his C drive. You also discover that his C drive is formatted as FAT. He executes DIR and tells you that the system is reporting only 235 files in the root directory. What could be causing this problem and what should the user do to fix it?

    A. This particular problem has no fix. The problem is with Windows NT and the only thing that can be done is to install a new hard drive and save the files on the new drive.

B. No problem here. Just tell the user to save the files to disk and then use File Manager to copy them over to the C drive.

C. Tell the user that his hard drive must be full and the only solution is to purchase a new hard drive.

D. The user must be using long file names. He probably has used all the directory entries in the root of the drive. The solution is to move some of these files to subdirectories. Remember that the FAT system is limited to a maximum of 512 directory entries at the root of every drive.

29. A user calls you and tells you that she is getting a syntax error while trying to copy a file from her FAT partition to a disk. She has booted the computer under MS-DOS and is using the DOS COPY command. The file that she is trying to copy has the file name C:\DOCS\THISISAFILE.TXT. The command that the user is entering is COPY C:\DOCS\THISISAFILE.TXT A:. Which one of the following command-line switches should she be using with the COPY command?

A. /N

B. /B

C. /L

D. -P

30. You want to further secure your system by storing all your files on an NTFS partition. How can you do this without losing all the data currently stored on your FAT partition?

A. You cannot.

B. Using Disk Administrator, format the FAT partition as NTFS.

C. Back up the current FAT partition and delete it in Disk Administrator. Then re-create the partition and restore the files from the backup.

D. Use the CONVERT.EXE utility to convert the partition to NTFS without losing the data already on the drive.

31. Recently, you have noticed that your server is running low on disk space. You do not have the budget to go out and purchase a new drive. What can you do as a temporary measure to give your users more disk space?

   A. Nothing.
   B. Reformat the drives and restore the data from a backup to minimize disk fragmentation, reducing the amount of wasted clusters on the drive.
   C. Convert your partitions to NTFS and then implement disk compression.
   D. Convert your partitions to FAT and then install the DriveSpace utility to compress the drive, giving your users more usable disk space.

32. To compress the files on your NTFS partition, you can use which of the following two utilities?

   A. COMPRESS.EXE and File Manager
   B. COMPACT.EXE and Windows NT Explorer
   C. COMPRESS.EXE and Windows NT Explorer
   D. DriveSpace and Windows NT Explorer

33. You copy a file from a folder that has its compression attribute checked to a new folder on the same drive. What attributes will the destination file have?

   A. The destination file will be compressed.
   B. The destination file will not be compressed.
   C. You cannot copy a compressed file without first uncompressing it.
   D. The destination file will inherit the compression attributes of its new parent directory.

34. You have been promoted to manager of a new project in another part of the country. Your replacement has asked you to turn over the current project files to him. Which of the following best describes the process for changing ownership of files and directories?

A. E-mail the files to him as attachments and have him save the files in a directory of his choice.

B. Have the system administrator make the new user the owner of the files and directories.

C. Give the user the Take Ownership permission and then have him take ownership of the files and directories.

D. It is not possible to change the ownership of files and directories.

35. Which of the following statements best describes what happens when ownership of files and directories is changed?

A. The user taking ownership of the files or directories becomes the current owner of the files and directories.

B. The groups to which the user taking ownership belongs become the current owner of the files and directories.

C. The user taking ownership of the files and directories becomes the current owner of the files and directories, as well as any groups to which the user belongs.

D. The user taking ownership of the files and directories becomes the current owner of the files and directories, except when the user is a member of the Administrators group. In this case, the Administrators group becomes the owner of the files and directories.

36. The default file and directory permissions on an NTFS partition are:

A. Everyone has Read.
B. Everyone has No Access.
C. Everyone has Full Control.
D. Administrators have Full Control.

37. The name of the Teachers group needs to be changed to Professors. Which statement best describes the process for changing the name of the group?

A. The name of the group cannot be changed.
B. Select the Rename option from the User menu in User Manager and enter the new group name.

C. Create a new group called Professors and then move the users from the Teachers group to the Professors group.

D. Create a new group called Professors and then delete the users from the Teachers group and add them to the Professors group.

38. A user belongs to the Sales group and the Marketing group. The user has the Read permission to a directory named DIR1. The Sales group has the Change permission to DIR1 and the Marketing group has no permissions to DIR1. What are the user's effective rights to DIR1?

A. The user has the Read and Change permission to DIR1.

B. The user has no permissions to DIR1, because the Marketing group has no permissions to the directory.

C. The user has only Read, because the user only gets what is assigned to the user directly.

D. The user has Full Control, because Read and Change added together equals Full Control.

39. A user belongs to the Sales group and the Marketing group. The user has the Read permission to a directory named DIR1. The Sales group has the Change permission to DIR1 and the Marketing group has No Access to DIR1. What are the user's effective rights to DIR1?

A. The user has the Read and Change permission to DIR1.

B. The user has no permissions to DIR1 because the Marketing group has no permissions to the directory.

C. The user has only Read, because the user only gets what is assigned to the user directly.

D. The user has No Access because the Marketing group has No Access.

40. Which one of the following statements best describes what happens to file permissions when files are copied and moved on NTFS partitions?

A. When you copy a file on an NTFS partition, the file inherits the permissions of the destination directory. When you move a file on an NTFS partition, the file retains the permissions that it had originally.

B. When you copy a file on an NTFS partition, the file retains the permissions that it had originally. When you move a file on an NTFS partition, the file inherits the permissions of the parent directory.

C. Whenever you move or copy a file on an NTFS partition, it always retains its original permissions.

D. Whenever you move or copy a file on an NTFS partition, it always inherits the permissions of the parent directory.

41. A user calls you and states that while running a disk diagnostic utility on his FAT partition, it was reporting errors relating to lost chains and clusters. Which of the following is most likely the problem?

A. The user is running a disk utility that does not recognize the existence of long file names and is incorrectly reporting errors.

B. The user is running a disk utility that does not recognize the existence of NT and its use should be discontinued immediately.

C. The user should restart the computer in DOS and then run the utility.

D. The user should contact the manufacturer of the utility and request a version that is compatible with NT.

Review Answers

1. C	10. A C D	19. C	28. D	37. D
2. A	11. C	20. B	29. A	38. A
3. B	12. D	21. A	30. D	39. D
4. D	13. A	22. C	31. C	40. A
5. C	14. A	23. A	32. B	41. A
6. D	15. C	24. C	33. D	
7. E	16. B	25. A	34. C	
8. A	17. D	26. C	35. D	
9. D	18. C	27. A	36. C	

Chapter 4

Stop! Before reading this chapter, test yourself to determine how much study time you will need to devote to this section.

1. A Microsoft Network computer that uses _____ can access NetWare resources through a GSNW gateway.

   A. SMB

   B. GSNW

   C. NWLink

   D. TCP/IP

2. A Windows NT computer must use _____ to access a client/server application on a NetWare server.

   A. GSNW

   B. CSNW

   C. FPNW

   D. None of the above

3. Windows NT Remote Access Service (RAS) uses _____ to combine several physical pathways into a single communications link.

   A. Link

   B. MultiConnect

   C. Multilink

   D. RASlink

4. To change the information in a Dial-up Networking phonebook entry, _____.

   A. click on the Edit button in the Dial-up Networking main screen.

   B. click on the More button in the Dial-up Networking main screen.

   C. right-click on the shortcut icon for the phonebook entry and choose Properties.

   D. Either A or C

Answers

1. A (see "Gateway Services for NetWare (GSNW)")
2. D (see "Server and Client/Server Applications")
3. C (see "Configuring Remote Access Service (RAS)")
4. B (see "Editing a Phonebook Entry and Other Options")

Connectivity

4

This chapter will help you prepare for the "Connectivity" section of Microsoft's Exam 70-67, "Implementing and Supporting Microsoft Windows NT Server." The "Connectivity" section includes the following objectives:

Test Objectives

> ▶ Configure Windows NT Server for interoperability with NetWare servers by using various tools. Tools include Gateway Services for NetWare and Migration Tool for NetWare.
>
> ▶ Install and configure Remote Access Service (RAS). Configuration options include configuring RAS communications, configuring RAS protocols, Configuring RAS security, and configuring Dial-up Networking clients.

Microsoft believes Windows NT is the best network operating system available, but Microsoft is aware of a strong NetWare presence. One of the driving forces behind the rapid acceptance of Windows NT is the ease with which it integrates into a NetWare environment.

Microsoft has gone to considerable trouble to make Windows NT compatible with Novell NetWare. Windows NT's NetWare-compatibility features include the NWLink network protocol, which is a clone of Novell's IPX/SPX, and a number of special services designed to help Windows NT and NetWare networks link up smoothly. This chapter describes the services you'll need to interoperate with NetWare. NetWare connectivity is extremely important to Microsoft, and you can bet they'll make it important to you when you sit down with the Windows NT Server exam.

Windows NT Remote Access Service (RAS) also offers some important connectivity features. This chapter will describe Windows

NT RAS, show you how to install and configure RAS, and show you how to configure Dial-Up Networking.

Interoperating with NetWare

Chapter 2 described how to install and configure NWLink, Microsoft's version of the once-secret IPX/SPX protocol suite. It is important to remember that NWLink by itself does not necessarily provide connectivity with NetWare resources. Microsoft provides a set of services that help Windows NT and NetWare systems interoperate. This section outlines the services and components you'll need to interoperate with NetWare for various purposes. You'll learn about these NetWare-related Windows NT services and tools:

▶ Gateway Services for NetWare (GSNW)

▶ Client Services for NetWare (CSNW)

▶ File and Print Services for NetWare (FPNW)

▶ Directory Service Manager for NetWare (DSMN)

▶ Migration Tool for NetWare

You then get a quick look at the components required for NT-based and NetWare-based client/server applications. This section finishes with a quick summary of NetWare connectivity issues.

As you prepare for the Windows NT Server exam, try to imagine these NetWare connectivity issues in the context of real networking situations.

Gateway Services for NetWare (GSNW)

Gateway Services for NetWare (GSNW) is available only with Windows NT Server. GSNW performs the following functions:

▶ Enables Windows NT Server systems to access NetWare file and print resources directly. (GSNW includes the functionality of Windows NT Workstation's Client Services for NetWare service, CSNW, described later in this chapter.)

▶ Enables a Windows NT Server to act as a gateway to NetWare resources. Non-NetWare clients on a Windows NT network then can access NetWare resources through the gateway as if they were accessing Windows NT resources (see fig. 4.1).

Figure 4.1

GSNW enables a Windows NT Server to act as a gateway to NetWare resources.

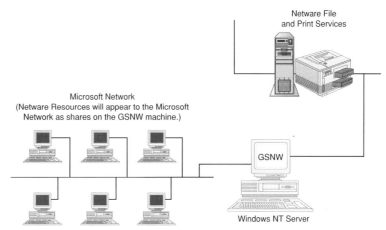

A GSNW gateway can provide Windows NT networks with convenient access to NetWare resources, but it isn't designed to serve as a high-volume solution for a busy network. Because all Windows NT clients must reach the NetWare server through a single connection, performance diminishes considerably with increased traffic. GSNW is ideal for occasional NetWare access—not for large-scale routing.

Network clients with operating systems that use Server Message Block (SMB)—Windows NT, Windows 95, and Windows for Workgroups—can access a share through a GSNW gateway. GSNW supports both NDS-based and bindery-based NetWare systems.

NetWare Directory Service (NDS) is a distributed database of network resources primarily associated with NetWare 4.x systems. Bindery-based NetWare networks are primarily associated with NetWare 3.x.

GSNW is a network service; you install it using the Services tab of the Control Panel Network application (see fig. 4.2). Before installing GSNW, you must remove any NetWare redirectors presently on your system (such as Novell' NetWare services for Windows NT) and reboot. To install GSNW, follow these steps:

1. Choose Start, Settings/Control Panel. Double-click on the Control Panel Network application icon.

2. In the Network application's Network dialog box, select the Services tab. Click on the Add button to open the Select Network Services dialog box.

3. Select Gateway (and Client) Services for NetWare in the Network Service list; then click on OK.

4. Windows NT prompts you for the location of the files (typically, the installation CD-ROM).

5. Windows NT asks if you want to restart your system. You must restart the system to enable the new service.

Figure 4.2

The Services tab of the Network dialog box.

The NetWare client features of GSNW are similar to the features of the CSNW service and are described in the next section.

For an exercise testing this information, see end of chapter.

To enable GSNW to act as a gateway to NetWare resources, you must perform the following steps:

1. Create a group called NTGATEWAY on the NetWare server.

2. Create a user account on the NetWare server for the gateway and add the gateway user account to the NTGATEWAY group.

note

You can use the NetWare Syscon utility to create the NTGATE-WAY group and the gateway's user account.

3. Double-click on the GSNW icon in the Control Panel. The Gateway Service for NetWare dialog box appears (see fig. 4.3). The Preferred Server, Default Tree and Context, Print Options, and Login Script Options frames are discussed in the following section.

4. To configure Windows NT to act as a gateway, click on the Gateway button. The Configure Gateway dialog box appears (see fig. 4.4).

Figure 4.3

The Gateway Services for NetWare dialog box.

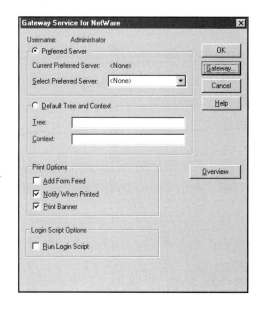

Figure 4.4

The Configure Gateway dialog box.

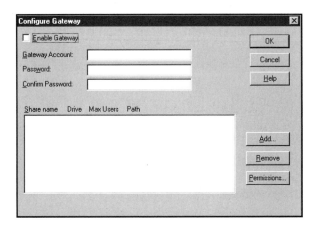

5. Select the Enable Gateway check box. In the Gateway Account text box, enter the name of the account you created on the NetWare server. Below the account name, enter the password for the account and retype the password in the Confirm Password text box.

GSNW essentially enables you to create a Windows NT share for a resource on a NetWare server. Microsoft network machines that use Server Message Block (SMB), such as Windows NT, Windows 95, and Windows for Workgroups, can then access the share even if they don't have NetWare client software. NetWare directories and volumes presently shared through a gateway appear in the Share name list at the bottom of the Configure Gateway dialog box.

To create a new share for a NetWare directory or volume, click on the Add button in the Configure Gateway dialog box. You are asked to enter a share name and a network path to the NetWare resource. You then can enter a drive letter for the share. The share appears to Windows NT, Windows 95, and Windows for Workgroups machines as a network drive on the gateway machine.

The Remove button in the Configure Gateway dialog box removes a gateway share. The Permissions button lets you set permissions for the share.

Client Services for NetWare (CSNW) and the GSNW Client

Client Services for NetWare (CSNW) enables a Windows NT Workstation to access file and print services on a NetWare server (see fig. 4.5). CSNW is incorporated into Windows NT Server's (described in the preceding section). GSNW and CSNW support both NDS-based and bindery-based NetWare servers.

Figure 4.5

CSNW, which is incorporated in GSNW, enables a Windows NT computer to access file and print services as a client on a NetWare network.

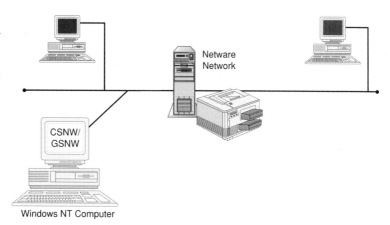

GSNW and CSNW support Novell's NetWare Core Protocol (NCP) and Large Internet Protocol (LIP).

CSNW, like GSNW, is a network service; you install it using the Services tab of the Control Panel Network application (refer to fig. 4.2). If you're running Windows NT Server, CSNW functions are installed automatically when you install GSNW.

To enable your Windows NT Server comptuer to act as a NetWare client, install GSNW (see the preceding section) and restart your system.

The first time you log on after you install CSNW or GSNW, Windows NT prompts you to enter a preferred server and attempts to validate your credentials for the NetWare network.

The Select Preferred Server for NetWare dialog box shows the name of the user attempting to log on and a drop-down list of available NetWare servers. As implied by the username parameter, this is a per-user configuration parameter. The selected server is stored in HKEY_CURRENT_USER, not HKEY_LOCAL_MACHINE.

Choose <None> in the Select Preferred Server for NetWare dialog box if you don't want to have a preferred server authenticate your logon request. Choosing the Cancel button just defers the decision until the next time you log on.

After you select a preferred server, Windows NT always tries to have that server authenticate the user. If the server is unavailable, the user is prompted for a new preferred server. A user can change his or her preferred server at any time via the new CSNW icon in Control Panel (which was added during installation of CSNW).

note

When Windows NT attempts to authenticate a user against the preferred server, the Windows NT-based computer passes the current username and password to the NetWare server. If both the server and the Windows NT-based computer contain the same username/password combination for that user, the user is authenticated immediately. If the preferred server cannot find a match, the user is prompted for a new username and password for the NetWare server.

At first, this is an easy problem to prevent; simply create identical accounts and passwords on each computer. CSNW does not synchronize NetWare passwords with Windows NT passwords, however. As time goes on and Windows NT users change their passwords, the only way users can keep their passwords in sync is to use the Novell SETPASS command to change their NetWare passwords each time they change their Windows NT passwords. This requires some user education on the part of the administrator and good practice on the part of the users.

Double-clicking on the GSNW icon in Control Panel opens the Gateway Service for NetWare dialog box (refer to fig. 4.3), which lets you select a preferred server and a default tree and context for the NetWare network.

You also can set printing options using the Gateway Service for NetWare dialog box, as follows:

▶ Add Form Feed completely ejects the last page from the printer when a job has completed.

▶ Notify When Printed causes a pop-up to appear on the user's display when the job has successfully completed.

▶ Print Banner prints a separator page before each job. The page includes the username of the person who sent the job to the printer as well as the date and time the job was submitted.

You also can choose to run a NetWare logon script.

Connecting to NetWare Servers

CSNW (and the client portion of GSNW) is a redirector implemented as a file system driver, just as is the traditional Windows NT redirector (RDR). As such, it is seamlessly integrated into the Windows NT environment. To connect to a NetWare server's directories, use Explorer or Network Neighborhood.

To connect to a NetWare server's printers, use the Add Printer Wizard in the Printers folder. Select Network Printer Server in the first screen. A display similar to Network Neighborhood then appears, and you can locate the printer on the appropriate server.

You also can use the traditional Windows NT NET USE command to connect to NetWare servers.

When you install GSNW or CSNW, it becomes the default network provider. To change the default back to Microsoft Windows Network, use the Network Access Order button on the Services tab of the Control Panel Network application (this button appears only when you have multiple network providers installed). Network Access Order button invokes the Network Access Order dialog box (see fig. 4.6).

Figure 4.6

The Network Access Order dialog box.

The default provider is listed at the top of the Network Access Order dialog box. You can expand any network provider's servers simply by double-clicking on its entry in Network Neighborhood.

NetWare servers don't appear under the umbrella of a workgroup or domain. That's intentional; after all, workgroups and domains are Microsoft network concepts.

When you double-click on a NetWare server, you will notice the final difference between the two type of networks. On a Windows NT server, directories must be explicitly shared for users to access them. On NetWare servers, however, all directories are public. When you expand a volume on a NetWare server, all the directories and subdirectories in that volume are accessible. If you continue to double-click down the hierarchy of directories, the tree continues to expand.

NetWare users are authenticated as soon as the server itself is selected. If the server's directories are accessible, the user has been authenticated. If the user's Windows NT password and NetWare password don't match, an Enter Network Credentials dialog box appears to give the user a chance to enter the correct NetWare password.

Command Prompt

You can browse the NetWare Network from the command prompt using the NET VIEW command almost as easily as you can browse the Microsoft Windows Network. You just need one extra switch:

```
NET VIEW /NETWORK:NW
```

This command returns a list of available NetWare servers.

To connect to a NetWare server's resource, use the NET USE command. This time, no additional parameters are necessary:

```
NET USE F: \\NWServer\Sys\Public
```

The preceding example would map drive F to the SYS\PUBLIC directory on NWServer. By design, the syntax is identical, whether connecting to a Windows NT server or a NetWare server (which underscores '"Universal"' in the Universal Naming Convention (UNC) syntax).

You can use the NET USE command as the equivalent of the NetWare CAPTURE command, too:

```
NET USE LPT1: \\NWServer\Queue
```

Compatibility Issues

Although NetWare commands now can be accessed from the command prompt, some executables cannot function unless a drive is mapped. For example, although you can access SYSCON by typing \\NWSERVER\SYS\PUBLIC\SYSCON at the command prompt, the program terminates with an error message unless you map a drive so that supporting files can be found as well.

You can run most NetWare utilities from a Windows NT Workstation running GSNW or CSNW, including SYSCON, PCONSOLE, and SETPASS. There are some specific application compatibility problems, however, and you should consult the documentation for GSNW or CSNW if you encounter problems.

File and Print Services for NetWare (FPNW)

File and Print Services for NetWare (FPNW) is an add-on utility that enables NetWare clients to access Windows NT file, print, and application services (see fig. 4.7).

Figure 4.7

The add-on service FPNW lets NetWare clients access resources on a Windows NT system.

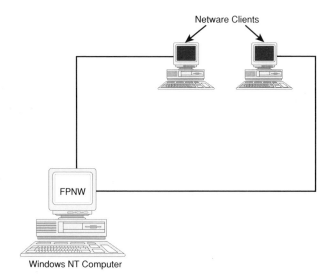

Netware Clients

FPNW

Windows NT Computer

FPNW doesn't require any additional software (such as Server Message Block support) on the NetWare client. In effect, FPNW enables the Windows NT Server to act like a NetWare 3.12 Server. The NetWare client can access the FPNW machine as it would a NetWare server.

Directory Service Manager for NetWare (DSMN)

Directory Service Manager for NetWare (DSMN) is an add-on utility that integrates NetWare and Windows NT user and group account information (see fig. 4.8).

DSMN copies NetWare user and group information to the Windows NT computer. You can use DSMN to manage NetWare accounts from Windows NT. DSMN also can merge server-based

NetWare accounts into a single account database, which the Windows NT computer can then propagate back to the NetWare servers. This enables a single network logon for server-based NetWare accounts.

Figure 4.8

DSMN integrates NetWare and Windows NT user and group accounts.

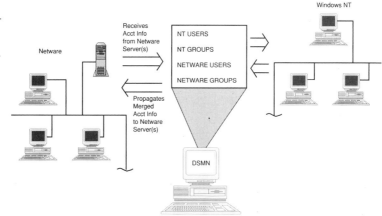

DSMN allows all network accounts (including NetWare accounts) to be managed from User Manager for Domains (see Chapter 3, "Managing Resources").

Migration Tool for NetWare

Microsoft is so eager for NetWare users to migrate to Windows NT that it developed a tool to automate the migration process. The Migration Tool for NetWare transfers file and directory information and user and group account information from a NetWare server to a Windows NT domain controller. The Migration Tool for NetWare also preserves logon scripts and directory and file effective rights. If you want, you can specify which accounts, files, or directories you want to migrate. Migration Tool for NetWare cannot preserve the original NetWare password, but it provides the capability of setting a new password from within the tool.

The Migration Tool for NetWare can migrate NetWare resources to the domain controller on which it is running, or it can execute from a separate NT Server or Workstation and migrate the Net-Ware resources to a domain controller somewhere else on the network (see fig. 4.9). NWLink and Gateway Services for NetWare must be running on both the computer running Migration Tool for NetWare and on the domain controller receiving the migration.

Figure 4.9

The Migration Tool for NetWare dialog box.

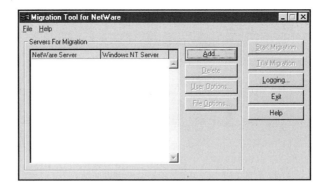

To run the Migration Tool for NetWare, choose Start, Run, and type **nwconv** in the Run dialog box.

The Migration Tool for NetWare provides a number of options for transferring file and account information. Always migrate files and directories to an NTFS partition if possible, because NTFS file and directory permissions provide an equivalent to the trustee rights specified for these resources in the NetWare environment.

Server and Client/Server Applications

A NetWare client that is equipped with Named Pipes, Windows Sockets, or IPX for NetBIOS can access a server-based application (such as Microsoft SQL Server) that is running on a Windows NT computer as long as the Windows NT computer has the NWLink protocol installed.

A Windows NT computer using NWLink can access a client/server application on a NetWare server without requiring any of the connectivity services described in this chapter.

NetWare Connectivity

For the Windows NT Server exam, you should have a good idea of what NetWare-connectivity components you'll need to interoperate with NetWare in various situations. The following list summarizes the preceding discussion of NetWare connectivity. You would do well to memorize this list and be ready to apply it:

▶ The NWLink protocol provides compatibility with Novell Netware IPX/SPX networks.

▶ A Windows NT Workstation computer running CSNW and the NWLink protocol or a Windows NT Server computer running GSNW and the NWLink protocol can connect to file and print services on a NetWare server.

▶ A Windows NT computer using the NWLink protocol can connect to client/server applications on a NetWare server (without requiring additional NetWare-connectivity services).

▶ Any Microsoft network client that uses Server Message Block (Windows NT, Windows 95, or Windows for Workgroups) can access NetWare resources through a NetWare gateway on a Windows NT Server computer that is running GSNW. The NetWare resources will appear to the Microsoft network client as Windows NT resources.

▶ A Windows NT Server system running the add-on utility DSMN can effectively integrate NetWare Server and Windows NT domain account information by copying NetWare account information to Windows NT and propagating the merged information back to the Windows NT Server system. This allows a single network login (across all servers) for NetWare accounts and management of all accounts from User Manager for Domains.

▶ A Windows NT computer running NWLink, GSNW, and the Migration Tool for NetWare can transfer user and group accouts, directories, files, and login scripts from NetWare servers to a Windows NT domain controller.

▶ A NetWare client running IPX can access a Windows NT Server system that is running the add-on utility FPNW.

▶ A NetWare client that supports Named Pipes, Windows Sockets, or IPX with NetBIOS can access a NWLink-enabled Windows NT computer running a server-based application, such as Microsoft SQL Server.

Configuring Remote Access Service (RAS)

Windows NT *Remote Access Service* (RAS) extends the power of Windows NT networking to anywhere you can find a phone line. Using RAS, a Windows NT computer can connect to a remote network via a dial-up connection and fully participate in the network as a network client. RAS also enables your Windows NT computer to receive dial-up connections from remote computers.

Microsoft specifies the following objective for the Windows NT Server exam:

Install and configure Remote Access Service (RAS). Configuration options include configuring RAS communications, configuring RAS protocols, Configuring RAS security, and configuring Dial-up Networking clients.

RAS supports SLIP and PPP line protocols, and NetBEUI, TCP/IP, and IPX network protocols. Because so many Internet users access their service providers using a phone line, RAS often serves as an Internet interface.

The dial-up networking application (in the Accessories program group) lets you create phonebook entries, which are preconfigured dial-up connections to specific sites. The Telephony application in the Control Panel enables the remote user to preconfigure dialing properties for different dialing locations.

RAS can connect to a remote computer using any of the following media:

- ▶ **Public Switched Telephone Network (PSTN).** (Also known as the phone company.) RAS can connect using a modem through an ordinary phone line.

- ▶ **X.25.** A packet-switched network. Computers access the network via a Packet Assembler Disassembler device (PAD). X.25 supports dial-up or direct connections.

- ▶ **Null modem cable.** A cable that connects two computers directly. The computers then communicate using their modems (rather than network adapter cards).

- ▶ **ISDN.** A digital line that provides faster communication and more bandwidth than a normal phone line. (It also costs more—that's why not everybody has it.) A computer must have a special ISDN card to access an ISDN line.

Windows NT 4 also includes a new feature called Multilink. Using Multilink, a Windows NT computer can form a RAS connection using more than one physical pathway. One Multilink connection, for example, could use two modems at once (or one modem line and one ISDN line) to form a single logical link. By using multiple pathways for one connection, Multilink can greatly increase bandwidth. Of course, the computer has to have access to more than one pathway (that is, it must have two modems installed) or you can't use it.

RAS Security

Like everything else in Windows NT, RAS is designed for security. Here are some of RAS's security features:

- ▶ **Auditing.** RAS can leave an audit trail, enabling you to see who logged on when and what authentication they provided.

- ▶ **Callback security.** You can enable RAS server to use callback (hang up all incoming calls and call the caller back), and you can limit callback numbers to prearranged sites that you know are safe.

▶ **Encryption.** RAS can encrypt logon information, or it can encrypt all data crossing the connection.

▶ **Security hosts.** In case Windows NT isn't safe enough, you can add an extra dose of security by using a third-party intermediary security host—a computer that stands between the RAS client and the RAS server and requires an extra round of authentication.

▶ **PPTP filtering.** You can tell Windows NT to filter out all packets except ultra-safe PPTP packets (described later in this chapter in the section "PPTP").

This chapter describes how to configure and use RAS server and dial-up networking.

RAS Line Protocols

RAS supports the following line protocols:

▶ SLIP

▶ PPP

The following sections describe these protocols.

SLIP

Serial Line Internet Protocol (SLIP) is a standard protocol for serial line connections over TCP/IP networks. SLIP is relatively old for the computer age—it was developed in 1984—and, though it hasn't "timed out" yet, it does lack some of the features that are available in PPP. Each node in a SLIP connection must have a static IP address; that is, you can't use nifty Windows NT features such as DHCP and WINS. Unlike PPP, SLIP does not support Net-BEUI or IPX; you must use TCP/IP with SLIP. Also, SLIP cannot encrypt logon information.

PPP

Point-to-Point Protocol (PPP) was originally conceived as a deluxe version of SLIP. Like SLIP, PPP is an industry standard for point-to-point communications, but PPP offers several advantages over SLIP. Most notably, PPP isn't limited to TCP/IP. PPP also supports IPX, NetBEUI, and several other network protocols, such as AppleTalk and DECnet.

Because PPP supports so many protocols, it allows much more flexibility in configuring network communications. Windows NT automatically binds RAS to TCP/IP, NetBEUI, and IPX if those protocols are installed at the same time as RAS.

Another advantage of PPP is that it supports encrypted passwords.

PPTP

Point-to-Point Tunneling Protocol (PPTP) is related to PPP, but is different enough, and important enough, to deserve its own section. PPTP is a protocol that lets you transmit PPP packets over a TCP/IP network securely. Because the Internet is a TCP/IP network, PPTP enables highly private network links over the otherwise highly public Internet. PPTP connections are encrypted, making them a nearly impenetrable to virtual voyeurs.

In fact, PPTP is part of an emerging technology called Virtual Private Networks (VPNs). The point of VPN is to provide corporate networks with the same (or close to the same) security over the Internet that they would have over a direct connection.

Another exciting advantage of PPTP (and another reason that it fits nicely into the scheme of the virtual private network) is that PPTP doesn't discriminate among protocols. Because PPP supports NetBEUI, IPX, and other network protocols, and because a PPTP operates on PPP packets, PPTP actually lets you transmit non-TCP/IP protocols over the Internet.

Because PPTP provides intranet privacy over the open Internet, it can significantly reduce costs in some situations. Networks that once would have depended on extravagant direct connections now can hook up via a local Internet service provider.

Routing with RAS

Windows NT RAS can perform some interesting routing functions. These functions are likely to make their way into the Windows NT Server exam, either as part of the connectivity section or as part of the protocols objective in the planning section.

RAS comes with a NetBIOS gateway. A RAS client using the NetBEUI protocol can connect to a RAS server and, using the NetBIOS gateway on the RAS server, can gain access to the remote LAN beyond the gateway regardless of what protocol the LAN is using (see fig. 4.10).

Figure 4.10

RAS can act as a NetBIOS gateway, connecting NetBEUI clients with networks using other protocols.

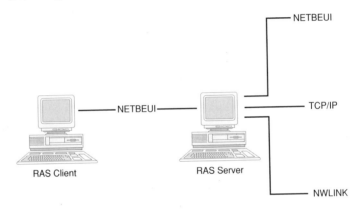

RAS can act as a TCP/IP or IPX router. RAS also is capable of serving as a Service Advertising Protocol (SAP) agent. (*SAP* is a NetWare protocol that lets servers advertise their services to the network.)

The Telephony API

The *Telephony Application Program Interface* (TAPI) provides a standard interface with telephony applications. (Telephony applications are applications that enable a computer to interact with telephone services, such as a network fax service or an online answering machine). TAPI oversees communication between the computer and the phone system, including initiating, answering, and ending calls. In effect, TAPI is a device driver for the phone system.

Windows NT's basic TAPI settings are set up in the Dialing Properties dialog box (see fig. 4.11). The Dialing Properties dialog box maintains location and area code settings, as well as calling card settings and a setting for the dialing type (tone or pulse). The first time you run a TAPI-aware application, you have a chance to set dialing properties. Or, you can reach the Dialing Properties dialog box directly in several ways, including through the Control Panel Telephony and Modems applications.

Figure 4.11

The Dialing Properties dialog box.

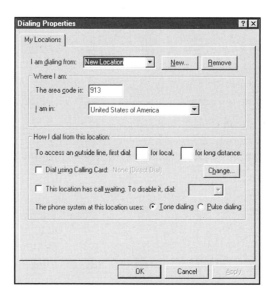

Installing and Configuring RAS

RAS is a network service, and, like other network services, is installed and removed using the Services tab of the Control Panel Network application.

Install RAS as follows:

1. In the Control Panel, double-click on the Network application icon.

2. In the Network dialog box that appears, click on the Services tab and then click on the Add button. The Select Network Service dialog box appears.

3. In the Select Network Service dialog box, choose Remote Access Service from the Network Service list and click on OK (see fig. 4.12). Windows NT prompts you for the path to the Windows NT Installation CD-ROM.

Figure 4.12

The Select Network Service dialog box.

4. Windows NT prompts you for name of an RAS-capable device and an associated communications port (see fig. 4.13). A modem installed on your system typically appears as a default value. Click on OK to accept the modem, or click on the down arrow to choose another RAS-capable device on your system. You also can install a new modem or an X.25 Pad using the Install Modem and Install X25 Pad buttons.

Figure 4.13

Selecting a RAS-capable device.

5. The Remote Access Setup dialog box appears (see fig. 4.14). Click on the Configure button to specify whether to use the port for dial-out connections, dial-in connections, or both (see fig. 4.15). The Port Usage options in figure 4.15 apply only to the port. In other words, you could configure COM1 for Dial out only and COM2 for Receive only. In the Remote

Access Setup dialog box, you also can add or remove a port entry from the list. The Clone button lets you copy a port configuration.

Figure 4.14

The Remote Access Setup dialog box.

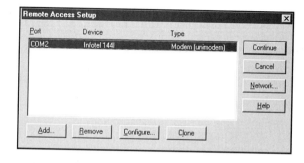

Figure 4.15

The Configure Port Usage dialog box.

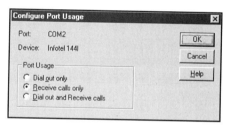

6. Click on the Network button in the Remote Access Setup dialog box to specify the network protocols for your Remote Access Service to support (see fig. 4.16). The Server Settings options in the lower portion of the Network Configuration dialog box appear only if you configure the port to receive calls. Select one or more dial-out protocols. If you want RAS to take care of receiving calls, select one or more server protocols, and choose an encryption setting for incoming connections. You also can enable Multilink. Multilink allows one logical connection to use several physical pathways.

Note in figure 4.15 that a Configure button follows each of the Server Settings protocol options. Each Configure button opens a dialog box that lets you specify configuration options for the protocol, as follows:

▶ The RAS Server NetBEUI Configuration dialog box lets you specify whether the incoming caller will have access to the entire network or to only the RAS server.

Figure 4.16

The Network Configuration dialog box.

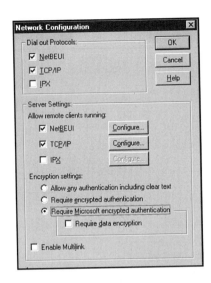

By confining a caller's access to the RAS server, you improve security (because the caller can access only one computer), but you reduce functionality because the caller can't access information on other machines.

▶ The RAS Server TCP/IP Configuration dialog box lets you define how the RAS server assigns IP addresses to dial-up clients (see fig. 4.17). You can use DHCP to assign client addresses, or you can configure RAS to assign IP addresses from a static address pool. If you choose to use a static address pool, input the beginning and ending addresses in the range. To exclude a range of addresses within the address pool, enter the beginning and ending addresses in the range you're excluding in the From and To boxes, then click on the Add button. The excluded range appears in the Excluded ranges box.

The RAS Server TCP/IP Configuration dialog box lets you specify whether a client can access the entire network or only the RAS server. By confining a caller's access to the RAS server, you improve security (because the caller can access only one computer), but you reduce functionality because the caller can't access information on other machines.

Figure 4.17

*The RAS Server
TCP/IP Configu-
ration dialog box.*

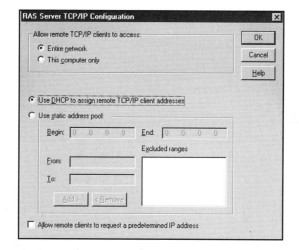

► The RAS Server IPX Configuration dialog box lets you
specify how the RAS server assigns IPX network numbers (see fig. 4.18).

Figure 4.18

*The RAS Server
IPX Configuration
dialog box.*

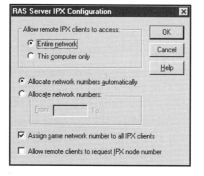

You also can specify whether a client can access the
entire network or only the RAS server. By confining a
caller's access to the RAS server, you improve security
(because the caller can access only one computer), but
you reduce functionality because the caller can't access
information on other machines.

7. After you define the RAS settings to your satisfaction, click
on OK.

8. The Network application's Services tab appears in the foreground. You should see Remote Access Service in the list of services. Click on the Close button.

9. Windows NT asks whether you want to Restart your computer. Choose Yes.

Changing the RAS Configuration

To view or change your RAS configuration, follow these steps:

1. Double-click on the Network icon in the Control Panel and select the Network application's Services tab.

2. Select Remote Access Service from the services list and click on the Properties button.

3. The Remote Access Setup dialog box appears (refer to fig. 4.13). Specify your new RAS configuration as described in steps 5 to 7 in the preceding section.

Dial-Up Networking

The Dial-Up Networking application lets you establish remote connections with other computers. The most common uses for Dial-Up Networking are as follows:

▶ Accessing an Internet service provider

▶ Accessing a remote Windows NT computer or domain

You can open the Dial-Up Networking application as follows:

1. Choose Start, Programs, Accessories.

2. Click on the Dial-Up Networking icon. Figure 4.19 shows the Dial-Up Networking dialog box.

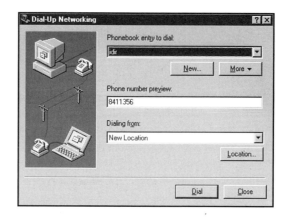

Dial-Up Networking maintains a list of phonebook entries. A *phonebook entry* is a bundle of information that Windows NT needs to establish a specific connection. You can use the Dial-Up Networking application to create a phonebook entry for your access provider, your Windows NT domain, or any other dial-up connection. When it's time to connect, select a phonebook entry from the drop-down menu at the top of the screen and click on the Dial button. If you access the phonebook entry often, you can create a Desktop shortcut that lets you access the phonebook entry directly.

You can create a new phonebook entry as follows:

1. Click on the New button in the Dial-Up Networking dialog box to open the New Phonebook Entry dialog box (see fig. 4.20).

2. In the New Phonebook Entry Basic tab, specify a name for the entry, an optional comment, and the phone number you want Windows NT to dial to make the connection. The Alternates button beside the phone number box lets you specify a prioritized list of alternative phone numbers. You also can specify a different modem or configure a modem from the Basic tab.

3. In the New Phonebook Entry Server tab, specify the communications protocol for the dial-up server (in the Dial-Up server type combo box) and the network protocol (see fig. 4.21). If you select the TCP/IP network protocol, click on the TCP/IP Settings button to configure TCP/IP settings (see fig. 4.22).

Figure 4.21

The New Phonebook Entry Server tab.

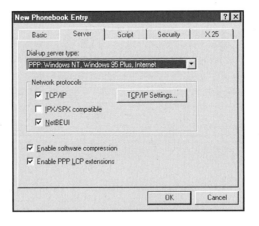

Figure 4.22

The PPP TCP/IP Settings dialog box.

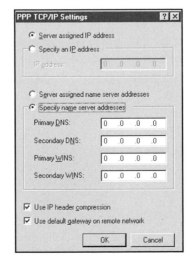

4. The New Phonebook Entry Script tab defines some of the
   connection's logon properties (see fig. 4.23). You can tell
   Windows NT to pop up a terminal window after dialing or to
   run a logon script after dialing. A terminal window enables
   you to interactively log on to the remote server in terminal
   mode. The Run this script radio button option automates
   the logon process. For more information on dial-up logon
   scripts, click on the Edit script button, which places you in a
   file that provides instructions and sample logon scripts,
   called SWITCH.INF. The Before dialing button lets you specify a terminal window or a logon script to execute before you
   dial.

Figure 4.23

*The New
Phonebook Entry
Script tab.*

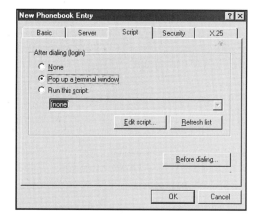

5. In the New Phonebook Entry Security tab, you can require
   encrypted authentication, or you can elect to accept any
   authentication including clear text (see fig. 4.24). You also
   can specify data encryption.

6. The New Phonebook Entry X.25 tab serves only for X.25
   service (described earlier in this chapter). Select an X.25
   access provider from the Network combo box and enter the
   requested information (see fig. 4.25).

Figure 4.24

The New Phonebook Entry Security tab.

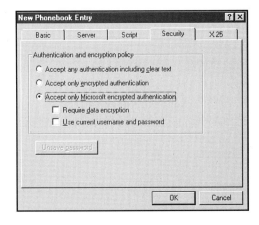

Figure 4.25

The New Phonebook Entry X.25 tab.

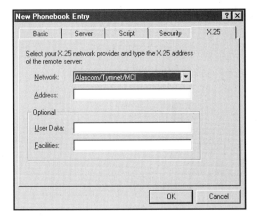

7. After you make changes to the New Phonebook Entry tab, click on OK. The new phonebook entry appears in the Dial-Up Networking dialog box.

Editing a Phonebook Entry and Other Options

The More button in the Dial-Up Networking dialog box offers several options. Figure 4.26 shows the More menu.

Figure 4.26

*The Dial-Up
Networking More
menu.*

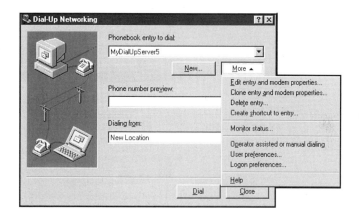

The following list describes the More menu options.

► **Edit entry and modem properties.** Returns you to the set-up tabs you configured in the preceding section (refer to figures 4.20 to 4.25).

► **Create shortcut to entry.** Creates a shortcut to the active phonebook entry (the Phonebook entry to dial drop-down list box in figure 4.19).

► **Monitor status.** Opens the Control Panel Dial-Up Networking Monitor.

► **User preferences.** Opens a User Preferences dialog box that presents the following four tabs:

   ► **Dialing.** Lets you specify dialing options, such as the number of redial attempts and the time between redial attempts. You also can use the Dialing tab to enable or disable Autodial (see the following section). Figure 4.27 shows the Dialing tab.

   ► **Callback.** Tells Windows NT what to do if the server you connect to offers callback. You can specify a number, you can elect to skip callback, or you can tell NT to prompt at the time callback is offered.

   ► **Appearance.** Offers some dial-time interface options (see fig. 4.28).

Figure 4.27

The User Prefer-
ences Dialing
tab.

Figure 4.28

The User Prefer-
ences Appear-
ance tab.

▶ **Phonebook.** Lets you specify a Dial-Up Networking
phonebook. Phonebook entries are stored in a file with
the .pbk extension. The default phonebook is the system phonebook. Using the Phonebook tab, you can
place an entry in your personal phonebook (a user-
specific phonebook), or you can choose a different
phonebook.

▶ **Logon preferences.** Configures Dialing, Callback, Appearance, and Phonebook settings for a remote Windows NT
logon. The Logon preferences options are very similar to the
User preferences options in the previous discussion. The
difference is that the User preferences options apply to a

user who is already logged on to Windows NT and is trying to connect to a remote machine. The Logon preferences apply to a user who isn't yet logged on to Windows NT and wants to log on directly to a Windows NT domain via a remote connection. The Windows NT Ctrl+Alt+Del logon dialog box includes the Logon using dial-up networking check box. If you enable this check box and log on using Dial-Up Networking, the preferences you set in the Logon preferences dialog box apply.

The Logon preferences dialog box doesn't appear unless you log on as an Administrator.

The Location button in the Dial-Up Networking dialog box lets you set a dialing prefix or suffix or specify a Telephony dialing location (refer to fig. 4.18).

AutoDial

For an exercise testing this information, see end of chapter.

Windows NT includes a feature called AutoDial. AutoDial automatically associates network connections with Phonebook entries. This means that if you attempt to access a file or directory that can be accessed only via a dial-up connection, Windows NT attempts to make the dial-up connection automatically.

AutoDial supports IP addresses, Internet host names, and Net-BIOS names. By default, AutoDial is enabled. You can enable/disable AutoDial for specific calling locations using the Dialing tab of the User Preferences dialog box (refer to fig. 4.24).

Exercise Section

Exercise 4.1:   Creating a Share with Gateway Services for NetWare

In Exercise 4.1, you learn how to create a gateway to a NetWare directory using GSNW.

Estimated time: 20 minutes

This chapter described how to create a gateway to a NetWare directory using Gateway Services for NetWare. If you have access to both a NetWare network and an NT network, it is helpful to try the process yourself as a learning exercise. If you don't have access to a NetWare network, take a moment to review the following procedure (also described in the chapter). Do as much as you can from the Windows NT end. For example, install the Gateway Services for NetWare service and start the GSNW application in control panel. Become familiar with the features of the Gateway Services for NetWare dialog box and the Configure Gateway dialog box.

1. Click on the Add button in the Services tab of the Control Panel Application and select Gateway (and Client) Services for NetWare in the Network Service list; then click on OK. Windows NT asks for the location of the files (typically, the installation CD-ROM). Windows NT then asks if you want to restart your system. Click on Yes to restart your system.

2. Create a group called NTGATEWAY on the NetWare server.

3. Create a user account on the NetWare server for the gateway and add the gateway user account to the NTGATEWAY group. You can use NetWare's Syscon utility to create the NTGATEWAY group and the gateway's user account.

4. Double-click on the GSNW icon in Control Panel. The Gateway Service for NetWare dialog box appears (refer to fig. 4.22). To configure Windows NT to act as a gateway, click on the Gateway button.

5. The Configure Gateway dialog box appears (refer to fig. 4.23). Click on the Enable Gateway check box. In the Gateway Account text box, enter the name of the account you created on the NetWare server. Below the account name, enter the password for the account and retype the password in the Confirm Password text box.

6. To create a new share for the NetWare directory or volume, click on the Add button. You are asked to enter a share name and a network path to the NetWare resource. You then can enter a drive letter for the share.

7. From another SMB-compatible computer on the Microsoft network (Windows NT, Windows 95, or Windows for Workgroups), access the gateway computer through Network Neighborhood. Look for the drive letter you entered in step 5 for the NetWare directory. Double-click on the drive letter and browse the NetWare files.

Exercise 4.2:   AutoDial

Exercise 4.2 shows you how to use Windows NT RAS in a practical situation and lets you try out Windows NT's AutoDial feature.

Estimated time: 20 minutes

1. Logon to a Windows NT domain using dial-Up networking. (Check the Logon using Dial-Up Networking check box below the domain name in the Windows NT Logon dialog box.) If you're already connected directly to the domain, unhook the network cable at the back of your computer so you will truly be remote.

When you logon using Dial-Up Networking, Windows NT will ask for a Dial-Up Networking phonebook entry. Make sure you have a phonebook entry for this connection. Also, be sure the RAS service is working on the domain. (This chapter described how to configure RAS and Dial-Up Networking.)

2. Locate a text file or a word processing document on a shared directory somewhere on the domain using Network Neighborhood icon in Explorer. (Use a file type that your computer is configured to recognize automatically—click on Options in the Explorer View menu and choose the File Types tab for a list or registered file types. A .txt file or a Write file should work.) If Explorer can't find the other computers in the domain, pull down the Explorer menu and click Find with the Computer option. Enter the name of the computer with the shared directory you want to access in the Find: Computer dialog and click on the Find Now button (see fig. 4.29). The computer will appear as an icon in the Find:Computer dialog box. Double-click on the icon for a list of shared resources.

Figure 4.29

The Find: Computer dialog box.

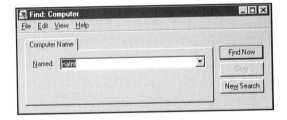

3. When you've located a file on the remote share, right-click on the file and choose Create Shortcut from the shortcut menu that appears. Create a shortcut to the file and drag the shortcut to the Desktop on your own computer.

4. Double-click on the shortcut to make sure it opens the file.

5. Shut down your system.

6. Logon again; this time, don't use dial-up networking. (Deselect the Logon Using Dial-up Networking check box.) You may get a message that says Windows NT could find the domain controller and logged you on using cached account information. Click on OK.

7. Wait until the logon process is finished. Double-click on the shortcut to the file on the remote domain.

8. If you selected the Always prompt before auto-dialing check box in the Appearances tab of the Dial-Up Networking User Preferences dialog box, Windows NT will ask if you want to initiate a connection with the remote file. Click on Yes. Auto-Dial will dial automatically dial the remote network and at-tempt to initiate a connection to the file referenced in the shortcut.

Review Questions

The following questions will test your knowledge of the information in this chapter. For additional questions, see MCP Endeavor and the Microsoft Roadmap/Assessment exam on the CD-ROM that accompanies this book.

1. Migration Tool for NetWare is not capable of preserving _____.

   A. accounts

   B. passwords

   C. files

   D. directories

   E. effective rights

2. A NetWare client machine running_____ can access Microsoft SQL Server on a Windows NT Server system.

   A. IPX with NetBIOS

   B. Client Services for NetWare (CSNW)

   C. File and Print Services for NetWare (FPNW)

   D. NWLink

3. After creating a NetWare gateway using GSNW, you can then create a share on the gateway machine for NetWare files using_____.

   A. GSNW

   B. Explorer or My Computer

   C. the Control Panel Server application

   D. Any of the above

4. Installing the _____service will enable your Windows NT Server machine to access file and print resources on a NetWare server.

    A. File and Print Services for NetWare (FPNW)

    B. Client Services for NetWare (CSNW)

    C. Gateway Services for NetWare (GSNW)

    D. Directory Service Manager for NetWare (DSMN)

5. What is the name of the utility that enables users to access the network through an NT Workstation or Server?

    A. Remote Control

    B. Remote Access Service

    C. Remote Network Service

    D. The Internet

6. The type of connections that RAS supports are (select all that apply):

    A. PSTN (Public Switched Telephone Network)

    B. X.25

    C. IEEE X.400

    D. Null Modem Cable

    E. ISDN

    F. RadioLan

7. What's the name of the feature that lets RAS use more than one communication channel at a time for the same connection?

    A. Multinet

    B. Multilink

    C. ISDN

    D. Multichannel

8. Identify the two serial protocols that RAS supports.

    A. IEEE 802.2 and X.25

    B. Ethernet and Token Ring

    C. SLIP and PPP

    D. ESLIP and PPTP

9. Which of the serial protocols supports the NetBEUI, IPX/SPX, and TCP/IP transport protocols over RAS?

    A. PPP

    B. SLIP

    C. PPTPS

    D. IEEE 802.2

10. You want to let users connect to your local area network using the Internet; however, you're concerned that security might be a problem. Which protocol should you use to ensure a reliable connection and a secure transmission of information?

    A. PPP

    B. SLIP

    C. IEEE 802.2

    D. PPTP

11. A user calls you and states that he's getting connected to his NT Workstation via RAS, but cannot see any resources on the network. What could be causing the problem?

    A. The user is using a userid that isn't configured to have network access via RAS.

    B. He's dialing in with a protocol configured for "This computer only" when it needs to configured for "Entire network."

    C. He needs to use a different protocol. NetBEUI isn't routable, so he can't see any other devices on the network if he's using it as his dial-in protocol.

    D. He needs to configure his RAS server to use ISDN because the PSTN can support only a limited amount of bandwidth.

12. A user is trying to dial in to the NT Server-based RAS server. The user is connecting but gets disconnected immediately and receives a message that says he isn't an authorized dial-in user. What is the first thing you should do?

A. Restart the NT Server, because one of the modems must be disabled.

B. Change the security configuration options on the RAS server to enable any authentication method including clear text.

C. Check to make sure the user has dial-in permissions in User Manager for Domains.

D. Tell the user to restart his remote system and try again.

13. You're trying to run a program from a NetWare server over your RAS connection. You have installed the NWLink-compatible transport protocol at your remote computer but you still cannot connect to the NetWare server. What did you forget to do?

A. You need to install the Client Service for NetWare (CSNW) so you can access a NetWare server using file and print services.

B. You need to install the FPNW (File and Print Services for NetWare) on the RAS Server to gain access to the NetWare servers.

C. You must dial in to the NetWare server directly.

D. You have to change your protocol to TCP/IP and install TCP/IP on the NetWare server.

14. You have several salespeople who dial in to your network via RAS. How can you configure the security options in RAS so the users can minimize long distance phone charges?

A. Configure the user's Dial-Up Networking software to use PPTP, which bypasses the PSTN billing computers, thus giving the users free long distance service.

B. Configure the RAS service to perform a callback based on the number specified by the user dialing in to the RAS server. The server authenticates the logon and then disconnects and calls the user back at the specified number.

C. Issue the users long distance calling cards and have their RAS calls billed directly to the company.

    D. Make sure the users are calling only from public tele-
phones and are making collect calls to the RAS server.
Then configure the RAS server to accept collect calls.

15. If you're having problems with the RAS server, what can you
do to have NT create a log?

    A. Under Remote Access Administrator, configure the
logging option.

    B. Under Control Panel, Network, Services, configure
RAS to write all connection information to the System
log.

    C. In the Registry, set the parameter Logging under the
following key to 1 to create a PPP.LOG file in the
<winnt root>\system32\Ras directory: HKEY_LOCAL_
MACHINE\System\CurrentControlSet\Services\Rasman\PPP\

    D. Run the program Raslog.exe, to create a RAS log in the
<winnt root>\system32\Ras directory.

16. Users would like to be able to connect to the Internet using
the company's T1 connection from home. You configure
RAS to allow your users to dial in. What protocol must they
use to dial in to the RAS server?

    A. IEEE 802.2

    B. Ethernet

    C. NetBEUI

    D. TCP/IP

17. Your management is concerned that accessing the network
via RAS may open up security problems. What features does
RAS support that help alleviate some of these concerns?

    A. RAS supports the U.S. Government DES (Data Encryp-
tion Standard) and encrypts all data going across the
communication channel.

    B. RAS, in fact, can be more secure than a LAN connec-
tion because of the Callback security, Encryption of
userid and password information, and PPTP features.

    C. RAS is not secure over standard PSTN connections unless data scrambling equipment is used on both ends of the connection.

    D. You can obtain a C2 level version the RAS product which meets U.S. Government standards for security.

18. Which statement below correctly identifies the differences between the RAS software running on Windows NT Workstation and RAS software running on Windows NT Server?

    A. When RAS is running on NT Workstation, you can access only the shared resources on that machine. When it is running on NT Server, you can access resources on the entire network.

    B. When RAS is running on NT Workstation you can access shared resources on the entire network, except for resources on NetWare Servers. Before you can do so, you must be running RAS on Windows NT Server.

    C. RAS running on Windows NT Workstation supports only one simultaneous connection whereas, if it is running on NT Server, it can support up to 256 connections.

    D. RAS running on Windows NT Workstation supports up to 256 simultaneous connections whereas if it's running on NT Server, it can support only one simultaneous connection, because the server is running other services that tie up the CPU.

19. You want remote TCP/IP RAS clients to have access to the entire TCP/IP network, but right now they can only connect to the RAS server machine. _____ will enable the client to reach the network.

    A. The Entire Network check box in the Server tab of the Dial-Up Networking Edit Phonebook Entry dialog box

    B. The Entire Network radio button in the Remote Access Permissions dialog box of the Remote Access Admin application

    C. The Entire Network radio button in the TCP/IP Configuration dialog box accessible via the Network button in the Remote Access Setup dialog box

    D. A, B, and C are all necessary

Review Answers

1. B	6. A B D E	11. B	16. D
2. A	7. B	12. C	17. B
3. A	8. C	13. A	18. C
4. C	9. A	14. B	19. C
5. B	10. D	15. C	

Chapter 5

Stop! Before reading this chapter, test yourself to determine how much study time you will need to devote to this section.

1. You are attempting to monitor disk performance statistics using Performance Monitor; however, all the statistics are showing 0. Why?

   A. Disk performance counters are not available on 486 computers because of the overhead they impose.

   B. Disk performance counters are usable only on SCSI controllers.

   C. Disk performance counters are usable only on IDE controllers.

   D. By default, disk performance counters are turned off unless you type **diskperf-y** at the command prompt.

2. By default, Windows NT Server is configured to work best as a file server for _____ users.

   A. 10

   B. 32

   C. 64

   D. 256

3. The Performance Monitor counter Bytes Total/sec measures the performance of _____.

   A. the physical disk

   B. the network segment

   C. the Server service

   D. the processor

Answers

1. D (see "The PhysicalDisk and LogicalDisk Objects")
2. C (see "Optimizing the Server Service")
3. C (see "The Server Object")

Chapter 5

Monitoring and Optimization

This chapter will help you prepare for the "Monitoring and Optimization" section of Microsoft's Exam 70-67, "Implementing and Supporting Windows NT Server 4.0." Microsoft provides the following specific objectives:

Test Objectives

- ▶ Monitor performance of various functions by using Performance Monitor. Functions include: processor, memory, disk, network.

- ▶ Identify performance bottlenecks.

The discussion of optimizing techniques (preceding the "Performance Monitor" section) provides a better understanding of Windows NT. You may see some of this material, such as the section on "Optimizing the Paging File," for either the "Optimizing" or the "Troubleshooting" sections of the Windows NT Server exam.

As with any computer solution, the performance of your applications on Windows NT depends on the combination of hardware and software on your system. A good match of the two provides a cost-effective computing solution. A mismatch of the two, however, results in inefficient use of resources or inadequate performance. Fortunately, Windows NT has many self-optimizing characteristics that don't require user intervention. With some careful planning, a typical installation can show some decent performance without the need for tinkering with obscure parameters in the Registry. This chapter looks at some of the steps you can take to make your Windows NT system (and your network) run more efficiently. You will also learn about a useful tool called Performance Monitor that will help you monitor and analyze what is going on within your system.

Performance Optimization

Optimal performance seems simple enough to define: completing a task in the shortest amount of time. Optimizing the performance of a system is a matter of arranging the resources of the system in such a way that the desired task is finished as quickly as possible. It means getting the best results with the hardware and software you have.

Optimization of a task on your system, then, consists of measuring and analyzing the resource demands of the task to determine what can be done to make it finish in a shorter period of time.

Before you can get truly optimal performance from your system, however, you need to answer some very important questions:

▶ What task or tasks on the system are most important?

▶ Do you want to optimize the utilization of the hardware, or the speed of a particular application or service?

The answers to these questions determine what you should measure and how to decide whether your performance is "optimal."

Performance Objectives

On a file server, for example, the objective could be to service requests from clients for files as quickly as possible. By measuring the number of bytes transferred to all the server's clients across the network in a given period of time, you can tell whether changes you made to the system's configuration made performance better or worse.

On the other hand, what would be "optimal performance" for a Primary Domain Controller (PDC) responsible for replicating a large account database to many Backup Domain Controllers (BDCs)? In such a case, the objective could be to achieve synchronization of the account database throughout the WAN in a timely manner with the minimum amount of network traffic. To know whether performance was optimal, you would need to measure two things: the amount of time it takes for changes to the account database to be implemented on all domain controllers, and the amount of network traffic that the domain synchronization generates.

Optimizing performance of a database server might include this objective: Provide the fastest response time for queries against the customer service database. If your goal is to make the database task complete as quickly as possible, regardless of the impact on other processes on the system, optimization could result in non-database tasks running more slowly than before.

Yet another performance goal could be to make the most efficient use of resources to get the greatest amount of work completed by all processes on the system. To achieve this goal, you need to optimize overall throughput and efficiency, making certain that processes do not get blocked by bottlenecks created by other processes.

After you optimize performance of your application (that is, get the best performance from the hardware and software you have), the next question is whether that level of performance meets your business goals. You may have the best performance possible with your existing system, but to get adequate performance you may need to upgrade one or more components, such as memory, disk, or processor.

The best way to know what you can do to improve performance is to measure it. Gathering data on how your system performs under various circumstances gives you the information you need to make appropriate changes to your system.

Windows NT Tunes Itself

One of Microsoft's design goals for Windows NT was that it should not require a user to make changes to Registry settings to get good performance. One of the problems with optimizing performance with any operating system is that what passes for "optimal configuration" changes as the demands on the system fluctuate. How large should the paging file be, for example? At one point in the day, a large paging file might be optimal, while a few hours or minutes later, a smaller paging file might be optimal.

Asking users and administrators to make these kinds of frequent configuration changes is not practical, and yet leaving a static configuration would inevitably lead to inefficiencies. So, Microsoft decided to let the operating system itself handle evaluating settings, such as the size of the disk cache and paging file, and adjust them dynamically as resource demands change.

As a result, Windows NT does most of the task of optimizing overall performance of the system without requiring manual changes to Registry parameters. Windows NT dynamically adjusts the balance between the size of the disk cache and the amount of RAM used for applications, for example, in response to resource demands on the system.

Reasons to Monitor Performance

Although there is little to tune in NT itself, you still have several reasons to monitor system performance.

Optimizing Specific Tasks

If you have a particular application on your server that you want to optimize, monitoring system performance can tell you whether changing your hardware would enable your application to run faster. It also can uncover contention by multiple applications for resources.

If you are setting up a database server, for example, performance data can tell you whether you have excess capacity to handle additional work, or whether you have a resource shortage affecting performance. If other applications are competing for the same resources as your database application, you can move the other applications to another server that is not as busy.

Troubleshooting Performance Problems

One of the most difficult kinds of performance problem to troubleshoot is diagnosing transient network problems. A sudden increase in interrupts generated by a malfunctioning network card can bring server performance to a screeching halt as the processor handles all the interrupts. If you monitor key indicators of network performance (number of errors, number of interrupts processed), you can be alerted of problems as they occur.

Planning for Future Needs

Another reason to monitor performance is that it enables you to detect changes in the way that the server is being used by users. If users are using a file server more frequently to store very large files, for example, the increased demands for file services can be measured and documented.

By anticipating changes in demand for the server's resources, you can take appropriate action before performance suffers.

Configuration Changes That Affect Performance

You can, however, change many things that affect overall system performance. All these strategies have the effect of shifting the demands for resources to achieve higher throughput.

Adding or Upgrading Hardware Components

This section furnishes examples of common hardware upgrades that may improve performance of their respective subsystems.

Processor

- ▶ Upgrade the speed of the processor.

- ▶ Add another processor (for example, two Pentium processors on an SMP system).

- ▶ Upgrade the secondary cache.

Memory

- ▶ You can never have too much RAM. Having adequate RAM reduces the need for paging memory to and from the hard disk.

▶ Shadowing of the ROM BIOS in RAM does not improve performance under Windows NT. Disabling this feature can, therefore, make more memory available to the system.

Disks

▶ Replace slow disks with faster ones.

▶ Use NTFS for partitions larger than 400 MB.

▶ Use a defragmentation tool if disks become fragmented.

▶ Upgrade from IDE to SCSI.

▶ Use a controller with the highest possible transfer rate and best multitasking functionality.

▶ Isolate disk I/O-intensive tasks on separate physical disks and/or disk controllers.

▶ Create a stripe set to gain the advantage of simultaneous writes to multiple disks if your hardware will support it.

Network

▶ Get a network card with the widest data bus available on your system. If your system has a PCI bus, for example, use a PCI network adapter rather than an ISA adapter. This consideration is especially important for network servers.

▶ Divide your network into multiple networks, attaching the server to each network with a different adapter. Allocating the server requests across the two separate interfaces alleviates congestion at the server.

Fault Tolerance

▶ If using software-based fault tolerance (such as striping with parity or RAID-5), use a hardware-based solution instead. Using RAID-5 implemented in hardware takes the burden of calculating the parity information off the processor.

▶ If the goal is the greatest availability of data, you could consider mirroring (via Windows NT fault tolerant drivers) two hardware-based RAID-5 arrays. There are also solutions for Windows NT for mirroring of entire servers, such as Octopus from Octopus Technologies.

Removing Unnecessary Software Components

To optimize your system, you can remove any software components that are using precious processor and memory resources. These software components fall into three categories: device drivers, network protocols, and services.

Device Drivers

Any drivers that are loaded into memory but not used should be removed. If you have a SCSI driver loaded for a non-existent adapter, for example, remove it. If you have an extra network adapter installed, but it is not currently connected to the network, remove the driver.

Be extremely careful when removing or disabling components in Windows NT. Removing the wrong components can make your system unstable or prevent it from booting. If you remove one of NT's standard drivers by mistake, you can run the Windows NT Setup program (WINNT32.EXE) to refresh the system files.

Network Protocols

Remove any unnecessary network protocols. If all your systems can communicate using NWLink, for example, remove NetBEUI. Loading protocols that are not necessary increases network traffic and processing overhead without improving performance.

You can remove the bindings for a protocol selectively, rather than removing the entire protocol component, by using the Bindings tab of the Control Panel Network application (see fig. 5.1). The Bindings tab in the Control Panel Network application enables you to enable and disable network bindings. In the figure, the circular mark beside NetBEUI Protocol indicates that it has been disabled for the Server service. This server will no longer service file and print requests that come via NetBEUI.

Figure 5.1

The Network dialog box.

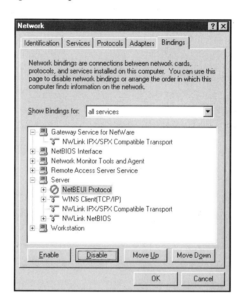

Services

Any services that this server does not need to provide should be disabled, or configured to start manually. If a server will not be providing print services, for example, you can disable the Spooler service.

You can display the list of installed services by choosing the Services application in the Control Panel, as shown in figure 5.2. You can free up wasted processor and memory resources by disabling unneeded services.

Figure 5.2

*The Services
dialog box.*

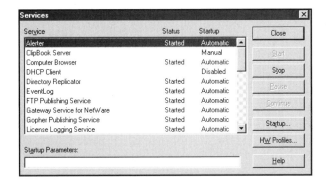

You can start and stop services from the command prompt. To
stop the Spooler service, for example, type the following command:

net stop spooler

To start the Spooler service, type this command:

net start spooler

You can combine the NET START command with the AT command to start and stop services as needed, locally or on another system:

at \\myserver 12:00 net start spooler

This technique is useful when you need certain services
across slow WAN links only at certain times of the day, such
as directory replication.

Replacing Inefficient Software

If your system has applications or drivers that use system resources
inefficiently, you may not be able to make a particular application
run faster. A poorly coded application or device driver can adversely affect performance of the entire system.

If your performance monitoring uncovers a software component
that makes unacceptably large resource demands, the solution is
to replace the offending software.

If the slow application is a 16-bit application, you may be able to find a faster 32-bit version.

Changing Windows NT Performance Parameters

Several relatively easy-to-change settings can make a substantial difference in performance.

Optimizing the Paging File

The Virtual Memory Manager in Windows NT is responsible for managing all the memory pages on the system, including physical memory (RAM) and virtual memory (the paging file). Whenever an application makes a reference to a page of memory that isn't currently located in physical RAM, a page fault occurs. Excessive paging activity dramatically affects overall system performance. Adding RAM reduces the need for paging, so when in doubt, add more RAM!

You configure the size of the paging file in the Virtual Memory dialog box (see fig. 5.3). To open the Virtual Memory dialog box, click on the Change button in the Performance tab of the Control Panel System application. When the system starts up, Windows NT creates a paging file (PAGEFILE.SYS) and sets its size to the minimum value in the Virtual Memory dialog box. The Virtual Memory Manager then monitors system activity and can increase the size of the paging file up to the maximum value if it determines that paging would be more efficient.

Figure 5.3

The Virtual Memory Manager.

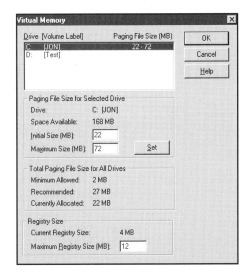

The following are general recommendations regarding the virtual memory settings:

▶ Consider spreading the paging file across multiple disks if your hardware supports writing to those disks at the same time.

▶ Move the paging file to the disk(s) with the lowest amount of total disk activity (see fig. 5.4).

Figure 5.4

Optimizing the paging file.

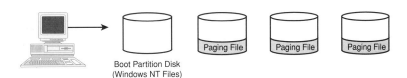

It's better to put the paging file on the disk(s) with the lowest amount of disk activity. If your system has two disks, consider putting the paging file on the disk that isn't the boot disk. (The boot disk contains Windows NT system files.) If you have multiple disks, try distributing the paging file among all disks except the boot disk.

▶ If you plan to use Windows NT's Recovery feature, which writes out debugging information if a stop error occurs to disk, your swap file must be larger than the amount of physical RAM present on the system.

▶ Monitor the size of the paging file under peak usage and then set the minimum size to that value. Making the minimum paging file size large enough eliminates the need for Virtual Memory Manager to increase its size (and saves processor cycles).

▶ To determine the amount of RAM to add to reduce paging activity, use a tool, such as Performance Monitor, to determine the amount of memory each application needs. Then remove applications (noting their working set sizes) until paging activity falls within acceptable limits. The amount of memory freed up by terminating those applications is the amount of physical RAM that the system requires.

Optimizing the Server Service

Another setting that can affect performance is the configuration of the Server service. To access the Server dialog box (see fig. 5.5), choose the Services tab in the Control Panel Network application, select the Server service, and click on the Properties button. By default, Windows NT Server is configured to work best as a file server for 64 or more users. Changing the Server service settings adjusts the amount of RAM and other resources allocated for the Server service to use. Table 5.1 provides a description of each of these settings.

Figure 5.5

The Server dialog box, accessible through the Services tab of the Control Panel Network application.

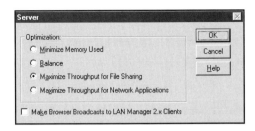

Table 5.1

Server Service Optimization

Setting	Description
Minimize Memory Used	Up to 10 connections
Balance	Up to 64 connections
Maximize Throughput for File Sharing	64 or more connections, large file cache (for file servers)
Maximize Throughput for Network Application	64 or more connections, small file cache (for servers)

Optimizing Other Services

Other services on your system may have Registry settings that you need to adjust for optimal performance. Table 5.2 lists some common values for standard Windows NT services that would be a good starting point for evaluation.

If you have installed additional services on your system, research the Registry parameters associated with those services for performance enhancement opportunities.

Table 5.2

Some Common Registry Values for Standard Windows NT Services

Service	Value
Net Logon	Pulse, Pulse Concurrency, Pulse Maximum, Replication Governor
Directory Replication	Interval, Guard Time
Computer Browser	Hidden, IsDomainMaster, MaintainServerList
Spooler	DefaultSpoolDirectory, PriorityClass

Rescheduling Resource-Intensive Tasks

Demands for resources on a server often fluctuate widely at different times of day. A server running an accounting package meets its greatest demands at the end of an accounting period. A logon server typically experiences a spike in authentication requests at the beginning of the day. Print servers often experience their heaviest demands during late morning and late afternoon. Shifting some of the demand from the peak period to other times can help alleviate the load on the server (see fig. 5.6). In addition, any task that competes for resources with your primary application should be scheduled to non-peak hours.

Figure 5.6

The Scheduling tab of the Printer Properties dialog box enables you to specify when a printer will be available.

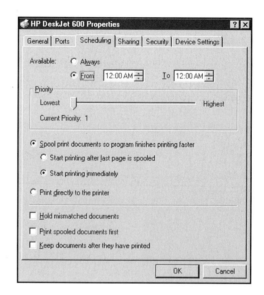

If you have a batch job that is processor-intensive, for example, do not schedule it to run on a domain controller at 8:00 a.m., when most users are logging on and logon authentication demands are at their greatest. Shift demands for resources to times when you have a surplus of the resource available.

Moving Tasks to Another System

If you find that you cannot resolve a resource shortage in an acceptable way on your system, you may be able to move the demand to another machine that has idle resources.

If you have two applications on a server, both of which are I/O-intensive, for example, you may be able to improve performance of both applications by moving one of them to another less busy server (see fig. 5.7).

Figure 5.7

Spreading out the workload.

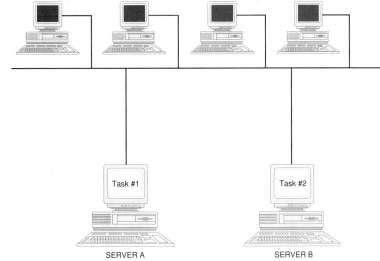

SERVER A   SERVER B

If you have two I/O-intensive applications running on a server, consider moving one application to a different server to even out the workload.

In a client/server application, you might also be able to spread out the load of your application by running portions of it using the idle processing capacity of other systems on the network.

Before You Change Anything

Before you can make any of these changes, you first must do some detective work. You have to be able to isolate which resource on the system has become the bottleneck; then you have to discover the source of the demand for that resource.

Suppose you find that while a certain task is being performed, the processor is busy 100 percent of the time. You cannot conclude that the problem is that you need a faster processor. You have to determine why the processor was busy. If your system has a memory shortage, for example, the processor could be busy handling the increased need to manage virtual memory. Alternatively, your task could have invoked another process that was ill-behaved and consumed the processor.

This kind of investigative work requires a measurement tool that can tell you what is really going on with your system.

Performance Monitor

For an exercise testing this information, see end of chapter.

By far the most useful tool for measuring performance on NT systems is Performance Monitor. Performance Monitor installs to the Administrative Tools program group by default. You can use Performance Monitor for the following tasks:

▶ Measuring the demand for resources on your system

▶ Identifying bottlenecks in your system performance

▶ Monitoring the behavior of individual processes

▶ Monitoring the performance of remote systems

▶ Generating alerts to inform you that an exception condition has occurred

▶ Exporting performance data for analysis using other tools

Figure 5.8 shows an example of a Performance Monitor chart measuring various aspects of a system's performance.

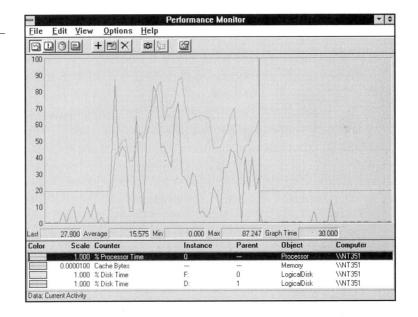

Performance Monitor is an essential tool for monitoring your system. You can use it to gather everything from general indicators of system health to details on individual processes on the system.

You can configure Performance Monitor to record a variety of statistical measurements (called *counters*) for a variety of system hardware and software components (called *objects*). Each object has its own collection of counters. The System object, for example, has counters that measure Processor Queue length, System Calls/sec, and so on. The Paging File object has counters that measure %Usage and %Usage Peak.

Windows NT Server exam objectives specify that you should be familiar with how to use Performance Monitor to measure processor, memory, disk, and network functions. Performance Monitor comes with Processor, Memory, and PhysicalDisk objects (all with associated counters) for measuring processor, memory, and disk functions. The Server object and the Network Segment object are two good indicators of network functions.

This section offers some guidelines on detecting bottlenecks and discusses some of the counters you can use to measure processor, memory, disk, and network activity. The exercises at the end of this chapter provide you with step-by-step instructions on how to use Performance Monitor to create charts, logs, and reports.

Microsoft lists the following objectives for the Monitoring and Optimizing section of the Windows NT Server exam:

▶ Monitor performance of various functions by using Performance Monitor. Functions include processor, memory, disk, network.

▶ Identify performance bottlenecks.

Bottleneck—The Limiting Resource

When you understand the tools you need for measuring your system's performance, you are ready to dig into the data to determine how to improve it.

This section presents a simple strategy for detecting the part of your system that has become the performance bottleneck.

The term *bottleneck* is a descriptive term that comes from a familiar phenomenon. If you take a bottle filled with your favorite beverage and turn it upside down, the rate at which the liquid pours out of the bottle depends on one thing: the width of the neck. In this sense, the limiting characteristic of the bottle, the characteristic that prevents a faster rate, is the neck of the bottle. If the neck were wider, you could pour the contents of the bottle more quickly.

The bottleneck on your system is the resource that limits the rate at which a task can complete. If the resource were faster, or you had more of it, the task would finish sooner. If your task uses processor, network, and disk resources, but mostly spends time using the disk, for example, the disk is the bottleneck. After you identify the bottleneck, you can resolve it by changing or reallocating your resources (such as adding a faster hard disk).

The simplest way to detect the bottleneck on your system is to examine the amount of time that the various components of your system consume in completing a task. The component that uses the most time to complete its portion of the task is the bottleneck.

Suppose that, using Performance Monitor, you determined that Windows NT consumed .5 seconds of processor time, .1 second accessing the network, and .8 seconds accessing the disk in executing your task. During most of the time the task is running, the processor and network are sitting idle waiting for the disk (see fig. 5.9). After you add a faster hard disk, the disk access is down to .4 seconds, but the processor still takes .5 seconds. Now the processor is the bottleneck.

Figure 5.9

Identifying a bottleneck.

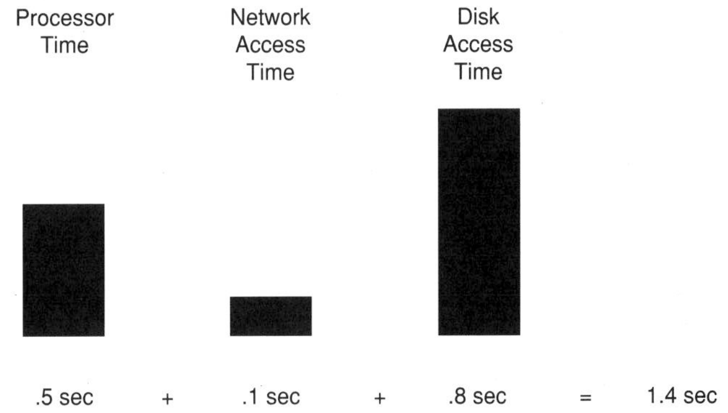

Processor Time	Network Access Time	Disk Access Time

.5 sec   +   .1 sec   +   .8 sec   =   1.4 sec

The subtask that consumes the greatest share of execution time is the bottleneck. In figure 5.9, the disk is the bottleneck.

Overall Performance Indicators

A reasonable place to start in monitoring performance for a server in Windows NT is to watch a number of general counters in Performance Monitor. These counters can provide a great deal of insight into the performance of the system as a whole. If you are not certain what to monitor, start with these and then gather more detail as you determine which component is the bottleneck.

Table 5.3 lists four counters that can give you a good indicator of overall system health.

Table 5.3

Counters that Provide an Indicator of Overall Performance	
Object	Counter
Processor	% Processor Time
Memory	Pages/sec
Physical Disk	% Disk Time
Server	Bytes Total/sec
Network Segment	% Network utilization

The following sections describe the counters in table 5.3, as well as some other important counters you may need to measure the performance of the processor, memory, physical disk, and server objects. You should be familiar with these counters for the Windows NT Server exam.

> You can use Performance Monitor to monitor these counters on your system regularly, including logging the activity to disk. If you have multiple servers to monitor, you can monitor all of them from one Performance Monitor session by adding counters from each of the systems.

The Processor Object

The following are useful counters for the processor object. In looking at the processor, be certain to remember that high levels of processor activity can result from two situations other than handling a processor-intensive task:

▶ A severe memory shortage with the processor busy managing virtual memory (swapping pages of memory to and from the disk).

▶ The system is busy handling a large number of interrupts.

In either of these cases, replacing the processor with a faster one does not address the real problem.

% Processor Time

This counter measures the amount of time the processor spent executing a non-idle thread. In effect, it is the percent of time that the processor was busy. If the average value exceeds 80 percent, the processor could be the bottleneck.

Interrupts/sec

This counter measures the number of interrupts the processor handles per second. An increase in the number of interrupts can indicate hardware failures in I/O devices such as disk controllers and network cards.

System: Processor Queue Length

This counter measures the number of threads waiting in the queue for an available processor. Generally, if the number of threads in the queue exceeds two, you have a problem with processor performance.

The Memory Object

In general, the symptoms of a memory shortage on the system are a busy processor (managing the virtual memory) and a high level of disk activity on the disk that contains the page file (accessing the disk to read and write memory pages).

Pages/sec

This counter measures the number of times that a memory page had to be paged in to memory or out to the disk. An increase in this value indicates an increase in paging activity.

Available Bytes

This counter measures the amount of physical memory available. When this value falls below 1 MB, you are getting excessive paging.

The PhysicalDisk and LogicalDisk Objects

Before you can use Performance Monitor to monitor disk activity, you must enable the disk performance counters. Otherwise, all values for the disk counters report zeroes in Performance Monitor.

To turn on the disk performance counters, log on as a user with administrative privileges and type the following:

```
diskperf -y
```

> To start the disk counters on a remote computer, add the computer name to the `diskperf` command:
>
> ```
> diskperf -y \\computername
> ```

The PhysicalDisk object measures the performance of a physical disk. The LogicalDisk object records parameters pertaining to a logical disk. A logical disk is a partition or logical drive that is accorded a drive letter (C, D, and so on).

PhysicalDisk: % Disk Time

This counter reports the percentage of time that the physical disk was busy reading or writing.

PhysicalDisk: Avg. Disk Queue Length

The average disk queue length is the average number of requests for a given disk (both read and write requests).

LogicalDisk: % Disk Time

This counter reports the percentage of time that the logical disk (for example, C) was busy. To monitor the total activity of all the partitions on a single disk drive, use the Physical Disk: % Disk Time counter.

LogicalDisk: Disk Queue Length

This counter measures the number of read and write requests waiting for the logical disk to become available. If this counter exceeds two, disk performance is suffering.

The Server Object

The Server component is responsible for handling all SMB-based requests for sessions and file and print services. If the Server service becomes the bottleneck, requests from clients are denied, forcing retries and creating slower response times and increased traffic.

Bytes Total/sec

This counter measures the number of bytes sent to and received from the network. It provides an overall indicator of how much information the Server service is handling. When the combined total of this counter for all your servers nears the maximum throughput for your network medium, you have run out of network capacity and need to subdivide the network.

Pool Nonpaged Failures and Pool Paged Failures

This counter measures the number of times that a request from the server to allocate memory failed. These failures are indicators of a memory shortage.

Establishing Baseline Performance Data

Many of the counters that Performance Monitor provides cannot be interpreted without some baseline data to which to compare it. The number of bytes read per second from the disk varies tremendously depending of the type of drive and controller that you have. The historical data for these counters, however, can provide a basis for comparison.

It is a good idea to log performance from your servers at various times of the day, regularly. Then if you do encounter a performance problem, you can look at the historical data to see how the demands on the server have changed over time. If you see changes in the percent of free space on the disk or the number of bytes that the Server component is handling, for example, you can make appropriate adjustments in the hardware before a performance problem develops.

With the right combination of hardware and software, Windows NT Server requires minimal to no tuning. Determining the right hardware for your needs, however, is critical in getting the best performance. Knowing how to interpret performance data for your system can help you understand how changes to your hardware will affect performance.

Exercise Section

Exercise 5.1: Creating a Chart in Performance Monitor

Exercise 5.1 will help you do the following: become familiar with the process of creating and reading a Performance Monitor chart; understand the basic components of the Performance Monitor main window and the Add to Chart dialog box; and learn how to turn on disk performance counters by using the `diskperf` command.

Estimated Time: 25 minutes

1. Choose Start, Programs, Administrative Tools, and click on Performance Monitor. The Performance Monitor window appears.

2. Choose Edit, Add to Chart (see fig. 5.10). The Add to Chart dialog box appears (see fig. 5.11). You also can open the Add to Chart dialog box by clicking on the plus sign in the toolbar of the Performance Monitor window.

Figure 5.10

The Performance Monitor window.

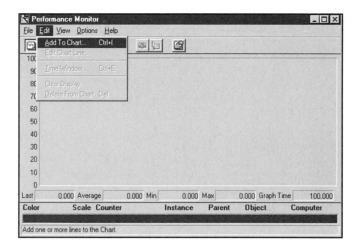

continues

Exercise 5.1: Continued

Figure 5.11

*The Add to Chart
dialog box.*

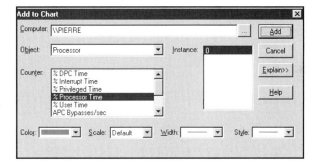

3a. The Computer text box at the top of the Add to Chart dialog box tells Performance Monitor which computer you want to monitor. The default is the local system. Click on the ellipses button to the right of the Computer text box for a browse list of computers on the network.

3b. The Object combo box tells Performance Monitor which object you want to monitor. As you learned earlier in this chapter, an object is a hardware or software component of your system. You can think of an object as a *category* of system statistics. Click on the down arrow to the right of the Object combo box to see a list of object options. Scroll through the list of objects. Look for the Processor, Memory, PhysicalDisk, LogicalDisk, Server, and Network Segment objects described earlier in this chapter. Choose the PhysicalDisk object. If you have more than one physical disk on your system, a list of your physical disks appears in the Instances box to the right of the Object box. The Instances box lists all instances of the object selected in the Object box. If necessary, choose a physical disk instance.

3c. The Counter list box displays the counters (the statistical measurements) available for the object in the Object box. Scroll through the list of counters for the PhysicalDisk object. If you feel like experimenting, select a different object in the Object box. Notice that the different object is accompanied by a different set of counters. Switch back to the PhysicalDisk object and choose the % Disk Time counter. Click on the Explain button. Notice that a description of the % Disk Time counter appears at the bottom of the dialog box.

3d. Click on the Done button in the Add to Chart dialog box. The dialog box closes and you see the Performance main window.

4. In the Performance Monitor main window, you'll see a vertical line sweeping across the chart from left to right. You also might also see a faint colored line at the bottom of the chart recording a % Disk Time value of 0. If so, this is because you have not enabled the disk performance counters for your system. (If the disk performance counters are enabled on your system, you should see a spikey line that looks like the readout from an electrocardiogram. Go on to step 5.)

If you need to enable the disk performance counters, choose click on the Start button go to the command prompt. Enter the command: diskperf –y. Reboot your system and repeat steps 1–4. (You do not have to browse through the Object and Counter lists this time.)

5. You should now see a spikey line representing the percent of time that the physical disk is busy reading or writing. Choose Edit, Add to Chart. Select the PhysicalDisk object and choose the counter Avg. Disk Queue Length. Click on the Add button; then choose the counter Avg. Disk Bytes/Read. Click on the Add button. Click on the Done button.

6. Examine the Performance Monitor main window. All three of the counters you selected should be tracing out spikey lines on the chart (see fig. 5.12). Each line is a different color. A table at the bottom of the window shows which counter goes with which color. The table also gives the scale of the output, the instance, the object, and the computer.

continues

Exercise 5.1: Continued

Figure 5.12

*Displaying perfor-
mance data.*

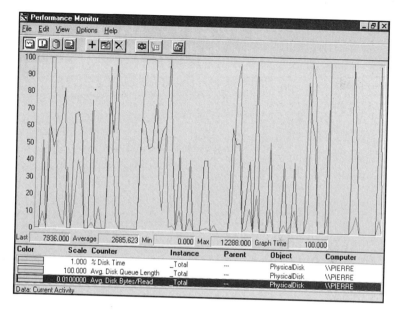

7. Below the chart (but above the table of counters) you will
find a row of statistical parameters labeled Last, Average,
Min, Max, and Graph Time. These parameters pertain to the
counter selected in the table at the bottom of the window.
Select a different counter and some of these values will
change. The Last value is the counter value over the last
second. Graph Time is the time it will take (in seconds) for
the vertical line that draws the chart to sweep across the
window.

8. Start Windows NT Explorer. Select a file (a graphics file or a
word processing document) and choose Edit, Copy. (This
will copy the file you selected to the Clipboard.) Go to another directory and choose Edit, Paste. (This will create a
copy of the file in the second directory.) Minimize Explorer
and return to the Performance Monitor main window. The
disk activity caused by your Explorer session will be reflected
in the spikes of the counter lines.

9. Choose Options, Chart. The Chart Options dialog box
appears (see fig. 5.13), providing a number of options

governing the chart display. The Update Time frame en-ables you to choose an update interval. The update interval tells Performance Monitor how frequently it should update the chart with new values. (If you choose the Manual Update option, the chart updates only when you press Ctrl+U or choose Options, Update Now.) Experiment with the Chart Options dialog box, or click on the Cancel button.

Figure 5.13

The Chart Options dialog box.

10. Choose File, Exit to exit Performance Monitor. The Save Chart Settings and Save Chart Settings As options in the File menu enable you to save the collection of objects and counters you are using now so you can monitor the same counters later without having to set them up again. The Export Chart option enables you to export the data to a file that you can open with a spreadsheet or database applica-tion. The Save Workspace option saves the settings for your chart as well as any settings for alerts, logs, or reports speci-fied in this session. You will learn more about alerts, logs, and reports in Exercise 5.2.

Exercise 5.2: Performance Monitor Alerts, Logs, and Reports

In Exercise 5.2, you will learn about the alternative views (Alert view, Log view, and Report view) available through the View menu of Performance Monitor, and you will learn how to log perfor-mance data to a log file.

continues

Exercise 5.2:   Continued

Estimated time: 25 minutes

1. Choose Start, Programs, Administrative Tools, and Performance Monitor. The Performance Monitormain window appears.

2. Open the View menu. You see the following four options:

   ▸ **The Chart option** plots the counters you select in a continuous chart (refer to Exercise 5.1).

   ▸ **The Alert option** automatically alert a network official if a predetermined counter threshold is surpassed.

   ▸ **The Log option** saves your system performance data to a log file.

   ▸ **The Report option** displays system performance data in a report format.

   The setup is similar for each of these view formats. All use some form of the Add to Chart dialog box (refer to Exercise 5.1). All have options configured through the first command at the top of the Options menu. (The name of the first command at the top of the Options menu changes depending on the active view. It was the Chart command in Exercise 5.1.)

3a. Choose View, Alert.

3b. Click on the plus sign in the toolbar or choose Edit, Add to Alert. The Add to Alert dialog box appears; it is similar to the Add to Chart dialog box, except you will notice two additional items at the bottom (see fig. 5.14).

   The options in the Alert If frame enable you to enter a threshold for the counter. The Over and Under radio buttons specify whether you should receive an alert if the counter value is over or under the threshold value. The Run Program on Alert text box enables you to specify a command line that will execute if the counter value reaches the threshold you specify in the Alert If box. Use the Run Program on

Alert text box to execute a command or script that will send a message to your beeper, send you an e-mail message, or notify your paging service.

Figure 5.14

The Add to Alert dialog box.

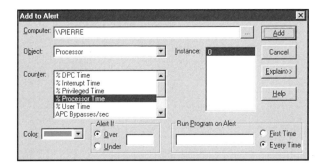

Do not specify a batch file in the Run Program on Alert text box. Performance Monitor uses Unicode format, which can confuse the command-prompt interpreter. (The < and > symbols, which are used in Unicode format, are interpreted as a redirection of input or output.)

3c. The default object in the Object combo box should be the Processor object. The default counter in the Counter list box should be % Processor Time. Enter the value **5%** in the Alert If box and select the Over radio button.

In the Run Program on Alert text box, type **SOL** and select the First Time radio button. This configuration tells Performance Monitor to execute Windows NT's Solitaire program when the % Processor Time exceeds five percent.

It is important to select the First Time radio button; otherwise, Performance Monitor will execute a new instance of Solitaire every time the % Processor Time exceeds five percent, which happens every time Performance Monitor executes a new instance of Solitaire. In other words, if you try this experiment without selecting the First Time radio button, you'll probably have to close Performance Monitor using the X button or reboot your system to stop the incessant shuffling and dealing.

continues

Exercise 5.2:   Continued

3d. Click on the Add button, and then click on the Done button.
The Alert Legend at the bottom of the Performance Moni-
tor window describes the active alert parameters. The Alert
Log shows every instance of an alert (see fig. 5.15).

Figure 5.15

*The Performance
Monitor Alert Log.*

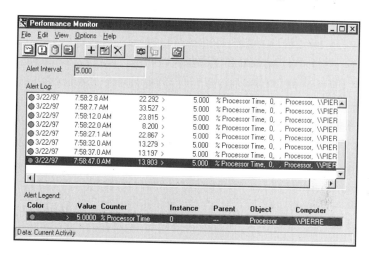

3e. Make some change to your Desktop. (Hide or reveal the
taskbar, change the size of the Performance Monitor window—anything that will cause a five percent utilization of
the processor.) The Solitaire program should miraculously
appear on your screen. In a real alert situation, Performance Monitor would execute an alert application instead
of starting a card game.

3f. Choose Edit, Delete Alert.

4a. Choose View, Log. The Log view saves performance data to
a log file instead of displaying it on-screen.

4b. Choose Edit, Add to Log. Notice that only the objects appear in the Add to Log dialog box. The counters and instances boxes do not appear because Performance Monitor
automatically logs all counters and all instances of the object to the log file.

Select the Memory Object and click on Add. If you want,
you can select another object, such as the Paging File object,
and then click on Add again. When you are finished adding
objects, click on Done.

4c. Choose Options Log. The Log Options dialog box appears (see fig. 5.16), enabling you to designate a log file that Performance Monitor will use to log the data.

In the File Name text box, enter the name **exer2**.

You also can specify an update interval. The update interval is the interval at which Performance Monitor records performance data to the log. The Manual Update radio button specifies that the file won't be undated unless you press Ctrl+U or choose Options, Update Now.

Click on the Start Log button to start saving data to the log. Wait a few minutes, and then return to the Log Options dialog box and click on the Stop Log button.

Figure 5.16

The Log Options dialog box.

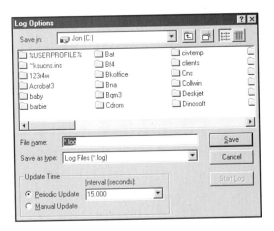

4d. Choose View, Chart.

4e. Choose Options, Data From. The Data From dialog box enables you to specify a source for the performance data that will appear in the chart. Note that the default source is Current Activity. (That is why the chart you created in Exercise 5.1 took its data from current system activity.)

The alternative to the Current Activity option is to use data from a log file. Click on the Log File radio button; click on the ellipses button to the right of Log File; and select the exer2 file you created in step 4c. Click on OK.

continues

Exercise 5.2: Continued

4f. Choose Edit, Add to Chart.

Click on the down arrow of the Object combo box. Notice that your only object choices are the Memory object and any other objects you selected in step 4b. Select the Memory object. Browse through the counter list and select Pages/sec. Click on the Add button. Select any other memory counters you want to display and click on the Add button. Click on Done.

4g. The log file's record of the counters you selected in 4f appear in the chart in the Performance main window. Notice that, unlike the chart you created in Exercise 5.1, this chart does not continuously sweep out new data. That is because this chart represents static data from a previous, finite monitoring session.

4h. Choose Edit, Time Window. A time window enables you to focus on a particular time interval within the log file (see fig. 5.17).

In this example (because you only collected data for a few minutes), the Time Window option might seem unnecessary. If you collected data for a longer period, however, and you want to zero in on a particular event, a time window can be very useful.

Set the beginning and end points of your Time Window by adjusting the gray start and stop sliders on the Time Window slide bar. The Bookmarks frame enables you to specify a log file bookmark as a start or stop point. (You can create a bookmark by choosing Options, Bookmark while collecting data to the log file or by clicking on the book in the Performance Monitor toolbar.)

Click on OK to view the data for the time interval.

Figure 5.17

*The Input Log
File Timeframe
dialog box.*

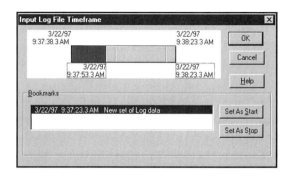

5a. Choose View, Report.

Choose Options, Data From.

In the Data From... dialog box, select the radio button labeled Current Activity. Report view displays the performance data in a report rather than in a graphics format.

5b. Choose Edit, Add to Report.

Select the processor object and choose the % Processor Time, % Interrupt Time, and Interrupts/sec counters (hold down the Ctrl key to select all three), and then click on Add. Select the PhysicalDisk object and choose the % Disk Time, Avg. Disk Queue Length, and Current Disk Queue Length counters. Click on the Add button. Select the Memory object and choose the Pages/sec, Page Faults/sec, and Available Bytes counters. Click on the Add button. Click on Done.

5c. Examine the main report window. Performance Monitor displays a report of the performance data in a hierarchical format, with counters listed under the appropriate object.

6. Choose File, Exit to exit Performance Monitor.

Review Questions

The following questions will test your knowledge of the information in this chapter. For additional questions, see MCP Endeavor and the Microsoft Roadmap/Assessment exam on the CD-ROM that accompanies this book.

1. For the most part, how much time should you spend tuning and optimizing Windows NT?

    A. At least an hour a day.

    B. You should plan on spending most of the first week after the initial installation.

    C. You should never have to.

    D. NT, for the most part, is self-tuning and requires very little user intervention.

2. Name the major tool for gathering information and identifying bottlenecks.

    A. Tune—T

    B. Monitor

    C. Performance Monitor

    D. Server Manager

    E. NT doesn't provide any tools for tuning and performance monitoring

3. Before you can tune a file server for optimum performance, which one of the following questions must you answer?

    A. How much money do you have to spend on new hardware?

    B. What types of tasks is the file server expected to perform?

    C. This question has no answer; simply put, tuning is the process of putting the fastest hardware in your computer.

    D. What type of business is the company using file server in? For certain companies, you cannot tune NT because of U.S. government restrictions.

4. A curious user tells you that while reading a major computer periodical, he came across this statement: "All computer systems have a bottleneck of some type." Why is this so?

   A. All computer systems are only as fast as their slowest component. You may remove one bottleneck, but you always expose another.

   B. The article was incorrect. For example, your file server has absolutely no bottlenecks.

   C. The article was referring to non-Windows NT systems. Microsoft has designed the system to continually self-adjust, thus eliminating bottlenecks.

   D. Because you always upgrade components as soon as new ones are available, you eliminate any potential bottlenecks before they become apparent.

5. Which statement is true regarding the type of hardware you should place in a heavily used file server?

   A. The equipment in the server is not important because nobody actually uses the server to run applications.

   B. You should always spend the most money on the server hardware.

   C. When designing a file server, always pick the hardware that exploits the full bus speed if possible (for example, SCSI hard drives, PCI bus network cards, and so on).

   D. You should use the same type of computer hardware as the workstations, so the users get good response time, because hardware from the same vendor works better together.

6. To optimize the network components in an NT Workstation or Server, which one of the following should you do?

   A. You do not need to do anything. NT automatically optimizes the network components.

   B. You should remove unused adapter cards and protocols.

C. You should always have TCP/IP, NetBEUI, and NWLink installed, even if your computers are using only one protocol. This leaves more paths open in case one protocol becomes unusable.

7. Select the name of the piece of software that automatically swaps data in physical RAM out to disk and back.

A. The Virtual Memory Manager

B. The Virtual Device Driver

C. Himem.exe

D. Emm386.exe

8. Name the paging file that Windows NT creates.

A. RAMPAGE.SYS

B. SYS$RAM.SYS

C. PAGEFILE.SYS

D. VIRAM.SYS

9. What are some of the things you can do to make the system use virtual memory more efficiently? Select all that apply.

A. Spread out the paging file across multiple hard drives.

B. Move the paging file to the drive where the Windows NT System files are located.

C. Move the paging file from the drive where the Windows NT System files are located.

D. Monitor the size of the paging file under peak usage and then set the minimum size of the paging file to that value, thereby saving time when the system has to expand the paging file.

10. Which Performance Monitor object and counter measures the amount of time that the CPU is busy?

A. Processor: % Busy Time

B. Processor: % Processor Time

C. System: % Processor Time

D. System: TotalProcessorUsage

11. While monitoring system performance in Performance Monitor, you notice that the number of interrupts per second have doubled. You haven't increased the number of users or added any new applications to the server. What does an increase of this counter mean?

   A. Nothing. It is normal for this counter to increase over time.

   B. It could mean that you have a potential hardware problem, and that a piece of hardware is generating many more interrupts than normal.

   C. It indicates that the network card is the bottleneck in the system and should be replaced.

   D. It indicates that the CPU is the bottleneck in the system and should be replaced or upgraded.

12. You're trying to explain the System: Processor Queue Length counter in Performance Monitor to a coworker. Which statement below best describes the purpose of this counter?

   A. It measures the amount of activity on the CPU.

   B. It indicates the number of threads waiting for CPU time.

   C. It indicates the number of users waiting to log on to the domain.

   D. It indicates the total CPU usage across all CPUs in the system. You see a number for this counter only if your computer has more than one CPU.

13. You're trying to get some statistics that measure the total amount of network traffic. Which Performance Monitor counter can you measure?

   A. Pool Nonpaged Failures

   B. Total Network Bytes/sec

   C. Bytes Total/sec

   D. Network: %Network Bytes

14. You notice an increase in the number of Pool Nonpaged Failures. What does that indicate?

   A. That you need to add more RAM to the server.

   B. That the hard disk is failing, and the system must continually retry to allocate page file space.

   C. That the system is using the RAM installed in the system, and is good sign that the server is running efficiently.

   D. That you need to upgrade the RAM in the system by installing faster EDO memory.

Review Answers

1. D	4. A	7. A	10. B	13. B
2. C	5. C	8. C	11. B	14. A
3. B	6. B	9. A C D	12. B	

Chapter 6

Test Yourself

Stop! Before reading this chapter, test yourself to determine how much study time you will need to devote to this section.

1. To boot with the LastKnownGood configuration _____.

    A. press F3 when the hardware profile screen appears.

    B. press Ctrl+Alt+Delete when prompted during the boot process.

    C. press the Escape key when prompted during the boot process.

    D. press the space bar when prompted during the boot process.

2. Which three of the following files are on the Windows NT emergency repair disk?

    A. DEFAULT.LOG

    B. CONFIG.NT

    C. SOFTWARE._

    D. NTUSER.DA_

3. Windows NT Server assigns a priority of _____ to the print spooler service.

    A. 5

    B. 7

    C. 9

    D. 12

4. Near the end of the logon process, your Windows NT Server system starts spontaneously dialing a phone number. The most likely cause for this is _____.

    A. a Dial-up Networking Phonebook entry was left minimized when you shut down your system.

    B. the AutoDial service is configured to start at Startup.

C. a remote user did not properly shut down a RAS connection before system shutdown.

D. Explorer is referencing a shortcut that requires an AutoDial connection.

Chapter

Troubleshooting

6

This chapter will help you prepare for the "Troubleshooting" section of Microsoft's Exam 70-67, "Implementing and Supporting Microsoft Windows NT Server 4.0." Microsoft provides for the Troubleshooting section:

Test Objectives

- ▶ Choose the appropriate course of action to take to resolve installation failures.

- ▶ Choose the appropriate course of action to take to resolve boot failures.

- ▶ Choose the appropriate course of action to take to resolve configuration errors.

- ▶ Choose the appropriate course of action to take to resolve printer problems.

- ▶ Choose the appropriate course of action to take to resolve RAS problems.

- ▶ Choose the appropriate course of action to take to resolve connectivity problems.

- ▶ Choose the appropriate course of action to take to resolve resource access problems and permission problems.

- ▶ Choose the appropriate course of action to take to resolve fault-tolerance failures. Fault-tolerance methods include: tape backup, mirroring, stripe set with parity, and disk duplexing.

The subject of Windows NT troubleshooting is as broad as the subject of Windows NT. Almost any task you perform in Windows NT may someday require troubleshooting. All the material in the preceding chapters is thus important to your achieving an understanding of troubleshooting. The more you know, the easier time you will have solving problems. The best tool for troubleshooting is an understanding of the underlying processes within NT. When something trips up, try to figure out what it tripped on, and you will be on your way to knowing why. In that vein, you may want to spend some time with Appendix A, overview of the "Overview of the Certification Process," which discusses Windows NT architecture and the ways that Windows NT supports various kinds of applications. You also may want to review some of the performance optimization techniques in Chapter 5, "Monitoring and Optimization," as you prepare for the "Troubleshooting" section of the NT Server exam.

This chapter describes some of the tips, tools, and techniques you need to find and solve problems in Windows NT.

General Troubleshooting Techniques

The following sections review some good solid general troubleshooting practices. You could consider these your troubleshooting fundamentals. Whatever other specific troubleshooting tips you have encountered are essentially meaningless if you don't integrate these basic habits into the fabric of your administrative being.

Document It

When a problem occurs, write it down. If it happened one time, it can happen again. Include the symptoms of the problem, configuration of the computer, and the diagnosis and resolution of the problem. Good troubleshooters build an incident reference library to save time and effort the next time the same problem occurs.

Back It Up

Experimentation can worsen a problem or introduce a new one. Always back up the system (if possible) before altering system files or configurations.

Test One Thing at a Time

If you suspect several possibilities as the cause of a problem, test only one suspicion at a time. If you change more than one item, you may solve the problem but still not know its exact cause or the exact solution.

Fix the Problem, Don't Remove It

If a component is not functioning correctly, going for the quick fix by just removing the malfunctioning device, driver, service, or application can feel highly enticing. You may, in fact, have to do just that to get the computer back up and running, but don't stop there. Follow through and fix the original problem so that you can restore the computer to its original configuration.

Troubleshooting Installation

The Windows NT installation process is remarkably easy for the user, but you still may occasionally experience problems (see Chapter 2, "Installation and Configuration"). Microsoft has identified the following common installation problems and solutions:

- ▶ **Media errors.** If there seems to be a problem with the Windows NT Installation CD-ROM or floppy disks, ask Microsoft Sales to replace the disk. Call 800-426-9400.

- ▶ **Insufficient disk space.** Delete unnecessary files and folders, compress NTFS partitions, reformat an existing partition or use Setup to create more space, create a new partition with more space.

- ▶ **Non-supported SCSI adapter.** Boot to a different operating system (that can use the SCSI adapter) and run WINNT from the installation CD-ROM, try a network installation, replace the unsupported adapter with a supported adapter on the Hardware Compatibility List.

▶ **Failure of dependency service to start.** Verify the protocol and adapter configuration in the Control Panel Network application, make certain that the local computer has a unique name.

▶ **Inability to connect to the domain controller.** Verify account name and password, make sure the domain name is correct, make sure the Primary Domain Controller is functioning properly, and verify protocol and adapter configuration settings in the Control Panel Network application. If you just finished installing or upgrading, make sure the domain account for the computer has been reset (added to the network again).

▶ **Error in assigning domain name.** Make certain that the domain name isn't identical to some other domain or computer name on the network.

Microsoft lists the following objective for the Windows NT Server exam:

Choose the appropriate course of action to take to resolve installation failures.

Troubleshooting Boot Failures

You usually know when you have a problem with the boot process: you can't boot. The boot process is one of the most common sources of problems in Windows NT. The cause may be a lost or corrupt boot file. Try booting from the Windows NT boot disk and perform an emergency repair if necessary. (The emergency repair process is described later in this chapter.)

Microsoft lists the following objective for the Windows NT Server exam:

Choose the appropriate course of action to take to resolve boot failures.

To diagnose a boot problem, you must understand the boot process. This section focuses on booting Windows NT and troubleshooting the boot process. It discusses various diagnostic and troubleshooting utilities useful to this end. Before you can use any of these Win32 programs, however, you need to be able to boot into Windows NT. If you can't do that, all Microsoft's tools are useless to you. Therefore, the first type of troubleshooting you should understand is how to deal with problems that you can encounter in booting the computer into Windows NT.

Booting Up

The boot process begins when your computer accesses the hard drive's Master Boot Record (MBR) to load Windows NT. If your system fails during the Power On Self Test (POST), the problem isn't NT-related; instead, it is a hardware issue. What happens after the MBR's program loads depends on the type of computer you are using.

The Intel Boot Sequence

On Intel x86-based computers, the boot sector of the active partition loads a file called NTLDR. Similar to IO.SYS for MS-DOS or Windows 95, NTLDR is a hidden, system, read-only file in the root of your system partition, responsible for loading the rest of the operating system. NTLDR carries out the following steps:

1. Switches the processor to the 32-bit flat memory model necessary to address 4 GB of RAM.

2. Starts the minifile system driver necessary for accessing the system and boot partitions. This minifile system driver contains just enough code to read files at boot time. The full file systems are loaded later.

3. Displays a Boot Loader menu that gives the user a choice of operating system to load, and waits for a response. The options for the Boot Loader menu are stored in a hidden, read-only file in the root of your system partition named BOOT.INI. This file is discussed in greater depth later in this chapter.

4. Invokes, if Windows NT is the selected system, the hardware detection routine to determine the hardware required. NTDETECT.COM (the same program that detects the hardware during NTSETUP) performs the hardware detection. NTDETECT.COM builds the hardware list and returns it to NTLDR. NTDETECT.COM is hidden, system, and read-only in the root of the system partition.

5. Loads the kernel of the operating system. The kernel is called NTOSKRNL.EXE, and you can find it in the <winnt_root>\SYSTEM32 directory. At this point, the screen clears and displays OS Loader V4.00.

6. Loads the Hardware Abstraction Layer (HAL). The HAL is a single file (HAL.DLL) that contains the code necessary to mask interrupts and exceptions from the kernel.

7. Loads SYSTEM, the HKEY_LOCAL_MACHINE\SYSTEM hive in the Registry. You can find the corresponding file in the <winnt_root>\SYSTEM32\CONFIG directory.

8. Loads the boot-time drivers. Boot-time drivers have a start value of 0. These values are loaded in the order in which they are listed in HKEY_LOCAL_MACHINE\SYSTEM\ CurrentControlSet\ Control\ServiceGroupOrder. Each time a driver loads, a dot is added to the series following the OS Loader V4.00 at the top of the screen. If the /sos switch is used in BOOT.INI, the name of each driver appears on a separate line as each is loaded. The drivers are not initialized yet.

9. Passes control, along with the hardware list collected by NTDETECT.COM, to NTOSKRNL.EXE.

After NTOSKRNL.EXE takes control, the boot phase ends and the load phases begin.

The RISC Boot Sequence

On a RISC-based computer, the boot process is much simpler because the firmware does much of the work that NTLDR and company does on the Intel platform. RISC-based computers maintain hardware configuration in their firmware (also called non-volatile RAM), so they don't need NTDETECT.COM. Their firmware also contains a list of valid operating systems and their locations, so they don't need BOOT.INI either.

RISC-based machines don't look for the Intel-specific NTLDR to boot the operating system; instead, they always look for a file called OSLOADER.EXE. This file is handed the hardware configuration data from the firmware. It then loads NTOSKRNL.EXE, HAL.DLL, and SYSTEM, and the boot process concludes.

Booting to Windows 95, MS-DOS, or OS/2

On Intel-based computers, you can install Windows NT over Windows 95 or MS-DOS. The boot loader screen offers the user a choice of Windows NT Workstation 4, Microsoft Windows, and MS-DOS. If the user chooses a non-Windows NT operating system, a file called BOOTSECT.DOS is loaded and executed. BOOTSECT.DOS is a hidden, system, read-only file in the root of the system partition. It contains the information that was present in the boot sector before Windows NT was installed. If a user chooses Windows 95 from the boot menu, for example, BOOTSECT.DOS loads IO.SYS and passes control to it.

BOOT.INI

NTLDR may invoke the Boot Loader menu, but BOOT.INI, an editable text file, controls it. (It is read-only, so you must remove that attribute before editing it.) BOOT.INI is the only INI file that Windows NT uses—if, indeed you can actually say that NT uses it. After all, Windows NT is not loaded when this file is called on.

BOOT.INI has only two sections: [boot loader] and [operating systems]:

ARC Sidebar

Because not all machines use MS-DOS-style paths (for example, c:\winnt) for referring to locations on a hard drive, Windows NT uses a cross-platform standard format called Advanced RISC Computer (ARC), within BOOT.INI. An ARC-compliant path consists of four parameters:

Parameter	Description
scsi(x) or multi(x)	indentifies the hardware adapter
disk(y)	SCSI bus number: always 0 if multi
rdisk(z)	Physical drive number for multi; ignored for SCSI
parition(a)	Logical partition number

The first three parameters are zero-based; that is, the first physical IDE drive is rdisk(0) and the second is rdisk(1). The partition parameter, however, is one-based, so the first partition on the drive is rdisk(0)partition(1).

All of the parameters—even the ones that are ignored—must be present in the path. For instance, multi(0)disk(0)rdisk(0)partition(1) is a valid path even though disk(0) is essentially unnecessary. multi(0)rdisk(0)partition(1) is not valid.

The first parameter almost always is multi, even for a SCSI controller. The only time you even see SCSI in a BOOT.INI file is if the BIOS on the controller is turned off. If this is the case, don't worry; an additional hidden, system, read-only file, NTBOOTDD.SYS, is present in the root of the system partition. NTBOOTDD.SYS is a device driver necessary for accessing a SCSI controller that doesn't have an on-board BIOS or doesn't use INT 13 to identify hard disks. If you have this file present, you probably see a scsi(x) entry in BOOT.INI. If you don't, you probably have upgraded from Windows NT 3.1 (where this setting was more common) without ever deleting the file.

The same holds true for a RISC-based computer; look at the firmware entries for the operating system paths, and you should see the same kind of ARC-compliant paths.

[boot loader]

The [boot loader] section of BOOT.INI defines the operating system that will be loaded if the user doesn't make a selection within a defined period of time. By default, you see something like this:

```
[boot loader]
timeout=30
default=multi(0)disk(0)rdisk(0)partition(1)\WINNT
```

The timeout parameter is the length of time (in seconds) that NTLDR has to wait for the user to make a decision. If timeout is set to 0, the default operating system loads immediately. If it is set to _1, the menu displays until the user makes a decision.

The default parameter defines the actual path, in ARC-compliant form, to the directory that contains the files for the default operating system, which usually is the last operating system installed, unless someone has changed this entry.

The easiest way to change the default operating system and the timeout is by using the Control Panel System application. Select the Startup/Shutdown tab and change the values in the System Startup frame (see fig. 6.1). You can edit BOOT.INI directly, but remember that a mistyped character in NOTEPAD.EXE or EDIT.COM could result in your system not booting properly.

Figure 6.1

Changing the default operating system in the System application's Startup/Shutdown tab.

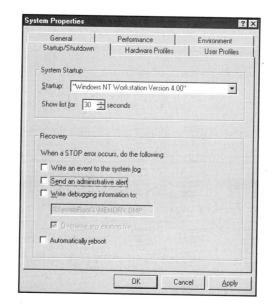

[operating systems]

The [operating systems] section contains a reference for every operating system available to the user from the Boot Loader menu, as well as any special switches necessary to customize the Windows NT environment. One of these entries must match the default= entry in the [boot loader] section. Otherwise, you end up with two entries for the same OS on-screen, one of which has "(default)" following it. In all likelihood, only one of these will work. Trial-and-error should quickly discern which one.

Note that the paths are in ARC format with a label in quotation marks, which displays as an on-screen selection. Here's an example of an [operating systems] section:

```
multi(0)disk(0)rdisk(0)partition(1)\WINNT="Windows NT Workstation
~Version 4.00"
multi(0)disk(0)rdisk(0)partition(1)\WINNT="Windows NT Workstation
~Version 4.00 [VGA mode]" /basevideo /sos
c:\="Windows 95"
```

There are two entries for the same Windows NT Workstation installation, but the second one includes two switches that customize the Windows NT boot and load process.

BOOT.INI Switches

The following sections delineate several useful switches that you can include in the [operating systems] section of BOOT.INI. The only way to include them is to manually edit the BOOT.INI file. If you decide to do so, be certain to take the read-only attribute off of the file before editing it, and be sure that you save the altered file as a text file if you use a word processor that normally saves in another format.

/basevideo

The /basevideo switch tells Windows NT to load the standard VGA driver rather than the optimized driver written for your video card, which is useful, for example, if your monitor breaks and is replaced by one that doesn't support the resolution or the refresh rate that your last one did. If you can't see, it is awfully hard to get into Control Panel to change the video settings. Selecting the VGA mode entry uses the standard VGA 640 × 480, 16-color driver that works with almost every monitor.

/sos

The /sos switch enumerates to the screen each driver as it loads during the kernel load phase. If Windows NT hangs during this phase, you can use the /sos switch to determine which driver caused the problem.

/noserialmice=[COMx|COMx,y,z_]

When Windows NT boots, NTDETECT.COM looks for, among other things, the presence of serial mice. Sometimes this detection routine misfires and identifies modems or other devices as serial mice. Then, when Windows NT loads and initializes, the serial port is unavailable and the device is unusable because Windows NT is expecting a serial mouse. In other instances, the serial mouse detection signal can shut down a UPS connected to the serial port.

The /noserialmice switch by itself tells NTDETECT.COM not to bother looking for serial mice. Used with a specific COM port(s), NTDETECT.COM still looks for serial mice, but not on the port(s) specified.

/crashdebug

The /crashdebug switch turns on the Automatic Recovery and Restart capability, which you can also configure using the Control Panel System application. In fact, when you configure this capability through Control Panel, what you are doing is merely adding this switch to the OS path in BOOT.INI.

/nodebug

Programmers often use a special version of Windows NT that includes debugging symbols useful for tracking down problems with code. This version of Windows NT runs slowly compared to the retail version, owing to the extra overhead in tracking every piece of executing code. To turn off the monitoring in this version of NT, add the /nodebug switch to the OS path in BOOT.INI.

/maxmem:n

Memory parity errors can be notoriously difficult to isolate. The /maxmem switch helps. When followed with a numeric value, this switch limits Windows NT's usable memory to the amount specified in the switch. This switch also is useful for developers using high-level workstations, who want to simulate performance on a lower-level machine.

/scsiordinal:n

If your system has two identical SCSI controllers, you need a way to distinguish one from the other. The /scsiordinal switch is used to assign a value of 0 to the first controller and 1 to the second.

Kernel Initialization Phase

After all the initial drivers have loaded, the screen turns blue and the text height shrinks; the kernel initialization phase has begun. Now the kernel and all the drivers loaded in the previous phase are initialized. The Registry begins to flesh out. The CurrentControlSet is copied to the CloneControlSet, and the volatile HARDWARE key is created. The system Registry hive then is scanned once more for higher-level drivers configured to start during system initialization. These drivers have a start value of 1 (like the keyboard and mouse) and then are loaded and initialized.

Services Load Phase

Here the session manager scans the system hive for a list of programs that must run before Windows NT fully initializes. These programs may include AUTOCHK.EXE, the boot-time version of CHKDSK.EXE that examines and repairs any problems within a file system, or AUTOCONV.EXE, which converts a partition from FAT to NTFS. These boot-time programs are stored in the following:

```
HKEY_LOCAL_MACHINE\SYSTEM\CurrentControlSet\Control\Session
Manager\BootExecute
```

Following these programs, the page file(s) are created based on the locations specified in

```
HKEY_LOCAL_MACHINE\SYSTEM\CurrentControlSet\Control\Session
Manager\Memory Management
```

Next, the SOFTWARE hive loads from <winnt_root>\SYSTEM32\
CONFIG. Session Manager then loads the CSR subsystem and any
other required subsystems from

```
HKEY_LOCAL_MACHINE\System\CurrentControlSet\Control\Session
Manager\SubSystems\Required
```

Finally, drivers that have a start value of 2 (Automatic) load.

The Windows NT Resource Kit includes a command-line utility
called DRIVERS.EXE that reports the name of all successfully
loaded drivers. If you have any doubts about a driver's capability to successfully load and initialize, try DRIVERS.EXE.

Windows Start Phase

After the Win32 subsystem starts, the screen then switches into
GUI mode. In other words, it looks like Windows. The Winlogon
process is invoked, which starts the Welcome dialog box appears.
Although users can go ahead and log on at this point, the system
might not respond for a few more moments while the Service
Controller initializes Computer Browser, Workstation, Server,
Spooler, and other automatic services.

The critical file at this point is SERVICES.EXE, which actually
starts Alerter, Computer Browser, EventLog, Messenger, Net-
Logon, NT LM Security Support Provider, Server, TCP/IP
NetBIOS Helper, and Workstation. A missing or corrupt
SERVICES.EXE cripples your Windows NT-based computer.

SERVICES.EXE starts its services by calling the appropriate DLLs:

Alerter	ALRSVC.DLL
Computer Browser	BROWSER.DLL
EventLog	EVENTLOG.DLL

Messenger	MSGSVC.DLL
Net Logon	NETLOGON.DLL
NT LM Security Support Provider	NTLMSSPS.DLL
Server	SRVSVC.DLL
TCP/IP NetBIOS Helper	LMHSVC.DLL
Workstation	WKSSVC.DLL

After a user successfully logs on to the system, the LastKnown-Good control set is updated and the boot is considered good. Until a user logs on for the first time, though, the boot/load process technically remains unfinished, so a problem that Windows NT cannot detect but that a user can see (such as a video problem) can be resolved by falling back on the LastKnownGood configuration.

Control Sets and LastKnownGood

A control set is a collection of configuration information used during boot by Windows NT. A special control set, called Last-KnownGood, plays a special role in troubleshooting the boot process.

After the system boots and a user logs on successfully, the current configuration settings are copied to the LastKnownGood control set in the Registry. These settings are preserved so that if the system cannot boot successfully the next time a user attempts to log on, the system can fall back on LastKnownGood, which, as the name implies, is the last configuration known to facilitate a "good" boot. LastKnownGood is stored in the Registry under

HKEY_LOCAL_MACHINE\SYSTEM\CurrentControlSet

The key to understanding LastKnownGood lies in recognizing that it updates the first (and only the first) time a user logs on to Windows NT after a reboot. If you notice something dicey—if, for example, you changed the settings for a driver that now refuses to load—you can power down and restart the system using the

LastKnownGood configuration. If you notice something wrong but still log on to the system, you are telling it that everything is okay, that this is a configuration that facilitates a good boot. The system then overwrites the LastKnownGood, and what you essentially end up with is a "LastKnownBad" configuration.

To boot with the LastKnownGood configuration, press the spacebar when prompted during the boot process. You are presented with the Hardware Profile/Configuration Recovery menu. Select a hardware profile and enter L for the LastKnownGood configuration.

Sometimes Windows NT boots using LastKnownGood of its own volition, but only if the normal boot process produces severe or critical errors in loading device drivers.

LastKnownGood does not do you any good if files are corrupt or missing. You must use the Emergency Repair Process for aid with that.

Troubleshooting the Boot Process

If one of the important boot files is missing or corrupt, Windows NT can't boot correctly. If NTLDR, NTDTECT.COM, BOOTSECT.DOS, or NTOSKRNL.EXE fail, NT displays a message that tells you the name of the missing file. Use the Emergency Repair Process to restore the system.

If BOOT.INI is missing, NTLDR tries to start Windows NT without consulting BOOT.INI or the boot menu. This works as long as Windows NT is installed in the default \Winnt directory. If Windows NT is installed in a different directory, however, NTLDR cannot find it and issues an error message stating that the file, \winnt root\system32\ntoskrnl.exe, is missing or corrupt.

If BOOT.INI contains an invalid path name, or if a BOOT.INI path includes an invalid device, the boot fails. Verify all BOOT.INI paths. If possible, boot from a floppy and edit BOOT.INI to fix the problem. The Emergency Repair Process described later in this chapter can restore BOOT.INI if the error stems from a recent change.

If you need to boot Windows NT from the floppy drive, you can use Setup Boot disks created using the Winnt.exe or Winnt32.exe utilities with the /ox switch (see Chapter 2). You need these disks to invoke the Emergency Repair Process, so it is nice to have them around.

The Emergency Repair Process

As you may recall from Chapter 2, the installation process enables you to create an emergency repair directory and emergency repair disk, both of which are backup copies of Registry information, (which come in handy if you can't boot Windows NT owing to missing or corrupt files). It is now time to take a look at ways in which the Emergency Repair Process can aid a troubled Windows NT installation.

Emergency Repair Directory Versus Emergency Repair Disk

Installation always creates the emergency repair directory. You can find it in <winnt_root>\REPAIR. You can create an emergency repair disk as well. Do you need both? Well, no, not really. The directory serves just as well as the disk unless the directory itself becomes corrupt, or the drive itself dies, in which case you're stuck. The disk serves as a backup in case of an extreme emergency.

Both the directory and disk are computer-specific, at least in part. Although you can sometimes borrow an emergency repair disk from another computer, you generally should assume otherwise. Keep a separate emergency repair disk for each computer and tag it with the serial number of the computer because names and locations change over time. Don't leave these disks in the hands of users. Keep them with an administrator in a secure but accessible location.

Table 6.1 lists and describes the files on the emergency repair disk.

Table 6.1

Files on the Emergency Repair Disk

Files	Description
SETUP.LOG	A text file that contains the names of all the Windows NT installation files, along with checksum values for each. If any of the files on your hard drive are missing or corrupt, the Emergency Repair Process should detect them with the aid of this hidden, system, and read-only file.
SYSTEM._	A compressed copy of the Registry's SYSTEM hive. This is the Windows NT control set collection.
SAM._	A compressed copy of the Registry's SAM hive. This is the Windows NT user accounts database.
SECURITY.__	A compressed copy of the Registry's SECURITY hive. This is the Windows NT security information, which includes SAM and the security policies.
SOFTWARE._	A compressed copy of the Registry's SOFTWARE hive. This hive contains all Win32 software configuration information.
DEFAULT._	A compressed copy of the system default profile.
CONFIG.NT	The VDM version of the MS-DOS CONFIG.SYS file.
AUTOEXEC.NT	The VDM version of the MS-DOS AUTOEXEC.BAT file.
NTUSER.DA_	A copy of the file NTUSER.DAT (which contains user profile information) from the directory winnt_root\profiles\Defaultuser.

RDISK.EXE

Both the emergency repair disk and directory are created during installation, but neither are updated automatically at anytime thereafter. To update the emergency repair information, use the hidden utility RDISK.EXE. To start RDISK, choose Start, Run and type **RDISK**. Because RDISK.EXE is in the search path

(\<winnt_root>\SYSTEM32), you do not have to specify the full path. Some administrators just add the RDISK program to the Administrative Tools group.

RDISK offers two options for administrators: Update Repair Info and Create Repair Disk (see fig. 6.2).

Figure 6.2

The RDISK utility.

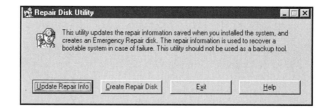

Update Repair Info

The Update Repair Info button updates only the emergency re-pair directory, although it does prompt for the creation/update of an emergency repair disk immediately following successful completion of the directory update. Always update the directory before creating the disk, because the disk will be created using the information in the directory.

Create Repair Disk

If the information in the repair directory is up-to-date, you may choose to create or update an emergency repair disk. You don't have to use a preformatted disk for the repair disk. RDISK formats the disk regardless.

A significant limitation of RDISK that you should definitely know about is that it will not update DEFAULT._, SECURITY, or SAM, in the repair directory (or disk). In other words, you may update your repair disk week-to-week, but none of your account changes are being backed up. To do a complete emergency repair update, you must run RDISK.EXE using the undocumented /S switch. This takes a while, especially if your account database is quite large. It is better, however, than losing all your accounts when disaster strikes. By the way, if you are wondering what happens if the emergency repair information requires more than one disk, rest easy, RDISK asks for an additional disk (or disks).

Starting the Emergency Repair Process

Whether you use the emergency repair directory or the emergency repair disk, you need to recognize that you can't boot from either or use either from within Windows NT. To actually invoke the Emergency Repair Process, you must access the original three Windows NT Setup disks. If you don't have the original disks handy, you generate them from the CD by using the WINNT /O or /OX switch. Chapter 2 includes more information on the WINNT.EXE program.

If you think way back to installation, you might recall that the Setup process actually gives you the initial choice either to install Windows NT or repair an existing installation. Pressing R on this screen invokes the Emergency Repair Process. Don't be concerned when the Setup process then continues apace through the rest of the three setup disks. This is normal.

The emergency repair process gives you several options. You can select any or all of the options in the emergency repair menu. (The default is to undertake all repair options.) After you select your repair options, Setup attempts to locate your hard drive. After Setup locates your hard drive, it asks you whether you want to use an emergency repair disk or whether you want Setup to search for your repair directory. You then encounter a series of restoration choices based on the repair options you selected and the problems Setup uncovers as it analyzes your system. The next few sections discuss the emergency repair options.

Inspect Registry Files

At this point, the process gets computer-specific. If your registry becomes corrupt, only your own emergency repair disk can save you—no one else's can. You granularly select to repair any combination of the SYSTEM, SOFTWARE, DEFAULT, and SECURITY/SAM hives, and these are copied directly from the repair directory/disk. You don't need the original source CD or disks for this procedure.

Inspect Startup Environment

The files required to boot Windows NT are discussed earlier in this chapter. If any of these files go AWOL or become corrupted, choose Inspect Startup Environment to repair them. You can use anyone's emergency repair disk for this option because these files are generic across all Windows NT installations (for the same platform, anyway). You do need to produce the original installation CD, however, before the repair process can replace the files.

Verify Windows NT System Files

This option often takes time, but systematically inspects every file in the Windows NT directory tree and compares them with the checksum values in SETUP.LOG. If it determines that any files are missing or corrupt, the repair process attempts to replace them. Again, you need the original disks or CD before you can do so.

Inspect Boot Sector

If you upgrade to a new version of DOS and suddenly find that you cannot boot to Windows NT anymore, your boot sector probably has been replaced. Using the MS-DOS or Windows 95 SYS command is notorious for trashing the Windows NT boot sector. The emergency repair disk solves this problem, and you don't even need a computer-specific ERD—you can borrow anybody's.

Troubleshooting Configuration Errors

Configuration errors are another common source of hardship for network professionals. Configuration errors are often introduced by a user or an administrator installing new software or a new device.

Microsoft lists the following objective for the Windows NT Server exam:

Choose the appropriate course of action to take to resolve configuration errors.

Some common device problems are resource conflicts (such as interrupt conflicts) and SCSI problems. Sometimes these problems manifest themselves at boot time. Sometimes they don't appear until you try to access the misconfigured device. Device error reports appear in the Event Log (described later in this chapter). Use Windows NT diagnostics to check resource settings. If the error is the result of a recent configuration change, you can reboot the system and boot to the LastKnownGood configuration.

If a Windows NT service doesn't start, check Event Viewer; or, check the Control Panel Services application to make sure the service is installed and configured to start.

Windows NT includes some important tools you can use to look for configuration errors. Those tool are as follows:

- ▶ Event Viewer

- ▶ Windows NT Diagnostics

- ▶ System Recovery

You will learn more about these tools in the following sections. You will also learn how to fend off a catastrophic misconfiguration by backing up your Registry.

Event Viewer

If your Windows NT-based computer manages to boot successfully, yet still isn't performing correctly, the first thing to check is the system event log, where all critical system messages are stored.

Windows NT includes the Event Viewer application in the Administrative Tool program group for viewing the messages stored in the system, security, and application log files (see fig. 6.3).

System Log

The system log, the default view in Event Viewer, is maintained by the operating system. It tracks three kinds of events:

▶ **Errors.** Symbolized by Stop signs, and indicative of the failure of a Windows NT component or device, or perhaps an inability to start. These errors are common on notebook computers when Windows NT fails to start the network components because PCMCIA network cards are not present.

▶ **Warnings.** Symbolized by exclamation points, and indicative of an impending problem. Low disk space on a partition triggers a warning, for example.

▶ **Information Events.** Symbolized by the traditional "I" in a blue circle, and indicative of an event that isn't at all bad but is still somehow significant. Browser elections often cause information events.

Figure 6.3

Event Viewer.

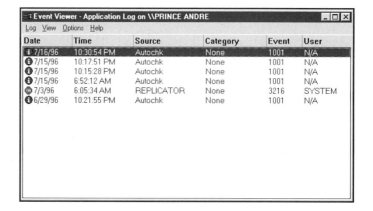

Security Log

The security log remains empty until you enable auditing through User Manager. After enabling auditing, the audited events reside here. The security log tracks two types of events:

▶ **Success Audits.** Symbolized by a key, and indicative of successful security access.

▶ **Failure Audits.** Symbolized by a padlock, and indicative of unsuccessful security access.

Application Log

The application log collects messages from native Windows NT applications (refer to fig. 6.3). If you aren't using any Win32 applications, this log remains empty. As you move toward native Windows NT programs, check this log occasionally, and certainly check it when you suspect a problem.

Securing Event Logs

Ordinarily, anyone can view the event log information. Some administrators, however, might not want guests to have this sort of access. There is one restriction, enabled through the Registry, that you can place on Event Viewer—you can prohibit guests from accessing the system or application logs from the following Registry location, where <log_name> is either System or Application:

```
HKEY_LOCAL_MACHINE\System\CurrentControlSet\Services\EventLog\~<log_name>
```

You need to add a value called RestrictGuestAccess of type REG_DWORD and set it equal to 1. To re-enable guest access to either log, set the appropriate RestrictGuestAccess value to 0 or just delete the value altogether.

Configuring Event Viewer

By default, log files can reach 512 KB, and events are overwritten after seven days. You can change these settings in the Event Log Settings dialog box, which you open by choosing Log Settings in the Event Viewer Log menu (see fig. 6.4).

Figure 6.4

The Event Log Settings dialog box.

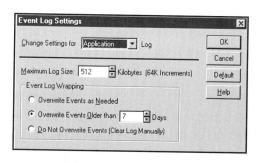

The Save As option in the Log menu enables you to save the log as an event log file (with an EVT extension), making it available for examination on another computer at a future time, or as a comma-separated value text file (also with a TXT extension) for importing into a spreadsheet or database. The format you select depends on the spreadsheet or database program you use for the text file you import. Choose the Select Computer command to view events on another computer (of course, you must have an administrator-level account on the remote Windows NT-based computer to succeed).

C2 environments require that all log information be retained. No information may be overwritten, because overwriting events may allow a security break to escape unnoticed after it is overwritten. This isn't the default setting, however; using it can result in the log file becoming quite large and unwieldy.

Using Event Viewer

At some point, every Windows NT user receives this infamous message:

```
One or more services failed to start. Please see the Event Viewer
for details.
```

This message appears when the first user logs on to the system after at least one Windows NT component fails to load successfully. As directed, you should immediately proceed to Event Viewer.

To find the source of the problem, look at the system log under the Event heading. Somewhere toward the top of the column, you should find an Event code of 6005. (By default, the logs list the most recent events at the top of the list, so start scanning at the top of the list or you may not find the most recent 6005 event.) If you look under the Source heading for this event, it should read EventLog, and it is an informational message. Event 6005 means that the EventLog service was successfully started. Any events that appear chronologically earlier than 6005 are events logged during system boot. Investigate these events, particularly the errors, because they may reveal the source of your problem.

To examine an event message, double-click on an event to open the Event Detail dialog box (see fig. 6.5).

Figure 6.5

The Event Detail dialog box.

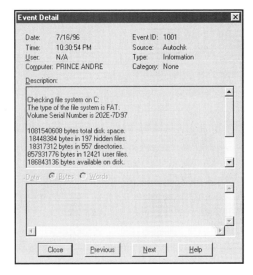

Note the identifying information for the event:

▶ Date of the event

▶ Time of the event

▶ User account that generated the event, if applicable (usually found in the security log)

▶ Computer on which the event occurred

▶ Event ID (the Windows NT Event code)

▶ Source Windows NT component that generated the event

▶ Type of event (Error, Warning, and so on)

▶ Category of event (Logon/Logoff audit, for example)

▶ Description of the event

▶ Data in hexadecimal format, useful to a developer or debugger

A note about the preceding items: the Event Descriptions have come a long way since the cryptic MS-DOS error messages. Some Windows NT messages tell you everything you need to know:

```
The D drive is almost full. The files will need to be backed up
and then deleted from the D drive.
```

Others perhaps tell you too much:

```
Could not look up the assoc block for an NBT association. Check
if the message read is corrupted. WINS looks at bit 11-14 of the
message to determine if the assoc. is from another WINS or from
an NBT node. It is possible that the bits are corrupted or that
there is a mismatch between what the two WINS servers expect to
see in those bits (maybe you changed the value to be put in code
and not increment the version number set during assoc. setup).
```

Sometimes progress seems to work in reverse:

```
A DosDevIoctl or DosFsCtl to NETWKSTA.SYS failed. The data shown
is in the format:DWORD approx CS:IP of call to ioctl or fsctlWORD
error code WORD ioctl or fsctl number.
```

Just write down the error message and call Microsoft's Product Support Services. They know what to do with the information.

If you want to save the hexadecimal data along with the event description, be certain to save the events as EVT files. The hex data doesn't save with TXT files.

You also can filter events so that only certain events report on-screen. Note that doing so doesn't delete messages from the event log, but rather, only controls which of the logged events appear in Event Viewer at any given time. To filter events, choose View, Filter Events. You may filter by the following:

▶ Event date and time

▶ Event type (Error, Warning, and so on)

▶ Source (Atdisk, Browser, and so on)

▶ User

▶ Computer

▶ Event ID

If you are filtering an event log imported from another computer, you can filter only for components installed on your own machine. In other words, the filters are read from your own Registry, not from the event log file itself.

Windows NT Diagnostics

Windows NT Diagnostics provides a tidy front end to much of the information in the HKEY_LOCAL_MACHINE Registry subtree. Like its ancestor, MSD from Windows 3.1, Windows NT Diagnostics can create incredibly detailed and valuable system configuration reports. One thing you cannot do with Windows NT Diagnostics is edit the system configuration. Figure 6.6 shows the Windows NT Diagnostics dialog box.

Figure 6.6

The Windows NT Diagnostics dialog box.

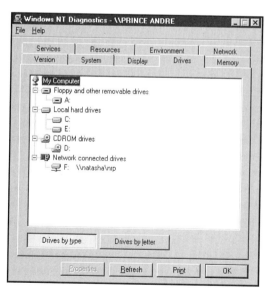

The Windows NT Diagnostics dialog box includes the following nine tabs:

▶ **Version.** Displays information stored under HKEY_LOCAL_
MACHINE\Software\Microsoft\Windows NT\CurrentVersion,
including the build number, registered owner, and Service
Pack update information.

▶ **System.** Displays information stored under HKEY_LOCAL_
MACHINE\Hardware, including CPU and other device identification information.

▶ **Display.** Displays information on the video adapter and
adapter settings.

▶ **Drives.** Lists all drive letters in use and their types, including
drive letters for floppy drives, hard disks, CD-ROM and opti-
cal drives, and network connections. Double-click on a drive
letter to display a drive Properties dialog box. The General
tab of the drive Properties dialog box shows byte and cluster
information for the drive (see fig. 6.7). The File System tab
shows file system information (see fig. 6.8).

Figure 6.7

*The drive Proper-
ties General tab.*

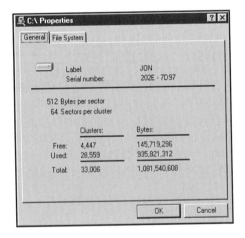

▶ **Memory.** Displays current memory load, as well as physical
and virtual memory statistics.

▶ **Services.** Displays service information stored under
HKEY_LOCAL_MACHINE\System\CurrentControlSet\Services,
including status. Click on the Devices button to display driver information stored under HKEY_LOCAL_MACHINE\
System\CurrentControlSet\Control, including status.

▶ **Resources.** Displays device information listed by interrupt and by port, and also by DMA channels and UMB locations in use.

▶ **Environment.** Displays environment variables for command prompt sessions (set under Control Panel System).

▶ **Network.** Displays network component configuration and status.

Figure 6.8

*The drive Proper-
ties File System
tab.*

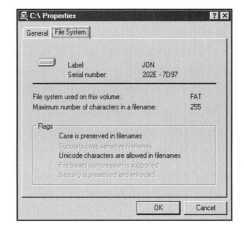

System Recovery

The Recovery utility is a tool you can use to record debugging information, alert an administrator, or reboot the system in the event of a Stop error. (A Stop error causes Windows NT to stop all processes.) To configure the Recovery utility, start the Control Panel System application and click on the Startup/Shutdown tab (see fig. 6.9).

The bottom frame of the Startup/Shutdown tab is devoted to Recovery options. The options are as follows:

▶ Write an event to the system log.

▶ Send an administrative alert.

▶ Write debugging information to (specify a file name). In the event of a Stop error, the Savedump.exe program dumps everything in memory to the pagefile and marks the location of the dump. When you restart your system, Windows NT copies the memory dump from the pagefile to the file specified in the Startup/Shutdown tab. You can then use a program called Dumpexam.exe in the \Support directory of the Windows NT CD-ROM to study the contents of the memory dump and determine the cause of the Stop error.

▶ Automatically reboot. You might not want to have your server sit idle after a Stop error. This option instructs Windows NT to automatically reboot after a Stop error.

Figure 6.9

The System application Startup/ Shutdown tab.

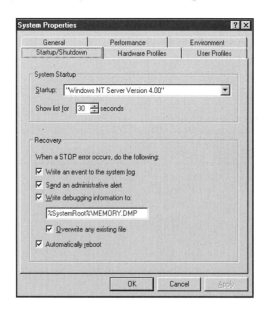

Backing Up the Registry

By now, you're more than aware of the danger of tampering with the Registry. Safety demands you back up the Registry before trying new Registry modification. It is useful to understand which files are involved during a backup of the Registry.

Before discussing Registry files, you should be familiar with the term hive. A hive is a binary file that contains all the keys and values within a branch of the Registry. Not every key is a hive.

Some keys are contained within hives, and others are never written to disk at all (such as HKEY_LOCAL_MACHINE\Hardware, which was examined earlier).

> You may be wondering why these files are called *hives*. Supposedly, one of the Windows NT developers thought the Registry resembled a massive beehive with all its tunnels and chambers, and so coined the term.

Two files are associated with each hive: one file is named after the hive and has no extension, and the other is identically named with a LOG extension (with the exception of SYSTEM, which has a SYSTEM.ALT counterpart for reasons to be explained shortly). Both files reside in the \<winnt_root>\SYSTEM32\CONFIG directory. Most of the hives loaded at any given time are residents of HKEY_LOCAL_MACHINE, and the others belong to HKEY_USERS. Here is a list of the Registry hives:

HKEY_LOCAL_MACHINE\SAM (SAM, SAM.LOG)

HKEY_LOCAL_MACHINE\SECURITY (SECURITY, SECURITY.LOG)

HKEY_LOCAL_MACHINE\SOFTWARE (SOFTWARE, SOFTWARE.LOG)

HKEY_LOCAL_MACHINE\SYSTEM (SYSTEM, SYSTEM.ALT)

HKEY_USERS\.DEFAULT (DEFAULT, DEFAULT.LOG)

HKEY_USERS\<user_sid> (<user_profile>, <user_profile>.LOG)

The LOG files provide fault tolerance for the Registry. Whenever configuration data is changed, the changes are written to the LOG file first. Then the first sector of the actual hive is flagged to indicate that an update is taking place. The data is transferred from the log to the hive, and the update flag on the hive is then lowered. If the computer were to crash after the flag had been raised but before it had been lowered, some, if not all the data, would quite possibly be corrupt. If that happened, when Windows NT restarted it would detect the flag still raised on the hive, and it would use the log to redo the update.

The only exception to this rule is the SYSTEM file. Because the SYSTEM hive contains critical information that must be loaded intact to load enough of the operating system to process the log files, a duplicate of SYSTEM is maintained as SYSTEM.ALT. This file functions identically to a log file, except that the entire file (rather than just the changes) is mirrored. If the computer were to crash during an update to the SYSTEM branch of the Registry, the integrity of the SYSTEM hive is still preserved. If the data had not yet been fully committed to SYSTEM.ALT, the SYSTEM hive is still preserved in its original configuration. If the data had not yet been fully committed to SYSTEM, SYSTEM.ALT would be used to redo the update.

Now that you know which files are involved in the Registry, do you need to back them all up? No. In fact, the LOG files are so transitory that they would be useless by the time the backup completes. You may want to back up the user profile information if you are going to alter user-specific information, but usually these settings are potentially harmless. SAM and SECURITY are off-limits for editing, so you can't hurt them at all.

The files of greatest import are SYSTEM and SOFTWARE, which usually are so small they can fit on a floppy disk. Consequently, just copying the files to a disk is rather tempting. Do not, however, give in to that temptation.

Registry files almost always are in a state of flux and are constantly open for read/write access. The Windows NT Backup program usually skips over these files for that reason. Probably the best way to back up the SYSTEM and SOFTWARE files is to use the Repair Disk application, another hidden application in the \<winnt_root>\SYSTEM32 directory. The section "RDISK.EXE," earlier in this chapter, discussed the Repair Disk utility, otherwise known as RDISK.EXE.

Backing Up Individual Keys

You can create your own hive files by saving an entire branch of the Registry starting from any key you choose. You do so by choosing Registry, Save Key in Registry Editor. To load the hive into the Registry of another Windows NT computer, choose Registry, Restore Key.

If you want to work with the key only temporarily, you can use the Restore Volatile command rather than the Restore Key command. The key still loads into the Registry at the selected location, but it doesn't reload the next time the system restarts.

Troubleshooting Printer Problems

Printing has always been troublesome, regardless of the operating system. Windows NT handles printing better than most systems do, but you still should make a concerted effort to avoid certain potential printing pitfalls.

If you can't print to a printer, try a different printer to see whether the problem also appears there. Try printing from a different account. Make certain that that the printer is plugged in, turned on, and so on. Make sure that the printer has paper. Remove and re-create the printer if necessary.

Microsoft lists the following objective for the Windows NT Server exam:

Choose the appropriate course of action to take to resolve printer problems.

When you try to isolate printing problems, the following guidelines can be helpful:

1. Check the cable connections and the printer port to verify that the printing device is on and the cables are all securely fitted. This precaution may seem rather obvious, but the simplest of things cause some of the most perplexing problems.

2. To verify that the correct printer driver is installed and configured properly, establish the type of printing device (such as PCL, PostScript, and so on) and verify that the correct driver type has been installed. If necessary, reinstall the printer driver. If a printer driver needs updating, use the Printers folder to install and configure the new printer driver.

3. Verify that the printer is selected, either explicitly in the application or as the default printer. Most Windows NT applications have a Printer Setup menu or toolbar button. When printing by means of OLE or some other indirect means, you need to specify a default printer.

4. Verify that enough hard disk space is available to generate the print job, especially on the partition that has the spooler directory specified, which, by default, is the system partition (that is, the winnt_root partition).

5. Run the simplest application possible (for example, Notepad) to verify that printing can occur from other applications within Windows NT. If problems are encountered printing from the application (other than a Win32-based application), check the appropriate application subsystem (for example, DOS, Win16, POSIX, and OS/2).

6. Print to a file (FILE:) and then copy the output file to a printer port. If this works, the problem is the spooler, or is data-transmission related. If this doesn't work, the problem is application- or driver-related.

Spooling Problems

By default, spooled print jobs reside in the \<winnt_root>\ SYSTEM32\SPOOL\PRINTERS directory until completely printed. If a Windows NT-based computer is acting as a print server for the network, make sure plenty of free disk space is available on the partition that contains the default spool directory. Spooled print jobs can be quite large and can eat up disk space more quickly than you might think, especially during peak printing periods. Also, keeping this partition defragmented improves printing performance. Because Windows NT doesn't include a defrag utility, you need to use a third-party utility (or boot to MS-DOS if you are using the FAT file system).

If you have more room on another partition, you may change the default spool directory in the Advanced tab of the Server Properties dialog box (as described earlier in this chapter). You can also change the spool directory in the Registry by adding a value called DefaultSpoolDirectory of type REG_SZ to the following and entering the path to the new spool directory:

```
HKEY_LOCAL_MACHINE\System\CurrentControlSet\Control\Print\
Printers
```

You need to restart the spooler service (or the computer itself) for the change to take effect.

You can also assign a separate spool directory for each individual printer. Enter the path to the new spool directory as the data for the value SpoolDirectory in the following, where <Printer> is the name of the printer you want to redirect:

```
HKEY_LOCAL_MACHINE\System\CurrentControlSet\Control\Print\~Printers\
<Printer>
```

Again, you need to restart the spooler service for this change to take effect.

Printing from Non-Windows-Based Applications

Non-Windows-based applications—for example, MS-DOS-based applications—require their own printer drivers if the application requires any kind of formatted output other than plain ASCII text. WordPerfect for MS-DOS, for example, does not even allow the user to print a document unless there is a WordPerfect-specific and printer-specific driver installed, for example, because non-Windows-based applications are not written to conform to or take advantage of the Windows APIs. Also, remember that you may need to use the NET USE LPT1: \\servername\printername command to enable the DOS-based application to print.

Handling the Computer Crashing

When a document prints, two files are created for the print job in the spool directory (by default, <winnt_root>\SYSTEM32\ SPOOL\PRINTERS). One of the files, which has an .SPL extension, is the actual print job spool file. The other file, which has an .SHD extension, is a shadow file that contains information about the job, including its owner and priority. These files remain in the spool directory until the jobs finish printing, at which point they are deleted.

In the event of a system crash, some spool and shadow files may be left over from jobs that were waiting to be printed. When the spooler service restarts (along with the rest of the system), the printer should process these files immediately. They are, however, sometimes corrupted during the crash and get stuck. Be certain, therefore, to check the spool directory every so often, and delete any spool and shadow files with old date/time stamps. How old is old depends on how long it takes to print a job on your printer. Certainly anything from days, weeks, or months ago should be deleted.

If a print job appears stuck in the printer and you cannot delete it, stop the spooler service in Control Panel Services and delete the SPL and/or SHD file for that job from the spool directory (match the date/time stamp on the files and in Print Manager to determine which files are causing the problem).

Printing Too Slow or Workstation Too Sluggish

Windows NT Workstation assigns priority 7 to the spooler service, which puts printing on an equal footing with other background applications. Windows NT Server, which favors printing over background applications, assigns priority 9 to the spooler, which puts it neck-and-neck with the foreground applications.

If a Windows NT-based workstation moonlighting as a print server appears to print too slowly, consider raising the priority by one or two classes. If the workstation is responding sluggishly to the user while printing, consider lowering the priority by a class or two. Don't alter the priority by more than two levels under any circumstances without a full understanding of the performance consequences involved.

To change the priority class for the Spooler service, add a value called PriorityClass of type REG_DWORD to HKEY_LOCAL_MACHINE\System\CurrentControlSet\Control\Print and set it equal to the priority class desired. If this value is set to 0 or isn't present, the default is used (7 for Windows NT Workstation, or 9 for Windows NT Server).

Troubleshooting RAS

If RAS isn't working, check the Event Viewer. Several RAS events appear in the system log.

You might also check the Control Panel Dial-Up Networking Monitor application. The Status tab of Dial-Up Networking Monitor displays statistics on current conditions, including connection statistics and device errors.

Microsoft lists the following objective for the Windows NT Server exam:

Choose the appropriate course of action to take to resolve RAS problems.

If you are having problems with PPP, you can log PPP debugging information to a file called PPP.Log in the \<winnt_root>\System32\Ras directory. To log PPP debugging information to PPP.Log, change the Registry value for the following subkey to 1:

```
\HKEY_LOCAL_MACHINE\System\CurrentControlSet\Services\Rasman\PPP\
Logging
```

Microsoft has identified the following common RAS problems and some possible solutions:

▶ **Authentication.** RAS authentication problems often stem from incompatible encryption methods. Try to connect using the `Allow any authentication including clear text` option (described earlier in this chapter). If you can connect using clear text and you can't connect using encryption, you know the client and server encryption methods are incompatible.

▶ **Callback with Multilink.** If a client makes a connection using Multilink over multiple phone lines, with Callback enabled, the server will call back using only a single phone line (in other words, Multilink functionality is lost). RAS can use only one phone number for callback. If the Multilink connection uses two channels over an ISDN line, the server can still use Multilink on the callback.

▶ **AutoDial at Logon.** At logon, when Explorer is initializing, it might reference a shortcut or some other target that requires an AutoDial connection, causing AutoDial to spontaneously dial a remote connection during logon. The only way to prevent this is to disable AutoDial, or to eliminate the shortcut or other target causing the AutoDial to occur.

Troubleshooting Connectivity Problems

Network problems often are caused by cables, adapters, or IRQ conflicts, or problems with transmission media. Protocol problems also can disrupt the network. Use a diagnostics program to check the network adapter card. Use a cable analyzer to check the cabling. Use Network Monitor (described in the next section) to check network traffic, or use a network protocol analyzer.

Microsoft lists the following objective for the Windows NT Server exam:

Choose the appropriate course of action to take to resolve connectivity problems.

If you are using TCP/IP, you often can isolate the problem by *pinging* the other computers on your network. Exercise 1.2 in Chapter 1 described a common diagnostic procedure:

1. Ping the 127.0.0.1 (the loopback address).

2. Ping your own IP address.

3. Ping the address of another computer on your subnet.

4. Ping the default gateway.

5. Ping a computer beyond the default gateway.

Check the Control Panel Services application to ensure that the Server service and the Workstation service (and any other vital services that might affect connectivity) are running properly. Check the Bindings tab in the Control Panel Network application to ensure that the services are bound to applications and adapters.

Network Monitor

Windows NT Server 4 includes a tool called Network Monitor. Network Monitor captures and filters packets and analyzes network activity. The Network Monitor included with Windows NT Server can monitor only the specific system on which it is installed, unlike the Network Monitor in Microsoft's Systems Management Server package, which can monitor other systems on the network.

To install Windows NT Server's Network Monitor, start the Network application in Control Panel and click on the Services tab. Click on the Add button and select Network Monitor from the network services list. After Network Monitor is installed, it appears in the Administrative Tools program group.

Figure 6.10 shows the Network Monitor main screen.

Figure 6.10

The Network Monitor main screen.

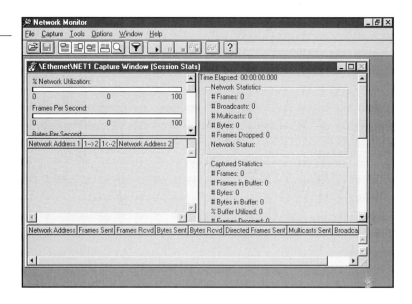

The Network Monitor window is divided into four sections, or *panes*. This section describes each of the four Network Monitor panes and discusses the various parameters and statistics you can monitor with Network Monitor.

The Graph pane (in the upper-left corner) shows the current network activity in a series of five bar charts. Note the scroll bar to the right of the Graph section. To view the bar charts (not shown in fig. 6.10), scroll down or drag the lower border down, exposing the hidden charts. The five bar graphs are as follows:

▶ % Network Utilization

▶ Frames Per Second

▶ Bytes Per Second

▶ Broadcasts Per Second

▶ Multicasts Per Second

Below the Graphs pane you see the Session Stats pane. The Session Stats pane indicates the exchange of information from two nodes on the network, the amount of data, and the direction of travel. This data is limited to a per-session basis.

The Session Stats pane reports only on the first 128 sessions it finds. You can specify a particular session creating a capture filter.

The Session Stats pane collects information on the following four areas:

▶ **Network Address 1.** The first node included in a network session.

▶ **1→2.** The number of packets sent from the first address to the second.

▶ **1←2.** The number of packets sent from the second address to the first.

▶ **Network Address 2.** The second node included in the network session.

On the right side of the display windows is the Total Stats pane, which reveals information relevant to the entire activity on the network. Whether statistics are supported depends on the network adapter. If a given network adapter isn't supported, Unsupported replaces the label.

The Total Stats information is divided into the following five categories:

▶ *Network Statistics*

Total Frames
Total Broadcasts
Total Multicasts
Total Bytes
Total Frames Dropped
Network Status

The Network Status value is always normal if you use an Ethernet network. If you use Token Ring, the Network Status value indicates the status of the ring.

▶ *Captured Statistics*

Captured Frames
Captured Frames in Buffer
Captured Bytes
Capture Bytes in Buffer
Percentage of Allotted Buffer Space in Use
Captured Packets Dropped

▶ *Per Second Statistics*

Frames
Bytes/second
Broadcasts/second
Multicasts/second
% Network Utilization

▶ *Network Card (MAC) Statistics*

Total Frames
Total Broadcasts
Total Multicasts
Total Bytes

▶ *Network Card (MAC) Error Statistics*

Total Cyclical Redundancy Check (CRC) Errors
Total Dropped Frames Due to Inadequate Buffer Space
Total Dropped Packets Due to Hardware Failure(s)

At the bottom of the display window, you see the Station Stats pane. The Station Stats pane displays information specific to a workstation's activity on the network. You can sort on any category by right-clicking on the column label.

The Station pane reports only on the first 128 sessions it finds. You can specify a particular session using a capture filter.

The following eight categories constitute the Station pane:

▶ Network Address

▶ Frames Sent

- ▶ Frames Rcvd

- ▶ Bytes Sent

- ▶ Bytes Rcvd

- ▶ Directed Frames Sent

- ▶ Multicasts Sent

- ▶ Broadcasts Sent

Troubleshooting Access and Permission Problems

If you can't log on, you may be using an incorrect username or password. Also, enable the check box beneath the password to make certain that you are logging on to the correct domain or workgroup (or the local machine). If you still can't log on, try logging on using another account. If other accounts are working normally, check the settings for your account in User Manager for Domains. If you can't log on from any account, repair the accounts database by using the emergency repair process. One of the worst culprits for logon problems is the Caps Lock key. Make certain that the user isn't typing the password in all caps.

Microsoft lists the following objective for the Windows NT Server exam:

Choose the appropriate course of action to take to resolve resource access problems and permission problems.

If a user can't access a file, a share, a printer, or some other resource, check the resource permissions. Try connecting using a different account. Try accessing a similar resource to see whether the problem also appears there. Make certain that the user has spelled the name of the resource correctly.

Check the Control Panel Services application to ensure that the NetLogon service, the Server service, and the Workstation service are running properly, and check the Bindings tab in the of the Control Panel Network application to ensure that the services are bound to applications and adapters.

You can also check User Manager for Domains to ensure that the user's group memberships haven't changed or that a change to a group rights setting hasn't inadvertently denied the user access to the resource.

Check System Policy Editor for restrictions on the user's access to computers or other resources.

Recovering from Fault-Tolerance Failures

Even if you are employing a high-tech RAID fault-tolerance system, a well planned backup routine is still your best defense against lost data. Windows NT includes a backup utility (NTBACKUP.EXE). Backup is part of the Administrative Tools group; figure 6.11 shows the Backup utility.

Figure 6.11

The Backup window.

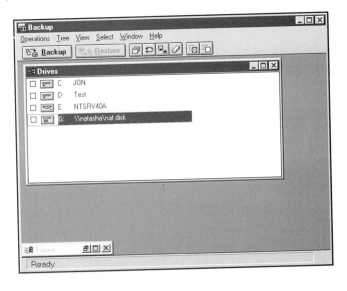

Microsoft lists the following objective for the Windows NT Server exam:

Choose the appropriate course of action to take to resolve fault-tolerance failures. Fault-tolerance methods include: tape backup, mirroring, stripe set with parity, disk duplexing.

Backing Up Files and Directories

The Backup main window shows the disk drives presently accessible to the Backup utility. Double-click on a drive and to see an Explorer-type directory tree (see fig. 6.12). Note that every directory or file has a small box beside it. Click on the box to back up the file or directory and all child files/directories beneath it.

Figure 6.12

Selecting a file or directory for backup.

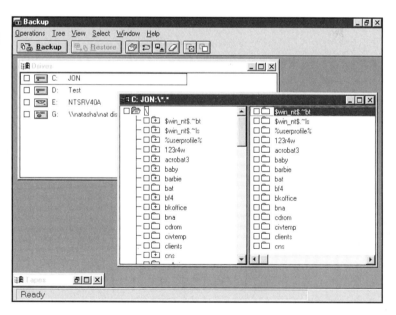

To start a backup, click on the Backup button in the toolbar or choose Operations, Backup. The Backup Information dialog box appears, offering a number of backup options (see fig. 6.13). Note the Log Information frame at the bottom of the Backup Information dialog box. You can write a summary or a detailed description of the backup operation to a log file.

Figure 6.13

The Backup Information dialog box.

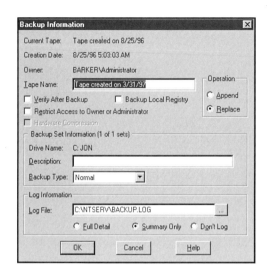

Restoring Files and Directories

To restore a file or directory using the Backuputility, open the Tapes window (if you don't see the Tapes window on your screen, pull down the Window menu and choose Tapes) and select the backup set you want to restore. Like the Drives window, the Tapes window enables you to expand directories and select individual files for restoration (see fig. 6.14).

Figure 6.14

The Tapes window.

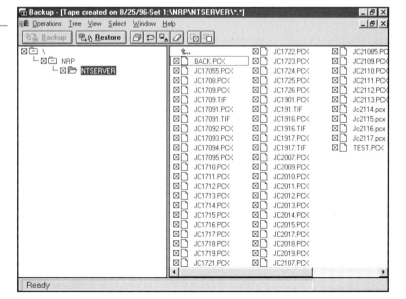

Select the files/directories you want to restore and click on the Restore button in the toolbar (or choose Operations, Restore). The Restore Information dialog box appears (see fig. 6.15). Select the desired restore options and click on OK to restore the files/directories.

Figure 6.15

The Restore Information dialog box.

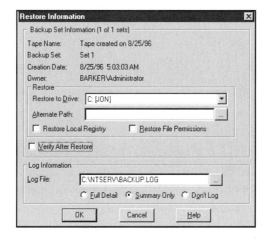

You also can run the NTBACKUP utility from the command prompt. This enables you to automate the backup process through batch files, so you can perform backups at regular intervals. You can only back up directories with the ntbackup command (not individual files). The syntax is as follows:

    ntbackup *operation path*

where *operation* is the name of the operation (backup, restore, and so on), and *path* is the path to the directory you're backing up. The NTBACKUP command includes a number of switches, including the following:

    /a cause the backup set to be appended after the last backup set. (If you don't specify /a will overwrite existing backup sets on the tape.)

    /v verifies the backup operation.

    /d "text" enables you to add a description of the data in the backup set.

    /t {option} enables you to specify the backup type (normal, incremental, daily, differential, copy).

For a complete description of NTBACKUP options, see Windows NT Online Help.

Breaking a Mirror Set

When a partitionin a mirror set fails, it becomes an orphan. To maintain service until the mirror is repaired, the fault-tolerant device directs all I/0 requests to the healthy partition. If the boot and/or system partitions are involved, a fault tolerant boot disk is required to restart the system. To create a fault tolerance boot disk, follow these steps:

1. Format a floppy disk using Windows NT.

2. If you are using an I386 system, copy NTLDR, NTDETECT.COM, NTBOOTDD.SYS (for SCSI disks not using SCSI BIOS), and BOOT.INI to the disk.

   If you're using a RISC-based computer, copy OSLOADER.EXE and HAL.DLL.

3. Modify the BOOT.INI file so that it points to the mirrored copy of the boot partition.

To fix a mirror set, you must first break it by choosing Fault Tolerance, Break Mirror. This action exposes the remaining partition as a separate volume. The healthy partition is given the drive letter that was previously assigned to it in the set, and the orphaned partition is given the next logical drive letter, or one that you manually selected for it.

After the mirror has been re-established as a primary partition, a new relationship can be formed by selecting additional free space and restarting the process of creating a mirror set.

Regenerating a Stripe Set with Parity

Like a mirror set, the partition that fails in a stripe set with parity becomes an orphan. Also, the fault-tolerant device redirects I/O requests to the remaining partitions in the set to enable reconstruction. So that this can be done, the data is stored in RAM by using the parity bits (which may affect the system's performance).

To regenerate a stripe set with parity, follow these steps:

1. Select the stripe set with parity by clicking on it.

2. Select an area of free space as large or larger than the stripe set.

3. Choose Fault Tolerance, Regenerate.

You must close the Disk Administrator and restart the system before the process can begin. After the system restarts, the information from the existing partitions in the stripe set are read into memory and re-created on the new member. This process completes in the background, so the stripe set with parity isn't active in the Disk Administrator until it finishes.

Troubleshooting Partitions and Disks

When you install Windows NT, your initial disk configuration is saved on the emergency repair disk and in the directory \<winnt_root>\Repair. The RDISK utility does update the disk configuration information stored on the repair disk and in the Repair directory. You can also save or restore the disk configuration by using Disk Adminstrator (see the section "Saving and Restoring Configuration Information," earlier in this chapter).

You should periodically update emergency configuration information in case you ever need to use the Emergency Repair Process or you ever want to you upgrade to a newer version of Windows NT. Otherwise, NT restores the original configuration that was saved when you first installed Windows NT.

Exercise Section

Exercise 6.1:   Booting with SOS

In Exercise 6.1, you learn how to initiate a Windows NT boot by using the /sos switch, which enumerates each driver as the drivers load during the kernel load phase.

Estimated time: 20 minutes

1. Start the Notepad accessory application and open the boot.ini file in the root directory of the system partition. In the Notepad Open dialog box, don't forget to select All Files in the box labeled Files of type. The extension may not appear in the browse list. (The file name may appear as *boot*, without the extension. If you aren't sure you have the right file, right-click on the file and select Properties.) Examine the MS-DOS name setting in the file Properties dialog box.

2. Figure 6.16 shows the boot.ini file in Notepad. Find the line with the text string "Windows NT Server Version 4.00 [VGA]." Make sure the string is followed by the switches /basevideo and /sos. If you're confident your system uses a VGA video driver, skip to step 6; otherwise, continue with step 4.

3. Save the boot.ini file to a different file name (such as boot.tmp) by using the File, Save As command.

4. Delete the /basevideo switch in the line with the text string "Windows NT Server Version 4.00 [VGA]." The /sos switch should remain. Change the text in the square brackets from "VGA" to "sos."

5. Save the file as boot.ini.

   You may have to use the Save As command to save boot.ini. Verify the file name in the File name box. Step 3 may have changed the default file name.

6. Close Notepad and shut down your system.

continues

Exercise 6.1: Continued

7. Reboot Windows NT. When the boot menu appears, choose the "sos" option (or the VGA option if you skipped steps 3–5).

8. Watch the drivers display on-screen as they load. (Watch carefully, they will disappear quickly from the screen.) The drivers, like the boot.ini entries, will appear in ARC format. If you experience a boot failure, you can use this technique to determine which driver crashed or hung the system.

9. Log on to Windows NT. Restore the boot.ini file to its original state, either by inserting "VGA" and "/basevideo" using Notepad or by copying the boot.tmp file back to boot.ini. When you're finished, open boot.ini and make sure it is back to normal.

Figure 6.16

A boot.ini file.

Step 9 is very important. You may not use the VGA boot option for months or even years, and when you do, you may not remember that you tried this exercise.

Review Questions

The following questions will text your knowledge of the information in this chapter. For additional questions, see MCP Endeavor and the Microsoft Roadmap/Assessment exam on the CD-ROM that accompanies this book.

1. A user calls and says that he can't log on to the system. He is getting a message that says NT cannot log you on. Check your userid and password information and try again, or something to that effect. What would you check?

   A. Make sure that the user types in the correct password and userid combination. Also check that the user has entered the password in the correct case and is specifying the correct domain name.

   B. Nothing. It's a normal message that the user would get when the server is down for maintenance.

   C. Log on as administrator and restart the domain controller to clear out any unused connections. When the server comes back up, the user should be able to log on.

2. You received a message during the boot process that a dependency service failed to start. Where should you check for more information?

   A. The file server error log

   B. In Event Viewer under the security log

   C. In Event Viewer under the system log

   D. In Server Manager, under the system log

3. You have turned on auditing, but cannot remember where the system puts the audit information. Where do you need to look?

   A. In Event Viewer under the security log

   B. In Event Viewer under the system log

    C. In Auditcon under the security section

    D. At the command prompt, type **NET** Show Audit

4. You're looking for a particular message in the system log under Event Viewer, but there are so many messages that you can't find the one you're looking for. How can you display messages of a certain type?

    A. You cannot. Event Viewer shows all the messages in the system log.

    B. You must set up Event Viewer to store only messages of the type you're looking for and then restart the system.

    C. You can filter the log by choosing View, Filter Events.

    D. You must first export the data to an ASCII file and then use the Edit program to find the specific data you seek.

5. Your manager informs you that an inventory of all company Computers running NT Workstation and NT Server needs to be done. Which NT utility can you use to safely determine the amount of RAM, type of CPU, and other information about the computers in question?

    A. You must purchase the 32-bit version of PC Tools. This program gives you the required information.

    B. No tools will run under NT because they would have to access the hardware directly, which isn't allowed under NT.

    C. You must manually edit the Registry and search for the information you need.

    D. Use the Windows NT Diagnostics utility.

6. A user calls you and says that while he was running Windows NT Diagnostics, he attempted to change the type of CPU that was reported but could not. Why?

A. NT Diagnostics only shows information. You cannot make any modifications using this tool.

B. The type of CPU cannot be changed with NT Diagnostics. The user must use Registry Editor to make the change manually.

C. The user must make the CPU change in CMOS setup, not in NT Diagnostics.

7. While on a telephone call with Microsoft, the support engineer asks you which version of the operating system you're running. How can you find this out? Choose all that apply.

A. You cannot. You must contact your network administrator for the information.

B. The support engineer should be able to look up your product registration information.

C. Run Windows NT Diagnostics and choose Version.

D. Check the Registry under the HKEY_LOCAL_MACHINE subtree.

8. You're having problems with Stop errors on a computer running Windows NT Server. How can you set the recovery options that tell the system what action to perform in the event of a Stop error?

A. You can set these options under Control Panel, System.

B. You cannot. The system automatically places an event in the system log and then restarts the computer.

C. You must configure a process to start whenever a Stop error is encountered by using the command-line utility AT.

D. Use the Control Panel, Network option to configure the action to be taken when a Stop error is encountered.

9. Which set of files are required to boot Windows NT on an Intel-x86 based computer?

   A. NTLDR
      BOOT.INI
      NTDETECT.COM
      NTOSKRNL.EXE
      NTBOOTDD.SYS

   B. NTLDR
      BOOT.MNU
      NTDETECT.EXE
      OSLOADER
      NTBOOTDD.SYS

   C. OSLOADER
      NTOSKRNL.EXE
      NTDETECT.COM
      NTBOOTDD.SYS

10. Which file is used on an Intel-x86 based computer for computers that have SCSI hard drive controllers with the BIOS disabled?

   A. OSLOADER.EXE

   B. BOOTSCSI.SYS

   C. NTBOOTDD.SYS

   D. NTBOOTSCSI.SYS

11. What is the best explanation of the function of the NTDETECT.COM program?

   A. It reads the hardware configuration data from a RISC-based computer and passes it on to the OSLOADER program.

   B. It reads the hardware configuration information from a computer with a Plug-and-Play BIOS and updates the Registry.

C. It scans the hardware in the computer and reports the list back to NTLDR for later inclusion in the Registry.

D. It initializes the hardware on a computer with a Plug-and-Play BIOS.

12. You receive a phone call from a user asking you whether she can somehow reduce the amount of time her computer takes to boot. She also would like to change the default operating system from MS-DOS to NT Workstation. Which utility would you advise her to use to accomplish this?

A. Control Panel, Boot

B. Control Panel, System

C. Server Manager

D. Configure on a user-by-user basis in the users' profiles

13. You receive a phone call from a user who accidentally changed the SCSI controller card driver and now the computer won't boot NT. It stops at the blue screen and gives him a system error. What would you suggest?

A. Tell the user to boot into DOS and rerun the Windows NT Setup program.

B. Suggest that the user go out and purchase and install the SCSI device that he selected.

C. Tell the user that he now needs to reinstall NT.

D. Suggest that the user select the LastKnowGood configuration during NT booting. Then have the user remove the incorrect driver.

14. You're trying to understand the ARC-naming conventions in your BOOT.INI file. What would the ARC name look like if your computer had an IDE drive as the boot device?

A. scsi(0)disk(1)rdisk(0)partition(1)

B. scsi(1)disk(1)rdisk(0)partition(1)

    C. multi(1)disk(0)rdisk(1)partition(1)

    D. multi(1)disk(1)rdisk(0)partition(2)

15. What does the /basevideo switch in the BOOT.INI file specify?

    A. To load NT, but not to use any upper memory blocks.

    B. To load NT, using the resolution specified by your last driver configuration for the display.

    C. To load NT, but to select the standard VGA mode 640 × 480.

    D. To load NT, but not in graphics mode. Load only the command-line version of NT.

16. You're having a problem loading NT on your workstation. It appears that a driver may not be loading correctly, but you can't tell which drivers are loading and which ones aren't. What command-line switch can you add to the BOOT.INI file to see a list of the drivers loading during the boot process?

    A. /sos

    B. /basevideo

    C. /crashdebug

    D. /listdrivers

17. Which utility enables you to create an emergency repair disk?

    A. Disk Administrator

    B. ERD.EXE

    C. BOOTNT.COM

    D. RDISK.EXE

18. If you receive the message `I/O Error accessing boot sector file multi(0)disk(0)rdisk(0)partition(1):\bootsect.dos`, which one of the critical boot files is missing?

    A. NTLDR

    B. NTDETECT.COM

    C. BOOTSECT.DOS

    D. MSDOS.SYS

19. What is the BOOTSECT.DOS file?

    A. A copy of the information that was originally on the boot sector of the drive before NT was installed. You use it to boot an operating system other than NT.

    B. A copy of the information needed to boot a RISC-based computer.

    C. The file that detects the hardware installed on a PC with a Plug-and-Play BIOS.

    D. The file that contains the boot menu selections.

20. If your BOOTSECT.DOS file becomes corrupted, can you copy this file from another NT-based computer?

    A. Yes

    B. No

    C. Yes, if the computer is configured exactly like yours

    D. No, but you can create it from DOS using the RDISK.EXE utility

21. The boot process is considered complete when?

    A. The WinLogon dialog box appears

    B. The user presses Ctrl+Alt+Del

    C. When the user logs on

    D. After the NTDETECT.COM program runs

22. You're concerned that your boot partition is filling up with print jobs and the disk may soon run out of disk space. What can you do?

   A. Change the Registry parameter DefaultSpoolDirectory to point to a hard disk partition that has more free disk space.
   B. There is nothing that you can do. You cannot change where NT puts the spooled print jobs.
   C. Install a larger hard disk in the system.
   D. Install another hard disk in the system and span the boot partition over the newly installed disk.

23. After you make changes to the disk partitioning scheme with the Disk Administrator program, what utility should you use to update the emergency repair disk?

   A. Disk Administrator
   B. BOOTUP.EXE
   C. FDISK
   D. RDISK

Review Answers

1. A	6. A	11. C	16. A	21. C
2. C	7. C D	12. B	17. D	22. A
3. A	8. A	13. D	18. C	23. D
4. C	9. A	14. C	19. A	
5. D	10. C	15. C	20. B	

Part

TCP/IP

2

Chapter 7

Introduction to TCP/IP

This chapter helps you prepare for the exam by covering the following objectives:

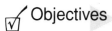 Objectives

- ▶ Install and configure TCP/IP

- ▶ On a Windows NT Server computer, configure Microsoft TCP/IP to support multiple network adapters

- ▶ Given a scenario, select the appropriate services to install when using Microsoft TCP/IP on a Microsoft Windows NT computers

The Exam

The "Internetworking with Microsoft TCP/IP on Microsoft Windows NT 4.0" exam (Exam 70-059) is one of the most crucial exams in the MCSE track. Although Microsoft does not require the exam, almost all MCSE candidates are choosing it as one of their electives. In fact, it is the most popular elective Microsoft offers. Furthermore, you can use the exam to obtain more than one certification. In addition to being an MCSE elective, the TCP/IP exam is one of three exams required to be a Microsoft Certified Product Specialist (MCPS) with an Internet Systems specialty.

In preparing for this exam, you learn some of the most useful networking skills you can have. TCP/IP is widely used on a variety of networks. Although TCP/IP has its roots in the Unix operating system and in the Internet, it often is used to connect different network operating systems into one heterogeneous network. Of course, a knowledge of TCP/IP is vital for establishing and maintaining Internet connections because TCP/IP is the Internet's protocol. However, a growing number of businesses are choosing to distribute vital internal information through intranets. Although intranets use mainly Web and FTP publishing (contained in Microsoft's Internet Information Server or IIS), once again, all these services depend on the TCP/IP protocol. (An intranet is a network intended strictly for internal use. For example, many companies use a Web server on a corporate intranet to distribute employee handbooks, phone lists, internal job listings, and shared work.)

Three Exam Preps in One Book

People prepare for exams in many ways. Some rely on their experience for the basic knowledge of a product and then fill in the details with a book such as this. Others take a Microsoft authorized course to learn the basics and the detailed information covered on the test. However, many Microsoft students end up buying additional materials to supplement the course information or to learn the material from a different point of view. Some people also purchase sample tests designed to duplicate the testing environment. Exam candidates who use a variety of sources to prepare for exams pass with higher scores and with fewer attempts, usually on the first try.

This book contains three different types of information that, when used together, can greatly improve your chances of passing the TCP/IP exam.

This book contains the same information that you would receive in Course 688, Internetworking Microsoft TCP/IP on Microsoft Windows NT 4.0, the Microsoft authorized course for this topic. Microsoft Certified Trainers, who present the authorized course each week, wrote this book. The authors explain TCP/IP in ways that are easy to understand. They also add information to provide a more thorough explanation of TCP/IP and the ways it is used in networking. These additional insights and explanations are typical of the type of information you receive from a top-notch Microsoft Certified Trainer. Therefore, you can read this book, answer the review questions, and do the exercises as a substitute for taking the Microsoft course. Microsoft has approved this book, certifying that the book contains all the information you need to know to pass the Microsoft TCP/IP test.

For those who have some experience with TCP/IP or who have taken the Microsoft course, this book is an excellent supplementary source. This book contains information not available in Microsoft courses, including a more detailed treatment of each topic. It has many more review questions that more thoroughly test your knowledge of each chapter. The exercises focus on the key concepts of TCP/IP, helping you review the most important principles with hands-on practice.

A set of sample exams is also included with this book. The test engine looks and feels like a Microsoft exam, complete with time limits and a score at the completion of the test. Authors well acquainted with the TCP/IP exam wrote the test questions, which are similar in scope and level of difficulty to those on the Microsoft TCP/IP exam. Each question in the sample test has a written explanation of the answers, which can be read only at the conclusion of the test. The answers can help you see the thinking required to correctly answer questions and to eliminate answers that don't apply.

Microsoft has made their tests extremely difficult. Test candidates must know material from the authorized Microsoft curriculum as well as information from other sources. Microsoft wants to pass only those candidates who truly know how to implement TCP/IP in a variety of environments. The *MCSE Training Guide: TCP/IP* was designed with one purpose in mind—to give all the resources you need to master TCP/IP and demonstrate your competence by passing the TCP/IP test.

What Is on the Test?

The Microsoft TCP/IP exam has questions from nine areas. Each chapter of this book is devoted to one of these areas. A test question can cover information from more than one area. In fact, test questions often cover several different areas to test your breadth of knowledge and your understanding of how the different components of TCP/IP work together.

Each chapter in this book includes appropriate references to other related components and how they work together, so you learn how all the pieces of TCP/IP work together. The review questions at the end of each chapter focus mainly on the material in that chapter; the sample test questions on the CD-ROM incorporate several sections into one question, more like actual test questions.

The following sections describe each part of the TCP/IP test and the type of information you are expected to know. The chapters that correspond to the test sections contain a thorough explanation of these concepts. You can use this summary as a useful final review to determine whether you are comfortable with all the topics listed here.

TCP/IP Architecture

This section covers the protocols and utilities that make up TCP/IP. These topics are covered in Chapter 8 of this book. The following list shows what you are expected to know from this area:

▶ What does each protocol in the TCP/IP suite do?

▶ How are these protocols combined to make a network connection?

▶ What are the TCP/IP utilities and how are they used? (Some tools are used for troubleshooting, which is covered in another section, but many utilities can be used to test your initial installation and to make various TCP/IP connections.)

▶ How was TCP/IP developed (its history) and how are changes made to the TCP/IP standards?

This section also covers the addressing scheme of TCP/IP and how it can be used to subnet a network. This is covered in Chapters 9 and 10. This list shows major topics you need to understand about addressing and subnetting:

▶ How are TCP/IP addresses structured?

▶ What do the four numbers (octets) that make up an address represent?

▶ How does the subnet mask divide the address into a network address and a host address?

▶ What type of subnet mask is needed to support a given number of subnets and hosts?

▶ What is supernetting and how does it work?

TCP/IP Routing and Name Resolution

This section covers how TCP/IP packets are sent from the host to the target and how this traffic can be directed with HOSTS and LMHOSTS files. This is covered in Chapters 11, 14, 15, and 16 of the book. (Chapters 17 and 18 more thoroughly describe WINS and DNS.) The following list shows what you need to know about TCP/IP routing:

▶ How does TCP/IP decide whether the target is a local or remote computer?

▶ How does TCP/IP decide if a computer is on a local or remote subnet?

▶ What role does the default gateway address play in routing?

▶ How do you configure LMHOSTS and HOSTS files to resolve TCP/IP addresses?

▶ How can you link information from a Unix HOSTS file into my Microsoft TCP/IP environment?

▶ If you don't use a static HOSTS or LMHOSTS file to resolve addresses, what other means are available to do this?

Installing TCP/IP on Windows NT Computers

This section covers installing TCP/IP on a Windows NT computer and how TCP/IP is configured through the Windows NT interface. Chapter 11 of this book describes this area. The following list shows what you need to know for this test section:

▶ Where in the NT interface is the new protocol installed?

▶ How do you configure TCP/IP with a manual IP address?

▶ How do you configure TCP/IP to automatically receive an IP address from a DHCP server?

▶ How do you configure other components of the TCP/IP address, such as using a DNS server or a WINS server?

▶ How do you assign multiple IP addresses to one network card?

The Dynamic Host Configuration Protocol (DHCP)

This section covers how clients can receive a TCP/IP address and other configuration information from a DHCP server. This is described in Chapter 12 of this book. The following list shows what you are expected to know from this area:

▶ How do you set up a DHCP server?

▶ What types of NT platforms can you install DHCP on?

▶ What clients can receive an address from DHCP?

▶ What additional configuration information can the client receive from DHCP?

▶ Where does a DHCP server have to be located on the network so clients can communicate with the server and receive an address?

▶ How do you set up a scope of TCP/IP addresses?

▶ How do you reserve an IP address for a specific client?

▶ What properties can you specify in addition to the address?

▶ How do you assign a Default Gateway, a WINS address, or a DNS server address along with the TCP/IP address?

▶ How do you set up scopes with multiple DHCP servers?

▶ How do you resolve the TCP/IP address for DHCP clients? (Chapters 14 and 15 more thoroughly describe WINS.)

▶ How often is a DHCP lease renewed?

▶ What happens on the client if a lease expires?

▶ How should you configure the lease life for various scenarios? (Using DHCP for a one-time assignment of addresses suggests a different lease life than using DHCP to manage a limited pool of addresses for brief Internet sessions.)

The Windows Internet Name Service (WINS)

This section covers how WINS automatically collects TCP/IP address and NetBIOS name mappings. This is described in Chapters 14 and 15 of the book. The following list shows what you need to know for the test:

▶ How do you install a WINS server?

▶ What NT platforms can WINS be installed on?

▶ How is a WINS database built?

▶ How can you view the WINS database?

▶ How can you add static entries to the WINS database?

▶ How can you import entries from a HOSTS file into the WINS database?

▶ How can you configure WINS to use a DNS server to resolve addresses that are not in its database?

▶ What clients can register their names and addresses with WINS?

▶ What clients can resolve addresses using WINS?

▶ How do clients need to be configured so they can use WINS?

▶ How can you configure WINS servers to replicate their databases?

▶ What are the two types of replication and when would I use each type?

▶ Where do you locate WINS servers on the network and how many WINS servers do you need?

▶ How does a client use a secondary WINS server?

The Domain Name System

This section covers how you can use DNS to resolve domain names or aliases to individual TCP/IP addresses. This is described in Chapters 17 and 18 of the book. You need to know the following:

▶ What does a DNS server do and what type of information is in a DNS database?

▶ How do you install a DNS server?

▶ What type of Windows NT platforms does DNS run on?

▶ Given a network configuration, where do you locate the DNS server so it is accessible to all DNS clients?

▶ Do you need more than one DNS server?

▶ How do you add entries to DNS?

▶ How do you add a zone and how do you add a record?

▶ How can you link DNS to WINS?

▶ How can you link your DNS server to other DNS servers?

▶ How does DNS resolve a name when other servers are linked to it?

▶ How does DNS server resolve Internet names?

▶ Can a non-Microsoft network (such as Unix) resolve names using a Microsoft DNS server?

Browsing in a TCP/IP Internetwork

This section covers the definition of browsing and how a browse list is built. This is described in Chapter 16 of the book. You should know the following for the test:

▶ How are different computers involved in the browsing process?

▶ How is browsing through TCP/IP different than browsing with other protocols?

▶ What is the difference between a Domain Master Browser and a Master Browser?

▶ What happens to browsing when a Master Browser goes down?

▶ What happens to browsing when a Domain Master Browser goes down?

▶ How do you configure the Domain Master Browser so you can browse other domains?

▶ How is the WINS server used to browse multiple domains?

▶ When do you have to create an LMHOSTS file to browse multiple domains?

- Does DNS play a role in browsing?

- What do you have to do when a Primary Domain Controller (PDC) goes down to preserve the browsing in my domain?

Implementing the Microsoft SNMP Service

This section covers what role SNMP (Simple Network Management Protocol) has in the TCP/IP suite of protocols and how you can use SNMP for troubleshooting. This is described in Chapter 21 of the book. For the test, you should know the following:

- What is SNMP used for?

- How do you install SNMP?

- What does SNMP expose in TCP/IP that can be used by troubleshooting and monitoring utilities?

- What Microsoft utilities use SNMP?

- What computers have to be running SNMP so they can be involved in troubleshooting?

- How can you customize a tool to extract SNMP information?

- How do I configure SNMP so troubleshooting information is available to other applications?

Performance Tuning and Optimization

This section covers what traffic TCP/IP generates as it is used for network communications. Once you understand that process, you can tune it to reduce network traffic and increase response time for clients. For the test, you should know the following:

- What are the steps involved in setting up a TCP/IP connection, such as the handshaking that connects a host to its target?

- When does TCP/IP use directed packets and when does it use broadcasts?

- Do broadcasts generate more traffic?

> ▸ How can I streamline communications?

> ▸ Where on different network segments can you locate DHCP, WINS, and DNS servers to improve response time and reduce network traffic?

> ▸ What tools are available to monitor TCP/IP communications and what information can each tool give me?

> ▸ What type of packets can I see using Network Monitor?

Troubleshooting TCP/IP

This chapter covers resolving TCP/IP communication problems, which can draw on any of the other chapters. The overall process is described in the Chapter 22. For the test, you should know the following:

> ▸ How can you use PING to verify a TCP/IP installation?

> ▸ What address do you PING to test basic functions of the TCP/IP stack on the computer?

> ▸ What address do you PING to test the capability to communicate with remote hosts?

> ▸ What information can you get using the IPCONFIG utility?

> ▸ How can you see if a client got a DHCP address and any additional configuration information it received?

> ▸ How can you fix name resolution with WINS or DNS servers?

> ▸ Why is the client getting a DHCP address from the wrong server?

How the Internetworking TCP/IP Test Differs from Other Microsoft Exams

In general, the Internetworking TCP/IP test is like other Microsoft tests; it has the same multiple-choice format. However, you need to know a few little quirks about this test to enhance your chances of passing. You can accustom yourself to these quirks as you take the sample tests so you will not falter under the time pressure of the real exam.

First, you need to know how to use the Windows Calculator. Each exam question provides access to the Calculator. This is the same Calculator located in the Accessories group in Windows 95 or Windows NT. Figure 7.1 shows a question from Microsoft's TCP/IP assessment test, available in the Microsoft Roadmap. Note the Calculator button at the top right of the question.

Figure 7.1

The Windows Calculator is accessed by selecting the Calculator button.

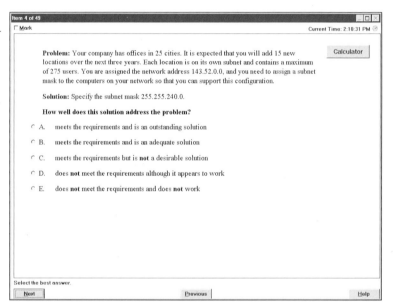

The Calculator is provided to help convert numbers easily from binary to decimal as you work with subnet masks and TCP/IP addresses. However, you can use only the Calculator's scientific mode to convert from decimal to binary. When you first open the Calculator, it is in standard mode. However, after you switch to scientific mode, the Calculator remains in that mode for the rest of the test. Figure 7.2 shows switching the Calculator from standard to scientific mode from the View menu.

Figure 7.2

*Switch from stan-
dard to scientific
mode from the
View menu.*

You should become comfortable with converting numbers from
binary to decimal and from decimal to binary. To convert a decimal number to binary, select the Dec button, then enter the number. Now select the Bin button. The binary number displays.
When you use this number for TCP/IP addresses or subnet masks,
be sure to add enough leading zeros to the number so you have
eight binary digits. You need to make sure you use eight digits
because you are dealing with octets. Figure 7.3 shows the final
step of converting decimal 240 to binary 11110000. In this figure,
the user has just selected Bin after entering 240 in decimal. A
complete description of binary arithmetic, the TCP/IP addressing
scheme, and subnet masking is contained in Chapter 9.

Figure 7.3

*The result of
converting deci-
mal 240 to binary.*

 Tip

Memorize the binary-to-decimal conversion tables in Chapter
9. Then you will know that a subnet mask of 255 indicates all
eight digits of that octet are the network ID whereas a subnet
of 240 uses only four digits for the network ID. I use the calculator on the test, but only as a tool to check my math. If you
know the conversion tables, you should be able to recognize
any mistakes you make with the calculator. You should be so
used to converting these numbers that you will know when
something just doesn't look right.

Microsoft has introduced a new type of question on many of the NT 4.0 exams. In these questions, you are presented with a scenario, a required result, and two optional results. The question also presents a proposed solution. You are asked to evaluate the solution as to whether it meets the required and optional results. The following is a sample question:

Scenario: It is a hot day and you are very thirsty. You want a drink.

Required results:

▶ Quench thirst.

▶ Replace fluids lost to heat.

Optional desired results:

▶ The drink should be cold.

▶ The drink should stimulate you.

Proposed solution:

▶ You drink a hot cup of coffee.

A. The proposed solution produces both the required result and the desired optional results.

B. The proposed solution produces the required result but only one of the desired optional results.

C. The proposed solution produces the required result but does not produce any of the desired optional results.

D. The proposed solution does not meet the required result.

In this question, the coffee would replace bodily fluids and quench the thirst (assuming you are a coffee drinker). The drink is hot, so it does not meet one of the optional results, but the caffeine in the coffee would stimulate the drinker, meeting the other optional result. The correct answer would be B.

This question has nothing to do with TCP/IP, but it does show the format of these types of questions. Often the same scenario is used for three or four consecutive questions. You should study the scenario carefully, because it is typically used again. However, each question usually presents a different proposed solution, so study the solution for each question carefully.

Once you understand the scenario and proposed solution, the trick is now to answer the test question correctly. Note that the required results can have more than one requirement. If any of the required results are not met by the solution, you can immediately choose answer D (the proposed solution does not produce the required results). There is no need to examine the optional desired results because the required result must work so you can move on to the optional ones.

If you have determined that the required result is produced, you can examine the optional desired results. Note that there are always two optional results. You merely need to decide how many of these are produced by the proposed solution. Answer A indicates both optional results are produced; answer B indicates only one is produced; and answer C indicates none of the optional results are produced. Remember that each of these answers depends on all the required results being produced. If the required results are completely fulfilled, then you should choose answer D.

Installing TCP/IP

 Objective   The rest of this book is dedicated to working with TCP/IP. It therefore seems that a logical place to start is installing the protocol.

To install TCP/IP protocol support, complete the following steps:

1. Open the Network Settings dialog box (double-click the Network icon in the Control Panel).

2. Click Add in the Protocols tab to open the Select Network Protocol dialog box.

3. Select TCP/IP Protocol in the Network Protocol list and choose OK.

4. The next prompt asks, "Do you wish to use DHCP?" If this computer will obtain its IP address from DHCP, choose Yes. If this computer will be configured with a static IP address, choose No.

5. When prompted, supply the path where Setup can locate the driver files.

6. Choose Close to exit the Network settings dialog box. After recalculating the bindings, Setup shows you a Microsoft TCP/IP Properties dialog box that will, at first, be blank.

7. If more than one adapter has been installed, select the adapter to be configured in the Adapter list. (You should configure each adapter with a valid IP address for the subnet they are on.)

8. If this computer will obtain its address configuration from DHCP for any of the network adapters, click the Obtain an IP address from a DHCP server radio button.

9. If this computer will be configured with static addresses, click the Specify an IP address radio button and complete the following fields:

IP Address (Required)

Subnet Mask (Required. Setup will suggest the default subnet mask appropriate for the IP address you enter.)

Default Gateway

10. Choose OK and restart the computer to activate the settings.

Services

Objective

After you have installed the TCP/IP protocol, you will be able to install several different services that work on the TCP/IP protocol. The following is a list of the services that you may need to install.

▶ **Internet Information Server (IIS).** IIS provides you the capability to share information to any type of computer that can use the TCP/IP protocol. IIS includes FTP, Gopher, and WWW servers.

- ▶ **Line Printer Daemon.** This server enables you to share printers with many different types of hosts, including main frames and Unix-based hosts.

- ▶ **Dynamic Host Configuration Protocol (DHCP).** DHCP provides automatic configuration of remote hosts, making management of a TCP/IP environment easy.

- ▶ **DHCP Relay Agent.** This extends the capabilities of the DHCP service by allowing it to work across various different subnets.

- ▶ **Windows Internet Name Service (WINS).** Without the ability to find another computer on the network, you would never be able to communicate. The WINS server provides a centralized method of name management that is both flexible and dynamic.

- ▶ **Simple Network Management Protocol Agent (SNMP).** In areas where you will use SNMP managers, or even if you want to track the performance of your TCP/IP protocols, you will want to install the SNMP agent.

- ▶ **Domain Name Server (DNS).** Whereas the WINS server provides the capability to find NetBIOS names, the DNS server works with host names to allow you to integrate your systems into the Internet or to resolve hosts on the Internet.

These services are covered in detail through the course of this book.

Architectural Overview of the TCP/IP Suite

8

This chapter will help you prepare for the exam by covering the basics of WINS. This information is the basis for all the information that will follow in this book.

STOP

Test Yourself! Before reading this chapter, test yourself to determine how much study time you will need to devote to this section.

1. You are trying to explain the architecture of TCP/IP to a fellow co-worker who has never used it. Your co-worker is familiar with other protocols and is also familiar with the OSI model. How many layers do you tell your co-worker TCP/IP has and to how many of them does it map in the OSI model?

2. The president of your company calls you into a meeting and asks you about the transition you're planning for the corporate-wide network to the TCP/IP protocol. The president expresses some concern about getting locked into a proprietary protocol that will put the company at the mercy of a software company. How do you respond?

3. Your network administrator has told you to integrate your IBM mainframes, NetWare servers, Macintosh clients, and Windows 95, and NT machines with a common protocol. Is TCP/IP able to connect all these different systems together?

4. During a test, you are asked which protocol in the TCP/IP suite is responsible for the routing and delivery of datagrams on the network. Which protocol do you say provides this functionality?

5. Your company has set up a streaming audio/video server that is accessible over your intranet. For some reason, you are unable to see any streaming content through your Web browser. You want to use Network Monitor to help determine whether the datagrams are actually being sent out onto the network. Which transport protocol is best suited for this type of data?

6. One of your users has been reading up on the Unix environment because the company is planning to migrate to the TCP/IP protocol. This user is worried that the Windows network is using the NetBIOS API, and that NetBIOS doesn't work over TCP/IP. Is this a valid concern?

Answers are located at the end of the chapter.

Introduction

Operating systems, networks, and protocols are all designed with a particular framework, or architecture, in mind. Although they may vary from vendor to vendor, it is this fundamental architecture that defines how all the components of a machine, operating system, and protocol fit together.

All computers in a network environment rely on network protocols to enable them to communicate with one another. Network protocols are designed and written to fit into the overall computing framework, or architecture, of the operating system running on a machine. Historically, and even today, defining how these protocols are developed is important. After operating systems such as Microsoft Windows NT began to support multiple protocols running on a machine at the same time, it became even more critical to have a clear idea of how various protocols function in relation to the operating system, and with each other.

This chapter begins with an introduction to physical network architectures. An understanding of the different types of networks is fundamental to understanding the benefits of TCP/IP, as well as many of the services provided by Microsoft, such as the Dynamic Host Configuration Protocol (DHCP) and the Windows Internet Name Service (WINS).

Without an understanding of networks in general, an appreciation of how TCP/IP works is much more difficult to reach. Therefore, this chapter briefly examines various physical network architectures before discussing the architecture of the TCP/IP protocol suite. Those readers not already familiar with physical network architectures may find this a welcome introduction, and those readers who are already familiar may find a review quickly puts points in perspective.

After a review of physical networks, the discussion turns to the Open Systems Interconnect (OSI) model, probably the most common industry architecture for defining how protocols interact with themselves and with each other. This chapter discusses the seven layers of the OSI model and the functionality of each of these layers.

After this, TCP/IP is introduced in terms of how it is managed and how it evolves through the use of Request For Comments (RFCs). It will introduce how TCP/IP maps to a four-layer model rather than a seven-layer model, while demonstrating how the functionality of each layer of the model is still maintained. Within these four layers, the reader discovers that TCP/IP is made up of more than just the TCP and IP protocols and consists of five primary protocols. This chapter serves as an introduction to these protocols as well as the Application Programming Interfaces (APIs) supported with Microsoft's implementation of TCP/IP.

Introductory Concepts—Network Basics

The subjects covered in this section represent the basic knowledge required to understand the architecture of TCP/IP. This section on network basics is intended to review basic network concepts and provide the larger picture within which to see how the TCP/IP architecture comes together.

The Components of a Network

Put simply, a *network* is a collection of machines that have been linked together both physically and through software components to facilitate communication and sharing of information among them. By this definition, a network might be as simple as the computers shown in figure 8.1. In fact, figure 8.1 shows the simplest kind of network that can be created: two machines connected by a piece of coaxial cable. This example is deceptively simple and hides a fairly complex arrangement of pieces that must work together to enable these two machines to communicate.

Figure 8.1

A network in the simplest terms.

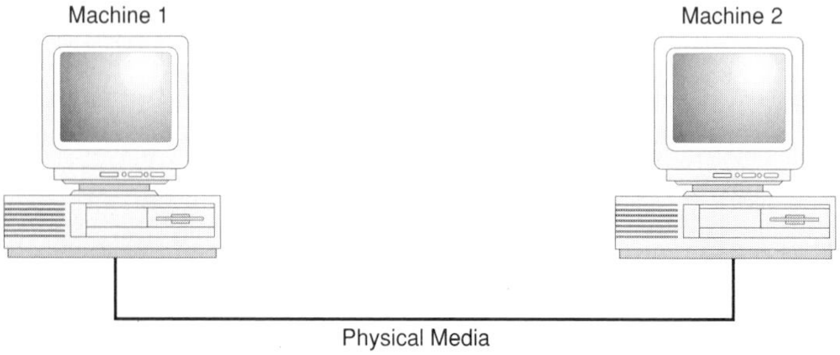

Machine 1   Machine 2

Physical Media

Look at figure 8.2, which shows each of the components, both hardware and software, required to enable communication between these two machines.

Figure 8.2

Network components.

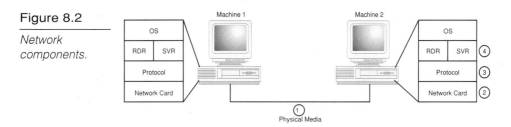

Observe that the first requirement for a network is a physical connection. A number of communication methods can be used to establish a physical connection: 10Base-T Ethernet, 10Base-2 Ethernet, Token Ring, FDDI, and others. Each connection type has pros and cons in terms of ease of installation, maintenance, and expense (see table 8.1). The following table reflects some generalizations about each type of media as a means to connect computers together. Unless you plan to run a wireless network, you need some kind of physical connection between machines for transferring data back and forth.

Table 8.1

Network Connection Types

Connection Type	Installation	Maintenance	Expense	Notes
10Base-2 Coaxial	Easy	Easy	Cheap	Traffic seen by all machines on a coax segment
10Base-T Unshielded Twisted Pair	Moderately easy	Easy	Moderately inexpensive	Traffic can be easily isolated
Token Ring	Moderately difficult	Difficult	Expensive	Traffic isolated, large data throughput
FDDI (Fiber)	Difficult	Difficult	Very expensive	Immune to electrical disturbances, very large data throughput

The second requirement for a network is appropriate hardware, such as a network card in the machine that acts as the interface to the network. The hardware provides the appropriate connection the machine needs to communicate with other machines across the wire. Physical networks can have different connection methods, depending on what has been installed. For example, if the physical network consists of coaxial cable, a BNC connector attaches the machines to the network; whereas if the physical network uses unshielded twisted-pair cabling, RJ-45 connectors connect the machines to the network. It is very difficult to connect an unshielded twisted pair network card to a network that uses coaxial cable and vice versa. Conversion devices and intermediary pieces can be purchased to allow for this kind of mixing, but you're generally better off buying a network card that supports your physical media inherently. This prevents an additional source of error when troubleshooting network connection problems.

Some network cards support multiple connection types for easy implementation. Naturally, a network card in the machine requires machine resources, including interrupts and memory addresses. These features need to be available for the network card to function.

Your third requirement in setting up a network is to install a network protocol. A network protocol is software installed on a machine that determines the agreed-upon set of rules for two or more machines to communicate with each other. One common metaphor used to describe different protocols is to compare them to human languages.

Think of a group of people in the same room who know nothing about each other. In order for them to communicate, this group has to determine what language to speak, how to handle identifying each other, whether to make general announcements or have private conversations, and so on. If machines are using different protocols, it is equivalent to one person speaking French and another person speaking Spanish. Machines that have different protocols installed are not able to communicate with each other. Common protocols in the Microsoft family include: NetBEUI (NetBIOS Extended User Interface), NWlink

(NDIS compliant version of Novell's IPX/SPX), DLC (Data Link Control), AFP (Appletalk File Protocol), and TCP/IP (Transmission Control Protocol/Internet Protocol).

The fourth and final key to the networking equation is having an operating system that is network-aware. Examples of operating systems that are network-aware include Windows NT, Windows 95, Windows for Workgroups, DOS, Unix, and Novell. Most operating systems are network-aware, but until now almost all applications were written to ask for local resources (hard drives) on the machine. Applications have only recently become fully network-aware and still generally use local drives to access resources.

Because applications still use local drives, it falls upon the operating system to be able to redirect (thus the name of the redirector) local resource requests to other machines out on the network. Figure 8.3 illustrates why you map or connect network drives to virtual local drives. The operating system knows the resources are on another machine, but the applications do not. In figure 8.3, the application thinks that drive x: is actually on the local machine. The operating system is responsible for acting on behalf of the application when a resource on the network is requested. Here the I/O manager redirects the save request from the application and sends it to the network redirector. To have a network, your operating system must have the appropriate networking components installed, otherwise the operating system cannot utilize resources that reside over a network connection.

Figure 8.3

A network redirection for an application.

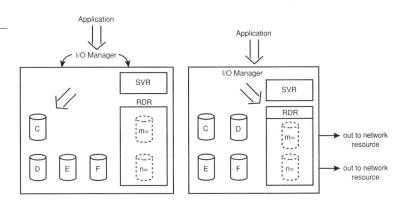

The Physical Address

As long as the four criteria discussed in the preceding section are met, creating a network is relatively simple. All that is necessary now is some way to distinguish machine A from machine B in a way the network cards can understand. This is done by using a physical address, the unique identifier assigned to a network card. This unique identifier is often referred to as the Mac address, the hardware address, or the ethernet address, but these all represent the same thing. For simplicity, this chapter refers to this identifier as the physical address.

A physical address is a 48-bit address represented by six sections of two hexadecimal values, for example 00-C0-DF-48-6F-13. It is assigned by the manufacturer of the network card before it is shipped to be sold. This identifier is designed to be unique and is often used to help identify a single machine on a network. At this level of the networking model, the Physical layer, data being passed over the network appears to be nothing more than the transmission and error-checking of voltage (1s and 0s) on the wire. These 1s and 0s are transmitted in a certain sequence based on the type of network used. This sequence is referred to as a frame. Within the frame, various pieces of information can be deciphered. The first active component to receive and process the voltage being transmitted onto the network is the network card. Figure 8.4 shows an example of what a standard ethernet frame looks like and the components to which an ethernet card is designed to pay attention.

Figure 8.4

A standard IEEE 802.3 (ethernet) frame.

The network card is responsible for determining whether the voltage is intended for it or some other machine. Each network card is given a set of rules that it must obey. First it listens to the preamble to synchronize itself so it can determine where the data within the frame begins. After it determines where the data begins, it discards both the Preamble and the Frame Check

Sequence before continuing to the next process. In the second process, the network card deciphers the data to determine for what physical address the frame is destined. If the destination address matches the physical address of the network card, it continues to process the information and pass the remaining data on for further action. If the destination address specifies some other machine's physical address, it silently discards the data within the frame and starts listening for other messages.

On a machine running Windows NT 4.0, it is relatively easy to determine its IP address. Complete the following steps:

1. From the Start menu, select Programs, Command Prompt.

2. After the command prompt window appears, type **IPCONFIG /all.**

3. Read the information provided by the IPCONFIG utility until you see a section called "Ethernet address." The value represented is the physical address of the machine.

If a network card discards the preamble and determines that the destination physical address is a broadcast, for example FF-FF-FF-FF-FF-FF, this means the message is intended for all machines connected on that network segment. Whenever a network card receives a broadcast, it assumes the data is relevant and passes the data to the rest of the system for further processing. Network protocols such as NetBEUI use broadcasts to begin communication with a single machine on the network, requiring all machines on the network segment to listen, process the frame, and allow higher layers in the networking model to discard the information. Network protocols such as TCP/IP, although capable of broadcasting, typically determine the specific physical address of the destination machine, eliminating a great deal of broadcast traffic.

Figures 8.5 and 8.6 illustrate the difference between the two types of methods in terms of the processing a machine initiates when receiving a broadcast or directed frame.

Figure 8.5

*A broadcast
frame using
NetBEUI.*

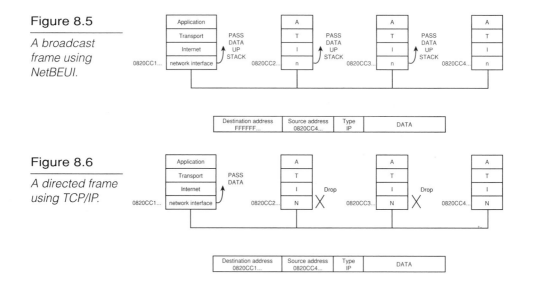

Figure 8.6

*A directed frame
using TCP/IP.*

In figure 8.5, each machine on the network opens up the frame
and discovers a broadcast address, indicating it must pass the data
up to higher layers for processing. In figure 8.6, only one machine
passes the data up to the higher networking layers, while the other machines silently discard the frame as uninteresting data.

It would be unfair to say that TCP/IP does not utilize any broadcasts to communicate, but in general, machines on a network
using NetBEUI spend more time deciphering broadcast traffic
than machines on a TCP/IP network. This is primarily because
NetBEUI is optimized for use on a local area network (LAN),
where bandwidth and resources are plenty. NetBEUI is also
enormously easy to install and configure and requires almost no
ongoing intervention on behalf of the user. It's only significant
weakness is that it is not a routeable protocol, meaning that it has
no addressing characteristics that allow packets to be moved from
one logical network to another.

TCP/IP, on the other hand, is designed for wide area network
(WAN) environments where routers are the common connection
method between two locations. Because of its routability and almost surgical (precise and efficient) use of bandwidth resources,
it is clearly the favorite for this type of environment. However, it
does require significantly more knowledge and experience on the
user's part to install and configure it correctly before it can be

utilized. This is probably why Microsoft deems it necessary to test user's and administrator's knowledge of this protocol (that is, they don't have a test dedicated to NetBEUI or NWLink).

Network Topologies

In the seemingly never-ending competition to maximize the amount of data that can be pushed through a piece of wire, numerous network topologies have been tried and tested. Initially, companies offered wholesale solutions for customers wanting to utilize various software packages. The problem was that these solutions typically required certain network protocols and certain hardware be in place before anything would work. This was often referred to as "monolithic" networking because these solutions were rarely interoperable with other applications or hardware.

After a company committed to a particular type of network, they were stuck with that network, and it was just too bad if a really useful application was released for a different network architecture. Accommodating a brand new application or suite of applications sometimes required removing the old network and installing another one. Administrators therefore wanted to make sure they were planning for the longest term possible. In an effort to sell administrators on the benefits of a particular networking package, companies developed network configurations for maximizing network performance. Performance was typically rated by how well a network architecture maximized available bandwidth. The strategies and implementation details for achieving these goals could be broken down into three general configurations. These evolved into the Bus, Ring, and Star configurations. It is helpful to understand how each of these developed.

The Bus Configuration

The bus configuration has its roots with coaxial cable in simple networks where desktop machines are simply connected together so that they can share information with each other. Traffic, here defined as voltage applied to the wire by any machine that needs to communicate, is applied to the bus, or the wire connecting the machines (see fig. 8.7).

Figure 8.7

*The bus configu-
ration.*

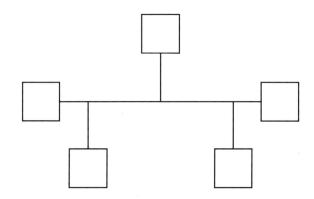

Any time a machine needs to access information from another machine, it simply sends out a sequenced variation of voltage in a frame that the destination machine can understand, process, and respond to. Notice in this configuration (fig. 8.7) that other machines on the network are also listening for frames and will open the frame up long enough to determine whether it is destined for them as well.

In this configuration, clients and servers can be randomly placed on the network, because they are all capable to listening to frames sent by a machine. The main selling point behind this type of network is that it is somewhat simple to set up, and can scale fairly well with the addition of relatively inexpensive hardware, such as repeaters or bridges. The keyword here is relatively. Remember, adding more machines to a bus type network simply adds more machines that will be competing for the wire to transmit.

One problem with this type of network architecture occurs when two machines try to communicate and send their frames on the wire at the same time. This is the electrical equivalent of a train wreck for 1s and 0s, or what is commonly referred to as a collision on the network. Any machine listening on the network for frames has no idea what to make of the chaotic confusion that results from a collision. Imagine trying to listen to fifteen or twenty people trying to talk at the same time to different people, and even possibly in different languages. Thankfully, network cards are designed with algorithms to alleviate some of the chaos surrounding collisions and ground rules for avoiding them in the future. One common design called Carrier-Sense Multiple Access with

Collision Detection (CSMA/CD) implements a standard set of rules for the transmission of frames on a network.

This simple concept (CSMA/CD) defines the relative politeness of machines on the network. When a network card wants to use the wire to transmit data, it listens first to determine whether another machine is already in the process of transmitting. If the network is idle (silent), the machine may transmit its own frames. If, in the course of transmitting, another network card also begins to transmit, a collision occurs. Each network card is instructed to stop transmitting, wait a random amount of time, and then listen again before trying to retransmit the data.

At the blazing speeds that data is transferred, it might seem that collisions are not a problem, and on small networks this is true; however, as networks grow in size and as the data being transferred between machines increases, the number of collisions also increases. It is possible to put so many machines on a network segment that the capability of machines to communicate is slowed down, if not stopped altogether. If too many machines try to communicate at the same time, it is nearly impossible for network cards to transmit data without collisions. This scenario is often referred to as saturating your bandwidth (the amount of sustainable data transfer rate) and should be avoided if at all possible.

To conceptualize this, just imagine the traffic on any rural road and how the traffic increases as the surrounding area becomes more developed. More and more people move into the area and use the roads until it becomes somewhat congested. A quick trip to the store may have taken five minutes initially, but now it takes fifteen minutes to run to the store, despite the fact that the distance hasn't changed. Further development and growth of the area into, say, a metropolitan city, leads to more people and more traffic, until eventually the trip to the store takes two hours because of the constant traffic jams. The usual effect of this is frustration and a commitment not to go to the store during rush hours.

The scenario described above can happen with computer networks as well. The inability to access resources in a timely manner because of saturated bandwidth can lead to productivity losses and frustrated users. One method that has been used to help reduce collisions is specifying a smaller frame size for sending data. By specifying small frame sizes, network cards must stop more often to allow other network cards the opportunity to transmit. This means computers can only send a small amount of data at any one time.

The Ring Configuration

The ring configuration (see fig. 8.8) provides an alternative method for the transmission of data from one computer to another over a network segment. This configuration relies on a token-passing method. In this type of network, one of the machines is designated to be the creator of a token. The token is the vehicle that carries all network communication, and it is sent from one machine to another in a circular loop, until it travels all the way around. A token has two basic states: In Use and Free. If a network card receives the token and the token is Free, it has permission to place data in the token, address the token for a destination address, and flag the token as In Use. This token is passed from network card to network card, each silently ignoring it, until it reaches its destination. After the destination address receives the frame, it formulates a reply, readdresses the token, and sends it back to the originator of the message. Again, the token is passed from one network card to another until the token reaches its origin. Assuming communication between the two machines is done, the originator of the communication releases the token by setting its flag to "Free" and passes it on to the next network card.

Figure 8.8

The ring configu-
ration.

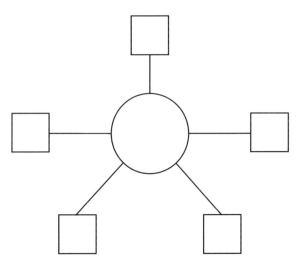

To conceptualize this method, think of a classroom of five students. At any one time a shoebox (the token) is in the hands of one of the students. It starts off empty (no lid, no tag) and is passed around from student to student. After a student decides to send a message, he or she assembles the message, places it inside the shoebox, and puts a lid on the shoebox with a tag indicating who is to receive the message.

Each time a student receives the shoebox, he or she checks to see whether the box has a lid and a tag. If it does have a lid, the student looks at the tag to determine for whom the message is intended. If the lid is on, but the tag isn't addressed to her, the student simply passes it to the next student. A student is only allowed to send a message to any of the others when he receives the shoebox and it is empty. Only if the shoebox is empty can a student put a message into the shoebox.

The only student that can remove the lid permanently is the original sender. After the communication is complete, the sender then removes the lid and passes the empty shoebox to the next student. Notice the absence of any type of collision detection. In a ring - based network, the only communication occurring on the network is by the machine that currently has control of the token. The risk of collisions has been completely eliminated. Not only that, but the lack of collisions means network cards don't have to be quite so polite and can send much larger frames. Larger frame sizes equate to much larger amounts of data being transmitted at any one time.

So where is the drawback? Look at our example again. Student four passes the shoebox with a message to student five. The shoebox is sitting on student five's desk, but student five actually skipped school that day. The ring has essentially been broken (machine crash) and the communications network is down. Without the capability to pass the token to student one, the other students are out of luck. Also, imagine the students are wearing blindfolds and can only identify the students to their immediate left and their immediate right through touch. Therefore, if a student (or machine) on a ring-based network is moved, the student has to learn who its neighbors are again before communications can be reestablished.

As with bus-based networks, software and hardware implementations have been developed to eliminate some of these problems, but ring networks are typically more expensive and more difficult to maintain and service. The main selling point behind this type of configuration is the amount of data that can be transferred at one time through the significantly larger frame sizes.

The Star Configuration

The star configuration (see fig. 8.9) is designed primarily to reduce the traffic with which any one machine has to compete to communicate on the network. It operates in almost the same way as the Bus configuration, with one exceptional difference. Through the implementation of smart hardware, in this case a fast switch in the center of the diagram, machines never have to worry about collisions with each other. The switch isolates the network segments so that collisions do not occur between network cards. All data is designed to flow through the switch. A virtual circuit is created between two machines to allow them to communicate with each other, and this virtual circuit lasts only as long as is necessary to transfer data. After the machines finish communicating, the virtual circuit is destroyed and the segments are isolated from each other once again.

Figure 8.9

The star configuration.

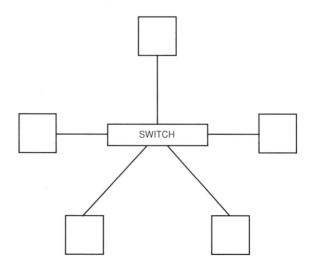

To visualize this, you might think of the switch in the middle acting as telephone operators did back in the days when connections were made between a caller and receiver by plugging the cables into their respective sockets. Switches are performing essentially the same task, just significantly quicker than a person can do it. Again, the connection lasts only as long as the two machines are communicating.

After the machines stop, the connection is broken, and the path between the two machines no longer exists. In a very small environment, each machine is assigned a port on the switch; in most situations, however, this is not terribly practical. Switches of this kind are typically very expensive and would not be used for a small number of machines. Most switches are used in hybrid configurations, where additional hubs are used to provide more available bandwidth to up to hundreds of machines.

The key characteristic of this type of configuration is that each machine with its own port receives the maximum sustainable bandwidth that the medium can carry, because each machine only sees the traffic for the connections it has established. This is one of the more expensive solutions to minimizing bandwidth bottlenecks, but it works very well when implemented.

Hybrid Configurations

These three basic network configurations have been modified and hybridized in the last couple of years so that each has several variations. But in the past, businesses had to chose which configuration they were going to use based not only on the merits of each implementation, but on which software they intended to use. This didn't make too many in the industry happy, understandably. A company producing network interface cards had to know exactly what kinds of programs would be run so that they could support those applications. At the same time, a programmer or software company couldn't complete the authoring of software until they knew what kind of physical network the software would be running on.

Hardware companies were unhappy; software companies were unhappy; and businesses faced with millions of dollars of upgrade investment every time there was a software or operating system conversion were decidedly unhappy.

All this unhappiness led the industry to develop several models for developing networks. These models typically include agreed-upon layers that distribute tasks among various manufacturers and programmers in the industry. This means that software companies can spend their time worrying about improving their software, not about network card standards. And for network card manufacturers, they can spend their time worrying about getting more throughput from their cards, rather than worrying about whether it can support the most popular application of the day. One of the most well-known of these models is the Open Systems Interconnect, or OSI model.

The OSI Model

The OSI model takes networking tasks and divides them into seven fundamentally different layers to make it easier for the industry to move forward and evolve (see figure 8.10). With the tasks segregated into functional units, a person writing the code for a network card doesn't have to worry about what applications are going to be run over it; conversely, a programmer writing an application doesn't have to worry about who manufactured the network card. How-ever, to make this work, everything must be written to comply with the boundary specifications between each of the seven layers of the model. Although the TCP/IP protocol suite only maps to a four-layer model, these four layers provide the same functionality as each of the seven layers of the OSI model.

This chapter examines the functionality of each of the seven layers first and then describes the function of the boundary layers between them. A good understanding of these layers will provide the proper background for looking at the four layers of the TCP/IP protocol suite.

The Physical Layer

The first layer is the Physical layer. This is the only layer that is truly connected to the network in the sense that it is the only layer concerned with how to interpret the voltage on the wire—the 1s and 0s. This layer is responsible for understanding the electrical rules associated with devices and for determining what kind of medium is actually being used (cables, connectors, and other mechanical distinctions). TCP/IP does not function at this level, leaving these tasks instead for the network cards to handle.

Figure 8.10

The seven layers of the OSI model.

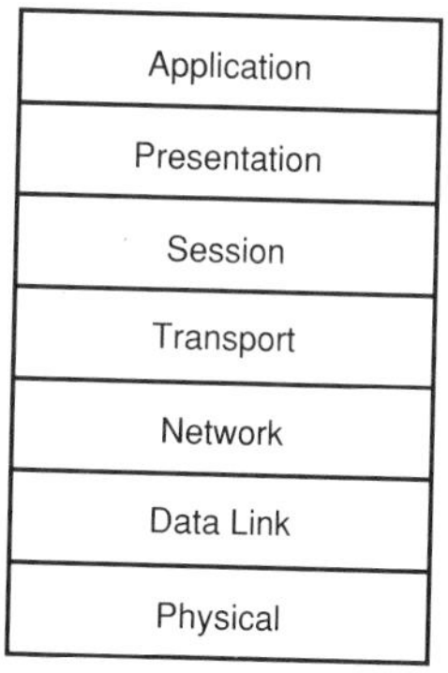

| Application |
| Presentation |
| Session |
| Transport |
| Network |
| Data Link |
| Physical |

The Data Link Layer

The second layer is the Data Link layer. This layer is responsible for the creation and interpretation of different frame types based on the actual physical network being used. For instance, ethernet and token-ring networks support different and numerous frame types, and the Data Link layer must understand the difference between them. This layer is also responsible for interpreting what it receives from the Physical layer, using low-level error detection and correction algorithms to determine when information needs to be re-sent. Network protocols, including the TCP/IP protocol suite, do not define physical standards at the physical or Data Link layer, but instead are written to make use of any standards that may currently be in use. The boundary layer in between the Data Link layer and Network layer defines a group of agreed-upon standards for how protocols communicate and gain access to these lower layers. As long as a network protocol is appropriately written to this boundary layer, the protocols should be able to access the network, regardless of what media type is being used.

The Network Layer

The third layer of the OSI model is the Network layer. This layer is mostly associated with the movement of data by means of addressing and routing. It directs the flow of data from a source to a destination, despite the fact that the machines may not be connected to the same physical wire or segment, by finding a path or route from one machine to another. If necessary, this layer can break data into smaller chunks for transmission. This is sometimes necessary when transferring data from one type of physical network to another, for instance, token-ring (which supports larger frame sizes) to ethernet (which supports smaller frame sizes). Of course, it is also responsible for reassembling those smaller chunks into the original data after the data has reached its destination. A number of protocols from the TCP/IP protocol suite exist in this layer, but the network protocol that is responsible for routing and delivery of packets is the IP protocol. More on this protocol and the others are discussed later in the chapter.

The Transport Layer

The fourth layer is the Transport layer. This layer is primarily responsible for guaranteeing delivery of packets transmitted by the Network layer, although it does not always have to do so. Depending on the protocol being used, delivery of packets may or may not be guaranteed. When it is responsible for guaranteeing the delivery of packets, it does so through various means of error control, including verification of sequence numbers for packets and other protocol-dependent mechanisms. TCP/IP has two protocols at this layer of the model, Transmission Control Protocol (TCP) and User Datagram Protocol (UDP). UDP may be used for non-guaranteed delivery of packets and TCP may be used to guarantee the delivery of packets.

The Session Layer

The fifth layer is the Session layer. This layer is responsible for managing connections between two machines during the course of communication between them. This layer is the one which determines whether it has received all pertinent information for the session and whether it can stop receiving or transmitting data. This layer also has built-in error correction and recovery methods. TCP/IP utilizes two Application Programming Interfaces (APIs)—Windows Sockets and NetBIOS—for determining whether all information has been sent and received between two connected machines.

The Presentation Layer

The sixth layer is the Presentation layer. This layer is primarily concerned with the conversion of data formats from one machine to another. One common example is the sending of data from a machine that uses the ASCII format for characters to a machine that uses the EBCDIC format for characters, typically IBM mainframes. The Presentation layer is responsible for picking up differences such as these and translating them to compatible formats. Both EBCDIC and ASCII are standards for translating characters to hexadecimal code. Letters, numbers, and symbols in one format must be translated when communicating with machines using a different format. This is the responsibility of the Presentation layer.

The Application Layer

The seventh layer is the Application layer. This is the last layer of the model and acts as the arbiter or translator between users' applications and the network. Applications that want to utilize the network to transfer data must be written to conform to networking APIs supported by the machine's networking components, such as Windows Sockets and NetBIOS. After the application makes an API call, the Application layer determines with which machine it wants to communicate, whether a session should be set up between the communicating machines, and whether the delivery of packets needs to be guaranteed.

The Layer Relationship

Between each layer is a common boundary layer. For instance, between the Network layer and the Transport layer is a boundary that both must be able to support. It is through these boundary layers that one layer of the networking model communicates and shares valuable and necessary information with the layer above or below it. In fact, each time a layer passes data to the layer below, it adds information to it, and each time a layer receives data it strips off its own information and passes the rest up the protocol stack. Figure 8.11 illustrates how each layer of the networking model adds and then strips away information.

Figure 8.11

Passing data up and down the model.

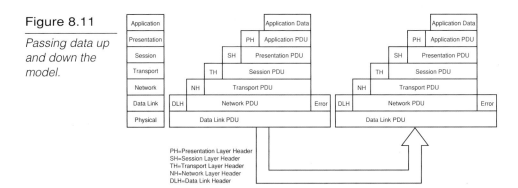

PH=Presentation Layer Header
SH=Session Layer Header
TH=Transport Layer Header
NH=Network Layer Header
DLH=Data Link Header

One of the most common and useful analogies used to describe the networking model is to imagine the process a letter goes through to get to its destination. Figure 8.12 shows a sample of the process.

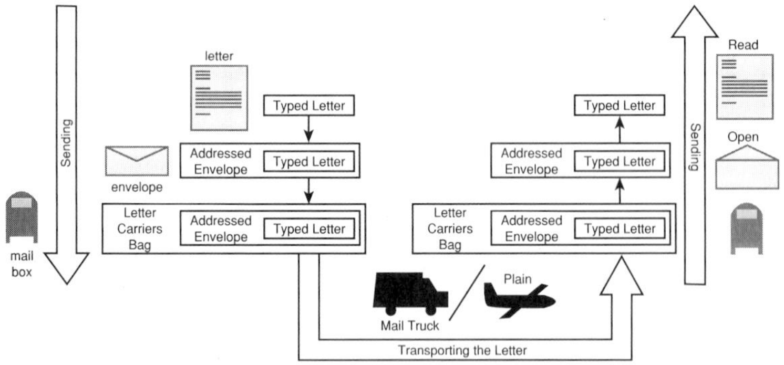

Figure 8.12

The process a letter goes through.

After looking at figure 8.12, what would happen if any of these steps broke down? The letter would not be received. The same thing happens on computer networks such as the one in figure 8.11. If any of the steps in the process break down, messages are not received. Error checking is applied to the model to keep the communications process from breaking down, just as the postal service runs in any kind of weather. But sometimes packets still get lost in the shuffle.

Messages sent from one computer to another move in the same manner. Messages from one layer are packaged and placed into the next layer. Each step of the process has little to do with the preceding or following step. The kind of envelope used has nothing to do with whether you wrote the message in English, French, or German, and it certainly doesn't matter what the message was. In the same way, where you actually address the envelope, California, Florida, or Hawaii, has absolutely nothing to do with what kind of envelope you use. The only common link between the address and the message is the envelope itself.

Lastly, it doesn't matter which vehicle: boat, plane or train, the postal service uses to deliver the envelope to its destination address, as long as it gets there. Each layer depends upon the other layers, but is only mildly related in terms of functionality to the others. With this introduction to networks and networking, the architecture of TCP/IP can be both more easily understood and appreciated.

Introduction to TCP/IP

The Transmission Control Protocol/Internet Protocol (TCP/IP) is an industry-standard suite of protocols designed to be routeable, robust, and functionally efficient. TCP/IP was originally designed as a set of wide area network (WAN) protocols for the express purpose of maintaining communication links and data transfer between sites in the event of an atomic/nuclear war. Since those early days, development of the protocols has passed from the hands of the government and has been the responsibility of the Internet community for some time.

The evolution of these protocols from a small four-site project into the foundation of the worldwide Internet has been extraordinary. But, despite more than 25 years of work and numerous modifications to the protocol suite, the inherent spirit of the original specifications is still intact.

Installing Microsoft's TCP/IP as a protocol on your machine or network provides the following advantages:

▶ **An industry-standard protocol.** Because TCP/IP is not maintained or written by one company, it is not proprietary or subject to as many compatibility issues. The Internet community as a whole decides whether a particular change or implementation is worthwhile. Naturally, this slows down the implementation of new features and characteristics compared to how quickly one directed company might make changes, but it does guarantee that changes are well thought out, that they provide functionality with most, if not all other implementations of TCP/IP, and that a set of specifications is publicly available that can be referenced at any time over the Internet, detailing how the protocol suite should be used and implemented.

▶ **A set of utilities for connecting dissimilar operating systems.** Many connectivity utilities have been written for the TCP/IP suite, including the File Transfer Protocol (FTP) and Terminal Emulation Protocol (Telnet). Because these utilities use the Windows Sockets API, connectivity from one machine to another is not dependent on the network operating system used on either machine. For example, a Unix FTP server could be accessed by a Microsoft FTP client to transfer files without either party having to worry about compatibility issues. This functionality also allows a Windows NT machine running a Telnet client to access and run commands on an IBM mainframe running a Telnet server, for example.

▶ **A scalable, cross-platform client-server architecture.** Consider what happened during the initial development of applications for the TCP/IP protocol suite. Vendors wanted to be able to write their own client/server applications, for instance, SQL server and SNMP. The specification for how to write applications was also up for public perusal. Which operating systems would be included? Users everywhere wanted to be able to take advantage of the connectivity options promised through utilizing TCP/IP, regardless of the operating system they were currently running. Therefore the Windows Sockets API was established, so that applications utilizing the TCP/IP protocol could write to a standard, agreed-upon interface. Because the contributors included everyone, and therefore every kind of operating system, the specifications for Windows Sockets on TCP/IP were written to make the operating system transparent to the application. Microsoft TCP/IP includes support for Windows Sockets and for connectivity to other Windows Sockets-compliant TCP/IP stacks.

▶ **Access to the Internet.** TCP/IP is the de facto protocol of the Internet and allows access to a wealth of information that can be found at thousands of locations around the world. To connect to the Internet, though, a valid IP address is required. Because IP addresses have become more and more scarce, and as security issues surrounding access to the Internet have been raised, many creative alternatives have been established to allow connections to the Internet. However, all these implementations utilize gateways or firewalls that act on behalf of the requesting machines.

Now that you understand the benefits of installing TCP/IP, you are ready to learn about how the TCP/IP protocol suite maps to a four-layer model.

The Four Layers of TCP/IP

TCP/IP maps to a four-layer architectural model. This model is called the Internet Protocol Suite and is broken into the Network Interface, Internet, Transport, and Application layers. Each of these layers corresponds to one or more layers of the OSI model. The Network Interface layer corresponds to the Physical and Data Link layers. The Internet layer corresponds to the Network layer. The Transport layer corresponds to the Transport layer, and the Application layer corresponds to the Session, Presentation, and Application layers of the OSI model. Figure 8.13 illustrates these relationships.

Figure 8.13

Layers in the TCP/IP protocol suite.

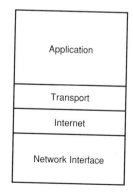

OSI Reference Model   Internet Model

Each of the four layers of the model is responsible for all the activities of the layers to which it maps.

The Network Interface layer is responsible for communicating directly with the network. It must understand the network architecture being used, such as token-ring or ethernet, and provide an interface allowing the Internet layer to communicate with it. The Internet layer is responsible for communicating directly with the Network Interface layer.

The Internet layer is primarily concerned with the routing and delivery of packets through the Internet Protocol (IP). All the protocols in the Transport layer must use IP to send data. The Internet Protocol includes rules for how to address and direct packets, fragment and reassemble packets, provide security information, and identify the type of service being used. However, because IP is not a connection-based protocol, it does not guarantee that packets transmitted onto the wire will not be lost, damaged, duplicated, or out of order. This is the responsibility of higher layers of the networking model, such as the Transport layer or the Application layer. Other protocols that exist in the Internet Layer are the Internet Control Messaging Protocol (ICMP), Internet Group Management Protocol (IGMP), and the Address Resolution Protocol (ARP). Each of these is described in more detail later in this chapter.

The Transport layer maps to the Transport layer of the OSI model and is responsible for providing communication between machines for applications. This communication can be connection-based or nonconnection-based. The primary difference between these two types of connections is whether there is a mechanism for tracking data and guaranteeing the delivery of the data to its destination. Transmission Control Protocol (TCP) is the protocol used for connection-based communication between two machines providing reliable data transfer. User Datagram Protocol (UDP) is used for nonconnection-based communication with no guarantee of delivery.

The Application layer of the Internet protocol suite is responsible for all the activities that occur in the Session, Presentation, and Application layers of the OSI model. Numerous protocols have been written for use in this layer, including Simple Network Management Protocol (SNMP), File Transfer Protocol (FTP), Simple Mail Transfer Protocol (SMTP), as well as many others.

The interface between each of these layers is written to have the capability to pass information from one layer to the other. Figure 8.14 illustrates how each layer adds its own information to the data and hands it down to the lower layers. It also illustrates how that data is then stripped off by the corresponding layer of the receiving machine, until what is left is only the information needed by that layer.

Figure 8.14

Layers in the TCP/IP protocol suite.

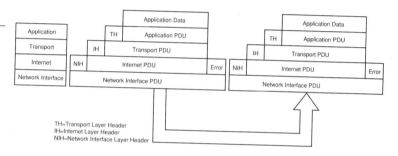

TH=Transport Layer Header
IH=Internet Layer Header
NIH=Network Interface Layer Header

The interface between the Network Interface layer and the Internet layer does not pass a great deal of information, although it must follow certain rules. Namely, it must listen to all broadcasts and send the rest of the data in the frame up to the Internet layer for processing, and if it receives any frames that do not have an IP frame type, they must be silently discarded.

The interface between the Internet layer and the Transport layer must be able to provide each layer full access to such information as the source and destination addresses, whether TCP or UDP should be utilized in the transport of data, and all other available mechanisms for IP. Rules and specifications for the Transport layer include giving the Transport layer the capability to change these parameters or to pass parameters it receives from the Application layer down to the Internet layer. The most important thing to remember about all of these boundary layers is that they must use the agreed upon rules for passing information from one layer to the other.

The interface between the Transport layer and the Application layer is written to provide an interface to applications, whether or not they are using the TCP or UDP protocol for transferring data. The interface utilizes the Windows Sockets and NetBIOS APIs to transfer parameters and data between the two layers. The Application layer must have full access to the Transport layer to change and alter parameters as necessary.

The layers provide only guidelines, though; the real work is done by the protocols that are contained within the layers. This chapter describes the TCP/IP protocol as being a suite of protocols, not just two (TCP and IP). In fact, six primary protocols are associated with TCP/IP:

▶ Transmission Control Protocol (TCP)

▶ User Datagram Protocol (UDP)

▶ Internet Protocol (IP)

▶ Internet Control Message Protocol (ICMP)

▶ Address Resolution Protocol (ARP)

▶ Internet Group Management Protocol (IGMP)

Figure 8.15 shows where each of these protocols resides in the architectural model. Each protocol has a graphic to help you visualize the type of communication that is being achieved through these protocols. The telephone is meant to represent TCP; the letter is meant to represent UDP; the security guard is meant to represent ICMP; the cable TV is meant to represent IGMP; the detective is meant to represent ARP; and the mail truck/phone operator is meant to represent IP. Each of these protocols and the details of their implementation is discussed in the following sections.

Transmission Control Protocol

The first protocol that lives in the Transport layer is the Transmission Control Protocol (TCP). This protocol is a connection-based protocol and requires the establishment of a session before data is transmitted between two machines. TCP packets are delivered to sockets or ports. Because TCP sets up a connection between two machines, it is designed to verify that all packets sent by a machine are received on the other end. If, for some reason, packets are lost, the sending machine resends the data. Because a session is established and delivery of packets is guaranteed, there is additional overhead involved with using TCP to transmit packets.

Figure 8.15

Protocols within the layers of the TCP/IP protocol suite.

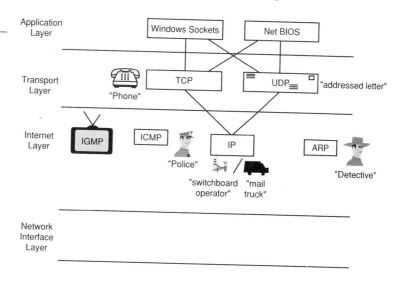

To understand TCP further, you must understand ports and sockets, connection-oriented communications, sliding windows, and acknowledgments. The following sections cover each of these areas.

Ports and Sockets

The communication process between the Transport layer and the Application layer involves identifying the application that has requested either a reliable or unreliable transport mechanism. Port assignments are the means used to identify application processes to the Transport layer. Ports identify to which process on the machine data should be sent for further processing. Specific port numbers have been assigned by the Internet Assigned Numbers Authority (IANA), specifically those from 1 to 1023. These port assignments are called the well-known ports and represent the ports to which standard applications listen. Defining these standard port numbers helps eliminate having to guess to which port an application is listening so that applications can direct their queries or messages directly. Port numbers above the well-known port range are available for running applications, and work in exactly the same way. In this case, however, the client or user has to be able to identify to which port the application is connecting. Ports can be used by both TCP and UDP for delivering data between two machines. Ports themselves do not care whether the data they receive is in order or not, but the applications running on those ports might.

To identify both the location and application to which a stream of data needs to be sent, the IP address (location) and the port number (application) are often combined into one functional address called a socket. Figure 8.16 illustrates the format for defining a socket. A socket can be defined for either TCP or UDP connections.

Figure 8.16

Definition of a socket.

IP address	+	Port	=	Select
131.107.2.200		137		131.107.2.200(137)

Connection-Oriented Communication

The Transmission Control Protocol (TCP) is a connection-based protocol that establishes a connection, or session, between two machines before any data is transferred. TCP exists within the Transport layer, between the Application layer and the IP layer, providing a reliable and guaranteed delivery mechanism to a destination machine. Connection-based protocols guarantee the delivery of packets by tracking the transmission and receipt of individual packets during communication. A session is able to track the progress of individual packets by monitoring when a packet is sent, in what order it was sent, and by notifying the sender when it is received so it can send more. Figure 8.17 illustrates how TCP sets up a connection-oriented session between two machines.

The first step in the communication process is to send a message indicating a desire to synchronize the systems. This is equivalent to dialing a phone number and waiting for someone to answer. The second step is for the machine to send an acknowledgment that it is listening and willing to accept data. This step is equivalent to a person answering the phone, and then waiting for the caller to say something. The third step is for the calling machine to send a message indicating that it understands the receiving machine's willingness to listen and that data transmission will now begin.

Figure 8.17

Connection-based communication.

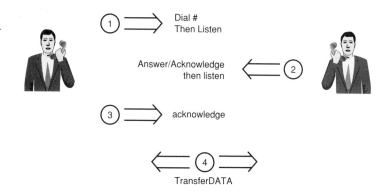

After the TCP session has been created, the machines begin to communicate just as people do during a phone call. In the example of the telephone, if the caller uses a cellular phone and some of the transmission is lost, the user indicates she did not receive the message by saying "What did you say? I didn't hear that." This indicates to the sender that he needs to resend the data.

Figure 8.18 illustrates the format of a TCP header. The header includes all the parameters that are used to guarantee delivery of packets and to provide error-checking and control. Notice that the header specifies a source and destination port for the communication. This tells the machine where it is supposed to send the data, and from where the data came.

Figure 8.18

The TCP datagram parameters.

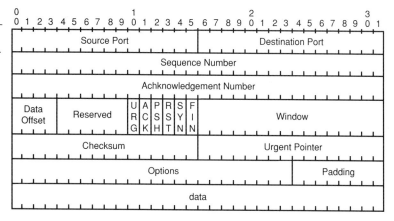

Included in the header are sections defining the sequence numbers and acknowledgment numbers that help verify the delivery of a datagram. A datagram or packet is simply the data that is being transferred to the destination machine. This data often has to be broken up into smaller pieces (datagrams) because the underlying network can only transmit so much data at one time. Other parameters include the SYN and FIN options for starting and ending communication sessions between two machines, the size of the window to be used in transferring data, a checksum for verifying the header information, and other options that can be specific implementations of TCP/IP. The last part of the frame is the actual data being transmitted. A full discussion of each of these parameters is beyond the scope of this book or the TCP/IP test. More academic texts and RFCs on the Internet describe in fuller detail the specifications for each parameter. I recommend looking for sources that speak to you in your language. Some resources are engineering texts; some are much too simple. Look for a happy medium to begin with and work your way into the more complex.

During the initialization of a TCP session, often called the "three-way handshake," both machines agree on the best method to track how much data is to be sent at any one time, acknowledgment numbers to be sent upon receipt of data, and when the connection is no longer necessary because all data has been transmitted and received. It is only after this session is created that data transmission begins. To provide reliable delivery, TCP places packets in sequenced order and requires acknowledgment that these packets reached their destination before it sends new data. TCP is typically used for transferring large amounts of data, or when the application requires acknowledgment that data has been received. Given all the additional overhead information that TCP needs to keep track of, the format of a TCP packet can be somewhat complex.

Try to visualize TCP as being similar to a phone call. Imagine Shey decides to call Kim on the phone. Shey picks up the phone and dials Kim's phone number. This is equivalent to TCP sending out a synchronization request to another machine. Kim happens to have caller ID and can identify Shey before picking up the phone. Kim decides to speak to Shey and picks up the phone with a greeting, something like "Hi," indicating her willingness to communicate.

This is equivalent to a machine sending an acknowledgment that it has received a synchronization request and is willing to respond. Shey now says "Hi," indicating that he has heard Kim and is ready to communicate, in the same way that a sending machine verifies that it has received the other machine's willingness to communicate. Now Shey and Kim can talk about anything they want, secure in the knowledge that their messages are being received.

After the transfer of data is complete, the TCP session is broken down in a similar three-step fashion. In the case of Shey and Kim, Shey may indicate his need to get off the phone because he's run out of things to say. Kim says, "Oh, no problem, goodnight." Shey ends the three step sequence by saying "Goodnight." Machines use the same type of process to break down a TCP session. The sending machine indicates that it has run out of data to send and wants to close the connection. The receiving machine indicates it has received all the data and that closing the connection is fine. The sending machine then simply closes the connection.

Sliding Windows

For an exercise covering this information, see end of chapter.

TCP uses the concept of sliding windows for transferring data between machines. Sliding windows are often referred to in the Unix environment as streams. Each machine has both a send window and a receive window that it utilizes to buffer data and make the communication process more efficient. A window represents the subset of data that is currently being sent to a destination machine, and is also the amount of data that is being received by the destination machine. At first this seems redundant, but it really isn't. Not all data that is sent is guaranteed to be received, so they must be kept track of on both machines. A sliding window allows a sending machine to send the window data in a stream without having to wait for an acknowledgment for every single packet.

A receiving window allows a machine to receive packets out of order and reorganize them while it waits for more packets. This reorganization may be necessary because TCP utilizes IP to transmit data, and IP does not guarantee the orderly delivery of packets. Figure 8.19 shows the send and receive windows that exist on machines that have TCP/IP installed. By default, window sizes in

Windows NT are a little more than 8 KB in size, representing eight standard ethernet frames. Standard ethernet frames are a little more than 1KB apiece.

Figure 8.19

Send and receive windows.

Packets do not always make it to their destination, though. TCP has been designed to recover in the event that packets are lost along the way, perhaps by busy routers. TCP keeps track of the data that has been sent out, and if it doesn't receive an acknowledgment for that data from the destination machine in a certain amount of time, the data is re-sent. In fact, until acknowledgment for a packet of data is received, further data transmission is halted completely.

Acknowledgments

Acknowledgments are a very important component necessary to ensure the reliable delivery of packets. As the receiving window receives packets, it sends acknowledgments to the sending window that the packets arrived intact. When the send window receives acknowledgments for data it has sent, it slides the window to the right so that it can send any additional data stored in memory. But it can only slide over by the number of acknowledgments it has received. By default, a receive window sends an acknowledgment for every two sequenced packets it receives. Therefore, assuming no network problems, if the send window in figure 8.20 sends eight packets to the receive window on the other machine, four acknowledgment packets come back. An acknowledgment for packets 1 and 2, 3 and 4, 5 and 6, and 7 and 8. The sending window slides over to the next eight packets waiting to be sent and sends those out to the receiving window. In this manner, the number of acknowledgments sent over the network is reduced, and the flow of traffic is increased.

Figure 8.20

Sliding after receiving acknowledgments.

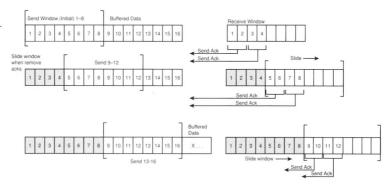

As long as the acknowledgments begin flowing back regularly from the receiving machine, data flows smoothly and efficiently. However, on busy networks, packets can get lost and acknowledgments may be delayed. Because TCP guarantees delivery and reliability of traffic flow, the window cannot slide past any data that has not been acknowledged. If the window cannot slide beyond a packet of data, no more data beyond the window is transmitted, TCP eventually has to shut down the session, and the communication fails.

Each machine is therefore instructed to wait a certain amount of time before either retransmitting data or sending acknowledgments for packets that arrive out of sequence. Each window is given a timer: the send window has the Retransmit Timer and the receive window has the Delayed Acknowledgment Timer. These timers help define what to do when communication isn't flowing very smoothly.

In the sending window, a Retransmit Timer is set for each packet, specifying how long to wait for an acknowledgment before making the assumption that the packet did not get to its destination. After this timer has expired, the send window is instructed to resend the packet and wait twice as long as the time set on the preceding timer. The default starting point for this timer is approximately 3 seconds but is usually reduced to less than a second almost immediately. Each time an acknowledgment is not received, the Retransmit Timer doubles. For instance, if the Retransmit Timer started at approximately 1 second, the second Retransmit Timer is set for 2 seconds, the third for 4 seconds, the fourth, 8 seconds, up to a fifth attempt that waits 16 seconds. The number of attempts can be altered in the Registry, but if after these attempts an acknowledgment still cannot be received, the TCP session is closed and errors are reported to the application. Figure 8.21 illustrates the resending of data after the first Retransmit Timer has expired.

The Registry location for changing the number of times to retry a transmission is in the following subkey:

`HKEY_LOCAL_MACHINE\SYSTEM\CurrentControlSet\Services\Tcpip\Parameters`

The Registry parameter and value is:

`TcpMaxDataRetransmissions (REG_DWORD)`.

The default value is 5.

Figure 8.21

Retransmission of data after the Retransmit Timer has expired.

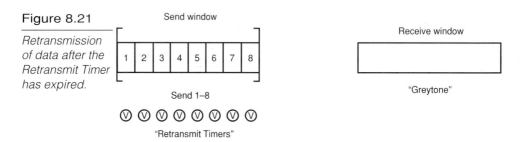

In the receiving window, a Delayed Acknowledgment Timer is set for those packets that arrive out of order. Remember, by default an acknowledgment is sent for every two sequenced packets, starting from the left-hand side of the window. If packets arrive out of order (if, for instance, 1 and 3 arrive but 2 is missing), an acknowledgment for two sequenced packets is not possible. When packets arrive out of order, a Delayed Acknowledgment Timer is set on the first packet in the pair. In the parenthetical example, a Timer is set on packet number 1. The Delayed Acknowledgment Timer is hard-coded for 200 milliseconds, or $\frac{1}{5}$ the Retransmit Timer. If packet 2 does not show up before the Delayed Acknowledgment Timer expires, an acknowledgment for packet 1, and only packet 1, is sent. No other acknowledgments are sent, including those for packets 3 through 8 that might have appeared. Until packet 2 arrives, the other packets are considered interesting, but useless. As data is acknowledged and passed to the Application layer, the receive window slides to the right, enabling more data to be received. Again though, if a packet doesn't show up, the window is not enabled to slide past it. Figure 8.22 illustrates the Delayed Acknowledgment Timer in action.

Figure 8.22

Setting of the Delayed Acknowledgment Timer for out-of-sequence packets.

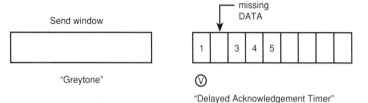

User Datagram Protocol

The second protocol that lives in the Transport layer is the User Datagram Protocol, or UDP. This protocol is a nonconnection-based protocol and does not require a session to be established between two machines before data is transmitted. UDP packets are still delivered to sockets or ports, just as they are in TCP. But because UDP does not create a session between machines, it cannot guarantee that packets are delivered or that they are delivered in order or retransmitted if the packets are lost. Given the apparent unreliability of this protocol, some may wonder why a protocol such as UDP was developed. Figure 8.23 illustrates the relative simplicity of the address format of UDP compared to TCP.

Figure 8.23

The UDP datagram format.

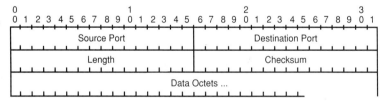

Notice that sending a UDP datagram has very little overhead involved. A UDP datagram has no synchronization parameters or priority options. All that exist are the source port, destination port, the length of the data, a checksum for verifying the header, and then the data.

There are actually a number of good reasons to have a transport protocol that does not require a session to be established. For one, very little overhead is associated with UDP, such as having to keep track of sequence numbers, Retransmit Timers, Delayed Acknowledgment Timers, and retransmission of packets. UDP is quick and extremely streamlined functionally; it's just not guaranteed. This makes UDP perfect for communications that involve broadcasts, general announcements to the network, or real-time data.

For an exercise covering this information, see end of chapter.

Try to visualize UDP as being similar to a postcard. In order for Shey to send a message to Kim, all Shey needs to know is Kim's address. Shey can write his message on the postcard, put Kim's address on it and put it in the mailbox to be sent. Shey does not have to verify that Kim is at home to send the postcard on its way. If Kim is at home when the mailman arrives, the postcard is read and the message is received. Notice that unless Kim responds back to Shey through mail or by phone, Shey can never really know whether the postcard was received. That is the nature of nonconnection-oriented protocols. Delivery is not guaranteed. If the mailman is eaten by the neighbor's dog, or the sorting machine at the post office eats the postcard, or a tornado takes out the mail truck, Shey may never know it, and Kim may never know there was a message intended for her.

In terms of applications, the same methodology is true. For instance, the Simple Network Management Protocol (SNMP) uses UDP ports 67 and 68 for occasionally polling for data from machines on the network and for initiating traps on machines when errors occur. These polls and traps are sent as UDP broadcasts and do not require a session to be established to communicate a message. Think about how useful that is. Does it make any sense for a machine that is having a catastrophic error of some sort to have to go through the business of establishing a TCP session, just to tell you the machine is going down? No, it doesn't. It makes perfect sense however, to let the last gasping breath of a machine be a broadcast message that it's in serious trouble.

Another really good use for UDP is in streaming video and streaming audio. Not only does the unguaranteed delivery of packets enable more data to be transmitted (because a broadcast has little to no overhead), but the retransmission of a packet is pointless, anyway. In the case of a streaming broadcast, users are more concerned with what's coming next than with trying to recover a packet or two that may not have made it. Compare it to listening to a music CD and a piece of dust gets stuck in one of the little grooves. In most cases, the omission of that piece is imperceptible; your ear barely notices and your brain probably filled in the gap for you anyway. Imagine instead that your CD player decides to guarantee the delivery of that one piece of data that it can't quite get, and ends up skipping and skipping indefinitely. It can definitely ruin the listening experience. It is easier to deal with an occasional packet dropping out to have as fulfilling a listening experience as possible. Thankfully, UDP was developed for applications to utilize in this very same fashion.

Internet Protocol

A number of protocols are found in the Internet layer, including the most important protocol in the entire suite, the Internet Protocol (IP). The reason that this is probably the most important protocol is that the Transport layer cannot communicate at all without communicating through IP in the Internet layer. Figure 8.24 illustrates that at one point or another all Transport layer traffic is passed through IP, with no exceptions. IP is responsible for the handling, addressing, and routing of packets on a network. It is a connection-less delivery system, and delivery of packets is not guaranteed. Reliability is provided by the higher layers, either through TCP or by higher-layer applications.

Figure 8.24

IP protocol layer.

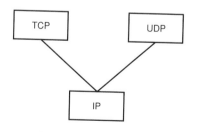

In figure 8.24, the IP protocol is referred to by a mail truck and a telephone operator icon, because IP is responsible for the delivery of packets whether they use connection-based or non-connection-based communications. Delivery and routing are not guaranteed, even though for the most part they work seamlessly.

IP also has a number of parameters that can be set. Figure 8.25 illustrates a sample datagram for IP and the various characteristics that can be configured.

Figure 8.25

An IP packet on the network.

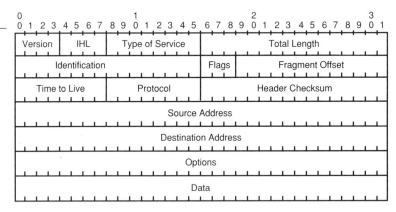

Of the parameters that can be controlled and set in the IP packet in figure 8.25, pay close attention to the Time to Live, the Protocol, Source Address, and the Destination Address. These parameters are what specify where a datagram is supposed to be sent, where it came from, how long a packet has to get to its destination before it is discarded by the network, and to what protocol (such as TCP or UDP) the data should be passed.

Addressing

The most fundamental element of the Internet Protocol is the address space that IP uses. Each machine on a network is given a unique 32-bit address called an Internet address or IP address. Addresses are divided into five categories, called classes. There are currently A, B, C, D, and E classes of addresses. The unique address given to a machine is derived from the Class A, B, or C addresses. Class D addresses are used for combining machines into one functional group, and Class E addresses are considered experimental and are not currently available. For now, the most important concept to understand is that each machine requires a unique address and IP is responsible for maintaining, utilizing, and manipulating it to provide communication between two machines. The whole concept behind uniquely identifying machines is to be able to send data to one machine and one machine only, even in the event that the IP stack has to broadcast at the Physical layer. Figure 8.26 illustrates how IP can distinguish between machines even when the frame is sent as a broadcast at the physical address layer.

Figure 8.26

An IP packet on the network.

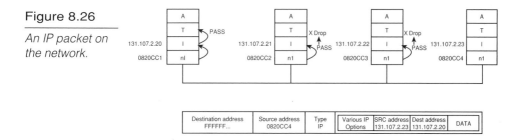

If IP receives data from the network interface layer that is addressed to another machine or is not a broadcast, its directions are to silently discard the packet and not continue processing it.

IP receives information in the form of packets from the Transport layer, from either TCP or UDP, and sends out data in what are commonly referred to as datagrams. The size of a datagram is dependent upon the type of network that is being used, such as token-ring or ethernet. If a packet has too much data to be transmitted in one datagram, it is broken into pieces and transmitted through several datagrams. Each of these datagrams has to then be reassembled by TCP or UDP. More on fragmentation and reassembly is discussed in the "Fragmentation and Reassembly" section later in this chapter.

Broadcasts

Despite the fact that IP was designed to be able to send packets directly to a particular machine, at times it is preferable to send a message to all machines connected to a physical segment. IP supports broadcasts at the Internet layer and if it receives a broadcast datagram from the Network Interface layer, it must process the packet as if it had been addressed to it.

Fragmentation and Reassembly

Fragmentation and reassembly occurs when data is too large to be transmitted on the underlying network. Combining a token-ring and ethernet network is the most common example. Token-ring networks support much larger frame sizes and therefore support larger datagram sizes. It may also be the case that the Transport layer sends the Internet layer more data than one datagram can handle. In either of these cases, IP must break down the data into manageable chunks through a process called fragmentation. After data is fragmented, each datagram gets a fragment ID, identifying it in the sequence so that each fragment can be reassembled at the destination machine. This whole process is transparent to the user. Figure 8.27 illustrates the fragmentation and reassembly process that can occur between two machines.

Figure 8.27

Fragmentation and reassembly.

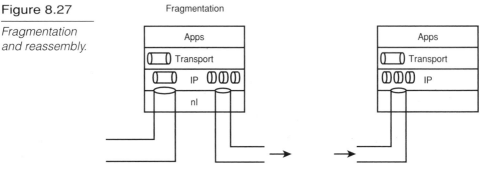

After the fragments have been received and reassembled at the destination machine, the data can be sent up to the higher layers for processing.

Routeability

IP is responsible for routing IP datagrams from one network to another. Machines on a network can be configured to support routing. With routing, when a machine receives a datagram that is neither addressed to it nor is a broadcast, it is given the additional responsibility of trying to find where the datagram should be sent so that it can reach its destination. Not all machines on a TCP/IP network are routers. But all routers have the capability to forward datagrams from one network to another. Connections to the Internet are often through one form of router or another.

Time To Live

The Time to Live (TTL) specification is set in Windows NT to a default of 128. This represents either 128 hops or 128 seconds, or a combination of the two. Each time a router handles a datagram, it decrements the TTL by one. If a datagram is held up at a router for longer than one second before it is transmitted, the router can decrement the TTL by more than one.

One way to visualize how the TTL works is to think of a deadly poison. Each time a datagram is sent out on to the network, it is injected with this deadly poison. The datagram has only the length of time specified in the TTL to get to its destination and receive the antidote for the poison. If the datagram gets routed through congested routers, traffic jams, narrow bandwidth communication avenues, and so on it just might not make it. If the TTL expires before the datagram reaches its destination, it is discarded from the network.

Although this concept may seem strange at first, in reality it prevents datagrams from running around a network indefinitely wreaking havoc with bandwidth and the synchronization of data. Imagine a scenario in which 100 datagrams are sent to a machine. Twenty-five of them have to be resent because the Retransmit Timer on the sending machine expired. After the communication is complete and the session broken down, suddenly 25 packets appear out of nowhere hitting the destination machine. It may be that these 25 packets got rerouted through some extremely slow network path and were never discarded. At least in this case the destination machine can just ignore the datagrams. However, in routed environments it would be pretty easy to set up infinite loops where packets would bounce in between two routers indefinitely.

So here we have TCP, UDP, and IP working together to provide both connection-oriented and non-connection-oriented communication. These three protocols work together to provide communication between two machines.

For an exercise covering this information, see end of chapter.

Consider an example that helps to illustrate exactly how each of these protocols works and the functionality required by them. In this illustration, Bob would like to send a message to Kim. The message is an invitation to a New Year's Eve party.

Think of TCP as being similar to a telephone call. Bob picks up the phone and dials Kim's number. If Kim is home and wants to receive calls, she picks up the phone, indicating that she is home and available to communicate. Kim answers with a greeting of some sort, such as "Hi," indicating to Bob that he should speak. Bob then chooses the appropriate response to Kim's "Hi," such as, "Hey, this is Bob, I'm glad you're home." After this pleasant exchange, the session has been created and Bob can send his message of friendship to Kim. If, however, Bob replies with a response such as "Goodbye," rather than "Hey," the communication breaks down because Kim would think, "How strange," and hang up the phone before any communication can occur. And certainly, if Kim is not at home, no data can be transferred.

Think of UDP now. Here communication can be achieved simply by Bob placing a written invitation in an envelope, addressing it properly, and placing the envelope in his mailbox with the flag up. Bob does not have to verify that Kim is currently at home to send the message. Delivery of the message is not guaranteed, however, because the only way for Bob to know whether the message got there would be for him to receive some indication from Kim, either by mail or by phone. Until Kim responds, Bob has no idea whether the mailman was attacked by a dog, or if perhaps the invitation is currently sitting under a stack of bills on Kim's desk. The point is, Bob has no way to know.

Now how did IP play into the picture? IP serves both kinds of communications methods, but in and of itself does not guarantee delivery of data. Consider how this applies to the example. For the telephone conversation, IP acts similarly to the old-style operator who connects the call. The operator can make the connection and deliver the available resources, but it's still up to Bob to say the correct things, and it's still up to Kim to answer the phone. For the mailed invitation, IP acts as the mailman. The mailman checks to see whether the address is properly formatted and routes it to the appropriate delivery method, until it eventually lands in Kim's mailbox. No guarantees are made here in terms of delivery of the mail.

Internet Control Message Protocol

Internet Control Message Protocol (ICMP) is part of the Internet layer and is responsible for reporting errors and messages regarding the delivery of IP datagrams. It can also send "source quench" and other self tuning signals during the transfer of data between two machines without the intervention of the user. These signals are designed to fine-tune and optimize the transfer of data automatically. ICMP is the protocol that warns you when a destination host is unreachable, or how long it took to get to a destination host. In figure 8.24, ICMP is represented by a policeman. If it helps, think of ICMP as the Internet Control Military Police, the protocol that's always watching over your shoulder.

ICMP messages can be broken down into two basic categories: the reporting of errors and the sending of queries. Error messages include the following:

▶ Destination unreachable

▶ Redirect

▶ Source quench

▶ Time exceeded

The Destination unreachable error message is generated by ICMP when an IP datagram is sent out and the destination machine either cannot be located or does not support the designated protocol. For instance, a sending machine may receive a Destination host unreachable message when trying to communicate through a router that does not know to which network to send a datagram.

The first important thing to realize about Redirect messages is that these are only sent by routers in a TCP/IP environment, not individual machines. A machine may have more than one default gateway defined for redundancy. If a router detects a better route to a particular destination, it forwards the first packet it receives, but sends a redirect message to the machine to update its route tables. In this way, the machine can use the better route to reach the remote network.

Sometimes a machine has to drop incoming datagrams because it has received so many it can't process them all. In this case, a machine can send a Source quench message to the source, indicating it needs to slow up transmission. The Source quench message can also be sent by a router if it is in between the source and destination machines and is encountering trouble routing all the packets in time. Upon receiving a Source quench message, the source machine immediately reduces its transmissions. However, it continues to try to increase the amount of data as time progresses to the original amount of data it was sending before.

The Time exceeded error message is sent by a router whenever it drops a packet due to the expiration of the TTL. This error message is sent to the source address to notify the machine of a possible infinite routing loop or that the TTL is set too low to get to the destination.

ICMP also includes general message queries. The two most commonly used are the following:

▶ Echo request

▶ Echo reply

The most familiar tool for verifying that an IP address on a network actually exists is the Personal Internet Groper (PING) utility. This utility uses the ICMP echo request and reply mechanisms. The echo request is a simple directed datagram that asks for acknowledgment that a particular IP address exists on the network. If a machine with this IP address exists and receives the request, it is designed to send an ICMP echo reply. This reply is sent back to the destination address to notify the source machine of its existence. The PING utility reports the existence of the IP address and how long it took to get there.

ICMP serves a number of functions, but primarily acts as the messenger for what is happening during the communication process. (Remember, you should think of ICMP as standing for the Internet Control Military Police.) For instance, in the mail example, if Bob improperly formats his address, ICMP (the police) come knocking on Bob's door to notify him of his error. Or if Bob sends so many letters to Kim that Kim's mailbox cannot hold them all, causing a considerable overflow at the post office, ICMP (the police) knock on Bob's door and politely ask him to reduce his transmissions. In the phone call scenario, if Bob dials the wrong number, ICMP (the police) are right there to warn Bob about the error of his ways. Or if Bob talks Kim's poor ear off and doesn't let her get a word in edgewise, ICMP (the police) kindly step in on Kim's behalf and remind Bob that conversations are supposed to work both ways.

Internet Group Management Protocol

For an exercise covering this information, see end of chapter.

Internet Group Management Protocol (IGMP) is a protocol and set of specifications that allow machines to be added and removed from IP address groups, utilizing the class D range of addresses mentioned earlier. IP allows the assignment of class D addresses to groups of machines so that they may receive broadcast data as one functional unit. Machines can be added and removed from these units or groups, or be members of multiple groups. The reason for assigning the cable television icon to this protocol in figure 8.24 is based on how both cable TV and IGMP work. Both work in fundamentally the same way.

For instance, when you want to receive the premium channels, you pay more money and the cable company alters your cable box so that you can receive the premium channels. You have therefore joined the group of people who receive the premium cable channels. All you have to do to remove yourself from this group is stop paying your bill. And presto, several months later, you no longer get the premium channels you once had. If you are not a subscriber, you never see the pay channels. But if you want premium channels you can get a wide range of choices, just as you can be a member of a number of Class D addresses, or IGMP groups, to receive broadcasts.

Most implementations of the TCP/IP protocol stack support this on the local machine; however routers designed to broadcast IGMP messages from one network to another are still in the experimental stage. Routers are designed to initiate queries for multicast groups on local network segments to determine whether they should be broadcasting on that segment. If at least one member of an IGMP group exists or responds with a IGMP response, the router processes IGMP datagrams and broadcasts them on the segment.

Address Resolution Protocol

Unless IP is planning to initiate a full broadcast on the network, it has to have the physical address of the machine to which it is going to send datagrams. For this information, it relies on Address Resolution Protocol (ARP). ARP is responsible for mapping IP addresses on the network to physical addresses in memory. This way, whenever IP needs a physical address for a particular IP address, ARP can deliver. But ARP's memory does not last indefinitely, and occasionally IP will ask for an IP address that is not in ARP's memory. When this happens, ARP has to go out and find one. This is why ARP is represented by the detective icon in figure 8.24.

ARP is responsible for finding a map to a local physical address for any local IP address that IP may request. If ARP does not have a map in memory it has to go find one on the network. ARP uses local broadcasts to find physical addresses of machines and maintains a cache in memory of recently mapped IP addresses to physical addresses. Although this cache does not last indefinitely, it enables ARP to not have to broadcast every time IP needs a physical address.

As long as the destination IP address is local, all ARP does is a local broadcast for that machine and returns the physical address to IP. IP, realizing that the destination IP address is local, simply formulates the datagram with the IP address above the physical address of the destination machine. Figure 8.28 shows how that process happens.

Figure 8.28

A datagram destined locally.

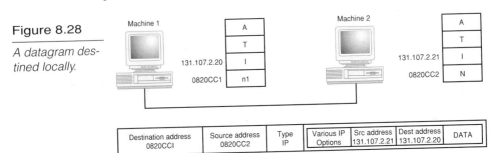

But IP does not always need to send datagrams to local IP address-es. In fact, often the destination address is on a remote network where the path may include several routers along the way. The hardest thing to realize conceptually is that ARP operates so close to the network interface layer that it is really only good for finding local physical addresses. This is true even in environments where routers exist. ARP never reports a physical address that exists on a remote network to IP. Figure 8.29 illustrates what would happen if ARP was capable of responding with a physical address from a remote network. IP datagrams specify exactly which physical ad-dress is supposed to listen to their message. In the example in figure 8.29, then, the datagram is sent out onto the network, and the router, which also has a physical address, simply ignores the packet. Not exactly what was intended.

Figure 8.29

IP asking ARP for a remote physical address.

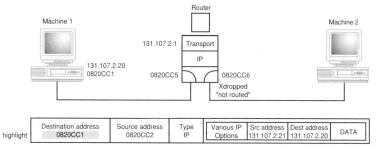

This packet is transmitted on segment A

To get the packet to the other network, the router is supposed to listen to the packet and forward it on. The only way to get it to listen to the packet, though, is to either do a broadcast, or send the packet to the router's physical address. IP is smart enough to realize that the destination IP address is on a remote network and that the datagram must be sent to the router. However, it has no idea what the physical address of the router is, and thus relies on ARP to discover that for it.

To route a packet, IP asks ARP whether it has the physical address of the router, not of the destination machine. This is one of the more subtle and elegant features of the TCP/IP suite, in that it cleverly redirects packets based upon what layer is being commu-nicated with. After IP receives the physical address of the router from ARP, it formulates the datagram, placing the destination IP address directly above the router's physical address. Figure 8.30 illustrates how this interaction actually works and how elegant this system of routing really is.

Figure 8.30

IP and ARP per-form sleight-of-hand.

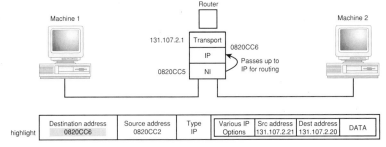

The Network APIs, Windows Sockets, and NetBIOS

Notice that in figure 8.31, the Application layer does not have protocols, but APIs. Recall that the Application layer provides the interface between applications and the transport protocols. Microsoft supports two APIs for applications to use: Windows Sockets and NetBIOS. This functionality is included because Microsoft networks still use NetBIOS for a number of internal mechanisms within the Windows NT operating system. It is also used because it provides a standard interface to a number of other protocols as well. TCP/IP, NetBEUI, and NWLink all have a NetBIOS interface to which applications can be written to use networking protocols. Strict Unix flavors of TCP/IP may not support the NetBIOS interface and may only support Windows Sockets as their API; Microsoft's implementation of TCP/IP therefore includes support for both.

The Windows Sockets interface defines an industry standard specification for how windows applications communicate with the TCP/IP protocol. This specification includes definitions for how to use the transport protocols and how to transfer data between two machines, including the establishment of connection-oriented sessions (TCP three-way handshake) and non-connection-oriented datagrams (broadcasts). The Windows Sockets API also defines how to uniquely address packets destined for a particular application on another machine. The concept of a socket (the combination of the TCP/IP address and the port

number) is a common example of the relative ease of uniquely
identifying a communications path. Because of the ease and
standardization of the Windows Sockets specifications, this API
is enjoying a tremendous amount of exposure and success, particularly in terms of its use in Internet applications.

Figure 8.31

*APIs in the Appli-
cation layer.*

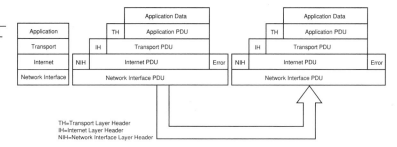

Windows Sockets uniquely identifies machines through their IP
address, so machine names in the TCP/IP environment are entirely
optional. Given that it is tremendously more difficult for users to
remember a hundred IP addresses over some form of an alias for
these machines, a name space was created to help identify machines on a TCP/IP network. A name space is a hierarchical naming scheme that uniquely identifies machine aliases to IP addresses.
This scheme allows two machines to have the same alias as long as
they are not in the same domain. This is very useful for people, but
entirely unnecessary for applications, since applications can use the
IP address. This is why you can use any alias you want to establish a
connection to a particular machine. As long as the name resolution
method (DNS, hosts file) returns a valid IP address, a communication path can be created. The IP address is what's most important.
With the NetBIOS API, the IP address is only part of the information necessary to establish communication between two machines,
and the name of the machine is required.

The NetBIOS API was developed on local area networks and has
evolved into a standard interface for applications to use to access
networking protocols in the Transport layer for both connection-
oriented and non-connection-oriented communications. NetBIOS
interfaces have been written for the NetBEUI, NWLink, and

TCP/IP protocols so that applications need not worry about which of these protocols is providing the transport services. Because each of these protocols supports the NetBIOS API, all the functionality for establishing sessions and initiating broadcasts is provided. Unlike Windows Sockets, NetBIOS requires not only an IP address to uniquely identify a machine, but a NetBIOS name as well.

Every machine on a network must be uniquely identified with a NetBIOS name. This name is required for establishing a NetBIOS session or sending out a broadcast. When utilizing names through a NetBIOS session, the sending machine must be able to resolve the NetBIOS name to an IP address. Because both an IP address and name are needed, all name resolution methods have to supply the correct IP address before successful communication can occur.

The Microsoft TCP/IP stack supports connection-oriented and non-connection-oriented communications established through either of these popular APIs. Microsoft includes NetBT (NetBIOS over TCP/IP) for applications that would like to utilize the NetBIOS API over a TCP/IP network. This small, seemingly insignificant piece of software is what prevents your machine from having to run two protocols, one for Windows Sockets, and one for NetBIOS. By providing NetBT with Microsoft's TCP/IP protocol stack, all NetBIOS calls an application may initiate are supported.

RFCs

Anyone interested in learning more about TCP/IP can find out more by reading the series of published standards called Request For Comments (RFCs). These standards can be thought of as the living documents of the Internet and are constantly under various stages of completion, acceptance, or planned obsolescence. Each enhancement or feature to the TCP/IP protocol is described by a particular RFC number. Whenever a significant change to a feature is recommended or suggested, and enough of the Internet community agrees on the change, a new RFC is created to discuss the new implementation and place it under further study.

RFCs are referred to as the living documents of the Internet because RFCs are never updated or deleted, much like the Constitution of the United States. Every addition or change is an amendment to the original. Therefore changes require the creation of a new RFC number, and always reference the original RFC they are intended to replace or enhance.

To keep track of whether RFCs are current, under progress, or no longer used, a classification system was created indicating the status of any individual RFC. These classifications are Required, Recommended, Elective, Limited Use, and Not Recommended. When you read an RFC, you may notice that different terminology is used. For instance, in the case of a particular implementation detail that is Required, the terminology used in the RFC says that this implementation must be used. In the case of a recommended implementation, the RFC uses the word "should." The elective portions are discussed in terms of how a protocol may do a particular feature. And of course, for those implementations that are not recommended, the use of "should not" is often seen. To view Internet RFCs, check out the following URL:

```
http://ds.internic.net/ds/dspg1intdoc.html
```

Exercises

Exercise 8.1: Using Netstat to Generate Statistics (TCP)

1. From the Start menu, choose Programs, Command Prompt.

2. At the command prompt, type **> netstat -s -p tcp**.

What appears is a statistics report for the TCP protocol as well as a display of any TCP sessions that are currently in use.

Exercise 8.2: Using Netstat to Generate Statistics (UDP)

1. From the Start menu, choose Programs, Command Prompt.

2. At the command prompt, type **> netstat -s -p udp**.

What appears is a statistics report for the UDP protocol.

Exercise 8.3: Using Netstat to Generate Statistics (IP)

1. From the Start menu, choose Programs, Command Prompt.

2. At the command prompt, type **> netstat -s -p ip**.

What appears is a statistics report for the IP protocol.

Exercise 8.4: Using Netstat to Generate Statistics (ICMP)

1. From the Start menu, choose Programs, Command Prompt.

2. At the command prompt, type **> netstat -s -p icmp**.

What appears is a statistics report for the ICMP protocol.

Review Questions

The following questions will test your knowledge of the information in this chapter:

1. You're talking with a few of the programmers in your department about an application they are working on. They tell you it is designed to use a connection-oriented protocol to communicate over the network. Which protocol in the TCP/IP protocol suite provides connection-oriented communications?

   A. Transmission Control Protocol

   B. User Datagram Protocol

   C. Internet Control Message Protocol

   D. Address Resolution Protocol

2. Several machines on the network utilize DHCP and WINS in order to get their IP address information and to resolve NetBIOS names to IP addresses, respectively. What protocol allows these machines to resolve an IP address to a hardware address?

   A. Internet Control Protocol

   B. DHCP address resolution manager

   C. WINS address resolution manager

   D. Address Resolution Protocol

3. An NT server in your environment needs to be able to communicate with other machines on the Internet using a DNS server to resolve names to IP addresses. Which command line utility displays whether a machine has been configured with the IP address of a DNS server?

   A. Netstat –N

   B. Nbtstat –N

   C. IPCONFIG

   D. PING

4. Several programmers are discussing the design of a new application to be written for your company and a heated debate ensues over whether the application should use Windows Sockets or NetBIOS. Half the programmers think TCP/IP supports Windows Sockets only and half think TCP/IP supports both Windows Sockets and NetBIOS. Who is correct in this argument?

   A. Programmers who say Windows sockets only

   B. Programmers who say NetBIOS only

   C. Programmers who say neither

   D. Programmers who say both are supported

5. The Dallas office is having trouble communicating with the Orlando office over the company's wide area networks links. There are several routers in between these two offices and you suspect some of them may be slow or not functioning at all. Which utility would be useful in determining the path and time that packets are taking to get from the Dallas office to the Orlando office?

   A. Tracert

   B. Netstat

   C. Nbtstat

   D. Ipconfig

6. You will be implementing DHCP in your environment and want to know how relay agents actually transmit DHCP requests from one network segment to another. What Internet resource is available to you for finding the specifications for a particular protocol or service?

   A. Request for Comments

   B. Netstat

   C. Nbtstat -Trace

   D. Network Monitor

7. One of your users calls and says that she cannot connect to the network. She can't logon to the NT domain and she can't use network neighborhood. As part of your trouble-shooting steps, you find out that the user can ping every IP address on the network successfully. Not only that but she seems to be able to FTP, HTTP, and Telnet wherever she wants to. Which of the following do you think might be the source of the error?

   A. NetBIOS API isn't functioning properly

   B. DNS isn't configured

   C. Telnet is an unpredictable program

   D. Windows sockets isn't functioning properly

8. Kristin is a user in the advertising department who is writing a document in Word. This is a very important document that must be transferred immediately to the remote office. If you had to select which protocol would be best for this type of transfer, which protocol would you choose?

   A. User Datagram Importance Protocol

   B. Internet Control Messaging Protocol

   C. Transmission Control Protocol

   D. Important Packet Protocol

9. Paul is a user who seems to be having some issues with connecting to another network segment on the other side of a router. Despite repeated attempts to route packets to the other side, Paul is unsuccessful. In an attempt to help Paul with his problem, you will need to determine which layer is responsible for the routing of IP packets. Which layer would that be?

   A. Network layer

   B. Transport layer

   C. Internet layer

   D. Application layer

10. Daphne works in the engineering department and is rather savvy with computers. She has informed you that you will be implementing a program that works at the Application layer and uses NetBIOS to communicate with a remote network computer. In order to test whether this application will work, which of the following would be a valid test?

   A. Ping destination computer

   B. Ping hostname of destination computer

   C. Tracert to destination machine

   D. NetView destination machine

11. During the troubleshooting of a problem, you take a trace to discover what is going on. As you are analyzing the packets, you discover a "Redirect" packet that appears to have come from a router. Which protocol is capable of generating such a packet?

   A. Transmission Control Protocol

   B. User Datagram Protocol

   C. Internet Group Management Protocol

   D. Internet Control Message Protocol

12. Some of the programmers in your environment are interested in writing a new program to communicate on the network. They have been studying IP and want to know if there is any way to direct packets to a group of users without having to send a broadcast to everyone. They don't want the program to keep lists. They want to be able to do this at the IP level. Which protocol would you suggest they take a closer look at?

   A. Internet Group Therapy Protocol

   B. Internet Group Protocol

   C. Internet Group Management Protocol

   D. Address Resolution Protocol

13. You've been given the task of troubleshooting a program failure because of your vast IP experience with ports and sockets. As part of this troubleshooting, you've been given access to the program code. This code seems to be having trouble communicating with its server component located on 7.23.70.1. The program uses TCP as its transport but still seems to not be running correctly. What additional piece of information is necessary in order for the client to communicate with the server?

   A. NetBIOS functionality

   B. 32-bit session utility

   C. Server Port definition

   D. Windows sockets Name resolution

Review Answers

1. A

2. D

3. C

4. D

5. A

6. A

7. A

8. C

9. C

10. D

11. D

12. C

13. C

Answers to the Test Yourself Questions at the Beginning of the Chapter

1. The TCP/IP protocol suite maps to a 4-layer networking model. Each of the layers corresponds to one or more of the OSI layers. These four layers map to all seven layers that exist in the OSI model. See "The Four Layers of TCP/IP."

2. Tell the president TCP/IP is an industry-standard suite of protocols that is not owned or developed by one company. The Internet community works on the establishment of these standards and the evolution of the protocols, and no implementation is considered mandatory until the whole community agrees upon a good implementation. See "RFCs."

3. TCP/IP has been developed as a cross-platform, client/server suite of protocols and enables IBM mainframes, NetWare servers, Macintosh clients, Windows 95, and Windows NT machines to be integrated together. See "Introduction to TCP/IP."

4. The IP protocol is responsible for routing and delivery of datagrams. See "Internet Protocol."

5. UDP is the best protocol for delivering streaming data, because it is much quicker and more streamlined, not requiring the overhead of verifying the delivery of datagrams. See "User Datagram Protocol."

6. This is an unnecessary concern, because Microsoft's TCP/IP protocol stack includes NetBT (NetBIOS over TCP/IP), which enables all NetBIOS API calls to utilize TCP/IP as a protocol. See "The Network APIs, Windows Sockets, and NetBIOS."

Chapter

IP Addressing

This chapter helps you prepare for the exam by covering the following objective:

Objective

▶ Diagnose and resolve IP addressing problems

STOP

Test Yourself! Before reading this chapter, test yourself to determine how much study time you will need to devote to this section.

1. How many layers does the OSI networking model have? The TCP/IP networking model?

2. How many classes of addresses are there?

3. What class of address can have 65,534 hosts per network?

4. How many bits long is a IPv6 address?

5. What two methods can you use to configure a TCP/IP address?

Answers are located at the end of the chapter.

Overview

A network protocol suite such as TCP/IP has to have a methodology by which devices on the network can identify each other at every level of the network model. TCP/IP provides identification at the Internet layer of the TCP/IP networking model in the form of IP addressing. Refer to Chapter 8 for a discussion of the four layers.

 Tip

Remember that the Internet layer of the TCP/IP networking model is equivalent to the Network layer of the OSI Reference Model.

Networked devices such as a computer or printer in a TCP/IP network rely on an identification scheme similar in concept to a postal system. In order for me to send a letter to you, I will have to submit the letter to my local postal system. For the system to deliver the correspondence, I will have to enclose it in an envelope clearly marked with the country, ZIP/postal code, city, street, and name identifying you and where you live. I will also include my return address, in order for the letter to be returned if you have changed your address or for you to write back.

In order to send information from one component to another through a TCP/IP network the information, like our correspondence, must contain the address of the recipient and the sender.

Instead of a letter this information is packaged, at the Internet Layer of the TCP/IP networking model, in units known as datagrams. The addresses are represented by 32-bit numbers called IP addresses.

TCP/IP Addressing Methods

When a device, such as a server or workstation, is attached to a TCP/IP network, it is commonly referred to as a *host*. Each host connected through a TCP/IP network must have the capability to communicate with every other host on the network as needed—security considerations notwithstanding. This capability to communicate is not just limited to the Internet layer of the TCP/IP architecture. Rather, a host has to be able to communicate at all four layers: the Process/Application layer, Host-to-Host layer, Internet layer, and Network Access layer. Each layer of the model uses its own addressing method to communicate with a remote TCP/IP host.

Addressing at the Process/Application layer is provided using host names. This naming method allows hosts to be configured with easily remembered names. This is a significant advantage, since the Process/Application layer is the level seen directly by users. Host naming will be discussed later in Chapter 17, "Host Name Resolution."

 Note

As a Windows NT administrator, you will undoubtedly be responsible for providing names for your servers. Please be kind to yourself and others. Use a name that makes sense in the context of your network and the location of your server. In a global economy, your network can easily expand beyond your wildest dreams. You might find it difficult to explain to your international colleague the significance of a domestically popular cartoon character. Check out RFC 1178 for recommended guidelines for naming a computer.

Port numbers are the addressing methods used at the Host-to-Host layer. These numbers are used to describe the interface to software processes operating on the host.

The Internet layer uses IP addresses. The current version of IP, IPv4, uses a 32-bit address. This amounts to a seemingly inexhaustible 4,294,967,296 addresses available. I emphasize "seemingly," because as the Internet and world markets continue to expand at incredible rates, the current method of IP addressing will not keep up. This chapter concentrates on IP addressing elements, in addition to future trends these elements will follow.

Table 9.1 summarizes the addressing method used in each of the TCP/IP architecture.

Table 9.1

Addressing Method in the TCP/IP Architecture	
TCP/IP Architecture	Addressing Method
Process/Application	Host name
Host-to-Host	Port number
Internet	IP address
Network Access	Hardware address (MAC address)

IP Addresses Defined

 Objective

Every device connected to a TCP/IP network requires at least one IP address and must be unique within that network. An IP address is commonly represented in dotted decimal notation. Here are some examples of IP addresses shown in dotted decimal form.

207.21.32.12

10.1.2.34

120.224.21.253

As in these examples, all IP addresses are 32 bits long and are comprised of four 8-bit segments known as *octets*. Representing IP addresses in dotted decimal notation makes them a lot easier to read than in the machine friendly binary format. As you will see in the next section, however, the capability to convert IP addresses to-and-from binary format is required for configuring your TCP/IP network and for the exam. The following is an example of an IP address shown in dotted decimal and its equivalent binary notation.

```
Dotted Decimal              Binary
207.21.32.12       11001111 00010101 00100000 00001100
```

Conversion Between Decimal and Binary Numbers

The term *bit* is commonly used to describe a 1 or 0 and is a contraction of the words *bi*nary digi*t*. Binary means a value of 2, and therefore bit patterns use a base 2 system, whereas decimal numbers us a base 10 system. For the purpose of converting IP addresses between decimal and binary, think of each decimal number as being mapped to an 8 digit binary number. For example, the IP address 207.21.32.12 can be represented as shown in table 9.2.

Table 9.2

Conversion of 207.21.32.12 to Decimal		
Decimal Value	Bits	Binary Value
207	128+64+0+0+8+4+2+1	11001111
21	0+0+0+16+0+4+0+1	00010101
32	0+0+32+0+0+0+0+0	00100000
12	0+0+0+0+8+4+0+0	00001100

Table 9.3 shows possible values of each bit in an octet.

Table 9.3

Possible Values of Each Bit in an Octet							
Bit	8	7	6	5	4	3	2	1
Value	128	64	32	16	8	4	2	1

 Note   This means that the binary number 11010 is the same as 16 + 8 + 2 or 26.

Network ID and Host ID

Although an IP address is a single value, it is divided into two pieces of information: the network ID and the host ID of the networked device.

The network ID identifies the systems that are located on the same physical network. All systems on the same physical network must have the same network ID, and the network ID must be unique to the local segment. In this case, local is defined as being on one side of a router.

The host ID identifies a workstation, server, router, or other TCP/IP device within a network. The host address for each device must be unique to the network ID. A computer connected to a TCP/IP network uses the network ID and host ID to determine which packets it should receive or ignore and to determine which devices are to have the opportunity of receiving its transmissions.

Throughout the world, TCP/IP networks vary greatly in size and scope. In order to accommodate the wide range of network design needs, IP addresses have been divided into classes.

IP Address Classes Defined

The IP address is 32 bits in length and is used to identify both the host address and the address of the network in which the host resides. An address class is defined to allocate the minimum number of bits that are to be used as the network ID. The remaining bits can be used to further subdivide the network using subnet masks and to define the host ID.

Table 9.4 illustrates the currently available IP address classes:

Table 9.4

Classes of IP Addresses Available Under IPv4					
IP Address Class	First Octet		Start in Binary	Number of	
	Minimum	Maximum		Networks	Hosts
Class A	1	126	1	126	16,777,214
Class B	128	191	10	16,384	65,534
Class C	192	223	110	2,097,152	254
Class D	224	239	1110		
Class E	240	247	11110		

 Note

Class D addresses are used for Multicasting (for example Real Audio broadcasts across the Internet. Class E are experimental. Neither of these address classes can be used as a host ID.

Let's revisit the one of the sample IP address shown in table 9.2. Based on our newly acquired knowledge of IP address classes, we see that IP address 207.21.32.12 is a Class C address. Note that the first octet is 207, and falls within the range of a Class C network. In addition, the binary equivalent of 207 is 1101111. Since the first three most significant bits are 110, we can again confirm that this is a Class C address.

Reasons for Using Specific Address Classes

If you are new to TCP/IP, you may be asking yourself "Why are there different classes of IP addresses, and how can I use them?" First of all, the Internet community has defined the different types of IP addresses in order to accommodate the needs of networks of different sizes. A network with less than 255 devices (workstations, routers, printers, and so) can be assigned a Class C network address. However, a large organization with up to 65,534 devices will need at least a Class B address.

Second, as long as you are not connecting your internal network directly to the public Internet, you can use any valid Class A, B, or C address you want. However, any device that is connected directly to the Internet, must be assigned a network ID from the Internet community. The organization responsible for administering the assignment of the network ID portions of IP addresses for network devices directly connected to the Internet is the Internet Network Information Center (InterNIC). They can be reached at www.internic.net.

 Note   RFC 1918 defines the methodology for IP address allocation for private networks.

For most private networks (intranets) on the border of the public Internet, IP addresses are either assigned dynamically (see Chapter 12, "Dynamic Host Configuration Protocol") or statically by an Internet Service Provider (ISP). The ISP maintains responsibility for administering IP network IDs assigned by InterNIC. Three examples of ISPs, which dynamically assign IP addresses, commonly used by individuals for dial-up access are CompuServe, America Online, and Prodigy. Typically, a private network requiring access to the Internet will use a direct connection to an ISP through a router. In these cases, the ISP will provide a network ID to the private network. This address will be a unique statically assigned address provided to the ISP from InterNIC. These commercial services are usually provided by larger ISPs, including MCI, AT&T, and GTE.

Classes Defined

We have already discussed the reason behind the provision of separate classes of IP addresses. Now we will discuss in more detail, the definition for each class of IP address. Before continuing, the following table and figure will help clarify the differences between host and network IDs. Table 9.5 illustrates the publicly available IP address classes (A to C) and their corresponding network and host ID components.

Table 9.5

Network and Host ID Assignments

IP Address Class	IP Address	Network ID	Host ID
Class A	a.b.c.d	a	b.c.d
Class B	a.b.c.d	a.b	c.d
Class C	a.b.c.d	a.b.c	d

Again, it is important to understand that the IP address consists of two parts: a network ID and a host ID. As shown in table 9.4, the most significant bits (MSBs) are used to determine how many bits are used for the network ID and the host ID. Figure 9.1 diagrams the placement of the MSBs within each of the five classes of IP addresses.

Figure 9.1

The placement of the most significant bits.

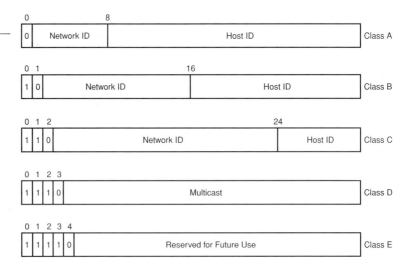

▶ **Class A** addresses are assigned to networks with extremely large numbers of hosts (networked devices). The MSB is set to 0, and is combined with the remaining seven bits of the first octet to complete the network ID. This leaves the last 3 octets, or 24 bits to be assigned to subnet masking and to hosts. As we saw in table 9.3, this allows for 126 (2^7-2) networks with up to 16,777,214 (2^{21}-2) hosts per network. An example of a Class A address is 10.1.2.34 where 10.0.0.0 is the network and 0.1.2.34 is the host.

▶ **Class B** addresses are assigned to networks with no more than 65,534 (2^{16}-2) hosts (networked devices). The MSBs are set to 10, and are combined with the remaining 14 bits of the first two octets to complete the network ID. This leaves the last 2 octets, or 16 bits to be assigned to subnet masking and to hosts and allows for 16,384 (2^{14}) networks. Each of these networks can have as many as 65+ thousand hosts. An example of a Class B address is 120.224.21.253 here the network is 120.224.0.0 and the host is 21.253.

▶ **Class C** addresses are assigned to small networks with a more limited number of hosts. The MSBs are set to 110, and are combined with the remaining 21 bits of the first three octets to complete the network ID. This leaves the last octet available to be assigned to subnet masking and to hosts, allowing for 2,097,152 (2^{21}) networks with up to 254 (2^8-2) hosts per network. An example of a Class B address is 207.21.32.12 which is a network of 207.21.32.0 with a host ID of 0.0.0.12.

▶ **Class D** addresses are reserved for multicast groups. Multicast addresses are assigned to groups of hosts that are cooperating, or are related in some manner. Each host in a multicast group has to be configured to accept multicast packets. The MSBs of a class D address are set to 1110. The remaining bits are uniquely assigned to each group of hosts. Microsoft NT supports class D addresses for applications such as Microsoft Net-Show.

▶ **Class E** addresses are an experimental class of IP addresses reserved for use in the future. The MSBs for class E addresses are 1111.

Note

You may be wondering why there are only 126 Class A networks, rather than 128 (2^8). As will be discussed in the next section: a network ID of all 0s is not allowed, and the Class A network ID of 127 is reserved. Read on to find out why!

IP Addressing Guidelines

As discussed earlier, a network administrator can choose to use any IP address he or she likes for an internal TCP/IP network (intranet). However, the following information should be kept in mind as these are notable exceptions:

▶ The network ID of 127 is reserved as the loopback address. It is also used in diagnostics.

▶ A network ID of all 1s or all 0s is never assigned to an individual network.

▶ A host ID of all 1s or all 0s is never assigned to an individual host.

▶ The value 255.255.255.255 represents the broadcast address.

The IP address 127.b.c.d, with b,c and d each being any number between 0 and 255, represents a software loopback address. Any packet sent to this address will be returned to the application without transmission to the network. That is, the information is returned to host from which it originates, without being sent out to the network. The packet is being copied from the transmit to receive buffer on the same host. Hence the name "loopback address." This address can be used as a check to see that TCP/IP software has been installed correctly. For example, executing a **ping 127.0.0.1** command on a Windows NT server will request a packet to be sent to itself. A return of this packet will imply a successful installation of TCP/IP. However, the return of this packet will not necessarily imply a successful configuration of TCP/IP. See Chapter 22, "Troubleshooting Microsoft TCP/IP," for more information.

Host ID values of all 0s are not assigned to individual hosts, because these addresses represent the network itself. For example, the IP address of 207.21.32.0 represents the Class C network 207.21.32. Similarly, the IP address of 10.0.0.0 represents the class A network 10. The IP address containing all 1s in the Host ID segment of the address, the address is known as a directed broadcast. For example, the IP address of 207.21.32.255 would be the address a packet is sent to if it is to be received by all hosts on the Class C network 207.21.32. Similarly, a packet sent to an address of 10.255.255.255 would be received by all hosts in the Class A network 10.

A network ID of all 0s is not defined. As seen in table 3.3, the valid range of Class A networks is 1 to 126, and not 0 to 126. Similarly, a network ID containing all 1s is not defined.

The address 255.255.255.255 is referred to as the local broadcast. This type of broadcast address can be used in a local area network, or intranet, where a broadcast will never cross a router boundary.

Assigning Network IDs

Whether you are configuring your TCP/IP LAN to connect to the public Internet, or not, you must follow specific guidelines for assigning IP addresses to networks and hosts.

Each and every physical network compliant with the TCP/IP protocol suite must have a unique network address. If the network is connected to the public Internet, the connecting network must have a network ID assigned by the InterNIC. However, all other networks may be assigned any valid network ID. Figure 9.2 provides an illustration of two intranets connected via a WAN link through the public Internet. Let's say that the network administrator of LAN A had already configured his network using a class A network ID. In this case, the network ID was 10.0.0.0. Meanwhile, his colleague in a separate physical location decides to use a Class B network address of 120.224.0.0 for her LAN. Fortunately for the two of them, they didn't have to change network IDs when management decided to connect these separate LANs via the public Internet. Instead, their company was assigned a class C address of 207.21.32.0 from the InterNIC, and they were able to connect LAN A with LAN B using a WAN link provided to them by an ISP.

Figure 9.2

A network addressing example of two TCP/IP LANs or intranets connected via a WAN link.

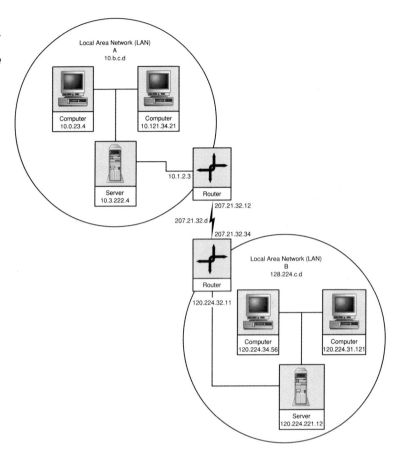

Assigning Host IDs

Just as every connected TCP/IP network must have a unique network ID, every IP addressed host within a network must be unique within that network. Figure 9.2 shows that all hosts have been assigned IP addresses unique within their networks. As can be seen, hosts do not just include computers and servers, but they also include ports on routers. By definition, a router allows for transmission of packets between different networks. As such, an IP router requires at least two network interfaces, or ports.

Note

An IP host with more than one network interface is called a *multi-homed host*.

Addressing with IP Version 6

As was discussed earlier in this chapter, 4,294,967,296 (2^{32}) may seem like an awful lot of IP addresses. However, we saw that many of these addresses are not available for private networks. And of those, many have been used up in the exponential growth of hosts connected to the public Internet. No fear! The Internet powers that be—Internet Engineering Task Force (IETF)—have risen to the challenge.

The current definition of the IP address is known as version 4, or Ipv4. This version has not been upgraded on the public Internet since 1970. However, the Internet community does not sleep. Indeed, there have been many proposals for extending the addressing scheme on the Internet. The winner is IP Version 6 (Ipv6), formerly referred to as IP next Generation (IpnG). What about Ipv5?—no such animal.

 Note   RFC 1883 specifies version 6 of the Internet Protocol (IPv6) as defined by the IETF.

The current version (Ipv4) of IP addressing uses a space of 4 octets. Ipv6 uses 16! These addresses are not commonly represented in dotted decimal form. Nor are they typically represented in binary form. But, to make things more challenging (yet take up less space) they are represented in 8 octet pairs in hexidecimal format! Here's an example:

```
3E0F:ACDE:11FE:2312:34A9:FE34: 1BAF:CABE
```

Not only does Ipv6 offer many times the address space of IPv4 (2^{128} addresses instead of just 2^{32}), but it boasts other benefits to take the Internet well into the future. These benefits include simplified header format, enhanced support for real-time data and built-in expandability through the use of extension headers.

By moving non-essential fields out of the base header and into extension headers allows for a significant increase in efficiency. For example, real-time data transmissions can be guaranteed a fixed band-width through a new field in the header.

Review Questions

1. Which of the following is the loopback address?

   A. 127.0.0.1

   B. 0.0.0.0

   C. 1.1.1.1

   D. 128.0.0.1

2. What class of address is 21.34.55.55?

   A. Class A

   B. Class B

   C. Class C

   D. Illegal

3. What class of address is 223.75.234.239?

   A. Class A

   B. Class B

   C. Class C

   D. Illegal

4. What class of address is 223.322.232.127?

   A. Class A

   B. Class B

   C. Class C

   D. Illegal

5. What class of address is 192.192.232.127?

   A. Class A

   B. Class B

   C. Class C

   D. Illegal

6. What class of address is 1.1.1.1?

    A. Class A

    B. Class B

    C. Class C

    D. Illegal

7. What class of address is 44.12.256.254?

    A. Class A

    B. Class B

    C. Class C

    D. Illegal

8. What class of address is 126.122.243.34?

    A. Class A

    B. Class B

    C. Class C

    D. illegal

9. By default, what is the Network ID for the address 201.102.21.12?

    A. 201.0.0.0

    B. 201.102.0.0

    C. 201.102.21.0

    D. 0.0.0.12

10. By default, what is the Network ID for the address 121.212.112.122?

    A. 121.0.0.0

    B. 121.212.0.0

    C. 121.212.112.0

    D. 0.0.0.122

11. By default, what is the Network ID for the address 198.81.91.119?

    A. 198.0.0.0

    B. 198.81.0.0

    C. 198.81.91.0

    D. 0.0.0.119

12. By default, what is the Host ID for the address 179.79.234.234?

    A. 179.0.0.0

    B. 0.0.234.234

    C. 0.79.234.234

    D. 0.0.0.234

13. By default, what is the Host ID for the address 41.1.6.222?

    A. 41.0.0.0

    B. 41.1.6.0

    C. 0.1.6.222

    D. 0.0.0.222

14. By default, what is the Network ID for the address 201.44.45.54?

    A. 0.0.0.54

    B. 0.0.45.54

    C. 201.44.0.0

    D. 201.44.45.0

15. By default, what is the Host ID for the address 201.44.45.54?

    A. 0.0.0.54

    B. 0.0.45.54

    C. 201.44.0.0

    D. 201.44.45.0

Review Answers

1. A

2. A

3. C

4. D

5. C

6. A

7. D

8. A

9. C

10. A

11. C

12. B

13. C

14. D

15. A

Answers to the Test Yourself Questions at the Beginning of the Chapter

1. The OSI model has seven layers whereas the TCP/IP model has four.
2. There are five classes of addresses: classes A–C are used for host addresses, class D addresses are for multicasting and class E is experimental.
3. Class B addresses provide 65.534 hosts per network.
4. Current IP addresses are 32 bits long, the new version of IP (IPv6) will use addresses 128 bits long.
5. Addresses can be configured manually or by using a DHCP server.

Chapter

Subnetting

This chapter helps you prepare for the exam by covering the following objectives:

 **Objectives**

▶ Configure subnet masks

▶ Given a scenario, identify valid network configurations

Test Yourself! Before reading this chapter, test yourself to determine how much study time you will need to devote to this section.

1. What are the three components of a TCP/IP Address?

2. How does the subnet mask divide a TCP/IP address into its components?

3. What subnet mask is used for a Class A network without subnets?

4. How can the wrong subnet mask prevent you from communicating with remote hosts?

5. How does a subnet mask determine the number of subnets that can be created on a network?

Answers are located at the end of the chapter.

Introduction

A TCP/IP address typically has two components: the *network ID* of the address, which specifies the general location of the host, and the *host ID*, which uniquely identifies an individual host after the network is located. In most cases, you will need to break your network into smaller more manageable pieces—notably you will segment your network for performance. If you are using TCP/IP these segments are referred to as subnets.

A subnet is really a subnetwork of a TCP/IP internetwork. An *internet* or *internetwork* is a group of computers linked together using TCP/IP technology. An internet can be either a portion of the Internet (the worldwide network of publicly interconnected TCP/IP networks) or a private corporate or enterprise internetwork. Such private internetworks are usually called intranets to show that they are internal to an enterprise and not part of the Internet.

The term *network* is used when it is not necessary to distinguish between individual subnets and internetworks. A subnet is simply a subdivision of a network. You create a subnet by carefully choosing the IP addresses and subnet masks for your hosts. This process is known as *subnet addressing* or *subnetting*. The term *subnetworking* or *subnetting* refers to the use of a custom subnet mask to subdivide a single network ID into multiple network IDs.

An IP address consists of four octets, which are numbers between 0 and 255. These are strung together with periods to look like this example 200.20.5.59. This number is a representation of a 32 binary number—made easier for humans to understand. Part of the address identifies the host's network or subnet, and part of the address identifies the host. The subnet mask specifies what portion of the TCP/IP address identifies which part. A subnet mask can also specify how much of the address will instead specify a subnet ID.

The subnet mask is used by the Internet layer (IP layer) to route a TCP/IP packet to its proper destination. When a TCP/IP address is combined with a subnet mask, the TCP/IP protocol determines whether the destination is on the local subnet or not.

If the destination address is on a different subnet than the sender is, then it is determined to be on a remote network and the packet is routed appropriately—normally through the default gateway. If the destination address is on the local subnet, the packet is not routed but sent directly to the destination host.

If a network has a small number of hosts that are all on the same segment that is no connection to any other network, they are all given the same network ID. Subnets are not needed in this case. If the network is larger, however, with remote segments connected by routers (an internetwork), then each individual subnet needs a different network ID. It is possible to assign a different network ID to each network segment, but organizations are usually given only one network ID for the entire organization. A subnet mask must then be used to use part of the host ID as the subnet ID. When assigning IP addresses and subnet masks, you must know how many subnets are required and the maximum number of hosts that are on each subnet. Then you can use a subnet mask that allows enough hosts on each subnet while allowing for enough subnets within the entire network.

Depending on the subnet mask selected, the internetwork can either have a lot of subnets with fewer hosts on each subnet, or a smaller number of subnets with a larger number of hosts on each subnet. The purpose of this chapter is to show how to determine the proper subnet mask to be used to meet the addressing requirements.

This chapter discusses the following topics:

- ▶ Subnet masks, host IDs, and network IDs

- ▶ The limitations of using a default subnet mask

- ▶ Subnetting—how to increase the number of subnets on the network by using a custom subnet mask

- ▶ Three different procedures for subnetting an internetwork

- ▶ Shortcuts to reduce the time it takes on the exam to subnet a network ID

The Purpose of Subnet Masks

A TCP/IP address is like a calendar date. The IP address has two components; a network ID and a host ID. The network ID may include a subnet ID. A date also has several components, such as a month, a day, and a year.

The subnet mask is used by the internet layer to determine which part of the IP address is the network ID and which part is the host ID. The subnet mask also can be used to determine whether a subnet is defined and to find the ID of that subnet. Calendar dates are also represented with a numbering scheme that communicates which part of the date is the month, day, and year.

As table 10.1 shows, dates are listed with the month first, then the day, then the year (in the United States, at least). If the year is in the 1900s, it is common to omit the first two digits in the year. Americans are so used to this type of date scheme that they rarely stop to think about it. The TCP/IP subnet mask specifies that the octets of the IP address marked as 255 are the network ID and octets marked by 0 are the host ID. When subnetting you will begin to see other numbers appear instead of just 0 and 255.

Table 10.1

IP Address:	200.20.16.5
Subnet Mask:	255.255.255.0
Network ID:	200.20.16
Host ID:	5
Date:	4/27/87
Date Scheme:	Month/Day/Year
Month:	4
Day:	27
Year:	1987

It's important to understand the correct date scheme when interpreting a date. For example, in Europe the orders of months and days are reversed. The date 12/6/69 is 12 June 1969 in Europe, whereas in the United States this date is interpreted as December 6, 1969. Similarly, with subnets, an understanding of the TCP/IP addressing scheme is necessary to decipher the IP address into the components of network ID, subnet ID, and host ID.

With a TCP/IP address, the address always follows the same format of four octets separated by periods. You can define different subnet masks, however, so that the address is interpreted differently. In table 10.2, the same IP address listed in table 10.1 is used, but with a different subnet mask. The address now specifies a subnet.

Table 10.2

IP Address:	11001000 00010100 00010000 00000101
Subnet Mask:	11111111 11111111 11111111 00000000
Network ID:	11001000 00010100 00010000 00000000
Host ID:	00000000 00000000 00000000 00000101

The TCP/IP address and subnet mask are made up of four 8-bit octets that, for ease of use, are viewed in decimal format rather than binary format. However, the address and subnet mask are actually binary so that IP understands them.

Any part of the subnet mask with 1s specifies the network portion of the address; 0s in the subnet mask specify the host portion of the address. The 1s are always at the first of the subnet mask, because an IP address always specifies the network portion of the address first. The host ID is specified by the remaining numbers of the IP address, which correspond to the 0s at the end of the subnet mask. In a subnet mask, note that the 1s are always grouped together and the 0s are always grouped together. The subnet mask basically divides the IP address into two pieces: the network ID and the host ID. The subnet mask simply indicates how many of the higher-order bits are devoted to the network ID and how many of the lower-order bits are devoted to the host ID.

The subnet mask determines how many host IDs are available. In the example in table 10.2, there is a maximum of 254 different hosts on the network 200.20.16 (200.20.16.1 through 200.20.16.254). If you want to have more hosts on one network, you have to use a different addressing scheme. For example, if you use a subnet mask of 255.255.0.0, the address is interpreted as shown in table 10.3.

Table 10.3

IP Address	200.20.16.5
Subnet Mask	255.255.0.0
Network ID	200.20
Host ID	16.5

With this subnet mask, two octets are available for the host ID. Using two octets allows you to have (256*256)-2 (you cannot use all 0s or all 1s) hosts on the network 200.20.

As noted, there are two cases that are not allowed for the host ID, these are where all bits are set to either 1 or 0. In these two cases the addresses are interpreted to mean a broadcast address (all 1s) or "this network only," (all 0s). Neither of these destinations is valid for a host ID. Thus, the number of valid addresses is $(2^n)-2$, where n is the number of bits used for the host ID.

The example in table 10.2 has fewer combinations of network IDs (because only two octets are used for the network) than in the example in table 10.1 (in which three octets are used for the network). Bear in mind that you cannot always chose the subnet mask that allows you the greatest number of host IDs. For example, if the hosts are on the Internet, you must use a certain set of IP addresses assigned by the Internet address assignment authority, InterNIC.

Because the number of IP addresses available today is limited, you usually do not have the luxury to choose an addressing scheme that gives exactly the combination of host and network ID you require. Suppose you are assigned the network ID 139.20 and have a total of 1,000 hosts on three remote networks. A Class B network using the default subnet mask of 255.255.0.0 only has one network (139.20) yet allows 65,534 hosts.

Using the Subnet Mask

This section will look at exactly how a subnet mask is used to determine which part of the IP address is the network ID and which part is the host ID. The IP layer performs binary calculations on the IP address and the subnet mask to determine the network ID portion of the IP address.

The computation TCP/IP performs is a logical bitwise "AND" of the IP address and the subnet mask. The calculation sounds complicated, but all it really means is that the address in its true 32-bit binary format is logically "ANDed" with the subnet mask (also a 32-bit binary number). This extracts the network ID.

Performing a bitwise AND on two bits results in 1 (or TRUE), if the two values are both 1. All other cases return a 0. In the examples (tables 10.1, 10.2 and 10.3) the numbers 255 or 0 are used for the subnet mask. In binary, 255 means all the bits in that octet are 1; 0 means they are 0.

1 AND 1 results in 1

1 AND 0 results in 0

0 AND 1 results in 0

0 AND 0 results in 0

In the example in table 10.1, the IP address 200.20.16.5 is "ANDed" with the subnet mask 255.255.255.0. Because 1 and "n" always returns "n" and because the first three octets are all 1s, this example simply duplicates the first three octets leaving the network ID of 200.20.16.

Table 10.4 illustrates the calculation that is performed.

Table 10.4

Example of a Bitwise AND Operation

	Decimal Notation	Binary Notation
IP address:	200.20.16.5	11001000 0001010000010000 00000101
Subnet mask:	255.255.255.0	11111111 1111111111111111 00000000
IP address AND Subnet mask:	200.20.16.0	11001000 0001010000010000 00000000

Determining the network ID is very easy if the subnet mask is made up of only 255 and 0 values. Simply "mask" or cover up the part of the IP address corresponding to the 0 octet(s) of the subnet mask. For example, if the IP address is 15.6.100.1 and the subnet mask is 255.255.0.0, then the resulting network ID is 15.6.

For more complicated subnet masks, you can use the Windows Calculator in scientific view to convert between decimal and binary numbers, and use the "AND" button to perform a logical "AND." For example, you can enter the number 240, select And, enter 35, and then select =. This gives you the decimal answer to the "AND." You can then convert the result to binary if desired. Or you can enter the numbers in binary, converting the result to decimal when you are finished. However, you must use the same number system for both of the operands in the "AND" process when using the Windows Calculator.

You may have to use a subnet mask with values other than 255 and 0 if you need to subdivide your network ID into individual subnets. If you are not using subnets, you can use the default subnet mask that Microsoft TCP/IP assigns when configuring the IP address.

Understanding Default Subnet Masks

Microsoft TCP/IP assigns a subnet mask to an IP address by default that can then be changed if needed. Table 10.5 shows the subnet mask that appears in the subnet mask field when an IP address is entered in the Microsoft TCP/IP Configuration dialog box.

Table 10.5

Default Subnet Masks

Class	IP Address	Default Subnet Mask
A	001.y.z.w to 126.y.z.w	255.0.0.0
B	128.y.z.w to 191.y.z.w	255.255.0.0
C	192.y.z.w to 223.y.z.w	255.255.255.0

In Chapter 9, the discussion of the TCP/IP addressing scheme focused on the different classes of IP addresses and the number of different networks and hosts per network that are available for each of the IP address classes. These values were based on the default subnet masks. See table 10.6 for a summary.

Table 10.6

Maximum Number of Networks and Hosts per Network in TCP/IP

Class	Using Default Subnet Mask	Number of Networks	Number of Hosts per Network
A	255.0.0.0	126	16,777,214
B	255.255.0.0	16,384	65,534
C	255.255.255.0	2,097,152	254

If the hosts on your internetwork are not directly on the Internet, you are free to choose the network IDs that you use. For the hosts and subnets that are a part of the Internet, however, the network IDs you use must be assigned by InterNIC.

 Note

> InterNIC—the Internet Network Information Center—is responsible for assigning network IDs for use on the Internet, among other things. You can visit InterNIC at `www.internic.net`.

If you are using network IDs assigned by InterNIC, you do not have the choice of choosing the address class you use. Using the address assigned by InterNIC, the number of subnets you use is normally limited by the number of network IDs assigned by InterNIC, and the number of hosts per subnet is determined by the class of address. Fortunately, if you are not assigned enough network addresses you can subdivide your network into a greater number of subnets by choosing the proper subnet mask. However, if you subnet your network, you have fewer possible hosts on each subnet.

Many companies today are avoiding the addressing constraints and security risks of having their hosts directly on the Internet by setting up private networks with gateway access to the Internet. Having a private network means that only the Internet gateway host needs to have an Internet address. For security, a firewall can be set up to prevent Internet hosts from directly accessing the company's network.

Subdividing a Network

Internetworks are networks comprised of individual segments connected by routers. The reasons for having distinct segments are as follows:

- ▶ They permit physically remote local networks to be connected.

- ▶ A mix of network technologies can be connected, such as ethernet on one segment and token ring on another.

▶ They allow an unlimited number of hosts to communicate by combining subnets, even though the number of hosts on each segment is limited by the type of network used.

▶ Network congestion is reduced as broadcasts and local network traffic are limited to the local segment.

Each segment is a subnet of the internetwork, and requires a unique network ID or specifically a subnet ID.

Subnetting

 The following are the steps involved in subnetting a network:

1. Determine the number of network IDs required for current use and also for planning future growth needs.

2. Determine the maximum number of host addresses that are on each subnet, again allowing for future growth.

3. Define one subnet mask for the entire internetwork that gives the desired number of subnets and allows enough hosts per subnet.

4. Determine the resulting subnet network IDs that are used.

5. Determine the valid host IDs and assign IP addresses to the hosts.

The following sections describe each of these steps in detail.

Step 1: Determine the Number of Network IDs Required

The first step in subnetting a network is to determine the number of subnets required while planning for future growth. A unique network ID is required for each subnet and each WAN connection.

Step 2: Determine the Number of Host IDs per Subnet Required

Determine the maximum number of hosts IDs that are required on each subnet. A host ID is required for:

▶ Each TCP/IP computer network interface card.

▶ Each TCP/IP printer network interface card.

▶ Each router interface on each subnet. For example, if a router is connected to two subnets, it requires two host IDs and therefore two IP addresses.

When determining the number of subnets and hosts per subnet that are needed in your internetwork, it is very important to plan for growth! The entire internetwork should use the same subnet mask; therefore the maximum number of subnets and hosts per subnet is predetermined when the subnet mask is chosen.

To illustrate the need for growth planning, consider an internetwork with two subnets. Each subnet has 50 hosts and the subnets are connected by a router. The network administrator is authorized by InterNIC to use the network ID 200.20.16 to put all the hosts on the Internet. As the following sections explain, a subnet mask of 255.255.255.192 creates two logical subnets on the internetwork, each allowing a maximum of 62 valid host IDs. In the future, if another segment is added or more than 62 hosts are needed on one segment, the network administrator needs to do the following: choose a new subnet mask, shut down every computer on the network to reconfigure the subnet mask, reconfigure a lot of the network software, and probably look for another job.

Note   When deciding on a subnet mask to use, make sure you allow for the number of subnets on the network and the number of hosts per subnet to increase substantially beyond current needs.

Step 3: Define the Subnet Mask

The next step is to define for the entire internetwork one subnet mask that gives the desired number of subnets and allows enough hosts per subnet.

As shown previously, the network ID of an IP address is determined by the "1s" of the subnet mask, shown in binary notation. To increase the number of network IDs, you need to add more bits to the subnet mask.

For example, you are assigned a Class B network ID of 168.20.0.0 by InterNIC. Using the default Class B subnet mask 255.255.0.0, you have one network ID (168.20.0.0) and about 65,000 valid host IDs (168.20.1.1 through 168.20.255.254). Suppose you want to subdivide the network into 4 subnets.

First, consider the host 168.20.16.1, using the subnet mask 255.255.0.0. In binary notation, it is represented as shown in table 10.7.

Table 10.7

IP address:	10101000.00010100.00010000.00000001
Subnet Mask:	11111111.11111111.00000000.00000000
Network ID:	10101000.00010100.00000000.00000000

Remember, the subnet mask 1 bits correspond to the network ID bit in the IP address.

By adding additional bits to the subnet mask, you increase the bits available for the network ID and thus create a few more combinations of network IDs.

Suppose that in the example in table 10.7 you add three bits to the subnet mask. The result increases the number of bits defining the network ID and decreases the number of bits that define the host ID. Thus, you have more network IDs, but fewer hosts on each subnet. The new subnet mask is:

```
Subnet Mask:     11111111     11111111     11100000     00000000
```

As you have three extra bits in the network ID, you now have six different network IDs. All 0s or all 1s are not allowed, because these are reserved for the broadcast-type addresses. All 0s mean "this network only," and all 1s mean broadcast. Table 10.8 shows all the possible subnet IDs using the network ID of 168.20.0.0 with a subnet mask of 255.255.224.0.

Table 10.8

Network IDs	Decimal Equivalent
10101000.00010100.001	168.20.32.0
10101000.00010100.010	168.20.64.0
10101000.00010100.011	168.20.96.0
10101000.00010100.100	168.20.128.0
10101000.00010100.101	168.20.160.0
10101000.00010100.110	168.20.192.0

Note that if you use only two additional bits in the subnet mask, you are only able to have two subnets. The network IDs that result in table 10.8 are as follows:

10101000.00010100.01	168.20.64.0
10101000.00010100.10	168.20.128.0

Therefore, you must use enough additional bits in the new subnet mask to create the desired number of subnets while still allowing for enough hosts on each subnet.

After you determine the number of subnets you need to create, calculate the required subnet mask as follows:

1. Add 1 to the number of subnets needed and convert the result to binary format. (Like the host ID, the subnet ID cannot be all 0s or all 1s—adding 1 avoids these possibilities.) You may want to use the Windows Calculator in Scientific view.

2. The number of bits you used to write the required subnets in binary is the number of additional bits that you add to the default subnet mask. You also need to include any 0 bits in the count. For example, if you need eight subnets that is the binary number 1000. This means you need four binary digits or bits in the subnet mask.

3. Place the number of binary digits needed at the beginning of the octet, and then fill the remaining eight digits in the octet with 0s.

4. Convert the subnet mask back to decimal format. This value replaces the first 0 octet in the subnet mask.

Suppose, for example, that you are assigned a Class B network ID of 168.20, and you need to create 5 subnets. Following the preceding steps, converting 5 into binary gives 00000101, or simply 101.

This means you need three bits to give enough combinations for 5 networks. Therefore, you need to add three bits to the default subnet mask. The default subnet mask for a Class B network is 255.255.0.0, or in binary is:

Default subnet mask
11111111.11111111.00000000.00000000

Adding the three bits creates the custom subnet mask:

Custom subnet mask
11111111.11111111.11100000.00000000

If you convert this to decimal, you will see the subnet mask is 255.255.224.0.

Step 4: Determine the Network IDs to Use

The next step is to determine the subnet IDs that are created, by applying the new subnet mask to the original assigned network ID. Any or all of the resulting subnet network IDs are used in the internetwork.

Three methods for determining the network IDs are given in this chapter. The first is a manual computation; the second is a short-cut for the first method; and the third uses tables with the values already calculated. As noted previously, you should become familiar with the manual calculations to understand the fundamentals of subnetting. All three methods are described in the following sections.

Defining the Network IDs Manually

For an exercise covering this information, see end of chapter.

The network ID for each subnet is determined using the same number of bits as were added to the default subnet mask in the previous step. Use the following steps to define each subnet network ID:

1. List all possible binary combinations of the additional bits added to the default subnet mask.

2. Discard the combinations with all 1s or all 0s. All 1s or all 0s are not valid as network IDs, because all 1s represents the broadcast address for the subnet and all 0s implies "this network only" as a destination.

3. Convert the remaining values to decimal notation. Remember you must use the full 8 bits of the octet for the binary number that is converted to decimal.

4. Finally, each value is appended to the original assigned network ID to produce a subnet network ID.

If you were assigned a Class B network ID of 168.20.0.0 and need to create at least 5 subnets. You need an additional 3 bits added to the default subnet mask to create the subnets. The new subnet mask is then 255.255.224.0, or in binary:

11111111   11111111   11100000   00000000

Listing all combinations of the additional bits gives the following:

000

001

010

011

100

101

110

111

Discarding the values 000 and 111, and converting the remaining combinations to decimal format, you have the following:

.32.	00100000
.64.	01000000
.96.	01100000
.128.	10000000
.160.	10100000
.192.	11000000

Appending the preceding values to the original assigned network ID gives the following new subnet network IDs:

168.20.32.0

168.20.64.0

168.20.96.0

168.20.128.0

168.20.160.0

168.20.192.0

All the new subnet network IDs use the subnet mask of 255.255.224.0.

A Shortcut for Defining the Network IDs

Defining the network IDs manually becomes tedious when more than three additional bits are added to the default subnet mask, because it requires listing and converting many bit combinations. The following is a shortcut method for defining the subnet network IDs:

1. After determining the new subnet mask you calculated for the required number of subnets and host IDs, list the additional octet added to the default subnet mask in decimal notation.

2. Convert the rightmost 1-bit of this value to decimal notation. This is the lowest order 1-bit in the octet you calculated. This decimal value is the incremental value between each subnet value, known as "Delta."

3. The maximum number of subnet network IDs that can be used with this subnet is 2 less than 2 to the power of n, where n is the number of bits you determined were needed for your subnet (# of subnets = $(2^\wedge n)-2$).

4. Append "Delta" as an octet to the original network ID to give the first subnet network ID.

5. Repeat Step 4 for each subnet network ID, incrementing each successive value by "Delta."

Again if you are assigned a Class B network ID of 168.20.0.0 and need to create at least 5 subnets. You needed an additional 3 bits added to the default subnet mask to create the subnets.

The additional bits added to the default subnet mask are 11100000.

The rightmost bit converted to decimal (00100000) is 32. Thus, the incremental value is 32. There will be $(2^\wedge 3)-2$ =6 subnets created.

The subnets created are as follows:

168.20.0.0 and 32 = 168.20.32.0

168.20.32.0 and 32 = 168.20.64.0

168.20.64.0 and 32 = 168.20.96.0

168.20.96.0 and 32 = 168.20.128.0

168.20.128.0 and 32 = 168.20.160.0

168.20.160.0 and 32 = 168.20.192.0

If you increment the last subnet network ID once more, the last octet matches the last octet of the subnet mask (224), which is considered a broadcast address and thus is an invalid network ID.

Defining the Network ID Using a Table

After you understand the previous two methods of defining subnet network IDs, you may want to instead use the tables found at the end of this chapter that have the appropriate values already calculated.

Step 5: Determine the Host IDs to Use

The final step in subnetting a network is to determine the valid host IDs and assign IP addresses to the hosts.

The host IDs for each subnet start with the value .001 in the last octet, and continue up to one less than the subnet ID of the next subnet. Keep in mind that the last octet cannot be .000 or .255, as these are reserved for broadcast addresses.

Finally, the valid IP addresses for each subnet are created by combining the subnet network ID with the host ID.

If once again you use the assigned address of 168.20.0.0 with five subnets, the range of IP addresses for each subnet is as follows:

Subnet	First IP Address	Last IP Address
168.20.32.0	168.20.32.1	168.20.63.254
168.20.64.0	168.20.64.1	168.20.95.254
168.20.96.0	168.20.96.1	168.20.127.254
168.20.128.0	168.20.128.1	168.20.159.254
168.20.160.0	168.20.160.1	168.20.191.254
168.20.192.0	168.20.192.1	168.20.223.254

Note in this example that the value of the third octet in the IP address can differ from the value calculated for the subnet. For example, the address 168.20.33.1 specifies a network ID of 168.20, a subnet of 32 (with a combined network address of 168.20.32), and a host ID of 1.1. The 1 in the third octet is added to the 32 to give a total value of 33 (binary 00100001). However, the subnet mask determines that the network portion of the address is 32, as indicated by the upper 3 bits, and the host ID is 1, as indicated by the lower 5 bits.

Using the Network Subnetting Tables

As mentioned earlier, after you understand how to use the previous manual calculations for subnetting a network, you may want to use the tables provided to avoid the lengthy calculations.

Tables 10.9, 10.10, and 10.11 show the number of subnets that are used with a given subnet mask for each of the Class A, B, or C addressing types.

Table 10.9

Class A Subnetting

Additional Bits Required (n)	Maximum Subnets (2^n-2)	Maximum Number Number of Hosts per Subnet ($2^{(24-n)}-2$)	Subnet Mask
0	0	16,777,214	255.0.0.0
1	invalid	invalid	invalid
2	2	4,194,302	255.192.0.0
3	6	2,097,150	255.224.0.0
4	14	1,048,574	255.240.0.0
5	30	524,286	255.248.0.0
6	62	262,142	255.252.0.0
7	126	131,070	255.254.0.0
8	254	65,534	255.255.0.0

Table 10.10

Class B Subnetting

Additional Bits Required (n)	Maximum Subnets (2^n-2)	Maximum Number Number of Hosts per Subnet ($2^{(16-n)}-2$)	Subnet Mask
0	0	65,534	255.255.0.0
1	invalid	invalid	invalid
2	2	16,382	255.255.192.0
3	6	8,190	255.255.224.0
4	14	4,094	255.255.240.0
5	30	2,046	255.255.248.0
6	62	1,022	255.255.252.0
7	126	510	255.255.254.0
8	254	254	255.255.255.0

Table 10.11

Class C Subnetting

Additional Bits Required (n)	Maximum Subnets (2^n-2)	Maximum Number Number of Hosts per Subnet ($2^{(16-n)}-2$)	Subnet Mask
0	0	254	255.255.255.0
1	invalid	invalid	invalid
2	2	62	255.255.255.192
3	6	30	255.255.255.224
4	14	14	255.255.255.240
5	30	6	255.255.255.248
6	62	2	255.255.255.252
7	invalid	invalid	255.255.255.254
8	invalid	invalid	255.255.255.255

In the preceding tables, the Additional Bits Required is the number of higher-order bits required to be added to the default subnet mask to achieve the required number of subnets and hosts per subnet. For convenience, the resulting subnet mask is shown in decimal notation rather than in binary.

As an example, suppose you are assigned a Class B network ID of 168.20 that must be subdivided into 3 subnets with a maximum of 500 hosts on any given subnet. Adding three bits to the subnet mask allows for 6 subnets with 8,190 hosts on each subnet. However, this subnet mask does not allow for much growth in the number of subnets, while allowing for more than ample growth in the number of hosts on each subnet. On the other extreme, adding 7 bits to the subnet allows 126 subnets with only 510 hosts on each subnet. This subnet mask allows for a great deal of growth in the number of subnets but very little growth in the number of hosts on each subnet. A more appropriate subnet mask is somewhere in the middle. A subnet mask with 4 additional bits allows 14 subnets with 4,094 hosts on each subnet. A subnet mask with 5 additional bits allows 30 subnets with 2,046 hosts on each subnet. Either of these choices is good. You can lean toward one or the other depending on whether you anticipate greater fragmentation on your network in the future, thus requiring more subnets, or greater growth on existing network segments, thus requiring more hosts on each subnet.

Exercises

Exercise 10.1:   Calculating Subnets

This exercise helps you use the Windows Calculator to calculate a custom subnet mask. You have been assigned a network address of 149.3.0.0. You want to set up a network with 45 subnets, and you expect no more than 1,000 hosts on each subnet.

1. Open the Windows Calculator (located under Programs, Accessories).

2. From the View menu, choose Scientific. Note the default numbering scheme is decimal, denoted by the Dec button.

3. Enter the number of subnets required plus 1.

4. Convert the number to binary by selecting the Bin button.

5. Write the number of bits required to express this number in binary.

6. Write an 8-bit binary number, with 1s for the upper digits and 0s for the lower digits. Use the number of 1s as determined in step 5 and the number of 0s remaining to make it an 8-bit number.

7. In the Windows Calculator, make sure the Bin button is selected.

8. Enter the 8-bit binary number.

9. Convert the number to decimal by selecting the Dec button.

10. Write down the decimal result.

11. Use this decimal result to specify a custom subnet mask for this network.

12. To determine the number of hosts possible for this network, in the Windows Calculator, enter 2, select x^y, then enter the number of bits remaining for the host IDs. Select = to calculate the result and subtract 2 to determine the total number of hosts possible on each subnet with this subnet mask.

Answers for Exercise 4.1:

4. The binary equivalent of 47 decimal is 101111.

5. This requires 6 bits.

6. The subnet mask for this octet is 11111100.

10. The decimal equivalent of 11111100 is 252.

11. The resulting subnet mask for a class B network is 255.255.252.0.

12. The number of hosts on each subnet is 1022, $2^{10} - 2$.

Exercise 10.2: Viewing Default Subnet Masks

This exercise notes the default subnet mask assigned to each TCP/IP address. You should have installed TCP/IP on your Windows NT computer.

1. Open the Network Properties by right-clicking Network Neighborhood and selecting Properties from the resulting menu.

2. Select the Protocols tab.

3. Select TCP/IP and then select Properties.

4. Write down any existing IP address so that you can restore this address when the exercise is over.

5. Select the Specify an IP Address button.

6. Type a Class A address in the IP address field, such as 9.36.108.45.

7. Note the subnet mask that appears by default.

8. Select Close to exit the Network Properties dialog box.

9. Repeat steps 1–3 to open the TCP/IP properties.

10. Type a Class B address in the IP address field, such as 131.107.2.200.

11. Note the subnet mask that appears by default.

12. Select Close to exit the Network Properties dialog box.

13. Repeat steps 1–3 to open the TCP/IP properties.

14. Type a Class C address in the IP address field, such as 200.20.5.16.

15. Note the subnet mask that appears by default.

16. Type your original IP address as noted in step 4.

17. Select Close to exit the Network Properties dialog box.

Review Questions

1. A default subnet mask allows for _____.

   A. The maximum number of network IDs

   B. The maximum number of host IDs

   C. A balance between the number of host IDs and network IDs

   D. 254 subnets

2. What devices require a unique host ID on a TCP/IP network?

   A. Each router

   B. Each PC

   C. Each network card

   D. Each network printer

3. What is the default subnet mask used for a Class B network?

   A. 255.0.0.0

   B. 255.255.0.0

   C. 255.255.255.0

   D. 255.255.255.255

4. How many different Class A networks are in the world?

   A. 126

   B. 128

   C. 254

   D. 256

5. How many hosts are on a Class C network with a default subnet mask?

   A. 126

   B. 128

C. 254

D. 256

6. A company is assigned the network ID 150.134.0.0 by InterNIC. The company wants to have 15 subnets and up to 1,000 hosts per subnet. How many bits are needed for the custom subnet mask?

A. 4

B. 5

C. 6

D. 7

7. In question 6, what should the company use for the subnet mask?

A. 255.255.0.0

B. 255.255.5.0

C. 255.255.31.0

D. 255.255.248.0

8. An organization is assigned the network ID 114.0.0.0 by Inter-NIC. The organization currently has 5 subnets with about 100,000 hosts per subnet. The management wants to divide the subnets into 25 new subnets to make each subnet more manageable. How many bits are used for the custom subnet mask?

A. 4

B. 5

C. 6

D. 7

9. In question 8, what should the organization use for the subnet mask?

A. 252.0.0.0

B. 255.0.0.0

C. 255.252.0.0

D. 255.255.252.0

Review Answers

1. B

2. C, D

3. B

4. A

5. C

6. B

7. D

8. C

9. C

Answers to the Test Yourself Questions at the Beginning of the Chapter

1. A TCP/IP address specifies the address of the network, the address of the host, and the subnet address. There may or not be a subnet address specified.

2. The portion of the subnet mask that converts to binary 1s shows the part of the IP address that is the network ID. The rest of the subnet mask, binary 0s, specifies which bits of the IP address designate the host address. If the subnet mask differs from the default for that class of network, then the binary 1s after the default 1s specify the subnet.

3. A class A address uses the first octet to specify the network ID. A subnet mask of 255.0.0.0 masks the first octet as the network ID and the remaining octets as the host ID.

4. If the subnet mask indicates that the host is local, the packet is not routed. However, if the host is remote and in incorrect subnet mask is used, the packet never reaches the remote host because IP will attempt to send it locally. At the other extreme, IP may attempt to route packets for a local host if the subnet mask is wrong.

5. By default, each network ID specifies only one network. The default subnet mask only designates this one network ID, leaving the remainder of the bits to indicate the host ID. By using additional bits to designate the network ID, a subnet mask can allow more than one network ID in the address. However, this results in a reduction in the number of hosts than can be on each subnet.

Chapter 11

Implementing IP Routing

This chapter helps you prepare for the exam by covering the following objective:

 Objective

▶ Configure a Windows NT Server computer to function as an IP router

Test Yourself! Before reading this chapter, test yourself to determine how much study time you will need to devote to this section.

1. When implementing TCP/IP on your wide area network, a user calls and asks why he cannot access the network. What are the three pieces of information a machine must have in a wide area network before it can communicate with other TCP/IP machines/hosts?

2. To update routing tables with an NT multihomed router, which dynamic routing protocol would have to be installed?

3. By default, does a static router know how to route packets to networks other than the ones to which it is physically connected?

4. During a test, you are asked which protocol in the TCP/IP suite is responsible for the routing and delivery of datagrams on the network. Which protocol would you say provided this function?

5. If network communications suddenly stopped between you and a remote network, what utility would best indicate whether a remote router had shut down or was non-functional?

6. You have been told that RIP is really good for small to mid-sized networks, but your network is very large. Does NT support the OSPF protocol as well as the RIP protocol, to help you scale up to enterprise network sizes?

Answers are located at the end of the chapter.

Introduction

Amazingly enough, many chapters and even whole books are dedicated to the concept of routing—discussing the types of routing, how routing works, different kinds of routers, problems encountered with routing, streamlining route tables, and so on. But very few discuss the most fundamentally important question of all: Why do you have to route in the first place? To help you fully understand routing, this chapter begins with a continuation of some of the networking concepts learned in Chapter 8. After the basics are covered, this chapter discusses the reasons for routing, and the benefits of doing so.

Recall from Chapter 8 on the architecture of networks that protocols are written to a standard networking model. Also recall that each layer of the networking model serves as an intermediary to higher layers of the model. Therefore, each layer knows how to communicate with another layer of its type, but has no idea what's going on in layers more than one level removed, either above or below it. In the mail example, the mailman has no clue what kind of message was written, what kind of paper was used, or whether the message was written in English. The only interface between the two layers is the address on the outside of the envelope, which is all the mailman needs. Looking at the networking model then, a frame at the network interface layer would look something like figure 11.1.

Figure 11.1

What the network interface layer sees.

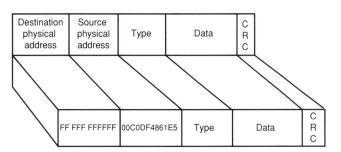

Notice in this example that the network interface layer can identify the destination hardware address, the source hardware address, the type of frame (802.3 ethernet, 802.5 token ring, and so on), and then data. The Network Interface layer has no idea what is in the data layer; it just knows that it's supposed to send the data to the destination hardware address indicated at the front of the packet. Based on the type of communication initiated, the destination address may be all FFs or an actual unique 6-byte physical address.

All this presupposes that the voltage including this information reaches its destination. Recall from Chapter 9 that on an ethernet network each machine transmits on a network segment to communicate. The number of machines that can communicate on a network segment is limited by the machines' capability to sense collisions and retransmit data. Networks are said to reach, or be close to, *bandwidth saturation*, when the machines are unable to avoid collisions while trying to communicate. The best way to avoid bandwidth saturation is to design your ethernet network so that traffic, in the form of voltage, is as segmented and isolated from other traffic as possible. Physical grouping of computers with devices such as bridges and routers minimizes the number of machines within a *collision domain*, or the physical part of the network that machines have to share to send and receive data.

Many network devices have been created to help in this process, to extend network segments and to isolate network traffic. To strengthen your understanding of these concepts, a review of each type of device follows. The author encourages those who are already familiar with these devices and how they work to feel free to skip these sections and move straight to the section titled "Understanding Routing." If these devices still raise some questions in your mind, the summary is provided to fill in conceptual gaps that may exist.

As this is a chapter devoted to IP routing, an in-depth discussion of routers as devices is reserved for later in the chapter, beginning with the "Understanding Routing" section.

Network Review

Discussions of networks to this point have been primarily focused on how they should be put together. In this following section, the review furthers this line of discussion on networks. Instead of covering the theory of network design, however, it provides an overview of the connection devices themselves.

Repeaters, Bridges, and Switches

How do repeaters, bridges, and switches factor into the networking equation? If you're installing a TCP/IP network, why do you have to understand these devices? Mostly because it's extraordinarily rare to run a network using one protocol and because these devices probably already exist on the network you work on. You need to understand how TCP/IP interacts or doesn't interact with these devices to fully understand the protocol suite. First, consider exactly what each device is designed to do.

Repeaters

Copper wire can carry voltage only so far before the integrity of that voltage begins to deteriorate. This deterioration of a voltage signal is referred to as *attenuation*. It more or less means that the difference between a clean 1 (voltage on) and a clean 0 (voltage off) becomes muddled. Figure 11.2 shows the distinction between fresh, clean signals and what the signals look like as the distance increases from where the voltage was applied. The big problem is that this seems to occur after only a couple of hundred feet, certainly not the distance that is necessary for very large networks to successfully communicate. Something had to be done to extend the length of a network segment.

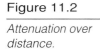
Figure 11.2

Attenuation over distance.

Extending the length of a network segment is difficult because distance is not the only factor that affects voltage. Other sources of interference can alter voltage on a wire. For instance, a copper wire can pick up voltage just from being in the same proximity as a magnetic or electrical source. This means that if a machine wants to communicate a "0" on the wire, but somewhere along the path of the wire it crosses another source of voltage, it picks up that voltage, resonating to that same frequency. Depending on the strength of that secondary source, this could make the "0" look like a "1" to the receiving machine(s). It may be easiest to think of the copper wire as a rambunctious partier who really likes to dance. If the wire hears music anywhere in the neighborhood, it picks up the beat and starts to dance. Imagine how chaotic it would seem to see a dancer try to do the waltz, the cha-cha, ballet, and disco all at the same time.

This troubled the engineers who were trying to design ethernet specifications; they had to figure out how to make sure only one dance was interpreted, while still being able to extend network segments. The network cards with which they were experimenting could transmit and interpret voltage very quickly (approx. 10 MB/sec, an enormous amount of data) and sat around idle most of the time, so speed didn't seem to be the problem. Interpreting whether the voltage was real, on the other hand, was much more difficult.

They experimented with twisting the copper wiring and shielding it from outside interference. They also wrote software to try to make the network devices "pseudo-smart" Along this line, special algorithms were written in the network card logic that basically stated, "If the voltage is close to a 1, make it a 1; if it's close to a 0, make it a 0. We'll have to perform some error checking afterward." After these algorithms were written and the wiring seemed fairly safe, engineers could finally turn to the task of extending the network.

This was fairly simple: design a piece of hardware between two wire segments; if the hardware hears voltage on one side, clean it up and retransmit it on the other side. String as many of these together as you want and you can extend a network for miles and miles, right? Well, no. Machines can't wait forever for a reply to figure out whether a machine receives the voltage; remember, the sending machine has no idea repeaters are on the network. So, after a certain time-out period, the network card just says, "Hey, forget it," or worse, "Hey let's retransmit!"

So, how many repeaters can be strung together, repeating voltage from one segment to another, before the time elapses for a response? The general networking rule is the 5-4-3 rule. This rule states that you can connect up to five network segments with four repeaters where only three of the segments are populated with machines. Standard rules for segment lengths of 100 feet or more, depending on the type of cable, such as coax or UTP, also had to be followed.

All this developed out of the necessity to weed garbage from the data. *Repeaters* were simply designed and implemented to freshen up the voltage on a network segment and retransmit it, all nice and clean again. This type of conditioning of the line occurs at the first layer of the networking model. Although no true error-correction and retransmission utilities are running here, algorithms determine how degraded a signal is, how best to boost the signal that will be rebroadcast, or whether to simply ignore the signal that's been received. Figure 11.3 illustrates at what layer of the networking model a repeater operates.

Figure 11.3

The repeater's role in the networking model.

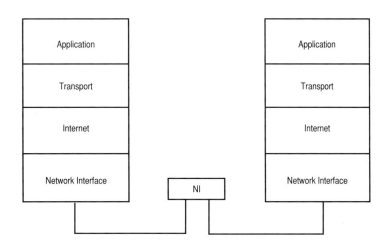

Given how low the repeater works in the networking model, it should be fairly clear that the TCP/IP protocol suite is not terribly concerned about whether there are repeaters in your networking environment—assuming of course, they're working. IP and ARP, the lowest working protocols in the suite, don't even care whether you're on an ethernet, token ring, or other type of network, so long as the underlying network infrastructure is functioning. The one important disadvantage of repeaters occurs when two machines are on the same network segment. When they need to communicate with each other, there is no need for every other segment to receive the same voltage. Figure 11.4 illustrates where repeaters fall a little short.

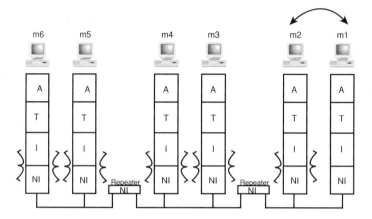

The great thing about repeaters is that they retransmit any kind of voltage, including broadcasts, throughout the network to any machine that is listening. Unfortunately, this is also one of their flaws. Repeaters retransmit—throughout the entire network—even when it is unnecessary. For instance, when two machines on the same network segment want to send directed packets between themselves, the repeater will still retransmit those signals throughout the network. This creates unnecessary traffic on the other network segments. Repeaters simply do not know any better. To correct this problem, a smarter device was needed.

Bridges

Repeaters ended up being exceptionally good at retransmitting data. So good, in fact, that when using a broadcast protocol like NetBEUI, the same bandwidth considerations discussed earlier became a problem again. Machines had a hard time trying to transmit data because they continued to collide with other machines trying to transmit data. This meant that the functional size of an ethernet network was really only a little over 100 machines or so. Numbers greater than this, and sometimes numbers even less than 100, on any segment or extended segment resulted in so many collisions that it usually hung up the entire network. The result was that you, as the network administrator, had to tell everyone to reboot—but please, not all at once! Repeaters were not going to be the only device necessary to make networking feasible.

Bridges were designed to be smarter than repeaters, transmitting data from one network segment to another only if absolutely necessary. Repeaters cannot serve this function because they simply regurgitate anything they see on one segment onto the other segment. Although useful, this is not always a terribly bright idea, as figure 11.5 demonstrates. The repeater correctly identifies that broadcasts are important to retransmit. In fact, most networking protocols provide for some way to implement a broadcast on the network, whether its purpose is to identify a server resource or find a physical address to initiate communication between two machines (even TCP/IP). Even though protocols typically use some form of broadcast to begin communicating with another machine, they are not broadcasting all the time. Besides announcing services, broadcasting is used usually only when you don't know the physical address of the machine with which you're trying to communicate, and have to ask the whole network. After both parties know each other's physical addresses, the machines no longer need broadcasts at this level to communicate. Designers needed a way to isolate the traffic to only the segments necessary for two machines to communicate after they knew the source and destination addresses. In this way, the previous downside to the repeater could be overcome, by only allowing traffic to be transmitted on the network segments where it was necessary, keeping unnecessary traffic to a minimum.

To understand how a bridge works, consider what you would have to know to pass broadcasts. For that matter, what information do you already have at your disposal? When you first turn on a bridge, it is basically blind. The bridge has no idea which machines are on the network and has to figure out which ports it is listening to. But it has memory and a set of rules by which it lives. A bridge only passes data from one segment or port to another based on the following conditions:

▶ If the destination physical address is on the same port as the source physical address, simply retransmit the request onto the same network segment.

▶ If the destination physical address is on a different port than the source physical address, transmit that packet to the port on which the destination physical address resides.

▶ If the destination physical address is unknown (not in the table) or it is a broadcast, pass the broadcast to the other ports, make a note of the source's physical address, and indicate in memory the port on which it resides.

Every time a packet is sent and received on a port, the bridge is responsible for identifying the port on which the source address lives. After this has been determined, that physical address is mapped to the port in the bridge's internal tables.

The advantage of being able to do this is that the number of machines on a network can essentially be doubled, tripled, and so on, depending on where the traffic patterns are and which machines communicate most with each other. Obviously, on some networks in which resources are centralized, this is not much help, but on networks in which resources are distributed in functional groups, it makes a great deal of difference.

Recall from the discussions on broadcasts that when a machine broadcasts a question, it also includes its source MAC address, or physical address. This is true regardless of the communications protocol being utilized. Why would NetBEUI or TCP/IP care about a source address if it is sending a broadcast? The initiator of the communication sends their physical address so that the receiver does not have to broadcast back. In terms of broadcast frames, bridges do not initially help much, because they simply retransmit the broadcast onto the segments and networks to which they are connected. They do come in handy after the source and destination addresses have been discovered. Bridges use the source addresses to build tables in memory of which addresses correspond to its ports. Look at the example shown in figure 11.5 to see how this works.

Figure 11.5

The bridge at work.

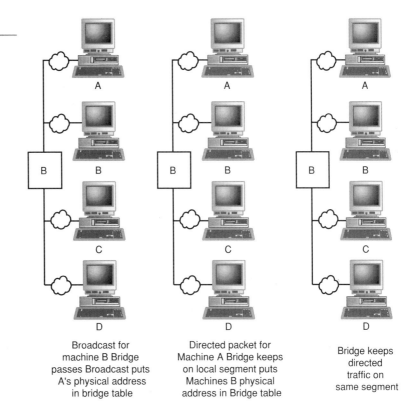

Broadcast for machine B Bridge passes Broadcast puts A's physical address in bridge table

Directed packet for Machine A Bridge keeps on local segment puts Machines B physical address in Bridge table

Bridge keeps directed traffic on same segment

As the example indicates, the bridge senses the voltage on the wire and decides whether it will rebroadcast the message based on its table. Bridges rebroadcast broadcasts by default; however, after they find source and destination addresses are on the same segment, they simply retransmit on that segment. If machine A tries to communicate with machine D, the router would mark machine D's physical address in network 2 and would know to pass any frames destined for physical address 5 to network 2. In this way, you can isolate local traffic from other segments, but when machines need to communicate with machines on another segment, they can do that as well. The tables that the bridges keep make them smart enough to look at the frames and determine where they are supposed to go. Different types of bridges learn their tables in different ways, but they all perform essentially the same task. Bridges are typically associated with bus-based and ring-based networks, and can serve as primitive gateways between these networks, reformatting frames from one and placing them on the network of the other.

Switches

Switches are devices that can be configured as bridges or routers and have a far more sophisticated means by which they approach movement of packets on a network. Most readily identified with the star and hybrid star networks, switches are designed to establish virtual circuits between two machines trying to communicate, so that the two machines see the traffic of only one, or at least only a few other, machines. Switches are primarily designed to reduce the number of machines within a collision domain. A *collision domain* is the logical grouping of machines that cannot avoid seeing each other's packets at the network interface layer. Ethernet networks using collision avoidance and detection techniques are designed to efficiently deal with this problem. Remember that the more machines on a particular network segment, the harder it is to communicate. Repeaters are not useful in restricting collisions because they retransmit everything they see. Bridges are more useful for directed packets, but still must transmit broadcasts. When properly configured, switches can establish point-to-point communications between two machines so that collision avoidance is no longer even necessary. Traffic between two machines will not interfere with other traffic that may be passing through the switch because the switch is sophisticated enough to isolate the traffic being transmitted from one port to another. Naturally, more than one machine can be added to a switch's port through the use of hubs. Figure 11.6 illustrates how a switch operates.

Figure 11.6

A look at a switch.

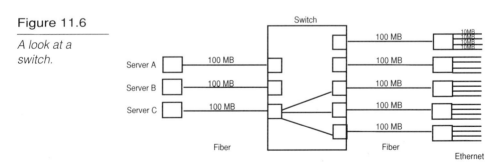

In this hybrid star configuration, the collision domain includes just the machines attached to that hub, not to any other ports. A full-scale discussion of switches is beyond the scope of this chapter. The important point to take away from this summary on switches is this: Although some switches can be configured to perform standard routing functions, most work at the Network Interface layer where IP is not involved yet. This means that if you have a digitally switched network, you may not need to break down your network IDs with subnet masks. The primary role of switches is to reduce the number of machines in your collision domains, thereby providing more sustained bandwidth to each machine on a network segment.

Looking at Broadcast Protocols

Before you can fully appreciate TCP/IP, you need to understand how each protocol in the suite works together. To gain this understanding, you need to spend some time looking at how broadcast protocols work. This section uses NetBEUI as an example protocol on a standard ethernet network. From this review of broadcast protocols, or non-routeable protocols, the discussion extends to the function of protocols that are point-to-point, or routeable protocols. You may be surprised to discover that although there are some significant differences between broadcast and point-to-point protocols, there are probably more similarities than differences.

A great deal of discussion on the networking model has focused up to this point on how each layer of the networking model on a sending machine needs to be able to communicate with its corresponding layer on the receiving machine. For instance, the Application layer knows how to communicate with the Application layer of another machine and the Session layer knows how to communicate with the Session layer of another machine. This function is fundamental to network architecture. At the bottom of the networking model is the Network Interface layer, and it necessarily follows that the Network Interface layer needs to communicate with the Network Interface layer, just as with each of the other layers. Part of the Network Interface layer includes the physical address of a machine, the 6-byte (48-bit) unique hexadecimal address assigned to a network card by the manufacturer.

NetBEUI is a broadcast protocol, but complies with the standard rules for networking in that NetBEUI's first task when trying to establish communication with another machine is to discover the physical address of the destination machine. With NetBEUI, each machine is uniquely identified by a name, called the NetBIOS name. This is the name of the machine given to it during installation of any Windows operating system using the NetBIOS interface. Even if the NetBEUI protocol is not loaded, the name is still a NetBIOS name and any protocol installed will have to support the NetBIOS interface. This is why Microsoft includes the NetBT (NetBIOS over TCP/IP) API in the protocol suite.

But back to NetBEUI; observe figure 11.7. This figure shows two machines in the state in which they would exist if they had never communicated with each other and the application on machine B wanted to communicate with machine A. The real conceptual bridge to cross here is that even though these machines may be sitting next to each other on the same piece of wire, they may not have a clue about how to communicate with each other. Remember that each layer of the networking model must be able to communicate or the whole process breaks down. So, even if the application layer of machine B knows it wants to speak to machine A, the lower layers may have no idea what the application layer is talking about.

Figure 11.7

Two machines that have not communicated before.

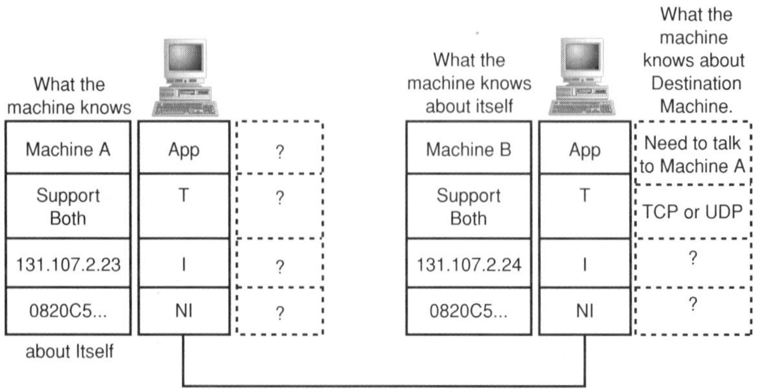

At this point, the lower layers have a choice. They can either report that they don't have a clue, or they can go out on the network and try find a machine with the appropriate name. In this case, machine B initiates a broadcast on the network using an ethernet frame in which the destination address is represented by 6 bytes of all FFs, as in figure 11.1. Recall that a broadcast utilizing all FFs indicates to every network interface card that it must pass this data up to the higher layers of the networking model. But, just as someone screaming incoherently does not tend to facilitate communication, it would behoove machine B to broadcast a meaningful question to those higher layers. In this case, the question is put very simply: "If you are machine A, what is your physical address?" This question also contains information about the sending machine, including the NetBIOS name and physical address. With NetBEUI, this question is sent all the way up to the Session layer of every machine on this network before the question is understood and possibly responded to. After a machine interprets the question and decides the message was intended for it, it sends back a directed message indicating its physical address. After these two machines have figured out each other's physical addresses, they can communicate with directed packets, meaning that they no longer need to use broadcasts that every machine listens to; they can place the physical addresses in the frames just as with a point-to-point protocol. Figure 11.8 illustrates the communication process between two machines using a broadcast protocol.

Figure 11.8

Communication with a broadcast protocol.

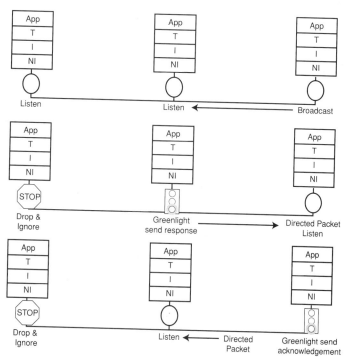

This is true any time a machine using a broadcast protocol attempts to communicate with another machine on the network. Part of the response given to any broadcast message is the destination machine's physical address. After a reply is sent, including the destination machine's physical address, broadcasts between the two machines are no longer necessary, and the actual physical address is placed in its appropriate location during data transfer.

So, if this is the case, what's the problem with NetBEUI? Why can't you use it on the Internet, too? In order to answer this question you need to look much further into the conceptual barriers imposed by this protocol. After you have uncovered and dissected the barriers, it should be fairly clear when NetBEUI is, and is not, useful as a protocol in the networking world.

First, NetBEUI was originally designed to be used on local area networks. This means that NetBEUI doesn't use an individual addressing scheme based on the important assumption that there is more than one network to worry about. This basic and fundamental design assumption lead to simple choices. For instance, as Chapter 8 discussed, it's important to be able to uniquely identify machines on a network. When using NetBEUI, a machine's uniqueness is defined by its physical address and its unique NetBIOS name, the name it received during installation of the operating system. Since its inception as a protocol, NetBEUI never had to worry about whether there was more than one network; it was not designed to worry about how to uniquely identify one network over another or how to move packets from one network to another, because it assumes there is only one network. That is why the question it asks during the broadcast for a physical address is somewhat simple: "If you're machine X, what is your physical address?" Notice the hidden assumption. Nowhere in the question does it ask what network the machine is on, because to NetBEUI, that is a meaningless question; of course we're all on the same network. Without the additional overhead of worrying about having to route packets, it has the advantage of being quick and efficient. It is not, however, routeable because it has no way to identify different networks, and requires each machine on the network segment to dedicate more resources due to its broadcast nature. Consider how far up the networking model a machine has to pass a random frame on the network before determining whether the frame was destined for it, during a broadcast. Figure 11.9 illustrates that process.

Figure 11.9

Session layer processing.

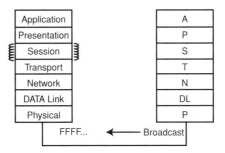

Using a broadcast protocol such as NetBEUI, the only fundamental restrictions in terms of networking are that multiple networks don't exist (remember, to a protocol such as NetBEUI, there's only one network, or LAN), and the functional number of computers you can put on that network is limited.

If you use the TCP/IP protocol, however, the destination for this data could be identified by the physical address assigned to the network card of that machine or the IP address given to that machine. As Chapter 9 indicated, the IP address has a lot of information. Not only does it contain the unique network identifier for that machine on a network, but it also has the unique host identifier as well. The capability to uniquely identify different network IDs is what makes TCP/IP a wide area network protocol, and is what separates it from broadcast protocols. Because IP recognizes the difference between unique machines and unique networks, the protocol had to be written with the capability to move data from one network to another by "routing" them from one network to another. This function is built into the IP protocol. In the case of a routed protocol, machines do not have to pass frames as high up in the networking model to determine if the packet is directed at them. Figure 11.10 illustrates the difference between a broadcast protocol and a directed, or routed, protocol.

Figure 11.10

Broadcast versus directed protocols.

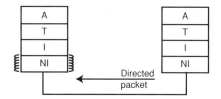

Because the network interface layer is responsible for checking the destination of frames, the determination of whether the data is for that machine occurs at a much lower layer on the networking model. TCP/IP was designed for use on a WAN in which multiple network segments are connected through devices called *routers*. Because TCP/IP uses several addressing schemes—IP addresses and physical addresses—it has the additional overhead of sorting through these and requires the administrator to have more knowledge of the protocol to implement it. However, this added overhead allows TCP/IP to be extraordinarily robust, routeable, and flexible. Figure 11.11 illustrates the addressing levels that TCP/IP uses, including physical address, IP address, and host naming conventions.

Figure 11.11

Unique addressing characteristics.

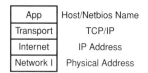

How did the source machine get the destination IP address in the first place? Recall from Chapter 8, that ARP (the detective) is the protocol responsible for going out and finding physical addresses of machines based on the IP address. ARP uses a small broadcast of its own on the network, somewhat similar to what NetBEUI does, except the packet is smaller. The ARP request frame is shown in figure 11.12.

Figure 11.12

Example of the ARP broadcast.

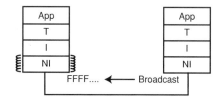

So you can see that even TCP/IP must use some sort of a broadcast to gain physical addresses, much like NetBEUI. These broadcasts just occur in a separate stage of communication. After ARP has negotiated the physical address between the two machines, it passes the physical address to IP so that it can create the directed frame necessary for communication. You can configure the TCP/IP suite with manual entries in the ARP cache so that ARP does not use broadcasts, but this adds a substantial amount of maintenance overhead on the administrator's part.

Refer to figure 11.10. Notice that each machine on the network in these examples still receives the initial frame and has to check it. Both examples in figures 11.9 and 11.10 use a standard ethernet network design using CSMA/CA, but they use a different protocol. Does this mean that a network has to be concerned with bandwidth issues regardless of which protocol is being used? Unfortunately, the answer is yes. Both examples indicate that on an ethernet network, frames (voltage) are applied to the wire segment that these machines are on, regardless of which protocol is being used. In fact, at this layer, the network cards have no idea which protocol is being used. All the network cards know at this level is that they listen and pass broadcasts up to the next layer and drop any packets that aren't broadcasts or aren't specifically addressed to them.

Now that the essential differences between broadcast and directed protocols has been covered, a more formal discussion of TCP/IP routing can be undertaken. The next section discusses what routing is, what a router is, and the routing process as a whole.

Understanding Routing

Recall from the IP addressing and subnetting sections that the first thing a machine does when initiating communication with another machine is try to figure out whether the destination address is local or remote. It carries out calculations on the source and destination address based on the given subnet mask and then compares the two results. If the results are the same, the destination address is on the local network and ARP is then asked to get the physical address of the destination machine. If, however, the results do not match, the destination host is remote, and ARP is asked to get the physical address of a router or the default gateway.

Routers are devices that work at the Internet layer of the TCP/IP protocol suite, and have been designed to transfer or forward packets of data to their destinations, even when the routers themselves are not the destination. Consider for a moment that during a broadcast at the Network Interface layer (for example, ARP broadcast) for an IP address, presumably all the machines except one ignore the broadcast. This is because only one machine has that unique IP address. All other machines pass this data up to IP and then silently discard the data because the data is not intended for them. Routers are special machines that are told not to silently discard these kinds of packets, but to try to find the correct route or path to send messages when they receive messages not destined for them. In this way, packets can traverse one network to another through a router, and because this routing process occurs at the Internet layer, it doesn't matter what kind of network you're running on, be it token ring, ethernet, or FDDI. Most machines are not designed to do this; only routers and gateways are. Figure 11.13 illustrates a simple routed network design with one router and three networks.

Figure 11.13

A simple routed network.

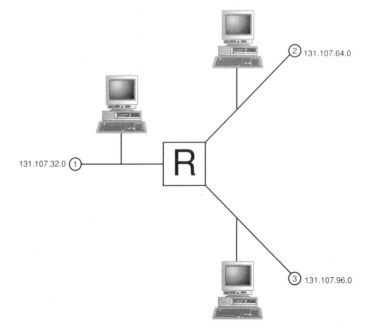

In this figure, the router separates the three network segments and keeps traffic on those network segments isolated from each other. Routers do not inherently support the passing of broadcasts, and must be specifically configured to do so on a network. This means that any machine broadcasting on network 1 will not be seen by machines on network 2 or 3. If a machine needs to communicate with a machine on the other side of a router, it needs to directly identify that machine and send those packets to the router to be forwarded.

How did this machine know the address of the router or default gateway? Host machines gain the IP address of the router in one of two ways. It is either manually configured in the network configuration of the machine, or the machine discovers the router address through a DHCP scope option. This information is stored in the registry and also appears in the machines internal route table.

This route table resides in memory and keeps track of networks and the physical interfaces that give access to those networks. On a local machine, the route table is fairly simple and usually contains no more than a few default entries, including the loopback address, the network on which the machine currently resides, and entries for various broadcasts. Figure 11.14 illustrates a common route table for a local machine.

Figure 11.14

A sample route table.

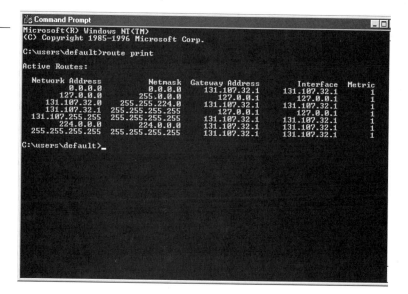

Every machine on a TCP/IP network consults its route table to determine what to do with addresses that are destined either locally or remotely. If a destination is on the local network, the route table informs IP to send the data to the local machine. If, however, the destination address is remote, IP consults the route table for an entry specific to that network. If an entry specific to that network exists, the packet is sent to the network interface identified by that route table entry. If no entry exists for that specific network and a default gateway has not been identified, the packet is dropped. It is only in the case that an entry does not exist and a default gateway for the machine has been configured, that IP will use the 0.0.0.0 route table entry (default gateway) to find a network interface address to send the data. Figure 11.15 has no specific networks identified and would therefore use the 0.0.0.0 entry, sending data destined for a remote network to 131.107.2.1 to be routed.

Dead Gateway Detection

Microsoft NT supports dead gateway detection when using TCP/IP. This means a machine can have more than one default gateway defined in its IP configuration. If, for some reason, the first default gateway is not responding, TCP/IP can switch to other default gateways to try to find a path to a particular destination. Dead gateway detection works only through the TCP protocol, so a utility such as ping does not initiate dead gateway detection when trying to communicate. A utility such as FTP, on the other hand, tries to establish a TCP connection and detects dead gateways. When TCP sends out data and no acknowledgments are received, it retransmits this data. But it only tries to retransmit data so many times before giving up on the connection. This number of times is defined by the registry entry called *TcpMaxData-Retransmissions*. When TCP reaches half of this value (default = 5), it asks IP to switch from the original default gateway, and to try to establish communication using the next default gateway configured on the machine. Dead gateway detection does not have to be turned on by the user; it is on automatically. After multiple default gateways are configured, dead gateway detection is initiated for any TCP connection, and the entries for the default gateways are placed in the routing table. The registry where you can configure this manually is as follows:

```
HKEY_LOCAL_MACHINE\SYSTEM\CurrentControlSet\Services\Tcpip\Parameters
```

Remember that by default, this selection is on. The only reason to edit this parameter would be if you do not want to use dead gateway detection. For more information on the exact registry entries and parameters, see Microsoft's online knowledge base.

After a machine determines where to send a packet destined for either a local or remote address, all other networking processes discussed earlier have to take place. Take a closer look at the packets that are created during these two processes, local and remote. The first example illustrates a command issued to a local machine and the second example illustrates the same for a remote machine. Both examples use figure 11.15, and the route table in figure 11.14 is the default route table for machine A on the network.

Figure 11.15

Example 1: From machine A, ping the address 131.107.32.20.

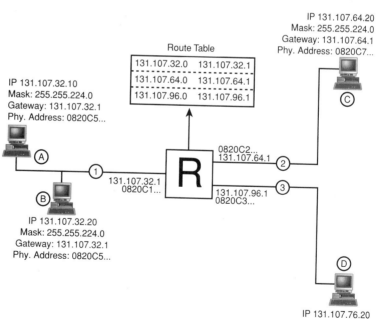

The first step is for machine A to use its subnet mask to determine whether this IP address is local or remote. After determining that the IP address is local, it consults the route table. Even though the destination is local, the machine still needs to figure out what interface to use to send out the data. Although this may seem somewhat trivial, keep in mind that a machine may have more than one IP address bound to a network card, or more than one network card attached to two networks. Either scenario provides a machine with more than one local interface to physical network segments. After the machine establishes the IP address of the interface, ARP is instructed to find the physical address of the local machine. A sample ARP broadcast for this address is shown in figure 11.16.

Figure 11.16

A sample ARP broadcast.

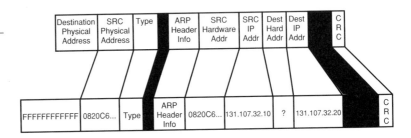

Once the destination address responds with its physical address, ARP relays this information to IP so that IP can formulate the directed packet shown in figure 11.17. Notice both the destination's physical address and IP address are used in the creation of this directed packet. After this packet is transmitted on the wire, only machine B's Network Interface layer responds to the physical address identified.

Figure 11.17

The completed frame.

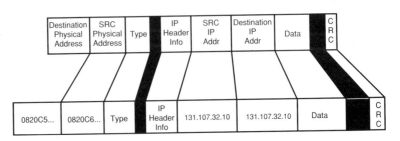

In this way, local communications are initiated. Observe the subtle differences between communicating with a local machine versus a remote machine.

The first step is for machine A to use its subnet mask to determine whether this IP address is local or remote. After determining that the IP address is remote, it consults the route table to determine where to send packets destined for this IP address. After consulting the default table, the machine does not find any entries specific to network 3. It does, however, have a default gateway defined at 131.107.32.1. Therefore, any packets destined for networks this machine does not know about should be sent to the default gateway at 131.107.32.1. IP asks ARP to find the physical address of the default gateway because that is where this packet will have to be sent. ARP consults the ARP cache and either returns a physical address stored in memory or initiates an ARP broadcast for the router. Figure 11.18 illustrates this ARP packet. There does not appear to be anything special about this packet except for the address that ARP is looking for.

Figure 11.18

An ARP broadcast for the router.

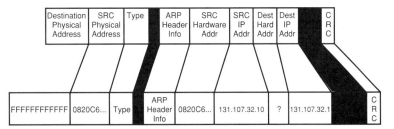

Once ARP locates the physical address of the router, it returns this physical address to IP so that IP can formulate the packet that will be sent. Figure 11.19 illustrates the packet that IP formulates. Take a close look at the destination physical address and the destination IP address.

Figure 11.19

A packet addressed to the router, but destined to a remote address.

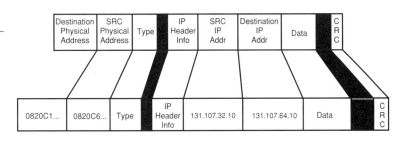

Notice how cleverly IP handles the routing of the packet. IP has to keep the destination IP address the same as that issued by the ping command, but send the packet in such a way that it can be forwarded by the router. It does this by creating a packet destined for the original IP address at the Internet layer, but sending the packet to the physical address of the router at the network interface layer. IP knows that the router is the only machine that will respond to a packet destined for this physical address, but that once the router passes this packet up to the IP layer, the router will be responsible for forwarding this packet to its destination.

After the packet resides on the router, the router has to go through the same process as any other host or machine on the network. The router must use its subnet mask to determine whether the packet's IP address is local or remote, access its route table to find the best possible route to the destination, and utilize ARP to find physical addresses to send the packet(s) to.

If this example had more routers and network segments, the first router would be responsible for figuring out the best route to the destination network. After it determined the best route, it would forward this data on to its next hop or router. This second router would go through the same motions, figuring out the best path to send the data along to its final destination.

Of course, discussion up to this point has focused on how the local machine gets a packet from itself to the first router along the path to a packet's destination. Both routers and machines keep a routing table. On a machine, this table is usually relatively short and simply defines the network that the machine is currently on and the machine's interface (IP address) to that network. On routers, these tables can be long and complex, but by default, a router knows only about the networks to which it has a physical interface. For instance, in figure 11.16, the router only knows about networks 1, 2, and 3, because it has a physical interface to each.

Static and Dynamic Routers

As the previous section discussed, routers have built-in tables used to determine where to send a packet destined for a particular network. By default, routers know only about networks to which they are physically attached. This section discusses how routers find out about networks to which they are not physically attached —either through manual configuration or dynamic configuration.

Static routers are routers that are not able to discover networks other than those to which they have a physical interface. If this type of router is to be able to route packets to any other network, it has to be told manually what to do, through either the assignment of a default gateway on the router, or by manually editing the route table. Microsoft NT enables the user to build a static router, or multihomed router, using multiple network cards and IP addresses. In a static router environment, new changes are not reflected in the routing tables on these routers.

Dynamic routers, on the other hand, utilize inter-routing protocols. These protocols simply provide a language for routers to communicate changes to their route tables to other routers in their environment. In this way, routing tables are built dynamically and the administrator does not have to manually edit route tables to bring up a new network segment.

Dynamic routers cannot provide this function without routing protocols, though. The most popular routing protocols are the Routing Information Protocol (RIP) and Open Shortest Path First protocol (OSPF). RIP is a broadcast-based protocol used primarily on small- to medium-sized networks. The more sophisticated OSPF protocol is used for medium to large networks.

Microsoft NT 4.0 supports the installation and use of RIP to provide dynamic routing for multihomed computers using NT as the operating system. In this way, routing tables can be updated whenever any additions to a network occur. If RIP or OSPF is used in a routed environment, it should help eliminate the need to have to manually edit route tables in your environment.

The Static Routing Environment

Take a look at how static routing works in an environment. Figure 11.20 shows a typical small network environment with two routers dividing three subnets. Each router has a standard routing table consisting of the networks to which they are attached. In the figure, router A is connected to subnet 1 and 2 and has a routing table that reflects this information. Router B is connected to subnet 2 and 3 and its routing table also reflects the networks on which it is currently configured. Take a look at what happens to a ping (echo request) packet when it is initiated by a machine on subnet 1.

Figure 11.20

A typical small network.

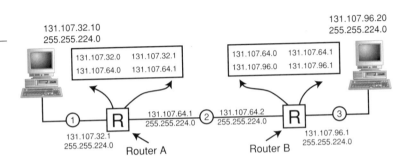

Combine everything you have learned from the previous chapters to isolate exactly how this ping request would flow. From the command prompt, or possibly a specific application on subnet 1, a ping command is issued to an IP address on subnet 3; let's say from IP address 131.107.32.10 to 131.107.96.20. First, IP takes the destination address and compares it to the source address using the subnet mask of that machine. After the comparison is done, IP determines that this destination address is on a remote network. IP checks its internal route table to determine where it's supposed to send packets destined for a remote network. Whenever a destination address is remote, IP knows to ask ARP for the physical address of the default gateway specified in the internal route table. ARP then either returns the physical address from the ARP cache or does a local ARP broadcast for the router's physical address. At this point, the ping request has not yet left the sending machine. IP gathers the physical address of the router, inserts the destination address into the ping packet and finally transmits the packet onto the wire of subnet 1.

Because IP very smartly sends the packet on the wire in such a way that only the router would not discard the packet, the packet safely arrives at the router. The network interface on the router passes the data up its network stack to IP, where IP discovers that this packet is not destined for it. Normally, IP on a machine would discard the packet. But this is a special kind of machine, a router, which has additional responsibilities including trying to forward packets it receives to the necessary network. Router A reads the IP address of the destination and compares this destination to its own source address using its subnet mask. At this point, IP determines the network to which this packet is supposed to be sent and checks its internal route table to see what to do with packets destined for the 131.107.96.0 network. Unfortunately, this router has no entries for this network and therefore drops this packet. ICMP reports an error to the machine on subnet 1, indicating that the destination address cannot be reached.

This seems like an awful lot of work to get an error message, especially if you know that the destination machine is working. There are two ways to get around this kind of scenario.

▶ Add a default gateway to the router's configuration

▶ Add a manual entry in the router's internal table

See what happens if you utilize one or both of these solutions on router A, picking up right where router A decided to drop the packet. Figure 11.21 illustrates the new routing table and default gateway assignment.

Figure 11.21

Adding a default gateway address.

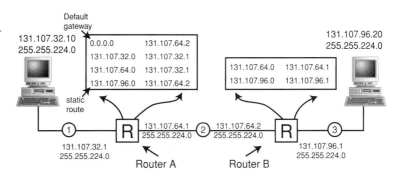

Router A has just figured out that the packet's destination address does not match its own IP address. It therefore checks its route table, looking for either a path to the 131.107.96.0 network or for the IP address of its default gateway. By configuring a default gateway, an administrator indicates to the router that if it handles a packet destined for a network that it has no idea about, the router should send it to the default gateway specified and hope for the best. This can be useful if you don't want to configure 37 route table entries on a network. Merely specifying default gateways can minimize the size of your route tables and minimize the number of manual entries you have to maintain. This, of course, comes with the possibility of making your network a little more inefficient. There are always tradeoffs when configuring a network.

Router A now figures out that it needs to send the ping request to the IP address of the other router based on its route table, in this case 131.107.64.2. Here is yet another conceptual gap. Router A really doesn't know whether the IP address represents a router or just another machine on the network. For that matter, it might be sending this packet into bit-space. Router A trusts that the administrator was wise enough to specify an IP address of a device that will help get the packet to its final destination. As an aside, this means that if you enter a route table entry incorrectly, the router just merrily starts sending packets to wherever you specified.

IP on router A now asks ARP to find the physical address of the next router in line. Just as on another machine, ARP either already has the physical address in cache or initiates an ARP broadcast to get it. After IP has the physical address, it reformulates the packet, addressing it to router B's physical address but leaving the original source address intact. It does not insert its own IP address as the source. If it did this, the destination address would never respond back to the original machine. The packet is transmitted onto the wire destined for router B.

Router B hears the transmission, goes through basically the same process, determines the destination address and discovers that it can send the packet directly to the destination machine. Utilizing the same ARP and IP procedures, the packet finally arrives at the destination machine on subnet 3. The ICMP echo request is acknowledged and ICMP formulates the ICMP echo response packet that must be sent back. Remember that up to this point, the original sending machine is just patiently waiting for a response.

The destination machine looks at the source address
(131.107.32.10), figures out that it's remote, finds the physical
address of router B to send the message back and transmits it
onto the wire.

 Note

In order for routing to work in a static routing environment, be
sure that each router is aware of all relevant networks. Otherwise, packets will be dropped unexpectedly on their return to
a destination.

Router B receives the packet, breaks it down and tries to figure
out what to do with a packet destined for the 131.107.32.0 subnet.
And, after all this work, router B drops the packet. Why? We made
all our changes to router A in terms of a default gateway and
route table entries, but we didn't do anything to router B. To
make static routing work, each router has to be updated and configured to know about other networks in the environment. It will
only be after a default gateway or manual entry in router B's route
table is configured, that the packets will successfully be transmitted between these two networks. Figure 11.22 illustrates the final
network configuration for the routers that enables successful communication between these subnets.

Figure 11.22

*The final network
routing tables.*

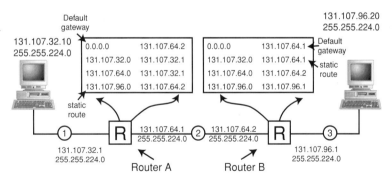

Default Gateways

You can easily identify default gateways on a machine. The two
easiest ways to identify default gateways for a machine or multihomed router is through manual configuration through the IP
properties sheet, or as a DHCP option. You can specify more than

one default gateway on a machine. Remember, however, that dead gateway detection will work only for machines initiating a TCP connection. In a routing table, the default gateway(s) is identified by the entry 0.0.0.0.

Route Tables

Route tables are used by machines/hosts on the network and by routers to determine where packets should be sent to reach their final destination. Each router builds an internal route table every time IP is loaded during system initialization. Take a closer look at a route table. Figure 11.23 illustrates an example of a route table built during the initialization of a machine configured to be a router.

Figure 11.23

Router's route table.

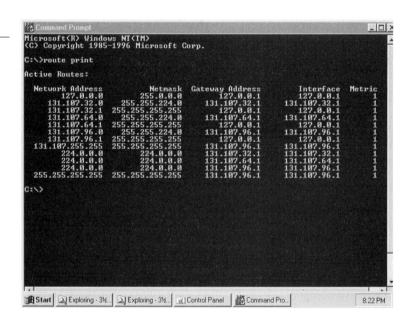

Notice the five columns of information provided within the route table.

> ▶ **Network Address.** This column represents all networks that this machine or router knows about, including entries for the default gateway, subnet and network broadcasts, the universal loopback address, and the default multicast address. In a route table, you can use names instead of IP addresses to identify networks. If you use names instead of

IP addresses, the names are resolved using the networks file found in the \%system drive%\system32\drivers\etc directory. While you can configure this option, the author strongly recommends against using such names, purely from a troubleshooting perspective. If, for some reason, the networks file was deleted or corrupted, name resolution would not be your only problem. Your router would suddenly find it difficult to route packets to these networks without knowing which IP addresses represented those network IDs.

▶ **Netmask.** This column simply identifies the subnet mask used for a particular network entry.

▶ **Gateway Address.** This is the IP address to which packets should be sent in order to route packets to their final destination. Each network address may specify a different gateway address in which to send packets. This may be particularly true if more than one router is connected to one network segment. This column may also have self-referential entries indicating the IP address to which broadcasts should be sent, as well as the local loopback entries. You can also use names to identify these IP addresses. Any names used here will be resolved using the local hosts file on the machine. Again, while this option is supplied, the author does not recommend introducing another source of possible error by using names in route tables.

▶ **Interface.** This IP address is used primarily to identify the IP address of the machine and to identify this IP address as the interface to the network. On a machine with one network card, only two entries appear. For any network address that is self-referential, the interface is 127.0.0.1, meaning that packets are not even sent onto the network. For all other communications, the IP address represents the network card interface used to communicate out onto the network. For multihomed machines, the interface IP address changes depending on which network address is configured on each network card. In this case, the interface identifies the IP address of the card connected to a particular network segment.

▶ **Metric.** The metric indicates the cost or hops associated with a particular network route. The router's job is to find the path representing the least cost or effort to get the packet to its destination. The lower the cost or hop count, the better or more efficient a particular route. On a static router, the metric for any network address will be one, indicating that the router thinks every network is only one router hop away. This is obviously not true, indicating that on static routers, this column is fairly meaningless. On dynamic routers, however, this column indicates to a router the best possible route to send packets.

Viewing the Route Table

To view the route table of an NT machine/router, two utilities can be used: the netstat utility and the route utility. To view the route table through netstat, go to the command prompt and type **netstat -r**.

This brings up the route table on your machine. However, all you can do is view the table. To view and manage the route table, including adding or changing entries, use the route utility. To view the route table using the route command, type **route print**.

This shows you the same table as before. When you type "route print" from the command prompt, the same table that displays with netstat -r appears. In both cases, the route table appears similar to the example shown in figure 11.22.

The entries that are in a route table on NT 40 by default include the following:

▶ **0.0.0.0.** Assuming, of course, that a default gateway is specified, this entry identifies the IP address of the default gateway, or the IP address to which packets will be sent if no other specific route table entry exists for a destination network. If multiple gateways are defined on an NT machine, you may notice more than one entry that looks like this, specifying each of the default gateways that is defined.

▶ **127.0.0.1.** This is the local loopback address used for diagnostic purposes, to make sure that the IP stack on a machine is properly installed and running.

- **Local network.** This is the identifier indicating the local network address. It indicates the gateway and interface, such as the machine's IP address, that is used whenever a packet needs to be transmitted to a local destination.

- **Local host.** This is used for self-referential purposes and points to the local loopback address as the gateway and interface.

- **Subnet broadcast.** This is a directed broadcast and is treated as a directed packet by routers. Routers support the transmission of directed broadcasts to the network that is defined by the broadcast. The packet is forwarded to the network, where it is broadcast to the machines on that network. In this case, the default entry specifies the IP address of the current machine for sending out subnet broadcasts to the network this machine is on.

- **224.0.0.0.** This is the default multicast address. If this machine is a member of any multicast groups, this and other multicast entries indicate to IP the interface used to communicate with the multicast network.

- **255.255.255.255.** This is a limited broadcast address for broadcasts destined for any machine on the local network. Routers that receive packets destined for this address may listen to the packet as a normal host, but do not support transmission of these types of broadcasts to other networks.

When a router looks for where to send a particular packet, it searches through the route table. After a route has been determined, meaning that an IP address has been found to send the data to, IP asks ARP for the physical address of that IP address. As soon as ARP replies, the frame can be constructed and transmitted onto the wire.

Building a Static Routing Table

The route command has a number of other switches that can be used to manage a route table statically. Up to this point, the print command is the only parameter that has been used. To manage a route table, however, an administrator must be able to add, delete, change, and clear route table entries. Each of these options is available; the following table shows each respective command:

To Add or Modify a Static Route	Function
route add [net id] mask [netmask] [gateway]	Adds a route
route -p add [net id] mask [netmask] [gateway]	Adds a persistent route
route delete [net id] [gateway]	Deletes a route
route change [net id] [gateway]	Modifies a route
route print	Displays route table
route –f	Clears all routes

For an exercise covering this information, see end of chapter.

Notice the entry that utilizes a -p (persistent) before the add parameter. By default, route table entries are kept only in memory. After a machine is rebooted, any entries that were manually added are gone and must be reentered. You can use batch files, startup scripts—or the persistent switch—to reenter static routes. The persistent entry switch writes route entries into the registry so that they survive a reboot of the machine. Naturally, this removes the need to create batch files or scripts, but requires manual deletion of the routes if they should change.

Note

Route table entries are kept only in memory and will not survive a reboot unless the -p switch is used.

The TRACERT Utility

Windows NT includes the TRACERT utility, which is used to verify the route a packet takes to reach its destination. To use the this utility, simply go to the command prompt and type **tracert <*IP address*>**.

The result of running this utility for a destination address will probably look similar to the following output :

```
C:\>tracert www.learnix.com

Tracing route to www.learnix.com [199.45.92.97]
over a maximum of 30 hops:

  1    156 ms    156 ms    141 ms  annex.intranet.ca [206.51.251.5]
  2    157 ms    156 ms    156 ms  cisco2.intranet.ca
[206.51.251.10]
  3    172 ms    156 ms    172 ms  spc-tor-6-Serial3-3.Sprint-
Canada.Net [206.186.248.85]
  4    156 ms    172 ms    187 ms  204.50.128.17
  5    171 ms    172 ms    157 ms  205.150.206.97
  6    172 ms    172 ms    297 ms  h5.bb1.tor2.h4.bb1.ott1.uunet.ca
[205.150.242.70]
  7    172 ms    171 ms    172 ms  max1.ott1.uunet.ca
[205.150.233.2]
  8    188 ms    203 ms    218 ms  router.learnix.ca
[199.71.122.193]
  9    203 ms    218 ms    235 ms  sparky [199.45.92.97]

Trace complete.
```

The result shows each router traversed to get to a destination as
well as how long it took to get through each particular router. The
time it takes to get through a particular router is calculated using
three algorithms, which are displayed for each router hop. The IP
address of each router traversed also displays. If a FQDN is available, this displays as well.

The TRACERT utility is useful for two primary diagnostic
purposes.

▶ It detects whether a particular router is not functioning
   along a known path. For instance, say a user knows that packets on a network always go through Texas to get from Florida
   to California, but communication seems to be dead. A tracert to a California address shows all the hops up to the point
   where the router in Texas should respond. If it does not
   respond, the time values are marked with "*"s, indicating a
   non-functioning path.

▶ This utility also determines whether a router is slow and possibly needs to be upgraded or helped by adding additional

routes on the network. You can determine this simply by looking at the time it takes for a packet to get through a particular router. If a particular router is deluged by packets, its return time may be significantly higher than that of any of the other hops, indicating it should be upgraded or helped in some way.

Dynamic Routing

For an exercise covering this information, see end of chapter.

The discussion to this point has focused on how to manually edit the route table to notify routers of the existence of networks to which they are not physically connected. This would be an enormously difficult task on large networks, where routes and networks may change on a frequent basis. It also makes redundant pathways horribly complex to manage, because you have to rely on each host to manage multiple default gateways and utilize dead gateway detection. Even utilizing these features on the client side does not guarantee timely reactions to the failure of links between routers.

These problems led to the development of routing protocols used specifically by routers to dynamically update each other's tables. Two of the most common protocols used by dynamic routers are RIP and OSPF. These protocols notify other routers that support these protocols of the networks they are attached to and of any changes that occur due to links being disconnected or becoming too congested to efficiently pass traffic. The standard rule of thumb when considering the use of either protocol is that RIP works well for small- to medium-sized networks, and OSPF works well for medium- to large-sized networks. The characteristics of RIP are discussed here because NT supports RIP on its multi-homed routers. The characteristics of OSPF are left to other reference sources. NT multihomed routers do not support the OSPF protocol out of the box.

Routing Internet Protocol

To understand RIP better on routers, first consider figure 11.22 (static routing), where routing tables had to be built manually. To pass packets from one network to another, each router had to be told where to send packets destined for a specific network (route table entry) or where to send packets it had no idea what to do with (default gateway). By default, routers know about the networks to which they are physically attached because their IP addresses on each of those networks give them the necessary information. The problem of remote networks is encountered almost immediately, though. For this reason, it became apparent that as networks grew in size, a more sophisticated way to update route tables would be necessary. From this need arose routing protocols, which enable routers to communicate with each other. The protocols enable one router to send information about the networks it knows about to any other router physically connected to the wire, and enable the router to receive information about other networks dynamically from other routers that also are able to communicate.

The RIP procedure for communicating between routers is through broadcasts over UDP port 520. RIP routers broadcast their route tables over this port and listen on this port for broadcasts from other routers that may be connected to the network. In this way, eventually all routers that are physically connected have up-to-date route tables and know where to send data for any network in the environment.

Not only do routers communicate the networks to which they are attached, but they also communicate how far away remote networks are from their particular location. This distance to another network is called a *hop*, or metric, and each router keeps track of this value within the route table. Each router along the path to a destination network represents a hop. For this reason, RIP is considered a distance-vector routing protocol. In this fashion, RIP can determine the route with the least number of hops necessary to get a packet to its final destination. Figure 11.24 illustrates how each hop count may be different within route tables on a network.

Figure 11.24

Hop counts in network route tables.

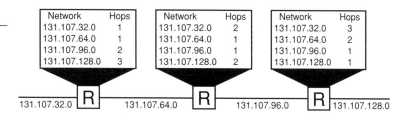

Network	Hops		Network	Hops		Network	Hops
131.107.32.0	1		131.107.32.0	2		131.107.32.0	3
131.107.64.0	1		131.107.64.0	1		131.107.64.0	2
131.107.96.0	2		131.107.96.0	1		131.107.96.0	1
131.107.128.0	3		131.107.128.0	2		131.107.128.0	1

131.107.32.0 R 131.107.64.0 R 131.107.96.0 R 131.107.128.0

As RIP was being developed, it was decided that routers would need to keep track of a maximum of 15 hops between networks. Therefore, any network address that had a hop count of 16 is considered unreachable. If a router's route table has two different hop counts for a particular network, the router sends the data to the route that has the least number of hops to the destination network.

Initially, it doesn't seem to make sense to limit the number of hops to a destination address, but this limitation is based primarily on how the RIP protocol works. Because RIP routers broadcast the networks they know about and how far away they are from those networks, certain precautions must be made in case any of these connections fail. After a router determines that a connection has failed, it must find a better route to that network from other route tables. This could create circular and upward-spiraling loops between routers, where the hop count continues to increase, ad infinitum.

If a redundant connection to that network exists with a higher hop count, eventually each router's tables increase to the point that the redundant route is chosen over the connection that died. But if no redundant route is available, the hop count could continue to increase indefinitely. To reduce this risk, several algorithms have been written to successfully react to connection failures, including the maximum hop count of 16, indicating an unreachable network. Administrators also have the ability to alter the hop count between routers, to encourage the use of some network routers over others that may be used purely for redundancy.

Broadcasts between routers occur every 30 seconds, whether the route table has changed or not. Figure 11.24 shows the original network in figure 11.22, but with dynamic tables instead of manual tables. In figure 11.24, router A sends a broadcast every 30 seconds, indicating the networks it knows about and how many hops it takes to get to those networks. Router B listens to this broadcast and checks router A's broadcast with its current route table. It enters any new information in its table and double-checks any entries that already exist. If router A indicates that it has a better route or hop count to a network, router B updates its table to reflect the better path. Router B initiates the same kind of broadcast to the networks to which it is attached, indicating its route table information as well.

Because RIP is the oldest routing protocol on the block and is widely used throughout the industry, several well-known problems exist when trying to implement this protocol in larger networks. These protocol deficiencies result in RIP being useful only in small to medium networks. RIP falls short in the following basic categories:

▶ Because RIP keeps track of every route table entry, including multiple paths to a particular network, routing tables can become large rather quickly. This can result in multiple RIP packets having to be broadcast in order to send a complete route table to other routers.

▶ Because RIP can allow hop counts only up to 15, with 16 representing an unreachable network, the size of networks on which RIP can be successfully implemented is necessarily restricted. Any large enterprise may need to achieve hop counts over and above this value.

▶ Broadcasts are sent by default every 30 seconds. This results in two fundamental problems. First, significant time delays occur between the times when a route goes down and all routers in the environment are notified of this change in the network. If a network goes down nine routers (hops) away, it can take up to $4 \frac{1}{2}$ minutes before that change makes it to the other end of the network. Meanwhile, packets sent in that direction can be lost and connections dropped. Second, while on a LAN, these broadcasts may not be significant in terms of bandwidth; but on an expensive WAN connection, these broadcasts may become bothersome, especially if the network is stable and the route tables are large. These broadcasts transmit redundant route table entries every 30 seconds without regard to whether it is necessary.

But these problems should not discourage the administrator of a small to medium network from using the RIP protocol. As long as you understand the benefits and limitations of the protocol, you should be able to use it quite successfully on a network.

Static and Dynamic Router Integration

Figure 11.25 illustrates a possible scenario in which a network consists of static routers and dynamic routers.

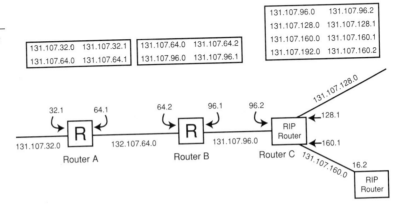

Figure 11.25

Integrating static and dynamic routers.

The best way to picture the integration of these two types of routers in an environment is to think of static routers as being dumb as a wall and dynamic routers as being a particularly chatty person. Think about it. Walls don't talk, thankfully, and no matter how much you talk to a wall, it's not going to respond. Now imagine a very chatty person standing in front of a wall, communicating a mile a minute about everything under the sun. The wall, no matter what incentives this person provides or promises, will simply return silence. Now extend this example to figure 11.25, which illustrates the default route tables for each of the routers.

Follow the path of a packet originating from the 131.107.32.0 network as it tries to reach the 131.107.128.0 network. By remembering our earlier example, it is fairly clear that router A will simply drop any packets destined for the 128 network. So, that fails, but you have come to expect that from static routers.

Therefore, you add static route table entries to router A. After you add the route table entries, the packet is again resent. Things seem to be running smoothly until router B gets hold of the packet and drops it. Oops, forgot! You must make static route table entries on all static routers in the environment. So, now, you add the appropriate route table entries on the static routers and the packet is ready to be sent again. Figure 11.26 illustrates the new route tables that have been created.

Figure 11.29

Static route table additions to the network.

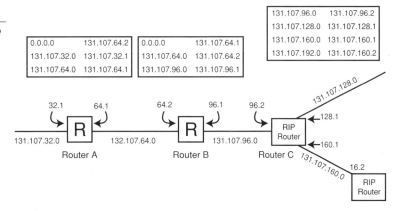

The packet is resent and makes it to Router B. Router B knows to send all packets destined for the 131.107.128.0 network to 131.107.96.1 and does so. However, the process of sending the packet does not result in router C having any idea where this packet comes from; the packet just lands on router C's doorstep. router C moves the packet to the 131.107.128.0 network. The machine that receives the packet tries to send a response to network 131.107.32.0 and sends its response to router C. Even though router C is a new RIP-enabled router, it has received no information about a 131.107.32.0 network from any of its friends. The packet gets dropped. So, when combining static and dynamic routers on a network, you have to enter static entries into the route table of your dynamic routers. Elegant, no; necessary, yes. To make matters worse, some dynamic routers do not propagate static route table entries, requiring all dynamic routers to have static route table entries added to them. Figure 11.27 illustrates the final route tables necessary to fulfill the communications requirements on the network.

Figure 11.27

Static route table additions to all routers on the network.

131.107.96.0	131.107.96.2
131.107.128.0	131.107.128.1
131.107.160.0	131.107.160.1
131.107.192.0	131.107.160.2
131.107.32.0	131.107.96.1
131.107.64.0	131.107.96.1

0.0.0.0	131.107.64.2
131.107.32.0	131.107.32.1
131.107.64.0	131.107.64.1

0.0.0.0	131.107.64.1
131.107.64.0	131.107.64.2
131.107.96.0	131.107.96.1

Building a Multihomed Router

☑ Objective

Windows NT enables an administrator to convert a machine into either a static or dynamic IP router. Static routers work well for extending a small network segment; dynamic routers using RIP work well on small to medium networks. A multihomed computer would probably not work well on large networks, however, based on RIP's limitations and the significant overhead associated with maintaining large route tables. Other considerations aside, however, building an NT router is fairly simple and easy to do.

Before continuing, let's define a or multihomed router. A multihomed router is simply a computer with more than one network card that has been configured to route packets from one network segment to another. The defining characteristic between a hardware router and a multihomed router is that on a multihomed computer, the operating system is the one that performs the routing. A hardware router is a device that is specifically manufactured and designed for routing only. You could think about it in more simple terms. For instance, you can run any Windows application, including Freecell, on a multihomed router; you cannot on a hardware router.

The first step toward building an NT router is to install two or more network cards in the machine. Anyone who has ever tried to do so will tell you this can often sound much easier than it is.

Each network card has to have its own IRQ and I/O address to use on the machine. These must be independent of other hardware cards you may be using in your machine, including video cards, sound cards, modems, hard disk controller cards, and so on. Basically, the machine needs to be stripped of any bells and whistles and other functions so that enough resources are available. Any resource conflicts result in significant headaches as your network cards don't appear and protocol drivers fail to load. The typical machine built for NT seminars and classes utilizes an NT router with three network cards and little else. After the machine successfully identifies the network cards, be careful of installing any additional third-party utilities. Sometimes they decide to steal the I/O addresses your network cards are using. The bottom line is that once this machine is built, try to leave it alone. Getting your machine stable will be the toughest part. Afterward, everything else is easy.

 Note

Be careful when installing third-party utilities after the router is configured. Sometimes they steal I/O addresses that may conflict with your network cards and cause routing problems.

After installing the network cards, make sure to assign separate IP addresses to each card, as follows:

1. In the network section of Control Panel under the protocol tab. Select TCP/IP and choose properties. Notice that where the network card is identified, the drop-down box reveals all the network cards you have installed, enabling you to choose a different IP address scheme for each network card.

2. After you give each network card its own IP address, indicating which network it is on, the machine can respond to packets coming from the networks to which it is attached. However, the machine is still not a router.

3. To turn the machine into a router, go back to TCP/IP properties and choose the routing Tab. Select the Enable IP Forwarding check box. After you select this box and have chosen OK to exit this configuration and the network configuration, you are asked to reboot your machine.

4. Reboot the machine. After the machine is rebooted, it is officially a router that can pass packets from one network to another.

The administrator then needs to decide whether the router will be static or dynamic. After IP forwarding is enabled, the router is a static router. If this is what is desired, no more configuration is necessary. If the administrator want to make this a dynamic router, then the RIP protocol needs to be installed.

This can be installed in the Services Tab through the network icon. After RIP is installed, this router listens for other RIP broadcasts, and broadcasts its own route table entries.

Although Windows NT supports the capability to create a static or dynamic router, the most important consideration for an administrator is probably whether he or she should spend the money to upgrade a machine for occasional routing of packets or spend the money for a hardware router. If the administrator plans to spend over $1,000 for a machine to route packets on a network, he may be better off spending it on hardware optimized for that purpose. Think of Windows NT routing versus hardware routing in much the same way as you would think about Windows NT RAID versus hardware RAID. Hardware implementation is usually a little more expensive, but is optimized for that specific task, whereas Windows NT implementations work well and are cheaper, but are not designed for constant pounding by a large network.

Exercises

Exercise 11.1:   Viewing the Route Table

Follow these steps to view your NT machines route table:

1. From the Start menu, select Command Prompt.

2. Type **route print**.

Exercise 11.2:   Adding an Entry to Your Route Table

Follow these steps to add a network to your route table:

1. From the Start menu, select Command Prompt.

2. Type **route add 131.107.64.0 mask 255.255.224.0** *IP address of your current gateway*.

3. Type **route print** to observe the addition.

Exercise 11.3:   Using the TRACERT Utility

1. From the Start menu, select Command Prompt.

2. Type **tracert** *ip_address* at the command prompt. For IP_address, chose a site that doesn't mind you hitting their server. Most sites won't mind an occasional hit, but it's bad form to continually do so.

3. Observe the results.

Review Questions

The following questions will test your knowledge of the information in this chapter:

1. In your environment, you have an NT machine that seems to not be responding to ping requests using an IP address. You would like to make sure that the machine's configuration is appropriate for the network. Which of the following options would you need to check?

   A. IP address

   B. Subnet mask

   C. Default gateway

   D. DNS

2. You've noticed a significant increase in the amount of time it takes to reach your remote offices. You think one of your routers may not be functioning. Which utility would you use to find the pathway a packet takes to reach its destination?

   A. WINS

   B. DNS

   C. TRACERT

   D. Network monitor

3. You have a machine that seems to be capable of communicating with other machines on its same local subnet, but whenever you try to reach destinations on a remote network, the communications fail. You run IPCONFIG /ALL and receive the information shown in figure 11.28. What is the problem?

   A. IP address

   B. Subnet mask

   C. Default gateway

   D. WINS

Figure 11.28

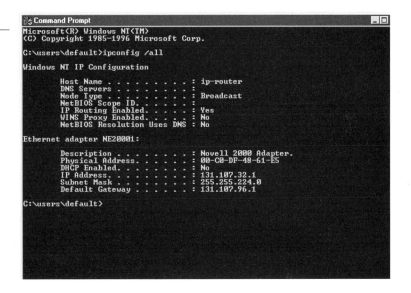

4. Your network is laid out like the one in figure 11.29. You seem to be having trouble with machine B in this environment. Although it seems to be able to communicate with machines on the same subnet, it can't communicate with machines on remote subnets. What seems to be the problem?

Figure 11.29

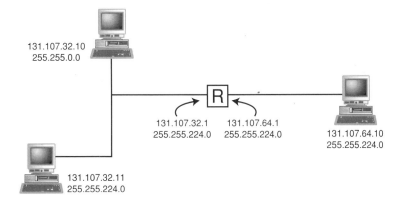

    A. IP address

    B. Subnet mask

    C. Default gateway

    D. DNS

5. You have set up a simple routed environment in which one router is central to three subnets, meaning that the router can see each of the three segments. No default gateway has been assigned because there does not seem to be any reason to do so. If a router does not know where to send a packet and no default gateway has been assigned, what will the router do with the packet?

    A. Drop the packet

    B. Store the packet for later processing

    C. Broadcast on the local network

    D. Use ARP to locate another pathway

6. Given the network shown in figure 11.30, will a packet from network 131.107.32.0 be able to reach network 131.107.96.0?

Figure 11.30

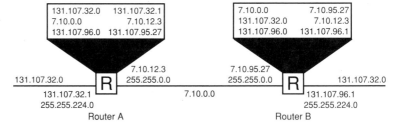

    A. Yes

    B. No

7. What would you have to change on the network in question 6 to make this scenario work?

    A. Change the default gateway address on router B

    B. Add a static ARP cache entry for 131.107.95.27 on router A

    C. Change the subnet mask for the 7.10 network to 255.255.255.0

    D. Change the gateway address for 131.107.96.0 on router A to 7.10.95.27

8. You want to have your NT routers share information on the network so that you don't have to continually update the route tables manually. What protocol do you need to install to allow this to happen?

   A. DNS

   B. RIP

   C. OSPF

   D. WINS

9. Ten machines on your network have stopped communicating with other machines on remote network segments. The router seems to be working properly, but you want to make sure the route table itself has not been modified. What utilities can you use to view the route table on your NT router?

   A. route

   B. netstat

   C. ping

   D. rttable

10. You set up an NT multihomed computer to be a router between two networks. You added multiple adapter cards and multiple IP addresses to the router. Because you are connecting only two subnets, you don't need to have a default gateway on your router. You do configure default gateways on all your clients to point to either side of the router based on what network they are on. You set up your network to look like the one in figure 11.31, but for some reason things are still not quite right. You can communicate on either side of the router, but not through the router. You must determine why machines on the 131.107.32.0 subnet seem to be having problems communicating with the 222.13.23.0 network. After you have figured out why your machines seem to be having trouble, what would you do to fix the problem?

Figure 11.31

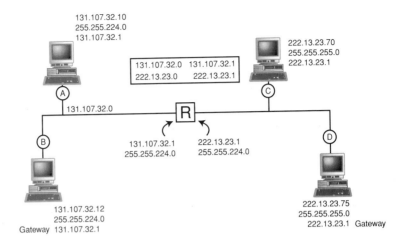

A. Change the subnet masks so that they are all the same

B. Add a default gateway to the router for the 222.13.23.0 network

C. Reconfigure the network so that both sides are on the 131.107.32.0 network

D. Enable IP forwarding on the router

11. Your environment consists of both LAN and WAN connections spread out over five continents. You've begun an expansion that has added a number of routers to your already large organization. Your network currently uses RIP as the routing protocol, but as new network segments are being added, routers on either end of your network insist that they cannot see each other and that they are unreachable. What seems to be the problem?

A. The routers were not made by Microsoft.

B. The RIP protocol cannot share route table information.

C. The RIP protocol cannot support more than 15 hops.

D. Routers are not designed for WAN connections.

12. When installing and testing a brand new NT router, you notice that the router routes packets to any network that it is physically attached to but drops packets to networks it is not attached to. There are seven of these networks that it cannot seem to route packets to. What would be the easiest way to make sure the router performs its function for those other networks?

    A. Disable IP routing

    B. Enable IP filtering on all ports

    C. Change the IP address bindings

    D. Add a default gateway

13. After adding a network segment (131.107.7.0) for a new wing, you discover that your route tables need to be altered. In this case, you simply need to add a new entry for this segment, but you want to make sure that the entry survives a reboot. What command would you choose for the addition?

    A. route change 131.107.2.0 131.107.7.0

    B. route add 131.107.7.0 mask 255.255.255.0 131.107.2.1

    C. route -p add 131.107.2.1 mask 255.255.255.0 131.107.7.0

    D. route -p add 131.107.7.0 mask 255.255.255.0 131.107.2.1

14. Last year, one of the big problems you encountered was a connectivity problem associated with only having one router in your environment that could route packets between subnets. This year your budget allowed you to add a second router to provide some backup for your primary router. Windows NT is smart enough to utilize dead gateway detection, but during your test of this feature it did not work at all. What might you have forgotten to configure for dead gateway detection to work?

A. Dead gateway detection must utilize RIP; therefore, RIP must be installed on each router.

B. Each host machine must be configured with the IP addresses of both routers before dead gateway detection is utilized.

C. Static route table entries must be configured on the routers so that they can communicate with each other.

D. Because they are initiating the communication, every application must be individually tailored to perform dead gateway detection.

15. After checking a route table, you notice that it is missing a very important route to one of your network segments. Before you can add the route to your routers table, however, you need to know what pieces of information to use the route utility?

A. Network ID

B. Netmask

C. MAC address

D. Gateway address

Review Answers

1. A, B, C

2. C

3. C

4. B

5. A

6. B

7. D

8. B

9. A, B

10. D

11. C

12. D

13. D

14. B

15. A, B, D

Answers to the Test Yourself Questions at the Beginning of the Chapter

1. IP address, subnet mask, and default gateway. The IP address, subnet mask, and default gateway are critical for a machine to know who it is, where it is, and how to send data to other networks.

2. RIP. RIP is the only routing protocol currently supported on Microsoft NT routers.

3. No, only the networks to which it is attached. To route to other networks, a static router would need to have manual entries placed in its routing table.

4. IP. This protocol is responsible for routing and delivering packets.

5. Tracert. The tracert utility is provided for troubleshooting slow or non-functioning routers.

6. No, NT routers do not support OSPF.

Chapter 12

Dynamic Host Configuration Protocol

This chapter will help you prepare for the exam by covering the following objectives:

 Objectives

▶ Configure scopes by using DHCP Manager

▶ Install and configure the DHCP relay agent

Test Yourself! Before reading this chapter, test yourself to determine how much study time you will need to devote to this section.

1. Which fields in the TCP/IP configuration will DHCP overwrite on a DHCP client that previously had TCP/IP manually configured?

2. What are three benefits of using DHCP to automatically configure a client for TCP/IP?

3. What extra steps should you take after installing two DHCP servers on a subnet?

4. What are the router requirements on an internetwork for enabling a DHCP client to communicate with a DHCP server on a remote subnet?

5. What steps should you take to ensure that DHCP does not assign an IP address that is already in use by a non-DHCP client?

6. Is it possible for two DHCP clients on an internetwork lease the same IP address at a given time? Why or why not?

7. A DHCP client is having difficulty communicating with hosts on an adjacent subnet. You do some troubleshooting and determine that the DHCP client is not using the default gateway that is set in the scope option for that subnet. What could be causing this problem?

8. How many DHCP servers are required on an internetwork of 10 subnets, each with 200 hosts and with BOOTP forwarding routers connecting the subnets? How many would you recommend and why?

9. Through which two methods can a DHCP client be configured to use DHCP for automatic TCP/IP configuration?

Answers are located at the end of the chapter.

Understanding DHCP

The configuration of Microsoft TCP/IP involves you knowing the correct values for several fields for each TCP/IP host and entering them manually. At the minimum, the host IP address, and subnet mask need to be configured. In most cases other parameters, such as WINS and DNS server addresses, also need to be configured on each host. DHCP relieves the need for manual configuration and provides a method of configuring and reconfiguring all the TCP/IP related parameters.

It is critical that the correct TCP/IP address is configured on each host; otherwise, hosts on the internetwork might:

▶ Fail to communicate

▶ Fail to initialize

▶ Cause other hosts on the internetwork to hang

The Dynamic Host Configuration protocol is an open industry standard that enables the automatic TCP/IP configuration of DHCP client computers. The use of Microsoft's DHCP server greatly reduces the administrative overhead of managing TCP/IP client computers by eliminating the need to manually configure clients. The DHCP server also allows for greater flexibility and mobility of clients on a TCP/IP network without administrator intervention. If used correctly, DHCP can eliminate nearly all the problems associated with TCP/IP. The administrator enters the valid IP addresses or ranges of IP addresses (called a scope) in the DHCP server database, which then assigns (or leases) the IP addresses to the DHCP client hosts.

Having all the TCP/IP configuration parameters stored on the DHCP server provides the following benefits:

▶ The administrator can quickly verify the IP address and other configuration parameters without having to go to each host. Also, reconfiguration of the DHCP database is accomplished at one central location, thereby eliminating the need to manually each host.

▶ DHCP does not lease the same IP address from a scope to two hosts at the same time; this can prevent duplicate IP addresses if used properly.

⚠ **Warning**
DHCP cannot detect which IP addresses are already being used by non-DHCP clients. If a host has a manually configured IP address and a DHCP scope is configured with that same address, the DHCP server may lease the address to a DHCP client, creating a duplicate IP address on the network. To prevent this situation, you must exclude all manually configured IP addresses from any scopes configured on the DHCP server.

▶ The DHCP administrator controls which IP addresses are used by which hosts. DHCP uses local network broadcasts to lease IP addresses to client hosts. If a second DHCP server resides on the same local network segment, the DHCP client can communicate with either server and may receive an IP address lease from the unintended DHCP server. See "Using Multiple DHCP Servers" later in this chapter for the ways to detect and prevent this situation.

▶ The chance of clerical and typing errors is reduced because the TCP/IP configuration parameters are entered in one place; the DHCP server database.

▶ Several options can be set for each DHCP scope (or globally for all scopes) that are configured on the client along with the IP address, for example, default gateway, WINS server addresses, and so on.

▶ An IP address may be leased for a limited time, which requires the DHCP client periodically to renew its lease before the lease expires. If the host is no longer using the IP address (is no longer running TCP/IP or is powered off), the lease expires and can then be assigned to another TCP/IP host. This feature is useful if the number of hosts requesting IP addresses is larger than the number of available valid IP addresses (such as when the network is part of the Internet).

> ▶ If a host is physically moved to a different subnet, the DHCP server on that subnet automatically reconfigures the host with the proper TCP/IP configuration information for that subnet.

What DHCP Servers Can Do

To enable automatic TCP/IP configuration by using DHCP, the DHCP administrator first enters the valid IP addresses as a scope in the DHCP server database and then activates the scope. The DHCP administrator now enters other TCP/IP configuration information that will be given to the clients. The administrator or user then selects the Enable Automatic DHCP Configuration option on the client (found in their network configuration).

When a DHCP client host starts up, TCP/IP initializes and the client requests an IP address from a DHCP server by issuing a Dhcpdiscover packet. The Dhcpdiscover packet represents the client's IP lease request.

After a DHCP server receives the Dhcpdiscover packet, the DHCP server offers (Dhcpoffer) one of the unassigned IP addresses from the scope of addresses that are valid for that host. This ensures that no two DHCP clients on that subnet have the same IP address. This Dhcpoffer information is sent back to the host. If your network contains more than one DHCP server, the host may receive several Dhcpoffers. In most cases, the host or client computer accepts the first Dhcpoffer that it receives. The client then sends a Dhcprequest packet containing the IP address offered by the DHCP server.

The DHCP server then sends the client an acknowledgment (Dhcpack) that contains the IP address originally sent and a lease for that address. The DHCP server leases the IP address to the DHCP client host for the specified period. The DHCP client must renew its lease before the lease expires. During the life of the lease, the client attempts to renew the lease.

The renewal request is sent automatically if the host still has TCP/IP initialized, can communicate with the DHCP server, and is still on the same subnet or network. After 50 percent of the lease time expires, the client attempts to renew its lease with the DHCP server that assigned its TCP/IP configuration. At 87.5 percent of the active lease period, the client, if unable to contact and renew the lease with the original DHCP server, attempts to communicate with any DHCP server to renew its configuration information. If the client cannot make contact with a DHCP server and consequently fails to maintain its lease, the client must discontinue use of the IP address and begin the entire process again by issuing a Dhcpdiscover packet.

Limitations of DHCP

Although DHCP can substantially reduce the headaches and time required to administer IP addresses, you should note a few limiting characteristics of DHCP:

▶ DHCP does not detect IP addresses already in use on a network by non-DHCP clients. These addresses should be excluded from any scopes configured on the DHCP server. This problem was fixed in service pack 2 for NT4.0.

▶ A DHCP server does not communicate with other DHCP servers and cannot detect IP addresses leased by other DHCP servers. Therefore, two DHCP servers should not use the same IP addresses in their respective scopes.

▶ DHCP servers cannot communicate with clients across routers unless BOOTP forwarding is enabled on the router, or the DHCP relay agent is enabled on the subnet.

▶ As with manually configured TCP/IP, incorrect values configured for a DHCP scope can cause unexpected and potentially disastrous results on the internetwork.

Other than the IP address and subnet mask, any values configured manually through the Network Control Panel Applet or Registry Editor of a DHCP client override the DHCP server scope settings. If you intend to use the server configured values, be sure to clear the values from the host TCP/IP configuration dialog boxes. Enabling DHCP on the client host does not automatically clear any preexisting values, although DHCP clears the IP address and subnet mask.

Planning a DHCP Implementation

As with all network services that you will use, you should plan the implementation of DHCP. There are a few conditions that must be met that will be covered in the next few sections.

Network Requirements

The following requirements must be met to implement Microsoft TCP/IP using DHCP:

▶ The DHCP server service must be running on a Windows NT server.

▶ The DHCP server must have a manually configured IP address.

▶ A DHCP server must be located on the same subnet as the DHCP clients, or the clients subnet must have a DHCP relay agent running, or the routers connecting the two subnets involved must be able to forward DHCP (BOOTP) datagrams.

▶ Pools of IP addresses known as *scopes* must be configured on the DHCP server.

It is easiest to implement DHCP with only one DHCP server on a subnet (local network segment). If more than one DHCP server is configured to provide addresses for a subnet then either could provide the address—there is no way to specify with server to use such as you can in WINS (Windows Internet Name Service). Because DHCP servers do not communicate with each other, a DHCP server has no way of knowing if an IP address is leased to a client from another DHCP server.

To prevent two DHCP servers from assigning the same IP address to two clients, you must ensure that each IP address is made available in a scope on only one DHCP server on the internetwork. In other words, the IP address scopes cannot overlap or contain the same IP addresses.

If no DHCP server is available to lease an IP address to a DHCP client—due to hardware problems, for example—the client cannot initialize. For this reason, you may want to have a second DHCP server, with unique IP address scopes, on the network. This scenario works best when the second DHCP server is on a different subnet connected by a router that forwards DHCP datagrams.

A DHCP client accepts the first IP address offer it receives from a DHCP server. This address would normally be from the DHCP server on the local network because the IP address request broadcast would reach the local DHCP server first. However, if the local DHCP server is not responding, and if the DHCP broadcasts were forwarded by the router, the DHCP client could accept a lease offer from a DHCP server on a remote network.

Finally, the DHCP server must have one or more scopes created by using the DHCP Server Manager application (Start, Programs, Administrative Tools, DHCP Manager). A *scope* is a range of IP addresses available for lease by DHCP clients; for example, 200.20.5.1 through 200.20.5.20 may be a scope for a given subnet, and 200.20.6.1 through 200.20.6.50 may be a scope for another subnet.

Installing the DHCP Relay Agent

 Essentially, the job of the DHCP relay agent is to forward DHCP broadcast messages between DHCP enabled clients and DHCP servers, across IP routers. The relay agent can be configure on any NT Server computer and adds very little load. The section deals with installing and configuring the DHCP relay agent.

 The DCHP relay agent that comes with NT 4.0 is a new service that will listen for DHCP broadcasts and forward them to one or more configured DHCP servers. This is different from an RFC1542 compliant router in that the system running the relay agent is not a router. The DHCP relay agent is similar to a WINS proxy agent—discussed in Chapter 15.

1. Open the Network configuration dialog box and select the Services tab.

2. Select Add and from the list that appears, select the DHCP relay agent. Click OK and when prompted, enter the path to the distribution files.

3. Click the Protocols tab and double-click the TCP/IP protocol.

4. On the DHCP Relay tab enter the IP address of a DHCP server and the maximum number of hops and seconds that the relay can take.

5. Close the TCP/IP configuration dialog box and the Network configuration dialog box.

6. Restart the computer when prompted.

Client Requirements

A Microsoft TCP/IP DHCP client can be any of the following Microsoft TCP/IP clients:

▶ Windows NT server 3.5 or later that is not a DHCP server

▶ Windows NT Workstation 3.5 or later

▶ Windows 95

▶ Windows for Workgroups 3.11 running the Microsoft TCP/IP-32 software from the Windows NT Server CD-ROM

▶ Microsoft Network Client for MS-DOS 3.0 from the Windows NT Server CD-ROM

▶ LAN Manager server for MS-DOS 2.2c from the Windows NT server CD-ROM

If some clients on the network do not use DHCP for IP address configuration—because they do not support DHCP or otherwise need to have TCP/IP manually configured—the IP addresses of these non-DHCP clients must not be made available for lease to the DHCP clients. Non-DHCP clients can include clients that do not support Microsoft DHCP (see the preceding list), and clients that must always use the same IP address, such as Windows Internet Name Service (WINS) servers, Domain Name Service (DNS) servers, and other DHCP servers.

⚠ Warning

You should not assign the addresses of servers (file and print, DNS, WINS, and so forth) by DHCP as the address could change. If you do you have to reconfigure the scope options every time one of these servers restarts.

Although you can use DHCP Manager to reserve an IP address for use by only a specific WINS or DNS server, this technique is not recommended. If a DHCP server with the proper address for these servers is not available on the network for some reason, the client is not assigned an IP address and cannot initialize TCP/IP.

(ᵠ) Tip

WINS servers, DNS servers, DHCP servers, multihomed IP routers, and any other computer that has its IP address specified in another host's TCP/IP configuration should have a static IP address. This method ensures that they always use the same IP address and that they can initialize even if the DHCP server is down.

The DHCP client must have DHCP enabled. For Windows NT and Windows 95, DHCP is enabled in the TCP/IP configuration dialog box by selecting "Obtain address automatically."

Using Multiple DHCP Servers

It is not recommended to have more than one DHCP server on a subnet because there is no way to control from which DHCP server a client receives an IP address lease. Any DHCP server that receives a client's DHCP request broadcast can send a DHCP offer to that client. The client accepts the first lease offer it receives from a DHCP server.

If more than one subnet exists on a network, it is generally recommended to have a DHCP server on each subnet. However, if the DHCP relay agent or routers that support the forwarding of BOOTP braodcasts are used then request for DHCP addresses can be handled by a single DHCP server.

A DHCP server has an IP address scope configured for each subnet to which it sends DHCP offers. If the DHCP server receives a relayed DHCP request from a remote subnet, it offers an IP address lease from the scope for that subnet. To ensure that a DHCP client can receive an IP address lease even if a DHCP server is not functioning, you should configure an IP address scope for a given subnet on more than one DHCP server. Thus, if a DHCP client cannot obtain a lease from the local DHCP server, the DHCP relay agent or router passes the request to a DHCP server on a remote network that can offer a DHCP lease to the client.

For example, consider a network with two subnets, each with a DHCP server, joined by a RFC 1542-compliant router. For this scenario, Microsoft recommends that each DHCP server contain approximately 75 percent of the available IP addresses for the subnet the DHCP server is on, and 25 percent of the available IP addresses for the remote subnet. Most of the IP addresses available for a subnet can be obtained from the local DHCP server. If the local DHCP server is unavailable, the remote DHCP server can offer a lease from the smaller range of IP addresses available from the scope on the remote DHCP server.

If the range of IP addresses available are 120.50.7.10 through 120.50.7.110 for Subnet A and 120.50.8.10 through 120.50.8.110 for Subnet B, you could configure the scopes on each DHCP server as follows:

Subnet	DHCP Server A	DHCP Server B
A	120.50.7.10 - 120.50.7.84	120.50.7.85 - 120.50.7.110
B	120.50.8.10 - 120.50.8.34	120.50.8.35 - 120.50.8.110

 **Warning**   You must ensure that no IP address is duplicated on another DHCP server. If two DHCP servers contain the same IP address, that IP address could potentially be leased to two DHCP clients at the same time. Therefore, IP address ranges must be split between multiple DHCP servers, as shown in the preceding example.

Using Scope Options

Each time a DHCP client initializes, it requests an IP address and subnet mask from the DHCP server. The server is configured with one or more scopes, each containing a range of valid IP addresses, the subnet mask for the internetwork, and additional optional DHCP client configuration information, known as scope options. For example, the default gateway for a subnet is often configured as a scope option for a given subnet. If any scope options are configured on the DHCP server, these are given to the DHCP client along with the IP address and subnet mask to be used by the client. The common scope options supported by Microsoft DHCP clients are shown in table 12.1.

Table 12.1

Scope Options Supported by Microsoft DHCP Clients

Scope Option	Option Number
Router	3
DNS server	6
DNS Domain Name	15
NetBIOS Name server (e.g. WINS)	44
NetBIOS Node Type	46
NetBIOS Scope ID	47

The Scope Options Configuration dialog box in the DHCP Manager application contains many other scope options (such as Time server) that can be sent to the clients along with the other TCP/IP configuration information. The Microsoft DHCP clients, however, ignore and discard all the scope option information except for the options listed in table 12.1.

Note It is possible to lease addresses to non-Microsoft clients, in this case you may have to add a client reservation. Then you will be able configure options for that single client.

How DHCP Works

DHCP client configuration is a four-part process, as follows:

1. When the DHCP client initializes, it broadcasts a request for an IP lease from a DHCP server called a DHCPDISCOVER.

2. All DHCP servers that receive the IP lease request respond to the DHCP client with an IP lease offer known as a DHCPOFFER. This includes DHCP servers on the local network and on remote networks when the relay agent is used or a router that passes BOOTP requests.

3. The DHCP client selects the first offer it receives and broadcasts an IP lease selection message specifying the IP address it has selected. This message is known as a DHCPREQUEST.

4. The DHCP server that offered the selected lease responds with a DHCP lease acknowledgment message known as a DHCPACK. The DHCP server then updates its DHCP database to show that the lease can no longer be offered to other DHCP clients. The DHCP servers offering leases that were not selected can offer those IP addresses in future lease offers.

DHCPACK Phase

After the server that offered the lease receives the DHCPREQUEST message, it checks its DHCP database to ensure that the IP address is still available. If the requested lease remains available, the DHCP server marks that IP address as being leased in its DHCP database and broadcasts a DHCPACK to acknowledge that the IP address has been leased to the DHCP client. The DHCPACK contains the same information as the DHCPOFFER sent, plus any optional DHCP information that has been configured for that scope as a scope option. If the requested lease is no longer available, the DHCP server broadcasts a DHCP negative acknowledgment (DHCPNACK) containing the DHCP client's hardware address. When the DHCP client receives a DHCPNACK, it must start the lease request process over with a DHCPDISCOVER message. After receiving a DHCPACK, the DHCP client can continue to initialize TCP/IP, and it updates its registry with the IP addressing information included with the lease. The client continues to use the leased IP address information until the command ipconfig/release is typed from a command prompt, or it receives a DHCPNACK from the DHCP server after unsuccessfully renewing its lease.

DHCP Lease Renewal

The DHCP client attempts to renew its IP address lease after 50 percent of its lease time has expired (or when manually requested to renew the lease by the ipconfig/renew command from a command prompt). To renew the lease, a DHCP client sends a DHCPREQUEST directly to the DHCP server that gave it the original lease. Again, the DHCPREQUEST contains the hardware address of the client and the requested IP address, but this time uses the DHCP server IP address for the destination and the DHCP client IP address for the source IP address in the datagram. If the DHCP server is available and the requested IP address is still available (has not been removed from the scope), the DHCP server responds by sending a DHCPACK directly to the DHCP client. If the server is available but the requested IP address is no longer in the configured scopes, a DHCPNACK is sent to the DHCP client, which then must start the lease process over with a DHCPDISCOVER. A DHCPNACK can be sent because of the following reasons.

▶ The IP address requested is no longer available because the lease has been manually expired on the server and has been given to another client.

▶ The IP address requested has been removed from the available scopes on the DHCP server.

▶ The DHCP client has been physically moved to another subnet that will use a different scope on the DHCP server for that subnet. Hence, the IP address changes to a valid IP address for the new subnet. If the server does not respond to the DHCPREQUEST sent after the lease is 50 percent expired, the DHCP client continues to use the original lease until it is seven-eighths expired (87.5 percent of the lease time has expired). Because this DHCPREQUEST is broadcast rather than directed to a particular DHCP server, any DHCP server can respond with a DHCPACK or DHCPNACK to renew or deny the lease.

Installing the DHCP Server Service

For an exercise covering this information, see end of chapter.

The DHCP server service can be installed on a computer running Microsoft TCP/IP and Windows NT Server version 3.5 or later. Exercise 6.1 demonstrates how to install the DHCP server service on a Windows NT Server 4.0 computer.

1. Open the Control Panel and double-click the Network icon.

2. From the Network settings dialog box, choose the services tab, click Add.

3. Choose the Microsoft DHCP Service from the list that appears and click OK. When prompted, enter the directory for the NT source files.

4. Click close on the Network settings dialog box and when prompted restart your computer.

The DHCP server must have a manually configured IP address, subnet mask, and default gateway. It cannot be assigned an address from another DHCP server, even if an address is reserved for the DHCP server.

Configuring the DHCP Server

After a DHCP server has been installed on an internetwork, you need to configure the following items:

▶ One or more IP address scopes (ranges of IP addresses to be leased) must be defined on the DHCP server.

▶ Non-DHCP client IP addresses must be excluded from the defined scopes.

▶ The options for the scope must be configured, for example, the default gateway for a subnet.

▶ IP address reservations for DHCP clients requiring a specific IP address to be assigned must be created.

▶ The DHCP clients must have automatic DHCP configuration enabled and should have unwanted manually configured TCP/IP parameters deleted.

Each of these is discussed in the following sections.

Creating Scopes

For an exercise covering this information, see end of chapter.

For a DHCP server to lease IP addresses to the DHCP clients, a range of valid IP addresses for those clients must be configured on the DHCP server. Each range of IP addresses is called a *scope*. One scope must be configured on the server for each subnet the DHCP server provides IP address leases to. The DHCP server is normally configured with a scope for the local subnet (the subnet the DHCP server is on) and, optionally, with a scope for each remote subnet that it will provide addresses for. The benefits of configuring scopes for remote subnets on a DHCP server are as follows:

▶ **The DHCP server can provide IP address leases to clients on remote subnets.** This feature is especially useful as a backup in case another DHCP server is not available. If no DHCP server is available with an IP address lease for a DHCP client, the client cannot initialize TCP/IP. To prevent this, you may want to have more than one DHCP server that can provide a DHCP client with a lease. You must ensure, however, that the scopes on each DHCP server have unique IP address ranges so that no duplicate IP addresses are on the internetwork.

▶ **You can create separate scope options for each subnet.** For example, each subnet would have a different default gateway that can be configured individually for each scope. After installing the DHCP server and restarting the computer, you must create an IP address scope. The following list demonstrates the creation of a scope. To perform this exercise, you must have the DHCP server service installed and running as shown in above. You should also know a range of IP addresses that you can use to create a DHCP scope, as well as the IP addresses that should be excluded out of that range.

The following list provides the steps that are required to configure a scope on the DHCP server.

1. Start the DHCP Manager (Start, Programs, Administrative Tools, DHCP Manager).

2. Select the local DHCP server "Local Machine" by clicking the entry, and then choose Create from the Scope menu item. The Create Scope dialog box is displayed. (Note: This will happen automatically the first time you run the DHCP Manager).

3. Type the starting and ending IP addresses for the first subnet in the Start Address and the End Address fields of the IP Address Pool.

4. Type the Subnet Mask for this scope in the Subnet Mask field.

5. If required, type a single IP address or a range of IP addresses to be excluded from the IP. The IP address that is not used in the Address Pool in the Exclusion Range Start Address scope is added to the Excluded Addresses list. Choose Add. Repeat if required.

 **Warning**

If any hosts are not using DHCP but have an IP address that falls within the IP address pool, the IP addresses of these hosts must be excluded from the scope. If the IP address is not excluded, DHCP does not know that the IP address is already in use and might assign the IP address to a DHCP client, causing a duplicate IP address on the network. If you want certain DHCP clients to use a specific IP address out of the scope, you can assign this address from the Add Reservations dialog box as described later in this section.

6. If you do not want the IP address leases to expire, select the Unlimited option under Lease Duration (if you do this then the configuration of the client will never be updated). If you want to force the DHCP clients to renew their leases periodically (to ensure that the client is still using the IP address), choose the Limited To: option and type the lease duration in days, hours, and minutes. By default, the Lease Duration is three days. If you have a large ratio of available IP addresses to hosts on the network, you may want to use a longer lease duration to reduce broadcast traffic. If hosts are regularly coming and going and changing subnets on the network,

such as with laptops and docking stations, you want a relatively short lease duration so the DHCP server recovers previously used IP addresses fairly quickly.

7. In the Name field, type the name to be used for referring to the scope in the DHCP Manager, for example, **subnet 200.20.1.0**.

8. In the Comment field, type an optional descriptive comment for the scope, for example, **Third floor – west side**.

Scope Options

For an exercise covering this information, see end of chapter.

Each DHCP scope can have several options set that are configured on the client along with the IP address, such as default gateway and WINS server addresses. DHCP Manager includes many scope options that can be configured and sent to the DHCP clients; it should be noted that if TCP/IP configuration has been manually entered, then the options (other than IP address and subnet mask) will be ignored by the client.

Two types of DHCP scope options are available:

▶ Global options, which are set for all scopes in the DHCP Manager

▶ Scope options, which are set for a selected scope in the DHCP Manager

The value set in a scope option overrides a value set for the same DHCP option in a global option. Any values manually configured on the DHCP client—through the Network Control Panel applet Microsoft TCP/IP Configuration dialog box, for example—override any DHCP configured options.

The following list outlines how to view and define global options for a DHCP server.

1. Start the DHCP Manager tool.

2. Choose either Scope or Global from the DHCP Options menu.

3. Configure the DHCP options required following these steps.

   1. From the unused Options list, select an option and click Add. The option is added to the Active Options list.

   2. Choose Value, the value for the option will now be displayed.

   3. You can now edit the value. There are three types of values that can be edited. Strings (such as Domain name), which you can simply enter. Hexadecimal values (such as NetBIOS node type), which you can enter. And finally IP address ranges—for these you click Edit Array and another dialog box appears allowing you to enter one or more IP addresses.

4. When all the required options are entered, click OK and exit the DHCP manager.

Address Reservations

For an exercise covering this information, see end of chapter.

If a DHCP client requires a specific IP address to be assigned to it each time it renews its IP address lease, that IP address can be reserved for the DHCP client through the DHCP Manager tool. Following are examples of clients that should have an IP address reservation:

▶ Servers on a network with non-WINS-enabled clients. If a server on such a network does not always lease the same IP address, the non-WINS clients might not be able to connect to the servers using NetBIOS over TCP/IP (NetBT).

▶ Any other host that is expected to have a specific IP address that hosts use to connect to.

The following list outlines how to reserve an IP address from a scope for a specific DHCP client.

1. Determine the hardware address for the DHCP client with the IP address to be reserved from the scope. This can be done by typing **ipconfig/all** at a client's command prompt. A sample ipconfig/all output is shown here:

```
Ethernet adapter NDISLoop1:
        Description . . . . . . . . : MS LoopBack Driver
        Physical Address. . . . . . : 20-4C-4F-4F-50-20
        DHCP Enabled. . . . . . . . : No
        IP Address. . . . . . . . . : 200.20.1.30
        Subnet Mask . . . . . . . . : 255.255.255.0
        Default Gateway . . . . . . : 200.20.1.1
```

2. Start the DHCP Manager, and select the DHCP server to be configured.

3. Select the scope containing the IP address to be reserved.

4. Choose Add Reservations from the Scope menu. The Add Reserved Clients dialog box is displayed.

5. In the IP Address field, type the IP address to be reserved for the DHCP client.

6. In the Unique Identifier field, type the hardware address of the network card for the IP address used. The hardware address should be typed without hyphens (-).

7. In the Client Name field, type a name for the client to be used only in DHCP Manager. This value is purely descriptive and does not affect the client in any way.

8. In the Client Comments field, optionally type any comments for the client reservation.

9. Choose Add. The reservation is enabled.

10. Choose Active Leases from the Scope menu of DHCP Manager. The Active Leases dialog box is displayed and the reservations are shown.

DHCP Clients

For a client to use DHCP to obtain IP address information, automatic DHCP configuration must be enabled at the client. The procedure is slightly different for Windows NT and Windows for Workgroups clients.

Windows NT and Windows 95 as DHCP Clients

You can enable Automatic DHCP configuration either before or after Microsoft TCP/IP is installed. To ensure that the DHCP TCP/IP parameters are used instead of any configured manually on the host, you should preferably enable automatic DHCP configuration before Microsoft TCP/IP is installed. To enable automatic DHCP configuration after TCP/IP is installed, follow these steps.

1. Double-click the Network icon in Control Panel. The Network settings dialog box will be displayed.

2. Select the Protocols tab. From the list of installed protocols, select TCP/IP and choose the Properties button. The TCP/IP configuration dialog box appears.

3. Select the Enable Automatic DHCP Configuration check box. The previous IP address and subnet mask values disappear. Ensure that all other configuration parameters you want DHCP to supply are cleared.

4. Close the TCP/IP configuration dialog box and the Network setting dialog box. Restart the system when prompted.

Windows for Workgroups as a DHCP Client

Configuring Windows for Workgroups as a DHCP client is simple.

1. Double-click the Network Setup icon in the Network program group of the Windows for Workgroups client.

2. Choose the Drivers button, select Microsoft TCP/IP- and choose the Setup button. The TCP/IP Configuration dialog box is displayed.

3. Select the Enable Automatic DHCP Configuration check box, and choose Continue. The dialog box closes and you are prompted to restart the computer.

4. Do not configure any other parameters, unless you want to override the options set in the DHCP scope, which is not recommended.

Using the **IPCONFIG** Utility

The IPCONFIG command-line utility is installed with Microsoft TCP/IP for Windows NT and Windows for Workgroups clients. This command-line utility and diagnostic tool can be used to

▶ Display detailed information about a computer

▶ Renew a DHCP IP address lease

▶ Release a DHCP IP address lease

Displaying Information

To display concise TCP/IP information about the local host, type **ipconfig** at a command prompt. This entry displays the IP address, subnet mask, and default gateway for each network interface card on the local host that uses TCP/IP. The following is an example of output displayed after ipconfig is typed from a command prompt:

```
C:\>ipconfig

Windows NT IP Configuration
Ethernet adapter NDISLoop1:
        IP Address. . . . . . . . . : 200.20.1.30
        Subnet Mask . . . . . . . . : 255.255.255.0
        Default Gateway . . . . . . : 200.20.1.1
```

For more detailed information, you can run the ipconfig/all command from a command prompt. The ipconfig/all command lists the following bits of information for each network interface card on the local host that is bound to TCP/IP:

▶ The Domain Name Service (DNS) host name, appended to the DNS domain name if one is configured

▶ The IP address of any DNS servers configured

▶ The NetBIOS name resolution node type, such as broadcast (b-node), hybrid (h-node), peer-to-peer (p-node), or mixed (m-node)

- ▶ The NetBIOS scope ID

- ▶ Whether IP Routing is enabled between two network interface cards, if on a multihomed computer

- ▶ Whether this host acts as a WINS proxy agent for non-WINS clients

- ▶ Whether NetBT on this host uses DNS for NetBIOS name resolution

Also, for each network interface card bound to TCP/IP on the host, ipconfig/all displays the following:

- ▶ A description of the type or model of network card

- ▶ The hardware or physical address of the network card

- ▶ Whether DHCP is enabled for automatic IP address configuration for the network card

- ▶ The IP address of the network card

- ▶ The subnet mask for the network card

- ▶ The default gateway for the network card

- ▶ The IP address for the primary WINS server for the network card, if configured

- ▶ The IP address for the secondary WINS server for the network card, if configured

The following example shows output after you type **ipconfig/all** at a command prompt:

```
C:\>ipconfig/all

Windows NT IP Configuration
        Host Name . . . . . . . . . : binky.gopherit.com
        DNS servers . . . . . . . . : 200.20.16.122
        Node Type . . . . . . . . . : Hybrid
        NetBIOS Scope ID. . . . . . :
        IP Routing Enabled. . . . . : No
```

```
                        WINS Proxy Enabled. . . . . : No
                        NetBIOS Resolution Uses DNS : Yes
Ethernet adapter NDISLoop1:
                        Description . . . . . . . . : MS LoopBack Driver
                        Physical Address. . . . . . : 20-4C-4F-4F-50-20
                        DHCP Enabled. . . . . . . . : No
                        IP Address. . . . . . . . . : 200.20.1.30
                        Subnet Mask . . . . . . . . : 255.255.255.0
                        Default Gateway . . . . . . : 200.20.1.1
                        Primary WINS server . . . . : 16.255.1.50
```

Renewing a Lease

The ipconfig/renew command, typed at a command prompt, causes the DHCP client immediately to attempt to renew its IP address lease with a DHCP server. The DHCP client sends a DH-CPREQUEST message to the DHCP server to receive a new lease duration and any options that have been updated or added to the scope. If a DHCP server does not respond, the DHCP client continues to use the current lease information.

The ipconfig/renew command is usually performed after scope options or scope address information has been changed on the DHCP server and you want the DHCP client to have these changes immediately.

By default, the ipconfig/renew command renews all leases for each network adapter on a multihomed computer. To renew the lease for only a specific network adapter, type **ipconfig/renew <adapter>**, where <adapter> is the specific adapter name.

Releasing a Lease

You can type the ipconfig/release command at a command prompt to have the DHCP client advise the DHCP server that it no longer needs the IP address lease. The DHCP client sends a DHCPRELEASE message to the DHCP server to have the lease marked as released in the DHCP database.

The ipconfig/release command is usually performed when the administrator wants the DHCP client to give up its lease, and possibly use a different lease. For example, the DHCP client's IP address can be reserved for another host or deleted from the DHCP database scope, and then the ipconfig/release command can be run to have the DHCP client give up that IP address lease and be forced to receive a different lease.

By default, the ipconfig/release command releases all leases for each network adapter on a multihomed computer. To release the lease for only a specific network adapter, type the **ipconfig/release <adapter>** command, where <adapter> is the specific adapter name.

Compacting the DHCP Database

Entries in the DHCP database are continually being added, modified, and deleted throughout the IP address leasing process. When entries are deleted, the space is not always completely filled with a new entry, due to the different sizes of each entry. After some time, the database contains unused space that can be recovered by compacting the database. This process is analogous to defragmenting a disk drive.

Microsoft recommends compacting the DHCP database from once every month to once every week, depending on the size of the internetwork. This compaction increases transaction speed and reduces the disk space used by the database.

The jetpack utility compacts the DHCP database (DHCP.mdb) into a temporary database, which is then automatically copied to DHCP.mdb and deleted. The command used is jetpack DHCP.mdb temp_name.mdb, where temp_name.mdb is any file name specified by the user, with extension .mdb.

The following shows how to compact the DHCP database:

1. Stop the DHCP server service by using the Control Panel, Server Manager, or a command prompt.

2. To stop the service from a command prompt, type **net stop dhcpserver service**. This stops the DHCP server.

3. Type **cd \systemroot\system32\dhcp**, where systemroot is
   WINNT35. This changes to the DHCP directory.

4. Type **jetpack dhcp.mdb temp.mdb**. This compacts dhcp.mdb
   into temp.mdb, then copies it back to dhcp.mdb, and automatically deletes temp.mdb.

5. Type **net start dhcpserver**. This restarts the DHCP server
   service.

Backing Up the DHCP Database

By default, the DHCP database is automatically backed up at a
specific interval. You can change the default interval by editing
the DHCP server BackupInterval parameter value contained in
the Registry.

```
SYSTEM\current\currentcontrolset\services\DHCPServer\Parameters
```

Backing up the DHCP database enables recovery from a system
crash or DHCP database corruption.

You can change the default backup interval of 15 minutes by performing the following steps:

1. Stop the DHCP server service from a command prompt by
   typing **net stop dhcpserver**.

2. Start the Registry Editor (REGEDT32.EXE).

3. Open the HKEY_LOCAL_MACHINE\SYSTEM\
   CurrentControlSet\Services\DHCPserver\Parameters key,
   and select BackupInterval.

4. In the Radix, make a selection, and configure the entry to
   the desired value. Close the Registry Editor.

5. Restart the DHCP server service from a command prompt by
   typing **net start dhcpserver**.

Restoring a Corrupt DHCP Database

If the DHCP database becomes corrupt, it can be restored from a backup in one of the following ways:

- ▶ It can be restored automatically.

- ▶ You can use the RestoreFlag key in the Registry.

- ▶ You can manually replace the corrupt database file.

Automatic Restoration

The DHCP server service automatically restores the backed-up copy of the database if it detects a corrupt database. If the database has become corrupt, stop and restart the DHCP server service. You can do this by typing **net stop dhcpserver** and then **net start dhcpserver** at a command prompt.

Registry RestoreFlag

If a corrupt DHCP database is not automatically restored from a backup when the DHCP server service is started, you can force the database to be restored by setting the RestoreFlag key in the Registry. To do this, perform the following tasks:

1. Stop the DHCP server service from a command prompt by typing **net stop dhcpserver**.

2. Start the Registry Editor (REGEDT32.EXE).

3. Open the HKEY_LOCAL_MACHINE\SYSTEM\ CurrentControlSet\Services\DHCPserver\Parameters key, and select RestoreFlag.

4. Change the value to **1** in the data field, and choose OK. Close the Registry Editor.

5. Restart the DHCP server service from a command prompt by typing **net start dhcpserver**. The database is restored from the backup, and the RestoreFlag entry in the Registry automatically resets to 0.

Copying from the Backup Directory

You can manually replace the corrupt database file with a backed-up version by performing the following tasks:

1. Stop the DHCP server service from a command by typing **net stop dhcpserver**.

2. Change to the DHCP directory by typing **cd \systemroot\ system32\dhcp\backup\jet**, where systemroot is WINNT, for example.

3. Copy the contents of the directory to the \systemroot\ system32\DHCP directory.

4. Type **net start dhcpserver** from a command prompt to re-start the DHCP server service.

Exercises

Exercise 12.1:   Installing the DHCP Server

In this exercise, you will install the DHCP service.

1. Open the Networking Setting dialog box, and choose Add from the Services tab.

2. Select Microsoft DHCP Server and click OK.

3. Enter the path for your Windows NT source files. Close the Network Setting dialog box and restart your computer.

4. From the Start menu, choose Programs, Administrative Tools. Verify that the DHCP Manager is installed.

Exercise 12.2:   Configuring a DHCP Scope

In this exercise, you will configure a scope on the DHCP server.

1. Start the DHCP Manager. Double-click the Local Machine to ensure you are connected to it.

2. Choose Scope, Create from the menu. The Create Scope dialog box appears.

3. Enter the following information for the IP Address Pool:

   Start Address   148.53.66.1

   End Address   148.53.127.254

   Subnet Mask   255.255.192.0

4. To add an Exclusion enter 148.53.90.0 into the Start Address and 148.53.90.255 in to the End Address. Click the Add button.

5. Leave the duration at default, and enter "Test Subnet 1" as the Name. Click OK.

6. You will be prompted to activate the scope; choose Yes.

Exercise 12.3: Adding Scope and Global Options in the DHCP Server

Now you will add options to the scope you configured.

1. Click the scope that was create in the previous exercise.

Note If you get an error click OK to continue, this is an undocument-ed feature (a bug). Close the DHCP Manager and reopen it to stop this.

2. From the menu choose DHCP Options, Scope.

3. From the list of Unused Options, choose 003 Router and click Add.

4. Click on the Values button to see the rest of the dialog box. Currently there is no router listed.

5. Choose Edit Array. In the dialog box that appears, enter 148.53.64.1 in the IP Address field. Click Add to add the address to the list.

6. Choose OK to close the IP Address Array Editor, and then choose OK to close the DHCP Options: Scope dialog box.

   The router option should appear in the Options Configuration panel.

7. Choose DHCP Options, Global from the menu, and add the following options:

   006 DNS Servers

   015 Domain Name

   044 WINS/NBNS Servers (You will get a message when you add this one.)

   046 WINS/NBT Node Type

8. Add the configuration for these options, using the following values:

DNS Server	148.53.64.8
Domain Name	scrimtech.com
WINS/NBNS Servers	198.53.64.8
WINS/NBT Node Type	0x8

9. Click OK.

Exercise 12.4:   Configuring a Second DHCP Scope

In this exercise, you will configure a second scope of addresses.

1. Add anther DHCP scope using the following values:

IP Address Pool

Start Address	148.53.140.0
End Address	148.53.191.255
Subnet Mask	255.255.192.0

2. Set the lease duration for 14 days, and the name the scope "Test Subnet 2."

There should be a number listed for each scope in the DHCP Manager. The number given is the subnet ID for the scope. This scenario used a Class B address, which is split into two subnets: 148.53.64.0 and 148.53.128.0.

3. Set the default gateway for this scope to 148.53.128.1.

4. This scope will not be used immediately, therefore you will deactivate it by choosing Scope, Deactivate.

Exercise 12.5:   Adding Client Reservations

Finally, you will add a client reservation.

1. Highlight the first subnet (148.53.64.0).

2. Choose Scope, Add Reservations from the menu.

3. In the Add Reserved Clients dialog box, change the IP address to 148.53.66.7.

4. Enter the unique identifier, 0000DE7342FA, and enter the client name as Rob.

5. Click Add.

6. Enter the IP address 148.53.66.9, with the unique identifier 00D4C9C57D34. The client name is Judy. Click add.

7. Choose Done.

Review Questions

1. Which of the following is not one of the five possible broadcasts in the DHCP process?

   A. DHCPNACK

   B. DHCPOFFER

   C. DHCPDISCOVER

   D. DHCPLEASE

2. Before a client can receive a DHCP address, what must be configured on the DHCP server?

   A. The DHCP relay agent

   B. A scope for the clients subnet

   C. A scope for the servers subnet

   D. A host name

3. What must a router support in order to pass DHCP broadcasts?

   A. RFC 1543

   B. BOOTP Relay

   C. RFC 1544

   D. This cannot be done

4. What is the recommended method of providing backup to the DHCP server?

   A. Configure two DHCP servers with the same scope

   B. Configure a BOOTP server

   C. Replicate the database using directory replication

   D. Configure two DHCP servers with different sections of the scope

5. What is the effect of a lease duration of unlimited?

    A. DHCP configuration options will never be update.

    B. There is no effect.

    C. There will be an increase in network traffic.

    D. Addresses cannot be shared dynamically.

6. In what environment is it advisable to have a short lease duration?

    A. In static environments where addresses don't change often

    B. When you have fewer hosts than IP addresses

    C. In environments where you have hosts moving and many changes to IP addresses

    D. When you have more hosts than IP addresses

7. What portions of the DHCP process are initiated by the server?

    A. Lease acquisition

    B. Lease renewal

    C. Lease release

    D. No processes are initiated by the server

8. How must an NT Server be configured before you install a DHCP server?

    A. The WINS server must be installed.

    B. The server requires a static IP configuration.

    C. TCP/IP must not be installed.

    D. None of the above.

9. What information is required to define a scope?

    A. Starting and ending address and the subnet mask

    B. Subnet ID and the number of addresses to lease

    C. Number of hosts to be leased

    D. The name of the scope

10. Which clients cannot use a DHCP server?

    A. MS LAN Manager for DOS 2.2c

    B. Windows NT Workstation

    C. MS LAN Manager for OS/2 2.2c

    D. Windows 95

11. How do you configure a client to use DHCP?

    A. Install the DHCP client service

    B. Select automatic configuration icon from the Control Panel

    C. DHCP automatically configures all clients

    D. Select Obtain IP address automatically in the TCP/IP configuration

12. What is the difference between a global and a scope option?

    A. Global options affect all system on the network whether DHCP clients or not.

    B. Scope options are set in the DHCP manager for individual scopes.

    C. Global options affect the clients on scopes where no scope options are configured.

    D. There is no difference in the options, just in how they are entered.

13. Why would you use a client reservation?

    A. To provide dynamic configuration of TCP/IP options with a static IP address.

    B. To be able to control all the IP addresses.

    C. This is required for any host that that cannot be a DHCP client but that uses an address in the scopes range.

    D. You cannot reserve addresses.

14. What is required for a client reservation?

    A. The NetBIOS name of the client

    B. The host name of the client

    C. The MAC address of the client

15. What happens to the client if you delete their lease?

    A. They immediately stop using the address.

    B. The will not be able to initialize at next startup.

    C. Nothing until they attempt to renew the address.

    D. The host will stop working.

Review Answers

1. D

2. B

3. B

4. D

5. A

6. C

7. D

8. B

9. A

10. C

11. D

12. B

13. A

14. C

15. C

Answers to the Test Yourself Questions at the Beginning of the Chapter

1. The IP address and subnet mask are no longer used when the Enable Automatic DHCP Configuration check box is selected.

2. The following are benefits of using DHCP:
   ► The administrator can quickly verify the IP address and other configuration parameters without having to check each host individually.
   ► DHCP does not lease the same IP address from a scope to two different hosts at the same time.
   ► The DHCP administrator controls which IP addresses are used by which hosts.
   ► Clerical and typing errors can be reduced.
   ► Multiple scope options can be set reducing the amount of manual configuration.
   ► An IP address may be leased for a limited time.
   ► A host can be automatically reconfigured when it moves to a different subnet.

3. These are the extra steps that should be taken after two DHCP servers have been installed on a subnet:
   ► You must ensure that the IP address ranges on each DHCP do not overlap. A given IP address must not be in a scope on more than one DHCP server in an internetwork.
   ► You should consider having the DHCP servers on separate subnets connected by a router configured as a DHCP relay agent.

4. To use a router on an internetwork that will enable a DHCP client to communicate with a DHCP server on a remote subnet, the router must possess the following characteristics:
   ► It must support RFC 1542.
   ► It must be configured to forward BOOTP packets between the subnets.

5. To ensure that DHCP does not assign an IP address that is already in use by a non-DHCP client, the non-DHCP client IP address should be excluded from that subnet's scope.

6. Yes, it is possible for two DHCP clients on an internetwork to lease the same IP address—if each received its lease from a different DHCP server and the DHCP server scopes contained overlapping IP addresses.

7. The DHCP client might still have a manually configured default gateway that is no longer correct.

8. Only one DHCP server is required, although it is usually recommended that each subnet have a DHCP server. Having one DHCP server on each subnet reduces DHCP lease broadcasts that have to be broadcast on a remote subnet. The DHCP servers can also be configured with ranges of unallocated IP addresses for each other's subnets so that another DHCP server can lease a DHCP client an IP address if the DHCP server on that client's subnet is unavailable. You must, however, ensure that the IP address scopes do not overlap so that any given IP address is found in only one scope on the internetwork.

9. You can select the Enable Automatic DHCP Configuration check box before or after Microsoft TCP/IP is installed and configured.

Chapter 13

NetBIOS Over TCP/IP

This chapter will help you prepare for the exam by covering the following objectives:

 Objectives

- ▶ Configure HOSTS and LMHOSTS

- ▶ Diagnose and resolve name resolution problems

STOP

Test Yourself! Before reading this chapter, test yourself to determine how much study time you will need to devote to this section.

1. What Winsock ports are used for NetBIOS communications?

2. Which node type(s) use a NetBIOS Name Server as the primary means of name resolution?

3. In all NetBIOS name resolution node types, which method of name resolution is first tried?

4. Describe the three main functions of NetBIOS.

5. What is an SMB?

6. Assuming Hybrid node resolution, in what order are the methods of name resolution attempted?

7. For what is the 16th character of the NetBIOS name used?

8. What is the use of the #BEGIN ALTERNATE tag in the LMHOSTS file?

9. In what scenario are you required to use the #DOM tag in an LMHOSTS file?

10. In what two ways can you configure a client to use a NetBIOS Name Server?

Answers are located at the end of the chapter.

Defining NetBIOS

Microsoft has been using NetBIOS for the upper layers of their networking architecture for years. This chapter looks at the NetBIOS standard and how it communicates. Mapping of NetBIOS functions to those found in TCP/IP also is discussed. This mapping is required for TCP/IP and any other network protocol installed in Windows NT so that the internal NetBIOS commands can traverse the network.

Although there are three main functions that need to be supported for NetBIOS to function—Name Management, Session Management and Data Transfer—there will be much emphasis given to the Name Management in this chapter. This is the key issue in using NetBIOS over TCP/IP because TCP/IP uses IP addressing, whereas NetBIOS uses computer names. The other functions present in NetBIOS are already present in TCP/IP.

NetBIOS is a networking standard based on the OSI (Open System Interconnect) model—also known as the seven-layer model. When referencing the OSI model, NetBIOS as implemented in Windows NT provides the services required for the top three layers: application, presentation, and session.

The application layer interacts with user programs (for example, Windows NT Explorer or Microsoft Word) and handles network access for those programs. When the application layer receives a request for network access, it turns the request into an SMB (Server Message Block). An SMB is a unit of work that tells the system at the other end what the user on this system wants to do (for example, read a file from the network). SMBs are considered Protocol Data Units (PDUs) and as such perform the work of moving requests and data between systems. All the other layers in the protocol stack simply serve to move the SMB from one system to another system.

After the SMB has been generated, the presentation layer prepares to deliver the information to the correct computer. This requires the services of the session layer, which creates or uses a session with the remote computer to deliver the information. In some cases (broadcasts), a session is not required. The presentation layer checks to see whether a session is required for the transmission—and, if a session is required, whether one already exists. If a session does not exist, the presentation layer uses the services of the session layer to create a session with the remote host. The presentation layer can then generate an NCB (Network Control Block) that tells the underlying layer what to do with the SMB (which is now the data to be transferred).

The session layer receives the NCB and acts on it normally by sending the data to the remote host. As already mentioned, the session layer is responsible for creating and terminating sessions with other hosts, as well as for controlling the flow of data. By using sessions, Windows NT adds a layer of security because the user's credentials (access token) are checked and verified when the session is created. In addition, sessions enables extra checking of the information flowing across the network to verify that it has arrived in good order.

NetBIOS Over TCP/IP (NBT)

When the OSI networking model, of which NetBIOS is a part, is compared to the TCP/IP networking model, it is essential to understand that the first layer in the TCP/IP stack is also the application layer. However, it encompasses the functions of the top three layers of the OSI model (see fig. 13.1). Because this is also where NetBIOS resides in the OSI model, some method is required to map the NetBIOS functions to the TCP/IP functions. Sitting between the TCP/IP application layer and the Transport layer is the Winsock interface. Winsock provides end points for communications. For example, to connect to a Web site, you call an IP address, protocol, and port number (for instance, 199.45.92.97:TCP:80 is a Web page address). The port number is the Winsock port on which the requested service lives.

Figure 13.1

Comparing the TCP/IP model to the OSI model.

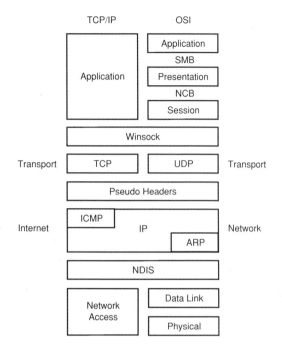

Therefore, for NetBIOS to function over TCP/IP, NetBIOS needs to use ports. Three ports have been assigned to NetBIOS on which to send information and listen for incoming traffic. Table 13.1 lists the three NetBIOS ports that are used.

Table 13.1

NetBIOS Port Numbers and Protocols			
Service	Nickname	Port	Protocol
NetBIOS Name Service	nbname	137	UDP
NetBIOS Datagram Service	Nbdatagram	138	UDP
NetBIOS Session Service	Nbsession	139	TCP

As shown in table 13.1, the ports for the NetBIOS Name Service and the NetBIOS Datagram Service use UDP (User Datagram Protocol). This means that no session is required to transmit information. NetBIOS is based heavily on broadcasts. This system dates to the time when NetBIOS was developed; the networks were smaller and typically only one segment, so broadcasts worked well. As this discussion on NetBIOS continues, you will discover that using broadcasts now represents a major problem.

Note

Most routers are configured not to forward broadcasts on ports 137 and 138 (although they can pass directed transmissions). NetBIOS uses broadcasts for many functions and the amount of broadcast traffic can congest routers. This can cause problems because functions such as domain validation and browser services require the use of broadcasts. These problems are addressed in Chapter 16, "IP Internetwork Browsing and Domain Functions."

NetBIOS Services

As previously established, Windows NT uses NetBIOS internally, and any protocol (not just TCP/IP) that works with NT must have some means of translating NetBIOS to a native format. You have already seen that three ports are used: 137, 138, and 139. This section looks at the NetBIOS services and maps them to TCP/IP services and the port numbers indicated.

Three main services need to be handled by the protocol to enable communications over the network. There is a requirement to find the remote computer, because NetBIOS uses computer names rather than IP addresses; this is probably the most critical service in enabling NetBIOS to function over TCP/IP. Name resolution is handled on port 137, which is the NetBIOS Name Service port.

Another function that needs to be handled by an underlying protocol (such as TCP/IP) is Session Management. NetBIOS creates a session with a remote computer when it wants to communicate. As previously noted, this provides better security because the user has to be identified, and also enables extra checking in the transfer of large files. TCP also has the capability to create a session (by use of the three-way handshake). Creating a NetBIOS session, therefore, first creates a TCP session that provides base-level communications. This requires TCP and therefore uses the Net-BIOS Session port, which is TCP port 139, as listed in table 13.1.

The last—and for users, most important—function is the capability to transfer data from one system to another (whether it is a print job going to the printer, or a file being saved on the network). Two types of Data Transfer are available to NetBIOS and therefore must be available in the underlying protocol: connection-oriented (for transferring files, and so on) and connectionless (for broadcasts, logon requests, and so forth). The first uses the services of a session, and therefore uses TCP and the NetBIOS session port (139). Connectionless transfer simply sends the information and doesn't care if the information is received; this suits the UDP transport protocol. As you may have guessed, connectionless transfers use the NetBIOS Datagram Service on UDP port 138.

As you can see, most of the functions map out easily. Session Management is a natural for TCP. Data Transfer is a basic network function, and TCP/IP already has connection-oriented and connectionless transfer methods available. The only function of NetBIOS that does not translate well is Name Management. Unfortunately, neither of the other functions works without the capability to resolve a NetBIOS name to a TCP/IP address.

Name Management

When a system is going to communicate with another computer on the network, some method of identifying the other computer is required. The identification is, of course, handled in the Net-BIOS world by the computer name (which can be up to 15 characters in length). When IBM and Microsoft developed the NetBIOS standard, fewer wide area networks (WANs) existed, and generally the local area networks (LANs) were small enough that they did not require the capability to be segmented. Generally, main frame and mini-computers were used when segmenting was required. Looking at other networking technologies, such as TCP/IP, that required computers to have numeric addresses, Microsoft and IBM decided that NetBIOS should use computer names to put a friendly face on the network because these could be resolved using broadcasts.

Because the identity of the system is the name, each name that you use for a computer must be unique on the network. However, as time has passed, networks became larger and it became desirable to group computers on the network and to be able to send information (messages) to users working on the computers. This lead to the requirement for multiple NetBIOS names. Currently, Windows NT enables you to register up to 250 NetBIOS names for any given computer. The common names that Windows NT registers are as follows:

▶ **Computer name.** This is the name that the computer uses on the network,; in all cases, this name must be unique. When a system starts and the name is already on the network, the networking portion of the system cannot initialize. (It is possible to duplicate a name in some multi-segment networks; however, the hosts can never communicate. This is because the name is checked on the local segment or on a NetBIOS Name Server).

▶ **User name.** The user name also is registered on the network. This enables the user to receive messages (such as printer notifications) that are sent to the user name. More than one instance of a user name can exist. However, only the first person to register the name receives messages; all other attempts to register that name fail until the person currently using the name shuts down. (The system continues to function correctly, but the user does not receive any messages.)

▶ **Workgroup or domain name.** This is a group name, and many different systems can register the name. This name is used to group computers into a single management area (a set of computers that are managed together).

Being as there are several different types of names, you may have more than one name registered on your computer. This is further complicated by the need to find a service that is running on a computer (for example, if you are trying to access network resources, the Workstation service in your system needs to communicate with the Server service on the remote system). If you think about sending a letter, simply addressing the letter to an apartment building does not get it to the person to whom you are writing. In the same way, sending an SMB to a computer does not guarantee that it reaches the correct service on the computer. Many services can use NetBIOS. The three most common services in Windows NT are as follows:

► **Server Service.** Provides the resources of your system for the other computers on the network to use

► **Workstation Service.** Enables you to use the services of another computer that is running the Server Service

► **Messenger Service.** Receives and displays messages for the names that are registered on your computer

As you can see, getting the information to the computer is half the battle. To make the network function, you need to connect to the correct service (end point). This means you require not only the name of the computer, but also the name that the service registered.

Thankfully, this is easy. When I noted previously that the names are 15 characters, I was referring to the portion you can enter. NetBIOS names are, in fact, 16 characters long; the last character identifies the service. Each service adds a 1-byte identifier to the end of the name when it is registered. The following is a list of some of the names that are registered and the services that they represent. (Note that the number the service uses is given in hexadecimal format—it is hard to see a space or a null in print.)

► **Computername[0x00].** The Workstation service on the computer being registered.

► **Computername[0x03].** The Messenger service registering on the computer.

► **Username[0x03].** The Messenger service registering the logged-on user on the network.

▶ **Computername[0x20].** The Server service registering the computer on the network.

▶ **Domainname[0x00].** Registers the computer as a member of the domain (or workgroup, as the case may be).

▶ **Domainname[0x1E].** Facilitates browser elections (also used in workgroup environments—browsing is covered in Chapter 16, "IP Internetwork Browsing and Domain Functions").

▶ **Domainname[0x1B].** Registers the computer as the Domain Master browser (covered in Chapter 15, "Administering a WINS Environment").

▶ **Domainname[0x1C].** Registers the computer as a domain controller, which enables your system to find a domain controller for logon validation.

▶ **Domainname[0x1d].** Registers the system as the local subnet's Master Browser.

Suppose, for example, that you are on a computer called WKS2399 and want to retrieve a file called exprep.xls from a server on a network called NTS94. In this case, an SMB is created by the application layer with a request to get the file, and your workstation service uses the NCB to get to a computer called NTS94[0x20]. After the server receives the SMB and wants to send the information back, it sends it to WKS2399[0x00].

Obviously, your system must have some way to find the server—that is, to resolve the name from NTS94[0x20] to a MAC address where it can send the information.

Name Resolution

Now that the naming of computers has been discussed, hopefully you can see the need for the system that has evolved. Up to this point, however, this chapter has discussed only theory. You now need to learn what happens with NetBIOS names. You can work with NetBIOS names in one of two ways: using broadcasts, or using the services of a NetBIOS Name Server. Either method can handle the four main functions required by the NetBIOS Name Service. The functions are as follows:

▶ **Name Registration.** As previously discussed, this is the process of registering a name for every service on the system on which you are working.

▶ **Name Query.** When your want to connect to another computer across the network, your system has to be able to find that computer's MAC address. This requires, in the case of TCP/IP, that you have the IP address (which TCP/IP resolves to a MAC address—the hardware address discussed in Chapter 8, "Architectural Overview of the TCP/IP Suite"). The Name Query is sent on the network (like the Address Resolution Protocol packet that follows) and requests a response from the computer that has this name registered.

▶ **Name Release.** As you shut down your system, a Name Release broadcast is sent on the wire. This informs hosts you are communicating with that you are shutting down. Notably, though, this releases your user name, which also is registered. By doing this, no problem with duplicate names arises if you log on at a different workstation.

▶ **Positive Name Query Response.** As implied, this is the response to the Name Query. Note that every host on the local network receives and accepts the Name Query packet that is sent as a broadcast packet. Each passes the packet to IP, which passes it to UDP, which passes it to the NetBIOS Name Service port. This means that every computer needs to spend CPU time checking whether the queried name is one of theirs.

Previously, it was mentioned that name services can be done using either a broadcast or a NetBIOS Name Server (NBNS). You should note that if a broadcast is used, the services are usable only on the local segment; in most multi-segment networks, an NBNS should be used to provide enterprise-wide name registration and resolution services. Name registration is handled using a local broadcast (actually a Name Query), and the name is registered if no local system responds with a Positive Name Query Response.

Windows NT has six methods for name resolution. The next few sections provide details of each of the methods and the order in which they are used. The six methods are as follows:

▶ NetBIOS Name Cache

▶ LMHOSTS file

▶ Broadcast

▶ NetBIOS Name Server

▶ HOSTS file

▶ DNS Server

NetBIOS Name Cache

The NetBIOS Name Cache is an area of memory containing a list of NetBIOS computer names and the associated IP address. An address in the Name Cache can get there in one of two ways: you have resolved that address or the address was preloaded from the LMHOSTS file (see "The LMHOSTS File"). The Name Cache provides a quick reference to frequently used IP addresses.

The NetBIOS Name Cache, however, cannot keep every address on your network. The cache (like ARP) only keeps entries for a short period of time—ten minutes by default. The exceptions are preloaded entries, which remain in cache.

You cannot directly modify the NetBIOS Name Cache. However, you can add preloaded entries in the LMHOSTS file. If you do this (or if you want to clear the Name Cache), use nbtstat -R. This purges and reloads the Name Cache. If you want to view the re-solved names, you can use nbtstat -r (the switches for nbtstat are, as you might have guessed, case sensitive).

A couple of registry entries affect the way the Name Cache works. The entries are found under the following registry key:

```
HKEY_LOCAL_MACHINE\SYSTEM\CurrentControlSet\Services\NetBT\Parameters
```

The entries are as follows:

▶ **Size: Small/Medium/Large.** The number of names kept in the Name Cache. The settings are Small (1—maintains only 16 names), Medium (2—maintains 64 names), and Large (3—maintains 128 names). The default is 1, which is sufficient for most client stations.

▶ **CacheTimeout.** The time in milliseconds that an entry remains in cache. The default is 927c0 (hex) or 600,000, which is ten minutes.

Broadcast

If the name cannot be found in the NetBIOS Name Cache, the system attempts to find the name using a broadcast on the local network. A broadcast is a necessary evil. It takes up bandwidth, but in many cases is the simplest way to find a system.

NetBIOS uses UDP (port 137) to send a Name Query to every computer on the local network. Every computer must then take the packet and pass it all the way up the protocol stack to NetBIOS so the name can be checked against the local name table. Two problems with using a broadcast are increased network traffic, and wasted CPU time on all the systems as the request is passed to NetBIOS to check names that don't exist.

You are going to see two methods that enable you to resolve names without broadcast traffic. You should note that broadcasts are a throwback to the early days of networks when computers were slower, networks tended to be single segments, and the bandwidth of networks was more than enough to cover the occasional broadcast.

You can use a couple of registry entries to customize the broadcast function. These are under the following registry key:

```
HKEY_LOCAL_MACHINE\SYSTEM\CurrentControlSet\Services\NetBT\Parameters
```

The entries are as follows:

- ▶ **BcastNameQueryCount.** The number of times the system retries the broadcast for the name. The default is three times.

- ▶ **BcastQueryTimeout.** The amount of time to wait before retrying the Name Query broadcast. The default is 7.5 seconds.

The LMHOSTS File

 Objective

For an exercise covering this information, see end of chapter.

Microsoft has been building network operating systems for a long time. Before Windows NT, Microsoft put out a product called LAN Manager. LAN Manager was based internally on NetBIOS and used NetBEUI as a protocol, which you may recall has one major problem—it cannot be routed from network to network. Microsoft choose NetBEUI in the first place because the NetBEUI protocol was compatible with the NetBIOS networking model that they were using.

To make LAN Manager more acceptable as a network operating system, Microsoft included TCP/IP as an alternate protocol for medium-to-large organizations wanting to use their product (which was based on Microsoft OS/2 version 1.3). But there was a problem: How do you resolve NetBIOS names using TCP/IP on a routed network? On the local network, the system could use the NetBIOS Name Service port and broadcast a request for the local name.

Note

Windows NT only checks the LMHOSTS file if a broadcast on the local network fails to resolve the address.

The solution was relatively easy: create a list of the systems to which the computer would have to talk. Given peer-to-peer networking had not become in vogue, only a limited number existed, anyway. In this file, you could put the IP address and the NetBIOS name of an systems you need to talk to. It was an obvious solution that does work. However, in some situations, the client would not be talking to a single machine, but rather searching for any machine with a particular service (the Netlogon service is a good example).

The list is the file LMHOSTS (no extension), which is located in the \%winroot%\system32\drivers\etc directory. A sample LMHOSTS file also was added during installation; this file is called lmhosts.sam. (If you use Notepad to create or edit the file, ensure that the file is saved as text and not as Unicode.)

 Note

> All the hosts on the Internet used to be listed in a single file at Stanford Research Institute's Network Information Center (SRI-NIC.) Whenever you tried to connect to another host, your system had to consult this file on the SRI-NIC server to find the IP address. The file was called hosts.txt.

The solution to the problem of finding a system running a particular service (such as Netlogon) rather than a particular computer was solved by including tags. Microsoft introduced several tags that enabled systems to send a request to all the computers that had a particular service running (for example, the #DOM tag tells your system that a particular system should be running the Netlogon service).

The result was a system that could communicate across routers even though it internally used NetBIOS. A workable compromise —sort of. As time went on, the amount of time that was spent updating the LMHOSTS file increased. In addition, because this file needs to be located on every host, the task became even more difficult.

Tags were a good solution once, and again proved to be able to resolve the issue. Microsoft added new tags that enabled computers to read a central LMHOSTS file. The client computer still needed a local LMHOSTS file so the system would know where and how to find the central one, however; this reduced the required number of lines from 70 or 80 or more, to 5 or 6.

Windows NT supports and uses several tags. Table 13.2 describes the tags available.

Table 13.2

Tags Available for Use by Windows NT

Tag	Use
#PRE	Tells the computer to preload the entry to the cache during initialization or after the nbtstat -R command has been issued. Entries with the #PRE tag have a life of −1 (static), meaning they are always in cache.
#DOM:domain_name	Indicates to the system that the computer is a domain controller and the domain that it controls. This enables Windows NT to handle domain functions, domain logon, and browsing services, among other things.
#NOFNR	Prevents the use of NetBIOS-directed name queries in the LAN Manager for a Unix environment.
#INCLUDE	Tells the computer the location of a central LMHOSTS file. The file is specified using a UNC (Universal Naming Convention)-type name such as \\MIS\Information\LMHOSTS. It is important that the computer name must be resolved to an IP address and must be included in the local LMHOSTS file as a preloaded entry.
#BEGIN_ALTERNATE	Used in conjunction with the #INCLUDE tag. Marks the beginning of a list of alternate locations for the centralized LMHOSTS file that can be used if the first entry is not available. Only one central LMHOSTS is used.

Tag	Use
#END_ALTERNATE	Ends the list of alternate locations for a central LMHOSTS file. Between the two entries, add as many alternates as you like. Windows NT tries each in sequence (remember, the names must resolve to IP addresses).
#MH	Multihomed computers may appear in the LMHOSTS file more that once. This tag lets the system know that this is a cases where it should not ignore the other entries in the list.

Note The LMHOSTS file is scanned from top to bottom. Therefore, your most frequently used servers should be listed first. Any entries to preload a server address should be at the bottom because they will already be in the NetBIOS Name Cache.

The following is an example of what an LMHOSTS file might contain:

```
152.42.35.2      victoria1   #DOM:MYCORP   #PRE
152.42.9.255     london2     #DOM:MYCORP
152.42.160.45    ottawa8     #PRE
152.42.97.56     houston4    #PRE
#INCLUDE \\victoria1\INFO\LMHOSTS
#BEGIN_ALTERNATE
#INCLUDE \\ottawa8\INFO\LMHOSTS
#INCLUDE \\houston4\INFO\LMHOSTS
#END_ALTERNATE
152.42.193.5     capetown4   #PRE #DOM:MYCORP
152.42.194.255   capetown8   #PRE #DOM:MYCORP
```

Note Use nbtstat -R to flush the NetBIOS Name Cache and reload from the LMHOSTS file. This enables you to test an LMHOSTS file as you create it.

Of course, nothing in this world is perfect, so you need to keep the following facts in mind when using the LMHOSTS file:

▶ If the IP address is wrong, then your system resolves the address. However, you cannot connect. Normally this shows up as a "Network Name not Found" error.

▶ Windows NT is good; however, if the NetBIOS name is spelled wrong in the LMHOSTS file, Windows NT can do nothing to resolve it. (Note the names are not case sensitive.)

▶ If the LMHOSTS file has multiple entries, the address for the first one is returned. If that entry is wrong, the result is the same as have a wrong IP address.

Only one registry entry affects LMHOSTS; however, you can easily change the entry in the Network Settings dialog box. The entry is Enable LMHOSTS, and if it is not selected, the system ignores the LMHOSTS file. This is selected by default in Windows NT and Windows 95, but deselected in Windows for Workgroups.

To change the Enable LMHOSTS setting, perform the following steps:

1. Open the Network Settings dialog box.

2. Select the Protocol tab and open the Properties for TPC/IP.

3. On the WINS Addressing tab, ensure there is a check in the Enable LMHOSTS Lookup check box to turn this on. Clear the check box to turn it off.

4. Close the TCP/IP Settings dialog box and the Network Settings dialog box.

5. Restart your computer.

NetBIOS Name Server

The LMHOSTS file has some limitations; even using a central LMHOSTS file requires a great deal of updating. If you don't use a central LMHOSTS file, and you attempt to update a host's address, you must visit every station on your network. In addition, the LMHOSTS file does not reduce broadcast traffic unless every entry is preloaded (meaning the system never has to perform a NetBIOS Name Query broadcast).

As the size of networks around the world began to increase, another method of name resolution had to be found. The method had to be able to reduce broadcast traffic and to update itself without intervention. TCP/IP already had a simple DNS service that computers could query to find the IP address for a given host name. The problem with DNS is it only resolves the basic host name; you are not be able to find services (such as Netlogon) that you sometimes seek.

In addition, DNS required a large—but, at least, centralized—file to be kept with a listing of all the IP-address-to-host name mappings. Of the three functions of NetBIOS naming—registration, resolution and release—the DNS service fit only one of the criteria.

So, a new type of name service had to be built that would enable systems to register their own IP addresses and that could respond to these systems' queries about the IP addresses of others. The system that emerged was the NetBIOS Name Server (NBNS). Windows NT implements this in the form of the WINS (Windows Internet Name Service) server discussed in Chapter 14, "Implementing Windows Internet Name Service."

Just as TCP/IP hosts had always had a DNS server entry, the NetBIOS world could now use an NBNS (such as WINS) server entry. The process was aided by the capability of the available routers to pass directed transmission over UDP port 137. A set of three basic commands was established, and NetBIOS networking was now capable of talking to the world.

You enter the WINS server address and a secondary WINS server address in the TCP/IP Settings page. This is all you need to do to use a WINS server as your NBNS.

The available commands include:

▶ **Name Registration.** The transmission registers a computer name with the NBNS. In this way, the NBNS is a dynamic system requiring little or no maintenance by the network administrators.

▶ **Name Query.** Normally, all the systems in an organization use the same NBNS. (Chapter 9 discusses replication, which makes a group of NBNS act as a single unit.) Then, it is easy to resolve a name—send the NetBIOS Name Query to the NBNS. The server responds with the IP address if the system has registered it.

▶ **Name Release.** Some names, such as user names, can move from one computer to another and, therefore, from one IP address to another. By including the capability to release a registered name, conflicts in the database are avoided.

Using an NBNS such as WINS has some major advantages if you use TCP/IP as your networking protocol with Windows products. The advantages include the following:

▶ Reduces broadcast traffic

▶ Reduces administrative overhead for maintenance

▶ Facilitates domain activity over a WAN

▶ Provides browsing services across multiple subnets

You can customize a couple of registry entries for the NBNS. These are under the following subkeys:

HKEY_LOCAL_MACHINE\SYSTEM\CurrentControlSet\Services\NetBT\Parameters

▶ **NameServerPort.** The UDP port used for NetBIOS Name Queries going to the NBNS. The default is 137 (89 hex).

▶ **NameSrvQueryCount.** Indicates the number of times your system should try each NBNS. The default is three times.

> ▶ **NameSrvQueryTimeout.** Indicates how long your computer should wait for a response from the NBNS. Default is 15 seconds (5dc hex milliseconds).

The HOSTS File

Because you are looking at NetBIOS name resolution, including the HOSTS file here might seem out of place. The HOSTS file is primarily associated with host name resolution. However, Windows NT uses the HOSTS file if all other methods of NetBIOS name resolution fail.

Host names are the TCP/IP names given to the computer. Usually, the host name is the same as the NetBIOS name (without the 16th character). However, it does not have to be. The host name may also include the Internet domain name; these parts together are the Fully Qualified Domain Name (FQDN). The host name can be any length. For example, thisisawebserver.mycorp.com is a valid FQDN; however, it is not a valid NetBIOS name. (More on this in Chapter 12, "Domain Name System.")

The HOSTS file that is located in the \%winroot%\system32\ drivers\etc directory is similar in makeup to the LMHOSTS file discussed earlier. The difference is that the HOSTS file is simpler in the following ways:

> ▶ No tags are in the HOSTS file.

> ▶ You can associate more than one name with a host by entering all the names on the same line, separated by spaces.

A sample HOSTS file might look like the following:

```
160.16.5.3      www www.scrimtech.com     # corporate web server
38.25.63.10     www.NTworld.com           # NT associate page
127.0.0.1       localhost
```

As noted, the first entry resolves www as well as www.scrimtech.com to the IP address 160.16.5.3. You may have noticed the # signs. These indicate comments in the HOSTS file that are always placed at the end of the line.

The entry for localhost at 127.0.0.1 is a default entry that Windows NT adds. This enables you to ping your computer by name to ensure the HOSTS file is working. (Ping is discussed in detail in Chapter 20, "Connectivity in Heterogeneous Environments.")

DNS

Just like using the HOSTS file, using DNS to resolve NetBIOS names may seem a little out of place. However, Windows NT can use a DNS server to resolve a host name. In environments that are working with the Internet almost exclusively, having a DNS server makes sense, and you can use it instead of WINS. If you want to do this, simply check the Enable DNS for Windows Resolution check box shown in figure 13.2.

Figure 13.2

The WINS Address tab in the TCP/IP Properties dialog box.

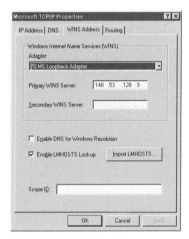

Configuring Windows NT to use a DNS server is simple, as you are shown in Chapter 15. All you need to do is enter a DNS server address in the DNS tab of the TCP/IP Properties dialog box (see fig. 13.3).

Order of Resolution

For an exercise covering this information, see end of chapter.

As you have just seen, there are six ways that Windows NT can resolve a NetBIOS name to an IP address. As discussed, each way works although some have limitations that make them impractical for a large-scale WAN. Thankfully, this does not matter because the methods of resolution back each other up and enable which-ever method that can resolve the name to resolve it.

Figure 13.3

The DNS tab in the TCP/IP Prop-erties dialog box.

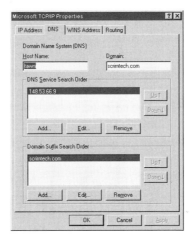

A problem could arise, though, if you are not careful. For instance, it makes sense for you to first read the HOSTS file, then broadcast the NetBIOS Name Query to the local subnet. Perhaps checking with the DNS server should be next. The point is, that the order in which you use the methods of resolution is more important than the resolution. You are fairly well-assured the name will be resolved (if you spelled it right); however, going through the resolution methods in the wrong order could slow down the process.

Remember that this is the resolution order for NetBIOS names only. Resolving host names uses a different method. Chapter 17, "Host Name Resolution," discusses that topic. For now, though, bear in mind that this is NetBIOS name resolution, which occurs when you use the NetBIOS interface instead of the Winsock interface. All the standard Microsoft products—Windows NT Explorer, User Manager, net.exe—use this method of resolution.

The NetBIOS node type sets the order of resolution. This can be set either by editing the registry, or by using the Dynamic Host Configuration Protocol (DHCP) server, if you are using DHCP to allocate IP addresses and services. You should note that the default is b-node (Broadcast)—unless a WINS server address is entered—in which case, it defaults to h-node (Hybrid). The node types that can be set are as follows:

▶ b-node (broadcast node)

▶ p-node (peer-to-peer node)—Uses an NBNS

▶ m-node (mixed node)—First tries b-node, then p-node

▶ h-node (hybrid node)—First tries p-node, then b-node

 Note

Microsoft's version of b-node is an enhanced form of the b-node standard. Because Microsoft already had an LMHOSTS file that had been used successfully with LAN Manager, Microsoft included searching this file in the b-node form of resolution.

b-node

The simplest way to resolve a name on the network is to ask everyone on the network if a name is his or her name. Obviously, this has to be done as a broadcast to the network with every host on the network responding to the broadcast.

NetBIOS Name Queries that are broadcast can take up a significant amount of bandwidth from the network, and also take CPU time from every host on the network. This causes the overall network performance to not only seem slower, but to be slower. Windows NT attempts three times to resolve the name using broadcasting, waiting 7.5 seconds between each.

The steps a b-node system goes through to resolve a name are as follows:

1. Checking the NetBIOS Name Cache

2. Broadcasting a NetBIOS Name Query

3. Checking the LMHOSTS file (Microsoft enhanced b-node only)

4. Checking a HOST file

5. Checking with a DNS server

p-node

As you saw, there are better ways to resolve a NetBIOS name. The best way is to ask a central system that has a list of every host's IP address and NetBIOS name, as well as special entries for systems from run services such as Netlogon. p-node does this for us.

p-node still uses a NetBIOS Name Query that is sent on the network. However, rather than being sent as a broadcast, the query is sent directly to an NBNS. In this way, the resolution is made quicker, and no CPU time is taken up on the other hosts on the network. Like the b-node, p-node makes three attempts to contact an NBNS, waiting 15 seconds each time.

The order of resolution for p-node is the following:

1. NetBIOS Name Cache

2. Asking a NetBIOS Name Server

3. HOSTS file

4. DNS

m-node

A Mixed Node system tries every method of resolution. This and h-node are combinations of the b-node and p-node systems. The only difference is the order in which Windows NT resolves the names.

For m-node, the order of resolution is the following:

1. NetBIOS Name Cache

2. Broadcasting a NetBIOS Name Query

3. Checking the LMHOSTS file

4. Asking a NetBIOS Name Server

5. Checking the HOSTS file

6. Consulting the DNS

h-node

The Hybrid Node, as stated, is a combination of the p-node and b-node resolution methods. Unlike m-node, h-node reduces broadcast traffic on your network by first consulting the NBNS before attempting a broadcast.

If you put a WINS address into the TCP/IP configuration, Windows NT automatically uses the h-node. The steps in h-node resolution are as follows:

1. Checking the NetBIOS Name Cache

2. Asking a NetBIOS Name Server

3. Broadcasting a NetBIOS Name Query

4. Checking the LMHOSTS file

5. Checking the HOSTS file

6. Consulting the DNS

Viewing and Setting the Node Type

Because the node type is important to the performance of the system that you are using, you can see the node type you are using and change it if a better method is available.

To check the current node type, you can use the command IPCONFIG /ALL, which you have seen several times already. In figure 13.4, you can see the output from this command; note that the node type is Hybrid (also note that a WINS server is listed).

Figure 13.4

*Output from the
IPCONFIG /ALL
command.*

You can set your node type manually. By default, you area b-node
system. If you want to become an h-node, simply add the address
of a WINS server into the TCP/IP configuration screen. If you
want to be a different node type, you have to edit the registry. The
entry is under the following subkey:

```
HKEY_LOCAL_MACHINE\SYSTEM\ CurrentControlSet\Services\NetBT\
Parameters
```

The entry is NodeType, which can be set to the following values:

- ▶ 1 (hex)—b-node

- ▶ 2 (hex)—p-node

- ▶ 4 (hex)—M-Mode

- ▶ 8 (hex)—h-node

On most networks, you automatically set the node type by using
the DHCP server. The DHCP options that you set are 044—
WINS/NBNS Server and 046—WINS/NBT Node Type. This enables an administrator to set the node type for all machines that
use DHCP.

nbtstat

 **Objective**

This chapter has made several references to the nbtstat command, which can be used to work with and diagnose NetBIOS over TCP/IP. This section looks at this command and the functions that you can perform using it. nbtstat is a diagnostic command that displays protocol statistics and current TCP/IP connections using NBT. The syntax is as follows:

```
nbtstat [-a remotename] [-A IP address] [-c] [-n] [-R] [-r] [-S]
[-s] [interval]
```

Although some of the command-line parameters for nbtstat have already been discussed, table 13.3 lists all the available switches.

Table 13.3

Switches for the nbtstat Command	
Switch	Description
-a remotename	Lists the names that another host has registered on the network. Remotename is the computer name of the other host.
-A IP address	Basically the same as the previous command; however, you can specify the IP address rather than the name.
-c	Displays all the names that are in the NetBIOS Name Cache and the IP address to which they map.
-n	Lists all the names that your computer has. If they have been registered, they are marked as such.
-R	Purges and reloads the NetBIOS Name Cache. The cache is reloaded from the LMHOSTS file, if one exists, using the entries marked with #PRE.
-r	Lists all the names that your computer has resolved and the IP address from them. The difference from the -c switch is that preloaded names are not listed.

Switch	Description
-S	Lists all the current sessions that have been established with your computer. This includes both the client and server sessions.
-s	Basically the same as the -S switch; however, the system attempts to resolve the IP addresses to a host name.
Interval	The interval in seconds at which the computer redisplays the information onscreen.

The following an example of the output from the nbtstat command:

```
NetBIOS Connection Table

Local  Name        State      In/Out  Remote Host  Input   Output
- - - - - - - - - - - - - - - - - - - - - - - - - - - - - - - - - - -
TAWNI       <03>  Listening
SCRIM       <03>  Listening
TAWNI       <00>  Connected  Out     198.53.147.2  0B      174B
```

The preceding example does not show all the possible columns, however. The column headings generated by the nbtstat utility listed along with their meanings are as follows:

- ▶ **Input.** The number of bytes of information that have been received.

- ▶ **Output.** The number of bytes of information that have been sent.

- ▶ **In/Out.** The direction in which the connection was made, with OUT to the other computer, or IN from it.

- ▶ **Life.** The time remaining before the cache entry is purged.

- ▶ **Local Name.** The local name used for the session.

- ▶ **Remote Host.** The name on the remote host being used in this session.

▶ **Type.** The type of name that was resolved.

▶ **State.** The state of the connection. Possible states include the following:

> ▶ **Connected.** A NetBIOS session has been established between the two hosts.

> ▶ **Associated.** Your system has requested a connection, and has resolved the remote name to an IP address. This is an active open.

> ▶ **Listening.** This is a service on your computer that is not being used. This is a passive open.

> ▶ **Idle.** The service that opened the port has since paused or hung. No activity is possible until the service resumes.

> ▶ **Connecting.** At this point, your system is attempting to create a NetBIOS session. The system is attempting to resolve the name of the remote host to an IP address.

> ▶ **Accepting.** A service on your system has been asked to open a session, and is negotiating the session with the remote host.

> ▶ **Reconnecting.** After a session has dropped (often due to time-out), your system is trying to reconnect.

> ▶ **Outbound.** The TCP three-way handshake is in progress. This establishes the transport layer session that is used to establish the NetBIOS session.

> ▶ **Inbound.** Same as outbound; however, this is a connection being made to a service on your system.

> ▶ **Disconnecting.** The remote system has requested a session be terminated, so the session is being shut down.

> ▶ **Disconnected.** Your system is requesting a session be terminated.

Exercises

Exercise 13.1:   Configuring an LMHOSTS file

This exercise takes you through the configuration of an LM-HOSTS file for a sample network. You then build the LMHOSTS file and verify that the preloaded entries are working.

1. Consider the diagram in figure 13.5.

Figure 13.5

The example network for the LMHOSTS exercise.

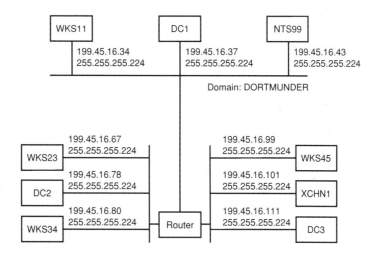

2. If all that is required is the capability to validate logon requests, which systems need to be configured with an LM-HOSTS file?

   None; there is a Domain Controller on each subnet.

3. For WKS23, what entries are required in the LMHOSTS file to enable DC1 or DC3 to validate the logon if DC2 is down?

   The following entries:

   ```
   199.45.16.37     DC1     #DOM:DORTMUNDER
   199.45.16.111    DC3     #DOM:DORTMUNDER
   ```

4. If all systems are required to work with NTS99 and XCHN1, what would be required in the LMHOSTS file? Which systems would need this file?

continues

The address of each server with its name would be required. All systems that are not on the same subnet should have these entries added.

5. To provide WKS11 with all the addresses it requires, what should be in its LMHOSTS file?

```
The LMHOSTS would look like this:
199.45.16.37     DC1    #DOM:DORTMUNDER
199.45.16.78     DC2    #DOM:DORTMUNDER
199.45.16.111    DC3    #DOM:DORTMUNDER
199.45.16.43     NTS99
199.45.16.101    XCHN1
```

6. If the workstations also provided services to the network, what additions would be required in the LMHOSTS file?

Each workstation's IP address and computer name would need to be added.

7. Assume each domain controller (DC) keeps a central copy of the LMHOSTS file. Write the LMHOSTS file that should now be on WKS45.

The file should look like the following.

```
199.45.16.37     DC1    #PRE    #DOM:DORTMUNDER
199.45.16.78     DC2    #PRE    #DOM:DORTMUNDER
199.45.16.111    DC3    #PRE    #DOM:DORTMUNDER
#INCLUDE   \\DC1\public\LMHOSTS
#BEGIN ALTERNATE
#INCLUDE   \\DC2\public\LMHOSTS
#INCLUDE   \\DC3\public\LMHOSTS
#END ALTERNATE
```

8. In the answers for questions 5 and 7, what lines are redundant?

Any line that includes a host that exists on the local subnet is redundant.

9. Using Notepad (or Edit), create the following file:

```
199.45.16.37     DC1    #PRE   #DOM:DORTMUNDER
199.45.16.78     DC2    #PRE   #DOM:DORTMUNDER
199.45.16.111    DC3    #PRE   #DOM:DORTMUNDER
199.45.16.43     NTS99  #PRE
199.45.16.101    XCHN1  #PRE
```

10. Save the file as %winroot%\SYSTEM32\Drivers\ETC\ LMHOSTS.

   (If one already exists, back it up first so you can return to your original settings.)

11. From a Command Prompt, enter the command nbtstat -c and note the names that are listed.

12. Enter the command nbtstat -R and then repeat step 11.

   The names should change.

13. Attempt to PING DC1. What happens?

   There should be a delay and then the name and address appear. The request should time out, or the host will be un-reachable.

Exercise 13.2:   Setting Node Types

In this exercise, you set your node type both by modifying the TCP/IP configuration and by editing the registry. (This exercise requires that you have a permanent address.)

1. Open the TCP/IP configuration dialog box (right-click Network Neighborhood, choose Properties. On the Protocols tab, double-click TCP/IP).

2. Select the WINS tab and clear the WINS entry.

3. Choose OK to close the TCP/IP Configuration dialog box and then Close to exit the Network Settings dialog box.

4. Restart your computer.

continues

Exercise 13.2: Continued

5. Start a DOS prompt and enter the command IPCONFIG / ALL. You should be set for Broadcast node.

6. Return to the WINS tab (see steps 1 and 2) and enter the IP address of your WINS server (any address will do).

7. Close the TCP/IP and Network configuration dialog boxes and restart your computer.

8. Start a DOS prompt and enter the command IPCONFIG / ALL. You NetBIOS node type should change.

9. Start the Registry Editor (Start, Run REGEDT32, OK).

10. Under HKEY_LOCAL_MACHINE, open the following keys and subkeys: SYSTEM, CurrentControlSet, Services, NetBT, Parameters.

11. NodeType is not listed in this key. Choose Edit, Add Value.

12. Enter NodeType as the name for the value and choose REG_DWORD as the type. Choose OK.

13. Enter 4 as the value. (Hex should be selected.)

14. From a command prompt, type IPCONFIG /ALL. Your node type should be Mixed.

15. Edit the value in the registry, changing NodeType to 0x2.

16. From a command prompt, type IPCONFIG /ALL. Your node type should be "Peer-Peer."

17. Delete the value and reset the network settings to their initial state, and then restart your computer.

Review Questions

1. Which of the following utilities will use NetBIOS name resolution?

    A. FTP

    B. NT Explorer

    C. Internet Explorer

    D. net.exe

2. What settings are available for the size of the NetBIOS Name Cache?

    A. Big

    B. Large

    C. Small

    D. Tiny

3. On a network with one segment, what benefit can be gained by using WINS?

    A. WINS can aid in the resolution of HOST names.

    B. WINS will facilitate Inter-Domain browsing.

    C. WINS will reduce network traffic.

    D. All of the above.

4. What command can you use to verify which sessions exist over NBT?

    A. net sessions

    B. nbtstat

    C. netstat -nbt

    D. netstat

5. In using the #INCLUDE statement, what is required for the server that contains the central LMHOSTS file?

   A. The server is listed in the LMHOSTS file with a #DOM tag.

   B. The server is listed in the LMHOSTS file with a #PRE tag.

   C. The server is listed in the LMHOSTS file.

   D. The server is on the local subnet.

6. Which port does a logon validation use?

   A. 136

   B. 137

   C. 138

   D. 139

7. Which layers in the OSI network model equate to the application layer in the TPC/IP network model?

   A. Application, presentation, and session

   B. Application and presentation

   C. Application only

   D. None of the above

8. What is the purpose of an NCB?

   A. Used for compatibility with NetWare

   B. Contains the request that is being sent to the remote system

   C. Controls where the SMB is sent

   D. An NCB is a Novell data structure

9. What port is used to transfer a file to a remote host?

    A. 136

    B. 137

    C. 138

    D. 139

10. At what point in broadcast node resolution is the LMHOSTS file checked?

    A. Second

    B. Third

    C. Fourth

    D. Fifth

11. What are the three basic names that are registered on a computer?

    A. Computername[0x00], Computername[0x03], Computername[0x1D]

    B. Computername[0x03], Computername[0x20], Computername[0x1D]

    C. Computername[0x00], Computername[0x20], Computername[0x1D]

    D. Computername[0x00], Computername[0x03], Computername[0x20]

12. Which name must be unique for every system on the network?

    A. The computer name

    B. The user name

    C. The workgroup name

    D. The domain name

13. When the messenger service registers a name, what is the value that identifies it with the messenger service?

    A. [0x00]

    B. [0x03]

    C. [0x20]

    D. [0x1D]

14. What two methods can be used to register a name on the network?

    A. Broadcast and the LMHOSTS file

    B. The LMHOSTS file and the HOSTS file

    C. Broadcast and an NBNS server

    D. The name is registered on the network when the computer is installed

15. If your organization uses WINS, how many hosts need to be configured with an LMHOSTS file?

    A. The WINS server only

    B. Domain controllers only

    C. All non-WINS capable workstations

    D. None

16. What are the three main functions of Name Management?

    A. Name resolution, renewal, and release

    B. Name queries, release, and renewal

    C. Name registration, renewal, and release

    D. Name registration, query, and release

17. Why are ports 137 and 138 normally configured not to pass broadcasts on most routers?

    A. For security purposes

    B. To prevent NetBIOS name conflicts

C. To prevent router congestion

D. These ports are not configured this way

18. By default, how long does a NetBIOS name remain in the Name Cache?

A. 2 minutes

B. 5 minutes

C. 10 minutes

D. 1 day

19. Can you change the size of the NetBIOS Name Cache?

A. Yes

B. No

C. Only by reinstalling NT

20. How many names can you register on a single Windows NT computer?

A. 16

B. 64

C. 128

D. 250

Review Answers

1. B, D

2. B, C

3. D

4. B

5. B

6. C

7. A

8. C

9. D

10. B

11. D

12. A

13. B

14. C

15. D

16. D

17. C

18. C

19. A

20. D

Answers to the Test Yourself Questions at the Beginning of the Chapter

1. NetBIOS communications are facilitated over TCP/IP using three ports: 137 (UDP) NetBIOS Name Service port, 138 (UDP) NetBIOS Datagram port, and 139 (TCP) NetBIOS Session Service Port.

2. Two node types use the NetBIOS Name Server as their main source of resolution: Peer-to-Peer node and Hybrid node.

3. For all methods of NetBIOS name resolution, the NetBIOS Name Cache is checked first.

4. The three main functions of NetBIOS are as follows:

   ▶ **Name Management.** Provides the capability to register and resolve names on the network, which provides a means of locating the target computer

   ▶ **Session Management.** Provides a method of communicating with a remote host, and provides security via user validation and error correction in large file transfers

   ▶ **Data Transfer.** Provides the capability to transfer data either using a session that already exists or, in the case of broadcasts, without a session

5. A Server Message Block (SMB) is a Protocol Data Unit; that is, the package that takes the request from the redirector to the server and back again. SMBs are usable only by the application layer in the OSI model, and are the data being transferred to all other layers.

6. In a Hybrid node environment, the order of resolution is as follows:

   NetBIOS Name Cache

   NetBIOS Name Server

   Local broadcast

   LMHOSTS file

   HOSTS file

   DNS server

7. The 16th character of the NetBIOS name identifies the service that is registering the name. For example, a registered name of NTS45[0x20] indicates Server service on a system with the computer name NTS45.

8. The #BEGIN ALTERNATE and #END ALTERNATE tags in the LMHOSTS file enclose a series of alternate locations for a centralized LMHOSTS file. A series of lines start with the #INCLUDE tag.

9. The #DOM tag identifies a domain controller. This tag facilitates the logon validation across a router when there is no local domain controller or the local domain controller is not available.

10. A client workstation can be configured manually by entering the address of a WINS server on the WINS tabs of the TCP/IP configuration dialog box, or it can be configured automatically from a DHCP server using the 044 NBNS server address and 046 NBNS node type options.

Chapter 14

Implementing Windows Internet Name Service

This chapter will help you prepare for the exam by covering the basics of WINS. This information is required to understand the next chapter.

Test Yourself! Before reading this chapter, test yourself to determine how much study time you will need to devote to this section.

1. What does a WINS server do?

2. How does the WINS server add entries to its database?

3. Where does a WINS client send its registration request?

4. What kind of platforms can be WINS clients?

5. How can non-WINS clients register their addresses with a WINS server?

6. How can non-WINS clients resolve addresses using the WINS server?

7. How many WINS servers should you install on a network?

8. How many names does a WINS client register with the WINS server?

9. What are the benefits of using a WINS server?

Answers are located at the end of the chapter.

The Windows Internet Name Service

The Windows Internet Name Service (WINS) provides name registration, renewal, release, and resolution services for NetBIOS names and IP addresses. It is implemented as an extension of RFCs 1001 and 1002.

A WINS server maintains a dynamic database linking NetBIOS names to IP addresses. The database is dynamic because each name registration has a *time to live* value—after its time to live has expired, the record is discarded from the database. The WINS server receives registration, renewal, and release requests from WINS clients, and updates its database based on this information. Name resolution queries from WINS clients are resolved using this database.

Using the WINS server for name registration, renewal, release, and resolution services provides a marked improvement over using broadcast messages or static mappings for these services. In the case of broadcast messages, rather than each computer sending a broadcast to all clients on its subnet for every name registration, each computer sends a unicast message to the WINS server. The same applies for name queries: rather than sending a broadcast message to all clients on its subnet, a WINS client sends a unicast message directly to the WINS server. For networks using static mappings, such as an LMHOSTS file, each computer has a fixed list of NetBIOS names and IP addresses, which can become difficult to manage—and impossible to manage when using dynamic IP address assignments, such as environments using DHCP (Dynamic Host Control Protocol). See Chapter 12 for more information on DHCP.

> **Note**
>
> A broadcast message is a TCP/IP packet sent from one computer to every other computer on a subnet. A unicast message is a TCP/IP packet sent from one computer directly to another computer.

The following section looks at how WINS works, and details the services that a WINS server provides to WINS clients.

How WINS Works

A WINS server provides name registration, renewal, release, and resolution services to client computers configured to use WINS. Just how these services are provided is an interesting combination of client and server processes. The four fundamental services provided by WINS are detailed in the following sections.

Name Registration

Name registration is the process by which the WINS server obtains information from WINS clients. Name registration occurs when a WINS client computer starts. The name registration process enables the WINS database to be maintained dynamically, rather than statically.

When a WINS client starts up, it sends a name registration to its configured WINS server. This registration provides the computer name and IP address of the WINS client to the WINS server. If the WINS server is running, and no other client has the same name registered, the server returns a successful registration message to the client. This message contains the name registration's time to live.

Each computer must have a unique name within the network. Without unique names, network communication would be next to impossible. After WINS clients send name registration requests to the WINS server, the server ensures that the name registration is unique—no other computer may have the same name. The following section looks at how the WINS server handles an attempt to register an existing name.

Note

At name registration, the WINS server detects a client's attempt to register a duplicate name—that is, a NetBIOS name already in use. If the name is already in use, the following occurs:

1. The server challenges the computer already holding the name registration to ensure that it is still active. If the

computer does not answer the challenge, the registration proceeds.

2. If the original host answers the challenge, the request receives a negative acknowledgment, and an error is registered in the System Event Log. The computer attempting to claim an existing name cannot communicate using NetBIOS on that adapter.

Name Renewal

Once a WINS client's name is registered, it is assigned a time to live, after which the name is removed from the WINS server's database. If there were no mechanism to renew leases, this would be an inefficient system, because at the end of each registration's time to live, the client computer would have to go through the entire registration process again. To avoid this, WINS clients can request a renewal to their name registration record.

This process is straightforward and similar to the initial name registration process. After one-eighth of the time to live value has passed, the client attempts to renew its name registration. If no response is received, the WINS client retries its renewal every two minutes, until half of its time to live has passed. The WINS client then tries to renew its lease with the secondary WINS server, as with the primary WINS server—the timer is reset to zero, and after one-eighth of its time to live value has passed, until it succeeds or half of its time to live has passed. If it is unsuccessful after half of its time to live has passed, it reverts to its primary WINS server.

After a name renewal succeeds at any point in the process—whichever WINS server accepts the renewal—the WINS client is provided with a new TTL value for its name registration.

Name renewal is a feature provided to the WINS client by the WINS server. The server does not provide this service to computers that are not WINS clients.

Name Release

WINS clients send a name release request to the WINS server during an orderly shutdown. This release message is a request to remove the IP address and NetBIOS name from the WINS server database. For computers that use broadcast name resolution, it sends a broadcast message indicating the name release to all computers on its subnet.

Upon receipt of the release request, the WINS server verifies that it has the IP address and NetBIOS name in its database. If an error occurs, the server sends a negative response to the WINS client. The following circumstances are possible errors that would cause the WINS server to send a negative response:

▶ If another client has a different IP address mapped to the same NetBIOS name

▶ If the WINS database is corrupted

▶ If the IP address or NetBIOS name specified does not exist within the WINS server's database

 Note

If a computer is not shut down correctly, the WINS server does not know that the name has been released, and the name is not released until the WINS name registration record expires.

Name Resolution

WINS clients send name resolution requests to the WINS server. A name resolution request typically occurs when the client computer tries to map a network drive. To connect to a network drive, the user needs to specify two things: a system name and a share name. The system name provided needs to be resolved to an IP address. The basic flow of a name resolution request is as follows:

1. When a client computer wants to resolve a name, it first checks its local NetBIOS name cache. (You can view the cache using the nbtstat command, which is covered in detail in Chapter 13.)

2. If the name is not in the local cache, a name query is sent to the primary WINS server. If the primary WINS server is unavailable, the request is re-sent twice before going to the secondary WINS server. If either WINS server resolves the name, a success message is sent to the client, containing the requested NetBIOS name and IP address.

3. If neither the primary nor secondary WINS server is available, or if neither server can resolve the query, a negative response is sent to the client. The WINS client then attempts to resolve the name using either an LMHOSTS file, a broadcast request, or DNS. Note that WINS clients can be configured to use many name resolution strategies.

 Note

WINS clients can be configured to use various methods of name resolution. These are referred to as b-node, h-node, m-node and p-node. Each method differs slightly.

These name resolution strategies are shown in the following list:

▶ **b-node name resolution** does not use WINS. It relies entirely on broadcast packets for name registration and resolution. This is the type of name resolution used in environments that do not have a WINS server, and can result in a large quantity of broadcast traffic.

▶ **p-node name resolution** uses WINS exclusively. The client does not fall back on broadcast messages when the WINS server cannot resolve the query or is unavailable.

▶ **m-node name resolution** is a combination of b-node and p-node. The client first uses b-node to attempt to resolve a query, and if the query is unsuccessful, the client resorts to p-node. The client computer can use WINS, but primarily uses broadcast messages.

▶ **h-node name resolution** also combines b-node and p-node strategies. Unlike m-node, the client uses p-node first and uses b-node as a last resort. This is the most efficient implementation because it reduces the reliance on broadcast messages, and still provides WINS clients with a backup method of name resolution if the WINS server is unavailable or cannot resolve the query.

 Note   WINS clients can be configured to use either method. Details on how to configure WINS clients are discussed in the "WINS Client Configuration" section of this chapter.

Implementation Considerations

Prior to implementing WINS, you need to examine a number of issues. These issues will largely determine the best implementation for your environment. Due to the scaleable nature of Windows NT networks, your environment could range from a network with one server and three workstations to a worldwide WAN with hundreds of servers and thousands of clients. The following sections examine these issues in more detail.

WINS Server Considerations

WINS servers are the most critical element of a WINS deployment. Determining how many WINS servers you need, where to place them, and how to configure them are important aspects of pre-deployment planning.

At an absolute minimum, you need one WINS server. Two WINS servers provide some degree of fault tolerance if the primary WINS server fails.

WINS servers don't have a built-in limit of the number of clients that can be served. A basic rule of thumb is that one WINS server can handle up to 1,500 name registrations per minute, and about 4,500 name queries per minute. As a good estimate, you would need to implement one primary and one secondary WINS server per 10,000 clients.

The WINS server must be running Windows NT Server; the WINS server cannot be installed on a Windows NT workstation. If the WINS server were a multiple processor system, this would increase performance considerably since the WINS server is a multi-threaded application, and can then run one thread on each processor.

One interesting component of the WINS server is that it supports database logging. *Database logging* is a fault-tolerance feature that maintains a log file in addition to the database. The log contains recent transaction information. If this feature is enabled, the database can be "rolled back" to a known state. However, this also decreases performance because all name registrations are processed twice. The tradeoff is fault tolerance: if logging is disabled, the most recent updates to the WINS database can be lost if the WINS server software crashes.

Finally, if your network spans multiple subnets, client computers can be configured to use WINS servers on the local subnet or on a different subnet. Clearly, this slows performance, and increases traffic through routers. Also, if WINS servers are located on a different subnet than the WINS client computers, the availability of the routers becomes paramount—if they are no longer available, neither are the WINS services.

Integrating WINS with DHCP

If your network is using DHCP to assign client IP addresses, integrating WINS is quite simple. Within your DHCP scope definitions, you can specify a number of WINS-related configuration parameters for client computers. DHCP client computers can be automatically configured to be WINS clients also. The following WINS-related configuration parameters can be specified within a DHCP scope:

▶ Primary WINS server IP address

▶ Secondary WINS server IP address

▶ Name resolution type (b-node, h-node, m-node, or p-node)

WINS Proxies

WINS servers provide name registration, renewal, release, and resolution services only to WINS clients. In environments with client systems that cannot use WINS, such as UNIX systems, there is a way to configure your network so that the WINS server can provide a subset of these services to non-WINS clients via a WINS proxy. The services that a WINS proxy provides are as follows:

▶ **Name registration.** A WINS proxy listens for name registration broadcasts from non-WINS clients and forwards the registration to the WINS server. Note that the name is not registered; it is only checked to ensure that no WINS client has the same name registered.

▶ **Name resolution.** WINS proxies also forward name resolution broadcasts to the WINS server for resolution. The WINS server processes the query and sends the information to the WINS proxy, which then forwards the query result to the non-WINS client.

▶ **Name renewal and release.** Because the non-WINS client does not have a database entry in the WINS server database, the server does not provide name renewal and release services to non-WINS clients.

Implementing a WINS proxy is straightforward: all you needs to do is modify one registry value on the computer that is to become the WINS proxy. WINS proxies *cannot be WINS servers*, and must be WINS clients. Also, no more than two WINS proxies can reside on one subnet. If your environment requires a WINS proxy, the installation procedure is shown below:

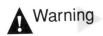 **Warning**   As with any other operations using the Registry Editor, please be careful. Making a recovery disk before using the Registry Editor is a good idea.

Note   To configure a client as a WINS proxy, start the Registry Editor, and change the `HKEY_LOCAL_MACHINE\System\CurrentControlSet\Services\NetBT\Parameters\EnableProxy` parameter to 1 (REG_DWORD value type).

WINS Client Considerations

Each WINS client must be configured to communicate with at least a primary WINS server. WINS client computers can be configured with both a primary and a secondary WINS server. This provides a certain degree of fault tolerance. If the primary WINS server is unavailable, the secondary WINS server can provide the same services.

Implementing WINS

The following two sections provide an overview of the implementation of a WINS server and a WINS client under Windows NT.

Implementing a WINS Server

To install a WINS server on a Windows NT server, simply select the Windows Internet Name Service from the Control Panel/Networks/Services screen, as shown in figure 14.1.

Figure 14.1

Installing a WINS server.

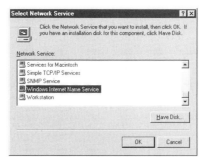

No other configuration information is required. The installation copies the required files for the WINS server, and also copies the WINS Administration utility. The WINS server is installed as a service, and starts after your server is restarted. Because WINS is installed as a service, it can be stopped and started from Control Panel/Services or from the command line using **NET START/ STOP/PAUSE/CONTINUE WINS**.

Configuring WINS Clients

WINS client configuration is equally straightforward. After the TCP/IP protocol has been installed on a client computer, such as a Windows NT computer, all you need to do is supply the address of the primary (and, if desired, secondary) WINS server by selecting Control Panel/Network, and then selecting the TCP/IP protocol's WINS Address tab (see fig. 14.2).

Figure 14.2

WINS client configuration.

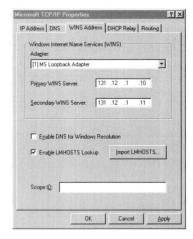

That's all! Next to no information is required to configure a WINS client.

Integrating WINS with DHCP

As would be expected, WINS and DHCP share a high level of integration. By definition, any DHCP client can have a different IP address at any time; this poses no problem for WINS, because both packages are tightly bound.

Within DHCP scope, global, or default settings, several WINS-related parameters can be specified. All of these parameters can be specified within the DHCP Manager; see Chapter 12 for more details. These parameters include the following:

▶ **044 WINS/NBNS Servers.** A list of the IP addresses of primary/secondary WINS servers for the DHCP client computers.

▶ **046 WINS/NBT Node Type.** Specifies the name resolution node for DHCP clients (see note earlier in this chapter regarding b-node, h-node, m-node, and p-node name resolution).

Note   If a WINS record is marked as released, and a name registration request arrives for the same host name, but with a different IP address, the WINS server registers the new request.

Review Questions

The following questions will test your knowledge of the information in this chapter.

1. What is the role of a WINS proxy?

   A. A WINS proxy is a secondary WINS server.

   B. A WINS proxy is any WINS server configured to provide name registration, renewal, release, and resolution services to non-WINS clients.

   C. A WINS proxy is any WINS client configured to provide name resolution services to non-WINS clients.

   D. A WINS proxy is a WINS server located on a different subnet than a WINS client.

2. Your network has client computers that are not WINS clients, and you have added a WINS proxy. Which services are not provided by the WINS proxy?

   A. Name registration

   B. Name resolution

   C. Name renewal

   D. Name release

3. Your Windows NT network has both a primary and a secondary WINS server. Which statement is accurate?

   A. If the primary WINS server is unavailable, the secondary WINS server can provide the same services to WINS clients.

   B. If the primary WINS server is unavailable, a WINS proxy agent is used to provide name services.

    C. If the primary WINS server is unavailable, and the secondary WINS server is also unavailable, a workstation automatically becomes a WINS proxy and provides name services.

    D. None of the above.

4. When does name renewal occur?

    A. Name renewal occurs when a WINS client is shut down in an orderly fashion.

    B. Name renewal occurs when the name registration's time to live expires.

    C. Name renewal occurs automatically before the name registration's time to live expires.

    D. Name renewal occurs only when initiated by a WINS proxy.

5. When does name registration occur?

    A. Name registration occurs whenever a WINS client sends a request to a WINS server to obtain the IP address of a NetBIOS host.

    B. Name registration occurs when a non-WINS client starts and sends a broadcast to a WINS proxy.

    C. Name registration occurs when a WINS client starts and sends a name registration request to a WINS server.

    D. Name registration occurs when a WINS client sends a name registration request to a WINS server, and then the WINS server sends a negative acknowledgment because the name is already registered.

6. Given a WINS client configured to use a primary and a secondary WINS server, if both servers are available, which statement is incorrect?

   A. The WINS client can perform name registration, renewal, release, and resolution operations.

   B. The WINS client cannot obtain the IP address associated with a given NetBIOS name.

   C. The WINS client can act as a WINS proxy.

   D. The WINS client is unable to resolve IP addresses associated with a given NetBIOS name unless broadcast name resolution is used.

7. Which features are not provided directly or indirectly by a WINS server?

   A. Name resolution for WINS clients

   B. Name release for non-WINS clients

   C. Name registration for WINS clients

   D. Name registration for non-WINS clients

   E. Name resolution for non-WINS clients

8. Your network presently has 100 client computers and 4 servers. Name resolution is handled by broadcast. By implementing a primary and a secondary WINS server to your network, and configuring all client computers to use WINS for name resolution, which of the following will not occur?

   A. Broadcast traffic will decrease.

   B. Broadcast traffic will increase.

   C. Non-WINS clients will be able to register their computer names on the WINS server.

   D. Non-WINS clients will be able to resolve name queries from both the primary and secondary WINS servers.

9. Your network has 50 client computers using WINS, and 2 servers acting as primary and secondary WINS servers. You want to add a WINS proxy to your network to provide name services to non-WINS clients. Which of the following statements would satisfy this requirement?

    A. Do nothing; non-WINS clients can use WINS servers directly.

    B. Configure the primary WINS server as a WINS proxy.

    C. Configure the secondary WINS server as a WINS proxy.

    D. Configure one of the WINS client computers as a WINS proxy.

10. Your network has 20 client computers configured as WINS clients using p-node name resolution. If the primary and secondary WINS servers are not available but a WINS proxy is available, how will names be resolved by clients?

    A. Clients will use broadcast name resolution.

    B. Clients will attempt to resolve names from a WINS proxy.

    C. One of the client computers will be promoted to the primary WINS server.

    D. Clients will be unable to resolve names.

11. Your network has 800 client computers configured as WINS clients using m-node name resolution. The client computers are split onto 4 subnets of 200 computers. Each subnet has a primary WINS server. You want to decrease broadcast traffic and increase reliability. Your solution is to add a secondary WINS server to each subnet and to change the client configuration from m-node to h-node. This solution:

    A. Accomplishes both of the objectives

    B. Accomplishes the first objective but not the second

    C. Accomplishes the second objective but not the first

    D. Accomplishes neither objective

12. In an environment having both a primary and a secondary WINS server, with clients configured accordingly, which of the following would be a consequence of the primary WINS server failing?

    A. Clients would be unable to resolve names from the secondary WINS server.

    B. Clients would be able to resolve names from the secondary WINS server.

    C. Name registrations would not be accepted by the secondary WINS server.

    D. Name registrations would be accepted by the secondary WINS server.

13. Which services are not provided by a WINS server?

    A. Resolving name queries sent from WINS clients

    B. Registering names based on name registration requests from WINS clients

    C. Dynamically assigning IP addresses to client computers

    D. Responding to broadcast name registrations

14. Which of the following is likely to occur when you add a WINS server to a network without one, and configure all network clients to use WINS?

    A. Broadcast traffic increases.

    B. Broadcast traffic decreases.

    C. Client computers send name requests to the WINS server.

    D. Client computers continue to send name requests using broadcast messages, but send name registration requests to the WINS server.

15. What is the role of the time-to-live value given to a WINS client after a successful name registration?

    A. The time to live indicates how long the name registration will be valid.

    B. The time to live indicates how long of an interval will pass before the client attempts to renew its name registration.

    C. The time to live indicates when the WINS client will attempt its first name renewal.

    D. The time to live indicates when the WINS server will attempt to renew the client name registration.

16. Which tasks do WINS proxies perform?

    A. WINS proxies act as secondary WINS servers.

    B. WINS proxies handle name renewal requests.

    C. WINS proxies handle name registration requests from non-WINS clients by ensuring the name is not registered in the WINS server.

    D. WINS proxies can forward non-WINS client name resolution requests to a WINS server.

17. What is the purpose of name renewal?

    A. Name renewal ensures no duplicate names exist on the network.

    B. Name renewal resolves NetBIOS names to IP addresses by WINS proxies.

    C. Name renewal reduces traffic generated on the network by allowing WINS clients to renew their name registrations rather than performing a full name registration.

    D. Name renewal removes the name registration from the WINS server's database when the WINS client shuts down.

18. Under what circumstances does name release occur?

   A. When a client sends a name registration for a name that is already registered

   B. When a client sends a name query, which cannot be resolved by the primary or secondary WINS server

   C. When a client computer shuts down

   D. Whenever a client computer sends a name renewal request that is not acknowledged

19. What is the purpose of a secondary WINS server?

   A. A secondary WINS server splits the database of name registrations between two WINS servers.

   B. A secondary WINS server handles only name release requests and name renewal requests; the primary WINS server handles only name registrations.

   C. A secondary WINS server acts as a backup in case the primary WINS server is unavailable for name queries and resolution.

   D. None of the above.

20. When a WINS client issues a request to access a network resource and needs to resolve a NetBIOS name to an IP address, which is the first step in the name resolution process?

   A. The WINS client issues a request directly to the primary WINS server.

   B. The WINS client first checks its local NetBIOS cache.

   C. The WINS client sends a broadcast message to all computers on the subnet.

   D. The WINS client sends its request directly to the secondary WINS server.

Review Answers

1. C

2. A, B, C, D

3. A

4. C

5. C

6. D

7. B, D

8. B, C, D

9. D

10. D

11. A

12. B, D

13. C, D

14. B, C

15. A

16. C, D

17. C

18. C

19. C

20. B

Answers to Test Yourself Questions at Beginning of Chapter

1. A WINS server automatically builds a database to resolve TCP/IP addresses. This database has entries that map TCP/IP addresses to NetBIOS computer names. WINS clients send name registrations to the WINS server. When validated, these registrations are added to the database. WINS clients also query WINS servers to resolve NetBIOS names to TCP/IP addresses. The WINS server uses its database to answer these queries.

2. Each time a WINS client boots, it registers its name with the WINS server. The WINS server verifies that the registration is unique, then sends a successful response to the client. If the mapping already exists, the WINS server queries the host of the original registration to see if the host is still active. If the host is still active, the WINS server sends a negative response to the WINS client requesting registration. If the WINS server doesn't receive a positive response from the existing host, then the WINS client is allowed to register and the WINS server sends the client a successful response.

3. A WINS client can register its NetBIOS name only with the WINS server specified in its TCP/IP settings. A WINS client can have two WINS server addresses, one for a primary WINS server and one for a secondary WINS server. However, only an address for a primary WINS server is required. The client first tries to register its name with its primary WINS server. If the client does not receive a response from the WINS server, it tries again until it has failed to register three times with the primary server. Then, if the WINS client has a secondary WINS server address configured, it also tries three times to register its name with the secondary WINS server. If successful, the client stops. If not, the client sends a broadcast in an attempt to register its name.

4. Basically, any Microsoft client capable of networking with TCP/IP can be a WINS client.

5. Non-WINS clients cannot register their names directly with a WINS server. However, you can manually add static entries to the WINS server for non-WINS clients. You can also import mappings from an LMHOSTS file. These imported mappings also become static entries. After you add static entries for all non-WINS clients, WINS clients should be able to resolve the name of any NetBIOS-based computer on the network.

6. A WINS proxy agent, configured on any Windows-based WINS client, can forward a request from a non-WINS client to the WINS server. Non-WINS clients usually request a name resolution through a broadcast. If a proxy agent is located on the same network segment as the non-WINS client, the proxy agent can hear the broadcast and forward it to the WINS server. The WINS server can be on a remote segment because the proxy agent sends the request directly to the TCP/IP address of the WINS server. The WINS server sends a response to the WINS proxy agent, which then sends a response to the non-WINS client that made the original request.

7. You should have at least two WINS servers. If one server goes down, clients can use the second server to continue to resolve addresses. If you have only one WINS server and that server goes down, WINS clients lose their capability to quickly resolve IP addresses. They may have to resort to broadcasts to resolve addresses, but because most b-node broadcasts are not forwarded, the clients have little chance of resolving addresses beyond their own network segment. As your network grows, you may need to add more WINS servers. Microsoft recommends that you have two WINS servers (one primary and one backup) for every 10,000 WINS clients.

8. A client registers a name for each service that has a networking component. For example, a client registers its own name, a name for the server service, a name for the workstation service, and a name for the messenger service. If additional networking services are installed, they are also registered. A domain controller also registers the name of its domain so domain controllers can be located for logon requests and for network browsing.

9. Because the WINS server builds its database automatically, the administrative burden of maintaining static mappings in an LMHOSTS file is greatly reduced. Also, you eliminate the chance of introducing errors in the LMHOSTS file because the WINS database is built dynamically with the exact TCP/IP addresses and NetBIOS names coming directly from the registering computer. Because WINS clients send their registration requests and address resolution requests directly to the WINS server, broadcast traffic is greatly reduced. Finally, because clients send registrations and queries directly to the server, you do not need to locate a WINS server on each network segment; directed packets can be routed directly to the WINS server.

C h a p t e r 15

Administering a WINS Environment

This chapter will help you prepare for the exam by covering the following objectives:

 Objectives

▶ Install and configure a WINS server

▶ Import LMHOSTS files to WINS

▶ Run WINS on a multihomed computer

▶ Configure WINS replication

▶ Configure static mappings in the WINS database

Test Yourself! Before reading this chapter, test yourself to determine how much study time you will need to devote to this section.

1. How often must WINS clients renew their name registrations with the WINS server?

2. How are entries removed from the WINS database?

3. How can a WINS client resolve addresses that are located in another WINS server's database?

4. How do you configure a WINS server to receive entries from another WINS server's database?

5. How do you configure two WINS servers so they have identical databases?

6. How can you back up a WINS server database?

7. How can you restore a WINS server database? Does this ever happen automatically?

8. On what platform can you install WINS, and how do you install it?

9. When does push replication occur and when does pull replication occur?

10. How is a WINS client configured to use a WINS server?

Answers are located at the end of the chapter.

Installing a WINS Server

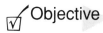
Objective

For an exercise covering this information, see end of chapter.

WINS must be installed on a Windows NT Server version 3.5x or 4.0. WINS servers on any version are compatible with the others; that is, you can mix an NT 3.51 WINS Server with an NT 4.0 WINS Server, including using them as replication partners. You can install WINS on any configuration of NT server—a member server, a Backup Domain Controller, or a Primary Domain Controller. The WINS server should have a static TCP/IP address with a subnet mask and default gateway along with any other TCP/IP parameters required for your network (such as a DNS server address). You can assign a DHCP address to the WINS server (the address should be reserved so the WINS server always receives the same address), but using a static address is the recommended option. Also, you should specify a WINS server address; in this case, the address would be the same machine. The exercises show you how to install a WINS server.

Note

Normally the WINS service should not be run on a computer that is multihomed (has two or more network cards). This is because the WINS server always registers its names in the local database. This is a problem if you will run DOS clients as they will always try the first address that they receive from the WINS server. Since the WINS server will register all of its card in order, the DOS client might not be able to reach resources on the WINS server from network other than the one on which the first card is located.

The WINS service is installed as a network service. After it is installed, it is immediately available for use. However, until WINS clients are configured with the TCP/IP address of the WINS server, they cannot register their names nor use the WINS server for name resolution. In fact, if there weren't any clients configured with this WINS server's address, the WINS database would remain empty unless you add static entries or set up replication with another WINS server.

WINS Clients

Any Microsoft client capable of networking can be a WINS client:

▶ Windows NT Server 3.5x, 4.0

▶ Windows NT Workstation 3.5x, 4.0

▶ Windows 95

▶ Windows for Workgroups with TCP/IP-32

▶ Microsoft Network Client 3.0 for MS-DOS

▶ LAN Manager 2.2c for MS-DOS

However, only the Windows-based clients can register their names with the WINS server. The DOS-based clients can use the WINS server for name resolution, but you must add static entries for DOS clients to the WINS server so their names can be resolved.

For an exercise covering this information, see end of chapter.

To enable these clients for WINS, the address of the primary WINS server must be specified on the client. The client can also have the address of a secondary WINS server configured. The client can either have this configuration information manually entered at the client or it can receive the configuration information with its TCP/IP address from a DHCP server. Exercises 11 and 12 at the end of the chapter show how to configure WINS clients manually and through a DHCP server.

Configuring WINS to be Used by Non-WINS Clients

A WINS server interacts in two ways with WINS clients. First, it registers the names of those clients. Second, it answers requests for name resolutions (name queries). You can enable both functions for non-WINS clients through additional configuration.

Registering Non-WINS Clients with Static Entries

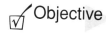

Objective

For an exercise covering this information, see end of chapter.

You can register a non-WINS client with a WINS server by adding a static entry to the WINS database. With entries added for non-WINS clients, a WINS client can resolve more names without resorting to looking up the entries in an LMHOSTS file. In fact, by adding entries for all non-WINS clients, you can eliminate the need for an LMHOSTS file. Static entries are added through the WINS Manager, as described in exercise 15.4 at the end of the chapter.

There are several types of static mappings. Table 15.1 summarizes the types you can add.

Table 15.1

Types of Static Mappings	
Type of Mapping	Explanation
Normal Group	Group names don't have an address rather the WINS server returns FFFFFFFF (the broadcast address). This forces the client to broadcasts on the local subnet to resolve the name.
Multihomed	A multihomed name is used to register a computer with more than one network card. It can contain up to 25 addresses.
Domain Name	In Windows NT 3.51, the Domain Name mapping was known as an Internet Group. The domain-name mapping contains up to a maximum of 25 IP addresses for the primary or backup domain controllers in a domain. This enables client computers and servers to locate a domain controller for logon validation and passthru authentication.
Internet Group	An Internet group mapping name is a user-defined mapping used to store addresses for members of a group other than a domain (such as a workgroup).

Adding Entries to WINS from an LMHOSTS File

Objective

You also can copy entries from an LMHOSTS file to a WINS server. Any entries copied this way are considered static entries. The exercises show you how to add static entries and how to import entries from an LMHOSTS file.

Resolving Names Through a WINS Server for Non-WINS Clients

For an exercise covering this information, see end of chapter.

You can also allow non-WINS clients to use a WINS server to resolve NetBIOS names by installing a *WINS proxy agent.* By definition, a non-WINS client cannot directly communicate with a WINS server to resolve a name. The non-WINS client resolves names by resorting to a b-node broadcast. If you install a WINS proxy agent, the proxy agent forwards any broadcasts for name resolution onto the WINS server. The proxy agent must be located on the same subnet as non-WINS clients so the proxy agent receives the broadcast for name resolution.

When a non-WINS client broadcasts a name resolution request, a proxy agent that hears the broadcast checks its own NetBIOS name cache to see whether an entry exists for the requested name. If the entry doesn't exist, the proxy agent adds to the cache an entry for that name with the status of pending. The proxy agent then sends a name resolution request for the same name to the WINS server. After the WINS server responds with the name resolution, the proxy agent adds the entry to its cache and then removes the pending status from the entry. The proxy agent does not forward the response to the non-WINS client making the request. When the non-WINS client broadcasts another request for the name resolution, the proxy agent now finds an entry for the name in its cache and the proxy agent can respond to the non-WINS client with a successful name resolution response.

The WINS proxy agent also forwards registration requests to the WINS server. However, registration requests for non-WINS clients are not added to the WINS server's database. The WINS server uses these forwarded registration requests to see whether there are any potential conflicts in its database with the requested name registration. You must still add static entries to the WINS database so names of non-WINS clients can be resolved.

You must place a WINS proxy agent on each subnet where non-WINS clients are located so those clients have access to the WINS server. Because those clients resolve names only by using broadcasts, which are not typically routed, those broadcasts never go beyond the subnet. With a proxy agent on each subnet, broadcasts on each subnet can then be forwarded to the WINS server. You can have two proxy agents on a subnet, but you shouldn't exceed this limit. Even having more than one proxy agent on a subnet can generate excessive work for the WINS server because each proxy agent forwards name resolution and name registration requests to the WINS server. The WINS server has to respond to duplicate messages from proxy agents if more than one proxy agent is on a subnet.

Any Windows-based WINS client can be a WINS proxy agent. To configure an NT server or workstation to be a proxy agent, you must turn on a parameter in the registry. This proxy agent cannot be a WINS server. Windows 95 and Windows for Workgroups computers are more easily configured by turning on a switch in the TCP/IP configuration. Exercise 15.13 at the end of the chapter shows how to configure a Windows NT computer and a Windows 95 computer to be a WINS proxy agent.

 Tip

To make an NT server or workstation into a proxy agent, open

`HKEY_LOCAL_MACHINE\System\CurrentControlSet\Services\NetBT`
`\Parameters`

and change the value of the EnableProxy parameter to 1.

After you configure a WINS client to be a proxy agent, you must reboot the machine for this change to take effect. No other configuration is needed for this proxy agent. This WINS client remains a proxy agent until you turn off the proxy agent parameter and reboot the computer.

Configuring a Client for WINS

To manually configure a WINS client, you specify the WINS server address as part of the TCP/IP configuration. Open the TCP/IP properties in the Protocol tab of the Network Properties dialog (opened with Control Panel, Network). Select the WINS tab in the TCP/IP properties dialog and simply specify the address of a primary WINS server. If you are using a secondary WINS server, you should also type in the IP address of the secondary WINS server.

You can also specify the address of a secondary WINS server. Figure 15.1 shows a client with manually configured WINS addresses.

Figure 15.1

Manually configuring a WINS client through TCP/IP properties.

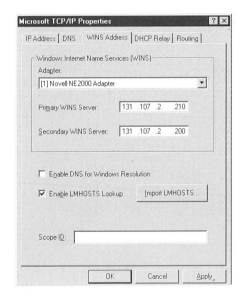

To configure a DHCP client to be a WINS client, you must add two properties to the DHCP scope created on the DHCP server. Installing and configuring DHCP is described in chapter 13. Under the DHCP scope options, add the following parameters:

▶ **044 WINS/NBNS Servers.** Configure this with the address of the primary WINS server and a secondary WINS server, if desired.

▶ **046 WINS/NBT Node.** By default, this is set to 2, a b-node broadcast. WINS clients use h-node broadcasts, so you must change the value of the this parameter to 8. Figure 15.2 shows these options added to a DCHP scope.

Figure 15.2

Configuring a DHCP scope to distribute WINS client configuration with a DHCP address.

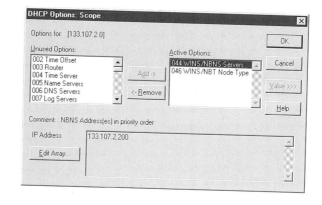

Replication

 Objective

Because WINS clients are configured to communicate only with specified WINS servers, the database on each WINS server may not have entries for all the WINS clients in the network. In fact, many TCP/IP implementations divide WINS clients among different WINS servers to balance the load. Unfortunately, WINS clients cannot resolve addresses registered with another WINS server unless the registrations from that server are somehow copied to the client's WINS server. *WINS replication* is the process used to copy one WINS server's database to another WINS server.

You can configure a WINS server so it replicates its database with another WINS server. This way, clients registered with one WINS server can be added to the database of another server. Static mappings entered on one server are also replicated to replication partners. In fact, you can enter static entries on only one WINS server and yet these entries can be propagated to any number of WINS servers through replication.

After you enable replication, clients seeking name resolution can see not only entries from their server but entries of the replication partners. Remember that clients register their names with the WINS server for which the clients are configured. WINS registrations are not done through broadcasts (in fact, one of main benefits of WINS is the reduction of broadcast traffic). Because one WINS server is collecting registrations just for its clients, the only way for its clients to resolve names registered with another WINS server is for replication to be configured between the servers.

For an exercise covering this information, see end of chapter.

To set up replication, you must configure a WINS server as a push partner or a pull partner. A *push partner* sends its entries to another server, such as if you want to send a copy of the database from this WINS server to the other WINS server. A *pull partner* receives entries from another server, such as if you want this server to receive a copy of the database from another WINS server. You must always configure WINS servers in pairs; otherwise, replication won't work. Figure 15.3 shows a WINS server that is configured to be a push and a pull partner.

Figure 15.3

Configuring a WINS server to be a push-pull partner.

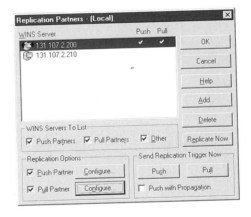

At the very least, one WINS server must be a push partner to send its entries out, while the other WINS server must be a pull partner to receive the entries. Replication does not occur unless both WINS servers are properly configured. If both WINS servers are configured as push and pull partners, then each server ends up with entries from the other server. In theory, the combined database on each WINS server should be the same. However, due to the lag time in replication, this doesn't always happen. Exercise 15.7 at the end of the chapter shows how to configure a WINS server as a replication partner.

Deciding which WINS server will be a push partner and which will be a pull partner is often driven by performance considerations. You often use a pull partner across slow WAN links because you can configure a pull partner to replicate only at certain times, such as at night when the WAN link is not as heavily utilized. In this case, you could make the WINS server on each side of the WAN link a pull partner with the other WINS server. This is known as pull-pull replication.

On faster links, you can use push partners. Push partners replicate when a specified number of changes are made to the database. These updates can happen fairly frequently, but are not too large because you are not waiting to replicate a whole day's worth of changes. If you want two WINS servers to have identical databases, you must configure each WINS server to be a push and a pull partner for the other server.

You can configure a replication partner to start replication in several ways:

1. When the WINS server starts, you can configure this startup replication for either a push or a pull partner.

2. At a specified interval, such as every 24 hours. This applies to pull replication.

3. When a push partner reaches a specified number of changes to the database. These changes include name registrations and name releases. When this threshold is reached, the push partner notifies all its pull partners that it has changes for replications.

4. You can manually force replication from the WINS Manager.

WINS can automatically replicate with other WINS servers if your network supports multicasting. By default, every 40 minutes, each WINS server sends a multicast to the address 224.0.1.24. Any servers found through this multicast are automatically configured as push and pull partners, with replication set to occur every two hours. If the routers on your network do not support multicasting, the WINS servers only see other servers on the same subnet.

You can turn off this multicasting feature by editing the registry in the following location:

```
HKEY_LOCAL_MACHINE\System\CurrentControlSet\Services\NetBT\Parameters
```

Change the value of UseSelfFndPnrs to 0. Change the value of McastIntvl to a large number.

The Replication Process

A WINS server replicates only its active and extinct entries; released entries are not replicated. A replication partner can have entries that are marked active even though they have been released by its partner. Released entries are not replicated, to reduce the traffic from computers booting and shutting down each day. However, if a registration changes, it is considered a new entry and it is replicated. The following example shows how records are replicated between replication partners.

Using the WINS Manager

As you install WINS, a WINS Manager tool is added to the Administrative Tools group. You can use this tool to manage the local WINS server and remote WINS servers as well. You can use WINS Manager to view the WINS database, add static entries to the database, configure push and pull partners for replication, and back up and restore the WINS database. Figure 15.4 shows the WINS Manager window that appears when you start WINS Manager.

Figure 15.4

The WINS Manager window.

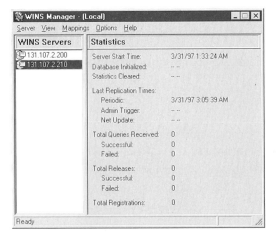

WINS Manager Configuration Dialog

For an exercise covering this information, see end of chapter.

You can use the WINS Server Configuration dialog box to configure how long entries stay in the WINS database. Figure 15.5 shows this dialog. The following four parameters control the life of entries:

Figure 15.5

The WINS Server Configuration dialog box.

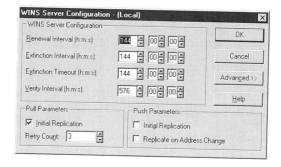

▶ **Renewal Interval.** This is the interval given to a WINS client after it successfully registers its name. The client begins renewing the name registration when half this time has expired. The default is six days.

▶ **Extinction Interval.** This is the amount of time that must pass before the WINS server marks a released entry as extinct. An extinct entry is not immediately deleted. The default is six days. The time until removal is controlled by the following parameter.

▶ **Extinction Timeout.** This is the amount of time WINS waits before removing (scavenging) entries that have been marked extinct. The default is six days.

▶ **Verify Interval.** This parameter applies if WINS servers are set up for replication. This is the interval at which the WINS server verifies that names in its database that came from other servers are still valid. The default is 24 days, and cannot be set below this value.

Initial Replication Configuration

You can configure whether the WINS server replicates with its replication partners it starts. Check the Initial Replication option under Pull Parameters on the WINS Server Configuration dialog to have a pull replication partner replicate on start up. You can also specify the number of times the pull partner tries to contact the other WINS server as the pull partner does the startup replication.

For a push partner, you can also configure it to replicate upon startup by checking the Initial Replication option under Push Parameters. You can also specify that the push partner replicates when it has an address change.

Advanced Configuration Options

You can turn on or turn off the logging of entries to the WINS database. This log file records changes that are made to the WINS database before they are made. By default, logging is on, which gives the WINS server a backup via the log file. If you turn off the logging, the WINS server registers names more quickly, but you lose the backup support of the log file. These settings are configured through the WINS Advanced Configuration dialog box, as shown in figure 15.6.

Figure 15.6

The WINS Advanced Configuration dialog box.

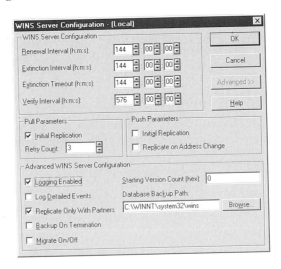

The following are the advanced settings you can configure:

▶ **Log Detailed Events.** If you turn this on, the logging of WINS events in Event Viewer is more verbose. This means that you get more useful troubleshooting information from the log file. However, some performance degradation occurs when verbose logging is turned on.

▶ **Replicate Only With Partners.** By default, WINS replicates only with other WINS servers that are specifically configured as push or pull partners. If you want the WINS server to replicate automatically, you must turn off this setting.

▶ **Backup On Termination.** If you set this option, the WINS database is automatically backed up when the WINS service is stopped. However, the database is not backed up when the NT server is shut down.

▶ **Migrate On/Off.** If this switch is on, static entries that have the same address as a WINS client requesting registration are overwritten. This option is helpful if you are converting a computer from a non-NT machine to an NT machine with the same TCP/IP address. To have addresses resolved for this non-NT machine in the past, you may have added a static entry to the WINS database. With the option on, the new dynamic entry can overwrite the old static entry. It is usually best to turn off this switch after you have migrated (upgraded) the new NT machine. This switch is off by default so static entries are not overwritten.

▶ **Starting Version Count.** This specifies the largest version ID number for the database. Each entry in the database is assigned a version ID. Replication is based on the version ID. A replication partner checks its last replicated entries against the version IDs of the records in the WINS database. The replication partner replicates only records with a later version ID than the last records it replicated from this partner. Usually, you don't need to change this parameter. However, if the database becomes corrupted, you may need to adjust this number so a replication partner replicates the proper entries.

▶ **Database Backup Path.** When the WINS database is backed up, it is copied to a local hard drive. This specifies the path to a directory on a local drive where the WINS backups are stored. This directory can also be used to automatically restore the WINS database. You must specify a local drive path.

Backing Up the WINS Database

For an exercise covering this information, see end of chapter.

The database can be backed up automatically when WINS shuts down. You also can schedule backups or manually start a backup. All these backups are copied to the backup directory specified in the Advanced Configuration options. You can manually start a WINS backup from the Mappings menu in the WINS Manager. To automatically schedule backups, configure the path for a backup directory. After you set this path, the WINS server automatically backs itself up every 24 hours.

You should also back up the WINS subkey in the registry. This subkey has the configuration settings for WINS, but does not contain any entries from the WINS database. The regular backup for WINS makes a copy of the database itself.

 Tip

To back up the WINS registry subkey, use the NT registry editor, REGEDT32. Then backup the HKEY_LOCAL_MACHINE\ System\CurrentControlSet\Services\WINS subkey. You can save this subkey in the same location you store the WINS database backups.

Restoring the WINS Database

For an exercise covering this information, see end of chapter.

You can restore the WINS database from the backups you made previously. To restore the database, from the Mappings menu in WINS Manager, choose Restore database.

WINS also can automatically restore the database. If the WINS service starts and detects a corrupted database, it automatically restores a backup from the specified backup directory. If you suspect the database is corrupt, you can stop and start the WINS service from Control Panel, Services to force this automatic restoration.

Files Used for WINS

The WINS database is stored in the path \WINNT\SYSTEM32\ WINS. Several files make up the WINS database:

- ▶ **WINS.MDB.** This is the WINS database itself.

- ▶ **WINSTMP.MDB.** This is a temporary working file used by WINS. This file is deleted when the WINS server is shut down normally, but a copy could remain in the directory after a crash.

- ▶ **J50.LOG.** This is the transaction log of the WINS database.

- ▶ **J50.CHK.** This is a checkpoint file used by the WINS database. This is equivalent to a cache for a disk drive.

Compacting the WINS Database

You can compact the WINS database to reduce its size. However, WINS under NT 4.0 is designed to automatically compact the database, so you shouldn't have to compact it. To force manual compacting of the database, use the JETPACK utility in the \WINNT\SYSTEM32\WINS directory. (The WINS database is a JET database, so this utility packs that database.) To pack the database, you must first stop the WINS service. You cannot pack an open database. Then type the following command:

jetpack WINS.mdb temp.mdb

This command compacts the database into the file temp.mdb, then copies the compacted database to WINS.mdb. The temporary file is deleted. After the database is compacted, you can restart the WINS service from Control Panel, Services.

Exercises

Exercise 15.1: Installing a WINS Server

With this exercise, you install the WINS service and configure your WINS server to use itself as the primary WINS server.

Prerequisites: You have installed Windows NT 4.0 Server with the TCP/IP protocol. The NT server can be a member server, a back-up domain controller, or a primary domain controller.

1. Right-click on Network Neighborhood, and choose properties from the menu. (Network properties can also be accessed from the Network icon in Control Panel.)

2. Select the Services tab, then choose Add. From the Network Service box, select Windows Internet Name Service and then choose OK.

3. Select the Protocols tab, select TCP/IP Protocol, then choose properties.

4. Select the WINS Address tab. Type the TCP/IP address of your Windows NT server as the primary WINS server.

5. Choose OK, then choose Close to close the Network properties dialog.

6. When prompted, choose Yes to reboot your server.

Exercise 15.2: Checking the Windows NT Application Log

With this exercise, you see where WINS writes its error messages.

Prerequisites: You have installed WINS on your Windows NT 4.0 server. You have rebooted the server since you installed WINS.

1. Choose Start, Programs, Administrative Tools.

2. From the Administrative Tools menu, choose Event Viewer.

3. From the Log menu in Event Viewer, choose Application.

4. Double-click on the top message.

5. Select Next to continue scrolling through the messages.

6. Note the messages generated by starting the database engine and checking its integrity upon startup.

7. Choose Close to return to the Application Log window.

8. Note the source of most of the messages, the JET database. WINS is a JET database, which is why WINS messages are recorded in the Application log of Event Viewer.

9. Close Event Viewer.

Exercise 15.3: Viewing the WINS Database Mappings

This exercise enables you to see the database mappings collected by the WINS server.

Prerequisites: You have installed WINS.

1. Choose Start, Programs, Administrative Tools.

2. From the Administrative Tools menu, choose WINS Manager.

3. In the WINS Manager window, note the statistics for your WINS server. The items listed are: the latest starting time of the WINS service (typically the last boot); the last registration time; and the total queries, releases, and registrations.

4. From the Server menu, choose Detailed Information.

5. Note you can see some total statistics about the WINS database from the Detailed Information window.

6. Choose Close.

7. From the Mappings menu in WINS Manager, choose Show Database. Note: If the menu is gray, select your WINS server in the WINS Manager window before choosing Show Database.

8. Note the different numbers registered for each machine name. See if you can find the registration for your computer's name, your computer's server service, your computer's

continues

Exercise 15.3: Continued

workstation service, and your user name. Use table 9.1 to find which numbers are used to register each service. Hint: Use the Set Filter button to view only your computer name in the database. When you are finished, use the Clear Filter button to reset the display to see the entire database.

9. Try the different sort order options to see how they affect the display.

10. Note the time stamp for each entry as well as the version ID. The time stamp specifies when the current status of the entry expires. The version ID is used to determine whether the record is replicated.

11. Close the Show Database window.

Exercise 15.4: Adding Static Entries to a WINS Database

In this exercise, you add static entries manually to the WINS database through WINS Manager. Figure 15.7 shows the static mappings after exercises 4 and 5 have been completed.

Prerequisites: You have installed WINS on a Windows NT 4.0 Server.

1. Choose Start, Programs, Administrative Tools.

2. From the Administrative Tools menu, choose WINS Manager.

3. From the Mappings menu in WINS Manager, choose Static Mappings.

4. Choose Add Mappings.

5. In the computer box, type **ABDCE**.

6. In the IP Address box, type **131.107.2.25**.

7. In the Type box, select Unique.

8. Choose Add to save the entry.

9. Add an entry for a computer named FGHIJ with an IP address of 133.107.4.53 and Type Group.

10. Add an entry for a computer named KLMNO with an IP address of 136.107.3.34 and Type Domain Name. Note with the Domain Name mappings you must also move the IP address down with the arrow before you can save it. This is because you can have multiple addresses (for multiple domain controllers) associated with a domain name.

11. Close the Add Static Mappings dialog. Note the mappings you have added in the Static Mappings dialog.

12. Try editing each of the entries. Note the type of each entry differs. Note also the Edit Static Mapping dialog for the domain mapping differs from the dialogs for the unique and group types.

13. Close the Static Mappings dialog box after exploring the Edit Static Mapping dialogs.

14. In the WINS Manager window, choose Show Database from the Mappings menu.

15. Scroll down the mappings database and note the static entries you added. The static mappings are marked with a check in the S column.

16. Sort the database by expiration date. Scroll to the bottom of the database and note the static mappings are there with a time stamp that won't let these entries expire.

17. Close the Show Database window.

Figure 15.7

Static mappings added manually and from an LMHOSTS file.

Exercise 15.5: Importing an LMHOSTS File into the WINS Database

In exercise 15.5, you add static mappings to a WINS database from an LMHOSTS file.

Prerequisites: You have installed WINS on a Windows NT 4.0 Server. You do not need an LMHOSTS file, although if you have written one or have one available, you can use it in this exercise.

Note

If you have your own LMHOSTS file you want to import, skip steps 1–4. Figure 15.7 shows the static mappings after labs 4–5 have been completed.

1. From Explorer, locate LMHOSTS.SAM. This file is located in the System32\Drivers\Etc subdirectory of your NT root directory.

2. Edit LMHOSTS.SAM with Notepad.

3. Remove the # comment characters in front of the lines registering IP addresses for rhino, appname, popular, and localsrv.

4. Save this file as LMHOSTS. Now the file is ready for importing.

5. Choose Start, Programs, Administrative Tools.

6. From the Administrative Tools menu, choose WINS Manager.

7. From the Mappings menu in WINS Manager, choose Static Mappings.

8. Choose the Import Mappings Button.

9. Browse to find the LMHOSTS file you modified, then choose that file.

10. Choose Open.

11. Note the names from the LMHOSTS file have been added to the static mappings.

12. Close the Static Mappings dialog.

13. From the Mappings menu, choose Show Database.

14. Note the mappings you added from the LMHOSTS file are now in the WINS database.

Exercise 15.6:   Configuring the WINS Server

In this exercise, you see the different configuration options in WINS Manager.

Prerequisites: You have installed WINS on a Windows NT 4.0 Server.

1. Choose Start, Programs, Administrative Tools.

2. From the Administrative Tools menu, choose WINS Manager.

3. From the Server menu, choose Configuration.

4. Note the default times for the Renewal Interval, the Extinction Interval, and the Extinction Timeout. Each of these values is six days (144 hours). These times dictate how quickly a WINS database entry moves from active to released (renewal interval), from released to extinct (extinction interval), and from extinct to being removed from the database (extinction timeout). Note that Microsoft recommends you do not modify these values.

5. Note the default time for the verify interval is 24 days (576 hours). This specifies when a WINS server verifies that entries that it does not own (entries added to the database due to replication) are still active. The minimum value you can set for this parameter is 24 days.

6. Note the check box to do push or pull replication when the WINS server initializes.

7. Choose the Advanced button.

8. Note two of the settings here that can affect WINS performance—Logging Enabled and Log Detailed Events.

continues

Exercise 15.6: Continued

With Logging Enabled, WINS must first write any changes to the WINS database to the JET.LOG file. Then, the changes are made to the database. This log file serves as an ongoing backup to the database should it crash during the write process. However, if a number of changes are being made to the database simultaneously, logging can slow WINS performance—for example, when everyone powers up their computers in the morning and the clients try to register at the same time. With Log Detailed Events turned on, more detailed messages are written to the Event Log. Note that both settings are turned on by default.

9. Note the default setting for Replicate Only With Partners. WINS replicates only with specified partners unless you turn this setting off. When turned off, WINS tries to replicate with all the WINS servers it can locate through broadcasts.

10. Choose OK to close the Configuration dialog.

Exercise 15.7: Configuring Replication Partners

In this exercise, you set up replication with another WINS server.

Prerequisites: You have installed WINS on a Windows NT 4.0 Server. Although it is ideal to have another WINS server to do this exercise, you can go through the steps of setting up replication without having another WINS server. However, you will not be able to see the results of replication.

1. Choose Start, Programs, Administrative Tools.

2. From the Administrative Tools menu, choose WINS Manager.

3. If you don't have another WINS server, skip to step 5. If you have another WINS server, do step 4.

4. From the Server menu, choose Add server. Type the TCP/IP address of the other WINS server, the choose OK.

5. Select your WINS server in the WINS Manager window.

6. From the Server menu, choose Replication Partners.

Note

If you do not have another WINS server, you cannot complete the remaining steps. However, you can see the interface for the remaining steps by referring to the figures in the section on "Replication" earlier in this chapter.

7. From the Replication Partners box, select the other WINS server.

8. In the Replication Options box, select the other WINS server to be both a push and a pull partner.

9. Choose Configuration for a Push Partner. Note that push replication is triggered when an Update Count is reached.

10. Choose Configuration for a Pull Partner. Note that pull replication is started at a specific time and then from an offset time after the initial replication time.

11. Note that in this dialog you can also manually trigger replication by choosing the Push or the Pull button in the Send Replication Trigger Now box.

Exercise 15.8: Backing Up the WINS Server

In exercise 15.8, you configure the WINS server for automatic backup and to manually back up the WINS server.

Prerequisites: You have installed WINS on a Windows NT 4.0 Server.

1. Choose Start, Programs, Administrative Tools.

2. From the Administrative Tools menu, choose WINS Manager.

3. From the Server menu in the WINS Manager windows, choose Configuration.

4. Choose Advanced.

5. In the Database Backup Path box, browse to find the System32\WINS subdirectory under the root of the NT installation.

continues

Exercise 15.8: Continued

6. Choose OK. A path similar to C:\WINNT\SYSTEM32\WINS should appear in the Database Backup Path box.

 Note With this path set, WINS backs up the database to this directory every 24 hours. This backup can be used for automatic recovery if WINS detects the database is corrupt. You can also restore the database manually from this directory.

7. Note the Backup On Termination option in the Advanced WINS Server Configuration box. When this option is checked, WINS automatically backs up the WINS database when the WINS service is stopped. However, the WINS server does not back up the database when the Windows NT server is shut down.

8. Choose OK to close the WINS Server Configuration dialog.

9. From the Mappings menu of the WINS Manager window, choose Backup Database.

10. Choose OK to back up the database to the path entered in the Advanced Configuration settings. You can also choose to save the backup in a different directory.

11. A message appears indicating the backup is successful.

Exercise 15.9: Restoring the WINS Database Backup

In this exercise, you manually restore a WINS database backup.

Prerequisites: You have installed WINS on a Windows NT 4.0 Server. You have completed exercise 15.8.

1. Choose Start, Settings, Control Panel.

2. From the Control Panel window, choose Services.

3. From the Services windows, select Windows Internet Name Service.

4. Choose Stop.

5. Choose Start, Programs, Administrative Tools.

6. From the Administrative Tools menu, choose WINS Manager.

7. From the Mappings menu in the WINS Manager windows, choose Restore Local Database.

Note   This option is grayed out if the WINS service is started. The WINS service must be stopped to restore the WINS database.

8. Choose OK to restore a backup from the path specified in the Advanced Configuration settings. You can also choose to restore a backup from a different directory.

9. A message indicating a successful restoration should appear.

10. Choose Start, Settings, Control Panel.

11. From the Control Panel window, choose Services.

12. From the Services dialog, choose Windows Internet Name Service.

13. Choose Start.

14. A message indicating WINS started successfully should appear.

Exercise 15.10:   Scavenging the WINS Database

This exercise initiates scavenging on the WINS server.

Prerequisites: You have installed WINS on a Windows NT 4.0 Server.

1. Choose Start, Programs, Administrative Tools.

2. From the Administrative Tools menu, choose WINS Manager.

3. From the Server menu in the WINS Manager window, choose Detailed Information. Note the last scavenging time, if any.

4. Choose Close.

5. From the Mappings menu, choose Initiate Scavenging.

continues

Exercise 15.10: Continued

6. A message appears indicating that the scavenging command has been queued.

7. Later, you can check the Detailed Information to see if scavenging has occurred.

Exercise 15.11: Manually Configuring a WINS Client

With this exercise, you manually configure a TCP/IP client to be a WINS client. You configure the WINS server to be a WINS client, but the same process is used to configure other WINS clients, that is, you specify the address of the primary WINS server in the specified box and if desired, the address of a secondary WINS server in the specified box.

Prerequisites: You have installed WINS on a Windows NT 4.0 Server.

1. Right-click on Network Neighborhood, then, from the menu, choose Properties. (You also can access the Network Properties dialog from Control Panel, Network.)

2. Select the Protocols tab.

3. Select TCP/IP Protocol, then choose Properties.

4. Select the WINS Address tab.

5. Type the address of your WINS server in the primary WINS Server box.

6. Choose OK, then choose Close.

7. Reboot your computer when prompted. You have now configured your computer manually to be a WINS client.

Exercise 15.12: Configuring a DHCP Client to be a WINS Client

The purpose of this exercise is to configure DHCP clients to automatically receive WINS client configuration through the DHCP scope.

Prerequisites: You have installed WINS on a Windows NT 4.0 Server. You have installed a DHCP server with a scope. See Chapter 12 for information on installing a DHCP server and adding a DHCP scope.

1. Choose Start, Programs, Administrative Tools.

2. From the Administrative Tools menu, choose DHCP Manager.

3. In the DHCP Manager window, choose the local machine.

4. Select the scope created under the local machine.

5. From the DHCP Options menu, select Scope.

Note   This option is grayed out unless you have selected the scope.

6. In the Unused Options box, select 044 WINS/NBNS Servers and choose Add.

7. In the Unused Options box, select 046 WINS/NBNS Node Type and choose Add.

8. From the Active Options box, select 044 WINS/NBNS Servers and choose Value.

9. Choose Edit Array, type the address of your WINS server, then choose Add.

10. Choose OK to close the IP Address Array Editor.

11. From the Active Options box, select 046 WINS/NBNS Node Type.

12. In the Byte box, change the value 0x2 (b-node broadcast) to 0x8 (h-node broadcast).

13. Choose OK. The scope options are now set for DHCP clients from this scope to automatically become clients of your WINS server.

Exercise 15.13: Configuring a WINS Proxy Agent

In exercise 15.13, you configure a Windows NT 4.0 computer to be a WINS proxy agent. In prior versions of Windows NT, configuring a computer to be a proxy agent was done through a check box in the advanced settings of TCP/IP. This is how Windows 95 and Windows for Workgroups machines are configured to be a proxy agent. However, this check box was removed in NT 4.0, so you must now go to the registry to configure a proxy agent.

Prerequisites: You have installed WINS on a Windows NT 4.0 Server.

1. Choose Start, Run.

2. Type **REGEDT32**, then choose OK.

3. In the window, HKEY_LOCAL_MACHINE, walk down the path:

`HKEY_LOCAL_MACHINE\System\CurrentControlSet\Services\NetBT\Parameters`

4. Notice the parameter called EnableProxy. To make this NT computer into a WINS proxy agent, you must change the value of this parameter to 1 and reboot the computer. However, because the computer you are working on is most likely your WINS server, and because you shouldn't have a proxy agent and a WINS server on the same machine, don't set the parameter.

5. Close the registry editor.

Review Questions

The following questions test your knowledge of the information in this chapter.

1. How does a WINS server gather entries to add to its database?

   A. It examines each packet sent on the network.

   B. It receives a copy of the browse list from the master browser on each network segment.

   C. WINS clients send a name registration to the WINS server.

   D. It retrieves a copy of the computer accounts in each domain.

2. Where does a client first look to resolve a NetBIOS name?

   A. In the NetBIOS cache on the WINS server

   B. In the NetBIOS cache on the WINS proxy agent

   C. In the NetBIOS cache on the primary Domain Controller

   D. In the NetBIOS cache on the client

3. What type of names are registered by WINS clients (select all that apply)?

   A. The computer name

   B. The domain name of a domain controller

   C. Share names created on that computer

   D. The names of network services

4. How do you configure automatic backup of the WINS database?

   A. Use the AT command to schedule the backup

   B. Specify the name of the backup directory in WINS Manager

    C. Specify the backup interval in WINS Manager

    D. Install a tape device through Control Panel, SCSI Adapters

5. When does a WINS client try to renew its registration?

    A. After three days

    B. One day before the registration expires

    C. Every 24 hours

    D. When one half of the registration life has expired

6. By default, where does the WINS server first write changes to the database?

    A. To the log file

    B. To the database

    C. To the registry

    D. To the temporary database

7. How do you configure replication to occur at specified intervals?

    A. Configure a WINS server to be a pull partner

    B. Use the AT command to schedule replication

    C. Configure a WINS server to be a push partner

    D. Edit the ReplIntrvl parameter in the registry

8. How can you add entries for non-WINS clients to a WINS server's database?

    A. Configure the WINS server to be a pull partner for a DNS server

    B. Import an LMHOSTS file

    C. Install the WINS proxy agent on the segment with non-WINS clients

    D. Add the entries with WINS Manager

9. When is an entry scavenged from the WINS database?

    A. When a WINS client requests a name release

    B. When a name registration expires without renewal

    C. When an entry has been marked extinct

    D. When the extinction interval has elapsed

10. Where can you see a record of WINS server error messages?

    A. In the Windows NT System Event Log

    B. In the ERROR.LOG file in the WINS directory

    C. In the Windows NT Application Event Log

    D. In the error log in WINS Manager

11. What does a WINS server do if it receives a name registration request for a host name already in its database?

    A. It replaces the old entry with the newer one.

    B. It queries the host of the existing registration to see whether the registration is still valid.

    C. It denies the registration request.

    D. It adds the registration as an alternate address for the existing name.

12. How do you install a WINS proxy agent?

    A. From Control Panel, Network, Services

    B. From Control Panel, Add Programs

    C. By changing a registry entry

    D. Running the Network Client Administration tool from the WINS program group

13. How can you configure a WINS server to automatically replicate its database with any other WINS servers?

    A. Specify All Servers as push partners for replication

B. Turn on the Migrate On/Off switch in WINS Manager

C. Change the UseSelfFndPnrs parameter in the registry to 0

D. Turn off the Replicate Only With Partners switch in WINS Manager

14. How does a client decide which WINS server to use?

A. The first WINS server that responds to a broadcast

B. The WINS server that WINS an election

C. The Initial WINS server configured in TCP/IP

D. The primary WINS server specified in the DHCP scope options

15. What happens to a name registration when the host crashes?

A. The WINS server marks the record as released after it queries the client at half of TTL

B. The name is marked as released after three renewal periods are missed

C. The name is scavenged after the registration expires

D. The name is released after the TTL is over

16. On which platform can you install a WINS server?

A. On a Windows NT 3.51 member server

B. On a Windows NT 4.0 workstation running the WINS proxy agent

C. On a Windows NT 4.0 Backup Domain Controller

D. On a Windows NT 4.0 Primary Domain Controller

17. How many WINS servers should be installed?

    A. One primary for each subnet and one secondary for every two subnets

    B. One primary for every 2,000 clients and one secondary for each additional 2,000 clients

    C. One primary and one secondary for every 10,000 clients

    D. One primary and secondary for each domain

18. How do you configure automatic address resolution for DHCP clients?

    A. Specify the Create WINS database option in the DHCP scope

    B. Install a WINS server with an address specified by the DHCP scope

    C. Schedule the active leases to be copied from DCHP manager to an LMHOSTS file

    D. Locate a DHCP relay agent on the same subnet as the WINS server

19. Where should a WINS proxy agent be located?

    A. On the same subnet as non-WINS clients

    B. On the same subnet as the DHCP server

    C. On the same subnet as the DNS server

    D. On the same subnet as the DHCP Relay Agent

20. To configure a DHCP scope to use WINS, the WINS/NBT Node type should be set to _____?

    A. 1

    B. 2

    C. 4

    D. 8

21. How can the WINS clients of one WINS server resolve the addresses of clients registered with another WINS server?

    A. The WINS server can be configured for recursive lookup to the other WINS server.

    B. The WINS server can be a replication partner of the other server.

    C. The client can be configured with the address of the other WINS server as its secondary WINS server.

    D. The WINS servers automatically synchronize their databases.

22. How can you remove entries from a WINS database that have been replicated from another WINS server?

    A. Select Delete Owner in WINS Manager.

    B. Stop WINS, restore the database backup, then start WINS.

    C. Remove the other WINS server as a replication partner.

    D. You must manually delete the entries.

23. How can you remove obsolete entries from the WINS database?

    A. Shorten the Extinction Timeout interval to 0

    B. Sort the entries by TTL and delete entries with TTL of 0.

    C. Select Initiate Scavenging from WINS Manager

    D. Set the Filter in WINS Manager to display only registrations with TTL > 0

24. Where is WINS configuration information stored?

    A. In the \WINNT\SYSTEM32\WINS directory

    B. In the registry

    C. In the WINS.CFG file in the WINNT directory

    D. In the J50.CHK file in the WINS directory

25. Which replication option is best for WINS servers separated by a slow WAN link?

    A. Pull replication configured to replicate after 100 changes

    B. Push replication configured to replicate after 100 changes

    C. Pull replication configured to replicate at 6 a.m. and 6 p.m.

    D. Push replication configured to replicate at 6 a.m. and 6 p.m.

Review Answers

1. C

2. D

3. A, B, D

4. B

5. D

6. A

7. A

8. B, D

9. D

10. C

11. B

12. C

13. D

14. D

15. D

16. A, C, D

17. C

18. B

19. A

20. D

21. B

22. A

23. C

24. B

25. C

Answers to Test Yourself Questions at Beginning of Chapter

1. Clients first register their names with the WINS server when they boot. Upon successful registration, they receive a time to live for their registration from the WINS server. Clients try to renew the registration when half this time has elapsed. The default time to live is six days, so the WINS client tries to renew its registration after three days. After the client renews its registration, the new time to live is, again, six days, so in another three days the client renews its registration.

2. Entries can be removed either when a client requests a release or when the registration expires. A client sends a registration release request when it shuts down normally. The WINS server marks released entries as inactive. If the client has not renewed its registration when its time to live expires (assuming the client has not released the registration), the WINS server marks the entry as released. After the specified extinction interval (the default is six days), the entry is marked extinct. The entry is not removed from the database until the extinction timeout interval is reached, which is also six days by default. In total, then, a client's address can remain in the WINS server database for 18 days after the initial registration, even if the client never renews its registration (six days for the time to live, six days for extinction interval, and six days for the extinction timeout).

3. A WINS client queries only WINS servers that are specified as its primary or secondary WINS servers. However, you can have a number of WINS servers on the network, with each server servicing a different set of clients. You can configure the WINS servers to copy their entries to another server through replication.

4. Configure the target WINS server as a replication partner of the source WINS server. To receive entries from another server, the WINS server must be a pull partner. You must also configure the source WINS server as a replication partner. To send entries to another WINS server, the local WINS server must be a push partner. You must configure both servers as replication partners of the other WINS server or replication does not happen.

5. You must configure each server as both a push and a pull replication partner for the other WINS server. Being a push partner sends a WINS server's entries to its partner. Being a pull partner lets a WINS server receive entries from its partner.

6. You must specify a backup directory path in WINS Manager. When the WINS server starts, it automatically backs up this directory. Every 24 hours after startup, it also automatically does a backup. You can also manually back up a WINS server through WINS Manager.

7. You can restore a WINS database backup manually through WINS Manager. A WINS server attempts to automatically restore a backup when it detects a corrupt database upon startup. You can force this automatic restoration when you suspect a corrupt database by stopping and starting the WINS service.

8. You can install a WINS server on an NT server, version 3.5x or 4.0. It can be on any variety of server—a member server, a backup domain controller, or a primary domain controller. You can install the WINS service during installation, but normally you install it later by configuring the network properties of the server through Control Panel, Network.

9. Push replication is configured to occur after a certain number of changes are made to the WINS database. This is usually used for replication partners on the same subnet, so replication can occur fairly often with only a small amount of traffic transmitted with each replication attempt.

   Pull replication is configured to take place at certain time intervals. Pull replication first occurs at a specified starting time and then at specified intervals after the starting time. Using the time setting for pull replication, you can schedule replication during hours when network traffic is at its lowest. This type of replication is typically used when a slow WAN link separates replication partners. During heavy traffic times on a WAN link, it is not usually desirable to have fairly constant traffic between servers, such as the traffic generated by push replication.

10. If the client is manually configured with a TCP/IP address, the address of a primary WINS server must also be configured. Although not required, you can also configure the address of a secondary WINS server.

    If the client receives its TCP/IP address from the WINS server, you must configure the options of the DHCP scope to include the address of a primary WINS server. You can also specify the address of a secondary WINS server. One additional parameter you must configure in the DHCP scope is the type of broadcasts used for WINS as h-node broadcasts.

IP Internetwork Browsing and Domain Functions

This chapter helps you prepare for the exam by covering the following objectives:

 Objectives

▶ Configure HOSTS and LMHOSTS file

▶ Configure and support browsing in a multiple-domain route environment

Test Yourself! Before reading this chapter, test yourself to determine how much study time you will need to devote to this section.

1. What is Windows NT internetwork browsing and what does it provide?

2. When is a WINS server not an adequate browsing solution?

3. What other browsing-related Windows NT services cause broadcasts?

Answers are located at the end of the chapter.

Browsing in Windows NT

The sharing of resources is the key to networking. For what other purpose does networking exist? Therefore, it is of utmost importance that there be an easy way of not only sharing a resource but of knowing what resources on the network are accessible. Figure 16.1 shows multiple networks, each with resources that need to be accessible by the other networks.

Figure 16.1

Browsing overview.

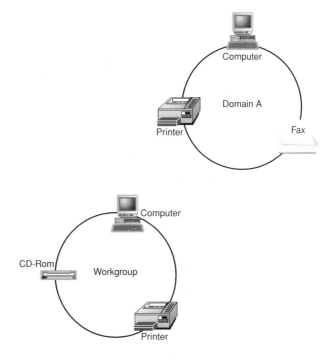

Microsoft has made this process of viewing network resources available through what may be referred to as *browsers*.

What these browsers do is actually collect a list (called the *browse list*) of the resources available on the network and pass this list out to requesting clients. One main computer is designated to collect and update the browse list. Having one computer keep track of the browse list frees the other systems to continue processing without the added overhead of constantly finding where everything is. It also cuts down on the network traffic by having a single source for this list of information rather than everyone needing a separate copy.

Browsing Tools

The next question you may ask is, "How do I browse and what am I browsing for?" The answer is easier than you might think and you have probably already used this browsing technique. One very simple example of browsing is the Network Neighborhood icon on your desktop. When you open up Network Neighborhood it provides a list of the network resources available in your local workgroup or domain. These network resources include but are not limited to: printers, fax, CD-ROM, and other drives or applications available on the network. This is the default list you should see when you first open it. The top icon, Entire Network, refers to just that, anything else that may be available on your network but not necessarily in your local workgroup or domain. This implies that there may be multiple workgroups and or domains in your network environment. Figure 16.2 illustrates the domain grouping.

Figure 16.2

Domain listing.

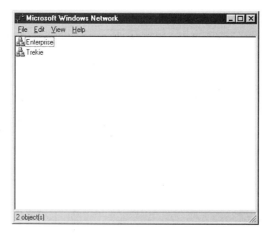

When you start opening up some of these remote domains or workgroups, you are in the process of browsing. This is much like window shopping. You go to the mall not knowing exactly what you need and so you browse through the shops until you find what you want.

The same applies to the network, but now you are browsing network resources—remote files, printers, CD-ROMs. Anything you need access to can be considered a resource. After you find the resource you want, you can utilize it—such as by printing a document to a network printer or by changing to a server-based database. By using the Network Neighborhood for browsing network resources, you are using the graphical view method or GUI (Graphical User Interface). You may also browse network resources from the command prompt by using the Net View command. After you specify the server name, a list appears showing the resources available on that specific server. Notice that you must use the correct Universal Naming Convention with the two backslashes (\\Server\Share).

For example

```
C:\users\default>net view \\instructor
```

results in the following:

```
Shared resources at \\instructor


Share name    Type        Used as  Comment

_ _ _ _ _ _ _ _ _ _ _ _ _ _ _ _ _ _ _ _ _ _ _ _ _ _ _ _ _ _
cdrom         Disk
MSDOS         Disk
NETLOGON      Disk                 Logon server share
Public        Disk
SQLSETUP      Disk
WGPO          Disk
The command completed successfully.
```

System Roles

Certain predefined roles must be addressed with certain names. The computer that has the resource you are trying to access may be referred to as the *host computer*. While you are trying to access its resources, this computer is also playing the role of a server because it is providing a service: the sharing of its resources. The person trying to access the host computer is in the role of a *client*.

Remember, a computer may play the roles of both client and server at once. If, for example, you are trying to access a printer on a remote computer while someone is utilizing your shared CD-ROM, you are then both client and server, because you are both sharing a resource and accessing a remote one.

Any time a resource—drive, printer, and so forth—is shared, it will appear on the browse list, which is available to everyone. Even if you have not been given permission to use the resource, it will still appear on the list you see. This is because it is an overall list of what network resources are available, not just the network resources that are available to you. There are ways of limiting access to the resource to the specific clients that you want, but there is not a way to just have the resources you have access to appear in your list, because your list is not specific to you, it is the entire list for either your workgroup, domain, or network. You limit access by setting permissions directly on the resource you are sharing.

You may have noticed that sometimes the browse list appears incomplete, or things are on the list that you cannot access, and have been given the correct permissions. If you do not have enough permissions to access this network resource, even though it appears in your browse list, you will still be denied access. The issues of proper permissions but no access and not appearing on the browse list at all happen because there is a delay on updating the browse list you are accessing. What happens is the resource you attempt to access is either not available anymore (which results in you being denied access to a resource you had previously been allowed to access), or does not appear in the browse list. Browse list timing issues are covered later in this section.

The Direct Approach

There is, however, a way around this problem of the browse list delay. One way is the direct approach, but this requires you to know the exact name of the network host that has the resource you desire to obtain, but not the resource itself. This is similar to the net view command but with a graphical interface.

The following steps show how to use the direct approach to access a computer:

1. Click the Start button.

2. Click Find.

3. Click Computer.

4. Type in the name of the server you are trying to find.

5. Click Find Now.

You should then see a list of resources that system has available (see fig. 16.3).

Figure 16.3

Computer browsing.

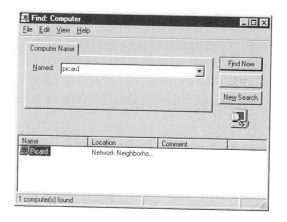

The direct approach bypasses browsing and does a broadcast for that host computer. It is especially helpful when a new resource has been made available but may not have appeared on any browse list, or when you want to see whether a resource to which you are getting denied access is really currently available on the network. You can also utilize the Net Use command at the command prompt to specify the remote resource you are going to access. The Net Use command is usually used in conjunction with the previously described Net View command (which just lists that servers shared resources), whereas the Net Use command actually attaches you to the resource.

Browsing Roles

Now that you understand what browsing itself is and what it can do for you, the next stage is to discuss the different browsing processes and the defined roles for browsing. The following are the browsing roles available. Figure 16.4 illustrates their placement and usage.

▶ **Master Browser.** Collects and maintains the master list of available resources in its domain or workgroup, and the list of names, not resources, in other domains and workgroups. Distributes the browse list to backup browsers.

▶ **Backup Browser.** Obtains its browse list from the Master Browser and passes this list to requesting clients.

▶ **Domain Master Browser.** Fulfills the role of a Master Browser for its domain as well as coordinating and synchronizing the browse list from all other Master Browsers for the domains that reside on remote networks.

▶ **Potential Browser.** A computer that could be a Master, Backup, or Domain Master Browser if needed, but currently does not fill a role nor hold a browse list.

▶ **Non-Browser.** A computer that does not maintain a browse list. It may have been configured not to participate, or it may possibly be a client computer.

Figure 16.4

Browsing roles.

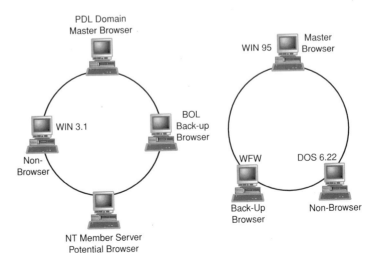

Filling Roles

Now that browsing roles are defined, who can fill them? Windows NT Workstation, Windows NT Server, Windows for Workgroups, and Windows 95 all can perform these browsing roles. However, only a Windows NT Server acting as a Primary Domain Controller (PDC) may occupy the role of the domain Master Browser. In a LAN, the Domain Master Browser is also the Master Browser.

Windows NT Workstation and Windows NT Member Servers can become backup browsers if there are at least three Windows NT server-based computers not already filling these roles for the workgroup or domain. Figure 16.5 shows how the browse list is distributed.

Figure 16.5

Distribution of the browse list.

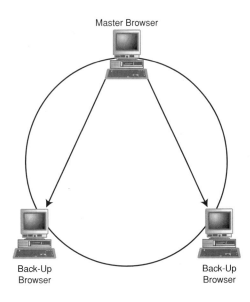

Master Browser

Back-Up Browser

Back-Up Browser

How do you know and control in which roles your computers are participating? Unfortunately, there is not a way to see what browsing role the computer is filling without looking in the Registry. By understanding some default rules and by a little user intervention, however, you can control the browsing environment to a certain extent. The first default to grasp is that Windows NT and Windows 95 are set to auto—meaning it potentially can fill a browsing role. The Master Browser is chosen through what is called an *election process*, which is based on the following criteria:

▶ A Windows NT-based computer takes precedence over a Windows 95 or Windows for Workgroups computer. Windows 95 will take priority over Windows for Workgroups. This is at any time. If a Windows 95 machine has been on for two years as soon as a Windows NT computer comes online an election will be held and the Windows NT computer will win because of its higher priority rating.

▶ The computer that has been turned on the longest wins the election and will become the new Master Browser. The idea behind this is that if it has been on the longest it has the most potential to not go down frequently, thus providing a more accurate and current browse list.

▶ If none of the preceding criteria fit, the server with a Net-BIOS name of lowest alphabetical lettering will win the election race of Master Browser. For example: a server with the name of Argyle will become the next Master Browser over a server with the name of Zot.

Controlling Your Browser Role

To control the browser role that your computer is playing for a Windows NT Server and Windows NT Workstation, you can change the IsDomainMaster Registry setting to a *true* or *yes* to force your computer to be the Master Browser This setting is found in the following Registry subkey:

```
\HKEY_LOCAL_MACHINE\SYSTEM\CurrentControlSet\Services\Browser\Parameters
```

To control your browser role for Windows 95, perform the following steps:

1. Right-click Network Neighborhood.

2. Choose Properties.

3. Select the File and Print Sharing for Microsoft Networks service if you have it installed. If it is not installed, you are not currently participating in browsing. You can install it by clicking on the Add button, selecting Microsoft, and then adding File and Print Sharing for Microsoft Networks.

4. Choose Properties.

5. Select Browse Master. This is set to Automatic by default; you can either enable or disable it (see fig. 16.6).

Figure 16.6

Windows 95 browsing control.

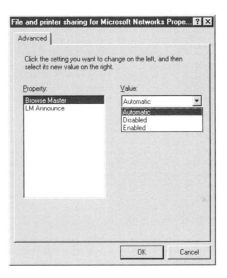

These are the only controls you have for configuring the browser roles of your computers. So you could turn it off on all but the specific machines that you want to participate in browsing, allowing you to at least narrow the possibilities. If one of those goes down, however, there goes your browsing. You cannot directly control backup browsers, only set them to auto with one set to IsDomainMaster.

Understanding the Cost of Browsing

Does being a Browse Master affect a computer's performance? Yes, it affects system performance. This performance degradation may be noticeable on slower systems, such as 486/66, but not as noticeable on most newer machines, such as a P5/100. Anything the computer does in some way affects its performance, but remember that being a Browse Master means keeping an updated list of network resources. The number of network resources with which the Browse Master needs to keep up obviously affects that computer's performance accordingly. The best you can do to minimize this performance degradation is to keep the amount of computers sharing network resources to a minimum. Doing so allows the Browse List to be short, relieving the strain on the Master Browser.

Windows NT Browsing Services

A lot is involved with browsing to make it do what it does—most of which happens automatically without any intervention. Sometimes, however, there are problems and it can help to understand the process involved to better understand the possible solutions to the problem.

The browsing services have three main break points, or sections, in Windows NT:

▶ Collecting information for the browse list

▶ Distributing the browse list itself

▶ Servicing browser client requests for the list

Each of these break points is discussed in the following sections.

Collecting the Browse List

The first important part of being able to browse network resources is the collection of the browse list itself. The Master Browser continually updates its browse list to include the current network resources available. This update process is continual, in that it is constantly having to revise its browse list as network resources appear and disappear. This process happens every time a computer is turned on that has something to share and every time one that is sharing resources is turned off. The Master Browser obtains a list of servers in its own domain or workgroup, as well as a list of other domains and workgroups and updates these servers with network resources to the browse list as changes are made. Much of this process has to do with browser announcements. Figure 16.7 shows the browser collection process.

When a computer that is running a server service is turned on, it announces itself to the Master Browser, which then adds this new resource to its browse list. This happens regardless of whether the computer has resources to share or not. When a computer is shut down properly, it announces to the Master Browser that it is leaving and again the Master Browser updates its list accordingly. If a Master Browser has an empty list, it can force domains to announce themselves so that it can add them to its list.

Figure 16.7

Browser collection.

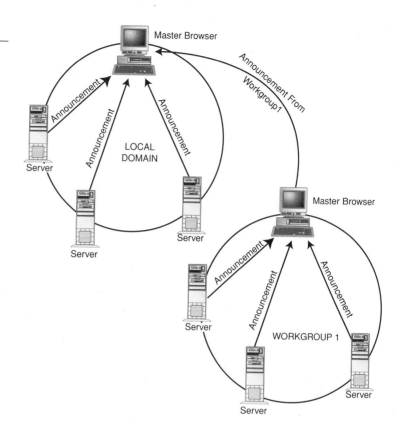

Master Browsers also receive what are called DomainAnnouncement packets that come from other domains and place these packets in their own local browse lists. These DomainAnnouncement packets contain the following information:

▶ The name of the domain.

▶ The name of the Master Browser for that domain.

▶ Whether the Browser is a Windows NT Server or Windows NT Workstation computer.

▶ If the Browser is a Windows NT Server computer, it is the Primary Domain Controller for that domain.

Distributing the Browse List

The next important part of browsing is the distribution of the previously collected browse list. The extent of this distribution depends largely on the size of the network. A Master Browser broadcasts a message every so often to let the backup browsers know the Master Browser is still around. This is important because if the Master Browser does not do this the network holds an election process to elect a new Master Browser.

The Master Browser holds the list of network resources. It is the Backup Browser that contacts the Master Browser and copies the list from the Master Browser. Therefore, the Backup Browsers are the active component, intermittently contacting the passive Master Browser for the updated list.

There can often be complications with distributing this browse list. The following sections discuss some of these difficulties and the corresponding solutions, such as browsing over subnets, announcement period timings, and Domain Master Browser failure.

Browsing Over Subnets

Within Windows NT, every local subnet, a collection of computers separated by a router, is its own browsing area. This browsing area is complete with its own Master Browser and Backup Browsers. Subnets hold Browser elections, for their own subnet, which demonstrates the need for a Domain Master Browser if you have multiple subnets on your internetwork to allow for browsing over more than just one subnet. Additionally, each subnet needs at least one Windows NT controller in each subnet to register with the Domain Master Browser. This allows for multi-subnet browsing.

Generally, broadcasts do not go through a router; the router needs to be BOOTP-enabled to allow passing of broadcasts. If a domain has multiple subnets, each Master Browser for each subnet uses a directed datagram called a MasterBrowserAnnouncement. The MasterBrowserAnnouncement lets the Domain Master Browser know it is available and what it has on its subnet list. These datagrams pass through the routers enabling these updates to occur. The Domain Master Browser adds all the subnet Master Browser lists to its own browse list, providing a complete browse list of the entire domain, including all subnets. This process occurs every 15 minutes to ensure regular list updates. The timing is not adjustable. Windows NT workgroups and Windows for

Workgroups are not able to send a MasterBrowserAnnouncement packet and therefore cannot span these multiple subnets or have a complete list—thus the need for Windows NT domain controllers to allow for multiple subnet browsing. Figure 16.8 illustrates what browsing over subnets might look like in a network design.

Figure 16.8

Browsing over subnets.

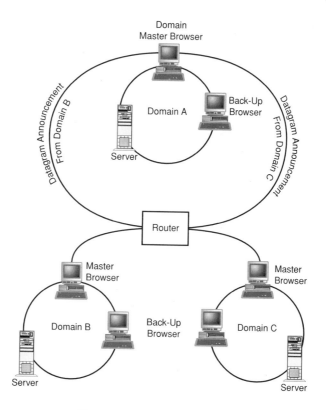

Announcement Periods

When the Master Browser first comes online it sends out a Domain-Announcement once a minute for the first 5 minutes and then only once every 15 minutes. If the domain does not respond by sending out its own DomainAnnouncement for three successive announcement periods, the domain is removed from the Master Browser list. A resource, therefore, might appear on your browse list but actually be unavailable, because it remains on the browse list until three full announcement periods have passed. It is then possible for a domain to appear up to 45 minutes after it is originally unavailable, which may be due to the Primary Domain Controller being off or having physical connectivity problems, such as a bad network card and or cable. You cannot change these announcement times or removal periods.

Domain Master Browser Failure

Based on the preceding information on browsers and subnets, notice what happens if a Domain Master Browser fails (see fig. 16.9). In the event of a failure, users on the entire network are limited to their own individual subnets, assuming they have a Master Browser for their subnet, of course. If there is not a Master Browser within your subnet, you are left with no browsing capabilities whatsoever. Without a Domain Master Browser, no complete overall browse list exists of the entire domain, and within three announcement periods all other servers not on the local subnet are removed from the browse list. You then need to either promote a Backup Domain Controller to perform the role of Domain Master Browser, or bring the downed Domain Master Browser back online before the time limit expires for its three announcements. Remember the Backup Domain Controller does not automatically promote itself, and once a new Domain Master Browser is elected it will take time to collect the browse list from all the different subnets. There is no way you can force the browse list.

Figure 16.9

Domain Master Browser failure.

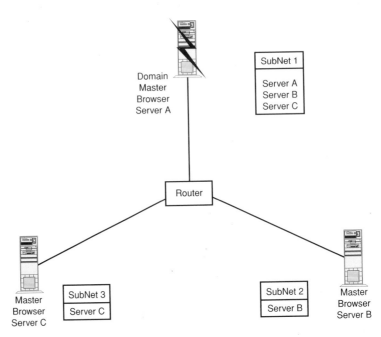

Servicing Client Requests

 **Objective**   The final browsing service process is the actual servicing of client requests. Now that a browse list exists and has been distributed, clients have something to access. Figure 16.10 illustrates what happens from the point when a client requests a resource to the actual connection of that resource.

Figure 16.10

Servicing clients.

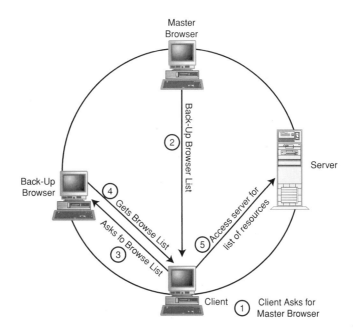

The process follows these steps:

1. The client tries to access a domain or workgroup using Explorer. In doing so, it contacts the Master Browser of the domain or workgroup that it is trying to access.

2. The Master Browser gives the client a list of three backup browsers.

3. The client then asks for the network resource from one of the backup browsers.

4. The Backup Browser gives the list of servers in that domain or workgroup for which the client is asking.

5. The client chooses a server and obtains a list of that server's shared resources.

This process can occasionally cause some conflict if the Master Browser has a resource in its list, but the Backup Browser has not updated itself yet, and the client connects to that Backup Browser and looks for the current list. The resource is not listed in the Backup Browse list yet. This is another reason why items that are not available may appear on the list, or may not be on the list at all.

Browsing in an IP Internetwork

 Objective

Now that you've learned about browsing itself and know how it works, you are ready to learn about browsing in an IP internetwork, meaning browsing over multiple subnets. This is not as easy as it sounds. Some has already been explained through the process of domain announcement. But this only allows for Master Browsers to talk to the Domain Master Browser. This requires a Windows NT domain controller to be in each subnet. It may not be feasible to put a domain controller at each subnet, thus, no browsing. The first major obstacle is that browsing relies on broadcast packets, which means they are actually sent to everyone on the network segment. However, routers do not generally forward these broadcast packets, creating a browsing problem for collecting, distributing, and servicing the client request for browse lists. If these packets are not forwarded, you are unable to browse in an internetwork environment without a local domain controller.

If the browse list cannot get distributed properly, then you have no browsing capability.

Solutions

There are a few possible solutions to the problem of being able to browse in an IP internetwork. There is the use of a BOOTP enabled router and an LMHOSTS file. The following section discusses the usefulness of the IP router.

IP Router

You can use a few solutions to get around the problem of routers and multiple subnets, not being able to browse without a Windows NT controller on each subnet. The first solution is to have a specific router that can forward these NetBIOS name broadcasts. This makes all the broadcasts and network resource requests appear to all client computers as if the broadcasts are all on the same subnet. Master browsers have their own lists as well as those of the other domains and workgroups, so when a client makes an inquiry for a browse list, the list can be provided for any domain or workgroup.

Having a BOOTP-enabled router, of course, fixes the browsing problem across routers. But this solution may not be perfect for every network layout and size. The reason having this BOOTP-enabled router is not the perfect solution is because if you do have the BOOTP-enabled router, all NetBIOS traffic is broadcast over the entire network, rather than limited to each subnet. This adds extremely high overhead to all the nodes of the network, degrading overall performance. The subnets are no longer isolated to their own specific areas, which causes a higher potential for browser election conflicts and excessive network traffic. Therefore, even though it does fix the problem of routers and multiple subnets, other problems, such as the excessive traffic that is generated, should be anticipated.

Directed Traffic

Additional solutions to the problem of browsing an IP internetwork without using a BOOTP-enabled router are available. The following section explains how to use directed IP traffic to service the client's browsing requests.

LMHOSTS File

An LMHOSTS file helps distribute the browsing information and service client requests. You can also use WINS to collect the browse lists and service client requests.

In the LMHOSTS file, the LM stands for LAN Manager; HOSTS is for the host computer. Its job is to resolve NetBIOS names to the corresponding IP address of remote hosts on different subnets. The purpose is to allow for communication between Master Browsers on remote subnets and the domain Master Browser. This sets up direct communication, enabling an updated list to be developed across a subnet. The one thing to remember about an LMHOSTS file is that it is your responsibility to create and maintain the file. Figure 16.11 illustrates using an LMHOSTS file in a network. A WINS service can dynamically provide this resolution for you.

Figure 16.11

Browsing using LMHOSTS.

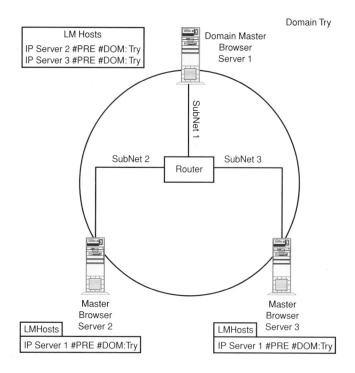

Using an LMHOSTS file is a workable solution, but be aware of some considerations. The LMHOSTS file must be on each and every subnet's Master Browser with an entry to the domain Master Browser to work. It must also be updated manually any time there are changes to the LMHOSTS list. The LMHOSTS file needs to be placed in the winntroot\system32\drivers\etc directory. There are sample TCP/IP files already you can use to reference. It is just a regular text file that can be created using any text editor. There is no file extension, and Windows NT will look and reference the file in this location whenever it needs to. The two items needed in the LMHOSTS file for it to work across a subnet are as follows:

▶ IP address and computer name of the domain Master Browser

▶ The domain name preceded by #PRE and #DOM:

For example:

```
129.62.101.5     server1        #PRE #DOM:try
129.62.101.17    server2        #PRE
129.62.101.25    server3        #PRE
```

The #PRE statement preloads the specific line it is on into memory as a permanent entry in the name cache making it easily available without having to first access the domain.

#DOM:<domain_name> allows for login validation over a router, account synchronization, and, in this case, browsing. Every time the computer sends a broadcast to a domain it also sends it to every computer that has a #DOM: in its LMHOSTS file. These types of broadcasts do go across routers, but are not sent to workgroups. There are many difficulties to watch out for, each of which shall be discussed in the following subsections.

Domain Master Browser

For the domain Master Browser you need an LMHOSTS file that is set up with entries pointing to each of the remote subnet Master Browsers. You should also have a #DOM: statement in each of the Master Browsers' LMHOSTS files pointing to each of the other subnet Master Browsers. If any of them gets promoted to the domain Master Browser, you then do not have to change all your LMHOSTS files.

Duplicate Names

If it finds duplicate LMHOSTS entries for a single domain, the Master Browser decides which relates to the domain Master Browser by querying each IP address for each entry it has. None of the Master Browser respond; only the domain Master Browser does that. Therefore it narrows down the list of duplicates and because only the real one responds it communicates with the one that responds and proceeds to exchange browse lists.

LMHOSTS File Placement

The placement of the LMHOSTS file is in the \etc directory of the client, as mentioned previously. For Windows NT, for example, it is placed in \systemroot\system32\drivers\etc. For Windows 95 and Windows for Workgroups, it is placed in \system_root (c:\windows).

LMHOSTS File Problems

The following are the most common problems you might have with the LMHOSTS file:

▶ The NetBIOS name is misspelled.

▶ The IP address is incorrect.

▶ An entry is not listed for that host.

▶ There are too many entries for a host whereas only the first entry is used. For example, if there are multiple entries in the LMHOSTS file for the same host computer, only the first one listed will be used.

▶ The LMHOSTS file is in the incorrect location and is not being read.

The LMHOSTS file certainly has its place in IP internetwork browsing, but it is certainly not the ultimate solution.

The WINS Solution

WINS (Windows Internet Naming Service) helps fix the problem of NetBIOS broadcast difficulties by dynamically registering the IP address and NetBIOS name, and keeping track of them in a database. Keeping these computer names in its database greatly enhances the network performance. Whenever they need to find a server, clients access the WINS server rather than broadcast on the network. Accessing the WINS server directly allows for a more direct approach when looking for network resources. Plus, it makes updating much easier, because you do not have to manually configure anything. Using a WINS server also provides easier browsing capability because you can freely use NetBIOS names in the place of IP address. The following is an example of using the PING utility with the NetBIOS name rather than specifying the entire IP address.

```
ping Server2
```

rather than

```
ping 207.0.58.33
```

See figure 16.12 for an example of the WINS implementation.

Figure 16.12

Browsing using WINS.

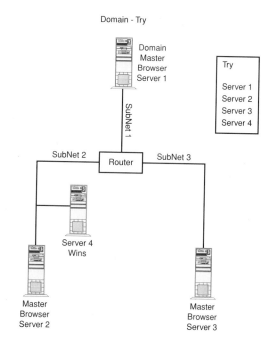

Domain Browser

If the computer is made a WINS client, the domain Master Browser periodically queries the WINS server to update its database of all the domains listed in the WINS database, thereby providing a complete list of all the domains and subnets including remote ones. This list has only domain names and their IP address, not the names of the Master Browsers of each particular subnet as before.

Client Access

When a client needs access to a network resource it calls up the WINS server directly and asks for a list of domain controllers in the domain. WINS provides a list of servers of up to 25 domain controllers, referred to as an *Internet group*. The client is then able to quickly access the domain controller it needs without a complete network broadcast.

Login and Domain Database Replication

Windows NT network services also performs other tasks that initiate broadcasts to all computers in the domain (see fig. 16.13). Two of these tasks are described as follows:

> ▶ **Logging on to a domain and password changes.** A broadcast message is sent out from the client computer to find a domain controller that can provide authentication of the login or find the primary domain controller to allow changing of the user's password.

> ▶ **Domain controllers replicating the domain user account database.** The primary domain controller sends a broadcast to the backup domain controllers, telling them it has changes to the account database they need to update to themselves.

Figure 16.13

Login and domain database replication.

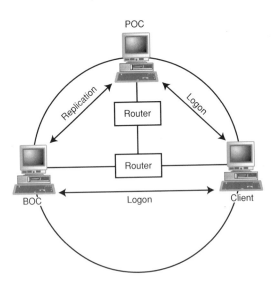

The preceding items are important to understand because they are broadcasts and therefore do not cross IP routers on their own. You have to utilize directed traffic instead. A broadcast initiated to perform these jobs is also given to the remote domain controllers. The list of remote domain controllers is decided by what is listed in either the LMHOSTS file or the WINS database.

When the client needs to access a domain controller, it broadcasts the message directly to the domain and looks for any #DOM:

entries in its LMHOSTS file that matches the domain name. If it finds an identical entry it sends the message specifically to that computer.

It is probably a good idea to add remote domain controller #DOM: entries into the LMHOSTS file with an identical domain name to each client. If the domain controller ever goes down, the users are still able to access remote domains and log on. This is also useful if there are no local domain controllers to enable users to log in to a domain controller on a remote subnet.

 Note

LMHOSTS files are generally for non-WINS clients. You can still reference these non-WINS clients by using a WINS proxy agent, enabling a WINS server to add a non-WINS client to its database through the use of an additional machine that updates the WINS server in place of the non-WINS client. Proxy servers are covered lightly in the following section but are not mentioned anymore as they are a topic all their own and not tested in this exam.

All the backup domain controllers should have #DOM: entries for the primary domain controller, as well as all other backup domain controllers. This way, if one gets promoted to the primary domain controller the backup domain controllers still have mappings to the new primary domain controller.

Overall, WINS provides the better solution for accessing multiple domains and workgroups over different subnets, provided, of course, that all systems are WINS-compliant: Windows 95, Windows NT, Windows for Workgroups with TCP/IP 32 add on.

WINS Proxy Agent

WINS proxy agents are Windows-based WINS clients, not WINS servers, that help non-WINS clients get NetBIOS name resolution. A non-WINS client cannot use a WINS server for its NetBIOS name resolution, so it sends out a name resolution broadcast. The WINS proxy agent listens for such broadcasts and, if it has the information needed, responds itself. If it doesn't have the resolution, it queries the WINS server to get the information and then pass it back to the non-WINS client, acting as a go-between.

Exercises

Exercise 16.1:   Implementing WINS

The following exercise shows how WINS works across routers. You need a network with a router and at least one Master Browser on each side of the router, a few WINS-capable clients on each side of the router, and one WINS server on one side (see fig. 16.14).

Figure 16.14

WINS lab layout.

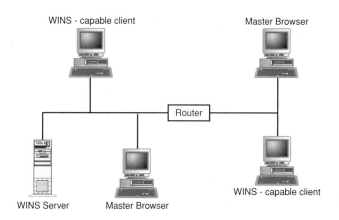

 Note   Don't worry if you currently do not have WINS set up or enabled; the first thing to do in the exercises is to disable WINS.

The first thing you need to do is disable the WINS server. This does not mean, however, to de-install it. Figure 16.15 shows using a manual implementation of WINS. Use the following steps:

1. Go to Control Panel and double-click on the Services icon.

2. Click Windows Internet Name service.

3. Click Startup and then select Manual.

4. Click OK and close all windows.

Figure 16.15

Starting WINS manually.

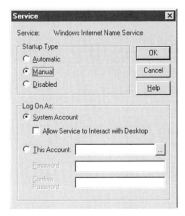

The next thing you need to do is make certain the clients are not enabled to access WINS. Use the following steps:

1. Go to Control Panel and double-click the Network icon.

2. Select Protocols, TCP/IP, Properties.

3. Click WINS Address.

4. Remove any WINS server address by highlighting the address listed and pressing the delete key.

5. Close the windows by clicking OK and then reboot.

6. After Windows NT reboots, use the Windows NT Explorer and find out who you see on the network.

With WINS disabled, no LMHOSTS, HOSTS, DNS, or an IP-enabled router can pass NetBIOS broadcasts, and you should only see what is on your local subnet. It may help to draw a diagram of your network design so that you can identify what systems you should be able to see. It may take a few minutes of updating before everyone appears on the browsing list in your subnet; have patience and keep refreshing or do a direct search.

Now that you have isolated your subnets, the next step is to set up WINS and watch it work.

continues

Exercise 16.1: Continued

If you had WINS set up prior to beginning this exercise and disabled it, all you need to do now is go back into the Services and tab enable the WINS service.

If you did not have WINS previously installed, don't worry. Now is a good time to install WINS.

With WINS newly enabled or installed, go to Network Neighborhood and browse the network. With WINS enabled, you should now see resources on both sides of the router. Figure 16.16 shows an example of what you might see in a WINS database. Sometimes WINS takes a minute to update its database so again keep refreshing before assuming you did something wrong.

Figure 16.16

WINS database.

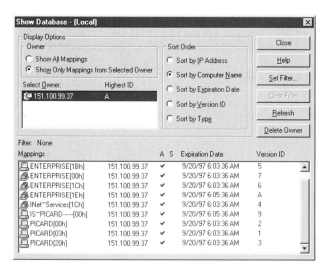

Exercise 16.2: Using an LMHOSTS File

In this exercise, you want to show how you can use an LMHOSTS file to browse across a router. You need the same configuration as in the previous exercise, except that this time you need to make certain that WINS is disabled. Figure 16.17 shows a diagram of the lab layout.

Figure 16.17

LMHOSTS lab layout.

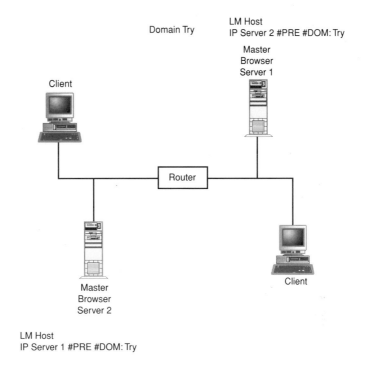

Domain Try

LM Host
IP Server 2 #PRE #DOM: Try

Master
Browser
Server 1

Client

Router

Client

Master
Browser
Server 2

LM Host
IP Server 1 #PRE #DOM: Try

First, you should browse using Network Neighborhood and notice what you see available. With everything disabled, you should only be able to see what is currently on your local subnet. If this is true, you can go on to create an LMHOSTS file. If this is not true, you will continue to be able to see other domains and workgroups in other subnets, which means that even if you implement the LMHOSTS file you will not be able to guarantee that it is actually the LMHOSTS file providing your resolution. This is why you need to check that there is no access before setting up the LMHOSTS file so that after you set it up you can prove the access to a remote subnet is provided by the LMHOSTS file and not some other means of resolution.

You now need to create an LMHOSTS file on each of the Master Browsers on each subnet, pointing specifically to the Master Browser on the other side of the subnet. Make sure you put the LMHOSTS file in the correct location. On Windows NT systems it goes in the \system_root\system32\drivers\etc directory. On Windows 95 and WFW it goes in the \system_root (c:\windows). Don't forget the #PRE and #DOM: statements.

continues

Exercise 16.2: Continued

After you have the files set up in the correct location, you need to enable LMHOSTS to be read by following these steps:

1. Go into the Windows NT Network Properties.

2. Select Protocols, TCP/IP, Properties.

3. Go to WINS address and click on Enable LMHOSTS lookup (see fig. 16.18).

4. Click OK and close all screens.

Figure 16.18

*Enabling
LMHOSTS
lookup.*

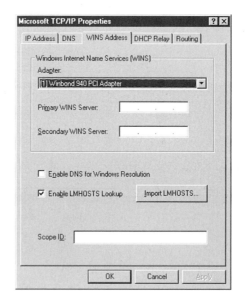

Now you should have LMHOSTS enabled. Go to Network Neighborhood and try exploring. You should see resources on both sides of the router now that you have enabled the usage of an LMHOSTS file. Again when browsing these remote resources through Network Neighborhood the browse list does take a few minutes to update.

Review Questions

The following questions test your knowledge of the information in this chapter.

1. What enables users to search for availability of network resources without knowing the exact location of the resources?

   A. Browsing through Network Neighborhood

   B. The Net Use command

   C. The Net View command

2. If a server name doesn't appear on the browse list, what are some possible causes?

   A. The server is on a different domain.

   B. The master domain hasn't updated the backup domain.

   C. The master domain hasn't updated the server.

3. If you are printing a file on your Windows NT workstation to a network printer and using your A: drive for a disk copy, while sharing your CD-ROM and writing a histogram report using performance monitor, can a remote system access your resources as a client to server?

4. Is there a way to access a network resource without browsing for the resource?

5. You are running a Windows NT 4.0 Server that is currently the primary domain controller, and you have a multiple domain network. What browser role(s) does the server have?

   A. Backup browser

   B. Master browser

   C. Potential browser

   D. Domain Master browser

   E. Potential browser

6. Which one of these situations is true regarding Master Browser to backup browser synchronization?

   A. The Master Browser copies the updates to the backup.

   B. The backup browser copies the updates to the master.

   C. The Master Browser copies the updates from the backup.

   D. The backup browser copies the updates from the master.

7. If I have a domain set up with two Windows 95 computers, three Windows NT workstations computers, three Windows NT server computers, and four Windows for Workgroup computers, who is the third backup browser for this domain?

   A. Windows 95

   B. Windows for Workgroups

   C. Windows NT workstation

   D. No one can fill this role

8. Who is in charge of continually updating the browse list and managing the database of network resources of domains and workgroups?

   A. Backup browser

   B. Master browser

   C. Potential browser

   D. Browser browser

9. Which of these statements is not true about the Domain-Announcement packet?

   A. It has the name of a domain.

   B. It has the name of the Master Browser for that domain.

   C. It specifies whether the Master Browser is a Windows NT server or workstation.

   D. If it is a Windows NT server it specifies the version number of the server.

10. You have a network with five different subnets, each with its own Master Browser. The network administrator wants to be able to see resources of each subnet at the same time. Which process allows for this?

    A. Directed datagram

    B. Directed telegram

    C. Replication

    D. Synchronization

11. If a domain announcement is sent out to a domain and the domain does not respond, how long is it before the remote domain is removed from the browse list?

    A. 4 announcement periods and 45 min

    B. 3 announcement periods and 45 min

    C. 4 announcement periods and 35 min

    D. 3 announcement periods and 35 min

12. You have a network with three subnets: Subnet A, Subnet B, and Subnet C. What happens if the domain Master Browser on Subnet A goes down?

    A. Browsing is restricted to each subnet.

    B. Subnet B can see C but not A.

    C. Subnet C can see B but not A.

    D. All subnets continue browsing normally.

13. How is it possible to browse across routers without the use of WINS, DNS, HOSTS, or LMHOSTS?

    A. You can browse using Network Neighborhood.

    B. You can use an IP-enabled router.

    C. You can use a bootp-enabled router.

14. The LMHOSTS file is mainly used on a network with non-WINS clients specifically for the job of _____.

    A. Resolving a NetBIOS name to MAC-level address.

    B. Resolving an IP address to NetBIOS name.

    C. Resolving an IP address to Internet names.

15. What does the #PRE statement in an LMHOSTS file do?

    A. Prepares a name to load into memory.

    B. Preloads an entry into cache.

    C. Permanently caches a preloaded file.

16. When should you put the other Master Browsers' domains into the LMHOSTS file as well as the domain Master Browser?

    A. If the Domain Master Browser is busy you have to change your LMHOSTS file to access the new Domain Master Browser.

    B. If the Domain Master Browser goes down you do not have to change your LMHOSTS file to access the new Domain Master Browser.

    C. If your LMHOSTS file is unavailable you have to update your Domain Master Browser list.

17. WINS can take the place of an LMHOSTS file over a network by _____ updating across routers?

    A. Dynamically

    B. Statically

18. If the Domain Master Browser is a WINS client, it can get automatic updates of remote domains.

    A. This is a true statement.

    B. This statement is false.

    C. This statement has nothing to do with the Master Browser and WINS.

19. What are two additional Windows NT network services that initiate a broadcast in a domain but not across routers?

    A. Logging in and passwords, PDC to PDC replication

    B. Directory replication and authentication

    C. Logging in and passwords, PDC to BDC replication

20. What is the purpose of a WINS proxy agent?

    A. To take the place of a WINS server

    B. To provide NetBIOS name resolution to non-WINS clients

    C. To provide host name resolution to non-WINS clients

Review Answers

1. A

2. B

3. Yes. The key is that you are sharing your CD-ROM, thus acting in the role of a server as well as a client while you are accessing other resources.

4. Yes, with either the Net View command or by choosing Start, Find, Computer.

5. B, D

6. D

7. C

8. B

9. D

10. A

11. B

12. A

13. C

14. B

15. B

16. B

17. A

18. A

19. C

20. B

Answers to the Test Yourself Questions at the Beginning of the Chapter

1. Windows NT internetwork browsing is a service that enables users to obtain a list of network resources available in their network environment. With internetwork browsing, users do not have to search for resources, nor does every machine need to maintain its own list. See "Browsing in Windows NT."

2. A WINS server does not provide an adequate browsing solution when there are clients that are unable to utilize the WINS services. These clients are commonly called *non-WINS clients*. The appropriate solution for these non-WINS clients is the use of an LMHOSTS file or a WINS proxy agent. See "Browsing in an IP Internetwork."

3. Browsing in an internetwork also contributes to the action of logging on to a domain, for authentication, and Domain controller replication. See "Login and Domain Database Replication."

17

Host Name Resolution

This chapter will help you prepare for the exam by covering the following objectives:

√ Objectives

► Configure HOSTS and LMHOSTS files

► Diagnose and resolve name resolution problems

Test Yourself! Before reading this chapter, test yourself to determine how much study time you will need to devote to this section.

1. The HOSTS file is an ASCII text file that statically maps _____.

   A. Host names and IP addresses

   B. NetBIOS names and IP addresses

   C. MAC addresses to IP addresses

   D. Fully Qualified Domain Names

2. The following entry is in the HOSTS file:

   ```
   197.197.197.5    MADONNA    rita
   ```

   When the command **PING MADONNA** is given, 197.197.197.5 responds successfully. When the command **PING RITA** is given, the host is not found. What is causing this problem?

   A. The line is not read after the MADONNA entry.

   B. An invalid IP address is used.

   C. Rita is not a valid server name.

   D. The file is case-sensitive.

Answers are located at the end of the chapter.

Host Names

Names are stored, and referenced, in many formats in TCP/IP. Although a host name is but one of many, it is one of the easiest to use. Problems, however, stem from the fact that Windows NT does not reference host names in the same manner as other operating systems.

In Unix, the host name is mapped directly to an IP address, and the IP address is mapped to a hardware address. Because NT uses NetBIOS internally, there is a stronger reliance on NetBIOS names than anything else. When a command is issued referencing a server, the NetBIOS name is resolved to an IP address, and then to a hardware address. For more information on this, please refer to Chapter 13, "NetBIOS over TCP/IP."

The primary advantage of using host names is that they are easy to remember and bound only by the limitation that they be under 255 characters in length. You can use more than one host name for a host.

 Note

The host name used does not have to match the NetBIOS name of the Windows NT machine.

Host name resolution, quite simply, is the process by which host names are mapped to IP addresses. You can do this in a number of ways, including:

▶ Local host name

▶ HOSTS files

▶ DNS (Domain Name System) servers

In the same way we saw that NetBIOS name resolution used host name resolution as a backup, NT uses NetBIOS name resolution to back up host name resolution. This means there are another three ways to resolve host names:

▶ WINS servers

▶ Local broadcast

▶ LMHOSTS file

Each of these methods, and corresponding utilities, is examined in the following pages.

Configure HOSTS Files

 Objective

The HOSTS file is an ASCII text file that statically maps local and remote host names and IP addresses. It is located in *systemroot*\ System32\Drivers\etc.

The HOSTS file is not case sensitive, however, some utilities that you will use may be. Entries in the HOSTS file are limited to 255 characters per entry. The HOSTS file is used by PING and other Winsock utilities to resolve host names locally and remotely. One HOSTS file must reside on each host, and the file is read from top to bottom. As soon as a match is found for a host name, the file stops being read. For that reason, when there are duplicate entries, the latter ones are always ignored, and the most commonly used names should be near the top of the file.

The following is an example of the default HOSTS file:

```
# Copyright (c) 1993-1995 Microsoft Corp.
#
# This is a sample HOSTS file used by Microsoft TCP/IP for Win-
dows NT.
#
# This file contains the mappings of IP addresses to host names.
Each entry should be kept on an individual line. The IP address
should be placed in the first column followed by the correspond-
ing host name.
# The IP address and the host name should be separated by at
least one space.
#
# Additionally, comments (such as these) may be inserted on indi-
vidual lines or following the machine name denoted by a '#' sym-
bol.
#
# For example:
#
```

```
#       102.54.94.97      rhino.acme.com       # source server
#        38.25.63.10      x.acme.com           # x client host

127.0.0.1        localhost
```

You should notice several things in this file. First, the pound sign (#) indicates a comment. When the system reads the file, every line beginning with a comment is ignored. When a # appears in the middle of a line, the line is read only up to the sign. If this file were in use on a live system, you would delete the first 17 lines or move them to the end of the file to keep them from being read every time the file is referenced.

The second thing to note is the entry:

```
127.0.0.1        localhost
```

This is a *loopback* address in every host. It references the internal card, regardless of the host address, and can be used for diagnostics to verify that connections are working properly internally, before testing that they are working properly down the wire.

Within the HOSTS file, fields are separated by white space that can be tabs or spaces. As mentioned earlier, a host can be referred to by more than one name—to do so, separate the entries on the same line with white space, as shown in the following example:

```
127.0.0.1        me loopback localhost
199.9.200.7      SALES7 victor
199.9.200.4      SALES4 nikki
199.9.200.3      SALES3 cole
199.9.200.2      SALES2 victoria
199.9.200.1      SALES1 nicholas
199.9.200.5      SALES5 jack
199.9.200.11     ACCT1
199.9.200.12     ACCT2
199.9.200.13     ACCT3
199.9.200.14     ACCT4
199.9.200.15     ACCT5
199.9.200.17     ACCT7
```

The aliases are other names by which the system can be referred. Here, "me" and "loopback" do the same as "localhost," and "nicholas" is the same as "SALES1." If an alias is used more than once, the search stops at the first match because the file is searched sequentially.

Exercise 17.2 allows you to practice editing this file.

Configure LMHOSTS File

 Objective

Whereas the HOSTS file contains the mappings of IP addresses to host names, the LMHOSTS file contains the mappings of IP addresses to Windows NT computer names. When speaking of Windows NT computer names, the inference is to NetBIOS names, or the names that would be used in conjunction with NET USE statements.

An example of the default version of this file follows:

```
# Copyright (c) 1993-1995 Microsoft Corp.
#
# This is a sample LMHOSTS file used by the Microsoft TCP/IP for
Windows NT.
#
# This file contains the mappings of IP addresses to NT computer
names # (NetBIOS) names.  Each entry should be kept on an indi-
vidual line.
# The IP address should be placed in the first column followed by
the # corresponding computername. The address and the comptername
# should be separated by at least one space or tab. The "#" char-
acter # is generally used to denote the start of a comment (see
the exceptions below).
#
# This file is compatible with Microsoft LAN Manager 2.x TCP/IP
lmhosts # files and offers the following extensions:
#
#       #PRE
#       #DOM:<domain>
#       #INCLUDE <filename>
```

```
#       #BEGIN_ALTERNATE
#       #END_ALTERNATE
#       \0xnn (non-printing character support)
#
# Following any entry in the file with the characters "#PRE" will
cause # the entry to be preloaded into the name cache. By de-
fault, entries are # not preloaded, but are parsed only after
dynamic name resolution fails.
#
# Following an entry with the "#DOM:<domain>" tag will associate
the # entry with the domain specified by <domain>. This affects
how the # browser and logon services behave in TCP/IP environ-
ments. To preload # the host name associated with #DOM entry, it
is necessary to also add a #PRE to the line. The <domain> is al-
ways preloaded although it will not be shown when the name cache
is viewed.
#
# Specifying "#INCLUDE <filename>" will force the RFC NetBIOS
(NBT) # software to seek the specified <filename> and parse it as
if it were local. <filename> is generally a UNC-based name, al-
lowing a # centralized lmhosts file to be maintained on a server.
# It is ALWAYS necessary to provide a mapping for the IP address
of the # server prior to the #INCLUDE. This mapping must use the
#PRE directive.
# In addition the share "public" in the example below must be in
the # LanManServer list of "NullSessionShares" in order for cli-
ent machines to # be able to read the lmhosts file successfully.
This key is under # \machine\system\currentcontrolset\services\
lanmanserver\ parameters\nullsessionshares # in the registry.
Simply add "public" to the list found there.
#
# The #BEGIN_ and #END_ALTERNATE keywords allow multiple #INCLUDE
# statements to be grouped together. Any single successful in-
clude will cause the group to succeed.
```

```
#
# Finally, non-printing characters can be embedded in mappings by
# first surrounding the NetBIOS name in quotations, then using
the \0xnn notation to specify a hex value for a non-printing
character.
#
# The following example illustrates all of these extensions:
#
# 102.54.94.97      rhino           #PRE #DOM:networking  #net
group's DC
# 102.54.94.102     "appname  \0x14"                      #special
app server
# 102.54.94.123     popular         #PRE                  #source
server
# 102.54.94.117     localsrv        #PRE                  #needed
for the include
#
# #BEGIN_ALTERNATE
# #INCLUDE \\localsrv\public\lmhosts
# #INCLUDE \\rhino\public\lmhosts
# #END_ALTERNATE
#
# In the above example, the "appname" server contains a special
# character in its name, the "popular" and "localsrv" server
names are preloaded, and the "rhino" server name is specified so
it can be used to later #INCLUDE a centrally maintained lmhosts
file if the "localsrv" system is unavailable.
#
# Note that the whole file is parsed including comments on each
lookup, so keeping the number of comments to a minimum will im-
prove performance.
# Therefore it is not advisable to simply add lmhosts file en-
tries onto the end of this file.
```

Once more, the pound sign (#) indicates comments, and the file is read sequentially on each lookup, so limiting the size of the comment lines at the beginning of the file is highly recommended.

You can use a number of special commands in the file to load entries into a name cache that is scanned on each lookup prior to referencing the file. (By default, entries are not preloaded, but are parsed only after dynamic name resolution fails). Using these commands decreases your lookup time and increases system efficiency.

Other Files to Be Aware Of

While the exam objectives specifically speak of the HOSTS and LMHOSTS files, these work in conjunction with other files copied to *systemroot*\\System32\\Drivers\\etc, namely the following:

- ▶ SERVICES

- ▶ NETWORKS

- ▶ PROTOCOL

A copy of each of these files is included for reference. Although you need not memorize them for the exam, be familiar with them for the real world.

SERVICES

The SERVICES file is used to identify the port numbers on which services operate. The following listing is the system default.

```
# Copyright (c) 1993-1995 Microsoft Corp.
#
# This file contains port numbers for well-known services as de-
fined by RFC 1060 (Assigned Numbers).
#
# Format:
#
# <service name>  <port number>/<protocol>  [aliases...]
[#<comment>]
#

echo            7/tcp
echo            7/udp
discard         9/tcp    sink null
discard         9/udp    sink null
```

```
systat          11/tcp
systat          11/tcp      users
daytime         13/tcp
daytime         13/udp
netstat         15/tcp
qotd            17/tcp      quote
qotd            17/udp      quote
chargen         19/tcp      ttytst source
chargen         19/udp      ttytst source
ftp-data        20/tcp
ftp             21/tcp
telnet          23/tcp
smtp            25/tcp      mail
time            37/tcp      timserver
time            37/udp      timserver
rlp             39/udp      resource       # resource location
name            42/tcp      nameserver
name            42/udp      nameserver
whois           43/tcp      nicname        # usually to sri-nic
domain          53/tcp      nameserver     # name-domain server
domain          53/udp      nameserver
nameserver      53/tcp      domain         # name-domain server
nameserver      53/udp      domain
mtp             57/tcp                     # deprecated
bootp           67/udp                     # boot program server
tftp            69/udp
rje             77/tcp      netrjs
finger          79/tcp
link            87/tcp      ttylink
supdup          95/tcp
hostnames       101/tcp     hostname       # usually from sri-nic
iso-tsap        102/tcp
dictionary      103/tcp     webster
x400            103/tcp                     # ISO Mail
x400-snd        104/tcp
csnet-ns        105/tcp
pop             109/tcp     postoffice
pop2            109/tcp                     # Post Office
pop3            110/tcp     postoffice
portmap         111/tcp
portmap         111/udp
sunrpc          111/tcp
```

```
sunrpc          111/udp
auth            113/tcp     authentication
sftp            115/tcp
path            117/tcp
uucp-path       117/tcp
nntp            119/tcp     usenet        # Network News Transfer
ntp             123/udp     ntpd ntp      # network time protocol (exp)
nbname          137/udp
nbdatagram      138/udp
nbsession       139/tcp
NeWS            144/tcp     news
sgmp            153/udp     sgmp
tcprepo         158/tcp     repository    # PCMAIL
snmp            161/udp     snmp
snmp-trap       162/udp     snmp
print-srv       170/tcp                   # network PostScript
vmnet           175/tcp
load            315/udp
vmnet0          400/tcp
sytek           500/udp
biff            512/udp     comsat
exec            512/tcp
login           513/tcp
who             513/udp     whod
shell           514/tcp     cmd           # no passwords used
syslog          514/udp
printer         515/tcp     spooler       # line printer spooler
talk            517/udp
ntalk           518/udp
efs             520/tcp                   # for LucasFilm
route           520/udp     router routed
timed           525/udp     timeserver
tempo           526/tcp     newdate
courier         530/tcp     rpc
conference      531/tcp     chat
rvd-control     531/udp     MIT disk
netnews         532/tcp     readnews
netwall         533/udp                   # -for emergency broadcasts
uucp            540/tcp     uucpd         # uucp daemon
klogin          543/tcp                   # Kerberos authenticated
rlogin
kshell          544/tcp     cmd           # and remote shell
new-rwho        550/udp     new-who       # experimental
```

```
remotefs          556/tcp     rfs_server rfs# Brunhoff remote filesystem
rmonitor          560/udp     rmonitord   # experimental
monitor           561/udp                 # experimental
garcon            600/tcp
maitrd            601/tcp
busboy            602/tcp
acctmaster        700/udp.
acctslave         701/udp
acct              702/udp
acctlogin         703/udp
acctprinter       704/udp
elcsd             704/udp                 # errlog
acctinfo          705/udp
acctslave2        706/udp
acctdisk          707/udp
kerberos          750/tcp     kdc         # Kerberos authentication—tcp
kerberos          750/udp     kdc         # Kerberos authentication—udp
kerberos_master   751/tcp                 # Kerberos authentication
kerberos_master   751/udp                 # Kerberos authentication
passwd_server     752/udp                 # Kerberos passwd server
userreg_server    753/udp                 # Kerberos userreg server
krb_prop          754/tcp                 # Kerberos slave propagation
erlogin           888/tcp                 # Login and environment pass-
ing
kpop              1109/tcp                # Pop with Kerberos
phone             1167/udp
ingreslock        1524/tcp
maze              1666/udp
nfs               2049/udp                # sun nfs
knetd             2053/tcp                # Kerberos de-multiplexor
eklogin           2105/tcp                # Kerberos encrypted rlogin
rmt               5555/tcp    rmtd
mtb               5556/tcp    mtbd        # mtb backup
man               9535/tcp                # remote man server
w                 9536/tcp
mantst            9537/tcp                # remote man server, testing
bnews             10000/tcp
rscs0             10000/udp
queue             10001/tcp
```

```
rscs1          10001/udp
poker          10002/tcp
rscs2          10002/udp
gateway        10003/tcp
rscs3          10003/udp
remp           10004/tcp
rscs4          10004/udp
rscs5          10005/udp
rscs6          10006/udp
rscs7          10007/udp
rscs8          10008/udp
rscs9          10009/udp
rscsa          10010/udp
rscsb          10011/udp
qmaster        10012/tcp
qmaster        10012/udp
```

To prevent services from running, or to alter their port assignments, you can edit the SERVICES file.

NETWORKS

The NETWORKS file holds mappings and aliases to network IP addresses. A copy of the default file follows:

```
# Copyright (c) 1993-1995 Microsoft Corp.
#
# This file contains network name/network number mappings for
# local networks. Network numbers are recognized in dotted
  decimal form.
#
# Format:
#
# <network name>   <network number>      [aliases...]  [#<comment>]
#
# For example:
#
#     loopback     127
#     campus       284.122.107
#     london       284.122.108

loopback                   127
```

Notice that the only active listing in the default file is to the loopback address.

PROTOCOL

The PROTOCOL file identifies protocols in the TCP/IP suite that are running and the assigned port number they are running on. A copy of the default file follows:

```
# Copyright (c) 1993-1995 Microsoft Corp.
#
# This file contains the Internet protocols as defined by RFC
1060 (Assigned Numbers).
#
# Format:
#
# <protocol name>  <assigned number>  [aliases...]    [#<comment>]

ip       0    IP        # Internet protocol
icmp     1    ICMP      # Internet control message protocol
ggp      3    GGP       # Gateway-gateway protocol
tcp      6    TCP       # Transmission control protocol
egp      8    EGP       # Exterior gateway protocol
pup      12   PUP       # PARC universal packet protocol
udp      17   UDP       # User datagram protocol
hmp      20   HMP       # Host monitoring protocol
xns-idp  22   XNS-IDP   # Xerox NS IDP
rdp      27   RDP       # "reliable datagram" protocol
rvd      66   RVD       # MIT remote virtual disk
```

The protocols listed along the left column should be very familiar to you from other chapters in this book.

DNS Servers

DNS (Domain Name System) servers can also be used by Windows NT 4.0 to resolve Fully Qualified Domain Names (FQDNs) to IP addresses. Although much more common in the Unix world, Windows NT utilizes the resolution in a two-step solution:

1. A DNS server is called to look up the FQDN supplied by the user.

2. ARP (Address Resolution Protocol) is used to find the hardware address or the address of the router that can deliver the request.

FQDNs are best exemplified by user addresses. For example, suppose that edulaney@iquest.net decides to use Internet Explorer to connect to www.mcp.com, which is running on Internet Information Server. The request is made at the application layer using information a user has entered.

The application layer sends it to the transport layer, which uses known ports (16-bit port addresses). The transport layer passes the data (request and information) to the network layer, which uses DNS lookup to find the addresses in 32-bit dotted decimal format.

Lastly, the interface (assume ethernet on both machines for simplicity) layer does an ARP broadcast to find the unique 48-bit hex address stamped into the NIC card.

The connection is now established and the two parties communicate—an immensely complicated procedure made possible by the DNS servers.

Diagnose and Resolve Name Resolution Problems

 Objective

Name resolution problems are easily identified as such with the PING utility. If you can ping a host using its IP address, but cannot ping it by its host name, then you have a resolution problem. If you cannot ping the host at all, then the problem lies elsewhere.

Problems that can occur with name resolution and their solutions fit into the following generalities:

1. The entry is misspelled. Examine the HOSTS or LMHOSTS file to verify that the host name is correctly spelled. If you are using the HOSTS file, capitalization is important because this file is case-sensitive whereas LMHOSTS is not case sensitive.

2. Comment characters prevent the entry from being read. Verify that a pound sign is not at the beginning of the line, or anywhere on the line prior to the host name.

3. There are duplicate entries in the file. Because the files are read in linear fashion, only the first entry is read and all others are ignored when duplication exists. Verify that all host names are unique.

4. A host other than the one you want is contacted. Verify that the IP address entered in the file(s) is valid and corresponds to the host name.

5. The wrong file is used. While similar in nature, HOSTS and LMHOSTS are quite different, and not all that interchangeable. HOSTS is used to map IP addresses to host names, and LMHOSTS is used to map NetBIOS names to IP addresses.

In addition to PING, the all-purpose TCP/IP troubleshooting tool, useful name resolution utilities include:

▶ nbtstat

▶ hostname

NBTSTAT

The nbtstat utility (NetBIOS over TCP/IP) displays protocol statistics and current TCP/IP connections. It is useful for troubleshooting NetBIOS name resolution problems, and has a number of parameters and options that can be used with it:

▶ **-a (adapter status).** Lists the remote machine's name table given its name.

▶ **-A (Adapter status).** Lists the remote machine's name table given its IP address.

▶ **-c (cache).** Lists the remote name cache including the IP addresses.

▶ **-n (names).** Lists local NetBIOS names.

▶ **-r (resolved).** Lists names resolved by broadcast and via WINS.

▶ **-R (Reload).** Purges and reloads the remote cache name table.

▶ **-S (Sessions).** Lists sessions table with the destination IP addresses.

▶ **-s (sessions).** Lists sessions table converting destination IP addresses to host names via the hosts file.

Hostname

The hostname.exe utility, located in *systemroot*\\System32 returns the name of the local host. This is used only to view the name, and cannot be used to change the name. You can change the host name from the Network Control Panel applet. Exercise 17.1 tests this utility.

Exercises

Exercise 17.1: Finding and Testing the Local Host Name

The following exercise shows you how to find the local host name and verify that you can ping it.

1. From the Start menu, choose Programs, MS-DOS prompt.

2. Type **HOSTNAME** to see the local host's name.

3. Type **PING {HOSTNAME}** where the {HOSTNAME} is the value returned in step two.

In this exercise, you found the local host name and were able to ping it.

Exercise 17.2: Editing the HOSTS File

This exercise shows you how to find and edit the HOSTS file.

1. From the Start menu, choose Programs, MS-DOS prompt.

2. Change directory to the appropriate location by typing **cd *systemroot*\\System32\\Drivers\\etc**. *Systemroot* is your Windows NT directory (normally \\WINNT).

3. Type **PING ME** and notice the error that comes back because the host is not found.

4. Type **EDIT HOSTS**.

   The last line of the file should read:

   `"127.0.0.1     localhost"`

5. Move one space to the right of the last character and type **ME**. The line now reads:

   `"127.0.0.1      localhost ME"`

6. Exit the editor and save the changes.

7. Type **PING ME** and notice the successful results.

In this exercise, you edited the HOSTS file and added an alias.

Review Questions

The following questions will test your knowledge of the information in this chapter. Questions 1–3 refer to the following HOSTS file:

```
127.0.0.1       localhost
192.200.2.4     karen     Kristin      #Evan
192.200.2.5     Spencer   Sales
192.200.2.6     #Lorraine Buis
192.200.2.7     Sales
```

1. Kristin, a user in the Finance department, calls to say that she is having trouble connecting to the host called Lorraine. When she pings 192.200.2.6, the result is successful, but when she pings Lorraine, the error message says the host is not found. What is causing this problem?

   A. Invalid IP address

   B. Duplicate entry

   C. Comment character in the wrong position

   D. Improper spelling of host name

2. Evan, in Accounting, needs to get into 192.200.2.7. He can ping the IP address, but if he tries to ping Sales, the results come back telling him that 192.200.2.5 is responding. What is causing this problem?

   A. Invalid IP address

   B. Duplicate entry

   C. Comment character in the wrong position

   D. Improper spelling of host name

3. Spencer, in Sales, needs to connect to the host, Karen. He can ping the IP address successfully, but if he attempts to ping Karen, the host is not found. What is causing this problem?

   A. Invalid IP address

   B. Duplicate entry

C. Comment character in the wrong position

D. Improper spelling of host name

4. Which utility is useful for troubleshooting NetBIOS name resolution problems?

    A. Nbtstat

    B. Netstat

    C. Ping

    D. Hostname

5. Which utility is useful for finding the local host name?

    A. Nbtstat

    B. Netstat

    C. Ping

    D. Hostname

6. Which utility is an all-purpose tool for troubleshooting TCP/IP problems?

    A. Nbtstat

    B. Netstat

    C. Ping

    D. Hostname

7. HOSTS file entries are limited to how many characters?

    A. 8

    B. 255

    C. 500

    D. Unlimited

8. The number of entries in the HOSTS file is limited to _____.

    A. 8

    B. 255

    C. 500

    D. Unlimited

9. Which file is used for host name resolution?

    A. HOSTS

    B. LMHOSTS

    C. ARP

    D. FQDN

10. Which file is used for NetBIOS name resolution?

    A. HOSTS

    B. LMHOSTS

    C. ARP

    D. FQDN

11. Which address is the loopback address?

    A. 0.0.0.1

    B. 127.0.0.0

    C. 127.0.0.1

    D. 255.255.255.255

12. HOSTS and LMHOSTS work in conjunction with what other files (select all correct answers)?

    A. NETWORKS

    B. PROTOCOL

    C. SERVICES

    D. RESL

Review Answers

1. C

2. B

3. D

4. A

5. D

6. C

7. B

8. D

9. A

10. B

11. C

12. A, B, C

Answers to the Test Yourself Questions at the Beginning of the Chapter

1. A. See "Configure HOSTS Files."

2. D. See "Diagnose and Resolve Name Resolution Problems."

Chapter 18

The Domain Name System

This chapter will help you prepare for the exam by covering the following objectives:

 Objectives

▶ Connect a DNS Server to a DNS root server

▶ Configure DNS Server roles

Test Yourself! Before reading this chapter, test yourself to determine how much study time you will need to devote to this section.

1. What is DNS?

2. How does DNS differ from other host resolution systems like WINS or HOSTS files?

3. Where are the records that make up the domain name space stored?

4. How does DNS on a Windows NT server differ from other implementations of DNS, such as on a Unix DNS Server?

5. How are DNS host names structured?

6. What are some of the top-level domains on the Internet, and what organization maintains zone files for these domains?

7. Should the DNS entries for one NT domain be in one zone file or placed in several zone files? Why?

8. What type of zone files are needed for DNS?

9. Can you register more than one host to the same name? Why would you want to do this?

10. Can a Windows NT DNS Server be used as a secondary server for a non-Microsoft primary server?

Answers are located at the end of the chapter.

History of DNS

The Domain Name System is one way to resolve host names in a TCP/IP environment. In non-Microsoft environments, host names are typically resolved through host files or DNS. In a Microsoft environment, WINS and broadcasts are also used. DNS is the primary system used to resolve host names on the Internet. In fact, DNS had its beginning in the early days of the Internet.

In its early days, the Internet was a small network established by the Department of Defense for research purposes. This network linked computers at several government agencies with a few universities. The host names of the computers in this network were registered in a single HOSTS file located on a centrally administered server. Each site that needed to resolve host names downloaded this file. Few computers were being added to this network, so the HOSTS file wasn't updated too often and the different sites only had to download this file periodically to update their own copies. As the number of hosts on the Internet grew, it became more and more difficult to manage all the names through a central HOSTS file. The number of entries was increasing rapidly, changes were being made frequently, and the server with the central HOSTS file was being accessed more and more often by the different Internet sites trying to download a new copy.

DNS was introduced in 1984 as a way to resolve host names without relying on one central HOSTS file. With DNS, the host names reside in a database that can be distributed among multiple servers, decreasing the load on any one server and also allowing more than one point of administration for this naming system. The name system is based on hierarchical names in a tree-type directory structure. DNS allows more types of registration than the simple host-name-to-TCP/IP-address mapping used in HOSTS files and allows room for future defined types. Because the database is distributed, it can support a much larger database than can be stored in a single HOSTS file. In fact, the database size is virtually unlimited because more servers can be added to handle additional parts of the database. The Domain Name System was first introduced in 1984.

History of Microsoft DNS

DNS was first introduced in the Microsoft environment as part of the Resource Kit for NT Server 3.51. It was not available as part of the NT source files. With version 4.0, DNS is now integrated with the NT source files. Although DNS is not installed by default as part of an NT 4.0 Server installation, you can specify DNS be included as part of an NT installation or you can add DNS later just as you would any other networking service that is part of NT.

Microsoft DNS is based on RFCs 974, 1034, and 1035. A popular implementation of DNS is called BIND (Berkeley Internet Name Domain), developed at UC Berkeley for their version of Unix. However BIND is not totally compliant with the DNS RFCs. Microsoft's DNS does support some features of BIND, but Microsoft DNS is based on the RFCs, not on BIND.

 Tip   You can read these RFCs, or any other RFC, by going to the InterNIC Web site at `http://ds.internic.net/ds/rfc-index.html`.

 Note   Microsoft is planning major enhancements to DNS for NT 5.0. Microsoft is planning to introduce an X.500-type directory structure for their networks in version 5.0. This directory structure will use DNS as the means to organize and control the network architecture. In current versions of NT, the only way to link domains together is through trust relationships. However, even though the domains are linked, you cannot easily manage all the domains. In NT 5.0, Microsoft is planning to keep trusts but manage them through DNS. In DNS an administrator will be able to see all the servers in the network in a hierarchy that brings all the resources in the network together in a more logical manner than the current interface for trust relationships provides.

Microsoft is planning a migration path to move existing trust relationships into DNS. Although administrators have been using DNS mostly to manage Internet or intranet connections, in the future administrators will use DNS to manage their entire network, both for local access and for Internet access.

The Structure of DNS

Some host-name systems, like NetBIOS names, use a flat database. With a flat database, all names exist at the same level, so there can't be any duplicate names. These names are like Social Security numbers: every participant in the Social Security program must have a unique number. The Social Security System is a national system that encompasses all workers in the United States, so it must use an identification system to distinguish between all the individuals in the United States.

DNS names are located in a hierarchical paths, like a directory structure. As figure 18.1 illustrates, you can have a file called TEST.TXT in C:\ and another file called TEST.TXT in C:\ASCII. In a network using DNS, you can have more than one server with the same name, as long as each is located in a different path.

Figure 18.1

Names in DNS are part of a logical tree structure called the domain name space. Each node in the space is called a domain and it can have subdomains.

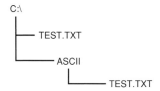

DNS Domains

The Internet Network Information Center (InterNIC) controls the top-level domains. These have names like "com" (for business-es), "edu" (for educational institutions like universities), "gov" (for government organizations), and "org" (for non-profit organizations). There are also domains for countries. You can visit the InterNIC web site at http://www.internic.com/. Table 18.1 summarizes common Internet domains.

Table 18.1

Common Internet Domains

Name	Type of Organization
com	Commercial organizations
edu	Educational institutions
org	Non-profit organizations
net	Networks (the backbone of the Internet)
gov	Non-military government organizations
mil	Military government organizations
num	Phone numbers
arpa	Reverse DNS
xx	Two-letter country code

Figure 18.2 shows the top-level domains on the Internet with some subdomains illustrated as well.

Figure 18.2

Domains of the Internet.

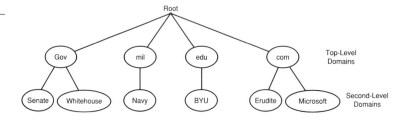

DNS Host Names

To refer to a host in a domain, use a fully qualified domain name (FQDN), which completely specifies the location of the host. An FQDN specifies the host name, the domain or subdomain the host belongs to, and any domains above that in the hierarchy until the root domain in the organization is specified. On the Internet, the root domain in the path is something like "com," but on a private network the top-level domains may be named according to some internal naming convention. The FQDN is read from left to right, with each host name or domain name specified by a period. The syntax of an FQDN follows:

```
host name.subdomain. … .domain
```

An example of an FQDN is www.microsoft.com, which refers to a server called "www" located in the subdomain called "microsoft" in the domain called "com." Referring to a host by its FQDN is similar to referring to a file by its complete directory path. However, a complete file name goes from general to specific, with the file name at the rightmost part of the path. An FQDN goes from specific to general, with the host name at the leftmost part of the name. Fully qualified domain names are more like addresses, as shown in figure 18.3. An address starts with the most specific information: who is to receive the letter. Then address specifies the house number in which the recipient lives, the street on which the house is located, the city where the street is located, and finally the most general location, the state where that city is located.

Figure 18.3

Addresses use a generic to specific naming scheme.

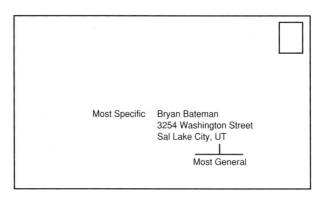

Most Specific   Bryan Bateman
3254 Washington Street
Sal Lake City, UT
Most General

Zone Files

The DNS database is stored in files called *zones*. It's possible, even desirable, to break the DNS database in a number of zones. Breaking the DNS database into zones was part of the original design goals of DNS. With multiple zones, the load of providing access to the database is spread among a number of servers. Also, the administrative burden of managing the database is spread out, because different administrators manage only the parts of the DNS database stored in their own zones. A zone can be any portion of the domain name space; it doesn't have to contain all the subdomains for that part of the DNS tree. Zones can be copied to other name servers through replication. With multiple zones, smaller amounts of information are copied when zone files are replicated than would be if the entire domain was located in one zone file.

Figure 18.4 shows a DNS domain, erudite.com, that is broken into several zones. Because this domain could be very large, splitting it into zones enables the administrators to manage smaller zone files that are located where the administrators work instead of in some central location. Also, because the files are smaller, less network traffic is generated as the zone files are copied from server to server. In fact, if the entire domain is located in one zone file, each time a change is made to the zone file the entire file must be copied to other DNS Servers that are configured to received a copy.

Figure 18.4

The domain erudite.com and its zones.

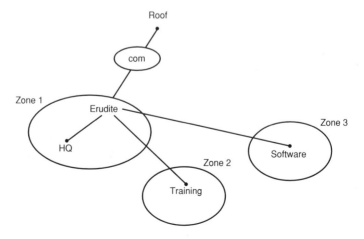

Types of DNS Servers

 Objective

A DNS Server has information about the domain name space that it has already obtained either from a local copy of a zone file or by making a query of another DNS Server. A name server can have more than one zone file installed on it. A name server can have the original copy of a zone, or it can receive a copy of a zone file from another name server. If a name server has any copy of a zone file, it has authority for that zone.

There are three types of name servers: Primary, Secondary, and Master.

A *primary server* has the original copy of a zone file. Any changes made to the zone file are made to the file on the primary server. When a primary server receives a query about a host name in its own zone, it retrieves the host resolution locally from its own zone files.

A *secondary server* gets a copy of zone files from another server. This secondary zone file is a read-only copy of the file; any changes made to the zone are made at the originating zone file. Then the changes are copied down to the secondary server through replication. When zone files are copied from another server it is called a zone transfer.

There are several reasons you should have a secondary server for each zone. A secondary server provides redundancy, enabling host names in the zone to be resolved even if the primary server goes down. A secondary server can also reduce the load on a primary server or reduce network traffic. For example, placing a secondary server on a remote site can reduce network traffic generated when clients cross the WAN link to resolve host names. With a secondary server at this remote site, client queries can be handled locally. The only traffic from DNS is generated when the zone file on the primary server changes and the secondary server downloads a new copy. Also, the primary server sees less activity because it communicates with only one host at the remote site (the secondary server) rather than resolve queries from all the clients at the site.

A server can have any number of zone files stored on it. The primary and secondary designation applies to each zone file rather than to the server itself. A server can be the primary for one zone (it has the master copy of that zone) and a secondary for another zone (it gets a read-only copy of the zone file through a zone transfer).

The server from which a secondary server receives a zone transfer is called the *Master Name Server*. The TCP/IP address of the Master Name Server is configured at the secondary server. The master server can be a primary or a secondary server. If the master is a primary, then the zone transfer comes directly from the source. If the master name server is a secondary server, the file received from the master server via a zone transfer is a copy of the read-only zone file. In this scenario, there can be a delay in receiving changes made to the zone file because the file must first be transferred to the master server and then transferred again to the next server in line.

As figure 18.5 illustrates, however, using secondary servers as master servers can reduce the load on a primary server by limiting the number of secondary servers to which the primary server must send zone transfers. In this figure, the primary server sends a copy of the zone to three servers in total while only communicating directly with one server. The master server for Secondary2 and Secondary3 is on the same side of a slow WAN link. The zone file is transferred once over the slow link to Secondary1, and then is transferred to the other servers on the same LAN.

Both primary and secondary servers are considered authoritative for their zones because they have the zone information. In other words, either the primary or the secondary can respond to a request for information about the part of the domain that is stored in that zone file.

A DNS Server doesn't have to have any zone files, either as a primary or a secondary server. If it has no zone files, the DNS Server is known as a *caching-only server*. The only responsibility of a caching server is to make DNS queries, return the results, and cache any results it obtains. Caching servers are not authoritative for any domains because they don't store copies of any zone files locally. When a caching-only server first starts, it does not have any DNS information stored. A caching server builds information only when it caches results of queries made after the server starts. However, installing DNS as a caching-only server may be a good choice across a slow WAN link, because entire zone files don't need to be transferred. The caching server can make a query across the link, but only one record is transmitted, not the full zone file. After the server has resolved a query, a future query for the same information can be resolved locally from the cache. Resolving locally eliminates the need to communicate across the WAN link (at least until the cached entry expires). The time to live of cached entries is determined by the server that answered the query. It returns a time to live for the query along with the name resolution.

Figure 18.5

Using a secondary server as a master server to reduce network traffic on a slow WAN link.

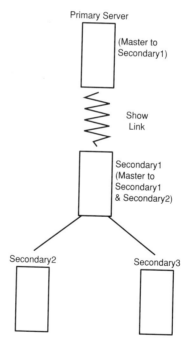

Resolving DNS Queries

A client querying a DNS Server is called a *resolver*, while a DNS Server is generically called a *name server*. DNS works at the Application layer of the OSI model, which is the top or seventh layer.

By working at this layer, DNS can more easily communicate with the client applications needing to resolve a host name. DNS can use either UDP or TCP for its communications. DNS tries to use UDP—which is more efficient—for better performance, but DNS resorts to TCP if can't communicate properly through UDP. TCP and UDP are discussed more completely in Chapter 8.

Three types of queries can be made to a DNS Server: recursive, iterative, and inverse. Some examples of queries include a web browser—such as Internet Explorer—requesting the IP address for a web site, a Microsoft client requesting a browse list, another DNS Server requesting a name query, or a WINS server unable to resolve a name from its own database.

A *recursive query* forces the DNS Server to respond to the request with either a failure or a successful response that includes the TCP/IP address for the domain name requested. Resolvers typically make recursive queries. With a recursive query, the DNS Server must contact any other DNS Servers it needs to resolve the request. When it receives a response from the other DNS Server(s), it then sends a response to the client. With a recursive query, the DNS Server is not allowed to pass the buck by simply giving the client the address of another DNS Server that might be able to handle the request. This type of query is made from a resolver to a name server, and also from a name server to its forwarder (another name server configured to handle requests forwarded to it).

An *iterative query* is one in which the name server is expected to provide the best information based on what the server knows from local zone files or from caching. If the name server doesn't have any information to answer the query, it simply sends a negative response. This is like playing the game, Go Fish. A player asks another player for a certain card: "Do you have any Jacks?" The player either answers yes and supplies the requested information (Jacks) or answers no and says, "Go Fish." In other words, I don't have what you're looking for; go try someone else. A forwarder makes this type of query as it tries to find names outside its local domain. It may have to query a number of outside DNS Servers in an attempt to resolve the name.

Figure 18.6 shows the entire query process, with a DNS client making an initial query of a DNS Server to resolve the name www.erudite.com. The client makes a recursive query; it expects to receive an answer without being referred to another server. The DNS Server receiving the query can't resolve the host name with its own information (cached or from zone files), so it makes an iterative query to a root name server. The root server sends back the address of the name server for the com domain. The DNS Server then sends an iterative query to the com name server. This server sends back the address of the name server authoritative for the erudite.com domain. The DNS Server then sends a query for www.erudite.com to this server, and the erudite.com name server finds a resolution for www and returns a reply. The local DNS Server can finally respond to the client that made the original request for the name resolution. The client was kept on hold while the DNS Server worked to find a response. Because the client sent a recursive query, the DNS Server was forced to go to this extra work until it could obtain an answer.

Figure 18.6

A resolver makes a recursive query, which forces the DNS Server to make several iterative queries so that it can return an answer to the client.

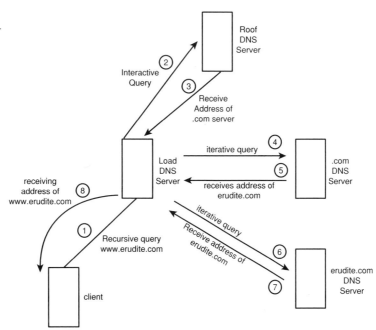

The third type of query, an *inverse query*, is used when the client wants to know the host name of a specified TCP/IP address. A special domain in the DNS name space resolves this type of query. Otherwise, a DNS Server would have to completely search all the DNS domains to make sure it found the correct name. This special domain is called in-addr.arpa. Nodes in this space are named after TCP/IP addresses rather than alphabetic host names. However, these node names have the TCP/IP names in reverse order.

Remember that TCP/IP addresses move from general to specific. The first octet(s) refers to the network; additional octets or portions of octets may be dedicated to defining a subnet as specified by the subnet mask; the remaining octets or parts of octets specify the host address of a specific computer. With DNS, however, host names are read from right to left, with the name of the domain on the right, the name of any subdomains moving from right to left, and finally the name of the host on the leftmost part of the fully qualified name. In order to make the node names of the inverse lookup zones compatible with DNS, the zone files are named with IP addresses, but the addresses are written in reverse order.

Inverse lookup queries are used when a client requests a service that only specified host names have been given permission to use. The server receiving the request only knows the IP address of the client, so the server must find out the host name to see whether the client is on the approved list. In this case, the server issues an inverse lookup query to find the host name matching the IP address of the client that requested the service.

A number of DNS Servers also have zones for inverse lookups. The highest levels of zone files, for Class A, B, and C networks, are maintained by InterNIC. Then individual network address owners can have zone files for subnets on their own networks.

A name server can return three types of responses to a query: a successful response with the IP address for the requested host name (or the host name for an inverse lookup), a pointer to another name server (only in an iterative query), or a failure message.

Time to Live for Queries

A name server caches all the information it receives when it resolves queries outside its own zone files. These cached responses can then be used to answer queries for the same information in the future. These cached entries don't stay on the DNS Server forever, however. There is a *time to live* (TTL) for the responses to make sure the DNS Server doesn't keep information for so long that it becomes out-of-date. The time to live for the cache can be set on each DNS Server.

There are two competing factors to consider when setting the time to live. One is the accuracy of the cached information. If the TTL is short, then the likelihood of having old information goes down considerably. If the TTL is long, then the cached responses could become outdated, meaning the DNS Server could give false answers to queries. The accuracy of the responses is also dependent on how stable your environment is. If names change often, then a short TTL is necessary. It is important, however, to consider the load on the server and the network. If the TTL is large, the server can answer more queries from cache and doesn't use local resources or network bandwidth to send out additional queries.

If a query is answered with an entry from cache, the TTL of the entry is also passed with the response. This way other DNS Servers that receive the response know how long the entry is valid. Other DNS Servers honor the TTL from the responding server; they don't set it again based on their own TTL. Thus entries truly expire rather than live in perpetuity as they move from server to server with an updated TTL. Resolvers (clients) also have a cache, and honor the TTL received from a name server that answered a query from the name server's cache.

Forwarders and Slaves

When a client contacts a DNS Server for name resolution, the DNS Server first looks in its local files to resolve the request. If the DNS Server is not authoritative for the zone pertaining to that request, it must look to another name server to resolve the request. When you are browsing the World Wide Web, resolving a domain name involves either making a request of a name server maintained by your ISP or going on the Internet to contact a name server there.

You may not want all DNS Servers to forward these requests. Thus DNS enables you to designate specific DNS Servers as forwarders. In general, only forwarders can communicate on the Internet or beyond the local network. The other DNS Servers are configured with the address of the forwarder. The forwarder is much like a gatekeeper, to which all outside requests are funneled. You can put some firewall software or other protective measures on the forwarder without having to do so to all the DNS Servers in your organization. An entire server is designated as a forwarder; this is not done on a zone-by-zone basis.

When a forwarder receives a request to resolve a name, it accesses outside resources and returns the response to the DNS Server that originated the request. If the forwarder can't answer the request, then the originating DNS Server can resort to other means to resolve the request.

Slaves are DNS Servers configured to use forwarders and also configured to return a failure message if the forwarder can't resolve the request. A slave does not try to contact other DNS Servers if its designated forwarder can't handle the request. In other words, a slave makes a recursive query to a forwarder.

Structure of Zone Files

Non-Microsoft name servers usually require manual editing of text files to create the zone files that comprise the domain name space. These files must be created with a specific syntax that can be read by DNS. Microsoft's DNS Server includes DNS Manager, a GUI interface that displays the settings from these files and enables you to make entries in these files via the interface rather than in the files themselves. DNS Manager also enables you to manage more than one DNS Server from one location. Although you can use DNS Manager to create or modify zone files even when you do not know their syntax, understanding the content and structure of the zone files is essential to your understanding of DNS. In fact, DNS Manager refers to many of the records in the zone file by their syntax name. So whether you use a text editor to modify zone files or do it through DNS Manager, you must still understand what the different records are used for.

The zone file is also known as the *database file*. It contains the resource records for the part of domain covered by the zone. These files are stored in the NT file structure, in the path \WINNT\SYSTEM32\dns. A DNS Server uses three types of zone files: database file (zone), cache, and reverse lookup. You can also have a boot file, which is used to initialize the DNS Server. However, a Microsoft DNS Server is usually initialized from values stored in the registry. The capability to initialize from a boot file is included in Microsoft DNS for compatibility with other types of DNS Servers.

Zone Files

Zone files have a .dns extension, like microsoft.com.dns. A sample zone file called place.dns in the dns\samples directory can be manually edited and used as a zone file. Of course, you can use DNS Manager with its windows interface to create zone files and the records within zone. On non-Microsoft DNS Servers, zone files are typically called db.zone.

You can use DNS Manager to create zone entries even when you do not know the syntax of the records. However, DNS Manager makes entries in zone files according to the syntax. It's important to know what each record is used for and what its parameters specify. The following sections examine the records that are usually found in a zone file.

SOA Record

For an exercise covering this information, see end of chapter.

Each database file starts with an SOA record, stating the *start of authority* for the file. This record specifies the primary server for this zone—the server that maintains the read/write copy of this file. The syntax of this record follows:

```
IN SOA <source host><contact e-mail><ser. No.><refresh
time><retry time><expiration time><TTL>
```

An example of the syntax follows:

```
@ IN SOA ns1.erudite.com kwolford.erudite.com. (
     101     ; serial number
     10800   ; refresh [3 hours]
     3600    ; retry [1 hour]
     604800  ; expire [7 days]
     86400 ) ; time to live [1 day]
```

The "@" symbol in this example indicates the local server; "IN" indicates an Internet record. The fully qualified name for the name server NS1 must end in a period. Note that the e-mail name for the administrator must have a period instead of the "@" symbol in the e-mail address. If the SOA record is on more than one line, an open parenthesis must end the first line and a close parenthesis must end the last line.

The following list explains the other parameters:

▶ **Source host.** The name of the host with the read/write copy of the file.

▶ **Contact e-mail.** The Internet e-mail address of the person who maintains this file. This address must be expressed with a period instead of the "@" that is usually found in e-mail addresses, such as kwolford.erudite.com instead of kwolford@erudite.com.

▶ **Serial number.** The version number of the database. This number should be changed each time the database changes. This number changes automatically if you use DNS Manager to change the zone file. If you use a text editor to modify the zone file, you must change this number yourself.

▶ **Refresh time.** The time a secondary server waits before checking the master server for changes to the database file. If the file has changed, the secondary server requests a zone transfer. This value is expressed in seconds.

▶ **Retry time.** The time a secondary server waits before trying again if a zone transfer fails. This value is expressed in seconds.

▶ **Expiration time.** The time a secondary server keeps trying to transfer a zone. After the expiration time passes, the old zone information is deleted. This value is expressed in seconds.

▶ **Time to live.** The time a server can cache resource records from this database file. The time to live is sent as part of the response for any queries that are answered from this database file. An individual resource record can have a TTL that overrides this value. This value is expressed in seconds.

If a resource record uses more than one line in a database file, you must end the first line with an open parenthesis and the last line with a close parenthesis.

Figure 18.7 shows the dialog box used in DNS Manager to modify the SOA record.

Figure 18.7

Editing the SOA record.

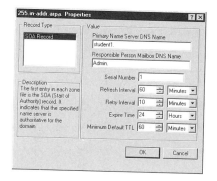

Name Server Record

The Name Server record specifies the other name servers for the specified domain. The syntax for a Name Server record follows:

```
<domain> IN NS <nameserver host>
```

An example of a Name Server record follows:

```
@ IN NS ns1.erudite.com
```

The "@" symbol indicates the local domain. The server NS1 in the domain erudite.com is the name server.

Figure 18.8 shows the interface used in DNS Manager to modify or add a Name Server record.

Figure 18.8

Adding a Name Server record.

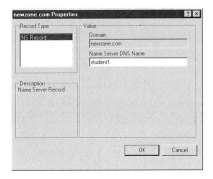

Mail Exchange Record

The Mail Exchange record specifies the name of the host that processes mail for this domain. If you list multiple mail servers, you can specify a preference number that specifies the order in which the mail servers should be used. If the first preferred mail server doesn't respond, the second one is contacted, and so on. The syntax of this record follows:

```
<domain> IN MX <preference><mailserver host>
```

Host Record

For an exercise covering this information, see end of chapter.

The Host Record is the record that actually specifies the TCP/IP address for a specified host. All hosts that have static TCP/IP addresses should have an entry in this database. Clients with dynamic addresses are resolved in other ways, such as through a WINS server. Most of the entries in a database file are host records. The syntax of this record follows:

```
<host name> IN A <ip address of host>
```

An example of some host records follows:

```
arthur      IN A 136.104.3.92
thomas      IN A 136.104.4.85
kathleen    IN A 136.104.1.38
```

In this example, three servers called "arthur," "thomas," and "kathleen" are registered with their corresponding IP addresses.

Figure 18.9 shows the dialog box used in DNS Manager to add a host record. Note that you can also create the corresponding PTR record at the same time. PTR or pointer records are used for reverse lookups, which are described later in this chapter.

Figure 18.9

Adding a Host record.

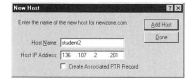

Local Host Record

The Local Host Record is simply a regular host record using a special host name and the normal TCP/IP loopback address (the address used to direct or "loop back" TCP/IP traffic back to the host generating the traffic). For example, the following record maps the name localhost to the loopback address of 127.0.0.1:

```
localhost IN A 127.0.0.1
```

This record enables a client to query for localhost.erudite.com and receive the normal loopback address.

CNAME Record

The CNAME record is an alias, enabling you to specify more than one name for each TCP/IP address. CNAME stands for *canonical name.* The syntax of a CNAME record follows:

```
<alias name> CNAME <host name>
```

Using CNAME records, you can combine an ftp and a web server on the same host, for example. The following example maps a server called InetServer to a TCP/IP address. Then the names FTP and WWW are aliased to this server.

```
InetServer IN A 136.107.3.43
FTP CNAME InetServer
WWW CNAME InetServer
```

These records illustrate how easy it is to change the server on which services are provided while still allowing access to the new server for clients that refer to its original name. For example, if you want move the Web server to another machine called New-Inet, you can modify the zone files to read as follows:

```
InetServer IN A 136.107.3.43
FTP CNAME InetServer
NewInet IN A 136.107.1.107
WWW CNAME NewInet
```

The only change required for access to the new server was to make entries at the DNS Server; changes do not have to be made at the clients. Any clients querying the DNS Server receive the updated address automatically in response to the query.

Figure 18.10 shows the dialog box used in DNS Manager to add or modify a CNAME record.

Figure 18.10

Adding a CNAME record.

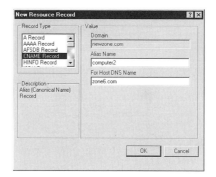

Using the Cache File to Connect to Root-Level Servers

 Objective

There is a cache file included with DNS that has entries for top-level servers of the Internet domains. If a host name can not be resolved from local zone files, DNS uses the cache file to look for a higher-level DNS Server to resolve the name. If your organization only has an intranet without any Internet access, you should replace this file with one that lists the top-level DNS Servers in your organization. This file is called cache.dns and is located at `\winnt\system32\dns`.

The latest version of this file can be downloaded from InterNIC at `ftp://rs.internic.net/domain/named.cache`.

Reverse Lookup File

The reverse lookup file has entries that enable IP addresses to be resolved to host names. Normally DNS is used to resolve host names to IP addresses, so the opposite process is called *reverse lookup*. The files are named according the Class of network, but with the octets in reverse order. Remember, a Class A network uses the first octet of the IP address for the network address, a Class B address uses the first 2 octets, and a Class C address uses the first 3 octets. The following examples are zone files for a Class A, Class B, and Class C network.

Network ID	Zone File Name
36.x.x.x	36.in-addr.arpa
138.107.x.x	107.138.in-addr.arpa
242.23.108.x	108.23.242.in-addr-arpa

Pointer Record

For an exercise covering this information, see end of chapter.

Pointer records are the reverse lookup entries. They specify the IP address in reverse order (like a DNS name with the most specific information first) and the corresponding host name. The syntax for a PTR record follows:

```
<ip reverse domain name> IN PTR <host name>
```

An example of this record follows:

```
43.3.107.136.in-addr.arpa. IN PTR InetServer.microsoft.com
```

This example is an entry for the server called InetServer with the IP address of 136.107.3.43.

Figure 18.11 shows a reverse lookup zone that includes DNS Server a PTR record as viewed in DNS Manager.

Figure 18.11

A reverse lookup zone with its PTR record.

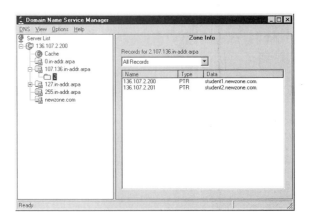

Arpa-127.rev File

The Arpa-127.rev file is included with every DNS Server. It provides reverse lookup for the local host, which is known as the loopback.

BIND Boot File

The BIND boot file is used if you do not plan to administer the DNS Server through windows interface but plan to edit text files instead. This file controls the startup of the DNS Server. The capability to use a BIND boot file is mainly provided for compatibility with BIND versions of DNS, which use boot files for startup. You can copy the files from these servers and with some editing use them to boot an NT DNS Server.

The commands that control the boot process in this file follow.

Directory Command

The directory command specifies the directory where the DNS files are found, including the files referenced by the boot file. The syntax of the directory command follows:

```
directory <directory>
```

An example of this command follows, showing that the files are located in the normal path of DNS files, which is also where NT is installed on C:\WINNT:

```
directory c:\winnt\system32\dns
```

Cache Command

The cache command specifies the cache file that is used to locate root servers for the domain. This command must be in the file. A cache file is part of Microsoft DNS. The syntax is as follows:

```
Cache . <filename>
```

An example of this command follows, which shows the name of the cache file, which is "cache" by default:

```
cache . cache
```

Remember the path for this file is already specified with the directory command.

Primary Command

The primary command specifies zone files for which this server is authoritative. For example, this server has the primary file for the zone. There can be more than one primary record in a file because a server can be the primary server for any number of zones. The syntax is as follows:

```
Primary <domain> <filename>
```

In the following example, the local server is primary for two zone files, erudite.dns and training.dns.

```
primary erudite.com erudite.dns
primary training.erudite.com training.dns
```

Secondary Command

The secondary command specifies those zones files for which this server is a secondary server. For example, it downloads a copy of the zone file from the primary server for the zone. The command specifies the zone file and also the address of the server where the secondary server is to download the zone file. Remember that a server can download the zone file from the primary server or from another secondary server. The file name specified identifies where the local copy of this file is to be stored. You can have more than one secondary command in a file because a server can be the secondary server for any number of zones. The syntax is as follows:

```
Secondary <domain> <hostlist> <local filename>
```

In this example, the local server is secondary for the zone software.dns, which can be transferred from the DNS Server with an IP address of 158.51.20.1.

```
secondary software.erudite.com 158.51.20.1 software.dns
```

Forwarders Command

For an exercise covering this information, see end of chapter.

The forwarders command specifies a server that can help resolve recursive queries if the local DNS Server cannot resolve them. The syntax is as follows:

```
Forwarders <hostlist>
```

In this example, two servers are configured as forwarders: 158.51.20.100 and 158.51.20.101:

```
forwarders 158.51.20.100 158.51.20.101
```

Slave Command

If a slave command is present, the local DNS Server must use the forwarders to resolve queries, the local server can't resolve the query using its own resources. The slave command must follow a forwarders command.

In this example, the local server is slave to the two servers listed in the forwarders command.

```
forwarders 158.51.20.100 158.51.20.101
slave
```

Review Questions

1. What are the benefits of DNS?

   A. It allows a distributed database that can be administered by a number of administrators.

   B. It allows host names that specify where a host is located.

   C. It allows WINS clients to register with the WINS server.

   D. It allows queries to other servers to resolve host names.

2. With what non-Microsoft DNS platforms is Microsoft DNS compatible?

   A. Only Unix DNS Servers that are based on BIND

   B. Only Unix DNS Servers that are based on the DNS RFCs

   C. Unix DNS Servers that are either BIND-based or RFC-based

   D. Only other Microsoft DNS Servers

3. In the DNS name www.microsoft.com, what does "microsoft" represent?

   A. The last name of the host

   B. The domain in which the host is located

   C. The IP address of the building in which the host is located

   D. The directory in which the host name file is located

4. If you do not specify the host name and domain in the TCP/IP configuration before installing DNS, what happens during the DNS installation?

   A. An NS record is not created on the server.

   B. DNS doesn't install.

    C. Default values are used to create NS and SOA records.

    D. You cannot create any zones on the server.

5. How do you create a Primary DNS Server?

    A. Install DNS on a Primary Domain Controller

    B. Configure the DNS Server to be a primary server in the Server Properties

    C. During DNS installation, specify that it is to be a primary server

    D. Create a primary zone

6. Where can a secondary server receive a copy of the zone file?

    A. Only from the primary server for the zone

    B. From any server that has a copy of the zone file

    C. Only from the master server for the zone

    D. Only from the top-level DNS Server for the domain

7. What record must be added to a zone file to alias a host to another name?

    A. An A record

    B. An SOA record

    C. A CNAME record

    D. A PTR record

8. How do you configure a client to use DNS to resolve a HOST name before using other methods?

    A. Query for a host name longer than 15 characters.

    B. Move DNS up in the Host Resolution Order dialog box.

    C. A client always searches DNS last.

    D. Configure the DNS to advertise itself to DNS clients.

9. How does a caching-only DNS Server build a database of host records?

A. The caching server downloads a copy of zone files into its cache from master servers when the caching server starts.

B. Entries from the local cache file are read into cache.

C. The server captures the results of queries as they are sent across the network.

D. The server makes queries.

10. What kind of query does a DNS client make to a DNS Server?

A. A reverse lookup query

B. An iterative query

C. A recursive query

D. A resolver query

11. Which server can be a master server for a Unix DNS Server that is the secondary server for a zone?

A. Any NT DNS Server with a primary zone

B. Any Unix server with a primary zone

C. Any NT DNS Server with a secondary zone

D. Any NT DNS Server with a zone that doesn't use WINS lookup

12. How can zone files be modified?

A. With NSLOOKUP

B. By editing the zone files with a text editor

C. With DNS Manager

D. With DNSCnfg

13. What is the use of the cache file on a DNS Server?

    A. It has records for DNS Servers at top-level domains.

    B. It provides initial values to the DNS cache.

    C. It specifies the TTL for cached entries.

    D. It specifies the amount of memory and its location for DNS caching.

14. What would the reverse lookup zone be called for a server with the IP address of 149.56.85.105?

    A. 105.85.56.149.in-addr.arpa

    B. 149.56.85.105.in-addr.arpa

    C. 56.149.in-addr.arpa

    D. 149.56.in-addr.arpa

15. How can you configure a secondary server to receive changes to zone files as soon as they are made?

    A. Decrease the refresh interval on the secondary server

    B. Turn on the Notify feature on the primary server

    C. Configure the primary server with push replication

    D. Make the primary server the master server for the secondary

16. How can you configure a DNS Server to send all queries to another DNS Server?

    A. Configure that server to use recursive queries

    B. Configure that server to be a cache-only server

    C. Configure that server to be a slave

    D. Configure that server to be a forwarder

17. You have several secondary DNS Servers on one side of a slow WAN link. How should you configure the master server for these secondary servers to minimize traffic over this slow WAN link?

   A. Have all the secondary servers on one side of link use one master server on the other side of the link.

   B. Have one secondary server use the primary server on the other side of the link as the master. Other secondary servers use the secondary on their side of the link as the master.

   C. Use a caching-only server as the master.

   D. Configure DNS for pull replication scheduled during low traffic times.

18. Where can you find the files needed to install DNS?

   A. On the NT 4.0 Server Resource Kit

   B. On the Backoffice CD

   C. On the NT 4.0 Server CD

   D. On the DNS CD

19. Which protocol does DNS try to use during its queries in order to minimize network traffic?

   A. UDP

   B. ARP

   C. IP

   D. TCP

Review Answers

1. A, B, D

2. C

3. B

4. A

5. D

6. B

7. C

8. A

9. D

10. C

11. B, D

12. B, C

13. A

14. C

15. B

16. C

17. B

18. C

19. A

Answers to the Test Yourself Questions at the Beginning of the Chapter

1. DNS stands for *Domain Name System*. It is a database that enables host names to be resolved to IP address-es. Entries to the database must be manually added; they are not dynamically built as in WINS.

2. The biggest difference between DNS and the other systems is that DNS uses a hierarchical name system that specifies the complete logical location of the host. With DNS, hosts can have common names, as long as they are located in a different portion of the DNS hierarchy, in much the same way that you can have two files with the same name located on different paths in a directory tree. WINS and HOST files use a flat database that simply registers the host name without any reference to where the host is located.

3. The DNS name space exists on a distributed database, in which different parts of the database are stored on different DNS Servers. These files in which the database records are stored are called *zone files*. DNS Serv-ers are configured to query each other when they are trying to resolve queries that can't be resolved in their own files. A DNS Server can access the entire database for the domain name space through these queries without having all the zone files stored locally. The hierarchical structure of DNS helps a DNS Server know where to send a query so it can resolve a host name.

4. Microsoft's implementation of DNS is based directly on the RFC's that define DNS. Some other versions of DNS are based on prior implementations of DNS, such as BIND, rather than directly on the RFC's. A Win-dows NT DNS Server is fully compatible with any other DNS Server based on the RFC's. The Microsoft DNS Server is also compatible with a BIND server. Microsoft has added enhancements to DNS to enable DNS and WINS to work together to resolve host names.

5. A DNS name is called a *fully qualified domain name* (FQDN). Reading from left to right, the name specifies the name of the host, the name of the domain or subdomain in which the host is located, the domain in which the subdomain is located, and so on until a top level domain is specified. For example, a FQDN like www.microsoft.com specifies a host named www in a domain called microsoft in a top-level domain called com.

6. InterNIC is the organization that assigns IP addresses for the Internet. InterNIC also maintains the zone files for the top-level domains. Some examples of top-level domains include .com for commercial organizations, .org for non-profit organizations, .edu for educational institutions, and .gov for non-military government organizations.

7. You can have all the records for the domain name space in one zone file. However, breaking a name space into more than one zone can offer several advantages. With multiple zones, different administrators can manage different zone files. Also, using different zones enables you to distribute the zone files to spread the load more evenly among servers and throughout the physical network.

8. A Microsoft DNS Server typically uses three types of zone files. A fourth type of file is typically used for non-Microsoft DNS Servers. A database zone file has the records for the zone, with the host name mappings to IP addresses. A cache file has addresses for top-level zones in the domain. The cache file that comes with DNS has addresses for those DNS Servers maintained by InterNIC that have zone files for the Internet. A reverse lookup file has IP address mappings to host names, so an IP address can be resolved to a host name. A fourth type of zone file is not required by DNS, the boot file. A boot file is used by a non-Microsoft DNS Server to specify the startup values for DNS. DNS on Windows NT starts up using values stored in the registry. However, it is possible to have a Microsoft DNS Server start up from a boot file.

9. Yes. In fact, this is done to spread the load for commonly accessed host names like www. When multiple IP addresses are registered to a single name, DNS uses a round-robin technique to resolve addresses. Each time a client queries the server for this name, the DNS Server gives out a different address in the list, return-ing to the beginning of the list when the server has given out all the names in the list.

10. Yes. Because Microsoft based its DNS on the RFCs, the NT DNS Server is compatible with other DNS Servers. However, if an NT DNS Server is using WINS lookup in a primary zone, this zone should not be copied to a non-Microsoft DNS Server because it doesn't know how to handle WINS records in a zone file.

Chapter 19

Implementing Microsoft DNS Servers

This chapter will help you prepare for the exam by covering the following objectives:

 Objectives

▶ Install and configure Microsoft DNS Server service on a Windows NT Server

▶ Configure DNS Server roles

▶ Integrate a DNS Server with other name servers

▶ Diagnose and resolve name resolution problems

Test Yourself! Before reading this chapter, test yourself to determine how much study time you will need to devote to this section.

1. What is an FQDN?

2. What is the purpose of a CNAME record?

3. What is the difference between a recursive and iterative query?

4. What purpose does an IP Forwarder serve?

5. For what two main roles can a DNS Server be configured?

6. What four main files are used to configure a DNS Server?

7. What is required to configure a Microsoft DNS Server to act as a Dynamic DNS Server?

8. What does reverse lookup provide?

9. Which type of applications use a DNS Server?

10. How do you configure Windows NT to use DNS to resolve NetBIOS names?

Answers are located at the end of the chapter.

Implementing Microsoft DNS Servers

In Chapter 18 you saw the steps involved in using DNS and looked at the configuration files and the types of configurations available; it is time to see how to implement DNS within Windows NT. This Chapter deals with setting up and configuring DNS within Windows NT.

Installing the DNS Server

Objective

For an exercise covering this information, see end of chapter.

The first item of business is to install the DNS Server. The system on which you install the DNS service must be running Windows NT Server and needs to have a static IP configuration (as seen in Chapter 7). Installing the DNS Server is simple given that, installing it is the same as installing any other network service. The steps are as follows:

1. Open the Network settings dialog box (right-click the Network Neighborhood and choose Properties).

2. On the Services tab, click Add, and select the Microsoft DNS Server (see fig. 19.1).

Figure 19.1

Adding the Microsoft DNS Server.

3. Click OK to add the service. When prompted, enter the directory in which your Windows NT source files are located.

4. Choose Close from the Network settings dialog box and, when prompted, restart your system.

You have now installed the DNS Server. To verify that the service is correctly installed, check the Services icon in Control Panel to ensure the Microsoft DNS Server is listed and has started.

Enabling DNS on the Client

Now that you have a DNS Server, you need to have your clients use the DNS Server. To enable Windows clients to use the DNS Server, you can add the address of the DNS Server to each station (manually), or you can set the DNS Server option on the DHCP server.

For Windows NT, you can use the following procedure to set the DNS Server address. (Setting the address on Windows 95 is the same.)

1. Open the TCP/IP settings dialog box. (Open the Network settings dialog box, and from the Protocol tab, double-click TCP/IP.)

2. On the DNS tab (see fig. 19.2), enter the required information. As a minimum, you need to enter the IP address of a DNS Server. The other options on this tab are described as follows:

   ▶ **Host Name.** This is the name of the local host. This is the same as the NetBIOS name by default; however, you can change it. (If you select a different name, you are warned that if the NetBIOS name is ever changed, the host name is set to the new NetBIOS name. If you use WINS to create a Dynamic DNS, the NetBIOS name and the host name must be the same.)

   ▶ **Domain.** This is the Internet domain to which the system belongs. This is combined with the Host Name to create the FQDN name that this system is known as.

   ▶ **DNS Service Search Order.** This is the IP address of one or more DNS Servers that you use. They are tried in the order given.

▶ **Domain Suffix Search Order.** When you search for another host—for example, if you enter **FTP sparky**—the system first looks for "sparky" as the name in the DNS Server. If "sparky" is not in your current domain, then that system will not be found and you would have to enter **FTP sparky.scrimtech.com**. If you work with servers at scrimtech.com frequently, you can add the domain scrimtech.com into this area, and if the address is not resolved from "sparky," a second query for "sparky.scrimtech.com" is automatically sent.

Figure 19.2

The DNS settings for the TCP/IP protocol.

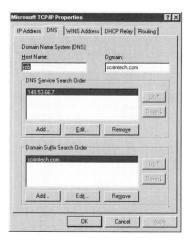

3. Click OK to close the TCP/IP settings. (If you are installing TCP/IP, you will need to enter the path to the Windows NT source files.)

4. Choose Close from the Network settings dialog box and restart your system. (This is not absolutely required, but generally it is recommended to ensure the values are correctly set.)

You can also use the DNS Server in place of the WINS server for resolving NetBIOS names. To do this, you need to change the settings on the WINS tab in the TCP/IP configuration. Specifically, you need to select the option to use DNS to resolve host names (see fig. 19.3).

Figure 19.3

Setting Windows NT to use DNS to resolve NetBIOS host names.

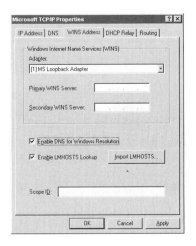

Using Existing BIND Files

If you already have a series of BIND files (as described in Chapter 18) set up on an existing DNS Server, you can use these files to configure the Microsoft DNS Server. The following are the steps you need to follow to configure Microsoft DNS Server to use these files:

1. Install the Microsoft DNS service (see the preceding section for instructions).

2. Stop the DNS service (from the Control Panel, choose the Services icon, click Microsoft DNS, and click the Stop button).

3. Copy the BIND files to the %winroot%\System32\DNS directory.

4. Start the DNS service (from the Control Panel, choose the Services icon, click Microsoft DNS, and click the Start button).

5. Use the DNS Manager to verify that your entries are there. (See "The DNS Administration Tool.")

Reinstalling Microsoft DNS Server

A quick note should be made here in case you need to reinstall the DNS Server. When you start adding zones to a Microsoft DNS Server, it by default switches to starting from the registry rather than the DNS files discussed earlier. It makes a note of this in the boot file. When you remove the server (before you reinstall) it does not remove this file; therefore, when you install the DNS Server again it assumes the boot file is valid and tries to read it. This causes several errors in the Event Log and causes the DNS not to start.

Therefore, if you need to remove the DNS Server, you should remove the boot file from the DNS directory. The original file is in the directory %winroot%\system32\dns\backup and you can copy the files back from there; however, the server continues to boot from the registry.

If you need to enable the system to boot from files, you must use the registry editor to open HKEY_LOCAL_MACHINE\SYSTEM\CurrentControlSet\Services\DNS\Parameters and delete the value EnableRegistryBoot.

The DNS Administration Tool

Adding the DNS Server adds the DNS administration tool. This tool makes configuring and maintaining the DNS Server very simple. It also provides single-seat administration as you can add several DNS Servers.

First, you need to add the DNS Server that you want to manage, as follows:

1. Start the DNS Manager by choosing Start, Programs, Administrative Tools, DNS Manager.

2. In the left pane of the DNS Manager, right-click Server List (see fig. 19.4).

3. Choose New Server from the menu.

4. In the DNS Server box (see fig. 19.5), enter the name or IP address of the server you wish to add.

Figure 19.4

The context menu from Server List.

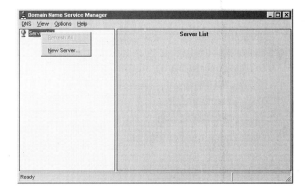

Figure 19.5

Adding a server to the DNS Manager.

Now that you have added the server, you can configure it and add entries. The DNS Server needs to be configured for the role that it plays in the overall system, and you should know what the server you are configuring will be used for.

Roles for a Microsoft DNS Server

The previous chapter discussed the roles that a server can take on Primary and Secondary. Mention also was made of using a DNS Server as a Caching-Only server; that is, a server that can only resolve addresses but which does not host any domains or sub-domains (zones).

The last chapter also discussed a DNS Server that acts as an IP Forwarder. That is, it receives the queries (recursive) from the other hosts on the network, and then attempts to resolve them using a recursive query to another DNS Server. This is useful if you wish to centralize the resolution of addresses at one server (which might be outside your firewall).

In the next few sections this chapter will focus on configuring Microsoft DNS Server for these different roles. The simplest role that a C„+ Server has is that of Caching-Only.

Configuring for Caching-Only

There is just about nothing you need to do to run a server as a Caching-Only server. As noted in the previous chapter, the Caching-Only server does not host any zones. If this is all you need, stop here.

Configuring as an IP Forwarder

An IP Forwarder is also a Caching-Only server; however, you need to configure it with the address of another DNS Server (another Microsoft DNS Server or any other DNS—for example, the one from your ISP). This configuration is fairly simple and the only information you require is the IP address of the server to use. Follow these steps:

1. Right-click the server in the Server List and select Properties.

2. On the Forwarders tab (see fig. 19.6), check the Use Forwarder(s) box.

Figure 19.6

Configuring as an IP Forwarder.

3. If the server is to only use the services of the other system, select Operate As Slave Server. (If you don't select this, the server attempts to resolve through the forwarder; however, it then uses an iterative query if that fails.)

4. Enter the address or addresses of the DNS Servers to which this one should forward queries.

5. If desired, set a time-out for the request.

6. Click OK to close the dialog box.

Creating a Primary DNS Server

For an exercise covering this information, see end of chapter.

The purpose of DNS is to resolve names to IP addresses. Therefore, you need to enter the addresses into the DNS server so other users can find your hosts. You do this by creating a zone in the DNS Server and entering the information that you want to make available to the world. The following list covers the steps required to create a zone:

1. Right-click the server that hosts the zone in the Server List.

2. Choose New Zone.

3. From the dialog box that appears, choose Primary (see fig. 19.7). Then choose Next.

Figure 19.7

Choosing the server's role in the domain.

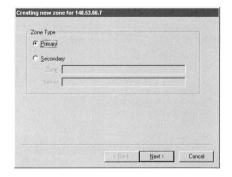

4. Enter the name of the domain (or sub-domain) for which you are creating a zone on the next screen (see fig. 19.8). Then press tab (this automatically enters a zone file name; if you are adding an existing zone file, enter the name of the file that has the information—it must be in the %winroot%\System32\DNS directory). When the information is in, click Next.

5. On the next screen, choose Finish.

Figure 19.8

Entering the zone name and file information.

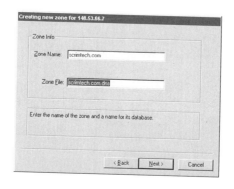

That is all there is to creating a zone. Now you can configure the zone and add the host (and other) records. When you have finished, the DNS Manager should look similar to figure 19.9.

Figure 19.9

The DNS Manager with a zone configured.

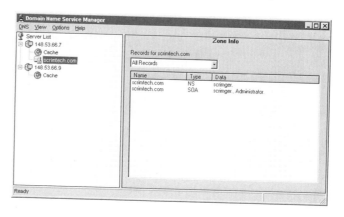

Setting Up and Reviewing the SOA Record

Configuring a zone is straightforward. Essentially, the information that you are entering here includes details for the Start of Authority (SOA) record and information about using WINS.

Setting up the information is easy. The following steps outline the process:

1. Right-click the zone you want to configure. Choose Properties from the menu. The Properties dialog box should appear and present the basic zone information (see fig. 19.10).

Figure 19.10

*The zone proper-
ties with the
General tab.*

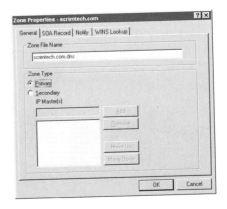

2. Click on the SOA Record tab to bring up the information about the SOA (see fig. 19.11).

Figure 19.11

*The Start of Au-
thority record.*

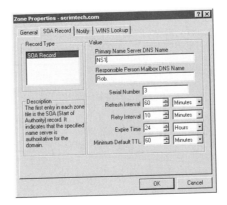

3. Edit the information in the SOA record. The fields that you can change here are as follows:

 ▶ **Primary Name Server DNS Name.** The name of the Primary name server that contains the files for the domain. Note that only the host name is entered, and then a "." that means this domain (for example, NS1 is NS1.ScrimTech.com.)

 ▶ **Responsible Person Mailbox DNS Name.** The e-mail address of the person who is in charge of the DNS. (Note, as in the Primary Name Server, you need to enter only the e-mail—followed by a period—if the e-mail address is within this domain.)

▶ **Serial Number.** A version ID that is assigned to the zone. The number is updated whenever you make changes to the database, so the secondary servers know that changes were made and can retrieve the new information.

▶ **Refresh Interval.** Tells the Secondary servers how often they should check their version number with the primaries to see if they need to transfer the zone information again.

▶ **Retry Interval.** Tells how long the Secondary server should wait before retrying the Primary server if it could not connect at the time given in Refresh Interval.

▶ **Expire Time.** Sets how long a Secondary server continues to give out information on this zone after not being able to connect with the Primary server.

▶ **Minimum Default TTL.** When a DNS Server performs an iterative query to resolve a name, the name is cached. This value sets how long other DNS Servers are allowed to keep the information about records that your DNS Server resolves for them.

4. Click the Notify tab (see fig. 19.12). (This is not really part of the SOA; however, it is added here because it deals with the Secondary servers.)

Figure 19.12

The Notify tab from the Zone Properties dialog box.

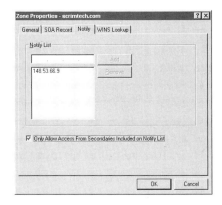

5. Enter the IP addresses of all the Secondary servers that should be notified when a change is made.

6. If desired, you can choose Only Allow Access From Secondaries Included on Notify List, which restricts which servers can retrieve your zone information.

7. Click OK to accept the changes you have made (the WINS tab is covered in the next section).

Integration with WINS

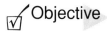 **Objective**

The last tab in the Zone Properties dialog box is the WINS Lookup tab (see fig. 19.13). You can use WINS to resolve DNS queries by telling the server to use the WINS server. Remember, for this to work, the hosts must use the same name for both their NetBIOS name and the host name, and they must register with the WINS server.

Figure 19.13

The WINS Lookup tab is used to configure DNS to use WINS for resolution.

Only a couple of options are available.

▶ **Use WINS Resolution.** Check this box to enable the DNS Server to query the WINS server for queries it receives that it cannot resolve from its own database.

▶ **Settings only affect local server.** Normally a temporary entry is added to the domain when this resolution method is used. Selecting this option only allows the current server to see these entries.

▶ **WINS Servers.** Here you need to enter the address of at least one WINS server. This server is queried in the order entered.

From the WINS Lookup tab, you can also open the Advanced Zone Properties dialog box (see fig. 19.14). You may need to use a couple of other settings in this dialog box.

Figure 19.14

The Advanced Zone Properties dialog box.

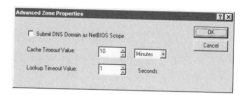

The options available are described in the following list:

▶ **Submit DNS Domain as NetBIOS Scope.** In some organizations, the NetBIOS scope ID is used to limit the number of hosts you can see using NetBIOS. The WINS server only responds with the address if matching scope IDs are used. Therefore, this option enables you to use the domain name as the NetBIOS scope.

▶ **Cache Timeout Value.** The length of time the DNS Server keeps the information that it gets from the WINS server.

▶ **Lookup Timeout Value.** The length of time the DNS Server waits for a resolution from the WINS server.

Adding HOSTS

Now that the domain has been created, and the WINS resolution is set up, you need to add the records that the WINS resolution cannot handle. Essentially, this is any non-WINS client that you have on your network, as well as any host that has an alias (discussed in the next section).

Adding a host record (or any record) is simple. All you need to do is right-click the domain (or sub-domain) to which you want to add the record. A menu (see fig. 19.15) appears from which you can choose New Host.

Figure 19.15

The context menu for a zone.

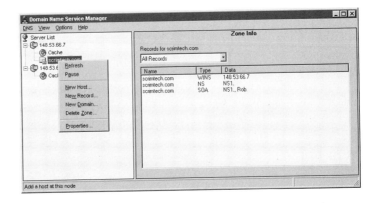

When you choose New Host, you see the dialog box shown in figure 19.16. Enter the host name and the IP address in this dialog box. You need only the host name because the domain or subdomain you clicked on is assumed.

Figure 19.16

The New Host dialog box.

An option to Create Associated PTR Record also exists. This enters the required information for the reverse lookup zone for this host. You need to create the reverse lookup zone before you can do this (see "Reverse Lookup").

Adding Other Records

For an exercise covering this information, see end of chapter.

The main purpose of a DNS Server is to resolve a host name to an IP address. There are, however, other types of information that other organizations may want, such as the address of your mail server. You can add several types of records to the DNS Server. The following list describes these other records:

▶ **A.** This is a host entry, exactly the same as was entered in the previous section.

▶ **AAAA.** This is also a host entry; the difference is that you can enter an IPng address (the new version of TCP/IP that will use 128-bit addresses rather than 32-bit).

▶ **AFSDB.** The AFSDB record gives the address of an AFS (Andrew File System) database server, or a DCE (Distributed Computing Environment) authenticated name server.

▶ **CNAME.** The canonical name is an alias that points one name such as WWW to another such as Web (see fig. 19.17). This is one of the most common records that you need to enter.

Figure 19.17

Adding an alias by creating a CNAME record.

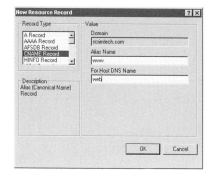

▶ **HINFO.** Enters machine information about a host, which allows other hosts on the network to find out CPU (Central Processing Unit) type and operating system information.

▶ **ISDN.** Integrated Services Digital Network allows you to map an entry to an ISDN phone number rather than an IP address. This is used in conjunction with an RT (Route Through) record to automate routing over dial-up ISDN.

▶ **MB.** This is an experimental record type used to associate an e-mail ID with a particular host *ID*.

▶ **MG.** Like an MB record, the MG is experimental; this associates an MB record with a Mail Group that could be used for mailing lists.

▶ **MINFO.** Another experimental record, MINFO enables you to enter the mail information about the person responsible for a given Mail record.

▶ **MR.** This is another experimental record. This provides for the Mail records the same service that CNAME entries provide for host names—aliases.

▶ **MX.** You need to enter at least one MX record (see fig. 19.18). The MX record takes incoming connections for mail and directs them to a mail server. You may enter more than one MX record. If you do, the system uses the Preference Number to determine the order in which to try them (lowest first).

Figure 19.18

Adding an MX record.

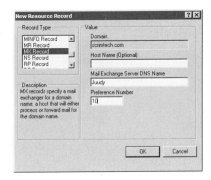

▶ **NS.** This is a name server record. It is used to find the other name servers in the domain.

▶ **PTR.** The Pointer record is part of the reverse lookup zone and is used to point the IP address at the host name.

▶ **RP.** This is where you enter the name (or names) of those people who are responsible for the domain that the server provides resolution for. There can be multiple entries of this type.

▶ **RT.** This points at another record in the DNS database. The Route Through provides information on how to get to a host using dial-up ISDN or X.25.

▶ **SOA.** As already discussed, the Start of Authority record provides the basic configuration for a zone.

▶ **TXT.** The Text record is a way of associating text information with a host. This can provide information about the computer (in addition to the information in an HINFO entry) or other information such as the location.

▶ **WKS.** Provides the capability to indicate which Well Known Services are running on a particular host. These match the service and protocols that are listed in the services file (%winroot%\System32\drivers\etc) below port 256.

▶ **X25.** Similar to the ISDN entry, this provides the capability to map a name to an X.121 name.

Adding these records is similar to adding a host record. Right-click the domain or sub-domain and choose New Record. Figure 19.19 shows a zone with several records defined.

Figure 19.19

A configured zone in the DNS Manager.

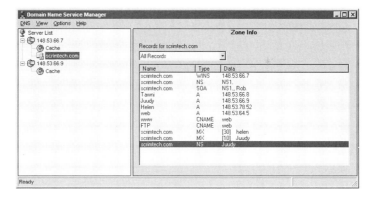

Creating a Sub-Domain

Many organizations are broken down into smaller groups that focus on one area of the business. Or perhaps the organization is dispersed geographically. In either case, the company may decide that they want break down their main domain into sub-domains. This is simple in Microsoft's DNS Server. Choose the parent domain (scrimtech.com, for example) and then right-click. Choose New Domain and enter the sub-domain name in the dialog box that appears (see fig. 19.20).

If the sub-domain is handled on another server, enter NS records for each of the other servers. If it is handled locally, simply add the records that are required.

Figure 19.20

Adding a Sub-Domain.

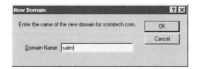

Setting Up the Secondary DNS Server

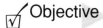

Objective

After you configure your server, you need to add a Secondary server. Adding this server provides redundancy and also splits the workload among the servers (you can have several Secondary servers if you wish). The following list outlines the steps involved:

1. In the DNS Manager, right-click the server to be configured as a Secondary server.

2. Choose New Zone from the context menu. From the New Zone dialog box, choose Secondary (see fig. 19.21).

Figure 19.21

Creating a Secondary Zone.

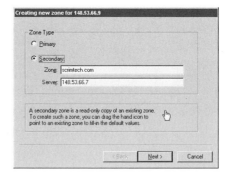

Note

On this screen, you are asked for the zone name and the server from which to get zone files. A handy option is the ability (as seen here) to drag the hand over another server listed in the DNS Manager to automatically pick up the information.

If the Primary DNS Server is not a Microsoft DNS Server, you will need to enter the information manually.

3. Click the Next button, and you can enter the information for the file. This should already be entered (see fig. 19.22), and you should click Next to accept the defaults.

Figure 19.22

Enter the zone file information.

4. The next screen asks you to identify the IP master for the zone. This should already be filled in for you (see fig. 19.23).

Figure 19.23

Setting the IP Master.

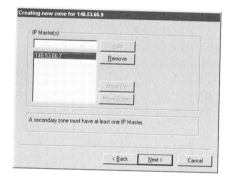

5. The last screen tells you that you are finished. Click Finish to close this screen.

Reverse Lookup

You should now understand the process of looking up an FQDN using a DNS Server. Looking up an IP address to find the host name is exactly the same (only backward). An FQDN starts with the specific host and then the domain; an IP address starts with Recall the dialog box used to add a host included an. To do this, choose DNS from the menu, then Update Server Data Files. This is done automatically when the server is shut down or when you exit the DNS Manager.

Now that the IP address is reversed, it is going the same way as an FQDN. Now you can resolve the address using DNS. Just like resolving www.scrimtech.com, you need to create a zone. This zone must have a particular name. To find the name, take the assigned portion of the address—for example, in 148.53.66.7 the portion that was assigned is 148.53, and for 204.12.25.3 it is 204.12.25. Now, create a zone in which these numbers are reversed and to which you add in-addr.arpa—that is, 53.148.in-addr.arpa or 25.12.204.in-addr.arpa, respectively.

Recall the dialog box used to add a host included an option to create a PTR record as you added hosts (refer to fig. 19.15). For this reason, you need to create the reverse lookup zone first, *before the other zones*, so these records can be automatically added. Note that you need to create a reverse lookup zone for each address you are assigned.

Updating DNS Startup Files

After you have added several records to the DNS Server, you need to update the information in the files on the system. Even if the server boots from the registry, the database (zone) files are stored. To do this, choose DNS from the menu, then Update Server Data Files. This is done automatically when the server is shut down or when you exit the DNS Manager.

DNS Manager Preferences

As a final note, you can set three options under Options, Preferences (see fig. 19.24) that affect the way the DNS Manager itself will behave.

These options include:

▶ **Auto Refresh Statistics.** Allows you to configure the statistics screen to automatically update information.

Figure 19.24

The Preferences dialog box.

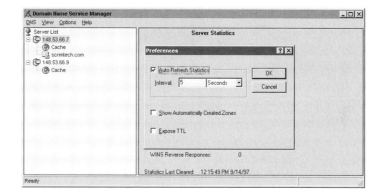

▶ **Show Automatically Created Zones.** Shows the zones that are automatically created. These are used for internal purposes only.

▶ **Expose TTL.** Allows you to expose the TTL for entries in your cache. (You can view these by double-clicking cache and then double-clicking the sub-folders.)

NSLOOKUP

 Objective

Along with the addition of a DNS Server, Windows NT 4.0 also has a tool that uses the DNS and enables you to verify that it is working. The NSLOOKUP command line is shown as follows:

```
nslookup [-option ...] [computer-to-find ¦ - [server]]
```

You can use NSLOOKUP to query the DNS Server from the command line (see table 19.1 for a list of switches) or you can start an interactive session with the server to enable you to query the database. For our purposes, only look at the command line.

Table 19.1

Command-Line Switches for the NSLOOKUP Command

Switch	Description
-option	Allows you to enter one or more commands from the command line. A list of the commands follows. For each option you wish to add, enter a hyphen (-) followed immediately by the command name. Note that the command line length needs to be less than 256 characters.
Computer-to-find	This is the host or IP address about which you wish to find information. It is processed using the default server, or if given, using the server that is specified.

The following list provides the options that are available with the NSLOOKUP command.

▶ **-t querytype.** Lists all records of a given type. The record types are listed under querytype.

▶ **-a.** Lists all the CNAME entries from the DNS Server.

▶ **-d.** Dumps all records that are in the DNS Server.

▶ **-h.** Returns information on the DNS Server's CPU and operating system.

▶ **-s.** Returns the well-known services for hosts in the DNS domain.

Exercises

Now that you have read about the DNS Server, it is time to practice working with the DNS Server and associated files. This section provides you with the steps to create and then test a domain called SunnyDays.com, which has been assigned the address 160.106.

Exercise 19.1:   Installing the Microsoft DNS Server

First, you need to install the DNS Server. This exercise assumes you have a network card in your system. If you do not, install the MS Loopback Adapter. This enables you to do the following exercises. If the system you are working on is running DNS, ensure that you back up the files before you proceed, just in case.

1. Open the Network Settings dialog box. Choose the Protocols tab and double-click the TCP/IP protocol.

2. On the DNS tab, enter your IP address as the DNS Server and click Add. Also add the domain **SunnyDays.com** into the domain field.

3. Click the Services tab and choose Add. From the list that appears, choose the Microsoft DNS Server and click OK.

4. Enter the directory for the Windows NT source files.

5. Close the Network Settings dialog box and restart your computer.

Exercise 19.2:   Configuring a DNS Domain

Now that the server is up and running, you need to create the domains that you will use. The first domain to be created is the reverse lookup domain. After that is in place, you create the SunnyDays.com domain.

1. From the Start menu, choose Programs, Administrative Tools, DNS Manager.

continues

Exercise 19.2: Continued

---

2. From the menu, choose DNS, New Server. Enter your IP address and click OK.

3. To create the reverse lookup domain, click your system's address. Choose DNS, New Zone.

4. Choose Primary and click Next.

5. For the Zone, enter **106.160.in-addr.arpa** and press tab (the file name is filled in for you).

6. Click Next to continue, then choose Finish.

7. Ensure "106.160.in-addr.arpa" is highlighted, and choose DNS, Properties from the menu.

8. On the WINS Reverse Lookup tab, check the box to Use WINS Reverse Lookup. Enter **SUNNYDAYS.COM** as the host domain, and choose OK. There should now be a new host record.

7. Select your DNS Server's address and select DNS, New Zone from the menu.

8. Select Primary and choose Next. Enter **SUNNYDAYS.COM** as the zone name. Press tab to have the system fill in the file name, then choose Next. Finally, click the Finish button.

9. Right-click the SunnyDays.com domain name. From the context menu that appears, select Properties.

10. Select the WINS Lookup tab.

11. Check the Use WINS Resolution box. Enter your IP address in the WINS server space and choose Add.

12. Choose OK to close the dialog box. A WINS record should be in the SunnyDays.com domain.

Exercise 19.3:   Adding Records

Now that you have created the reverse lookup domain and the SunnyDays.com domain, add some records to the database.

1. Right-click the SunnyDays.com and choose Add Host.

2. In the New Host dialog box, add Rob as the Host Name and 160.106.66.7 as the Host IP Address.

3. Check the Create Associated PTR Record to create the reverse lookup record at the same time.

4. Choose Add Host. Now, enter Judy as the Host Name and 160.106.66.9 as the Host IP Address.

5. Click Add Host. Then click the Done button to close the dialog box. You should see the two new records in the DNS Manager.

6. Click on the 106.160.in-addr.arpa domain and press F5 to refresh. Notice there is now a 66 sub-domain.

7. Double-click the 66 sub-domain. What new hosts are there? There should be PTR records for the two hosts you just added.

8. Select the SunnyDays.com domain again. Add the following hosts, ensuring that you add the associated PTR records.

Mail1	160.106.92.14
Mail2	160.106.101.80
Mail3	160.106.127.14
Web1	160.106.65.7
Web2	160.106.72.14
FTP_Pub1	160.106.99.99
FTP_Pub2	160.106.104.255
DEV	160.106.82.7

continues

9. Close the New Host dialog box. Verify that the records were added to the SunnyDays.com and the reverse lookup domains.

10. Highlight SunnyDays.com, and choose DNS, New Domain from the menu.

11. Enter **DEV** as the Name for the new domain and choose OK.

12. Right click on the DEV sub-domain. Choose New Record. Select CNAME as the record type.

13. Enter **WWW** as the alias, and **web2.SunnyDays.com** as the Host. (This entry sets up WWW.DEV.SUNNYDAYS.COM to point to WEB2.SUNNYDAYS.COM.)

14. Click OK to add the record. (It should appear in the Zone Info window.)

15. Create the following CNAME entries in the SunnyDays.com domain. Right-click SunnyDays.com, each time choosing New Record.

Alias	Host
WWW	web1.SunnyDays.com
FTP	FTP_PUB1.SunnyDays.com
DEV_FTP	FTP_PUB2.SunnyDays.com

16. Create a new record in the SunnyDays.com domain. This time, choose MX as the Record Type.

17. Leave the Host blank for this record, and enter **mail1.SunnyDays.com** as the Mail Exchange Server DNS Name. Enter **10** as the Preference.

18. Choose OK to add the record. Add a second MX record for the SunnyDays.com using **mail2.SunnyDays.com** as the Mail Server and **20** as the Preference.

19. Now add the MX record for dev.SunnyDays.com. To do this, right click on SunnyDays.com and choose New Record; again, this is an MX record.

20. The difference is that you include the Host name. Enter **DEV** as the Host, add **mail3.SunnyDays.com** as the Mail Exchange Server DNS Name, and **10** as the preference.

21. Ensure that all the records appear to be in place, and then close the DNS Manager.

Exercise 19.4:   Testing the DNS Server

This exercise gives you a chance to test the information you entered and to check that everything is working correctly.

1. Start a command prompt.

2. Type the command **NSLOOKUP 160.106.101.80** and press enter. What response did you get? (The response should show that 160.106.101.80 is mail2.SunnyDays.com. Here you have done a reverse lookup on the IP address.)

3. Using the **NSLOOKUP** command, find out what responses the following entries give you:

    160.106.66.7

    160.106.99.99

    www.SunnyDays.com

    www.dev.SunnyDays.com

    ftp.SunnyDays.com

continues

The results should be:

160.106.66.7	rob.SunnyDays.com
160.106.99.99	ftp_pub1.SunnyDays.com
www.SunnyDays.com	160.106.65.7 (web1.SunnyDays.com)
www.dev.SunnyDays.com	148.55.72.14 (web2.SunnyDays.com)
ftp.SunnyDays.com	160.106.99.99 (ftp_pub1.SunnyDays.com)

4. Start an interactive session with the name server by typing **NSLOOKUP** and pressing enter.

5. Try the following commands:

    ls SunnyDays.com

    ls -t mx SunnyDays.com

    ls -d

    q=soa

    SunnyDays.com

    q=mx

    SunnyDays.com

    Where is the third mail server?

    dev.SunnyDays.com

6. Press Ctrl+C to exit the interactive query.

7. Close the command prompt.

Review Questions

The following questions will test your knowledge of the information in this chapter:

1. Your organization uses primarily Microsoft operating systems; you want to be able to provide reverse DNS lookup for the hosts in your organization for servers on the Internet. Your organization uses DHCP to assign IP addresses. What do you need to do to provide reverse lookup capabilities?

    A. Reserve a DHCP address for each client and enter this information into the DNS server.

    B. Set up the clients to use DNS for WINS resolution.

    C. Add @ IN WINS record in the DNS database.

    D. This is not possible.

2. Your organization wants to be able to control the entries that are in your DNS Server. You currently have a domain registered with the InterNIC and your ISP is providing your DNS resolution. You have a 128Kbps link to your ISP and don't want to use all of the band width resolving DNS queries. Which of the following would best suit your needs?

    A. Increase your line speed to a T1 and set up two DNS Servers.

    B. Set up a DNS Server in your organization and arrange for your ISP to transfer your zone to their servers.

    C. Have your ISP continue to handle DNS for your organization.

    D. Use WINS to handle all name resolution.

3. Which of the following are roles that you can configure your DNS Server for?

   A. Primary

   B. Tertiary

   C. Backup

   D. IP Forwarder

4. You had Microsoft DNS Server installed and had tested the configuration. Later you remove and reinstall the Service in preparation for configuring the DNS Server with the real information. What must you do to make sure the DNS Server starts cleanly?

   A. Remove the files from the %winroot%\system32\dns directory.

   B. Reinstall Windows NT.

   C. Also remove and reinstall the WINS server.

   D. Nothing, the configuration will work fine.

5. Your Organization currently uses a Unix server for DNS. The server is fully configured using BIND files. In which two ways can you configure your Microsoft DNS Server so you will not need to re-enter any information?

   A. Set up Microsoft DNS as the Primary and transfer the zone to the Unix system.

   B. Set up Microsoft DNS as the Secondary and transfer the zone from the Unix system.

   C. Configure the Microsoft DNS server as an IP Forwarder.

   D. Configure the Microsoft DNS server as a Caching Only server.

6. Which of the following statements about DNS are true?

    A. DNS resolves NetBIOS names to TCP/IP addresses.

    B. DNS resolves host names to TCP.IP addresses.

    C. DNS resolves IP addresses to hardware addresses.

    D. DNS resolves IP addresses to host names.

7. You have a computer called WEBSERVER with a TPC/IP address of 148.53.66.45 running Microsoft Internet Information Server. This system provides the HTTP and FTP services for your organization on the Internet. Which of the following sets of entries are correct for your database file?

    A. www IN A 148.53.66.45

       ftp IN A 148.53.66.45

    B. www IN A 148.53.66.45

       ftp IN A 148.53.66.45

       webserver CNAME www

    C. webserver IN A 148.53.66.45

       www CNAME webserver

       ftp CNAME webserver

    D. 45.66.53.148 IN PTR webserver

8. Which of the following is *not* part of a Fully Qualified Domain Name?

    A. Type of Organization

    B. Host name

    C. Company name

    D. CPU type

9. Your organization uses a firewall and inside the firewall, you have five subnets. You intended to provide a DNS Server on each subnet, but want them to query the main DNS server that sits outside the firewall. What configuration should you choose for the DNS Servers that you will put on each subnet?

   A. Configure the DNS Server outside the firewall to use a WINS server on each local subnet, then configure the DNS Servers on the local subnets to use WINS resolution.

   B. Set up the DNS Servers on the local subnets as IP Forwarders to the DNS Server outside the firewall.

   C. Create a Primary zone on each of the DNS Servers inside the firewall and configure the DNS Server outside the firewall to transfer each zone.

   D. This is not possible.

10. When you are configuring your DNS server, where do you configure the length of time that an entry will be cached on your server?

    A. Set the TTL in the DNS Manager properties on your server.

    B. Set the TTL in the Cache file on the remote server.

    C. Set the TTL in the registry under HKEY_LOCAL_MACHINE\SYSTEM\ CurrentControlSet\Services\TCPIP\Parameters.

    D. Set the TTL in the remote server in the SOA record.

11. Which of the following will enable a client computer to use a DNS Server for NetBIOS name resolution?

    A. Configure the WINS Server to use DNS lookup.

    B. Do nothing; this will happen automatically.

    C. On the WINS configuration tab enable DNS for NetBIOS name resolution.

    D. Add a DNS entry in the LMHOSTS file.

12. Which of the following NSLOOKUP commands will provide a list of all the mail servers for the domain nt.com?

    A. NSLOOKUP -t MX nt.com

    B. NSLOOKUP -a MX nt.com

    C. NSLOOKUP -h nt.com

    D. NSLOOKUP -m nt.com

13. In which of the following scenarios will a recursive query *not* be used?

    A. Your system querying the DNS Server

    B. Your DNS Server querying the Root-Level servers

    C. Your DNS Server querying the WINS Server

    D. Your DNS Server querying when configured as an IP forwarder

14. Your user is at a computer called "prod172." The IP address of the computer is 152.63.85.5, and the computer is used to publish to the World Wide Web for the domain "gowest.com." Which entries should you find in the database file?

    A. prod172 IN MX 152.63.85.5

    B. www cname 152.63.85.5

    C. prod172 IN A 152.63.85.5

       www CNAME 152.63.85.5

    D. prod172 IN A 152.63.85.5

       www CNAME prod172

15. What is the purpose of a HINFO record?

    A. Provides host information including the user name

    B. Provides host information including CPU type

    C. Provides host information including BIOS version

    D. Provides host information including hard disk size

16. Which of the following files is *not* required for compliance with the DNS RFCs?

    A. The Cache file

    B. The Database file

    C. The Boot file

    D. The Reverse Lookup file

17. What is the purpose of the Domain Suffix Search Order?

    A. When you look for host name entries, it can be used to complete the FQDN.

    B. When you look for NetBIOS name entries, it can be used as the NetBIOS Scope ID.

    C. Allows your computer to be in more than one domain at a time.

    D. Tells your systems which NT domains to search when looking for a log on server.

18. Which of the following best describes the order in which you should configure the DNS server?

    A. Install the server, create the zone, enter all the records, then create the reverse lookup zone and add the WINS records.

    B. Install the server, create the reverse lookup zone, then add the zone information followed by the WINS lookup records and the other hosts.

   C. Create the DNS Server database files using a text editor, install the server, then verify the information.

   D. Install the DNS Server and then transfer the zone from the WINS Server.

19. What information is contained in an MX record?

   A. A Preference entry.

   B. The mail server name.

   C. The WWW server name.

   D. There is no such record.

20. What is the purpose of the Cache file?

   A. Stores the names of hosts that your server has resolved.

   B. Allows you to enter commonly used hosts that will be loaded to the cache.

   C. Stores the addresses of Root Level servers.

   D. Is used to temporarily build the DNS Server information as the server starts.

Review Answers

   1. C

   2. B

   3. A, D

   4. A

   5. B, C

   6. B, D (Note: A is also correct given the fact that NetBIOS name resolution will use host name resolution as a backup.)

   7. C

   8. D

9. B

10. D

11. C (Note: B is also correct given the fact that NetBIOS name resolution will use host name resolution as a backup.)

12. A

13. B

14. D

15. B

16. C

17. A

18. B

19. A, B

20. C

Answers to the Test Yourself Questions at the Beginning of the Chapter

1. An FQDN is a Fully Qualified Domain Name. This name identifies a TCP/IP host and the domain to which it belongs.

2. A CNAME record or conical name is an alias in a DNS Server that points to a host. Normally this is used to point WWW and/or FTP to the correct server.

3. When a client application is attempting to locate another host, the resolver that is part of the client sends a recursive query to the local DNS Server. If the DNS knows the address, it returns it; otherwise, it queries several servers to find a definitive address for the target host. This series of queries is considered an iterative query.

4. An IP Forwarder is in essence a Caching-Only server; however, rather than doing an iterative query to resolve names it doesn't know, it will perform a recursive query to a central DNS Server. This enables you to have one or two main DNS Servers connected to the Internet and many IP Forwarders that distribute the load or improve performance over slow WAN links.

5. The two main roles for a DNS Server are Primary and Secondary. The Primary maintains the DNS files and the Secondaries retrieve these files from the Primary.

6. The four main files are database file, reverse lookup file, cache file, and boot file.

7. In a Microsoft network, you can configure the DNS Server to use WINS to resolve names. Assuming that NetBIOS names and the host names are the same, this lets the DNS Server dynamically resolve addresses.

8. Reverse lookup provides the capability to look up a host name for a given IP address.

9. DNS is used by applications that work directly with the Winsock interface. This may include Internet Explorer, FTP, or Telnet.

10. On the WINS tab in the TCP/IP configuration, you can select Enable DNS for NetBIOS name resolution. This tells Windows NT to use the DNS Servers to resolve NetBIOS names rather than WINS.

Chapter 20

Connectivity in Heterogeneous Environments

This chapter helps you prepare for the exam by covering the following objectives:

Objectives

- ▶ Configure a Windows NT Server computer to support TCP/IP printing

- ▶ Given a scenario, identify which utility to use to connect to a TCP/IP based Unix host

- ▶ Use Microsoft TCP/IP utilities to diagnose IP configuration problems

- ▶ Given a scenario, identify which tool to use to monitor TCP/IP traffic

- ▶ Identify which Microsoft TCP/IP utility to use to diagnose IP configuration problems

Test Yourself! Before reading this chapter, test yourself to determine how much study time you will need to devote to this section.

1. What must be supported by a remote host system in order to use FTP connect to network resources?

2. What is the role of an SMB server service on a remote host?

3. Which remote execution utility can establish a terminal session with a remote host?

4. Which file transfer utility does not require user authentication?

5. Which utility would be used to send a binary file from a Windows NT computer to a remote host?

6. Which file transfer protocols is not implemented as a server service in Windows NT Server without using a third-party product?

7. Which common winsock utilities use the connection-oriented features of TCP/IP?

Answers are located at the end of the chapter.

Connectivity in Heterogeneous Environments

It is common to have different operating systems and platforms within a network. One way to achieve connectivity between platforms is to use the TCP/IP protocol. TCP/IP is available as a network protocol on most network operating systems, including Windows NT, Novell NetWare, almost all Unix operating systems, and many more. This chapter examines ways to connect different systems using the TCP/IP protocol.

Although you can interconnect different systems without using TCP/IP, TCP/IP provides a large number of utilities and services that are not available when using other protocols. Among others, the following are available:

▶ **Connectivity using Microsoft networking.** Remote host systems that support the requirements of Microsoft networking can easily be accessed by other client computers. This is not strictly provided by TCP/IP, but is supported under TCP/IP.

▶ **Remote execution.** Using standard utilities provided with Windows NT, you can execute commands on remote computers. These utilities such as RSH (Remote Shell) and REXEC (Remote Execute) require TCP/IP.

▶ **File transfer.** When direct connectivity using Microsoft networking is impossible, file transfer utilities are available to transmit and receive files to or from a remote host system. These utilities such as FTP (File Transfer Protocol) and RCP (Remote Copy Protocol) require TCP/IP to operate.

▶ **Printing.** Integration between Microsoft Windows NT and remote host system print sub-systems can be achieved using standard utilities and services available with Windows NT. These utilities LPR (Line Printer Request), and LPQ(Line Printer Query) and the LPD (Line Printer Deamon) service require TCP/IP to operate.

In addition to the preceding list, the TCP/IP protocol supports a large variety of other utilities for troubleshooting and debugging such as netstat and nbtstat.

Varying degrees of connectivity and transparency are possible depending on your requirements and the TCP/IP options your other systems can support.

The remainder of this chapter discusses the options available, depending on your environment.

Communicating Over TCP/IP

You can use standard Microsoft networking commands, such as the **NET USE** command or NT Explorer, to connect to remote hosts if the following requirements are met:

▶ Your computer and the remote host must be using the same transport driver (such as TCP/IP, IPX/SPX, or NBF).

▶ The remote host must provide an SMB server, because the Workstation service in Windows NT communicates with an SMB (server message block—for an overview of SMB communications refer back to Chapter 13) server process.

▶ The remote host must provide the standard suite of NetBIOS services as discussed in Chapter 13 "NetBIOS Over TCP/IP."

Effectively, connectivity using Microsoft networking is available when the remote host can provide the equivalent to a Windows NT *Server service*. To connect to resources on a remote system, you don't need to change the configuration of the Windows NT system; however the remote computer needs to be configured to act as an SMB server on a protocol used by your Windows NT system.

This option provides the greatest degree of integration between Microsoft client computers and remote host systems. Many systems support connectivity through Microsoft networking. These include LAN Manager for OS/2, LAN Manager for Unix, DEC PATHWORKS and IBM LAN Server for OS/2. In cases where this is impossible, you have other options.

For file services, Windows NT includes several utilities, including an FTP client and server, a TFTP (Trivial File Transfer Protocol) client, and a RCP client. Third-party options also exist, such as

NFS (Network File System) clients for Windows NT. Windows NT does not provide a TFTP server, and cannot accept Telnet sessions without third party utilities.

Printing services can also be provided, using the LPD/LPR print model. The LPD service can be run on Windows NT, and an LPR client is available with Windows NT.

Third-party utilities are available to provide an NFS (Network File System) server via a Windows NT server. These utilities can provide NFS services to PCs, Unix systems, or any other NFS client system. All standard Windows NT file systems are supported.

If the remote host system does not have an SMB client available, a series of TCP/IP utilities are available to connect between a remote host and a Windows NT computer. These utilities are discussed later in this chapter.

Microsoft TCP/IP Utilities

 Objective

Windows NT includes TCP/IP utilities that provide many options for connecting to foreign systems using the TCP/IP protocol. In cases where it is impossible to connect to remote host systems using Microsoft networking, these utilities provide a variety of network services.

These utilities allow Microsoft clients to perform remote execution, data transfer, printing services, and much more. The following sections examine these utilities in more detail.

Remote Execution Utilities

Windows NT includes a series of remote execution utilities that enable a user to execute commands on a Unix host system. These utilities provide varying degrees of security. Note that varying subsets of these utilities are available with Windows NT Server and Workstation. The resource kit includes all of these utilities.

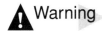**Warning**

Any of these utilities that require passwords transmit the password as plain text. Unlike the Windows NT logon sequence, the logon information is not encrypted before being transmitted. Any unscrupulous user with access to network monitoring software could intercept the user name and password for the remote host. If you use the same user name and password on the remote host and on your Windows NT system, your Windows NT account could be compromised.

Windows NT provides three remote execution utilities. Each is discussed in more detail in the following sections.

The REXEC Utility

REXEC enables a user to start a process on a remote host system, using a user name and password for authentication. If the host authenticates the user, REXEC starts the specified process and terminates. Command-line options are as follows:

```
D:\>rexec /?
Runs commands on remote hosts running the REXEC service. REXEC
authenticates the user name on the remote host before executing
the specified command.

REXEC host [-l username] [-n] command
```

host	Specifies the remote host on which to run command
-l username	Specifies the user name on the remote host
-n	Redirects the input of REXEC to NULL
command	Specifies the command to run

You can specify the remote host as an IP address or as a host name. After REXEC connects to the specified host, it prompts for a password. If the host authenticates the user, the specified command is executed, and the REXEC utility exits. REXEC can be used for command line programs—interactive programs such as text editors would not be usable with REXEC.

This utility provides a reasonable degree of security because the remote host authenticates the user. The down side is that the user name and password are not encrypted prior to transmission.

The RSH Utility

RSH provides much the same function as REXEC, but user authentication is handled differently. Unlike with REXEC, you do not need to specify a user name. The only validation performed by RSH is to verify that the user name is in a hidden file on the Unix system (the .rhosts file). If the remote host is configured to allow any user to use RSH, no user name needs to be provided.

> On Unix systems, the .rhosts and the hosts.equiv files are used for authentication. Because these files can be used to grant access to either all users on a computer or some users on a computer, be careful. Refer to *Internet Firewalls and Network Security*, also by New Riders Publishing, for the formatting and contents of these files and related security issues.

However, because it is extremely unlikely a system would be configured in this way, the RSH utility provides the logged-on user name if no user name is provided. This can be overridden if desired. RSH has the following command-line options:

Runs commands on remote hosts running the RSH service.

```
C:\>rsh /?
rsh: remote terminal session not supported

Runs commands on remote hosts running the RSH service.

RSH host [-l username] [-n] command
```

host	Specifies the remote host on which to run command.
-l username	Specifies the user name to use on the remote host. If omitted, the logged on user name is used.
-n	Redirects the input of RSH to NULL.
command	Specifies the command to run.

After you start RSH, it connects to the remote system's RSH daemon (Unix-speak for a service). The RSH daemon ensures that the user name is in the .rhosts file on the remote host, and if authentication succeeds, the specified command is executed.

Like REXEC, RSH provides a certain degree of security insofar as the remote host validates the access.

The Telnet Utility

Telnet is defined in RFC 854 as a remote terminal emulation protocol. It provides terminal emulation for DEC VT100, DEC VT52, and TTY terminals. Telnet uses the connection-oriented services of the TCP/IP protocol for communications.

The remote host system must be running a telnet daemon. After you start telnet, you can connect to a remote host using the Connect/Remote system option. You are prompted for the following information (see fig. 20.1):

▶ **Host name.** The IP address or host name of the remote host

▶ **Port.** One of the ports supported by the telnet application—telnet, daytime, echo, quotd, or chargen

▶ **Terminal type.** One of VT100, ANSI (TTY), or VT52

Figure 20.1

The telnet utility.

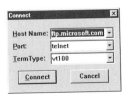

As with REXEC and RSH, telnet provides some security, insofar as access to the remote system requires a user name and password.

 Warning   Telnet does not encrypt any information whatsoever. The password and user name are sent as clear text, as is your entire terminal session. If you are using telnet to perform remote administration on a Unix system, your root password could be intercepted by an unscrupulous user.

Data Transfer Utilities

Several utilities are available to allow file transfer between Windows NT systems and remote hosts. As with remote execution utilities, the same caveat applies when dealing with user names and passwords. These utilities are examined in greater detail in the following sections.

RCP

The RCP command copies files from a Windows NT system to a remote host, and handles authentication in much the same way as RSH. To communicate with the RCP daemon on the remote system, the user name provided must be in the remote host's .rhosts file. The following command-line options are available:

```
C:\>rcp ?

Copies files to and from computer running the RCP service.

RCP [-a ¦ -b] [-h] [-r] [host][.user:]source [host][.user:]
path\destination
```

-a	Specifies ASCII transfer mode. This mode converts the EOL characters to a carriage return for Unix and a carriage return/line feed for personal computers. This is the default transfer mode.
-b	Specifies binary image transfer mode.
-h	Transfers hidden files.
-r	Copies the contents of all subdirectories; destination must be a directory.
host	Specifies the local or remote host. If host is specified as an IP address, you must specify the user.
.user:	Specifies a user name to use, rather than the current user name.
source	Specifies the files to copy.
path\destination	Specifies the path relative to the logon

directory on the remote host. Use the escape
characters (\ , ", or ') in remote paths to
use wildcard characters on the remote host.

As with RSH, RCP provides security by matching the user name
provided with a user name in the .rhosts file. Unlike RSH, RCP
does not prompt for a password.

FTP

FTP, or the file transfer protocol, provides a simple but robust
mechanism for copying files to or from remote hosts using the
connection-oriented services of TCP/IP. FTP is a component of
the TCP/IP protocol, and is defined in RFC 959. To use FTP to
send or receive files, the following requirements must be met:

▶ The client computer must have FTP client software, such as
the FTP client included with Windows NT.

▶ The user must have a user name and password on the remote system. In some cases, a user name of *anonymous* with
no password suffices.

▶ The remote system must be running an FTP daemon.

▶ Your system and the remote system must be running the
TCP/IP protocol.

You can use FTP in either a command line mode or in a command interpreter mode. The following options are available from
the command line:

Transfers files to and from a computer running an FTP server
service (sometimes called a daemon). FTP can be used
interactively.

FTP [-v] [-d] [-i] [-n] [-g] [-s:filename] [-a] [-w:windowsize]
[host]

    -v   Suppresses display of remote server responses.
    -n   Suppresses auto-login upon initial connection.

-i	Turns off interactive prompting during multiple file transfers.
-d	Enables debugging.
-g	Disables filename globbing (see GLOB command).
-s:filename	Specifies a text file containing FTP commands; the commands will automatically run after FTP starts.
-a	Use any local interface when binding data connection.
-w:buffersize	Overrides the default transfer buffer size of 4096.
host	Specifies the host name or IP address of the remote host to connect to.

If you use FTP in a command interpreter mode, some of the more frequently used options are as follows:

▶ **open.** Specifies the remote system to which you connect.

▶ **close.** Disconnects from a remote system.

▶ **ls.** Obtains a directory listing on a remote system, much like the dir command in DOS. Note that the ls –l command provides file size and time stamps.

▶ **cd.** Changes directories on the remote system. This command functions in much the same way as the DOS cd command.

▶ **lcd.** Changes directories on the local system. This command also functions in much the same way as the DOS cd command.

▶ **binary.** Instructs FTP to treat all files transferred as binary.

▶ **ascii.** Instructs FTP to treat all files transferred as text.

▶ **get.** Copies a file from the remote host to your local computer.

▶ **put.** Copies a file from your local computer to the remote host.

▶ **debug.** Turns on debugging commands that can be useful in diagnosing problems.

Because remote host systems typically are based on Unix, you encounter a number of nuances relating to Unix such as the following:

▶ The Unix operating system uses the forward slash in path references, not the backward slash. In Windows NT, the file name \WINNT40\README.TXT would be /WINNT40/README.TXT.

▶ Unix is case sensitive at all times—the command *get MyFile* and the command *get MYFILE* are not the same. User names and passwords are also case-sensitive.

▶ Unix treats wild card characters, such as the asterisk and the question mark, differently. The glob command within FTP changes how wild card characters in local file names are treated.

You can also install a Windows NT FTP server, which can provide FTP file transfer services to other systems.

TFTP

TFTP provides similar functions as FTP. Unlike FTP, TFTP uses the connectionless communication features of TCP/IP. The features available in FTP are complex; those in TFTP are simpler. Unlike FTP, TFTP can be used only in a command line mode—no command interpreter mode is available. For command-line mode, the following options are available:

```
C:\>tftp /?
```

```
Transfers files to and from a remote computer running the TFTP
service.
```

```
TFTP [-i] host [GET ¦ PUT] source [destination]
```

```
    -i              Specifies binary image transfer mode (also
                    called octet). In binary image mode the file is
                    moved literally, byte by byte. Use this mode
                    when transferring binary files.
    host            Specifies the local or remote host.
```

```
GET                Transfers the file destination on the remote
                   host to the file source on the local host.
PUT                Transfers the file source on the local host to
                   the file destination on the remote host.
source             Specifies the file to transfer.
destination        Specifies where to transfer the file.
```

There is no TFTP server included with Windows NT, however third party TFTP servers are available.

Why use TFTP instead of FTP? Some platforms don't support FTP, notably devices that require firmware updates. Routers typically require the use of TFTP to update firmware information, such as micro-kernels.

Note

Many network devices such as routers and concentrators use an operating system stored in firmware. As such, upgrades are usually handled using TFTP; the process is known as a firmware update.

HTTP and Web Browsers

The explosive growth of the Internet in recent years is largely due to its flexibility. One of the Internet's building blocks is the HyperText Transfer Protocol, HTTP. It defines a way of transferring hypertext data across TCP/IP networks. The hypertext data is formatted in HTML (HyperText Markup Language). An HTML document can have a link to any other HTML document. This enables Web page designers to include text, audio files, graphics, and video within the same page.

HTTP and HTML are comprehensive standards, and a full discussion is outside the scope of this chapter. However, a discussion of Web browsers is in order. Web browsing software is used to download and view HTML documents using the HTTP protocol, but can also be used to download documents using FTP, gopher, or other protocols.

Unlike the other file transfer utilities mentioned in this section, HTTP does not use a user name or password. Information on the

World Wide Web is typically destined for access by any user, and therefore usually does not require authentication.

Many Web browsers are available; however, they all function in much the same way.

Printing Utilities

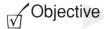 **Objective**

Printing within Windows NT is a remarkably complex process. The same is true of remote host systems, such as Unix platforms. The Windows NT and host system print models can interact to a large extent. The following sections describe how clients and servers on Windows NT and remote host systems can interact.

Windows NT Client Printing to a Remote Host System

You can use two methods to print to a remote host from a Windows NT client: using the LPR command from the Windows NT client computer, or creating an LPR printer on a Windows NT client computer.

Using the LPR Command-Line Utility

One of the utilities included with Microsoft TCP/IP is the LPR utility. This program allows a Windows NT computer to send a print job to a remote host printer. The remote host system must be running the LPD daemon, and you must know the name of the remote host and the printer. This utility has the following command-line options:

```
Sends a print job to a network printerUsage: lpr -S server -P
printer [-C class] [-J job] [-o option] [-x] [-d] filename

Options:
    -S server   Name or IP address of the host providing lpd
                service
    -P printer  Name of the print queue
    -C class    Job classification for use on the burst page
    -J job      Job name to print on the burst page
    -o option   Indicates the type of file (by default assumes a
                text file)
```

```
                        Use "-o l" for binary (for example, postscript)
                        files
        -x              Compatibility with SunOS 4.1.x and prior
                        versions
        -d              Sends data file first
```

Creating an LPR Printer on a Windows NT Computer

By creating an LPR printer on the Windows NT client computer, a higher degree of transparency is provided. If the printer is shared, the Windows NT client can act as a print gateway for other Windows NT computers.

To create an LPR printer under Windows NT, simply follow the procedure shown below:

1. Select Settings/Printers, then click Add Printer. Select My Computer, because you need to add a new printer port, as shown in figure 20.2.

Figure 20.2

Creating an LPR printer on a Windows NT system.

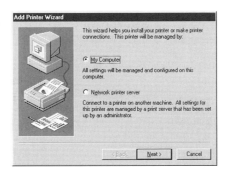

2. At this point, select Add Port, and select LPR port, as shown in figure 20.3.

Figure 20.3

Adding an LPR port.

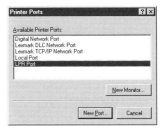

3. You are then prompted to provide the host name (or IP address) of the remote host system, along with the printer name, as shown in figure 20.4.

Figure 20.4

LPR printer information.

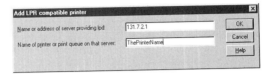

4. If you choose to share the printer, any client computer that can print to your Windows NT computer can also print to the LPR printer on the remote host system.

Remote Host Client Printing to a Windows NT Server

Remote hosts also can print to a Windows NT printer, because Windows NT can provide an LPD service. The LPD service (lpdsvc) provides the same service that an LPD daemon on a Unix host. Because it is implemented as a service, it is controlled through Control Panel, Services. This service automatically installs when you opt to install TCP/IP print services.

Remote host systems use different commands for printing. One command that works on most systems is the LPR command. A sample command line which would work on most systems is as follows:

```
lpr -s NTSYSTEM -p NTPRINTER filename
```

For the lpr command on the remote system, specify the DNS name (or IP address) of your NT system, along with the printer name. Windows NT internally directs the print job to the specified printer.

Please refer to the documentation for your remote host system for more information.

Troubleshooting Utilities

 **Objective**

The previously discussed utilities provide basic connectivity services between Windows NT systems and remote host systems. The following utilities are diagnostic and troubleshooting tools for connectivity between heterogeneous systems.

 Note

Most of these utilities are discussed elsewhere in the book. For example, the NBTSTAT utility is discussed in detail in Chapter 13, and NSLOOKUP is discussed in detail in Chapter 19.

These utilities provide debugging and troubleshooting information to determine the cause of a connectivity failure between Microsoft clients and remote host computers. This section does not cover all possible debugging tools—indeed, a separate book could be written on this topic.

In addition to debugging utilities, the following suggestions can be of considerable use when troubleshooting:

▶ If TCP/IP cannot communicate from a Microsoft host to a remote host system, the utilities discussed in this chapter will not work correctly.

▶ If the systems are on different subnets, and cannot communicate, remember that TCP/IP requires routing to communicate between subnets.

▶ If the systems previously were able to communicate, but can no longer communicate, suspect either your router(s) or changes in software configuration.

▶ Utilities that require user names and passwords on the remote host need a user account on the remote system. If you have an account on a Windows NT system, the remote host system does not know or care. Trust relationships are not the same as achieving connectivity.

▶ On Windows NT computers, never forget to consult the Event Viewer. Any messages that are out of the ordinary may provide valuable clues to the cause of the problem.

Although the following tools are not strictly related to connectivity in heterogeneous environments, these tools are useful in trouble-shooting almost any TCP/IP network.

PING

The PING command is one of the most useful commands in the TCP/IP protocol. It sends a series of packets to another system, which in turn sends back a response. This utility can be extremely useful in troubleshooting problems with remote hosts.

The PING utility is used as a command-line program, and accepts the following parameters:

```
Usage: ping [-t] [-a] [-n count] [-l size] [-f] [-i TTL] [-v TOS]
            [-r count] [-s count] [[-j host-list] ¦ [-k host-
            list]] [-w timeout] destination-list
Options:
    -t              Pings the specified host until interrupted
    -a              Resolves addresses to host names
    -n count        Number of echo requests to send.
    -l size         Sends buffer size
    -f              Sets Don't Fragment flag in packet
    -i TTL          Time to Live
    -v TOS          Type of Service
    -r count        Records route for count hops
    -s count        Time stamp for count hops
    -j host-list    Loose source route along host-list
    -k host-list    Strict source route along host-list
    -w timeout      Time-out in milliseconds to wait for each reply
```

The PING command indicates whether the host can be reached, and how long it took for the host to send a return packet. On a local area network, the time is indicated as less than 10 milliseconds, but across wide area network links, this value can be much greater.

TRACERT

The TRACERT utility determines the intermediary steps involved in communicating with another IP host. It provides a road map of all the routing an IP packet takes to get from host A to host B.

```
Usage: tracert [-d] [-h maximum_hops] [-j host-list] [-w timeout]
            target_name
```

```
Options:
    -d                    Does not resolve addresses to host names
    -h maximum_hops       Maximum number of hops to search for
                          target
    -j host-list          Loose source route along host-list
    -w timeout            Wait time-out milliseconds for each reply
```

As with the PING command, TRACERT returns the amount of time required for each routing *hop*.

IPCONFIG

One of the key areas that causes problems with TCP/IP is configuration. Windows NT provides a utility that will allow you to view the configuration of a workstation so you can verify the configuration. The following listing provides a summary of the usage of IPCONFIG:

```
C:\>ipconfig /?Windows NT IP Configuration
Usage: ipconfig [/? ¦ /all ¦ /release [adapter] ¦ /renew [adapter]]
Options:
       /?        Display this help message.
       /all      Display full configuration information.
       /release  Release the IP address for the specified adapter.
       /renew    Renew the IP address for the specified adapter.

The default is to display only the IP address, subnet mask and
default gateway for each adapter bound to TCP/IP.

For Release and Renew, if no adapter name is specified, then the
IP address leases for all adapters bound to TCP/IP will be released
or renewed.
```

NETSTAT

Once you have determined that your base level communications are working you will need to verify the services on your system. This involves looking at the services that are listening for incoming traffic and/or verifying that you are creating a session with a remote station. The NETSTAT command will allow you to do this.

```
C:\>netstat /?

Displays protocol statistics and current TCP/IP network connections.

NETSTAT [-a] [-e] [-n] [-s] [-p proto] [-r] [interval]
```

```
    -a              Displays all connections and listening ports.
                    (Server-side connections are normally not shown).
    -e              Displays Ethernet statistics.  This may be
                    combined with the -s option.
    -n              Displays addresses and port numbers in numerical
                    form.
    -p proto        Shows connections for the protocol specified by
                    proto; proto may be tcp or udp.  If used with the
    -s              option to display per-protocol statistics, proto
                    may be tcp, udp, or ip.
    -r              Displays the contents of the routing table.
    -s              Displays per-protocol statistics.  By default,
                    statistics are shown for TCP, UDP and IP; the
    -p              option may be used to specify a subset of the
                    default.
    interval        Redisplays selected statistics, pausing interval
                    seconds between each display.  Press CTRL+C to
                    stop redisplaying statistics.  If omitted,
                    netstat will print the current configuration
                    information once.
```

NBTSTAT

Whereas NETSTAT deals with all the connections that your system has with other computers, NBTSTAT deals with only the NetBIOS connections. NBTSTAT also allows you to verify that name resolution is taking place by providing a method to view the name cache.

```
C:\>nbtstat /?

Displays protocol statistics and current TCP/IP connections using
NBT (NetBIOS over TCP/IP).

NBTSTAT [-a RemoteName] [-A IP address] [-c] [-n]
        [-r] [-R] [-s] [-S] [interval] ]

    -a   (adapter status) Lists the remote machine's name table
         given its name
    -A   (Adapter status) Lists the remote machine's name table
         given its IP address.
```

-c	(cache)	Lists the remote name cache including the IP addresses
-n	(names)	Lists local NetBIOS names.
-r	(resolved)	Lists names resolved by broadcast and via WINS
-R	(Reload)	Purges and reloads the remote cache name table
-S	(Sessions)	Lists sessions table with the destination IP addresses
-s	(sessions)	Lists sessions table converting destina tion IP addresses to host names via the hosts file.

RemoteName	Remote host machine name.
IP address	Dotted decimal representation of the IP address.
interval	Redisplays selected statistics, pausing interval seconds between each display. Press Ctrl+C to stop redisplaying statistics.

NSLOOKUP

One of the key issues in using TCP/IP is the capability to resolve a host name to an IP address. This is usually done by a DNS server (see Chapters 12 and 13). In order to test the capability to resolve names, Windows NT comes with a utility called NSLOOKUP.

```
Usage:   nslookup [-opt ...]
    # interactive mode using default server   nslookup [-opt
    ...] - server
    # interactive mode using 'server'   nslookup [-opt ...] host
    # just look up 'host' using default server   nslookup [-opt
    ...] host server
    # just look up 'host' using 'server'
```

ROUTE

Occasionally it is necessary to check how a system will route packets on the network. Normally your system will simply send all packets to the default gateway, however, in cases where your are having problems communicating with a group of computers, the ROUTE command may provide an answer.

```
C:\>route Manipulates network routing tables.ROUTE [-f] [command
[destination] [MASK netmask] [gateway] [METRIC metric]]
    -f          Clears the routing tables of all gateway entries.
                If this is used in conjunction with one of the
                commands, the tables are cleared prior to running
                the command.

    -p          When used with the ADD command, makes a route
                persistent across boots of the system. By default,
                routes are not preserved when the system is
                restarted. When used with the PRINT command,
                displays the list of registered persistent
                routes. Ignored for all other commands, which
                always affect the appropriate persistent routes.

    command     Specifies one of four commands
                PRINT    Prints a route
                ADD      Adds a route
                DELETE   Deletes a route
                CHANGE   Modifies an existing route

    destination Specifies the host.

    MASK        If the MASK keyword is present, the next parameter
                is interpreted as the netmask parameter.

    netmask     If provided, specifies a sub-net mask value to be
                associated with this route entry.  If not
                specified, it defaults to 255.255.255.255.

    gateway     Specifies gateway.

    METRIC      specifies the metric/cost for the destination
```

All symbolic names used for destination are looked up in the network database file NETWORKS. The symbolic names for gateway are looked up in the host name database file HOSTS. If the command is print or delete, wildcards may be used for the destination and gateway, or the gateway argument may be omitted.

ARP

As has been discussed, once the name has been resolved to an IP address, you computer must resolve the IP address to a MAC address. This is handled Address Resolution Protocol (ARP). The ARP utility will allow you to view the addresses that have been resolved.

C:\>arp /?Displays and modifies the IP-to-Physical address translation tables used by address resolution protocol (ARP).

```
ARP -s inet_addr eth_addr [if_addr]
ARP -d inet_addr [if_addr]
ARP -a [inet_addr] [-N if_addr]
```

-a	Displays current ARP entries by interrogating the current protocol data. If inet_addr is specified, the IP and Physical addresses for only the specified computer are displayed. If more than one network interface uses ARP, entries for each ARP table are displayed.
-g	Same as -a.
inet_addr	Specifies an internet address.
-N if_addr	Displays the ARP entries for the network interface specified by if_addr.
-d	Deletes the host specified by inet_addr.
-s	Adds the host and associates the Internet address inet_addr with the Physical address eth_addr. The Physical address is given as 6 hexadecimal bytes separated by hyphens. The entry is permanent.

```
eth_addr      Specifies a physical address.
if_addr       If present, this specifies the Internet address of
              the interface whose address translation table
              should be modified. If not present, the first
              applicable interface will be used.
```

Performance Monitor

To tune or optimize Windows NT you will need to be able to look at the performance of the server on many different levels. NT provides an integrated tool that provides information about your system on many different levels. The Performance Monitor will allow you to check not only track the flow of traffic in and out of the system but will also allow you to look at the performance of the various service and programs that are running on your system.

Network Monitor

There are two version of the Network Monitor the basic version that comes with Windows NT and the full version that comes with the SMS (Systems Management Server). Both versions will allow you to capture the packets that are flowing into and out of your computer. The Full version that comes with SMS will also allow you extra functionality such as the capability to capture all packets on the local network or on remote networks, edit those packets, derive statistics about protocols and users on the network.

There are two pieces to the Network Monitor. The Agent which will capture the data. There is also the Monitor Tool which can be used to view the data.

The Network Monitor can be used to diagnose more complex issue with connectivity by allowing you see the actual packets that are flowing on the network verifying which steps are being used to resolve names or which port numbers are being used to connect.

Review Questions

1. Which utility can you use to transfer a file to a remote host using the connection-oriented services of TCP/IP?

    A. TFTP

    B. HTML

    C. FTP

    D. Telnet

2. Which remote execution utility encrypts user names and passwords before transmission?

    A. REXEC

    B. RSH

    C. Telnet

    D. None of the above

3. Which of the following statements about REXEC are incorrect?

    A. REXEC can start processes on Windows NT computers.

    B. REXEC does not require a user name or password.

    C. REXEC can establish terminal sessions on a remote host.

    D. REXEC requires an SMB server on the remote host.

    E. All of the above.

4. Given a remote host system running TCP/IP and having an SMB server service, which of the following provides the most transparent network connectivity for file transfer?

    A. Using an NFS client on a Windows NT computer

    B. Using Microsoft networking functions on a Windows NT computer

    C. Using FTP to copy files from the remote host to your local computer

    D. Using telnet to establish a remote terminal session with the remote host

5. Which of the following statements about telnet are incorrect?

    A. Telnet can be used to remotely administer Windows NT computers.

    B. Telnet encrypts user names and passwords for enhanced security.

    C. Telnet can be used to provide terminal emulation when connecting to remote host systems.

    D. Telnet can be used to view HTML documents with graphical images.

6. A user on a Windows NT computer wishes to run an interactive text editor on a remote host computer. Which utilities would be suitable for use?

    A. Telnet

    B. FTP

    C. REXEC

    D. RSH

    E. HTTP

    F. LPR

7. A user at a Windows NT computer running the TCP/IP protocol wishes to send a print job to an LPR printer on a remote host system. Which methods enable the user to send the print job to the remote host?

    A. Using the LPD command-line utility from the Windows NT system, specifying the host name, printer name and file name

B. Using the LPR command-line utility from the Windows NT system, specifying the host name, printer name and file name

C. Creating an LPR printer in Control Panel/Printers, specifying the host name and printer name required for the creation of an LPR port

D. Creating an LPR printer in Control Panel/Printers, specifying the host name and printer name required for the creation of an LPD server on the Windows NT computer

8. Which procedure enables a remote computer to send a print job to a Windows NT printer in the fewest steps?

A. Creating an LPR printer on the Windows NT computer, sharing the printer, and running the LPR command from the remote host system specifying the required information

B. Creating the LPR printer on the Windows NT computer, and running the LPR command from the remote host system specifying the required information

C. Running the LPR command on the remote system— Windows NT automatically routes the print job to the printer with no further configuration on the Windows NT computer

D. Running the LPD command from the remote host, because the LPD command spawns a copy of the LPDSVC command on the Windows NT computer whether or not TCP/IP printing support is installed

9. Which of the following allows a Windows NT computer to act as a print gateway to an LPR printer on a remote host?

A. Creating an LPR printer on the Windows NT computer, sharing the printer, and connecting to the newly created printer from any other computer on the network.

B. Creating an LPR printer on the Windows NT computer, and installing an LPR printer on every other computer on the network because Windows NT computers cannot act as print gateways to LPR printers.

C. Creating an LPR printer on the Windows NT computer, and installing the LPDSVC service on every other computer on the network.

D. None of the above—Windows NT automatically routes print jobs to any printer, including LPR, without any configuration.

10. Your network includes a number of NT Servers, workstations and TCP/IP host systems. If you want to establish a secure terminal session to a host system from a Windows NT client, which of the following utilities would be adequate?

A. Telnet

B. FTP

C. TFTP

D. None of the above

11. You have a client computer using TCP/IP on a local subnet, and you want to transfer a file to a remote system overseas. Which of the following utilities would provide the most reliable file transfer?

A. Telnet

B. TFTP

C. TCP

D. FTP

12. In a network which has a mixture of Windows NT and remote host systems, you want to administer remote host systems from a Windows NT computer by running remote

system jobs. Which of the following utilities would allow you to execute a job on a remote system without requiring a log-in password?

A. TFTP

B. REXEC

C. RSH

D. Telnet

13. Which of the following statements about FTP are INCORRECT?

A. FTP encrypts user names and passwords.

B. FTP does not encrypt user names and passwords, but uses MD5 and CHAP to encrypt data transfer.

C. FTP does not perform any encryption whatsoever.

D. None of the above.

14. Your network provides a Web server to the Internet through a firewall. Which of the following protocols would usually NOT be available to a client on the other side of your firewall?

A. HTTP

B. FTP

C. TFTP

D. Telnet

15. HTML documents are transferred using the HTTP protocol. Of the following statements, which accurately describes the HTTP protocol?

A. HTTP uses the non-connection-oriented communication features of TCP/IP for data transfer.

B. HTTP requires a user name and password for all HTML documents.

    C. The HTTP protocol uses the connection-oriented communication features of TCP/IP for data transfer.

    D. HTTP can only be used for text files.

16. Which parameters are required when using the LPR command on a Windows NT computer to send a print job to a remote host?

    A. The remote host name

    B. User name and password for the remote system

    C. The remote printer name

    D. The name of the file to be printed

    E. The remote system's SMB server name

17. By creating an LPR printer on a Windows NT computer, and sharing the newly created printer, which of the following statements describes the added functions?

    A. Remote host systems can print to the LPR printer, and Windows NT client computers can print to the LPR printer, but only by using the LPR command.

    B. Remote host systems can print to the LPR printer, and Windows NT computers can print to the LPR printer using Windows NT printing, but other Windows NT computers cannot print to the LPR printer.

    C. Remote host systems can print to the LPR printer, Windows NT computers can print to the LPR printer using Windows NT printing, and other Windows NT computers can print to the LPR printer.

    D. Remote host systems cannot print to the LPR printer, Windows NT computers can print to the LPR printer using Windows NT printing, and other Windows NT computers can print to the LPR printer.

Review Answers

1. C

2. D

3. E

4. B

5. A, B, D

6. A, D

7. B, C

8. B

9. A

10. D

11. D

12. C

13. A, B

14. D

15. C

16. A, C, D

17. C

Answers to the Test Yourself Questions at the Beginning of the Chapter

1. The remote host must be using the same transport protocol as the Microsoft client and the remote host must be configured as an FTP server.

2. The SMB server communicates with the workstation service on a Windows NT computer.

3. Telnet can be used to establish a remote terminal session.

4. The only file transfer utility that does not require authentication is HTTP.

5. Files can be transferred to another station using RCP, FTP, and TFTP.

6. The Internet Information Server has FTP, Gopher and HTTP services. This means TFTP and RCP are not implemented as services in NT.

7. FTP, Telnet, and HTTP are the common winsock applications that use TCP (connection oriented) transfers.

Implementing the Microsoft SNMP Service

21

This chapter will help you prepare for the exam by covering the following objective:

 Objective

▶ Configure SNMP

1. What is the purpose of SNMP?

2. To what extent does SNMP resolve host names?

3. At what level does SNMP fit into the TCP/IP architecture?

4. What levels of security exist for SNMP?

Answers are located at the end of the chapter.

The Usefulness of SNMP

SNMP (Simple Network Management Protocol) is part of the TCP/IP protocol suite. It corresponds to the Application layer in the Internet Protocol Suite.

SNMP enables network administrators to remotely troubleshoot and monitor hubs and routers (see fig. 21.1). Much of SNMP is defined within RFCs 1157 and 1212, though there are many more RFCs on SNMP. SNMP can be found, along with other RFCs, on various web sites, including `http://ds.internic.net`. You can also do a search on SNMP or RFC and find more specific information related to a specific part of SNMP—for example, on just ethernet and SNMP.

Figure 21.1

Hubs and routers.

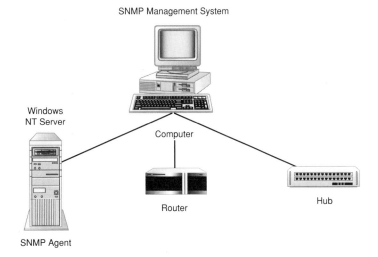

Using SNMP, you can find out information about these remote devices without having to physically be at the device itself. This can be a very useful tool if understood and used properly. You can find a wide variety of information about these devices, depending on the device itself, of course. Some examples include the following:

▶ IP address of a router

▶ Number of open files

▶ Amount of hard drive space available

▶ Version number of a Windows NT host

Before you set up SNMP, you need the IP address or host names of the systems that will either be the initiators or those that will respond to the requests. Microsoft's SNMP Service uses the regular Windows NT host name resolution, such as HOSTS, DNS, WINS, and LMHOSTS. Therefore, if you are using one of these resolution methods, add the correct host name to IP address resolution for the computers that you are setting up with SNMP.

The types of systems on which you can find data include the following:

▶ Mainframes

▶ Gateways and routers

▶ Hubs and bridges

▶ Windows NT servers

▶ LAN Manager servers

▶ SNMP agents

SNMP uses a distributed architecture design to facilitate its properties. This means that various parts of SNMP are spread throughout the network to complete the task of collecting and processing data to provide remote management.

Because SNMP is a distributed system, you can spread out the management of it in different locations so as not to overtax any one PC, and for multiple management functionality (see fig. 21.2).

Figure 21.2

SNMP in the works.

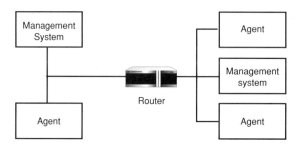

An SNMP Service by Microsoft enables a machine running Windows NT to be able to transfer its current condition to a computer running an SNMP management system. However, this is only the agent side, not the management tools. This chapter's Labs use an SNMPutil.exe that is a basic command prompt utility. Various third-party management utilities are available, including the following:

▶ IBM NetView

▶ Sun Net Manager

▶ Hewlett-Packard OpenView

This chapter focuses primarily on the SNMP protocol rather than the management utilities; the management utilities are a product of their own and not included in Microsoft training material or exam.

SNMP Agents and Management

There are two main parts to SNMP: the agent and the management side.

▶ The management station is the centralized location from which you can manage SNMP.

▶ The agent station is the piece of equipment that you are trying to extract data from.

Each part is discussed in the following sections.

The SNMP Management System

The management system is the key component for obtaining information from the client. You need at least one management system to even be able to use the SNMP Service. The management system is responsible for "asking the questions." As mentioned earlier, there are a certain number of questions it can ask each device, depending upon the type of device. The management system is, of course, a computer running one of the various software components mentioned earlier (see fig. 21.3).

Figure 21.3

Agents and management systems.

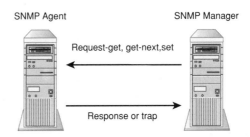

SNMP Agent   SNMP Manager

Request-get, get-next,set

Response or trap

There are also certain commands that can be given specifically at the management system. These are generic commands not specific to any type of management system directly:

▶ **get.** Requests a specific value. For example, it can query how many active sessions are open.

▶ **get-next.** Requests the next object's value. For example, you can query a client's arp cache and then ask for each subsequent value.

▶ **set.** Changes the value on an object that has the properties of read-write. This command is not often used due to security, and the fact that the majority of objects have a read-only attribute.

Usually, you have only one management system running the SNMP Service per group of hosts. This group is known as a *community*. Sometimes, however, you may want to have more. Some of these reasons are discussed in the following list:

▶ You may want to have multiple management systems inquire different queries to the same agents.

▶ There might be different management sites for one community.

▶ As the network grows and becomes more complex, you may need to help differentiate certain aspects of your community.

The SNMP Agent

You have seen so far what the SNMP management side is responsible for and can specifically do. For the most part, the management side is the active component for getting information. The SNMP agent, on the other hand, is responsible for complying with the requests and responding to the SNMP manager accordingly. Generally, the agent is a router, server, or hub. The agent is usually a passive component only responding to a direct query.

In one particular instance, however, the agent is the initiator, acting on its own without a direct query. This special case is called a *trap*. A trap is set up from the management side on the agent. But the management does not need to go to the agent to find out if the trap information has been tripped. The agent sends an alert to the management system telling it that the event has occurred. Most of the time, the agent is passive except in this one occasion. A trap is similar to a father and son fishing with a net on a stream. The dad sets up the net on the stream. The net has certain sized holes in it, just the right size for catching a certain type and size of fish. The dad then goes downstream to set up more, leaving his son to tend to the net. When the fish comes along, it gets caught in the net and the son runs to tell his father.

The stream is the traffic going through the router. The net is the trap set by the management system. The son is the one responding to the trap and running to tell his father they have caught the fish without the father having to go back and check on his trap. The special fish that is caught might be an alert that a particular server's hard drive is full or a duplicate IP address. Although this is a rough analogy, it gets the basic idea across. What happens, however, if a spare tire comes down the stream and gets caught in the trap? Sometimes invalid packets can set off the trap without it being what you are looking for. These are rare events and the traps set are very specific in what they are looking for.

Management Information Base

Now that you've learned a little about the management system and agents, you can delve into the different types of query databases.

The data that the management system requests from an agent is contained in a *Management Information Base* (MIB). This is a list of questions that the management system can ask. The list of questions depends on what type of device it is asking. The MIB is the database of information that can be queried against.

A variety of MIB databases can be established. The MIB is stored on the SNMP agent and is similar to the Windows NT Registry in its hierarchical structure. These MIBs are available to both the agents and management system as a reference that both can pull information from.

The Microsoft SNMP Service supports the following MIB databases:

▶ Internet MIB II

▶ LAN Manager MIB II

▶ DHCP MIB

▶ WINS MIB

These databases are discussed in the following sections.

Internet MIB II

Internet MIB II defines 171 objects for fault troubleshooting on the network and configuration analysis. It is defined in RFC 1212, which adds to, and overwrites, the previous version, Internet MIB I.

LAN Manager MIB II

LAN Manager MIB II defines about 90 objects associated with Microsoft Networking, such as:

- ▶ Shares

- ▶ Users

- ▶ Logon

- ▶ Sessions

- ▶ Statistical

The majority of LAN Manager MIB II's objects are set to read-only mode due to the limited security function of SNMP.

DHCP MIB

The DHCP MIB identifies objects that can monitor the DHCP server's actions. It is set up automatically when a DHCP server service is installed and is called DHCPMIB.DLL. It has 14 objects that can be used for monitoring the DHCP server activity, including items such as the following:

- ▶ The number of active leases

- ▶ The number of failures

- ▶ The number of DHCP discover requests received

WINS MIB

WINS MIB (WINSMIB.DLL) is a Microsoft-specific MIB relating directly to the WINS server service. It is automatically installed when WINS is set up. It monitors WINS server activity and has approximately 70 objects. It checks such items as the number of resolution requests, success and failure, and the date and time of last database replication.

MIB Structure

As mentioned previously, the name space for MIB objects is hierarchical. It is structured in this manner so that each manageable object can be assigned a globally unique name. Certain organizations have the authority to assign the name space for parts of the tree design.

The MIB structure is similar to TCP/IP addresses. You get only one address from the InterNIC and then subnet it according to your needs. You do not have to contact "InterNIC" for each address assignment. The same applies here. Organizations can assign names without consulting an Internet authority for every specific assignment. For example, the name space assigned to Microsoft's LAN Manager is 1.3.6.1.4.1.77. More recently, Microsoft has been assigned 1.3.6.1.4.1.311; any new MIB would then be identified under that branch. Figure 21.4 illustrates the hierarchical name tree.

Figure 21.4

Hierarchical name tree.

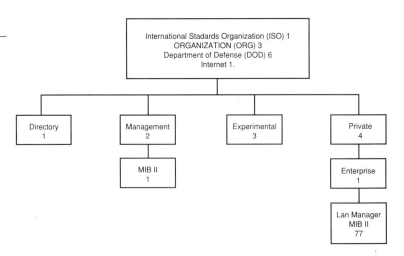

The object identifier in the hierarchy is written as a sequence of labels beginning at the root and ending at the object. It flows down the chart, starting with the International Standards Organization (ISO) and ending with the object MIB II. Labels are separated by periods. The following is an example of this labeling technique:

The object identifier for a MIB II:

Object Name	Object Number
Iso.org.dod.internet. management.mibii	1.3.6.2.1

The object identifier for LAN Manager MIB II:

Object Name	Object Number
iso.org.dod.internet. private. enterprise. lanmanger	1.3.6.1.4.77

 Note   The name space used here for the object identifiers is completely separate from that used with Unix domain names.

Microsoft SNMP Service

The SNMP Service is an additional component of Windows NT TCP/IP software. It includes the four supported MIBs; each is a dynamic-link library and can be loaded and unloaded as needed. It provides SNMP agent services to any TCP/IP host running SNMP management software. It also performs the following:

▶ Reports special happenings, such as traps, to multiple hosts

▶ Responds to requests for information from multiple hosts

▶ Can be set up on any system running Windows NT and TCP/IP

▶ Sets up special counters in Performance monitor that can be used to monitor the TCP/IP performance related to SNMP

▶ Uses host names and IP addresses to recognize which hosts it receives, and requests information

SNMP Architecture

The MIB architecture can be extended to enable developers to create their own MIB libraries, called *extension agents*. Extension agents expand the list of objects that an MIB can report on, making it not only more expansive but also directed to be specifically related to network setup and devices. Figure 21.5 illustrates the SNMP architecture.

Figure 21.5

SNMP architecture.

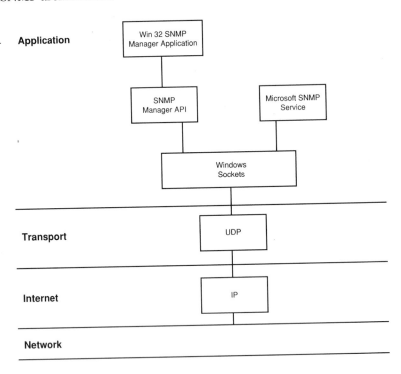

Although the Microsoft SNMP Service doesn't have management software included, it does have a Microsoft Win32 SNMP Manager API that works with the Windows Sockets. The API can then be used by developers to create third-party SNMP management utilities.

The Microsoft SNMP uses User Datagram Protocol (UDP port 161) to send and receive messages, and IP to route messages.

SNMP Communities

A *community* is a group of hosts running the SNMP Service to which they all belong. These usually consist of at least one management system and multiple agents. The idea is to logically organize systems into organizational units for better network management. Figure 21.6 illustrates SNMP communites.

Figure 21.6

SNMP communities.

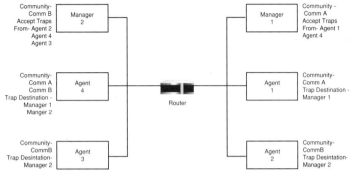

Communities are called by a *community name.* This name is case sensitive. The default community name is public and generally all hosts belong to it. Also by default, all SNMP agents respond to any request using the community public name. By using unique community names, however, you can provide limited security and segregation of hosts.

Agents do not accept requests nor respond to hosts that are not from their configured community. Agents can be members of multiple communities at the same time, but they must be explicitly configured as such. This enables them to respond to different SNMP managers from various communities.

In this example, two separate communities are defined: CommA and CommB. Only the managers and agents that are members of the same community can communicate.

> ▶ Agent1 can send and receive messages to Manager1 because they are both members of the CommA community.

> ▶ Agent2 and Agent3 can send and receive messages to Manager2 because they are all members of the CommB community.

> ▶ Agent4 can send and receive messages to Manager1 and Manager2 because Agent4 is a member of the CommA and CommB communities.

Security

There really is no established security with SNMP. The data is not encrypted, and there is no setup to stop someone from accessing the network, discovering the community names and addresses used, and sending fake requests to agents.

A major reason most MIBs are read-only is so that unauthorized changes cannot be made. The best security you can have is to use unique community names. Choose Send Authentication Trap and specify a Trap Destination, and stipulate Only Accept SNMP Packets from these Hosts.

You might also set up traps that let you know whether the agents receive requests from communities or addresses not specified. This way, you can track down unauthorized SNMP activity.

Installing and Configuring SNMP

 The SNMP Service can be installed for the following reasons:

- ▶ You want to monitor TCP/IP with Performance Monitor.

- ▶ You want to monitor a Windows NT-based system with a third-party application.

- ▶ You want to set up your computer as an SNMP agent.

The following are steps on installing the SNMP Service, assuming you already have TCP/IP installed and set up. These steps also assume you have administrative privileges to install and utilize SNMP.

1. Click on Start, Settings, Control Panel.

2. Double-click Network to bring up the Network properties dialog box.

3. On the Network Settings dialog box, click Add.

4. Click the Services tab (see fig. 21.7) and click Add.

Figure 21.7

The add services screen.

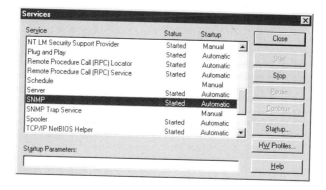

5. The Select Network Service dialog box appears (see fig. 21.8).

Figure 21.8

SNMP Service.

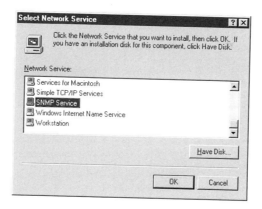

6. Click SNMP Service and then click on OK.

7. Specify the location of the Microsoft Windows NT distribution files.

8. After the files are copied, the Microsoft SNMP Properties dialog box appears (see fig. 21.9). The parameters shown in table 21.1 need to be configured:

Figure 21.9

*The Microsoft
SNMP Properties
dialog box.*

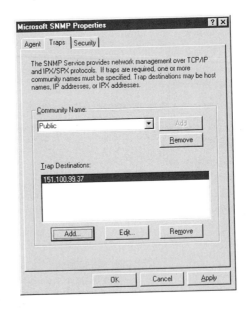

Table 21.1

SNMP Configuration Options

Parameter	Definition
Community Name	The community name to which traps are sent. Remember, it is public by default. There must be a management system in that community to receive and request information.
Trap Destination	The IP addresses of hosts to which you want the SNMP Service to send traps. Note that you can use IP addresses, host names (as long as they are resolved properly), and IPX addresses.

9. Now choose OK to close the SNMP Properties dialog box. Then choose Close to exit the Network properties dialog box. When prompted, Restart your computer.

SNMP Security Parameters

There are several options that you can set that affect the security of the SNMP agent (see fig. 21.10). By default the agent will respond to any manager using community name public. Because this can be inside or outside your organization you should at the very least change the community name.

Figure 21.10

*SNMP security
settings.*

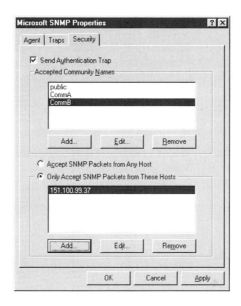

Table 21.2 describes the available options.

Table 21.2

Security Options for the SNMP Agent

Parameter	Description
Send Authentication Trap	Sends information back to the trap initiator responding that the trap failed. This could be because of an incorrect community name or because the host is not specified for service.
Accepted Community Names	When a manager sends a query, a community name is included, this is a list of community names that the agent will respond to.
Accept SNMP Packets from Any Host	Responds to any query from any management system in any community.
Only Accept SNMP Packets from These Hosts	Responds to only the hosts listed.

SNMP Agent

In some cases you will configure other aspects of the SNMP agent. These set the type of devices that you will monitor and who is responsible for the system.

The options available are as follows:

▶ The contact name of the person you want to be alerted about conditions on this station—generally, this is the user of the computer.

▶ The location is a descriptive field for the computer to help keep track of the system sending the alert.

▶ The last part of the screen identifies the types of connections/devices this agent will monitor. These include:

  ▶ Physical—You are managing physical devices like repeaters or hubs.

  ▶ Applications—Set if the Windows NT computer uses an application that uses TCP/IP. You should check this box every time, because just by using SNMP you should have TCP/IP set up.

  ▶ Datalink/Subnetwork—For managing a bridge.

  ▶ Internet—Causes the Windows NT computer to act as an IP gateway, or router.

  ▶ End-to-End—Causes the Windows NT computer to act as an IP host. You should check this box every time because you are most likely an IP host.

Any errors with SNMP will be recorded in the system log. The log records any SNMP activity. Use Event Viewer to look at the errors and to find the problem and possible solutions.

Using the SNMP Utility

The SNMP utility does not come with Windows NT. It is included in the Windows NT Resource Kit and called SNMPUTIL.EXE. Basically, it is a command line management system utility. It checks that the SNMP Service has been set up and is working correctly. You can also utilize it to make command calls. You cannot do full SNMP management from this utility but, as you will see, you would not want to due to, the complex syntax.

The following is the general syntax structure:

```
snmputil command gent community object_identifier_(OID)
```

The following are the commands you can use:

- ▶ **walk.** Moves through the MIB branch identified by what you have placed in the object_identifer

- ▶ **get.** Returns the value of the item specified by the object_identifier

- ▶ **getnext.** Returns the value of the next object after the one specified by the get command

To find out the time the WINS server service began, for example, providing WINS is installed and the SNMP agent is running, you query the WINS MIB with the following command:

```
c:\>snmputil getnext localhost public .1.3.6.1.4.1.311.1.1.1.1
```

In this example, the first part refers to the Microsoft branch: .1.3.6.1.4.1.311 (or iso.org.dod.internet.private.enterprise. microsoft). The last part of the example refers to the specific MIB and object you are querying: .1.1.1.1 (or .software.Wins.Par.Par WinsStartTime). A returned value might look like the following:

```
Value = OCTET STRING - 01:17:22 on 11:23:1997.<0xa>
```

What SNMP Is Really Doing

The following example tracks a sample of SNMP traffic between a manager and an agent. Remember in real life you will use management software (such as HP's Openview, which allows you to see the MIBs and query without knowing all the numbers).

1. The SNMP management system makes a request of an agent using the agent's IP address or host name.

   a. Request sent by the application to UDP port 161.

   b. Host name resolved to an IP address, if host name was used, using host name resolution methods: localhost, HOSTS file, DNS, WINS, broadcast, LMHOSTS file.

2. SNMP packet gets set up with the listed information inside, and routes the packet on the agent's UDP port 161:

   a. The command for the objects: get, get-next, set.

   b. The community name and any other specified data.

3. An SNMP agent gets the packet and puts it into its buffer.

   a. The community name is checked for validity. If it is not correct or is corrupted, the packet is rejected.

   b. If the community name checks out, the agent checks to see whether the originating host name or IP address is correct as well. If not, it is thrown out.

   c. The inquiry is then passed to the correct DLL as described in the preceding section on MIBs.

   d. The object identifier gets mapped to the specific API and that call gets made.

   e. The DLL sends the data to the agent.

4. The SNMP packet is given to the SNMP manager with the requested information.

Exercises

First, you need to install TCP/IP, then SNMP agent and monitor tools. Refer to "Installing and Configuring SNMP" earlier in this chapter for information on installing SNMP.

Exercise 21.1: Exploring Performance Monitor Counters

After you have installed SNMP, you may want to look at the Performance Monitor utility and notice the TCP/IP objects available for monitoring. To do this, use the following steps:

1. Choose Start, Programs, Administrative Tools and select Performance Monitor.

2. Click on the Edit menu and click Add to Chart.

3. Look at the list of available TCP/IP objects.

An example exercise monitoring SNMP using one of the TCP/IP related objects is as follows:

1. Follow the previous exercise.

2. Select the ICMP object from the list.

3. Click on Messages/sec in the counter box.

4. For the Scale, set to 1 and click Add.

5. Select another object IP.

6. From the Counter list, click Datagrams sent/sec.

7. Set the scale to 1 and then click Add.

8. Select Done.

9. Make certain you are using the chart view.

10. Change Vertical Maximum to 10 and click OK.

11. Go to a command prompt and ping another computer.

12. Go back to Performance Monitor and notice what happened.

continues

Exercise 21.1: Continued

13. There should be two messages for ICMP and one IP datagram (two ICMP messages—one request, one reply).

14. Shut down Performance Monitor and go to the next exercise.

Exercise 21.2: Using SNMPUTIL to Access MIB Objects

This exercise is dependent on DHCP, WINS, TCP/IP, and SNMP being set up and you performing these exercises from that host machine. You may want to use the F3 key to bring up similar commands and check your number sequence carefully.

1. Copy the SNMPUtil.exe to winnt_root.

2. Go to a command prompt.

3. Type the following to find out the number of IP addresses leased by your DHCP server by querying the DHCP MIB:

```
snmputil getnext your_ip_address community_name
.1.3.6.1.4.1.311.1.3.2.1.1.1
```

4. Type the following to find out how many failed queries have been done by your WINS server by querying the WINS MIB:

```
snmputil getnext your_ip_address community_name
.1.3.6.1.4.1.311.1.2.1.18
```

5. Type the following to find out how many successful queries have be done by your WINS server by querying the WINS MIB:

```
snmputil getnext your_ip_address community_name
.1.3.6.1.4.1.311.1.2.1.17
```

6. Type the following to find out the version of Windows NT server that you are using. Notice this requires queries; you combine the results to get your full response. Notice here you are querying the LAN Manager MIB, as noted by the change in the hierarchical format.

```
snmputil getnext your_ip_address community_name
.1.3.6.1.4.1.77.1.1.1
snmputil getnext your_ip_address community_name
.1.3.6.1.4.1.77.1.1.2
```

Review Questions

The following questions test your knowledge of the information in this chapter:

1. When using an SNMP management system to query an agent, you can find out which of the following when querying the WINS MIB?

   A. The number of WINS servers available on your network

   B. The number of successful queries made on the WINS proxy server

   C. The number of unsuccessful queries processed by the WINS server

2. Through the use of SNMP, you can find out remote management information on which of the following items?

   A. Hub

   B. Router

   C. Bridge

   D. Windows NT Server

   E. Windows NT Workstation

3. When using SNMP in a TCP/IP network across a router with Unix hosts, Windows NT Servers, and LAN Manager stations, how would SNMP be able to resolve a host name?

   A. HOSTS file

   B. LMHOSTS file

   C. DNS

   D. DHCP

   E. WINS

4. The commands that you are able to implement on the management system side when making requests to the agents consist of which of the following?

A. get, set, go

B. walk, get, get-next

C. get, get-next, walk

D. set, get-next, get

5. The active component of the SNMP system that performs the trap is which of the following?

A. Management system

B. Agent

6. The part of SNMP that has specific objects related to the type of item that the management system is able to make queries against and is stored on the agent is called what?

A. MIIB

B. Management Information Base

C. MHB

D. Management Internet Information Base

7. Which of the following statements regarding the activity of SNMP and its actions are false?

A. Reports traps to multiple hosts

B. Responds to requests from multiple hosts

C. Sets up counters in Performance Monitor for SNMP

D. Uses host names and IP addresses to identify source and destination

8. A community is a group of hosts running SNMP, to which they all belong and respond to requests from a management system to agents. The default community name for all communities is _____.

A. punic

B. comm

C. community

D. public

9. When setting up security in SNMP, what is the most secure option you can select without limiting the potential for additional communities?

   A. Have a community name other than public, select Only Accept SNMP Packets from These Hosts, and set a trap to alert invalid inquiries.

   B. Have a community name of public, select Only Accept SNMP Packets from These Hosts, and set a trap to alert invalid inquiries.

   C. Have a community name of public, select Accept SNMP Packets from These Hosts.

10. When setting up an SNMP management system on a Windows NT host machine, what MIBs are supported by default under Windows NT 4.0?

   A. Internet MIB I, LAN Manager MIB II, WINS MIB, DHCP MIB

   B. Internet MIB II, LAN Manager MIB I, WINS MIB, DHCP MIB

   C. Internet MIB II, LAN Manager MIB II, WINS MIB, DHCP MIB

   D. Internet MIB II, LAN Manager MIB II, WINS MIB I, DHCP MIB

11. In order for SNMP agents and management systems to communicate with each other, they need to be set up with the same _____ name.

   A. public

   B. unity

    C. group

    D. community

12. If you are having problems with SNMP, where in Windows NT should you look?

    A. Event Viewer in Windows NT Administrative Tools

    B. Performance Monitor

    C. The SNMP log

13. Which agent services are enabled by default when setting up the Windows NT SNMP agent?

    A. Internet

    B. Physical

    C. End to End

    D. Application

14. Which SNMP operation is instituted by the agent instead of the management system?

    A. walk

    B. set

    C. trap

    D. get

15. The message sent by an SNMP agent to warn an SNMP management system of an error or specific event is known as a _____.

    A. net

    B. trap

    C. get

    D. warning event

16. What is the name of the utility found in the Windows NT Resource Kit that can be used to check if the SNMP Service

is configured correctly and working with the SNMP management system?

    A. SNMPCHECK

    B. SNMPSTAT

    C. SNMPUTIL

    D. SNMPMANG

17. What is the object identifier for a MIB II?

    A. iso.org.dod.internet.management.mib2

    B. iso.org.dod.internet.management.mibii

    C. 1.3.6.2.2

18. The MIB architecture can be extended to enable developers to create their own MIB libraries by using _____.

    A. Extension agents

    B. Extendor agents

    C. Additional dynamic link libraries

19. Why would you install the SNMP Service?

    A. You want to monitor TCP/IP with Performance Monitor.

    B. You want to remotely manage a proxy agent.

    C. You want to monitor a Windows NT-based system with a third-party application.

    D. You want to set up your computer as an SNMP agent.

20. Is it possible to have an SNMP Management utility manage multiple community names, and if so, why would you want to?

    A. Yes, for security reasons.

    B. No, it is not possible.

    C. Yes, but only for organizational purposes.

Review Answers

1. C

2. A, B, C, D

3. A, B, C, E

4. D

5. B

6. B

7. C

8. D

9. A

10. C

11. D

12. A

13. A, C, D

14. C

15. B

16. C

17. B

18. A

19. A, C, D

20. A

Answers to the Test Yourself Questions at the Beginning of the Chapter

1. SNMP provides remote management of routers, hubs, and Windows NT hosts. See "The Usefulness of SNMP."

2. SNMP uses the same host name resolution as TCP/IP: HOSTS file, DNS, WINS, broadcast, and LMHOSTS file. See "Microsoft SNMP Service."

3. SNMP fits at the application level and integrates using a socket similar to Windows sockets. See "SNMP Architecture."

4. There are none. The only type of security is to limit specific agents to the particular management systems to which they will respond and the read-write permissions on community strings.

Chapter 22

Troubleshooting Microsoft TCP/IP

This chapter helps you prepare for the exam by covering the following objectives:

 Objectives

▶ Diagnose and resolve IP addressing problems

▶ Use Microsoft TCP/IP utilities to diagnose IP configuration problems

▶ Identify which Microsoft TCP/IP utility to use to diagnose IP configuration problems

▶ Diagnose and resolve name resolution problems

 **Test Yourself! Before reading this chapter, test yourself to determine how much study time you will need to devote to this section.**

1. What addresses can you Ping to test a TCP/IP configuration?

2. What is one address you can Ping to prove complete TCP/IP connectivity?

3. How can you determine whether a DHCP client got an IP address? If the client didn't get an address, how can you force the client to again try to get an address?

4. You can Ping an NT server's IP address but you cannot connect to a share on the server. Where are possible sources of this problem?

5. What problems can occur if a client does not have the proper address configured for the default gateway?

6. What is the effect on TCP/IP if the wrong IRQ is specified for the network card? Where do you see an indication of this problem?

7. How can you test the resolution of host names?

Answers are located at the end of the chapter.

Introduction

Your ability to successfully troubleshoot connectivity problems with TCP/IP depends upon your mastery of all the concepts of TCP/IP. For example, you must know how TCP/IP addresses work, how host names are resolved, and how routers are used to direct TCP/IP traffic. Without understanding how TCP/IP traffic makes its way from one host to another, you cannot know which tools to use to diagnose the problem and how to solve the problem itself. All the skills you mastered in prior chapters come into play as you troubleshoot TCP/IP problems.

As a client makes a TCP/IP connection, the packet prepared by TCP/IP must work its way through the TCP/IP architecture. Figure 22.1 shows the TCP/IP architecture. An incoming packet must first connect to the adapter card, as specified by the MAC address of the network card. This is the Network Interface layer. Then the packet works its way to the Internet layer, as specified by the TCP/IP address. The Transport layer is next, using the UDP or TCP protocols. The last layer is the Application layer, where the user actually sees a connection via a drive connection, printer connection, FTP session (File Transfer Protocol, a TCP/IP utility to copy files from an FTP server), Web session, or a Telnet session.

Figure 22.1

The TCP/IP architecture.

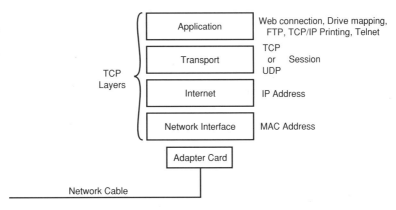

Although TCP/IP works through four layers, troubleshooting TCP/IP can be divided into just two main areas: TCP/IP address configuration and host name resolution. When configuring TCP/IP, you specify the addresses of the various components of TCP/IP that are used to route IP traffic from one host to another. With the correct configuration, TCP/IP can move a packet from one location to another through a clearly defined path. If there are configuration errors, the road for TCP/IP communications is a jumbled path, with no clear way for packets to reach other hosts. In fact, with an improper configuration, you could be telling TCP/IP to make a U-turn to route a packet while a traffic sign clearly states, "No U-turns Allowed."

If TCP/IP is configured correctly, you can contact another host by using the remote host's IP address. However, to make a connection you typically refer to another computer by its host name. If you cannot resolve host names to IP addresses, you can't establish a session with the other host, such as connecting a network drive, connecting to a Web server, or logging on to a domain. Even though TCP/IP may be configured correctly, allowing a smooth path from one host to another, if you can't resolve host names you can't accomplish the day-to-day networking tasks that almost always depend on using host names.

TCP/IP Configuration

The correct configuration of TCP/IP depends not only on entering correct TCP/IP parameters, but also on the underlying configuration of the operating system. Because TCP/IP is a networking protocol, the networking components of the operating system must be working correctly in order for TCP/IP to work. Let's examine the network configuration on a Windows NT machine to determine the underlying components that must be in place for TCP/IP to properly function.

Windows NT Network Configuration

Figure 22.2 shows the Network Properties for a Windows NT computer installed as a Windows NT Workstation or a Windows NT Server. You can access this box through Control Panel, Network. A number of things can be configured in the Network Properties dialog box that affect the capability of Windows NT to communicate over the network, and thus use TCP/IP. As Figure 22.2 shows, one of properties you can configure through this dialog box is the NetBIOS name of the computer. This name is used for any NetBIOS-related communication. When you connect to other Microsoft computers, you use NetBIOS names, which must be resolved to a TCP/IP address if you are using TCP/IP.

Figure 22.2

The Identification tab of Network Properties.

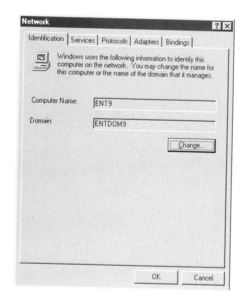

The Services tab of the dialog box shows the networking services are installed on the computer. For TCP/IP connections, you need at the very least the Workstation Service (client software). Additional services are installed by default, however, such as the Server service and the Computer Browser service. Figure 22.3 shows the Services tab of the Network Properties dialog box, with the default services that are part of a typical Windows NT installation.

The Protocols tab of the dialog box (see fig. 22.4) shows the networking protocols that are installed and enables you to configure them. TCP/IP configuration is discussed in the section "TCP/IP Configuration Parameters." If you need to add TCP/IP or simply want to see whether it is installed, however, this is the place to look.

Figure 22.3

The Services tab of Network Properties.

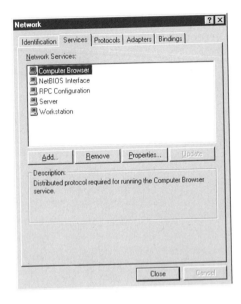

Figure 22.4

The Protocols tab of Network Properties.

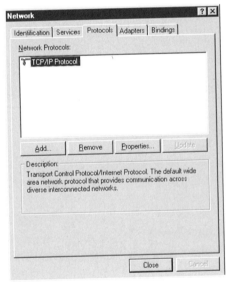

Adapter card drivers are installed and configured in the Adapters tab (see fig. 22.5). Without a properly configured adapter card driver, you cannot communicate on the network, regardless of the protocol you are using. Figure 22.5 shows the configuration for an

NE2000 adapter card. Both the IRQ and I/O Address must be correct. For other adapter cards, you may have other types of parameters, such as a slot number or port type (twisted pair or coax connection).

Figure 22.5

The Adapters tab of Network | Properties.

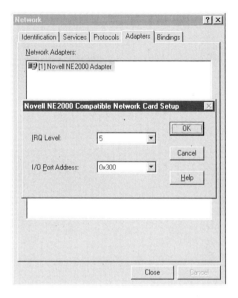

The Bindings tab (see fig. 22.6) specifies how the installed network protocols are used for the various networking services. The bindings affect performance by the order they are listed. The top binding is the one NT tries to use, and NT waits for a timeout period before using another protocol if it can't establish a session with the highest-priority protocol. In addition to changing the priority of the bindings, you can also disable the bindings of a protocol. You can turn off the TCP/IP protocol for the Workstation Service (or any other service, for that matter). With TCP/IP disabled for the Workstation Service (as shown in fig. 16.6), this computer cannot function as a Microsoft client using TCP/IP. The computer cannot, for example, map a drive to a server using TCP/IP. (Other client software, such as FTP or a Web browser, can still use TCP/IP, however.) If the binding is active for the Server service, the computer can respond to incoming requests for drive mappings from other TCP/IP clients.

Figure 22.6

*The Bindings tab
of Network
Properties.*

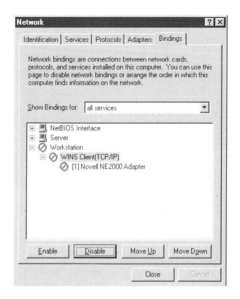

Verifying a Windows NT Network Configuration

*For an exercise
covering this
information, see
end of chapter.*

You should check the Network Properties on the NT computer to
verify that operating system settings are not hindering TCP/IP
from connecting. You can also check the System Log in NT Event
Viewer for possible error messages coming from network configuration errors. Problems with the network card configuration are
usually announced in two types of messages. First, when NT boots,
you should see a message saying A Dependency Service Failed to
Start. This means the adapter card, on which other services depend, failed. Because the adapter card failed, these other services
couldn't start. Second, you should see an error in the System Log
from the adapter card. There should be other errors following it
as other services that depend on the adapter card fail to start. In
some cases, however, you won't see any error messages; TCP/IP
simply won't connect, even with a Ping command. You should not
depend on an error message to remind you to verify that the
adapter card settings are correct.

In checking the Network properties, a number of things must be
in place for TCP/IP to work properly. The computer must have a
unique NetBIOS name. If a computer uses a duplicate name, the
networking services do not start. The error generated from the

duplicate name is the first chronological error in the list, at the bottom of the screen. The subsequent errors, moving from bottom to top, are a result of the duplicate name. Without a unique name, the other networking services don't start. And without networking services, TCP/IP does not work because this computer has no way to communicate on the network.

You must have client software (the Workstation service) installed on the computer to initiate TCP/IP communications. To respond to incoming requests you must have the Server service installed. You can verify their installation on the Services tab of the Network Properties dialog box. You should also check to make sure the services are started. In Control Panel, Services you can see whether services are started and how they are configured to start. The Startup parameters shown in figure 22.7 are configured to have the Workstation service start automatically when NT boots.

Figure 22.7

The Service dialog box with the Workstation service configured for automatic startup.

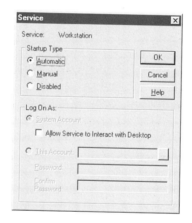

You can also check the Network properties to make sure TCP/IP is installed. Because you configure TCP/IP through the Protocols tab, you can quickly see whether TCP/IP is installed because it is listed on the Protocols tab.

You should check the configuration of the network adapter driver. If the driver is not configured properly, without the correct driver for the adapter card or without the proper settings that match the configuration of the card, you cannot communicate on the network. Figure 16.8 shows the System Log with an error resulting from the wrong adapter card parameters. The first chronological error comes from the adapter card problems. Any subsequent errors are generated from the network card not starting. Remember that by default new entries in the log are added at the top of the display.

Figure 22.8

Error messages from incorrect adapter card settings.

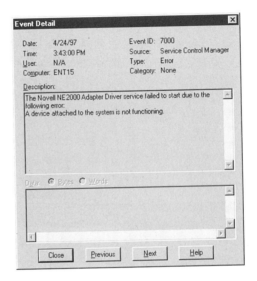

Finally, the bindings must be configured properly. All the protocols installed on the computer should be bound to the various networking services. You can check the bindings on the Bindings tab of Network Properties. Make sure TCP/IP is not disabled on any of the services.

 Tip

You can also move TCP/IP up in the binding order if you have multiple protocols installed. The binding order does not affect the computer's capability to connect using TCP/IP, but it does make TCP/IP connections faster than if TCP/IP is lower in the binding order.

TCP/IP Configuration Parameters

 **Objective**

Three main parameters specify how TCP/IP is configured: the IP address, the subnet mask, and the default gateway, which is the address of the router. These parameters are configured through the Protocols tab of the Network Properties dialog box. Figure 22.9 shows TCP/IP manually configured on a Windows NT client. Although it is possible to receive an IP address from a DHCP server, for the moment this discussion focuses on parameters that are manually configured. (DHCP is discussed in the section "DHCP Configuration Problems.")

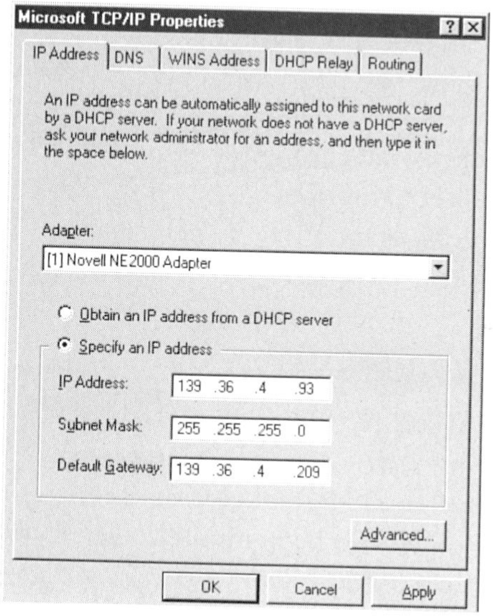

Figure 22.9

TCP/IP Properties with a manual TCP/IP address.

These TCP/IP parameters must be configured correctly or you cannot connect with TCP/IP. An incorrect configuration can result from typos; if you type the wrong IP address, subnet mask, or default gateway you may not connect properly or even be able to connect at all. To illustrate, if you dial the wrong number when making a telephone call, you can't reach the party you're calling. If you read the wrong phone number out of the phone book, you won't ever make a correct call even if you dial the number you think is correct time and time again.

Whether the TCP/IP configuration parameters are wrong due to a typo or due to a mistaken number, the incorrect parameters affect communications. Different types of problems occur when each of these parameters has a configuration error.

IP Address Configuration Problems

An incorrect TCP/IP address might not even cause any problems. If you configure an IP address that is on the correct subnet, but uses the wrong host ID, and is not a duplicate, the client may be able to communicate just fine. If, however, the correct IP address has been entered in a static file or database that resolves host names to IP addresses, such as an LMHOSTS file or a DNS database file, there are some communication problems. Typically, therefore, an incorrect IP address does cause some problems.

Incorrect configuration of the TCP/IP parameters can cause different symptoms for each type of parameter. The following sections examine the effects that each TCP/IP parameter can have on IP communications.

IP Address

A TCP/IP address has two or possibly three components that uniquely identify the computer the address is assigned to. At the very least, the IP address specifies the network address and host address of the computer. Also, if you are subnetting (using part of the host address to specify a subnet address), the third part of the address specifies the subnet address of the host.

Figure 22.10 shows the effect of an incorrect network address. In this example, the TCP/IP address assigned to a client is typed incorrectly. The address assigned to the client is 143.168.3.9, whereas the correct address was supposed to be 133.168.3.9. The network ID for the incorrect address is 143.168.x.x, whereas the network ID for the correct address is 133.168.x.x. With this incorrect address (143.168.3.9), the client is not able to communicate with any other TCP/IP hosts. Because the network address is incorrect, any packets this client sends will be routed to the wrong location.

If the incorrect host (143.168.3.9) sends a message to a local client (133.168.3.20), the TCP/IP configuration of the sending host indicates this is a remote address because it doesn't match the network address of the host initiating the communication. The packet won't ever reach the local client, because the address 133.168.3.20 is interpreted as a remote address.

Figure 22.10

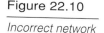

Incorrect network address.

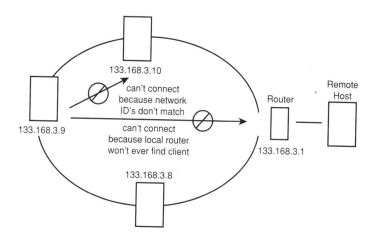

If a local client (133.168.3.6) sends a message to the incorrect host (143.168.3.9), the message never reaches its intended destination. The message is either routed (if the local client sends the message to the IP address as written) or it stays on the local subnet (if the local client sends it to what should have been the address, 133.168.3.9). If the message is routed, the incorrect client does not receive the message because it is on the same segment of the network as the local client. If the message is not routed, the message still does not reach the incorrect client because the IP address for the destination host (133.168.3.9) does not match the address as configured on the incorrect client (143.168.3.9).

Figure 22.11 gives another example of an incorrect IP address. In this case, a class A address is used, 33.x.x.x. The subnet mask (255.255.0.0) indicates the second octet is also being used to create subnets. In this case, even though the client has the same network address as the other clients on the same subnet, the client has a different subnet number because the address was typed incorrectly. This time the incorrect address specifies the wrong subnet ID. The client 33.5.8.4 is on subnet 5 while the other clients on the subnet have the address 33.4.x.x. In this case, if the client 33.5.8.4. tries to contact other clients on the same subnet, the message is routed because the subnet id doesn't match the subnet number of the source host. If the client 33.5.8.4 tries to send a message to a remote host, the message is routed, but the message isn't returned to the client because the router doesn't handle subnet 5, only subnet 4.

Figure 22.11

Incorrect subnet address.

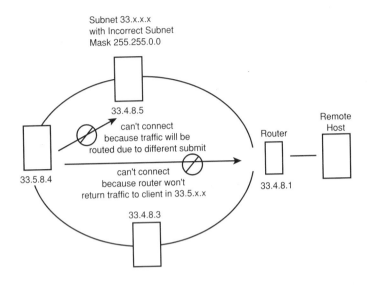

Subnet 33.x.x.x
with Incorrect Subnet
Mask 255.255.0.0

33.4.8.5

can't connect
because traffic will be
routed due to different submit

Remote
Host

Router

33.5.8.4

can't connect
because router won't
return traffic to client in 33.5.x.x

33.4.8.1

33.4.8.3

If a local client tries to send a message to 33.5.8.4, the message doesn't reach the client. If the local client uses the address as configured, the message is routed, which isn't the correct solution because the destination host is local. If the local client sends the message to what should have been the IP address, 33.5.8.4 doesn't receive the message because the IP address isn't configured correctly.

The last component of an IP address that can cause communication problems is the host address. An incorrect host address may not always cause a problem, however. In figure 22.12, a local client has the wrong IP address, but only the host address portion of the address is wrong. The network address and subnet match the rest of the clients on the subnet. In this case, if a client sends a message to the client with the incorrect address, the message still reaches the client. However, if someone tries to contact the client with what should have been the address, he doesn't contact the client. In fact, he could contact another host that ended up with the address that was supposed to be given to the original host. If the original host ends up with the same IP address as another host through the configuration error, the first client to boot works, but the second client to boot may note the address conflict and not load the TCP/IP stack at all. In this case, the second client to boot isn't able to make any TCP/IP communications.

Figure 22.12

Incorrect host address.

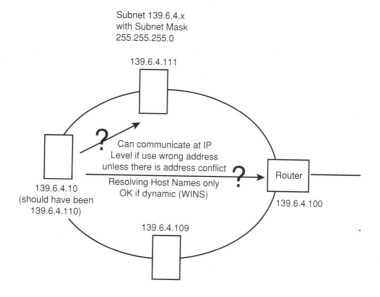

Subnet 139.6.4.x
with Subnet Mask
255.255.255.0

139.6.4.111

Can communicate at IP
Level if use wrong address
unless there is address conflict

Router

Resolving Host Names only
OK if dynamic (WINS)

139.6.4.10
(should have been
139.6.4.110)

139.6.4.100

139.6.4.109

Another problem comes in when the correct address was registered in static files, such as an LMHOSTS file or a DNS database. In this case, no one can communicate with this client by name because the name resolution for this host always returns the correct address, which can't be used to contact the host because the address has been typed incorrectly. Basically, the problems you encounter with an incorrect host address are intermittent. However, if the host was configured to be a WINS client, the host name is registered along with the incorrect address. Another WINS client trying to connect with this computer receives an accurate mapping for the host name.

Subnet Mask

The subnet mask indicates which portion of the IP address specifies the network address and which portion of the address specifies the host address. Also, the subnet mask can be used to take part of what would have been the host address and use it to further divide the network into subnets. If the subnet mask is not configured correctly, your clients may not be able to communicate at all, or you may see partial communication problems.

Figure 22.13 shows a subnet on a TCP/IP network. The network uses a Class B network address of 138.13.x.x. However, the third octet is used in this case for subnetting, so all the clients in the figure should be on subnet 4, as indicated by the common addresses 138.13.4.x. Unfortunately, the subnet mask entered for one client is 255.255.0.0. When this client tries to communicate with other hosts on the same subnet, it should be able to contact them because the subnet mask indicates they are on the same subnet, which is correct. However, if the client tries to contact a host on another subnet, such as 138.13.3.x, the client fails. In this case, the subnet mask still interprets the destination host to be on the same subnet and the message is never routed. Because the destination host is on another subnet, the message never reaches the intended destination. The subnet mask is used to determine routing for outgoing communications, so the client with the incorrect subnet mask can receive incoming messages. However, when the client tries to return communications, the message isn't routed if the source host is on the same network but on a different subnet. So in actuality, the client really can establish communications with only one side of the conversation. Contact with hosts outside the local network still works because those contacts are routed.

Figure 22.13

Incorrect subnet mask—missing third octet.

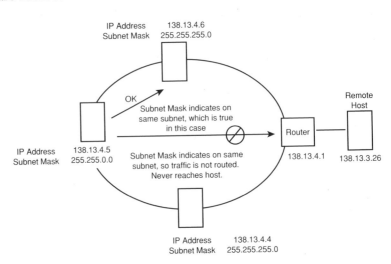

Figure 22.14 shows a subnet mask that masks too many bits. In this case, the subnet mask is 255.255.255.0. However, the network designers had intended the subnet mask to be 255.255.240.0, with four bits of the third octet used for the subnet and four bits as part of the host address. If the incorrect client tries to send a message to a local host and the third octet is the same, the message is not routed and thus reaches the local client. However, if the local client has an address that differs in the last four bits of the third octet, the message is routed and never reaches its destination. If the incorrect client tries to send a message to another client on another subnet, the message is routed because the third octet is different.

Figure 22.14

Incorrect subnet mask—incorrect third octet.

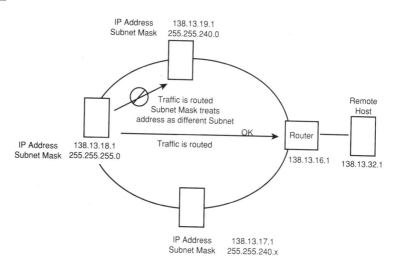

Subnet 138.13.16-31.x

IP Address   138.13.19.1
Subnet Mask 255.255.240.0

Traffic is routed
Subnet Mask treats
address as different Subnet

Remote
Host

OK

Router

IP Address   138.13.18.1   Traffic is routed
Subnet Mask 255.255.255.0

138.13.16.1   138.13.32.1

IP Address   138.13.17.1
Subnet Mask 255.255.240.x

Note

Problems with the subnet mask also lead to intermittent connections. Sometimes the connection works, sometimes it doesn't. The problems show up when the IP address of the destination host causes a packet to be routed when it shouldn't or to remain local when the packet should be routed.

Default Gateway

The default gateway address is the address of the router, the gateway to the world beyond the local subnet. If the default gateway address is wrong, the client with the wrong default gateway address can contact local hosts but is not able to communicate at all beyond the local subnet. It is possible for the incorrect client to receive a message, because the default gateway is used only to send packets to other hosts. However, as soon as the incorrect client attempts to respond to the incoming message, the default gateway address doesn't work and the message doesn't reach the host that sent the original message.

DHCP Client Configuration Problems

All the TCP/IP parameters mentioned previously can cause communication problems if they are not configured correctly. Using a DHCP server can greatly reduce these configuration problems. If the DHCP scope is set up properly, without any typos or other configuration errors, DHCP clients shouldn't have any configuration problems. It is impossible to completely eliminate human error, but using DHCP should reduce the points of potential errors to just the DHCP servers rather than every client on the network.

Even when there are no configuration problems with DHCP addresses, DHCP clients can get a duplicate IP address from a DHCP server. If you have multiple DHCP servers in your environment, you should have scopes on each DHCP server for different subnets. Usually you have scopes with a larger number of addresses for the local subnet where the DHCP server is located and smaller scopes for other subnets. Creating multiple scopes on one server provides backup for giving clients IP addresses. If the server on the local scope is busy or down, the client can still receive an address from a remote DHCP server. When the router forwards this DCHP request to another subnet, it includes the address of the subnet it came from so that the remote DHCP server knows from which scope of addresses to lease an address to the remote client. Using this type of redundancy, however, can cause problems if you don't configure the scopes on all the DHCP servers correctly.

The most important part of the configuration is to make sure you don't have duplicate addresses in the different scopes. On one server, for example, you could have a scope in the range 131.107.2.100 to 131.107.2.170. On the remote DHCP server, you could have a scope of 131.107.2.171 to 131.107.2.200. By setting up the scopes without overlap, you should not have any problems with clients receiving duplicate IP addresses. DHCP servers do not communicate with each other, so one server does not know anything about the addresses the other server has leased. Therefore, you must ensure the servers never give out duplicate information by making sure the scopes for one subnet on all the different DHCP servers have unique IP addresses.

Another common problem with having multiple scopes on one server is entering the configuration parameters correctly. For example, if you enter the default gateway as 131.107.3.1 (instead of 131.107.2.1) for the scope 131.107.2.100 to 131.107.2.170, the clients receiving these addresses will not be able to communicate beyond the local subnet, because they have the wrong router address. With one scope on a DCHP server, you are usually quite sure of what all the configuration parameters should be. With multiple scopes on one server, however, it is easy to get confused about which scope you are editing and what the parameters should be for that scope. To avoid this type of problem, check each scope's parameters very carefully to make sure the parameters match the address of the scope, not the subnet where the DHCP server is located.

Also, if the client doesn't receive an address because the server is down or doesn't respond in a timely manner, the client is not able to contact anyone. Without an IP address, the IP stack does not initialize and the client can't communicate at·all with TCP/IP.

Tools Used to Troubleshoot TCP/IP Configuration Problems

 Objective

A number of tools come with TCP/IP when the protocol is installed on a Windows NT computer. After you have resolved any problems caused by the Windows NT network configuration, you can then focus on using the TCP/IP tools to solve IP problems.

Some tools can be used to verify the configuration parameters. Other tools can be used to test the connectivity capabilities of TCP/IP as configured.

Using IPCONFIG to Verify a TCP/IP Configuration

If you configure the TCP/IP address and other TCP/IP parameters manually, you can always verify the configuration through the Network Properties dialog box. However, if the client receives an address from a DHCP server, the only information available in the Network Properties dialog box is that the client is receiving its address from DHCP. Because the configuration information for a DHCP client is received dynamically, you must use a utility that can read the current configuration to verify the settings.

The command-line utility IPCONFIG can be used to see how the local host is configured—whether the parameters come from manual configuration or from a DHCP server. Figure 22.15 shows the results of using IPCONFIG in a command prompt. The basic configuration parameters are displayed: the IP address, the subnet mask, and the default gateway. You can see additional information by using IPCONFIG with the /all switch. Figure 22.16 shows the results of IPCONFIG /all executed in a command prompt. In this case, not only are the standard parameters shown, but additional information, such as the WINS server address and the DNS server address, is also displayed. In the example shown in the figure the client received its IP address from a DHCP server, so additional information like the address of the DHCP server and the lease life of the IP address is also shown.

Note   A Windows version of IPCONFIG, called WNTIPCFG.EXE, is included with the Windows NT Resource Kit. WNTIPCFG reports the same information as the IPCONFIG command-utility. WNTIPCFG can also be used to release and renew DCHP addresses, as described in the following section.

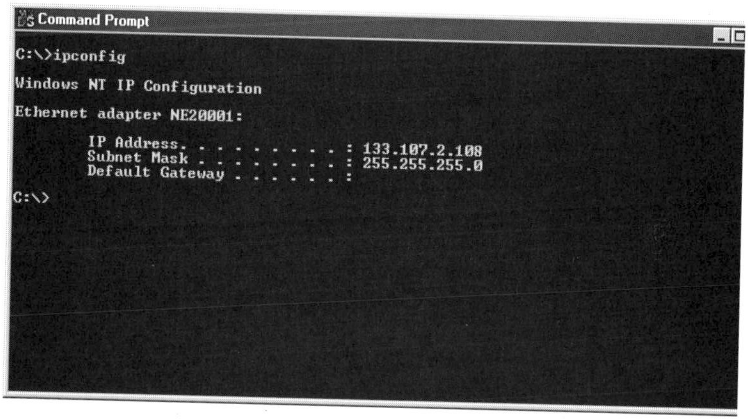

Figure 22.15

The results of the IPCONFIG command.

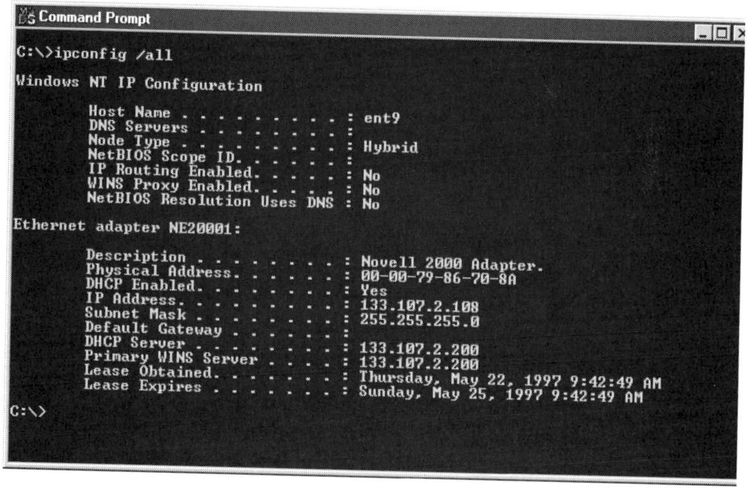

Figure 22.16

The results of the IPCONFIG /all command.

Using IPCONFIG to Resolve DHCP Address Problems

When a DHCP client gets an IP that is not configured correctly or if the client doesn't get an IP address at all, IPCONFIG can be used to resolve these problems. If the client gets incorrect IP parameters, that should be apparent from the results of IPCONFIG /all. You should be able to see that some of the parameters don't match the IP address or that some parameters are completely blank. For example, you could have the wrong default gateway, or the client might not be configured to be a WINS client.

When a DHCP client fails to receive an address, the results of IPCONFIG /all are different. In this case, the client has an IP address of 0.0.0.0—an invalid address—and the DHCP server is 255.255.255.255—a broadcast address. Figure 22.17 shows the results of IPCONFIG /all when the client fails to obtain an address from a DHCP server.

Figure 22.17

DHCP client never received an IP address as indicated by results of IPCONFIG /all.

```
Command Prompt                                                    _ □ X

C:\>ipconfig /all

Windows NT IP Configuration

        Host Name . . . . . . . . . . : ent9
        DNS Servers . . . . . . . . . :
        Node Type . . . . . . . . . . : Hybrid
        NetBIOS Scope ID. . . . . . . :
        IP Routing Enabled. . . . . . : No
        WINS Proxy Enabled. . . . . . : No
        NetBIOS Resolution Uses DNS : No

Ethernet adapter NE20001:

        Description . . . . . . . . . : Novell 2000 Adapter.
        Physical Address. . . . . . . : 00-00-79-86-70-8A
        DHCP Enabled. . . . . . . . . : Yes
        IP Address. . . . . . . . . . : 0.0.0.0
        Subnet Mask . . . . . . . . . : 0.0.0.0
        Default Gateway . . . . . . . :
        DHCP Server . . . . . . . . . : 255.255.255.255
        Primary WINS Server . . . . . : 133.107.2.200

C:\>
```

To fix this problem, you can release the incorrect address with IPCONFIG /release and then try to obtain a new IP address with IPCONFIG /renew. The IPCONFIG /renew command sends out a new request for a DHCP address. If a DHCP server is available, the server responds with the lease of an IP address. Figure 22.18 shows the results of using IPCONFIG /release to release an address and using IPCONFIG /renew to acquire a new address.

 Note

In many cases, the DHCP client will acquire the same address after releasing and renewing. That the client receives the same address indicates the same DHCP server responded to the renewal request and gave out the address that had just been released back into the pool of available addresses. If you need to renew an address because the parameters of the scope are incorrect, you must fix the parameters before releasing and renewing the address. Otherwise, the client could receive the same address again with the same incorrect parameters.

Tip

Occasionally, a DHCP client will not acquire an address regardless of how many times you release and renew the address. One way to try to fix the problem is to manually assign the client a static IP address. Once the client is configured with this address, which you can verify by using IPCONFIG, switch back to DHCP.

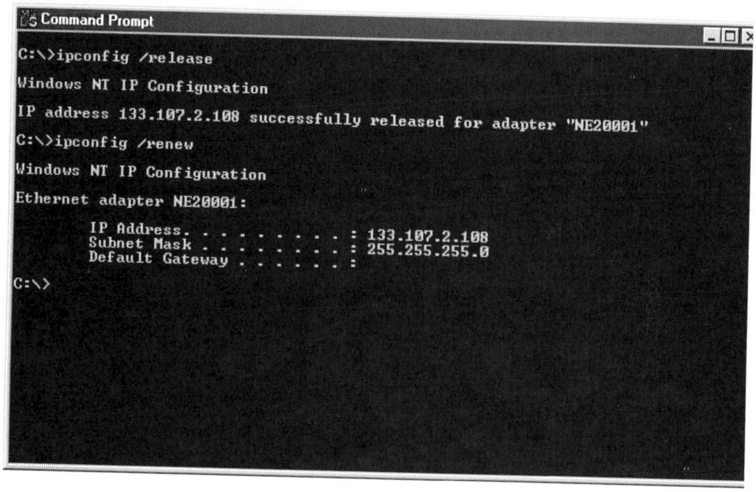

Figure 22.18

Using IPCONFIG /release to release an address and IPCONFIG /renew to get a new address.

```
Command Prompt                                                          _ □ ×
C:\>ipconfig /release
Windows NT IP Configuration
IP address 133.107.2.108 successfully released for adapter "NE20001"
C:\>ipconfig /renew
Windows NT IP Configuration
Ethernet adapter NE20001:

        IP Address. . . . . . . . . : 133.107.2.108
        Subnet Mask . . . . . . . . : 255.255.255.0
        Default Gateway . . . . . . :

C:\>
```

Using Ping to Test an IP Configuration

For an exercise covering this information, see end of chapter.

Ping is a command-line tool included with every Microsoft TCP/IP client (any DOS or Windows client with the TCP/IP protocol installed). You can use Ping to send a test packet to the specified address and then, if things are working properly, the packet is returned. Figure 22.19 shows the results of a successful Ping command. Note that four successful responses are returned. Unsuccessful Pings can result in different messages, depending on the type of problem Ping encounters while trying to send and receive the test packet.

Although Ping is a simple tool to use (from the command prompt simply type Ping with the IP address or host name you want to Ping), choosing what to Ping is the key to using it for successful troubleshooting. The remainder of this section covers which IP addresses or hosts you should Ping to troubleshoot TCP/IP connectivity problems.

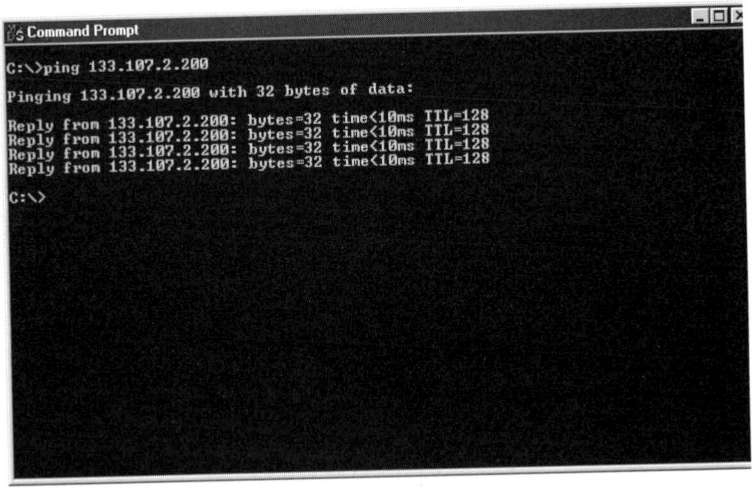

Figure 22.19

The results of a successful Ping command.

Troubleshooting IP Protocol Installation by Pinging the Loopback Address

The first step in troubleshooting many problems is to verify that TCP/IP installed correctly on the client. You can look at the configuration through the Network Properties dialog box or with IPCONFIG, but to actually test the working status of the protocol stack you should try to Ping the loopback address. The loopback address is 127.0.0.1. When you Ping this address, a packet is not sent on the network. Ping simply sends a packet down through the layers of the IP architecture and then up the layers again. If TCP/IP is installed correctly, you should receive an immediate successful response as shown in figure 22.20. If IP is not installed correctly, the response fails (see fig. 22.21).

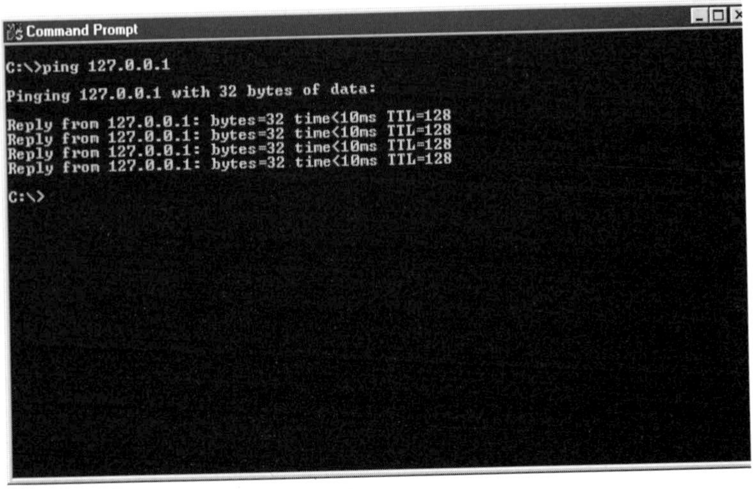

Figure 22.20

A successful loopback Ping.

Figure 22.21

A failed loopback Ping.

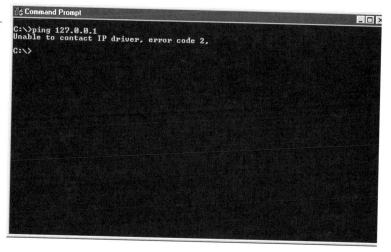

```
Command Prompt                                    _ □ x
C:\>ping 127.0.0.1
Unable to contact IP driver, error code 2,

C:\>
```

To correct problems of this type, you should verify the NT network configuration and the protocol installation. You can check the following items:

▶ Make sure TCP/IP is listed on the installed protocols.

▶ Make sure the network adapter card is configured correctly.

▶ Make sure TCP/IP shows up in the bindings for the adapter card and that the bindings are not disabled for TCP/IP.

▶ Check the system log for any errors indicating that the network services didn't start.

If you try the preceding steps, including rebooting the system, and have no success, you may have to remove TCP/IP and install it again. Sometimes NT gets hung up somewhere and it thinks things are really installed when they are not. Removing the protocol and then installing it again can often resolve this half-way state.

Troubleshooting Client Address Configuration by Pinging Local Address

Another step in verifying the TCP/IP configuration, after you have verified that TCP/IP is installed correctly, is to Ping the address of the local host. Simply Ping the IP address that you think is configured for the client. You should receive an immediate successful reply if the client address is configured as specified in the Ping command. You can also Ping the name of the local host, but problems with name resolution are discussed later in the section "Name Resolution Problems." For the moment, you are concerned with raw TCP/IP connectivity—the capability to communicate with another IP host by using its IP address. Figure 22.22 shows a successful local Ping; figure 22.23 shows a failed Ping.

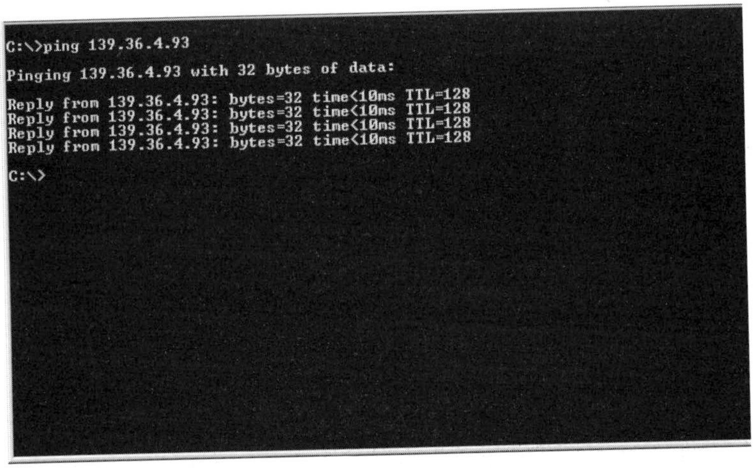

Figure 22.22

Successful Ping of the local address.

```
C:\>ping 139.36.4.93

Pinging 139.36.4.93 with 32 bytes of data:

Reply from 139.36.4.93: bytes=32 time<10ms ITL=128
Reply from 139.36.4.93: bytes=32 time<10ms ITL=128
Reply from 139.36.4.93: bytes=32 time<10ms ITL=128
Reply from 139.36.4.93: bytes=32 time<10ms ITL=128

C:\>
```

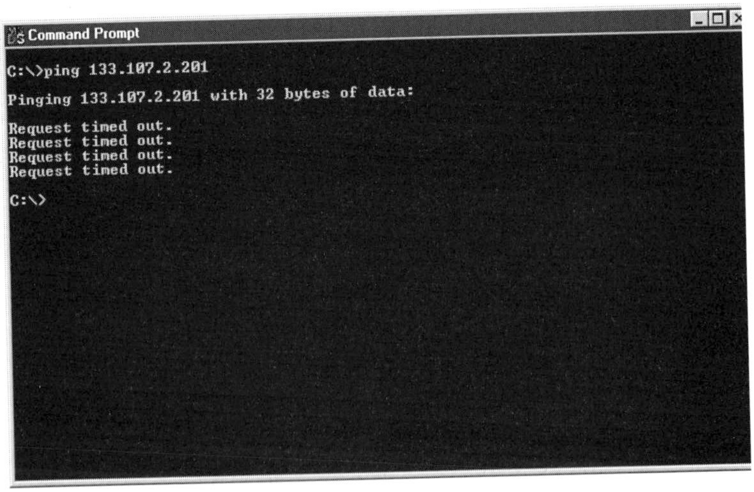

Figure 22.23

Failed Ping of the local address.

```
Command Prompt
C:\>ping 133.107.2.201

Pinging 133.107.2.201 with 32 bytes of data:

Request timed out.
Request timed out.
Request timed out.
Request timed out.

C:\>
```

Correcting a failure at this level concerns checking the way the client address was configured. Was the address typed in correctly? Did the client receive the IP address from the DHCP server that you expected? Also, does the client have a connection on the network? Pinging the local host address does not cause a packet to be sent on the network, so if you have lost network connectivity, this Ping won't indicate a network failure.

Troubleshooting Router Problems by Pinging the Default Gateway

If you can communicate with hosts on the same subnet but cannot establish communications with hosts beyond the subnet, the problem may be with the router or the way its address is configured. To communicate beyond the subnet, a router must be enabled with an address that matches the subnet address for the clients on the local subnet. The router also has other ports configured with different addresses so it can send packets out to the network at large. Pinging the default gateway address tests the address you have configured for the router and also tests the router itself. Figure 22.24 shows a successful Ping to the default gateway. Figure 22.25 shows a failed Ping.

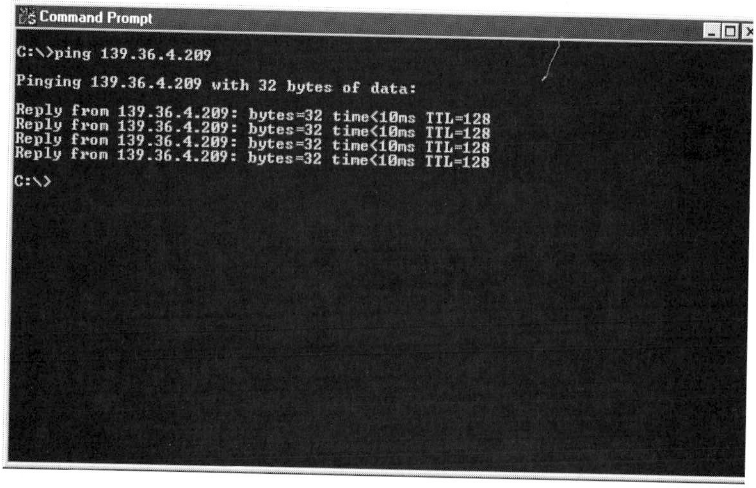

Figure 22.24

Successful Ping of the default gateway.

```
Command Prompt                                                    _ □ x

C:\>ping 139.36.4.209

Pinging 139.36.4.209 with 32 bytes of data:

Reply from 139.36.4.209: bytes=32 time<10ms TTL=128
Reply from 139.36.4.209: bytes=32 time<10ms TTL=128
Reply from 139.36.4.209: bytes=32 time<10ms TTL=128
Reply from 139.36.4.209: bytes=32 time<10ms TTL=128

C:\>
```

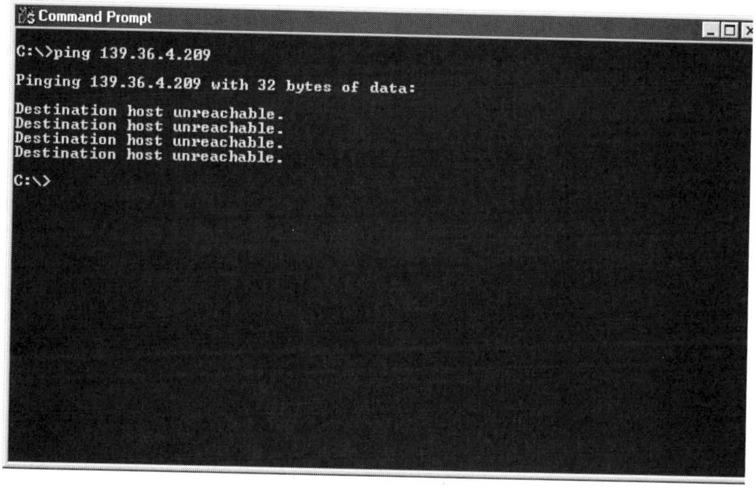

Figure 22.25

Failed Ping of the default gateway.

```
Command Prompt                                                    _ □ x

C:\>ping 139.36.4.209

Pinging 139.36.4.209 with 32 bytes of data:

Destination host unreachable.
Destination host unreachable.
Destination host unreachable.
Destination host unreachable.

C:\>
```

If the default gateway Ping fails, there are several possible sources for the error:

▶ **The router has failed or is down.** In this case, you cannot make connections outside the subnet until the router is brought up again. However, you should be able to communicate with hosts on the same subnet.

▶ **The client has lost a physical connection with the router or with the network.** You can test a network connection at a hardware level and also through the software by trying to establish a session with a server with another protocol, such as NetBEUI, for example. If you only have TCP/IP on your network, you can temporarily install NetBEUI on the client and on another computer on the same subnet. Test connectivity by connecting to a file share on the other computer. Remember, the computer should be on the same subnet because NetBEUI packets don't usually route.

▶ **The IP address on the router may be configured incorrectly.** The router address must match the client's default gateway address so that packets can move outside the subnet.

▶ **The client has the wrong router address.** Of course, if you Ping the correct router address and it works, you also want to make sure the default gateway address configured on the client matches the address you successfully Pinged.

▶ **The wrong subnet mask is configured.** If the subnet mask is wrong, packets destined for a remote subnet may not be routed.

You should also Ping each of the IP addresses used by the different ports on your router. It's possible that the local interface for your subnet is working but other interfaces on the router, which actually connect the router to the other subnets on the network, have some type of problem.

Pinging a Remote Host

As a final test in using Ping, you can Ping the IP address of a remote host, a computer on another subnet, or even the IP address

of a Web server or FTP server on the Internet. If you can successfully Ping a remote host, your problem doesn't lie with the IP
configuration; you are probably having trouble resolving host
names. Figure 22.26 shows the results of a successful remote host
Ping, in this case a Web server at Microsoft. Figure 22.27 shows a
failed remote host Ping.

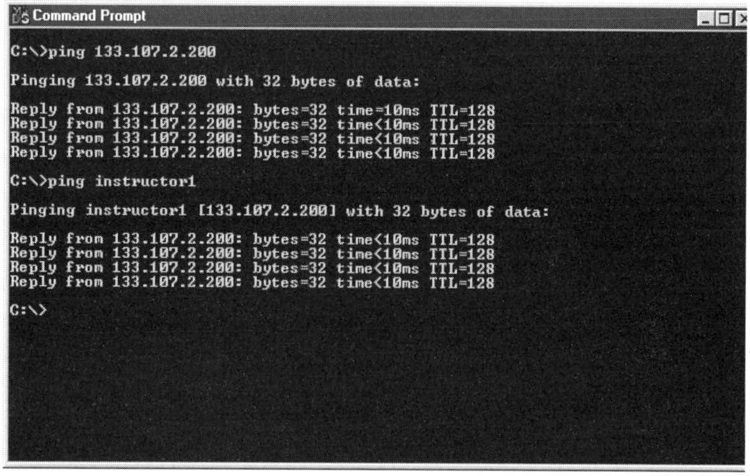

Figure 22.26

*Successful Ping
of a remote host.*

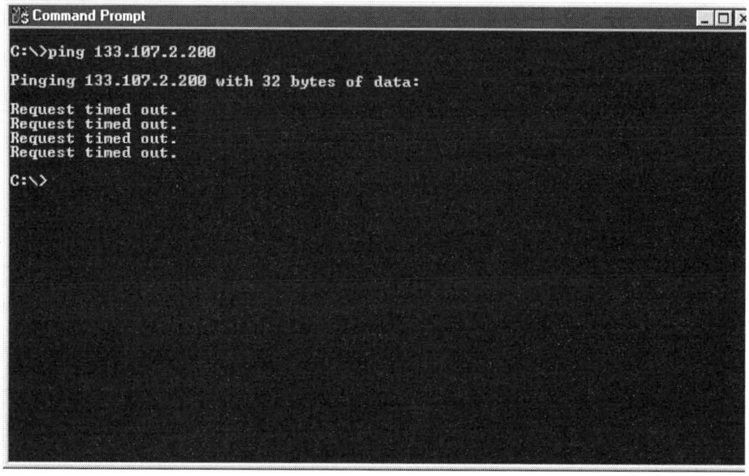

```
Command Prompt                                                   _ □ ×

C:\>ping 133.107.2.200

Pinging 133.107.2.200 with 32 bytes of data:

Reply from 133.107.2.200: bytes=32 time=10ms TTL=128
Reply from 133.107.2.200: bytes=32 time<10ms TTL=128
Reply from 133.107.2.200: bytes=32 time<10ms TTL=128
Reply from 133.107.2.200: bytes=32 time<10ms TTL=128

C:\>ping instructor1

Pinging instructor1 [133.107.2.200] with 32 bytes of data:

Reply from 133.107.2.200: bytes=32 time<10ms TTL=128
Reply from 133.107.2.200: bytes=32 time<10ms TTL=128
Reply from 133.107.2.200: bytes=32 time<10ms TTL=128
Reply from 133.107.2.200: bytes=32 time<10ms TTL=128

C:\>
```

Figure 22.27

*Failed Ping of a
remote host.*

```
Command Prompt                                                   _ □ ×

C:\>ping 133.107.2.200

Pinging 133.107.2.200 with 32 bytes of data:

Request timed out.
Request timed out.
Request timed out.
Request timed out.

C:\>
```

If Pinging the remote host fails, your problems may be with the
router, the subnet mask, or the local IP configuration. However, if
you have followed the earlier steps of Pinging the loopback, local
host address, and the default gateway address, you have already
eliminated many of the problems that could cause this Ping to fail.

When a remote host Ping fails after you have tried the other Ping options, the failure may be due to other routers beyond the default gateway used for your subnet. If you know the physical layout of your network, you can Ping other router addresses along the path to the remote host to see where the trouble lies. Remember to Ping the addresses on both sides of the router: the address that receives the packet and the address that forwards the packet on. You can also use the Route command, as described in the following section, to find the path used to contact the remote host.

It is also possible that there is not a physical path to the remote host due to a router crash, a disruption in the physical network, or a crash on the remote host.

 Note

Many troubleshooters prefer to simply try this last step when using Ping to troubleshoot IP configuration and connectivity. If you can successfully Ping a remote host, then the other layers of TCP/IP must be working correctly. In order for a packet to reach a remote host, IP must be installed correctly, the local client address must be configured properly, and the packet must be routed. If a Ping to the remote host works, then you can look to other sources (usually name resolution) for your connection problems. If the Ping fails, you can try each preceding step until you find the layer where the problem is located. Then you can resolve the problem at this layer. Figure 22.28 shows the methodology used to test IP with Ping. You can either start by Pinging the loopback address and working up through the architecture, or you can Ping the remote host. Of course, if Pinging the remote host works you can stop. If not, you can work back through the architecture until you find a layer where Ping succeeds. The problem must therefore be at the next layer.

Other Tools

You can use a number of tools to help troubleshoot and isolate the source of TCP/IP problems. Each tool gives you a different view of the process used to resolve an IP address to a hardware address, and then routes the IP packet to the appropriate destination.

Figure 22.28

Using Ping to test the TCP/IP configuration.

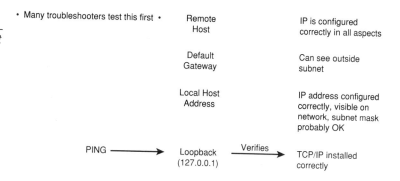

For an exercise covering this information, see end of chapter.

▶ **ARP.** ARP (Address Resolution Protocol) can be used to see the entries in the Address Resolution table, which maps network card addresses (MAC addresses) to IP addresses. You can check to see whether the IP addresses you believe should be in the table are there and whether they are mapped to the computers they should be. Usually, you do not know the MAC addresses of the hosts on your network. However, if you cannot contact a host, or if a connection is made to an unexpected host, you can check this table with the ARP command to begin isolating which host is actually assigned an IP address.

For an exercise covering this information, see end of chapter.

▶ **ROUTE.** ROUTE is a command-line utility that enables you to see the local routing table and add entries to it. Execute the ROUTE PRINT command to see the contents of the route table. Execute the ROUTE ADD command to add entries to the route table, and make these entries permanent with the -p switch. Execute the ROUTE DELETE command to remove entries from the route table. Execute the ROUTE command without any switches to see a help file describing all the switches for the command.

For an exercise covering this information, see end of chapter.

▶ **NBTSTAT.** NBTSTAT is a command-line utility that enables you to check the resolution of NetBIOS names to TCP/IP addresses. With NBTSTAT, you can check the status of current NetBIOS sessions. You can also add entries to the NetBIOS name cache from the LMHOSTS file or check your registered NetBIOS name and the NetBIOS scope assigned to your computer, if any. Execute NBTSTAT -c to display the contents of the NetBIOS name cache. Execute NBTSTAT -R to empty the NetBIOS name cache and reload it from the

LMHOSTS file. Execute NBTSTAT -S to display the current NetBIOS sessions with their status. Execute NBTSTAT /? for a complete description of the NBTSTAT command options.

For an exercise covering this information, see end of chapter.

▶ **NETSTAT.** NETSTAT is a command-line utility that enables you to check the status of current IP connections. Executing NETSTAT without switches displays protocol statistics and current TCP/IP connections. Executing NETSTAT with the -a switch (NETSTAT -a) displays all connections and listening ports, even those ports not currently involved with a connection. NETSTAT -r displays the route table along with active connections. Execute NETSTAT /? for a full description of the NETSTAT command options.

For an exercise covering this information, see end of chapter.

▶ **TRACERT.** TRACERT is a command-line utility that enables you to verify the route to a remote host. Execute TRACERT *hostname*, where *hostname* is the computer name or IP address of the computer whose route you want to trace. TRACERT will return the different IP addresses the packet was routed through to reach the final destination. The results also include the number of hops needed to reach the destination. Execute TRACERT without any options to see a help file that describes all the TRACERT switches.

▶ **NSLOOKUP.** NSLOOKUP is a command-line utility that enables you to verify entries on a DNS server. You can use NSLOOKUP in two modes: interactive and non-interactive. In interactive mode, you start a session with the DNS server in which you can make several requests. In non-interactive mode, you specify a command that makes a single query of the DNS server. If you want to make another query, you must type another non-interactive command. NSLOOKUP is described more completely in Chapter 18, "The Domain Name System."

▶ **SNMP.** The SNMP protocol enables TCP/IP to export information to troubleshooting tools like Performance Monitor or other third-party tools. By itself, SNMP does not report any troubleshooting information. If you are using tools that depend on SNMP, however, you cannot see all the information available from these tools until you install SNMP. To install SNMP, open Control Panel, Network, and then add SNMP from the Services tab.

▶ **Performance Monitor.** Performance Monitor is a Windows tool you can use to monitor TCP/IP performance on the local computer and also on the local network segment. Performance Monitor is included in the Administrative Tools menu on any Windows NT computer. You must also install SNMP to see more complete troubleshooting information for the TCP/IP protocol.

▶ **Network Monitor.** Network Monitor is a Windows tool that enables you to see network traffic that is sent or received by a Windows NT computer. Network Monitor is included with Windows NT 4.0. To install Network Monitor, open Control Panel, Network, and then add the Network Monitor Tools and Agent from the Services tab. The version of Network Monitor that comes with Windows NT 4.0 is a simple version; it only captures traffic for the local machines (incoming and outgoing traffic). Microsoft's System Management Server, a network management product, comes with a more complete version of Network Monitor that enables you to capture packets on the local machine for the entire local network segment. You can also filter out traffic that isn't important to the troubleshooting process.

Name Resolution Problems

If you have configured TCP/IP correctly and the protocol is installed and working, then the problem with connectivity is probably due to errors in resolving host names. When you test connectivity with TCP/IP addresses, you are testing a lower-level of connectivity than users generally use. When users want to connect to a network resource, such as mapping a drive to a server or connecting to a Web site, they usually refer to that server or Web site by its name rather than its TCP/IP address. In fact, users do not usually know the IP address of particular server. The name used to establish a connection must be resolved down to an IP address so that the networking software can make a connection. After you've tested the IP connectivity, the next logical step is to check the resolution of a name down to its IP address. If a name cannot be resolved to its IP address or if it is resolved to the wrong address, users will not be able to connect to the network resource with that name, even if you can connect to it using an IP address.

Two types of computer names are used when communicating on the network. A NetBIOS name is assigned to a Microsoft computer, such as a Windows NT server or a Windows 95 client. A host name is assigned to non-Microsoft computer, such as a Unix server. (Host names can also be assigned to a Windows NT server running Internet Information Server. For example, the name www.microsoft.com refers to a Web server on the Microsoft Web site. This server is running on Windows NT.) In general, when using Microsoft networking, such as connecting to a server for file sharing, print sharing, or applications, you refer to that computer by its NetBIOS name. When executing a TCP/IP-specific command, such as FTP or using a Web browser, you refer to that computer by its host name.

A NetBIOS name is resolved to a TCP/IP address in several ways. Figure 22.29 shows how NetBIOS names are resolved. The TCP/IP client initiating a session first looks in its local name cache. If the client cannot find the name in a local cache, it queries a WINS server, if configured to be a WINS client. If the WINS server cannot resolve the name, the client tries a broadcast that only reaches the local subnet, because routers, by default, are not configured to forward broadcasts. If the client cannot find the name through a broadcast, it looks for any LMHOSTS or HOSTS files, if it has been configured to do so. Finally, if the client cannot resolve a name in any other way, it queries a DNS server if it has been configured to be a DNS client. However, if the client specifies a name longer than 15 characters (the maximum length of a NetBIOS name), the client first queries DNS before trying a HOSTS file or WINS.

Host names are resolved in a similar manner. The client, however, checks sources that are used solely to resolve host names before trying sources that are using to resolve NetBIOS names. In resolving host names, the client first checks the HOSTS file, then the DNS server, if configured to be a DNS client. These two sources only resolve host names. If the client cannot resolve the name, it checks the WINS server, if configured as a WINS client, tries a broadcast, and then looks in the LMHOSTS file. The last three methods to resolve a name are used to resolve NetBIOS names, but it is possible for a host name to be listed in these sources.

Figure 22.29

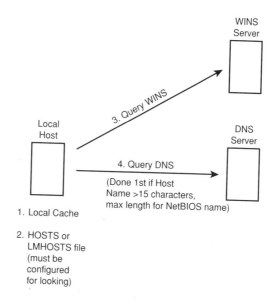

Resolving
NetBIOS names.

Several tools are available to test name resolution. They are discussed in the following sections.

Testing Name Resolution with Ping

Just as you can use Ping to verify the TCP/IP configuration, you can also use Ping to verify host name resolution. If you can successfully Ping a host name, then you have verified TCP/IP communication from the Network Interface layer of the TCP/IP architecture to the Transport layer. The layers of TCP/IP were reviewed in figure 22.1, earlier in this chapter. When you Ping a host name, a successful reply shows the IP address of the host. This shows that the name has been successfully resolved to an IP address and that you can communicate with that host.

Testing NetBIOS Name Resolution by Establishing a Session

The ultimate test of connectivity is to establish a session with another host. If you can establish a session through mapping a drive or by executing a Net Use command (which is the command-line equivalent of mapping a drive), you have made a NetBIOS connection. If you can FTP, Telnet, or establish a Web session with another host, you have made a Sockets connection. A NetBIOS connection or a Sockets connection are the two main types of connections made by a TCP/IP client.

After the drive has been mapped with Net Use, you can switch to the new drive letter, view files and directories, and do any other things that are specified in the permissions of the share mapped to the drive letter. To get more information about the syntax of the Net Use command, type **net help use** in a command prompt.

A common problem in making NetBIOS connections is that the wrong NetBIOS name is used. Verify that the destination host has the same name that you are using to make the connection. Another potential problem with the name configuration occurs when NetBIOS scope IDs are used. Only NetBIOS hosts with the same scope ID can communicate with each other. The scope ID is configured through the advanced TCP/IP parameters. Incorrect share permissions can prevent you from establishing a NetBIOS session. When you try to connect a drive to a share where you have No Access, you receive an Access Denied message. This message indicates that you can connect to the server, but your rights did not allow you to make a connection to this specific share. This type of failure has nothing to do with TCP/IP connectivity. Remember that if the administrator changes your permissions to give you access, and you want to try again, you must log out and log in again to receive a new access token with the updated permissions.

To resolve NetBIOS connectivity problems, you must know what sources are used to resolve NetBIOS names. The first place a client looks to resolve a NetBIOS name is the local cache. You can view the contents of the NetBIOS cache with the NBTSTAT command. You should verify that no incorrect entry is in the cache that maps the NetBIOS name to an incorrect IP address. If there is, however, you can remove the entry and then try to make another connection.

The next place to attempt NetBIOS name resolution is in a query to a WINS server. The client must be configured to be a WINS client. You can verify the address of the WINS server through the Advanced properties of TCP/IP or by using IPCONFIG /all. You can view the contents of the WINS database by using WINS Manager on the WINS server. Verify that the host name is in the database and, if so, make sure it is mapped to the correct IP address.

If the WINS server is configured to do a DNS lookup, you have another way to get NetBIOS resolution. The WINS server queries DNS if the WINS server cannot resolve the name from its own database. You can view the contents of the DNS database files by using DNS Manager on the DNS server or by using the NSLOOKUP utility from any client.

The client next tries a broadcast to resolve NetBIOS names, although you cannot configure what the client finds through the broadcast. The next place the client looks for NetBIOS name resolution is the LMHOSTS file. You can configure the contents of this file. The client must be configured for LMHOSTS lookup in the advanced TCP/IP configuration. Also, the LMHOSTS file must be located in the correct directory path. On an NT computer, the LMHOSTS file must be in the path <winnt root>\system32\etc.

Next, verify the entries in the LMHOSTS file. The correct host name and IP address must be entered in this file. If you have multiple entries in the file for a host name, only the first entry is used. If you added another entry for a host in the file, you must delete the other entry listed earlier in the file so that it will not be used.

Domain names are another source of potential problems with LMHOSTS files. The domain name must be registered with the IP address of the Primary Domain Controller (PDC) and #DOM (a switch that registers the server as a domain controller) on the same line. This entry is necessary to log on to the domain as well as to see the domain in a browse list.

Another problem with LMHOSTS files doesn't prevent connectivity, but it can greatly delay it. If you have #INCLUDE statements at the top of the LMHOSTS file, the files specified by #INCLUDE are included first before any other entries lower in the LMHOSTS file are searched. You can speed connections to hosts entered in the LMHOSTS file by moving the #INCLUDE entries to the bottom of the LMHOSTS file.

Testing TCP Name Resolution by Establishing a Session

Typical TCP/IP connections from a Microsoft client, such as FTP or Telnet, use Windows Sockets. To test connectivity at this level, try establishing an FTP or Telnet session or try to connect to a Web server. When you successfully connect to a Web server, you see the site's Web page, and you can navigate through the page. When the connection fails, you receive a message on your Internet browser that the connection failed.

To resolve problems with a Windows Sockets connection, you must understand how a client resolves TCP host names. The first place a client looks to resolve a host name is the local host name. You can see what TCP/IP thinks is the local host name by executing the Hostname command. Verify that if the local host is what you expect it to be. You can modify the host name in the DNS tab of the TCP/IP properties.

The next place the client looks is in a HOSTS file. This file must be located in the path <winnt root>\system32\etc. Verify that any entry in the file for the host is correct, with the correct host name and IP address. If multiple entries for the same host name are in the file, only the first name is used. The HOSTS file can also have links to HOSTS files on other servers. If links are specified in the local HOSTS file, you should make sure entries in the other HOSTS files are also correct.

The final place a client can use for host name resolution is a DNS server. The client must be configured to use DNS in the advanced properties of TCP/IP. The DNS server must have a zone file corresponding to the domain name specified in the host name, or it must be able to query another DNS server that can resolve the name. DNS is discussed in detail in Chapter 18.

Other Symptoms of TCP/IP Configuration Problems

Other symptoms can indicate problems with TCP/IP connectivity or its configuration.

Default Gateway Does Not Belong to Configured Interfaces

When you configure TCP/IP manually, you can receive the message `The Default Gateway does not belong to configured interfaces`. This message occurs when the address of the default gateway cannot logically belong to the same subnet as the host IP address. This can happen because the subnet mask is wrong, the default gateway address is wrong, or the local host address is wrong.

The TCP/IP Host Doesn't Respond

If a connection to a remote TCP/IP host is hung, you can check the status of the connection with the NETSTAT -a command. This command shows all the connections established with TCP. Successful connections should have 0 bytes in the send and receive queues. If there are bytes in the queues, then there are problems with the connection. If the connection appears to be hung but there aren't any bytes in the queues, there is probably a delay in the connection.

The Connection Is Made to the Wrong Host

You've checked everything in the IP configuration on the host and the client, yet the client connects to the wrong host. (This can happen when you establish a session using an IP address rather than a host name, such as when using Telnet.) This symptom can occur when duplicate IP addresses are on the network. You have to find the computer with the duplicate address and modify the address so it is unique. With duplicate addresses, connections are inconsistent—clients sometimes connect to one host, sometimes to another.

Error 53 Is Returned When Trying to Make a NetBIOS Session

You are trying to establish a NetBIOS session, such as mapping a drive by using the Net Use command, but Error 53 is returned. This happens because the computer name cannot be found on the network. In other words, TCP/IP can't find a computer name to resolve to an IP address. You can use the normal NetBIOS host resolution troubleshooting to resolve this problem. If the host names are correct, it's possible you are using NetBIOS scopes. If NetBIOS scopes are configured (non-blank), only hosts with the same scope ID can communicate with each other.

An FTP Server Does Not Seem to Work

FTP must be installed correctly before any clients can make connections to the server. Just as you can ping the loopback address to test a TCP/IP installation, you can also FTP the loopback address on the FTP server to test the FTP installation.

Exercises

Exercise 22.1: Correcting a Network Configuration Error

Use this exercise to see the effects that an improperly configured network card has on other networking services and protocols. Before starting, make sure you have installed Windows NT Server with a computer that has a network adapter card and that TCP/IP has been installed.

1. Clear the System Log in Event Viewer.

2. From the desktop, right-click Network Neighborhood and choose Properties from the resulting menu.

3. From the Network Properties dialog box, select the Adapters tab.

4. Select your adapter card from the list and choose Properties.

5. Change the IRQ of your adapter card to an incorrect setting.

6. Close this dialog box and choose to reboot your computer when prompted.

7. When your computer reboots, note the message received after the Logon prompt appears. The message should indicate A Dependency Service Failed to Start.

8. Log on and open Event Viewer.

9. Note the error message generated from the adapter card. Note the other error messages generated after the adapter card error.

10. Clear the System Log in Event Viewer.

11. From the command prompt, type **ping 127.0.0.1**. This Ping fails because TCP/IP doesn't start if the adapter doesn't start.

12. From the Network Properties dialog box, change the IRQ of your adapter card back to its proper setting and reboot.

continues

Exercise 22.1: Continued
---

13. Log on and check the System Log. There should be no adapter card errors or errors from networking services.

14. From the command prompt, type **ping 127.0.0.1**. This Ping succeeds because TCP/IP is started now.

Exercise 22.2: Using Ping to Test an IP Configuration

This exercise uses Ping to verify a TCP/IP installation and configuration. You should have installed Windows NT Server and TCP/IP.

1. From the desktop, right-click on Network Neighborhood and choose Properties from the resulting menu.

2. From the Bindings tab, expand all the networking services.

3. Select TCP/IP and choose Disable.

4. Repeat step 3 until you have disabled TCP/IP for all the listed networking services.

5. Close the dialog box and when prompted choose to reboot your computer.

6. When the computer reboots, log in.

7. From a command prompt, type **ping 127.0.0.1**. This Ping works because TCP/IP is installed.

8. From a command prompt, type **ping x.x.x.x**, where x.x.x.x is your default gateway address. This Ping fails because you have disabled TCP/IP from all the networking services. There isn't a way for TCP/IP packets to be sent on the network.

9. From the Bindings tab in Network Properties, enable TCP/IP for all the networking services.

10. Close the dialog box and when prompted, choose to reboot your computer.

11. When the computer reboots, log in.

12. From a command prompt, Ping your default gateway. The Ping works this time because a path now exists by which TCP/IP communications can reach the network.

Exercise 22.3:   Using ARP to Examine the ARP Cache and Add Entries

---

This exercise uses the ARP command to examine and modify the ARP cache.

1. From a command prompt, type **arp -g**. The contents of the ARP cache appear.

2. From a command prompt, type **arp -s 143.42.16.9 0800026c139f**. This adds a static entry to the ARP cache.

3. From a command prompt, type **arp -g** to view the revised contents of the ARP cache.

4. From a command prompt, type **arp -d 143.42.16.9**. This removes the static entry you added in step 2.

5. From a command prompt, type **arp /?** to see all the switches for the ARP command.

Exercise 22.4:   Using the Route Command to View the Routing Table and Add Entries

---

This exercise is used to display the contents of the local route table and to see how this table lists the default gateway address. You should have installed TCP/IP and have a default gateway address configured.

1. From a command prompt, type **route -p print**. This displays the local route table. Note the address of your client as well as the address of the default gateway in the route table.

2. Open Control Panel, Network, and then select the Protocols tab.

3. Open the TCP/IP Properties dialog box.

4. Delete the Default Gateway address.

5. Choose Apply and close the dialog box.

6. From a command prompt, type **route -p print**. Note the default gateway address is missing from the table.

continues

Exercise 22.4: Continued

7. Follow steps 2–5 to restore the default gateway address.

8. From a command prompt, type **route** /? to see all the switches available with the Route command.

Exercise 22.5: Using NBTSTAT to View the Local NetBIOS Name Cache and Add Entries to the Cache from an LMHOSTS File

Exercise 22.5 examines the contents of the local NetBIOS name cache and loads entries into the cache from an LMHOSTS file. You should have installed TCP/IP and have another Windows client with TCP/IP installed and fire sharing enabled.

1. Use Notepad to open the file \WINNT\SYSTEM32\DRIVERS\ETC\LMHOSTS.SAM.

2. Add an entry to the bottom of the file for the other Windows client, specifying the NetBIOS name and the IP address of the Windows client. Make sure there is not a comment (#) in front of this line.

3. Save the file in the same directory as LMHOSTS (without an extension).

4. From a command prompt on your NT computer, type **nbtstat -c**. This displays the local cache.

5. From a command prompt, **type nbtstat -R**. This purges the cache and loads the contents of the LMHOSTS file into the local cache.

6. From a command prompt, type **nbtstat -c** to display the new contents of the local cache.

7. Using Windows NT Explorer, map a network drive to the other Windows client. The local cache was used to resolve the NetBIOS name for this connection.

8. From a command prompt, type **nbtstat** /? to see all the switches available with the NBTSTAT command.

Exercise 22.6: Using NETSTAT to Examine TCP/IP Connections

You can perform this exercise to see the information returned by the Netstat command. You should have installed TCP/IP and have access to other TCP/IP servers, such as Internet access.

1. Connect to another TCP/IP server through a Web browser or by mapping a network drive.

2. From a command prompt, type **netstat**. This displays the statistics about your current connections.

3. From a command prompt, type **netstat -a**. Note that this command also displays any listening ports.

4. From a command prompt, type **netstat -r**. Note that this command also displays the route table in addition to the connection information.

5. From a command prompt, type **netstat /?** to display all the switches available for the NETSTAT command.

Exercise 22.7: Using TRACERT to Display the Path Used to Establish a TCP/IP Connection

Exercise 22.7 displays the route used to establish a TCP/IP connection. You should have installed TCP/IP and have access to the Internet.

1. Open your Web browser and connect to www.microsoft.com.

2. From a command prompt, type **tracert www.microsoft.com**. Note the route used to connect to the Microsoft Web site and the number of hops used for the connection.

3. Connect to www.microsoft.com/train_cert.

4. From a command prompt, type **tracert www.microsoft.com/train_cert**. See if the path is the same as that used for the prior connection.

continues

5. Connect to `home.microsoft.com`.

6. From a command prompt, type **tracert**. See if the path is different than connecting to `www.microsoft.com`.

7. Try connecting to other Web sites and viewing the path to these sites.

8. Reconnect to some of the same sites and view the path with TRACERT. Is the path the same each time you connect?

Review Questions

1. How can you see the address of the DHCP server from which a client received its IP address?

   A. Advanced properties of TCP/IP

   B. Using IPCONFIG /all

   C. Using DHCPINFO

   D. Pinging DHCP

2. Which should you do to verify that your router is configured correctly?

   A. Ping a remote host

   B. Ping 127.0.0.1

   C. Execute the ROUTE command

   D. Execute IPCONFIG /all

3. Your IP address is 136.193.5.1, your subnet mask is 255.255.240.0, and you are trying to Ping a host with the command "ping 136.193.2.23". The Ping doesn't work. What could cause the Ping to fail?

   A. The default gateway is not configured correctly.

   B. The subnet mask interprets the IP address as being on another subnet and the packet is routed.

   C. The subnet mask interprets the address as being on the local subnet and the packet is not routed.

   D. You must Ping the local host first.

4. You are using Performance Monitor but very few TCP/IP statistics are available. How can you increase the number of TCP/IP objects and counters to monitor?

   A. Install a promiscuous mode adapter card.

   B. Configure the correct default gateway in Performance Monitor.

    C. Bind TCP/IP to the Monitor service.

    D. Install the SNMP service.

5. TCP/IP is not working. You recall that when Windows NT first booted the message `A Dependency Service Failed to Start` appeared. What is a possible cause of the problem?

    A. The SNMP service is not installed.

    B. The network card is not configured correctly.

    C. The secondary WINS server is down.

    D. The PDC of your domain is down.

6. You can Ping a remote host's IP address, but you cannot connect to a share on that host. What is a possible cause of this problem?

    A. The share must be configured to enable anonymous connections.

    B. The Host Name Resolution Protocol must be installed.

    C. The LMHOSTS file does not have any entry for this server.

    D. The client has not been configured to use DHCP.

7. You made a mistake in configuring an IP address and typed the client's address as 96.82.49.208 rather than 196.82.49.208. What is the most likely result of this configuration error?

    A. The client can communicate only with hosts having the network address 96.x.x.x.

    B. The client cannot communicate with hosts beyond the local subnet.

    C. The client cannot communicate with hosts on the local subnet.

    D. The client cannot communicate with any hosts.

8. You are using NWLink and TCP/IP. How can you reduce the time that is needed to establish a TCP/IP session with another host?

   A. Move TCP/IP to the top of the bindings for the Workstation service.

   B. Configure the default gateway address to point to a faster router.

   C. Decrease the TTL for WINS registrations.

   D. Use SNMP to tune the TCP/IP cache size.

9. A DHCP client has failed to lease an IP address. What is the best way to have the client try again to get a lease?

   A. Issue a REQUEST command to the DHCP server.

   B. Reserve an address for the client on the DHCP server.

   C. Use IPCONFIG /release, then IPCONFIG /renew.

   D. Reboot the client.

10. What is the effect if you do not configure a router address on a TCP/IP client?

    A. You cannot communicate with any other TCP/IP hosts.

    B. You can only communicate with hosts connected to the default gateway.

    C. You can only communicate with hosts on the local subnet.

    D. TCP/IP doesn't initialize.

11. You have several entries for a host name in an LMHOSTS file. Which entry is used to resolve the host name to an IP address?

    A. The entry with the most current time stamp

    B. The first entry in the file

    C. The last entry in the file

    D. The entry with the largest IP address

12. A DHCP client has been configured to use the wrong DNS server. How can you correct the problem?

    A. Change the scope options on DHCP, then renew the lease on the client.

    B. Use IPCONFIG /update:DNS to make the change.

    C. Enter the address of the DNS server in the advanced properties of TCP/IP.

    D. Add an entry for the DHCP client on the other DNS server.

13. A TCP/IP client had a drive mapped to an NT server. You have just changed the IP address of the server and rebooted. Now the client can't connect to the new server, even though the server is configured to be a WINS client. What is the most likely cause of this problem?

    A. The WINS server hasn't copied the new registration to all its clients.

    B. The client has the old IP address cached.

    C. The LMHOSTS file on the NT Server needs to be updated.

    D. The DNS server needs to be updated.

14. On an NT computer, where does TCP/IP display its error messages?

    A. In the TCP/IP log file

    B. In the SNMP log file

    C. In the System Log

    D. In the TCP.ERR file

15. How can you test the installation of an FTP server?

    A. Ping the FTP loopback address.

    B. Ping another FTP server.

    C. FTP another server.

    D. FTP the loopback address.

Review Answers

1. B

2. A

3. C

4. D

5. B

6. C

7. D

8. A

9. C

10. C

11. B

12. A

13. B

14. C

15. D

Answers to the Test Yourself Questions at Beginning of Chapter

1. Pinging the loopback address 127.0.0.1 verifies that TCP/IP is installed correctly. Pinging the local host address verifies that the host has a network connection and the TCP/IP stack works all the way down to the Network Interface layer. Pinging the default gateway confirms that packets can be routed to the router. Pinging a remote host verifies that the client can communicate with any client on the network.

2. Ping a remote host. If the client can communicate with a remote host, it proves that the stack is installed and configured correctly and that the router is working properly.

3. Use the IPCONFIG /all command in a command prompt. If the client received an address, the address along with the lease life and the address of the DHCP server that leased the address is listed. If the client did not acquire an address, the IP address of 0.0.0.0 is specified for the client. You can use the IPCONFIG /release command to free up any IP leases and then use the IPCONFIG /renew command to force the client to try to get an IP address.

4. Pinging the server proves you have connectivity at the IP level. When you connect to a share on the server, you are establishing a NetBIOS session with the server. NetBIOS names can be resolved by the client requesting the connections by looking in the local NetBIOS cache, looking in an LMHOSTS file if the client is configured for LMHOSTS lookup, and querying a WINS server. You can check each of these sources of name resolution for possible conflicts or incorrect entries.

5. The client can communicate with any local hosts, because those packets don't need to be routed. However, whenever the client tries to communicate with a remote host, the packet isn't routed because the address specified on the client for the default gateway isn't correct.

6. TCP/IP doesn't work, because it depends on other networking services that don't start if the adapter card isn't properly configured. You might see the `Dependency Service Failed to Start` message when NT first boots. This indicates networking services that depend on the adapter card are failing because the adapter card driver can't start based on its current configuration. After logging on, you might also see messages when you check the System Log of Event Viewer. If the messages are written to the event log, you will see an error message indicating the adapter card failed followed by error messages from other networking services that also failed to start. You might, however, see a failure of network connections as the only visible symptom of this problem.

7. One solution is to Ping the host name rather than the IP address of the host. However, the ultimate test of name resolution is to connect to the host with FTP, Telnet, or through a Web browser. If you can connect, then the name is being resolved properly and you have total connectivity with the host.

TCP/IP and Remote Access Service

This chapter helps you to prepare for the exam by covering the following objective:

 Objective

▶ Configure a RAS server and dial-up networking for use on a TCP/IP network

Test Yourself! Before reading this chapter, test yourself to determine how much study time you will need to devote to this section.

1. What service does RAS provide?

2. How many inbound RAS connections can Windows NT Workstation handle? Windows NT Server?

3. What dial-in protocols does Windows NT support?

4. When a user dials in, can she talk just to the system that she dials into?

5. What is multilink?

6. What is callback security, and what configurations can you have?

7. What are the three options that can be set for Port Usage?

8. What network protocols will the RAS server support?

9. Can a user who dials in with NetBEUI use the services of a remote server that communicates with TCP/IP?

10. What is the purpose of the Telephony API?

Answers are located at the end of the chapter.

Overview of RAS

RAS essentially enables users to connect to your network and act as if they are directly connected to it. RAS has two main components: the server (Remote Access Service) and the client (Dial Up Networking.) The RAS server can be Windows NT Server, Workstation, or Windows 95 (either with Service Pack 1 or OEM Service Release 2) and will enable users to connect to the network from a remote location. The Microsoft RAS server always uses the PPP (Point to Point Protocol) when users are dialing in to the network as the line protocol.

In addition to connecting to a Microsoft RAS server, Windows Dial-Up Networking can connect with other forms of RAS (other dial-in servers such as Unix terminal servers) by using either SLIP (Serial Line Internet Protocol) or PPP. All that is required is a communications device.

PPP versus SLIP

When clients connect to a server by using a modem, they must do so through something other than the frames that normally traverse a network (such as IEEE802.3 discussed in Chapter 9). Some other transport method is needed. In the case of dial-up servers (or terminal servers), two line protocols are popular. Serial Line Internet Protocol, or SLIP, is used frequently in Unix implementations. SLIP is the older of the two line protocols and is geared directly for TCP/IP communications. Windows NT can use the services of a SLIP server. However, it does not provide a SLIP server. Microsoft's RAS server uses Point to Point Protocol (PPP) because SLIP requires a static IP address and does not provide facility for secured logon (passwords are sent as clear text).

PPP was developed as a replacement for SLIP and provides several different advantages over the earlier protocol. PPP can automatically provide the client computer with an IP address and other configurations. It provides a secure logon and has the capability to transport protocols other than TCP/IP (such as AppleTalk, IPX, and NetBEUI.)

PPP has two important extensions: Multilink Protocol (MP) and Point to Point Tunneling Protocol (PPTP). Windows NT supports both of these extensions to the original PPP.

Multilink Protocol enables a client station to use more than one physical connection to connect to a remote server. This capability provides better throughput over standard modems. You will, however, need multiple phone lines and modems to enable this protocol. This setup can be an easy interim solution if you need to temporarily connect to offices and don't have the time or budget to set up a leased line or other similar connection.

Point to Point Tunneling Protocol facilitates secure connections across the Internet. By using PPTP, users can connect to any Internet Service Provider (ISP) and can use the ISP's network as a gateway to connect to the office network. During the session initialization, the client and server negotiate a 40-bit session key. This key can be used to encrypt all packets that will be sent back and forth over the Internet. The packets are encapsulated into PPP packets as the data.

Modems

Modems have been around for years and provide a cheap and relatively reliable method of communications over the Public Switched Telephone Network (PSTN). Installing a modem in a computer is a straightforward process. This section covers the configuring, testing, and troubleshooting of modems.

There are two main types of modems: internal and external. Internal modems are slightly cheaper, but you must open the computer to install it, and they require a free interrupt (IRQ). If you elect to go with an external modem, you should check that you have an available communications (COM) port that will be able to handle the speed of the modem.

Ports

Whether you have an internal or external modem, you will need to install the modem as a communications port. Normally, this is no problem; however, there are cases (most notably with internal modems) in which you will need to change the settings for the port. This also can cause problems with an external modem. If you cannot talk to the modem, you should check the port settings.

To check the port settings, open the Control Panel (Start, Settings, Control Panel) and double-click on the Ports Icon. The Ports dialog box appears (see fig. 23.1).

Figure 23.1

The Ports dialog box.

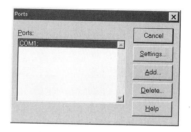

Select the port whose settings you want to check and click Settings. Another dialog box appears, showing you the settings for the port (see fig. 23.2).

Figure 23.2

The Settings for COM1 are shown in this dialog box.

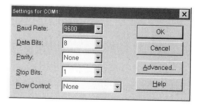

Five settings are available, but these are general settings that only deal with applications that don't set these parameters. The following list provides a description of the parameters.

▶ **Baud Rate.** The rate at which the data will flow. Serial communications move your data one bit at a time. In addition, for every byte that is sent there are (normally) 4 bits of overhead. To find the transfer rate in bytes, therefore, divide the baud rate number by 12.

▶ **Data Bits**. Not all systems use 8 bits to store one character. Some only use seven. The data bits setting allows the computer to adjust the number of bits used in the transfer.

▶ **Parity.** Parity is used to verify that information that is being transferred is getting across the line successfully. The parity can be Even, Odd, Mark, or Space, or you can set No Parity, which is what is normally used.

▶ **Stop Bits.** In some systems stop bits are used to mark the end of the transmission.

▶ **Flow Control.** This option can be set to Xon/Xoff, Hardware or None. Flow Control, as the name implies, is used to control the movement of the data between the modem and your computer. Hardware flow control uses Request to Send (RTS) and Clear to Send (CTS). The system sends a signal through the RTS wire in the cable telling the modem it wants to send. When the modem has finished transmitting what is in its buffer and signals that it has space, it will signal the computer that it can send the data using the CTS wire. Xon/Xoff is a software form of flow control where the modem sends Xon (ASCII character 17) when it is ready for data from the computer and Xoff (ASCII character 19) when it has too much data (this type of flow control does not work well with binary transfers because the Xon and Xoff characters can be part of a file).

In most cases, you can ignore these settings. They will be set and reset by the application that you will use. However, if you click the Advanced button (see fig. 23.3), you will find some settings that you do need to be aware of.

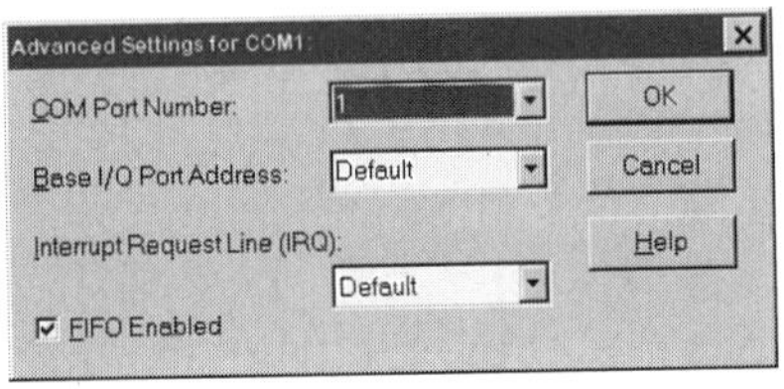

Figure 23.3

The Advanced Settings for COM1.

Advanced Settings for COM1

COM Port Number:
Base I/O Port Address: Default
Interrupt Request Line (IRQ): Default
☑ FIFO Enabled

OK
Cancel
Help

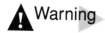 **Warning**

> If you make changes in this dialog box, the system will no longer be a standard system. Many applications can be affected if you make changes here.

The options that you can set here affect all applications that use the communications port. The following list provides an overview of the options that you can set.

- ▶ **COM Port Number.** Here you will select the port that you want to configure.

- ▶ **Base I/O Port Address.** When information is received from a hardware (physical) device, the information is placed in RAM by the BIOS. This setting changes where in RAM you will place the information. Unless your hardware requires a different address, do not change this.

- ▶ **Interrupt Request Line (IRQ).** After the BIOS places the information in RAM, it alerts the CPU to the presence of the data by using a hardware interrupt. Interrupts are a prime source for conflicts and one of the main causes of system failures. As was stated before, unless your hardware requires it, do not change this option.

- ▶ **FIFO Enabled.** This enables the on-chip buffering available in 16550 UARTs. Note that on some of the older revisions of the 16550, there were problems with random data loss when using FIFO. If you are experiencing unexplained problems, try disabling FIFO. With FIFO enabled, there can be a slight increase in throughput.

When you are attempting to troubleshoot a serial problem, always check that these settings are correct. Making sure that the port options are correct allows you to communicate with the modem smoothly.

Configuring Modems

Users can connect to the office network or the Internet in many ways. The most common method is to use a modem. This section deals with installing and troubleshooting modems.

Installing a Modem

Installing a modem is simple in Windows NT. After the hardware is connected, go to the Control Panel and double-click the Modems icon. If there is no modem installed, the modem installer will start automatically (see fig. 23.4). This wizard steps you through the installation of the modem. If you already have a modem, you will need to click Add.

Figure 23.4

The Install New Modem wizard.

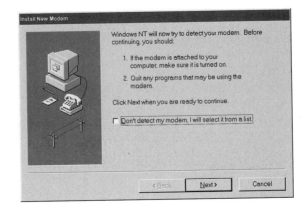

If you have already used the installer once and it was unable to detect the modem, you probably have one of two problems. Either the modem cannot be detected and you will have to install it manually, or the system can't see the modem, in which case you should check the port. If you need to install the modem manually, check the box, "Don't detect my modem; I will select it from a list." This displays a screen that enables you to select the modem (see fig. 23.5.)

Figure 23.5

The Install New Modem dialog box that lists available modems.

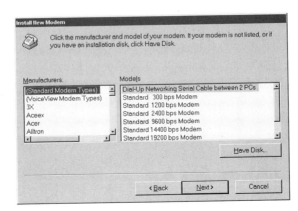

After you have the modem installed, you can check your modem properties by using the Modems icon in the Control Panel. When you open the icon, you will see a dialog box that lists all of the available modems (see fig. 23.6).

Figure 23.6

The Modems Properties dialog box, which, in this case, lists only one modem.

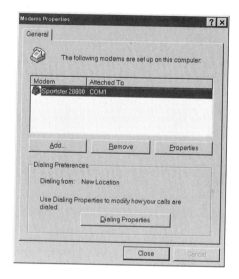

From here you will be able to check and set the properties for the modems that are installed in the computer. Several different options are of interest. Select Modem, Properties to bring up the General properties for the modem (see fig. 23.7).

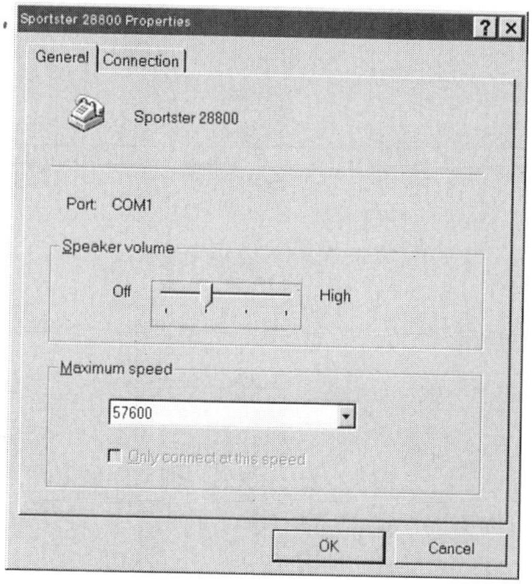

Figure 23.7

The General Properties tab for a modem.

You need to set only a couple of settings on the General tab. The following list provides the properties and what you should check for.

▶ **Port.** Displays the port that the modem was installed on. You should check the port if the hardware has been changed and the port settings if the modem is not working.

▶ **Speaker Volume.** Determines the volume of the speaker during the connection phase. Turned up the volume enough to allow you to verify that you are getting dial tone and that the other end is in fact a modem.

▶ **Maximum Speed.** Sets the fastest rate that the system will attempt to communicate with the modem. If this is set to high, some modems will not be able to respond to the system. If this is the case, lower the rate.

▶ **Only connect at this speed.** Instruct the modem that it must connect to the remote site at the same speed you set for communications with the modem. If the other site is unable to support this speed, you will not be able to communicate.

The other tab in the modem properties dialog box is the Connection tab (see fig. 23.8), which deals with the way that the modem connects. There are a couple of settings you can check when attempting to troubleshoot modems.

Figure 23.8

The Connection tab in the Modem Properties dialog box.

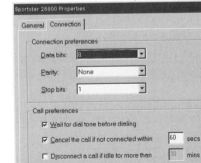

The Connection tab lets you control two properties: the Connection preferences and the Call preferences. The Connection preferences are the communications settings (which were discussed previously in the "Ports" section). These settings override the port settings. The three items from the Call preferences are listed below.

- ▶ **Wait for tone before dialing.** Normally, this should be selected; however, some phone systems in the world still do not have a dial tone. Make sure that this is set correctly for your area.

- ▶ **Cancel the call if not connected within.** This option sets the maximum amount of time that it will take for the call to be established. If line conditions are very bad, you may have to bump up this number to allow the modem more time to establish a connection and negotiate the line speed that will be used.

- ▶ **Disconnect a call if idle for more than.** This option enables you to set the maximum amount of time that a call can sit idle. Windows NT 4 provides an autodial service that automatically calls back a server when you get disconnected and then attempts to use a network service. This feature reduces the amount of time a user can tie up a line and can prevent massive long-distance charges. However, users need to be made aware of the time limit. If they are required to enter information for a terminal login, they should be told because the terminal screen will appear unexpectedly when the system tries to autoconnect.

    Also, if a user is not aware and is using an ISP for e-mail, she needs to be told that setting the e-mail program to check for new mail at period intervals will cause the system to automatically dial the server and check—possibly using up the allowed number of hours with their ISP.

The final thing to check when doing modem configurations and troubleshooting is the Advanced Connection information (see fig. 23.9). These settings can adversely affect communications.

Figure 23.9

The Advanced Connection Settings dialog box.

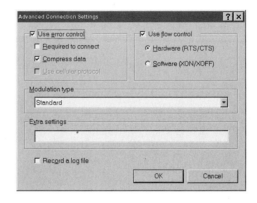

You will want to verify a few options in the advanced modem options. The following list describes the different options and things that you should look for.

▶ **Use Error control.** This turns on or off some common settings that affect the way the system will deal with the modem. The specific options are listed here:

   ▶ **Required to connect.** This forces the modem to establish that an error correcting protocol (such as MNP class 5) be used before the connection is established. Do not use it as the default. If the modem on the other end of the connection does not support the same class of error detection, the connection will fail.

   ▶ **Compress data.** This tells the modem to use data compression. Microsoft RAS automatically implements software compression between the client and workstation if both are Microsoft. Turn on this option only if you are talking to a non-Microsoft server; otherwise, the modem will try to compress data that is already compressed.

   ▶ **Use cellular protocol.** Lets the system know that the modem you are using is a cellular modem.

▶ **User flow control.** This overrides the flow control setting for the port. Both types of flow control are available. In most cases, you should use hardware flow control. The use of flow control enables you to set the speed of the transmission between the computer and the modem. The choices are Xon/Xoff and hardware.

▶ **Modulation Type.** This enables users to set the type of frequency modulation for the modem to that of the phone system they are using. The modulation is either standard or Bell and deals with the sound frequency that is used for the send and receive channels for the communicating hosts.

▶ **Extra settings.** This enables you to enter extra modem initialization strings that you want to have sent to the modem whenever a call is placed.

▶ **Record a log file.** This probably is the most important setting from the perspective of troubleshooting. It enables you to record a file that lets you see the communications that took place between the modem and the computer during the connection phase of the communications. An example of the log is shown in figure 23.10.

Figure 23.10

The modem log as shown in Notepad.

```
ModemLog_Sportster 28800 - Notepad                                    _ □ ×
File  Edit  Search  Help
07-25-1997 09:59:53.203 - Recv: <cr><lf>OK<cr><lf>
07-25-1997 09:59:53.203 - Interpreted response: OK
07-25-1997 09:59:53.203 - Send: ATS7=60S19=0L0M1&M4&K1&H1&R2&I0B0X4<cr>
07-25-1997 09:59:53.437 - Recv: <cr><lf>OK<cr><lf>
07-25-1997 09:59:53.437 - Interpreted response: OK
07-25-1997 09:59:53.437 - Waiting for a call.
07-25-1997 09:59:53.437 - Send: ATS0=0<cr>
07-25-1997 09:59:53.718 - 57600,N,8,1
07-25-1997 09:59:53.953 - Initializing modem.
07-25-1997 09:59:53.953 - Send: ATE0Q0U1<cr>
07-25-1997 09:59:54.234 - Recv: <cr><lf>OK<cr><lf>
07-25-1997 09:59:54.234 - Interpreted response: OK
07-25-1997 09:59:54.234 - Send: AT &F1 E0 U1 &C1 &D2 Q0 S0=0 &B1 &A3<cr>
07-25-1997 09:59:54.453 - Recv: <cr><lf>OK<cr><lf>
07-25-1997 09:59:54.453 - Interpreted response: OK
07-25-1997 09:59:54.453 - Send: ATS7=55S19=0L0M1&M4&K1&H1&R2&I0B0X4<cr>
07-25-1997 09:59:54.625 - Recv: <cr><lf>OK<cr><lf>
07-25-1997 09:59:54.625 - Interpreted response: OK
07-25-1997 09:59:54.625 - Dialing.
07-25-1997 09:59:54.625 - Send: ATDT#######<cr>
07-25-1997 10:00:11.781 - Recv: <cr><lf>CONNECT 28800/ARQ/U34/LAPM/U42BIS<cr
07-25-1997 10:00:11.781 - Interpreted response: Connect
07-25-1997 10:00:11.781 - Connection established at 28800bps.
07-25-1997 10:00:11.781 - Error-control on.
```

Note

You might notice in figure 23.10 that the phone number is not shown as the modem called it. This provides added security.

Dialing Properties

From the Modem Properties dialog box (refer to fig. 23.6), you can also click the Dialing Properties button. You can the config- ure the system so that it knows where you are dialing from. This information is used in conjunction with Dial-Up Networking to allow the system to determine whether your call is long distance, if it should use a calling card, how to disable the call waiting feature, and so on.

When you click the Dialing Properties dialog box, the dialog box shown in figure 23.11 appears. You may create a single location or multiple locations.

Figure 23.11

The Dialing Prop-erties dialog box.

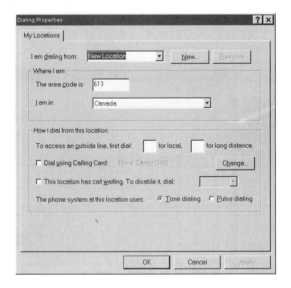

Several different items are available, and if this information is not set correctly, the client computer may attempt to connect to a local server as a long-distance call (or vice versa). The following list describes the entries that you can make:

▶ **I am dialing from.** The name of the location. To create a new entry, click the New button and enter a name in the text box. The user will need to know which entry to use when dialing.

▶ **The area code is.** The computer uses this information to determine whether it is required to dial the number as a long distance or as a local number.

- ▶ **I am in.** Sets the country code for dialing purposes so the system can connect to international numbers.

- ▶ **To access an outside line, first dial.** Set the access code for dialing out from a location. There is an entry for local calls and one for long distance.

- ▶ **Dial using Calling Card.** Enables you to have the computer enter the calling card information to make the connection with the remote host. Click the Change button to review or change calling card information.

- ▶ **This location has call waiting.** The call waiting tone often causes a connection to be dropped. You can enter the information here to disable call waiting for the location that you are dialing from.

- ▶ **The phone system at this location uses.** Enables you to select whether the system that you are calling from will use tone or pulse dialing.

If there are problems trying to connect, you should always verify the information in the Dialing Properties.

Other Communications Technologies

As stated previously, you will be able to connect to the Windows NT server in different ways. There are two principal methods by which you will be able to connect: ISDN (Integrated Services Digital Network) and X.25 (which is a wide-area networking standard.)

ISDN

One of the most common choices for connecting remote sites or even for individuals or small organizations to connect to the Internet, ISDN is becoming a very common method of communications.

Whereas a standard phone line can handle transmission speeds of up to 9,600 bits per second (compression makes up the rest of the transmission speed in most modems, such as those that transfer data at 33.6 Kbps), ISDN transmits at speeds of 64 or 128 kilobits per second, depending on whether it is one or two channels.

ISDN is a point-to-point communications technology, and special equipment must be installed at both the server and the remote site. You will need to install an ISDN card, which acts as a network card, in place of a modem in both computers. As you may have guessed by now, ISDN connections are more expensive than modems. However, if there is a requirement for higher speed, the cost will most likely be justified. Be aware, though, that in some parts of the world, this is a metered service—the more you use, the more you pay.

X.25

The X.25 protocol is not an actual device, but rather a standard for connections. It is packet-switching communication protocol that was designed for WAN connectivity.

RAS supports X.25 connections using Packet Assemblers/ Disassemblers (PADs) and X.25 smart cards. These are installed as a network card, just like with ISDN.

Dial-In Permissions

As with all other aspects of Windows NT, security is built into the RAS Server. At a minimum, a user will require an account in Windows NT, and that account will need to have dial-in permissions set.

You can grant users dial-in permission by using the User Manager (or User Manager for Domains) or through the Remote Access Admin program. If you are having problems connecting to the RAS server, this is one of the first things to check. Following are the steps to set or check dial-in permissions.

1. Open the User Manager (Start, Programs, Administrative Tools, User Manager.)

2. Select the account that you are using and choose User, Properties. You will see the User Properties dialog box, like the one shown in figure 23.12.

Figure 23.12

*The User Proper-
ties dialog box.*

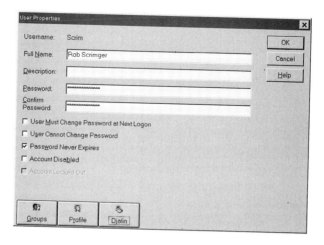

3. Click the Dial in button. The Dialin Information dialog box
   appears (see fig. 23.13).

Figure 23.13

*The Dialin Infor-
mation dialog
box.*

4. Check the "Grant dialin permission to user" box to allow the
   user to dial in.

You can also check the permissions from the Remote Access Admin utility. The following list provides the steps to do this.

1. Start the Remote Access Admin (Start, Programs, Administrative tools, RAS Admin.)

2. From the menu choose Users, Permissions.

3. In the Permissions dialog box, select the user and ensure
   that Dialin permission is granted (see fig. 23.14).

Figure 23.14

Dialin permission can be set in the Remote Access Admin.

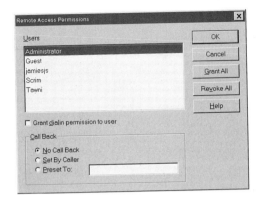

Callback Security

You probably noticed in both of the methods that there was a setting for Call Back. Call Back means that the server will do just that, call the user back. You have three options:

▶ **No Call Back.** This is the default and means that the Call Back feature is disabled.

▶ **Set By Caller.** By using this option, the user can set the number that should be used when the server calls back, which is useful if you have many users who travel and want to centralize long distance.

▶ **Preset To.** This enhances the security of the network by forcing the user to call from a specific phone number. If this is set, the user may call only from that one location.

PPP Problems

As was mentioned previously, Windows NT acts as a PPP server, which means that the client station and the server undergo a negotiation during the initial phase of the call.

During the negotiation, the client and server decide on the protocol to be used and the parameters for the protocol. If there are problems connecting, you may want to set up PPP logging to actually watch the negotiation between the server and client.

This is set up on the server by changing the Logging option under the following:

```
HKEY_LOCAL_MACHINE\SYSTEM\CurrentControlSet\Services\RASMAN\
PPP\Parameters
```

The log file will be in the system32\RAS directory and, like the modem log, can be viewed by using any text editor.

Some of the problems that you may encounter are given in the following list.

▶ You must ensure that the protocol that you are requesting from the RAS client is available on the RAS server. There must be at least one common protocol or the connection will fail.

▶ If you are using NetBEUI, ensure that the name you are using on the RAS client is not in use on the network that you are attempting to connect to.

▶ If you are attempting to connect by using TCP/IP, then the RAS server must be configured to provide you with an address.

Dial-Up Networking

 Objective

This section steps through the configuration of the client computer and points out the important areas. The component that is used to connect to the RAS server is Dial-Up Networking. Before you can configure Dial-Up Networking, you must install a modem or other means of communications.

By using Dial-Up Networking, you will create a phonebook entry for each of the locations you will call. The steps that are required to create an entry are given in the following list.

1. Open the My Computer icon and then open Dial-Up Networking. (If you do not have an entry, a wizard appears that will step you through creating a phonebook entry.)

2. Click the New button to create an entry. You can also select an entry in the list and click More and choose Edit the Entry.

If you choose New, the New Entry Wizard appears. You can choose to enter the information manually. Because this chapter is concerned with troubleshooting, this section covers the manual entries because they provide more options.

3. The New (or Edit) Phonebook Entry dialog box appears (see fig. 23.15). By default, it opens to the Basic tab, the options for which are discussed below. Enter or verify the information.

Figure 23.15

The Basic tab for a phonebook entry.

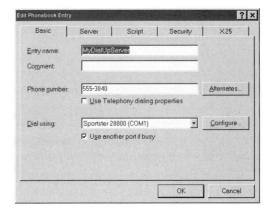

- ▶ **Entry name.** The name of the entry.

- ▶ **Comment.** Any comment you want to make about the entry.

- ▶ **Phone number.** The phone number for the entry; you should verify this. You can enter multiple entries by selecting the Alternates button. These numbers are tried in the sequence in which they are entered; you also have the option to move the most successful number to the top of the list.

- ▶ **Use telephony-dialing properties.** This tells the system to use the properties that you set for your location when dialing the number. When you are troubleshooting, turn this off.

- ▶ **Dial using.** Informs the system which modem you want to use when dialing. Verify that the modem exists and, if Multilink is selected, choose configure and verify the phone numbers that are entered for each of the modems that are listed.

▶ **Use another port if busy.** This tells the system to dial using another modem if the modem specified is busy.

4. Select the server tab and enter or verify the information (see fig. 23.16). The entries are described below.

Figure 23.16

The Server properties for a phonebook entry.

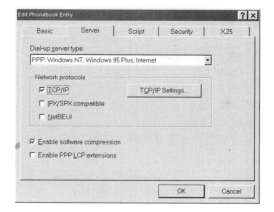

▶ **Dial-up server type.** Tells the system what type of server you are trying to connect to. You can use three different types of servers: PPP, such as Windows NT, SLIP, and Windows NT 3.1 RAS. Make sure the correct type is selected or your computer will attempt to use the wrong line protocol.

▶ **Network protocols.** Here you can select the protocols that you want to be able to use. If the client computer will be using the Internet, TCP/IP needs to be selected. If the client is going to use the services of a remote NetWare server, IPX/SPX must be selected. If you will be using only the services from a Windows NT network, then you can choose any of the protocols (remembering that the server must also use this protocol.)

▶ **Enable software compression.** If you are working with a Windows NT server, you can select this to turn on the software compression. For troubleshooting purposes, you should turn this off.

▶ **Enable PPP LCP extensions.** Tells the system that the PPP server will be able to set up the client station and will be able to verify the user name and password. This also should be turned off when you are troubleshooting.

5. If you are using TCP/IP for this connection, you should also set or verify the TCP/IP Settings. The TCP/IP setting screen will appear, the screen will be different depending on the type of server you selected. The PPP settings are shown in figure 23.17 and a description of the options is given below.

Figure 23.17

The PPP TCP/IP Settings dialog box.

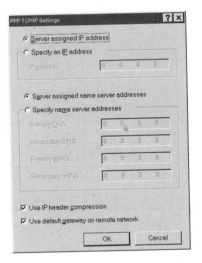

▶ **Server assigned IP address.** Tells the computer that the server assigns the IP address for this station. The server must have some means of assigning IP addresses to use this option.

▶ **Specify an IP address.** Enables you to give the station an IP address. The address need to be unique and must be correct for the servers network. The server must also allow the client to request an IP address.

▶ **Server assigned name server addresses.** Tells the system that the server assigns the IP addresses for DNS and WINS server.

▶ **Specify name server addresses.** Lets you set the addresses for DNS and WINS servers. This option enables you to see whether the server is giving you correct addresses.

▶ **Use IP header compression.** The use of IP header compression reduces the overhead that is transmitted over the modem. Disable this when troubleshooting.

▶ **Use default gateway on the remote network.** If you are connected to a network and dialed in to a service provider, this option tells Windows NT to send information that is bound for a remote network to the gateway on the dial in server.

6. Set the script options on the Script tab (see fig. 23.18).

Figure 23.18

The Script tab for a phonebook entry.

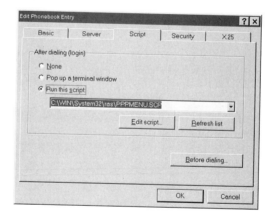

▶ **After dialing (login).** There are three different settings here. Make sure you use the correct one. For NT-to-NT communications, select None. For other connections, you may have to enter information. For troubleshooting, try the terminal window, which lets you enter the information manually, rather than using the script. If this works, then you should verify the script.

▶ **Before dialing.** If you click this button, you are presented with basically the same options. You can use this to bring up a window or run a script before you dial the remote host.

7. Check or enter the security information on the security tab (see fig. 23.19). This should be set to the same level as the security on the server or the connection will probably fail.

Figure 23.19

Setting security options for the phonebook entry.

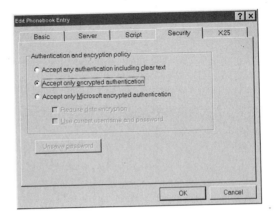

▶ **Authentication and encryption policy.** Here you can set the level of security that you want. For troubleshooting, you can try "Accept any authentication including clear text," which should be set to match the setting on the server.

▶ **Require data encryption.** If you are using Microsoft-encrypted authentication, you will have the option to encrypt all data that is being sent over the connection. Set this to match the server.

▶ **User current name and password.** Enables Windows to send the current user name and password as your login information. If you are not using the same name and password on the client as you do on the network, do not check this box. You will be prompted for the user name and password to log on just like when you attempted to connect (see fig. 23.20).

Figure 23.20

The prompt for logon information.

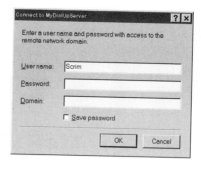

▶ **Unsave password.** If you told the system to save the logon password for a connection, you can clear it by clicking on this button. You should do this in the case of a logon problem.

8. Finally, you can enter or check the information for X.25 connections (see fig. 23.21).

Figure 23.21

X.25 settings for a phonebook entry.

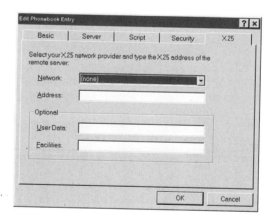

Because there are so many different options to configure, there are great potential for errors. Client errors tend either to be validation problems or errors in the network protocols. Remember that you may need to check the configuration of the server.

The RAS Server

This section covers the RAS server and the configuration of that server. Probably the best place to start would be the installation of the RAS server. After a short description of the installation, this section moves on to the configuration of the server.

Installing the RAS Server

The following steps describe the process of installing RAS.

1. Open the Network Setting dialog box (Start, Settings, Control Panel, Network).

2. From the Services tab, choose Add.

3. From the list that appears, choose Remote Access Service and click OK.

4. When prompted, enter the path to the Windows NT source files.

5. RAS asks you for the device that it should use at that point. (This includes ISDN and X.25.)

6. The Remote Access Setup dialog box appears (see fig. 23.22). Click Continue (the options for this dialog box are discussed soon).

7. From the Network settings dialog box, click Close.

8. When prompted, shut down and restart your system.

Figure 23.22

The Remote Access Setup dialog box.

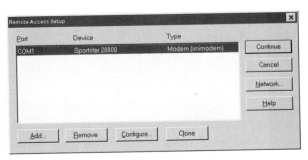

Configuring the RAS Server

If several users are all having problems connecting to your RAS server, check the modem first, and then check the configuration of the server. This section covers the basic configuration for a RAS server, which is done when you install RAS or when you verify it after installation by going to the Network settings dialog box and double-clicking Remote Access Service from the Services tab.

You will see the dialog box shown in figure 23.22. You will be able to configure each port and set the overall network preferences. Four buttons are concerned with the port settings:

▶ **Add.** Enables you to add another port to the RAS server. This could be a modem, X.25 PAD, or a PPTP Virtual Private Network.

▶ **Remove.** Removes the port from RAS.

▶ **Configure.** Brings up the Configure Port Usage dialog box, in which you can configure how this port is to be used (see fig. 23.23). Check this if no users are able to dial in.

▶ **Clone.** This setting lets you copy a port. Windows NT Server has been tested with up to 256 ports.

Figure 23.23

Configuring port usage.

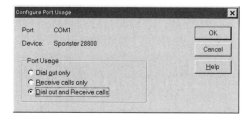

 Windows NT Workstation and Windows 95 (with service pack 1 or the OSR2 release) allow only one client to dial in).

After the ports are configured, you will need to configure the network settings, which affect what users will be able to see, how they will be authenticated, and what protocols they will be able to use when they dial in to the network. When you click the Network button, the Network Configuration dialog box appears (see fig. 23.24).

Figure 23.24

*The Network
Configuration
dialog box.*

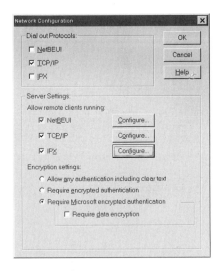

This dialog box has three main areas: the first is Dial Out Protocols, which sets which protocols you can use to dial into another server. Then there are the dial in protocols that will set the protocols that users can use to connect to you.

Finally there are the Encryption settings. The level of security that you choose must also be set on the client computer. If the client cannot use the same level of security, they will not be validated by the server.

Each of the server-side protocols has a Configuration button. The following sections deal with the configuration of each. Before you can use a protocol with RAS, it must be installed on the server.

Configuring TCP/IP on the RAS Server

If you run a mixed network that includes Unix-like hosts, then you should enable the TCP/IP protocol on the RAS server. This allows your clients to use an Internet connection on your network. The RAS Server TCP/IP Configuration dialog box includes the capability to restrict network access to the RAS server (see fig. 23.25).

Figure 23.25

*RAS Server TCP/
IP Configuration
dialog box.*

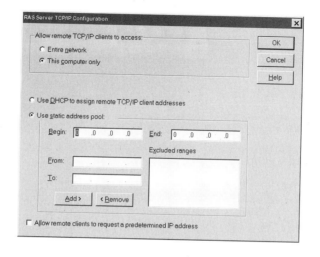

The other options all deal with the assignment of TCP/IP address
to the clients that are dialing in. By default, the RAS server uses
the services of a Dynamic Host Configuration Protocol (DHCP)
server to assign the addresses. If your DHCP server has a long
lease period, you may want to assign the numbers from a pool of
addresses that are given on the server. If you allow the client to
request an address, you must configure the client stations for all
the other parameters.

If your clients are having problems connecting, assign a range of
addresses to the RAS server; this eliminates any problems related
to the DHCP server and still allows you to prevent clients from
requesting specific IP addresses.

Monitoring the RAS Connection

After you have made the RAS connection, you will be able to monitor the connection. The client side and the server side each has a
tool of its own. This section looks at both of them because they
can be used to see what is happening with the connection.

Monitoring from the RAS Server

From the server, you can use the Remote Access Admin tool to
monitor the ports. From the Start menu, choose Programs, Administrative tools, RAS Admin. You will see the Admin tool (see
fig. 23.26).

Figure 23.26

*The Remote
Access Admin
tool.*

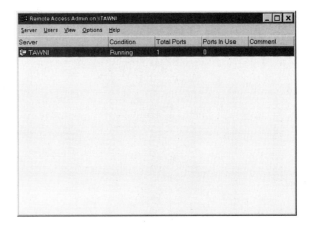

Select the server you want to look at and double-click the server.
A list of the communications ports appears (see fig. 23.27). For
every port that is available on the server, you will see the current
user's name and the time of his initial connection.

Figure 23.27

*Communications
Ports on a RAS
server.*

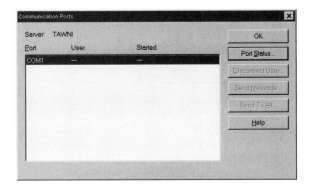

From here you can disconnect users or send a message to a single
user or all users who are connected to the server. You can also
check the Port Status, which shows you all the connection information for the port (see fig. 23.28).

Figure 23.28

The port status display.

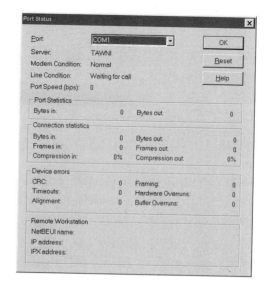

Dial-Up Networking Monitor

On the client side, there is an application called the Dial-Up Networking Monitor, which you can use to check the status of the communications. There are three tabs in the monitor.

The Status Tab

The Status tab provides you with basic information about the connection (see fig. 23.29). You have the option to hang up the connection or to view its details.

Figure 23.29

The Status tab from the Dial-Up Networking Monitor.

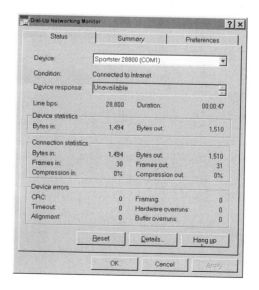

Clicking the Details tab brings up another screen (see fig. 23.30), which provides the details about the client's names on the network.

Figure 23.30

Connection Details showing the clients network identification.

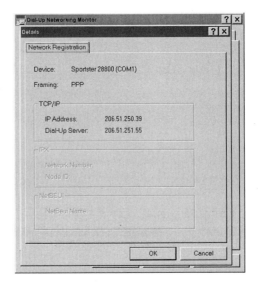

The Summary Tab

The Summary tab summarizes all the connections that the client currently has open (see fig. 23.31). It is useful only cases where you have multiple connections.

Figure 23.31

The Summary tab.

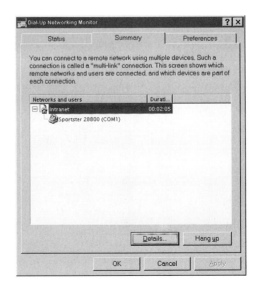

The Preferences Tab

The Preferences tab allows you to control the settings for dial-up networking (see fig. 23.32). The options break down into two main areas. You can control when a sound is played and how the Dial-Up Networking monitor will look.

Figure 23.32

Setting Dial-Up Networking preferences.

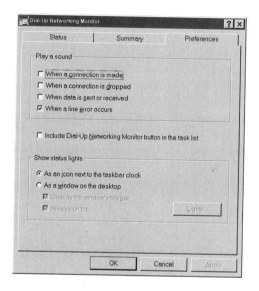

Common RAS Problems

Clients experience two common problems with RAS, which are covered here.

Authentication

Authentication can be a problem in two areas. The first is obvious. The client may attempt to connect by using the incorrect user name and password. This can easily happen if the user is dialing from a home system. The RAS client may be set to attempt the connection using the current user name and password.

The other authentication problem occurs if the security settings on the server and the client do not match. You can get around this by using the "Allow any authentication" setting or possibly by using the "After Dial terminal window."

Callback with Multilink

There is currently no way to configure Call Back security with Multilink setup. If you attempt to do this, the initial connections will be made, but then the server will hang up. The server only has one number for the client and will therefore only call back to one port.

Exercises

Exercise 23.1: Adding a Null Modem

In this exercise, you will install a Null modem that will allow those of you without a modem to proceed through some of the remaining exercises.

1. Open the Control Panel and double-click the Modems icon

2. Click the Add button to bring up the modem installer.

3. Choose "Don't detect my modem, I will select it from a list and then click next."

4. The list of manufacturers and models appears. From the Standard Modem Types, choose Dial-Up Networking Serial Cable between 2 PCs and click Next.

5. Choose any available port and click Next. NT installs your modem. When the next screen appears, choose Finish.

6. Choose OK to close the modem installer.

Exercise 23.2: Installing Remote Access Service

In this exercise, you will install the Remote Access Service. If you already have this installed, skip to exercise 3.

1. Open the Network Setting dialog box and choose Add from the Services tab.

2. Choose the Remote Access Service from the list, click OK, and enter the source files directory when prompted.

3. Choose Close on the Network Settings dialog box. When prompted, select the Null modem or the modem you already had.

4. From the RAS Setup Dialog box, choose Configure and select Dial Out. Click OK to return to the RAS Setup dialog box.

continues

Exercise 23.2: Continued

    5. Click the Continue button.

    6. When prompted, restart your system.

Exercise 23.3: Creating Phonebook Entries

You will now create a new phonebook entry. This exercise walks you through all the information that would be required to create a real phonebook entry.

1. Open the My Computer icon and double-click the Dial-Up Networking.

2. Because this is the first time you have run Dial-Up Networking, you are informed that the phone book is empty and asked to add a new entry.

Note

If you have already used Dial-Up Networking, you can click the New button, and you will be in the same position.

3. For the Name, enter **Test Entry Number 1** and click Next.

4. Select the first (I am calling the internet) and third (The non-Windows NT server) check boxes. Then click Next.

5. Enter **555-3840** as the phone number and click Next.

6. Select PPP as the protocol and click Next.

7. Choose "Use a terminal window from the next screen" and click Next.

8. Assuming the server provides you an address, click Next.

9. Enter **148.53.66.7** as the DNS server and click Next.

10. Now that you have entered all the information, click Finish.

Exercise 23.4:   Editing Phone Book Entries

In this exercise, you will edit a phone book entry and tinker with the preferences.

1. To create a shortcut to the entry, choose More, Create a shortcut to the entry.

2. Accept the default name (Test Entry Number 1.rnk).

3. Close the Dial-Up Networking dialog box.

4. On the desktop, right-click the icon and choose Edit entry and modem properties.

5. Add the alternate numbers **555-9930** and **555-6110**. To do this, click the Alternates button, type the first number in the New phone number field and click Add. Do the same for the second number.

6. Click OK to save the changes.

7. You have created a script for this entry and want to use it. Right-click the icon on the desktop and choose Edit entry and modem properties.

8. Select the Script tab and click Run this Script.

9. From the drop down list box, choose PPPMENU.SCP.

10. Click the Server tab and Enable software compression.

11. Click OK to save the changes.

Exercise 23.5:   Configuring RAS as a Server

In this exercise, you will set up the Remote Access Service to act as a RAS server; this will allow others to dial in to your machine.

1. Open the Network Setting dialog box and choose the Services tab.

2. Click on the Remote Access Service and click the Properties button.

continues

Exercise 23.5: Continued

3. In the dialog box that appears, select the Null Modem cable (or the modem you are using) and select Configure.

4. Click the Dial Out and Receive Calls option and then OK to close the dialog box.

5. Click the Network button. From here, ensure that TCP/IP is configured in the Server Settings.

6. Click the Configure button beside TCP/IP and choose Use static address pool.

7. Enter **148.53.90.0** as the Begin address and **148.53.90.255** as the end address. Click OK to close the dialog box and OK again to close the Server settings.

8. Click Continue to return to the Network Settings dialog box and then choose Close.

9. Restart your computer.

Exercise 23.6: Assigning Permissions

You will now provide your users with dial-in Permissions and review the Remote Access Admin program.

1. Start the User Manager for Domains (User Manager will work well in this case.)

2. Choose User, New user and enter the following information:

Username	Bilbo
Full name	Bilbo Baggins
Description	Hobbit (small with fury feet)
Password	Blank

3. Click the Dial-in icon and check the "Grant dial in permission."

4. Click OK to close the dial-in screen and OK to add the user.

5. Close User Manager for Domains.

6. Open the Remote Access Admin program from the Administrative Tools group.

7. Choose Users, Permissions from the menu. Click on Bilbo's name in the list. Does he have dial-in permission? (He should.)

8. Choose the account you logged on as; if you do not have dial-in permission, grant it to yourself.

Review Questions

1. Where can you enable a log that will record all of the communications between the modem and the system?

    A. In the Telephony API advanced options

    B. In the RAS Administration tool under advanced options

    C. In the Modem advanced properties

    D. In the Port Settings Advanced dialog box

2. Can the Telephony API be set to turn off the call waiting?

    A. Yes

    B. No

3. What types of security does the RAS Server accept?

    A. Clear text

    B. Kerberos

    C. Shiva

    D. Microsoft

4. Can you enter more than one phone number per phone-book entry?

    A. Yes

    B. No

5. How do you create a shortcut to a phonebook entry?

    A. From the RAS administrator

    B. From the Dial-Up Networking icon

    C. From the RAS Administrator

    D. By using Drag and Drop

6. What do you have to change in order to use a different DNS for a phone book entry?

    A. Change the Dial-Up networking properties

    B. Change the TCP/IP properties

    C. Change the settings in RAS administrator

    D. Dial-up networking will always use the default

7. What condition must be met before you can select a frame size of 1,006 or 1,500 bytes?

    A. You must use PPP.

    B. You must use PPTP.

    C. You must use SLIP.

    D. You must use CSLIP.

8. If your dial-in server requires you to log on, and this cannot be scripted, what can you do?

    A. Use NT logon

    B. Bring up a terminal window

    C. Use Client Services for Netware

    D. You will not be able to dial in

9. How can the Dial-Up Networking Monitor be displayed?

    A. As a icon on the Task Bar (beside the clock)

    B. As a regular icon on the Task Bar

    C. As a window

    D. All of the above

10. What does Auto dial do for you?

    A. Enables you to dial users from the User Manager

    B. Enables you to connect to your ISP using Windows Messaging

    C. Reconnects network resources when accessed

    D. Automatically dials at a given time

11. What events can cause the Dial-Up Networking Monitor to make a sound?

    A. On connection

    B. On errors

    C. When the program starts

    D. When the program terminates

12. Where can you grant a user dial-in permissions?

    A. From the command prompt

    B. From the User Manager

    C. From the RAS administrator

    D. From Server Manager

13. From where does the IP address for a client come?

    A. From the client

    B. From the DHCP Server

    C. From a scope of addresses on the RAS Server

    D. All of the above

14. What is the purpose of PPTP?

    A. New form of the PPP protocol

    B. Allows Tuned connections

    C. Allows secured connections across the Internet

    D. Enables the user to dial in using more than one line

15. How does PPTP show up in the Remote Access Admin?

    A. RPN

    B. VPN

    C. SPN

    D. DPN

Review Answers

1. C

2. A

3. A, D

4. A

5. B

6. A

7. C

8. B

9. D

10. C

11. A, B

12. B, C

13. D

14. C

15. B

Answers to the Test Yourself Questions at the Beginning of the Chapter

1. RAS provides dial-up networking for Windows NT Workstation and Server.

2. There is a one connection limit on inbound RAS when you are working with NT Workstation; Windows NT Server has been tested with up to 256 inbound connections.

3. Windows NT allows you to dial out using either PPP (Point to Point Protocol) or SLIP (Serial Line Internet Protocol). The dial-in for Windows NT only supports PPP.

4. Depending on the configuration of the protocol that she uses to dial in, she will be allowed to see either the one computer that she dials into or the entire network.

5. Multilink is a special protocol that allows a user to use more than one modem to connect to a RAS server. Note that the multilink protocol does not work with the callback security.

6. Callback security causes the RAS server to call back the client. There are three forms of callback security: None (no callback is done); Set by Caller (this allows the caller to enter the number they are at; though this does not necessarily increase security, it reduces the long-distance charges for the user); and Preset (this requires that the users be at a specific phone number, so they can call only from a known location.)

7. A port can be used for Dial Out, Receive Calls, or both.

8. The RAS server enables you to call in by using NetBEUI, NWLink, and TCP/IP, which are configured in the RAS Setup under the Network button.

9. If the server is using NetBIOS, then the user will be able to call in by using NetBIOS (or anything else). The RAS Server uses a system called a *NetBIOS Gateway* to forward the SMB request to the other server over the TCP/IP protocol.

10. The Telephony API allows Windows NT to be set up with different locations. You will be able to choose the location that you are calling from, and the system will know whether the call is local or long distance, what the dialing codes are, and even what calling card to use.

P a r t **3**

Internet Information Server 4

Chapter 24

Planning

This chapter helps you prepare for the exam by covering the following objectives:

 **Objectives**

▶ Choose a security strategy for various situations. Security considerations include the following:

   ▶ Controlling anonymous access

   ▶ Controlling access to known users and groups

   ▶ Controlling access by a host or network

   ▶ Configuring SSL to provide encryption and authentication schemes

   ▶ Identifying the appropriate balance between security requirements and performance requirements

▶ Choose an implementation strategy for an Internet site or an intranet site for standalone servers, single-domain environments, and multiple-domain environments. Tasks include the following:

   ▶ Resolving host header name issues by using a HOSTS file or DNS, or both

   ▶ Choosing the appropriate operating system on which to install IIS

▶ Choose the appropriate technology to resolve specified problems. Technology options include the following:

   ▶ WWW service

continues

- ► FTP Service
- ► Microsoft Transaction Server
- ► Microsoft SMTP Service
- ► Microsoft NNTP Service
- ► Microsoft Index Server
- ► Microsoft Certificate Server

Test Yourself! Before reading this chapter, test yourself to determine how much study time you will need to devote to this section.

1. What is the name of the user account set up by default for the anonymous account to use?

2. DNS can be used for dynamic resolution of host names to IP addresses. If you want to use static name resolution, such as at a small site, you use the HOSTS file. The length of each entry in the HOSTS file is how many characters?

3. You are concerned about security at your site and implement the use of certificates. All of your clients are using Microsoft's Internet Explorer browser. What is the minimum version they can use now that certificates are employed at your site?

Answers are located at the end of the chapter...

The topics for this chapter simply reflect the Planning objectives. They include the following:

▶ Choosing a Security Strategy

▶ Implementation Strategies

▶ Choosing Appropriate Technologies

Choosing a Security Strategy

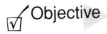 Objective

Microsoft Internet Information Server (IIS) 4.0 incorporates a number of security features into its service—and builds on Windows NT 4.0's security. There are five sub-objectives for this category:

▶ Controlling anonymous access

▶ Controlling access to known users and groups

▶ Controlling access by host or network

▶ Configuring SSL to provide encryption and authentication schemes

▶ Identifying the appropriate balance between security requirements and performance requirements

Each of these sub-objectives is examined in the following sections.

Controlling Anonymous Access

Anonymous access enables clients to access your servers (FTP or WWW) without giving a name, or using the name *anonymous*. Traditionally, WWW access has been completely anonymous. FTP began as a service requiring usernames, but later anonymous access was added. When a user has entered *anonymous* as his username, he can log on to your site by using his email address as his password.

IIS uses the default IUSR_*computername* account for all anonymous logons. This account, like all other user accounts, appears in the User Manager for Domains utility (shown in Figure 24.1) and can be administered from there.

Figure 24.1

The anonymous user account can be administered from User Manager for Domains.

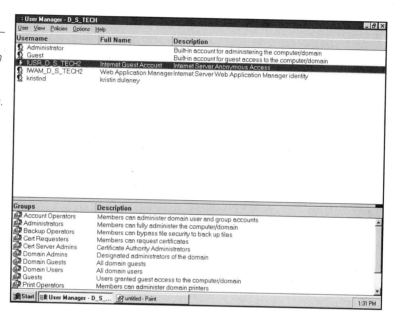

Permissions set up for this account determine an anonymous user's privileges. The default properties are shown in Figure 24.2, including the fact that the user cannot change the password and that the password does not expire.

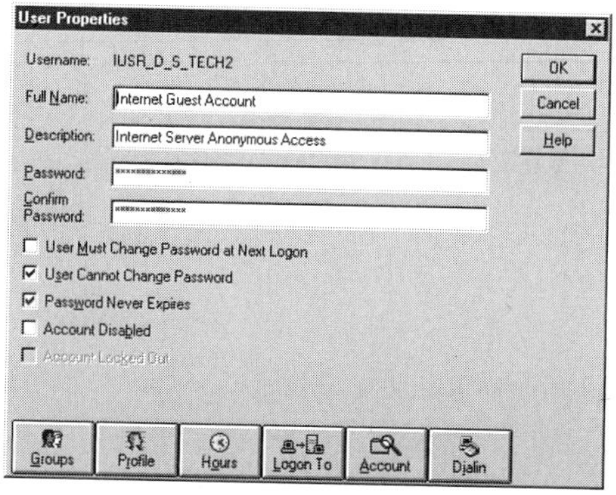

Figure 24.2

The default anonymous user account properties.

Anonymous FTP

On the FTP Accounts Security tab, you can configure the following options:

- ▶ **Allow Anonymous Connections.** Select this for anonymous connections.

- ▶ **Username.** Displays the IUSR_*computername* name as set up by IIS in Windows NT User Manager for Domains and in Internet Service Manager.

- ▶ **Password.** A randomly generated password was created by User Manager for Domains and Internet Service Manager. You must have a password; no blanks are allowed. If you change this password, make sure it matches the one in User Manager for Domains and Internet Service Manager for this user.

- ▶ **Allow only anonymous connections.** Click this option to limit access to your FTP server to only those who log on as anonymous. This restricts users from possibly logging on with an account that has administrative rights.

 The Enable Automatic Password Synchronization option was added to eliminate accidental password inconsistencies between IIS 4 and User Manager.

- ▶ **Administrator.** Select those accounts that are allowed to administer this virtual FTP site. To administer a virtual FTP site, a user should first be a member of the Administrative group under Windows NT. Click the Add button to add a user account to this list. Remove an account by selecting the account and clicking Remove.

 FTP passwords are ALWAYS transmitted as clear text, and because of that FTP should be limited to anonymous access only.

Anonymous WWW

IIS 4.0 can be set up to verify the identify of clients who access your Web site. On public Web sites on which non-critical or public domain information and applications are available, authentication of users connecting to your Web site may not be important. However, if you have secure data or want to restrict Web access to specific clients, logon and authentication requirements become very important.

Use the following steps to set authentication and logon requirements:

1. Open Internet Service Manager.

2. Right-click on a Web site, file (NTFS systems only), or directory you want to configure.

3. Click on Properties. The property sheet for that item is displayed, as shown in Figure 24.3.

Figure 24.3

The properties for a Web site are available through Internet Service Manager.

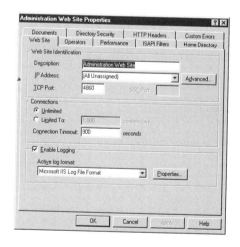

4. Click the Directory Security (or File Security if you want to set file-specific properties) tab.

5. Click the Edit button under Anonymous Access and Authentication Control. The Authentication Methods dialog box appears, as shown in Figure 24.4.

Figure 24.4

The authentication methods can be defined for each Web site.

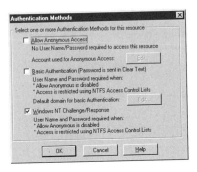

6. Select an authentication method from the following options:

> **Allow Anonymous Access**. Enables clients to connect to your Web site without requiring a username or password. Click the Edit button to select the Windows NT user account used to access your computer. By default the account IUSR_*computername* is used. This account is granted Log on Locally user rights by default and is necessary for anonymous logon access to your Web site. Click OK to return to the Authentication Methods dialog box.

> **Basic Authentication**. Use this method if you do not specify anonymous access and you want a client connecting to your Web site to enter a valid Windows NT username and password to log on. This sends a password in clear text format (the passwords are transmitted in an unencrypted format). Click the Edit button to specify a default logon domain for users who do not explicitly name a domain.

> **Windows NT Challenge/Response**. This setting is used if you want the Windows NT Challenge/Response feature to authenticate the client attempting to connect to your Web site. The only Web browsers that support this feature include Internet Explorer 2.0 and higher. During the challenge/response procedure, cryptographic information is exchanged between the client and server to authenticate the user.

Note   Basic Authentication transmits the username and password in encrypted text when using SSL.

7. Click OK.

Preventing Anonymous WWW Access

Normally, you want anonymous WWW access at most sites. This isn't the case, however, if you're dealing with sensitive data. In this situation, you can prevent the use of anonymous access by requiring IIS to authenticate users. Authentication can be done on the basis of known users and groups, by host or network, or by Secure Socket Layer authentication.

Authentication of users takes place only if you have disabled anonymous access, or anonymous access fails because there isn't an anonymous account with appropriate permissions in NTFS.

Controlling Access to Known Users and Groups

As opposed to the anonymous model, you can use NTFS (NT File System) permissions to limit access to your site to a defined set of users or groups. In this situation, all users must have a Windows NT account that is valid, and they must provide the user ID and password to establish the connection. When connected, the permissions set for the user govern what he can and cannot access.

NTFS permissions can be broken into five categories:

▶ **Change**—Assigns Read (R), Execute (X), Write (W), and Delete (D) permissions.

▶ **Full Control**—Assigns R, X, W, and D permissions (also includes the ability to change permissions and take ownership).

▶ **No Access**—No Access overrides all other permissions. It still enables users to connect, but nothing shows up except the message `You do not have permission to access this directory`.

▶ **Read**—Assigns only R and X permissions.

▶ **Special Access**—Whatever you define.

As with all Windows NT permissions, user and group permissions accumulate, with the exception of No Access, which instantly overrides all other permissions.

Controlling Access by Host or Network

In addition to limiting access to your site on the basis of users or groups, you also can limit it based upon the host or network the access is coming from. In so doing, there are two models you can operate under. The first is where you select a group of networks or hosts and grant them access. In so doing, you are saying that only they can come in, while everyone else is denied access.

The other model is to select a group of networks or hosts and deny them access. In so doing, you are saying that this group is not allowed access, while everyone else is. The solution to your situation is dependent upon your individual site and needs.

To grant access to only a few, do the following:

1. Start Internet Service Manager, select the Web site (or file or directory), and open the properties.

2. Choose either Directory Security or File Security, based upon which one you want to assign access for, as shown in Figure 24.5.

Figure 24.5

The Directory Security property choices for the Web site.

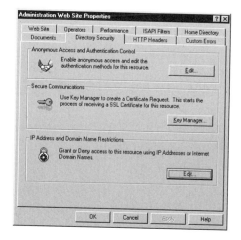

3. Click Edit under IP Address and Domain Name Restrictions.

4. Select Denied Access from the IP Address and Domain Name Restrictions dialog box.

5. Click Add.

6. Select either Single Computer, Group of Computers, or Domain Name from the Grant Access On dialog box, shown in Figure 24.6.

Figure 24.6

The three methods of denying access to a Web site.

7. Type in the IP address of those to whom you're giving access, or click the DNS Lookup button to browse for them by name.

8. Click OK twice.

Exercise 1 illustrates the opposite of this action and shows how to deny access to a select group of hosts or networks. To pass this exam, you must memorize the subnet mask table shown in Table 24.1. Pay particular attention to the number of hosts available with each subnet.

Table 24.1

Valid Subnet Range Values	
Last Digits of Subnet Address	Number of Addresses in Range
128	128
192	64
224	32
240	16
248	8
252	4
254	2
255	1 (not used)

Configuring SSL

Secure Sockets Layer—or SSL—enables you to protect communications over a network whether that network be an intranet or the Internet. It does so by establishing a private (and encrypted) communication link between the user and the server.

As an interesting aside, SSL can be used to authenticate not only specific users, but also the anonymous user. If SSL is enabled and a user attempts anonymous access, the Web server looks for a valid certificate on the client and rejects those lacking such.

Note Never use SSL on a server with a processor that cannot afford the extra load. The processor impact of SSL is substantial because everything must be encrypted.

To enable SSL on your server, implement the following steps:

1. Start Internet Service Manager and click the Key Manager icon. The Key Manager utility is displayed, as shown in Figure 24.7.

Figure 24.7

The Key Manager utility enables you to generate certificate requests.

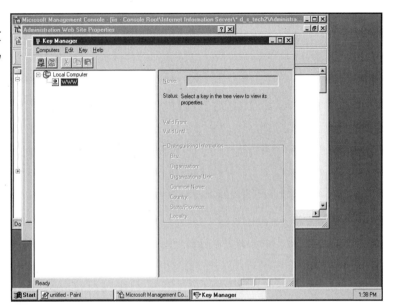

2. Use Key Manager to generate a certificate request file by choosing Create New Key.

3. Submit the request for a certificate to an online authority and obtain their approval (which can take between days and months).

4. Save the certificate, which is returned as an ASCII file.

5. Start Internet Service Manager once more and click on Key Manager. Select the key from the window and choose Install Key Certificate. You have now completed this part and must assign it to a Web site.

6. Select a Web site in Internet Service Manager and open the properties.

7. Go to Advanced under Web Site Identification.

8. Assign the Web site IP address to port 443 under the Multiple SSL identities of this Web Site dialog box.

9. Click Edit on the Secure Communications option of the property sheet. This opens the Secure Communications dialog box.

10. On the Secure Communications dialog box, set the Web server to require a secure channel and enable the Web server's SSL client certificate authentication.

Identifying the Appropriate Balance Between Security and Performance Requirements

In the absence of security, users can access resources without any difficulties. In the presence of absolute security, users cannot access resources at all. Somewhere between the two extremes lies the security-to-usability equilibrium you are striving for. Determining where that equilibrium rests at each site is the responsibility of the administrator.

Common sense plays a large part in the decision on how much security to implement. For example, security should be tighter at any financial institution or site conducting financial transactions than at a user's home page. Likewise, site security should be tighter at any site involving medical or employment information than one containing sports scores.

For an intranet, you should consider creating a group of users who need to access your documents and assigning the Log on Locally right to the group. Use Windows NT Challenge Response for authentication, and make certain that only the selected group has permission to read and access the documents.

For a public Web site, consider using Microsoft Certificate Server in combination with Secure Sockets Layer (SSL).

Understanding Implementation Strategies

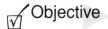 When implementing IIS, there are several factors to consider: the environment, the method of host name resolution, and the operating system. One of the following sections examines the host name issues, while another looks at operating system possibilities. The following paragraphs concentrate on the issues of environment.

There are three possibilities for IIS environments in the Windows NT world: on a standalone server, in a single-domain environment, and in a multiple-domain environment.

On a standalone server, it is important that IIS be able to interact with the LAN, WAN, or other network architecture that you're seeking. Confining IIS to a standalone server adds a level of security in that users who penetrate the security of the server are able to access only that server and nothing more. At the same time, in a single-domain environment, placing IIS on the PDC can add a considerable (additional) load on an already busy server. The balance must be weighed at each site, and it may indeed be more beneficial to place IIS on a Windows NT Server that has been installed as a Server Role instead of a Domain Controller. This would allow the server to be a member of the domain, for security, while not taxing it with authentication duties.

In a single-domain environment, IIS is often installed on the Primary Domain Controller. In so doing, IIS is able to capitalize upon the security of the PDC and user/resource authentication there.

In a multiple-domain environment, it is important that IIS be accessible to all of the domains. Bandwidth becomes extremely important as the server faces the limitations of the "wire." Thought should be given to using the best (fastest) Network Interface Card possible, with an ample amount of RAM and a fast processor to service all of the traffic the IIS server will face.

Resolving Host Name Issues with HOSTS or DNS

There are two methods of resolving host names in a Windows NT environment—with static HOSTS files and with dynamic DNS. This section looks at both solutions.

Understanding HOSTS

The HOSTS file is an ASCII text file that statically maps local and remote host names and IP addresses. It is located in *\systemroot*\System32\Drivers\etc.

In most operating systems (such as UNIX) and prior to Windows NT version 4.0, HOSTS is case sensitive. Regardless of operating system, the file is limited to 255 characters per entry. It is used by PING and other utilities that need it to resolve host names locally and remotely. One HOSTS file must reside on each host, and the file is read from top to bottom. As soon as a match is found for a host name, the file stops being read. For that reason, when there are duplicate entries, the latter ones are always ignored, and the most commonly used names should be near the top of the file.

An example of the default HOSTS file is shown in the following code listing:

```
# Copyright (c) 1993-1995 Microsoft Corp.
#
# This is a sample HOSTS file used by Microsoft TCP/IP for
# Windows NT.
#
# This file contains the mappings of IP addresses to host names.
# Each entry should be kept on an individual line. The IP address
# should be placed in the first column followed by the
# corresponding host name. The IP address and the host name
# should be separated by at least one space.
#
# Additionally, comments (such as these) may be inserted on
# individual lines or following the machine name denoted by a '#'
# symbol.
```

```
#
# For example:
#
#      102.54.94.97      rhino.acme.com          # source server
#      38.25.63.10       x.acme.com              # x client host

127.0.0.1        localhost
```

There are several things to notice in this file. The first is that the pound sign (#) indicates a comment. When the file is read by the system, every line beginning with a comment is ignored. When a # appears in the middle of a line, the line is only read up to the sign. If this were in use on a live system, the first 17 lines should be deleted or moved to the end of the file to keep them from being read every time the file is referenced.

The second thing to note is the following entry:

```
127.0.0.1        localhost
```

This is a *loopback* address in every host. It references the internal card, regardless of the actual host address, and can be used for diagnostics to verify that things are working properly internally, before testing that they are working properly down the wire.

Within the HOSTS file, fields are separated by white space that can be either tabs or spaces. As mentioned earlier, a host can be referred to by more than one name—to do so, separate the entries on the same line with white space, as shown in the following example:

```
127.0.0.1        me loopback localhost
199.9.200.7      SALES7 victor
199.9.200.4      SALES4 nikki
199.9.200.3      SALES3 cole
199.9.200.2      SALES2 victoria
199.9.200.1      SALES1 nicholas
199.9.200.5      SALES5 jack
199.9.200.11     ACCT1
199.9.200.12     ACCT2
```

```
199.9.200.13    ACCT3
199.9.200.14    ACCT4
199.9.200.15    ACCT5
199.9.200.17    ACCT7
```

The aliases are other names by which the system can be referenced. Here, me and loopback do the same as localhost, while nicholas is the same as SALES1. If an alias is used more than once, the search stops at the first match because the file is searched sequentially.

Understanding DNS

The Domain Name System is one way to resolve host names in a TCP/IP environment. In non-Microsoft environments, host names are typically resolved through HOSTS files or DNS. In a Microsoft environment, WINS and broadcasts are also used. DNS is the primary system used to resolve host names on the Internet. In fact, DNS had its beginning in the early days of the Internet.

In its early days, the Internet was a small network established by the Department of Defense for research purposes. This network linked computers at several government agencies with a few universities. The host names of the computers in this network were registered in a single HOSTS file located on a centrally administered server. Each site that needed to resolve host names downloaded this file. Few computers were being added to this network, so the HOSTS file wasn't updated too often, and the different sites only had to download this file periodically to update their own copies.

As the number of hosts on the Internet grew, it became more and more difficult to manage all the names through a central HOSTS file. The number of entries was increasing rapidly, changes were being made frequently, and the server with the central HOSTS file was being accessed more and more often by the different Internet sites trying to download a new copy.

DNS was introduced in 1984 as a way to resolve host names without relying on one central HOSTS file. With DNS, the host names reside in a database that can be distributed among multiple servers, decreasing the load on any one server and also allowing more than one point of administration for this naming system. The name system is based on hierarchical names in a tree-type directory structure. DNS enables more types of registration than the simple host-name-to-TCP/IP-address mapping used in HOSTS files and enables room for future defined types.

Because the database is distributed, it can support a much larger database than can be stored in a single HOSTS file. In fact, the database size is virtually unlimited because more servers can be added to handle additional parts of the database. The Domain Name System was first introduced in 1984.

History of Microsoft DNS

DNS was first introduced in the Microsoft environment as part of the Resource Kit for Windows NT Server 3.51. It wasn't available as part of the Windows NT distribution files. With version 4.0, DNS is now integrated with the Windows NT source files. Although DNS is not installed by default as part of a Windows NT 4.0 Server installation, you can specify DNS to be included as part of a Windows NT installation or you can add DNS later, just as you would any other networking service that's part of Windows NT.

Microsoft DNS is based on RFCs (Requests for Comments) 974, 1034, and 1035. A popular implementation of DNS is called BIND (Berkeley Internet Name Domain), developed at UC Berkeley for its version of UNIX. However BIND isn't totally compliant with the DNS RFCs. Microsoft's DNS does support some features of BIND, but Microsoft DNS is based on the RFCs, not on BIND.

 Note

You can read these RFCs, or any other RFC, by going to the InterNIC Web site at `http://ds.internic.net/ds/rfc-index.html`.

The Structure of DNS

Some host-name systems, like NetBIOS names, use a flat database. With a flat database, all names exist at the same level, so there can't be any duplicate names. These names are like Social Security numbers: Every participant in the Social Security program must have a unique number. The Social Security system is a national system that encompasses all workers in the United States, so it must use an identification system to distinguish between all the individuals in the United States.

DNS names are located in a hierarchical path, like a directory structure. You can have a file called TEST.TXT in C:\ and another file called TEST.TXT in C:\ASCII. In a network using DNS, you can have more than one server with the same name, as long as each is located in a different path.

Because of DNS's hierarchical structure, there can be two hosts with the same name, so long as they're not at the same place in the hierarchy. For instance, there's a server named (or probably aliased) at microsoft.com, and one at compaq.com, but because they're at different places in the domain tree they're still unique.

DNS Domains

The Internet Network Information Center (InterNIC) controls the top-level domains. These have names like com (for business-es), edu (for educational institutions like universities), gov (for government organizations), and org (for non-profit organiza-tions). There are also domains for countries. You can visit the InterNIC Web site at http://www.internic.com/. Table 24.2 sum-marizes common Internet domains.

Table 24.2

Common Internet Domains	
Name	Type of Organization
com	Commercial organizations
edu	Educational institutions
org	Non-profit organizations
net	Networks (the backbone of the Internet)
gov	Non-military government organizations

Name	Type of Organization
mil	Military government organizations
num	Phone numbers
arpa	Reverse DNS
xx	Two-letter country code

DNS Host Names

To refer to a host in a domain, use a fully qualified domain name (FQDN), which completely specifies the location of the host. An FQDN specifies the host name, the domain or subdomain the host belongs to, and any domains above that in the hierarchy until the root domain in the organization is specified. On the Internet, the root domain in the path is something like com, but on a private network the top-level domains may be named according to some internal naming convention. The FQDN is read from left to right, and each host name or domain name is specified by a period. The syntax of an FQDN follows:

```
host name.subdomain. … .domain
```

An example of an FQDN is www.microsoft.com, which refers to a server called www located in the subdomain called microsoft in the domain called com. Referring to a host by its FQDN is similar to referring to a file by its complete directory path. However, a complete filename goes from general to specific, with the filename at the rightmost part of the path. An FQDN goes from specific to general, with the host name at the leftmost part of the name.

Fully qualified domain names are more like addresses. An address starts with the most specific information: who is to receive the letter. Then the address specifies the house number in which the recipient lives, the street on which the house is located, the city where the street is located, and finally the most general location, the state where that city is located.

Zone Files

The DNS database is stored in files called *zones*. It's possible, even desirable, to break the DNS database into a number of zones. Breaking the DNS database into zones was part of the original design goal of DNS. With multiple zones, the load of providing access to the database is spread between a number of servers. Also, the administrative burden of managing the database is spread out, because different administrators manage only the parts of the DNS database stored in their own zones. A zone can be any portion of the domain name space; it doesn't have to contain all the subdomains for that part of the DNS tree. Zones can be copied to other name servers through replication. With multiple zones, smaller amounts of information are copied when zone files are replicated than would be if the entire domain was located in one zone file.

 Note
Splitting a DNS database into zones doesn't always guarantee that it will be distributed. Another approach to this is with subdomains being handled by separate DNS servers.

Reverse Lookup

Looking up an IP address to find the host name is exactly the same as the process of looking up an FQDN using a DNS Server (only backwards). An FQDN starts with the specific host and then the domain; an IP address starts with the network ID and then the host ID. Because you want to use DNS to handle the mapping, both must go the same way, so the octets of the IP address are reversed. That is, 148.53.66.7 in the inverse address resolution is 7.66.53.148.

 Note
In actuality, the final octet of the IP address is rarely reversed into an Inarpa address.

Once the IP address is reversed, it is going the same way as an FQDN. Now you can resolve the address using DNS. Just as with resolving www.scrimtech.com, you need to create a zone. This zone must have a particular name. To find the name, take the assigned portion of the address—for example, in 148.53.66.7 the portion that was assigned is 148.53, and for 204.12.25.3 it is 204.12.25. Now, create a zone in which these numbers are reversed and to which you add in-addr.arpa—that is, 53.148.in-addr.arpa or 25.12.204.in-addr.arpa, respectively.

Choosing an Appropriate Operating System

There are three operating systems that Internet Information Server 4.0 will run on: Windows NT Server, Windows NT Workstation, and Windows 95.

 Note

> IIS runs as itself only on Windows NT Server. On Windows 95 and Windows NT Workstation, it runs as Peer Web Services, a chopped up/scaled down version of IIS.

Windows 95 should not be considered a practical choice for a production environment because it—in and of itself—is not a server operating system. Windows 95 is limited to only one connection at a time and has no built-in method of true, secure, user authentication. Windows 95, however, is an excellent platform for a mobile development workforce to use on laptops while fine-tuning IIS applications that aren't yet live.

Windows NT Workstation 4.0 includes Peer Web Services, a limited version of IIS 2.0. Windows NT Workstation can be used with IIS for a very small intranet implementation. The number of concurrent connections Workstation can support is limited to 10, and that makes the product less than minimal for an Internet Server service. Like Windows 95, it is ideal for a laptop operating system that a mobile development workforce can use for tuning applications.

Windows NT Server 4.0 supports an unlimited number of concurrent connections, up to 256 phone connections (RAS), and is fine-tuned for a production server environment. As such, there is no better operating system on which to run IIS, and this should be the one used in all production Internet environments.

Choosing Appropriate Technologies

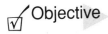 Objective

There are a number of servers and services that come with the basic Internet Information Server 4.0 product. Many of these have been with IIS since version 2.0 or before, while several are new to this release. Choosing the right server or service to add can only be accomplished by understanding the purpose behind each.

WWW

While the World Wide Web is often used synonymously with the term Internet, the World Wide Web is but one of the Internet's components. The Internet has been in existence for years but never gained fame with the masses until the World Wide Web was created to place a graphical service on it.

Use the World Wide Web if you want to include HTML (Hypertext Markup Language) documents on your site, as illustrated in Figure 24.8, and allow remote clients and browsers to reach them.

FTP

An FTP (File Transport Protocol) server enables clients attaching to your server to transmit files to and from the server, as illustrated in Figure 24.9.

Although FTP is one of the oldest Internet services, it is still one of the most popular ways to transfer files over the Internet.

Figure 24.8

An example of a WWW site.

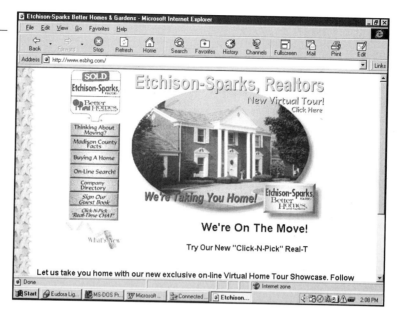

Figure 24.9

An example of an FTP site.

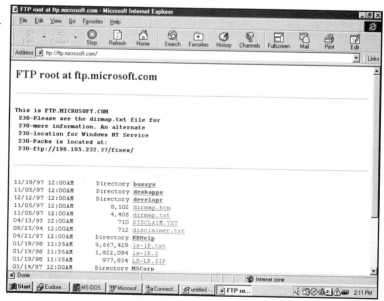

Microsoft Transaction Server

Microsoft Transaction Server—acronymed as MTS—is a transaction processing system for managing and developing server applications. It enables you to keep track of transactions that occur on the server.

Microsoft SMTP Service

Microsoft SMTP Service uses the Simple Mail Transfer Protocol to send and receive email using TCP port 25 for operations. Once installed, it can be managed and administered through Internet Service Manager or Internet Service Manager for SMTP Service. The two function almost identically, with the difference being that the latter enables you to administer SMTP through HTML, while the former requires administration from the server.

Microsoft NNTP Service

The Microsoft NNTP Service supports the Network News Transport Protocol and enables clients to access newsgroups. You can reach and interact with existing newsgroups or create new ones.

Microsoft NNTP supports MIME, HTML, GIF, and JPEG. Like SMTP, when installed it can be managed and administered through Internet Service Manager or Internet Service Manager for SMTP Service.

Microsoft Index Server

Microsoft Index Server indexes Web content at your Internet or intranet site to enable clients to quickly find information through queries. It includes a query engine that can find the results and has the ability to format the results to meet specifications you define.

Index Server can work with HTML documents as well as Excel and Word documents.

Microsoft Certificate Server

Microsoft Certificate Server enables you to increase the security of your site by issuing certificates (digital identifiers) that use public-key encryption. Certificates enable you to verify that you have secure communication across the network, whether that network is an intranet or the Internet. The server certificates are issued from a third-party organization and contain information about the organization and the public key.

With public-key encryption, there are actually two keys involved, forming a key pair. The first is the public key, which is a known value and the one used to establish a secure HTTP connection. The second key is a private key, known only by the user. The two are mathematical opposites of each other and are used to negotiate a secure TCP/IP connection.

When the connection is established, a session key (typically 40-bits in length) is used between the server and client to encrypt and decrypt the transmissions.

Certificate Server is an integral component of the Microsoft Internet Security Framework (ISF) model. This integration means that Windows NT users and groups can be mapped to certificates, and the users still receive the benefit of a single logon to the network.

Requests for certificates come into Microsoft Certificate Server across HTTP, email, or as Remote Procedure Calls. Every request is verified against a policy before being responded to in X.509 format (used for authentication with the SSL protocol). Different policies can be in place for different groups of users, and policy modules can be written in Microsoft Visual Basic, C++, or Java.

The browser that requests the certificates must be Microsoft Internet Explorer 3.0 or greater or Netscape Navigator 3.0 or greater.

Exercises

Exercise 24.1: Denying Access to a Select Group of Hosts or Networks

To deny access to only a few networks or hosts, do the following:

1. Start Internet Service Manager, select the Web site (or file or directory) and open the properties.

2. Choose either Directory Security or File Security, based upon which you want to assign access for.

3. Click Edit under TCP/IP and Domain Name Restrictions.

4. Select Granted Access from the IP Address and Domain Name Restrictions dialog box.

5. Click Add.

6. Select either Single Computer, Group of Computers, or Domain Name from the Deny Access On dialog box.

7. Type in the IP address of those to whom you're denying access, or click the DNS Lookup button to browse for them by name.

8. Click OK twice.

Exercise 24.2: Find the Local Host Name and Test It

The following exercise steps show you how to find the local host name and verify that you can ping it:

1. From the Start menu, choose Programs, MS-DOS prompt.

2. Type **HOSTNAME** to see the local host's name.

3. Type **PING {HOSTNAME}** (the {HOSTNAME} is the value returned in step two).

Exercise 24.3:   Edit the HOSTS File

The following exercise steps show you how to find and edit the HOSTS file on a Windows NT Server machine.

1. From the Start menu, choose Programs, MS-DOS prompt.

2. Change the directory to the appropriate location by typing:

   cd*systemroot*\\System32\\Drivers\\etc

   (*systemroot* is your Windows NT directory.)

3. Type **PING ME** and notice the error that comes back because the host isn't found.

4. Type **EDIT HOSTS**.

   The last line of the file should read:

   127.0.0.1localhost

5. Move one space to the right of the last character and enter

   ME

   so the line now reads:

   127.0.0.1localhost ME

6. Exit the editor and save the changes.

7. Type **PING ME** and notice the successful results.

Exercise 24.4:   Viewing Internet Explorer Certificates

To view the certificates presently in Internet Explorer 4.0, do the following:

1. In Explorer, select Internet Options from the View menu.

2. Select the Content tab, and click Personal.

continues

Exercise 24.4:   Continued

3. If any certificates are there, they will be displayed in the list box. You can then select one and click the button marked View Certificates.

4. Select each Field to view the details in the Details box.

Exercise 24.5: Turning on Windows NT Challenge/Response

To turn on the Windows NT Challenge/Response authentication, do the following:

1. Choose a Web site in Internet Service Manager and choose the property sheet.

2. Click Edit under Anonymous Access and Authentication Control.

3. Choose Windows NT Challenge/Response from the Authentication Methods dialog box.

Review Questions

1. The Internet Information Server provides you with the ability to share information with any type of computer that can use the TCP/IP protocol. IIS includes which servers?

    A. FTP

    B. SNMP

    C. TCP/IP

    D. WWW

2. Zachary wants to create a Web site to which the public is not allowed access. Instead, only the internal hosts that fall within a specified IP address range can get to it. He sets the IP and Domain Name Restriction specifications to an IP address of 192.2.2.0 and the subnet mask to 255.255.255.240. Which host addresses can access Zachary's site?

    A. 192.2.2.0 through 192.2.2.3

    B. 192.2.2.0 through 192.2.2.7

    C. 192.2.2.0 through 192.2.2.15

    D. 192.2.2.0 through 192.2.2.31

    E. 192.2.2.0 through 192.2.2.61

3. Which service resolves host names to IP addresses?

    A. DNS

    B. DHCP

    C. WINS

    D. BDC

4. Your organization currently uses a UNIX server for DNS. The server is fully configured using BIND files. In what two ways can you configure your Microsoft DNS Server so that you won't need to re-enter any information?

   A. Set up Microsoft DNS as the primary and transfer the zone to the UNIX system

   B. Set up Microsoft DNS as the secondary and transfer the zone from the UNIX system

   C. Configure the Microsoft DNS server as an IP Forwarder

   D. Configure the Microsoft DNS server as a Caching Only server

5. Which of the following is *not* part of a Fully Qualified Domain Name? (Choose all options that apply.)

   A. Type of organization

   B. Host name

   C. Company name

   D. CPU type

6. What are the benefits of DNS? (Select all options that apply.)

   A. It allows a distributed database that can be administered by a number of administrators.

   B. It allows host names that specify where a host is located.

   C. It allows WINS clients to register with the WINS server.

   D. It allows queries to other servers to resolve host names.

7. With what non-Microsoft DNS platforms is Microsoft DNS compatible?

   A. Only UNIX DNS servers that are based on BIND

   B. Only UNIX DNS servers that are based on the DNS RFCs

C. UNIX DNS servers that are either BIND-based or RFC-based

D. Only other Microsoft DNS servers

8. In the DNS name www.microsoft.com, what does microsoft represent?

A. The last name of the host

B. The domain in which the host is located

C. The IP address of the building in which the host is located

D. The directory in which the host name file is located

9. Evan wants to install a service or server on his IIS system that will enable users to upload files to his site. Which server/ service should he consider?

A. WWW

B. FTP

C. Microsoft Transaction Server

D. SMTP

E. NNTP

10. Kristin wants to install a service or server on her IIS system that will enable users to upload files to newsgroups. Which server/service should she consider?

A. WWW

B. FTP

C. Microsoft Transaction Server

D. SMTP

E. NNTP

11. Spencer wants to install a service or server on his IIS system that will enable users to send email to the Internet. Which server/service should he consider?

    A. WWW

    B. FTP

    C. Microsoft Transaction Server

    D. SMTP

    E. NNTP

12. Microsoft NNTP supports which of the following file types?

    A. MIME

    B. UUENCODE

    C. HTML

    D. GIF

    E. PDF

Review Answers

1. **A,D**. Of those listed, IIS includes FTP and WWW servers.

2. **C**. Setting an IP address of 192.2.2.0 and subnet mask to 255.255.255.240 will make the valid host range 192.2.2.0 through 192.2.2.15.

3. **A**. The DNS server resolves host names to IP addresses.

4. **B,D**. Set up DNS as the secondary and transfer the zone from the UNIX system and configure the DNS server as a Caching Only server.

5. **D**. CPU type is not a component of an FQDN.

6. **A,B,D**. Although DNS on a Windows NT server can be configured to query the WINS server for a name resolution, WINS clients do not register themselves directly with the DNS server.

7. **C**. Windows NT DNS is based on the RFCs for DNS, but it is designed to be compatible with DNS servers based on BIND as well.

8. **B**. The path specifies a host named www in a domain microsoft. The domain microsoft is located in the top-level domain com.

9. **B**. FTP is used to enable clients to upload and download files.

10. **E**. NNTP is used to communicate with newsgroups.

11. **D**. SMTP is used to send email to the Internet.

12. **A,C,D**. NNTP accepts HTML, MIME, JPEG, and GIF.

Answers to Test Yourself Questions at Beginning of Chapter

1. IUSR_computername is the name of the anonymous account automatically created during the installation of IIS. See "Controlling Anonymous Access."

2. Each line in the HOSTS file is limited to 255 characters in length. See "Understanding HOSTS."

3. Internet Explorer 3.0 is the earliest version of that browser that will work with certificates. See "Microsoft Certificate Server."

Installation and Configuration

This chapter helps you prepare for the exam by covering the following objectives:

 Objectives

▶ Install IIS. Tasks include

- ▶ Configuring a Microsoft Windows NT Server 4.0 computer for the installation of IIS

- ▶ Identifying differences to a Windows NT Server 4.0 computer made by the installation of IIS

▶ Configure IIS to support the FTP service. Tasks include

- ▶ Setting bandwidth and user connections

- ▶ Setting user logon requirements and authentication requirements

- ▶ Modifying port settings

- ▶ Setting directory listing style

- ▶ Configuring virtual directories and servers

▶ Configure IIS to support the WWW service:

- ▶ Setting bandwidth and user connections

- ▶ Setting user logon requirements and authentication requirements

continues

- Modifying port settings

- Setting default pages

- Setting HTTP 1.1 host header names to host multiple Web sites

- Enabling HTTP Keep-alives

▶ Configure and save consoles by using Microsoft Management Console.

▶ Verify server settings by accessing the metabase.

▶ Choose the appropriate administration method.

▶ Install and configure Certificate Server.

▶ Install and configure Microsoft SMTP Service.

▶ Install and configure Microsoft NNTP Service.

▶ Customize the installation of Microsoft Site Server Express Content Analyzer.

▶ Customize the installation of Microsoft Site Server Express Usage Import and Report Writer.

Test Yourself! Before reading this chapter, test yourself to determine how much study time you will need to devote to this section.

1. As an IIS consultant, a client asks you to outline the features of IIS 4 that should be installed for search documents, providing digital certificates and newsgroup capabilities. What features should you install with IIS?

2. You are setting up an IIS installation in your client's office. The client wants to have Basic Authentication enabled. What two conditions must be met for Basic Authentication to work?

3. After setting up IIS on your client's server, the client wants to know how he should administer IIS. What do you say?

4. To keep inactive connections or slow connections from consuming network resources, describe the technique you should use to limit this resource problem.

5. You've set up the FTP Service on a client's IIS server. What is the default authentication method used by the FTP Service?

6. What is the metabase, and why is it used by IIS?

7. You're asked by another administrator in your office to provide a copy of your MMC console of your Web site. Can you do this? If so, how?

Answers are located at the end of the chapter...

Microsoft makes it fairly easy to install Internet Information Server 4.0 (IIS) under Windows NT Server 4.0. During installation, setup wizards walk you through the process. Although you don't need to know a whole lot about IIS before jumping into the IIS setup, you should know the requirements of IIS and how your Windows NT Server 4.0 system should be set up. This chapter covers these points.

After you install IIS, you need to know how to configure its World Wide Web and FTP services, along with setting up Microsoft Management Console (MMC) consoles and how to choose the appropriate administration method. You learn how in this chapter. The following topics are covered:

- ▶ Installing IIS

- ▶ Configuring IIS to support the FTP service

- ▶ Configuring IIS to support the WWW service

- ▶ Configuring and saving consoles by using Microsoft Management Console

- ▶ Verifying server settings by accessing the metabase

- ▶ Choosing the appropriate administration method

- ▶ Customizing the Installation of Microsoft Site Server Express Analysis Content Analyzer

- ▶ Customizing the Installation of Microsoft Site Server Analysis Report Writer and Usage Import

 Note

The Microsoft Certificate Server, Microsoft SMTP Service, and Microsoft NNTP Service can be automatically installed when you install IIS 4. The following section covers how to install these three services, along with any configuration concerns for the services. Because the installation is automatic, separate sections for the objectives "Install and Configure Certificate Server," "Install and Configure Microsoft SMTP Service," and "Install and Configure Microsoft NNTP Service" are not included in this chapter.

Installing IIS

 **Objective**   Microsoft Internet Information Server (IIS) 4 is the newest Internet and Web server designed to run under Windows NT Server 4.0. Setting up and configuring IIS is the first step in setting up an Internet or intranet site.

IIS 4 includes the following features:

- ▶ Authentication Server
- ▶ SMTP Mail Server
- ▶ Microsoft Management Console
- ▶ NNTP News Server
- ▶ Script Debugger
- ▶ Site Analyst
- ▶ Transaction Server
- ▶ Usage Analyst
- ▶ Web Publishing Wizard
- ▶ Windows Scripting Host
- ▶ FrontPage Server Administrator

After you install IIS 4, you can add Hypertext Markup Language (HTML) files to your server for users to connect to and view.

Configuring a Microsoft Windows NT Server 4 Computer for the Installation of IIS

IIS 4 is available only as part of the Windows NT 4.0 Option Pack. Currently, IIS 4 is available on CD-ROM from Microsoft or as a large download from Microsoft's Web site. You can download it as part of the Windows NT 4.0 Option Pack from Microsoft at the following address:

`http://www.microsoft.com/downtrial/optionpack.asp`

You also can order an Option Pack CD-ROM from Microsoft from the same site. With this download, you're provided with IIS 4, Microsoft Site Server Express 2.0, Transaction Server 2.0, Microsoft Message Queue Server 1.0, Certificate Server 1.0, Index Server Express, Internet Explorer 4.0, remote-access services for virtual networking, and Windows NT Service Pack 3.

 Note
The version of IIS provided with Windows NT 4.0 Server is IIS 2.0. This book covers how to install IIS 4.

Before you set up IIS 4, your system must meet or exceed the hardware requirements summarized in Tables 25.1 and 25.2. Table 25.1 shows requirements for a system running an Intel *x*86 processor. Table 25.2 lists requirements for a system running a DEC Alpha processor.

Table 25.1

IIS 4 hardware requirements for an Intel system.	
Hardware Device	Requirements
CPU	Minimum of a 90MHz 486DX processor. For better performance, you need a Pentium 133-or-higher processor.
Hard disk space	Minimum of 50MB, but it is recommended you have at least 120MB. This does not include storage needed for files you plan to distribute via IIS.
Memory	Minimum of 32MB. For Web site on which you will store multimedia files or expect a great deal of traffic, 48MB is the recommended minimum.
Monitor	Super VGA monitor with 800×600 resolution.

Table 25.2

IIS 4 hardware requirements for an Alpha system.	
Hardware Device	Requirements
CPU	Minimum of 150MHz processor.
Hard disk space	Minimum of 120MB, but you should allocate up to 200MB for best performance.
Memory	Minimum of 48MB. For better performance, have at least 64MB.
Monitor	Super VGA monitor with 800×600 resolution.

 Tip

If you install all the components that ship with IIS 4, you need over 355MB of hard disk space.

Before you install IIS 4, remove any installations of a previous version of IIS. You also should disable other versions of FTP, Gopher, or World Wide Web services you have installed under Windows NT Server 4.0. This includes the Windows Academic Centre (EMWAC) service included with the Windows NT Resource Kit.

You also should have the following software installed:

▶ Windows NT Server 4.0

▶ Service Pack 3 for Windows NT Server 4.0

▶ Internet Explorer 4.01 or higher

You also must be logged on to the Windows NT Server computer with Administrator privileges.

Another consideration before installing IIS 4 is to install TCP/IP (Transmission Control Protocol/Internet Protocol) on your Windows NT 4.0 computer. TCP/IP is used to provide Internet connectivity to retrieve data from the Internet.

For systems in which file-level security is needed, configure Windows NT Server with the NT File System (NTFS). NTFS enables you to limit access to files and directories. Systems running FAT do not allow you to limit access at the file level, only the directory level.

Finally, you should consider installing DHCP (Dynamic Host Configuration Protocol) if you plan to run IIS 4 on an Intranet. DHCP automatically assigns IP (Internet Protocol) addresses to computers connecting to the server and those that are set up to use DHCP. For systems connecting to the Internet, you need to acquire a TCP/IP address from the InterNIC or from an Internet Service Provider (ISP).

 Note

For load balancing purposes, it is recommended that you install DHCP on a different server within your intranet than the one IIS is running on.

 Tip

To help secure your IIS installation, you should perform the following tasks in addition to the tasks described previously:

▶ Turn on auditing (which requires NT to be running on NTFS and not FAT for files and directories).

▶ Limit the Guest account and other accounts to specific directories on the server.

▶ Limit who has membership to the administrators group.

▶ Start only those services and protocols required by your system.

▶ Use complex password schemes.

▶ Review network share permissions.

 Note

Disable NetBIOS over TCP/IP for additional security.

Installing IIS 4

After you get Windows NT Server 4.0 set up to receive IIS 4, you're ready to start the IIS 4 setup program. Make sure you are connected to the Internet or to your intranet before installing IIS.

Tip

If you decide you don't want to install IIS 4 and you've already started the IIS 4 setup program, don't cancel it. This will leave files on your system that the uninstall program cannot remove. Finish the entire installation process, then uninstall IIS 4 if you don't want it on your system.

To start IIS 4 setup, insert the Option Pack CD-ROM and locate the Setup icon in Explorer. Double-click the Setup icon. Or, if you downloaded IIS 4 from the Internet, double-click the setup file.

Note

IIS 4 relies on Internet Explorer 4.0 for many of its management and configuration tasks. If you do not already have IE 4.0 installed, you'll be prompted to install it when you start the IIS 4 setup routine. Be sure to click Yes if prompted to install IE 4.0. Windows NT will need to shut down and restart before continuing with the IIS installation.

Next, perform the following steps:

1. Click Next on the Welcome to the Windows NT 4.0 Option dialog box. The End User License Agreement screen appears.

2. Click Accept.

3. Click Custom. A dialog box with components will appear. You also can click Minimum or Typical, but these steps assume you want to have control over the components that are installed.

4. Click the component you want to install. If you want to change the specific options (called *subcomponents*) that install with the components, click the Show Subcomponents button. This displays a dialog box with the specific options that fall under a component heading. Selected components and subcomponents have check marks next to them.

Specific components and their subcomponents are listed in Table 25.3.

Table 25.3

IIS 4 setup options.

Component	Subcomponents	Description
Certificate Server	Certificate Server Certificate Authority	Enables you to create Certificate Authority on the IIS server to issue digital certificates to users accessing your Web.
	Certificate Server Documentation	Documents to help you install and configure Certificate Authorities.
	Certificate Server Web Client	Enables you to post Web pages on your server to submit requests and retrieve certificates from a Certificate Authority.
FrontPage 98 Server Extensions	FrontPage Server Extensions files	Enables you to author Web pages and administer Web sites using Microsoft FrontPage and Visual InterDev.
Visual InterDev RAD	Visual InterDev RAD Remote Deployment Support	Enables you to deploy applications remotely on the Web server.

Component	Subcomponents	Description
Internet Information Server (IIS)	Common Program Files	Files used by several IIS components.
	Documentation	Product documentation for IIS.
	File Transfer Protocol(FTP) Server	Provides FTP support to set up an FTP site to allow users to upload and download files from your site.
	Internet News Server	Installs the Microsoft Internet News Server for NNTP news.
	Internet Service Manager	Provides a snap-in for the Microsoft Management Console (MMC) to administer IIS.
	Internet Service Manager (HTML)	Provides an HTML-based administrative tool for IIS. You use IE 4.0 with this manager to administer IIS.
	SMTP Server	Installs the SMTP (Simple Mail Transfer Protocol) Server for email.
	World Wide Web samples	Installs sample IIS Web sites and other samples.
	World Wide Web Server	Installs the Web server so clients can access your Web site.
Microsoft Data Access Components 1.5 (MDAC, ADO, ODBC, and OLE)	ActiveX Data Objects (ADO) 1.5	Installs the ActiveX Data Objects and other OLE DB and ODBC files.

continues

Table 25.3   Continued

Component	Subcomponents	Description
	Data Sources	Installs the drivers and providers to access common data sources, including Jet and Access (ODBC), Oracle, and SQL Server data sources.
	Remote Data Service 1.5 (RDS/ADC)	Installs Remote Data Service. Click the Show Subcomponents button to see options for this subcomponent.
Microsoft Index Server	Index Server System Files	Installs the files for the the Index Server system.
	Language Resources	Installs Index Server language resources. Click the Show Subcomponents button to see a list of these languages. US English Language is the default setting.
	Online Documentation	Installs Index Server documentation.
	Sample Files	Installs sample files on how to use the Index Server.
Microsoft Message Queue (MSMQ)	Administration Guide	Installs the MSMQ Administration Guide.
	Administration Tools	Enables you to control and monitor your message queuing enterprise.
	Microsoft Message Queue Server	Installs the required MSMQ files.

Component	Subcomponents	Description
	Software Development Kit	Installs the MSMQ SDK for creating MSMQ applications with C or C++ APIs or with ActiveX components.
Microsoft Script Debugger	Microsoft Script Debugger	Installs the Microsoft Script Debugger to debug Active Server Pages scripts and applications.
Microsoft Site Server Express 2.0	Analysis—Content	Enables you to analyze your site with content, site visualization, link management, and reporting tool.
	Analysis—Usage	Enables you to analyze your site usage.
	Publishing— Posting Acceptor 1.01	Enables IIS to receive files uploaded to it using the HTTP POST protocol.
	Publishing— Web Publishing Wizard 1.52	Automatically uploads new or revised content to Web servers.
Internet Connection Services for RAS (Remote Services)	Connection Manager Administration Kit	Sets up dial-up profiles in Access Connection Manager.
	Connection Point Services	Provides administration and services to phonebooks.
	Internet Authentication Services	Installs the Internet Authentication Service.
	Product Documentation	Installs documentation for Remote Access Services.

continues

Table 25.3 Continued

Component	Subcomponents	Description
Transaction Server	Microsoft Management Console	Installs MMC, which is an interface for systems management applications.
	Transaction Server (MTS) Core Components	Installs MTS files.
	Transaction Server Core Documentation	Installs MTS product documentation.
	Transaction Server Deployment	Installs headers, libraries, and samples to help you create transaction components.
Windows Scripting Host	Windows Scripting Host Files	Installs executable files for the Windows Scripting Host.
	Windows Scripting Host Sample Scripts	Provides sample scripts.

The following steps assume all components and subcomponents are selected. Depending on your choices, you may not see all the dialog boxes shown in these steps.

5. Click Next. A dialog box showing the default publishing folders appears. The following list summarizes these folders:

   ▶ Web services are installed in the `C:\Inetpub\wwwroot` folder.

   ▶ FTP services are installed in the `C:\Inetpub\ftproot` folder.

   ▶ Applications are installed in the `C:\Program Files` folder.

You can change any of these default folders by typing over them or clicking the Browse button next to them.

6. Click Next. The Transaction Server dialog box displays. The MTS Install Folder field shows where Transaction Server will be installed. By default, this folder is named C:\Program Files\Mts. You can change this folder if you like.

7. Click Next. A dialog box to set remote administration features displays. You can choose to administer IIS from a Local account, in which no other account information is needed, or from a Remote account on another machine, which requires the Administrator Account name and its password. You can click the Browse button to locate the Administrator Account.

8. Click Next. The Index Server dialog box displays the default folder for the index. This default directory is C:\Inetpub. You can change this folder if you like.

9. Click Next. The Mail Server dialog box displays the default folder for the mailroot directory. Other folders (mail queue, mailbox, and badmail) will be created under this folder. The default for this folder is C:\Inetpub\Mailroot.

10. Click Next. The News Server dialog box displays the default folder for the nntpfile directory. Articles and data files used by the news server will be stored under this folder. The default for this folder is C:\Inetpub\nntpfile.

11. Click Next. Select from one of the following types of MSMQ servers:

   ▶ **Primary Enterprise Controller (PEC).** Installs only one PEC on the network and contains the master copy of the MSMQ Information Store. This PEC will act as the Primary Site Controller for one site. You must have SQL Server installed to choose this option.

   ▶ **Primary Site Controller (PSC).** Installs one PSC for each site, which is a physical set of computers communicating with each other, usually paralleling the

physical location of the computers. You must have SQL
Server installed to choose this option.

▶ **Backup Site Controller (BSC).** BSCs provide a backup
of the PSC in case the PSC fails. You must have SQL
Server installed to choose this option.

▶ **Routing Server.** Provides routing services, remote message store, and store-and-forward services. These servers are spread across the network to enable messages to
reach a target queue via different paths. Each PEC,
PSC, and BSC also acts as a Routing Server.

12. Click Next. The Microsoft Certificate Server Setup—Introduction dialog box displays. This wizard shows how to create
a new Certificate Authority.

13. Click Next. In the Certificate Server—Choose Storage Location dialog box, enter the location to store configuration
files and certificate files. Unless the Windows NT domain
controller is available for use, enter a shared folder.

14. Click Next. Fill in your identification information, including
name, state, country, locality, and other items.

15. Click Next. In the Choose Key Storage Location dialog box,
enter the names you want for the System Store and Container for your keys.

16. Click Next. In the Choose Database Location dialog box, you
are shown the default folder in which the certificate information will be stored.

17. Click Next. The Choose CSP and Hashing dialog box shows
the Cryptographic Services Providers (CSP) you can select.
You also can choose the hash algorithms from the Hash list.

18. Click Next. The Choose Certificate Output File Names dialog box shows the signature and key exchange certificate
names. You can change these if necessary; however, the default names should suffice for most installations.

19. Click Next. You can enter a comment to identify the certificate later.

20. Click Next. Setup now completes the installation process and installs the IIS files on your hard disk. This process may take a long time to complete.

21. Click Finish when all the files are installed to your system.

22. Click Yes when prompted to restart your computer.

Identifying Changes to a Windows NT Server 4.0 Computer Made by the Installation of IIS

When you install IIS 4, your Windows NT Server 4.0 computer will include some new components:

▶ Microsoft Management Console (MMC) is the host for the Internet Service Manager. Internet Service Manager is IIS's administrative program.

▶ Registry changes can be viewed by selecting Start | Programs | Windows NT 4.0 Option Pack | Microsoft Site Server Express 2.0 | Documentation. Expand the Microsoft Internet Information Server option and click Administrator's Reference in the left pane (see Figure 25.1) and click Registry. Click the topic you want to read, such as WWW Service Registry Entries.

▶ New services include the FTP Publishing Service, IIS Administration Service, Content Index, and World Wide Web Publishing Service.

Note

The three services added during IIS 4 installation—FTP Publishing Service, IIS Administration Service, and World Wide Web Publishing Service—are set to start when you start Windows NT Server. You can change the default settings for each service from the Services dialog box.

Figure 25.1

You can view the different Registry changes from the Windows NT 4.0 Option Pack Documentation.

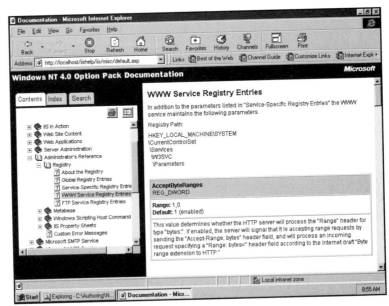

- ▶ User Manager for Domains lists a new username in the list of user accounts. This username is IUSR_*computername* and allows anonymous access to Internet services on your computer.

- ▶ Performance Monitor can now be used to track several IIS services, including Content Index, Content Index Filter, FTP Service, HTTP Content Index, HTTP Service, and Internet Information Services Global. Some of the over 75 counters added to Performance Monitor enable you to track connections, bytes transferred, and cache information.

Configuring IIS to Support the FTP Service

Objective

An FTP (File Transport Protocol) server provides clients attaching to your server the capability of transmitting files to and from the server. Although FTP is one of the oldest Internet services, it is still one of the most popular ways to transfer files over the Internet.

Before you go live with your IIS 4 server, you may want to configure some of the settings relating to FTP. These include

▶ Setting bandwidth and user connections

▶ Setting user logon requirements and authentication requirements

▶ Modifying port settings

▶ Setting directory listing style

▶ Configuring virtual directories and servers

Setting User Connections

To conserve bandwidth for other clients accessing your FTP site, consider limiting the number of connections that can be made to your FTP server. When connection limits are maxed out, those attempting to connect to your server will be rejected and must try again later. Another task you should consider for your FTP site is to limit the bandwidth used by the WWW server. You are shown how to do this in the "Setting Bandwidth and User Connections" section later in this chapter. This will provide more bandwidth for your FTP service.

To set user connections, perform the following steps:

1. Select Start | Programs | Windows NT 4.0 Option Pack | Microsoft Internet Information Server | Internet Service Manager.

2. Expand the Internet Information Server folder.

3. Expand the FTP server that you want to modify.

4. Right-click the Default FTP Site entry. Your Web site may be named something different.

5. Click Properties. The FTP Site Properties sheet appears.

6. On the FTP Site tab, click the Limited To option (see Figure 25.2.

Figure 25.2

Use the FTP Site tab to set the number of simultaneous connections to your site.

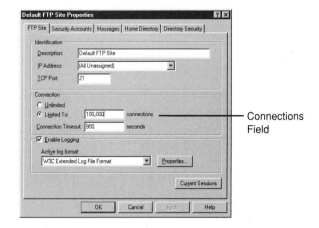

Connections Field

7. Enter a value in the connections field. The default is 100,000, but you may want to lower this if your resources are limited.

8. In the Connection Timeout field, enter a value for the amount of time your server should automatically disconnect an idle session. The default is 15 minutes (900 seconds), but an average setting is five minutes (300 seconds). For an infinite amount of time, enter all 9s in this field.

Note

Even if a connection is lost or a client stops working, your site will continue to process data until the timeout value is reached. Setting an appropriate timeout value will limit the loss of resources due to these lost connections.

9. Click OK, or keep open if you want to continue changing FTP site settings.

Setting User Logon Requirements and Authentication Requirements

To enable clients to access your FTP server, you need to set up user logon and authentication requirements. If you want to allow all users access to your FTP server, you must allow anonymous connections. Users with the name *anonymous* can then log into your site by using their email address as their password.

IIS uses the default IUSR_computername account for all anonymous logons. Permissions set up for this account determine an anonymous user's privileges.

On the FTP Site Properties sheet, Security Accounts tab, you can configure the following options:

- ▶ **Allow Anonymous Connections.** Select this for anonymous connections.

- ▶ **Username.** Displays the IUSR_computername name as set up by IIS in the Windows NT User Manager for Domains and in the Internet Service Manager.

- ▶ **Password.** A randomly generated password was created by User Manager for Domains and Internet Service Manager. You must have a password here; no blanks are allowed. If you change this password, make sure it matches the one in the User Manager for Domains and Internet Service Manager for this user.

- ▶ **Allow only Anonymous Connections.** Click this option to limit access to your FTP server to only those who log on as anonymous. This restricts users from logging on with an account that has administrative rights.

- ▶ **Administrator.** Select those accounts who are allowed to administer this virtual FTP site. Click the Add button to add a user account to this list. Remove an account by selecting the account and clicking Remove.

- ▶ **Enable Automatic Password Synchronization.** Select this option to automatically synchronize the IUSR_Computername account password seen here with the IUSR_computername account password contained in the Windows NT User Account database.

Modifying Port Settings

Port settings are used by clients to connect to your FTP site. By default, the FTP server is set up with a port setting of 21. You can change this setting to a unique TCP port number, but you must announce this setting to all clients who want to access your server.

Perform the following steps to change the port number:

1. Choose the following: Start | Programs | Windows NT 4.0 Option Pack | Microsoft Internet Information Server | Internet Service Manager.

 Tip

You can use the HTML version of Internet Service Manager if you want to administer IIS from Internet Explorer 4.0. The procedures shown in this chapter, however, show how to use the Microsoft Management Console (MMC) to run the Internet Service Manager.

2. Expand the Internet Information Server folder.

3. Expand the server in which you want to modify the port value (see Figure 25.3).

Figure 25.3

The Microsoft Management Console provides access to the Internet Service Manager to administer your FTP site.

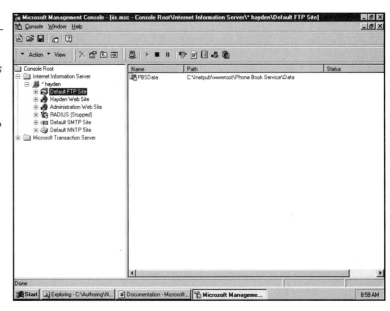

4. Right-click the Default FTP Site entry. Your FTP site may be named something different.

5. Click Properties. The FTP Site Properties sheet displays (see Figure 25.4).

Figure 25.4

Use the FTP Site Properties sheet to change the port setting.

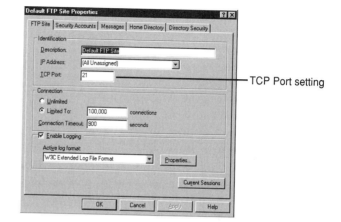

TCP Port setting

6. Change the TCP Port value to a new setting.

7. Click OK.

Setting Directory Listing Style

A directory listing style is the way in which your server will display a directory listing. Because Windows NT Server uses a listing style similar to DOS (such as C:\folder\subfolder), you can change this to display in UNIX format. UNIX format (such as /c/directory/subdirectory/) is commonly found on the Internet and is expected by most Web browsers. Use UNIX format for the greatest compatibility on the Internet.

To change your server's directory listing style, perform the following steps:

1. From the FTP Site Properties sheet (see the preceding section), click the Home Directory tab (see Figure 25.5).

2. Under Directory Listing Style, select UNIX. The default is MS-DOS.

3. Click OK, or keep open if you want to continue changing FTP settings.

Figure 25.5

The Home Directory tab includes settings for changing the directory listing style, as well as other default FTP directory settings.

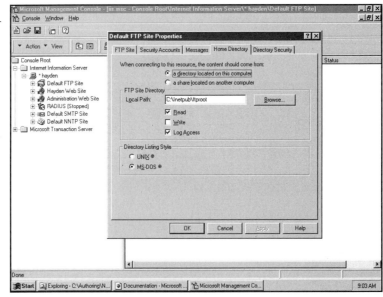

Configuring FTP Home Directory

IIS 4 enables you to change the home directory for your virtual server. When you install the FTP service, IIS 4 creates a default home directory called \inetpub\ftproot. This directory, which has no name and is indicated by a slash (/) in a URL, is the primary location for FTP files.

You place files in the home directory and its subdirectories to enable clients to access them (the files).

To change your home directories, perform the following steps:

1. From the FTP Site Properties sheet (see the preceding section), make sure the Home Directory tab appears (refer to Figure 25.5).

2. In the When connecting to this resource, the content should come from area, select one of the following paths:

   ▶ **A Directory Located on This Computer.** Select this option to specify a local directory.

> ▶ **A Share Located on Another Computer.** Select this option to specify a directory on another computer on the network.

3. In the Local Path field (or Network Share if you select the second option from the preceding list), enter the path to the directory you want to specify as the home directory. For local directories, use standard syntax, such as C:\directory\subdirectory. However, network paths must follow the Universal Naming Convention (UNC), such as *computername**sharename*. For shares, enter the username and password to access that computer, if prompted.

4. Set the home directory access controls from the following options:

> ▶ **Read.** Lets clients read and download files you store in the home directory or in virtual directories. You must select Read permissions for FTP directories, or every request for a file stored in the home directory will result in an error message being returned to the client. By default, this option is selected.

> ▶ **Write.** Lets clients upload files to the home directory on your FTP server. This option should be selected only for FTP servers in which users must upload files. By default, this option is not selected.

Note   Directory settings for home directories set up on NTFS drives must match NTFS settings. If settings do not match, IIS uses the most restrictive settings.

> ▶ **Log Access.** Provides a record of visitors to the home directory. By default, this option is selected.

5. Click OK.

IIS 4 also enables you to create Virtual Directories, which enable you to set up directories located on other servers for your visitors to access. You set up Virtual Directories from Internet Service

Manager. Perform the following steps to create Virtual Directories for your FTP service:

1. Right-click on the FTP server and select New | Virtual Directory. The New Virtual Directory Wizard displays (see Figure 25.6).

Figure 25.6

Assign a name to your new Virtual Directory.

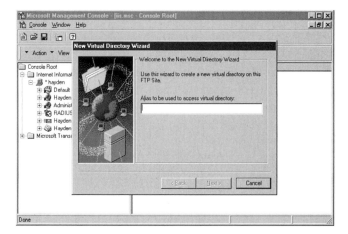

2. Enter a name for the Virtual Directory. The name you enter here will be the name placed in the URL to access this directory.

3. Click Next. Enter the path to the directory to which you want the Virtual Directory to point. Use UNC notation for directories on another system.

4. Click Next. Set the following permissions to the Virtual Directory:

   ▶ **Allow Read Access.** Enables visitors to read files on the Virtual Directory.

   ▶ **Allow Write Access.** Enables visitors to write files to the Virtual Directory.

5. Click Finish.

Configuring IIS to Support the WWW Service

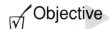 Objective

After you install IIS 4, you can configure the WWW service for your Web site. The configuration changes you can make include the following:

► Setting bandwidth and user connections

► Setting user logon requirements and authentication requirements

► Modifying port settings

► Setting default pages

► Setting HTTP 1.1 host header names to host multiple Web sites

► Enabling HTTP keep-alives

Setting Bandwidth and User Connections

In order to conserve bandwidth for other clients accessing your Web site, consider limiting the number of connections that can connect to your site. When connection limits are maxed out, those attempting to connect to your server will be rejected and must try again later. You can limit the number of connections to your Web site, email, or news servers.

Another task you should consider for your Web site is to limit the bandwidth used by the Web server. This leaves bandwidth available for other services, such as email or news services. Limiting bandwidth is known as *throttling bandwidth*, and it limits only the bandwidth used by static HTML files. If you have multiple sites set up, you can throttle the bandwidth used by each site.

Tip

If you want to view your Web site's connection activity, open Windows NT Performance Monitor and set it to view FTP Service or Web Service from the Object list. You then can view Anonymous Users/sec, Bytes Received/sec, and other counters. Use this information to help you set the bandwidth and user connections.

To set user connections and set bandwidth throttling, follow Exercise 25.2 at the end of the chapter.

Setting User Logon Requirements and Authentication Requirements

IIS 4 can be set up to verify the identity of clients who access your Web site. On public Web sites on which noncritical or public domain information and applications are available, authentication of users connecting to your Web site may not be important. However, if you have secure data or want to restrict Web access to specific clients, logon and authentication requirements become very important.

Perform the following steps to set authentication and logon requirements:

1. Open Internet Service Manager.

2. Right-click a Web site, file (NTFS systems only), or directory you want to configure.

3. Click Properties. The property sheet for that item will appear.

4. Click the Directory Security (or File Security if you want to set file-specific properties) tab (see Figure 25.7).

5. Click the Edit button under Anonymous Access and Authentication Control. The Authentication Methods dialog box appears (see Figure 25.8)

Figure 25.7

You can set logon and authentica-tion requirements from the Directory Security tab.

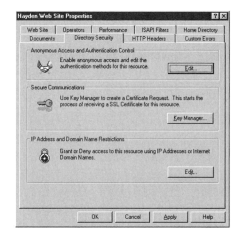

Figure 25.8

Select one or more authentica-tion methods from the Authentica-tion Methods dialog box.

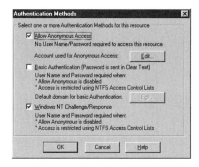

6. Select an authentication method from the following options:

   ▶ **Allow Anonymous Access.** This option enables clients to connect to your Web site without requiring a username or password. Click the Edit button to select the Win-dows NT user account used to access your computer. The default account IUSR_computername is used. This account is granted Log on Locally user rights by default and is necessary for anonymous logon access to your Web site. Click OK to return to the Authentication Methods dialog box.

   ▶ **Basic Authentication.** Use this method if you do not specify anonymous access and you want a client con-necting to your Web site to enter a valid Windows NT username and password to logon. This sends a pass-word in clear text format with the passwords being transmitted in an unencrypted format. Click the Edit button to specify a default logon domain for users who do not explicitly name a domain.

▶ **Windows NT Challenge/Response.** This setting is used if you want the Windows NT Challenge/Response feature to authenticate the client attempting to connect to your Web site. The only Web browsers that support this feature include Internet Explorer 2.0 and higher. During the challenge/response procedure, encrytped information is exchanged between the client and server to authenticate the user.

> **Tip**
>
> IIS 4 uses the Basic and Windows NT Challenge/Response to authenticate users if anonymous access is denied either through the dialog box or via NTFS permissions.

7. Click OK.

If you have a server certificate installed, you also can use the Secure Sockets Layer (SSL) to authenticate users logging on to your Web site.

Modifying Port Settings

In a process similar to setting the port for FTP sites, you can change the default port setting for your Web site to any unique TCP port number. If you do this, however, you must let all clients know of your port setting before they can connect to your Web site. For a port setting other than the default, which is 80, the user must enter the port value as part of the URL.

To set the port setting, perform the following steps:

1. In the Web Site Properties dialog box, click the Web Site tab (see Figure 25.9).

2. In the TCP Port field, enter a new value for the port address. This must be a unique TCP value for your server.

Figure 25.9

The default port setting is usually the best for public Web sites, but you can change it by modifying the TCP Port setting on the Web Site tab.

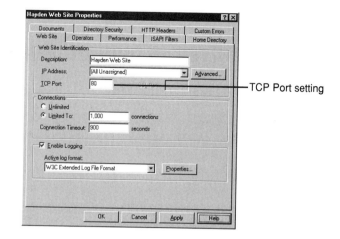

TCP Port setting

3. Click OK, or keep open if you want to continue changing Web site settings.

Setting Default Pages

If you have any experience browsing the Web, you know that for many sites you do not have to enter a specific document name (such as index.html) when accessing the Web site's home page. You can set IIS 4 to display a default page when clients access your site without a specified document in the URL. From this default page (usually your home page or index page), you can direct users to other documents or resources on your site.

IIS 4 enables you to specify more than one default document and list the documents in order of preference. When a client connects to your site, IIS searches for the topdocument and displays it if found. If it can't be found—for example, it is being updated or edited—the next default document is displayed.

To set default pages, perform the following:

1. From the Web Site Properties sheet, click the Documents tab (see Figure 25.10).

2. Select the Enable Default Document button. This option is enabled by default.

Figure 25.10

Setting a default document enables users to connect to your Web site without specifying a document name.

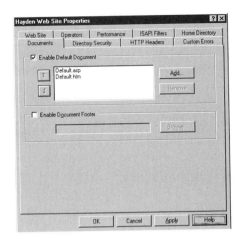

3. Click the Add button to specify a different default document.

4. In the Add Default Document dialog box, specify a new default document. An example of one that many Web sites use is index.htm.

5. Click OK.

6. Click the up or down arrows on the Documents tab to modify the search order for the default documents.

7. Click the Enable Document Footer option if you want IIS to insert an HTML file (which is really a short HTML document with formatting tags for footer content) to the bottom of your Web documents.

8. Enter the path and filename for the footer file.

9. Click OK, or keep open if you want to continue changing Web site settings.

Setting HTTP 1.1 Host Header Names to Host Multiple Web Sites

IIS 4 provides support for HTTP 1.1 host headers to allow multiple host names to be associated with one IP address. With this feature, a separate IP address is not needed for every virtual server you support. Microsoft Internet Explorer 3.0-and-later and Netscape Navigator 2.0-and-later support this feature, but many other browsers do not.

To set host header names for multiple Web sites, perform the following steps:

1. From the Web Site Properties sheet, click the Web Site tab.

2. Click the Advanced button. The Advanced Multiple Web Site Configuration dialog box displays (see Figure 25.11).

Figure 25.11

Add multiple host header names for hosting multiple Web sites.

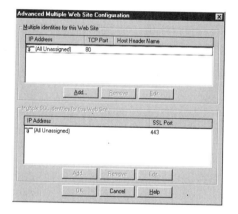

3. Click the Add button. The Advanced Web Site Identification dialog box displays (see Figure 25.12).

Figure 25.12

Fill in the information to identify the multiple host name.

4. Fill in the IP Address, TCP Port, and Host Header Name fields. The IP Address field must include an IP address that has already been defined by the DHCP Server. The Host Header Name field must include a registered DNS value.

5. Click OK.

6. Click OK to close the Advanced Multiple Web Site Configuration dialog box, or click Add to continue adding new multiple host header names to this site.

7. Click OK to close the Web Site Properties sheet.

Enabling HTTP Keep-Alives

You can enable IIS 4's Keep-Alive feature to enable clients to maintain open connections. This way a client does not need to re-establish connections for each request. By enabling Keep-Alive, you decrease the amount of time a client waits to connect to another document or application on your site. But you also increase the amount of resources devoted to this client.

To enable HTTP keep-alives, perform the following steps:

1. From the Web Site Properties sheet, click the Performance tab (see Figure 25.13).

Figure 25.13

Enable the HTTP keep-alive setting on the Performance tab.

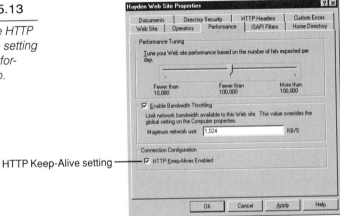

HTTP Keep-Alive setting

2. Select HTTP Keep-Alives Enabled. This option is enabled by default. If a checkmark already appears in this checkbox, no changes are needed.

3. Click OK.

Configuring and Saving Consoles by Using Microsoft Management Console

☑ Objective ▶ Microsoft Management Console (MMC) is used to organize and perform management tasks for IIS 4. MMC does not actually administer any part of IIS or your network; rather, it provides a framework for other applications (called *snap-ins*) to administer parts of the network. Internet Service Manager, for instance, is a snap-in. When Internet Service Manager starts (not the HTML version), an MMC console appears with the Internet Service Manager displayed as a snap-in.

In the future, Microsoft BackOffice and Windows NT will offer MMC snap-in administration tools. Other vendors are expected to provide snap-ins as well.

When you start a snap-in in MMC, a console displays. Consoles have one or more windows. The Internet Service Manager, for instance, includes two windows. On the left side, called the *scope pane*, a tree view is shown. The right pane, which shows the results of selecting something on the left page, is called the *results pane*.

You can view multiple windows in a console and then save that view for later. You might, for instance, create one window to show a snap-in for changing settings and another window to display a Web page with program updates. You can then display that window view or share it with other users via email, floppy disk, or network.

Verifying Server Settings by Accessing the Metabase

☑ Objective ▶ The *metabase* is a memory-resident data storage area that stores your IIS 4 configuration values. The metabase is analogous to, but not identical to, the Windows NT Registry. It is also faster and more flexible than the Registry. The metabase has keys that correspond to IIS elements; each key has properties that affect the configuration of that element. The hierarchy of the NNTP service keys, for example, is shown in Figure 25.14.

Figure 25.14

The hierarchy of the NNTP service keys.

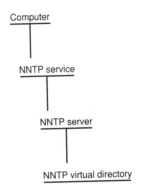

You can use the IIS Administration Objects to configure your IIS 4 installation, as well as change settings that affect the operation of your IIS Web server, FTP site, virtual directories, and other components. One application that uses the IIS Administration in Objects is the Internet Service Manager (HTML) that you use in Internet Explorer 4.0 (see Figure 25.15).

Figure 25.15

The HTML version of Internet Service Manager uses IIS Administration Objects to configure IIS components.

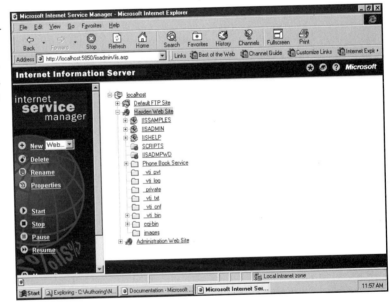

Choosing the Appropriate Administration Method

 **Objective**

IIS 4 provides two main ways to administer your IIS installation. You still must use the common Windows NT administration tools to set file and directory rights and user accounts, and to view performance measurements. But to administer IIS 4, you use Internet Service Manager, either as a snap-in to MMC or as an HTML application in Internet Explorer 4.0.

With Internet Service Manager (HTML), you can manage your Web site remotely using a standard Web browser (IE 4.0 is recommended). This makes it convenient for administrators to manage a Web site when physically away from the Web site. An administrator, for instance, may be located in a different building than where the Web server is housed. By using Internet Service Manager (HTML), the administrator can connect to the server and administer it from the remote location.

Internet Service Manager (HTML) can be customized using Active Server Pages and the IIS Administration Objects. By customizing Internet Service Manager (HTML), or by creating new HTML-based administration tools, ISPs and administrators can create pages for customers or users to modify settings on the Web.

For administration tasks on the server, administrators can use familiar Windows NT Server administration tools, including the following:

- ▶ **User Manager for Domains.** Create a new user for your system to access file, print, and Web services.

- ▶ **Event Viewer.** Monitor systems events and log application and security events used by the Web server. Event Viewer also can be used to audit access to secure files.

- ▶ **Performance Monitor.** Monitor the performance of IIS 4, including FTP and Web services, including HTTP and indexing counters. Use Performance Monitor to get a view of server load.

Customizing the Installation of Microsoft Site Server Express Analysis Content Analyzer

☑ Objective

The Site Server Express Analysis Content Analyzer (Content Analyzer for short) enables you to create WebMaps to give you a view of your Web site, helping you manage your Web site. WebMaps are graphical representations of resources on your site. These resources can include HTML documents, audio and video files, Java applets, FTP resources, and applications.

Content Analyzer also enables you to manage your links. You can ensure links are included in the resources and that they all work correctly.

When you install IIS 4, you have the option of installing all or part of the Microsoft Site Server Express 2.0 tool. If you choose the Content Analyzer option (refer to Table 25.3), the Analysis-Content subcomponent should be selected if you want to install the Content Analyzer.

The system requirements and recommendations for installing Content Analyzer are shown in Table 25.4.

Table 25.4

Content Analyzer system requirements.		
Component	Requirement	Recommendation
CPU	Intel 486 66MHz	120MHz Pentium
RAM	16MB	32MB
Hard disk space	14MB	
Internet connection	Modem	Direct
Browser	IE 3.0 or above Netscape Navigator 3.0 or above	IE 4.0
Authoring tools	Not required	Recommended
Multimedia applications	Not required	Recommended

After IIS 4 is installed, you start Content Analyzer by selecting Start I Programs I Windows NT 4.0 Option Pack I Site Server Express 2.0 I Content Analyzer. Click the Open WebMap button to display WebMaps in Content Analyzer. A sample WebMap is included, named SAMPLE.WMP. The Content Analyzer displays as shown in Figure 25.16. This screen shows an example of a Web-Map created by Content Analyzer and displayed in tree and Cyberbolic views.

Figure 25.16

Most Web site administrators use the tree and Cyberbolic views to view WebMaps.

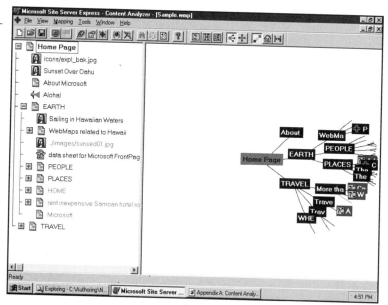

Customizing the Installation of Microsoft Site Server Analysis Report Writer and Usage Import

Site Server Express includes two types of usage components: the Usage Import (see Figure 25.17) and Report Writer (see Figure 25.18). These tools enable you to gather and review IIS 4 log files from a server. With the data you collect from nine different reports, you can chart and identify trends on the usage of your IIS server.

Figure 25.17

Usage Import enables you to log data about your IIS 4 site.

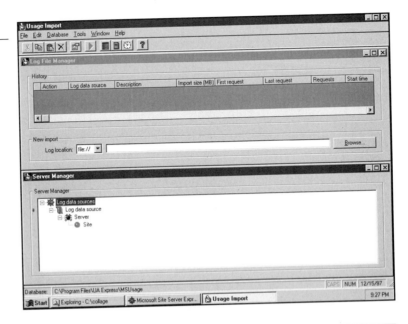

Figure 25.18

Report Writer is used to create reports from site data collected by Usage Import and saved in a database.

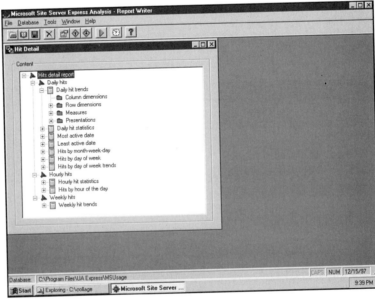

When you plan to use Usage Import and Report Writer, you should also install a relational database. The database is used to store imported log file data so each of the Site Server Express components can interact with the database to process, organize, and analyze the data. Usage Import is used to filter and configure the data in the database. Report Writer then uses that information to create reports based on the activity on your IIS site.

You can install Report Writer if you select to install the Site Server Analysis Usage Import component. The system requirements and recommendations for installing Usage Import and Report Writer are shown in Table 25.5.

Table 25.5

Usage Import and Report Writer system require-ments.

Component	Requirement	Recommendation
CPU	90MHz Pentium	133MHz Pentium
RAM	16MB	32MB
Hard disk space	15MB	Additional space for log files needed
Internet connection	Modem	Direct
Browser	HTML 2-compatible browser that supports tables	IE 4.0

 Tip You can use the Internet connection to resolve IP addresses, run Whois inquiries, and conduct HTML title lookups.

You also may want to install the following optional reporting applications:

▶ Microsoft Word version 7 (or later) to create Word reports

▶ Microsoft Excel version 7 (or later) to create spreadsheet reports

▶ Microsoft Access or the Access runtime version

▶ Microsoft SQL Server if the total size of your databases are more than 75MB per month

▶ Precompiled DLL for Microsoft ISAPI

▶ Source code for Apache and Netscape NSAPI server extensions

Note

When Access is used with Usage Import and Report Writer, a default database by the name of ANALYST.MDB is created by the installation program. A compressed copy of ANALYST.MDB in its original format (no Internet sites or log file data are contained in this file) is created in a zip file called TEMPLATE.ZIP. Use this file if you need to create a new database.

Exercises

Exercise 25.1: Installing IIS

The following exercise walks you through a simple installation of IIS:

1. Insert the Option Pack CD-ROM and locate the Setup icon in Explorer. Double-click on the Setup icon. If you downloaded IIS 4 from the Internet, double-click on the setup file.

2. Click Next on the Welcome to the Windows NT 4.0 Option dialog box. The End User License Agreement screen appears.

3. Click Accept.

4. Click Custom.

5. Click the components you want to install. Click Next. A dialog box showing the default publishing folders appears. A list summarizing folder locations appears.

6. Click Next. Walk through the dialog boxes adding the components you selected in step 5.

7. After installing the components, click Next. Setup now completes the installation process and installs the IIS files on your hard disk.

8. Click Finish when all the files are installed to your system.

9. Click Yes when prompted to restart your computer.

Exercise 25.2: Setting User Connections and Bandwidth Throttling

The following exercise walks you through setting user connections and setting bandwidth throttling:

1. Select Start | Programs | Windows NT 4.0 Option Pack | Microsoft Internet Information Server | Internet Service Manager.

2. Expand the Internet Information Server folder.

3. Expand the server that you want to modify.

4. Right-click the Default Web Site entry. Your Web site may be named something different.

5. Click Properties. The Web Site Properties sheet appears.

6. On the Web Site tab, click the Limited To option (see Figure 25.19).

Figure 25.19

Use the Web Site tab to set the number of simultaneous connections to your site.

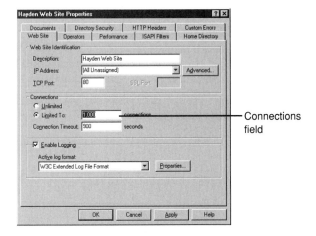

Connections field

7. Enter a value in the connections field. The default is 1,000, but you may want to lower this if your resources are limited.

8. In the Connection Timeout field, enter a value for the amount of time your server should automatically disconnect an idle session. The default is 15 minutes (900 seconds), but an average setting is five minutes (300 seconds). For an infinite amount of time, enter all 9s in this field.

Note

Even if a connection is lost or a browser stops working, your site will continue to process data until the timeout value is reached. Setting an appropriate timeout value will limit the loss of resources due to these lost connections.

9. Click the Performance tab (see Figure 25.20).

Figure 25.20

Set the band-width throttling value to limit the bandwidth available to your Web site.

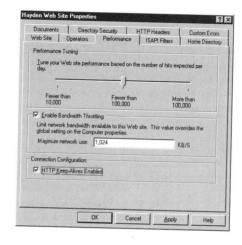

10. Click the Enable Bandwidth Throttling option.

11. In the Maximum network use field, enter a value for the amount of bandwidth (measured in KB/S) you want IIS to use.

 Tip

The value you set on the Performance tab overrides settings for bandwidth throttling set on the Computer Properties sheet. This is true even if the value on the Performance tab is set higher than that on the Computer Properties sheet.

12. Click OK, or keep open if you want to continue changing Web site settings.

Exercise 25.3:   Configuring Views

The following exercise shows you how to copy a window view, create a view with a different root, and close the scope pane:

1. Select Start|Programs|Windows NT 4.0 Option Pack|Microsoft Internet Information Server|Internet Service Manager. MMC displays with Internet Service Manager (see Figure 25.21).

2. Select Window|New Window. A copy of the window displays.

Figure 25.21

MMC with Internet Service Manager snap-in displayed.

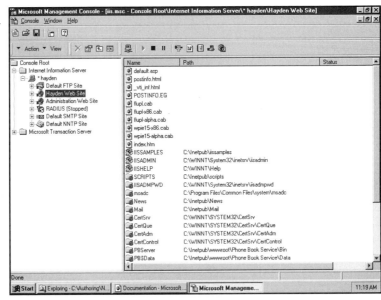

3. To create a view with a different root, click the node you want to view as the root.

4. Click the Action menu.

5. Click New window from here. A new window will appear with the node you select as the root node (see Figure 25.22).

Figure 25.22

A node selected as the root node.

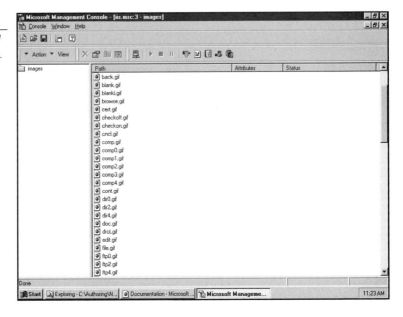

6. To view only the results pane, click the Action menu.

7. Click the Scope Pane option. The scope pane (the left pane) is removed so only the results pane shows.

8. To save this console, select Console | Save As.

9. Fill out the Save As dialog box. Consoles have an MSC extension.

10. Click Save.

Review Questions

1. As an IIS consultant, you're asked to install IIS on an intranet in your client's company. From the following choices, what are two changes to Windows NT you should make before installing IIS?

   A. Install TCP/IP and WINS

   B. Install DHCP and NTFS

   C. Install FAT32 and WINS

   D. None of the above

2. IIS 4 introduces the Microsoft Management Console (MMC) for managing and administering IIS tasks and resources. What types of applications can you run in MMC?

   A. DHTML pages

   B. Plug-ins

   C. Snap-ins

   D. All of the above

3. You are the administrator for an Internet site in a small publishing firm. The firm wants visitors to be able to enter the firm's domain name without a specific document to access the home page. What must you enable in IIS to allow this?

   A. A default page

   B. An index page

   C. home.html

   D. A virtual server with index.html

4. You are the administrator of your company's Internet and intranet site. You are away from the office and must access the IIS server for administration concerns. What is the best administration method for this situation?

   A. Connect to your FTP server as administrator.

   B. Use Internet Explorer 4.0 to access the default page.

   C. Use Internet Service Manager (HTML) to connect to the server via the Internet.

   D. All of the above.

5. You are an IIS consultant. A client wants to install ISS to support email, Web and FTP services, and database access. What are the minimum components that you must install?

   A. SMTP Service, WWW Service, FTP Service, Site Server Express, Index Server

   B. Full install

   C. NNTP Service, Web and FTP Services, ODBC support

   D. SMTP Service, WWW Service, FTP Service, Microsoft Data Access Components 1.5 with Data Sources

6. You're hired by a client to install IIS. The client wants to ensure that the WWW service is as secure as possible. Pick three choices from the following that will help provide a secure environment for IIS:

   A. Limit the Guest account and other accounts to specific directories on the server.

   B. Turn off auditing.

   C. Review network share permissions.

   D. Limit who has membership to the administrators group.

7. As the administrator of your company's intranet site, you need to connect to the server remotely for administration concerns. You plan to use Internet Service Manager (HTML). What privileges are required to do this?

    A. Guest rights

    B. Local user rights

    C. Administrator rights

    D. None of the above

8. You are an IIS administrator in an accounting firm. You are asked to install IIS on a server and you start the installation process. During the IIS Setup routine, you decide to end the installation to start it again the following day. What is your best course of action?

    A. Click the Cancel button to stop Setup.

    B. Finish Setup and then uninstall IIS.

    C. Shut down and restart Windows NT Server 4.0 and edit the Metabase.

    D. None of the above.

9. You are using Internet Service Manager and want to hide the scope pane. Select the correct sequence of steps from the following answers to complete this task:

    A. Select Console | Hide Scope Pane.

    B. Select Window | Panes | Hide Scope Pane.

    C. Select View | List.

    D. Select Action | Scope Pane.

10. As an IIS consultant, you're requested to set up IIS in a man-
    ufacturing firm. The firm would like IIS to be set up so Inter-
    net users must log in using a username and password. The
    firm wants the Windows NT Challenge/Response authenti-
    cation feature to be used to authenticate the user. Which of
    the following answers is the best for this situation?

    A. The user must use an HTML 3.2–compatible browser.

    B. The user must use Internet Explorer 2.0 or later.

    C. The user must invoke Challenge/Response authentica-
       tion on his/her client.

    D. None of the above.

11. When setting up the FTP Service in IIS, you want to enable
    anonymous users to upload files to the FTP server. What
    permission is needed to do this?

    A. Write Only

    B. Execute

    C. Read

    D. Both A and C

12. You are an IIS administrator and need to install IIS on a new
    server. During IIS installation, what services can be installed?
    (Choose three.)

    A. Certificate Server

    B. Transaction Server

    C. Message Queue

    D. Gopher

13. You've installed IIS on your Windows NT Server 4.0 server. What are two changes that have been made to this server after IIS has been installed?

    A. You'll no longer be able to use IE 4.0 as a client application.

    B. Performance Monitor will have Web Service objects available.

    C. User Manager for Domains lists a new username in the list of user accounts.

    D. The Metabase replaces the Windows NT Registry.

14. You are an Internet administrator in a small foam packaging firm. You've set up IIS to run an Internet site. What is the name of the new user created by IIS during installation? (computername is the computer name on which IIS is installed)

    A. IISR_computername

    B. anon_computername

    C. IWAM_computername

    D. IUSR_computername

15. You use Performance Monitor to monitor activity on your IIS server. Pick three counters that you can add to Performance Monitor to track the Web Service object:

    A. Anonymous Users/sec

    B. Bytes Created/sec

    C. Files/sec

    D. Total Head Requests

Review Answers

1. **B**. For systems in which file-level security is needed, configure NTFS so you can limit access to files and directories. Also, you should consider installing DHCP if you plan to run IIS 4 on an Intranet.

2. **C**. MMC does not actually administer any part of IIS or your network; rather, it provides a framework for other applications (called snap-ins) to administer parts of the network. Internet Service Manager, for instance, is a snap-in. When Internet Service Manager starts (not the HTML version), an MMC console appears with the Internet Service Manager displayed as a snap-in.

3. **A**. You can set IIS 4 to display a default page when clients access your site without a specified document in the URL. From this default page (usually your home page or index page), you can direct users to other documents or resources on your site.

4. **C**. With Internet Service Manager (HTML), you can manage your Web site remotely using a standard Web browser, such as IE 4.0. This makes it convenient for administrators to manage a Web site when physically away from the Web site. An administrator, for instance, may be located in a different building than where the Web server is housed.

5. **D**. Table 2.3 describes the different services and components you can install with IIS 4.

6. **A, C, D**. To help secure your IIS installation, you should perform the following tasks:

   ▶ Turn on auditing.

   ▶ Limit the Guest account and other accounts to specific directories on the server.

   ▶ Limit who has membership to the administrators group.

> ▶ Start only those services and protocols required by your system.

> ▶ Use complex password schemes.

> ▶ Review network share permissions.

7. **C.** By using Internet Service Manager (HTML), the administrator can connect to the server and administer it from the remote location.

8. **B.** If you decide you don't want to install IIS 4 and you've already started the IIS 4 setup program, don't cancel it. This will leave files on your system that the uninstall program cannot remove. Finish the entire installation process, then uninstall IIS 4 if you don't want it on your system.

9. **D.** To view only the results pane, click the Action menu and click the Scope Pane option. The scope pane (the left pane) is removed, so only the results pane shows.

10. **B.** Windows NT Challenge/Response feature authenticates the client attempting to connect to your Web site. The only Web browsers that support this feature include Internet Explorer 2.0 and higher. During the challenge/response procedure, encrypted information is exchanged between the client and server to authenticate the user.

11. **A.** Write enables clients to upload files to the home directory on your FTP server. This option should be selected only for FTP servers in which users must upload files. By default, this option is not selected.

12. **A, B, C.** Table 2.3 describes the different services and components you can install with IIS 4.

13. **B, C.** When you install IIS 4, your Windows NT Server 4.0 compute will change. The following are the changes that occur:

> ▶ Microsoft Management Console (MMC) is the host for the Internet Service Manager. Internet Service Manager is IIS's administrative program.

▶ Registry changes can be viewed by selecting
Start I Programs I Windows NT 4.0 Option
Pack I Microsoft Site Server Express 2.0 I Documentation. Click on Administrator's Reference in the left
pane and click Registry. Click on the topic you want to
read, such as WWW Service Registry Entries.

▶ New services include the FTP Publishing Service, IIS
Administration Service, Content Index, and World
Wide Web Publishing Service.

▶ User Manager for Domains lists a new username in the
list of user accounts. This username is IUSR_*computername*
and allows anonymous access to Internet services on
your computer.

▶ Performance Monitor can now be used to track several
IIS services, including Content Index, Content Index
Filter, FTP Service, HTTP Content Index, HTTP Service, and Internet Information Services Global. Some
of the over 75 counters added to Performance Monitor
enable you to track connections, bytes transferred, and
cache information.

14. **D**. User Manager for Domains lists a new username in the
list of user accounts. This username is IUSR_*computername* and
allows anonymous access to Internet services on your computer.

15. **A, C, D**. Performance Monitor can now be used to track
HTTP Services. Some of the over 75 counters added to Performance Monitor enable you to track connections, bytes
transferred, and cache information. Chapter 6 discusses
Performance Monitor in more detail.

Answers to Test Yourself Questions at Beginning of Chapter

1. Microsoft Index Server 3.0, Microsoft Certificate Server, and Internet News Server. See "Installing IIS 4."

2. Anonymous access must be disabled, and anonymous access is denied because Windows NT permissions are set requiring the user to log on with a username and password. See "Setting User Logon Requirements and Authentication Requirements."

3. The client can use standard Windows NT Server administration tools, including Performance Monitor and User Manager for Domains. In addition, Internet Service Manager can be used as a snap-in to the Microsoft Management Console (MMC). For remote administration, Internet Service Manager (HTML) can be used in Internet Explorer 4.0. See "Choosing the Appropriate Administration Method."

4. Set the connection timeout period to a reasonable amount. See "Setting Bandwidth and User Connections."

5. Anonymous authentication. See "Setting User Logon Requirements and Authentication Requirements."

6. The metabase is a hierarchical database that stores IIS 4 settings. The metabase has keys that correspond to IIS elements; each key has properties that affect the configuration of that element. It is analogous to the Windows NT Registry, but it is much faster and more flexible then the Registry. See "Verifying Server Settings by Accessing the Metabase."

7. Yes, you can. Create a console view of the Web server you want to share and select Action I New Window From Here. When the new window displays, select Console I Save As and save the console with an MSC extension. Send the file to the other administrator. See "Configuring and Saving Consoles By Using Microsoft Management Console."

C h a p t e r 26

Configuring and Managing Resource Access

This chapter helps you prepare for the exam by covering the following objectives:

 Objectives

- ▶ Create and share directories with appropriate permissions. Tasks include the following:

    - ▶ Setting directory-level permissions

    - ▶ Setting file-level permission

- ▶ Create and share local and remote virtual directories with appropriate permissions. Tasks include the following:

    - ▶ Creating a virtual directory and assigning an alias

    - ▶ Setting directory-level permissions

    - ▶ Setting file-level permissions

- ▶ Create and share virtual servers with appropriate permissions. Tasks include the following:

    - ▶ Assigning IP addresses

- ▶ Write scripts to manage the FTP service or the WWW service

- ▶ Manage a web site by using Content Analyzer. Tasks include the following:

    - ▶ Creating, customizing, and navigating WebMaps

continues

- ▶ Examining a Web site by using the various reports provided by Content Analyzer

- ▶ Tracking links by using a WebMap

▶ Configure Microsoft SMTP Service to host personal mailboxes

▶ Configure Microsoft NNTP Service to host a newsgroup

▶ Configure Certificate Server to issue certificates

▶ Configure Index Server to index a web site

▶ Manage MIME types

▶ Manage the FTP service

▶ Manage the WWW service

Test Yourself! Before reading this chapter, test yourself to determine how much study time you will need to devote to this section.

1. What is the default port used for the WWW service?

2. Where should virtual directories always be stored?

3. Virtual servers allow one server to alias multiple what?

4. What utility included with the Windows NT Resource Kit can be used to count the number of lines in a log file?

5. What are two views that can be seen of a web site with Web-Maps?

6. What is the default port used for the SMTP service?

7. By default, and in the absence of SSL, what is the TCP port that the NNTP service uses?

8. After using Key Manager to generate a digital certificate request file for use with SSL, what must you do next?

9. With Index Server, what percentage of disk space does the data require?

10. MIME is an acronym for what?

11. In terms of increments of time, FTP log files can be created on what basis?

12. What is the process used to make a WWW site hidden?

Answers are located at the end of the chapter....

This chapter is a broad collection of assorted topics, many of which are addressed elsewhere in this book, but not in the context of configuration and management. Much of the configuration and management of services is done during the initial planning, installation, or troubleshooting phases. This chapter looks at the topics from a fine-tuning standpoint and accentuate what has already been addressed.

The topics covered in this chapter include the following:

- ▶ Creating and Sharing Directories

- ▶ Creating and Sharing Virtual Directories

- ▶ Creating and Sharing Virtual Servers

- ▶ Writing Scripts for Service Management

- ▶ Using Content Analyzer

- ▶ Configuring SMTP

- ▶ Configuring NNTP

- ▶ Configuring Certificate Server

- ▶ Configuring Index Server

- ▶ Managing MIME Types

- ▶ Managing the FTP Service

- ▶ Managing the WWW Service

Creating and Sharing Directories

To create and share a new WWW or FTP directory, start the Internet Service Manager and select the server on which you want to create the directory. After that, implement the following steps:

1. Right-click and select New. This brings up the choice of creating an FTP or WWW site. Make the appropriate selection and the corresponding wizard starts. (WWW is used for the rest of this discussion.)

2. Enter the Web site description and select Next.

3. Select or verify the IP address to use. If you are creating a new site, make certain you use an address that is not currently being used, or it will create a conflict with the current one.

4. The TCP port defaults to 80. This is the default used for all WWW services. If you want to offer the service but hide it from most browsers, choose another port.

5. If SSL is to be used, enter the appropriate port for it (default is 443), and click Next.

6. Enter the path for what will appear as the home directory (you also can use the Browse button to specify).

7. By default, the checkbox appears, allowing anonymous access to the Web site (see Figure 26.1). If you do not want anonymous access, remove the check. Choose Next.

8. Select the access permissions for the directory. Choices include the following:

   ▶ Allow Read Access—Assigned by default

   ▶ Allow Script Access—Assigned by default

   ▶ Allow Execute Access—Includes Script access

   ▶ Allow Write Access

   ▶ Allow Directory Browsing

9. Choose Finish.

Figure 26.1

Selecting the home directory path and whether or not anonymous access is allowed.

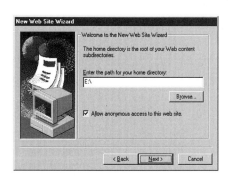

Choosing the Access Rights

The five rights that you can select for IIS access work in conjunction with all other rights. Like share rights, the IIS rights are *in addition to* NTFS rights and of greatest value when you are using anonymous access. Allowing Read access lets a user view a file if their NTFS permissions also allow it. Taking away Read, however, prevents the user from viewing the file regardless of what NTFS permissions are set.

As listed previously, the names of the rights are pretty self-explanatory. The only caveats to note are that Read and Script access are assigned by default, and Execute is a superset of Script access.

Note

> The Execute permission allows for CGI & ISAPI scripts to execute, while Script is sufficient for IDC, IDQ, and ASP. These topics are explored further in Chapter 27, "Integration and Interoperability," and Chapter 28, "Running Applications."

Changing Permissions and Access for Directories

After the wizard has been run and the directory is configured for site access, you can change permissions and access for individual directories by selecting the directory in Internet Service Manager, right-clicking, and choosing Properties.

Figure 26.2 shows the properties for a directory. Notice that access permissions have now been set to read and write, or any combination thereof, and permissions are now None, Script, or Execute (which includes script).

Click the Directory Security tab of the directories properties and you see that you have three items that you can configure:

▶ Anonymous Access and Authentication Control

▶ Secure Communications

▶ IP Address and Domain Name restrictions

Figure 26.2

The properties for a WWW directory.

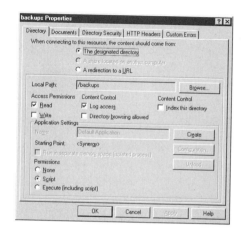

The latter two options are discussed later in this chapter. Selecting Edit on the enabling anonymous access portion brings up the screen shown in Figure 26.3. From this screen you can choose to allow or disallow anonymous access, and (by choosing Edit) the name of the anonymous access account (which defaults to `IUSR_{computername}`).

Figure 26.3

The Authentication methods dialog box for the WWW anonymous user.

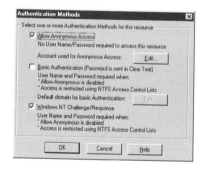

Changing Permissions and Access for Files

You also can control the permissions for specific files in a similar manner. First, select the file and choose its properties. A screen similar to Figure 26.4 is displayed. Choosing the File Security tab, you can set the same options for the file as were illustrated in Figure 26.3 for the directory.

Figure 26.4

The properties for a WWW file.

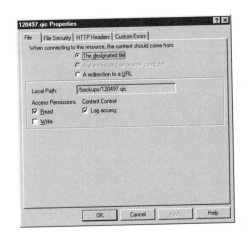

Creating and Sharing Virtual Directories

Objective

As the name implies, virtual directories are entities that do not exist, but give you the ability to reference relative file locations to make it appear as if they are in a directory. By so doing, you can get around issues such as disk space and determining where best to store files.

Note

If you are uncertain as to why you would want to create an additional shared directory, think of the example of an Internet Service Provider giving their clients the ability to have their own web page. Their personal Web site, in some cases, is added to the host's domain name. (For example `http://www.flash.net/~andrew.`)

The disadvantage to using virtual directories is a slight decrease in performance if they reside on a different server because files must be retrieved from the LAN. The only other downside is that virtual directories are not visible in directory listings and must be accessed through explicit links within HTML files.

Virtual directories must exist on servers that all reside within the same NT domain and within the domain in which the IIS server resides. Aside from this restriction, the directories can be either local or remote.

Creating a Virtual Directory

If you choose to create the virtual directory on a local computer, the Internet Service Manager can be used to assign an alias to it. To do so, implement the following steps:

1. Start the Internet Service Manager from the Programs portion of the Start menu.

2. Open a web site, right-click the left pane, and choose New.

3. Select Virtual Directory (as shown in Figure 26.5). This starts the New Virtual Directory Wizard.

Figure 26.5

Select Virtual Directory from the New menu.

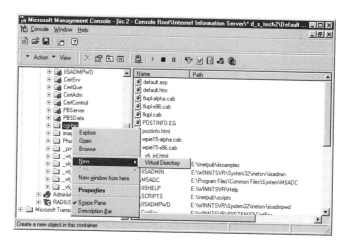

4. Enter an alias to be used for the virtual directory name, and click Next (as shown if Figure 26.6).

Figure 26.6

Enter an alias to be used for the virtual directory.

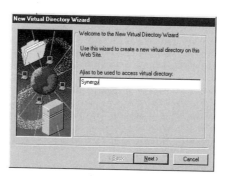

5. Enter the physical path to the virtual directory, as shown in Figure 26.7 (you also can select the Browse button), and click Next.

Figure 26.7

Enter the physical path for the virtual directory to use.

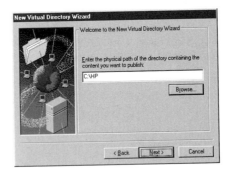

6. Select the access permissions for the virtual directory. Choices include the following:

▶ Allow Read Access

▶ Allow Script Access

▶ Allow Execute Access

▶ Allow Write Access

▶ Allow Directory Browsing

The choices, and defaults, are shown in Figure 26.8.

Figure 26.8

Selecting Access rights for the new virtual directory.

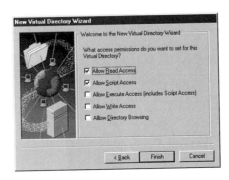

7. Select Finish.

Making Changes After Setup

After the wizard has been run and the virtual directory is configured for site access, you can change permissions and access for individual directories or files by selecting the directory\file in Internet Service Manager, right-clicking, and choosing Properties.

Creating and Sharing Virtual Servers

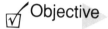 The major benefit of virtual servers is that they enable you to expand your site beyond the limitations of a single site per server. You can combine a number of different sites (domain names) on a single server through the implementation of virtual servers.

Also known as multi-homed hosts, multi-homed servers, or just plain multi-homing, virtual servers enable one host to respond to requests for the following totally three different sites:

```
http://www.synergy.com
```

```
http://www.synergy_technology.com
```

```
http://www.st.com
```

All of the previous domain names are Fully Qualified Domain Names (FQDNs). A fully qualified domain name completely specifies the location of the host. An FQDN specifies the host name, the domain or subdomain the host belongs to, and any domains above in the hierarchy until the root domain in the organization is specified. On the Internet, the root domain in the path is something like com, but on a private network the top-level domains may be named according to some internal naming convention. The FQDN is read from left to right, with each host name or domain name specified by a period. The syntax of an FQDN follows:

```
host name.subdomain. … .domain
```

An example of an FQDN is www.microsoft.com, which refers to a server called www located in the subdomain called microsoft in the domain called com. Referring to a host by its FQDN is similar to referring to a file by its complete directory path. However, a complete file name goes from general to specific, with the file name at the rightmost part of the path.

An FQDN goes from specific to general, with the host name at the leftmost part of the name. Fully qualified domain names are more like addresses. An address starts with the most specific information: who is to receive the letter. The address specifies the house number in which the recipient lives, the street on which the house is located, the city where the street is located, and finally the most general location, the state where that city is located.

Assigning an IP Address

Each site is specified by a unique IP address, and the absence of a unique IP address makes the site visible to all virtual servers.

Creating a Virtual Server

To create a virtual server, you must first have created a directory to publish (local or virtual). Then implement the following steps:

1. Start Internet Service Manager.

2. From the Action menu, select New, and then WWW Site (see Figure 26.9).

Figure 26.9

Creating a virtual server begins with choosing to create a new site.

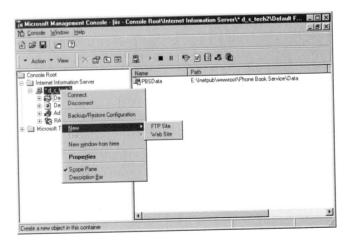

3. Enter an IP address to use for the site and the TCP port, as shown in Figure 26.10. Click on Next.

Figure 26.10

Enter the IP address and port for the virtual server.

4. Enter the path for the home directory and whether or not anonymous access is allowed. Click Next.

5. Configure the appropriate rights and click Finish.

 Note   Permissions for directories and sites on virtual servers can be configured the same as in the previous sections.

Writing Scripts for Service Management

 **Objective**   New to IIS 4.0 is the MicrosoftScript Debugger. It can be used to debug scripts written in Jscript, Visual Basic Scripting Edition (VBScript), and a number of other languages. If you know one of these languages, you can simply manage administrative tasks by writing scripts to manage your services (FTP or WWW).

Management tasks to automate should include the inspection of log files (described in the sections "Managing the FTP Service" and "Managing the WWW Service" later in this chapter). The log files can be examined for statistical information such as the number of hits, errors, and so on.

One way of exploring the log files is with the large number of UNIX-type utilities (all POSIX-compliant) found in the Windows

NT Resource Kit. These utilities also can be useful in creating scripts to examine the log files. The utilities include the following:

- `find`—Enables you to find a file according to specified criteria, such as date, size, and so on.

- `grep`—Enables you to locate an entry within a file. Possibly the most powerful search tool ever written; parameters enable you to search according to case (default is yes), count the entries, find only those that do not match, and more.

- `touch`—Enables you to change the extended attributes of a file, such as the date and time associated with the file, without ever opening it.

- `wc`—Enables you to count the entries in a file in terms of lines, words, or characters. This is most useful when trying to determine the number of entries in a file.

Using Content Analyzer

 **Objective**

Content Analyzer is a new method of managing your Web site in a simplified manner. It enables you to create WebMaps, as shown in Figure 26.11, that let you see a graphical representation of your entire site.

The graphical representation includes all HTML pages, audio and video files, as well as graphic images and links to other services. The left side of the WebMap display (as shown in Figure 26.11) is a tree view of the site, while the right pane shows Cyberbolic view. You can choose to see either of the two or both—whichever is most convenient for you.

In addition to the graphical representation, Content Analyzer can be used to create a set of links to your site in a report that you can use for troubleshooting. You also can save the maps of your site (to a database, spreadsheet, or HTML file) for comparison at later points in time to see what has changed as time has progressed.

Figure 26.11

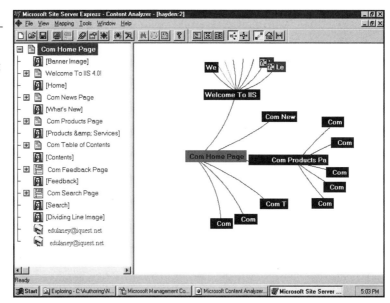

The WebMap view available in Content Analyzer.

Configuring SMTP

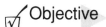 **Objective**

SMTP, an acronym for Simple Mail Transfer Protocol, enables you to send mail to others on your network as well as to the Internet. The SMTP Site property sheet is used to set the basic connection parameters, such as the port to use (default port is 25), number of simultaneous connections (default is 1000), and length of inactivity before disconnect (default is 60 seconds).

 Note

Another great use for the SMTP service is to link its abilities to a web page. In other words, if you have a web site that requires some type of response by the visitor, then you can provide a resource for them to use to send you e-mail, without the visitor needing a mail client on their end. So, you've given the visitor the power to e-mail you something without requiring them to have an e-mail client, such as Outlook, installed on their machine.

Regardless of its size, each site has only one Microsoft SMTP site for the service. You cannot create additional sites or delete existing ones. To display the SMTP property sheets, implement the following steps:

1. Expand the SMTP tree in Internet Service Manager.

2. Highlight and right-click the SMTP site, then choose Properties.

3. The following five tabs are displayed:

   ▶ The SMTP Site tab enables you to determine how this server connects to, sends, and receives messages with other servers.

   ▶ The Operators tab enables you to determine which groups have operator status.

   ▶ The Messages tab lets you configure limits on message size and decide what to do with undeliverable mail; you also can specify a maximum number of recipients who can receive a single message (the default is 100).

   ▶ The Delivery tab specifies how many messages should be sent per connections, the route to use, and so on.

   ▶ The Directory Security tab enables you to specify other servers to accept only, or restrict only.

Configuring NNTP

 Objective

NNTP, an acronym for Network News Transport Protocol, enables you to configure a server for clients to read newsgroups. The Microsoft NNTP Service included with IIS 4.0 is the server side of the operation, whereas Microsoft Internet Mail and News is a common client (now being replaced in the market by Outlook Express).

The default port for NNTP is 119, although this changes to 563 if SSL is used. When the client connects to the service, it requests a list of available newsgroups. The NNTP service authenticates the user, then sends the list of newsgroups.

The client picks a newsgroup to view and requests the list of articles. Authentication takes place again by the NNTP service, and then the list of articles is sent. The client then picks articles they want to see and the NNTP Service sends them.

Posting Articles

Posting of articles works in a similar fashion: NNTP verifies that the client is allowed to post to the newsgroup, and then takes the article, adds it to the newsgroup, and updates the index.

Every newsgroup has its own directory (with the same name as the newsgroup), and every article is stored as a separate file within that directory (with an .NWS extension). By default, %SystemRoot%\Inetpub\nntproot is the main directory.

Creating a New Newsgroup

When you create a new newsgroup (through the Groups property sheet of Internet Service Manager), NNTP automatically creates the new directory. Within the newsgroup directory, indexes are also stored. They have an extension of .XIX and one is created for every 128 articles.

The NNTP service starts automatically when the NT Server starts but can be paused, stopped, or started from the Services icon of the Control Panel (where it appears as Microsoft NNTP Service). It, like other IIS-related services, also can be paused, stopped, or started from the Microsoft Management Console.

Configuring Certificate Server

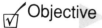 Objective

Microsoft Certificate Server enables you to generate, create and use keys for digital authentication. To use, you must first obtain a valid server certificate (generated with Key Manager) from a certificate authority. The following table lists the Web sites of several certificate authorities within the United States.

Note   You can generate a certificate with certificate server without getting certified by an agency, but they aren't considered valid.

BankGate	`http://www.bankgate.com`
GTE CyberTrust	`http://www.cybertrust.gte.com`
Thawte Consulting	`http://www.thawte.com`
Verisign	`http://www.verisign.com`

Once you've created a certificate or a certificate authority has issued you a valid certificate, use Key Manager to activate the certificate.

Configuring Index Server

 **Objective**   Index Server is configured based upon the size of the site and the number of documents it contains. Four items should be taken into consideration when configuring Index Server:

▶ Number of documents in the corpus

▶ Size of the corpus

▶ Rate of search requests arriving at the server

▶ Complexity of queries

Increasing the amount of memory and going with the fastest CPU available increases Index Server performance. The disk space needed for the data is always roughly 40 percent the size of the corpus.

Index Server can be used to index multiple servers by sharing a folder on the remote volume and creating a virtual directory on the indexing server. The biggest difficulty in doing this is maintaining link integrity.

Managing MIME Types

 Objective
MIME is an acronym for Multipurpose Internet Mail Extension, and is used to define the type of file sent to the browser, based upon the extension. If your server is supplying files in multiple formats, it must have a MIME mapping for each file type or browsers will most likely be unable to retrieve the file.

MIME mappings for IIS 4.0 are different than they were in previous versions. The mappings are kept in the Registry under KEY_LOCAL_MACHINE\SOFTWARE\Classes\MIME\Databases\ Content Type, and can be viewed, edited, or have new ones added by using Regedit, or Regedt32. Figure 26.12 shows an example of the MIME mapping for text files in Regedt32.exe.

Figure 26.12

The MIME mapping for text files.

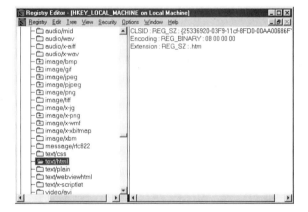

 Note
These mappings occur whether or not IIS is installed. It appears to be a Windows common registry of Mime types.

If you aren't comfortable with editing the Registry directly (and you probably should not be), you also can add entries to the Registry through the HTTP Headers tab of any directory or virtual directory. The File Types button at the bottom of the properties page enables you to enter MIME maps in a much simpler way than editing the Registry. The button is shown in Figure 26.13.

Selecting this button enables you to specify new MIME types by giving the associated extension and the content type, as shown in Figure 26.14.

Figure 26.13

The MIME Map option appears on the HTTP Headers tab.

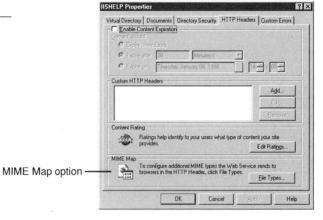

MIME Map option

Figure 26.14

The MIME Map option enables you to specify file type extensions and content type.

Managing the FTP Service

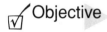 Objective ▶ Once installed and running, the FTP service can be managed through two main utilities:

- ▶ The Services icon of the Control Panel

- ▶ Internet Service Manager

Using the Control Panel Method

The first utility of note is the Services icon in the Control Panel. From here you can start, pause, or stop the FTP Publishing Service, as well as configure it for startup in three ways:

- ▶ Automatic (the default)—The service is started when all of IIS starts.

- ▶ Manual—Requiring interaction from the administrator to actively start it.

- ▶ Disabled—It does not start at all.

Once started, the service can be stopped or paused (as well as started again after either of the other two). When the service is stopped, it is unloaded, whereas when it is paused, it remains loaded with the intention of it being restarted again.

FTP Site Options with Internet Service Manager

From the Internet Service Manager, you can select your FTP site and choose to stop, pause, or start the site by right-clicking it. You also can manage all properties of the site from here, as shown in Figure 26.15.

Figure 26.15

The Properties sheets for an FTP site.

There are five tabs to the properties, each containing specific information on the Web site. Each tab is discussed in the paragraphs that follow in the order, which are arranged in the order that they appear by default.

FTP Site Tab

The FTP Site tab enables you to change the description (name) of the FTP site, the IP address, and the TCP port. As has been pointed out before, port 21 is the default TCP port, but changing it to another value enables the site to become hidden. Additional settings on this tab enable you to specify a number of seconds for a connection timeout, limit the number of connections allowed (if bandwidth is an issue; the default is limited to 1,000 connections) and enable logging. By default, the logs are written to %SystemRoot%\System32\Logfiles.

You can choose for the log files to be created in a number of different time periods. The way in which you choose for them to be created governs the name of the log files created (which always consist of some combination of variables.) The table that follows summarizes the log files.

Log Time Period	Log File Name
Daily	inyymmdd.log
Weekly	inyymmww.log
Monthly	inyymm.log
Unlimited File Size	inetsv#.log
When file size reaches (19MB is the default, but another MB can be specified)	inetsv#.log

Security Accounts Tab

The Security Accounts tab enables you to allow or disallow anonymous access, and define which Windows NT user accounts have operator privileges. You also can choose to allow only anonymous connections and enable automatic password synchronization.

 Tip

An important point when studying for the exam—it is a two-stepped approach—you cannot configure only anonymous access until you have first enabled anonymous access.

Messages Tab

The Messages tab enables you to specify a message to be displayed when users access the site. This can be done in three ways:

▶ Upon welcome

▶ Upon exit

▶ Upon there being too many users (maximum connections reached)

Home Directory Tab

The Home Directory tab enables you to specify a home directory in either of two ways:

▶ On this computer (the default)

▶ As a share on another computer

If you are specifying a directory on this computer, you must give the path. If you are specifying a share on another computer, you must give the UNC path (\\server\share). In either scenario, you then assign permissions for that directory of Read and/or Write, and choose if you want to log access. You also must specify whether directory listings should appear in UNIX style or MS-DOS style. UNIX is the default and should be left as such in most implementations for maximum compatibility.

Directory Security Tab

The Directory Security tab enables you to configure IP address and Domain Name restrictions. When configuring, you have two choices:

▶ Specify all addresses that are prohibited

▶ Specify all addresses that are allowed access

Recall that the three ways to enter addresses are as a single computer (by IP address), a group of computers (by IP address), or by domain name. Refer to Chapter 24, "Planning," for more information about entering addresses.

Managing the WWW Service

 Objective ▶ Once installed and running, the WWW service can be managed through two main utilities:

- ▶ The Services icon of the Control Panel

- ▶ Internet Service Manager

Using the Control Panel Method

The first utility of note is the Services icon in the Control Panel. From here, you can start, pause, or stop the World Wide Web Publishing Service, or configure it for startup in three ways:

- ▶ Automatic (the default)—The service is started when all of IIS starts.

- ▶ Manual—Start it.

- ▶ Disabled—It does not start at all.

WWW Site Options with Internet Service Manager

From the Internet Service Manager, you can select your Web site (or any Web site if you have multiples) and choose to stop, pause, or start the site by right-clicking it.

You also can manage all properties of the site from here, as shown in Figure 26.16.

There are nine tabs to the properties, each containing specific information about the Web site. In the order that they appear by default, each tab is discussed in the paragraphs that follow.

Figure 26.16

The Properties sheets for a Web site.

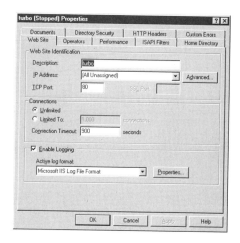

Web Site Tab

The Web Site tab enables you to change the description (name) of the Web site, the IP address, and the TCP port. As has been pointed out before, port 80 is the default TCP port, but changing it to another value allows the site to become hidden. This is useful in a situation where you want to create an intranet and avoid traffic from the Internet. The Advanced tab enables you to assign multiple identities for the Web site. Additional settings on this tab enable you to configure the SSL port, limit the number of connections allowed (if bandwidth is an issue; the default is unlimited) and enable logging. By default, the logs are written to the following directory:

%SystemRoot%\System32\Logfiles

Note

What is presented here is an example. There's no good reason for changing a port number, unless you want to use blind security. The best way to handle filtering Internet traffic would be to change the host security settings for the site, rather than changing the port.

You can choose for the log files to be created in a number of different time periods. The way in which you choose for them to be created governs the name of the log files created (which always consist of some combination of variables). The table that follows summarizes this process.

Log Time Period	Log File Name
Daily	inyymmdd.log
Weekly	inyymmww.log
Monthly	inyymm.log
Unlimited File Size	inetsv#.log
When file size reaches 19MB (19MB is the default, but another MB can be specified)	inetsv#.log

Operators Tab

The Operators tab simply enables you to define which Windows NT user accounts have operator privileges.

Performance Tab

The Performance tab enables you to tune the Web site according to the number of hits you expect each day. There are three settings:

- ▶ Fewer than 10,000

- ▶ Fewer than 100,000 (the default)

- ▶ More than 100,000

You also can enable bandwidth throttling from the Performance tab to prevent the entire network from being slow to service the Web site. By default, bandwidth throttling is not enabled. Finally, on the Performance tab you can configure HTTP Keep-Alives to be enabled. This maintains the open connection and uses it for the next account so that a new connection doesn't have to be created each time a user accesses the site.

ISAPI Filters Tab

The ISAPI Filters tab enables you to add or remove filters for the site. ISAPI filters are discussed in great detail in Chapter 28.

Home Directory Tab

The Home Directory tab enables you to specify a home directory in three ways:

▶ On this computer (the default)

▶ As a share on another computer

▶ As an URL to be redirected to

If you are specifying a directory on this computer, you must give the path. If you are specifying a share on another computer, you must give the UNC path (\\server\share). In either scenario, you then assign permissions for that directory. If you go with the third option and redirect the home directory to an URL, you must specify the URL and choose how the client will be sent. You can send the client as one of the following:

▶ The exact URL you enter

▶ A directory below the URL you enter

▶ A permanent redirection for the resource

Documents Tab

The Documents tab enables you to define the default documents to display if a specific document is not specified in the URL request. Multiple files can be listed, and the first one in the list is always used unless it is unavailable. If it is unavailable (or unable to be found), then the next one in the list is used.

Directory Security Tab

The Directory Security tab enables you to configure anonymous access and authentication, as well as secure communications and IP address and domain name restrictions. When configuring the latter, you have two choices:

▶ Specify all addresses that are prohibited

▶ Specify all addresses that are allowed access

The three ways to enter addresses are as a single computer (by IP address), a group of computers (by IP address), or by domain name.

HTTP Headers Tab

The HTTP Headers tab enables you to specify an expiration time for your content (the default is none), set custom headers, assign a rating to your content (to alert parents to pornography, and so on) and configure MIME maps (see the section "Managing MIME Types," earlier in this chapter).

Custom Errors Tab

The last tab, Custom Errors, enables you to configure the error message returned to the user when an event occurs. For example, error 400 is, by default, a Bad Request, and the file 400.htm is used to return the message 404 is Not Found, and so on.

Exercises

Exercise 26.1:   Changing Permissions for a File

The following exercise illustrates how to add Write permissions to a file:

1. Start Internet Service Manager.

2. Select a file, right-click it, and choose Properties.

3. Beneath Access Permissions, check the Write check box.

4. Click OK.

Exercise 26.2:   Creating a Virtual Directory

The following exercise walks you through the steps of creating a virtual directory named Scott:

1. Start Internet Service Manager.

2. Double-click the Internet Information Server until servers are displayed.

3. Double-click a server.

4. Highlight Default Web Site and right-click.

5. Choose New, Virtual Directory.

6. For a directory alias, enter **Scott**. Press Next.

7. Click the Browse button for a physical path, and find My Briefcase. Select it and then click Next.

8. Change the permissions for the virtual directory so that only Read access is allowed.

9. Select Finish.

10. Double-click the Default Web Site. Scott should now appear as a directory.

Exercise 26.3: Preventing a Host from Accessing Your Site

The following exercise walks you through the steps of denying access to a host based upon its IP address:

1. Start Internet Service Manager.

2. Double-click the Internet Information Server until servers are displayed.

3. Double-click a server.

4. Highlight Default Web Site and right-click.

5. Choose Properties and select the Directory Security tab.

6. Beneath the IP Address and Domain Name Restrictions frame, click the Edit button.

7. Make certain the active radio button on the IP Address and Domain Name Restrictions screen is Granted Access, and click Add.

8. With the active option button on the Deny Access On screen being on Single Computer, enter the IP address 195.200.200.001 and click OK.

9. The word Deny should appear on the IP Address and Domain Name Restrictions screen beside the IP address entered. Click OK.

10. Back at the Directory Security tab, click either OK or Apply and you have now restricted host 195.200.200.001 from accessing your site.

Exercise 26.4: Allow only a Set of Hosts to Access Your Site

The following exercise walks you through the steps of restricting access to your site to only 128 hosts based upon their IP address:

1. Start Internet Service Manager.

2. Double-click the Internet Information Server until servers are displayed.

3. Double-click a server.

4. Highlight Default Web Site and right-click.

5. Choose Properties and select the Directory Security tab.

6. Beneath the IP Address and Domain Name Restrictions frame, click the Edit button.

7. Make certain the active radio button on the IP Address and Domain Name Restrictions screen is Denied Access, and click Add.

8. With the active option button on the Grant Access On screen being on Group of Computers, enter the IP address 195.200.200.001 and the subnet value 255.255.255.128.

9. Click OK.

10. The word Grant should now appear on the IP Address and Domain Name Restrictions screen beside the IP address entered, with the subnet value in parentheses beside it.

11. Click OK.

12. Back at the Directory Security tab, click either OK or Apply and you have now restricted access to your site to 128 hosts only, beginning with 195.200.200.001 and progressing incrementally.

Exercise 26.5: Set a Default Document

The following exercise walks you through the steps of enabling a default document to be displayed when someone accesses your site without specifying a file name:

1. Start Internet Service Manager.

2. Double-click the Internet Information Server until servers are displayed.

3. Double-click a server.

continues

Exercise 26.5: Continued

4. Highlight Default Web Site and right-click.

5. Choose Properties and select the Documents tab.

6. Click the Enable Default Document check box.

7. Click the Add button.

8. Enter the name of your default document (such as DEAULT.HTM or DEFAULT.ASP) in the Default Document Name field and click OK.

9. The document now appears in the text field. Following steps 7 and 8, you can enter multiple documents to be displayed in successive order if the first document is unavailable (the first one in the list will always be displayed if it is available).

Exercise 26.6: Disable HTTP Keep-Alives

The following exercise walks you through the steps of disabling HTTP Keep-Alives:

1. Start Internet Service Manager.

2. Double-click the Internet Information Server until servers are displayed.

3. Double-click a server.

4. Highlight Default Web Site and right-click.

5. Choose Properties and select the Performance tab.

6. Beneath the Connection Configuration frame, click the HTTP Keep-Alives Enabled check box to remove the default checkmark.

7. Click the OK or Apply buttons.

Exercise 26.7:   Change the Web Service TCP Port

This exercise walks you through the steps of changing the TCP port of the Web service to hide it from browsers not specifically pointed to it:

1. Start Internet Service Manager.

2. Double-click the Internet Information Server until servers are displayed.

3. Double-click a server.

4. Highlight the Web site you want to hide and right-click.

5. Choose Properties and select the Web Site tab.

6. At the TCP Port field, change the default value of 80 to the new port number (such as 7500).

7. Click the OK or Apply buttons.

Review Questions

1. TCP port 80 is the default for which service?

   A. NNTP

   B. SMTP

   C. WWW

   D. FTP

2. By default, anonymous access is enabled for which of the following services following installation?

   A. WWW

   B. FTP

   C. SMTP

   D. NNTP

3. What permissions are assigned to a WWW directory by default during the site creation by the wizard?

   A. Allow Read Access

   B. Allow Write Access

   C. Allow Directory Browsing

   D. Allow Script Access

4. Rob is having difficulty with users properly accessing resources on an intranet Web site that he created. For the directory in question, NTFS permissions allow Read for everyone, but he has removed the Read permission for IIS. What is the effect of this action?

   A. no one can read the files in the directory.

   B. only those users recognized by NT are allowed to read the files in the directory.

   C. all users can read the files because NTFS overrides IIS permissions.

   D. only users coming from NT Workstation or NT Server can read the files in the directory.

5. The default user name for the anonymous account on a computer named SPENCER for the WWW service is which of the following?

    A. SPENCER

    B. IUSR

    C. IUSR_SPENCER

    D. SPENCER_IUSR

6. When creating virtual directories, they should reside where?

    A. on the server

    B. in the domain

    C. on the WAN

    D. anywhere

7. Karen has created a number of virtual directories at her site, but cannot get them to appear in directory listings. This is most likely caused by which of the following?

    A. inappropriate permissions

    B. a port other than 80 being used

    C. virtual directories beyond the server

    D. a failure to use links in HTML files

8. Multi-homing is also known as creating which of the following?

    A. virtual files

    B. virtual directories

    C. virtual servers

    D. virtual private networks

9. In the DNS name www.microsoft.com, what does microsoft represent?

   A. the last name of the host

   B. the domain in which the host is located

   C. the IP address of the building in which the host is located

   D. the directory in which the host name file is located

10. The wc utility included in the Windows NT Resource Kit can be used to count which of the following items in a log file?

    A. words

    B. characters

    C. lines

    D. paragraphs

11. TCP port 25 is the default for which service?

    A. NNTP

    B. SMTP

    C. WWW

    D. FTP

12. How many SMTP sites are allowed for the SMTP service?

    A. 0

    B. 1

    C. 2

    D. unlimited

13. By default in SMTP, how many users can receive a single message?

    A. 1

    B. 100

    C. 256

    D. 512

14. Allan, a new administrator, notices traffic on TCP port 563. SSL is in use. What service is using port 563, by default?

    A. NNTP

    B. SMTP

    C. WWW

    D. FTP

15. By default, into what directory are FTP log files written to?

    A. %SystemRoot%

    B. %SystemRoot%\Inetpub

    C. %SystemRoot%\Inetpub\Logfiles

    D. %SystemRoot%\System32\Logfiles

Review Answers

1. **C.** The default TCP port for the WWW Service is 80.

2. **A, B.** By default, anonymous access is enabled for WWW and FTP during installation.

3. **A, D.** Allow Read Access and Allow Script access are selected by default.

4. **A.** Taking away the Allow Read Access permission in IIS prevents users from viewing files in the directory.

5. **C.** The default anonymous account user name is always IUSR_computername.

6. **B**. Virtual directories should always be stored on servers within the same NT domain as the IIS server resides.

7. **D**. Virtual directories do not appear in directory listings, and must be accessed through explicit links within HTML files.

8. **C**. Multi-homing is another word for using virtual servers.

9. **B**. The path specifies a host named www in a domain microsoft. The domain microsoft is located in the top-level domain com.

10. **A, B, C**. The wc utility can be used to count characters, words, or lines in a log file.

11. **B**. The default TCP port for the SMTP Service is 25.

12. **B**. Regardless of the size of the site, only one SMTP service is allowed.

13. **B**. By default, in SMTP 100 users can receive a single message.

14. **A**. By default, NNTP operates at TCP port 563 with SSL.

15. **D**. By default, FTP log files are written to the %SystemRoot%\System32\Logfiles directory.

Answers to Test Yourself Questions at Beginning of Chapter

1. The default TCP port used for the WWW service is 80. See "Creating and Sharing Directories."
2. Virtual directories should always be stored on servers within the same NT domain as the IIS server resides. See "Creating and Sharing Virtual Directories."
3. Virtual servers allow one server to alias multiple domain names. See "Creating and Sharing Virtual Servers."
4. The wc utility can be used to count the number of lines in a log file, as well as the number of words or characters. See "Writing Scripts for Service Management."
5. WebMaps enable you to view your site with a tree view, or Cyberbolic view (or both). See "Using Content Analyzer."
6. The default TCP port for the SMTP service is port 25. See "Configuring SMTP."
7. By default, and in the absence of SSL, NNTP uses TCP port 119. See "Configuring NNTP."
8. After generating the digital certificate, it must be registered with a certificate authority. See "Configuring Certificate Server."
9. The Index Server data, in all cases, is approximately 40 percent of the size of the corpus. See "Configuring Index Server."
10. MIME is an acronym for Multipurpose Internet Mail Extension. See "Managing MIME Types."
11. FTP logs can be created on a Daily, Weekly, or Monthly basis. See "Managing the FTP Service."
12. A WWW site can be made hidden by changing the default TCP port. See "Managing the WWW Service."

Chapter **27**

Integration and Interoperability

This chapter helps you prepare for the exam by covering the following objectives:

 Objectives

▶ Configure IIS to connect to a database. There is only one task. Configuring ODBC.

▶ Configure IIS to integrate with Index Server. The tasks include the following:

    ▶ Specifying query parameters by creating the .IDQ file

    ▶ Specifying how the query results are formatted and displayed to the user by creating the .HTX file

 **Test Yourself! Before reading this chapter, test yourself to determine how much study time you will need to devote to this section.**

1. What are the two file extensions used by ODBC to determine how the database is accessed and how the output Web page is constructed?

2. What is the conditional expression that can be used in an .IDQ file to see if one entry is a subset of a second entry?

Answers are located at the end of the chapter....

This chapter examines integration between the WWW service of IIS and other servers and services. The other servers and services discussed fall into one of two categories: databases or Index Server. Connecting IIS to a database enables you to pull or update information from a server dedicated to such a task—such as SQL. Integrating with Index Server enables you to make the available data visible and searchable by those accessing your site. The chapter is organized as follows:

 Objectives

▶ Configuring IIS to Connect to a Database

▶ Configuring Integration with Index Server

Configuring IIS to Connect to a Database

With the expansion of the World Wide Web into homes around the United States came the expectation that Web browsers would allow users to retrieve data specific to a need. Users grew frustrated at looking at static screen pages and wanted to be able to pull up data and forms based on their requests. From an HTML coding standpoint, creating a Web page for every conceivable request is impractical. The sheer volume of pages would be incomprehensible, and the action of updating the pages each time a piece of data changed would be more than any one person could handle.

To solve the problem, such databases as Oracle or Microsoft SQL (Structured Query Language) Server can be used with Microsoft Internet Information Server (IIS) 4. The databases can supply the information to fulfill a query, update information, and add new data through the Web almost as easily as if a user were sitting at a PC on a Local Area Network.

Databases have been around since the early days of computing, and Web servers have been around for a number of years. What is new is the integration of the two to create the dynamic Web sites expected today.

Because Windows NT Server is growing in popularity exponentially, and it is the platform on which Internet Information Server runs, it is not uncommon to expect the database to which you connect to be Microsoft SQL Server. This is the expectation for the exam and the thrust of the discussion that follows.

Understanding ODBC

Open Database Connectivity (ODBC) is an API (Application Programming Interface) that provides a simple way to connect to an existing database (whether that database be SQL or any ODBC-compliant database). It was designed by Microsoft to address the issue of any number of applications needing to interface with SQL server.

The greatest advantage that ODBC offers is that it defines a clear distinction between the application and the database, and thus does not require any specific programming. To use it, you create a query and template for how the output will look.

There are four major components to IIS's implementation of ODBC:

> ▶ **.HTM**—The file containing the hyperlink for a query. The request comes from the browser and merely specifies the URL for the .IDC (Internet Database Connector) file on IIS.

> ▶ **.IDC**—The file containing the data source file information and SQL statement.

> ▶ **.HTX**—A file of HTML extensions containing the template document with placeholders for the result.

Figure 27.1 illustrates the processes involved in answering a query request.

Figure 27.1

The process of resolving a database query in IIS.

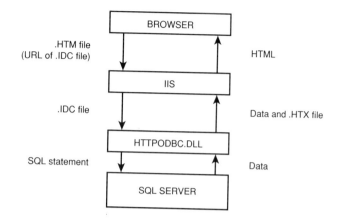

Implementing ODBC

Implementing ODBC is extremely easy and can be broken into the following steps:

1. Double-click the ODBC icon in the Control Panel.

2. Select the System DSN tab from the ODBC Data Source Administrator dialog box (shown in Figure 27.2).

Figure 27.2

The System DSN tab enables you to configure data sources.

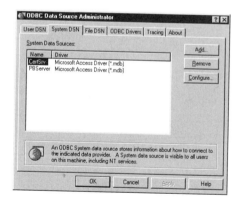

3. Choose Add and select the driver (SQL, Access, and Oracle appear as choices). This is illustrated by Figure 27.3.

4. Specify the name and description of the data source on the Create a New Data Source dialog box shown in Figure 27.4.

Figure 27.3

Select the new data sources.

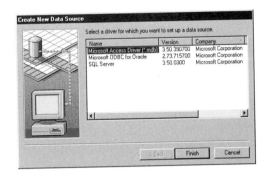

Figure 27.4

You must specify a name, description, and server for the data source.

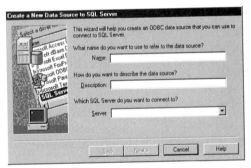

5. Specify the server to connect to and click Next.

6. If you are using a data source that can perform authentication, such as SQL Server, then specify how authentication is to be done (shown in Figure 27.5).

Figure 27.5

Specify how authentication will be handled.

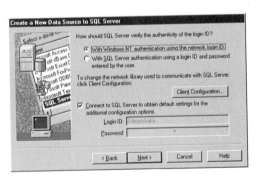

Authentication can be done by Windows NT or SQL Server. If SQL Server is chosen, it uses standard logon security and a SQL Server user ID and password must be given for all connections. If you choose to use Windows NT authentication, the Windows NT user account is associated with a SQL Server user account, and integrated security is used to establish the connection.

> **Note**
>
> In reality, to get Windows NT logins to work, three things must be done:
>
> ▶ SQL Server security must be set to Integrated (NT only) or Mixed (NT & SQL).
>
> ▶ Named Pipes or Multiprotocol must be set up as the connection type—this is because NT refuses to send your password as clear text.
>
> ▶ You must use SQL Security Manager to assign NT users to SQL users.
>
> The security mode on the server is critical.

Figure 27.5 also shows a Client Configuration button. This can be used to customize the configuration if you are using nonstandard pipes.

The Login ID and Password boxes at the bottom of Figure 27.5 are used only if you have selected SQL Server authentication, and become grayed out if you are using Windows NT authentication.

Other ODBC Tabs

Other tabs in the ODBC Data Source Administrator dialog box include the following:

▶ User DSN

▶ File DSN

▶ ODBC Drivers

▶ Tracing

▶ About

The User DSN tab, shown in Figure 27.6, is used to add, delete, or change the setup of data source names (DSNs). The data sources specified here are local to a computer and can only be used by the current user.

Figure 27.6

The User DSN tab enables you to configure data sources specific to a user.

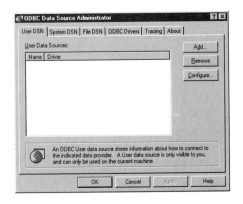

The File DSN tab is used to add, delete, or change the setup of data sources with file data source names. File-based data sources can be shared between all users that are using the same drivers and are not dedicated to individual users or local machines.

The ODBC Drivers tab shows information about the ODBC drivers that are currently installed. The information given includes the name, version, filename, and created date of every ODBC driver (and the name of the company responsible for it.)

The Tracing tab, shown in Figure 27.7, enables you to configure how the ODBC Driver Manager will trace ODBC calls to functions. Choices include all of the time, dynamically, by a custom DLL, or for one connection only (as well as not at all.)

Figure 27.7

The Tracing tab of the ODBC Data Source Administrator.

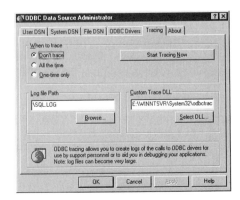

The About tab lists the ODBC core components, as well as the actual files they consist of, and the versions. An example of the information it provides is shown in Figure 27.8.

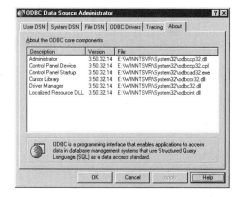

Creating and Developing Files

Once the registration has been completed and ODBC has been configured, the remaining steps involve creating and developing the files to be used.

The .IDC File

The .IDC file contains the SQL command used to interface between IIS and the Httpodbc.dll library. There are four required parameters to the file:

- ▶ Datasource

- ▶ Username

- ▶ Template

- ▶ SQLStatement

The Datasource is simply the name of the ODBC data source that has been defined in the ODBC Data Source Administrator dialog box available from the Control Panel.

The Username is the username required to access the data source, and can be any valid logon name for the SQL Server database. This (as well as the Password field, if used) is ignored if you use integrated security or if the database doesn't have security installed.

The Template specified the name of the file (.HTX) that will be used as a template to display (and do any necessary interpretation) of the SQL results.

The SQLStatement is the list of commands you want to execute. Parameter values can be used if they are enclosed in percent signs (%). If multiple lines are required, a plus sign (+) must be the first character on each line.

An example of an .IDC file follows:

```
Datasource: Synergy
Username:    sa
Template:    syn_temp.htx
SQLStatement:
+SELECT employeeno, dob, doh
+FROM pubs.dbo.synergy
+WHERE salary>50000
```

The preceding code pulls the employee number, date of birth, and date of hire information from the pubs.dbo.synergy database for every employee exceeding $50,000 in salary. Once the data has been extracted, it is combined with an .HTX file (in this case syn_temp.htx) for formatting.

Optional fields that can be used in the .IDC file include the following:

▶ DefaultParameters—To specify default values in the event nothing is specified by the client

▶ Expires—The number of seconds to wait before refreshing

▶ MaxFieldSize—The maximum buffer space per field (beyond this, truncation takes place)

▶ MaxRecords—The maximum number of records to return per query

▶ ODBCConnection—Can either be set to POOL to add the connection to the connection pool (keeping open for future requests) or NONPOOL to not do so

▶ Password—The password for the username given

▶ RequiredParameters—Parameters that have to be filled in by the client before you can do the query. Parameters are separated by a comma, and if the user does not provide them all, then Httpodbc.dll returns an error message to them.

▶ Translationfile—The path for non-English characters to be found before being returned to the browser

▶ Content-type—A valid MIME type describing what goes back to the client. If the .HTX file has HTML, then this usually is text/html.

The .HTX File

The .HTX file is an HTML template that fills in its blanks with information returned from a query. It accepts SQL information in, and returns HTML information out. A quick look at an .HTX file shows that it looks very much like an HTML file, and contains many of the same fields.

Database fields that it receives are known as containers and are identified by field names surrounded by percent signs (%) and angle brackets (<>). Thus the employeeno field that comes from the SQL database is known as <%employeeno%> in an .HTX file.

All processing is done in loops that start with <%begindetail%> and end with <%enddetail%>. Logic can be included with <%if…%> and <%endif%>, as well as <%else%> statements. You also can use the four standard programming operators:

▶ EQ—Equal to

▶ GT—Greater than

▶ LT—Less than

▶ CONTAINS

An example of an .HTX file would be

```
<HTML>
<HEAD>
<TITLE>Welcome to Synergy</TITLE>
</HEAD>
<H2>Employees with Salaries greater than $50,000</H2>
<%begindetail%>
<b>Employee number:</b><%employeeno%> <b>Date of birth and hire:
➥</b><%dob%>, <%doh%><P>
<%enddetail%>
</HTML>
```

Some useful samples of .HTX files can be found on your system, and located by using the NT Find utility from the Start menu to look for files ending in that extension. Three useful ones for working with Index Server are located in the %systemroot%\system32\inetsrv\iisadmin\isadmin directory of your system, and an example of one is given at the end of this chapter.

Configuring Integration with Index Server

 Objective

Index Server has already been examined several times in this book, including the explanation of it in Chapter 24, "Planning," and details about how to configure it in Chapter 26, "Configuring and Managing Resource Access." This section covers how it handles queries and returns results. For most intents and purposes, this discussion is very much like the earlier discussion of .HTX files (used to format and return the query results to the user).

The difference exists in the files used to hold the queries. Rather than using the .IDC file previously discussed, Index Server uses an .IDQ (Internet Data Query) file. The .IDQ file should always be placed in the Scripts directory, and it requires Execute or Script permission to function properly.

There are two sections to the file and it begins with a tag of <Query> (the first section) and is followed by the [Names] section. The Names section is purely optional and not used most of the time.

If it is used, it defines nonstandard column names that are referred to in a query. The Query section of the file is all that is required, and it can contain parameters, variables, and conditional expressions.

Restrictions are that lines must start with the variable you are trying to set, and only one variable can be set per line. Additionally, percent signs (%) are used to identify the variables and references.

Using Variables in .IDQ Files

The variables that can be used in .IDQ files are as follows:

- ▶ CiCatalog—Sets the location for the catalog. If the value is already set, the value here overrides that one.

- ▶ CiCodepage—Sets the server's code page. Again, if the value is already set, the entry here overrides the previous one.

- ▶ CiColumns—Defines a list of columns that will be used in the .HTX file.

- ▶ CiDeferNonIndexedTrimming—By default is not used, but can be set if the scope of the query must be limited.

- ▶ CiFlags—Query flags can be set to DEEP or SHALLOW to determine if only the directory listed in CiScope is searched.

- ▶ CiForceUseCi—By setting to TRUE, you can force the query to use the content index even if it is out of date.

- ▶ CiLocale—Specifies the locale used to issue the query.

- ▶ CiMaxRecordsInResultSet—Specifies the maximum number of results that can be returned from the query.

- ▶ CiMaxRecordsPerPage—Specifies the maximum number of records that can appear on a display page.

- ▶ CiRestriction—A restriction that you are placing on the query.

- ▶ CiScope—Specifies the starting directory for the search.

▶ CiSort—Specifies whether the results should be sorted in an order of ascending, or descending.

▶ CiTemplate—Specifies the full path of the .HTX file from the root. Index Server is bound by the Windows NT shell limit of 260 characters per path.

As with most script files, a pound sign (#) can be used to specify a comment. At whatever point the # sign is in the line, from there on the line will be ignored.

Using Conditional Expressions in .IDQ Files

The following conditional expressions can be used in .IDQ files:

▶ CONTAINS—Is true if any part of the first value is found in the second value

▶ EQ—Equal to

▶ GE—Greater than or equal to

▶ GT—Greater than

▶ ISEMPTY—Is true if the value is null

▶ LE—Less than or equal to

▶ LT—Less than

▶ NE—Not equal to

An Example of the .IDQ File

The following is an example of an .IDQ file:

```
[Query]
CiColumns=employeeno,dob,doh
CiMaxRecordsInResultSet=50
CiMaxRecordsPerPage=20
#20 used for compatibility with most browsers
```

```
CiScope=/
CiFlags=DEEP
CiTemplate=/scripts/synergy.htx
```

In the example, three columns are queried in the database: employeeno, dob, and doh. The maximum number of records that will be returned is 50, with up to 20 on each page of display. The fifth line is a comment line added by the person who created the file. It has no effect on operation whatsoever. The CiScope is set to the root directory with the search (CiFlags) set to go through all subdirectories. The template to use is then specified by the CiTemplate variable.

The Scan .IDQ File

One of the best examples of an efficient .IDQ file is SCAN.IDQ, located in the %systemroot%/system32\inetsrv\iisadmin\isadmin folder of your system. It is used with QUERY.HTM as a query file, and printed in its entirety here (line numbers have been added to help explain how it works):

```
1.  [Names]
2.  #
3.  # Query Metadata propset
4.  MetaVRootUsed(DBTYPE_BOOL)      = 624c9360-93d0-11cf-a787-
➥00004c752752 2
5.  MetaVRootAuto(DBTYPE_BOOL)      = 624c9360-93d0-11cf-a787-
➥00004c752752 3
6.  MetaVRootManual(DBTYPE_BOOL)    = 624c9360-93d0-11cf-a787-
➥00004c752752 4
7.  MetaPropertyGuid(DBTYPE_GUID)   = 624c9360-93d0-11cf-a787-
➥00004c752752 5
8.  MetaPropertyDispId(DBTYPE_I4)   = 624c9360-93d0-11cf-a787-
➥00004c752752 6
9.  MetaPropertyName(DBTYPE_WSTR)   = 624c9360-93d0-11cf-a787-
➥00004c752752 7
10. StorageType(DBTYPE_UI4)         = b725f130-47ef-101a-a5f1-
➥02608c9eebac 4

11. # This is the query file for the query.htm query form.
12. #

13. [Query]
```

```
14. # The CiCatalog variable must point to where the catalog
➥(index) files
15. # are stored on your system.  You will probably have to
➥change this
16. # value.  If this value is not specified, a default value is
➥read from
17. # the registry from:
18. # HKEY_LOCAL_MACHINE\System\CurrentControlSet\Control\
➥ContentIndex\IsapiDefaultCatalogDirectory

19. # CiCatalog=d:\

20. # These are the columns that are referenced in the .htx files
21. # when formatting output for each hit.

22. CiColumns=vpath, path, metavrootused, metavrootauto,
➥metavrootmanual, storagetype

23. # The CiRestriction is the query.  Here, it's just pass in
➥from the
24. # form in the .htm file.

25. CiRestriction=#vpath *

26. # Don't allow more than 300 total hits in the result set. It
➥can be
27. # expensive for the server to allow this value to get too
➥large.

28. CiMaxRecordsInResultSet=300

29. # Display CiMaxRecordsPerPage hits on each page of output

30. CiMaxRecordsPerPage=%CiMaxRecordsPerPage%

31. # CiScope is the directory (virtual or real) under which
➥results are
32. # returned.  If a file matches the query but is not in a
➥directory beneath
33. # CiScope, it is not returned in the result set.
34. # A scope of \ means all hits matching the query are
➥returned.
```

```
35. CiScope=VIRTUAL_ROOTS

36. # This is the .htx file to use for formatting the results of
➡the query.

37. CiTemplate=/iisadmin/isadmin/scan.htx

38. # This is the list of property names to use in sorting the
➡results.
39. # Append [a] or [d] to the property name to specify ascending
➡or
40. # descending.  Separate keys in multi-key sorts with commas.
41. # For example, to sort on file write date ascending, then
➡file size
42. # descending, use CiSort=write[a],filesize[d]

43. CiSort=%CiSort%

44. # Setting CiForceUseCi to true means that the index is
➡assumed to be
45. # up to date, so queries that might otherwise force a walk of
➡the
46. # directory structure (find files older than X), will instead
➡use
47. # the index and run more quickly.  Of course, that means that
➡the results
48. # might miss files that match the query.

49. CiForceUseCi=true
```

Lines 1 and 13 set up the two required sections of the file. Lines 2 and 12 are blank, used for aesthetic purposes when reading the file. All lines beginning with the pound character (#) are comment lines and are ignored during execution. Lines 4 through 10 define nonstandard column names that are referred to in the query.

Line 22 lists the columns referenced in the .HTX file, while line 25 really does not set a restriction, as the restriction itself is preceded by the pound sign (#), commenting it out. The maximum number of records returned is limited to 300 by line 28, and the number of records per page is set by line 30.

The search begins at the virtual roots—per line 35—and the template used for formatting the results is scan.htx, per line 37 (listed in the following section). Line 43 defines the sort, while line 49 forces the index to be assumed to be up to date.

After the data has been returned, SCAN.HTX comes into play, so that file is examined next.

The Scan .HTX File

After SCAN.IDQ has performed its function, results are returned to SCAN.HTX, also located in the %systemroot%/system32\inetsrv\iisadmin\isadmin folder of your system. It is printed in its entirety here (line numbers have been added to help explain how it works):

```
1.   <HTML>

2.   <!--
3.   <%CiTemplate%>

4.   This is the formatting page for query results. This file
 ➥defines
5.   how the result page header, rows, and footer will appear.
6.   -->

7.   <HEAD>
8.   <!-- The title lists the # of documents -->

9.   <%if CiMatchedRecordCount eq 0%>
10.  <TITLE><%escapeHTML CiRestriction%> - no documents matched.</
 ➥TITLE>
11.  <%else%>
12.  <TITLE><%escapeHTML CiRestriction%> - documents
 ➥<%CiFirstRecordNumber%> to <%CiLastRecordNumber%></TITLE>
13.  <%endif%>
14.  </HEAD>

15.  <BODY BGCOLOR="#FFFFFF" TEXT="#000000" LINK="#000066"
 ➥VLINK="#808080" ALINK="#FF0000" TOPMARGIN=0>

16.  <TABLE>
```

```
17. <TR>
18. <TD><IMG SRC ="/iisadmin/isadmin/64x_book.jpg"
➡ALIGN=Middle></TD>
19. <TD VALIGN=MIDDLE><H1>Index Server</H1><br><center><h2>Search
➡Results</h2></center></TD>
20. </TR>
21. </TABLE>

22. <!-- Print a header that lists the query and the number of
➡hits -->

23. <H5>
24. <%if CiMatchedRecordCount eq 0%>
25. No virtual roots matched the query "<%EscapeHTML
➡CiRestriction%>".
26. <%else%>
27. Virtual roots <%CiFirstRecordNumber%> to
➡<%CiLastRecordNumber%> of
28. <%CiMatchedRecordCount%> matching the query
29. "<%EscapeHTML CiRestriction%>" for catalog <%CiCatalog%>
30. <%endif%>
31. </H5>

32. <!--
33. This table has a link to a new query page, a previous button,
➡and
34. a next page button.  The buttons are only displayed when
➡appropriate.
35. -->

36. <TABLE WIDTH=80%>

37. <!--
38. Query.htm set HTMLQueryForm as the name of the page to return
➡to
39. for a new query.
40. -->

41. <!-- Define a "previous" button if this isn't the first page
➡ -->

42. <%if CiContainsFirstRecord eq 0%>
43. <TD ALIGN=LEFT>
44. <FORM ACTION="/iisadmin/isadmin/scan.idq" METHOD="GET">
45. <INPUT TYPE="HIDDEN"
```

```
46. NAME="CiBookMark" VALUE="<%CiBookMark%>" >
47. <INPUT TYPE="HIDDEN"
48. NAME="CiBookmarkSkipCount" VALUE="-<%EscapeRAW
➥CiMaxRecordsPerPage%>" >
49. <INPUT TYPE="HIDDEN"
50. NAME="CiRestriction" VALUE="<%CiRestriction%>" >
51. <INPUT TYPE="HIDDEN"
52. NAME="CiMaxRecordsPerPage" VALUE="<%EscapeRAW
➥CiMaxRecordsPerPage%>" >
53. <INPUT TYPE="SUBMIT"
54. VALUE="Previous <%CiMaxRecordsPerPage%> documents">
55. </FORM>
56. </TD>
57. <%endif%>

58. <!-- Define a "next" button if this isn't the last page -->

59. <%if CiContainsLastRecord eq 0%>
60. <TD ALIGN=RIGHT>
61. <FORM ACTION="/iisadmin/isadmin/scan.idq" METHOD="GET">
62. <INPUT TYPE="HIDDEN"
63. NAME="CiBookMark" VALUE="<%CiBookMark%>" >
64. <INPUT TYPE="HIDDEN"
65. NAME="CiBookmarkSkipCount" VALUE="<%EscapeRAW
➥CiMaxRecordsPerPage%>" >
66. <INPUT TYPE="HIDDEN"
67. NAME="CiRestriction" VALUE="<%CiRestriction%>" >
68. <INPUT TYPE="HIDDEN"
69. NAME="CiMaxRecordsPerPage" VALUE="<%EscapeRAW
➥CiMaxRecordsPerPage%>" >
70. <INPUT TYPE="SUBMIT"
71. VALUE="Next <%CiRecordsNextPage%> documents">
72. </FORM>
73. </TD>
74. <%endif%>
75. </TABLE>

76. <HR>

77. <!--
78. The begindetail/enddetail section describes how each row of
➥output
79. is be formatted.  The sample below prints:

80. record number
```

81. document title (if one exists) or virtual path of the file
82. the abstract for the file
83. the url for the file
84. the file's size and last write time
85. -->

86. <FORM ACTION="/iisadmin/isadmin/scan.ida" METHOD="GET">
87. <table>
88. <tr>
89. <th width=147 align="left">Virtual Root</th>
90. <th width=147 align="left">Physical Root</th>
91. <th width=147 align="left">Type</th>
92. <th colspan = 3 width=450 align="center">Type Of Scan</th>
93. </tr>

94. <!--
95. NAME: PROOT_<virtual root> VALUE: physical path to root
96. NAME: SCAN_<virtual root> VALUE: "NoScan".
➡ Implies no scan will be performed
97. NAME: SCAN_<virtual root> VALUE: "FullScan".
➡Implies full scan will be performed
98. NAME: SCAN_<virtual root> VALUE: "IncrementalScan".
➡Implies incremental scan will be performed

99. -->

100. <%begindetail%>
101. <INPUT TYPE="HIDDEN" NAME="PROOT_<%if StorageType eq
➡1%>NNTP_<%endif%><%vpath%>" VALUE="<%path%>">
102. <%if metavrootused ne 0%>
103. <tr>
104. <td><%vpath%></td>
105. <td><%path%></td>
106. <td><%if StorageType eq 1%>News<%else%>Web<%endif%></td>
107. <td><input type=radio checked name="SCAN_<%if StorageType eq
➡1%>NNTP_<%endif%><%vpath%>" value="NoScan"> No Scan </td>
108. <td><input type=radio name="SCAN_<%if StorageType eq
➡1%>NNTP_<%endif%><%vpath%>" value="IncrementalScan">
➡Incremental Scan </td>
109. <td><input type=radio name="SCAN_<%if StorageType eq
➡1%>NNTP_<%endif%><%vpath%>" value="FullScan"> Full Scan </td>
110. </tr>

```
111. <%endif%>
112. <%enddetail%>
113. </table>

114. <INPUT TYPE="SUBMIT"
115. VALUE="Submit changes">
116. </FORM>
117. <P>

118. <!-- Only display a line if there were any hits that
➥matched the query -->

119. <%if CiMatchedRecordCount ne 0%>
110. <HR>
111. <%endif%>

112. <TABLE WIDTH=80%>

113. <!--
114. Query.htm set HTMLQueryForm as the name of the page to
➥return to
115. for a new query.
116. -->

117. <TD> <A HREF="/iisadmin/isadmin/admin.htm">Administration
➥Main Menu</A> </TD>

118. <!-- Define a "previous" button if this isn't the first page
➥-->

119. <%if CiContainsFirstRecord eq 0%>
120. <TD ALIGN=LEFT>
121. <FORM ACTION="/iisadmin/isadmin/scan.idq" METHOD="GET">
122. <INPUT TYPE="HIDDEN"
123. NAME="CiBookMark" VALUE="<%CiBookMark%>" >
124. <INPUT TYPE="HIDDEN"
125. NAME="CiBookmarkSkipCount" VALUE="-<%EscapeRAW
➥CiMaxRecordsPerPage%>" >
126. <INPUT TYPE="HIDDEN"
127. NAME="CiRestriction" VALUE="<%CiRestriction%>" >
128. <INPUT TYPE="HIDDEN"
129. NAME="CiMaxRecordsPerPage" VALUE="<%EscapeRAW
➥CiMaxRecordsPerPage%>" >
130. <INPUT TYPE="SUBMIT"
```

```
131.  VALUE="Previous <%CiMaxRecordsPerPage%> documents">
132.  </FORM>
133.  </TD>
134.  <%endif%>


135.  <!-- Define a "next" button if this isn't the last page -->


136.  <%if CiContainsLastRecord eq 0%>
137.  <TD ALIGN=RIGHT>
138.  <FORM ACTION="/iisadmin/isadmin/scan.idq" METHOD="GET">
139.  <INPUT TYPE="HIDDEN"
140.  NAME="CiBookMark" VALUE="<%CiBookMark%>" >
141.  <INPUT TYPE="HIDDEN"
142.  NAME="CiBookmarkSkipCount" VALUE="<%EscapeRAW
➥CiMaxRecordsPerPage%>" >
143.  <INPUT TYPE="HIDDEN"
144.  NAME="CiRestriction" VALUE="<%CiRestriction%>" >
145.  <INPUT TYPE="HIDDEN"
146.  NAME="CiMaxRecordsPerPage" VALUE="<%EscapeRAW
➥CiMaxRecordsPerPage%>" >
147.  <INPUT TYPE="SUBMIT"
148.  VALUE="Next <%CiRecordsNextPage%> documents">
149.  </FORM>
150.  </TD>
151.  <%endif%>
152.  </TABLE>


153.  <P><BR>


154.  <!--
155.  If the index is out of date (for example, if it's still
➥being created
156.  or updated after changes to files in an indexed directory)
➥let the
157.  user know.
158.  -->
159.  <%if CiOutOfDate ne 0%>
160.  <P><BR>
161.  <I><B>The index is out of date.</B></I>
162.  <%endif%>


163.  <!--
164.  If the query was not executed because it needed to enumerate
➥to
165.  resolve the query instead of using the index, but
➥CiForceUseCi
```

```
166. was TRUE, let the user know
167. -->

168. <%if CiQueryIncomplete eq 1%>
169. <P><BR>
170. <I><B>The query is too expensive to complete.</B></I>
171. <%endif%>

172. <!-- Output a page number and count of pages -->

173. <%if CiTotalNumberPages gt 0%>
174. <P>
175. Page <%CiCurrentPageNumber%> of <%CiTotalNumberPages%>
176. <P>
177. <%endif%>
178. </HTML>
```

The preceding file is too long for a discussion of every line. Fortunately, it's necessary only to look at the lines of greatest interest to this discussion.

Lines 9 through 13 look for the number of total matches found, and return a title corresponding to zero or more than zero. Lines 24 to 30 fashion the results based on the number of virtual servers found.

Other lines continue to format the display based on the results found (should there be a Next button, and so on). Notice the constant checks for results (finds, pages, and so on) greater than zero: lines 119, 146, 183, and so on. An example of how this screen looks is shown in Figure 27.9.

Figure 27.9

*An example of
the SCAN.HTX
page.*

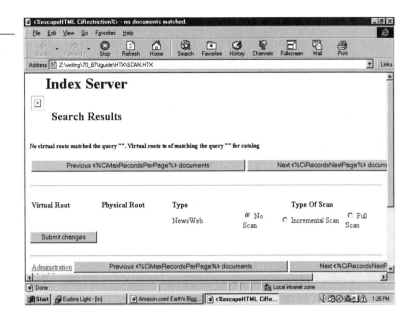

The Query .HTM File

The two preceding sections discussed the .IDQ file that gathers
results and the .HTX file that formats those results. Missing from
the equation is the .HTM file, which first queries for the results.
One of the best examples of this file is QUERY.HTM, located in
%systemroot$\InetPub\iissamples\ISSamples. It is this file which
sends the query to the IDQ file. The following is the complete list
of the Query .HTM code lines:

```
1.  <!DOCTYPE HTML PUBLIC "-//IETF//DTD HTML 3.0//EN" "html.dtd">
2.  <HTML>

3.  <HEAD>

4.  <!--
```

```
5. *****      INSTRUCTIONS FOR CUSTOMIZING THIS FORM      *****

6. To customize this form, look for remarks in the file
➥beginning with
7. 5 stars ("*****"). These lines contain instructions for
➥easily
8. customizing the most common query form elements.

9. -->

10. <TITLE>Index Server 2.0 Sample HTM/IDQ/HTX Search Form</
➥TITLE>
11. <META NAME="DESCRIPTION" CONTENT="Sample query form for
➥Microsoft Index Server">
12. <META NAME="AUTHOR"      CONTENT="Index Server Team">
13. <META NAME="KEYWORDS"    CONTENT="query, content, hit">
14. <META NAME="SUBJECT"     CONTENT="sample form">
15. <META NAME="MS.CATEGORY" CONTENT="Internet">
16. <META NAME="MS.LOCALE"   CONTENT="EN-US">
17. <META HTTP-EQUIV="Content-Type" CONTENT="text/html;
➥charset=Windows-1252">
18. </HEAD>

19. <!-- ***** To change the form's background pattern, simply
save your background pattern
20. using the name IS2BKGND.GIF in the same directory as this
➥form. ***** -->
21. <BODY background="is2bkgnd.gif">

22. <TABLE>

23. <TR><TD><A href="http://www.microsoft.com/ntserver/search"
➥target="_top" style="text-decoration: none">

24. <!-- ***** To change the form's logo, simply save your logo
➥ using the name IS2LOGO.GIF
25. in the same directory as this form. -->
26. <IMG SRC ="is2logo.gif" VALIGN=MIDDLE ALIGN=LEFT>

27. </A></TD></TR>
28. <TR><TD ALIGN="RIGHT"><H3>
```

```
29. <!-- ***** The following line of text is displayed next to
➡the form logo. -->
30. Sample HTM/IDQ/HTX Search Form

31. </H3></TD></TD></TR>
32. </TR>
33. </TABLE>

34. <FORM ACTION="query.idq" METHOD="GET">
35. <TABLE WIDTH=500>
36. <TR>
37. <TD>Enter your query below:</TD>
38. </TR>
39. <TR>
40. <TD><INPUT TYPE="TEXT" NAME="CiRestriction" SIZE="80"
➡ MAXLENGTH="100" VALUE=""></TD>
41. <TD><INPUT TYPE="SUBMIT" VALUE="Go"></TD>
42. </TR>
43. <TR>
44. <TD ALIGN="RIGHT"><A HREF="ixqlang.htm">Tips for searching</
➡A></TD>
45. </TR>
46. <TR>
47. <TD>
48. <P><INPUT NAME="FreeText" TYPE=CHECKBOX>Search for any
➡combination of words entered above.
49. </TD>
50. </TR>
51. </TABLE>

52. <!-- The CiScope parameter allows you to control which
➡documents are searched. To search
53. the entire document set, use a value of "/", which
➡corresponds to the root of your web
54. virtual namespace. To search a subset of your documents,
➡set the value equal to the
55. virtual directory you want to search.  -->
56. <INPUT TYPE="HIDDEN" NAME="CiScope" VALUE="/">

57. <INPUT TYPE="HIDDEN" NAME="CiMaxRecordsPerPage" VALUE="10">
58. <INPUT TYPE="HIDDEN" NAME="TemplateName" VALUE="query">
```

```
59. <INPUT TYPE="HIDDEN" NAME="CiSort" VALUE="rank[d]">
60. <INPUT TYPE="HIDDEN" NAME="HTMLQueryForm" VALUE="query.htm">
61. </FORM>


62. <!-- BEGIN STANDARD MICROSOFT FOOTER FOR QUERY PAGES -->


63. <hr width=500 align=left>
64. <p>
65. <table border="0" cellpadding="0" cellspacing="0"
➡width="500">
66. <tr>
67. <!-- IIS GIF -->
68. <td>
69. <a href="http://www.microsoft.com/iis"><img src="/IISSamples/
➡Default/nts_iis.GIF" alt="Learn more about Internet Information
➡Server!" width="88" height="31" border="0"></font></a>
70. </td>


71. <!-- Microsoft Legal Info -->
72. <td align=center>
73. <font size="1" face="Verdana, Arial, Helvetica"> (c)1997
➡Microsoft Corporation. All rights reserved.<br></font><a
➡href="http://www.microsoft.com/misc/cpyright.htm"><font size="1"
➡face="Verdana, Arial, Helvetica">Legal Notices.</font></a>
74. </td>


75. <!-- Best with IE GIF -->
76. <td align=right>
77. <a href="http://www.microsoft.com/ie"><img src="/IISSamples/
➡Default/IE.GIF" alt="Download Internet Explorer!" width="88"
➡height="31" border="0"></a>
78. </td>
79. </tr>
80. </table>


81. <!-- END STANDARD MICROSOFT FOOTER FOR QUERY PAGES -->


82. </BODY>
83. </HTML>
```

The results of running the file are shown in Figure 27.10. They are self-explanatory in nature.

Figure 27.10

An example of the QUERY.HTM page.

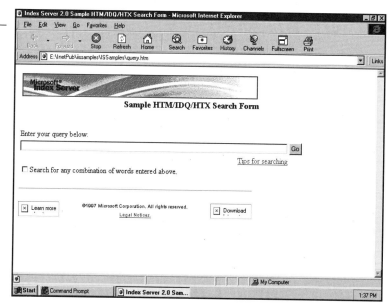

Exercises

Exercise 27.1: Examine the ODBC Core Components

To see which ODBC core components are installed on your system, follow these steps:

1. Double-click the ODBC icon in the Control Panel.

2. Select the About tab from the ODBC Data Source Administrator dialog box.

3. Note the core components installed and the version number of each.

Exercise 27.2: Edit the QUERY.HTM File

To modify the QUERY.HTM file to perform a query based upon your database, follow these steps:

1. Start a word processing application such as Microsoft Word 97.

2. Select the File, Open menu, switch to All Files, and find the existing copy of QUERY.HTM (by default, in InetPub\iissamples\ISSamples.

3. What appears is the HTML result. Select View, HTML Source and the code is displayed.

4. Make the changes to reflect your system and database.

5. Choose File, Save, and then Exit. Lastly, confirm that it is saved as an .HTM file.

Exercise 27.3:   Examine the Sample Files on Your System

To examine the sample .HTM, .IDQ, and .HTX files on your system, follow these steps:

1. Start a word processing application such as Microsoft Word 97.

2. Select the File, Open menu and go to InetPub\iissamples\ISSamples. You may need to change the file type to All Files in order to see the listings.

3. What appears is a number of sample files to use in creating your own scripts. Bring each one up and you will see the HTML result. Select View, HTML Source and the code is displayed.

Review Questions

1. When specifying a template path, how many characters can be used in the path specification?

    A. 8

    B. 255

    C. 256

    D. 260

2. Of the following file extensions, which can be used to contain queries?

    A. HTM

    B. IDC

    C. IDQ

    D. HTX

3. Which of the following files can be used to contain templates?

    A. HTM

    B. IDC

    C. IDQ

    D. HTX

4. Where can Login Authentication to a SQL Server accessed through IIS be done?

    A. On the NT Server

    B. On the SQL Server

    C. On the IIS Server

    D. On the Index Server

5. In which file would the `<Query>` tag be found

    A. Sample.htm

    B. Sample.idc

    C. Sample.idq

    D. Sample.htx

6. In which file would the SQL Statement parameter be found?

    A. Sample.htm

    B. Sample.idc

    C. Sample.idq

    D. Sample.htx

7. What is the comment character used as the first character in script files to prevent the line from being processed?

    A. %

    B. <

    C. [

    D. #

8. Joe calls Steve, the new administrator, and says that he is doing some deletion of unnecessary files and has come across one called HTTPODBC.DLL. How could this file be explained?

    A. It is the dynamic link library providing ODBC support on the server

    B. It is the file used to install ODBC support on the server

    C. It is needed for HTTP operations

    D. It should be deleted after installation

9. In which file would the MaxRecords parameter be found?

   A. Sample.htm

   B. Sample.idc

   C. Sample.idq

   D. Sample.htx

10. In which file would the CiCodePage variable be found?

   A. Sample.htm

   B. Sample.idc

   C. Sample.idq

   D. Sample.htx

Review Answers

1. **D.** The limit is 260 characters on any NT-based pathname.

2. **B, C.** Queries can be in either .IDC or .IDQ files.

3. **D.** .HTX files signify templates.

4. **A, B.** SQL Server Login Authentication can be done by SQL Server or NT Server.

5. **C.** The <Query> tag is used in .IDQ files.

6. **B.** SQLStatement is one of required parameters of the .IDC file.

7. **D.** The pound sign (#) is used to signify comments.

8. **A.** HTTPODBC.DLL is the dynamic link library providing ODBC support on the server.

9. **D.** MaxRecords is a parameter that can be used in .HTX files.

10. **C.** CiCodePage is one variable that can be used in .IDQ files.

Answers to Test Yourself Questions at Beginning of Chapter

1. Files with .IDC extensions stipulate how the data is accessed, while those with .HTX extensions stipulate how the data is presented. See "Configuring IIS to Connect to a Database."

2. The CONTAINS expression in an .IDQ file checks to see if one entry is a subset of another entry. See "Configuring Integration with Index Server."

Chapter 28

Running Applications

This chapter helps you prepare for the exam by covering the following objectives:

✓ Objectives ▶

▶ Configure IIS to support server-side scripting

▶ Configure IIS to run ISAPI applications

▶ Configure IIS to support ADO associated with the WWW service

Test Yourself! Before reading this chapter, test yourself to determine how much study time you will need to devote to this section.

1. What are the three items that can be contained within Active Server Pages?

2. What are the two ways that ISAPI can be implemented?

3. What three types of files can ADO be used to access?

Answers are located at the end of the chapter...

This chapter addresses the scripting side of IIS and other servers and services. The topics discussed are ways that scripts can be created and implemented to automate tasks on the IIS server—primarily in conjunction with the WWW service. It is imperative that you understand the material in Chapter 26, "Configuring and Managing Resource Access," and Chapter 27, "Integration and Interoperability," before attempting to understand scripting.

The sample Web site included with IIS 4.0, "Exploration Air," includes some examples of scripting and Active Server Pages. This material is highly recommended. The files are very useful and can provide you with a lot of insights into IIS 4.0 capabilities.

The specific topics covered in this chapter include the following:

▶ Configuring IIS to support server-side scripting

▶ Configuring IIS to run ISAPI applications

▶ Configuring ADO support

Configuring IIS to Support Server-Side Scripting

√ Objective ▶ Microsoft Internet Information Server (IIS) 4.0 enables an administrator or Webmaster to use Active Server Pages (ASP) to do Web application programming. ASP simplifies server-side programming and offers support for ActiveX objects (also known as server-side objects), as well as HTML tags and all Active scripting commands.

The .ASP extension is assigned to all ASP scripts, and the files include text, HTML tags, and ASP script commands. While HTML tags begin with < and end with >, ASP tags begin with <% and end with %>. The tags also are known as *delimiters*, and it is the delimiters that signal the server that processing is required at that point. Look at the following example:

```
It is now <%= Time %>
```

Once the server processes the script command, the following is displayed:

It is now 14:52:10

The easiest way to create ASP files is to start with standard HTML files and add the script commands to them (as well as rename the file from .htm to .asp).

 Tip

For purposes of passing the exam, also know that *primary script commands* are those within <%%>.

Active Server Pages can be used with VBScript, Jscript, PerlScript, or any other recognized scripting language. Not only can you use a variety of languages, but you also can use multiple languages within the same script. The syntax for doing so follows:

```
<SCRIPT LANGUAGE="VBScript" RUNAT=SERVER>
routine
</SCRIPT>
<SCRIPT LANGUAGE="PerlScript" RUNAT=SERVER>
routine
</SCRIPT>
```

In addition to defining variables by an operation (such as DATE, TIME, and so on), you also can set variables and reference them within the scripts. This is done through the use of the SET command, and the variable is then referenced in a manner similar to how the Time variable was referenced. You can also create an array of data to reference through use of the Session variable if you wanted the value to persist between scripts, which is unique for the life of the session. Look at the following example:

```
Session ("City") = "Anderson"
Set Session ("State") = "IN"
How is the weather in <%= Session("City") %>?
```

This is displayed as the following:

How is the weather in Anderson?

As mentioned, the Session variables are kept for the entire duration of the session, and abandoned afterward. To force the purging of the variables, you can use the Session.Abandon call. This loses the variables (and ends the session).

The Use of Cookies

Clients using ASP first establish unique session keys, a process carried by the use of HTTP cookies. No buffering is used, by default, so all operations that take place are immediately sent to the browser. This causes a session cookie to be sent for every browser interaction, but you can elect to turn on buffering and prevent the sending of some unnecessary cookies.

 Note

Cookies are components of a session or information stored on the client's machine.

A Walkthrough of the Steps Involved in Active Server Pages

The following is a simplified example of how ASPs work:

1. The browser sends an HTTP request for an Active Server Page. The server knows it to be an Active Server Page due to the .ASP extension.

2. The server sends the file to ASP.DLL for execution of all code.

3. Processing is done and the server sends back an HTML page.

4. If there is any client-side code, it is executed on the client, and the page is displayed in the browser.

Note that during this process, no server-side scripting is sent to the client, so the clients can't view the script.

Scripting Hosts

Scripting hosts are designed to improve Operating System operations, and there are two scripting hosts available with IIS:

▶ A command-based scripting host

▶ A Windows-based scripting host

The hosts are very similar in nature. The command-based one is called by Cscript.exe, and the Windows-based host is called by Wscript.exe.

Parameters that can be used with Cscript.exe are as follows:

▶ //?—Shows the command line parameters.

▶ //B—Places the engine in batch mode.

▶ //C—Causes Cscript to be the default engine used by running scripts.

▶ //I—The opposite of //B, it places the engine in interactive mode.

▶ //logo—Shows a logo at execution time.

▶ //nologo—Does not display a logo at execution time.

▶ //R—Registers known script extensions with the engine. Known script extensions include .js, .vbs, and .tcl. This operation is done by default and you need not use the parameter.

▶ //S—Saves the current command line options for the user

▶ //T:nn—The timeout specified in number of seconds. The default is no limit, but you can specify a value to prevent excessive script execution.

Figure 28.1 shows the Wscript configuration screen (available from the Run command or any command line).

Figure 28.1

The Wscript con-
figuration box.

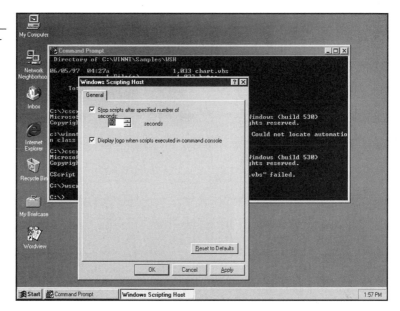

The options for Wscript configuration enable you to specify a
number of seconds after which to stop script execution (equivalent to //T:nn in Cscript), and enable you to toggle the banner on
and off (//logo and //nologo in Cscript). Wscript does not have the
capability for interactive or batch modes.

Adding Conditions

You can add conditional processing to your scripts by using
IF..Then..Else logic. The syntax is as follows:

```
If {condition exists} Then
{action to perform}
Else
{another action to perform
End If
```

You also can run an operation a number of times by using
For..Next loops:

```
For Each {variable} in {set}
{action to perform}
Next
```

As with most scripting languages, indentation is not required, but it is used to make it easier to read and debug the script. Additionally, ASP itself is not case sensitive, but the language used to execute the commands may be.

An Example of Server-Side Scripting

The following is an example based on a script file included with IIS. The Shortcut.vbs file uses Wscript to create a NotePad shortcut on the desktop:

```
' Windows Script Host Sample Script
'
' ------------------------------------------------------------
'            Copyright (C) 1996 Microsoft Corporation
'
' You have a royalty-free right to use, modify, reproduce and
distribute
' the Sample Application Files (and/or any modified version) in
any way
' you find useful, provided that you agree that Microsoft has no
warranty,
' obligations, or liability for any Sample Application Files.
' ------------------------------------------------------------
'
' This sample demonstrates how to use the WshShell object.
' to create a shortcut on the desktop


Dim WshShell, MyShortcut, MyDesktop, DesktopPath

' Initialize WshShell object
  Set WshShell = WScript.CreateObject("WScript.Shell")

' Read desktop path using WshSpecialFolders object
  DesktopPath = WshShell.SpecialFolders("Desktop")

' Create a shortcut object on the desktop
  Set MyShortcut = WshShell.CreateShortcut(DesktopPath &
➥"\Shortcut to notepad.lnk")
```

```
' Set shortcut object properties and save it
  MyShortcut.TargetPath =
➡WshShell.ExpandEnvironmentStrings("%windir%\notepad.exe")
  MyShortcut.WorkingDirectory =
➡WshShell.ExpandEnvironmentStrings("%windir%")
  MyShortcut.WindowStyle = 4
  MyShortcut.IconLocation = WshShell.ExpandEnvironmentStrings
➡("%windir%\notepad.exe, 0")
  MyShortcut.Save
```

Configuring IIS to Run ISAPI Applications

 Objective

ISAPI—Internet Server API (Application Programming Inter-face)—applications are an alternative to Active Server Pages. In fact, the ASP scripting engine is an ISAPI filter. Like ASP, ISAPI can be used to write applications that Web users can activate by filling out an HTML form or clicking a link in an HTML page on your Web server. The user-supplied information can then be re-sponded to and the results returned in an HTML page or posted to a database.

ISAPI was a Microsoft improvement over popular CGI (Common Gateway Interface) scripting, and offers much better performance than CGI because applications are loaded into memory at server run-time. This means that they require less overhead and each request does not start a separate process. Additionally, ISAPI applications are created as DLLs on the server, and allow pre-pro-cessing of requests and post-processing of responses, permitting site-specific handling of HTTP requests and responses.

ISAPI filters can be used for applications such as customized au-thentication, access, or logging. You can create complex sites by combining ISAPI filters and applications.

ISAPI works with OLE connectivity and the Internet Database Connector. This allows ISAPI to be implemented as a DLL (in essence, an executable) or as a filter (translating another execut-able's output). If ISAPI is used as a filter, then it is not called when the browser accesses an URL, but is summoned by the server in response to an event (which could easily be an URL request). Common uses of ISAPI filters include the following:

- ► Tracking URL usage statistics

- ► Performing authentication

- ► Adding entries to log files

- ► Compression

For the Exam

If you want to become an ISAPI programmer, then you'll need a book three times the length of this one to learn the language. If you want to pass the exam, (the purpose of this book), then there are several things you need to know:

- ► ISAPI applications effectively extend server applications to the desktop.

- ► ISAPI is similar to CGI but offers better performance.

- ► Although created by Microsoft, ISAPI is an open specification that third parties can write to.

- ► ISAPI filters can do pre- or post-processing.

Configuring ADO Support

 The newest enhancement to Microsoft's Web service offering is ADO—ActiveX Data Objects. ADO combines a set of core functions and unique functions for each implementation. ADO was designed to replace the need for all other data access methods, and Microsoft recommends migration of all applications to ADO when it is feasible.

ADO can access the following:

- ► Text

- ► Relational databases

- ► Any ODBC-compliant data source

ADO grew out of ASP (Active Server Pages) and offers the following benefits:

- Low memory overhead

- Small disk footprint

- Ease of use

- De-emphasis on object hierarchy

- Ability to use ODBC 3.0 connection pooling

Connection pooling enables you to open database connections and manage sharing across different user requests while reducing the number of idle connections. In order to use it, you must set a timeout property in the Registry. When a user times out, rather than the connection being totally lost, it is saved into a pool. When the next request comes in, that connection is used, rather than a whole new connection being created each and every time.

While ADO has a number of benefits, its greatest downside is that it is mostly read-only on the browser. All filtering and processing must be done on the server, and when it reaches the browser, it is in its final state. Although there are ways around this, they are more cumbersome and difficult than other options.

For the Exam

As with ISAPI, if you want to become an ADO programmer, you'll need to purchase a book specific to that end. If you want to pass the exam then there are only a few things you need to know:

- ADO objects are small, compact, and easy to write to.

- ADO knows what data to access through DSN (Data Source Name) files.

- It is the DSN that contains the user security, database configuration, and location information.

- ▶ The DSN can be an actual file (text) or merely an entry in the Registry. ODBC enables you to create three types of DSNs—User (in Registry), System (in Registry) or File (text file).

- ▶ A system DSN applies to all users logged into the server.

- ▶ A user DSN applies to a specific user (or set of).

- ▶ A file DSN gives access to multiple users and can be transferred between servers by copying the file.

- ▶ DSN files are created through the ODBC icon of the Control Panel.

- ▶ ADO connections are written in the files with variable names such as *cn*. Look at the following example:

```
Set cn = Server.CreateObject("ADODB.Connection")
Cn.Open "FILEDSN=Example.dsn"
```

- ▶ A RecordSet is a table or query from a subset of the object that you wish to retrieve. Rather than retrieving the entire Access or SQL database, you retrieve a component of it, known as a RecordSet object.

- ▶ ADO commands are written in the files as variables, such as *cm*. Look at the following example:

```
Set cm = Server.CreateObject("ADODB.Command")
Cm.CommandText = "APPEND INTO Array (X, Y) VALUES"
```

Exercises

Exercise 28.1:   Run the Chart.VBS program

This exercise illustrates how to run a script program in Cscript and Wscript.

1. Open a command line

2. Enter:

    Cscript {*root path*}\Samples\Wsh\Chart.VBS

3. Enter:

    Cscript //logo {*root path*}\Samples\Wsh\Chart.VBS

4. Enter:

    Cscript //nologo {*root path*}\Samples\Wsh\Chart.VBS

5. From the Run command, enter:

    Wscript {*root path*}\Samples\Wsh\Chart.VBS

Review Questions

1. What file extension is used to signify, and required for, Active Server Pages?

   A. ASP

   B. EXE

   C. COM

   D. HTM

2. Which of the following would not be a component of Active Server Pages?

   A. HTML

   B. text

   C. access data

   D. script commands

3. The line of code "*<BODY>*" would be considered:

   A. an Active Server tag

   B. an HTML tag

   C. an ADO tag

   D. an ISAPI tag

4. Which variable in Active Server Pages is erased from existence when a connection is no longer there?

   A. BROWSER

   B. USER

   C. USERSESSION

   D. SESSION

5. What are the scripting hosts included with IIS?

    A. Cscript

    B. Wscript

    C. Uscript

    D. Pscript

6 Which of the following commands would make PerlScript active to process the .ASP file?

    A. `</SCRIPT="PerlScript">`

    B. `<SCRIPT="PerlScript">`

    C. `</SCRIPT LANGUAGE="PerlScript">`

    D. `<SCRIPT LANGUAGE="PerlScript">`

7. What command can be used to force the purging of variables?

    A. `Session.purge`

    B. `Session.abandon`

    C. `Abandon.session`

    D. `Purge.session`

8. Which Cscript parameter is the opposite of the `//B` parameter?

    A. `//T`

    B. `//R`

    C. `//S`

    D. `//I`

    E. `//C`

9. Conditional script commands in .ASP files that begin with IF must end with:

    A. FI

    B. END IF

    C. ENDIF

    D. IF END

10. Which type of processing can ISAPI filters do?

    A. pre-processing only

    B. post-processing only

    C. both pre- and post-processing

    D. neither pre- nor post-processing

11. ISAPI is implemented as

    A. a TSR

    B. a DLL

    C. an EXE

    D. as ASP

12. It would be Microsoft's recommendation that all sites with the time and resources to do so convert Web\data interaction to what type?

    A. ISAPI

    B. CGI

    C. ADO

    D. ASP

13. Which of the following are benefits of ADO?

    A. small disk footprint

    B. high memory overhead

    C. improved authentication

    D. emphasis on object hierarchy

14. What are the two types of DSNs?

    A. HTML files

    B. text files

    C. registry entries

    D. executables

15. To what group does a System DSN apply?

    A. specific users

    B. specific groups

    C. all users logged on the server

    D. multiple users

16. Which of the following variable names is recommended by Microsoft to use when specifying a connection in an ADO file?

    A. `cm`

    B. `cn`

    C. `co`

    D. `recordset`

Review Answers

1. **A.** Active Server Pages must have the .asp file extension.

2. **C.** Access data would not be Active Server Pages.

3. **B.** `<BODY>` is an HTML tag.

4. **D.** The *SESSION* variable goes away when the session (or connection) is no longer there.

5. **A, B**. Both Cscript and Wscript are included with IIS.

6. **D**. `<SCRIPT LANGUAGE="PerlScript">` would make PerlScript active for that portion of the .asp file.

7. **B**. `Session.abandon` can be used to force the purging of variables.

8. **D**. `//I` places the engine in interactive mode—the opposite of `//B`, which places it in batch mode.

9. **B**. Conditional script commands in .asp files that begin with `IF` must end with `END IF`.

10. **C**. ISAPI filters can do both pre- and post-processing.

11. **B**. ISAPI is implemented as a DLL.

12. **C**. It would be Microsoft's recommendation that all sites with the time and resources to do so convert Web\data interaction to ADO.

13. **A**. A benefit of ADO is its use of a small disk footprint.

14. **B, C**. DSNs can be text files or Registry entries.

15. **C**. A System DSN applies to all users logged on to the server.

16. **B**. `Cn` is used to specify a connection in an ADO file.

Answers to Test Yourself Questions at Beginning of Chapter

1. Active Server Pages can contain text, HTML code, and script commands. See "Configuring IIS to Support Server-Side Scripting."

2. ISAPI can be implemented as a DLL or a filter. See "Configuring IIS to Run ISAPI Applications."

3. ADO can be used to access text files, relational databases, or ODBC-compliant data sources. See "Configuring ADO Support."

Chapter 29

Monitoring and Optimization

This chapter will help you prepare for the exam by covering the following objectives:

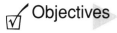

Objectives

▶ Maintain a log for fine-tuning and auditing purposes. Tasks include

  ▶ Importing log files into a Usage Import and Report Writer Database

  ▶ Configuring the logging features of the WWW service

  ▶ Configuring the logging features of the FTP service

  ▶ Configuring Usage Import and Report Writer to analyze logs created by the WWW service or the FTP service

▶ Monitor performance of various functions by using Performance Monitor. Functions include HHTP and FTP sessions.

▶ Analyze performance. Performance issues include

  ▶ Identifying bottlenecks

  ▶ Identifying network-related performance issues

  ▶ Identifying disk-related performance issues

  ▶ Identifying CPU-related performance issues

continues

- ▶ Optimize performance of IIS

- ▶ Optimize performance of Index Server

- ▶ Optimize performance of Microsoft SMTP Service

- ▶ Optimize performance of Microsoft NNTP Service

- ▶ Interpret performance data

- ▶ Optimize a Web site by using Content Analyzer

Test Yourself! Before reading this chapter, test yourself to determine how much study time you will need to devote to this section.

1. As the administrator for your IIS 4 Web site, you're asked to produce a report showing the daily Web traffic to your site. Which tool do you use and can you automate this task?

2. You are a consultant for a company that uses IIS 4. IIS 4 runs a Web site and FTP site under IIS 4. You are asked to track the number of anonymous users currently attached to the site. What do you do?

3. When administering IIS 4, you want to keep an eye out for hardware bottlenecks that may occur. What are some of the tools you can use to watch for these?

4. You're the administrator of your IIS 4 Web site. The Web site is responding sluggishly, and you notice some inactive clients are staying connected to your server. How can you change this?

5. On your company's Web site, you run Microsoft Index Server. You have between 100,000 and 150,000 documents stored on it. How much RAM is recommended for this number of documents?

6. You are an IIS 4 consultant working with a large company that has asked you to set up a smart host. What is this?

7. The Microsoft NNTP news server you administer allows too many clients to connect to it simultaneously, resulting in a poorly performing server. How can you change it so only a specific number of clients can connect at the same time?

8. What are the statistical measurements called that are used in Performance Monitor?

9. To help you manage your company's Web site, you use the Content Analyzer. Name three ways you can use this tool to optimize your site.

Answers are located at the end of the chapter...

Microsoft makes it very easy to monitor and optimize your IIS 4 Web site. Each time a user interacts with your Web site and requests resources from it, such as a Web page, image file, or similar item, a hit is recorded in a log file. You can log each IIS 4 service to help you fine-tune and optimize your site, plan for future expansion, and review the security of your site. IIS 4 enables you to send log data to a text file or to an Open Database Connectivity (ODBC)–compliant database, such as Microsoft SQL Server or Microsoft Access.

In this chapter you learn how to monitor and optimize your site, including the WWW and FTP services, the Index Service, and the Microsoft SMTP and NNTP services. Specific topics covered include

▶ Maintaining IIS 4 logs

▶ Monitoring performance of various functions using Performance Monitor

▶ Analyzing performance

▶ Optimizing the performance of IIS

▶ Optimizing the performance of Index Server

▶ Optimizing the performance of Microsoft SMTP Service

▶ Optimizing the performance of Microsoft NNTP Service

▶ Interpreting performance data

▶ Optimizing a Web site using Content Analyzer

Maintaining IIS 4 Logs

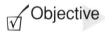 Objective

Maintaining IIS 4 logs is one of the most important tasks in fine-tuning and auditing an IIS site. In the following sections, you learn how to configure WWW and FTP services logging, configure Report Writer and Usage Import to analyze logs created by these services, and automate the Report Writer and Usage Import.

Importing Log Files into a Report Writer and Usage Import Database

The Report Writer and Usage Import Database help you analyze and create reports based on logs created by IIS. Report Writer creates analysis reports based on the log file data. Usage Import, on the other hand, reads the log files and places the data into a relational database.

To begin using these tools, you import the log file or files you want to analyze into a Report Writer and Usage Import database. The database is essentially a container that holds imported data from a log file.

Both Report Writer and Usage Import connect to this database when they start. You can see the name of the database each tool connects to by looking at the bottom of its screen on the status bar (see Figure 29.1). If Report Writer or Usage Import cannot find the database it is configured to connect to, you are prompted to enter the name of a valid database.

Figure 29.1

You can view the database that Report Writer connects to by looking at the status bar.

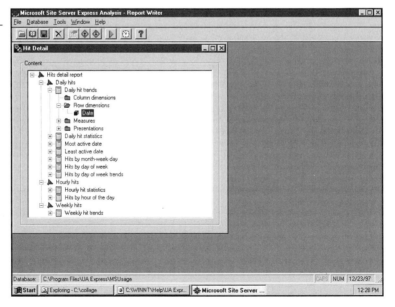

Relational databases are used because of their efficient use of data storage. Relational databases do not require redundant information from your log file to be stored. This results in smaller databases and less required disk space. In some cases, the database may be 10–20 percent smaller than the original log file.

Relational databases are also used because they enable you to analyze your data in a more flexible way. You can cross-reference over 200 different Internet server usage data properties.

To import log files into Usage Import so that you can analyze your site's data in Report Writer, perform the following steps:

1. Make sure you can access the Internet server log file on the local computer.

2. Select Start | Programs | Windows NT 4.0 Option Pack | Microsoft Site Server Express 2.0 | Usage Import. Usage Import starts. The first time you start Usage Import, you need to configure an Internet site in a database, because no sites are configured yet. Usage Import displays the Microsoft Site Server Express Analysis dialog box (see Figure 29.2), which informs you that you must use the Server Manager to configure your Internet site.

Figure 29.2

The Microsoft Site Server Express Analysis dialog box.

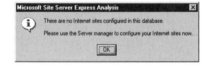

 Tip

If the Microsoft Site Server Express Analysis dialog box does not display, you've already configured a site under Usage Import. You can start Server Manager again by selecting File | Server Manager after Usage Import starts. Right-click on the Log Data Source item in the Server Manager and click on New Server. The Server Properties dialog box displays, which is explained in step 5.

3. Click OK. The Log data source Properties dialog box displays (see Figure 29.3).

Figure 29.3

The Log data source Properties dialog box.

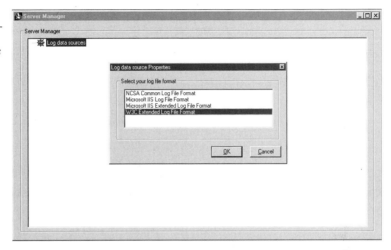

4. From the Log data source Properties dialog box, click the log file format for your log data source. Some of the file formats include NCSA Common Log File Format, Microsoft IIS Log File Format, Microsoft IIS Extended Log File Format, W3C Extended Log File Format, and others. The options available here correspond to the type of server you are analyzing. You can read more about the log file types supported in the "Configuring the Logging Features of the WWW Service" and "Configuring the Logging Features of the FTP Service" sections, later in this chapter.

Tip

To create customizable log files, use the W3C Extended Log File Format. Compared to other log file formats, such as NCSA Common Log File Format and Microsoft IIS Log Format, the W3C Extended Log File Format also records the greatest amount of information about your Web site, including referring URL and cookie information.

5. Click OK. The Server Properties dialog box displays (see Figure 29.4). Set the following items on this dialog box:

▶ **Server type.** Sets the type of server for which your log file is configured. You can select World Wide Web, FTP, Gopher, or RealAudio servers.

▶ **Directory index files.** Enter your server's index file, such as default.asp, index.html, home.htm, or other name. This is the name of the file that is displayed in the client when the URL ends in a slash (/).

▶ **IP address.** Enter the IP address of the server. This field is optional.

▶ **IP port.** Enter the server's IP port number. The default is 80.

▶ **Local timezone.** Enter the local time zone where your content is stored.

▶ **Local domain.** Enter the domain name for the local network that is hosting your content. This setting is used to distinguish hits from internal and external clients. If you use a hosting service (such as IQuest), enter the domain of that service, such as **iquest.net**.

Figure 29.4

The Server Properties dialog box.

6. Click OK. The Site Properties dialog box displays (see Figure 29.5).

7. Enter the URL of the home page in the Home page URLs field on the Basic tab. This information is required. As an

optional entry, fill in the Server filesystem paths for this Site field. If you have multiple URLs, list them all in this field.

Figure 29.5

The Site Proper-ties dialog box.

8. Click the Excludes tab (see Figure 29.6). Here you can set log file information that should be excluded from the database. These settings are optional. You can enter the name of hosts you want to exclude in the Hosts to exclude from import field. To exclude log file information based on inline image requests, enter the image file types in the Inline images to exclude from import field. Some common file types you might enter here include gif, jpg, jpeg, and png. You might opt to exclude these entries to decrease the time it takes to import the log file and make the database smaller.

 Tip

Although you have excluded inline images, you will still get accurate bandwidth calculations.

9. Click OK. The Usage Import window displays with the Log File Manager and Server Manager windows (see Figure 29.7). The Log File Manager organizes, filters, and imports log files for analysis. The Server Manager, on the other hand, sets up the site structure for which the logs are imported. Before any data can be imported into a database, the servers and sites that created the log data must be configured in the Service Manager.

Figure 29.6

The Excludes tab on the Site Properties dialog box.

Figure 29.7

The Usage Import window.

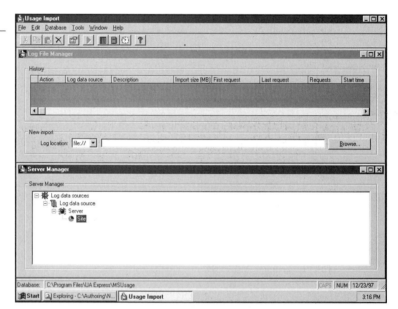

10. In the Log File Manager window, enter the complete path for your log file in the Log location field. Click Browse to locate the file graphically.

11. Click the Start Import button on the Usage Import window toolbar (this tool is a green right-facing arrow). After Usage Import finishes importing the log file, the Microsoft Site Server Express Analysis dialog box displays, telling you the import is completed and how long the import process took (see Figure 29.8).

Figure 29.8

The Microsoft Site Server Express Analysis dialog box.

12. Click OK. The Usage Import Statistics dialog box displays (see Figure 29.9).

Figure 29.9

The Usage Import Statistics dialog box.

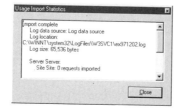

13. Click Close.

When you are ready to create a report of a log file in Report Writer, perform the following steps:

1. Select Start | Programs | Windows NT 4.0 Option Pack | Microsoft Site Server Express 2.0 | Report Writer. Report Writer starts and displays the Report Writer opening dialog box (see Figure 29.10).

Figure 29.10

The Report Writer dialog box.

2. Select the From the Report Writer catalog option on the Report Writer dialog box. You can create your own report using the From scratch option. However, you should use the Report Writer catalog option the first few times you run Report Writer to see how the tool works.

3. Click OK. The Report Writer dialog box with the Report Writer catalog field displays (see Figure 29.11).

Figure 29.11

*The Report Writer
catalog field
displaying in the
Report Writer
dialog box.*

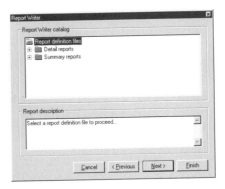

4. Select the plus sign next to the Detail reports or Summary reports folders, depending on the type of summary you want to create.

5. Click a report type, such as Hits detail report. To read about each type of report, click on it and view a description in the Report Description area at the bottom of the Report Writer dialog box.

6. Click Next. The Report Writer dialog box shown in Figure 29.12 displays. You set the date range of the data to analyze from this dialog box. The default is Every request you've imported. You also can narrow the date ranges, such as This week, This year, or a specific range (Before 12/25/98, for example).

Figure 29.12

*Set the date
range of the log
file data to ana-
lyze from this
Report Writer
dialog box.*

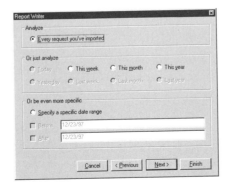

7. Click Next. The Report Writer dialog box shown in Figure
   29.13 displays. From this dialog box, you can filter log file
   data using Boolean expressions and items included in the
   Filter name reference drop-down list. To use an item in the
   drop-down list, select the down arrow, click on the item, and
   drag the item to the Filter field. This enables you to create
   expressions and drag and drop Filter name reference items
   into your expressions.

Figure 29.13

*You can filter log
file data using
this Report Writer
dialog box.*

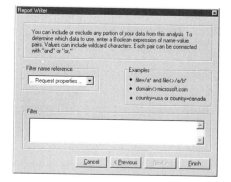

8. Click Finish. The Detail window for the report you want to
   generate displays (see Figure 29.14). From this window you
   can see the types of information that will be included in your
   new report. You can delete items from this window by selecting the item and pressing Delete.

Figure 29.14

*The Hit Detail
window.*

9. Click the Create Report Document toolbar button on the
   Report Writer toolbar. The Report Document dialog box
   displays (see Figure 29.15).

Figure 29.15

*The Report docu-
ment dialog box.*

10. Enter a filename and select the format of the report. The
    default report format is HTML, which automatically displays
    in your Web browser. You also can select Microsoft Word and
    Microsoft Excel, which you can display in those applications.
    Click the Template button if you want to specify a report
    template that you have created.

11. Click OK. The report document is created. The Report Writ-
    er Statistics dialog box displays as well. Click Close to close
    this dialog box. If you specified the HTML format in step 10,
    your registered Web browser will launch with the report dis-
    played (see Figure 29.16).

Figure 29.16

*A Report Writer
document dis-
playing in Internet
Explorer 4.0.*

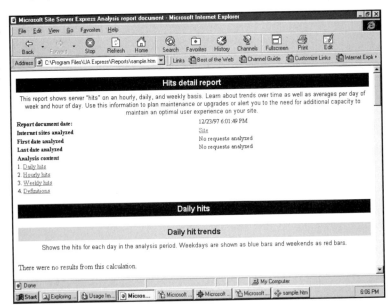

Configuring the Logging Features of the WWW Service

Probably one of the first actions you want to do when administering your IIS 4 site is to configure the logging features of the WWW and FTP services. When looking at log file information, you should keep in mind that this information does not show definitive information about users and visitors to your sites. Because Internet protocols are stateless, there cannot be sustained connections between clients and servers.

Log file data can give you a historical record of who has visited your site (based on visiting IP addresses), content exchanges (client downloads and uploads), which pages are the most popular ones on your site, and other information. A log file can be studied, for example, to see what traffic patterns develop on your site for maintenance issues (when you can perform daily, weekly, and monthly maintenance).

 Tip

Your log file can be accessed only after you stop your site. You can do this by starting Internet Service Manager, selecting the site, and clicking the Stop button on the Internet Service Manager toolbar. Click the Start button to start the site again.

 Note

See the next section, "Configuring the Logging Features of the FTP Service," for information on configuring logging features for the FTP service.

To configure logging features for your WWW service, perform the following steps:

1. Select Start | Programs | Windows NT 4.0 Option Pack | Microsoft Internet Information Server | Internet Service Manager. Internet Service Manager opens in the Microsoft Management Console (MMC) (see Figure 29.17).

Figure 29.17

Internet Service Manager displayed in MMC.

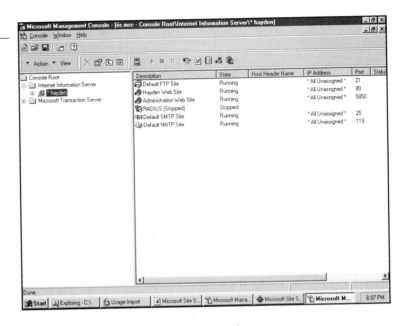

2. Right-click the Web site you want to configure.

3. Click Properties. The Web Site Properties dialog box displays (see Figure 29.18).

Figure 29.18

The Web Site Properties dialog box.

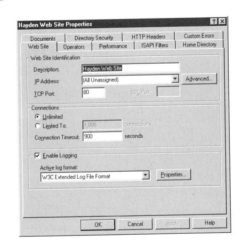

4. Click the Enable Logging option.

5. Click the Active log format drop-down list and select the type of log format you want to create. The following are the supported log file formats:

▶ **Microsoft IIS Log Format.** This is a fixed ASCII format that records basic logging items, including username, request date, request time, client IP address, number of bytes received, HTTP status code, and other items. This is a comma-delimited log file, making it easier to parse than other ASCII formats.

▶ **NCSA Common Log File Format.** This is a fixed ASCII format endorsed by the National Center for Supercomputing Applications (NCSA). The data it logs includes remote hostname, username, HTTP status code, request type, and the number of bytes received by the server. Spaces separate different items logged.

▶ **ODBC Logging.** This is a fixed format that is logged to a database. This log includes client IP address, username, request date, request time, HTTP status code, bytes received, bytes sent, action carried out, and the target. When you choose this option, you must specify the database for the file to be logged to. In addition, you must set up the database to receive that log data.

▶ **W3C Extended Log File Format.** This is a customizable ASCII format endorsed by the World Wide Web Consortium (W3C). This is the default setting. You can set this log format to record a number of different settings, such as request date, request time, client IP address, server IP address, server port, HTTP status code, and more. Data is separated by spaces in this format.

The following steps show how to configure the W3C Extended Log File Format.

6. Click the Properties button. The Extended Logging Properties dialog box displays (see Figure 29.19). If you selected a log format other than W3C Extended Log File Format from the Active log format drop-down list, the properties dialog box for that format displays.

7. In the New Log Time Period section, set the period when you want IIS to create a new log file for the selected Web site.

The default is Daily, but you can select Weekly, Monthly, Unlimited file size, or When file size reaches. If you select the last option, you need to set a maximum file size the log file can reach before a new file is created. The default here is 19MB. For active Web sites, the log file can reach sizes of over 100MB very quickly.

Figure 29.19

The Extended Logging Properties dialog box for the W3C Extended Log File Format.

8. Enter the directory in which you want to store the log file. The default is %WinDir\System32\LogFiles. Click the Browse button to locate a new directory graphically.

Note

The log filename syntax is shown next to the Log file name label; an example of the syntax is exyymmdd.log. The first two characters in the name, *ex*, denote the type of log file format you selected in step 5. These characters include *in* for Microsoft IIS Log File Format, *nc* for NCSA Common Log File Format, and *ex* for W3C Extended Log File Format.

The remaining characters in the log filename syntax correspond to the date the file is created: *yy* is the year, *mm* is the month, and *dd* is the day.

If you select the ODBC Logging format, you must specify a Data Source Name (DSN), which does not follow these naming schemes.

9. Click the Extended Properties tab to display the logging options (see Figure 29.20) you can set (this tab is available

only when you select the W3C Extended Log File Format option). On this tab, you can set the options described in Table 29.1.

Figure 29.20

The Extended Properties tab.

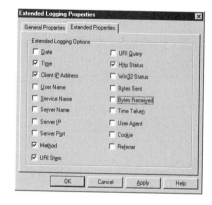

Table 29.1

W3C Extended Log File Format logging options.

Option	Description
Date	Date the activity occurred
Time	Time the activity occurred
Client IP Address	IP address of the client attaching to your server
User Name	Name of user who accessed your server
Service Name	Client computer's Internet service
Server Name	Server name where the log entry was created
Server IP	Server IP address where the log entry was created
Server Port	Shows the port number to which the client is connected
Method	Shows the action the client was performing
URI Stem	Logs the resource the client was accessing on your server, such as an HTML page, CGI program, and so on

continues

Table 29.1 Continued

Option	Description
URI Query	Logs the search string the client was trying to match
HTTP Status	Shows the status (in HTTP terms) of the client action
Win32 Status	Shows the status (in Windows NT terms) of the client action
Bytes Sent	Shows the number of bytes sent by the server
Bytes Received	Shows the number of bytes received by the server
Time Taken	Shows the amount of time to execute the action requested by the client
User Agent	Reports the browser used by the client
Cookie	Shows the content of any cookies sent or received by the server
Protocol Version	Shows the protocol used by the client to access the server (HTTP or FTP)
Referrer	Shows the URL of the site from where the user clicked on to get to your site

Note The default Extended Logging Options for the W3C Extended Log File Format include Time, Client IP Address, Method, URI Stem, and HTTP Status.

10. Click OK to close the Extended Logging Properties dialog box.

11. Click OK to close the Web Site Properties dialog box.

Log files can grow very large, so be sure your server on which the log file resides has plenty of free disk space. Logging shuts down if your server runs out of disk space when trying to add a new log entry to a file. When this happens, you'll see an event logged in the Windows NT Event Viewer. Another event will be logged when IIS is able to continue logging IIS activities (when disk space is freed up, for example).

Configuring the Logging Features of the FTP Service

As with the WWW service, you can configure the logging features of the FTP service in IIS 4. To do this, perform the following steps:

1. Select Start | Programs | Windows NT 4.0 Option Pack | Microsoft Internet Information Server | Internet Service Manager. Internet Service Manager opens in the Microsoft Management Console (MMC) (refer to Figure 29.17).

2. Right-click on the FTP site you want to configure.

3. Click Properties. The Default FTP Site Properties dialog box displays (see Figure 29.21).

Figure 29.21

The Default FTP Site Properties dialog box.

4. Click the Enable Logging option.

5. Click the Active log format drop-down list and select the type of log format you want to create. You can choose from Microsoft IIS Log File Format, ODBC Logging, and W3C Extended Log File Format. NCSA Common Log File Format is not supported on FTP sites. See step 5 in the preceding section for an explanation of these formats.

The following steps show how to configure the W3C Extended Log File Format.

6. Click the Properties button. The Extended Logging Properties dialog box displays (see Figure 29.22). If you selected a log format other than W3C Extended Log File Format from the Active log format drop-down list, the properties dialog box for that format displays.

Figure 29.22

The Extended Logging Properties dialog box for the W3C Extended Log File Format.

7. In the New Log Time Period section, set when you want IIS to create a new log file for the selected FTP site. The default is Daily, but you can select Weekly, Monthly, Unlimited file size, or When file size reaches. If you select the last option, you need to set a maximum file size the log file can reach before a new file is created. The default here is 19MB.

8. Enter the directory in which you want to store the log file. The default is %WinDir\System32\LogFiles. Click the Browse button to locate a new directory graphically.

9. Click the Extended Properties tab to display the logging options (see Figure 29.23) you can set (this tab is available only when you select the W3C Extended Log File Format option). On this tab, you can set the options described in Table 29.1.

10. Click OK to close the Extended Logging Properties dialog box.

11. Click OK to close the FTP Site Properties dialog box.

Figure 29.23

The Extended Logging Proper-ties tab.

Configuring Report Writer and Usage Import to Analyze Logs Created by the WWW Service or the FTP Service

You learned earlier how to import a log file into Usage Import and how to create a report in Report Writer. You learn here how to configure Report Writer and Usage Import to analyze logs that are created by your WWW or FTP service.

The Usage Import Options

In Usage Import, you can access the Usage Import Options dialog box by selecting Tools|Options. This dialog box (see Figure 29.24) enables you to configure several settings and save them as your default settings or use them only during the current Usage Import session. If you opt not to save them as default settings, the next time you start Usage Import the previous settings are used.

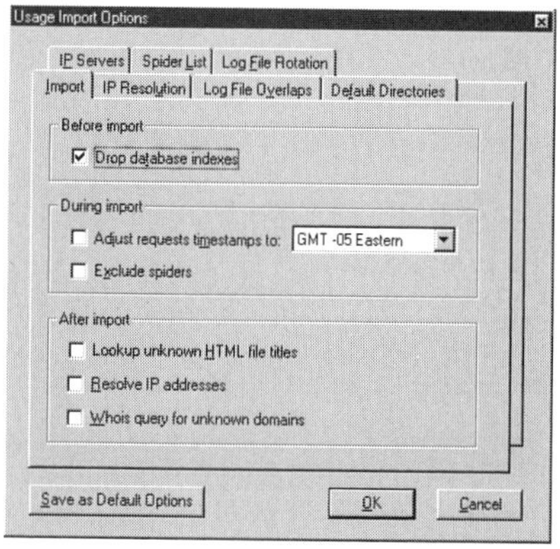

Figure 29.24

The Usage Im-port Options dialog box.

On the Import tab, you can set the following options:

▶ **Drop database indexes.** For analysis purposes, database indexes must be created. After you have a large amount of data in a database, however, you can enable this option and drop indexes during the import process.

▶ **Adjust requests timestamps to.** Turn on this option if you want all time stamps in log files to adjust to the time zone shown in the drop-down list. This is handy if you have Web sites in servers in multiple time zones.

▶ **Exclude spiders.** By selecting this option, you tell IIS to disregard hits from Internet search engines (which use spiders to search the Internet) and other agents shown on the Spider List tab.

▶ **Lookup unknown HTML file titles.** Performs HTML title lookups on HTML files added to the database during the log file import.

▶ **Resolve IP Addresses.** Resolves unresolved IP addresses found in log files during the import process.

▶ **Whois query for unknown domains.** Tells Usage Import to perform a Whois query for unknown organization names.

 Tip On any of the Usage Import Options tabs, click the Save As Default Options button if you want your changes to be saved.

The IP Resolution tab (see Figure 29.25) includes the following options:

▶ **Cache IP resolutions for *n* days.** Enables you to set the number of days between IP lookups.

▶ **Timeout a resolution attempt after *n* seconds.** Enables you to set the number of seconds for Usage Import to attempt to resolve an IP address. After this time, Usage Import will stop attempting to resolve the IP address. Higher values mean better results, but will slow down the import process.

Figure 29.25

The IP Resolution tab.

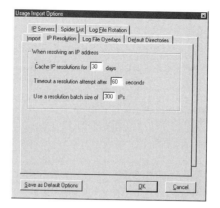

▶ **Use a resolution batch size of *n* IPs.** Specifies the batch size Usage Import uses for IP resolution.

 Tip

A large number setting in the Use a Resolution Batch Size of *n* IPs option may cause your DNS server to crash. Report Writer may also show a large number of unresolved addresses, which may not be correct.

The Log File Overlaps tab (see Figure 29.26) includes the following two options:

Figure 29.26

The Log File Overlaps tab.

▶ **To be considered an overlap, records must overlap by at least *n* minutes.** Sets the overlap period by the import module. Overlap periods are redundancies introduced in your log file database because of log files being accidentally reimported, resuming interrupted logging actions, concatenating two log files, and running logs on separate servers. If you specify shorter periods, overlaps may be reduced, but later analysis may be adversely affected.

▶ **If an overlap is detected.** Enables you to choose an action Usage Import should do when an overlap is detected. You can choose from these options: Import All Records, Stop the Import, Stop All Imports, and Discard Records and Proceed.

The Default Directories tab (see Figure 29.27) includes one option, the Log Files field. Use this field to specify the default directory for log files and import files.

Figure 29.27

*The Default
Directories tab.*

The IP Servers tab (see Figure 29.28) includes these two options:

Figure 29.28

*The IP Servers
tab.*

▶ **HTTP Proxy**. Import uses the proxy server host name (if specified) and port number for all HTML title lookups.

 Tip

For proxy servers that require usernames and passwords, use the syntax *username:password@hostname.*

▶ **Local domain of DNS server.** Clarifies hosts returned from IP resolutions. Enter your DNS server here, or, if an ISP maintains your DNS server, enter your ISP's setting here.

The Spider List tab (see Figure 29.29) includes common spider agents you want to exclude if the Exclude spiders option is selected on the Import tab. You can delete any agent here by selecting it and pressing Delete. Or you can add to the list by placing an asterisk (*) after the Freeloader item and then entering the word **and**, followed by the name of the agent. No spaces are allowed between words.

Figure 29.29

The Spider List tab.

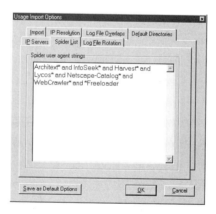

Finally, the Log File Rotation tab (see Figure 29.30) includes the item At the end of an import. This option enables you to control the treatment of data that is cut off due to file rotation. This is data that is divided at the end of one file and begins again at the start of a new log. You can select from these options: commit open visits to database, discard open visits, and store open visits for next import.

Figure 29.30

*The Log File
Rotation tab.*

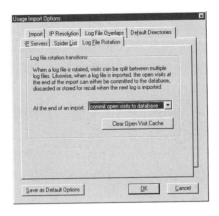

Click OK on the Usage Import Options dialog box to close it and
to use the settings you've configured.

The Report Writer Options

You can configure Report Writer options by opening Report Writ-
er and selecting Tools|Options. The Report Writer Options dia-
log box displays (see Figure 29.31).

Figure 29.31

*The Report Writer
Options dialog
box.*

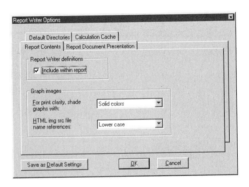

 Tip

On any of the Report Writer Options tabs, click the Save As
Default Options button if you want your changes to be permanently saved.

On the Report Contents tab (refer to Figure 29.31), you can set
the following options:

▶ **Include within report.** Use this option to have Report Writer include usage definitions at the bottom of every report. You may, after you become more familiar with Report Writer documents, want to disable this option so your reports don't have these definitions.

▶ **For print clarity, shade graphs with.** Use this option to specify Solid colors and Pattern lines for graph shading. For printed reports on noncolor printers, select the Pattern lines option.

▶ **HTML img src file name references.** Select which case to use when naming image and source files. For UNIX systems, use the correct case option for your system. In most situations, lowercase is the best choice.

On the Report Document Presentation tab (see Figure 29.32), you can set the following options on how the report is styled:

Figure 29.32

The Report Document Presentation tab.

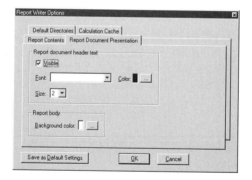

▶ **Visible.** Specify this option so Report Writer displays header information, including analysis time period, site analyzed, and report sections.

▶ **Font, Color, and Size options.** Use these options to specify the font, color, and size of the header information text.

▶ **Background color.** Click the ... button to display the Color dialog box in which to specify a background color for your report.

The Default Directories tab (see Figure 29.33) includes these two options:

Figure 29.33

*The Default
Directories tab.*

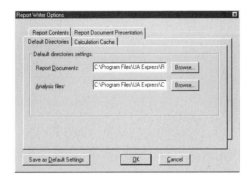

> ▶ **Report Documents.** Set the path for your completed reports
>   in this field.

> ▶ **Analysis files.** Set the path for your completed analysis files
>   in this field.

Finally, the Calculation Cache tab (see Figure 29.34) includes
these options:

Figure 29.34

*The Calculations
Cache tab.*

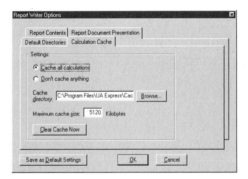

> ▶ **Cache all calculations.** Enables you to cache report calcula-
>   tions in the Cache folder for future use. By using cache cal-
>   culations, you can speed up report generations.

> ▶ **Don't cache anything.** Turns off the calculation cache fea-
>   ture.

> ▶ **Cache directory.** Sets the directory in which calculations are
>   cached.

> ▶ **Maximum cache size.** Sets the maximum amount of cached material the Cache directory can hold. This setting is in kilobytes.

> ▶ **Clear Cache Now.** Click this button when you want to clear the calculations cache.

Click OK in the Report Writer Options dialog box to close it and to use the settings you've configured.

Automating the Use of Report Writer and Usage Import

A handy feature of the Report Writer and Usage Import is the automation capability. Automating Report Writer and Usage Import is done by using the Scheduler tool. You can set up Scheduler so that a report is generated every day when you arrive at work or a report is created at the end of the week to be dispersed to your Internet site administration team.

When you use Scheduler, you create jobs that have tasks scheduled to begin at specific times and days. Tasks are simply activities, such as importing a log or creating a report. After you set up a job, Scheduler creates a batch file that will run to execute the specific tasks.

To create a new job in Usage Import, perform the following steps:

1. Open Usage Import and click on the Scheduler toolbar button (or select Tools | Scheduler). The Scheduler window displays (see Figure 29.35).

Figure 29.35

The Scheduler window.

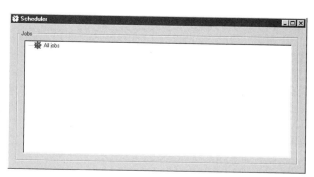

2. Double-click the All jobs item. The Job Properties dialog box displays (see Figure 29.36).

Figure 29.36

*The Job Proper-
ties dialog box.*

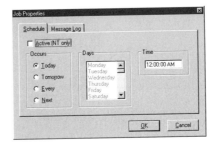

3. Click the Active (NT only) check box. If this is cleared, the Scheduler does not run the specified job. This is handy if you want to disable a specific job without deleting it entirely. This way you have the option of enabling it again without going through the process of setting up the job again.

4. In the Occurs area, select when you want the job to start.

5. If you chose Every or Next in the preceding step, select the day(s) you want the job to run in the Days area. Press Ctrl to select multiple days.

6. Enter the time you want the job to run in the Time field.

 Tip

Times are entered in 24-hour format, so 3:00 p.m. is denoted as 15:00 hours.

7. Click the Message Log tab (see Figure 29.37). You can save messages about the results of each task in a log file by entering the path and filename for the log file in the Message Log field. From the drop-down list, you can select variables to be added to the filename. When the file is created, the variables, such as *$d(23)*, are replaced by actual values.

8. Click OK to save your new job to the Scheduler window (see Figure 29.38).

Figure 29.37

The Message Log tab.

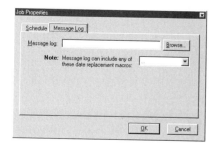

Figure 29.38

Your new job added to the Scheduler window.

 Tip

You can click on the New job name twice (do not double-click it) to rename the job.

You now need to add tasks to your new job. Perform the following steps:

1. Right-click your new job and select New Task. The Task Properties dialog box displays (see Figure 29.39).

Figure 29.39

The Task Properties dialog box.

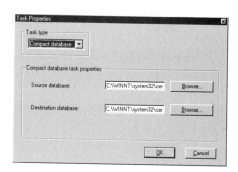

2. Select the type of task you want to add to your job by clicking on the Task type drop-down list. If you want to automate the

database compacting tasks, for instance, select Compact database. The options available on the Task Properties dialog box change when you pick a different task.

3. Fill out the fields (if any are shown) for the task you select.

4. Click OK to save your new task. The Scheduler window shows the new task under your new job (see Figure 29.40). Again, you can rename the new task by clicking on it twice.

Figure 29.40

A new task added to your new job.

5. Continue adding tasks to your job by repeating steps 1–4.

6. When finished, close the Scheduler window and click Yes when prompted to start the job.

Monitoring Performance of Various Functions Using Performance Monitor

 Objective ▶ IIS 4 provides several powerful tools to monitor and administer your Internet server, but you can still use common Windows NT administration tools to monitor IIS 4's performance. One such tool that is indispensable for IIS 4 monitoring is Performance Monitor.

Note ▶ You should already be familiar with Performance Monitor before proceeding with this objective. You can learn more about Performance Monitor in *Inside Windows NT 4.0 Server*, New Riders Publishing.

With Performance Monitor you can monitor functions relating to HTTP and FTP sessions. Performance Monitor is used when you want to see trends and patterns in your site's usage. When you install IIS 4, new objects relating to Web and FTP services are added to Performance Monitor along with specific counters for those services. Objects are individual occurrences of a system resource, such as Web Service, FTP Service, Active Server Pages, Browser, and other items. Counters, on the other hand, are statistics relating to the objects, such as Debugging Requests, Memory Allocated, and Request Wait Time (all of which relate to the Active Server Pages object).

Performance Monitor can be started from the Administrative Tools (Common) folder. To specify the object and counter(s) you want to track, select Edit|Add to Chart. The Add to Chart dialog box displays (see Figure 29.41).

Figure 29.41

Add objects and counters to Performance Monitor from the Add to Chart dialog box.

The Performance Monitor screen shown in Figure 29.42 is monitoring functions relating to Web and FTP service. The following objects and counters are used:

▶ Web Services object with Anonymous User/sec, Bytes Sent/sec, and Maximum NonAnonymous Users counters selected

▶ FTP Server object with Bytes Total/sec, Current Anonymous Users, and Maximum Connections counters selected

Table 29.2 lists the objects and counters available in Performance Monitor to help you monitor IIS 4.

Figure 29.42

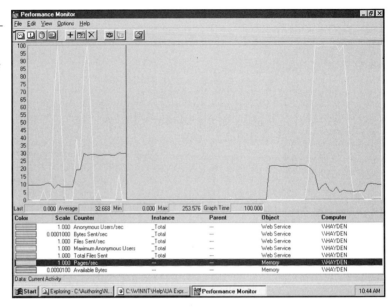

An example of monitoring Web and FTP services in Performance Monitor.

Table 29.2

IIS 4-related objects and counters in Performance Monitor.

Object	Counter
Active Server Pages	Debugging Requests
	Errors During Script Runtime
	Errors From ASP Preprocessor
	Errors From Script Compilers
	Errors/Sec
	Memory Allocated
	Request Bytes In Total
	Request Bytes Out Total
	Request Execution Time
	Request Wait Time
	Requests Disconnected
	Requests Executing
	Requests Failed Total

Object	Counter
	Requests Not Authorized
	Requests Not Found
	Requests Queued
	Requests Rejected
	Requests Succeeded
	Requests Timed Out
	Requests Total
	Requests/Sec
	Script Engines Cached
	Session Duration
	Sessions Current
	Sessions Timed Out
	Sessions Total
	Template Cache Hit Rate
	Template Notifications
	Templates Cached
	Transactions Aborted
	Transactions Committed
	Transactions Pending
	Transactions Total
	Transactions/Sec
FTP Service	Bytes Received/Sec
	Bytes Sent/Sec
	Bytes Total/Sec
	Current Anonymous Users
	Current Connections
	Current NonAnonymous Users
	Maximum Anonymous Users

continues

Table 29.2 Continued

Object	Counter
	Total Anonymous Users
	Total Connection Attempts
	Total Files Received
	Total Files Sent
	Total Files Transferred
	Total Logon Attempts
	Total NonAnonymous Users
Internet Information Services Global	Cache Flushes
	Cache Hits
	Cache Hits %
	Cache Misses
	Cached File Handles
	Current Blocked Async I/O Requests
	Directory Listings
	Measured Async I/O Bandwidth Usage
	Objects
	Total Allowed Async I/O Requests
	Total Blocked Async I/O Requests
	Total Rejected Async I/O Requests
NNTP Server	Article Map Entries
	Article Map Entries/Sec
	Articles Deleted
	Articles Deleted/Sec
	Articles Posted
	Articles Posted/Sec
	Articles Received
	Articles Received/Sec

Object	Counter
	Articles Sent
	Articles Sent/Sec
	Articles Total
	Bytes Received/Sec
	Bytes Sent/Sec
	Bytes Total/Sec
	Control Messages Failed
	Control Messages Received
	Current Anonymous Users
	Current Connections
	Current NonAnonymous Users
	Current Outbound Connections
	Failed Outbound Logons
	History Map Entries
	History Map Entries/Sec
	Maximum Anonymous Users
	Maximum Connections
	Maximum NonAnonymous Users
	Moderated Postings Failed
	Moderated Postings Sent
	Sessions Flow Controlled
	Total Anonymous Users
	Total Connections
	Total NonAnonymous Users
	Total Outbound Connections
	Total Outbound Connections Failed
	Total Passive Feeds
	Total Pull Feeds

continues

Table 29.2 Continued

Object	Counter
	Total Push Feeds
	Total SSL Connections
	Xover Entries
	Xover Entries/Sec
SMTP Server	% Recipients Local
	% Recipients Remote
	Avg Recipients/Msg Received
	Avg Recipients/Msg Sent
	Avg Retries/Msg Delivered
	Avg Retries/Msg Sent
	Bytes Received Total
	Bytes Received/Sec
	Bytes Sent Total
	Bytes Sent/Sec
	Bytes Total
	Bytes Total/Sec
	Connection Errors/Sec
	Directory Drops Total
	Directory Drops/Sec
	Directory Pickup Queue Length
	DNS Queries Total
	DNS Queries/Sec
	ETRN Messages Total
	ETRN Messages/Sec
	Inbound Connections Current
	Inbound Connections Total
	Local Queue Length
	Local Retry Queue Length

Object	Counter
	Message Bytes Received Total
	Message Bytes Received/Sec
	Message Bytes Sent Total
	Message Bytes Sent/Sec
Message Bytes Total	Message Bytes Total/Sec
	Message Delivery Retries
	Message Received/Sec
	Message Send Retries
	Messages Delivered Total
	Messages Delivered/Sec
	Messages Received Total
	Messages Refused for Address Objects
	Messages Refused for Mail Objects
	Messages Refused For Size
	Messages Retrieved Total
	Messages Retrieved/Sec
	Messages Sent Total
	Messages Sent/Sec
	NDRs Generated
	Number of MailFiles Open
	Number of QueueFiles Open
	Outbound Connections Current
	Outbound Connections Refused
	Outbound Connections Total
	Remote Queue Length
	Remote Retry Queue Length
	Routing Table Lookups Total
	Routing Table Lookups/Sec
	Total Connection Errors

continues

Table 29.2 Continued

Object	Counter
Web Service	Anonymous Users/Sec
	Bytes Received/Sec
	Bytes Sent/Sec
	Bytes Total/Sec
	CGI Requests/Sec
	Connection Attempts/Sec
	Current Anonymous Users
	Current Blocked Asyn I/O Requests
	Current CGI Requests
	Current Connections
	Current ISAPI Extension Requests
	Current NonAnonymous Users
	Delete Requests/Sec
	Files Received/Sec
	Files Sent/Sec
	Files/Sec
	Get Requests/Sec
	Head Requests/Sec
	ISAPI Extension Requests/Sec
	Logon Attempts/Sec
	Maximum Anonymous Users
	Maximum CGI Requests
	Maximum Connections
	Maximum ISAPI Extension Requests
	Maximum NonAnonymous Users
	Measured Async I/O Bandwidth Usage
	NonAnonymous Users/Sec

Object	Counter
	Not Found Errors/Sec
	Other Request Methods/Sec
	Post Requests/Sec
	Put Requests/Sec
	System Code Resident Bytes
	Total Allowed Async I/O Requests
	Total Anonymous Users
	Total Blocked Async I/O Requests
	Total CGI Requests
	Total Connection Attempts
	Total Delete Requests
	Total Files Received
	Total Files Sent
	Total Files Transferred
	Total Get Requests
	Total Head Requests
	Total ISAPI Extension Requests
	Total Logon Attempts
	Total Method Requests
	Total Method Requests/Sec
	Total NonAnonymous Users
	Total Not Found Errors
	Total Other Request Methods
	Total Post Requests
	Total Put Requests
	Total Rejected Async I/O Requests
	Total Trace Requests

Analyzing Performance

 **Objective** As the IIS 4 administrator, you are responsible for analyzing the performance of the Internet site. But you also need to pay close attention to other server performance issues. These performance issues include the following:

- ▶ Identifying Bottlenecks

- ▶ Identifying Network-Related Performance Issues

- ▶ Identifying Disk-Related Performance Issues

- ▶ Identifying CPU-Related Performance Issues

Identifying Bottlenecks

Bottlenecks occur when one (or several) hardware resources is being used too much, sometimes resulting in the draining of another hardware resource. The result is a performance reduction over the entire network. A bottleneck may occur as a result of insufficient server memory or because of too little bandwidth available to the connected users. A bottleneck is the largest source of delay that can be reduced. You need to know how to recognize bottlenecks on your system before you can even attempt to remedy them.

Finding a bottleneck can be a slow and arduous task at times. You must don your "detective" hat when looking for the combination of hardware and software that is creating the bottleneck. Start looking for bottlenecks by running Performance Monitor to create a baseline of activities for your site.

You also can use Event Viewer to record events and audit situations on your computer that may require your attention. Another useful tool to use to locate bottlenecks is the Task Manager. Task Manager shows you all the ongoing tasks and threads on your computer.

Note One performance bottleneck you should be aware of is logging to a database. As IIS 4 logs activities to a database, an ODBC connection must be established. This connection process may take a relatively long time, causing a performance bottleneck to occur. If you cannot speed up the ODBC connection time, consider switching to file-based logging. File-based logging is faster than database logging.

The following sections explore some common bottlenecks that you should become familiar with when administering IIS 4.

Identifying Network-Related Performance Issues

Because IIS 4 may reside on your local area network server, you should become aware of some of the network-related performance issues that can affect the performance of your Internet site.

According to Microsoft, for medium-to-very-busy sites, you can expect IIS to saturate a 10Mbps ethernet network adapter. If this happens, it will certainly cause bottlenecks to occur that are network-related. However, it is almost impossible for a Web server to saturate a 10Mbps ethernet adapter. It *could* saturate a 56KB link or a T1. Remember that a T1 line provides 15 percent of the speed of an ethernet connection. To check for network saturation, check for CPU % Utilization on both the client and server. To prevent the server from becoming network-bound, increase network bandwidth to the server by using one of the following solutions:

▶ Use multiple 10MB Ethernet cards

▶ Install a 100MB Ethernet or FDDI network card

Identifying Disk-Related Performance Issues

You may encounter hard disk bottlenecks if you have a very large file set, such as an application in the range of 5MB or larger, that is being accessed by clients in a random pattern. To identify a bottleneck of this sort, perform the following steps:

1. Start Performance Monitor.

2. Select Edit | Add To Chart.

3. From the Add to Chart dialog box (see Figure 29.43), select the PhysicalDisk item from the Object drop-down list object.

Figure 29.43

Select the PhysicalDisk object and % Disk Time counter from the Add to Chart dialog box.

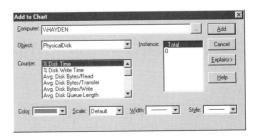

4. From the Counter list, select % Disk Time.

5. Click Add.

6. Click Done.

The % Disk Time counter shows the percentage of elapsed time the disk is busy servicing read or write requests. If there is a bottleneck involving disk access, the PhysicalDisk % Disk Time counter will be high, because the percentage of the CPU utilization will remain low and the network card will not be saturated.

When you notice a disk-related bottleneck, you can improve performance in a few ways. The best answer to a disk bottleneck is striping or mirroring. You also can use a redundant array of inexpensive drives (RAID).

Identifying CPU-Related Performance Issues

You can identify CPU bottlenecks by measuring the amount of the server CPU that is being utilized. Perform the following steps to measure this value:

1. Start Performance Monitor.

2. Select Edit | Add To Chart.

3. From the Add To Chart dialog box, select the Processor item from the Object drop-down list object.

4. From the Counter list, select % Processor Time.

5. From the Instance list, select the number of instances you want to view.

6. Click Add.

7. Click Done.

You'll notice CPU bottlenecks if you notice very high CPU % Processor Time numbers while the network card remains well below capacity. If the CPU % Processor Time value is high, try the following remedies:

▶ Upgrade the CPU to a faster one.

▶ Add additional CPUs to your server.

▶ Move other applications (such as database applications) you run on the Web server to another computer.

▶ Add more computers on which you replicate your site and then distribute traffic across them.

Optimizing the Performance of IIS

Objective

One of the greatest improvements to IIS 4 is the inclusion of the Microsoft Management Console (MMC) to help you manage and administer IIS. With MMC, you can make global performance changes (such as limiting bandwidth usage), set service master properties, and configure other IIS properties to help optimize its performance.

To change global performance properties under IIS, perform the following steps:

1. Open Internet Service Manager in MMC.

2. Right-click the server you want to modify.

3. Select Properties to display the Server Properties dialog box for that server (see Figure 29.44).

Figure 29.44

The Server Properties dialog box.

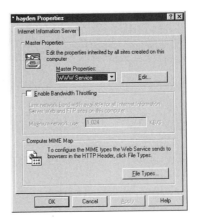

4. Click the Performance tab, then the Enable Bandwidth Throttling option to control the amount of bandwidth consumption by all IIS services. You may want to do this if your network card is set up to handle multiple services, such as email and Web services. In the Maximum network use field, enter a bandwidth value in KB/S (kilobytes/second).

 Tip

To get a bandwidth value for your server, begin with a value that is 50 percent of your connection bandwidth. You can then increase or decrease this value to tweak your system requirements.

5. Click the Master Properties drop-down list. This displays the services (WWW and/or FTP) you have installed and those for which you can customize default master properties. Master properties are standard settings for all the Web sites or FTP sites hosted on your server. After you set master properties for all your sites, you can still modify settings for individual sites. Master Properties provides you with an easy and quick way to set common parameters for all your sites.

6. Select the service you want to modify.

7. Click Edit. The Service Master Properties dialog box for your site displays (see Figure 29.45).

Figure 29.45

The Service Master Properties dialog box.

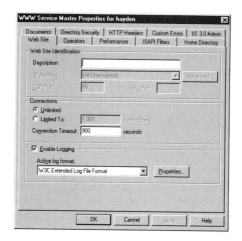

From this dialog box you can set the following performance parameters:

▶ Connections

▶ Performance Tuning

▶ Enable Bandwidth Throttling

▶ HTTP Keep-Alives

These parameters are discussed in more detail in the following sections.

Connections

You find the Connections area on the Web Site tab of the Service Master Properties dialog box. This area includes the Unlimited and Limited To options that control the number of simultaneous connections your Web or FTP sites allow. Click the Limited To option to specify the number of simultaneous connections to your sites. Then enter a value in the connection field (the default is 1,000). If you do not want to limit the number of connections, select the Unlimited option (which is the default setting).

You also can set the timeout value for each inactive connection. This value is set in seconds and will automatically disconnect a client after that client has been inactive on your site for the set number of seconds. In the Connection Timeout field, enter a value for the amount of time your server should automatically disconnect an idle session. The default is 15 minutes (900 seconds), but an average setting is five minutes (300 seconds). For an infinite amount of time, enter all 9s in this field.

 Note

Even if a connection is lost or a browser stops working, your site will continue to process data until the timeout value is reached. Setting an appropriate timeout value will limit the loss of resources due to these lost connections.

Performance Tuning

The Performance tab (see Figure 29.46) on the Service Master Properties dialog box includes the Performance Tuning option. This option is set to the estimated number of connections you anticipate for your site. Move the slider to the appropriate value. If you anticipate fewer than 10,000 visitors each day, move the slider to the far left; for a site with fewer than 100,000 visitors, keep the slider in the middle; and for a busy site that has over 100,000 visitors, move the slider to the far right.

Figure 29.46

The Performance tab on the Service Master Properties dialog box.

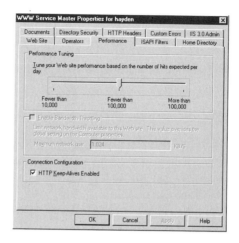

When you move the slider to a setting, IIS 4 alters the resources allocated to the service. Settings that are higher than the actual number of connections will result in faster connections and will improve Web server performance. This is because more resources are allocated to fewer connections. On the other hand, if you set the Performance Tuning slider to a number that is much higher than the actual number of connections, you will notice a decrease in overall server performance, because server memory is being wasted (basically it is not being utilized). This setting will devote more resources to your Web service and fewer resources to other server applications. You should compare your daily hit logs with the Performance Tuning setting to ensure this setting closely matches the actual connections to your site.

Enable Bandwidth Throttling

Another performance option you can set is also on thePerformance tab. The Enable Bandwidth Throttling option, which you were shown how to set at the server level in the "Optimizing the Performance of IIS" section, sets the global bandwidth used by your Web site.

Click the Enable Bandwidth Throttling option and set a bandwidth setting based on kilobytes per second (KB/S).

Note   The value you set on the Performance tab overrides settings for bandwidth throttling set on the Computer Properties sheet. This is true even if the value on the Performance tab is set higher than that on the Computer Properties sheet.

HTTP Keep-Alives

The final performance optimization setting you can modify on the Performance tab is the Connection Configuration option. This includes the HTTP Keep-Alives Enable option. You can enable IIS 4's keep-alive feature to enable clients to maintain open connections. This way a client does not need to re-establish connections for each request, such as for each request for an image, document, or other resource. By enabling keep-alive, you not only decrease the amount of time a client waits to connect to another document or application on your site, but also increase the amount of resources devoted to this client.

Click the HTTP Keep-Alives Enabled option to turn on this feature to ensure that clients with slower connections are not prematurely closed. You should enable this feature for better server performance so that repeated requests from an individual client are not necessary when a page containing multiple elements is accessed.

Inheritance Overrides

If you make any changes to the Service Master Properties options, you also affect all individual sites under that service. When you click OK to save settings on the Service Master Properties dialog box (see Figure 29.47), the Inheritance Overrides dialog box will appear if a value you've changed will be overridden based on values of an individual site, or *child node.*

Select the child node(s) from the Descendants with overridden defaults for the current property that you want to change to match the new value you set on the Service Master Properties dialog box. Click OK.

Figure 29.47

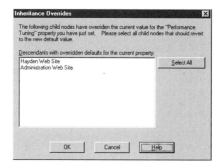

The Inheritance Overrides dialog box.

Optimizing the Performance of Index Server

 Objective

Microsoft Index Server is used to index the contents and proper-ties of Internet or intranet documents stored on an IIS server. You are shown how to install Index Server in earlier chapters, but one way to optimize its performance is to run it on a system with an optimum configuration. By and large, the basic Windows NT Serv-er configuration provides adequate Index Server performance. This situation is probably best suited, however, for a small organi-zation or an Internet site that does not expect a large amount of daily traffic.

To optimize the performance of Index Server, you should start by looking at the configuration of the computer on which it resides. The following are the factors that you need to measure to set this configuration:

▶ Number of documents in the corpus, which is the collection of documents and HTML pages indexed by Index Server

▶ Corpus size

▶ Rate of search requests

▶ Kind of queries

You'll find that the amount of memory you have installed will greatly affect the performance of Index Server. For sites that have fewer than 100,000 documents stored in the corpus, a minimum of 32MB is required and recommended. However, if you have

100,000 to 250,000 documents, the recommended amount of memory jumps to 64–128MB, whereas the minimum required still is 32MB. For sites with 250,000 to 500,000 documents, you need a minimum of 64MB of RAM, but it is recommended that you have 128–256MB. Finally, if you have over 500,000 documents, you must have 128MB of RAM installed, but at least 256MB is recommended.

 Note

Keep in mind that complex search queries will run faster when Index Server is installed on a computer with a faster CPU. Also, a faster CPU and additional memory will improve indexing performance.

Another system configuration setting you should pay attention to is the amount of free hard disk space where the Index Server catalog is stored. If less than 3MB of free space is available on the index disk, indexing and filtering are temporarily paused until additional disk space is made available. The event log records a message that `Very low disk space was detected on drive` *drive*`. Please free up at least` *number*`MB of space for content index to continue`.

 Tip

The minimum amount of disk space should be at least 30 percent of the corpus. However, during a master merge (which deletes redundant data and enables queries to run faster), you may need up to 45 percent of the corpus.

Optimizing the Performance of Microsoft SMTP Service

 **Objective**

The Microsoft SMTP service enables IIS 4 to deliver messages over the Internet. Microsoft SMTP supports basic SMTP (Simple Mail Transfer Protocol) delivery functions and is compatible with SMTP mail clients.

When you install IIS 4, you also can install Microsoft SMTP. The default settings for Microsoft SMTP can be used, but you also can customize your SMTP Service to optimize it for your system. The following are some of the ways you can optimize Microsoft SMTP:

▶ Set connection limits

▶ Set message limits

▶ Specify a smart host

Setting Connection Limits

You can set the number of simultaneous connections for incoming and outgoing connections. To set this number, open Microsoft Manager Console (MMC), right-click on the SMTP site you want to modify, and select Properties. The SMTP Site Properties dialog box displays (see Figure 29.48).

Figure 29.48

The SMTP Site Properties dialog box.

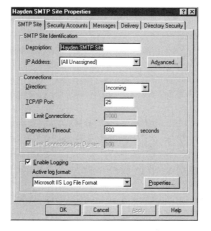

On the SMTP Site tab, perform the following steps to set the connection limit:

1. Click the Limit Connections option.

2. In the Limit Connections option field, enter the number of simultaneous connections for your SMTP Service. For incoming messages, the default is 1,000 and the minimum is 1. For outgoing messages, the default is 500 and the minimum is 1. *Outgoing messages* refers to the number of concurrent outbound connections to all remote domains.

3. In the Connection Timeout field, enter the period of time an inactive connection is disconnected. The default is 600 seconds for both incoming and outgoing messages.

4. In the Limit Connections per Domain field, enter the number of outgoing connections to a single remote domain. This option is available only with outgoing connections. The default is 100 connections and should be less than or equal to the value set in the Limit Connections field.

5. Click Apply.

Message Limits

You can set limits on the size and number of messages each connection can have. To do this, click the Messages tab of the SMTP Site Properties dialog box (see Figure 29.49) and perform the following steps:

Figure 29.49

The Messages tab of the SMTP Site Properties dialog box.

1. Click the Limit Messages option.

2. In the Maximum Message Size field, enter the value for the maximum size of a message (in kilobytes). The minimum size is 1KB; the default is 2048KB (2MB).

Note   If a single message exceeds the Maximum Message Size, it can still be processed by SMTP Server if it does not exceed the Maximum Session Size.

3. In the Maximum Session Size field, enter the value for the maximum size of a message before the connection will be closed. Set this value to the same or higher than the Maximum Message Size. The default is 10MB.

4. Click the Limit Messages per Connections option to specify the number of messages that can be sent in one connection. You can use this value to increase system performance by enabling SMTP Server to use multiple connections to deliver messages to a remote domain. When the limit is reached, a new connection is opened and the transmission continues until all messages are delivered.

 Tip   To determine a value for the Limit Messages per Connections option limit, run Performance Monitor and select the SMTP Server object. In the Counter list, select Messages Sent/Sec. The Limit Messages per Connection value should be less than the value indicated by the performance counter.

5. Click Apply.

Specifying a Smart Host

Instead of sending all outgoing messages directly to a remote domain, you can route all messages through a smart host. A smart host enables you to route messages over a more direct or less costly connection than other routes.

Note   Smart hosts are similar to the route domain option for remote domains. With a remote domain, however, only messages for that remote domain are routed to a specific server. On the

continues

other hand, with smart hosts, all outgoing messages are routed to that server. If you set up a smart host, you can still designate a different route for a remote domain. The route domain
setting overrides the smart host setting.

To set up a smart host, do the following:

1. Select the Delivery tab (see Figure 29.50) on the SMTP Site
    Properties dialog box.

Figure 29.50

*The Delivery tab
on the SMTP Site
Properties dialog
box.*

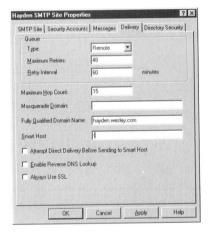

2. In the Smart Host field, enter the name of the smart host
    server. You can enter a string or enter an IP address in this
    field. To increase system performance when using an IP ad-
    dress here, enclose the address in brackets. Microsoft SMTP
    will then look at the IP address as an actual IP address with-
    out looking at it as a string value first.

3. Select the Attempt Direct Delivery Before Sending to Smart
    Host option. This option is used if you want SMTP Service to
    attempt to deliver remote messages locally before forwarding
    them to the smart host server. The default is to send all re-
    mote messages to the smart host, not to attempt direct delivery.

4. Click OK.

Optimizing the Performance of Microsoft NNTP Service

 Objective

The Microsoft NNTP Service is used to let users exchange communications via the Internet Network News Transport Protocol (NNTP). Users can post and view articles, much like they can when attached to the Usenet news service available on the Internet.

Similarly to the Microsoft SMTP Server, you can run Microsoft NNTP Service without modifying its default settings. However, you may want to tweak some of its properties to get better performance out of it. Two optimization tasks you can perform are changing connection settings and modifying client postings.

Changing Connection Settings

You can limit the number of simultaneous news client connections to a virtual server. You can set a value up to 2 billion, in other words, a relatively unlimited number of connections. To do this, open the Microsoft Management Console and right-click on the NNTP Site you want to modify. Select Properties to display the NNTP Site Properties dialog box (see Figure 29.51).

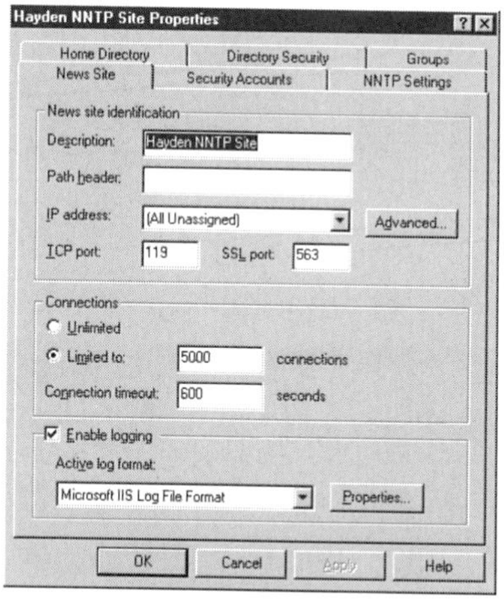

Figure 29.51

The NNTP Site Properties dialog box.

On the News Site tab, perform the following steps:

1. Click the Unlimited option if you want to specify that there is no limit to the number of simultaneous connections.

2. Click the Limited to option and fill in the connections field with the number of simultaneous connections you want to limit NNTP to handling. The default is 5,000. Increase or decrease this value depending on your server size and needs.

3. In the Connection timeout field, enter a value for NNTP Server to automatically disconnect inactive clients. The default is 600 seconds.

4. Click Apply.

Modifying Client Postings

The NNTP Settings tab (see Figure 29.52) includes options for modifying client posting parameters. This tab enables you to set the maximum size of news articles posted to your NNTP Server.

Figure 29.52

The NNTP Settings tab.

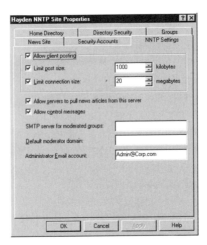

To modify client postings, perform the following steps:

1. Select the Limit post size option.

2. Enter a value to indicate the maximum size of a news article that a client can post to your NNTP Server. The default is 1,000KB. However, you may want to decrease this value if you want your news server to be set up to handle smaller articles. Increase this value, on the other hand, to allow larger articles to be posted. If an article exceeds this value, it still will be posted if the article does not surpass the Limit connection size value.

3. Click the Limit connection size option.

4. Enter a value to indicate the maximum size for articles that a news client can post to your news server. The default is 20MB.

5. Click OK.

Interpreting Performance Data

 Objective

There are two tools primarily used for monitoring TCP/IP traffic, and these are the primary tools for gathering data for interpretation:

▶ Performance Monitor

▶ Network Monitor

Performance Monitor

The Performance Monitor is Windows NT's all-around tool for monitoring a network using statistical measurements called counters. It has the capability of collecting data on both hardware and software components, called objects, and its primary purpose is to establish a baseline from which everything can be judged. It offers the ability to check/monitor/identify the following:

▶ The demand for resources

▶ Bottlenecks in performance

▶ The behavior of individual processes

▶ The performance of remote systems

It also can

▶ Generate alerts to exception conditions

▶ Export data for analysis

Every object has a number of counters, and you should be familiar with those for the Paging File object - %Usage and %Usage Peak, which will tell whether a paging file is reaching its maximum size.

To get numerical statistics, use the Report (columnar) view. To see how counters change over a period of time, use the log feature. To spot abnormalities that occur in data over a period of time, use the Chart view.

To monitor a number of servers and be alerted if a counter exceeds a specified number, create one Performance Monitor alert for each server on your workstation. Enter your username in the Net Name on the Alert Options dialog box (below Send Network Message tab), and you will be alerted when the alert conditions arise. Only one name can be placed here, and the name can be that of a user or group, but not multiple users or groups.

If you are monitoring a number of performance counters and that monitoring is slowing down other operations on your workstation, the best remedy is to increase the monitoring interval.

To tune or optimize Windows NT, you need to be able to look at the performance of the server on many different levels.

Note

Two important pieces of information to remember: You *must* install the Network Monitor Agent to be able to see several of the network performance counters, and SNMP service *must* be installed in order to gather TCP/IP statistics.

Network Monitor

Network Monitor is a Windows tool that enables you to see network traffic that is sent or received by a Windows NT computer. Network Monitor is included with Windows NT 4.0, but it must be installed to be active.

To install Network Monitor, open Control Panel|Network and then add the Network Monitor Tools and Agent from the Services tab. The version of Network Monitor that comes with Windows NT 4.0 is a simple version; it captures traffic only for the local machines (incoming and outgoing traffic).

Microsoft's System Management Server, a network management product, comes with a more complete version of Network Monitor that enables you to capture packets on the local machine for the entire local network segment. Both versions enable you to capture the packets that are flowing in and out of your computer. The Full version that comes with SMS also gives you extra functionality, such as the ability to capture all packets on the local network or on remote networks, edit those packets, and derive statistics about protocols and users on the network.

There are two pieces to the Network Monitor. The Agent captures the data. The Monitor Tool can be used to view the data. You also can filter out traffic that isn't important to the trouble-shooting process.

The Network Monitor can be used to diagnose more complex issues with connectivity by enabling you to see the actual packets that are flowing on the network, verifying which steps are being used to resolve names or which port numbers are being used to connect.

 Note

As with ISAPI, filters enable you to limit what you are viewing and keep the data from being overwhelming. The most commonly used filters are INCLUDE and EXCLUDE, which capture, or avoid capturing, specific data. The Network Monitor included

continues

with Windows NT Server can monitor only the specific system on which it is installed, unlike the Network Monitor in SMS, which can monitor other systems on the network.

Optimizing a Web Site Using Content Analyzer

☑ Objective ▶   The Site Server Express Analysis Content Analyzer (Content Analyzer for short) enables you to create WebMaps to give you a view of your Web site, helping you manage your Web site. WebMaps are graphical representations of resources on your site. These resources can include HTML documents, audio and video files, Java applets, FTP resources, and applications. Content Analyzer also enables you to manage your links. You can ensure that links are included in the resources and that they all work correctly.

You can use Content Analyzer to optimize your Web site. Here are some of the ways you can do this:

- ▶ Import usage data to review how users are using your site (see Figure 29.53). Important data you can view here includes how many hits a page receives, which pages are being hit the most, and from which URLs those hits are coming.

- ▶ Export the Tree view of your site's WebMap to be an HTML index or table of contents for your site. You also can use the index report from the Content Analyzer site report to serve as an HTML index of your site's contents.

- ▶ Assign helper applications to file types to edit source files. From Content Analyzer you can set helper applications to create and view site resources. This enables you quickly to check a broken link and fix it in an HTML editor, such as Microsoft FrontPage.

- ▶ View resource properties from within Content Analyzer. You can view name, size, load size, modification date, URL, MIME type, HTTP status, and other properties.

Figure 29.53

Content Analyzer provides a report of your site.

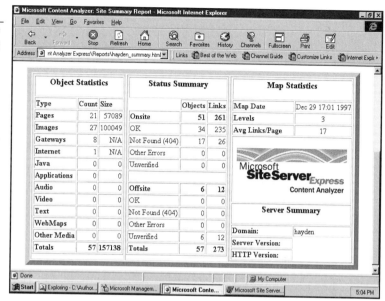

▶ View a resource's links in Content Analyzer. When viewing links within a resource, you can see the hyperlink text, MIME type, size, order, HTTP status, number of links, location of the linked document, hits, and other link information. Use this information to fine-tune or fix link-related problems in your documents.

▶ Verify onsite and offsite links. Links that are unavailable are shown in red. These links may be broken, or an offsite link may not have been available when you attempted to verify it.

Note

This chapter does not teach you how to use Content Analyzer. For information on Content Analyzer, read the *Content Analyzer User's Guide*.

Exercises

In the following exercise, you make a report of a log file in Report Writer:

1. Select Start | Programs | Windows NT 4.0 Option Pack | Microsoft Site Server Express 2.0 | Report Writer. Report Writer starts and displays the Report Writer opening dialog box.

2. Select the From the Report Writer Catalog option on the Report Writer dialog box.

3. Click OK. The Report Writer dialog box with the Report Writer Catalog field appears.

4. Select the plus sign next to Detail Reports.

5. Click Hits detail report.

6. Click Next. The Report Writer dialog box displays. Set the date range of the data to analyze for a one-month time period.

7. Click Next. The Report Writer dialog box displays.

8. Click Finish. The Detail window for the report you want to generate displays.

9. Click the Create Report Document toolbar button on the Report Writer toolbar. The Report Document dialog box displays.

10. Enter a filename and keep the default report format of HTML.

11. Click OK. The report document is created.

The following exercise shows how to configure the logging features of the FTP service in IIS 4:

1. Select Start | Programs | Windows NT 4.0 Option Pack | Microsoft Internet Information Server | Internet Service Manager. Internet Service Manager opens in the MMC.

2. Right-click the FTP site you want to configure.

3. Click Properties. The FTP Site Properties dialog box displays.

4. Click the Enable Logging option.

5. Click the Active Log Format drop-down list and select the type of log format you want to create. The following steps show how to configure the W3C.

7. In the New Log Time Period section, set when you want IIS to create a new log file for the selected FTP site.

8. Enter the directory in which you want to store the log file. The default is %WinDir\System32\LogFiles.

9. Click the Extended Properties tab to display the logging options you can set (this tab is available only when you select the W3C Extended Log File Format option). On this tab, you can set the options described earlier in Table 29.1.

10. Click OK to close the Extended Logging Properties dialog box.

11. Click OK to close the FTP Site Properties dialog box.

Exercise 29.3:   Creating Automatic Jobs in Usage Import

The following exercise shows how create a new job in Usage Import:

1. Open Usage Import and click on the Scheduler toolbar button. The Scheduler window displays.

2. Double-click on the All Jobs item. The Job Properties dialog box displays.

3. Click the Active (NT Only) check box. If this is cleared, the Scheduler does not run the specified job.

4. In the Occurs area, select when you want the job to start.

5. If you chose Every or Next in the preceding step, select the day(s) you want the job to run in the Days area. Press Ctrl to select multiple days.

6. Enter the time you want the job to run in the Time field.

7. Click the Message Log tab. You can save messages about the results of each task in a log file by entering the path and filename for the log file in the Message Log field. From the drop-down list, you can select variables to be added to the filename. When the file is created, the variables, such as *$d(23)*, are replaced by actual values.

8. Click OK to save your new job to the Scheduler window.

Review Questions

1. You administer an Internet site with IIS 4's Web and FTP service running. You have Microsoft Index Server installed and have a corpus with over 500,000 documents stored. What is the recommended amount of RAM your server should have?

    A. 32MB

    B. 64MB

    C. 128MB

    D. 256MB

2. On the same Index Server computer as discussed in Question 1, what is the minimum amount of RAM you need?

    A. 32MB

    B. 64MB

    C. 128MB

    D. 256MB

3. You are an IIS 4 consultant. Your client runs IIS 4 and needs a weekly report summarizing the number of users who access its site and the number of hits every hour. What tool should you use to generate this report?

    A. Microsoft Excel

    B. Microsoft Site Server Express Analysis—Report Writer

    C. Microsoft Site Server Express Analysis—Usage Import

    D. Crystal Reports

4. When setting up IIS 4 logging, you want to customize the type of data that is logged. Which logging option should you choose?

    A. NCSA Common Log File Format

    B. W3C Extended Log File Format

    C. ODBC Logging

    D. SQL Logging

5. IIS 4 is installed on a server with all IIS 4's default settings used. When you examine the Web Site tab on the Service Master Properties dialog box, what is the number of maximum connections listed in the Limited To field under the Connections area?

    A. 0

    B. 500

    C. 1000

    D. 100

6. The IIS 4 Web site you administer does not receive a large number of hits each day, but the server's performance is sluggish. Which one of the following statements is true?

    A. The Performance Tuning slider setting on the WWW Service Master Properties Performance tab is too high.

    B. The Performance Tuning slider setting on the WWW Service Master Properties Performance tab is too low.

    C. The site could be operating at a TCP port other than the default.

    D. You are probably using IDE drives rather than SCSI.

7. The IIS 4 server you manage performs slowly and has numerous hits reported for every client that connects to your site. Which one of the following may need to be enabled to alleviate this problem?

    A. Enable Bandwidth Throttling

    B. Enable Logging

    C. Connection Timeout

    D. HTTP Keep-Alives Enabled

8. To optimize the performance of your FTP site, you can set which of the following option(s) that you can also set for your Web site?

   A. Connection Timeout

   B. Enable Bandwidth Throttling

   C. Connection Limited To Value

   D. Home Directory Redirection to URL

9. Your company has IIS 4 installed with the Microsoft SMTP and Microsoft NNTP Services running. What is the default maximum size of news articles that can be posted to a Microsoft NNTP Service news server?

   A. Unlimited

   B. 2MB

   C. 1000KB

   D. 512KB

10. You run Performance Monitor periodically to check your IIS 4's performance. Which of the following counters is not a valid item under the Internet Information Services Global object?

   A. Current Blocked Async I/O Requests

   B. File Listings

   C. Measured Async I/O Bandwidth Usage

   D. Objects

11. You are an IIS 4 consultant. A client calls to report that Microsoft Index Server has stopped running, and a message says that there is not enough free disk space available. From the following choices, you know what about the amount of disk space at this point?

   A. The free disk space has dropped to 100MB.

   B. The free disk space has dropped to 3MB.

C. The free disk space is not 20 percent of the corpus.

D. The free disk space is not 50 percent of the corpus.

12. When installing Microsoft Index Server, you need to calculate the amount of free disk space to set aside for it. What is the amount you should set aside?

A. 20 percent of the corpus

B. 30 percent of the corpus

C. 45 percent of the corpus

D. 50 percent of the corpus

13. You administer your company's IIS 4's Internet site. You need to create a report based on your server's data logs using Report Writer. Before running Report Writer, what should you do?

A. Enable logging and install SQL Server or MS Access

B. Enable ODBC Logging file format

C. Run Usage Import and import the log file

D. Use Edit from the command line to convert the file to TXT

14. You use the Scheduler in Report Writer and Usage Import. What is the name of the items placed in a new job?

A. Job items

B. Categories

C. Subjobs

D. Tasks

15. You are a consultant for a company that uses IIS 4 to run its Web and FTP sites. You are asked to track the number of nonanonymous users currently attached to the site. Which Performance Monitor counter do you use to track this value?

    A. Current Anonymous Users

    B. Logged In Users

    C. Current NonAnonymous Users

    D. Users

16. You're the administrator of your IIS 4 Web site. The Web site is responding sluggishly, and you notice some inactive clients are staying connected to your server. What is an appropriate response?

    A. From the Web site's Service Master Properties dialog box, set the Connection Timeout field to a higher number.

    B. From the Web site's Service Master Properties dialog box, enable the Unlimited Connection option.

    C. From the Web site's Service Master Properties dialog box, set the Connection Timeout field to a lower amount.

    D. From the Web site's Service Monitor Properties dialog box, set the Connection Timeout field to a lower amount.

17. On your company's Web site, you run Microsoft Index Server. You have between 100,000 and 150,000 documents stored on it. How much RAM is recommended for this number of documents?

    A. 32MB

    B. 64MB

    C. 128MB

    D. 256MB

18. You are an IIS 4 consultant working with a large company that has asked you to set up a smart host. What should you do to increase performance if you enter an IP address for the smart host?

   A. Use brackets to surround the IP address.

   B. Use commas to separate octets.

   C. Use percent signs to surround the IP address.

   D. Use semicolons to separate octets.

Review Answers

1. **D.** If you have over 500,000 documents, you must have 256MB.

2. **C.** If you have over 500,000 documents, you must have 128MB of RAM installed.

3. **B.** Microsoft Site Server Express Analysis–Report Writer is the recommended tool for generating this report.

4. **B.** W3C Extended Log File Format enables you to customize the type of data that is logged.

5. **C.** 1000 is the default in the Limited To field.

6. **A.** The Performance Tuning slider on the WWW Service Master Properties Performance tab is set too high.

7. **D.** HHTP Keep-Alives Enabled can help alleviate the problem.

8. **A,C.** The Connection Timeout and Connection Limited To value pertain to both FTP and WWW sites.

9. **C.** The default maximum size of news articles that can be posted to a Microsoft NNTP Service news server is 1000KB.

10. **A,C,D.** Only File Listings is a valid IIS Global object.

11. **B.** When free space drops below 3MB, Index Server will stop running.

12. **B.** The amount of free space should be 30 percent of the corpus.

13. **C.** Run Usage Import and import the file in question.

14. **D.** Items placed in a new job are called Tasks.

15. **C.** Current NonAnonymous Users in Performance Monitor will track the number of nonanonymous users.

16. **C.** From the Web site's Service Master Properties dialog box, set the Connection Timeout field to a lower amount.

17. **B.** A minimum of 64MB is recommended for this many documents.

18. **A.** Use brackets to surround the IP address and increase performance.

Answers to Test Yourself Questions at Beginning of Chapter

1. To create a report of daily Web site activity, enable logging for your site, and use Report Writer to create a detailed report of the activity. You can use Scheduler in Report Writer or Usage Analyst to automate this task. See "Importing Log Files Into a Report Writer and Usage Import Database" for details.

2. Run Performance Monitor, select Edit I Add To Chart, and select the FTP Service from the Objects list. From the Counter list, select Current Anonymous Users and click Add. Click Done. See "Monitoring Performance of Various Functions by Using Performance Monitor."

3. You can use Performance Monitor, Event Viewer, and Network Monitor. See "Analyzing Performance" for more information.

4. From the Web site's Service Master Properties dialog box, set the Connection Timeout field to a lower amount. See "Optimizing the Performance of IIS."

5. If you have between 100,000 and 150,000 documents, you should have 64–128MB of RAM. The minimum required is only 32MB, but the higher number is recommended. See "Optimizing the Performance of Index Server."

6. Instead of sending all outgoing messages in Microsoft SMTP Service directly to a remote domain, you can route all messages through a smart host. A smart host enables you to route messages over a more direct or less costly connection than via other routes. See "Optimizing the Performance of Microsoft SMTP Service."

7. On the NNTP Site Properties dialog box, click the Limited To option and fill in the connections field with the number of simultaneous connections you want to limit NNTP to handle. The default is 5,000. See "Changing Connection Settings."

8. Performance Monitor uses statistical measurements called counters. See "Interpreting Performance Data."

9. You can import usage data to review how users are using your site, export the Tree view of your site's WebMap to be an HTML index or table of contents for your site, and assign helper applications to file types to edit source files. See "Optimizing a Web Site Using Content Analyzer."

Chapter 30

Troubleshooting

This chapter helps you prepare for the exam by covering the following objectives:

 Objectives

> ▶ Resolve IIS configuration problems
>
> ▶ Resolve security problems
>
> ▶ Resolve resource access problems
>
> ▶ Resolve Index Server query problems
>
> ▶ Resolve setup issues when installing IIS on a Windows NT 4.0 computer
>
> ▶ Use a WebMap to find and repair broken links, hyperlink texts, headings, and titles
>
> ▶ Resolve WWW service problems
>
> ▶ Resolve FTP service problems

Test Yourself! Before reading this chapter, test yourself to determine how much study time you will need to devote to this section.

1. The three main values that must be entered to configure TCP/IP on a host with the ability to communicate beyond their network ID are what?

2. What NTFS permission enables a user to view any documents that are stored in a share, but does not enable them to make any changes to the documents?

3. Which command-line command should be given at a client to see the address of the DHCP server from which the client received its IP address?

4. By default, when does Index Server start?

5. To upgrade IIS 3.0 to IIS 4.0, what must you do?

6. What tool, new to IIS 4.0, can be used to administer Web site content to help you keep your Web site up-to-date and functioning correctly?

7. What is the default TCP control port for the WWW service?

8. What is the default TCP control port for the FTP service?

Answers are located at the end of the chapter...

This chapter covers the troubleshooting of IIS 4 problems in a number of areas, including the following:

- ▶ Resolving IIS configuration problems

- ▶ Resolving security problems

- ▶ Resolving resource access problems

- ▶ Resolving Index Server problems

- ▶ Resolving setup issues when installing IIS on a Windows NT Server 4.0 computer

- ▶ Using a WebMap to find and repair broken links, hyperlink texts, headings, and titles

- ▶ Resolving WWW Service problems

- ▶ Resolving FTP Service problems

Resolving IIS Configuration Problems

IIS configuration problems can usually be diagnosed rather quickly by the fact that nothing works. If the problem isn't with configuration (such as security, Index Server, and so on), then the problem is isolated to those services. If the problem is configuration, however, everything ceases to operate.

Configuration problems can be related to the installation of IIS or the configuration of TCP/IP. We will look at each of these in the following sections.

Installation Problems

Before you set up IIS 4, your system must meet or exceed the hardware requirements summarized in Tables 30.1 and 30.2. Table 30.1 shows requirements for a system running an Intel x86 processor; Table 30.2 lists requirements for a system running a DEC Alpha processor.

Table 30.1

IIS 4 hardware requirements for an Intel system

Hardware Device	Requirements
CPU	Minimum of a 90 MHZ 486 DX processor. For better performance, you need a Pentium 133 or higher processor.
Hard disk space	Minimum of 50 MB, but it is recommended you have at least 120 MB. This does not include storage needed for files you plan to distribute via IIS.
Memory	Minimum of 32 MB. For a Web site on which you will store multimedia files or expect a great deal of traffic, 48 MB is the recommended minimum.
Monitor	Super VGA monitor with 800x600 resolution.

Table 30.2

IIS 4 hardware requirements for an Alpha system

Hardware Device	Requirements
CPU	Minimum of 150 MHZ processor.
Hard disk space	Minimum of 120 MB, but you should allocate up to 200 MB for best performance.
Memory	Minimum of 48 MB. For better performance, have at least 64 MB.
Monitor	Super VGA monitor with 800x600 resolution.

Before you install IIS 4, remove any installations of a previous version of IIS. You'll also need to disable other versions of FTP, Gopher, or World Wide Web services you have installed under Windows NT Server 4.0. This includes the Windows Academic Center (EMWAC) service included with the Windows NT Resource Kit.

You also should have the following software installed:

▶ Windows NT Server 4.0

▶ Service Pack 3 for Windows NT Server 4.0

▶ Internet Explorer (4.01 or higher)

You also must be logged on to the Windows NT Server computer with Administrator privileges. Failing to have proper permissions or the required software installed almost always guarantees a failed installation.

TCP/IP Problems

Three main parameters specify how TCP/IP is configured on a host with the ability to communicate beyond its network ID: the IP address, the subnet mask, and the default gateway, which is the address of the router. These parameters are configured through the Protocols tab of the Network Properties dialog box. Although it's possible to receive an IP address from a DHCP server, for the moment this discussion focuses on parameters that are manually configured. DHCP related issues are discussed later, in the section "DHCP Client Configuration Problems."

These three TCP/IP parameters must be configured correctly or you cannot connect with TCP/IP. An incorrect configuration can result from typographical errors; if you type the wrong IP address, subnet mask, or default gateway, you may not connect properly or even be able to connect at all. To illustrate, if you dial the wrong number when making a telephone call, you can't reach the party you're calling. If you read the wrong phone number out of the phone book, you won't ever make a correct call, even if you dial the number you think is correct time and time again.

Whether the TCP/IP configuration parameters are wrong due to a typo or due to a mistaken number, the incorrect parameters affect communications. Different types of problems occur when each of these parameters has a configuration error.

IP Address Configuration Problems

While an incorrect TCP/IP address almost always causes problems, there are some instances when it does not. If you configure an IP address that's on the correct subnet but uses the wrong host ID and isn't a duplicate, the client may be able to communicate just fine. If, however, the correct IP address has been entered in a static file or database that resolves host names to IP addresses, such as an LMHOSTS file or a DNS database file, there can be some communication problems. Typically, therefore, an incorrect IP address does cause some problems.

Each TCP/IP parameter reacts differently if configured incorrectly. The following sections examine the effects that each TCP/IP parameter can have on IP communications.

IP Address

A TCP/IP address has two and sometimes three components that uniquely identify the computer the address is assigned to. At the very least, the IP address specifies the network address and host address of the computer. Also, if you are subnetting (using part of the host address to specify a subnet address), the third part of the address specifies the subnet address of the host.

▶ If the incorrect host (for example, 143.168.3.9) sends a message to a local client (for example, 133.168.3.20), the TCP/IP configuration of the sending host indicates that this is a remote address because it doesn't match the network address of the host initiating the communication. The packet won't ever reach the local client, because the address 133.168.3.20 is interpreted as a remote address.

▶ If a local client (133.168.3.6) sends a message to the incorrect host (143.168.3.9), the message never reaches its intended destination. The message is either routed (if the local client sends the message to the IP address as written) or it stays on the local subnet (if the local client sends it to what should have been the address, 133.168.3.9).

1. If the message is routed, the incorrect client does not receive the message because it is on the same segment of the network as the local client.

2. If the message is not routed, the message still doesn't reach the incorrect client because the IP address for the destination host (133.168.3.9) doesn't match the address as configured on the incorrect client (143.168.3.9).

Figure 30.1 gives an example of an incorrect IP address. In this case, a class A address is used, 33.x.x.x. The subnet mask (255.255.0.0) indicates the second octet is also being used to create subnets. In this case, even though the client has the same network address as the other clients on the same subnet, the client has a different subnet number because the address was typed incorrectly. The incorrect address specifies the wrong subnet ID. The client 33.5.8.4 is on subnet 5 while the other clients on the subnet have the address 33.4.x.x. If the client 33.5.8.4. tries to contact other clients on the same subnet, the message is routed because the subnet ID doesn't match the subnet number of the source host. If the client 33.5.8.4 tries to send a message to a remote host, the message is routed, but the message isn't returned to the client because the router doesn't handle subnet 5, only subnet 4.

Figure 30.1

An incorrect subnet address.

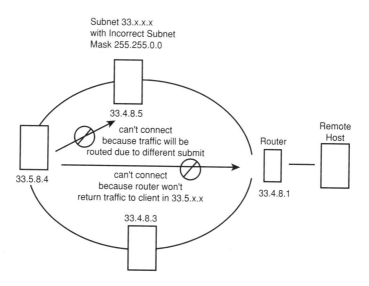

If a local client tries to send a message to 33.5.8.4, the message doesn't reach the client. If the local client uses the address as configured, the message is routed, which isn't the correct solution because the destination host is local. If the local client sends the message to what should have been the IP address, 33.5.8.4 doesn't receive the message because the IP address isn't configured correctly.

The last component of an IP address that can cause communication problems is the host address. An incorrect host address may not always cause a problem, however. In Figure 30.2, a local client has the wrong IP address, but only the host address portion of the address is wrong. The network address and subnet match the rest of the clients on the subnet. In this case, if a client sends a message to the client with the incorrect address, the message still reaches the client. However, if someone tries to contact the client with what should have been the address, he doesn't contact the client. In fact, he could contact another host that ended up with the address that was supposed to be given to the original host. If the original host ends up with the same IP address as another host through the configuration error, the first client to boot works, but the second client to boot may note the address conflict and not load the TCP/IP stack at all. In this case, the second client to boot isn't able to make any TCP/IP communications and this disrupts communications for both workstations (in a best-case scenario).

Figure 30.2

Incorrect host address.

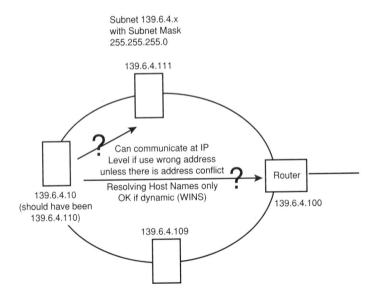

Subnet 139.6.4.x
with Subnet Mask
255.255.255.0

139.6.4.111

Can communicate at IP
Level if use wrong address
unless there is address conflict

Resolving Host Names only
OK if dynamic (WINS)

139.6.4.10
(should have been
139.6.4.110)

Router

139.6.4.100

139.6.4.109

Another problem comes in when the correct address was registered in static files, such as an LMHOSTS file or a DNS database, but an incorrect address is entered elsewhere. In this case, no one can communicate with this client by name because the name resolution for this host always returns the correct address, which can't be used to contact the host because the address has been typed incorrectly. Basically, the problems you encounter with an incorrect host address are intermittent. However, if the host was configured to be a WINS client, the host name is registered along with the incorrect address. Another WINS client trying to connect with this computer receives an accurate mapping for the host name.

Subnet Mask

The subnet mask specifies which portion of the IP address specifies the network address and which portion of the address specifies the host address. The subnet mask also can be used to take part of what would have been the host address and use it to further divide the network into subnets. If the subnet mask isn't configured correctly, your clients may not be able to communicate at all, or you may see partial communication problems.

Figure 30.3 shows a subnet on a TCP/IP network. The network uses a class B network address of 138.13.x.x. However, the third octet is used in this case for subnetting, so all the clients in the figure should be on subnet 4, as indicated by the common addresses 138.13.4.x. Unfortunately, the subnet mask entered for one client is 255.255.0.0. When this client tries to communicate with other hosts on the same subnet, it should be able to contact them because the subnet mask indicates they are on the same subnet, which is correct.

If the client tries to contact a host on another subnet, however, such as 138.13.3.x, the client fails. In this case, the subnet mask still interprets the destination host to be on the same subnet and the message is never routed. Because the destination host is on another subnet, the message never reaches the intended destination. The subnet mask is used to determine routing for outgoing communications, so the client with the incorrect subnet mask can receive incoming messages. However, when the client tries to return communications, the message isn't routed if the source host is on the same network but on a different subnet. So in actuality, the client really can establish communications with only one side of the conversation. Contact with hosts outside the local network still works because those contacts are routed.

Figure 30.3

An incorrect subnet mask—missing the third octet.

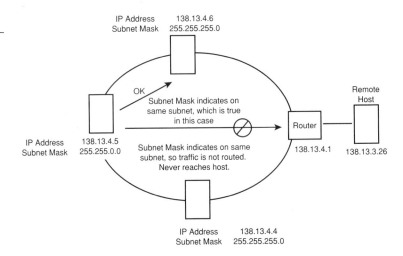

Figure 30.4 shows a subnet mask that masks too many bits. In this case, the subnet mask is 255.255.255.0. However, the network designers had intended the subnet mask to be 255.255.240.0, with four bits of the third octet used for the subnet and four bits as part of the host address. If the incorrect client tries to send a message to a local host and the third octet is the same, the message is not routed and thus reaches the local client. However, if the local client has an address that differs in the last four bits of the third octet, the message is routed and never reaches its destination. If the incorrect client tries to send a message to another client on another subnet, the message is routed because the third octet is different. The whole problem can be summed up by the incorrect subnet mask in the third octet.

Figure 30.4

Incorrect subnet mask—incorrect third octet.

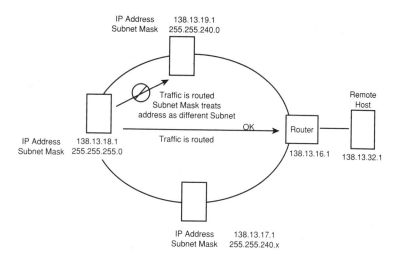

Subnet 138.13.16-31.x

IP Address   138.13.19.1
Subnet Mask   255.255.240.0

Traffic is routed
Subnet Mask treats
address as different Subnet

OK

Remote
Host

Router

IP Address   138.13.18.1
Subnet Mask   255.255.255.0

Traffic is routed

138.13.16.1   138.13.32.1

IP Address   138.13.17.1
Subnet Mask   255.255.240.x

Note

Problems with the subnet mask might appear as intermittent connections. Sometimes the connection works, sometimes it doesn't. The problems show up when the IP address of the destination host causes a packet to be routed when it shouldn't or to remain local when the packet should be routed.

Default Gateway

The default gateway address is the address of the router, the gateway to the world beyond the local subnet. If the default gateway address is wrong, the client with the wrong default gateway address can contact local hosts but isn't able to communicate at all beyond the local subnet. It's possible for the incorrect client to receive a message, because the default gateway is used only to send packets to other hosts. However, as soon as the incorrect client attempts to respond to the incoming message, the default gateway address doesn't work and the message doesn't reach the host that sent the original message. In many cases, the Default Gateway doesn't show up in an IPCONFIG/ALL (all variables of IP configuration) response if it hasn't been entered correctly.

DHCP Client Configuration Problems

All the TCP/IP parameters mentioned previously can cause communication problems if they're not configured correctly. Using a DHCP server can greatly reduce these configuration problems. If the DHCP scope is set up properly, without any typos or other configuration errors, DHCP clients shouldn't have any configuration problems. It's impossible to completely eliminate human error, but using DHCP should reduce the points of potential errors to just the DHCP servers rather than every client on the network.

Even when there are no configuration problems with DHCP addresses, DHCP clients can get a duplicate IP address from a DHCP server. If you have multiple DHCP servers in your environment, you should have scopes on each DCHP server for different subnets. Usually you have scopes with a larger number of addresses for the local subnet where the DHCP server is located and smaller scopes for other subnets. Creating multiple scopes on one server provides backup for giving clients IP addresses. If the server on the local scope is busy or down, the client can still receive an address from a remote DHCP server. When the router forwards this DHCP request to another subnet's server, it includes the address of the subnet it came from so that the remote DHCP server knows from which subnet scope of addresses to lease an address to the remote client. Using this type of redundancy, however, can cause problems if you don't configure the scopes on all the DHCP servers correctly.

The most important part of the configuration is to make sure you don't have duplicate addresses in the different scopes. On one server, for example, you could have a scope in the range 131.107.2.100 to 131.107.2.170. On the remote DHCP server, you could have a scope of 131.107.2.171 to 131.107.2.200. By setting up the scopes without overlap, you should not have any problems with clients receiving duplicate IP addresses. DHCP servers don't communicate with each other, so one server doesn't know anything about the addresses the other server has leased. Therefore, you must ensure that the servers never give out duplicate information by making sure the scopes for one subnet on all the different DHCP servers have unique IP addresses.

Another common problem with having multiple scopes on one server is entering the configuration parameters correctly. For example, if you enter the default gateway as 131.107.3.1 (instead of 131.107.2.1) for the scope 131.107.2.100 to 131.107.2.170, the clients receiving these addresses won't be able to communicate beyond the local subnet because they have the wrong router address. With one scope on a DHCP server, you're usually quite sure of what all the configuration parameters should be. With multiple scopes on one server, however, it's easy to get confused about which scope you're editing and what the parameters should be for that scope. To avoid this type of problem, check each scope's parameters very carefully to make sure the parameters match the address of the scope, not the subnet where the DHCP server is located.

Also, if the client doesn't receive an address because the server is down, or doesn't respond in a timely manner, the client isn't able to contact anyone. Without an IP address, the IP stack doesn't initialize and the client can't communicate at all with TCP/IP.

Resolving Security Problems

 Security problems relate to a user or users being unable to utilize the resources you have made available to them—or to too many users being able to access what only one or two should be able to access. There are an unlimited number of reasons why these situations could occur, based upon what the resources are and how users access them.

Problem Areas

A number of different problem areas are examined in the following sections through the presentation of various issues involving server technologies.

In most Web server operations, you want to make the service available to the public, and to as many users as possible. Unfortunately, this can lead to the risk of allowing unwanted traffic in. Solutions to solving this problem are to use a firewall to restrict traffic, disable anonymous usage, or move the Web server service to a port other than its default 80—essentially hiding it from the outside world (discussed in more detail in this chapter's section on resolving WWW service problems).

▶ **Firewalls** can be used to restrict incoming traffic to only those services you are choosing to allow in. Additionally, a firewall can be used to prevent all traffic from coming in. If you're attempting to make data available on the Web, consider putting the Web server outside the firewall and allowing traffic to pass to it but to nothing else on your network.

▶ **Anonymous usage** is a staple of most public Web sites. If you don't wish to have a public Web site, however, consider disabling the logon. You can configure the Web server to use user authentication to verify that everyone accessing it has a valid Windows NT user account (they must give a username and password before being allowed to interact with the server).

▶ **Secure Sockets Layer (SSL) 3.0** is included with IIS and its use should be mandatory on any site holding sensitive data (such as medical information, credit card information, and so on). SSL enables a secure connection to be established between the browser and the server, and encryption to be used between them.

▶ **Server Certificates**, a part of SSL, can be created (unique digital identifications) to authenticate your Web site to browsers. This is used for public and private key (key pair) interactions of a secure nature.

▶ **NTFS permissions** can be used in conjunction with IIS to secure individual files and directories from those who should not access them. The five permission types follow:

▶ Change—Users can read and modify files, including deleting them and adding new ones to a directory.

▶ Full Control—The default for the Everyone group. Users can modify, move, delete, take ownership, and even change permissions.

- ► No Access—Overrides everything else and gives absolutely no access to the resource.

- ► Read—As the name implies, users can read the data.

- ► Special Access—User permissions have been set to something specific by the administrator.

Far and away, the No Access permission is the most powerful permission. When it is implemented, the user that has been assigned this permission has no access to that resource. It doesn't matter what other permissions have been assigned. The No Access permission overrides any other assigned permissions.

The Basic Steps in the Access Control Process

Solving most security problems involves using a great deal of common sense (if passwords are used, make them more than one character in length, and so on) and understanding what is taking place. The following steps illustrate the access control process:

1. The Web server receives a request from the browser to perform an operation.

2. The Web server checks to see if the IP address is permitted. If there are no restrictions on IP address ranges, or the request is coming from a valid range, processing continues.

3. The Web server checks to see if the user is permitted.

4. The Web server checks to see if its own permissions will enable access.

5. A check is made to see if the NTFS permissions will enable access.

If any of the preceding steps fail, then the access is denied. If they all succeed, then access is granted.

Resolving Resource Access Problems

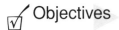 Objectives

Resource access problems are identified by a user or users being unable to access a resource. This problem can be caused by a lack of appropriate security or the TCP/IP configuration of the host or clients as discussed in the following section.

Using IPCONFIG to Resolve DHCP Address Problems

When a DHCP client gets an IP that isn't configured correctly, or if the client doesn't get an IP address at all, IPCONFIG can be used to resolve these problems. If the client gets incorrect IP parameters, it should be apparent from the results of IPCONFIG/all. You should be able to see that some of the parameters don't match the IP address or that some parameters are completely blank. For example, you could have the wrong default gateway (in which case the entry would not appear), or the client might not be configured to be a WINS client.

When a DHCP client fails to receive an address, the results of IPCONFIG /all are different. In this case, the client has an IP address of 0.0.0.0—an invalid address—and the DHCP server is 255.255.255.255—a broadcast address.

To fix this problem, you can release the incorrect address with IPCONFIG /release and then try to obtain a new IP address with IPCONFIG /renew. The IPCONFIG /renew command sends out a new request for a DHCP address. If a DHCP server is available, the server responds with the lease of an IP address. If there is no response, then it sends a request for a new one.

In many cases, the DHCP client acquires the same address after releasing and renewing. That the client receives the same address indicates the same DHCP server responded to the renewal request and gave out the address that had just been released back into the pool of available addresses. If you need to renew an address because the parameters of the scope are incorrect, you must fix the parameters in DHCP configuration before releasing and renewing the address. Otherwise, the client could receive the same address again with the same incorrect parameters.

Note

> Occasionally, a DHCP client won't acquire an address regardless of how many times you release and renew the address. One way to try to fix the problem is to manually assign the client a static IP address. Once the client is configured with this address, which you can verify by using IPCONFIG, switch back to DHCP.

Microsoft IP Configuration Troubleshooting Utilities

A number of tools come with TCP/IP when the protocol is installed on a Windows NT computer. After you have resolved any problems caused by the Windows NT network configuration, you can then focus on using the TCP/IP tools to solve IP problems. Some tools can be used to verify the configuration parameters. Other tools can be used to test the connectivity capabilities of TCP/IP as configured.

Using Ping to Test an IP Configuration

Ping is a command-line tool included with every Microsoft TCP/IP client (any DOS or Windows client with the TCP/IP protocol installed). You can use Ping to send a test packet to the specified address. If things are working properly, the packet is returned. Figure 30.5 shows the results of a successful Ping command. Note that four successful responses are returned. Unsuccessful pings can result in different messages, depending on the type of problem Ping encounters while trying to send and receive the test packet.

Although Ping is a simple tool to use (from the command prompt simply type Ping with the IP address or host name you want to ping), choosing what to ping is the key to using it for successful troubleshooting. The remainder of this section covers which IP addresses or hosts you should ping to troubleshoot TCP/IP connectivity problems.

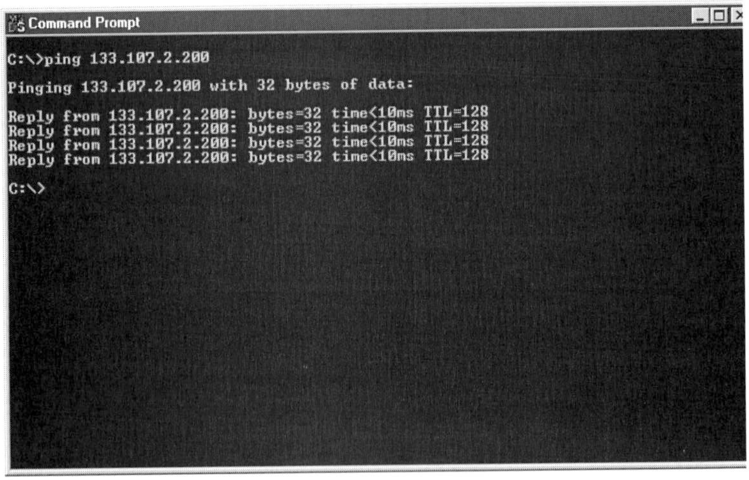

Figure 30.5

The results of a successful Ping *command.*

```
Command Prompt                                          _ □ ×

C:\>ping 133.107.2.200

Pinging 133.107.2.200 with 32 bytes of data:

Reply from 133.107.2.200: bytes=32 time<10ms TTL=128
Reply from 133.107.2.200: bytes=32 time<10ms TTL=128
Reply from 133.107.2.200: bytes=32 time<10ms TTL=128
Reply from 133.107.2.200: bytes=32 time<10ms TTL=128

C:\>
```

Troubleshooting IP Protocol Installation by Pinging the Loopback Address

The first step in troubleshooting many problems is to verify that TCP/IP installed correctly on the client. You can look at the configuration through the Network Properties dialog box or with IPCONFIG, but to actually test the working status of the protocol stack you should try to ping the loopback address. The loopback address is 127.0.0.1. When you ping this address, a packet isn't sent on the network. Ping simply sends a packet down through the layers of the IP architecture and then up the layers again. If TCP/IP is installed correctly, you should receive an immediate successful response. If IP isn't installed correctly, the response fails.

To correct problems of this type, you should verify the NT network configuration and the protocol installation. You can check the following items:

▶ Make sure TCP/IP is listed on the installed protocols.

▶ Make sure the network adapter card is configured correctly.

▶ Make sure TCP/IP shows up in the bindings for the adapter card and that the bindings aren't disabled for TCP/IP.

▶ Check the system log for any errors indicating that the network services didn't start.

If you try the preceding steps, including rebooting the system, and have no success, you may have to remove TCP/IP and install it again. Sometimes Windows NT gets hung up somewhere and thinks things are really installed when they are not. Removing the protocol and then installing it again can often resolve this halfway state.

Troubleshooting Client Address Configuration by Pinging Local Addresses

Another step in verifying the TCP/IP configuration, after you have verified that TCP/IP is installed correctly, is to ping the address of the local host. Simply ping the IP address that you think is configured for the client. You should receive an immediate successful reply if the client address is configured as specified in the Ping command. You also can ping the name of the local host, but problems with name resolution are discussed later in this chapter's section "Name Resolution Problems." For the moment, you are concerned with raw TCP/IP connectivity—the capability to communicate with another IP host by using its IP address.

Correcting a failure at this level concerns checking the way the client address was configured. Was the address typed in correctly? Did the client receive the IP address from the DHCP server that you expected? Also, does the client have a connection on the network? Pinging the local host address doesn't cause a packet to be sent on the network, so if you have lost network connectivity, this ping won't indicate a network failure.

Troubleshooting Router Problems by Pinging the Default Gateway

If you can communicate with hosts on the same subnet but cannot establish communications with hosts beyond the subnet, the problem may be with the router or the way its address is configured. To communicate beyond the subnet, a router must be enabled with an address that matches the subnet address for the clients on the local subnet. The router also has other ports configured with different addresses, so it can send packets out to the network at large. Pinging the default gateway address tests the address you have configured for the router and also tests the router itself.

If the default gateway ping fails, there are several possible sources for the error:

▶ **The router has failed or is down.** In this case, you cannot make connections outside the subnet until the router is brought up again. However, you should be able to communicate with hosts on the same subnet.

▶ **The client has lost a physical connection with the router or with the network.** You can test a network connection at a hardware level and also through the software by trying to establish a session with a server with another protocol, such as NetBEUI, for example. If you only have TCP/IP on your network, you can temporarily install NetBEUI on the client and on another computer on the same subnet. Test connectivity by connecting to a file share on the other computer. Remember, the computer should be on the same subnet because NetBEUI packets don't route (but may be bridged).

▶ **The IP address on the router may be configured incorrectly.** The router address must match the client's default gateway address so that packets can move outside the subnet.

▶ **The client has the wrong router address.** Of course, if you ping the correct router address and it works, you also want to make sure the default gateway address configured on the client matches the address you successfully pinged.

▶ **The wrong subnet mask is configured.** If the subnet mask is wrong, packets destined for a remote subnet may not be routed.

You should also ping each of the IP addresses used by the different ports on your router. It's possible that the local interface for your subnet is working but other interfaces on the router, which actually connect the router to the other subnets on the network, have some type of problem.

Pinging a Remote Host

As a final test in using Ping, you can ping the IP address of a remote host, a computer on another subnet, or even the IP address

of a Web server or FTP server on the Internet. If you can successfully ping a remote host, your problem doesn't lie with the IP
configuration; you're probably having trouble resolving host
names.

If pinging the remote host fails, your problems may be with the
router, the subnet mask, or the local IP configuration. However, if
you have followed the earlier steps of pinging the loopback, local
host address, and the default gateway address, you have already
eliminated many of the problems that could cause this Ping to fail.

When a remote host Ping fails after you have tried the other Ping
options, the failure may be due to other routers beyond the default gateway used for your subnet. If you know the physical layout
of your network, you can ping other router addresses along the
path to the remote host to see where the trouble lies. Remember
to ping the addresses on both sides of the router: the address that
receives the packet and the address that forwards the packet on.
You also can use the Route command, as described in the following
section to find the path used to contact the remote host.

It is also possible that there is not a physical path to the remote
host due to a router crash, a disruption in the physical network,
or a crash on the remote host.

Many troubleshooters prefer to simply try this last step when using
Ping to troubleshoot IP configuration and connectivity. If you can
successfully ping a remote host, then the other layers of TCP/IP
must be working correctly. In order for a packet to reach a remote
host, IP must be installed correctly, the local client address must
be configured properly, and the packet must be routed. If a Ping
to the remote host works, then you can look to other sources (usually name resolution) for your connection problems. If the Ping
fails, you can try each preceding step until you find the layer
where the problem is located. Then you can resolve the problem
at that layer. You can either start by pinging the loopback address
and working up through the architecture, or you can ping the
remote host. Of course, if pinging the remote host works, you can
stop. If not, you can work back through the architecture until you
find a layer where Ping succeeds. The problem must therefore be
at the next layer.

Diagnosing and Resolving Name Resolution Problems

Name resolution problems are easily identified as such with the PING utility. If you can ping a host using its IP address, but cannot ping it by its host name, then you have a resolution problem. If you cannot ping the host at all, then the problem lies elsewhere.

Problems that can occur with name resolution and their solutions fit into the following categories:

▶ **The entry is misspelled.** Examine the HOSTS or LMHOSTS file to verify that the host name is correctly spelled. If you're using the HOSTS file on a system prior to Windows NT 4.0, capitalization is important, as this file is case sensitive, because while LMHOSTS is not case sensitive (regardless of the Windows NT version number).

▶ **Comment characters prevent the entry from being read.** Verify that a pound sign is not at the beginning of the line (with the exception of entries such as #PRE and #DOM in LMHOSTS only), or anywhere on the line prior to the host name.

▶ **There are duplicate entries in the file.** Beacause the files are read in linear fashion, with any duplication, only the first entry is read and all others are ignored. Verify that all host names are unique.

▶ **A host other than the one you want is contacted.** Verify that the IP address entered in the file(s) is valid and corresponds to the host name.

▶ **The wrong file is used.** While similar in nature, HOSTS and LMHOSTS are really quite different, and not all that interchangeable. HOSTS is used to map IP addresses to host names, and LMHOSTS is used to map NetBIOS names to IP addresses.

In addition to PING, the all-purpose TCP/IP troubleshooting tool, useful name-resolution utilities include the following:

▶ NBTSTAT

▶ HOSTNAME

NBTSTAT

The NBTSTAT utility (NetBIOS over TCP/IP) displays protocol statistics and current TCP/IP connections. It is useful for troubleshooting NetBIOS name resolution problems, and has a number of parameters and options that can be used with it:

▶ -a (adapter status)—lists the remote machine's name table given its name

▶ -A (Adapter status)—lists the remote machine's name table given its IP address

▶ -c (cache)—lists the remote name cache, including the IP addresses

▶ -n (names)—lists local NetBIOS names

▶ -r (resolved)—lists names resolved by broadcast and via WINS

▶ -R (Reload)—purges and reloads the remote cache name table

▶ -S (Sessions)—lists sessions table with the destination IP addresses

▶ -s (sessions)—lists sessions table converting destination IP addresses to host names via the LMHOSTS file

Hostname

The HOSTNAME.EXE utility, located in *systemroot*\System32 returns the name of the local host. This is used only to view the name and cannot be used to change the name. The host name is changed from the Network Control Panel applet.

If you have configured TCP/IP correctly and the protocol is installed and working, then the problem with connectivity is probably due to errors in resolving host names. When you test connectivity with TCP/IP addresses, you are testing a lower-level of connectivity than users generally use. When users want to connect to a network resource, such as mapping a drive to a server or connecting to a Web site, they usually refer to that server or Web site by its name rather than its TCP/IP address. In fact, users do not usually know the IP address of a particular server.

The name used to establish a connection must be resolved down to an IP address so that the networking software can make a connection. Once you've tested the IP connectivity, the next logical step is to check the resolution of a name down to its IP address. If a name cannot be resolved to its IP address or if it is resolved to the wrong address, users won't be able to connect to the network resource with that name, even if you can connect to it using an IP address.

Two types of computer names are used when communicating on the network. A NetBIOS name is assigned to a Microsoft computer, such as a Windows NT server or a Windows 95 client. A host name is assigned to a non-Microsoft computer, such as a UNIX server. (Host names also can be assigned to a Windows NT server running Internet Information Server. For example, the name www.microsoft.com refers to a Web server on the Microsoft Web site. This server is running on Windows NT.) In general, when using Microsoft networking, such as connecting to a server for file sharing, print sharing, or applications, you refer to that computer by its NetBIOS name. When executing a TCP/IP-specific command, such as FTP or using a Web browser, you refer to that computer by its host name.

A NetBIOS name can be resolved to a TCP/IP address in several ways. Figure 30.6 shows an example of how NetBIOS names are resolved. The TCP/IP client initiating a session first looks in its local name cache. If the client cannot find the name in a local cache, it then queries a WINS server if it is configured to be a WINS client. If the WINS server cannot resolve the name, the client tries a broadcast that only reaches the local subnet, because routers, by default, aren't configured to forward broadcasts. If the client cannot find the name through a broadcast, it looks for any LMHOSTS or HOSTS files, if it has been configured to do so. Finally, if the client cannot resolve a name in any other way, it queries a DNS server if it has been configured to be a DNS client. However, if the client specifies a name longer than 15 characters (the maximum length of a NetBIOS name), the client first queries DNS before trying a HOSTS file or WINS.

Figure 30.6

Resolving NetBIOS names.

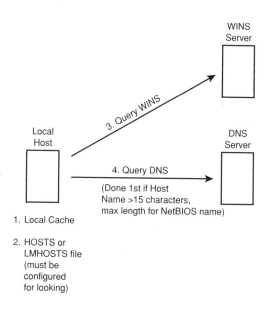

Host names are resolved in a similar manner. The client, however, checks sources that are used solely to resolve host names before trying sources that are used to resolve NetBIOS names. In resolving host names, the client first tries the local host name, then checks the HOSTS file next, followed by the DNS server (if it is configured to be a DNS client). These two sources only resolve host names. If the client cannot resolve the name, it checks the WINS server, if configured as a WINS client, tries a broadcast, then looks in the LMHOSTS file. The last three methods to resolve a name are used to resolve NetBIOS names, but it is possible for a host name to be listed in these sources.

Several tools are available to test name resolution. They are discussed in the following sections.

Testing Name Resolution with `Ping`

Just as you can use `Ping` to verify the TCP/IP configuration, you can also use `Ping` to verify host name resolution. If you can successfully ping a host name, then you have verified TCP/IP communication from the Network Interface layer of the TCP/IP architecture to the Transport layer. When you ping a host name, a successful reply shows the IP address of the host. This shows that the name has been successfully resolved to an IP address and that you can communicate with that host.

Testing NetBIOS Name Resolution by Establishing a Session

The ultimate test of connectivity is to establish a session with another host. If you can establish a session through mapping a drive or by executing a `Net Use` command (which is the command-line equivalent of mapping a drive), you have made a NetBIOS connection. If you can FTP, Telnet, or establish a Web session with another host, you have made a Sockets connection. NetBIOS connection and Sockets connection are the two main types of connections made by a TCP/IP client.

After the drive has been mapped with `Net Use`, you can switch to the new drive letter, view files and directories, and do any other things that are specified in the permissions of the share mapped to the drive letter. To get more information about the syntax of the `Net Use` command, type `net help use` in a command prompt.

A common problem in making NetBIOS connections is that the wrong NetBIOS name is used. Verify that the destination host has the same name that you are using to make the connection.

Another potential problem with the name configuration occurs when NetBIOS scope IDs are used. Only NetBIOS hosts with the same scope ID can communicate with each other. The scope ID is configured through the advanced TCP/IP parameters. Incorrect share permissions can prevent you from establishing a NetBIOS session. When you try to connect a drive to a share where you have No Access, you receive an Access Denied message. This message indicates that you can connect to the server, but your rights did not enable you to make a connection to this specific share. This type of failure has nothing to do with TCP/IP connectivity. Remember that if the administrator adds your account to a group that has access, and you want to try again, you must log out and log in again to receive a new access token with the updated permissions.

To resolve NetBIOS connectivity problems, you must know what sources are used to resolve NetBIOS names. The first place a client looks to resolve a NetBIOS name is the local cache. You can view the contents of the NetBIOS cache with the NBTSTAT command. You should verify that no incorrect entry is in the cache that maps the NetBIOS name to an incorrect IP address. If there is, however, you can remove the entry and then try to make another connection.

The next place to attempt NetBIOS name resolution is in a query to a WINS server. The client must be configured to be a WINS client. You can verify the address of the WINS server through the Advanced properties of TCP/IP or by using IPCONFIG/all. You can view the contents of the WINS database by using WINS Manager on the WINS server (or any computer where the management tools are installed). Verify that the host name is in the database and, if so, make sure it is mapped to the correct IP address.

If the WINS server is configured to do a DNS lookup, you have another way to get NetBIOS resolution. The WINS server queries DNS if the WINS server cannot resolve the name from its own database. You can view the contents of the DNS database files by using DNS Manager on the DNS server or by using the NSLOOKUP utility from any client.

The client next tries a broadcast to resolve NetBIOS names, although you cannot configure what the client finds through the broadcast. The next place the client looks for NetBIOS name resolution is the LMHOSTS file. You can configure the contents of this file. The client must be configured for LMHOSTS lookup in the advanced TCP/IP configuration. Also, the LMHOSTS file must be located in the correct directory path. On a Windows NT computer, the LMHOSTS file must be in the path <winnt root>\system32\drivers\etc.

Next, verify the entries in the LMHOSTS file. The correct host name and IP address must be entered in this file. If you have multiple entries in the file for a host name, only the first entry is used. If you added another entry for a host in the file, you must delete it so that it will not be used.

Domain names are another source of potential problems with LMHOSTS files in a non-WINS environment. The domain name must be registered with the IP address of the Primary Domain Controller (PDC) and #DOM (a switch that registers the server as a domain controller) on the same line. This entry is necessary to log on to the domain as well as to see the domain in a browse list.

Another problem with LMHOSTS files doesn't prevent connectivity, but it can greatly delay it. If you have #INCLUDE statements at the top of the LMHOSTS file, the files specified by #INCLUDE are included before any other entries lower in the LMHOSTS file are searched. You can speed connections to hosts entered in the LMHOSTS file by moving the #INCLUDE entries to the bottom of the LMHOSTS file.

Testing TCP Name Resolution by Establishing a Session

Typical TCP/IP connections from a Microsoft client, such as FTP or Telnet, use Windows Sockets. To test connectivity at this level, try establishing an FTP or Telnet session or try to connect to a Web server. When you successfully connect to a Web server, you see the site's Web page, and you can navigate through the page. When the connection fails, you receive a message on your Internet browser that the connection failed.

To resolve problems with a Windows Sockets connection, you must understand how a client resolves TCP host names. The first place a client looks to resolve a host name is the local host name. You can see what TCP/IP thinks the local host name is by executing the Hostname command. Verify the host name if the results of the Hostname command confirm that the local host is what you expect it to be. You can modify the host name in the DNS tab of the TCP/IP properties.

The next place the client looks is in a HOSTS file. This file must be located in the path <winnt root>\system32\drivers\etc. Verify that any entry in the file for the host is correct, with the correct host name and IP address. If multiple entries for the same host name are in the file, only the first name is used. The HOSTS file can also have links to HOSTS files on other servers. If links are specified in the local HOSTS file, you should make sure entries in the other HOSTS files also are correct.

The final place a client can use host name resolution is a DNS server. The client must be configured to use DNS on the DNS tab in the TCP/IP properties dialog box. The DNS server must have a zone file corresponding to the domain name specified in the host name, or it must be able to query another DNS server that can resolve the name.

Resolving Index Server Problems

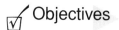 Objectives

Index Server works with IIS through queries that come in the form of .IDQ (Internet Data Query) files. It responds to those queries in the form of .IDQ files as well. In order to function properly, .IDQ files should always be placed in the Scripts directory, and they require Execute or Script permission.

As discussed in Chapter 4, there are two sections to .IDQ files with [Query] being required, and [Names] being optional (used only to define nonstandard column names that are referred to in a query). Refer to Chapter 4 for a listing of parameters, variables, and conditional expressions.

Most troubleshooting/trouble correction is implemented automatically with Index Server. For example, if the cache becomes corrupted, Index Server begins a recovery operation, and no administrator interaction is required. In all events, messages are written to the event log indicating the actions taking place, and administrators can monitor their Index Server installations from there.

Query Errors

Errors can, and often do, occur when improper syntax is used in queries, when files are corrupt, or when other problems occur. There is a series of standard messages returned to alert you that this is the cause of the problem, and this section examines those.

Syntax Errors

According to Microsoft's online documentation (file ixerrysn.htm), the error messages, as shown in Table 30.3, can be returned when executing a query.

Table 30.3

The ixerrysn.htm file.

Message	Explanation
Expecting closing parenthesis	Occurs when parentheses are mismatched.
Expecting closing square bracket	An opening square bracket was not followed by a closing square bracket. Usually the result of an ill-formed weight.
Expecting comma	Occurs when a reserved token or end-of-string occurs before the closing brace of a vector property. Example: @VectorString = {A1, B@}.
Expecting currency	A currency value was expected but not found. Occurs when a property of type DBTYPE_CY is fed incorrect input. Correct format for currency is #.#.
Expecting date	A date was expected but not found. Occurs when a property of type DBTYPE_DATE is fed incorrect input. Allowed formats for dates are yyyy/mm/dd, yyyy/mm/dd hh:mm:ss, and relative dates (-#y, -#m, -#w, -#d, -#h, -#n, -#s).

Message	Explanation
Expecting end of string	A complete restriction has been parsed, and there is still more input. Example: (@size = 100) sample.
Expecting GUID	A GUID (Globally Unique Identifier) was expected but not found. Occurs when a property of `DBTYPE_GUID` is fed incorrect input. Property format for a GUID is XXXXXXXX-XXXX-XXXX-XXXX-XXXXXXXXXXXX.
Expecting integer	An integer was expected but not found. Occurs when a property of an integer type (`DBTYPE_I4`, for example) is fed a nonnumeric value, or a nonnumeric vector weight is entered.
Expecting phrase	A textual phrase was expected and not found. This error occurs in a variety of situations where the query parser is expecting plain text and is given a special token instead.
Expecting property name	Occurs when a correctly formed property name is not found after an @ sign.
Expecting real number	A real number was expected but not found. Occurs when a property of a real type (`DBTYPE_R4`, for example) if fed a nonnumeric value.
Expecting regular expression	Similar to Expecting phrase error. Used when in regular-expression parsing mode.
The file *<file>* is on a remote UNC share. .IDQ, .IDA, and .HTX files cannot be placed on a remote UNC share	An .IDQ, .IDA, or .HTX file was found on a remote UNC share. None of these files can be on a remote UNC share.

continues

Table 30.3   Continued

Message	Explanation
Invalid literal	Occurs only when a query property is formatted poorly. Almost all conditions are covered by the Expecting Integer, Expecting Date, and other errors.
No such property	Property specified after @, #, or $ does not exist. It is not a default property and is not specified in the [Names] section of the .IDQ file.
Not yet implemented	An unimplemented feature of Index Server.
Out of memory	The server ran out of memory processing the `CiRestriction`.
Regular expressions require a property of type string	A property of a nontextual type (`DBTYPE_I4`, `DBTYPE_GUID`, and so on) was selected for regular-expression mode. For example, `#size 100*` would cause this error.
Unexpected end of string	There is a missing quotation mark in your query.
Unsupported property type	For future expansion. Will occur when a display-only property type is used in a query restriction.
Weight must be between 0 and 1000	Occurs when a query term weight is outside the legal range of 0 to 1000.

IDQ File Errors

According to Microsoft's online documentation in file ixerridg.htm, the messages in Table 30.4 are returned by use of the `CiErrorMessage` variable, accessible from .htx error pages.

Table 30.4

The ixerridq.htm file.

Message	Explanation
The catalog directory cannot be found in the location specified by 'CiCatalog=' in file <file>.	The catalog location specified by the CiCatalog parameter did not contain a valid content index catalog.
DBTYPE_BYREF must be used with DBTYPE_STR, DBTYPE_WSTR, DBTYPE_GUID, or DBTYPE_UI1 types.	DBTYPE_BYREF must always be used in conjunction with an indirect type in the [Names] section.
DBTYPE_VECTOR or DBTYPE_BYREF used alone.	The VECTOR and BYREF property modifiers must always be used with a type. Example: DBTYPE_I4 | DBTYPE_VECTOR
Duplicate column, possibly by a column alias, found in the 'CiColumns=' specification in file <file>.	The same property was named more than once in the CiColumns line. It may have been mentioned with different friendly names that refer to the same property.
Duplicate property name.	The same property was defined twice in the [Names] section.
Expecting closing parenthesis.	Opening parenthesis in [Names] section is not followed by closing parenthesis in .IDQ file.
Expecting GUID.	Incorrectly formatted entry in the [Names] section of .IDQ file.
Expecting integer.	Incorrectly formatted entry in the [Names] section of .IDQ file.
Expecting property name.	Incorrectly formatted entry in the [Names] section of .IDQ file.
Expecting property specifier.	Invalid or missing property specifier in [Names] section. Property is named either by PROPID (integer) or string.

continues

Table 30.4 Continued

Message	Explanation
Expecting SHALLOW or DEEP in .IDQ file *<file>* on line 'CiFlags='.	The CiFlags parameter has a value other than SHALLOW or DEEP.
Expecting TRUE or FALSE in .IDQ file *<file>* on line 'CiForceUseCi='.	The CiForceUseCi parameter has a value other than TRUE or FALSE.
Expecting type specifier.	Incorrectly formatted entry in the [Names] section of .IDQ file.
Failed to set property name.	A resource failure. Usually out of memory.
The file *<file>* is on a network share. .IDQ, .IDA, and .HTX files cannot be placed on a network share.	You must put these files into a virtual root on the local computer.
The .HTX file specified could not be found in any virtual or physical path.	The file specified in the CiTemplate parameter could not be located.
The .IDQ file *<file>* contains a duplicate entry on line *<line>*.	A parameter in the [Query] section of the .IDQ file was given more than once.
The .IDQ file *<file>* could not be found.	Check the path to the .IDQ file and then make sure the .IDQ file is in that path.
An invalid 'CiScope=' or 'CiCatalog=' was specified in file *<file>*.	The .IDQ file cannot contain invalid parameters. Correct the condition and try again.
Invalid GUID.	A poorly formatted GUID was found in the [Names] section.
An invalid locale was specified on the 'CiLocale=' line in .IDQ file *<file>*.	The locale ID specified by the CiLocale parameter was not recognized as a valid locale ID.
Invalid property found in the 'CiColumns=' specification in file *<file>*.	A property specified in the CiColumns parameter is not a standard property and is not listed in the [Names] section of the .IDQ file.

Message	Explanation
Invalid property found in the 'CiSort=' specification in file *<file>*.	A property specified in the CiSort parameter is not a standard property and is not listed in the [Names] section of the .IDQ file.
An invalid sort order was specified on the 'CiSort=' line in file *<file>*. Only [a] and [d] are supported.	A sort-order specification following a property name in the CiSort parameter was unrecognized. Only [a] (for ascending) and [d] (for descending) are allowed.
One or more output columns must be specified in the .IDQ file *<file>*.	The CiColumns parameter is missing or empty. At least one output column must be specified for the query.
Operation on line *number* of .IDA file *<file>* is invalid.	An unrecognized keyword was found in the .IDA file.
The query failed because the Web server is busy processing other requests.	The limit on the number of queries has been exceeded. To allow more queries to wait in the queue for processing, increase the value of the Registry key IsapiRequest QueueSize, and to allow more queries to be processed simultaneously, increase the value for the Registry key IsapiRequest ThresholdFactor.
Read error in file *<file>*.	I/O error occurred reading the file. Generally caused by hardware failure.
A restriction must be specified in the .IDQ file *<file>*.	The CiRestriction parameter is missing or empty. Every query must have a restriction. A restriction such as #vpath *.* will match all pages.

continues

Table 30.4 Continued

Message	Explanation
A scope must be specified in the .IDQ file *<file>*.	The CiScope parameter is missing or empty. Every query must have a scope. The scope / (forward slash) will match every page in all virtual directories and the scope \ (backslash) will match every page on every physical path.
The template file cannot be found in the location specified by 'CiTemplate=' in file *<file>*	An attempt to open a .HTX file at the location specified by the CiTemplate parameter failed. The path may be invalid, it may specify a directory, or it may resolve to NULL after parameter replacement.
A template file must be specified in the .IDQ file *<file>*.	The CiTemplate parameter is missing or empty. Every query must have a template (.HTX) file.
Template for .IDA file *<file>* cannot have detail section.	A <%BeginDetail%> was found in the .IDA file. Please remove it and the entire detail section.
Unrecognized type.	Type specifed is not one of the valid types (DBTYPE_I4, DBTYPE_GUID, and so on).
You must specify 'MaxRecordsPerPage' in the .IDQ file *<file>*.	The CiMaxRecordsPerPage parameter is missing or empty. Every query must specify the number of records per page.

Event Log Messages

Index Server system errors are reported in the application event log under the Ci Filter Service category. System errors reported here include page filtering (indexing) problems, out-of-resource conditions, index corruption, and so on.

The messages in Table 30.5 are written to the Windows NT application event log. This information comes from Microsoft's online documentation, file ixerrlog.htm.

Table 30.5

The ixerrlog.htm file.	
Message	Explanation
Account *user-id* does not have interactive logon privileges on this computer. You can give *user-id* interactive logon privileges on this computer using the user manager administrative tool.	The specified *user-id* does not have interactive logon privileges on the computer running Index Server. Give the *user-id* interactive logon privileges through the User Manager for Domains.
The CI filter daemon has prematurely stopped and will be subsequently restarted.	The filter daemon (Cidaemon.exe) stopped unexpectedly. It will be automatically restarted. This can be caused by poorly written filters, or experimentation with the Windows NT Task Manager.
CI has started on *<catalog>*.	An informational message logged when Index Server is started successfully.
Class for extension *<extension>* unknown. Sample file: *<file>*	This is a warning that files with the specified extension are being filtered with the default (text) filter. This can lead to the addition of unnecessary data in the index. Consider turning off filtering for this extension. The full physical path of a representative file is included in the message. Generation of this message can be disabled by turning on a special flag in `ContentIndex` Registry key.
Cleaning up corrupted content index metadata on *<catalog>*. Index will be automatically restored by refiltering all documents.	A catastrophic data corruption error was detected on the specified catalog. The catalog will be rebuilt. This is usually caused by hardware failure, but also can occur in rare circumstances because of abrupt shutdown or power failure. Recovery will occur automatically.

continues

Table 30.5 Continued

Message	Explanation
Content index on *<catalog>* could not be initialized. Error *<number>*.	Unknown, possibly catastrophic error. Please report the error number to Microsoft Technical Support. To recover, delete all files under *<catalog>* and re-index.
Content index on *<catalog>* is corrupted. Please shut down restart Web server.	A catastrophic data corruption error and was detected on the specified catalog. The catalog will be rebuilt. This is usually caused by hardware failure, but also can occur in rare circumstances because of abrupt shutdown or power failure. You must shut down and restart the Web server for recovery to occur.
Content index corruption detected in component *<component>*. Stack trace is *<stack>*.	The content index is corrupted. Delete the catalog and start over. If you keep getting this error, remove and reinstall Index Server.
Content index corruption detected in component *<component>* in catalog *<catalog>*. Stack trace is *<stack>*.	The content index is corrupt. Delete the catalog and start over. If you keep getting this error, remove and reinstall Index Server.
The content index could not filter file *<file>*. The filter operation was retried *<number>* times without success.	The specified document failed to successfully filter *<number>* times. This usually indicates a corrupted document or corrupted properties. In rare cases, filtering may fail because the document was in use for a long period of time.
Content index on drive is corrupted. Please shut down and restart the Content Index service (cisvc).	In the Windows NT Control Panel under Services, stop the Content Index service, and then restart it.

Message	Explanation
The content index filter for file "*<file>*" generated content data more than *<size>* times the file's size.	Filtering of the specified document generated more than the allowed maximum amount of output. This is usually caused by a poorly written filter, a corrupted document, or both.
The content index filter stopped while filtering "*<file>*". The CI daemon was restarted. Please check the validity of the filter for objects of this class.	Filtering of the specified document was started, but did not finish before the timeout period expired. This is usually caused by a poorly written filter, a corrupted document, or both.
A content scan has completed on *<catalog>*.	A content scan of the catalog has been completed successfully.
An error has been detected on *<catalog>* that requires a full content scan.	The catalog lost a change notification, usually due to lack of resources (disk space) or hardware failure. The complete scope of the catalog will be scanned, and all documents will be refiltered. This action is deferred until a suitable time.
An error has been detected in content index on *<catalog>*.	The content index is corrupted. Delete the catalog and start over. If you keep getting this error, remove and reinstall Index Server.
An error has been detected on *<catalog>* that requires a partial content scan.	The catalog lost a change notification, usually due to lack of resources (disk space) or hardware failure. A partial scope of the catalog will be scanned, and some documents will be refiltered. This action is deferred until a suitable time.
Error *<number>* detected in content index on *<catalog>*.	Unknown, possibly catastrophic error. Please report error number to Microsoft Techical Support. To recover, delete all files under *<catalog>* and start over.

continues

Table 30.5   Continued

Message	Explanation
File change notifications are turned off for scope "*<scope>*" because of error *<number>*. This scope will be periodically rescanned.	An error prevented reestablishing automatic change notifications for the specified directory scope. To determine documents that changed in the scope, periodic incremental scans will be done by Index Server. The rescan interval is specified in the registry.
File change notifications for scope "*<scope>*" are not enabled because of error *<number>*. This scope will be periodically rescanned.	An error prevented establishment of automatic change notifications for the specified directory scope. This usually happens with virtual roots that point to remote shares on file servers that do not support automatic change notifications. To determine which documents changed in the scope, periodic incremental scans will be done by Index Server. The rescan interval is specified in the registry.
The filter service could not run since file *<file>* could not be found on your system.	An executable or DLL required for filtering cannot be found, usually because Cidaemon.exe is not on the path.
A full content scan has started on *<catalog>*.	A complete rescan of the catalog has been initiated.
<number> inconsistencies were detected in PropertyStore during recovery of catalog *<catalog>*.	Corruption was detected in the property cache during startup. Recovery is automatically scheduled. Usually the result of hardware failure or abrupt shutdown.
Master merge cannot be restarted on *<catalog>* due to error *<number>*.	A master merge cannot be restarted on the specified catalog. The error code gives the reason.

Message	Explanation
Master merge cannot be started on *<catalog>* due to error *<number>*.	A master merge cannot be started on the specified catalog. The error code gives the reason.
Master merge has been paused on *<catalog>*. It will be rescheduled later.	A master merge has been temporarily halted on the specified catalog. Often occurs when a merge runs out of system resources (disk space, memory, and so on).
Master merge has completed on *<catalog>*.	A master merge has been completed on the specified catalog. This is an informational message.
Master merge has restarted on *<catalog>*.	A paused master merge has been restarted.
Master merge has started on *<catalog>*.	A master merge has been initiated on the specified catalog. This is an informational message.
Master merge was started on *<catalog>* because the amount of remaining disk space was less than *<number>*%.	A master merge was started because the amount of free space on the catalog volume dropped below a minimum threshold. The total free disk space should be increased after the master merge completes.
Master merge was started on *<catalog>* because more than *<number>* documents have changed since the last master merge.	A master merge was started because the number of documents changed since the last master merge exceeded the maximum thresh old.
Master merge was started on *<catalog>* because the size of the shadow indexes is more than *<number>*% the disk.	A master merge was started because the amount of data in shadow indexes exceeded the maximum threshold.

continues

Table 30.5 Continued

Message	Explanation
Notifications are not enabled on *<pathname>* because this is a DFS aware share. This scope will be periodically scanned.	If a virtual root points to a distributed file system (DFS) share, notifications are disabled for the entire DFS share because DFS does not support notifications.
One or more embeddings in file *<file>* could not be filtered.	The specified file was filtered correctly, but several of the embedded objects could not be filtered. This is usually caused by embedded objects without a registered filter. Text within unfiltered embedded objects is not searchable. Generation of this message can be disabled by turning on a special flag in key registry.
The path *<pathname>* is too long for Content Index.	The Content Index service detected a path that was longer than the maximum number of characters allowed for a path name as determined by the constant MAX_PATH (260 characters). As a result, no documents from that path will be returned or indexed.
Please check your system time. It might be set to an invalid value.	This event is generated when the system time is invalid, for example, when set to a date before January 1, 1980. When the system time is invalid, the date may appear as 2096.

Message	Explanation
<Process-Name> failed to logon *<UserId>* because of error *<number>*.	The specified process (Index Server SearchEngine or CiDaemon) failed to log on the specified user because of an error. The remote shares for which the UserId is used will not be filtered correctly. This can happen if either the password is wrong or the validity of the password could not be verified due to network errors.
PropertyStore inconsistency detected in catalog *<catalog>*.	Corruption was detected in the property cache. Recovery is automatically scheduled. Usually the result of hardware failure or abrupt shutdown.
Recovery is starting on PropertyStore in catalog *<catalog>*.	Corruption was detected in the property cache. Recovery is starting on the property cache. This can take a long time, depending upon the size of the property cache.
Recovery was performed successfully on PropertyStore in catalog *<catalog>*.	Corruption was detected in the property cache. The error has been fixed. Usually the result of hardware failure or abrupt shutdown.
Very low disk space was detected on drive *<drive>*. Please free up at least *<number>* MB of space for content index to continue.	Free space has fallen below the minimum threshold required for successful merge. This is just a warning, but no merges will be initiated until space is freed up. Filtering will also stop.

Virtual Roots

Table 30.6, which follows, is from the ixerrlog.htm as well, and it describes the error messages that occur when virtual root problems are the cause of the error.

Table 30.6

The virtual roots component of ixerrlog.htm.	
Message	Explanation
Added virtual root <*root*> to index.	The message "Mapped to <*path*>" is added to the event log when a virtual root is indexed.
Removed virtual root <*root*> from index.	This message is written to the event log when a virtual root is deleted from the index.
Added scope <*path*> to index.	This message is added to the event log when a new physical scope is indexed.
Removed scope <*path*> from index.	This message is written to the event log when a new physical scope is deleted from the index.

Other Index Server Issues

Other issues to be aware of with Index Server include the following:

- ▶ Index Server starting and stopping
- ▶ Word weighting
- ▶ Disk filling

Index Server Starting and Stopping

Index Server, by default, is set to automatically start when IIS does. If this is set to another value, such as manual, then IIS can be started from the Services icon in the Control Panel. This is the same utility that can be used to stop the Index Server service, although it automatically shuts down when IIS does.

If Index Server isn't running and a query comes in, Index Server automatically starts. Therefore, as an administrator, the starting of Index Server is not something you should ever need to do manually. The stopping of Index Server is something you should never need to do, either, but you can do it from the Services utility.

Word Weighting

Word weighting determines how words in the data are indexed. This process is done by the Waisindx.exe utility. It determines what to index, how much to weight words, how to optimize the server, and where to find the actual data. As a rule of thumb, seven indexes are created for each data file, with the combined size of the seven indexes being equal to 110% of the size of the data file.

The weighting factors that Waisindx.exe uses are as follows:

- ▶ **The actual weight of the word.** Whether it appears in a headline, capitalized, etc., or just in the body of the data.

- ▶ **The term of the weight.** How many times does it appear, and thus, how important is it to the data?

- ▶ **The proximity.** How close do multiple words always appear to each other? For example, computer publishing.

- ▶ **The density of the word.** This is computed by taking the number of times the word appears and dividing it by the total number of all words in the data.

When Waisindx.exe is run, it creates the indexes that are then used to locate the data. As you add new records to the data, the indexes are not updated, and you must rerun Waisindx.exe to create new indexes incorporating the new data.

Running Out of Disk Space

One of the most common problems with using Index Server is that of running out of disk space. If the drive fills, indexing is paused, and the only method of knowing this is by a message written to the event log. The event log should be monitored routinely by an administrator for this and similar occurrences.

Resolving Setup Issues When Installing IIS on a Windows NT Server 4.0 Computer

 Objectives ▶

Before you install IIS 4.0, you must remove any installations of a previous version of IIS, and disable other versions of FTP, Gopher, or World Wide Web services running under Windows NT Server 4.0.

You must be logged on to the Windows NT Server computer with Administrator privileges, and need to have the following software installed:

▶ Windows NT Server 4.0

▶ Service Pack 3 for Windows NT Server 4.0

▶ Internet Explorer (4.01 or higher)

If all of the above conditions have been met, and problems exist, then you should know where to turn for assistance. There are a number of places to find help, and they include the following:

▶ The Windows NT Resource Kit

▶ Online help in both Windows NT and IIS

▶ Microsoft Technet

▶ CompuServe

▶ The Microsoft Internet site

The Microsoft Windows NT Resource Kit includes three volumes of in-depth information and a CD of utilities. The Resource Kit utilities add a large number of troubleshooting utilities and can help you isolate problems much easier.

The online help in NT is available from the Start Menu, Help, or from almost anywhere else in the product by pressing F1. The IIS help is available at several locations, but most notably by selecting Product Documentation from the IIS section of the Programs menu.

Microsoft Technet is a monthly CD subscription that includes the latest service packs, drivers, and updates for all operating system products. Once installed, you can run it at any time by choosing Microsoft TechNet from the Programs menu.

The CompuServe forums are not as well supported as they once were and almost everything is shifting to the Web, but they are still a good location to find interaction among users experiencing similar problems. The easiest method to use to find a forum supporting the problem you're experiencing is to click the stoplight icon on the main CompuServe menu (or type GO at a command prompt) and enter NDEX. This brings up an index of all the forums currently available. You can select a choice from the list, or—depending upon your version of CompuServe—choose GO again, and enter the abbreviation for the forum you want.

The Microsoft Internet site at http://www.microsoft.com makes all software updates and patches available. It also serves as an entry point to the KnowledgeBase where you can find documentation on all known problems.

Use a WebMap to Find and Repair Broken Links, Hyperlink Texts, Headings, and Titles

 Objectives

Content Analyzer's WebMaps can be used to administer Web site content to help you keep your Web site up-to-date and functioning correctly. You use the Link Info window, searches, and properties to help manage your site's content. In this section you are shown how to use the Link Info windows to find and repair the following:

▶ Broken links

▶ Hyperlink text

▶ Headings

▶ Titles

To show the Link Info window, create a WebMap of your Web site. Click the Object Links toolbar button, or right-click the page you want to view and select Links. The Link Info window is displayed (see Figure 30.7). In this window, you can display different types of links on a page.

Figure 30.7

The Link Info window.

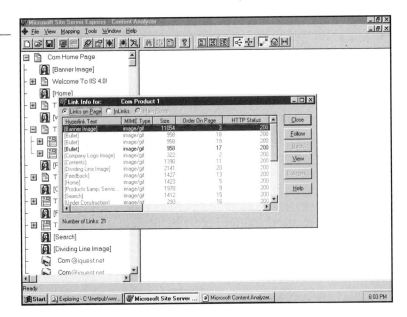

Click the Links on Page option to display all links on a selected page. This is handy if you want to review navigational paths on a page.

Click the InLinks option to display links that reference the page you are reviewing. These are called InLinks, and can be from pages on the same site as the page you're viewing or from another site.

When you click the Main Route option, the Link Info window displays all ancestor links from the main page to the selected page. If the page you're reviewing is your site's home page, for instance, you won't see any other ancestors. However, if the page is one level below the home page (that is, you can link to the page from the home page), you'll see the home page displayed when selecting the Main Route option. This is because the home page is the *parent* of the page you're reviewing. Pages one level below the child page are considered *grandchildren* to the home page, and so on. You'll find this option handy when you're viewing a page that is buried deep in the hierarchy and ancestry is not easy to discern.

Finally, to see the number of links for each type of link option you can display, look at the bottom of the Link Info window.

Fix Broken Links

As your Web site matures and content is upgraded, deleted, moved, and renamed, you'll need to update links on your pages. Over time, however, some of your page may contain broken links, those references that lead nowhere. You can use a WebMap to discover broken links and then launch your Web page editor to fix the link.

You can use two methods to search for broken objects in your pages. One way is to conduct a search for all links that are broken. Another way is to search for broken objects or for objects based on a specific HTTP status.

To search for broken links, use these steps:

1. Create a WebMap and select Tools, Custom Search (or click the Search toolbar button). The Search dialog box is displayed.

2. Configure the Search dialog box using the following parameters:

   ▶ Object Type set to Links

   ▶ Field set to Broken

   ▶ Modifiers set to Equals

   ▶ Value set to True

Note
There is also an option to select TOOLS, QUICK SEARCH, and BROKEN LINKS.

3. Click Search. The Search Results window displays all broken links, if any.

Note

Sometimes links are shown as broken (shown in red) but really aren't broken at all. A site may be unavailable because of repairs it is going through. Or there may be too much network traffic to enable you to connect to the server. You may need to try the site later to establish a connection to it.

To fix a broken link from the Search Results window, implement the following steps:

1. Select the link.

2. Select the parent page (the page that includes the broken link) of the page you just selected.

3. Select Tools, Launch Helper App.

Checking and Modifying Hyperlink Text

Text that is used to describe a link (that is, the text that is hyperlinked to another object) also can be viewed using the Content Analyzer. Many sites use consistent wording and spellings for hyperlink text pointing to the same object. You can check the In-Links text to a particular object quickly with Content Analyzer. Then, if necessary, launch your editor to modify this text.

To review the hyperlink text, perform the following steps:

1. Select the object that you want to see the InLinks text for.

2. Click the Object Links toolbar button. The Link Info window is displayed.

3. Click the InLinks option.

4. Scroll through the list of InLinks and view the hyperlink text in the Hyperlink Text column.

Note   If Hyperlink Text is not a column in the Links Info window, add it by right-clicking any column header in the Links Info window. Use the Configure Columns dialog box to add the Hyperlink Text column to the Links Info window. Click Done.

5. Select a link you want to change and click Follow. The page you want to change is displayed.

6. Right-click a page you want to modify and select Launch Helper App and the specific application to modify the page. Change the hyperlink text on that page.

Checking and Changing Headers

Content Analyzer can be used to check header information in pages. Headers are HTML tags used to set up sections in your Web pages.

To view headers on a page in Content Analyzer, implement the following steps:

1. Create a WebMap.

2. Right-click a page you want to check.

3. Select Properties to display the Properties dialog box.

4. Click the Page tab and review the Headings area.

5. Click OK to close the Properties dialog box.

If the page you just checked includes a header you want to change, or does not include headers but you want to add them to the page, right-click the page in the WebMap and select Launch Helper App. Select the helper application that enables you to edit the source code of the page. Modify the page to include headers.

Checking Page Titles

You can use Content Analyzer to check page titles. Page titles are referenced by many index servers, and also are used by some browsers (such as Internet Explorer) in bookmark lists.

You'll probably want to check page titles as your Web page content changes or evolves. To check page titles, implement the following steps:

1. Create a WebMap and perform a Custom Search for all pages.

2. Add the Title column to the Search Results window. This shows you the titles for each page displayed.

3. Double-click an object in the Search Results window. The associated browser launches, with the page displayed. Review the page to see if the title for it describes the content of the page. If a title is not shown, create a title for the page based on its content. You can then launch a helper application for editing Web pages to add or modify a page's title.

Resolving WWW Service Problems

 Objectives

HTTP is currently the most used protocol on the Internet. The default control port assignment is 80, and you can hide the service by moving it to any other available port above 1023.

By default, all configured IIS services (WWW, FTP, etc.) start automatically and stop automatically when IIS does. To start, stop, or pause the service manager by site, perform the following steps:

1. Start Internet Service Manager and select the site.

2. Right-click the mouse and choose which of the three options you want (Start, Stop, or Pause).

3. Alternatively, after selecting the site, you can choose the action to take from the toolbar.

If users experience problems viewing your Web site, it can be an indication of permission problems. Make certain that Read permission is assigned to all users for the directory containing the site.

The Anonymous Access and Authentication Control field of the site's property sheet enable you to choose among anonymous access, basic authentication permissions, or Windows NT Challenge/Response. Work backwards in selecting an option from the list until you hit the combination allowing all of your clients to connect to the site without difficulty.

Resolving FTP Service Problems

As discussed elsewhere in this book, you can install a Windows NT FTP server that can provide FTP file transfer services to other systems. This allows the server to serve clients in the same manner that has traditionally been done on UNIX machines. The FTP service is a component of IIS.

FTP, or file transfer protocol, provides a simple but robust mechanism for copying files to or from remote hosts using the connection-oriented services of TCP/IP. FTP is a component of the TCP/IP protocol, and is defined in RFC 959. To use FTP to send or receive files, the following requirements must be met:

▶ The client computer must have FTP client software, such as the FTP client included with Windows NT.

▶ The user must have a username and password on the remote system. In some cases, a username of *anonymous* with no password suffices.

▶ The remote system must be running an FTP daemon or service (depending upon whether it is UNIX or NT).

▶ Your system and the remote system must be running the TCP/IP protocol.

You can use FTP in either a command line mode or in a command interpreter mode. The following options are available from the command line:

```
C:\>ftp ?
Transfers files to and from a computer running an FTP server
                service (sometimes called a daemon). Ftp can be
                used interactively.

FTP [-v] [-d] [-i] [-n] [-g] [-s:filename] [-a] [-w:windowsize]
➥[host]

   -v            Suppresses display of remote server responses.
   -n            Suppresses auto-login upon initial connection.
   -i            Turns off interactive prompting during multiple
                 file transfers.
   -d            Enables debugging.
   -g            Disables filename globbing (see GLOB command).
   -s:filename   Specifies a text file containing FTP commands;
                 the commands will automatically run after FTP
                 starts.
   -a            Use any local interface when binding data
                 connection.
   -w:buffersize Overrides the default transfer buffer size of
                 4096.
   host          Specifies the host name or IP address of the
                 remote host to connect to.
```

If you use FTP in a command interpreter mode, some of the more frequently used options are as follows:

▶ open: Specifies the remote system to which you connect.

▶ close: Disconnects from a remote system. Bye or Quit work as well.

▶ ls: Obtains a directory listing on a remote system, much like the dir command in DOS. Note that the ls -l command provides file size and time stamps. In Windows NT you can use the old DOS DIR as well.

▶ `cd`: Changes directories on the remote system. This command functions in much the same way as the DOS `cd` command.

▶ `lcd`: Changes directories on the local system. This command also functions in much the same way as the DOS `cd` command.

▶ `binary`: Instructs FTP to treat all files transferred as binary.

▶ `ascii`: Instructs FTP to treat all files transferred as text. You need to choose a transfer type because certain files cannot be read correctly as binary, while ASCII is universally accepted.

▶ `get`: Copies a file from the remote host to your local computer.

▶ `put`: Copies a file from your local computer to the remote host.

▶ `debug`: Turns on debugging commands that can be useful in diagnosing problems.

Because remote host systems typically are based on UNIX, you will encounter a number of nuances relating to UNIX if you interact with these hosts in your FTP connections:

▶ The UNIX operating system uses the forward slash in path references, not the backward slash. In UNIX, the filename \WINNT40\README.TXT would be /WINNT40/README.TXT.

▶ UNIX is case sensitive at all times—the command `get MyFile` and the command `get MYFILE` are not the same. Usernames and passwords also are case sensitive.

▶ UNIX treats wild card characters, such as the asterisk and the question mark, differently. The `glob` command within FTP changes how wild card characters in local filenames are treated.

The biggest problems with FTP typically involve permissions in uploading and downloading files. To upload files, a user (whether specified by name or anonymous) must have change permission to the directory. To download files, a user (again, either by name or anonymous) must have read permission. These represent the very bare bones permissions required to perform these operations. If an anonymous user cannot get connected, verify that the anonymous user password is the same in both User Manager for Domains and Internet Service Manager. These are distinct logons and passwords, and unified logons work only if their values are the same.

To prevent anonymous users from logging on to your site, you can take advantage of this information about FTP. When FTP is running on the server it constantly looks for activity on control port 21—its pre-assigned number. If you wish to offer the service, yet hide its availability, you can do so by changing the port assignment from 21 to any open number greater than 1023. Alternatively, or additionally, you can disable anonymous access by unchecking the Allow Anonymous Access checkbox in the Authentication Methods dialog box for each site.

FTP usage statistics can be gathered from Performance Monitor using the Connection Attempts and Logon Attempts counters. The former reports when a host attempts to connect to a target anonymously, while the latter indicates those times a connection other than anonymous was attempted.

Exercises

Exercise 30.1: Examine your Windows 95 TCP/IP configuration

To become familiar with how TCP/IP is configured, examine your TCP/IP configuration information on a Windows 95 system and implement the following steps:

1. Choose Run from the Start menu.

2. Type WINIPCFG and press Enter.

3. Select the More Info >> button.

4. Note the Host and Adapter information that appears.

Exercise 30.2: Examine your Windows NT TCP/IP configuration

To become more familiar with how TCP/IP is configured, examine your TCP/IP configuration information on a Windows NT Workstation or Server system that is manually configured. Implement the following steps:

1. Right-click Network Neighborhood and choose Properties.

2. Select the Protocols tab.

3. Highlight TCP/IP and choose Properties.

4. Note the configuration information presented.

Exercise 30.3: Setting NTFS Permissions

To set the NTFS Permissions on a directory or file object, the following steps must be completed:

1. Right-click the NTFS Resource.

2. Select Properties from the pop-up menu for the object.

3. Switch to the Security Page of the object. This only appears if the resource is on an NTFS volume.

continues

Exercise 30.3: Continued

4. Click the Permissions button.

5. Click the Add Button to add new groups and users to assign NTFS permissions to the resource.

6. Click the local group or user that you want to assign permissions to and choose the NTFS permission you wish to assign from the bottom drop list.

7. Click the OK button to return to the Directory Permissions dialog box. From the top of the dialog box, choose whether you want to replace the permissions on all existing files in the directory and whether you want the changes to propagate to all subdirectories.

8. Click OK to make your changes to NTFS permissions effective.

9. Answer Yes to the dialog box that questions whether you want the change in security information to replace the existing security information on all files in all subdirectories.

10. Click OK to exit the Directory's properties dialog box.

Exercise 30.4: Using NBTSTAT to view the local NetBIOS name cache and add entries to the cache from an LMHOSTS file

You should have installed TCP/IP and have another Windows client with TCP/IP installed and file sharing enabled.

1. Use Notepad to open the file \WINNT\SYSTEM32\DRIVERS\ETC\LMHOSTS.SAM.

2. Add an entry to the bottom of the file for the other Windows client, specifying the NetBIOS name and the IP address of the Windows client. Make sure that there's not a comment (#) in front of this line.

3. Save the file in the same directory as LMHOSTS (without an extension).

4. From a command prompt on your NT computer, type nbtstat -c. This displays the local cache.

5. From a command prompt, type `nbstat -R`. This purges the cache and loads the contents of the LMHOSTS file into the local cache.

6. From a command prompt, type `nbtstat -c` to display the new contents of the local cache.

7. Using Windows NT Explorer, map a network drive to the other Windows client. The local cache was used to resolve the NetBIOS name for this connection.

8. From a command prompt, type `nbtstat /?` to see all the switches available with the `NBTSTAT` command.

Exercise 30.5: Examine your Windows NT TCP/IP configuration

To examine your TCP/IP configuration information on a Windows NT Workstation or Server system that is configured through static or dynamic IP addresses (DHCP), implement the following steps:

1. From the Start menu, select Programs, and then Command Prompt.

2. Type in `IPCONFIG`.

3. Note the information that appears. Now type `IPCONFIG /ALL`.

4. Note the information that appears.

Exercise 30.6: Examine your Windows NT configuration with the Resource Kit

To examine your TCP/IP configuration information if the Windows NT Resource Kit CD has been installed on your system, implement the following steps:

1. From the Start menu, Choose Programs, then Resource Kit 4.0.

2. Choose Internet Utils and then IP Configuration.

continues

Exercise 30.6: Continued

3. Select the More Info >> button.

4. Note the Host and Adapter information that appears.

Exercise 30.7: Correcting a network configuration error

Use this exercise to see the effects that an improperly configured network card has on other networking services and protocols. Before starting, make sure you have installed Windows NT Server with a computer that has a network adapter card and that TCP/IP has been installed.

1. Clear the System Log in Event Viewer.

2. From the desktop, right-click on Network Neighborhood and choose Properties from the resulting menu.

3. From the Network Properties dialog box, select the Adapters tab.

4. Select your adapter card from the list and choose Properties.

5. Note the correct setting as it is and change the .IRQ of your adapter card to an incorrect setting.

6. Close this dialog box and choose to reboot your computer when prompted.

7. When your computer reboots, note the message received after the Logon prompt is displayed. The message should indicate A Dependency Service Failed to Start.

8. Log on and open Event Viewer.

9. Note the error message generated from the adapter card. Note the other error messages generated after the adapter card error.

10. Clear the System Log in Event Viewer.

11. From the command prompt, type ping 127.0.0.1. This Ping fails because TCP/IP doesn't start if the adapter doesn't start.

12. From the Network Properties dialog box, change the .IRQ of your adapter card back to its proper setting and reboot.

13. Log on and check the System Log. There should be no adapter card errors or errors from networking services.

14. From the command prompt, type `ping 127.0.0.1`. This `Ping` succeeds because TCP/IP is started now.

Exercise 30.8: Using `Ping` to test an IP configuration

This exercise uses `Ping` to verify a TCP/IP installation and configuration. You should have installed Windows NT Server and TCP/IP.

1. From the desktop, right-click on Network Neighborhood and choose Properties from the resulting menu.

2. From the Bindings tab, expand all the networking services.

3. Select TCP/IP and choose Disable.

4. Repeat Step 3 until you have disabled TCP/IP for all the listed networking services.

5. Close the dialog box and, when prompted, choose to reboot your computer.

6. When the computer reboots, log in.

7. From a command prompt, type `ping 127.0.0.1`. This `Ping` works because TCP/IP is installed.

8. From a command prompt, type `ping x.x.x.x`, where x.x.x.x is your default gateway address. This `Ping` fails because you have disabled TCP/IP from all the networking services. There isn't a way for TCP/IP packets to be sent on the network.

9. From the Bindings tab in Network Properties, enable TCP/IP for all the networking services.

10. Close the dialog box and, when prompted, choose to reboot your computer.

continues

Exercise 30.8: Continued

11. When the computer reboots, log in.

12. From a command prompt, ping your default gateway. The
    Ping works this time because a path now exists by which
    TCP/IP communications can reach the network.

Review Questions

1. Which of the following NTFS Directory permissions enables the user to view the contents of a directory and to navigate to its subdirectories?

    A. No Access

    B. List

    C. Read

    D. Add

    E. Change

2. Which of the following NTFS Directory permissions over-rides all other permissions?

    A. No Access

    B. List

    C. Read

    D. Add

    E. Change

3. Which of the following NTFS Directory permissions enables the user to do the most data manipulation?

    A. No Access

    B. List

    C. Read

    D. Add

    E. Change

4. Which of the following NTFS Directory permissions enables the user to navigate the entire directory structure, view the contents of the directory, view the contents of any files in the directory, and execute programs?

    A. No Access

    B. List

    C. Read

    D. Add

    E. Change

5. Which of the following NTFS Directory permissions enables the user to add new subdirectories and files to the directory, but not to access files within the directory?

    A. No Access

    B. List

    C. Read

    D. Add

    E. Change

6. Which set of permissions enable a user to add new files to the directory structure and, once the files have been added, ensures that the user has read-only access to the files?

    A. No Access

    B. List

    C. Read

    D. Add

    E. Change

7. HOSTS file entries are limited to how many characters?

    A. 8

    B. 255

    C. 500

    D. unlimited

8. The number of entries in the HOSTS file is limited to

    A. 8

    B. 255

    C. 500

    D. unlimited

9. Which of the following files are case sensitive on NT 3.5 systems?

    A. HOSTS

    B. LMHOSTS

    C. ARP

    D. FQDN

10. Which of the following files is used for NetBIOS name resolution?

    A. HOSTS

    B. LMHOSTS

    C. ARP

    D. FQDN

11. Index Server error messages can be viewed with

    A. Server Manager

    B. User Manager for Domains

    C. Event Viewer

    D. Disk Administrator

12. Index Server error messages are written to what log file?

    A. System

    B. Server

    C. Security

    D. Application

13. To run IIS 4.0 on NT, which Service Pack must be installed?

    A. none

    B. 1

    C. 2

    D. 3

14. What version of Internet Explorer is required on the IIS Server for IIS version 4.0?

    A. 2.0

    B. 3.0

    C. 3.01

    D. 4.01

15. Which of the following server services operates, by default, at control port 80:

    A. WWW

    B. FTP

    C. Gopher

    D. Index Server

Review Answers

1. **B**. List enables the user to view the contents of a directory and to navigate to its subdirectories.

2. **A**. No Access overrides all other permissions.

3. **E**. Change enables the user to do the most data manipulation.

4. **C**. Read enables the user to navigate the entire directory structure, view the contents of the directory, view the contents of any files in the directory, and execute programs.

5. **D**. Add enables the user to add new subdirectories and files to the directory, but not to access files within the directory.

6. **C, D**. Read and Add enable a user to add new files to the directory structure and, once the files have been added, the user then has only read-only access to the files.

7. **B**. HOSTS file lines are limited to 255 characters in length.

8. **D**. The HOSTS file can be an unlimited number of lines long.

9. **A**. The HOSTS file, prior to NT 4.0, was case sensitive and remains so on non-NT systems.

10. **B**. LMHOSTS is the static file used for NetBIOS name resolution.

11. **C**. Index Server system errors can be viewed with Event Viewer.

12. **D**. Index Server error messages are written to the application log.

13. **D**. To run IIS 4.0 on NT, Service Pack 3 must be installed.

14. **D**. Internet Explorer 4.01 or greater is required on the IIS Server for IIS version 4.0.

15. **A**. The WWW server services operates, by default, at control port 80.

Answers to Test Yourself Questions at Beginning of Chapter

1. The IP address, the subnet mask, and the default gateway are the three values that must be entered at each host to configure TCP/IP. See "Resolving IIS Configuration Problems."

2. With the Read permission, users can view any documents that are stored in the share, but they cannot make any changes to the documents. See "Resolving Security Problems."

3. IPCONFIG/ALL shows the DHCP server as well as all IP configuration information. See "Resolving Resource Access Problems."

4. By default, Index Server starts when IIS starts. If, for some reason, it has not started, Index Server starts with the first query. See "Resolving Index Server Query Problems."

5. To upgrade IIS 3.0 to IIS 4.0, you must first delete all traces of the IIS 3.0 operating files before installing 4.0. See "Resolving Setup Issues When Installing IIS on a Windows NT Server 4.0 Computer."

6. Content Analyzer's WebMap can be used to administer site content. It is new to IIS 4.0 and can help you keep your site up-to-date and functioning correctly. See "Use a WebMap to Find and Repair Broken Links, Hyperlink Texts, Headings, and Titles."

7. The default TCP control port for the WWW service is 80. See "Resolving WWW Service Problems."

8. The default TCP control port for the FTP service is 21. See "Resolving FTP Service Problems."

P a r t 4

Appendixes

Appendix

Overview of the
Certification Process

A

You must pass rigorous certification exams to become a Microsoft Certified Professional. These certification exams provide a valid and reliable measure of your technical proficiency and expertise. The closed-book exams are developed in consultation with computer industry professionals who have on-the-job experience with Microsoft products in the workplace. These exams are conducted by an independent organization—Sylvan Prometric—at more than 1,200 Authorized Prometric Testing Centers around the world.

Currently Microsoft offers six types of certification, based on specific areas of expertise:

▶ **Microsoft Certified Professional (MCP).** Qualified to provide installation, configuration, and support for users of at least one Microsoft desktop operating system, such as Windows NT Workstation. In addition, candidates can take elective exams to develop areas of specialization. MCP is considered the initial or first level of expertise leading to a premium certification.

▶ **Microsoft Certified Professional—+Internet (MCP+Internet).** Qualified to plan security, install and configure server products, manage server resources, extend service to run CGI scripts or ISAPI scripts, monitor and analyze performance, and troubleshoot problems.

▶ **Microsoft Certified Systems Engineer (MCSE).** Qualified to effectively plan, implement, maintain, and support information systems with Microsoft Windows NT and other Microsoft advanced systems and workgroup products, such as Microsoft Office and Microsoft BackOffice. MCSE is a second level of expertise.

▶ **Microsoft Certified Systems Engineer—+ Internet (MCSE+Internet).** Qualified in the core MCSE areas, plus qualified to enhance, deploy, and manage sophisticated intranet and Internet solutions that include a browser, proxy server, host servers, database, and messaging and commerce components. In addition, an MCSE+Internet-certified professional will be able to manage and analyze Web sites.

▶ **Microsoft Certified Solution Developer (MCSD).** Qualified to design and develop custom business solutions by using Microsoft development tools, technologies, and platforms, including Microsoft Office and Microsoft BackOffice. MCSD is a second level of expertise.

▶ **Microsoft Certified Trainer (MCT).** Instructionally and technically qualified by Microsoft to deliver Microsoft Education courses at Microsoft-authorized sites. An MCT must be employed by a Microsoft Solution Provider Authorized Technical Education Center or a Microsoft Authorized Academic Training site.

Note

For up-to-date information about each type of certification, visit the Microsoft Training and Certification World Wide Web site at `http://www.microsoft.com/train_cert`. You must have an Internet account and a WWW browser to access this information. You also can call the following sources:

▶ Microsoft Certified Professional Program: 800-636-7544

▶ Sylvan Prometric Testing Centers: 800-755-EXAM

▶ Microsoft Online Institute (MOLI): 800-449-9333

How to Become a Microsoft Certified Professional (MCP)

Becoming an MCP requires you to pass one operating system exam. The following list shows the names and exam numbers of all the operating systems from which you can choose to qualify for your MCP certification:

▶ Implementing and Supporting Microsoft Windows 95, #70-063*

▶ Implementing and Supporting Microsoft Windows 95, #70-064

▶ Implementing and Supporting Microsoft Windows NT Workstation 4.02, #70-073

▶ Implementing and Supporting Microsoft Windows NT Workstation 3.51, #70-042

▶ Implementing and Supporting Microsoft Windows NT Server 4.0, #70-067

▶ Implementing and Supporting Microsoft Windows NT Server 3.51, #70-043

▶ Microsoft Windows for Workgroups 3.11-Desktop, #70-048*

▶ Microsoft Windows 3.1, #70-030*

▶ Microsoft Windows Architecture I, #70-160

▶ Microsoft Windows Architecture II, #70-161

Note   Exams marked with an asterisk (*)are scheduled to be retired. Check the Microsoft Training and Certification World Wide Web site at http://www.microsoft.com/train_cert for details.

How to Become a Microsoft Certified Professional+Internet (MCP+Internet)

Becoming an MCP with a specialty in Internet technology requires you to pass the following three exams:

▶ Internetworking Microsoft TCP/IP on Microsoft Windows NT 4.0, #70-059

▶ Implementing and Supporting Microsoft Windows NT Server 4.0, #70-067

▶ Implementing and Supporting Microsoft Internet Information Server 3.0 and Microsoft Index Server 1.1, #70-077

OR, Implementing and Supporting Microsoft Internet Information Server 4.0, #70-087

How to Become a Microsoft Certified Systems Engineer (MCSE)

MCSE candidates must pass four operating system exams and two elective exams. The MCSE certification path is divided into two tracks: the Windows NT 3.51 track and the Windows NT 4.0 track.

The following lists show the core requirements (four operating system exams) for both the Windows NT 3.51 and 4.0 tracks, and the elective courses (two exams) you can choose from for either track.

The four Windows NT 3.51 Track Core Requirements for MCSE certification are as follows:

▶ Implementing and Supporting Microsoft Windows NT Server 3.51, #70-043

▶ Implementing and Supporting Microsoft Windows NT Workstation 3.51, #70-042

▶ Networking Essentials, #70-058

▶ Microsoft Windows 3.1, #70-030*

   OR Microsoft Windows for Workgroups 3.11, #70-048*

   OR Implementing and Supporting Microsoft Windows 95, #70-063*

   OR Implementing and Supporting Microsoft Windows 95, #70-064

The four Windows NT 4.0 Track Core Requirements for MCSE certification are as follows:

▶ Implementing and Supporting Microsoft Windows NT Server 4.0, #70-067

▶ Implementing and Supporting Microsoft Windows NT Server 4.0 in the Enterprise, #70-068

▶ Networking Essentials, #70-058

▶ Microsoft Windows 3.1, #70-030*

   OR Microsoft Windows for Workgroups 3.11, #70-048*

   OR Implementing and Supporting Microsoft Windows 95, #70-063*

   OR Implementing and Supporting Microsoft Windows 95, #70-064

   OR Implementing and Supporting Microsoft Windows NT Workstation 4.0, #70-073

For either the Windows NT 3.51 and or the 4.0 track, you must pass two of the following elective exams for MCSE certification:

▶ Implementing and Supporting Microsoft SNA Server 3.0, #70-013

   OR Implementing and Supporting Microsoft SNA Server 4.0, #70-085

▶ Implementing and Supporting Microsoft Systems Management Server 1.0, #70-014*

OR Implementing and Supporting Microsoft Systems Management Server 1.2, #70-018

OR Implementing and Supporting Microsoft Systems Management Server 1.2, #70-086

▶ Microsoft SQL Server 4.2 Database Implementation, #70-021

OR Implementing a Database Design on Microsoft SQL Server 6.5, #70-027

OR Implementing a Database Design on Microsoft SQL Server 7.0, #70-029

▶ Microsoft SQL Server 4.2 Database Administration for Microsoft Windows NT, #70-022

OR System Administration for Microsoft SQL Server 6.5, #70-026

OR System Administration for Microsoft SQL Server 7.0, #70-028

▶ Microsoft Mail for PC Networks 3.2-Enterprise, #70-037

▶ Internetworking with Microsoft TCP/IP on Microsoft Windows NT (3.5-3.51), #70-053

OR Internetworking with Microsoft TCP/IP on Microsoft Windows NT 4.0, #70-059

▶ Implementing and Supporting Microsoft Exchange Server 4.0, #70-075*

OR Implementing and Supporting Microsoft Exchange Server 5.0, #70-076

OR Implementing and Supporting Microsoft Exchange Server 5.5, #70-081

▶ Implementing and Supporting Microsoft Internet Information Server 3.0 and Microsoft Index Server 1.1, #70-077

OR Implementing and Supporting Microsoft Internet Information Server 4.0, #70-087

▶ Implementing and Supporting Microsoft Internet Explorer 4.0 by Using the Internet Explorer Resource Kit, #70-079

How to Become a Microsoft Certified Systems Engineer + Internet (MCSE+I)

MCSE+Internet candidates must pass seven operating system exams and two elective exams.

The following lists show the core requirements and the elective courses (two exams). The seven MCSE+Internet core exams required for certification are as follows:

▶ Networking Essentials, #70-058

▶ Internetworking with Microsoft TCP/IP on Microsoft Windows NT 4.0, #70-059

▶ Implementing and Supporting Microsoft Windows 95, #70-063

OR Implementing and Supporting Microsoft Windows NT Workstation 4.0, #70-073

▶ Implementing and Supporting Microsoft Windows NT Server 4.0, #70-067

▶ Implementing and Supporting Microsoft Windows NT Server 4.0 in the Enterprise, #70-068

▶ Implementing and Supporting Microsoft Internet Information Server 3.0 and Microsoft Index Server 1.1, #70-077

OR Implementing and Supporting Microsoft Internet Information Server 4.0, #70-087

▶ Implementing and Supporting Microsoft Internet Explorer 4.0 by Using the Internet Explorer Resource Kit, #70-079

You must also pass two of the following elective exams:

▶ System Administration for Microsoft SQL Server 6.5, #70-026

▶ Implementing a Database Design on Microsoft SQL Server 6.5, #70-027

▶ Implementing and Supporting Microsoft Exchange Server 5.0, #70-076

   OR Implementing and Supporting Microsoft Exchange Server 5.5, #70-081

▶ Implementing and Supporting Microsoft Proxy Server 1.0, #70-078

   OR Implementing and Supporting Microsoft Proxy Server 2.0, #70-088

How to Become a Microsoft Certified Solution Developer (MCSD)

MCSD candidates must pass two core technology exams and two elective exams. The following lists show the required technology exams, plus the elective exams that apply toward obtaining the MCSD.

You must pass the following two core technology exams to qualify for MCSD certification:

▶ Microsoft Windows Architecture I, #70-160

▶ Microsoft Windows Architecture II, #70-161

You must also pass two of the following elective exams to become an MSCD:

▶ Microsoft SQL Server 4.2 Database Implementation, #70-021

   OR Implementing a Database Design on Microsoft SQL Server 6.5, #70-027

   OR Implementing a Database Design on Microsoft SQL Server 7.0, #70-029

▶ Developing Applications with C++ Using the Microsoft Foundation Class Library, #70-024

▶ Microsoft Visual Basic 3.0 for Windows-Application Development, #70-050

   OR Programming with Microsoft Visual Basic 4.0, #70-065

   OR Developing Applications with Microsoft Visual Basic 5.0, #70-165

▶ Microsoft Access 2.0 for Windows-Application Development, #70-051

   OR Microsoft Access for Windows 95 and the Microsoft Access Development Toolkit, #70-069

▶ Developing Applications with Microsoft Excel 5.0 Using Visual Basic for Applications, #70-052

▶ Programming in Microsoft Visual FoxPro 3.0 for Windows, #70-054

▶ Implementing OLE in Microsoft Foundation Class Applications, #70-025

Becoming a Microsoft Certified Trainer (MCT)

To understand the requirements and process for becoming a Microsoft Certified Trainer (MCT), you must obtain the Microsoft Certified Trainer Guide document (MCTGUIDE.DOC) from the following WWW site:

```
http://www.microsoft.com/train_cert/download.htm
```

On this page, click on the hyperlink MCT GUIDE (mctguide.doc) (117k). If your WWW browser can display DOC files (Word for Windows native file format), the MCT Guide appears in the browser window. Otherwise, you need to download it and open it in Word for Windows or Windows 95 WordPad. The MCT Guide explains in detail the following four-step process to becoming an MCT:

1. Complete and mail a Microsoft Certified Trainer application to Microsoft. You must include proof of your skills for presenting instructional material. The options for doing so are described in the MCT Guide.

2. Obtain and study the Microsoft Trainer Kit for the Microsoft Official Curricula (MOC) course(s) for which you want to be certified. Microsoft Trainer Kits can be ordered by calling 800-688-0496 in North America. Other regions should review the MCT Guide for information about how to order a Trainer Kit.

3. Pass the Microsoft certification exam for the product for which you want to be certified to teach.

4. Attend the Microsoft Official Curriculum (MOC) course for the course for which you want to be certified. This must be done so you can understand how the course is structured, how labs are completed, and how the course flows.

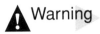 Warning

You should consider the preceding steps as a general overview of the MCT certification process. The precise steps that you need to take are described in detail in the MCTGUIDE.DOC file on the WWW site mentioned earlier. Do not misconstrue the preceding steps as the actual process you need to take.

If you are interested in becoming an MCT, you can receive more information by visiting the Microsoft Certified Training (MCT) WWW site at http://www.microsoft.com/train_cert/mctint.htm; or call 800-688-0496.

Appendix

Study Tips

Self-study involves any method that you employ to learn a given topic, with the most popular being third-party books, such as the one you hold in your hand. Before you begin to study for a certification exam, you should know exactly what Microsoft expects you to learn.

Pay close attention to the objectives posted for the exam. The entire set of objectives is listed in the introduction to this book. The relevant subset of objectives also appears at the beginning of each chapter. The objectives can always be found on the WWW site at http://www.microsoft.com/train_cert. As well, you should notice at the beginning of the book a handy tear-out card with an objective matrix that lists all objectives and the page you can turn to for information on that objective.

Another thing to think about is this: humans vary in their learning styles. Some people are visual learners, others are textual, and still others learn best from aural sources. However, there are some basic principles of learning that apply to everyone. For example, students who take notes on lectures have better recall on exam day—even if they did not study the notes later—because they encoded the information as well as decoded it, they processed it in a deeper, more active fashion than those who simply listened to the lecture.

Hence, use the study techniques that you know work for you, but also take advantage of more general principles of learning. For example, if you are a visual learner, pay special attention to the figures provided in this book. Also create your own visual cues by doing things like diagramming processes and relationships.

A general principle of learning that you might take advantage of has to do with studying the organization and the details of information separately. Cognitive learning research has demonstrated that if you attempt to focus on learning just the organization of the information, followed by a focus on just learning the specific details, you will retain the information better than if you attempt to take in all of the information at once. Use your study materials to prepare a detailed outline of the material on the exam. Study it first by learning the organization of the material. Then, in your next pass through the outline, focus on memorizing and understanding the detail. Trying to do both at once only leads to the two types of information interfering with your overall learning.

Finally, follow common-sense practices in your studying as well. These basic sorts of studying strategies are listed below:

▶ Study in bright light to reduce fatigue and depression.

▶ Establish a regular study schedule and stick as close to it as possible.

▶ Turn off all forms of distraction, including radios and televisions; or try studying in a quiet room.

▶ Always study in the same place so your materials are always readily at hand.

▶ Take short (approximately 15-minute) breaks every two to three hours or so. Studies have proven that your brain assimilates information better when these rest periods are taken.

Pre-Testing Yourself

Before taking the actual exam, verify that you are ready to do so by testing yourself many times in a variety of ways. Within this book, there are questions at the beginning and end of each chapter. On the accompanying CD-ROM, there is an electronic test engine that emulates the actual Microsoft exam and enables you to test your knowledge of the subject areas. Use this repeatedly until you are consistently scoring in the 90 percent range (or better).

Note

This means, of course, that you can't start studying five days before the exam begins. You will need to give yourself plenty of time to read, practice, and allow for testing yourself several times.

The New Riders' TestPrep electronic testing engine, we believe, is the best test preparation tool on the market, unparalleled by other engines. TestPrep is described in detail in Appendix D, "All About TestPrep."

Hints and Tips for Doing Your Best on the Tests

When you go to take the actual exam be prepared. Arrive early and be ready to show two forms of identification. Expect wordy questions. Although you have 90 minutes to take each of the exams, there are about 50 questions you must answer. This gives you less than two minutes to answer each question. This may sound like ample time for each question, but remember that many of the questions can involve lengthy word problems, exhibits that must be referred to, and, more recently, even simulations. Your 90 minutes of exam time can be consumed very quickly.

It has been estimated that approximately 85 percent of the candidates taking their first Microsoft exam fail it. It is not so much that they are unprepared and lack the knowledge they need. It is more the case that they don't know what to expect and are immediately intimidated by the wordiness of the questions and the ambiguity they feel is implied in the answers.

Things to Watch For

When you take the exam, read very carefully! Make sure that you understand just what the question requires, and take notice of the number of correct choices you need to make. Remember that some questions require that you select a single correct answer; other questions have more than one correct answer. Radial buttons next to the answer choices indicate that the answers are mutually exclusive—there is but one correct answer. On the other hand, check boxes indicate that the answers are not mutually exclusive and there are multiple correct answers.

Again, read the questions fully. With lengthy questions, the last sentence often dramatically changes the scenario. When taking the exam, you are given pencils and two sheets of paper. If you are uncertain of what the question requires, map out the scenario on the paper until you have it clear in your mind. You must turn in the scrap paper at the end of the exam.

Choosing the Right Answer

Adopt a strategy for evaluating possible answers. Eliminate those answers that are impossible or implausible. Carefully evaluate those that remain. Be careful: some answers are true statements as they stand on their own, but in the context of the question, might not makes sense as correct answers. The answers must match or relate to the question before they can serve as correct choices.

Marking Answers for Return

You can mark questions on the actual exam and refer back to them later. If you encounter a wordy question that will take a long time to read and decipher, mark it and return to it when you have completed the rest of the exam. This will prevent you from wasting time on it and running out of time on the exam—there are only 90 minutes allotted for the exam and it ends when those 90 minutes expire, whether or not you are finished with the exam.

Changing Answers

The rule of thumb here is *don't!* If you have read the question carefully and completely, and you felt like you knew the right answer, you probably did. Don't second-guess yourself! If, as you check your answers, one stands out as clearly marked incorrectly, however, of course you should change it in that instance. But if you are at all unsure, go with your first impression.

Attaching Notes to Test Questions

At the conclusion of the exam, before the grading takes place, you are given the opportunity to attach a message to any question. If you feel that a question was too ambiguous, or tested on knowledge you do not need to know to work with the product, take this opportunity to state your case. Unheard of is the instance in which Microsoft changes a test score as a result of an attached message. However, it never hurts to try—and it helps to vent your frustration before blowing the proverbial 50-amp fuse.

Good luck!

Appendix

What's on the CD-ROM

This appendix is a brief rundown of what you'll find on the CD-ROM that comes with this book. For a more detailed description of the newly developed TestPrep test engine, exclusive to Macmillan Computer Publishing, please see Appendix D, "All About TestPrep."

TestPrep

TestPrep is a new test engine developed exclusively for Macmillan Computer Publishing. It is, we believe, the best test engine available because it closely emulates the actual Microsoft exam, and enables you to check your score by category, which helps you determine what topics you need to study further. Before running the TestPrep software, be sure to read CDROM.hlp (in the root directory of the CD-ROM) for late-breaking news on TestPrep features. For a complete description of the benefits of TestPrep, please see Appendix D.

Exclusive Electronic Version of Text

Also contained on the CD-ROM is the electronic version of this book. You can use this to help you search for terms or areas that you need to study. The electronic version comes complete with all figures as they appear in the book.

Copyright Information and Disclaimer

Appendix

All About TestPrep

The TestPrep software included on the CD-ROM accompanying this book enables you to test your +Internet exams knowledge in a manner similar to that employed by the actual Microsoft exam. There are actually three applications included: Practice Exams, Study Cards, and Flash Cards. Practice Exams provide you with simulated multiple-choice tests. Study Cards provide the same sorts of questions (but enable you to control the number and types of questions) and provide immediate feedback to you. This format enables you to learn from your testing and control the topics on which you want to be tested. Flash Cards provide this same sort of feedback and allow the same sort of control but require short answer or essay answers to questions; you are not prompted with multiple choice selections or cued as to the number of correct answers to provide.

While it is possible to maximize the TestPrep applications, the default is for them to run in smaller mode so you can refer to your Windows NT or 95 desktop while answering questions. TestPrep uses a unique randomization process to ensure that each time you run the programs you are presented with a different sequence of questions—this enhances your learning and helps prevent you from merely memorizing the expected answers over time without reading the question each and every time.

Question Presentation

TestPrep Practice Exams and Study Cards emulate the actual Microsoft exams, in that radial (circle) buttons are used to signify only one correct choice, while check boxes (squares) are used to indicate multiple correct answers. Whenever more than one answer is correct, the number you should select is given in the wording of the question.

Scoring

The TestPrep Practice Exam Score Report uses actual numbers from the three exams. That is, the number of questions, number of correct answers needed, and time limit are the same as the Microsoft exams.

Index

E

J

K

L

O

W

Notes...

Notes...

Notes...

Notes...

Notes...